the
deliberate
dumbing
down
of america

the deliberate dumbing down of america

C 2

A Chronological Paper Trail

by Charlotte Thomson Iserbyt

‖ CONSCIENCE
PRESS

RAVENNA, OHIO

Published in 1999.
Printed in the United States of America.
Acid-free paper. Archival quality.

Library of Congress Catalog Card Number: 98–89726
ISBN: 0–9667071–0–9

Conscience Press • P.O. Box 449 • Ravenna, Ohio • 44266–0449

Printed by The Athens Printing Company, Athens, Georgia
Graphic design by Colin Leslie
Cover design by 3–D Research Company
Index compiled by Kari Miller
Cartoons created by Joel Pett, *Herald Leader* of Lexington, Kentucky

This book is dedicated to my late mother and father, Charlotte and Clifton Thomson, wonderful parents who devoted much of their lives to public service, and to my late great aunt, Florence Stanton Thomson, whose generosity enabled the writer to undertake the research, writing, and publishing of this book.

It is also dedicated to my husband, Jan, and two sons, Robert and Samuel, whose tolerance of Mom's activism and frequent absences from home over a period of thirty years allowed the writer to pursue her search for the truth. Jan's gourmet cooking lifted our spirits and kept us all from starving! Without the men's patience, humor, and moral support, this book could not have been written.

IN MEMORIAM

This book is a small tribute to the late Honorable John M. Ashbrook, 17th Congressional District of Ohio, whose work in Congress during the 1960s and 1970s exposed the treasonous plans which ultimately led to the internationalization and deliberate dumbing down of American education.

TABLE OF CONTENTS

The human brain should be used for processing, not storage.

—Thomas A. Kelly, Ph.D.
The Effective School Report

FOREWORD

Charlotte Iserbyt is to be greatly commended for having put together the most formidable and practical compilation of documentation describing the "deliberate dumbing down" of American children by their education system. Anyone interested in the truth will be shocked by the way American social engineers have systematically gone about destroying the intellect of millions of American children for the purpose of leading the American people into a socialist world government controlled by behavioral and social scientists.

Mrs. Iserbyt has also documented the gradual transformation of our once academically successful education system into one devoted to training children to become compliant human resources to be used by government and industry for their own purposes. This is how fascist-socialist societies train their children to become servants of their government masters. The successful implementation of this new philosophy of education will spell the end of the American dream of individual freedom and opportunity. The government will plan your life for you, and unless you comply with government restrictions and regulations your ability to pursue a career of your own choice will be severely limited.

What is so mind boggling is that all of this is being financed by the American people themselves through their own taxes. In other words, the American people are underwriting the destruction of their own freedom and way of life by lavishly financing through federal grants the very social scientists who are undermining our national sovereignty and preparing our children to become the dumbed-down vassals of the new world order. It reminds one of how the Nazis charged their victims train fare to their own doom.

One of the interesting insights revealed by these documents is how the social engineers use a deliberately created education "crisis" to move their agenda forward by offering radical reforms that are sold to the public as fixing the crisis—which they never do. The new reforms simply set the stage for the next crisis, which provides the pretext for the next move forward. This is the dialectical process at work, a process our behavioral engineers have learned to use very effectively. Its success depends on the ability of the "change agents" to continually deceive the public which tends to believe anything the experts tell them.

And so, our children continue to be at risk in America's schools. They are at risk academically because of such programs as whole language, mastery learning, direct instruction, Skinnerian operant conditioning, all of which have created huge learning problems that inevitably lead to what is commonly known as Attention Deficit Disorder and the drugging of four million children with the powerful drug Ritalin. Mrs. Iserbyt has dealt extensively with the root causes of immorality in our society and the role of the public schools in the teaching of moral relativism (no right/no wrong ethics). She raises a red flag regarding the current efforts of left-wing liberals and right-wing conservatives (radical center) to come up with a new kid on the block—"common ground" character education—which will, under the microscope, turn out to be the same warmed-over values education alert parent groups have resisted for over fifty years. This is a perfect example of the Hegelian Dialectic at work.

The reader will find in this book a plethora of information that will leave no doubt in the mind of the serious researcher exactly where the American education system is headed. If we wish to stop this juggernaut toward a socialist-fascist system, then we must restore educational freedom to America. Americans forget that the present government education system started as a Prussian import in the 1840's–'50's. It was a system built on Hegel's belief that the state was "God" walking on earth. The only way to restore educational freedom, and put education back into the hands of parents where it belongs, is to get the federal government, with its coercive policies, out of education. The billions of dollars being spent by the federal government to destroy educational freedom must be halted, and that can only be done by getting American legislators to understand that the American people want to remain a free people, in charge of their own lives and the education of their children.

SAMUEL L. BLUMENFELD

PREFACE

Coexistence on this tightly knit earth should be viewed as an existence not only without wars... but also without [the government] *telling us how to live, what to say, what to think, what to know, and what not to know.*
> —Aleksandr Solzhenitsyn, from a speech given September 11, 1973[1]

Educated men are as much superior to uneducated men as the living are to the dead.
> —Aristotle, 384–322 B.C.[2]

For over a twenty-five-year period the research used in this chronology has been collected from many sources: the United States Department of Education; international agencies; state agencies; the media; concerned educators; parents; legislators, and talented researchers with whom I have worked. In the process of gathering this information two beliefs that most Americans hold in common became clear:

1) If a child can read, write and compute at a reasonably proficient level, he will be able to do just about anything he wishes, enabling him to control his destiny to the extent that God allows (remain free);

2) Providing such basic educational proficiencies *is not and should not be* an expensive proposition.

Since most Americans believe the second premise—that providing basic educational proficiencies is not and should not be an expensive proposition—it becomes obvious that it is only a radical agenda, the purpose of which is to change values and attitudes (brainwash), that is the *costly* agenda. In other words, brainwashing by our schools and universities is what is bankrupting our nation and our children's minds.

In 1997 there were 46.4 million public school students. During 1993–1994 (the latest years the statistics were available) the average per pupil expenditure was $6,330.00 in 1996

xiii

constant dollars. Multiply the number of students by the per pupil expenditure (using old-fashioned mathematical procedures) for a total K–12 budget per year of $293.7 billion dollars. If one adds the cost of higher education to this figure, one arrives at a total budget per year of *over half a trillion dollars.*[3] The sorry result of such an incredibly large expenditure—the performance of American students—is discussed in *Pursuing Excellence—A Study of U.S. Twelfth Grade Mathematics and Science Achievement in International Context: Initial Findings from the Third International Mathematics and Science Study* (TIMMS), a report from the U.S. Department of Education (NCES 98–049). *Pursuing Excellence* reads:

> Achievement of Students, Key Points: U.S. twelfth graders scored below the international average and among the lowest of the 21 TIMSS nations in both mathematics and science general knowledge in the final year of secondary school. (p. 24)

Obviously, something is terribly wrong when a $6,330 per pupil expenditure produces such pathetic results. This writer has visited private schools which charge $1,000 per year in tuition which enjoy superior academic results. Parents of home-schooled children spend a maximum of $1,000 per year and usually have similar excellent results.

There are many talented and respected researchers and activists who have carefully documented the "weird" activities which have taken place "in the name of education." Any opposition to change agent activities in local schools has invariably been met with cries of "Prove your case, document your statements," etc. Documentation, when presented, has been ignored and called incomplete. The classic response by the education establishment has been, "You're taking that out of context!"—even when presented with an entire book which uses their own words to detail exactly what the "resisters" are claiming to be true. "Resisters"—usually parents—have been called every name in the book. Parents have been told for over thirty years, "You're the *only* parent who has ever complained." The media has been convinced to join in the attack upon common sense views, effectively discrediting the perspective of well-informed citizens.

The desire by "resisters" to prove their case has been so strong that they have continued to amass—over a thirty- to fifty-year period—what must surely amount to *tons* of materials containing irrefutable proof, in the education change agents' own words, of deliberate, malicious intent to achieve behavioral changes in students/parents/society which have nothing to do with commonly understood educational objectives. Upon delivery of such proof, "resisters" are consistently met with the "shoot the messenger" stonewalling response by teachers, school boards, superintendents, state and local officials, as well as the supposedly objective institutions of academia and the press.

This resister's book, or collection of research in book form, was put together primarily to satisfy my own need to see the various components which led to the dumbing down of the United States of America assembled in chronological order—in writing. Even I, who had observed these weird activities taking place at all levels of government, was reluctant to accept a malicious intent behind each individual, chronological activity or innovation, unless I could connect it with other, similar activities taking place at other times. This book, which makes such connections, has provided for me a much-needed sense of closure.

the deliberate dumbing down of america is also a book for my children, grandchildren, and great-grandchildren. I want them to know that there were thousands of Americans who may not have died or been shot at in overseas wars, but *were* shot at in small-town "wars" at school board meetings, at state legislative hearings on education, and, most importantly, in the media. I want my progeny to know that whatever intellectual and spiritual freedoms to which they may still lay claim were fought for—are a result of—the courageous work of incredible people who dared to tell the truth against all odds.

I want them to know that there will always be hope for freedom if they follow in these people's footsteps; if they cherish the concept of "free will"; if they believe that human beings are special, not animals, and that they have intellects, souls, and consciences. I want them to know that if the government schools are allowed to teach children K–12 using Pavlovian/Skinnerian animal training methods—which provide tangible rewards only for correct answers—there can be no freedom.

Why? People "trained"—not educated—by such educational techniques will be fearful of taking principled, sometimes controversial, stands when called for because these people will have been programmed to speak up only if a positive reward or response is forthcoming. The price of freedom has often been paid with pain and loneliness.

In 1971 when I returned to the United States after living abroad for 18 years, I was shocked to find public education had become a warm, fuzzy, soft, mushy, touchy-feely experience, with its purpose being socialization, not learning. From that time on, from the vantage point of having two young sons in the public schools, I became involved—as a member of a philosophy committee for a school, as an elected school board member, as co-founder of Guardians of Education for Maine (GEM), and finally as a senior policy advisor in the Office of Educational Research and Improvement (OERI) of the U.S. Department of Education during President Ronald Reagan's first term of office. OERI was, and is, the office from which *all* the controversial national and international educational restructuring has emanated.

Those ten years (1971–1981) changed my life. As an American who had spent many years working abroad, I had experienced traveling in and living in socialist countries. When I returned to the United States I realized that America's transition from a sovereign constitutional republic to a socialist democracy would not come about through warfare (bullets and tanks) but through the implementation and installation of the "system" in *all* areas of government—federal, state and local. The brainwashing for acceptance of the "system's" control would take place in the school—through indoctrination and the use of behavior modification, which comes under so many labels: the most recent labels being Outcome-Based Education, Skinnerian Mastery Learning or Direct Instruction.[4] In the 1970s this writer and many others waged the war against values clarification, which was later renamed "critical thinking," which regardless of the label—and there are bound to be many more labels on the horizon—is nothing but pure, unadulterated destruction of absolute values of right and wrong upon which stable and free societies depend and upon which our nation was founded.

In 1973 I started the long journey into becoming a "resister," placing the first incriminating piece of paper in my "education" files. That first piece of paper was a purple ditto sheet entitled "All About Me," next to which was a smiley face. It was an open-ended questionnaire beginning with: "My name is _____." My son brought it home from public school in fourth grade. The questions were highly personal; so much so that they encouraged my son to lie, since he didn't want to "spill the beans" about his mother, father and brother. The purpose of such a questionnaire was to find out the student's state of mind, how he felt, what he liked and disliked, and what his values were. With this knowledge it would be easier for the government school to modify his values and behavior at will—without, of course, the student's knowledge or parents' consent.

That was just the beginning. There was more to come: the new social studies textbook *World of Mankind*. Published by Follett, this book instructed the teacher how to instill humanistic (no right/no wrong) values in the K–3 students. At the text's suggestion the teacher was encouraged to take little tots for walks in town during which he would point out big and small houses, asking the little tots who they thought lived in the houses: Poor or Rich? "What do you think they eat in the big house? ...in the little house?" When I complained about this non-educational activity at a school board meeting I was dismissed as a censor and the press did its usual hatchet job on me as a misguided parent. A friend of mine—a very bright gal who had also lived abroad for years—told me that she had overheard discussion of me at the local co-op. The word was out in town that I was a "kook." That was not a "positive response/ reward" for my taking what I believed to be a principled position. Since I had not been "trained," I was just mad!

Next stop on the road to becoming a "resister" was to become a member of the school philosophy committee. Our Harvard-educated, professional change agent superintendent gave all of the committee members a copy of "The Philosophy of Education" (1975 version) from the Montgomery County schools in Maryland, hoping to influence whatever recommendations we would make. (For those who like to eat dessert before soup, read the entry under 1946 concerning *Community-Centered Schools: The Blueprint for Education in Montgomery County, Maryland*. This document was in fact the "Blueprint" for the nation's schools.) When asked to write a paper expressing our views on the goals of education, I wrote that, amongst other goals, I felt the schools should strive to instill "*sound* morals and values in the students." The superintendent and a few teachers on the committee zeroed in on me, asking "What's the definition of 'sound' and whose values?"

After two failed attempts to get elected to the school board, I finally succeeded in 1976 on the third try. The votes were counted three times, even though I had won by a very healthy margin!

My experience on the school board taught me that when it comes to modern education, "the end justifies the means." Our change agent superintendent was more at home with a lie than he was with the truth. Whatever good I accomplished while on the school board— stopping the Planning, Programming and Budgeting System (PPBS) now known as Total Quality Management (TQM) or Generally Accepted Accounting Procedures/Generally Accepted Federal Funding Reporting (GAAP/GAFFR), getting values clarification banned by the board, and demanding five (yes, 5!) minutes of grammar per day, etc.—was tossed out two weeks after I left office.

Another milestone on my journey was an in-service training session entitled "Innovations in Education." A retired teacher, who understood what was happening in education, paid for me to attend. This training program developed by Professor Ronald Havelock of the University of Michigan and funded by the United States Office of Education taught teachers and administrators how to "sneak in" controversial methods of teaching and "innovative" programs. These controversial, "innovative" programs included health education, sex education, drug and alcohol education, death education, critical thinking education, etc. Since then I have always found it interesting that the controversial school programs are the only ones that have the word "education" attached to them! I don't recall—until recently—"math ed.," "reading ed.," "history ed.," or "science ed." A good rule of thumb for teachers, parents and school board members interested in academics and traditional values is to question any subject that has the word "education" attached to it.

This in-service training literally "blew my mind." I have never recovered from it. The presenter (change agent) taught us how to "manipulate" the taxpayers/parents into accepting controversial programs. He explained how to identify the "resisters" in the community and how to get around their resistance. He instructed us in how to go to the highly respected members of the community—those with the Chamber of Commerce, Rotary, Junior League, Little League, YMCA, Historical Society, etc.—to manipulate them into supporting the controversial/non-academic programs and into bad-mouthing the resisters. Advice was also given as to how to get the media to support these programs.

I left this training—with my very valuable textbook, *The Change Agent's Guide to Innovations in Education,* under my arm—feeling *very* sick to my stomach and in complete denial over that in which I had been involved. This was not the nation in which I grew up; something seriously disturbing had happened between 1953 when I left the United States and 1971 when I returned.

Orchestrated Consensus

In retrospect, I had just found out that the United States was engaged in war. People write important books about war: books documenting the battles fought, the names of the generals involved, the names of those who fired the first shot. This book is simply a history book about another kind of war:

- one fought using psychological methods;
- a one-hundred-year war;
- a different, more deadly war than any in which our country has ever been involved;
- a war about which the average American hasn't the foggiest idea.

The reason Americans do not understand this war is because *it has been fought in secret*—in the schools of our nation, targeting *our children* who are captive in classrooms. The wagers of this war are using very sophisticated and effective tools:

- Hegelian Dialectic (common ground, consensus and compromise)
- Gradualism (two steps forward; one step backward)
- Semantic deception (redefining terms to get agreement without understanding).

The Hegelian Dialectic[5] is a process formulated by the German philosopher Georg Wilhelm Friedrich Hegel (1770–1831) and used by Karl Marx in codifying revolutionary Communism as dialectical materialism. This process can be illustrated as:

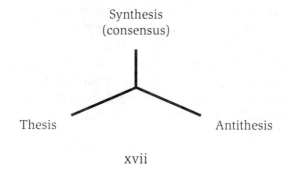

Synthesis
(consensus)

Thesis   Antithesis

The "Thesis" represents either an established practice or point of view which is pitted against the "Antithesis"—usually a crisis of opposition fabricated or created by change agents—causing the "Thesis" to *compromise* itself, incorporating some part of the "Antithesis" to produce the "Synthesis"—sometimes called *consensus*. This is the primary tool in the bag of tricks used by change agents who are trained to direct this process all over the country; much like the in-service training I received. A good example of this concept was voiced by T.H. Bell when he was U.S. Secretary of Education: "[We] need to *create a crisis to get consensus in order to bring about change.*" (The reader might be reminded that it was under T.H. Bell's direction that the U.S. Department of Education implemented the changes "suggested" by *A Nation at Risk*—the alarm that was sounded in the early 1980s to announce the "crisis" in education.)

Since we have been, as a nation, so relentlessly exposed to this Hegelian dialectical process (which is essential to the smooth operation of the "system") under the guise of "reaching consensus" in our involvement in parent-teacher organizations, on school boards, in legislatures, and even in goal setting in community service organizations and groups—including our churches—I want to explain clearly how it works in a practical application. A good example with which most of us can identify involves property taxes for local schools. Let us consider an example from Michigan—

The internationalist change agents must abolish local control (the "Thesis") in order to restructure our schools from academics to global workforce training (the "Synthesis"). Funding of education with the property tax allows *local control*, but it also enables the change agents and teachers' unions to create higher and higher school budgets paid for with higher taxes, thus infuriating homeowners. Eventually, property owners *accept* the change agents' radical *proposal* (the "Anti- thesis") to reduce their property taxes by transferring education funding *from* the local property tax *to* the state income tax. Thus, the change agents accomplish their ultimate goal; the transfer of funding of education from the local level to the state level. When this transfer occurs it increases state/federal control and funding, leading to the federal/internationalist goal of implementing global workforce training through the schools (the "Synthesis").[6]

Regarding the power of "gradualism," remember the story of the frog and how he didn't save himself because he didn't realize what was happening to him? He was thrown into cold water which, in turn, was gradually heated up until finally it reached the boiling point and he was dead. This is how "gradualism" works through a series of "created crises" which utilize Hegel's dialectical process, leading us to more radical change than we would ever otherwise accept.

In the instance of "semantic deception"—do you remember your kindly principal telling you that the new decision-making program would help your child make better decisions? What good parent wouldn't want his or her child to learn how to make "good" decisions? Did you know that the decision-making program is the same controversial values clarification program recently rejected by your school board and against which you may have given repeated testimony? As I've said before, the wagers of this intellectual social war have employed very effective weapons to implement their changes.

This war has, in fact, become the war to end all wars. If citizens on this planet can be brainwashed or robotized, using dumbed-down Pavlovian/Skinnerian education, to accept what those in control want, there will be no more wars. If there are no rights or wrongs, there will be no one wanting to "right" a "wrong." Robots have no conscience. The only permissible conscience will be the United Nations or a global conscience. Whether an action is good or bad will be decided by a "Global Government's Global Conscience," as recommended by Dr. Brock Chisholm, executive secretary of the World Health Organization, Interim Commission, in 1947—and later in 1996 by current United States Secretary of State Madeline Albright. (See quotes in entry under 1947.)

You may protest, "But, no one has died in this war." Is that the only criteria we have with which to measure whether war is war? Didn't Aristotle say it well when he said, "Educated men are as much superior to uneducated men as the living are to the dead"? To withhold the tools of education can kill a person's spirit just as surely as a bullet his body. The tragedy is that many Americans have died in other wars to protect the freedoms being taken away in *this* one. This war which produces the death of intellect and freedom is not waged by a foreign enemy but by the silent enemy in the ivory towers, in our own government, and in tax-exempt foundations—the enemy whose every move I have tried to document in this book, usually in his/her/its own words.

Ronald Havelock's change agent in-service training prepared me for what I would find in the U.S. Department of Education when I worked there from 1981–1982. The use of taxpayers' hard-earned money to fund Havelock's "Change Agent Manual" was only one out of hundreds of expensive U.S. Department of Education grants each year going everywhere, even overseas, to further the cause of internationalist "dumbing down" education (behavior modification) so necessary for the present introduction of global workforce training. I was relieved of my duties after leaking an important technology grant (computer-assisted instruction proposal) to the press.

Much of this book contains quotes from government documents detailing the real purposes of American education:

- to use the schools to change America from a free, individual nation to a socialist, global "state," just one of many socialist states which will be subservient to the United Nations Charter, not the *United States Constitution*
- to brainwash our children, starting at birth, to reject individualism in favor of collectivism
- to reject high academic standards in favor of OBE/ISO 1400/9000[7] egalitarianism
- to reject truth and absolutes in favor of tolerance, situational ethics and consensus
- to reject American values in favor of internationalist values (globalism)
- to reject freedom to choose one's career in favor of the totalitarian K–12 school-to-work/OBE process, aptly named "limited learning for lifelong labor,"[8] coordinated through United Nations Educational, Scientific, and Cultural Organization.

Only when all children in public, private and home schools are robotized—and believe as one—will World Government be acceptable to citizens and able to be implemented without firing a shot. The attractive-sounding "choice" proposals will enable the globalist elite to achieve their goal: the robotization (brainwashing) of all Americans in order to gain their acceptance of lifelong education and workforce training—part of the world management system to achieve a new global feudalism.

The socialist/fascist global workforce training agenda is being implemented as I write this book. The report to the European Commission entitled *Transatlantic Co-operation in Inter-*

national Education: Projects of the Handswerkskammer Koblenz with Partners in the United States and in the European Union by Karl-Jurgen Wilbert and Bernard Eckgold (May 1997) says in part:

> In June, 1994, with the support of the Handswerkskamer Koblenz, an American-German vocational education conference took place... at the University of Texas at Austin. The vocational education researchers and economic specialists... were in agreement that an economic and employment policy is necessary where a systematic vocational training is as equally important as an academic education, as a "career pathway." ...The first practical steps along these lines, which are also significant from the point of view of the educational policy, were made with the vocational training of American apprentices in skilled craft companies, in the area of the Koblenz chamber.

Under section "e) Scientific Assistance for the Projects," one reads:

> The international projects ought to be scientifically assisted and analyzed both for the feedback to the transatlantic dialogue on educational policy, and also for the assessment and qualitative improvement of the cross-border vocational education projects. As a result it should be made possible on the German side to set up a connection to other projects of German-American cooperation in vocational training; *e.g.*, of the federal institute for vocational training for the project in the U.S. state of Maine. On the USA side an interlinking with other initiatives for vocational training—for example, through the Center for the Study of Human Resources at the University of Texas, Austin—would be desirable.

This particular document discusses the history of apprenticeships—especially the role of medieval guilds—and attempts to make a case for nations which heretofore have cherished liberal economic ideas—i.e., individual economic freedom—to return to a system of cooperative economic solutions (the guild system used in the Middle Ages which accepted very young children from farms and cities and trained them in "necessary" skills). Another word for this is "serfdom." Had our elected officials at the federal, state, and local levels read this document, they could never have voted in favor of socialist/fascist legislation implementing workforce training to meet the needs of the *global* economy. Unless, of course, they happen to support such a totalitarian economic system. (This incredible document was accessed at the following internet address: http://www.kwk-koblenz.de/ausland/trans-uk.doc)

Just as Barbara Tuchman or another historian would do in writing the history of the other kinds of wars, I have identified chronologically the major battles, players, dates and places. I know that researchers and writers with far more talent than I will feel that I have neglected some key events in this war. I stand guilty on all counts, even before their well-researched charges are submitted. Yes, much of importance has been left out, due to space limitations, but the overview of the battlefields and maneuvers will give the reader an opportunity to glimpse the immensity of this conflict.

In order to win a battle one must know who the "real" enemy is. Otherwise, one is shooting in the dark and often hitting those not the least bit responsible for the mayhem. This book, hopefully, identifies the "real" enemy and provides Americans involved in this war—be they plain, ordinary citizens, elected officials, or traditional teachers—with the ammunition to fight to obtain victory.

Preface

Endnotes:

1 Noted Soviet dissident, slave labor camp intern, and author of *The Gulag Archipelago* and numerous other books.

2 *The Basic Works of Aristotle*, Richard McKeon, Ed., from *Familiar Quotations by John Bartlett, 14th ed.* (Little, Brown & Co.: Boston, Toronto, 1968).

3 Statistics taken from *The Condition of Education, 1997*, published by the National Center for Educational Statistics, U.S. Department of Education (NCES 97–388). Internet address: http://www.ed/gov/NCES.

4 OBE/ML/DI or outcomes-based education/mastery learning/direct instruction.

5 Dean Gotcher, author of *The Dialectic & Praxis: Diaprax and the End of the Ages* and other materials dealing with dialectical consensus building and human relations training, has done some excellent work in this area of research. For more detailed information on this process, please write to Dean Gotcher of the Institution for Authority Research, 5436 S. Boston Pl., Tulsa, Oklahoma 74105, or call 918-742-3855.

6 See Appendix XXII for an article by Tim Clem which explains this process in much more detail.

7 ISO stands for International Standards of Operation for manufacturing (9000) and human resources (1400), coordinated through the United Nations Educational, Social and Cultural Organization (UNESCO).

8 "Privatization or Socialization" by C. Weatherly, 1994. Delivered as part of a speech to a group in Minnesota and later published in *The Christian Conscience* magazine (Vol. 1, No. 2: February 1995, pp. 29–30).

ACKNOWLEDGMENTS

In particular I want to thank a handful of government officials who provided me with important documents. They must remain anonymous for obvious reasons.

I would also like to mention several incredibly fine Americans who are unfortunately no longer with us, who provided me with the priceless research and necessary resources to write this book. They are: Jo-Ann Abrigg, Rexford Daniels, Norman Dodd, Ruth Feld, Mary Larkin, Judge Robert Morris, Walter Crocker Pew and Mary Royer.

Very special thanks go to the following education researchers and writers with whom I have worked and who have contributed to and made this book possible (in alphabetical order): Mary Adams, Polly Anglin, Marilyn Boyer, Shirley Correll, Peggy and Dennis Cuddy, Janet Egan, Melanie Fields, Ann Frazier, Betty Freauf, Jeannie Georges, Peggy Grimes, Rosalind Haley, Karen Hayes, Tracey Hayes, Maureen Heaton, Mary Jo Heiland, Ann Herzer, Anita Hoge, Betsy Kraus, Jacqueline and Malcolm Lawrence, Mina Legg, Bettye and Kirk Lewis, Joanne Lisac, Joan Masters, Nancy Maze, Janelle Moon, Opal Moore, Barbara Morris, LuAnne Robson, Patricia Royall, Elisabeth Russinoff, Cris Shardelman, Debbie Stevens, Rose Stewart, Elisabeth Trotto, Georgiana Warner, Geri Wenta, and Jil Wilson. Thanks are also extended to their respective spouses who made their contributions possible.

Obviously, the job of editing this book was monumental! Cynthia Weatherly, who is one of the nation's finest education researchers and talented writers and with whom I have worked for twenty years, took my rough manuscript and turned it into a mammoth historical presentation. Her incredible work on this book represents a true labor of love for this nation and for our children and grandchildren. I will forever be grateful to Cindi and her husband, Neal, who extended a gracious welcome to me each time I descended upon them, including a four-month stay last winter!

In addition, my deepest thanks go to the Leslie family of Conscience Press—Sarah, Lynn and Colin, and Sarah's parents, Paul and Jean Huling, each of whom contributed in his own vital way to the publication of this book in such a professional manner. How this family published this book and managed at the same time to make three moves in and out of different houses during this one-year period is beyond belief. There are no words to express this writer's gratitude for this one family's contribution to the preservation of liberty for all Americans.

Of course, the book would never have seen the light of day without the very professional job delivered by Tim and Janet Fields of The Athens Printing Company of Athens, Georgia. Tim's unbelievable patience with interminable delays was beyond the call of duty.

And last, but not least, thanks to the folks at the reference desk of the University of Georgia Library, who cheerfully and professionally assisted the writer and editor with critical documentation, and to Air Tran, whose extremely reasonable airfare from Boston to Atlanta allowed Cindi and me to collaborate on the most important stages of this book's production.

Deepest apologies to whomever I have neglected to mention. You will find a special place in Heaven.

INTRODUCTION

In the fall of 1972 a small group of students in an introduction to educational psychology class at a midwestern university saved every single soul in the lifeboat.

The professor became agitated. "No! Go back and do the exercise again. Follow the instructions."

The students, products of the radical 1960s culture, expected this to be a small group assignment in creativity and ingenuity. They had worked out an intricate plan whereby everyone in the lifeboat could survive. When the professor persisted, the students resisted—and ultimately refused to do the exercise. Chalk up a victory to the human spirit.

However, it was a short-lived victory. This overloaded "lifeboat in crisis" represented a dramatic shift in education. The exercise—in which students were compelled to choose which humans were expendable and, therefore, should be cast off into the water—became a mainstay in classrooms across the country. Creative solutions? Not allowed. Instructions? Strictly adhered to. In truth, there is to be only one correct answer to the lifeboat drama: death.

The narrowing (dumbing down) of intellectual freedom had begun. Lifeboat exercises epitomize the shift in education from academic education (1880–1960) to values education (1960–1980). In *the deliberate dumbing down of america* writer Charlotte Iserbyt chronicles this shift and the later shift to workforce training "education" (1980–2000). The case is made that the values education period was critical to the transformation of education. It succeeded in persuading (brainwashing? duping?) Americans into accepting the belief that values were transient, flexible and situational—subject to the evolution of human society. Brave new values were integrated into curricula and instruction. The mind of the average American became "trained" (conditioned) to accept the idea that education exists solely for the purpose of getting a good paying job in the global workforce economy.

"Human capital," a term coined by reformers to describe our children, implies that humans are expendable. This explains why the lifeboat exercise has been used so rampantly, and why it was so critical to the education reformers' plans. Is it any wonder, then, that we witnessed the horror of the Littleton, Colorado shootings, and that other violence in schools across the country is increasing? Death education in the classroom may be linked to deaths in the classroom. The dumbing down of a nation inevitably leads to the death of a culture.

The premise of Charlotte Iserbyt's chronological history of the "deliberate dumbing down" of America is borne out by the author's extensive documentation, gathered from the education community's own sources. Iserbyt isolates the public policy end of education and sticks with it from decade to decade, steadfastly documenting the controversial methodology that has been institutionalized into legislation, public documents and other important papers setting forth public agenda. By choosing to focus on public policy in the context of academic theory, Iserbyt fills an important void in anti-reform literature. Her most important contribution is demonstrating how theory influenced public policy, public policy influenced theory, and how this ultimately affected practice—how policy and theory played out in the classroom.

Iserbyt skillfully demonstrates the interconnections between the international, national, regional, state and local plans for the transformation of American society via education. Iserbyt connects the evolution of education in the twentieth century to major significant geopolitical, social and economic events which have influenced education policy. This attention to detail adds important context to the events chronicled in the book, a dimension not found in other books critiquing education reform.

For too many years the late Harvard psychologist B.F. Skinner has been virtually ignored by conservative leaders, who focused their criticism exclusively on pervasive cultural influences of the humanistic psychologists (Rogers, Maslow, et al.). Skinner was written off as a utopian psychologist who represented no threat. Iserbyt's premise, proven well, is that B.F. Skinner is comfortably alive and well—embedded within modern education methods. Direct Instruction, Mastery Learning and Outcome-Based Education are irrefutably the current incarnation of Skinner's 1960s Programmed Instruction—a method of instruction which linked children to the computer and turned learning into a flow chart of managed behaviors.

Interwoven throughout the book is the important theme of operant conditioning in education. Surprisingly, Iserbyt never debates the effectiveness of the method. Entry after entry in the book substantiates Iserbyt's premise that the method is purposefully used to create a robotic child—one who cannot make connections, repeat an act, nor recall a fact unless provided with the necessary stimuli and environment (like a dog who learns to sit after the immediate receipt of a dog biscuit). Iserbyt reaches the inescapable conclusion that the method perfectly complements the reformers' agenda for a dumbed-down global workforce.

Iserbyt so effectively nails down her case that the debate noticeably shifts to the ethics of implementing such a method on children. The late Christian apologist and theologian, Dr. Francis Schaeffer, when discussing the evils of B.F. Skinner in his little booklet *Back to Freedom and Dignity* (1972), warned: "Within the Skinnerian system there are no ethical controls; there is no boundary limit to what can be done by the elite in whose hands control resides." There is intriguing evidence in Iserbyt's book that the "democratic" society of the near future will be managed via systematized operant conditioning—a startling proposition with ramifications which reach far beyond the scope of simple education reform.

Inevitably, questions and controversy will arise after publication of this book. How many popular computer games, programs, and curricula for children are heavily dependent upon this method—a method which requires immediate rewards? To what extent have home school and Christian school leaders, authors, and curriculum companies endorsed and utilized this method? How many child rearing (training) programs, workbooks and seminars are based upon these Skinnerian methods? After reading this book parents will no longer be duped into accepting behaviorist methods—in whatever guise, or by whatever name they come.

Publication of *the deliberate dumbing down of america* is certain to add fuel to the fire in this nation's phonics wars. Ever since publication of her first work (*Back to Basics Reform or OBE Skinnerian International Curriculum*, 1985), Iserbyt has been trumpeting the fact that the Skinnerian method applied in the Exemplary Center for Reading Instruction (ECRI) is the very same method applied in Siegfried Engelmann's DISTAR (Direct Instruction System for Teaching and Remediation, now known as Reading Mastery). In her latest work, Iserbyt provides exhaustive documentation that Direct Instruction (a.k.a. systematic, intensive phonics)—which is being institutionalized nationally under the guise of "traditional" phonics thanks to the passage of *The Reading Excellence Act of 1998*—relies on the Skinnerian method to teach reading.

Charlotte Iserbyt is the consummate whistle-blower. The writer describes her own personal experiences as a school board director and as senior policy advisor in the U.S. Department of Education's Office of Educational Research and Improvement—from which emanated most of the dumbing down programs described in this book. There are no sacred cows in Iserbyt's reporting of the chronological history of education reform. With little fanfare, the agendas and methods of key reform leaders (conservative and liberal) are allowed to unmask themselves in their own words and by their own actions. Of particular interest is Iserbyt's material on the issue of school "choice"—abundant evidence from both sides of the political spectrum. The reader will learn that private, Christian and home schools are all neatly tied into the reform web via computer technology, databanking, assessment testing and, ultimately, the intention to use rewards and penalties to enforce compliance to the "transformed" system of education in this country.

The careful researcher will appreciate the fact that the book is heavily documented but user-friendly. Citations are designed for the average reader, not just the academician. The chronological format of the book allows one to read forward or backward in time, or one entry at a time, according to personal preference. The accompanying appendices provide a source of in-depth topical material, which frees up the chronological text from becoming bogged down in details. The index and glossary are such valuable research tools that they are worth the price of the book.

Iserbyt does very little hand-holding throughout the book. Commentary is sparse; readers can make their own connections and insert their own personal experiences. Iserbyt has strategically laid down key pieces to a giant jigsaw puzzle. The overall picture is purposefully arranged to portray one point of view. However, readers will be hard-pressed to come up with an alternative view. Just when it seems that one piece of the puzzle is an isolated, insignificant event, suddenly one comes across a stunning new entry that puts the pieces tightly together to form a vivid picture of the overall plan. Try as one might, the reader cannot escape the consistent, deliberate, 100-year plan to dumb down the populace.

Amidst all of the policy documents and historical data in the book, one can easily identify the heart of the writer. Iserbyt gently reminds the reader that the real issue at hand is the child. It is America's children who are experiencing the full brunt of the new methods, new curricula and new agendas in the classroom. Many readers will experience the "light bulb" turning on as they fully come to understand how the innovations which have occurred in education during the last century affected their parents, themselves, their children and grand-children.

Teachers may find the contents of this book particularly enlightening and refreshing. Iserbyt takes the reader behind the scenes to reveal the true nature of many popular classroom curricula. The truth will be comforting to those who have utilized certain programs or methods, and perhaps were troubled by them, but didn't know the full scope or plan behind them. Iserbyt does not ignore or soft-peddle the ethical issues, but encourages the reader to take the high moral ground.

The other day a caller phoned into Rush Limbaugh's daily radio talk show. The caller's wife earns $25,000 per year as a teacher. She has 30 students. Her school district receives $9,000 per year per student. This totals $270,000 per year. "Why isn't my wife being paid more?" he asked. The caller—and people like him—should be referred to *the deliberate dumbing down of america*. In this book they will find the scandalous answer. It has something to do with why we have a generation of—as Limbaugh describes it—"young skulls full of mush."

SARAH LESLIE

the
deliberate
dumbing
down
of america

1

THE SOWING OF THE SEEDS:
late eighteenth and nineteenth centuries

"The Sowing of the Seeds: late eighteenth and nineteenth centuries" is the shortest chapter of *the deliberate dumbing down of america*. Undoubtedly, this chapter may be one of the most important since the philosophies of Jean-Jacques Rousseau, Wilhelm Wundt, and John Dewey et al., reflect a total departure from the traditional definition of education like the one given in *The New Century Dictionary of the English Language* (Appleton, Century, Crofts: New York, 1927):

> The drawing out of a person's innate talents and abilities by imparting the knowledge of languages, scientific reasoning, history, literature, rhetoric, etc.—the channels through which those abilities would flourish and serve.[1]

A quantum leap was taken from the above definition to the new, dehumanizing definition used by the experimental psychologists found in *An Outline of Educational Psychology* (Barnes & Noble: New York, 1934, rev. ed.) by Rudolph Pintner et al. That truly revolutionary definition claims that

> learning is the result of modifiability in the paths of neural conduction. Explanations of even such forms of learning as abstraction and generalization demand of the neurones only growth, excitability, conductivity, and modifiability. The mind is the connection-system of man; and learning is the process of connecting. The situation-response formula is adequate to cover learning of any sort, and the really influential factors in learning are readiness of the neurones, sequence in time, belongingness, and satisfying consequences.[2]

An in-depth understanding of the deplorable situation found in our nation's schools today is impossible without an understanding of the redefinition in the above statements. Education in the twenty-first century will, for the majority of youth, be workforce training. Thus, the need for Pavlovian/Skinnerian methodology based on operant conditioning which, in essence, is at the heart of the above dehumanizing definition of education. This "sowing of the seeds" through redefinition will reap the death of traditional, liberal arts education through the advent of mastery learning, outcome-based education, and direct instruction—all of which will be performance-based and behaviorist.

1762

EMILE BY JEAN-JACQUES ROUSSEAU (CHEZ JEAN NEAULME DUCHESNE: A. AMSTERDAM [Paris], 1762) was published. Rousseau's "Social Contract" presented in *Emile* influenced the French Revolution. In this book Rousseau promoted child-centered "permissive education" in which a teacher "should avoid strict discipline and tiresome lessons." Both Rousseau (1712–1788) and Swiss educator Johann Heinrich Pestalozzi (1746–1827) believed that the "whole child" should be educated by "doing," and that religion should not be a guiding principle in education, a theme we shall see repeated over the next 238 years.

1832

WILHELM WUNDT, FOUNDER OF EXPERIMENTAL PSYCHOLOGY AND THE FORCE BEHIND ITS dissemination throughout the Western world, was born in 1832 in Neckarau, southern Germany. The following excerpts concerning Wundt's contribution to modern education are taken from *The Leipzig Connection: The Systematic Destruction of American Education* by Paolo Lionni and Lance J. Klass[3] (Heron Books: Portland, Ore., 1980):

> To Wundt, a thing made sense and was worth pursuing if it could be measured, quantified, and scientifically demonstrated. Seeing no way to do this with the human soul, he proposed that psychology concern itself solely with experience. As Wundt put it... Karl Marx injected Hegel's theories with economics and sociology, developing a "philosophy of dialectical materialism."... (p. 8)
>
> From Wundt's work it was only a short step to the later redefinition of education. Originally, education meant drawing out of a person's innate talents and abilities by imparting the knowledge of languages, scientific reasoning, history, literature, rhetoric, etc.—the channels through which those abilities would flourish and serve. To the experimental psychologist, however, education became the process of exposing the student to "meaningful" experiences so as to ensure desired reactions:
>
> > [L]earning is the result of modifiability in the paths of neural conduction. Explanations of even such forms of learning as abstraction and generalization demand of the neurones only growth, excitability, conductivity, and modifiability. The mind is the connection-system of man; and learning is the process of connecting. The situation-response formula is adequate to cover learning of any sort, and the really influential factors in learning are readiness of the neurones, sequence in time, belongingness, and satisfying consequences.[4]

If one assumes (as did Wundt) that there is nothing there to begin with but a body, a brain, a nervous system, then one must try to educate by inducing sensations in that nervous system. Through these experiences, the individual will learn to respond to any given stimulus, with the "correct" response. The child is not, for example, thought capable of volitional control over his actions, or of deciding whether he will act or not act in a certain way; his actions are thought to be preconditioned and beyond his control, he is a stimulus-response mechanism. According to this thinking, he is his reactions. Wundt's thesis laid the philosophical basis for the principles of conditioning later developed by Pavlov (who studied physiology in Leipzig in 1884, five years after Wundt had inaugurated his laboratory there) and American behavioral psychologists such as Watson and Skinner; for laboratories and electroconvulsive therapy; for schools oriented more toward socialization of the child than toward the development of intellect; and for the emergence of a society more and more blatantly devoted to the gratification of sensory desire at the expense of responsibility and achievement. (pp. 14–15)

[Ed. Note: The reader should purchase *The Leipzig Connection: The Systematic Destruction of American Education*, a slim paperback book which, in this writer's opinion, is the most useful and important book available regarding the method used to change children's behavior/values and to "dumb down" an entire society. The authors, Lionni and Klass, have made an outstanding contribution to the history of American education and to the understanding of why and how America, which up until the 1930s had the finest education system in the world, ended up with one of the worst education systems in the industrialized world in a short period of fifty years.

Another commentary on the importance of Wundt's theories comes from Dennis L. Cuddy, Ph.D., in an excellent article entitled "The Conditioning of America" (*The Christian News*, New Haven, Mo., December 11, 1989).[5] An excerpt follows:

The conditioning of modern American society began with John Dewey, a psychologist, a Fabian Socialist and the "Father of Progressive Education." Dewey used the psychology developed in Leipzig by Wilhelm Wundt, and believed that through a stimulus-response approach (like Pavlov) students could be conditioned for a new social order.]

1862

THE FIRST EXPERIMENT WITH "OUTCOME-BASED EDUCATION" (OBE) WAS CONDUCTED IN England in 1862. Teacher opposition resulted in abandonment of the experiment. Don Martin of University of Pittsburgh, George E. Overholt and Wayne J. Urban of Georgia State University wrote *Accountability in American Education: A Critique* (Princeton Book Company: Princeton, N.J., 1976) containing a section entitled "Payment for Results" which chronicles the English experiment. The following excerpt outlines the experiment:

The call for "sound and cheap" elementary instruction was answered by legislation, passed by Parliament during 1862, known as The Revised Code. This was the legislation that produced payment [for] results, the nineteenth century English accountability system.... The opposition to the English payment-[for]-results system which arose at the time of its introduction was particularly interesting. Teachers provided the bulk of the resistance, and they based their objections on both educational and economic grounds.... They abhorred the narrowness and mechanical character the system imposed on the educational process. They also objected to the economic burden forced upon them by basing their pay on student performance.

[Ed. Note: "Payment for Results" and Outcome-Based Education are based on teacher accountability and require teaching to the test, the results of which are to be "measured" for accountability purposes. Both methods of teaching result in a narrow, mechanistic system of education similar to Mastery Learning. Teachers in the United States in 1999, as were teachers involved in the experiment in England, will be judged and paid according to students' test scores; i.e., how well the teachers teach to the test. Proponents of Mastery Learning believe that almost all children can learn if given enough time, adequate resources geared to the individual learning style of the student, and a curriculum aligned to test items (teach to the test). Mastery Learning uses Skinnerian methodology (operant conditioning) in order to obtain "predictable" results. Benjamin Bloom, the father of Mastery Learning, says that "the purpose of education is to change the thoughts, actions and feelings of students." Mastery Learning (ML) and its fraternal twin Direct Instruction (DI) are key components of Outcome-Based Education (OBE) and Effective Schools Research (ESR). The reader is urged to study the definitions of all these terms, including the behaviorist term section found in the glosssary of this book prior to reading further. The one common thread running through this book relates to these terms and their importance in the implementation of workforce training and attitude and value change.]

1874

EDWARD LEE THORNDIKE WAS BORN AUGUST 31, 1874 IN WILLIAMSBURG, MASSACHUsetts. Thorndike was trained in the new psychology by the first generation of Wilhelm Wundt's protegés. He graduated from Wesleyan University in 1895 after having studied with Wundtians Andrew C. Armstrong and Charles Judd. He went to graduate school at Harvard and studied under psychologist William James. While at Harvard, Thorndike surprised James by doing research with chickens, testing their behavior, and pioneering what later became known as "animal psychology." As briefly stated by Thorndike himself, psychology was the "science of the intellect, character, and behavior of animals, including man."[6] To further excerpt *The Leipzig Connection*'s excellent treatment of Thorndike's background:

Thorndike applied for a fellowship at Columbia, was accepted by Cattell, and moved with his two most intelligent chickens to New York, where he continued his research and earned his Ph.D. in 1893. Thorndike's specialty was the "puzzle box," into which he would put various animals (chickens, rats, cats) and let them find their way out by themselves. His doctoral dissertation on cats has become part of the classical literature of psychology. After receiving his doctorate, he spent a year as a teacher at Western Reserve University, and it wasn't long before Cattell advised Dean [James Earl] Russell to visit Thorndike's first classroom at Western Reserve: "Although the Dean found him 'dealing with the investigations of mice and monkeys,' he came away satisfied that he was worth trying out on humans."

Russell offered Thorndike a job at Teachers College, where the experimenter remained for the next thirty years. Thorndike was the first psychologist to study animal behavior in an experimental psychology laboratory and (following Cattell's suggestion) apply the same techniques to children and youth; as one result, in 1903, he published the book *Educational Psychology*. In the following years he published a total of 507 books, monographs, and articles.

Thorndike's primary assumption was the same as Wundt's: that man is an animal, that his actions are actually always reactions, and that he can be studied in the laboratory in much the same way as an animal might be studied. Thorndike equated children with the rats, monkeys, fish, cats, and chickens upon which he experimented in his laboratory and was prepared to apply what he found there to learning in the classroom. He extrapolated "laws" from his research into animal behavior which he then applied to the training of teachers, who took what they had learned to every corner of the United States and ran their classrooms, curricula, and schools, on the basis of this new "educational" psychology.

In *The Principles of Teaching Based on Psychology* (1906), Thorndike proposed making "the study of teaching scientific and practical." Thorndike's definition of the art of teaching is

> the art of giving and withholding stimuli with the result of producing or preventing certain responses. In this definition the term stimulus is used widely for any event which influences a person—for a word spoken to him, a look, a sentence which he reads, the air he breathes, etc., etc. The term response is used for any reaction made by him—a new thought, a feeling of interest, a bodily act, any mental or bodily condition resulting from the stimulus. The aim of the teacher is to produce desirable and prevent undesirable changes in human beings by producing and preventing certain responses. The means at the disposal of the teacher are the stimuli which can be brought to bear upon the pupil—the teacher's words, gestures, and appearance, the condition and appliances of the school room, the books to be used and objects to be seen, and so on through a long list of the things and events which the teacher can control.

1896

PSYCHOLOGY BY JOHN DEWEY, THE FATHER OF "PROGRESSIVE EDUCATION," WAS PUBLISHED (University of Chicago Press: Chicago, 1896). This was the first American textbook on the "revised" subject of education. *Psychology* would become the most widely-read and quoted textbook used in schools of education in this country. Just prior to the publication of his landmark book, Dewey had joined the faculty of the Rockefeller-endowed University of Chicago as head of the combined departments of philosophy, psychology and pedagogy (teaching). In that same year, 1895, the university allocated $1,000 to establish a laboratory in which Dewey could apply psychological principles and experimental techniques to the study of learning. The laboratory opened in January 1896 as the Dewey School, later to become known as The University of Chicago Laboratory School.[7] Dewey thought of the school as a place

> where his theories of education could be put into practice, tested, and scientifically evaluated....
>
> ...Dewey... sought to apply the doctrines of experience and experiment to everyday life and, hence, to education... seeking via this model institution to pave the way for the "schools of the future." There he had put into actual practice three of the revolutionary beliefs he had culled from the new psychology: that to put the child in possession of his fullest talents,

education should be active rather than passive; that to prepare the child for a democratic society, the school should be social rather than individualist; and that to enable the child to think creatively, experimentation rather than imitation should be encouraged.[8]

Samuel Blumenfeld in his book, *The Whole Language/OBE Fraud* (Paradigm Co.: Boise, Idaho, 1996), further explains Dewey's perspective:

What kind of curriculum would fit the school that was a mini-cooperative society? Dewey's recommendation was indeed radical: build the curriculum not around academic subjects but around occupational activities which provided maximum opportunities for peer interaction and socialization. Since the beginning of Western civilization, the school curriculum was centered around the development of academic skills, the intellectual faculties, and high literacy. Dewey wanted to change all of that. Why? Because high literacy produced that abominable form of independent intelligence which was basically, as Dewey believed, anti-social.

Thus, from Dewey's point of view, the school's primary commitment to literacy was indeed the key to the whole problem. In 1898, Dewey wrote an essay, "The Primary-Education Fetish," in which he explained exactly what he meant:

There is... a false education god whose idolators are legion, and whose cult influences the entire educational system. This is language study—the study not of foreign language, but of English; not in higher, but in primary education. It is almost an unquestioned assumption, of educational theory and practice both, that the first three years of a child's school life shall be mainly taken up with learning to read and write his own language. If we add to this the learning of a certain amount of numerical combinations, we have the pivot about which primary education swings.... It does not follow, however, that conditions—social, industrial and intellectual—have undergone such a radical change, that the time has come for a thoroughgoing examination of the emphasis put upon linguistic work in elementary instruction.... The plea for the predominance of learning to read in early school life because of the great importance attaching to literature seems to me a perversion.

Endnotes:

1 Paolo Lionni and Lance J. Klass. *The Leipzig Connection: The Systematic Destruction of American Education* (Heron Books: Portland, Ore., 1980).
2 Ibid.
3 *The Leipzig Connection* may be obtained by sending a check for $11.45 to: Heron Books, P.O. Box 503, Sheridan, OR, or by calling 1–503–843–3834.
4 Rudolph Pintner et al. *An Outline of Educational Psychology, Revised* (Barnes & Noble: New York, 1934), p. 79.
5 Dr. Cuddy's important publications on the history of American education, from which this writer has frequently quoted, can be obtained by writing: Florida ProFamily Forum, Inc., P.O. Box 1059, Highland City, FL 33846–1059; or by calling 1–914–644–6218. Cuddy's newly revised edition of *Chronology of Education with Quotable Quotes* and *Secret Records Revealed: The Men, the Money and the Methods Behind the New World Order* should be in the library of every serious education researcher.
6 *The Leipzig Connection*, pp. 36–39.
7 Ibid.
8 These quotes taken from Ida B. DePencier's book, *The History of the Laboratory Schools: The University of Chicago, 1896–1965* (Quadrangle Books: Chicago, 1967) and *A History of Teachers College: Columbia University* by Lawrence A. Cremin, David A. Shannon, and Mary Evelyn Townsend (Columbia University Press: New York, 1934), as cited in *The Leipzig Connection*.

2

THE TURNING OF THE TIDES*:
early twentieth century

For a nation that had been able to point with pride to extraordinary advances in all areas of endeavor carried out by *individuals*, with no assistance whatsoever from the government, the early years of the twentieth century surely reflected a "Turning of the Tides." An alien collectivist (socialist) philosophy, much of which came from Europe, crashed onto the shores of our nation, bringing with it radical changes in economics, politics, and education, funded—surprisingly enough—by several wealthy American families and their tax-exempt foundations.

The goal of these wealthy families and their foundations—a seamless non-competitive global system for commerce and trade—when stripped of flowery expressions of concern for minorities, the less fortunate, etc., represented the initial stage of what this author now refers to as *the deliberate dumbing down of america*.

Seventy years later, the carefully laid plans to change America from a sovereign, constitutional republic with a free enterprise economic base to just one of many nations in an international socialist (collectivist) system (New World Order) are apparent. Only a dumbed down population, with no memory of America's roots as a prideful nation, could be expected to willingly succumb to the global workforce training planned by the Carnegie Corporation and the John D. Rockefellers, I and II, in the early twentieth century which is being implemented by the United States Congress in the year 1999.

---

* "The Turning of the Tides" is the title of a report submitted to Congress by Hon. Paul W. Shafer (Mich.) and John Howland Snow. The original text was delivered in the House of Representatives on March 21, 1952.

1902

THE GENERAL EDUCATION BOARD (GEB) WAS INCORPORATED BY AN ACT OF THE UNITED
States Congress. Approved January 12, 1902, the General Education Board was endowed by
Mr. John D. Rockefeller, Sr., for the purpose of establishing an educational laboratory to
experiment with early innovations in education.

1905

IN 1905 THE INTERCOLLEGIATE SOCIALIST SOCIETY (ISS) WAS FOUNDED IN NEW YORK CITY
by Upton Sinclair, Jack London, Clarence Darrow and others. Its permanent headquarters
were established at the Rand School of Social Studies in 1908 and ISS became the League for
Industrial Democracy (LID) in 1921. John Dewey became president of the League for Industrial Democracy in 1939.

THE CARNEGIE FOUNDATION FOR THE ADVANCEMENT OF TEACHING WAS FOUNDED IN 1905.
Henry S. Pritchett served as the Foundation's first president. Pritchett was the author of *What
Is Religion and Other Student Questions* (Houghton Mifflin Company: Boston, 1906), *Relations
of Denominations to Colleges* (1908), and *A Woman's Opportunities in Christian Industry and
Business* (1907).

1906

NATIONAL EDUCATION ASSOCIATION (NEA) BECAME A FEDERALLY CHARTERED ASSOCIATION
for teachers in 1906 under the authority of H.R. 10501. Originally founded in 1857, it was
known as the National Teachers Association until 1870.

1908

IN 1908 ITALIAN EDUCATOR, THE LATE MARIA MONTESSORI (1870–1952), DEVELOPED A
method of teaching—relying on guidance and training of senses rather than more rigid control
of children's activities—which would be very influential throughout the rest of the century.
Montessori was a doctor who, after graduating from medical school in Rome, took a position
at a psychiatric clinic and became interested in helping retarded children. Her pedagogical
mentor became Edouard Seguin, a French physician who worked with retarded children and
who promoted the idea that having the children work with concrete objects helped their
physical and mental development.

Montessori opened her first Casa dei Bambini (Montessori school) in Rome in 1907. She
created a classroom climate in which her belief that a child's "individual liberty" would be

violated "if two children want the same material" and are not "left to settle the problem for themselves" or by forcibly removing a misbehaving child from a group. Montessori, much like Rudolph Steiner of Germany, taught that each child is already a perfectly developed adult human being and that through her educational process "the incarnating child" can find his own place in the cosmos. It should be noted that at one time Benito Mussolini was president of the Montessori Society of Italy.

The Montessori Method was published in 1912 and much of Montessori's work was printed by the Theosophical Publishing House. Montessori once lived with the Theosophists in India and earned the praise of Mahatma Gandhi with her "Cosmic Education" which was popular with Hindus and Theosophists worldwide. Elizabeth Clare Prophet, the cultic head of the Church Universal and Triumphant, founded a group called Montessori International, and Robert Muller, the celebrated author of the New Age *World Core Curriculum*, in a Costa Rica speech claimed that the Montessori Method was one of the educational programs which would greatly benefit global children for the New Age.

In her *Education for a New World* Montessori wrote that "The world was not created for us to enjoy, but we are created to evolve the cosmos." In an issue of the *North American Montessori Teachers Association Journal* one finds the following revealing comment:

> Maria Montessori, along with many other enlightened thinkers of our time, foresaw nothing less than the emergence of a new human culture. This new culture, a global, planetized humanity, would be based on a new consciousness of the unity and interdependence of all being, the interconnectedness of all forms of energy and matter. It is a culture of the present paradigm shift, by which we are beginning to align ourselves to educate the human potential for conscious cooperation with the evolution of life on the planet.[1]

1913

JOHN D. ROCKEFELLER, JR.'S DIRECTOR OF CHARITY FOR THE ROCKEFELLER FOUNDATION, Frederick T. Gates, set up the Southern Education Board (SEB), which was later incorporated into the General Education Board (GEB) in 1913, setting in motion "the deliberate dumbing down of America." *The Country School of Tomorrow: Occasional Papers No. 1* (General Education Board: New York, 1913) written by Frederick T. Gates contained a section entitled "A Vision of the Remedy" in which he wrote the following:

> Is there aught of remedy for this neglect of rural life? Let us, at least, yield ourselves to the gratifications of a beautiful dream that there is. In our dream, we have limitless resources, and the people yield themselves with perfect docility to our molding hand. The present educational conventions fade from our minds; and, unhampered by tradition, we work our own good will upon a grateful and responsive rural folk. We shall not try to make these people or any of their children into philosophers or men of learning or of science. We are not to raise up from among them authors, orators, poets, or men of letters. We shall not search for embryo great artists, painters, musicians. Nor will we cherish even the humbler ambition to raise up from among them lawyers, doctors, preachers, politicians, statesmen, of whom we now have ample supply.

1914

A RESOLUTION WAS PASSED BY THE NORMAL SCHOOL SECTION OF THE NATIONAL EDUCATION ASSO-ciation at its annual meeting in St. Paul, Minnesota in the year 1914. An excerpt follows:

> We view with alarm the activity of the Carnegie and Rockefeller Foundations—agencies not in any way responsible to the people—in their efforts to control the policies of our State educational institutions, to fashion after their conception and to standardize our courses of study, and to surround the institutions with conditions which menace true academic free-dom and defeat the primary purpose of democracy as heretofore preserved inviolate in our common schools, normal schools, and universities.

1917

THE 1917 *CONGRESSIONAL RECORD OF THE UNITED STATES SENATE* PUBLISHED THE FOL-lowing excerpt from a booklet containing articles by Bishop Warren A. Candler, Chancellor of Emory University in Atlanta:

> This board [the General Education Board] was authorized to do almost every conceivable thing which is anywise related to education, from opening a kitchen to establishing a univer-sity, and its power to connect itself with the work of every sort of educational plant or enterprise conceivable will be especially observed. This power to project its influence over other corporations is at once the greatest and most dangerous power it has. (p. 2831)

THE UNITED STATES ENTERED WORLD WAR I IN 1917.

1918

IN THE JANUARY 13, 1918 ISSUE OF *NEW YORK WORLD* WILLIAM BOYCE THOMPSON, FED-eral Reserve Bank director and founding member of the Council on Foreign Relations, stated that

> Russia is pointing the way to great and sweeping world changes. It is not in Russia alone that the old order is passing. There is a lot of the old order in America, and that is going, too.... I'm glad it is so. When I sat and watched those democratic conclaves in Russia, I felt I would welcome a similar scene in the United States.

[Ed. Note: M. Maxine Tremaine of Massachusetts, recognized for her careful research related to international affairs, made the following statements regarding Willian Boyce Thompson before the National Convention of Women for Constitutional Government in a July 1983 speech entitled "Russia Is the Model Country of International Bankers and Industrialists Ad-ministered by the United Nations Headquarters in Geneva, Switzerland": "William Boyce Thompson personally contributed $1 million to the Russian Revolution. He also arranged for the transfer of money from the United States to (the Communist revolutionaries)."]

CARNEGIE AND ROCKEFELLER FOUNDATIONS PLANNED THE DEMISE OF TRADITIONAL ACADEMIC education in 1918. Rockefeller's focus would be national education; Carnegie would be in charge of international education.

1919

THE INSTITUTE OF INTERNATIONAL EDUCATION (IIE) WAS FOUNDED IN 1919 THROUGH A grant from the Carnegie Endowment for International Peace. The Institute's purpose was to operate a student exchange program. This process of "exchanges" grew in concept and practice with the IIE administering visitor exchange programs for the U.S. Information Agency (USIA) in the 1990s. The U.S.-Soviet Education Agreements were negotiated by the Carnegie Endowment's parent organization, the Carnegie Corporation, fostering exchanges of curriculum, pedagogy and materials as well as students.

THE PROGRESSIVE EDUCATION ASSOCIATION (P.E.A.) WAS FOUNDED IN 1919 AND ORGAnized by John Dewey, even though he would not become a member in its early years. P.E.A.'s goals and aims were projected for the last half of this century at a board meeting held November 15–17, 1943 in Chicago, Illinois. Attendees included: Harold Rugg, Marion Carswell, Arthur Gould, Theodore Brameld, Prudence Bosterick, and Carson Ryan. Speaking of their plans for the period following World War II, the board published a statement in its journal *Progressive Education* (December 1943, Vol. XX, No. 8) which included the following excerpt:

> This is a global war, and the peace now in the making will determine what our national life will be for the next century. It will demonstrate the degree of our national morality. We are writing now the credo by which our children must live....
>
> Your Board unanimously proposes a broadening of the interests and program of this Association to include the communities in which our children live. To this end, they propose additions to the governing body to include representatives of welfare services, health, industry, labor and the professions. In short, a cross-section body to give scope to our program....
>
> Yes, something happened around a table in Chicago. An organization which might have become mellowed with the years to futility, in three short days again drew a blueprint for children of the world.

[Ed. Note: For what "our national life will be for the rest of this century" and perhaps on into the next, see the 1946 *Mongomery County Blueprint* and 1999 *Gwinnett Daily* entries.]

1921

IN 1921 THE LEAGUE FOR INDUSTRIAL DEMOCRACY CHANGED ITS NAME FROM THE INTERCOLlegiate Socialist Society (ISS) and stated its purpose as: "Education for a new social order based on production and not for profit" ("A Chronology of Education," Dorothy Dawson, 1978).

HAROLD RUGG, WRITER OF SOCIAL STUDIES TEXTBOOK SERIES ENTITLED *THE FRONTIER Thinkers* which was published by the Progressive Education Association, in 1921 became president of the National Association of Directors of Education Research which would later become known as the American Educational Research Association.

THE COUNCIL ON FOREIGN RELATIONS WAS ESTABLISHED IN 1921 THROUGH THE EFFORTS OF Col. Edwin Mandell House, *confidant extraordinaire* to President Woodrow Wilson and about whom Wilson said, "Mr. House is my second personality... His thoughts and mine are one." House was the initiator of the effort to establish this American branch of the English Royal Institute of International Affairs. Prior to 1921, House's group, "the Inquiry," called the CFR the "Institute of International Affairs." In 1912 House had authored *Philip Dru: Administrator* which promoted "socialism as dreamed of by Karl Marx" about which book Wilson's Secretary of the Interior Franklin Lane wrote to a personal friend: "All that book has said should be, comes about. The President comes to Philip Dru in the end."

Walter Lippmann, member of the Fabian Society and Intercollegiate Socialist Society, was a founding member of the CFR. Whitney Shepardson was a director of the CFR from 1921 until 1966. Shepardson had been an assistant to Col. House in the 1918 peace conference following World War I and served as secretary of the League of Nations committee. Shepardson later became a director of the Carnegie Corporation British and Colonies fund. Other early CFR members included: Charles E. (Chip) Bohlen, first secretary to the American embassy in Moscow during World War II and President Franklin Roosevelt's interpreter for his meeting with Josef Stalin at the Teheran conference; Frank Aydelotte, a trustee of the Carnegie Foundation, president of Swarthmore College, American secretary to the (Cecil) Rhodes Trustees (of the Rhodes Scholarship Fund), and director of the Institute for Advanced Study at Princeton; Secretary of War Henry Stimson, who initiated George Bush into "Skull and Bones" and whose special consultant Bernadotte Schmitt had also been a special advisor to Alger Hiss when he had served as secretary-general of the United Nations Conference on International Organization in San Francisco in 1945; and William Paley, founder of the Columbia Broadcasting System (CBS) whose chief advisor was Edward Bernays, Sigmund Freud's nephew who wrote *Propaganda,* in which Bernays reveals:

> Those who manipulate the organized habits and opinions of the masses constitute an invisible government which is the true ruling power of the country.... It remains a fact in almost every act of our daily lives, whether in the sphere of politics or business, in our social conduct or our ethical thinking, we are dominated by this relatively small number of persons.... As civilization has become more complex, and as the need for invisible government has been increasingly demonstrated, the technical means have been invented and developed by which opinion may be regimented.

The late Professor Carroll Quigley of Georgetown University described the CFR as "a front for J.P Morgan and Company in association with the very small American Round Table Group." Quigley further commented:

> The board of the CFR have carried ever since the marks of their origin.... There grew up in the 20th century a power structure between London and New York which penetrated deeply into university life, the press, and the practice of foreign policy.... The American branch of

this "English Establishment" exerted much of its influence through five American newspapers (*New York Times*, *New York Herald Tribune*, *Christian Science Monitor*, *Washington Post*, and the late lamented *Boston Evening Transcript*).[2]

Arthur Schlesinger, Jr., penned a tome entitled *A Thousand Days* in 1965 in which he wrote that

> the New York financial and legal community was the heart of the American establishment.... Its front organizations [were] the Rockefeller, Ford and Carnegie foundations and the Council on Foreign Relations.

1922

ON DECEMBER 15, 1922 THE COUNCIL ON FOREIGN RELATIONS endorsed world government.

1925

THE INTERNATIONAL BUREAU OF EDUCATION, FORMERLY KNOWN AS THE INSTITUTE JEAN-Jacques Rousseau, was established in 1925 with a grant from the Rockefeller Foundation. The Bureau became part of the United Nations Educational, Scientific and Cultural Organization (UNESCO).

IN 1925 *TENNESSEE VS. JOHN THOMAS SCOPES*, OR THE SCOPES "MONKEY TRIAL," TOOK place in Dayton, Tennessee. This trial was an important educational milestone regarding the teaching of the theory of evolution in public schools. *Scopes* pitted two famous barristers of the day—William Jennings Bryan and Clarence Darrow—against each other. The basic argument of the American Civil Liberties Union (ACLU) and the evolutionists' was that evolutionary theory should not be censored from the public schools. After this trial, Fabian Socialist and first head of UNESCO Sir Julian Huxley claimed that humanism's "keynote, the central concept to which all its details are related, is evolution."

[Ed. Note: Huxley could have continued by predicting that educational and training methods in the future would be based on the theory of evolution—that man is an animal to be trained as Pavlov, Thorndike and Skinner trained animals, as with outcome-based education, mastery learning and direct instruction.]

1927

THE *CHRISTIAN SCIENCE MONITOR* OF AUGUST 8, 1927 QUOTED FROM AN ADDRESS TO THE World Federation of Education Associations (WFEA) at their Toronto, Canada conference delivered by Dr. Augustus Thomas, commissioner of education for the state of Maine. Excerpts from Dr. Thomas's revealing address follow:

> If there are those who think we are to jump immediately into a new world order, actuated by complete understanding and brotherly love, they are doomed to disappointment. If we are ever to approach that time, it will be after patient and persistent effort of long duration. The present international situation of mistrust and fear can only be corrected by a formula of equal status, continuously applied, to every phase of international contacts, until the cobwebs of the old order are brushed out of the minds of the people of all lands. This means that the world must await a long process of education and a building up of public conscience and an international morality, or, in other words, until there is a world-wide sentiment which will back up the modern conception of a world community. This brings us to the international mind, which is nothing more or less than the habit of thinking of foreign relations and business affecting the several countries of the civilized world as free co-operating equals.

1928

A DELIBERATE MATH "DUMB DOWN" WAS SERIOUSLY DISCUSSED IN 1928. A TEACHER NAMED O.A. Nelson, John Dewey, Edward Thorndike (who conducted early behavioral psychology experiments with chickens), and other Council on Foreign Relations members attended a Progressive Education Association meeting in 1928 at which O.A. Nelson was informed that the purpose of "new math" was to dumb down students. Nelson revealed in a later interview with Young Parents Alert that the Progressive Education Association was a communist front. According to the *National Educator* (July, 1979):

> Mr. O.A. Nelson, retired educator, has supplied the vitally important documentation needed to support the link-up between the textbooks and the Council on Foreign Relations. His letter was first printed in "Young Parents Alert" (Lake Elmo, Minnesota). His story is self-explanatory.

> I know from personal experience what I am talking about. In December 1928, I was asked to talk to the American Association for the Advancement of Science. On December 27th, naïve and inexperienced, I agreed. I had done some special work in teaching functional physics in high school. That was to be my topic. The next day, the 28th, a Dr. Ziegler asked me if I would attend a special educational meeting in his room after the AAAS meeting. We met from 10 o'clock [p.m.] until after 2:30 a.m.
>
> We were 13 at the meeting. Two things caused Dr. Ziegler, who was Chairman of the Educational Committee of the Council on Foreign Relations, to ask me to attend... my talk on the teaching of functional physics in high school, and the fact that I was a member of a group known as the Progressive Educators of America, which was nothing but a Communist front. I thought the word "progressive" meant progress for better schools. Eleven of those attending the meeting were leaders in education. Drs. John Dewey and Edward Thorndike, from Columbia University, were there, and the others were of equal rank. I checked later and found that ALL were paid members of the Communist Party of Russia. I was classified as a member of the Party, but I did not know it at the time.
>
> The sole work of the group was to destroy our schools! We spent one hour and forty-five minutes discussing the so-called "Modern Math." At one point I objected because there was too much memory work, and math is reasoning; not memory. Dr. Ziegler turned to me and said, "Nelson, wake up! That is what we want... a math that the pupils

cannot apply to life situations when they get out of school!" That math was not introduced until much later, as those present thought it was too radical a change. A milder course by Dr. Breckner was substituted but it was also worthless, as far as understanding math was concerned. The radical change was introduced in 1952. It was the one we are using now. So, if pupils come out of high school now, not knowing any math, don't blame them. The results are supposed to be worthless.

[Ed. Note: Mr. Nelson was formerly assistant principal at Wilson High School, Minneapolis, Minnesota, as well as Johnson High School in St. Paul. This writer was fortunate enough to verify the above story by calling a teacher colleague of the late Mr. Nelson. Also, members of the "Young Parents Alert" in Lake Elmo, Minnesota provided the writer with an audiocasette of the speech he gave at a Young Parents Alert education conference on April 28, 1979.]

Endnotes:

1 The referenced *North American Association for Montessori Teachers Association Journal* is published by the North American Association for Montessori Teachers Association (Cleveland Heights, Ohio, 1988, 4th quarter).
2 Much of the information in the entry concerning the formation of the Council on Foreign Relations, including Prof. Quigley's quote, is taken from the recently updated edition of Dr. Dennis Laurence Cuddy's *Secret Records Revealed: The Men, the Money, and the Methods Behind the New World Order* (Hearthstone Publishing, Ltd.: Oklahoma City, 1999).

3

THE TROUBLING THIRTIES

"And the builder of this new world must be education.... Plainly, the first step in the case of each country is to train an elite to think, feel, and act internationally." The preceding words of Paul Mantoux of Paris, France are taken from the foreword to *International Understanding* by John Eugene Harley, published by the Stanford University Press in 1931.

A flock of individuals of collectivist persuasion jumped on Monsieur Mantoux's bandwagon in "The Troubling Thirties." Aldous Huxley brought along his *Brave New World*; Professor George Counts contributed his *Dare the School Build a New Social Order?*; William Z. Foster (national chairman of the Communist Party of the United States of America) wrote his *Toward a Soviet America*; John Dewey co-authored *The Humanist Manifesto I*; the Carnegie Corporation added its *Conclusions and Recommendations for the Social Studies* and its Eight-Year Study (which was in the 1990s referred to by the Education Commission of the States as the model for Outcome-Based Education); and surprisingly, Herbert Hoover proposed a Research Committee on Recent Social Trends to Implement the Planned Society.

The thirties were indeed troubling. Unfortunately, the average American was unaware of the important steps being taken to collectivize (socialize) this nation, particularly that of utilizing the schools as the vehicle through which Mantoux's "new world" could be brought into being.

1931

INTERNATIONAL UNDERSTANDING BY JOHN EUGENE HARLEY (STANFORD UNIVERSITY PRESS:

Stanford, Calif., 1931) was published. Excerpts from the foreword by Paul Mantoux of Paris, France follows:

> And the builder of this new world must be education. Education alone can lay the foundation on which the building is to rest. On this point a kind of consensus has been reached by those who trust the future of international cooperation and those who refuse to believe in it. When the latter go about repeating that to succeed in such a task one would have to change human nature, they do but exaggerate the acknowledged need for a gradual and patient reshaping of the public mind.... How can a well-prepared elite be raised throughout the world to spread its influence over the masses, who can then support them in their turn?... Here we encounter the real problem, and it is essentially a problem of education.... During the last decade of the nineteenth century, in England, a group of men devoted to the study of economic problems endeavored to prepare the public mind for broad changes which, in their view, must be effected if social peace is to be preserved. To this end they founded the London School of Economics and Political Science, which today ranks among the most famous institutions of education. In our day, the problem has become more far-reaching still. Brutal events have supplied evidence of a truth that had been slowly gaining ground, namely, the interdependence of nations and the need for establishing in the world an order and harmony hitherto lacking.
>
> Some [undertakings] have specialized in one branch of knowledge, like the Institute of Pacific Relations; others cover the whole field of political science, like the Ecole des Sciences Politiques, the London School of Economics, and the Deutsche Hochschule fur Politik. Some are debating or research centers, widely differing in character from one another according as their tendency is scientific rather than political; such are the Royal Institute of International Affairs, the Council on Foreign Relations, the Social Science Research Council, and the American Academy of Political and Social Science.... the World Education Association and the International Bureau of Education are endeavoring to compare education in civilized countries and to bridge differences by a process of mutual borrowing of methods.... Plainly, the first step in the case of each country is to train an elite to think, feel, and act internationally.

1932

BRAVE NEW WORLD (DOUBLEDAY, DOTAN: GARDEN CITY, N.Y., 1932) BY ALDOUS HUXLEY, the renowned English novelist and essayist, was published. In this famous work Huxley satirized the mechanical world of the future in which technology replaced much of the everyday activities of humans.

PROFESSOR GEORGE COUNTS OF COLUMBIA UNIVERSITY TEACHERS COLLEGE WROTE *DARE the School Build a New Social Order?* (John Day Company: New York, 1932). He and many other American educators traveling back and forth to Russia became completely convinced that the Soviet Communist system was the ultimate system. Counts was deeply involved in, and a member of, the Carnegie Foundation-financed Commission on the Social Studies which produced the American Historical Association's *Conclusions and Recommendations: Report of the Commission on the Social Studies* in 1934. He was also the author of *The American Road to Culture* series (Quinn and Broden, Co., Inc.: Rahway, N.J., 1930–1934) and *The Soviet Chal-*

lenge to America (John Day Co.: New York, 1931). Excerpts from this entry's major focus, Counts's *Dare the School Build a New Social Order?*, follow:

> If property rights are to be diffused in industrial society, natural resources and all important forms of capital will have to be collectively owned.... This clearly means that, if democracy is to survive in the United States, it must abandon its individualistic affiliations in the sphere of economics.... Within these limits, as I see it, our democratic tradition must of necessity evolve and gradually assume an essentially collectivistic pattern.
>
> The important point is that fundamental changes in the economic system are imperative. Whatever services historic capitalism may have rendered in the past, and they have been many, its days are numbered. With its dedication [to] the principle of selfishness, its exaltation of the profit motive, its reliance upon the forces of competition, and its placing of property above human rights, it will either have to be displaced altogether or changed so radically in form and spirit that its identity will be completely lost.

TOWARD A SOVIET AMERICA (ELGIN ENTERPRISES, INC.: LOS ANGELES, 1932) BY WILLIAM Z. Foster, national chairman of the Communist Party of the United States, was published. Foster died in 1961 in Moscow and was given a state funeral in the Kremlin. His book called for

> a U.S. Department of Education; implementation of a scientific materialist philosophy; studies revolutionized, being cleansed of religious, patriotic and other features of the bourgeois ideology; students taught on the basis of Marxian dialectical materialism, internationalism and general ethics of a new socialist society; present obsolete methods of teaching will be superseded by a scientific pedagogy. The whole basis and organization of capitalist science will be revolutionized. Science will become materialistic, hence truly scientific. God will be banished from the laboratories as well as from the schools.

[Ed. Note: Everything called for by Foster has taken place. "Scientific pedagogy" is OBE/mastery learning/direct instruction (Pavlov/Skinner). See the 1973 entry for *Foundations of Behavioral Research, Second Edition*, for some of the implications of implementing "a scientific materialistic philosophy."]

PRESIDENT HERBERT HOOVER APPOINTED A RESEARCH COMMITTEE ON RECENT SOCIAL TRENDS to implement the planned society in 1932. (In 1919 Franklin Roosevelt had told a friend that he personally would like to see Hoover in the White House.) The Research Committee was not approved nor funded by Congress; it became an Executive Action and was underwritten by the Rockefeller Foundation. No report was made to Congress or to the people during the time it functioned. The work of that committee has been called "a monumental achievement by the largest community of social scientists ever assembled to assess the social condition of a nation."[1]

THE NATIONAL EDUCATION ASSOCIATION CREATED THE EDUCATIONAL POLICIES COMMISSION (EPC) in 1932 for the purpose of changing the Goals for American Education. In 1944 the EPC prepared a volume of extreme importance entitled *Education for All American Youth*. This highly promoted document told, in fictional format and as though it were a *fait accompli*, how the "Planners" would solve all the problems; not just of youth, but of two imaginary communities—a village and a city—through involving citizens in cooperation for the goals of the planners. The following goals are laid out in this book:

- federal programs for health, education and welfare combined in one giant bureau
- Head Start programs
- getting pre-school children into the system
- teacher participation in curriculum decisions
- federal funds without federal control
- youth services through a "poverty program"
- removal of local control of political and educational matters "without seeming to do so"
- sex education

[Ed. Note: The involvement of "citizens in cooperation for the goals of the planners" is "participatory democracy," unheard of publicly until twenty years later.[2]]

THE EIGHT-YEAR STUDY WAS INITIATED BY THE COMMISSION ON RELATION OF SCHOOL AND College of the Progressive Education Association in 1932. Chairman of the Commission and author of *The Story of the Eight-Year Study* (Harper & Brothers: New York, 1942) Wilford M. Aikin chronicled the study's beginnings and purposes. Recounting the proceedings at the 1930 annual meeting of the Progressive Education Association, Aikin wrote:

> In the course of... discussion many proposals for improvement of the work of our secondary schools were made and generally approved. But almost every suggestion was met with the statement, "Yes, that should be done in our high schools, but it can't be done without risking students' chances of being admitted to college. If the student doesn't follow the pattern of subjects and units prescribed by the colleges, he probably will not be accepted." ...[S]omeone with courage and vision proposed that the Progressive Education Association should be asked to establish a Commission on the Relation of School and College to explore possibilities of better co-ordination of school and college work and to seek an agreement which would provide freedom for secondary schools to attempt fundamental reconstruction.... All members agreed that secondary education in the United States needed experimental study and comprehensive re-examination in the light of fuller knowledge of the learning process and the needs of young people in our society.... (p. 2)
>
> It has been assumed that physical and emotional reactions are not involved in the learning process, but if they are, they are not very important. The newer concept of learning holds that a human being develops through doing those things which have meaning to him; that the doing involves the whole person in all aspects of his being; and that growth takes place as each experience leads to greater understanding and more intelligent reaction to new situations.
>
> Holding this view, the participating schools believed that the school should become a place in which young people work together at tasks which are clearly related to their purposes.... The school should stimulate his whole being. It should provide opportunities for the full exercise of his physical, intellectual, emotional and spiritual powers as he strives to achieve recognition and a place of usefulness and honor in adult society. (p. 17)

Beginning in 1933 and continuing through 1941, the Eight-Year Study laid the groundwork for many of the education "reforms" and innovations we are encountering today. Most of the funding for the study came from the Carnegie Corporation of New York and the General Education Board. Commission and working committee members of note who participated in the study are: Wilford Aikin, Bruno Bettelheim, Burton P. Fowler, Frances Knapp, Louis Raths, Harold Rugg, Ralph Tyler, Hilda Taba, and Goodwin Watson.

Over the eight years of the study five volumes were published: *The Story of the Eight-Year Study* by Wilford Aikin; *Exploring the Curriculum: The Work of the Thirty Schools from the Viewpoint of Curriculum Consultants* by H.H. Giles, S.P. McCutcheon, and A.N. Zechiel; *Appraising and Recording Student Progress: Evaluation Records and Reports in the Thirty Schools* by Eugene R. Smith, Ralph W. Tyler and the evaluation staff; *Did They Succeed in College?: The Follow-up Study of the Graduates of the Thirty Schools* by Neal E. Drought and William E. Scott with preface by Max McConn; and *Thirty Schools Tell Their Story: Each School Writes of Its Participation in the Eight-Year Study.*

[Ed. Note: As will be seen in later entries in this book, the Eight-Year Study was foundational to outcome-based education and proposals to remove the Carnegie Unit. The Carnegie Unit has traditionally been the measure of participation; a certain number of units—hours in each class—in various disciplines have been required of the student in order to graduate or be accepted at a college. The Carnegie Unit measure is representative of the educational philosophy reflected in most state constitutions—that the state is responsible *to provide and make available educational opportunities* to all its citizens. The removal of this unit has been a central feature of current OBE/ML reform plans which reflect the philosophy that the state must guarantee that all citizens *receive and achieve an educational outcome determined by the state.* A change from "inputs" to "outputs."]

1933

HUMANIST MANIFESTO I WAS ORIGINALLY PUBLISHED IN 1933 IN THE *NEW HUMANIST* (VOL. VI, #3, 1933: Yellow Springs, Ohio), the main publication of the American Humanist Association. Co-author John Dewey, the noted philosopher and educator, called for a synthesizing of all religions and a "socialized and cooperative economic order." The following are excerpts taken from *Secular Humanism and the Schools: The Issue Whose Time Has Come* by Onalee McGraw, Ph.D. (Critical Issues, Series 2, The Heritage Foundation: Washington, D.C., 1976):

> The basis of humanist belief is that there is no Almighty God, the Creator and Sustainer of life. Humanists believe that man is his own god. They believe that moral values are relative, devised according to the needs of particular people, and that ethics are likewise situational.
>
> Humanists reject Judeo-Christian moral and ethical laws, such as those contained in the Ten Commandments, calling them "dogmatic," "outmoded," "authoritarian," and a hindrance to human progress. In humanism, self-fulfillment, happiness, love, and justice are found by each man individually, without reference to any divine source. In the Judeo-Christian ethic, there is and can be no real self-fulfillment, happiness, love, or justice on earth that can be found which does not ultimately issue from Almighty God, the Creator and Sustainer.
>
> Several main differences between the humanist ethic and the Judeo-Christian ethic

become clear upon reading the Humanist Manifestos I and II (1933 and 1973) and comparing them to the tenets of the Judeo-Christian ethic contained in the Old and New Testaments.... At issue is the basic concept concerning the nature of man and the "rules" by which men govern themselves individually, in society, and in government. In the Judeo-Christian ethic, man's ultimate deliverance and salvation—his finding a means of living together on this planet, in peace, harmony, justice, and love—is through God's given "rules."

For the humanist, man's greatness, his coming of age, his total fulfillment is found when he no longer needs the idea of God. Man gets rid of God, not just to do what he wills but to regain possession of human greatness.

Is Humanistic Education unconstitutional? Inasmuch as humanistic curriculum programs and "values clarification" and "moral education" teaching strategies are based upon materialistic values found only in man's nature itself, they reject the spiritual and moral tradition of theistic faith and religion. Thus, many parents who subscribe to Judeo-Christian belief oppose humanistic education in the tax-supported schools on grounds that such programs promote and advocate the religion of secular humanism in violation of the First Amendment to the *United States Constitution*.

The U.S. Supreme Court cited Secular Humanism as a religion in the 1961 case of *Torcaso v. Watkins* (367 U.S. 488). Roy Torcaso, the appellant, a practicing Humanist in Maryland, had refused to declare his belief in Almighty God, as then required by State law in order for him to be commissioned as a notary public. The Court held that the requirement for such an oath "invades appellant's freedom of belief and religion." The Court declared in *Torcaso* that the "no establishment" clause of the First Amendment reached far more than churches of theistic faiths, that it is not the business of government or its agents to probe beliefs, and that therefore its inquiry is concluded by the fact of the profession of belief.

The Court stated: "We repeat and again reaffirm that neither a State nor the Federal Government can constitutionally force a person to profess a belief or disbelief in any religion. Neither can constitutionally pass laws or impose requirements which aid all religions as against non-believers, and neither can aid those religions based on a belief in the existence of God as against those religions founded on different beliefs."

The Court has also stated "Among religions in this country which do not teach what would generally be considered a belief in the existence of God are Buddhism, Taoism, Ethical Culture, Secular Humanism and others." The *Torcaso* and *Abington* cases defined secular humanism as a religion and prohibited the government from establishing a religion of secularism by affirmatively opposing hostility to theistic religion, values, and beliefs.[3]

IN 1933 DR. PAUL MORT, CHAIRMAN OF THE PROGRESSIVE EDUCATION ASSOCIATION'S COMmittee on the Emergency in Education and one of the foremost authorities in the U.S. on school finance, wrote an article entitled "National Support for Our Public Schools," which was published in the December issue of *Progressive Education* (The Progressive Education Association: Washington, D.C., 1933). An excerpt follows:

> At a time when schools should be particularly alert in helping to meet new conditions [Depression era], far too many of the individuals equipped to help in meeting these conditions have been removed from the payrolls, and in a vast number of communities schools have been reduced to the task of dishing out traditional subject matter.

[Ed. Note: Read this quote at the next school budget meeting when taxpayers are being manipulated into paying more and more taxes to pay for controversial programs that have nothing to do with "traditional subject matter." You might point out that children were compelled to receive a better academic (traditional subject matter) education during the Depression due to hard times (less money). See the 1946 entry dealing with *Community-Centered Schools: The Blueprint* for another quote by Paul Mort regarding how long it takes to implement "change."]

DR. GEORGE HARTMANN, PROFESSOR OF EDUCATIONAL PSYCHOLOGY AT PENNSYLVANIA STATE College, wrote "A New Definition of the Educated Man" for the December 1933 issue of *Progressive Education*. Hartmann was active in the League for Independent Political Action, the Farmer-Laborer Political Federation, and the Socialist Party. He was co-author of *Readings in Industrial Psychology* (Appleton) and a frequent contributor to psychological journals. Excerpts from "A New Definition of the Educated Man" follow:

> Some may at once protest, "What? Is education to have as one of its symptoms the acceptance of radical views?" The answer is "Yes," if "radicalism" means any serious endeavor to alter our social arrangements for the better. We must consciously adopt and foster the position that it is the prime business of education to remake our institutions and our traditions—and learn to recognize the possession of this spirit as one of the main earmarks of the educated man.... The principal obstacle to the acceptance of this outcome is the persistence of a set of "inert" ideas (to use Whitehead's phrase) which lingers to afflict our civilization. One of the most subtle and pernicious of these inherited and unexamined postulates is the view that the aim of education (or life, for that matter) is the development of the individual's personality as such....
>
> ...For good or for ill, we must cease training people for what they are going to do, and point out instead what they should do. It will probably fall to our generation to resurrect the word "ought" to its rightful status in the affairs of men—for what else are values if not areas of experience with an imperious push or pull emanating from them?
>
> There are some purists who will be frightened by the indoctrination which must inevitably follow if this recommendation is effective.... Such an objection is silly, for since indoctrination of attitudes occurs anyhow, our sole concern must be to ensure that the right ones are established....
>
> How any one with the least pretensions to higher education can fail to be thrilled by the ultimate prospects of a single world government, the abolition of war and poverty, the enhancement of beauty in daily life, and the enlightened practice of eugenics and euthenics, is a riddle which can be explained only by a blind, exclusive regard for the immediately practicable.... What nobler and more enlightened aim for education in this century can possibly be proposed than that it enlists the enthusiasms of youth for the attainment of more rational forms of group living.

1934

CONCLUSIONS AND RECOMMENDATIONS FOR THE SOCIAL STUDIES (CHAS. SCRIBNER'S SONS: New York, 1934) compiled by the American Historical Association was published. This book was the result of a project funded to the tune of $340,000 by the Carnegie Corporation of New York called "Investigation of the Social Studies in the Schools," and was carried out by the American Historical Association. Professor Harold Laski, a philosopher of British socialism, said of this report: "At bottom, and stripped of its carefully neutral phrases, the report is an educational program for a Socialist America."[4] Important excerpts from *Conclusions* follow:

> [Preface] The Commission is under special obligation to its sponsor, the American Historical Association. Above all, it recognizes its indebtedness to the Trustees of the Carnegie Corporation, whose financial aid made possible the whole five-year investigation of social science instruction in the schools, eventuating in the following *Conclusions and Recommendations.*
>
> The Commission could not limit itself to a survey of textbooks, curricula, methods of instruction, and schemes of examination, but was impelled to consider the condition and prospects of the American people as a part of Western Civilization merging into a world order. (p. 1)

Of utmost importance is the following admission of the planners' goals to change our free enterprise/representative republic:

> The Commission was also driven to this broader conception of its task by the obvious fact that American civilization, in common with Western civilization, is passing through one of the great critical ages of history, is modifying its traditional faith in economic individualism, and is embarking upon vast experiments in social planning and control which call for large-scale cooperation on the part of the people.... (pp. 1–2)
>
> Cumulative evidence supports the conclusion that in the United States as in other countries, the age of *laissez faire* in economy and government is closing and a new age of collectivism is emerging.... (p.16)
>
> The implications for education are clear and imperative: (a) the efficient functioning of the emerging economy and the full utilization of its potentialities require profound changes in the attitudes and outlook of the American people, especially the rising generation—a complete and frank recognition that the old order is passing, that the new order is emerging.... (pp. 34–35)
>
> Organized public education in the United States, much more than ever before, is now compelled, if it is to fulfill its social obligations, to adjust its objectives, its curriculum, its methods of instruction, and its administrative procedures to the requirements of the emerging integrated order.
>
> If the school is to justify its maintenance and assume its responsibilities, it must recognize the new order and proceed to equip the rising generation to cooperate effectively in the increasingly interdependent society and to live rationally and well within its limitations and possibilities.... Signed: A.C. Krey, Chairman; Charles A. Beard; Isaiah Bowman (signed with reservations printed as Appendix C); Ada Comstock; George S. Counts; Avery O. Craven; Guy Stanton Ford; Carlton J.H. Hayes; Henry Johnson; A.C. Krey; Leon C. Marshall; Jesse H. Newton; Jesse F. Steiner. (Frank A. Ballou, Edmund E. Day, Ernest Hom, and Charles E. Merriam declined to sign these *Conclusions.*) (p. 35)

1939

MEIN KAMPF BY ADOLPH HITLER (STACKPOLE SONS PUBLISHERS: GERMANY, 1939) WAS published. Excerpts follow:

> Academic school training, which today is the be-all and end-all of the State's entire educational work, can be taken over by the populist state with but slight changes. These changes are in three fields....

In the first place, the childish brain must in general not be burdened with things ninety-five per cent of which it does not need, and which it therefore forgets [emphasis in original]. The curriculum of primary and grammar schools, in particular, is a hybrid affair. In many of the individual subjects the material to be learned has increased to such an extent that only a fraction of it sticks in the individual's head, and only a fraction of this abundance can be used, while on the other hand it is not enough for the purpose of a man working and his living in a certain field. Take for instance the ordinary civil servant who has graduated from secondary school or from the upper *realschule*, when he is thirty-five or forty; and test the school learning which he once so painfully acquired. How little of all the stuff that was then drummed into him still remains! One will, indeed, be answered: "Yes, but the object of the amount that was learned was not simply to put a man in possession of a great deal of information later, but to train his power of intellectual absorption, and the thinking power, particularly the power of observation of the brain." This is true in part. But still there is danger that the youthful brain may be drowned in a flood of impressions which it is very seldom able to master, and whose individual elements it can neither sift nor judge according to their greater or less importance; and on top of that, it is usually not the inessential but the essential which is forgotten and sacrificed. Thus the main object of learning so much is lost; for after all it cannot consist in making the brain able to learn by unmeasured piling-up of instruction, but in creating for later life a fund of knowledge which the individual needs, and which through him once more benefits society....

Summing up: the populist state will have to put general scholastic instruction into a shortened form, including the very essentials. Outside of that, opportunity must be offered for thorough, specialized scholarly training. It is enough if the individual person is given a store of general knowledge in broad outline, receiving a thorough detailed and specialized training only in the field which will be his in later life.... The shortening of the schedule and of the number of classes thus attained would be used for the benefit of the development of the body, the character, of will and resolution....

There should be a sharp distinction between general and specialized knowledge. As the latter threatens, especially today, to sink more and more into service of Mammon, general cultivation, at least so far as its more idealistic approach is concerned, must be preserved as a counter-weight. Here too the principle must be incessantly pounded in that industry and technology, trade and commerce can flourish only so long as an idealistically-minded national community provides the necessary conditions. These conditions are founded not on materialistic egoism, but on self-denying readiness for sacrifice.

[Ed. Note: This author has quoted extensively from *Mein Kampf*'s chapter on education in order that the reader may see the similarity between Hitler's views on education and workforce training and those of American government officials implementing OBE and school-to-work programs in the 1990s. The above quotations also bear a striking resemblance to Theodore Sizer's Coalition of Essential Schools' philosophy of "less is more" and to the 1988 Association for Supervision and Curriculum Development's Robert Muller *World Core Curriculum* in use in Eugene, Oregon and elsewhere.]

WORLD WAR II BEGAN IN 1939.

Endnotes:

1 This material has been excerpted from *The Impossible Dream* by K.M. Heaton (Hart Publications: Bellingham, Wash., 1990). This important book may be ordered from K.M. Heaton by sending a check for $17.50 to: Hart Publications, 1507 Lincoln

Street, Bellingham, WA. 98226. The Hon. John R. Rarick, former member of Congress, says of Mrs. Heaton's *The Impossible Dream*: "This is a dynamic volume of must reading for every American who loves this country and our system of government. Her in-depth writing arouses an awareness of the greatness this nation has achieved, a fear as to where we are heading, and of how far we must fall before it will all come to a halt.... There is an obvious, concerted program to irrevocably change our USA, yet many go on day after day, taking for granted what they didn't earn, and presuming the USA will go on forever. The change of our system from one of individual rights and freedoms to a one-world collective is taking place right before our very eyes."

2   Ibid, p. 215.

3   See 1988 entry for Supreme Court Justice Clarence Thomas's ruling on protection in the workplace from "abusive and intrusive" training, rendered when Thomas served as chairman of the Equal Employment Opportunity Commission (EEOC).

4   "A New Education for a New America"(*The New Republic*, July 29, 1936) carried quote by Prof. Harold Laski.

4

THE FOMENTATION
of the forties and fifties

Most *Webster's* dictionaries define the word "fomentation" as follows: "to stir up trouble, instigate; incite (as to foment a riot)." The forties and fifties will be remembered for the radical, un-American activities and views of some Americans and their paid staffs who, having risen to the highest levels in the tax-exempt foundations and government, were unfortunately accepted by the man on the street as having the best interests of this nation at heart.

Had these individuals been dressed in dirty, ragged clothes, worn old shoes and funny felt hats, they would likely have been accused of "fomenting" or instigating trouble—planning the transformation of our nation from a sovereign, free constitutional republic to only one of many socialist democracies subservient to an internationalist world government. However, the fact that many of these gentlemen and their paid staffs were associated with Ivy League colleges, major industries, and prestigious civic and religious institutions, wore Brooks Brothers suits and button-down-collared shirts, and many had served with distinction in World War II worked to obscure the fact that their goals were alien to those of the average Main Street American—for that matter, alien to the *Constitution of the United States of America* and its *Bill of Rights*.

United States membership in the United Nations Educational, Scientific and Cultural Organization (UNESCO) in 1946 set in motion the destabilization of our society through the rejection of absolute morals and values, Judeo-Christian tradition, and Roman law. Legislation authorizing United States membership in UNESCO marked the end of United States autonomy in a very crucial area: that of education. From this time on UNESCO would dictate education policy to our government and others. This legislation was accompanied by President Harry Truman's remarkable statement: "Education must establish the moral unity of mankind." Truman's recommendation was bolstered by General Brock Chisholm, a Canadian psychiatrist and friend of Soviet agent Alger Hiss. Chisholm redefined health to include "mental" health, and presented a paper entitled "The Psychiatry of Enduring Peace and Social Progress" to the United Nations World Health Organization (WHO) in 1946 which "reinterpreted" (eradicated) the word "morality." Chisholm asserted that

> The reinterpretation and eventually eradication of the concept of right and wrong... these are
> the belated objectives of practically all effective psychotherapy.

Brock Chisholm went on to recommend that teachers all over the world be trained in "no right/ no wrong" psychotherapeutic techniques found in the schools today. The use of these techniques has resulted in (1) a high percentage of the populace (60% if the polls taken during the summer of 1998 related to the public's approval of President William Jefferson Clinton are to be believed) responding that lying under oath is not sufficient reason for a president's removal from office, and (2) incredibly immoral/amoral and violent behavior of American youth.

Has the reader ever seen a more exquisite illustration of the dialectic at work? Create the chaos; people naturally call for help. The next step is to impose the totalitarian solution. The "New World Disorder" (chaos), evident on the nightly news, will ultimately require the same totalitarian control described so well by George Orwell in his novel *1984*. Orwell said, "If you want a picture of the future, imagine a boot stamping on the human face—forever... and remember, that is forever."

If one believes, as does this writer, that the well-being of mankind and the stability of this world and its institutions depend on the rule of law, then the 1940s and 1950s will be remembered as the commencement of the unraveling of civic order in the United States of America and throughout the world. The rule of law is usually based on concepts of right and wrong, grounded in some very widely accepted values that have been laid down since earliest times, and even spelled out in Roman law. Since the end of World War II, instead of the concept of law nations have been basing their actions on the United Nations' humanistic (non-absolutist) situational ethics philosophy set forth in the statements of General Brock Chisholm and President Harry Truman.

In 1948, shortly after General Chisholm made his recommendation to banish the concept of right and wrong, Professors B.F. Skinner and Alfred C. Kinsey published their books, *Walden Two* and *Sexual Behavior in the Human Male*, respectively. Skinner's novel, *Walden Two*, recommended— amongst other radical things—that "children be reared by the state, to be trained from birth to demonstrate only desirable characteristics and behavior." Kinsey, as a taxonomic scientist, wrested human sexuality from the constraints of love and marriage in order to advance the grand scheme to move America and the world toward the eugenic future envisioned by the elite scientists of the "New Biology," a shift which would affect the legal and medical professions.[1]

In 1953 Professor Skinner published *Science and Human Behavior* in which he said, "Operant conditioning shapes behavior as a sculptor shapes a lump of clay."[2] Also, in 1953, as if commissioned by Skinner and Kinsey to come up with a system to facilitate the necessary "changes" in behavior through operant conditioning and restructuring of the human personality (taxonomizing it), Professor Benjamin Bloom with the assistance of Professor David Krathwohl completed *Taxonomy of Educational Objectives*—a classification of learning behavior encompassing the cognitive, affective and psychomotor "domains" of learning.[3] *Webster's Dictionary* defines "taxonomy" as follows: "the study of the general principles of scientific classification: systematics." It should be noted that "scientific classification" related to education of a human being involves breaking behavior down into categories—to be measured and observed—behavior (actions) which can be isolated from the human personality with its important spiritual dimension.

Bloom said in *Taxonomy* that "the philosopher, as well as the behavioral scientist must find ways of determining what changes (values) are desirable and perhaps what changes are necessary." He stated that for the schools to attempt to change values is a virtual "Pandora's Box," but that

> [O]ur "box" must be opened if we are to face reality and take action, and that it is in this "box" that the most influential controls are to be found. The affective domain contains the forces that determine the nature of an individual's life and ultimately the life of an entire people.

Kinsey and Bloom, as scientists, were involved in the breaking down of man (taxonomizing) into units of behavior which Skinner, as a behaviorist, could identify, measure and change. This breaking down or "deconstructing of Man" was intended to separate man from his God-given, freedom-providing identity. This opened the door to the study of methods to control man and society: enter Skinner, representing the Behaviorist School of the non-science "science" of psychology. Bloom changed the focus of education from a general, liberal arts education which benefited *man as a whole* to a narrow training which would be based on the behavioral psychologists' determination of what changes in "thoughts, feelings, and actions" would be desirable and, perhaps, necessary for the benefit of *society as a whole*.[4] Bloom's *Taxonomy* provided the finishing and crucial touch to the foundation laid by Dewey and others of the bedrock of today's education and teacher training.

The work of Bloom, Kinsey and Skinner provided the ingredients for future moral chaos with which we are struggling today at the national and international levels. *People Weekly*'s cover story for the week of June 23, 1997, "Heartbreaking Crimes: Kids without a Conscience? Rape, murder, a baby dead at a prom: A look at young lives that seem to have gone very, very wrong," offers vivid examples of incredibly immoral/amoral and violent behavior. Melissa Drexler, 18—baby was found dead at the prom; Daphne Abdela, 15—accused of a Central Park murder; Jeremy Strohmeyer, 18—accused of killing a 7-year-old; Corey Arthur, 19—accused of murdering Jonathan Levin; and Amy Grossberg, 18—accused of killing her newborn. In addition, the past few years have provided Americans with news of tragedy after tragedy involving young people shooting their peers and teachers at schools across the country in Arkansas, Kentucky, Oregon, Washington state, Georgia, and with the most tragic of all because of the numbers involved, in Littleton, Colorado where twelve students and one teacher were murdered, two perpetrators committed suicide, and many others were critically injured.

President Dwight D. Eisenhower signed the first agreements with the Soviet Union in 1958, including an education agreement—something that would not come as a surprise to those familiar with the White House-directed plan to merge the United States and the Soviet Union explained to Norman Dodd in 1953 by Rowan Gaither, president of the Ford Foundation. Similar agreements have been signed from that time forward. The most important education agreements negotiated between the Carnegie Corporation and the Soviet Academy of Science, and those signed by Presidents Reagan and Gorbachev in 1985, remain in effect to this day.

The forties and fifties set all the essential ingredients in place for implementation in the sixties of a system of education geared to behavior and values change.

1941

EDUCATION FOR DESTRUCTION WAS WRITTEN BY DR. B.R. BURCHETT AND PUBLISHED BY her in Philadelphia, Pennsylvania in 1941. The promotional flyer for Dr. Burchett's book read as follows:

> *Arresting... Disturbing... Exciting*
>
> NOW for the First Time—the AMAZING STORY OF COMMUNISTS' INIQUITOUS CORRUPTION OF AMERICA'S SCHOOL CHILDREN
>
> HOW does the small Sovieteer minority control loyal teachers in our schools and colleges?
> HOW are anti-American, anti-religious, anti-Christ textbooks forced upon teachers and students?
> WHY are Washington and Jefferson ridiculed, while Marx and Lenin are canonized in the schools?
> WHY are boys and girls of 13 taught free love, sexual promiscuity, and other degrading subjects?
>
> WHAT'S GOING ON IN OUR AMERICAN SCHOOLS ANYWAY?
>
> The answers to these and other dismaying questions are all found in
> *Education for Destruction*
>
> [A]n eyewitness account by Dr. B.R. Burchett, former Head of Department of Latin in the Philadelphia public school system. It is a fearless and devastating exposé of Communism in America's schools, its concealed objectives, hidden motives, serpent-like power, and its vicious demoralization of children and adolescents. EVERY parent... EVERY educator... EVERY clergyman should read this book! [emphasis in original]

Dr. Burchett has included, opposite the title page of her book, a photograph of one of the classrooms in the school in which she taught. Under the photo are the words "No communism in the public schools?" accompanied by the following comments:

An observer, seeing that the largest poster in sight bears the letters U.S.S.R., might think that this is a picture of a school room in Russia. It is a picture of a room in a public school in Philadelphia. Did Superintendent Broome know about this? Did the Board of Education know about it? The picture is taken from Dr. Broome's Annual Report to the Board of Education, for the year ended June 30, 1936....

There had been a branch of the Young Communist League meeting in the South Philadelphia High School. According to the papers Miss Wanger made a great virtue of having disbanded it. Strangely, there was no "investigation" as to how it came to be meeting here in the first place, with a regularly assigned room and with a teacher as sponsor.

In spite of the facts presented in Mr. Allen's circular, and in spite of such an amazing thing as the meeting of the Young Communist League in the school, Dr. Broome, Superintendent of Schools, according to the *Philadelphia Record* of May 7, 1936, said: "I don't propose to investigate any general statement; if she (myself, Burchett) has anything specific to say I will be glad to hear her and investigate."... Recently, a special committee was appointed to consider the attacks on the "books of Harold O. Rugg and others on the ground of subversive teaching." Dr. Edwin C. Broome was a member of that Committee. It is not surprising, therefore, that the Rugg books were white-washed in the Committee report of February 26, 1941.

According to the above quotes, Dr. Edwin Broome, under whom Dr. Burchett worked, was deeply involved in curriculum changes favorable to indoctrination of the students in communism. Of special interest is the fact that Dr. Edwin Broome is the same Dr. Edwin Broome about whom Dorothy Dawson wrote in her article entitled "The Blueprint: Community-Centered Schools" for the Montgomery County, Maryland *Advertiser*, April 11, 1973. Mrs. Dawson personally typed the original *Blueprint for Montgomery County Schools* for Dr. Broome to present to the board of education in 1946. An additional excerpt from Mrs. Dawson's article follows:

In 1946 Dr. Edwin W. Broome was Superintendent of Schools.... From the *Maryland Teacher*, May 1953: "Dr. Edwin W. Broome announces retirement from Superintendency" by Mrs. Florence Massey Black, BCC High School. "Edwin W. Broome, the philosopher who took John Dewey out of his writings and put him to work in the classrooms of Montgomery County, is being honored upon his retirement this year by various groups in the State of Maryland and in his own county. He has served thirty-six years as superintendent of schools and forty-nine years in the county system. Greatly influenced by the late John Dewey, Edwin W. Broome set to work to show by analogy, specific example, and curriculum development, how each teacher could bring that philosophy into his work. And so it was that John Dewey came into the classrooms of Montgomery County."

[Ed. Note: Additionally, the *Maryland Teacher* did not mention that Dr. Broome had also served a controversial term as superintendent in the Philadelphia, Pennsylvania public school system. One might add that John Dewey not only came into the classrooms of Montgomery County, but also into all the classrooms of the United States, since the Montgomery County Plan was a pilot for the nation. This writer, when serving on her school's Philosophy Committee in 1973, had an updated copy of the "Montgomery County Philosophy" given to her by her Harvard-educated, change-agent superintendent. He recommended it as one philosophy statement to which our committee might wish to refer as we drew up a new philosophy for our school district. (See Appendix I for further excerpts from the *Blueprint for Montgomery County Schools*.)]

1942

IN 1942 *TIME* MAGAZINE (MARCH 16, 1942) RAN AN EXTENSIVE ARTICLE IN ITS RELIGION section dealing with a proposal by Protestant groups in the United States for a plan of action toward "a just and durable peace" for the years following the end of World War II. Excerpts from *Time*'s "American Malvern" follow:

These are the high spots of organized U.S. Protestantism's super-protestant new program for a just and durable peace after World War II:

- Ultimately, "a world government of delegated powers."
- Complete abandonment of U.S. isolationism.
- Strong immediate limitations on national sovereignty.
- International control of all armies and navies.
- A universal system of money... so planned as to prevent inflation and deflation.
- Worldwide freedom of immigration.
- Progressive elimination of all tariff and quota restrictions on world trade.
- "Autonomy for all subject and colonial peoples" (with much better treatment for Negroes in the U.S.).
- "No punitive reparations, no humiliating decrees of war guilt, no arbitrary dismemberment of nations."
- A "democratically controlled" international bank "to make development capital available in all parts of the world without the predatory and imperialistic aftermath so characteristic of large-scale private and governmental loans."

This program was adopted last week by 375 appointed representatives of 30-odd denominations called together at Ohio Wesleyan University by the Federal Council of Churches. Every local Protestant church in the country will now be urged to get behind the program. "As Christian citizens," its sponsors affirmed, "we must seek to translate our beliefs into practical realities and to create a public opinion which will insure that the United States shall play its full and essential part in the creation of a moral way of international living."...

The meeting showed its temper early by passing a set of 13 "requisite principles for peace" submitted by Chairman John Foster Dulles and his inter-church Commission to Study the Basis of a Just and Durable Peace. These principles, far from putting all the onus on Germany or Japan, bade the U.S. give thought to the short-sightedness of its own policies after World War I, declared that the U.S. would have to turn over a new leaf if the world is to enjoy lasting peace....

Some of the conference's economic opinions were almost as sensational as the extreme internationalism of its political program. It held that "a new order of economic life is both imminent and imperative"—a new order that is sure to come either "through voluntary cooperation within the framework of democracy or through explosive political revolution." Without condemning the profit motive as such, it denounced various defects in the profit system for breeding war, demagogues and dictators, "mass unemployment, widespread dispossession from homes and farms, destitution, lack of opportunity for youth and of security for old age." Instead, "the church must demand economic arrangements measured by human welfare... must appeal to the Christian motive of human service as paramount to personal gain or governmental coercion."

"Collectivism is coming, whether we like it or not," the delegates were told by no less a churchman than England's Dr. William Paton, co-secretary of the World Council of Churches, but the conference did not veer as far to the left as its definitely pinko British counterpart, the now famous Malvern Conference (*Time*, Jan. 20, 1941). It did, however, back up Labor's demand for an increasing share in industrial management. It echoed Labor's shibboleth that the denial of collective bargaining "reduces labor to a commodity." It urged taxation designed "to the end that our wealth may be more equitably distributed." It urged experimentation with government and cooperative ownership....

The ultimate goal: "a duly constituted world government of delegated powers: an international legislative body, an international court with adequate jurisdiction, international administrative bodies with necessary powers, and adequate international police forces and provision for enforcing its worldwide economic authority." (pp. 44, 46–47)

1943

THE AMERICAN FEDERATION OF TEACHERS (AFT) PUBLISHED THE BOOK *AMERICA, RUSSIA and the Communist Party in the Postwar World* by John L. Childs and George S. Counts (The John Day Co., New York). (The reader will recall previous entries in this book relating to George S. Counts's role in the promotion of collectivism in the early part of this century and a similar agenda mapped out by the Federal Council of Churches referenced earlier.)

Prior to reading excerpts from this remarkably naïve book, the reader is reminded that it was written *after* Stalin's mass terror of the 1930s, which included purges, trials, self-denunciations, disappearances, imprisonments and executions. Excerpts taken from the book's jacket follow:

> This book is the first in a series projected for publication by The Commission on Education and the Postwar World of the American Federation of Teachers.... It demonstrates beyond all argument that if this war is to be followed by a just and lasting peace, America and Russia must find a way to get along together. For the United Nations, including America and Russia, is the only agency that can establish such a peace. Russia's stupendous achievements, and her vast area, population, and resources, make her a world power second to none. We are blind if we think we can continue half grateful ally, half suspicious rival, of Russia. What then, stands in the way of good relations between America and Russia? It is not differences in social systems and ideologies, for these *can* [emphasis in original] exist side by side.... It is a twenty-five year legacy of mutual suspicion, fear, and active hostility. The removal of this legacy requires concessions on both sides.

The preface states in part:

> Among the subjects already chosen (by the Commission) for study are the problems of American youth, education for world-citizenship, and the kind of educational program required to meet the demands of our technological society.

Excerpts from chapter X, "Bases of Collaboration," are revealing:

> 6. The United States, on her side, will have to make profound readjustments in her historical policy with regard to the rest of the world in general and with regard to the Soviet Union in

particular.... The following constitute the bare minima of readjustments required of our country:

 a. She must abandon the notion that she can enjoy security and maintain her democratic way of life by adhering to her historic policy of no "entangling alliances." She cannot have peace if she continues to disregard the fact of world-wide interdependence—economic, political, military, and cultural. (p. 80)

 c. She must enter unreservedly into the partnership of the United Nations....

 e. She must revise her estimate of the enduring character of a collectivist state. She must banish from her mind the naïve doctrine, which controlled her relations with the Soviet Union in the early years of the Russian Revolution, that a collectivist state, being contrary to the laws of human nature, economics, and morality, must sooner or later collapse. (p. 81)...

 g. She must repudiate her earlier policy toward the Soviet Union. She must convince the Russian people she will have no part whatsoever in any effort to isolate, to encircle, and to destroy their collectivist state.... She must show by word, deed, and spirit that she is prepared to collaborate with nations of different traditions, different ideologies, and different economic and political systems in the organization of the world for peace and progress.... All of this means that those privileged groups in our own society which are fearful of any change in our property relations [free enterprise system] and which were primarily responsible for the shaping of the earlier policy must not be permitted to determine our postwar relations with Russia. (p. 82)

 h. She must, finally, have a vivid consciousness of the weaknesses in her own domestic economy. She must realize that, in spite of the very real advances made in recent years, we have only begun to face the problem of rebuilding the economic foundations of our democracy. In the process of rebuilding perhaps we may be able to learn something from the experiences of the Russian people. (p. 83)

1945

IN 1945 WORLD WAR II ENDED. THE PREPARATION OF A "JUST AND DURABLE PEACE" TO produce "a duly constituted world government" began.

UNITED NATIONS CHARTER BECAME EFFECTIVE ON OCTOBER 24, 1945. PLAYING AN IMPORTANT role in the creation of the United Nations was the United States Chamber of Commerce. In 1999 when parents find their local Chamber of Commerce deeply involved in the highly controversial, socialist/fascist, dumbing-down workforce training—necessary for a planned, global economy—the fact that the U.S. Chamber was a prime mover in establishing the United Nations should not be forgotten. The following information is excerpted from an important research paper by Erica Carle entitled "The Chamber of Commerce: Its Power and Goals" (December, 1983):

> Two slogans were popularized in order to gain backing for Chamber leadership: "World peace through world trade" and "More business in government and less government in business."
>
> The Chamber sought to commercialize the world under its own direction. To do this it needed to find ways to affect and bypass operating policies of various states and nations. To

change national policies, and even laws, required popular support and collective action. A new type of blanket organization was needed, one that could blanket not only governments, but professions, unions, educational institutions, farms, industries, sciences, religions and even families. An organization was sought which could bring about the cooperation and commercialization of all of these. A strong controllable international blanket organization was needed.

By the 1930's plans for the new blanket organization to serve the Chamber's purposes, the United Nations, were already well under way. The Chamber had the cooperation of tax-exempt foundations, some of which, such as the Carnegie Foundation for International Peace and the Rockefeller Foundation, had been set up early in the century. Large banks and trusts could see future profits for themselves if they cooperated with the Chamber; and the cooperation of international corporations was assumed, especially since Thomas J. Watson was President of the International Chamber of Commerce and a Trustee of the Carnegie Foundation for International Peace.

World War II aided... efforts to establish a "rational" international commercial system.... The United Nations organization could be used to gain governments' compliance with the Chamber's plans for a unified, controlled world economy, and also the cooperation of various non-Governmental organizations.

The following are some of the measures the Chamber of Commerce has supported to aid in the transfer of power from individuals and independent governments, groups, businesses and professions to the Chamber-advocated management system:

1. Creation of the United Nations.
2. Creation of the Organization for Economic Cooperation and Development.
3. Regional Government or "New Federalism."
4. Medicare (Commercialization of medical professions).
5. Postal reorganization.
6. Organized Crime Control Act.
7. Contracting for school services with private industry.
8. Voucher system for education.
9. Management and human relations techniques for handling personnel in industry.
10. Health care planning councils.
11. Prepaid medical practice (HMOs).
12. Federal land use planning.
13. Federally-imposed career education.
14. Equal Rights Amendment.
15. Cross-town busing for desegregation.[5]

INDIANA UNIVERSITY ADDED TWO NEW FACULTY MEMBERS TO ITS ROSTER IN 1945. DR. Burrhus Frederic (B.F.) Skinner became chairman of the Psychology Department and continued work on his forthcoming book, *Walden II*. Dr. Hermann J. Muller (future Nobel Prize winner), zoologist and private advocate of forced sterilization and selective eugenics, arrived in the Zoology Department to join long-time faculty member Alfred C. Kinsey. A publicly-allied communist, Muller had authored the book *Out of the Night: A Biologist's View of the Future* (The Vanguard Press: New York, 1935), which dealt with selective breeding and the advocacy of cloning of masses of human "resources." (Thirteen years after Muller's death in 1967 a sperm bank was established in California in Muller's honor, the Repository for Germinal Choice, which stores and distributes the sperm of Nobel Prize winners and others of "exceptional" ability.)

1946

"THE PSYCHIATRY OF ENDURING PEACE AND SOCIAL PROGRESS" IN THE WILLIAM ALANSON *White Memorial Lectures by Major General G.B.* [Brock] *Chisholm, C.B.E., M.D., Deputy Minister of Health, Dept. of National Health and Welfare, Canada* (Vol. 9, No. 1) was published in 1946. The book contained a foreword by Abe Fortas, former U.S. secretary of state. The article "The Psychiatry of Enduring Peace and Social Progress" was re-published in the March 1948 (No. 437) issue of *International Conciliation* published by the World Health Organization and Carnegie Endowment for International Peace. This last version included a preface written by Alger Hiss, former president of the Carnegie Endowment who would later be convicted of spying for the Soviet Union. It is important also to remember that Dr. David Hamburg, former president of the Carnegie Corporation of New York who signed the Carnegie Corporation/Soviet Academy of Science education agreement in 1985, is a psychiatrist. Excerpts from Brock Chisholm's article follow:

> The re-interpretation and eventually eradication of the concept of right and wrong which has been the basis of child training, the substitution of intelligent and rational thinking for faith in the certainties of the old people, these are the belated objectives of practically all effective psychotherapy. Would it not be sensible to stop imposing our local prejudices and faiths on children and give them all sides of every question so that in their own time they may have the ability to size things up, and make their own decisions? ...If the race is to be freed from its crippling burden of good and evil it must be psychiatrists who take the original responsibility.... The people who matter are the teachers, the young mothers and fathers, the parent-teacher associations, youth groups, service clubs, schools and colleges, the churches and Sunday schools—everyone who can be reached and given help toward intellectual freedom and honesty for themselves and for the children whose future depends on them....
>
> The battle, if it is to be undertaken, will be long and difficult but the truth will prevail—whenever enough people want it to. With luck we have perhaps fifteen or twenty years before the outbreak of the next world war if we remain as we are, twenty years in which to change the dearest certainties of enough of the human race, twenty years in which to root out and destroy the oldest and most flourishing parasitical growth in the world, the tree of the knowledge of good and evil, so that man may learn to preserve his most precious heritage, his innocence and intellectual freedom, twenty years in which to remove the necessity for the perverse satisfactions to be found in warfare.

If the reader is inclined to dismiss the above statements by Brock Chisholm as statements from an individual biased by his psychiatric profession and spoken at a point in time remote from today, please read the following statement by U.S. Ambassador to the United Nations Madeline Albright in Atlanta, Georgia, September of 1996, as it appeared in *The Congressional Digest* for January 1997:

> Setting Global Standards. The United Nations is one instrument that we use to make this world a little less inhumane, a little less brutal, a little less unfair than it otherwise would be.

This brings us to another important, and basic, function of the United Nations. And that is its role in creating a global consensus about what is right and what is wrong. (p. 14)

[Ed. Note: The reader should refer back to the preface of this book, *the deliberate dumbing down of america*, for discussion of the need to create robots who do not know right from wrong and who do not have a conscience—leaving the determination of right and wrong to the proposed United Nations "Global Conscience."]

C.S. LEWIS WROTE *THAT HIDEOUS STRENGTH* (COPYRIGHT BY CLIVE STAPLES LEWIS: Macmillan Company: New York, 1946). Lewis's uncanny ability to predict accurately how society would be manipulated into acceptance of totalitarian control was displayed in the following excerpt taken from a conversation Lewis's fictitious Lord Feverstone had with a young man named Mark:

> [Feverstone] "Man has got to take charge of Man. That means, remember, that some men have got to take charge of the rest—which is another reason for cashing in on it as soon as one can. You and I want to be the people who do the taking charge, not the ones who are taken charge of. Quite."
>
> "What sort of thing have you in mind?"
>
> "Quite simple and obvious things, at first—sterilization of the unfit, liquidation of backward races (we don't want any dead weights), selective breeding. Then real education, including pre-natal education. By real education I mean one that has no 'take-it-or-leave-it' nonsense. A real education makes the patient what it wants infallibly: whatever he or his parents try to do about it. Of course, it'll have to be mainly psychological at first. But we'll get on to biochemical conditioning in the end and direct manipulation of the brain...."
>
> "But this is stupendous, Feverstone."
>
> "It's the real thing at last. A new type of man: and it's people like you who've got to begin to make him."
>
> "That's my trouble. Don't think it's false modesty, but I haven't yet seen how I can contribute."
>
> "No, but we have. You are what we need: a trained sociologist with a radically realistic outlook, not afraid of responsibility. Also, a sociologist who can write."
>
> "You don't mean you want me to write up all this?"
>
> "No. We want you to write it down—to camouflage it. Only for the present, of course. Once the thing gets going we shan't have to bother about the great heart of the British public. We'll make the great heart what we want it to be." (p. 42)

[Ed. Note: Appendix XXVI contains an example of Brian Rowan's literary fulfillment of Feverstone's request for "a trained sociologist who can write." It is also interesting to note that William Spady, the "father of OBE," is a sociologist as well. The definition by Feverstone of "real education" not being "take-it-or-leave-it nonsense" reflects the 1990s outcome-based education reform call for emphasis on "outputs" rather than on constitutionally supported "inputs" discussed in chapter 1.]

COMMUNITY-CENTERED SCHOOLS: THE BLUEPRINT FOR MONTGOMERY COUNTY SCHOOLS, Maryland, was proposed by Dr. Nicholaus L. Englehardt and Associates, Consultants, and written by Dr. Walter D. Cocking of New York City on April 1, 1946. This material was provided by the late Dorothy Dawson who was secretary to the superintendent of schools of Montgomery County, Maryland, Dr. Edwin Broome. Mrs. Dawson typed this *Blueprint* for presentation to the Montgomery County Board of Education. (See Appendix I.) The Letter of Transmittal that accompanied *The Blueprint* said:

> Dr. Paul Mort and others have accumulated evidence which shows a period of almost fifty years between the establishment of need [needs assessment] and the school programs geared to meet it... if the school as an agency of society is to justify itself for the period ahead of us, it must be accepted that its fundamental function is to serve the people of the entire community, the very young children, the children of middle years, early adolescent youth, older youth and the adults as well.

"LEARNING AND PEACE: UNESCO STARTS ITS WORK" BY RICHARD A. JOHNSON WAS PRINTED in the October 1946 (No. 424) issue of *International Conciliation* published by the Carnegie Endowment for International Peace. This booklet gives the history of UNESCO (United Nations Education, Scientific, and Cultural Organization) from the Conference of Allied Ministers of Education in 1943–45, through legislation authorizing United States membership in UNESCO (P.L. 565, 79th Congress) approved July 30, 1946. President Harry Truman's remarkable statement of the same date accompanied this legislation: "[E]ducation must establish the moral unity of mankind."

THE EDUCATIONAL TESTING SERVICE (ETS) OF PRINCETON, NEW JERSEY, WAS FUNDED with an initial endowment of $750,000 from the Carnegie Corporation in 1946.

[Ed. Note: For further amplification and understanding of the far-reaching implications of the relationship between Educational Testing Service and the Carnegie Corporation, the reader should be sure to read: 1964 entry regarding the National Assessment of Educational Progress (NAEP) which ETS administers; two 1995 entries for articles from *The Bismarck* (North Dakota) *Tribune* dealing with NAEP; and Appendix IV.]

1947

NATIONAL TRAINING LABORATORY (NTL) WAS ESTABLISHED IN 1947. THE FIRST LABORATORY session on human relations and group processes was held at Gould Academy in Bethel, Maine. Founders of the National Training Laboratory had important connections with the Office of Strategic Services (OSS)—World War II forerunner to the Central Intelligence Agency (CIA). The NTL would become—with the National Education Association (NEA)—a premiere agency for human relations training (change agent/brainwashing).

A 1962 book published jointly by NTL and the NEA entitled *Five Issues in Training* addressed the process of "unfreezing, changing, and refreezing" attitudes in order to bring about change by stating the following: "The Chinese communists would remove the target person from those situations and social relationships which tended to confirm and reinforce the validity of the old attitudes." (p. 49)

This process is widely used in education, theology, medicine, business, government, etc., by pressuring individuals to participate in "retreats," removing them from familiar surroundings to "unfreeze" their attitudes and values. People have been coming from all over the world to attend these retreats at NTL in Bethel, Maine since its founding. An excerpt from the 1977 issue of *NTL Newsletter* follows:

> From the New Britain workshop dialogues of the founders emerged the notions of "action research laboratory" and "change agent" which were terms coined to denote a very vigorous proactive social change kind of posture, a merging of radical education, deviant behavioral science, and humanistic democracy.

HIGHER EDUCATION FOR AMERICAN DEMOCRACY; V. 3, ORGANIZING HIGHER EDUCATION, report of the President's Commission on Higher Education (U.S. Government Printing Office: Washington, D.C., 1947) was circulated. It revealed that:

> The role which education will play officially must be conditioned essentially by policies established by the State Department in this country and by ministries of foreign affairs in other countries. Higher education must play a very important part in carrying out in this country the program developed by the United Nations Educational, Scientific, and Cultural Organization and in influencing that program by studies and reports bearing upon international relations.... The United States Office of Education must be prepared to work effectively with the State Department and with the UNESCO. (p. 48)

1948

SEXUAL BEHAVIOR IN THE HUMAN MALE BY ALFRED C. KINSEY WITH WARDELL POMEROY, Clyde Martin and Paul Gebhard (W.B. Saunders: Philadelphia, PA, 1948) was published. This book and the controversial "research" it represented became a lightning rod around which much social turmoil was generated in this country and abroad.

As Judith Reisman, Ph.D., has described in her book, *Kinsey: Crimes and Consequences*[6] (Institute for Media Education: Arlington, Va., 1998):

> Three books written by leading legal, scholarly, and scientific authorities and assisted by Kinsey, were published in 1948 in tandem with Kinsey's *Sexual Behavior in the Human Male*. All three books called for legal implementation of Kinsey's "grand scheme" to loosen, alter and/or overturn America's laws concerning sexual behavior.

Those books were: (1) *Sexual Habits of American Men: A Symposium on the Kinsey Report*, edited by Albert Deutsch (Prentice Hall: New York, 1948); (2) *American Sexual Behavior and the Kinsey Report* by Morris Ernst and David Loth (W.W. Norton: New York, 1948); and (3) a re-publication of the 1933 book *The Ethics of Sexual Acts* (Alfred A. Knoff: New York, 1948) by René Guyon, French jurist and pedophile noted for having coined the phrase in reference to children: "Sex before eight or it's too late." To further elaborate on the connections of these books and ideas generated by them, Reisman wrote on page 189 of her book:

Dr. Harry Benjamin, an endocrinologist and international sexologist, and close friend and correspondent of both Kinsey and Guyon, wrote of their collaboration in his Introduction to Guyon's 1948 book:

> Many... sex activities, illegal and immoral, but widely practiced, are recorded by both investigators... Guyon speaking as a philosopher, and Kinsey, judging merely by empirical data... [are] upsetting our most cherished conventions. Unless we want to close our eyes to the truth or imprison 95% of our male population, we must completely revise our legal and moral codes.... It probably comes as a jolt to many, even open-minded people, when they realize that chastity cannot be a virtue because it is not a natural state.

[Ed. Note: The above extraordinary statement revealed the depth of some very perverse thinking in the area of human sexuality—thinking which would become institutionalized to the extent that in 1999 the American Psychological Association (APA) felt comfortable publishing in its *Journal* a study suggesting that pedophilia is harmless and even beneficial if consensual. According to an article in the June 10, 1999 issue of *The Washington Times*, entitled "Psychology Group Regrets Publishing Pedophilia Report: Practice Not Always Harmful, Article Said," the APA was taken by surprise when "its report provoked angry public reaction, including a House of Representatives resolution condemning it. It followed up with an abrupt about-face in an apologetic letter to House Majority Whip Tom DeLay" which expressed regret—not that it supported the idea of acceptable adult-child sex—but that the article had been published in a public journal.]

To prove the march toward sexual revolution had, indeed, reached the courts, Reisman further quotes Manfred S. Guttmacher, M.D., author of *The Role of Psychiatry and Law* (Charles C. Thomas: Springfield, Ill., 1968) and special consultant to the American Law Institute Model Penal Code Committee:

> In 1950 the American Law Institute began the monumental task of writing a Model Penal Code. I am told that a quarter of a century earlier the Institute had approached the Rockefeller Foundation for the funds needed to carry out this project, but at that time, Dr. Alan Gregg, man of great wisdom, counseled the Foundation to wait, that the behavioral sciences were on the threshold of development to the point at which they could be of great assistance. Apparently, the Institute concluded that the time has arrived.

WALDEN TWO, A NOVEL BY B.F. SKINNER (THE MACMILLAN COMPANY: NEW YORK, 1948) was published. Skinner recommended in this novel that children be reared by the state; to be trained from birth to demonstrate only desirable characteristics and behavior. He also wrote on page 312 of the paperback edition:

> What was needed was a new conception of man, compatible with our scientific knowledge, which would lead to a philosophy of education bearing some relation to educational practices. But to achieve this, education would have to abandon the technical limitations which it had imposed upon itself and step forth into a broader sphere of human engineering. Nothing short of a complete revision of a culture would suffice.

The late Professor Skinner died before his ideal school described in *Walden II* would become somewhat of a reality—a "Model School for the 21st Century." The following excerpts from *Walden Two* contain some restructuring terminology and resemble in many ways what a "restructured" school is supposed to look like in the 1990s:

> A much better education would cost less if society were better organized.
>
> We can arrange things more expeditiously here because we don't need to be constantly re-educating. The ordinary teacher spends a good share of her time changing the cultural and intellectual habits which the child acquires from its family and surrounding culture. Or else the teacher duplicates home training, in a complete waste of time. Here we can almost say that the school *is* the family, and vice versa. [emphasis in original]
>
> ...We don't need "grades." Everyone knows that talents and abilities don't develop at the same rate in different children. A fourth-grade reader may be a sixth-grade mathematician. The grade is an administrative device which does violence to the nature of the developmental process. Here the child advances as rapidly as he likes in any field. No time is wasted in forcing him to participate in, or be bored by, activities he has outgrown. And the backward child can be handled more efficiently too.
>
> We also don't require all our children to develop the same abilities or skills. We don't insist upon a certain set of courses. I don't suppose we have a single child who has had a "secondary school education," whatever that means. But they've all developed as rapidly as advisable, and they're well educated in many useful respects. By the same token, we don't waste time in teaching the unteachable. The fixed education represented by a diploma is a bit of conspicuous waste which has no place in Walden Two. We don't attach an economic or honorific value to education. It has its own value or none at all.
>
> Since our children remain happy, energetic, and curious, we don't need to teach "subjects" at all. We teach only the techniques of learning and thinking. As for geography, literature, the sciences—we give our children opportunity and guidance, and they learn them for themselves. In that way we dispense with half the teachers required under the old system, and the education is incomparably better. Our children aren't neglected, but they're seldom, if ever, *taught* anything. [emphasis in original] (pp. 118–120)

In the United States, 1990s teachers are instructed to act as facilitators and guidance counselors. Computer technology will take care of workforce training and whatever "education" remains. Wisconsin history teacher Gene Malone wrote a short review of *Walden Two*. Some of Malone's excerpts follow:

> *Walden Two* is fiction based on a Utopian community named after Henry David Thoreau's nature-Utopia, Walden Pond. Burris... telling the story of a planned society appears to be B.F. Skinner speaking. Frazier is the planner/manager/founder of the Utopia.... The Utopia/ Walden Two is presented in the United States. Burris and his friends are given a tour of Walden Two and Castle is unimpressed. Burris, at the end, joins Walden Two. Quotes follow from pages:
>
> 92—"Community love"
> 245—"We not only can control human behavior, we MUST."
> 219—"The new order."
> 189—"Psychologists are our priests."
> 188—"Walden Two is not a religious community."
> 282—"Their behavior is determined, yet they're free."

286—"What is love, except another name for the use of positive reinforcement?"
278—"Let us control the lives of our children and see what we can make of them."
274—"Behave as you ought!"
186—"We can make men adequate for group living.... That was our faith."
134—"Our goal is to have every adult member of Walden Two regard our children as his own, and to have every child think of every adult as his parent."
135—"No sensible person will suppose that love or affection has anything to do with blood."
112—"Education in Walden Two is part of the life of the community.... Our children begin to work at a very early age."
108—"History is honored in Walden Two only as entertainment."
105—"We are always thinking of the whole group."
160—"We are opposed to competition."
139—"The community, as a revised family"

Conclusion: This fictional presentation of Skinner's ideal community is much like the language and laws in use today by the behavioral elite—describing their plans for your children, your schools, your country. It is behavior management by the unchosen.

During the year of 1948, Dr. Skinner moved his family from Indiana University to Cambridge, Massachusetts to join the faculty of Harvard University.

DURING 1948 ALGER HISS, WHO LATER WOULD BE CONVICTED OF SPYING FOR THE SOVIET Union, wrote the preface to Gen. Brock Chisholm's lecture, "The Psychiatry of Enduring Peace and Social Progress," which was re-published in *International Conciliation* (No. 437, March, 1948, p. 109). Alger Hiss was at that time president of the Carnegie Endowment for International Peace, the publisher of *International Conciliation*. The preface to Chisholm's lecture, which redefined the word "health," follows:

The World Health Organization came into formal existence early in February. For nearly a year and a half its most urgent functions have been performed by an Interim Commission.

The new specialized agency carries on one of the most successful parts of the work of the League of Nations. The Constitution of the World Health Organization, however, has a far wider basis than that established for the League organization, and embodies in its provisions the broadest principles in public health service today. Defining health as a "state of complete physical, mental, and social well-being, and not merely the absence of disease or infirmity," it includes not only the more conventional fields of activity but also mental health, housing, nutrition, economic or working conditions, and administrative and social techniques affecting public health. In no other field is international cooperation more essential and in no other field has it been more effective and political difference less apparent.

The present issue of *International Conciliation* reviews the history of the Interim Commission through its last meeting in February. The first World Health Assembly will convene in June 1948. A brief introductory article has been prepared by Dr. Brock Chisholm, Executive Secretary, World Health Organization, Interim Commission. Dr. Chisholm is an eminent psychiatrist and served during the war as Director-General of Medical Services of the Canadian Army. The main discussion of the World Health Organization has been contributed by C.E.A. Winslow, Professor Emeritus of the Yale University and Editor of the American Journal of Public Health. Dr. Winslow has been a member of the Board of Scientific Directors of the International Health Division of the Rockefeller Foundation, Medical Director of the League of the Red Cross Societies, and Expert Assessor of the Health Committee of the League of Nations.

> Alger Hiss, President
> New York, New York
> February 21, 1948

1949

BASIC PRINCIPLES OF CURRICULUM AND INSTRUCTION (UNIVERSITY OF CHICAGO PRESS: Chicago, 1949) by Professor Ralph Tyler, chairman of the Department of Education at the University of Chicago, was published. Tyler stated that:

> Since the real purpose of education is not to have the instructor perform certain activities but to bring about significant changes in the student's pattern of behavior, it becomes important to recognize that any statement of the objective... should be a statement of changes to take place in the student.

1950

IN 1950 "MAN OUT OF A JOB: PASADENA TRIES TOO LATE TO HOLD ONTO ITS SCHOOL Superintendent" was carried in *Life Magazine* (December 11, 1950). An excerpt follows:

> Last month criticism of [Willard] Goslin took a serious turn. A militant citizens' group accused him of permitting Communistic influences in the schools—because he continued already established classes in sex education and favored the elimination of report cards. Then while Goslin was in New York City on business, the school board sent him a telegram asking him to resign.

1951

"THE GREATEST SUBVERSIVE PLOT IN HISTORY: REPORT TO THE AMERICAN PEOPLE ON UNESCO" from *The Congressional Record, Proceedings and Debates of the 82nd Congress, First Session* in 1951 included the extended remarks of Hon. John T. Wood (Idaho) in the U.S. House of Representatives, Thursday, October 18. Excerpts follow:

> Mr. Speaker, I am herewith appending an article published by the American Flag Committee... bearing the title "A Report to the American People on UNESCO." Just how careless and unthinking can we be that we permit this band of spies and traitors to exist another day in this land we all love? Are there no limits to our callousness and neglect of palpable and evident treason stalking rampant through our land, warping the minds and imaginations of even our little children, to the lying propaganda and palpable untruths we allow to be fed to

them through this monstrous poison?...

UNESCO's scheme to pervert public education appears in a series of nine volumes, titled *Toward World Understanding* which presume to instruct kindergarten and elementary grade teachers in the fine art of preparing our youngsters for the day when their first loyalty will be to a world government, of which the United States will form but an administrative part....

The program is quite specific. The teacher is to begin by eliminating any and all words, phrases, descriptions, pictures, maps, classroom material or teaching methods of a sort causing his pupils to feel or express a particular love for, or loyalty to, the United States of America. Children exhibiting such prejudice as a result of prior home influence—UNESCO calls it the outgrowth of the narrow family spirit—are to be dealt an abundant measure of counter propaganda at the earliest possible age. Booklet V, on page 9, advises the teacher that:

> The kindergarten or infant school has a significant part to play in the child's education. Not only can it correct many of the errors of home training, but it can also prepare the child for membership, at about the age of seven, in a group of his own age and habits—the first of many such social identifications that he must achieve on his way to membership in the world society.

WHILE YOU SLEPT: OUR TRAGEDY IN ASIA AND WHO MADE IT BY JOHN T. FLYNN (THE Devin-Adair Co., New York, 1951) was published. This Cold War treatise on the connections between the American left-wing elite and Communist organizers concludes with the following statement and significant quotation which served as an early warning, heralded again and again throughout this book:

> While we arm against Russia, we remain defenseless against the enemies within our walls. It is they, not Stalin's flyers or soldiers or atomic bombers, who will destroy us. One of the greatest of all Americans once made a speech on the "Perpetuation of our Political Institutions." It is these institutions from which we draw our great strength and promise of survival. It was Abraham Lincoln who said:
>
> > Shall we expect a transatlantic military giant to step the ocean and crush us at a blow? Never! All the armies of Europe, Asia and Africa combined with all the treasure of the earth (our own excepted) in their military chest, with a Bonaparte for a commander, could not by force take a drink from the Ohio or make a track on the Blue Ridge in a trail of a thousand years.... At what point then is the approach of danger to be expected? I answer: If it [should] ever reach us it must spring up amongst us; it cannot come from abroad. If destruction be our lot, we must ourselves be its author and finisher. As a nation of freemen we must live through all times or die by suicide.[7]

IMPACT OF SCIENCE UPON SOCIETY BY BERTRAND RUSSELL (COLUMBIA UNIVERSITY PRESS: New York, 1951; Simon and Schuster: New York, 1953) was published. What follows calls to mind the extensive use of behavior modification techniques on students, causing them to question and reject traditional values, and preparing them to willingly submit to totalitarian controls:

Education should aim at destroying free will so that after pupils are thus schooled they will be incapable throughout the rest of their lives of thinking or acting otherwise than as their school masters would have wished.... Influences of the home are obstructive; and in order to condition students, verses set to music and repeatedly intoned are very effective.... It is for a future scientist to make these maxims precise and discover exactly how much it costs per head to make children believe that snow is black. When the technique has been perfected, every government that has been in charge of education for more than one generation will be able to control its subjects securely without the need of armies or policemen.

1952

Subversive Influence in the Educational Process: Hearings before the Subcommittee to Investigate the Administration of the Internal Security Act and Other Internal Security Laws of the Committee on the Judiciary: United States Senate, Eighty-Second Congress, Second Session on Subversive Influence in the Educational Process was printed for the Committee on the Judiciary (Printing Office: Washington, D.C., Sept. 9, 10, 23, 24, 25 and October 13, 1952). Robert Morris was counsel and Benjamin Mandel was director of research for this project. Excerpts from the testimony of Bella V. Dodd, New York, who was accompanied by her attorney Godfrey P. Schmidt, follow:

> Mr. Morris: Dr. Dodd, how recently have you been associated with the Communist Party?
>
> Mrs. Dodd: June 1949.
>
> Mr. Morris: Do you mean you severed your connection with the Communist Party at that time?
>
> Mrs. Dodd: They severed their connection with me. I had previously tried to find my way out of the Communist Party. In 1949 they formally issued a resolution of expulsion....
>
> Mr. Morris: Dr. Dodd, will you tell us what relationship you bore to the Communist Party organization while you were the legislative representative for the Teachers' Union?
>
> Mrs. Dodd: Well, I soon got to know the majority of the people in the top leadership of the Teachers' Union were Communists, or, at least, were influenced by the Communist organization in the city.
>
> Sen. Homer Ferguson (Mich.): In other words, the steering committee, as I take your testimony, was used for the purpose of steering the teachers along the line that communism desired?
>
> Mrs. Dodd: On political questions, yes.... I would say also on certain educational questions. You take, for instance, the whole question of theory of education, whether it should be progressive education or whether it should be the more formal education. The Communist Party as a whole adopted a line of being for progressive education. And that would be carried on through the steering committee and into the union.[8]

[Ed.Note: Let us look ahead to 1985 to the U.S.-Soviet Education Agreement signed by Presidents Reagan and Gorbachev, and the Carnegie-Soviet Education Agreement. It was the same Robert Morris who served as counsel for the Senate Judiciary Committee's investigation who later, in 1989 as the new president of America's Future, Inc., permitted the publication of this writer's pamphlet "Soviets in the Classroom: America's Latest Education Fad"—four years after the agreements were signed. At that time, Mr. Morris—as politically knowledgeable and astute a person as one could hope to meet—was completely unaware of the agreements! The major conservative organizations and media had refused to publicize these treasonous agreements, with the exception of two well-known organizations which gave them "once over lightly" treatment.]

COOPERATIVE PROCEDURES IN LEARNING (COLUMBIA UNIVERSITY PRESS: NEW YORK, 1952) by Alice Miel, professor of education at Teachers College of Columbia University, and associates at the Bureau of Publications at Teachers College of Columbia University was published. Excerpts follow:

> [Foreword] As is true of most of the publications of the Horace Mann-Lincoln Institute of School Experimentation, *Cooperative Procedures in Learning* represents the work of many people and emphasizes the experimental approach to curriculum improvement.
> Having just completed a unit in social studies, we spent today's class period planning the procedure for a new unit. I started the discussion by pointing out the three methods by which we had studied other units: (1) individual project work, (2) group project work, (3) textbook work. I asked the class to consider these three methods and then to decide which they preferred, or suggest another method for studying our coming work.
> It was here that I noticed that most of those who seemed in favor of group projects were students who were well developed socially and had worked well with others in the past, whereas those favoring individual projects were almost entirely the A students who obviously knew they were capable of doing good work on their own and would receive more recognition for it through individual work.

[Ed. Note: The collectivist philosophy that the group is more important than the individual got off the ground in education in the 1950s as a result of the experimental research of educators conducting work similar to that of Alice Miel. By the 1990s egalitarian dumbing-down, outcome-based education—with its cooperative learning, mastery learning, group grades, total quality management, etc.—is the accepted method in the schools of education and in the classroom.]

IN 1952 "MODERN MATH" WAS INTRODUCED TO DUMB DOWN MATH STUDENTS SO THAT THEY couldn't apply the math concepts to "real life situations when they get out of schools," according to a "Dr. Ziegler" who served as chairman of the Education Committee of the Council on Foreign Relations in 1928. (Refer to 1928 entry concerning O.A. Nelson, math teacher, for background of this entry.)

1953

NORMAN DODD, A YALE GRADUATE, INTELLECTUAL AND NEW YORK CITY INVESTMENT BANKER, was chosen to be the research director for the Reece Committee of the U.S. House of Representatives in 1953. The Reece Committee was named for its creator, Rep. Carroll Reece of

Tennessee, and was formed to investigate the status of tax-exempt foundations. Dodd sent committee questionnaires to numerous foundations, and as a result of one such request, Joseph E. Johnson, president of the Carnegie Endowment for International Peace, invited Dodd to send a committee staffer to Carnegie headquarters in New York City to examine the minutes of the meetings of the foundation's trustees. These minutes had long since been stored away in a warehouse. Obviously, Johnson, who was a close friend of former Carnegie Endowment's president and Soviet spy Alger Hiss, had no idea what was in them.

The minutes revealed that in 1910 the Carnegie Endowment's trustees asked themselves this question: "Is there any way known to man more effective than war, to so alter the life of an entire people?" For a year the trustees sought an effective "peaceful" method to "alter the life of an entire people." Ultimately, they concluded that war was the most effective way to change people. Consequently, the trustees of the Carnegie Endowment for International Peace next asked themselves: "How do we involve the United States in a war?" And they answered, "We must control the diplomatic machinery of the United States by first gaining control of the State Department." Norman Dodd stated that the trustees' minutes reinforced what the Reece Committee had uncovered elsewhere about the Carnegie Endowment: "It had already become a powerful policy-making force inside the State Department."

During those early years of the Carnegie Endowment, war clouds were already forming over Europe and the opportunity of enactment of their plan was drawing near. History proved that World War I did indeed have an enormous impact on the American people. For the first time in our history, large numbers of wives and mothers had to leave their homes to work in war factories, thus effectively eroding woman's historic role as the "heart" of the family. The sanctity of the family itself was placed in jeopardy. Life in America was so thoroughly changed that, according to Dodd's findings, "[T]he trustees had the brashness to congratulate themselves on the wisdom and validity of their original decision." They sent a confidential message to President Woodrow Wilson, insisting that the war not be ended too quickly.

After the war, the Carnegie Endowment trustees reasoned that if they could get control of education in the United States they would be able to prevent a return to the way of life as it had been prior to the war. They recruited the Rockefeller Foundation to assist in such a monumental task. According to Dodd's Reece Committee report: "They divided the task in parts, giving to the Rockefeller Foundation the responsibility of altering education as it pertains to domestic subjects, but Carnegie retained the task of altering our education in foreign affairs and about international relations."

During a subsequent personal meeting with Mr. Dodd, President Rowan Gaither of the Ford Foundation said, "Mr. Dodd, we invited you to come here because we thought that perhaps, off the record, you would be kind enough to tell us why the Congress is interested in the operations of foundations such as ours?" Gaither answered his own rhetorical question with a startling admission:

> Mr. Dodd, all of us here at the policy making level of the foundation have at one time or another served in the OSS [Office of Strategic Services, CIA forerunner] or the European Economic Administration, operating under directives from the White House. We operate under those same directives.... The substance under which we operate is that we shall use our grant making power to so alter life in the United States that we can be comfortably merged with the Soviet Union.

Stunned, Dodd replied, "Why don't you tell the American people what you just told me and you could save the taxpayers thousands of dollars set aside for this investigation?" Gaither responded, "Mr. Dodd, we wouldn't think of doing that."

In public, of course, Gaither never admitted what he had revealed in private. However, on numerous public occasions Norman Dodd repeated what Gaither had said, and was neither sued by Gaither nor challenged by the Ford Foundation. Dodd was subsequently warned that "If you proceed with the investigation as you have outlined, you will be killed."[9]

The Reece Committee never completely finished its work of investigating and receiving testimony in open hearings involving the representatives of the major tax-exempt foundations. The process was completely disrupted and finally derailed by the deliberately disruptive activity of one of its members, Congressman Wayne Hays of Ohio. According to general counsel for the Reece Committee, Renee A. Wormser's account in *Foundations: Their Power and Influence* (Devin-Adair: New York, 1958, p. 341), "[Hays] was frank enough to tell us that he had been put on the committee by Mr. [Sam] Rayburn, the Democratic Leader in the House, as the equivalent of a watchdog. Just what he was to 'watch' was not made clear until it became apparent that Mr. Hays was making it his business to frustrate the investigation to the greatest extent possible."

[Ed. Note: The Cox Committee, created by Congress as a result of Rep. E.E. Cox of Georgia submitting a resolution to the House of Representatives in the 82nd Congress, was a forerunner of the Reece Committee. The Cox Committee was created to "direct a thorough investigation of foundations." However, just as the Reece Committee which followed, the Cox Committee was unable to get to the bottom of tax-exempt foundation affairs. Again, according to Mr. Wormser, "The Cox Committee did find that there had been a Communist, Moscow-directed plot to infiltrate American foundations and to use their funds for Communist purposes."]

SCIENCE AND HUMAN BEHAVIOR BY B.F. SKINNER (MACMILLAN & CO.: NEW YORK, 1953) was published. To quote Skinner again, "Operant conditioning shapes behavior as a sculptor shapes a lump of clay."

ALFRED C. KINSEY, ALONG WITH WARDELL POMEROY, CLYDE MARTIN, AND PAUL GEBHARD, published *Sexual Behavior in the Human Female* (W.B. Saunders: Philadelphia, Pa., 1953). According to Professor David Allyn, lecturer in the Department of History at Princeton University, this book, along with Kinsey's *Sexual Behavior in the Human Male*, served to solidify the move which

> changed the way social scientists studied sexuality by breaking from the accepted social hygienic, psychoanalytic, psychiatric and physiological approaches.... [Kinsey's work] played [a] critical role in the mid-century privatization of morality. In the post-WWII era, experts abandoned the concept of "public morals," a concept which had underpinned the social control of American sexuality from the 1870's onward.... In the 1950's and 60's, however, sexual morality was privatized, and the state-controlled, highly regulated moral economy of the past gave way to a new, "deregulated" moral market.... Kinsey's [work] argued against government interference in private life.

[Ed. Note: The above statement by Allyn was made during a presentation entitled "Private Acts/Public Policy: Alfred Kinsey, the American Law Institute and the Privatization of American Sexual Morality" at the 1995 Chevron Conference on the History of the Behavioral and Social Sciences as part of a special symposium on Alfred Kinsey. Allyn acknowledged the Charles Warren Center at Harvard University and the Rockefeller Archive Center as providing grants which made his research possible.]

DR. LEWIS ALBERT ALESEN PUBLISHED A FASCINATING BOOK ENTITLED *MENTAL ROBOTS* (The Caxton Printers, Ltd.: Caldwell, Idaho, 1953). Dr. Alesen, distinguished physician and surgeon, served as president of the California Medical Association from 1952–1953, and also wrote *The Physician's Responsibility as a Leader*. Some excerpts from Dr. Alesen's chapter 7 of *Mental Robots*, "The Tools of Robotry," follow:

Herbert A. Philbrick [double agent and author of *I Led Three Lives*] has been recently quoted as stressing that Soviet psychiatry is the psychiatry of Pavlov, upon whose original work on dogs the theory of the conditioned reflex is based. This conditioned reflex is the principle underlying all of the procedures employed by the Soviets in their brain-washing and brain-changing techniques. Under its skillful use the human can be, and has been in countless instances, so altered as completely to transform the concepts previously held and to prepare the individual so treated for a docile acceptance of all manner of authoritarian controls. The psychiatrist boasts that he possesses the power to alter human personality, and he has certainly made good his boast in many respects, at least to the extent of being able to force phony confessions out of men like Cardinal Mindszenty, Robert Vogeler, and a host of others who have been subjected to all manner of torture during their period of conditioning.

In a book entitled *Conditioned Reflex Therapy* by Andrew Salte, published in 1949 by the Creative Age Press, individual free will, freedom of choice, and, of course, individual responsibility are categorically denied in these words:

> We are meat in which habits have taken up residence. We are a result of the way other people have acted to us. We are the reactions. Having conditioned reflexes means carrying about pieces of past realities.... We think with our habits, and our emotional training determines our thinking. Where there is a conditioned reflex, there is no will. Our "will power" is dependent on our previously learned reflexes.

Certainly it is true that the Communists, both in Russia, China, and the Iron Curtain countries, have accomplished spectacular changes in the thinking of millions of their citizens. Whether or not this mass changing is altogether sincere or durable is not for the moment as significant as the fact that it has taken place, and that based upon it there has been, apparently, a ready acceptance of revolutionary doctrines radically defying former custom and accepted usage, and transforming the individual under this spell of persuasion or compulsion into an individual possessing entirely different characteristics from those formerly exhibited. And thus, whole new social, economic, political, and even religious regimes have been accepted in a comparatively short time.

In order to comprehend at all adequately what has been and what is happening to the mental processes and attitudes of the American people during recent years, and in order most particularly to be aware of and alert to the carefully planned goals of the inner and hard-core sponsors of the so-called mental health program, it is pertinent to explore briefly the science and art of cybernetics. Cybernetics, according to Gould's medical dictionary, "The science dealing with communication and communication-control theory as applied to mechanical devices and animals; and including the study of servo-mechanisms, that is, feed-back mechanicisms; Josiah Macy, Jr. Foundation, 565 Park Avenue, N.Y. 21, N.Y., has published a series of symposia on cybernetics 'Circular Causal and Feed-Back Mechanisms in Biology and Social Systems.'"

In a Freedom Forum presentation entitled "Inside U.S. Communism" by Herbert Philbrick, at Harding College, Searcy, Arkansas, April 16, 1954, and distributed by the National Education Program, Mr. Philbrick had this to say about cybernetics:

> The Communists, I have discovered, have a favorite term for their system of influencing people in devious ways. The word they use as an over-all title of this technique is "cybernetics." Cybernetics as a pure science has a very legitimate and worth-while function. It has to do with how to improve conduits and cables, how to make better coaxial cables for television, how to improve telephone service, how to make more efficient electronic brains, etc. It has a very legitimate service as a pure science.
>
> But since a human being, to a Communist, is simply another machine; since human nerve centers have exactly the same function as an electronic circuit; since a human has not a soul—he is only a mechanical apparatus—the Communists have decided that this particular science has a very useful application—not on machines but on humans.
>
> Now we've heard a great deal more recently about brain-washing. Back in 1940 that word wasn't familiar to us, but what was going on inside these Young Communist League cells was a technique of cybernetics, a technique of brain-washing, if you will; the highly developed science of *demolishing the minds and the spirits of men*. [emphasis in original] The Communists brag that theirs is a "technique of Soviet psychiatry." Now Soviet psychiatry is based on the same basic principles as that of our own doctors and psychiatrists except that the Communists have a different purpose in their psychiatry. Our doctors work with unhealthy minds and try to make them healthy and whole again. The Communists have decided that cybernetics provides a very wonderful way to go to work on healthy minds and to destroy them. And of course we are now getting a bit of that picture from our own prisoners of war who were jailed and imprisoned by the North Koreans and the Red Chinese. One of my good friends is Robert Vogeler. We've learned a great deal from Bob Vogeler about the technique of brain-washing. It's a horrifying story.
>
> I would suggest that you folks who are interested in this subject, perhaps some of you students, could adopt for special study this field of cybernetics. It is brand new. I don't know of a single book on the subject in connection with what the Communists are doing with it. As a matter of fact, my own knowledge is very limited because the only facts I have are those few things which we have gathered from inside the Communist Party which indicate that the Reds have been working around the clock in this study of the scientific manipulation and control of information. It is based on the findings of Pavlov which say that a man, like an animal, conditioned to respond to certain impulses, can be conditioned to respond to words, phrases and symbols. Therefore you pour in the words, phrases and symbols to which he will respond *without thinking* [emphasis in original]. And then you withhold other certain words which will cause him to respond in a way which you may not desire. It is the scientific control of human beings by means of control [of] information.

As the pattern for the international robot of the future, so meticulously drawn to scale by our condescending planners and masters, becomes increasingly clear, it behooves us to study that plan carefully, to determine to just what extent it has already been effectuated, to appraise the multitudinous forces aiding and abetting its adoption, and to determine, finally, whether we as individuals do, in fact, possess characteristics of sufficient value to justify any resistance to this seemingly almost overwhelming juggernaut of collectivism which is rushing headlong upon us. Have we in America, the greatest land upon which God's sun has ever shone, succumbed to the fleshpots of a modern Egypt? Have we become so softened by bellies lined with rich food, wives clad in rich raiment, and housing and appurtenances designed to shield us from every intellectual endeavor that we are no longer interested in making any effort to reclaim and to reinvigorate the one economic, social, and political system which has made all of this possible for us?

1954

ALICE A. BAILEY, AN AMERICAN THEOSOPHIST, WROTE *EDUCATION IN THE NEW AGE* (LUCIS Trust: New York and London, 1954).[10] The following information was written in the front of the book: "The publication of this book is financed by the Tibetan Book Fund which is established for the perpetuation of the teachings of the Tibetan and Alice A. Bailey. This fund is controlled by the Lucis Trust, a tax-exempt, religious, educational corporation. It is published in Dutch, French, Spanish, German, Italian and Portugese. Translation into other languages is proceeding." Following are some excerpts from chapter 3, "The Next Step in the Mental Development of Humanity":

The Mental Transition Period

There are three immediate steps ahead of the educational system of the world, and some progress has already been made towards taking them. First: The development of more adequate means of understanding and studying the human being. This will be made possible in three ways:
1. The growth and the development of the Science of Psychology. This is the science of the essential man, and is at this time being more generally recognised as useful to, and consistent with, the right development of the human unit. The various schools of psychology, so numerous and separative, will each eventually contribute its particular and peculiar truth, and thus the real science of the soul will emerge from this synthesis.
2. The growth and the development of the *Science of the Seven Rays*. This science will throw light upon racial and individual types; it will clearly formulate the nature of individual and racial problems; it will indicate the forces and energies which are struggling for expression in the individual and in the race; and when the two major rays and the minor rays (which meet in every man) are recognised and studied by the educator in connection with the individual, the result will be right individual and group training, and correct vocational indications.
3. The acceptance of the *Teaching anent* [about] *the Constitution of Man* given by the esotericists, with the implied relation of soul and body, the nature of those bodies, their qualities and purpose, and the interrelation existing between the soul and the three vehicles of expression in the three worlds of human endeavors.
    In order to bring this about, the best that the East has to offer and the knowledge of the West will have to be made available. The training of the physical body, the control of the emotional body, and the development of right mental apprehension must proceed sequentially, with due attention to the time factor, and also to that period wherein planned coordination of all aspects of the man should be carefully developed. (pp. 69–70)

[Ed. Note: After returning from a stint in the U.S. Department of Education in the early 1980s, this author attended a school board meeting and noticed the change agent superintendent's scrawlings on a blackboard, which had evidently been used as part of some sort of in-service training. He had divided a circle into the following sections: physical, mental, creative, and "spiritual." My reaction was "Hmmm," since it was he with whom I had sparred over the use of values clarification—which destroyed any real Judeo/Christian spirituality—when I served on the board in the late 1970s.]

1955

THE NEW YORK TIMES REPORTED ON AUGUST 6, 1955 THAT PRESIDENT DWIGHT D. Eisenhower called for the first White House Conference on Education. The announcement follows:

> WASHINGTON, D.C.—Reservations have been made in eight hotels here for 2045 rooms to be occupied November 20 through December 1 by participants in the White House Conference on Education. This conference, first of its kind to be called by a President, will be unusual in many ways. The ground rules call for two or more noneducators to each educator in order to stir up the widest possible education support by citizenry in the States.... However, the really unusual part of the conference plan lies in its sharp departure from the conventional, somewhat haphazard way of conducting big conferences. The President's committee has set up six subjects to be discussed; five of them to be thrashed out at the conference, and one to be taken home. Each of the five questions to be gone into here will be discussed in successive all-delegate sessions of 200 tables of 10 persons plus a discussion leader. The five questions under mass consideration will be:
>   1. What should our schools accomplish?
>   2. In what ways can we organize our school system more effectively and economically?
>   3. What are our school building needs?
>   4. How can we get good teachers—and keep them?
>   5. How can we finance our schools—build and operate them?
>   The question to be taken home is: How can we obtain a continuing interest in education?
>   At the close of each all-delegate session a stenographic pool will be on hand to compile the consensus at each table and to jot down the dissents. The 200 discussion leaders will convene around 20 tables in a smaller room, further refine the results and give their "consensus" and "dissents" to a second flight of stenographers. The mass of delegates then proceed to another question. The leaders of the 20 tables subsequently move to two tables. Their findings, set down by stenographers, will be forwarded to the conference committee for incorporation in the final report.

[Ed. Note: This conference was probably one of the first national conferences to use the manipulative and non-representative group dynamics/Delphi Technique to orchestrate the participants into reaching consensus on pre-determined goals. Anyone who has participated in local or state goal-setting committees should recognize the drill. This conference provided an excellent example of the dialectical process at work.]

1956

TAXONOMY OF EDUCATIONAL OBJECTIVES: THE CLASSIFICATION OF EDUCATIONAL GOALS, *Handbook II, Affective Domain* by David Krathwohl, Benjamin Bloom, and Bertram Massie (Longman: New York/London, 1956) was published. This *Taxonomy* provided the necessary tool for the schools of education to restructure education from academics to values (behavior) change. The swinging door was finally propped open to incorporate attitudes, values and beliefs into the definition of education. It is impossible to overestimate the *Taxonomy*'s importance. An excerpt follows:

> In fact, a large part of what we call "good teaching" is the teacher's ability to attain affective objectives [attitudes, values, beliefs] through challenging the students' fixed beliefs and getting them to discuss issues. (p. 55)

1958

IN 1958 AT THE PEAK OF THE COLD WAR PRESIDENT DWIGHT D. EISENHOWER SIGNED THE first United States-Union of Soviet Socialist Republics (U.S.S.R.) agreements. These agreements included education.

NATIONAL DEFENSE EDUCATION ACT WAS PASSED IN 1958 BY THE U.S. CONGRESS AS A result of Soviet success in space, demonstrated by the launching of *Sputnik*. This *Act*, which set the stage for incredible federal control of education through heavy financing for behavior modification, science, mathematics, guidance counseling, and testing, etc., involved "modern techniques developed from scientific principles," the full weight of which would be felt at the end of the century. Title I, General Provisions, Findings and Declaration of Policy, Sec. 101 of this *Act* reads:

> The Congress hereby finds and declares that the security of the Nation requires the fullest development of the mental resources and technical skills of its young men and women. The present emergency demands that additional and more adequate educational opportunities be made available. The defense of this nation depends upon the mastery of modern techniques developed from complex scientific principles. It depends as well upon the discovery and development of new principles, new techniques, and new knowledge.

Endnotes:

1   For a thorough treatment of this subject, please read Dr. Judith A. Reisman's book *Kinsey: Crimes and Consequences—The Red Queen and the Grand Scheme* (The Institute for Media Education, Inc.: Arlington, Va., 1998). To order call 1–800–837–0544.

2   B.F. Skinner. *Science and Human Behavior* (Macmillan & Co.: New York, 1953).

3   The *Taxonomy* involves: Cognitive—how a student perceives or judges knowledge or facts; Affective—how a student feels or what he believes about a subject; Psychomotor—what a student does as a result of what he perceives or believes; converting belief to action.

4   See Appendix XIX for an excellent critique of Bloom's *Taxonomy*.

5   This document may be ordered from: Education Service Council, P.O. Box 271, Elm Grove, WI 53122. Erica Carle's latest and very important book, *Why Things Are the Way They Are* (Dorrance Publishing Co.: Pittsburgh, Pa., 1996), can be ordered in hardcover from: Dorrance Publishing Co., 643 Smithfield Street, Pittsburgh, PA 15222.

6   To order Dr. Reisman's book, call 1–800–837–0544.

7   Speech before Young Men's Lyceum, Springfield, Illinois, January, 1837.

8   For further information, purchase *School of Darkness: The Record of a Life and of a Conflict between Two Faiths* by Bella V. Dodd (P.J. Kennedy & Sons: New York, 1954. Copyright transferred in 1963 to Bella V. Dodd, Devin-Adair Publishers).

9   This section dealing with the Dodd Report was written by Robert H. Goldsborough and published in his book *Lines of Credit: Ropes of Bondage*, (The American Research Foundation, Inc.: Baltimore, 1989). This fascinating book may be obtained by sending a check for $8.00 to: Robert H. Goldsborough, P.O. Box 5687, Baltimore, MD 21210.

10   The offices of Lucis Trust (formerly Lucifer Publishing) which were previously located across from the United Nations Building in New York have offered for sale the Robert Muller *World Core Curriculum* (a New Age elementary education curriculum), written by Muller who served as the under secretary of the UN. The *World Core Curriculum* states that it is based on the teachings of Alice Bailey's spirit guide, the Tibetan teacher Djwhal Khul. The present address for Lucis Trust is: 120 Wall St., New York, NY. Muller's curriculum can also be ordered from: Robert Muller School, 6005 Royaloak Dr., Arlington, TX. It should be noted that the Robert Muller School is a member of the UNESCO Associated Schools Project, certified as a United Nations Associated School.

5

THE SICK SIXTIES:
psychology and skills

Presidents Eisenhower, Kennedy and Johnson, while ostensibly concerning themselves with racial injustice, economic inequities, and equal educational opportunities, were, in fact, responsible for installing the lifelong control system—the Planning, Programming, Budgeting Management System (PPBS)—into all departments of government. This was accomplished during what would become "The Sick Sixties" under the guise of "accountability to the taxpayers," a theme which will be repeated throughout the remainder of this century.

American education would henceforth concern itself with the importance of the *group* rather than with the importance of the individual. This would be true in spite of the push towards individualized education (mastery learning and computers), leading people to believe that concern for the individual was the driving force behind change.

Like "accountability," another common thread running through "The Sick Sixties" was the idea that for the first time in America the purpose of education would be to focus on the student's *emotional health* rather than on his academic learning. In order to change society, it was essential to identify the attitudinal changes needed in each student; then, modify the student's behavior according to the preconceived model approved by government social engineers known as "change agents." This model did not allow for competition or individual thought, belief, etc., but was conceived to standardize (robotize) human beings—particularly Americans—so that the entire populace would be in general agreement with government policy and future planning for world government.

Removal of the last semblance of local control would come through the passage of the *Elemen-*

tary and Secondary Education Act of 1965 (ESEA), the most important piece of legislation to pass during Lyndon Johnson's administration.

Two of the major federal initiatives developed with funding from *The Elementary and Secondary Education Act of 1965* which have contributed to the "deliberate dumbing down" of not only students but teachers as well, are listed below:

1. the 1965–1969 Behavioral Science Teacher Education Program (BSTEP), and

2. the 1969 publication by the federal government of *Pacesetters in Innovation*, a 584-page catalogue of behavior modification programs to be used by the schools.

Pacesetters provided evidence of a concerted effort to destroy the last vestiges of traditional academic education, replacing it with a behavior and mind control system guaranteed to create the "New Soviet Man" who would be unlikely to challenge totalitarian policies emanating from his local, state or federal/international government. Professor John Goodlad, the nation's premiere change agent who has been receiving federal and tax-exempt foundation grants for at least thirty years, said in 1969:

> The most controversial issues of the twenty-first century will pertain to the ends and means of modifying human behavior and who shall determine them. The first educational question will not be "what knowledge is of the most worth?" but "what kinds of human beings do we wish to produce?" The possibilities virtually defy our imagination.[1]

Behavior change on such a massive scale necessitated the creation of many agencies and policy devices which would oversee the implementation of the necessary innovations. Three agencies were: (1) the National Assessment of Educational Progress (NAEP), which tested students at various grade levels; (2) the Education Commission of the States (ECS), which enabled the states to become unified regarding education and its outreach—one entity supposedly controlled by its member states, but in reality controlled by its consensus policy which invariably reflected federal policy—and (3) the National Diffusion Network (NDN) which served as the transmission belt and advertising agency for federally funded programs, the majority of which were intended to destroy traditional right/wrong absolutist values through psychotherapeutic and behavioral techniques.[2]

Congressman John M. Ashbrook of Ohio, to whose memory the writer has dedicated this book, expressed his concern over the above-described radical shift in the direction of education before the U.S. House of Representatives on July 18, 1961 in a speech he delivered entitled "The Myth of Federal Aid to Education without Control." With extraordinary foresight, John Ashbrook warned that:

> In the report *A Federal Education Agency for the Future* we find the vehicle for Federal domination of our schools. It is a real and present danger.... The battle lines are now being drawn between those who seek control and uniformity of our local schools and those who oppose this further bureaucratic centralization in Washington. It is my sincere hope that the Congress will respond to this challenge and defeat the aid to education bills which will implement the goals incorporated in *A Federal Education Agency for the Future*.

Unfortunately, Congressman Ashbrook's words of wisdom did not convince his fellow colleagues and, therefore, did not influence the burgeoning sentiment of the majority in Congress. Had Ashbrook's views prevailed, the citizens of this great nation would be in a far better position to deal with the problems we face at home and abroad in 1999.

1960

UNITED NATIONS EDUCATIONAL, SCIENTIFIC AND CULTURAL ORGANIZATION'S *CONVENTION Against Discrimination* was signed in Paris, France in 1960. This *Convention* laid the groundwork for control of American education—both public and private—by U.N. agencies and agents.

SOVIET EDUCATION PROGRAMS: FOUNDATIONS, CURRICULUMS, TEACHER PREPARATION BY William K. Medlin (specialist in Comparative Education for Eastern Europe, Division of International Education), Clarence B. Lindquist (chief of Natural Sciences and Mathematics, Division of Higher Education), and Marshall L. Schmitt (specialist for Industrial Arts, Division of State and Local School Systems) was published in 1960 under the auspices of U.S. Department of Health, Education and Welfare Secretary Arthur S. Flemming and Office of Education Commissioner Lawrence G. Derthick (OE–14037, Bulletin 1960, No. 17). Americans familiar with the details of American school-to-work restructuring will see that the United States is adopting the Soviet polytechnic system described in the following paper. The "Pavlovian conditioned reflex theory" discussed is the Skinnerian mastery learning/direct instruction method required in order to implement outcome-based education and school-to-work. Excerpts from this extraordinarily important report follow:

> HIGHLIGHTS
>   In the school classroom and workshop, in the machine building plant, at the countryside, and wherever we went, we felt the pulse of the Soviet Government's drive to educate and train a new generation of technically skilled and scientifically literate citizens. Such is the consensus of the three specialists who are authors of this volume.
>   The ideas and practices of Soviet education form a philosophy of education in which the authoritarian concept predominates.... With 60 percent of the adult male population illiterate in 1900, a massive educational effort was deemed necessary to transform this situation into one where new skills and scientific inquiry could meet national needs.
>   The curriculum is unified and is the same for all schools throughout the U.S.S.R. with but slight variations in non-Russian nationality areas.... Principles of Darwinism, which are studied in grade 9 of U.S.S.R. schools, teach children about the origin of life together with the history of evolution in the organic world. The main theme of the course is evolution.
>   Major efforts of U.S.S.R. schools during the past 30 years have been to train youngsters for the Government's planned economic programs and to inculcate devotion to its political and social system.... Science and mathematics occupy 31.4 percent of the student's time in the complete U.S.S.R. 10-year school.
>   According to school officials, all work of pupils in these subjects has to be done in pen and ink in order to inculcate habits of neatness and accuracy.
>   U.S.S.R. plans are to bring all secondary school children into labor education and

training experiences through the regular school program. The "school of general education" is now named the "labor-polytechnic school of general education."

Industrial and agricultural sciences and technical developments are causing Soviet educators to be concerned about future needs for readapting the schools to give more appropriate instruction for the coming age of automation, atomic power, and space.... The authors consider the polytechnic program in the Soviet elementary-secondary schools "as an integral part of the Soviet philosophy of education." It is not a subject but in fact a *type* [emphasis in the original] of education, and other subjects... contribute to the polytechnic area.

Soviet patriotism—fidelity to the Soviet land and to the ideas of communism—occupies a leading place in this educational conditioning, and in this sense gives the school a political character as well as a moral one. Employing primarily the conditioned reflex theory as elaborated by Pavlov (1849–1936), Soviet psychologists have worked out a system of didactics which are strict and fixed in their conception and application; one might even use the term "narrow" to distinguish them from the broad scope of methods employed, for example, in most U.S. schools. Soviet psychologists maintain that fundamentally all (except physically disturbed or handicapped) children can learn the standardized subject matter through the teaching methods devised for all schools. By definition, therefore, they exclude from practical consideration many educational techniques.... The curriculum, dominated until now by the so-called "hard" subjects, is designed to give all future citizens an intellectual foundation that is, in form, a traditional European one. This systematic approach to education tends to give Soviet teachers a classroom control that appears complete.

Certain of their psychological research findings in the past are not the only explanation that we observe for this principle, however, and it is well to point out that Soviet psychologists have only recently been in a position to try out new methods in connection with a more diversified curriculum. As one Moscow educator pointed out to us in a discussion on methods, the researchers are not always successful in getting their results and viewpoints adopted in school programs. Psychologists and other researchers are busily engaged in work on such areas as development of the cognitive activity of pupils in the teaching process (especially in relation to the polytechnic curriculum); simplification in learning reading and arithmetic skills in the lower grades; the formation of character and teaching moral values, including Soviet patriotism; psychological preparation of future teachers; the principles and methods for meeting individual children's needs (such as "self-appreciation"),[3] in terms of handicaps and as regards a child's particular attitudes, peculiarities, and maturity; and understanding the internal, structural integrity of each school subject and its interrelationships with other branches of knowledge. These research activities are carried out under Soviet conditions and exemplify some of the major problems which educators there now face.

Soviet educators define their system as an all-round training whereby youth can participate in creating the conditions for a socialist, and ultimately, Communist society. Such participation can become possible, they hold, only as students cultivate all the basic disciplines and only through a "steady rise in the productivity of labor"... which is linked closely with the educative process. School children and students are engaged in a total educational program which aims to teach all the same basic subjects, morals and habits in order to provide society with future workers and employees whose general education will make them socialist (Communist) citizens and contribute to their productivity upon learning a vocation (profession). (pp. 10–11)

IN 1960 PRESIDENT DWIGHT D. EISENHOWER RECEIVED A FINAL REPORT FROM HIS COM-mission on National Goals entitled *Goals for Americans*. The 372-page volume recommended carrying out an international, socialist agenda for the United States. This report, following on the heels of the 1955 White House Conference on Education's use of the Delphi technique,[4] served to carve in stone the use of dialectic methods in public policy making through the use of results-based "planning" by consensus, not consent. This also may have marked the beginning of restructuring America from a constitutional republic to a socialist democracy.

Before listing an excerpted version of *Goals for Americans*, the writer would like to point out that although on their face these goals may sound legitimate, they are, in fact, blatantly socialistic. Only those recommendations which lean towards socialism have been included in this entry.

GOALS FOR AMERICANS

II. EQUALITY. Every man and woman must have equal rights before the law, and an equal opportunity to vote and hold office, to be educated, to get a job and to be promoted when qualified, to buy a home, to participate fully in community affairs.

III. THE DEMOCRATIC PROCESS. ...With firm faith in individual American responsibility, the Commission answered these questions with a confident and yet measured "yes." While stressing private responsibility, the Commission also forthrightly favors government action at all levels whenever necessary to achieve the national goals.... The Commission adopted as its own his [Professor Wallace S. Sayre of Columbia University] principal recommendations, that "the President be given unequivocal authority and responsibility to develop a true senior civil service," and that the pay of top government employees should be drastically increased.

IV. EDUCATION. Annual Public and Private Expenditure for Education by 1970 Must Be Approximately $40 Billion—Double the 1960 Figure.... There must be more and better teachers, enlarged facilities, and changes in curricula and methods. Above all, schooling should fit the varying capacities of individuals; every student should be stimulated to work to his utmost; authentic concern for excellence is imperative.

Among specific steps, the Commission recommended that:

1. Small and inefficient school districts should be consolidated, reducing the total number from 40,000 to about 10,000.[5]
2. Teachers' salaries at all levels must be improved.
3. Two-year colleges should be within commuting distance of most high school graduates.
4. Adult education should provide a new emphasis on education throughout life....

VI. DISARMAMENT. Disarmament should be our ultimate goal.

VII. LESS DEVELOPED NATIONS. The success of the underdeveloped nations must depend primarily on their own efforts. We should assist by providing education, training, economic and technical assistance, and by increasing the flow of public and private capital.... Doubling their rate of economic growth within five years is a reasonable objective.... The U.S. share of such an effort would require by 1965 an outflow of $5 to $5.5 billion per year of public and private capital, as compared with

$3.4 billion per year in the 1956–59 period....

> X. THE UNITED NATIONS. A key goal in the pursuit of a vigorous and effective foreign policy is the preservation and strengthening of the United Nations.

At the end of the Commission on National Goals report is the following:

> [A]ttributed to American Assembly, founded by Dwight D. Eisenhower in 1950 when he was President of Columbia University.

Attached to the report was a pamphlet entitled "Suggestions for Holding a Local Assembly on National Goals." The process for arriving at "consensus" explained in the pamphlet is actually group dynamics. Consensus is *not* consent! These documents prove there has been a well-formulated and funded plan to change the American system of government through decision-making by unelected task forces, Soviet-style five-year plans, Delphi-type discussion groups, etc. This type of participatory decision making called for by regional government—involving partnerships and unelected councils—is taking place in every state of the nation today. It is rarely challenged since few Americans understand our constitutional form of government, and are, therefore, unable to recognize the important differences between a representative republic and the parliamentary form of government found in socialist democracies.

TEACHING MACHINES AND PROGRAMMED LEARNING: A SOURCE BOOK (DEPARTMENT OF Audio-Visual Instruction, National Education Association: Washington, D.C., 1960), edited by A.A. Lumsdaine (program director of the American Institute for Research and professor of education at the University of California in Los Angeles) and Robert Glaser (professor of psychology at the University of Pittsburgh and research advisor at the American Institute for Research) was published. Extensive excerpts from this document can be found in Appendix II Some interesting selections follow:

[Chapter entitled] The Science of Learning and the Art of Teaching by B.F. Skinner

> Recent improvements in the conditions which control behavior in the field of learning are of two principal sorts. The "law of effect" has been taken seriously; we have made sure that effects *do* occur and that they occur under conditions which are optimal for producing the changes called learning. Once we have arranged the particular type of consequence called a reinforcement, our techniques permit us to shape the behavior of an organism almost at will. It has become a routine exercise to demonstrate this in classes in elementary psychology by conditioning such an organism as a pigeon. (pp. 99–100)...
> In all this work, the species of the organism has made surprisingly little difference. It is true that the organisms studied have all been vertebrates, but they still cover a wide range. Comparable results have been obtained with rats, pigeons, dogs, monkeys, human children, and most recently—by the author in collaboration with Ogden R. Lindsley—with human psychotic subjects. In spite of great phylogenetic differences, all these organisms show amazingly similar properties of the learning process. It should be emphasized that this has been achieved by analyzing the effects of reinforcement and by designing techniques which manipulate reinforcement with considerable precision. Only in this way can the behavior of the individual organism be brought under such precise control. It is also important to note that through a gradual advance to complex interrelations among responses, the same degree of

rigor is being extended to behavior which would usually be assigned to such fields as perception, thinking, and personality dynamics. (p. 103)

1961

PROGRAMMED LEARNING: EVOLVING PRINCIPLES AND INDUSTRIAL APPLICATIONS (Foundation for Research on Human Behavior: Ann Arbor, Mich., 1961) edited by Jerome P. Lysaught was published. Appendix III contains significant material from this book. An excerpt from the introduction by Thomas H. Miller follows:

> To introduce the subject, we would like to have each of you work through the first lesson of Dr. B.F. Skinner's course in psychology. We would hope, incidentally, that a portion of the material is somewhat new to you so that some learning will actually take place in your encounter with the subject matter. Further, we hope it will demonstrate certain phenomena that will be spoken of repeatedly today, such as effective reinforcement of the learner and progress at the individual rate.
>
> Imagine yourself to be a freshman student at Harvard. You are taking, for the first time, a college course in psychology. This is your first day in that course. Your introduction to the course consists of the presentation of the programmed learning sequence on the next pages.
>
> The directions are simple. You should read the first stimulus item, S-1, consider it, and then construct in your own words the best possible answer. As soon as you have done this, turn the page and compare your answer with the answer listed at R-1, the first response item. Proceed through the program, going on to S-2 on the next page.

Under the section entitled "Principles of Programming," written by Robert Glaser, we find the following excerpts to be revealing:

> It is indeed true that this book would never have been conceived without the well-known and perhaps undying work of Professor Skinner.... It is largely through Professor Skinner's work that all this theory and excitement about teaching machines and programmed learning has come about.
>
> The essential task involved is to evoke the specific forms of behavior from the student and through appropriate reinforcement bring them under the control of specific subject matter stimuli. As a student goes through a learning program certain of his responses must be strengthened and shaped from initial unskilled behavior to subject matter competence.... Our present knowledge of the learning process points out that through the process of reinforcement, new forms of behavior can be created with a great degree of subtlety. The central feature of this process is making the reinforcement contingent upon performances of the learner. (Often the word "reward" is used to refer to one class of reinforcing events.)...
>
> The term "programming" refers to the process of constructing sequences of instructional material in a way that maximizes the rate of acquisition and retention and enhances the motivation of the student.... A central process for the acquisition of behavior is reinforcement. Behavior is acquired as a result of a contingent relationship between the response of an organism and a consequent event. In order for these contingencies of reinforcement to be effective, certain conditions must be met. Reinforcement must follow the occurrence of the behavior being taught. If this is not the case, different and perhaps unwarranted behavior will be learned.

ON JULY 18, 1961, CONGRESSMAN JOHN M. ASHBROOK DELIVERED A SPEECH BEFORE CONgress entitled "The Myth of Federal Aid to Education without Control" (*Congressional Record*: pp. 11868–11880). Excerpts from his very important speech, which documented and exposed the plans for the internationalization and transformation of American education, follow:

> That there was any doubt of the Federal bureaucrats' intentions in this matter was laid to rest with the discovery of a Health, Education, and Welfare publication, *A Federal Education Agency for the Future*, which is a report of the Office of Education, dated April 1961.... I feel that its pronouncements are a blueprint for complete domination and direction of our schools from Washington. The publication was not popularly distributed and there was some difficulty in obtaining a copy.
>
> Fifty-six pages of findings contain recommendations which call for more and more Federal participation and control and repeatedly stress the need for Federal activity in formulating educational policies. It recommends a review of teacher preparation, curriculum and textbooks. It calls for an implementation of international education projects in cooperation with UNESCO in the United Nations, and ministries of education abroad. Of course, it recommends an enlarged office of education and the use of social scientists as key advisers.... It places stress on "implementing international educational projects in the United States and bringing maximum effectiveness to the total international educational effort." Would not the Communists, with their footholds and infiltrations in these organizations, love this? No detail has been overlooked—"curriculum will have to undergo continual reshaping and upgrading; and new techniques and tools of instruction will have to be developed" and "teacher preparation, textbooks, and the curriculum in these subject fields must be improved in the decade ahead." In the report... we find the vehicle for Federal domination of our schools.
>
> ...The battle lines are now drawn between those who seek control and uniformity of our local schools and those who oppose this further bureaucratic centralization in Washington. It is my sincere hope that the Congress will respond to this challenge and defeat the aid to education bills which will implement the goals incorporated in *A Federal Education Agency for the Future*.

Ashbrook went on to point out that

> [Under] The Mission [as stated in the report]... the basic mission of the Office [of Education] to "promote the cause of education" remains unchanged since its establishment in 1867.
>
> ...What is meant when he [Sterling M. McMurrin, Commissioner of Education] says, "I anticipate that much of this activity will take place through normal administrative processes within the Office and the Department"? In the jargon of Washington bureaucracy this means that the report will be largely implemented on the administrative level without Congressional action and approval.
>
> The House Committee on Education and Labor recently voted out H.R. 7904 which would extend the *National Defense Education Act*.... It is evident that the administration has chosen this vehicle for enacting piecemeal the recommendations of *A Federal Education Agency for the Future*.

Ashbrook continued to quote from *Agency for the Future* which he said "laid bare the real nemesis of the Federal bureaucrats—the tradition of local control." The report stated, "The tradition of local control should no longer be permitted to inhibit Office of Education leadership." The Committee on Mission and Organization called for

[An] Office of Educational Research that would administer a separate program of extra-mural contracts and grants for basic and experimental research in disciplines bearing upon the educational situation, and would serve the other parts of the Bureau with advice on research problems.... Since it is presumed that the Centers, oriented to education as it is organized and administered, will deal with educational problems directly confronting schools and colleges, it is believed desirable that extra-mural research be significantly attentive to basic problems of human development, training and teaching, regardless of whether or not they are acknowledged as immediately pressing problems by educators. In short, some research should be conducted precisely because it challenges the assumptions upon which practicing educators are proceeding.

The above is obviously a reference to behavioral sciences research which, until that time, had not found a permanent home at the local school educator level nor was there the need to conduct such research in order to challenge the "assumptions upon which practicing educators are proceeding." Attached to the Committee's report were appendices from which the following excerpts are taken:

Appendix B
The Mission of the Office of Education in the 1960s

The schools of tomorrow must prepare their students for living in a world of continuous and rapid change, presenting them with unprecedented social, economic, and political problems. We must, in fact, give to education a character that will initiate and support a process of lifelong learning if Americans are to keep abreast of the accelerating advent of new knowledge and of the increasing complexity of modern life. These prospective conditions are already suggested in part by the rapidly increasing demand for highly specialized and professional skills. During the coming decade, new means must be developed for identifying and releasing student potential; curriculums will have to undergo continual reshaping and upgrading; and new techniques and tools of instruction will have to be developed....

- Education is basic to effort to bring about an enduringly peaceful world.
- Next decade will bring closer and multiple relationships with Ministries of Education abroad and international organizations, such as UNESCO, the Organization of American States, International Bureau of Education.
- Variations among States and school districts in standards of instruction, facilities, staff, and services expose serious inadequacies. Our progress toward the ideal of equality of educational opportunity is tragically uneven.
- In the area of international educational cooperation, in particular, it must play the major role, since only the Federal Government can enter into agreements with other governments. Along with these responsibilities should be included that of stimulating and participating activity in the process of formulation, examination, and reformulation of the goals of our national society in terms of educational objectives.
- The development of uniform, consistent and compatible statistical data in all States and in all institutions of higher education will call for both technical and financial assistance to these sources from the Office of Education....
- Economists, sociologists, and other social scientists will be needed on the staff to assist in dealing with educational problems in their total context.

National Defense Education Act (NDEA) *Amendment of 1961—Additional Views,* which accompanied H.R. 7904, included very important testimony regarding the dangers of the

NDEA and the recommendations made in the above *Agency for the Future* report. A discussion of the dangers of federal control follows:

> We [the undersigned] reject, furthermore, the philosophy that there can exist Federal aid to any degree without Federal control. We further hold that there should not be Federal aid without Federal control. It is the responsibility of the Federal Government to so supervise and control its allocations that waste and misuse is kept to a minimum. Since we do not desire such federal control in the field of public education, we do not desire Federal aid to education.
>
> We should never permit the American educational system to become the vehicle for experimentation by educational ideologues. A careful analysis of the writings and statements of vocal and influential spokesmen in the governmental and educational fields indicates a desire on the part of some of these individuals to utilize the educational system as a means of transforming the economic and social outlook of the United States.
>
> We point to a statement by Dr. Harold Rugg, for many years professor of education at Teachers College, Columbia University, who declared in *Frontiers of Democracy* on May 15, 1943 (pp. 247–254) concerning the teachers' colleges:

> > Let them become powerful national centers for the graduate study of ideas and they will thereby become forces of creative imagination standing at the very vortex of the ideational revolution. Let us make our teacher education institutions into great direction finders for our new society, pointers of the way, dynamic trailblazers of the New Frontiers.

> We could supply pages of documentation analyzing the type of new frontier planned. It is indeed a Socialist frontier. It had been hoped that the philosophy of education expressed by Dr. Rugg and his cohorts back in the early forties, had long since been repudiated. However, in April of 1961, the U.S. Department of Health, Education, and Welfare published a booklet entitled *A Federal Education Agency for the Future*. Anyone who doubts that the Federal aid to education bills now before Congress would mean eventual Federal control of education, should carefully read and analyze for himself what the Office of Education is planning for tomorrow's schools. They openly predict their "need" for new powers on the passage of the multimillion-dollar aid legislation now before us. They recommend that their Office of Education be elevated to the status of U.S. Education Agency, "to reflect the more active role of this unit of Government." They envision the new Agency's mission as one of "leadership" (p. 42), "national policymaking" (p. 43), "national planning" (p. 47), "to prepare students to understand the world of tomorrow" (p. 40). The Office of Education writers further say "along with these responsibilities should be included that of stimulating and participating in the process of formulation, examination, and reformulation of the goals of our society in the terms of educational objectives" (p. 43).

[Ed. Note: A careful warning was sounded through the *National Defense Education Act Amendment of 1961—Additional Views* when the Congressmen said, "We reject that there can exist Federal aid to any degree without Federal control. We further hold that there should not be Federal aid without Federal control." This applies as well to all of the voucher and tax credit proposals before us today (in 1999) flying under the banner of "choice."

The Mission Statement of the Office of Education clearly called for the establishment of the National Center for Education Statistics, the National Assessment of Educational Progress, and the "wholistic" approach to education through the inclusion of social scientists in the education process—a clear departure from academically oriented educational pursuits into intrusive areas totally unrelated to education.

Even taking into account the collectivist direction taken by radical educators in the first half of this century, this movement could not have borne fruit had it not been for President Dwight Eisenhower's Commission on National Goals which produced *Goals for Americans* in 1960. These goals, along with the implementation of PPBS and Bloom's *Taxonomy of Educational Objectives*, seem to have provided the catalyst for the "planned economy" being implemented in the United States in 1999.]

ON SEPTEMBER 2, 1961 THE 87TH CONGRESS PASSED THE *ARMS CONTROL AND DISARMAMENT Act* (P.L. 87–297, H.R. 9118) which established a United States Arms Control and Disarmament Agency. Following is the statement of purpose for this important *Act*:

Public Law 87–297
87th Congress, H.R. 9118
September 26, 1961

AN ACT

To establish a United States Arms Control and Disarmament Agency.
Be it enacted by the Senate and House of Representatives of the United States of America in Congress Assembled,

TITLE 1—SHORT TITLE, PURPOSE, AND DEFINITIONS
SHORT TITLE

SECTION 1. This Act may be cited as the "Arms Control and Disarmament Act."
SECTION 2. As used in this Act—

(a) The Terms "arms control" and "disarmament" mean the identification, verification, inspection, limitation, control, reduction, or elimination, of armed forces and armaments of all kinds under international agreement including the necessary steps taken under such an agreement to establish an effective system of international control, or to create and strengthen international organizations for the maintenance of peace.

As partial fulfillment of the provision to take "the necessary steps... to establish an effective system of international control, or to create and strengthen international organizations for the maintenance of peace," President John F. Kennedy's U.S. Department of State simultaneously issued *State Department Publication 7277: The United States Program for General and Complete Disarmament in a Peaceful World*. The following are excerpts from Publication 7277:

[a] world in which adjustment to change takes place in accordance with the principles of the United Nations.

In order to make possible the achievement of that goal, the program sets forth the following specific objectives toward which nations should direct their efforts.

- The disbanding of all national armed forces and the prohibition of their reestablishment in any form whatsoever other than those required to preserve internal order and for contributions to a United Nations Peace Force.
- The elimination from national arsenals of all armaments including all weapons of mass destruction and the means for their delivery, other than those required for a United Nations Peace Force and for maintaining internal order.

- The manufacture of armaments would be prohibited except for those of agreed types and quantities to be used by the U.N. Peace Force and those required to maintain internal order. All other armaments would be destroyed or converted to peaceful purposes.

During the Congressional debate over the *Arms Control and Disarmament Act*, those favoring the establishment of the agency called it the "Peace Agency." Congressman John Ashbrook, an opponent of the measure and its implications, called it the "Surrender Agency" and further expressed his concern that the agency "may well be the back door for the one-worlders to accomplish their goal of an International World Court." Additionally, Senator Joseph S. Clark of Pennsylvania declared on the floor of the U.S. Senate March 1, 1962 that this new international focus was "the fixed, determined and approved policy of the government of the United States," much to his sorrow.

[Ed. Note: The goal perceived by Ashbrook, Clark and others of the *Arms Control and Disarmament Act* was to further extend the influence and control of the United Nations through United States contributions to the power of the UN regional alliances such as the North Atlantic Treaty Organization (NATO) and Southeast Asia Treaty Organization (SEATO). The development of education curriculum by United Nations Educational, Scientific, and Cultural Organization (UNESCO) and its outreach to the youth and communities throughout the world, coupled with the international political and economic weight of the UN through NATO and the UN's treaty-making capacity, lends credence to the concerns voiced in Congress and elsewhere that a one-world government has been in the making since the end of World War II.]

"HARRISON BERGERON," ONE OF THE SEVERAL SHORT STORIES BY KURT VONNEGUT, JR., included in his book *Welcome to the Monkey House* (Delacorte Press/Seymour Lawrence: New York, 1961), provided uncanny insight into the nature of America's dumbed-down society in the year 2081. How the elitist "planners, managers" deal with Americans whose intellects and independence create problems for the smooth functioning of a society controlled for the benefit of all is the focus of the story.[6] An excerpt follows:

> The year was 2081, and everybody was equal. They weren't only equal before God and the law. They were equal every which way. Nobody was smarter than anybody else. Nobody was stronger or quicker than anybody else. All this equality was due to the 211th, 212th, and 213th Amendments to the Constitution, and to the unceasing vigilance of agents of the United States Handicapper General.

[Ed. Note: The reader will, later in this book, recall this fictional forecast when encountering outcome-based education, Individual Education Plans (IEP's) for ALL—not just the handicapped—and the *Reading Excellence Act* passed by Congress October 16, 1998, which will provide federal tax support for Skinnerian phonics instruction programs developed and used with special education children for over 25 years. In 1999 House Education and Workforce Committee Chairman William Goodling (PA) will also propose the removal of funding from present titles of the *Elementary and Secondary Act* (ESEA) in order to completely fund the *Individuals with Disabilities in Education Act* (IDEA). Vonnegut's office of "Handicapper General" may not wait until 2081!]

1962

IN THE SEPTEMBER 3, 1962 EDITION OF *THE DAN SMOOT REPORT*[7] (VOL. 8, NO. 36) SMOOT'S article "Stabbed in the Back on the Fourth of July" dealt with an Independence Day speech given in Philadelphia by President John F. Kennedy in which he said:

> But I will say here and now on this day of independence that the United States will be ready for a Declaration of Interdependence—that we will be prepared to discuss with a United Europe the ways and means of forming a concrete Atlantic Partnership—a mutually beneficial partnership between the new union now emerging in Europe and the old American Union founded here 175 years ago.
> Today Americans must learn to think intercontinentally.

On July 11, 1961, according to Smoot's report:

> James Reston (a member of the Council on Foreign Relations and an admirer of President Kennedy) commented on the President's speech in a *New York Times* article :

> > This year... President Kennedy went to Independence Hall, of all places, and on the Fourth of July, of all days, and virtually proposed to repeal the *Declaration of Independence* in favor of a declaration of interdependence.... Maybe it is just the drowsy indolence of the summer, but American opinion seems remarkably receptive, or at least acquiescent, to President Kennedy's proposal for a partnership of the Atlantic nations.... In Washington, there was not a whisper of protest from a single national leader.

1963

THE ROLE OF THE COMPUTER IN FUTURE INSTRUCTIONAL SYSTEMS WAS PUBLISHED AS THE March/April, 1963 supplement of *Audiovisual Communication Review* (Monograph 2 of the Technological Development Project of the National Education Association [Contract #SAE9073], U.S. Office of Education, Dept. of Health, Education and Welfare: Washington, D.C., 1963). James D. Finn of Los Angeles was the principal investigator and Donald P. Ely was the consulting investigator for this project. (Donald Ely also became project director for the U.S. Department of Education's *Project BEST: Basic Educational Skills through Technology*, which will be discussed in a later entry in this book.) Excerpts from a chapter entitled "Effortless Learning, Attitude Changing, and Training in Decision-Making" follow:

> Another area of potential development in computer applications is the attitude changing machine. Dr. Bertram Raven in the Psychology Department at the University of California at Los Angeles is in the process of building a computer-based device for changing attitudes. This device will work on the principle that students' attitudes can be changed effectively by using the Socratic method of asking an appropriate series of leading questions designed to right the balance between appropriate attitudes, and those deemed less acceptable. For instance, after first determining a student's constellation of attitudes through appropriate testing procedures, the machine would calculate which attitudes are "out of phase" and which of these are amenable to change. If the student were opposed to foreign trade, say, and a favorable disposition were sought for, the machine would select an appropriate series of

statements and questions organized to right the imbalance in the student's attitudes. The machine, for instance, would have detected that the student liked President Kennedy and was against the spread of Communism; therefore, the student would be shown that JFK favored foreign trade and that foreign trade to underdeveloped countries helped to arrest the Communist infiltration of these governments. If the student's attitudes toward Kennedy and against Communism were sufficiently strong, Dr. Raven would hypothesize that a positive change in attitude toward foreign trade would be effectively brought about by showing the student the inconsistency of his views. There is considerable evidence that such techniques do effectively change attitudes.

Admittedly, training in decision-making skills is a legitimate goal of education in this age of automation, but the problem remains—does the educator know what values to attach to the different outcomes of these decisions?... What about students whose values are out of line with the acceptable values of democratic society? Should they be taught to conform to someone else's accepted judgment of proper values? Training in decision-making is ultimately compounded with training in value judgment and, as such, becomes a controversial subject that needs to be resolved by educators before the tools can be put to use.

UNIVERSITY OF PITTSBURGH'S LEARNING RESEARCH AND DEVELOPMENT CENTER introduced in 1963 the Individually Prescribed Instruction (IPI) model which would allow for the implementation of continuous progress programs necessary for value change and school-to-work training. A good example of what Individually Prescribed Instruction is designed to do is given in *Planned Change in Education: A Systems Approach*, edited by David S. Bushnell of Project Focus and Donald Rappaport of Price Waterhouse & Co. (Harcourt, Brace and Jovanovich, Inc.: New York, 1971). Excerpts from chapter 7, "Individualizing Instruction" by Robert G. Scanlon, program director for the Individualizing Learning Program of Research for Better Schools, Inc., and Mary V. Brown, assistant program director to the project, are reprinted below:

IPI is an instructional system that permits the teacher to plan and conduct a program of studies tailored to the needs and characteristics of each student. Its procedures have been designed to enable the school to meet more of the needs of more individual pupils and take a new direction in the continuing search for ways to adapt instruction to individual pupils. The rate of learning, amount of practice, type of materials, and mode of instruction are the parameters of individual differences emphasized in IPI.

During the school year 1963–64, the Learning Research and Development Center and the Baldwin-Whitehall public schools (a suburban Pittsburgh school system) initiated an experimental project to investigate the feasibility of a system of individualized instruction in an entire K–6 school (Oakleaf). This came as a result of a series of exploratory studies begun in 1951–1962 designed to test preliminary notions in a single classroom. The work started with the use of programmed instruction in an intact classroom.

As work proceeded, it became apparent that the significant individualization feature of programmed instruction could not be augmented unless the organization of the classroom was changed to permit a more flexible context. Out of this experience grew the current Individually Prescribed Instruction project in which various combinations of instructional materials, testing procedures, and teacher practices are being used to accommodate individual student differences.

IPI is a system based on a set of specified objectives correlated with diagnostic instruments, curriculum materials, teaching techniques, and management capabilities. The objectives of the system are:

1. to permit student mastery of instructional content at individual learning rates;
2. to ensure active student involvement in the learning process;
3. to encourage student involvement in learning through self-directed and self-initiated activities;
4. to encourage student evaluation of progress toward mastery and to provide instructional materials and techniques based on individual needs and styles. (pp. 93–95)

[Ed. Note: IPI is necessary to the success of outcome-based education because it does away with norm-referenced testing and the traditional grading system. The Carnegie Unit is also jeopardized by the introduction of IPI. The federally funded laboratory Research for Better Schools, Inc., in Philadelphia, Pennsylvania field-tested IPI, thus setting the stage for Skinnerian mastery learning/direct instruction and the use of Skinner's "box" (the computer) to be incorporated into curriculum. Homeschoolers and Christian educators should be reminded that this project is reflected in many of the curricular and organizational designs advocated for their use.]

IN 1963 A NATIONAL PROJECT WAS INITIATED WHICH WAS THE FORERUNNER OF THE National Assessment of Educational Progress (NAEP) and became the model for individual state assessments which have created enormous controversy due to their focus on attitudinal and value change. This study was presented in *A Plan for Evaluating the Quality of Educational Programs in Pennsylvania: Highlights of a Report from Educational Testing Service to the State Board of Education of the Commonwealth of Pennsylvania* (Educational Testing Service: Princeton, N.J., June 30, 1965). The combination of the Skinnerian method of training and the assessments' emphasis on change in attitudes, values and beliefs resulted in what the average parent considered a "lethal concoction," absolutely guaranteed to create a "robotized citizen for the New Pagan Age." Although Appendix IV of this book includes verbatim text from the *Plan*, the following excerpts provide a fairly clear picture of the intent of those involved in this seminal project:

This Committee on Quality Education sought the advice of experts [including Dr. Urie Bronfenbrenner of the Department of Sociology, Cornell University; Dr. David R. Krathwohl of the College of Education, Michigan State University [a co-author with Benjamin Bloom of *The Taxonomy of Educational Objectives: Affective Domain*]; and Dr. Ralph Tyler, director of the Center for Advanced Study in the Behavioral Sciences in Palo Alto, California. These experts constituted a Standing Advisory Committee for the project....

It [the Committee] concluded that an educational program is to be regarded as adequate only if it can be shown to contribute to the total development of pupils.... The Committee recognizes that many of the desirable qualities that schools should help pupils acquire are difficult to define and even more difficult to measure. It feels, nevertheless, that any evaluation procedure that leaves these qualities out of account is deficient as a basis for determining whether the program of any school district is educationally adequate....

The first step in judging the quality of educational programs is to decide on the purposes of education. What should children *be* and *do* and *know* [emphasis in original] as a consequence of having gone to school? What are the goals of the schools? These questions have been high on the agenda of the Committee on Quality Education. Its members wanted a set of goals that would reflect the problems society faces in the world of today.... Measures of conventional academic achievement, for instance, are at a more advanced stage of development than measures of attitude and values.

Measures of progress toward the ten goals are unequally developed. Some are more dependable and valid than others. For example, tests of reading comprehension are relatively well developed and reasonably well understood while tests of such qualities as self-understanding and tolerance are less well developed and poorly understood.... Where the available measures are clearly inadequate, intensive research and development should be undertaken immediately to bring them to the point where they can have full effect in the evaluation program.

JAMES CLAVELL WROTE *THE CHILDREN'S STORY* (DELACORTE PRESS/ELEANOR FRIEDE: NEW York, 1963). In this book Clavell, author of *King Rat, Tai-Pan, Shogun* and *Noble House,* explains most eloquently how little children can have their minds manipulated into believing anything the teacher wants them to believe, even to the point of believing their parents are old-fashioned and should go back to school to unlearn bad thoughts, and that God does not exist. On the dust jacket of the book we learn:

It was a simple incident in the life of James Clavell—a talk with his young daughter just home from school—that inspired this chilling tale of what could happen in twenty-five quietly devastating minutes. He [Clavell] writes: *"the children's story* came into being that day. It was then that I really realized how vulnerable my child's mind was—any mind for that matter—under controlled circumstances."

Some excerpts from the last pages of this remarkable book follow:

"Sit down, Johnny, and we'll start learning good things and not worry about grown-up bad thoughts. Oh yes," she said when she sat down at her seat again, brimming with happiness. "I have a lovely surprise for you. You're all going to stay overnight with us. We have a lovely room and beds and lots of food, and we'll all tell stories and have such a lovely time."

"Oh, good," the children said.

"Can I stay up till eight o'clock?" Mary asked breathlessly.

"Well, as it's our first new day, we'll all stay up to eight-thirty. But only if you promise to go right to sleep afterward."

The children all promised. They were very happy. Jenny said, "But first we got to say our prayers. Before we go to sleep."

The New Teacher smiled at her. "Of course. Perhaps we should say a prayer now. In some schools that's a custom, too." She thought a moment, and the faces watched her. Then she said, "Let's pray. But let's pray for something very good. What should we pray for?"

"Bless Momma and Daddy," Danny said immediately.

"That's a good idea, Danny. I have one. Let's pray for candy. That's a good idea, isn't it?"

They all nodded happily.

So, following their New Teacher, they all closed their eyes and steepled their hands together, and they prayed with her for candy.

The New Teacher opened her eyes and looked around disappointedly. "But where's our candy? God is all-seeing and is everywhere, and if we pray, He answers our prayers. Isn't that true?"

"I prayed for a puppy of my own lots of times, but I never got one," Danny said.

"Maybe we didn't pray hard enough. Perhaps we should kneel down like it's done in church."

So the New Teacher knelt and all the children knelt and they prayed very, very hard. But there was still no candy.

Because the New Teacher was disappointed, the children were very disappointed. Then she said, "Perhaps we're using the wrong name." She thought a moment and then said, "Instead of saying 'God,' let's say 'Our Leader.' Let's pray to Our Leader for candy. Let's pray very hard and don't open your eyes till I say."

So the children shut their eyes tightly and prayed very hard, and as they prayed, the New Teacher took out some candy from her pocket and quietly put a piece on each child's desk. She did not notice Johnny—alone of all the children—watching her through his half-closed eyes.

She went softly back to her desk and the prayer ended, and the children opened their eyes and they stared at the candy and they were overjoyed.

"I'm going to pray to Our Leader every time," Mary said excitedly.

"Me, too," Hilda said. "Could we eat Our Leader's candy now, teacher?"

"Oh, let's, please, please, please."

"So Our Leader answered your prayers, didn't he?"

"I saw you put the candy on our desks!" Johnny burst out. "I *saw* you.... I didn't close my eyes, and I saw you. You had 'em in your pocket. We didn't get them with praying. *You* put them there."

All the children, appalled, stared at him and then at their New Teacher. She stood at the front of the class and looked back at Johnny and then at all of them.

"Yes, Johnny, you're quite right. You're a very, very wise boy. Children, *I* put candy on your desks. So you know that it doesn't matter whom you ask, whom you shut your eyes and 'pray' to—to God or anyone, even Our Leader—no one will give you anything. Only another human being." She looked at Danny. "God didn't give you the puppy you wanted. But if you work hard, I will. Only I or someone like me can *give* you things. Praying to God or anything or anyone for something is a waste of time." [all emphases in original]

1964

AN ARTICLE ENTITLED "ETHICAL EDUCATION" WAS PUBLISHED IN *FREE MIND*, THE JOURNAL of the American Humanist Association, in its June/July 1964 issue. The following is an excerpt:

> At the 1962 Humanist meeting in Los Angeles four women attended a workshop on humanist family services and began to lay the groundwork for the AHA's widespread involvement in ethical education for children.... The purpose of a humanist ethical education program should be to provide the child with tools by which he can make his own decisions.

[Ed. Note: From this time on efforts would be made to develop and implement humanistic (no right/no wrong) values education under many labels, just a few of which were/are: values clarification; decision making; critical thinking; problem solving; and moral, character, citizenship and civic education.]

IN 1964 THE CARNEGIE CORPORATION APPOINTED RALPH TYLER CHAIRMAN OF THE COM-
mittee on Assessing the Progress of Education which continued the project begun in 1963 that
would in 1969 become the National Assessment of Educational Progress (NAEP).

[Ed. Note: In 1999 NAEP is funded by the federal government and widely used across the
United States. Individual states are passing legislation to use NAEP as a state test and parents
and legislators are mistakenly believing that these "tests" (assessments) will give them information about the performance of their children in academic subjects. This is a misconception;
NAEP tracks conformity to government-generated goals.]

1965

THE BEHAVIORAL SCIENCE TEACHER EDUCATION PROGRAM (BSTEP), FUNDED BY THE U.S.
Department of Health, Education and Welfare, was initiated in 1965 at Michigan State University and carried out between the years 1965 and 1969. BSTEP's purpose was to change the
teacher from a transmitter of knowledge/content to a social change agent/facilitator/clini-
cian. Traditional public school administrators were appalled at this new role for teachers. (For
more extensive reading of the BSTEP proposal, see Appendix V.)

ELEMENTARY AND SECONDARY EDUCATION ACT (ESEA) *OF 1965* WAS PASSED BY CONGRESS.
This marked the end of local control and the beginning of nationalization/internationaliza-
tion of education in the United States. Use of goal-setting, Management by Objectives (MBO),
Planning, Programming, Budgeting Systems (PPBS) and systems management for accountability purposes would be totally funded by and directed from the federal level. The table of
contents for ESEA included:

- Title I—Financial Assistance to local educational agencies for education of children
  from low-income families
- Title II—School library resources, textbooks, and other instructional materials
- Title III—Supplementary educational centers and services, guidance counseling, and
  testing
- Title IV—Libraries, learning resources, educational innovation, and support
- Title V—Grants to strengthen State Departments of Education
- Title VI—Vacant
- Title VII—Bilingual education programs
- Title VIII—General provisions
- Title IX—Ethnic heritage program

ESEA targeted low income/minority students for experimentation with Skinnerian "basic skills" programs; i.e., Follow Through [mastery learning/direct instruction], Right-to-Read,
Exemplary Center for Reading Instruction (ECRI), Project INSTRUCT, etc. By the end of the
1980s state departments of education would be receiving between 60–75% of their operating
budget from the U.S. Department of Education—which was not even in existence at the time
of passage of the *ESEA*!

PRESIDENT LYNDON B. JOHNSON ISSUED AN EXECUTIVE ORDER IN 1965 INTRODUCING THE Planning, Programming and Budgeting System (PPBS) into use throughout all departments of the entire federal government.

THE EDUCATION COMMISSION OF THE STATES (ECS) WAS CREATED IN 1965 "IN ORDER TO bring some degree of order out of this chaos," wrote Harvard University President James B. Conant in 1964 in reference to education policy making in the United States. ECS was to be made up of dues-paying "members" comprising representatives of each participating state's legislative Education Committees and their governors. The Competency-Based Education (CBE) movement—which evolved into outcome-based education (OBE), both using mastery learning as a base—was orchestrated by ECS. Since ECS served as the resource and coordinator of information flowing to state legislative committees and governors' offices across the land, it is no wonder that all states ended up having the same curriculum.

A very important article, entitled "E.C.S. at 20: The Compact's Potential Is Still To Be Realized" by Thomas Toch which covered the history of ECS, was printed in *Education Week* (October 24, 1984). Excerpts follow:

> "Some degree of order needs to be brought out of this chaos," wrote James B. Conant, the President of Harvard University, in 1964 in reference to education policy making in the nation. "We cannot have a national educational policy," he added in his book *Shaping Educational Policy*, "but we might be able to evolve a nationwide policy." The solution, Mr. Conant concluded, was a "new venture in cooperative federalism," a compact among the states to create an organization to focus national attention on the pressing education issues of the day. The following spring, the Carnegie Corporation and the Ford Foundation awarded a grant to Terry Sanford, who had recently left the governorship of North Carolina, to transform the Conant idea into reality. John W. Gardner was Carnegie's president at the time. A preliminary draft of the compact was completed by July and endorsed by representatives from all 50 states and the territories in September. Within five months, 10 states had ratified the agreement, giving it legal status. Out of the compact was born the Education Commission of the States (E.C.S.)....
>
> "We invented a little device to get the compact approved quickly," Mr. Sanford, now the President of Duke University, said recently. "We didn't need money from the legislatures, we had plenty of foundation funding, so we agreed that the governors could ratify it by executive order."...
>
> But since the establishment under Governor James B. Hunt of the Commission's Task Force on Education for Economic Growth two years ago, ECS's role has begun to change. The task force's report *Action for Excellence* joined *A Nation at Risk* and the Carnegie Foundation for the Advancement of Teaching's *High School* acted as principal voices in the chorus of reform. It gained Gov. Hunt and several other "education governors" who were linked to ECS wide national publicity, and, in making a series of specific reform recommendations, thrust ECS into the policy-making arena.

PSYCHOSYNTHESIS: A MANUAL OF PRINCIPLES AND TECHNIQUES (PSYCHOSYNTHESIS Research Foundation: Crucible imprint of Aquarian Press, Thorsons Publishing Group: Northamptonshire, England, 1965) by Dr. Roberto Assagioli, a practicing psychiatrist in Florence, Italy, was published.

Roberto Assagioli defined "psychosynthesis" as the "formation or reconstruction of a new personality—the transpersonal or 'spiritual Self.'" An excerpt from *Psychosynthesis* explained:

> What distinguishes psychosynthesis from many other attempts at psychological understanding is the position we take as to the existence of a spiritual Self.... We consider that the spiritual is as basic as the material part of man... essentially we include within the study of psychological facts all those which may be related to the higher urges within man which tends to make him grow towards greater realization of his spiritual essence. Our position affirms that all the superior manifestations of the human psyche, such as creative imagination, intuition, aspiration, genius, are facts which are as real and as important as are the conditioned reflexes, and therefore, are susceptible to research and treatment just as scientifically as conditioned reflexes.

As psychology began to assert itself as an "acceptable science" in the "sick sixties," Assagioli's "psychosynthesis" concept is credited with creating a paradigm that enabled an integration (synthesis) of psychology with spirituality. Assagioli emphasized a holistic worldview, laying the groundwork for the future educational pedagogy of "holistic education" of the 1990s—teaching the "whole child." He was also the originator of a group of exercises for "Spiritual Psychosynthesis" based on what we now call "role playing." These include: "on the *Legend of the Holy Grail*," "on Dante's *Divine Comedy*," and "on the *Blossoming of the Rose*."

Assagioli's view of the human psyche included a progression from lower to higher order "consciousness" (or thinking) which is similar to "New Age" ideas about the evolution of man into a "collective consciousness." These ideas laid the philosophical foundation for character education, values clarification, and consciousness-altering techniques used in the classroom. For example, the "sick sixties" were hallmarked by the emergence of "transpersonal psychology," a designation typified today by the statement, "I'm OK, you're OK." One of its promoters—and a disciple of Roberto Assagioli—was Jack Canfield. Canfield's name appears on many education curricula and training programs utilizing behavior modification for values clarification.

Significantly, Roberto Assagioli's selected appendices in *Psychosynthesis* include an article entitled "Initiated Symbol Projection" (ISP) written by a German psychiatrist named Hanscarl Leurner. According to a note by Assagioli, "Dr. Leurner now prefers to call his method 'Guided Affective Imagery'"—a form of guided imagery widely practiced in elementary and secondary classrooms, business training sessions, counseling sessions, and religious services. A description of what Leurner called his "psycho-diagnostic and psycho-therapeutic technique" is provided:

> The subject is seated in a comfortable chair or on a couch (lying down), asked to close his eyes, and induced to relax...a light hypnoid state has proved valuable. Deep and regular breathing...[t]hen, in a psychological state characterized by diminished consciousness of the outer world, reduced conscious criticism and self-control, the subject is asked to visualize.... In the phenomenology of medical psychology, they are similar to "hypnogic visions."

[Ed. Note: The fact that guided imagery is a psychological technique raises a question regarding its use in the classroom by teachers who are not professional therapists.]

1966

PSYCHOLOGY BY WILBERT JAMES MCKEACHIE OF THE UNIVERSITY OF MICHIGAN AND CHARlotte Lackner Doyle of Cornell University (Addison-Wesley Publishing Co., Inc.: New York, 1966) was published. An excerpt from a chapter entitled "What Does a Psychologist Observe?" follows:

Watson's approach to psychology, with its emphasis on *observable* behavior, became known as behaviorism. The major problem with this approach was that it excluded from psychology some of its major concerns. No one can directly observe the motives, feelings, perceptions, thoughts, and memories of others. Re-defining thought in terms of muscle movements made thought a measurable event, but ignored some of the properties of thought that make it psychologically interesting. The behaviorists became committed to the study of muscle movements in place of an analysis of thought. (pp. 4–5)

1967

THE COMPUTER IN AMERICAN EDUCATION EDITED BY DON D. BUSHNELL AND DWIGHT W. Allen (John Wiley & Sons: New York, 1967) was published. Excerpts follow:

The technology for controlling others exists and it will be used, given the persistence of power-seeking motives. Furthermore, we will need to use it, since the necessary social changes cannot come about if the affected people do not understand and desire them.... How do we educate "run-of-the-mill" citizens for membership in a democratic society?... How do we teach people to understand their relationship to long range planning?... And how do we teach people to be comfortable with the process of change? Should we educate for this? We shall probably have to. But how?...

The need for educating to embrace change is not limited to youngsters.... Education for tomorrow's world will involve more than programming students by a computer; it will equally involve the ways in which we program... parents to *respond* to the education... children get for this kind of world. To the extent we succeed with the youngsters but not with the parents, we will have... a very serious consequence: an increasing separation of the young from their parents.... It will have psychological repercussions, probably producing in the children both guilt and hostility (arising from their rejection of their parents' views and values in lifestyles). (p. 7)

PROJECT FOLLOW THROUGH WAS INITIATED IN 1967, FUNDED UNDER THE *ECONOMIC OPportunity Act of 1964*, and carried out as a part of President Lyndon Johnson's "War on Poverty." Follow Through was administered by the U.S. Office of Education in the Department of Health, Education and Welfare. One of the models of instruction examined in trial under Follow Through was the Direct Instruction (DI) model developed by W.C. Becker and Siegfried Engelmann. Direct Instruction is based on the work of the late B.F. Skinner of Harvard, Edward Thorndike of Columbia University, and Ivan Pavlov of Russia, even though their works are not directly quoted in the DI literature.

Alice M. Rivlin,[8] a member of the Brookings Institute staff, in a lecture entitled "Systematic Thinking for Social Action" for the institute's H. Rowan Gaither Lectures Series at the University of California at Berkeley (under the sponsorship of the Graduate School of Business Administration and the Center for Research in Management Science, 1970), critically evaluated Project Follow Through and its results. Following are excerpts from Rivlin's speech:

> The Follow Through program is another example of a current attempt to use federal funds to learn how to produce services effectively—in this case, services for young children. Follow Through is a quasi-experiment, with a statistical design far less sophisticated than that of the New Jersey income maintenance experiment. There was evidence that children could move ahead rapidly in a good preschool program, but that when they were dumped back into the same dismal slum school the gains were lost. The objective of Follow Through was to determine whether the gains achieved through Head Start could be maintained through special programs in the early years of elementary school.... The approaches were extremely varied. The Becker-Engelmann program [Direct Instruction], developed at the University of Illinois, emphasized intensive work with small groups of children on the cognitive skills that deprived children often lack—verbal expression, reading, math skills. The methods involve rapid-fire questioning of students by instructors with rewards in the form of praise and stars for the right answers. It is a highly-disciplined approach and has been described as an intellectual "pressure cooker."...
>
> Since Follow Through was not a scientifically designed experiment, there is reason to question whether valid conclusions can be drawn from it about the relative effectiveness of the various approaches.... In any case, there are not enough projects of any type to support definitive statements about what works best with different kinds of populations.

[Ed. Note: Although the evaluation of Follow Through cited some academic and self-esteem gains at some Direct Instruction model sites, it would have been virtually impossible for these gains *not* to have been made considering the models with which they were compared—the non-academic focus of the "touchy-feely" open classroom. Had the Direct Instruction model been in competition with a traditional phonics program which was not based on animal behavioral psychology ("scientific, research-based"), it is most unlikely it would have been able to point to any gains at all. Unsuspecting parents in the 1990s seeking more structured academic education for their children than can be found in schools experimenting with constructivistic developmental programs (whole language, etc.) are turning to DI, not realizing they are embracing a method based on mastery learning and animal psychology.]

PLANNING, PROGRAMMING, BUDGETING SYSTEM (PPBS) WAS APPLIED TO EDUCATION IN 1967. During Ronald Reagan's tenure as governor of California, PPBS was installed in the California school system. The California Assembly passed AB 61 (1967) which authorized a pilot study of PPBS; ACR 198 (1970) created the Joint Committee on Educational Goals and Evaluation; AAB 2800 (1971) and SB 1526 (1971) set up the essential PPBS subsystems to facilitate federal funding and centralized control of state schools' goals, evaluation and management of all school programs and people; AB 293 (1971), the "Stull Bill," provided for teacher evaluation; the California State Board of Education approved Program Budgeting in a new *California School Accounting Manual* (Phase I of PPBS); and Reagan signed AB 1207 (1973), giving the accounting manual legal mandate in districts throughout the state. PPBS implementation in education (and in other governmental functions) was given considerable impetus by Governor Reagan who "strongly expressed" the intent of his administration to activate PPBS, a management tool of political change through funding, in *Implementing PPB in State, City and County: A Report on the 5–5–5 Project*. (State-Local Finances Project of The George Washington University: Washington, D.C., June, 1969). This entry summarizes this *Report*, published in cooperation with: The Council of State Governments, The International City Managers Association, The National Association of Counties, The National Governors' Conference, The National League of Cities, and The United States Conference of Mayors.

1968

B.F. Skinner: The Man and His Ideas by Richard I. Evans was published (Dutton and Company: New York, 1968). Evans's excellent critique of the totalitarian views of Professor Skinner was funded by the National Science Foundation. Extensive quotes from this book are included in Appendix XXIV. A few pertinent excerpts follow:

> "I could make a pigeon a high achiever by reinforcing it on a proper schedule.".... His [Skinner's] concern for what he believes to be the inadequacy of our formal education system led to applying the principles of operant conditioning to a learning system which he called the teaching machine, but Skinner's approach is concerned with more than merely methods and techniques. He challenges the very foundations by which man in our society is shaped and controlled. (p. 10)...
>
> ..."[F]or the purpose of analyzing behavior we have to assume man is a machine. (p. 24) ...You can induce him to behave according to the dictates of society instead of his own selfish interest." (p. 42)...
>
> ..."I should not bother with ordinary learning theory, for example. I would eliminate most sensory psychology and I would give them no cognitive psychology whatsoever [meaning the students, ed.]." (p. 91)" ...It isn't the person who is important, it's the method. If the practice of psychology survives, that's the main objective. It's the same with cultural practices in general: no one survives as a person." (p. 96) "...It does bother me that thousands of teachers don't understand, because immediate gains are more likely in the classroom than in the clinic. Teachers will eventually know—they must [understand]—and I am more concerned with promoting my theories in education [operant conditioning]." (p. 96) "...I should like to see our government set up a large educational agency in which specialists could be sent to train teachers." (p. 109)

In 1953 Skinner wrote *Science and Human Behavior* (Macmillan & Co.: New York, 1953), within which is found the following quote:

> A rather obvious solution is to distribute the control of human behavior among many agencies which have so little in common that they are not likely to join together in a despotic unit. In general this is the argument for democracy against totalitarianism. In a totalitarian state all agencies are brought together under a single super-agency.

[Ed. Note: Obviously, even before the U.S. Department of Education was established and organized teacher in-service training had taken a behaviorist (performance-based) turn, Skinner was advocating these very operant conditioning methods in all phases of education. Beginning in 1965, the federal government implemented several teacher education programs based on performance—performance-based teacher education—which would fulfill Skinner's plan. Skinner was always more concerned with "how" teachers teach than with "what" teachers teach. The reader should refer to Bettye Lewis's fine summary of the establishment of the *Behavioral Science Teacher Education Program* (BSTEP) in Appendix V for descriptions of these programs.]

THE MAY 1968 ISSUE OF THE EDUCATIONAL JOURNAL *THE INSTRUCTOR* RAN AN ARTICLE BY Dr. Paul Brandwein, adjunct professor at University of Pittsburgh, entitled "School System of the Future" which outlined the changes on the horizon relative to the relationship between children, parents and schools. The following quotes will be of interest:

> [Parents] often have little, if any knowledge of the rudiments of the human enterprise we call teaching and learning, or even the elements of the behavioral sciences undergirding child development.... The most formative years are what we call pre-kindergarten years.... Television can be utilized to provide the proper instruction [indoctrination] to the parent... a minimum of an hour a day... continuing over four or five years... aimed at the parent to equip him as "teacher."
>
> Learning is synonymous with environmental behavior change.... Learning... is the modification of behavior through interaction with the environment.... [New school system structure] would maintain continuity over some nineteen years, with three carefully articulated periods of schooling... 1. *Primary*, with the first four or five years in the home with "informed" parents as teachers; 2. *Secondary*, with parents as teacher aides; 3. *Preparatory*, to be used differently for children with varying gifts and destinations.... The student would be able to choose vocational training, studies related to semi-skilled occupation, or collegiate work for the next four years, with one year given over to public service....
>
> [P]rimary education with the parents as teacher has the aim of making the home a healthy and healing environment.... Education must heal. If it does not heal and make strong, it is not education.
>
> Assume with me that education, as profession and enterprise, would join forces with government and industry to support education of the parent in the mode, manner, and morality befitting the early education of children. Teachers and behavioral scientists—psychologists, psychiatrists, sociologists, students of child development—would be called upon. We have common, indeed universal, communication with the home through radio, television, and printed materials; and soon other aspects of electronic technology will be available.
>
> The Secondary Years, beginning with kindergarten, concern themselves with the concepts and skills required for effective participation in our society.... In *structure* [emphasis in original], the curriculum might well be organized in terms of continuous and progressive experience (synonyms: non-graded curriculum, continuous progress).... Grades (marks, scores) as we know them would not be used, but there would be reports to the parents of child's progress, similar to what some schools are doing now.
>
> Each boy and girl would choose an area of public service coordinated with his gifts and destination. Care of children, care of the aged and infirm, assisting in schools and in hospitals, conserving our natural resources, could well be among such tasks. The major peace-seeking and peace-keeping strategy of society is education. Peace is inevitable.

LEARNING AND INSTRUCTION, A CHICAGO INNER CITY SCHOOLS POSITION PAPER PRESENTED in June of 1968 to the Chicago Board of Education, was produced by the planning staff in

Chicago made up of: Dr. Donald Leu, William Farquhar, Lee Shulman, and the Chicago and Michigan State universities in collaboration. One reference used was *Soviet Preschool Education*, translated by Henry Chauncey (Educational Testing Service, Princeton, N.J.). Excerpts from the Chicago Mastery Learning Project position paper, *Learning and Instruction*, follow:

> We view the child with his defined characteristics as input to a school organization which modifies his capabilities toward certain goals and objectives as output. The school organization is an optimal deployment of teachers employing a special subject matter who attempt through instruction, with the aid of selected elements of the community, to achieve specified outputs. The joint participation of the children, school and community leave none of these elements unchanged....
>
> This emphasis should be accomplished within the context of a truly ungraded structure which we shall denote by the terms Continuous Development-Mastery Learning. This approach has the following characteristics: (a) Beginning with Chicago's present concept of Continuous Development, the objectives of the language arts curriculum must be much further differentiated and articulated in the manner currently being conducted by Sophie Bloom [wife of the late Benjamin Bloom] in Chicago, and Pittsburgh's Individually Prescribed Instruction Project. In the Continuous Development-Mastery Learning approach, a large number of sequentially designated objectives, tied into specific capabilities to be mastered by pupils, are identified. This is done by curriculum development specialists in collaboration with instructional personnel. [References used in this paper were from the late Benjamin Bloom, John Carroll, Robert Gagne, Robert Glaser and Henry Chauncey, ed.]

The following is an excerpt from an article published in *Education Week*, March 6, 1985 entitled "Half of Chicago Students Drop out, Study Finds: Problem Called Enormous Human Tragedy":

> Calling the dropout problem in Chicago "a human tragedy of enormous dimensions," a recent study has found that almost half of the 39,500 public school students in the 1980 freshman class failed to graduate, and that only about a third of those who did were able to read at or above the national 12th grade level. "These statistics about the class of 1984 reflect the destruction of tens of thousands of young lives, year in and year out," says the study, released in January by Designs for Change, a nonprofit research and child-advocacy organization in Chicago.... "Most of these young people are permanently locked out of our changing economy and have no hope of continuing their education or getting a permanent job with a future," the authors wrote.

Professor Lee Shulman's involvement in the Chicago Mastery Learning disaster was, however, quickly forgotten or considered unimportant. According to *Education Daily* of May 21, 1987—two years later:

> Shulman, who heads Stanford's Education Policy Institute, last week was awarded $817,000 by Carnegie Corporation to develop over the next 15 months new forms of teacher assessment materials that would be the basis of standards adopted by a national teacher certification board.

The *Education Daily* article further discussed the requirement for teacher critique of the way two textbooks treat photosynthesis and how they (teachers) developed a lesson plan based on each one:

The teacher then would be directed to use the textbooks to tell the examiners how he or she would teach students with varying religious, cultural and ethnic backgrounds.

Nine years later *Education Week* of October 23, 1996 reported Shulman again leading the outcome-/performance-based teacher education bandwagon of social change agents:

His successful performance as developer of new forms of teacher assessment materials leads to his being named President of the Carnegie Foundation for the Advancement of Teaching, filling the vacancy created by the death last year of Ernest L. Boyer.

An excerpt from an October 21, 1996 *New York Times* article entitled "Carnegie Foundation Selects a New Leader" emphasized Shulman's importance in the field of behavioral psychology:

He [Shulman] has been a Guggenheim Fellow, a Fellow of the American Psychological Association and a Fellow of the Center for Advanced Study in the Behavioral Sciences. He is the immediate past president of the National Academy of Education and a former president of the American Education Research Association.

IN A 1968 SPEECH ENTITLED "THE UNITED NATIONS AND ALTERNATIVE FORMULATIONS— The Hard Road to World Order," Richard Gardner, former U.S. deputy assistant secretary of state and U.S. ambassador to Italy, provided an accurate forewarning and picture of the environment in which Americans and citizens of other countries live today, explaining how the elitist planners would, through the use of gradualism, succeed in their century-long plan to create a One World Government. In an excerpt from the speech Gardner explains the following:

In short, we are likely to do better by building our "house of world order" from the bottom up rather than the top down. It will look like a great, "booming, buzzing confusion," to use William James's famous description of reality, but an end run around national sovereignty, eroding it piece by piece, is likely to get us to world order faster than the old-fashioned frontal attack.

ETHNA REID OF THE GRANITE SCHOOL DISTRICT, SALT LAKE CITY, UTAH RECEIVED $848,536 in federal grants under Title III of the *ESEA* in 1968 to develop the Exemplary Center for Reading Instruction (ECRI), a Mastery Learning program. This grant far exceeded the legal cap on federal education program funding at that time. In 1982 Reid claimed that her mastery learning program "is undoubtedly one of those in greatest use today in the United States at all grade levels, K–12."[9]

The 120-page teacher pre-service training manual from ECRI was devoted to the training of teachers in stimulus-response-stimulus/operant conditioning techniques (Skinner), and materials on the "adaptation of birds, monitoring forms before and after instruction" (observation data sheet records). *How to Teach Animals* by B.F. Skinner and *How to Teach Animals: A Rat, a Pigeon, a Dog* by Kathleen and Shauna Reid are both listed as teacher and resource materials. The *ECRI Teacher Training Manual* cites the work of Siegfried Engelmann, the developer of DISTAR (Direct Instruction System for Teaching and Remediation)/Reading Mastery, and Direct Instruction in instructing teachers how to use operant conditioning, stimulus-response-stimulus to get desired behaviors. Reviewed by the U.S. Department of Education's Joint Dissemination Review Panel (JDRP) and approved as an exemplary education program in 1974, ECRI was promoted throughout the National Diffusion Network (NDN), the federally funded transmission belt for controversial and mostly non-academic programs.

On May 5, 1984 the officers of the Arizona Federation of Teachers unanimously passed a resolution—spearheaded by Ann Herzer, an Arizona teacher—which stated in part that members of the Arizona affiliate

> oppose such programs as ECRI, Project INSTRUCT and/or any other programs that use operant conditioning under the guise of Mastery Learning, Classroom Management, Precision Teaching, Structured Learning and Discipline, and petition the U.S. Congress for protection against the use of such methods on teachers and students without their prior consent.

The Arizona resolution was supported by Dr. Jeanette Veatch, internationally known expert in the field of reading, who in a July 1980 letter to Ann Herzer called the ECRI program "a more modern version of breaking children to the heel of thought control.... It is so flagrantly dangerous, damaging and destructive I am appalled at its existence." Unfortunately, Albert Shanker, then president of the national American Federation of Teachers (AFT), tabled the Arizona affiliate's resolution at AFT's August, 1984 national convention in Washington, D.C.

With this historical perspective in mind, consider an article which appeared in *Education Week* September 6, 1997 entitled "New AFT President Urges Members to Help Floundering Schools." The late Albert Shanker would be pleased that the AFT continues to support Skinnerian mastery learning/direct instruction, for the article states in part: "Also featured [at AFT's QUEST Conference] was Direct Instruction, a scripted set of lessons used for teaching at-risk students."

JOHN GOODLAD'S ARTICLE, "LEARNING AND TEACHING IN THE FUTURE," WAS PUBLISHED by the National Education Association's journal *Today's Education* in 1968. Excerpts from Goodlad's article follow:

> The most controversial issues of the twenty-first century will pertain to the ends and means of modifying human behavior and who shall determine them. The first educational question will not be "what knowledge is of the most worth?" but "what kinds of human beings do we wish to produce?" The possibilities virtually defy our imagination.

TECHNOLOGY OF TEACHING BY B.F SKINNER WAS PUBLISHED (PRENTICE HALL: NEW YORK, 1968) and became part of the educational lore of the day. An excerpt follows:

> Absolute power in education is not a serious issue today because it seems out of reach. However, a technology of teaching will need to be much more powerful if the race with

catastrophe is to be won, and it may then, like any powerful technology, need to be contained. An appropriate counter control will not be generated as a revolt against aversive measures but by a policy designed to maximize the contribution which education can make to the strength of the culture. The issue is important because the government of the future will probably operate mainly through educational techniques. (p. 260)

[Ed. note: Skinner was 100% correct. The government in 1999 "operates mainly through educational techniques." Those individuals and agencies conforming with government policies, criteria, etc., are rewarded, whereas those who do not conform are either ignored or denied special privileges and funding. In the late twentieth century, following the philosophy of B.F. Skinner that the "environment is all," all evil is attributed to the environment and no one is held responsible for his actions.]

"THE FOUNDATION MACHINE" BY EDITH KERMIT ROOSEVELT WAS PUBLISHED IN THE DEcember 26, 1968 issue of *The Wanderer*. In this important article Mrs. Roosevelt discussed problems that had been created by the Carnegie Corporation's new reading program as follows:

Even now the Carnegie Corporation is facing protests from parents whose children are exposed to the textbooks financed by the foundation under its "Project Read." This project provides *programmed* textbooks for schools, particularly in "culturally deprived areas." An estimated five million children throughout the nation are using the material in the programmed textbooks produced by the Behavioral Research Laboratories, Palo Alto, California. This writer has gone over these textbooks in the "Reading" series financed by the Carnegie Corporation and authored by M.W. Sullivan, a linguist. These foundation-funded books reveal a fire pattern that amounts to an incitement to the sort of arson and guerilla warfare that took place in Watts, Washington, D.C., and elsewhere. On one page in the series we find a torch next to a white porch. The caption reads invitingly, "a torch, a porch." Further along there is a picture of a man smiling while he holds a torch aloft. The caption beneath it reads: "This man has a t_rch in his hand." The children are required as an exercise to insert the missing letter to fill in the word torch. The next picture shows the burning torch touching the porch, with a caption, "a torch on a porch." Thus, the children are led in stages to the final act that suggests itself quite naturally. The picture in the series shows a hand moving the hands of a clock to twenty-five minutes past one, while this same shack is being devoured by flames. The message is plain: an example of a man who deliberately commits the criminal act of setting a home on fire. Tragically, these young children are being indoctrinated with a pattern of anti-social ideas that will completely and violently alienate them from the mainstream of American middle-class values.... Other pictures in the Carnegie-funded supposedly educational texts include a comparison of a flag with a rag, the ransoming of an American soldier in a Chinese prison, a picture that shows people kneeling in a church to say their prayers beside a picture of a horse being taught to kneel in the same way, a reference to a candidate elected to public office as a "ruler," a picture of a boy stealing a girl's purse, and another boy throwing pointed darts at a companion whom he uses as target practice.

Understandably, the Carnegie-financed books are causing concern to local law-enforcement officials, many of whom have to cope with riot or near-riot conditions. Ellen Morphonios, prosecutor for Florida in its attorney's office, and a chief of its Criminal Court Division, said recently: "It's a slap in the face and an insult to every member of the Negro community, saying that the only way to communicate with Negro children is to show a robber or violence. It's like subliminal advertising. If this isn't subversive and deliberately done as part of a master plan.... Only a sick mind could have produced it."

Repeated instances of this type of anti-social activity obviously constitute a strong argument for removing the tax-exempt status of these educational foundations, and for curbing their activities by Federal regulations and Congressional oversight.

[Ed. Note: The programmed textbooks used in Project Read are based on Skinnerian animal psychology. Programmed instruction calls for individualized instruction/self-instruction (programmed books and or teaching machines) and differs from the lecture/discussion method of teaching where the teacher, not the program, is the dispenser of knowledge.]

AGENDA FOR THE NATION, EDITED BY KERMIT GORDON (BROOKINGS INSTITUTION: WASHington, D.C., 1968) and funded by the Ford Foundation, was published. Ralph Tyler's article "Investing in Better Schools" (pp. 207–236) was included in the compilation of articles which were written as a contribution to public discussion and debate as a new president and a new Congress assumed their responsibilites. Other contributors included: Stephen K. Bailey, Kenneth B. Clark, Clark Kerr, Henry A. Kissinger, Edwin O. Reischauer, and Charles L. Schultze. The following excerpted recommendations from Tyler's article which refer to the Certificate of Initial Mastery, no more Carnegie Units, the Eight-Year Study and outcome-based education, read like pages out of *Goals 2000: Educate America Act* and reports prepared by Marc Tucker's National Center on Education and the Economy, the Secretary's Commission on Achieving Necessary Skills (SCANS), etc.—all of which are involved in the socialistic restructuring of the nation's schools and economy:

> What is required is a major effort to furnish high school students with significant adult activities—job programs, community service corps experience, work in health centers, apprentice experience in research and development, and in staff studies conducted by public agencies. It will be necessary to redesign the high school in order to open it to the community and to utilize many kinds of persons in education. The school will need to serve a wider range of ages and allow students to vary the amount of time devoted to studies. To supply a substitute for grades and credits as qualification for employment opportunities, a certification system will need to be developed to validate the student's competence in various major areas. This will also tend to reduce the emphasis upon purely formal requirements such as class attendance and the completion of prescribed courses.

1968–1969. *NARRATIVE REPORT OF PROJECT FUNDED UNDER TITLE III, ELEMENTARY AND Secondary Education Act (FY 1969)—Title of Project: OPERATION PEP, a Statewide Project to Prepare Educational Planners for California* (U.S. Office of Education Grant Award No. OEG 3–7-704444410-4439, 7-1-68 to 6-30-69. $299,457 grant to San Mateo County Superintendent of Schools, Redwood City, California, Project Director: Donald R. Miller) was compiled and registered with the U.S. Office of Education in the Department of Health, Education and Welfare. An excerpt from this report follows:

> Major Objectives: The objectives of Operation PEP have been specified with respect for the educational needs of society and the role requirements of professional educators. They in-

clude: (1) to plan, develop, validate, and implement an instructional program for educational planners and managers featuring a system approach to educational management; (2) to establish an orderly diffusion process for system approach concepts, principles, and procedures involving key agencies, organizations, and individuals; (3) to provide assurance that the program developed by Operation PEP will be continuously renewed and presented, and (4) to promote the utilization and adoption of a system approach to educational management and educational leaders in California.

[Ed. Note: Mastery learning/direct instruction fits into PPBS systems management, Management by Objectives (MBO) and computer-assisted instruction as a hand fits into a glove. OBE in 1999 is Operation PEP in 1968. California's teachers' union was adamantly opposed to its enabling legislation and to Operation PEP in general.]

1969

PACESETTERS IN INNOVATION: CUMULATIVE ISSUE OF ALL PROJECTS IN OPERATION AS OF *February 1969 under Title III, Supplementary Centers and Services Program, Elementary and Secondary Education Act of 1965* (U.S. Department of Health, Education and Welfare: Washington, D.C.,1969) was published. This incredible 584-page catalog of education programs gives abstracts of innovative programs dealing with humanistic education; i.e., values clarification, self-esteem programs, individualized education, open classroom, etc. Shirley Correll, Ph.D., president of Florida's Pro-Family Forum, wrote "An Evaluation of HEW's Publication *Pacesetters in Innovation*" which said in part:

> A thorough evaluation of HEW's 584-page publication, *Pacesetters in Innovation*, is alarming, even to one accustomed to the thrust of today's public schools, and even more interesting when placed in its proper perspective of total HEW funding. It is described as a program "to support supplementary education centers and services, guidance counseling and testing" on state and local levels. These PACE programs (Projects to Advance Creativity in Education) describe "Psychotherapy," "Behavior Modification," "Psychoeducation Clinics," "Changed Parent-Student Relationships," "Total Environmental Control," "Humanistic Curriculum," "Sensitivity Training," and attitudinal measuring devices, ad nauseam. One program discusses "Experimental Buses featuring multichannel programming, individual receivers and active response opportunities (allowing audio presentations of cognitive and/or affective [emotional] instructional materials." Could it be that there's more to this busing than integration?
>
> I found that PACE's direction was to "organize the process of change to restructure and reorganize the school system." Many different methods were used to accomplish this. Teachers are subjected to "Sensitivity Training" and "Change Agentry" training (an educational term used to describe the role of group leader as that of changing the attitude of students and others), not only to condition the teachers to new philosophies, but to "spread their influence to others in their own district and throughout the state via various visitation programs."
>
> Through the influences of these and various other programs, "structured or graded classes are systematically phased out and replaced by ungraded individualized instruction" (which ultimately becomes the opposite of individualized instruction as all children eventually are fit to a pre-conceived mold or norm by computerized assessment).

THE ROLE OF THE SCHOOL IN THE COMMUNITY WAS PUBLISHED (PENDELL PUBLISHING CO.:
Midland, Michigan, 1969). This slim 136-page book, edited by Dr. Howard W. Hickey, Dr.
Curtis Van Voorhees, and associates, was "written to serve as a much-needed textbook for
teachers and students in Community Education; and to serve as a handbook on Community
Education for school officials and community education leaders." The following excerpts are
from *The Role of the School in the Community*:

> Chapter III. An Overview by Jack D. Minzey and Clarence R. Olsen
> As the social forces have sought to bring action to bear on community problems, the need for
> a vehicle of action has become apparent. Not all groups have identified the most effective
> means of implementing their programs structured about community problems, but a num-
> ber of influential persons and groups are aware of the community education concept and are
> extremely optimistic about its possibilities as the means by which their goals of social engi-
> neering can be accomplished. (p. 40)

> Chapter VI. A Developmental Process by Curtis Van Voorhees
> When a community school director attempts to identify courses to be included in the ques-
> tioning process it is important to remember, as previously mentioned, that people are typi-
> cally unable to identify many of their own problems and needs. While they may sometimes
> be able to identify what they want in the way of a class, it is unlikely that many people who
> need assistance in preparing nutritious meals are aware of that fact. And parents who are in
> need of information about child health practices are unlikely to recognize that they need
> such help. So it must be remembered that the simple existence of a problem does not guar-
> antee its recognition by the person with the problem. Community school coordinators must,
> therefore, develop a questioning form which will get at the unidentified problems of people
> without unduly alarming or offending the respondent; they must seek to solicit information
> from people which will allow community school coordinators to plan better programs for the
> people they attempt to serve—programs that will hopefully change, in a positive way, the
> attitude, behavior and life style of the community residents.

[Ed. Note: The term "community education" is rarely used today due to its socialistic philosophy causing extreme controversy in the 1960s, 1970s and early 1980s. The average American
rejected the notion that the community was there to serve his/her needs and that decision-
making by unelected councils was acceptable or perhaps preferable to decision-making by
elected officials. The change agents wisely dropped the label and now use terms such as
"communitarianism," "participatory democracy," "site-based management," "school-based
clinics," "year-round schools," Hillary Clinton's *It Takes a Village to Raise a Child* concept, all
of which are individually or collectively Community Education. As Anita Hoge, a well-known
education researcher, says, "It doesn't take a village to raise a child unless you live in a
commune." At a Community Education Conference held in Washington, D.C. in 1976 a community educator from Alaska stated that "community education could be likened to the system in Russia and China."[10]]

MASTER PLAN FOR PUBLIC EDUCATION IN HAWAII—TOWARD A NEW ERA FOR EDUCATION IN
Hawaii was published in 1969 by the State of Hawaii Department of Education, Honolulu,
Hawaii. This publication was partially funded under Title V, Sec. 503, P.L. 890–10 (U.S. Office
of Education). Excerpts follow from this extraordinarily frank *Master Plan* which would serve
as a model for the rest of the nation:

Implications for Education... Second, the computer will enhance learning.... The teacher will operate as a manager.... The teacher will have a ready record of each student's performance and a ready access to the information the student needs during each stage of his progress. (p. 36)

Perhaps we must go significantly beyond the present, minimum family educational programs that candidly discuss interpersonal relationships, family conflicts and tensions, counseling and rehabilitation services and the many areas that need to be explored between a man, a woman, and their children. (p. 46)

The task of the schools during the past stable, relatively unchanging world was to emphasize fixed habits, memorization of facts, and development of specific skills to meet known needs. But for a future which will include vast changes, the emphasis should be on how to meet new situations, on the skills of research, observation, analysis, logic and communication, on the development of attitudes appropriate to change, and on a commitment to flexibility and reason. (p. 50)

Behavioral sciences subject matter should form a part of our modern curriculum to provide a basis for self knowledge and behavioral concepts.... Study of ethical traditions, concepts and changes in value structure should be emphasized.... Department of Education should experiment with the group therapy, role playing and encounter group approach that are professionally planned and conducted, as a basis for understanding other people, races, cultures and points of view. (pp. 51–52)

From the point of view of the teacher, individualized instruction should provide for opportunities to diagnose the learning styles, and strengths and weaknesses of pupils; direct assistance by skilled counselors, psychologists, social workers and physicians will assist in accurate and meaningful diagnosis.... The Department should adopt team teaching and non-gradedness as the basic approach to classroom instruction. The present system of age and grade classification of students is excessively rigid and not conducive to individualized instruction. A non-graded approach, therefore, on a K–12 basis, is sought as an ultimate goal. (p. 54)

The school system will seek financial support of educational programs on the basis of educational outputs, that is, the improvement, growth and changes that occur in the behavior of the pupil as a result of schooling. (p. 55)

This school system will systematically study the benefits of any promising non-educational input to enhance learning. Recent discoveries from the field of bio-chemistry suggest that there already exists a fairly extensive class of drugs to improve learning such as persistence, attentiveness, immediate memory, and long term memory.... The application of biochemical research findings, heretofore centered in lower forms of animal life, will be a source of conspicuous controversy when children become the objects of such experimentation. Schools will conceivably be swept into a whole new area of collaboration in research with biochemists and psychologists to improve learning. The immediate and long-term impact on teaching as well as on learning and the ethical and moral consequences of extensive use of chemicals to assist in the learning process must be studied extensively.... The Department should initiate a long term, continuing series of discussions with individuals directly associated with these research efforts. Lay persons from our community should be an integral part of these discussions. (p. 56)

The Department should take the initiative to establish a state compact of all agencies with responsibilities in education in this state. The purpose of such a compact will be to coordinate planning and execution of educational programs.... Assuming that the basic period of schooling required for the youth of Hawaii may remain at twelve years, extending the school day and the school year may be the solution to this pressing problem. Some of the benefits which can be anticipated from an extended school year and a school day are: An improvement in economic and professional status of our teachers,... an increased use of facilities and equipment. School facilities will be in use throughout the year.... (p. 62)

That our system of values should change as the conditions in which these values find their expression change is evident in history.... Our past also has shown that society courts trouble when it clings stubbornly to outmoded values after experience has clearly shown that they need to be revised. For example, developments in our society have now cast considerable doubts on the worth of such deep-seated beliefs, still held strongly in some quarters, as extreme and rugged individualism or isolationism in international affairs. While values tend to persist, they are tentative. They provide the directions basic to any conscious and direct attempt to influence pupil behavior.... Some will argue, of course, that direct and purposeful effort at changing value orientations of pupils is no concern of the schools. But from what we know of the pupil and his development, the school is inescapably involved in influencing his moral values and ethical structure. (p. 63)

The roles and responsibilities of teachers will change noticeably in the years ahead. By 1985 it should be more accurate to term a teacher a "learning clinician" for the schools will be "clinics" whose purpose is to provide individualized educational and psychological "services" to the student.[11] (p. 69)

However, in the spring of 1967, the Department undertook to install a new "System," more commonly referred to as "PPBS." This sophisticated system of budgeting was crystalized in the federal defense agency during the early 1960's, and has, since 1965, been formally adopted by all departments within the federal government.... From a long-range standpoint, PPBS is surely the direction we must move toward if we are to do more than survive in a rapidly approaching computerized world.... However, operationally, there are several reasons why the entire PPBS anatomy cannot be totally... operable at this time. Although some of the problems are due to the system itself, most are due to the present undeveloped state of the educational industry. Some of these factors are: While we accept the PPBS concept, we must constantly be mindful that the system is a tool of management, not an end in itself, not a panacea or solution for all our management problems. Further, it should never be considered a replacement for experienced human judgment, but only an aid in arriving at sound judgments... in the field of education, which deals primarily in human behavior, there is almost no reliable research data on causal relationships. We do not know exactly why or how students learn.... Cost/effectiveness analysis which lies at the heart of PPBS is virtually impossible without this kind of data.... As can readily be seen, the multiplicity and complexity of objectives and the difficulty of quantifying human behavior makes it exceedingly difficult to state our objectives in the manner specified by PPBS.... Another significant problem—this time to do with PPBS—is that it does not formally allow for value consideration. And yet, values—academic, economic, political, social, esthetic—appear to play a crucial role in the decision-making process. But how do we quantify values? How do we negotiate conflicting values? What will be the proper mix of values and how do we factor it into the array of alternatives and the decision-making process? These are vital questions that must be answered if we are to rationalize the decision-making process. (pp. 96–97)

Mount a comprehensive and continuing effort to develop standards and a system of measurement that will permit effective evaluation of student and Department of Education performance. (p. 98)

[Ed. Note: PPBS and MBO are essentially the same as TQM. At a 1992 Total Quality Manage-
ment (TQM) in Education Conference in St. Paul, Minnesota—sponsored by the National
Governors' Association and attended by the writer—a representative from IBM stated that
TQM is a more "sophisticated, refined form of PPBS."]

IN 1969 DON DAVIES, FORMER DEPUTY COMMISSIONER OF EDUCATION FOR THE U.S. OFFICE
of Education and editor of *Communities and Their Schools*, wrote "Changing Conditions in
American Schools" as part of the "Elementary Teacher Training Models," a section of the
Behavioral Science Teacher Education Program (U.S. Office of Education, Department of Health,
Education and Welfare [developed at Michigan State University under HEW grant]: Washing-
ton, D.C., 1969). The following are excerpts from "Changing Conditions in American Schools":

> (1) Moving from a mass approach to an individual approach in education;
> (2) Moving from an emphasis on memorizing to an emphasis on the non-cognitive,
>   non-intellectual components of life;
> (3) Moving from a concept of a school isolated from the community;
> (4) Moving from a fear of technology to using machinery and technology for educa-
>   tional purposes;
> (5) Moving from a negative to a positive attitude towards children who are different;
> (6) Moving from a provincial perspective of the world in education to a multicultural
>   perspective;
> (7) Moving from a system characterized by academic snobbery to one which recog-
>   nizes and nurtures a wide variety of talents and values; and
> (8) Moving from a system based on serving time to one which emphasizes perfor-
>   mance.

[Ed. Note: 1, 2, 4, 7, and 8 should be familar to the reader. They represent OBE/ML/DI and
technology. Numbers 5 and 6 are global education/values education.]

PROFESSOR DEAN CORRIGAN, IN A 1969 SPEECH BEFORE THE 22ND ANNUAL TEACHER EDUCA-
tion Conference at the University of Georgia, predicted that "teaching machines will pace a
student's progress, diagnose his weaknesses and make certain that he understands a fundamental concept before allowing him to advance to the next lesson."

[Ed. Note: Skinner said "computers are essentially sophisticated versions of the teaching
machines of the 1960s... programmed learning." (See *Education Week* 8/31/83.)]

A REPORT FROM THE STATE COMMITTEE ON PUBLIC EDUCATION TO THE CALIFORNIA STATE
*Board of Education—Citizens for the 21st Century—Long-Range Considerations for California
Elementary and Secondary Education* (California State Assembly: Sacramento, California, 1969)
was prepared by Professor John I. Goodlad. Funded by the *Elementary and Secondary Education Act of 1965*, the *Report* states:

Experimentation, Innovation, Implementation.

We have seen that mechanisms are needed for systematically determining the appropriate responsibilities of local, state, and federal education agencies. Similarly, we need mechanisms for systematically determining the kinds of human beings to be developed in our schools. Such mechanisms do not now exist in this state or any state. We need, too, mechanisms for appraising the quality of innovations and for systematically determining how a full range of projects might be put in a single school. (p. 471)

IMPROVING EDUCATIONAL ASSESSMENT AND AN INVENTORY OF MEASURES OF AFFECTIVE Behavior by Walcott H. Beatty, chairman and editor (Association for Supervision and Curriculum Development Commission on Assessment of Educational Outcomes [NEA Stock No. 611–17804]: Washington, D.C., 1969) was published. A chapter entitled "The Purposes of Assessment" by Ralph Tyler, "the father of educational assessment," was included in this important book. The following excerpts relate primarily to the principle of transfer in learning:

The function of the school's teaching is to develop young people whose behavior outside the classroom is effective and significant. Therefore, in appraising the relative effectiveness of curriculum materials or programs, one goes beyond a checking of program and purpose to consider whether the learnings are generalizable to life outside the school. The Progressive Education Association's Eight-Year Study, for example, followed a group of high school graduates into college and occupational roles to learn the extent to which they were able to utilize ways of thinking, feeling, and acting that the school had tried to develop....

We are all familiar with the general principle that any measures of education should be based upon educational objectives—what kind of learning are we seeking? Thirty-eight years ago, when Paul Diederich and I began some of these efforts in the Progressive Education Association, much was said about determining educational objectives. We talked about educational objectives at a level so general that such objectives represented desirable and attainable human outcomes. Now, as the people from conditioning have moved into an interest in learning in the schools, the notions of behavioral objectives have become much more specific....

As far as I know, one cannot very well teach a pigeon a general principle that he can then apply to a variety of situations. The objectives for persons coming out of the Skinnerian background tend to be highly specific ones. When I listen to Gagne, who is an intelligent and effective conditioner, talk about human learning objectives, I wince a good deal because he sets very specific ones. I know that we can attain levels of generalization of objectives that are higher than that....

As a graduate student at Chicago 42 years ago, I did a study with Judd, who was at that time arguing with Thorndike over the principle of transfer in learning. Thorndike had demonstrated that transfer was not automatic among the formal disciplines; a person could take a course in Latin and not be able to handle other kinds of languages any more effectively. Thorndike reached the conclusion that every objective had to be very specific, like conditioning objectives. His first treatise on the psychology of arithmetic established some 3,000 objectives for elementary school arithmetic. Judd, however, had come out of the social psychology tradition, having studied with Wundt at Leipzig. His view was that generalization was not only possible but was essential in education. The task he assigned me was to check on Thorndike's view that the addition of every one of the 100 pairs of one-digit combinations had to be practiced by the learner before he could add all of the pairs. The design of my study was to take the principles of grouping for addition and help pupils see them. I noted that five and two, and six and one, and zero and seven and three and four all total seven and had the students practice 21 out of the 100, emphasizing that each operation illustrated a general principle. I found that the youngsters in the experimental group who had practiced on only 21 illustrations did just as well on the average over the sample of the total 100 as the pupils who had practiced systematically every one of the 100....

The possibility of generalization is of course not new to the reader of this booklet. In curriculum development we now work on the principle that human beings can generalize, so they do not have to practice every specific. The question is at what level of generalization do we set up objectives. There are overgeneralizations you can immediately see; for example, the use of "you" for both singular and plural forms often confuses students in grammar exercises. The problem of the effective curriculum maker and teacher is to figure out the level of generalization that is possible with a certain child or a certain group, then to establish objectives based on reaching that level of generalization. You will have twenty objectives perhaps, but not more. The conditioning view, based upon specific situations and practices, may involve several hundred objectives for a course because specific practices must be used to accomplish each aspect of the conditioning. (pp. 8–9)

"U.S. PLAN TO 'TAKE OVER' GRADE SCHOOLS INTIMATED" BY JOHN STEINBACHER WAS AN article which appeared in the *Anaheim Bulletin* (Anaheim, California) in 1969. Excerpts follow:

Is the U.S. Office of Education, a division of the Department of Health, Education and Welfare, poised for a total takeover of every elementary school in the nation?

That was indicated Thursday in a federally funded project at Cal State, Fullerton by Bernard Kravett, a professor at the school who took part last year in a federally funded project at the University of Washington. Known as the Tri-University Project, three universities were involved in a massively funded federal project to restructure the entire higher education system for training teachers, which, in effect, would make local elementary schools only a subsidiary arm of the federal government.... This system, to be called Teacher Preparation Experienced Systematically, is to be instituted at once.... All teacher training institutions will operate jointly with local school districts and teacher organizations to "establish performance criteria which become behavioral objectives." ...Students in colleges who are studying to be teachers will be placed in "clinical settings," where there will be a clinical counselor for each 12 students....

As the teacher trainees progress through the four-year course, they will be constantly assessed by testing and performance criteria, as well as constantly counseled by the trained psychologists.... At the end of each year, the teacher trainee will either pass on to the next level or will be recycled to take additional work in the areas in which he is found deficient.... The new approach is to stress attitudinal changes on the part of the teachers and the students....

Built into the system is a strong emphasis on the findings of the behavioral scientists. Teacher trainees will be counseled into becoming a "good team member on the faculty," and those who cannot adapt to "teamstanding" will be washed out of the teacher courses. The teacher is to learn how to "carry out the order of the team and the team leader." ...The purpose of the so-called college activities will be to "build on behavioral objectives in order to help children find out who they are and help the child in his quest for identity. All education will be built on behavioral tasks rather than on course credits and grade point averages," he said. Kravett said the federal government had financed nine universities to come up with "programs" and it is from these programs, largely developed in behavioral science laboratories, that the new elementary program will come. California, he said, has a long way to go to catch up with the rest of the nation in accepting this new program. However, he said the government was spending "fantastic amounts of money and the Federal Government is totally behind it, pushing it and providing all the money you can possibly need." (p. 4)

THE NATIONAL ASSESSMENT OF EDUCATIONAL PROGRESS (NAEP), MANDATED BY THE U.S. Congress, was initiated in 1969. NAEP has periodically "assessed" (monitored the knowledge, skills, and performance of) students aged 9, 13, and 17, as well as various grade levels. The subject areas assessed have included: reading, writing, mathematics, science, citizenship, U.S. history, geography, social studies, art, music, literature, computer competence, and career and occupational development. NAEP also has collected background information from students, teachers, and administrators, and has related these data to student achievement. The Educational Testing Service (ETS) in 1983 took over the contract to administer the NAEP from the Carnegie Corporation-spawned Education Commission of the States. This move effectively kept Carnegie in control of educational assessment, since it was the Carnegie Foundation for the Advancement of Teaching (a subdivision of the Carnegie Corporation) which had provided the $750,000 initial endowment (start-up funds) to launch ETS in 1947. Through an agreement between the American Council on Education, the Carnegie Foundation and the College Entrance Examination Board, all of whom turned over their testing programs and a portion of their assets to ETS, the move to establish Educational Testing Service as the primary provider of testing material was accomplished.

In 1988 Congress established the National Assessment Governing Board (NAGB). The purpose of NAGB was to provide policy guidance for the execution of NAEP. The board was composed of nationally and locally elected officials, chief state school officers, classroom teachers, local school board members, and leaders of the business community, among others. Specifically, NAGB has been charged by Congress to perform the following duties: select subject areas to be assessed; identify appropriate achievement goals for each age group; develop assessment objectives; design a methodology of assessment; and produce guidelines and standards for national, regional, and state comparisons.

OVER A PERIOD OF THREE DECADES RESEARCH FOR *EDUCATION FOR RESULTS: IN RESPONSE to A Nation at Risk, Vol. 1: Guaranteeing Effective Performance by Our Schools* was conducted by Robert E. Corrigan, Ph.D., and Betty O. Corrigan.[12] This final publication was published in 1983 for the Reagan Administration's use. Rather than being the protection from harmful innovations that concerned parents had been promised, this report actually served as a springboard for implementing OBE. This writer is including it under the "Sick Sixties" since most of the programs comprising experimentation history (pilot OBE/ML/DI programs, including one in Korea) were, in the words of the Corrigans, implemented "across our country over a period of 22 + years (1960–1983)." (For more complete understanding of the impact of this study, see Appendix VI.)

Endnotes:

1   John Goodlad, "A Report from the State Committee on Public Education to the California State Board of Education—Citizens for the Twenty-first Century—Long Range Considerations for California Elementary and Secondary Education," 1969.

2 The function of the National Diffusion Network has been distributed throughout the U.S. Department of Education's organizational subdivisions. The dissemination process is now carried on by individual offices and their projects. This was done as a result of the "Reorganization of Government according to the Malcolm Baldridge Award criteria" (TQM) under Vice President Al Gore's supervision.

3 This is another term, used in this publication, for today's "self-esteem."

4 The writer recommends that those readers interested in the radical, leftist substance of "Recommendations for Delphi Discussion Groups," contact K.M. Heaton whose *Road to Revolution* contains information on this subject. See Resources for Heaton's address.

5 The reader should turn to the inside cover of this book for the excellent cartoon by Joel Pett which carries the title "Consolidation."

6 "Harrison Bergeron" has been made into a video, available at your local video store.

7 Dan Smoot was a former Harvard professor who served for 9–1/2 years in the Federal Bureau of Investigation.

8 Alice Rivlin later became director of the Congressional Budget Office, and presently serves as the chairman of the Board of Control for the District of Columbia.

9 Ethna Reid was quoted in Dennis Bailey's article "Learning to Read the ECRI Way" for the January 8, 1982 issue of *The Maine Times*.

10 Audio tape of meeting from personal file of researcher who attended conference.

11 In the January 1969 issue of *Today's Education*, journal of the National Education Association, two professors of education at Indiana University refer to schools of the 1970s as "clinics, whose purpose is to provide individualized psychosocial 'treatment' for the student."

12 The Corrigans' organization is: SAFE Learning Systems, Inc., P.O. Box 5089, Anaheim, CA 92804.

6

THE SERIOUS SEVENTIES

"Concerned with grave, important, or complex matters, problems" and "giving cause for concern" are two out of five definitions given in *Webster's Dictionary* for the word "serious" which definitely apply to this chapter, "The Serious Seventies." Unfortunately, since the average American was purposely kept in the dark about what was taking place, being able "to be concerned" was an impossibility. To the change agents roaming the education landscape, "change" was the goal, and the end justified the means, even if it meant misleading through semantic deception the parents and taxpayers who paid the bills and provided the resources—the children and teachers upon whom the change agents would experiment.

"The Serious Seventies" contains excerpts from important government documents, education journal articles, professional papers, and critiques by key educationists regarding the major components of reform planned for the end of the century as a result of federal legislation passed in the 1960s. From a study of the key documents one detects a vigorous tug-of-war taking place at the highest decision-making levels in education. Stringent debate was carried on regarding the pros and cons of the use of systematic planning and technology in an area of human endeavor (education) which until this time had had relatively little interference from political, social and economic planners (social engineers). State commissioners of education, local education agency superintendents, and especially teachers and school boards had been able to make decisions at the state and local level—decisions which they considered to be in the best interest of students and the communities in which they lived and worked. But "change" was the name of this serious new game.

A careful reading of "The Serious Seventies" documents, especially the 1972 Association for

Educational Computing and Technology (AECT) report entitled *The Field of Educational Technology: A Statement of Definition* (October, 1972), has convinced this writer that significant resistance to goal setting, systems management, computer-assisted instruction, etc., which existed at the beginning of the 1970s was, unfortunately, overcome. For instance, the above-referenced document contained the following most important warning regarding the use of technology in the classroom; a warning that, evidently, was not heeded in the years to come. The warning read in part:

> It should be clear that the concerned professional does not have to be a "liberal," or a "conservative." The concerned professional must, however, show moral sensitivity to the effect of what he or she does [in the field of technology]. It does not matter what position an individual comes to as long as it is not "I'll do it because it can be done."

The above recommendation relating to the ethical use of technology in the classroom was evidently ignored by the change agents who decided instead that "We'll do it because it can be done."

In 1971 *Phi Delta Kappan* published a paper entitled *Performance-Based Teacher Education* [PBTE]: *What Is the State of the Art?* This paper spelled out the *raison d'etre* for the transition from teacher education based on knowledge of subject matter to teacher education based on the ability to "perform" in the classroom. Skinnerian methods adopted by Madeline Hunter and others would become the foundation for future teacher training and accreditation, and ultimately the method for workforce training. This paper makes it all too clear that the purpose of PBTE was to "lower standards" so that the teaching profession could be more "inclusive"—or so "they" said. However, this writer believes inclusion was more than likely the cover (excuse acceptable to those who believed in equal opportunity) to install the performance-based system necessary for the eventual implementation of the school-to-work polytech system planned in 1934 and activated in the 1990s. From this time forward, the deliberate dumbing down would proceed with a vengeance.

During "The Serious Seventies" the ship of education set a new course. Navigating these new waters would require a new chart, one entirely different from that used in the past.

1970

A PROHIBITION AGAINST FEDERAL CONTROL OF EDUCATION, SECTION 432, *GENERAL EDUcation Provisions Act* (GEPA), was enacted in 1970 and reads as follows:

> Sec. 432. No provision of any applicable program shall be construed to authorize any department, agency, officer, or employee of the United States to exercise any direction, supervision, or control over the curriculum, program of instruction, administration, or personnel of any educational institution, school, or school system, or over the selection of library resources, textbooks, or other printed or published instructional materials by any educational institution or school system, or to require the assignment or transportation of students or teachers in order to overcome racial imbalance. (20 U.S.C. 1232a) Enacted April 18, 1970, P.L. 91–230, Title IV, sec. 401(a)(10), 81 Stat.169.

[Ed. Note: The interpretation of the above prohibition lies in the eyes of the beholder. Parents and traditional teachers have held that all curriculum and teaching based on the federally funded Northwest Regional Educational Laboratory Goals Collection, National Diffusion Network Programs, and "scientific research-based" reading programs funded under the *Reading Excellence Act of 1998* should be covered by GEPA and are consequently illegal. Educrats, on the other hand, have held that the only way for a program to be covered by GEPA would be for the secretary of education to sit on the sidewalk outside the U.S. Department of Education, developing curriculum, and passing it out to interested passersby.]

THE SHREVEPORT [LOUISIANA] *JOURNAL* OF JANUARY 20, 1970 CARRIED AN ARTICLE EN-titled "And It Came to Pass" in its Views from Other Newspapers section in which the author asked:

JACKSON (MISS.) DAILY NEWS—Has HEW Replaced NRA [*National Recovery Act*]?

Thirty-seven years ago an unbelieving editor sat down and wrote an editorial for his paper, *The Monroe Evening News* of Monroe, Michigan, USA. The date was Wednesday, September 13, 1933.

   Under the Lead Line, "Not That!", that incredulous American newspaper editor went on to ask his readers of three decades ago, "Are the schools of America to be used as a propaganda agency to mould public opinion into conformity with the policies of the administration?"

   Still in a tone of utter disbelief that editor went on to quote from an interview with one Louis Alber, chief of the speakers division of the National Recovery Act. "Just read these astounding utterances by Mr. Alber," the editor challenges his subscribers.

> The rugged individualism of Americanism must go, because it is contrary to the purposes of the New Deal and the NRA which is remaking America.
>   Russia and Germany are attempting to compel a new order by means of their nationalism-compulsion. The United States will do it by moral persuasion. Of course we expect some opposition, but the principles of the New Deal must be carried to the youth of the nation. We expect to accomplish by education what dictators in Europe are seeking to do by compulsion and force.
>   Mr. Alber went on to explain that a "primer" outlining methods of teaching to be used, along with motion pictures on the subject, were being prepared for distribution to all public and parochial schools and commented that: "NRA is the outstanding part of the President's program, but in fact it is only a fragment. The general public is not informed on the other parts of the program, and the schools are the places to reach the future builders of the nation."

From our vantage point in history we know that the notorious NRA was laid to rest early in its incubation period by the United States Supreme Court.

   What is important to each and all of us today is what has transpired in the intervening years since 1933. That editor of long ago remarked, "So as sweeping and revolutionary as NRA is, it is only a fragment of a greater program of which the public knows nothing, and this unknown program is to be inculcated into the minds of pupils in the schools everywhere, by official efforts and at government expense.... Now our schools are to become—like those of Germany and Russia—an agency for the promotion of whatever political, social, and economic policies the administration may desire to carry out. And the taxpayers, whether they like it or not, are to pay for having their children converted to those policies."

The Editor closed by stating: "The whole proposition is so amazing, and so alarming in its implications, that we refuse to take it seriously."

Take a look about you today, with the Washington-directed school policies. Is the Health, Education and Welfare Department doing exactly what the defunct NRA started out to do?

REPORT OF THE STUDY, TITLE III, ESEA BY EMERY STOOF WAS PRODUCED BY THE EDUCA-tional Innovation Advisory Commission and the Bureau of Planning and Development of the California State Department of Education in 1970. Excerpts follow:

> Origin of the Bureau... An Instructional Program Planning and Development Unit was estab-lished by State Board action in 1965 and was funded through a Title V, ESEA project. This unit was comprised of persons responsible for the state level administration of Title III, ESEA, and co-ordination of Title V, ESEA. A general conceptual model for effective planned change in education, as well as a management model for the administration of Title III, ESEA, was submitted to the State Board's Federal Aid Committee in 1965, with November 10, 1965 as the first deadline for receiving applications for funds....
>
> Two significant developments early in the state administration of Title III, ESEA, were (1) the project to Prepare Educational Planners (Operation PEP), and (2) the funding of twenty-one regional planning centers. "PEP" sessions trained administrators in systematic planning procedures, systems analysis techniques, "planning, programming and budgeting system" and cost-benefit analysis. PACE (Projects to Advance Creativity in Education) was to encourage school districts to develop imaginative solutions to educational problems, to uti-lize more effectively research findings, to translate the latest knowledge about teaching and learning into widespread educational practice, and to create an awareness of new programs. Through the regional centers, the Bureau has endeavored to (1) encourage the development of creative innovations, (2) demonstrate worthwhile innovations in educational practice through exemplary programs, and (3) supplement existing programs and facilities.

[Ed. Note: This is an example of how the Federal government began its takeover of all state and local education agencies, removing any semblance of what could be considered local control. The California report explains exactly what happened in every single state due to our elected officials' inability to resist taking federal money and their trust of education change agents (administrators, principals, superintendents, etc.). How many American children have been severely handicapped academically and morally by experimental, "innovative" programs which had absolutely nothing to do with academics, but everything to do with attitude, value and belief change?]

IN 1970 LEONARD S. KENWORTHY, PROFESSOR OF EDUCATION AT BROOKLYN COLLEGE OF the City of New York, wrote *The International Dimension of Education: Background Paper II Prepared for the World Conference on Education* (Asilomar, California, March 5–14, 1970), edited by Norman V. Overly. The conference was sponsored by the Association for Supervi-sion and Curriculum Development, National Education Association, and the Commission on International Cooperation in Education. Excerpts from the report follow:

> III. The International Dimensions of Our Schools: Some Overall Considerations
> Here and there teachers have modified individual courses.... Schools have rewritten syllabi

or added courses.... But nowhere has there been a rigorous examination of the total experiences of children and/or youth in schools and the development of a continuous, cumulative, comprehensive curriculum to create the new type of people needed for effective living in the latter part of the 20th century....

...All the work we do in developing internationally minded individuals should be directed to improved behavior.

That means that all the efforts in this dimension of education must be predicated on the research in the formation, reinforcement, and change of attitudes and on the development of skills. Knowledge is tremendously important, but we should be clear by now that it must be carefully selected knowledge, discovered by the learners rather than told to them, and organized by them with the help of teachers or professors around concepts, generalizations, or big ideas. Teaching, therefore, becomes the process of helping younger people to probe, discover, analyze, compare, and contrast rather than telling.

There is a rich mine of data now on attitude formation, change, and reinforcement which teachers need to study carefully and apply to this dimension of education as well as to others. For example, we know that most basic attitudes are learned very early but that attitudes can be changed at any age. We know that times of personal and societal crisis are the best times to bring about change. But we also know that people must not be threatened by changes. They must be relatively secure and much of their resistance to change recognized and tolerated as a manifestation of an inner struggle to reject the old and accept the new. Therefore, the acceptance of the old views with equanimity is important, so that the threat to a person is minimal. We know, too, that appeals to pride and self-interest may be helpful in bringing about change. So are the statements and actions of prestige persons. Membership in new groups is often helpful in insulating a person from slipping back into old patterns. We also know that changing a total group is easier and more likely to produce results than trying to change individuals. And it is clear that concentration upon specific areas of change rather than general approaches is usually most effective....

Changed behavior is our goal and it consists in large measure of improved attitudes, improved skills, and carefully selected knowledge—these three—and the greatest of these is attitudes....

The program emphasizes feelings as well as facts. In some parts of the world in the field of education today, the emphasis is upon cognitive learning or intellectual development. This is especially true in the United States.... But in the international dimensions of education, as in other dimensions, the affective domain or emotional development is just as important....

We need to get at the "gut level" in much of our teaching. We need to use music, art, powerful literature, films and other approaches which get at the feeling level of learning. For example, the writer has found tremendously effective a 10-minute film on the United Nations, entitled "Overture." There is no narrative in this film; the pictures are shown against a background of music, with the Vienna Symphony Orchestra playing the *Egmont Overture*. It is a powerful learning device and moves its viewers in a way few other approaches touch them. (pp. 23–39)

1971

EDUCATION: FROM THE ACQUISITION OF KNOWLEDGE TO PROGRAMMED, CONDITIONED RE-*sponses* was submitted by Assemblyman Robert H. Burke (70th California Assembly District) to the California Legislature in 1971. An excerpt follows:

INTRODUCTION
Several months ago, my office began accumulating material which had particular significance in the area of Planning, Programming, Budgeting Systems because of its potential use
as a tool of fiscal accountability in the field of education. As we searched into the information available on the application of this subject in education, it became increasingly difficult
to see any relationship between the proposed programs and fiscal accountability. It was
apparent after a study of the methods proposed for use by the schools for accountability
purposes that fiscal accountability was being minimized and that techniques were being
promoted for achieving behavioral objectives. Other seemingly unrelated organizations,
projects, and programs were uncovered because of their influence on the application of
accountability methods. They were as parts in a puzzle—analyzed by themselves, each of
these projects appeared to be either harmless or an expression of someone's "dream." When
linked together with other "harmless" programs, they were no longer formless but could be
seen as an entire package of plans outlining methods of implementation, organization structures (including flow-charts), computerization, use of behavioral profile catalogs, and goals
and objectives determination.

CONTROVERSIAL SEXOLOGISTS LESTER A. KIRKENDALL AND RUTH F. OSBORNE DEVELOPED
in 1971 a program entitled "Sex Education—Student Syllabus No: 216786, correlated with
M.I.P. 180800" which was one of the first sex education programs to use a mastery learning
approach. This program was published by the National Book Company, owned by Carl W.
Salser, executive director of Educational Research Associates, a non-profit educational research corporation in Portland, Oregon. Mr. Salser is also the owner of Halcyon Press and is a
long-time advocate of individualized instruction and mastery learning.

Carl Salser is the author of a pamphlet entitled "The Carnegie Unit: An Administrative
Convenience, but an Educational Catastrophe" and is a supporter of outcome-based educa-
tion/mastery learning. Full implementation of OBE/ML calls for the removal of the Carnegie
Unit—the "seat time" measure of subject exposure for students which determines graduation
and college entry eligibility. Salser was a member during 1981–1982 of the presidentially
appointed National Council on Educational Research which had oversight of the activities at
the former National Institute of Education of the U.S. Department of Education.

IN 1971 THE SECRETARIAT OF THE UNITED NATIONS EDUCATIONAL, SCIENTIFIC, AND CUL-
tural Organization (UNESCO) called upon George W. Parkyn of New Zealand to outline a
possible model for an education system based on the ideal of a continuous education process
throughout the lifetime of the learner—a means of bringing an existing national school system
into line with lifelong learning. The result of this effort was a book entitled *Towards a Conceptual Model of Life-Long Education*, published in 1973 by UNESCO (English Edition ISBN 92-
3-101117-0). The preface of the book contained the following interesting biographical sketch
of the little-known Dr. Parkyn:

> The Secretariat called on George W. Parkyn of New Zealand to prepare this first study. Dr.
> Parkyn has rendered extensive service to education in many parts of the world: in New
> Zealand, as a teacher in primary and secondary schools, as a senior lecturer at the University
> of Otago, and as director of the New Zealand Council for Educational Research, 1954–1967;

at UNESCO, where he made substantial contributions to the *World Survey of Education*; at Stanford University, California, as a visiting professor; in New Zealand again, as a visiting lecturer in Comparative Education at the University of Auckland; and as Professor of Comparative Education at the University of London, Institute of Education.... Dr. Parkyn was asked to review the available literature in this field and to involve several of his colleagues at Stanford University, California, in discussions on the basic concept. Psychologists, sociologists, and anthropologists, as well as professional educators took part in the conceptual stage, contributing a rich variety of views. Among those who helped the author in the preparation of the study were his research assistants, Mr. Alejandro Toledo and Mr. Hei-tak Wu, and his colleagues, Dr. John C. Bock, Dr. Martin Carnoy, Dr. Henry M. Levin and Dr. Frank J. Moore.

[Ed. Note: The Dr. Henry M. Levin mentioned above is the same Henry Levin whose K–8 Accelerated Schools Project is one of the seventeen reform models that schools may adopt to qualify for their share of nearly $150 million in federal grants, according to the January 20, 1999 edition of *Education Week* (p. 1). The article "Who's In, Who's Out" listed Accelerated Learning as being used in urban schools. It is based on a constructivist philosophy which has echoes of and references to Maria Montessori's and John Dewey's philosophies of education and incorporates the controversial Lozanov method of Superlearning.]

PSYCHOLOGY APPLIED TO TEACHING BY ROBERT F. BIENTER (HOUGHTON MIFFLIN CO.: Boston, 1971) was published. This popular psychology text was recommended for use in Introduction to Educational Psychology courses in universities in the early 1970s. Chapter 5, under the sub-heading of "S-R Associationism and Programmed Learning," is excerpted here:

Watson [John B.] (who did the most to popularize Pavlovian theory in the United States) based one of his most famous experiments (Watson and Rayner, 1920) on the observation that young children have a "natural" fear of sudden loud sounds. He set up a situation in which a two-year-old boy named Albert was encouraged to play with a white rat. After this preliminary period, Watson suddenly hit a steel bar with a hammer just as Albert reached for the rat, and the noise frightened the child so much that he came to respond to the rat with fear. He had been conditioned to associate the rat with the loud sound. The success of this experiment led Watson to believe that he could control behavior in almost limitless ways, by arranging sequences of conditioned responses. He trumpeted his claim in this famous statement:

> Give me a dozen healthy infants, well formed, and my own special world to bring them up in, and I'll guarantee to take any one at random and train him to become any type of specialist I might select—doctor, lawyer, artist, merchant-chief and yes, even beggarman and thief—regardless of his talents, penchants, tendencies, abilities, vocations, and race of his ancestry. (pp. 152–3)

Later on in the chapter, Skinner's contributions are discussed:

An even more striking example of Skinner's overwhelming enthusiasm for programmed learning is his claim that mere manipulation of the teaching machine should be "reinforcing enough to keep a pupil at work for suitable periods every day."... Thus it is apparent that Skinner's enthusiasm has prevented him from seeing some of the deficiencies of programmed instruction. Many critics have been especially dissatisfied with his attempt to refute the charge that programs limit creativity. Clearly when the person composing a program decides in advance what is to be learned and how it is to be learned, a student has no opportunity to develop in his own way. He is limited by what the programmer knows and by how the programmer learned....

It is true that the student might use the material in an original way *after* he had finished the program, but there is the possibility that programmed instruction interferes with this process. For example, some students who have completed programs report that although they have progressed quickly and satisfactorily and feel that they have learned something, they aren't sure where to go from here. Typically, the next step is to take an exam, usually of the multiple-choice type, which is highly similar to the program in which that stimuli are presented and responses are chosen. But what happens after the exam? If the student cannot respond unless he is stimulated in the same way he was in the program or exam, he will rarely be able to apply what he has learned to real life situations.

What we are dealing with here is the subject of transfer... which is basic to education. Ellis has pointed out that little research has been done on the transferability of programmed learning; in almost all studies the experimenter determines the degree of learning solely on the basis of each child's performance on a test given immediately after the completion of the program. Skinner maintains that the student can be taught to transfer ideas through separate programs designed for this purpose and that a properly written program will wean the student from the machine, but there is little evidence to back up this contention. On logical grounds alone it seems reasonable to question the transfer value of programmed instruction.

Markle notes that in order to ensure that approximately 95 percent of the answers will be correct, as Skinner suggests, programmers are forced to keep revising programs for the lowest common denominator—the slowest students in the group. This eventually leads to programs which most students can complete fairly easily, but it also leads to programs which are oversimplified and repetitious. (pp. 168–171)

THE INDIVIDUALIZED LEARNING LETTER (T.I.L.L.): ADMINISTRATOR'S GUIDE TO IMPROVE *Learning; Individualized Instruction Methods; Flexible Scheduling; Behavioral Objectives; Study Units; Self-Directed Learning; Accountability, Vol. I* (February 22, 1971: T.I.L.L., Huntington, N.Y.)[1] was published and circulated. Excerpts follow:

Opting to become a greater force in promoting I.I. (Individualized Instruction), The Northeast Association for Individualization of Instruction (Wyandanch, N.Y.) has gone national—by substituting the word "national" for "northeast.".... The enlarged 2–1/2 day convention is geared to give registrants more time to watch I.I. in action in live classrooms. Several of the nation's I.I. leaders already lined up to run workshops include: Dr. Lloyd Bishop, NYU; Dr. Sid Rollins, Rhode Island College; Dr. Robert Scanlon, Research for Better Schools [Research for Better Schools and University of Pittsburgh Learning Research and Development Center (Robert Glaser) were instrumental in development of IPI in the early 1960s, ed.]; Dr. Edward Pino, Superintendent of Cherry Creek Schools (Englewood, CO); Dr. Robert Anderson, Harvard University; Dr. Leon Lessinger, Georgia State University; Dr. Robert Sinclair, University of Massachusetts; Jane Root, Stanford Research Associates; and Dr. Glen Ovard, Brigham Young University. Representatives of USOE, NEA, NY State Department of Education will be present. (The latter supports the conference with an annual grant.)....

QUOTES YOU CAN USE:
DOWN WITH BOOKS. "Textbooks not only encourage learning at the wrong level (imparting

facts rather than telling how to gather facts, etc.), they also violate an important new concern in American education—individualized instruction.... Textbooks produce superficially knowledgeable students... who know virtually nothing in depth about anything.... A good start would be to... declare a moratorium on textbook use in all courses." Dwight D. Allen, Dean of Education, University of Massachusetts, writing on "The Decline of Textbooks, Change."[2]

RECOMMENDED BOOKS: *Behavioral Objectives: A Guide for Individualized Learning*. Four-volume set covering more than 4000 objectives representing four years' work of more than 200 teachers. Arranged by subject area. Covers language arts, social studies, math and science. A comprehensive collection. Westinghouse Learning Corp., 100 Park Avenue, New York, N.Y. 10017.

MEETINGS STRESSING INDIVIDUALIZED INSTRUCTION: Ninth National Society for Programmed Instruction Convention, March 31–April 3, 1971. University of Rochester, Rochester, N.Y. Heavy emphasis on applying principles and processes of individualized instruction. Session on redesigning schools of tomorrow. Contact Dr. Robert G. Pierleone, College of Education, University of Rochester, Rochester, N.Y. First Educational Technology Conference. April 5–8, 1971. Americana Hotel, N.Y. City, N.Y. Conference seminars and workshops will cover curriculum design, use of computers, programmed instruction, simulation, innovation theory, etc.

IN FORTHCOMING ISSUES: Update of 46 Case Studies of Individualized Instruction as originally reported by Jack V. Edling, Oregon State System of Higher Education.

"REVISED REPORT OF POPULATION SUBCOMMITTEE, GOVERNOR'S ADVISORY COUNCIL ON Environmental Quality" for the State of Michigan, to be used at the April 6, 1971 meeting of the subcommittee, was filed in the Library, Legislative Service Bureau in Lansing, Michigan. Excerpts from this disturbing report follow:

I. Concept of a Population Goal

In general, the Subcommittee was in agreement with *U.S. Senate Resolution No. 214*, as follows:

> That it is the policy of the United States to develop, encourage, and implement at the earliest possible time, the necessary policies, attitudes, social standards, and actions which will by voluntary means consistent with human rights and individual conscience, stabilize the population of the United States and thereby promote the future well-being of the citizens of this Nation and the entire world.

It was the feeling of the Subcommittee that the intent of the above Resolution should be encouraged by voluntary means and due consideration given to human rights. However, in order to accomplish the above goal, state and federal legislation must accompany this intent to provide disincentives.

II. Optimum Goal

An optimum goal is to be considered in preference to a maximum carrying capacity. As a starting point, zero population growth is the recommended goal for the citizens of Michigan.... That the human population on a finite "space ship" cannot increase indefinitely is obvious. What is not so obvious is what constitutes an "optimum" level of population and the methods by which it is to be limited....

III. How Does Society Obtain Population Control?

Constraints on population size can be divided into two types, biological and social. Biological constraints include the limitation of those energies and chemicals required to drive human society as a biological system.... Societal constraints are more appropriate since the human population explosion is basically a social problem. There are three classes of social institutions which can be utilized to obtain population control. These are the political, economic and education systems. Each of these represent powerful control systems which help to regulate the behavior of our society.

A wide range of public policies are available by which man can affect population size. Some policies can seek to change man's basic values and attitudes with respect to the issues of population size. Other policies can seek to directly affect man's behaviors which have consequences for population size. Some suggested policy goals are listed.

General Public Understanding
Having children is a public interest as well as a private interest. Likewise, the use of the environment must be understood to be a collective responsibility rather than a private or individual responsibility, since the costs and the benefits of the use of the environment are indivisible to all members of the collectivity. This idea runs counter to the underlying ethic of individualism and privateness of our society, but is basic if we are to mobilize the collective will which is necessary for social action. To change such a basic set of attitudes and values requires cooperation from the full range of opinion leaders in the society. A program of education for leaders in all sectors of society, such as religious, economic, political, educational, technical, etc., is therefore called for.

Since basic attitudes and values are formed early in life, and since it is the youth of society who are yet capable of determining the size of future families, a program for all levels of formal education can be a powerful way to change society's attitudes and values on the question of population size as outlined above.

The idea that family size is a collective, social responsibility rather than just an individual responsibility can be fostered both directly by exhortations by opinion leaders and in the schools, and indirectly by the actions that government and other institutions in society take. For example, the proposal to eliminate the income tax exemption for children in excess of the two-child family limit can be a powerful way for government to symbolize its determination that family size is a collective responsibility.

Public understanding of the interdependent nature of our natural and man-made environment is also important for enlightened public support for population control policies. A state-wide education program concerning ecology and population biology is needed for both student and adult segments of our society. This will require vigorous action to remove the topic of sex from the closets of obscurity in which conservative elements in our society have placed it....

Cultural Changes
Two types of cultural changes are needed in order to reduce the population increase: reduce the desired size of families, and reduce the social pressure to marry and have a family.

Large families can be changed from an economic asset to an economic liability if all members of society can be offered the prospect that through work, saving, and deferred spending they can achieve economic security for themselves and their children. For the already affluent middle class, larger families can be made an economic liability by increasing the incentives for and the costs of advanced education for their children....

Cultural changes to reduce the social pressure to marry and have a family can be pursued by changing educational materials which glorify married life and family life as the only "normal" life pattern, by granting greater public recognition to non-married and non-family life styles, by facilitating careers for single women....

[Ed. Note: The above recommendation regarding reducing the social pressure to marry and have a family was successfully carried out over a period of 25 years according to an article entitled "Institution in Transition" by Michelle Boorstein which appeared in *The Maine Sunday Telegram*'s August 30, 1998 issue, Home and Family Section, G–1. This Associated Press article said in part:

They [Pam Hesse and Rob Lemar] share a home and a future but not a formal vow—just one couple caught up in the seismic shifts taking place in American attitudes toward marriage and childbearing.

A soon-to-be-released Census Bureau report shows Hesse is far from an exception; in fact, she's in the majority. The report, the bureau's first compilation of all its 60 years of data on childbearing and marriage, finds that for the first time, the majority of "first births"—someone's first child—were either conceived by or born to an unmarried woman. That is up from 18 percent in the 1930s.

This is connected to an erosion of the centrality of marriage, said Stephanie Coontz of Evergreen State College in Olympia, Washington, who studies the family and its role in history.]

Returning to the Population Subcommittee's report:

Direct Behavior Changes
Two general types of public policies are distributive policies and regulative policies. Distributive policies involve the distribution of resources and opportunities to people who choose to modify their behavior to conform with the socially desired patterns. They thus operate as incentives rather than as official constraints. Examples include the elimination of tax incentives for larger families, monetary incentives for sterilization or adopted families, and removing the income tax discrimination against single citizens....

Regulative policies involve direct constraints on behavior and necessarily generate greater political conflict than distributive policies. This is because regulative policies eliminate the element of voluntary choice and apply automatically and categorically to a whole class of people or of behaviors. Examples of such regulative policies designed to control population growth include forced sterilization and restrictive licensing procedures to marry and to have children. However, it does not seem necessary, desirable, or feasible to involve regulative policies for population control at this time. One regulative type policy which is now in effect and which allows population increase is the law forbidding abortion. Restrictions against abortions should be removed to allow individual choice in the use of this back-up method of birth control....

A general acceptance of birth control to obtain population stability will create a more static ethnic, cultural and racial structure in society. Minority groups will continue to stay at a numerical minority. Minority problems are basically social and should be solved in that manner. An equilibrium condition will also alter the structure of our economic relationship both within our society (a shift from an expanding economy to a competitive displacement economy) and between other countries that will still be experiencing increasing populations....

Immediate consideration must be given to (1) the development of an integrated social control of our population size and growth, and (2) the impact of a steady stable condition on our society. The scope and complexity of this task requires the attention of a highly professional team whose talents and professional training are equal to the challenge. It is the recommendation of the Council that such a team be brought together and charged with the prompt development of the details of this program and reporting back to the Council.

Approved by the Population Subcommittee, March 30, 1971.

Present: Dr. C.T. Black, Mr. Robert Boatman, Professor William Cooper, Dr. Ralph MacMullan, and M.S. Reisen, M.D., Chairman

Surely it is no coincidence that the above-mentioned Michigan and U.S. Senate recommended policies on population control were being discussed at the same time (1971) that the United States was engaged in "Ping Pong" diplomacy with Communist China, the international leader in mandatory population control. Some excerpts follow from "The Ping Heard Round the World" which appeared in the April 26, 1971 issue of *Time* magazine:

> Dressed in an austere gray tunic, Premier Chou En-Lai moved along a line of respectfully silent visitors in Peking's massive Great Hall of the People.... Finally he stopped to chat with the 15-member U.S. team and three accompanying American reporters, the first group of U.S. citizens and journalists to visit China in nearly a quarter of a century. "We have opened a new page in the relations of the Chinese and American people," he told the U.S. visitors.
>
> ...Yet in last week's gestures to the United States table tennis team, the Chinese were clearly indicating that a new era could begin. They carefully made their approaches through private U.S. citizens, but they were responding to earlier signals that had been sent by the Nixon Administration over the past two years.
>
> ...Probably never before in history has a sport been used so effectively as a tool of international diplomacy.

[Ed. Note: Back to family planning, Michigan-style. *Population and Family Planning in the People's Republic of China, 1971*, a book published by the Victor-Bostrom Fund and the Population Crisis Committee, has a table of contents that includes: "A Letter from Peking" by Edgar Snow, author of *Red Star Over China*; "Family Planning in China" by Han Suyin, M.D.; and "Why Not Adopt China's Population Goals?" In other words, it looks like Ping Pong Diplomacy may have been used to open up the dialogue between Communist China and "private" American groups supporting population control. These would, in turn, lobby in Congress for more liberal family planning policies and for the legalization of abortion as recommended in the *U.S. Senate Journal Resolution #214* and the Michigan paper. Here again, as was the case with the 1985 Carnegie Corporation-Soviet Academy of Sciences education agreement, diplomacy is being conducted by private parties: table tennis teams and groups such as the nonprofit Victor-Bostrom Fund and the Population Crisis Committee.]

***PERFORMANCE-BASED TEACHER EDUCATION: WHAT IS THE STATE OF THE ART?* BY STANLEY** Elam, editor of Phi Delta Kappa Publications (AACTE Committee on Performance-Based Teacher Education, American Association of Colleges for Teacher Education: Washington, D.C., 1971), was published. This paper was originally prepared in 1971 pursuant to a contract with the U.S. Office of Education through the Texas Education Agency, Austin, Texas. Excerpts follow:

> The Association is pleased to offer to the teacher education community the Committee's first state of the art paper.... In performance-based programs... he [the teacher] is held accountable, not for passing grades, but for attaining a given level of competency in performing the essential tasks of teaching.... Acceptance of this basic principle has program implications that are truly revolutionary.
>
> The claim that teacher education programs were not producing people equipped to teach minority group children and youth effectively has pointed directly to the need for reform in teacher education.... Moreover, the claim of minority group youth that there should be alternative routes to professional status has raised serious questions about the suitability of generally recognized teacher education programs.

[Ed. Note: The above paper was one of the first—and perhaps the most influential—professional papers setting the stage for full-blown implementation of Skinnerian outcome-based/performance-based education. The definitions, criteria, assessment, etc., are identical to those found in present professional OBE literature. (See Appendix VII for fuller excerpts from this paper.)]

CONCERN REGARDING THE DELIBERATE DUMBING DOWN OF AMERICA IS NOT CONFINED TO this author according to an article entitled "Young People Are Getting Dumber," by David Hawkins, editorial staff writer, in the August 26, 1971 issue of *The Dallas Morning News.* Excerpts from this interesting article, which discusses the importance of acquiring a large vocabulary, follow:

> John Gaston, who bosses the Fort Worth branch of the Human Engineering Laboratory (half his clients are from Dallas), dropped a bomb on me as we discussed aptitude testing.
> "Do you know," he said, "that the present generation knows less than its parents?"
> "You mean to say that young people aren't smarter than we are—that all we've heard about this generation being the last and best isn't so?"
> Gaston nodded solemnly: "Young people know fewer words than their fathers. That makes them know less." He fixed me with a foreboding eye: "Can you imagine what a drop in knowledge of 1 per cent a year for 30 years could do to our civilization?"
> The question answered itself. And though I could hardly believe what Gaston was saying, I knew it wasn't instant sociology.
> What he says is based on hundreds of thousands of tests given in several parts of the country since 1922 by what is probably the most prestigious non-profit outfit in the field of vocational research. The Human Engineers don't even advertise.
> But Gaston wasn't through: "We also believe," he was saying, "that the recent rise in violence correlates with the drop in vocabulary. Long [range] testing has convinced us that crime and violence predominate among people who score low in vocabulary. If they can't express themselves with their tongues, they'll use their fists."
> "We test many gifted people who are low in vocabulary and we tell them all—we tell the world—to learn the words. Swallow the dictionary. Brilliant aptitudes aren't worth much

without words to give them wings."

Gaston paused and then dropped another bomb. "The one thing successful people have in common isn't high aptitudes—it's high vocabulary, and it's within everybody's reach. Success actually correlates more with vocabulary than with the gifts we're born with."

"Aptitudes will only show them which road to take. Vocabulary will determine how high they climb. Right now, the present generation is headed downwards."

SOME IMPORTANT STATEMENTS BY PROFESSOR JOHN I. GOODLAD, PRESIDENT OF EDUCA-tional Inquiry, Incorporated, appeared in *A Report to the President's Commission on School Finance (Schooling for the Future: Toward Quality and Equality in American Precollegiate Education)* October 15, 1971. Goodlad makes the following comments under "Issue #9—Educational Innovation: What changes in purposes, procedures or institutional arrangements are needed to improve the quality of American elementary and secondary education?":

> The literature on how we socialize or develop normative behavior in our children and the populace in general is fairly dismal.... [T]he majority of our youth still hold the same values as their parents....
>
> In the second paradigm... the suggestion is made that there are different targets for the change agent. For example, in a social system such as a school probably five to fifteen percent of the people are open to change. They are the "early majority" and can be counted on to be supportive. A second group, sixty to ninety percent, are the resisters. They need special attention and careful strategies need to be employed with them. Also, there are the leaders, formal and informal, and their support is critical. In his research, for example, Demeter noted some time ago the special role of the school principal in innovation:

> > Building principals are key figures in the (innovation) process. Where they are both aware of and sympathetic to an innovation, it tends to prosper. Where they are ignorant of its existence, or apathetic if not hostile, it tends to remain outside the bloodstream of the school.

> Few people think in these ways today. Rather, as a people, we tend to rely upon common sense or what might be called conventional wisdom as we make significant decisions which, in turn, seriously affect our lives.... More often than not, school board members, parents and the public make important decisions about what should happen in their schools based upon these past experiences or other conventional wisdom.... The use of conventional wisdom as a basis for decision-making is a major impediment to educational improvement....
>
> The child of suburbia is likely to be a materialist and somewhat of a hypocrite. He tends to be a striver in school, a conformist, and above all a believer in being "nice," polite, clean and tidy. He divides Humanity into the black and white, the Jew and the Christian, the rich and the poor, the "smart" and the "dumb." He is often conspicuously self-centered. In all these respects, the suburban child patterns his attitudes after those of his parents.... If we do not alter this pattern, if we do not resocialize ourselves to accept and plan for change, our society may decay. What may be left in the not too distant future is what other formerly great societies have had, reflections on past glories....
>
> In the social interaction model of change, the assumption is made that the change agent is the decision-maker about the innovation. That is, it is assumed that he decides what the adopter will change to. This is a serious problem for two very good reasons. First, as we have shown, people cannot be forced to change until they are psychologically ready. Thus, at

every stage, each individual is, in fact, deciding how far he is ready or willing to move, if at all.

[Ed. Note: As a former school board member, this writer can relate to the above quote. Principals who resisted innovation eventually ended up being forced out of the system undergoing radical change. Their trials and tribulations were known only to them, and what they underwent during the change agents' activities in their schools could be described as inhumane treatment.]

THE TRI-COUNTY K–12 COURSE GOAL PROJECT, THE RESULTS OF WHICH WERE LATER PUB-lished by the Northwest Regional Laboratory of the U.S. Department of Education and used extensively throughout the nation as the formulaic sample for "goals setting," was initiated in 1971. In the appendix entitled "Classification System for the School Curriculum" for her *Practitioner's Implementation Handbook* [series]: *The Outcome-Based Curriculum* (Outcome Associates: Princeton, N.J., 1992), Charlotte Danielson, M.A., a prominent educator and proponent of outcome-based education, said: "The knowledge and inquiry and problem-solving skills sections of this taxonomy were first developed by the Tri-County Goal Development Project, Portland, Oregon."[3] Assistant superintendent Victor W. Doherty, Evaluation Department of the Portland Public Schools in Portland, Oregon, in a November 2, 1981 letter to Mrs. Opal Moore, described this Goal Development Project as follows:

> The Tri-County Goal Development Project was initiated by me in 1971 in an effort to develop a resource for arriving at well-defined learning outcome statements for use in curriculum planning and evaluation. At that time the only language available was the behavioral objective, a statement which combined a performance specification with a learning outcome often in such a way as to conceal the real learning that was being sought. By freeing the learning outcome statements from performance specification and by defining learning outcomes of three distinctly different types (information, process skills, and values), we were able to produce outcome statements that served both the planning and evaluation functions. The project was organized to include 55 school districts in Multnomah, Clackamas, and Washington Counties and writing was done initially by teachers whose time was donated to the project by member districts.

[Ed. Note: The writer believes that this very controversial project which provided the goals framework for OBE was illegal—in clear violation of the 1970 GEPA prohibition against federal government involvement in curriculum development.]

1972

THE NEWPORT HARBOR ENSIGN OF CORONA DEL MAR, CALIFORNIA CARRIED AN ARTICLE entitled "Teachers Are Recycled" in its January 20, 1972 issue. The following are excerpts from this important article:

> Education in California is finally going to catch up with the "innovative" Newport-Mesa Unified School District. With the passage of the Stull Bill, AB 293, all school districts are mandated to evaluate their classroom teachers and certificated personnel through new guide-

lines. Another portion of the bill will allow a district to dismiss a teacher with tenure, without going to court.

A teacher will no longer have the prerogative of having his own "style" of teaching, because he will be held "accountable" to uniform expected student progress. His job will depend on how well he can produce "intended" behavioral changes in students.

"School districts just haven't had time to tool up for it," explained Dr. William Cunningham, Executive Director of the Association of California School Administrators (ACSA). Until recently, he was superintendent of the Newport-Mesa district.

The Newport-Mesa district, under the guidance of Dr. Cunningham, accomplished this task years ago. In fact we have warned of this appraisal plan in many of our columns throughout the past 2 years. Its formal name is "staff performance appraisal plan," at least in this district, and was formulated as early as 1967.

In 1968 five elementary schools in our district (California, Mariners, Presidio, Victoria, Monte Vista) and one high school (Estancia) were selected from schools that volunteered for the project. They were accepted on the basis that at least 60% of the teachers were willing to participate in the "in-service training sessions" and to "apply" the assessment processes learned at these sessions in their own classroom situations. A total of 88 teachers participated in all aspects of the pilot study....

FORMAL TRAINING SESSIONS: participants attended two 2–1/2 hour sessions to acquire the prerequisite tools. Evidence was collected to show that by the end of the final training session, 80% of the participants had acquired a minimal level of ability to apply these competencies.

PREREQUISITE TOOLS: Teachers learning how to identify or diagnose strengths and weaknesses, learning to write and use behavioral objectives, learning new teaching techniques and procedures, etc. Teachers learn these through workshops and in-service training, having acquired these skills, teachers had to go through the "appraisal" technique.

APPRAISAL TECHNIQUE: During the observation phase, observation teams composed of teacher colleagues and a resource person from UCLA or the District collected data regarding the execution of the previously planned lessons. The observation team recorded both the verbal behavior of pupils and teacher (e.g., teacher questions and pupil responses) and non-verbal behavior which could be objectively described....

What all this amounts to is "peer group" analysis. Group dynamics would be the term used in other circles. To be more blunt, others would call it sensitivity training in its purest form—role-playing, to say the least....

The teacher must cooperate and learn the new methods of teaching, writing behavioral objectives, playing psychologist.

THE NEW YORK TIMES CARRIED A LENGTHY FRONT PAGE ARTICLE ON APRIL 30, 1972 BY William K. Stevens entitled "The Social Studies: A Revolution Is on—New Approach Is Questioning, Skeptical—Students Examine Various Cultures." This article explained the early history of the twenty-six-year controversy which has raged across the United States between those desiring education for a global society versus those desiring education in American History and Western Civilization; i.e., the question of "social studies" versus traditional history, and "process" education versus fact-based education. Excerpts follow:

When C. Frederick Risinger started teaching American History at Lake Park High School near Chicago, he operated just about as teachers had for generations. He drilled students on names and dates. He talked a lot about kings and presidents. And he worked from a standard text whose patriotic theme held that the United States was "founded on the highest principles that men of good will and common sense have been able to put into practice."

That was ten years ago, but it might as well be 50. For the social studies curriculum at Lake Park has changed almost beyond recognition. The 32-year-old Mr. Risinger, now head of the department, has abandoned the traditional text and set his students to analyzing all revolutions, not just the American, and from all points of view, including the British one that George Washington was both a traitor and an inept general.

AN ARTICLE ENTITLED "PEOPLE CONTROL BLUEPRINT" BY CAROL DENTON WAS PUBLISHED in the May, 1972 issue (Vol. 3, No. 12) of *The National Educator* (Fullerton, CA). Recommendations made in the top secret paper discussed in this article echo those mentioned in the April 6, 1971 Michigan Governor's Advisory Council on Population paper. Excerpts follow:

A "Top Secret" paper from the Center for the Study of Democratic Institutions, now in the hands of *The National Educator,* reveals a plan for total control of the people of the United States through behavioral modification techniques of B.F. Skinner, the controversial behaviorist author of *Beyond Freedom and Dignity....*

According to the "Dialogue Discussion Paper," marked "Top Secret" across the bottom of the cover page, a conference was held at the Center on January 17 through 19, 1972, at which time a discussion on "The Social and Philosophical Implications of Behavior Modification" was held. The paper in question is the one prepared [by] four individuals for presentation at that conference entitled "Controlled Environment for Social Change." The authors are Vitali Rozynko, Kenneth Swift, Josephine Swift and Larney J. Boggs....

The second page of the paper carries the inscription, "To B.F. Skinner and James G. Holland.".... Page 3 of the paper states that the "Top Secret" document was prepared on December 31, 1971....

The authors of this tome are senior staff members of the Operant Behavior Modification Project located at Mendocino State Hospital in California and the project is partially supported by a grant from the National Institute on Alcohol Abuse....

On page 5 of this blueprint for totalitarianism, the authors state that "we are presently concerned with controlling upheavals and anarchic behavior associated with social change and discontent.".... The authors go on to say that they believe an "Orwellian world" is more likely under presently developing society than under the kind of rigorous controls of a society envisioned by Skinner....

On page 6, the authors deplore the growing demands for "law and order," stating that the population is now more apt to support governmental repression than previously, in response to "their own fears."...

They add that "with the rising population, depletion of natural resources, and the increase of pollution, repressive measures may have to be used to guarantee survival of our species. These measures may take the form of forced sterilization, greatly restricted uses of energy and limits on population movement and living location."...

Skinner, on the other hand, they allege—"advocates more sophisticated controls over the population, since punishment (by the government) for the most part works only temporarily and only while the punishing agent is present."...

On the other hand, the authors allege, operant conditioning (sensitivity training) and other behavioral techniques can be used to control the population through "positive reinforcement."

MARY THOMPSON, SECRETARY AND MEMBER OF THE SPEAKERS' BUREAU OF THE SANTA CLARA, California Republican Women's Federation, gave a very important speech regarding Planning, Programming, Budgeting Systems (PPBS) on June 11, 1972. Following are key excerpts:

When I was first asked to speak to you about PPBS (Planning, Programming, Budgeting Systems), I inquired whether it was to be addressed to PPBS as applied to education. I shall deal with it at the education level today, however you should remember that PPBS is a tool for implementing the very restructuring of government at all levels in every area of governmental institutions. What is involved is the use of government agencies to accomplish mass behavioral change in every area....

PPBS is a plan being pushed by Federal and State governments to completely change education....

The accountability involved in PPBS means accountability to the state's predetermined education goals....

One leader of education innovation (Shelly Umans—Management of Education) has called it "A systematic design for education revolution."...

In a systems management of the education process, the child himself is the product. Note: the child... his feelings, his values, his behavior, as well as his intellectual development....

PPBS is the culmination of the "people planners" dreams....

Then in 1965 the means for accomplishing the actual restructuring of education was provided in the *Elementary and Secondary Education Act* (ESEA). President Johnson has said that he considered the ESEA the most significant single piece of legislation of his administration. Recall that it was also the same year of 1965 when the presidential order was given to introduce PPBS throughout the entire federal government. 1965 was the year which unleashed the actual restructuring of governmental processes and formally included education as a legitimate Federal government function....

PPBS is the systems management tool made possible by technology of computer hardware to affect the planned change....

In order to make an explanation of PPBS intelligible, you must also know that education itself has been redefined. Simply put, it has become the objective of education to measure and diagnose the child in order to prescribe a program to develop his feelings and emotions, values and loyalties toward predetermined behavioral objectives.... Drawing it right down to basics, we are talking about conditioned responses in human terms. Pavlov experimented on dogs!...

Taking each element of PPBS will show how the process is accomplished. PLANNING—Planning phase (please note that the process involved with a systems approach is always described in terms of "phases") always includes the establishment of goals committees, citizens committees, needs assessment committees.... These are referred to as "community involvement." The committees are always either self appointed or chosen—never elected. They always include guidance from some trained "change agents" who may be administrators, curriculum personnel or local citizens. Questionnaires and surveys are used to gather data on how the community "feels" and to test community attitudes. The ingeniousness of the process is that everybody thinks he is having a voice in the direction of public schools. Not so... for Federal change agencies, specifically regional education centers established by ESEA, influence and essentially determine terminology used in the questionnaires and surveys. The change agents at the district level then function to "identify needs and problems for change" as they have been programmed to identify them at the training sessions sponsored by Federal offices such as our Center for Planning and Evaluation in Santa Clara County. That is why the goals are essentially the same in school districts across the country.

It also explains why three years ago every school district was confronted with the Family Life Education issue at the same time....

Unknowing citizens' committees are used by the process to generate acceptance of goals already determined. What they don't realize is that professional change agents are operating in the behaviorist's framework of thought and Mr. or Mrs. Citizen Parent is operating in his traditional education framework of thought. So, the local change agents are able to facilitate a group to a consensus in support of predetermined goals by using familiar, traditional terms which carry the new behaviorist meanings....

Another name for this process is Participatory Democracy, a term by the way, which was coined by Students for a Democratic Society in their *Port Huron Manifesto* to identify the process for citizen participation in destruction of their own political institutions....

Richard Farson of Western Behavioral Sciences Institute made a report to the Office of Education in Sacramento in 1967. He said it this way:

> The application of systems analysis is aided by several phenomena that would be of help in almost any situation of organizational change. First, it is relatively easier to make big changes than to make small ones—and systems changes are almost always big ones. Because they are big, it is difficult for people to mount resistance to them, for they go beyond the ordinary decision-making, policy-making activities of individual members of an organization. It is far easier to muster argument against a $100 expenditure for partitions than against a complete reorganization of the work flow....

Teachers, you have professional organizations to protect your professional interests. Use them to protect your personal privacy and professional integrity. Encourage organizations of teachers to take positions publicly in opposition to PPBS....

We believe the time has come to establish private schools to keep our children from falling victim to the behaviorists while there is still opportunity to do so. BE AWARE OF THE FACT THAT THE VOUCHER SYSTEM IS LURKING IN THE WINGS TO BRING THE PRIVATE SCHOOLS INTO THE NATIONAL CONTROL [emphasis in original].

THE LEDGER OF TALLAHASSEE FLORIDA ON JULY 27, 1972 IN AN ARTICLE ENTITLED "SCHOOLS to Try New Program" quoted Florida state education officials as saying that a new program being field-tested in Florida will tell teachers and parents not only why Johnny can't read, but why the school can't teach him and how much it's costing to try. Excerpts follow:

> "We're putting all the various components together now," said Associate Education Commissioner Cecil Golden. "What we're doing should soon become very visible." However, he estimates it will take seven to ten years before the program is completely operational....
>
> Golden says it may sound like a lot of gibberish at this point, but "when we bring it all together" it should produce a more flexible and relevant educational system....
>
> He said many people in the State Department of Education are working independently on various facets and aspects of the program and, like those assembling the atom bomb, "very few of them understand exactly what they are building, and won't until we put all the parts together."

[Ed. Note: This article refers to PPBS/MBO—the early years. *The Atlanta Constitution* published an article entitled "Georgia Schools OK Tracking System" in its July 1, 1998 issue which describes later PPBS implementation and which is included in this book's entry of the same date.]

THE DON BELL REPORT OF SEPTEMBER 8, 1972 REPORTED ON A WHITE HOUSE CONFER-ence on the Industrial World held February 7 of that year. The conference title was "A Look at Business in 1990." Excerpts follow:

As one of the participants in that conference, Roy Ash, President of Litton Industries and Chairman of the President's Advisory Council on Executive Organization, later appeared before the Los Angeles Chamber of Commerce to tell West Coast businessmen what was decided at the White House Conference. The billing for this latter event is impressive reading:

The Los Angeles Chamber of Commerce in cooperation with the U.S. Department of Commerce and the White House Staff, is presenting The White House Conference, The World Ahead: A Look at Business in 1990, Thursday, May 18, 1972. Los Angeles Hilton. 3:00–6:30 p.m.

Following is part of what Roy Ash told his Los Angeles audience:

The answer is that increasing economic and business interdependence among nations is the keynote of the next two decades of world business—decades that will see major steps toward a single world economy....
Some aspects of individual sovereignty will be given over to international authority....
As importantly, international agreements between the socialist and the private property economies add a different dimension to the problems for which solutions need to be found over the years ahead. But as Jean Frere, Managing Partner of Banque Lambert, Brussels, forecasts, the socialist countries will take major steps toward joining the world economy by 1990. He goes so far as to see them becoming members of the International Monetary Fund, the *sine qua non* for effective participation in multilateral commerce. Then also, by 1990 an imaginative variety of contractual arrangements will have been devised and put into operation by which the socialist countries and the private capital countries will be doing considerable business together, neither being required to abandon its base idea....
These powerful factors of production—that is, capital, technology and management—will be fully mobile, neither contained nor containable within national borders....
As a framework for their [multinational corporations] development and application will be the establishment of more effective supranational institutions to deal with intergovernmental matters and matters between governments and world industry. A key intergovernmental institution that needs to work well in a world economy is the International Monetary Fund. The IMF will become, in Robert Roosa's [Brown Bros. Harriman & Co.] words, the most advanced embodiment of the aspirations that so many have for a world society, a world economy. The IMF, he forecasts for 1990, is going to be the source of all of the primary reserves of all the banking systems of the world....
For, in the final analysis, we are commanded by the fact that the economies of the major countries of the world will be interlocked. And since major economic matters in all countries are also important political matters in and between countries, the inevitable consequence of these propositions is that the broader and total destinies—economic, political, and social—of all the world's nations are closely interlocked. We are clearly at that point where economic issues and their related effects can be considered only in terms of a total world destiny, not just separate national destinies, and certainly not just a separate go-it-alone destiny for the United States.

"THE FIELD OF EDUCATIONAL TECHNOLOGY: A STATEMENT OF DEFINITION" BY DONALD P. Ely, editor and chairman of the Definition and Terminology Committee of the Association for Educational Computing and Technology (AECT, a spin-off of the National Education Association), was circulated in October, 1972. In this paper leading specialists in the field of educational technology warn of the potential dangers of computers and the need for ethics in programming. One of the participants in the production of this position paper said: "If it is decided the work will bring about negative ends, the concerned professional refuses to perform it." (See Appendix VIII for fuller excerpts.)

DR. CHESTER M. PIERCE, M.D. OF HARVARD UNIVERSITY WROTE AN ARTICLE ENTITLED "Becoming Planetary Citizens: A Quest for Meaning" which appeared in the November 1972 issue of *Childhood Education*. Excerpts follow which include alarming recommendations for "education":

Creative Altruism
In the past forty years social science experimentation has shown that by age five children already have a lot of political attitudes. Regardless of economic or social background, almost every kindergartner has a tenacious loyalty to his country and its leader. This phenomenon is understandable in the psychological terms of loyalty to a strong father-figure and of the need for security. But a child can enter kindergarten with the same kind of loyalty to the earth as to his homeland....

Systems Analysis
Children can be taught to integrate knowledge of systems in ever-widening circles. I don't know how to tell you to do it, but as professionals you will be challenged to find ways. Just because no one yet knows how doesn't mean it can't be done....

New Views of Parenting
Another essential curricular decision you will have to make is what to teach a young child about his future role as a man or a woman. A lot will depend on what you know and what your philosophy is about parenting.... Already we are hearing about experiments that are challenging our traditional views of monogamous marriage patterns....

Learning to Relinquish
Finally—perhaps most difficult of all—you will have to teach children how to unlearn, how to re-learn and how to give up things....

Public Problem Number One
If we truly accept that today's child must grow [up] to be a cosmopolite and "planetary citizen," we face major problems. How do you get a child to see that the whole world is his province when every day on television he sees people who can't live next door to their neighbors, who argue about things like busing?... Before the horizon I think the major problem to be solved in America if we are to enable people to grow as super-generalists and "planetary citizens" is the elimination of racism. Paradoxically, both the two chief deterrents and the two chief facilitators to this goal are the public school system and the mass media.... Early childhood specialists have a staggering responsibility but an unrivaled importance in producing "planetary citizens" whose geographic and intellectual provinces are as limitless as their all-embracing humanity.

BRUCE JOYCE AND MARSHA WEIL OF COLUMBIA TEACHERS' COLLEGE WROTE *MODELS OF Teaching* (Prentice Hall, Inc.: Englewood Cliffs, New Jersey, 1972). The book was the product of research funded by the U.S. Office of Education's Bureau of Research under a contract with Teachers' College, Columbia University, in 1968. *Models of Teaching*'s importance lay not only in the fact that the book itself would be used extensively for in-service teacher training in behavior modification, but that the book would serve as the foundation from which Joyce would develop his "Models of Teacher Repertoire Training," which has been used extensively (since the 1970s to the present) in order to change the teacher from a transmitter of knowledge (content) to a facilitator of learning (behavior modifier). Several excerpts from *Models of Teaching* follow:

> Principles of teaching are not conceived as static tenets but as dynamically interactive with social and cognitive purpose, with the learning theory underlying procedures, with available support technology, and with the personal and intellectual characteristics of learning groups. What is emphasized is the wide range of options the teacher may adopt and adapt to his unique situation.

In the preface, which has a subtitle, "We Teach by Creating Environments for Children," Joyce and Weil explain:

> In this book we describe models which represent four different "families" of approaches to teaching. Some of the models focus on the individual and the development of his unique personality. Some focus on the human group and represent ways of teaching which emphasize group energy, interpersonal skills, and social commitment. Others represent ways of teaching concepts, modes of inquiry from the disciplines, and methods for increasing intellectual capacity. Still others apply psychological models of operant conditioning to the teaching-learning process. For the teacher we provide some advice on how to learn the various models based on our experiences in the Preservice Teacher Education Program at Teachers College, Columbia University. For curriculum and materials designers we include chapters on systematic planning using a variety of models of teaching. For both, we present a system for deciding what approaches to teaching are appropriate for what ends and how models can be selected to match the learning styles of children. (pp. *xiii–xiv*)

Excerpts from the table of contents of *Models of Teaching* include:

> (2) Group Investigation—Democratic Process as a Source. The school is considered as a model of an ideal society. This chapter explores a variety of democratic teaching designed by Herbert Thelen to bring about a new type of social relationship among men....

> (5) The Laboratory Method—The T-Group Model. The National Training Laboratory has developed approaches to train people to cope with change through more effective social relationships. This model is the father of the encounter-group strategies.

> (6) Concept Attainment—A Model Developed from a Study of Thinking. This model was developed by the authors from a study of work by Jerome S. Bruner and his associates. [Bruner will be encountered in a later entry as a developer, along with B.F. Skinner, of the humanistic social studies curriculum, *Man: A Course of Study*, ed.]

> (7) An Inductive Model—A Model Drawn from Conceptions of Mental Processes and General

Theory-Building. The late Hilda Taba developed a series of models to improve the inductive thinking ability of children and adults. Her strategies are presented in this chapter.... [In 1957 a California State Senate investigative committee exposed the work of Hilda Taba as harmful to children, ed.]

(12) Non-Directive Teaching—Rogerian Counseling as a Source. From his studies of counseling and therapy, Carl Rogers has developed a flexible model of teaching emphasizing an environment which encourages students to create their own environments for learning.

(13) Classroom Meeting Model—A Model Drawn from a Stance toward Mental Health. Another therapist, [William] Glasser, has also developed a stance toward teaching—one which emphasized methods easily applicable to the classroom situation.... [In 1971 the Citizens Committee of California, Inc., presented "A Bill of Particulars" for the abolition of Dr. William Glasser's theory from the Orange County Unified School District which stated in part: "Dr. Glasser has developed a method of education which negates a desire to achieve and compete; destroys respect for authority; expounds a 'situational ethics' philosophy; and develops group thinking." William Glasser's philosophy is a component of Outcome-Based Education, ed.]

(15) Awareness Training—A Model to Increase Human Awareness. Gestalt therapists and other humanistic psychologists have focused on strategies for increasing the awareness and sense of possibilities of individuals. A number of models for sensitivity training have been developed by William Schutz.

(16) Operant Conditioning—The pioneering work of B.F. Skinner has been followed by a mass of approaches to teaching and training based on the shaping of learning tasks and use of reinforcement schedules. Several such models are explored here.

(17) A Model for Matching Environments to People—The psychologist David Hunt has generated a "model of models"—an approach to teaching which suggests how we can match teaching styles to learning styles so as to increase growth toward personal flexibility.

(18) The Models Way of Thinking—An Operational Language. The chapter explores the philosophical and practical implications of a stance toward education and includes a spectrum of models which have different uses for different students.

One finds the following information in chapter 16 under the title "Operant Conditioning":

The person most responsible for applying behavioral principles to education is B.F. Skinner, whose Theory of Operant Conditioning provided the basis for programmed instruction.

The Theory of Operant Conditioning represents the process by which human behavior becomes shaped into certain patterns by external forces. The theory assumes that any process or activity has observable manifestations and can be behaviorally defined, that is, defined in terms of observable behavior. Either or both of the theory's two major operations, reinforcement and stimulus-control, are emphasized in the educational applications of operant conditioning theory.

Conditioning refers to the process of increasing the probability of occurrence of existing or new behavior in an individual by means of reinforcement. In operant conditioning the response (behavior) operates upon the environment to generate consequences.

The consequences are contingent upon the emission of a response, and they are reinforcing. For example, the response "Pass the butter" operates upon the environment, another person, to obtain the butter. The response is reinforced by the receipt of the butter. In other words, the probability that a future desire for butter will elicit the same response is increased by its initial success.... The stimulus and reinforcement are independent variables upon which the response is dependent. As Skinner phrases it "the stimulus acting prior to the emission of the response, sets the occasion upon which the response is likely to be reinforced." (1) A stimulus is "any condition, event or change in the environment of an individual which produces a change in behavior." (2) It may be verbal (oral, written) or physical. A response may be defined as a unit of behavior.... According to Skinner, reinforcement must immediately follow a response if it is to be effective. Delayed reinforcement is much less effective in modifying behavior. (pp. 271–273)

An official overview of the "Models of Teacher Repertoire Training" program, made available to the author while working in the U.S. Department of Education, states under "Brief Description of Intervention" the following:

The objective of the intervention is to prepare teachers who can choose from a number of available alternatives the most appropriate strategy to be used with a particular group of students in a particular situation at a particular time. "Most appropriate" refers to the effectiveness of the strategy selected vs. the alternatives in terms of the probability that the students will learn what the teacher has predicted for them. The feasibility of achieving this objective in a clinical, or controlled situation has been long established. This intervention establishes that feasibility in the real world of the elementary and secondary school settings and offers a reliable, cost effective plan to do so.... The models which have been selected for this system are ones for which there is empirical evidence and/or theoretical grounding which supports the probability that students will learn what is predicted from them. Teachers learn to select the models and match them to the objectives they seek.... The families include: (1) Behavior Modification and Cybernetic Models which have evolved from attempts to develop efficient systems for sequencing learning tasks and shaping behavior by manipulating reinforcement.... Clinical analysis guides are useful to provide feedback about performance and to support on-site coaching. In addition to print material there are more than thirty hours of video tapes to support the training system.... The principal criterion of effectiveness rests upon existing empirical evidence that pre-specified changes in teaching behavior will produce predictable changes in pupil performance.

This information suggests that Skinner—and, evidently, Joyce and Weil—believe that man is truly only a response organism with no intrinsic soul or intellect, definitely a product of evolution. During a U.S. Department of Education Joint Dissemination Review Panel meeting at which Bruce Joyce and Jim Stefansen submitted application for funding, some of the participants made the following statements:

JOYCE: "It has been difficult in the past to bring about curriculum change, behavior change. In California we are establishing a network of 100 school districts. New strategies for teaching and exporting programs."

COULSON: "Couldn't agree more that what you are doing needs to be done. Maybe we are not ready yet to talk about selective use of repertoire. You must gather data supporting selective use of methods."

STEFANSEN: "Primary claim is we do know how to train teachers to make ultimate choices so that when those behaviors take place students are affected. Question is, can you train teachers to accept strategies each of which we know are the better of two or more choices?"

JACKSON: "No question in my mind that Joyce is onto something of great importance. Problem here has to do with claims of effectiveness rather than evidence of effectiveness. Relationship between teacher behavior and student achievement."

(UNKNOWN PANEL MEMBER) "There are thousands of investigations to support Skinner strategies."

The following excerpt from the "Models of Teacher Repertoire Training"—which includes most of the highly controversial behavior modification methods in existence—is taken from *Models of Teaching* by Joyce and was furnished to this writer by the Maine Facilitator Center in Auburn, Maine in 1985.[4]

(1) Information Processing—how do students acquire and act on information?
Concept Attainment—Jerome Bruner, Goodnow, Austin
Inductive Thinking—Hilda Taba
Direct Instruction—Benjamin Bloom, Madeline Hunter, James Block and Ethna Reid [How interesting that Joyce identifies the four most influential developers and promoters of Skinnerian "Mastery Learning/Teaching" with "Direct Instruction," which is the method attributed to Siegfried Engelmann and called for in the *Reading Excellence Act of 1998*, ed.]

(2) Personal Family—How does each person develop his/her unique possibilities?
Nondirective Teaching—Carl Rogers
Synectics—Thomas Gordon
Classroom Meetings—William Glasser

(3) Social Models—How does the individual relate to society or other people?
Jurisprudential Inquiry—Oliver and Shaver
Role Playing—Shaftel, Chesler and Fox

(4) Behavioral Models—How is visible behavior changed?
Training Model
Stress Reduction—Decker
Assertiveness Training—Wolpe, Lazarus

[Ed. Note: The writer has given extensive coverage to *Models of Teaching* since these teacher behavior modification training programs have been in effect for thirty years and are probably the most inclusive. It includes many, if not all of the controversial methods about which parents complain, if they are lucky enough to find out they are being used. Most parents are unaware of these manipulative methods intended to change their children's behavior. Considering the prevalence of behavior modification in the schools it is a wonder our schools and our children are not in worse shape than they are. There has obviously been immense teacher and student resistance to this type of manipulation.]

PRESIDENT RICHARD NIXON CREATED THE NATIONAL INSTITUTE OF EDUCATION (NIE) IN 1972. Serving as a presidential assistant at that time, Chester Finn (who would later be appointed assistant secretary of education, Office of Educational Research and Improvement under Secretary William Bennett in the Reagan administration) was one of the principal authors of Nixon's proposal for NIE. The December 8, 1982 issue of *Education Week* contained an interesting article on the history and purpose of NIE entitled "Success Eludes 10-Year-Old Agency." An excerpt which pertains to the redefinition of education from academic/content-based to scientific, outcome-/performance-based follows:

> "The purpose of a National Institute of Education," said Daniel P. Moynihan who was the agency's principal advocate in the Nixon Administration, "is to develop the art and science of education to the point that equality of educational opportunity results in a satisfactory equivalence of educational achievement."

For those who have difficulty understanding Daniel Moynihan's education jargon, "develop the art and science of education to the point that equality of educational opportunity results in a satisfactory equivalence of educational achievement" means that education from that time on would be considered a "science." In other words, with education becoming a "science," behavioral psychology (Pavlov/Skinner) would be used in the classrooms of America in order to equalize results which would be predictable and could be scientifically measured. The teacher and student would be judged not on what they know, but on how they perform— like rats and pigeons—facilitating the "redistribution of brains." Professor James Block, a leader in Skinnerian/mastery learning circles, discussed this redistribution of brains in an article published in *Educational Leadership* (November 1979) entitled "Mastery Learning: The Current State of the Craft." Block explained that:

> One of the striking personal features of mastery learning, for example, is the degree to which it encourages cooperative individualism in student learning as opposed to selfish competition. Just how much room is there left in the world for individualists who are more concerned with their own performance than the performance of others? One of the striking societal features of mastery learning is the degree to which it presses for a society based on the excellence of all participants rather than one based on the excellence of a few. Can any society afford universal excellence, or must all societies make most people incompetent so that a few can be competent?

Returning to the *Education Week* article referenced above, the story of NIE continued:

> Among the serious, continuing obstacles to the Institute's attainment of its goals, those interviewed for this article cited the following three: Understanding, Funding, and Leadership.... Under "Understanding" one reads: "Because educational research is a relatively young area of social science, it does not enjoy wide respect among scholars, and its relationship to teaching and learning is poorly understood by many of those who work in the schools."
>
> The first director chosen by the current [Reagan] Administration to head the institute, Edward A. Curran, articulated the conservatives' position in a memorandum to the President last May that called for dismantling the institute. "NIE is based on the premise that education is a science whose progress depends on systematic 'research and development.' As a professional educator, I know that this premise is false," wrote Mr. Curran, who was dismissed from the agency shortly thereafter.

[Ed. Note: Ed Curran was the first "shoe to drop"; he would be followed by some of the nation's finest academic teachers who also held Curran's view that education is *not* a science.

Of interest to this writer is the extensive influence NIE's research has on local classroom practice considering its rather paltry budget. The reason for this lies in the fact that 90% of all education research is federally funded, thus guaranteeing that NIE controls 90% of the national research product—teaching and learning. When the National Institute of Education was finally abolished none of its functions were eliminated since it was subsumed by the Office of Educational Research and Improvement.

"Equivalence of educational achievement," described by Patrick Moynihan, equals Performance-Based Education (PBE) and Outcome-Based Education (OBE), which in turn equal a deliberate dumbing down of American teachers and youth—necessary in order to implement the performance-based workforce training agenda planned since the early nineteen hundreds.

Good academic- and content-oriented teachers understand that education is not social science. In 1999 efforts are being made to encourage these good teachers to get out of the way so that teachers trained in performance-based Skinnerian teaching and Total Quality Management can be hired to replace them.]

1973

Schooling in the United States by John Goodlad, M. Frances Klein, and Jerrold M. Novotney (Charles F. Kettering Foundation Program: McGraw-Hill Co., New York, 1973) was published. Excerpts follow:

CONDITIONING OR BEHAVIOR MODIFICATION:

Several experimental preschool programs make extensive use of behaviorist theory (now called "operant conditioning" or "behavior modification") as a means of instruction in both the cognitive and socioemotional realms. [Professor Lawrence] Kohlberg notes:

> In general, such a program implies a play for shaping the child's behavior by successive approximation from responses. At every step, immediate feedback or reward is desirable and immediate repetition and elaboration of the correct response is used. A careful detailed programming of learning is required to make sure that (a) each response builds on the preceding, (b) incorrect responses are not made since once made they persist and interfere with correct responses, and (c) feedback and reward are immediate.

The Liverpool Laboratory School at the Research and Development Center in Early Childhood Education at Syracuse University is a program based directly on reinforcement theory.... The school is to determine whether children can learn cognitive skills during the preschool years and to identify techniques which will be successful in bringing about such learning. The program is built around a highly detailed schedule of reinforcement. Skills to be taught are broken down into specific components, each of which is immediately reinforced when it appears correctly. Teachers reinforce in four steps: in the first, raisins or candies are awarded for each correct response; in the second, the candies are replaced by tokens which can be traded for a small prize; the third involves distributing tokens which can be exchanged for more valuable tokens. Two or more of the latter may be traded for a prize. In the fourth step, four valuable tokens are required to receive a prize....

Bereiter and Engelmann [Direct Instruction/DISTAR/Reading Mastery (SRA)] also use operant conditioning in their program. Their reinforcement program contains both verbal and tangible rewards. Weber describes a rapid-fire sequence in language training in which the teacher verbally reinforces each response of the students:

> Teacher: What is the same as beautiful?
> Children: Pretty.
> Teacher: Good. You are so good. If someone is beautiful they are pretty. What is the opposite of pretty?
> Children: Ugly.
> Teacher: I'll have to shake everyone's hand....

She also speaks of an arithmetic lesson in which the children were given a cracker for each correct response....

Teaching and managing behavior by means of operant conditioning does not appeal to all and raises several moral issues. In the first place, it postulates an image of the learner as passive and receptive and leaves little room for individuality and creative thinking. According to William E. Martin in *Rediscovering the Mind of the Child*:

> A science of behavior emphasizes the importance of environmental manipulation and scheduling and thus the mechanization and routinization of experience. Similarly, it stresses performance in the individual. Doing something, doing it efficiently, doing it automatically—these are the goals. It is the mechanization of man as well as the mechanization of the environment. The result is the triumph of technology: a push button world with well-trained button-pushers. (pp. 40–43)

[Ed. Note: Surely, if American parents understood this dehumanizing method being implemented in the nation's schools under whatever label—OBE, ML, DI in conjunction with computers—they would see the many dangers to their children. One of those dangers being that after twelve years of rewards for correct answers, will their children ever have the courage or be motivated to do anything on their own—to take a stand when what is left of their "principles" is challenged? If this method is implemented in *all schools of the nation*, and I mean ALL—public, private, religious and home school (in many cases due to the use of computers or "Skinner's box") as is happening right now—our nation will become a nation of robotic drones responding to whomever wishes to control them for whatever purpose.]

RONALD G. HAVELOCK'S *THE CHANGE AGENT'S GUIDE TO INNOVATION IN EDUCATION* WAS published (Educational Technology Publishing: Englewood Cliffs, New Jersey, 1973). This *Guide*, which contains authentic case studies on how to sneak in controversial curricula and teaching strategies, or get them adopted by naïve school boards, is the educator's bible for bringing about change in our children's values. Havelock's *Guide* was funded by the U.S. Office of Education and the Department of Health, Education and Welfare, and has continued to receive funding well into the 1980s. It has been republished in a second edition in 1995 by the same publishers.

[Ed. Note: Why is it that the change agents' plans and their tools to "transform" our educational system *never* change, while parents and teachers are told, repeatedly, that they must be ready and willing *to change*?]

FOUNDATIONS OF BEHAVIORAL RESEARCH, SECOND EDITION BY FRED N. KERLINGER OF New York University (Holt, Rinehart and Winston, Inc.: New York, 1973) was published. Describing the purpose of writing this textbook, Dr. Kerlinger wrote in his preface:

> The writing of this book has been strongly influenced by the book's major purpose: to help students understand the fundamental nature of the scientific approach to problem solution.... All else is subordinate to this. Thus the book, as its name indicates, strongly emphasizes the *fundamentals or foundations* of behavioral research [emphasis in original].
>
> To accomplish the major purpose indicated above, the book... is a treatise on scientific research; it is limited to what is generally accepted as the scientific approach.

Kerlinger's treatise on scientific research, from which the writer quotes, would have been strengthened considerably had he included the following description of Wilhelm Wundt's theory:[5]

> A thing made sense and was worth pursuing if it could be measured, quantified, and scientifically demonstrated. Seeing there was no way to do this with the human soul, he proposed that psychology concern itself solely with experience.

Hence, behavioral psychology and scientific research were born. With such a heavy emphasis on quantifiable, measurable, and scientifically demonstrable performance as a base for psychological research, the writer felt it important to use an instructive text which would help the reader understand the complexities of what is known as "the scientific method," since it is being so widely proclaimed as the be-all and end-all of educational curriculum development and methodology today. Fred Kerlinger states in his *Foundations of Behavioral Research* textbook that:

> Scientific research is a systematic, controlled, empirical and critical investigation of hypothetical propositions about... the presumed relations among natural phenomena.... If such and such occurs, then so-and-so-results....
>
> The scientist... systematically builds his theoretical structures, tests them for internal consistency, and subjects aspects of them to empirical test. Second, the scientist systematically and empirically tests his theories and hypotheses.

These statements lead one to believe that the true scientific method so often employed by scientists dealing with experimental material which can be replicated and tested is being employed by behavioral psychologists. However, the following quotes from Kerlinger's textbook will quickly dispel this misconception:

> Many people think that science is basically a fact-gathering activity. It is not. As M. Cohen says:
>
> > There is... no genuine progress in scientific insight through the Baconian method of accumulating empirical facts without hypotheses or anticipation of nature. Without some guiding idea we do not know what facts to gather... we cannot determine what is relevant and what is irrelevant. [From *A Preface to Logic* (Meridian: New York, 1956) by M. Cohen.]
>
> The scientifically uninformed person often has the idea that the scientist is a highly objective individual who gathers data without preconceived ideas. Poincare pointed out how wrong this idea is. He said:

It is often said that experiments should be made without preconceived ideas. That is impossible. Not only would it make every experiment fruitless, but even if we wished to do so, it could not be done. [From *Science and Hypothesis* (Dover: New York, N.Y., 1952) by H. Poincare.] (p. 16)

In other words, if we as parents and citizens believe that the same "scientific, research-based" standards applied to research in education and psychology are those applied to medicine, geology, or engineering, we are sadly mistaken. If we believe that objective criteria are employed when evaluating educational curriculum or behavioral analysis, we are likewise mistaken. Therefore, when presented with proposals in academic curricula that purport to be founded in "scientific, research-based" evaluation, we should take them with a grain of salt! For instance, Kerlinger, as a psychological researcher, wrote about "Science and Common Sense":

Common sense may often be a bad master for the evaluation of knowledge.... [One] view would say that science is a systematic and controlled extension of common sense, since common sense, as [J.] Conant points out, is a series of concepts and conceptual schemes satisfactory for the practical uses of mankind. But these concepts and conceptual schemes may be seriously misleading in modern science—and particularly in psychology and education. It was self-evident to many educators of the last century... to use punishment as a basic tool of pedagogy. Now we have evidence that this older common sense view of motivation may be quite erroneous. Reward seems more effective than punishment in aiding learning.

The reader by now may recognize the fact that B.F. Skinner's behavioral theories have conclusively influenced psychological and educational theory, based on the last statement above—the fact that "rewards are more effective than punishment in aiding learning." This is vintage Skinner, who also did not believe in punishment. Skinner thought that a person could be controlled by the environment—psychologically facilitative "school climate"—to do what is best for him. Bad behavior should be ignored, according to Skinner. Good behavior should be rewarded. A very good method of dog training!

Kerlinger went on to point out that:

A final difference between common sense and science lies in explanations of observed phenomena. The scientist, when attempting to explain the relations among observed phenomena, carefully rules out what have been called "metaphysical explanations." A metaphysical explanation is simply a proposition that cannot be tested. To say, for example, that people are poor and starving because God wills it, that studying hard subjects improves the child's moral character, or that it is wrong to be authoritarian in the classroom is to talk metaphysics.

The New World Dictionary (Merriam Webster: New York, 1979) defines "metaphysics" as follows: "the branch of philosophy that deals with first principles and seeks to explain the nature of knowledge, nature of being or reality; metaphysical; beyond the physical or material; incorporeal, supernatural, transcendental." Most parents and even teachers are very well acquainted with what behavioral scientists call "metaphysics" in this context. The fact that behavioral researchers discount this important aspect of man's personality and being is consistent with what this writer perceived when gathering the research for this book—particularly in the chapter entitled "The Fomentation of the Forties and Fifties" when Kinsey, Bloom and Skinner brought together the powerful tools for the deconstruction of the God-fearing, educated man of the early twentieth century. There is no place for this brand of "science" when dealing with educational theories and methods which will influence forever the character and concept of man.

The bottom line for understanding this conflict between science and psychology is that the application of statistical methods to human behavior in the name of science is misdirected and inappropriate. When we measure natural phenomena, we get results that will vary depending upon the environmental factors affecting the thing being measured. For example, we can measure the speed at which a rock falls from a certain height. Although the rock's speed may be affected by external factors, such as air resistance, there is nothing the rock can do, no decision it can make that will change the speed at which it falls. However, when we attempt to measure a person's attitudes or opinions, that person can change his or her attitude, opinion, or belief at any time—often because of a conscious, deliberate decision to do so, as an act of will. Such deliberate assertion of a person's will is extremely difficult, if not impossible to measure.

The social "sciences" and psychology have long yearned for the respectability of scientific disciplines, and have touted themselves as science for many decades. However, both fields emerged from the same humanistic cesspools of the last century. In discussing the shift to modern "naturalistic" or "materialistic" science, the late Dr. Francis Schaeffer warned:

> When psychology and social science were made a part of a closed cause-and-effect system, along with physics, astronomy and chemistry, it was not only God who died. Man died. And within this framework love died. There is no place for love in a totally closed cause-and-effect system. There is no place for morals in a totally closed cause-and-effect system. There is no place for the freedom of people in a totally closed cause-and-effect system. Man becomes a zero. People and all they do become only a part of the machinery.[6]

1974

THE NATIONAL DIFFUSION NETWORK (NDN), THE TRANSMISSION BELT FOR FEDERALLY FUNDED and developed innovative and/or behavior modification programs, was established in 1974. This network, which bears much of the blame for the dilution of absolute values of those children and parents exposed to NDN programs from the mid-seventies to the present, was created to facilitate the adoption by local schools of innovative programs which had been approved by the Joint Dissemination Review Panel (JDRP), a federal panel of educators.

Most, if not all, states received funding from the U.S. Department of Education to set up Facilitator Centers staffed by educators familiar with NDN programs. These individuals who had contacts in school districts throughout the individual states promoted the programs and arranged for the "developers," or other staff associated with the program, to visit the state to conduct in-service training at schools which had adopted the programs.

Often these programs were described in benign NDN program terms and flew under the banner of "basic skills." Local school boards accepted them since they were subsidized and less expensive to implement than programs developed by private sector textbook companies. The NDN's penetration of the national educational landscape in the early 1980s is exemplified by the fact that Texas alone had approximately seventeen NDN offices which facilitated the adoption of programs. The State of Maine received some sort of "gold medal" for being the number one state in its number of program adoptions.

There is no question that the National Diffusion Network programs have caused more controversy among parents than any other programs developed with federal funds. The regional hearings held by the U.S. Department of Education in 1984 to take testimony from citizens regarding the need for regulations to enforce the *Protection of Pupil Rights Amendment* (PPRA) consisted of emotional and angry testimony from teachers and parents regarding the value-destroying programs in the NDN. The two most destructive programs developed prior to 1984 were *Curriculum for Meeting Modern Problems*, which contained *The New Model Me* for the high school level, and *Positive Attitude toward Learning*. Both of these curricula employed behavior modification techniques, values clarification, role playing and, specifically, such games as "The Survival Game"—sometimes known as "The Lifeboat Game"— where students were enlisted to decide who is worthy of survival in a shipwreck: the priest, the lawyer, the pregnant mother, angry teenager, etc.—pure humanistic curricula.[7]

[Ed. Note: Critiques of many of the most controversial NDN programs can be found in the testimonies given during the hearings for proposed regulations for the *Hatch Amendment* in 1984 contained in *Child Abuse in the Classroom* edited by Phyllis Schlafly (Pere Marquette Press: Alton, Illinois, 1984).[8] Mrs. Schlafly took it upon herself to publish these important testimonies due to the U.S. Department of Education's unwillingness to do so. As late as 1994 the NDN continued to list *The New Model Me* as an "exemplary program" in its *Educational Programs that Work*, the catalog of the National Diffusion Network.[9] Such blatant continuation of programs designed to destroy children's values, no matter which administration is in office, is shocking.]

A PERFORMANCE ACCOUNTABILITY SYSTEM FOR SCHOOL ADMINISTRATORS (PARKER PUBlishing Co., Inc.: West Nyack, N.Y., 1974) by T.H. Bell, Ph.D., was published. T.H. Bell later served as secretary of education during President Ronald Reagan's first term in office, 1981–1985. Excerpts from Bell's book follow:

USE OF TESTS IN NEEDS ASSESSMENT:

The economic, sociological, psychological and physical aspects of students must be taken into account as we look at their educational needs and accomplishments, and fortunately there are a number of attitude and inventory scales that can be used to assess these admittedly difficult to measure outcomes. (pp. 33–34)

Most of these efforts to manage education try to center in one place an information center that receives reports and makes available to all members of the management team various types of information useful to managers. (p. 45)

[Ed. Note: There is no question in this writer's mind that this one man bears much of the responsibility for the deliberate dumbing down of our schools. He set the stage for outcome-based education through his early support for systems management—Management by Objectives and Planning, Programming, Budgeting Systems. These systems later evolved into full-blown Total Quality Management for education, having gone through the initial stage of Professor Benjamin Bloom's Mastery Learning and ending up in 1984 as William Spady's Transformational OBE. Outcome-Based or results/performance/competency-based education requires mastery learning, direct instruction, individualized instruction, systems management and computer technology.

Bell's earlier activities in the 1970s as U.S. Commissioner of Education, including his role in promoting and supporting dumbed-down life role competencies for K–12 (see 1975 Adult Performance Level Study and the 1983 Delker article) and his testimony before the U.S. Congress in favor of a U.S. Department of Education, should have kept his name off of any list of potential nominees presented to President Reagan. Concerns regarding this nomination expressed by Reagan supporters were proved well-founded when: Bell spearheaded the technology initiative in 1981 (see Project BEST, Better Education Skills Through Technology); funded in 1984 William Spady's infamous Far West Laboratory (Utah OBE) grant which promised to (and did!) put OBE "in all schools of the nation"; predicted that schools would be bookless by the year 2000; recommended that all students have computers; and fired Edward Curran, the director of the National Institute of Education, when Curran recommended to President Reagan that his office (the NIE) be abolished.

According to a former member of the Utah Education Association who was a close friend of Bell's in the 1970s, had the Senate Committee that confirmed T.H. Bell as secretary of education read Bell's book, *A Performance Accountability System for School Administrators*, it is unlikely he would have been confirmed. (See Appendix IX quotes from Bell's book.)]

"PARENTS FEAR 'BIG BROTHER' ASPECT OF NEW CONCEPT" BY MONICA LANZA WAS WRIT-ten for the Passaic, New Jersey *The Herald News* on March 20, 1974. Excerpts follow from the first of a two-part series:

> Questioning the purpose of modern educational *goals* by parents has brought to light the possibility that a new curriculum ultimately could force all school children to fit a preconceived mold or norm by computerized evaluation [emphasis in original]. And, students who don't could be branded misfits and sent to a school psychologist for therapy. The threat, they say, is in the form of a bill before the state legislature that would take effect July 1, if passed. This bill would provide for two new Educational Improvement Centers in New Jersey, bringing the total of such centers in the state to four. The centers are currently being used by the federal government to reach the grass-roots level through its *Elementary and Secondary Education Act*.... Under the stated aim of developing "critical thinking skills" in children, the centers, as agents for the Planning, Programming, Budgeting System (PPBS), have been charged with using behavior modification and sensitivity training to develop those skills....
>
> At the Cedar Knolls center in Morris County, Joseph T. Pascarelli, program developer, recently conducted a workshop which was attended by a number of teachers who reviewed one method of sensitivity training, known as the "Who Shall Survive" game.[9] Participants in the game are given the sexes, backgrounds and capabilities of 15 people in a bomb shelter that supports only seven people, and are asked to decide which seven are the best equipped to re-populate the earth. The answer that none should be put to death is not accepted. This type of training, according to opponents, changes the values of the students who may have been taught at home that murder is wrong under all circumstances.

From the second article in the series, "Teachers Taught to Be 'Agents of Social Change,'" the reader is informed that:

> Educational Improvement Centers (EICs) provide training to prepare teachers to become agents for social change....
>
> A publication entitled *Education: From the Acquisition of Knowledge to Programmed Conditioned Response* states: "Teachers who are seemingly impervious to change will be sought out and trained on an individual basis, and forces which block the adoption of new ideas will be identified and ways to overcome these forces will be explored."...
>
> Behavior modification was the theme of a learning center at a workshop at the Northwestern New Jersey EIC recently. A teacher rattled off the three domains of behavior modification as propounded by a Benjamin Bloom, who more than a dozen years ago, redefined the purpose of education as "behavior modification."....
>
> The multitude of programs available is mind-boggling. Programs filter down from entities like the Educational Resource Information Center [ERIC] and are presented to local school systems with a flourish. They are praised by gullible administrators and put into action by unwitting teachers....
>
> One of the reasons for their current success is that the language used in the presentation of new programs is almost unintelligible. There are teachers who will admit to not understanding the jargon, but not publicly—and those who do see underlying dangers say nothing for fear of losing their jobs....
>
> The father of the myriad federally financed programs is "Projects to Advance Creativity in Education" (PACE). The PACE programs are described in a 584–page publication entitled *Pacesetters in Innovation* which lists such "subjects" as psychotherapy, sensitivity training, behavior modification, and humanistic curriculum....
>
> According to the Department of Health, Education and Welfare (HEW) *Catalog of Assistance*, the PACE program reached seven million children during 1971 and 1972 at a cost of $250 million. The Office of Education has more than 100 such programs, and HEW funded 70,000 behavioral research programs—some among prison inmates which were soundly criticized and are being withdrawn from the prison system....
>
> Mr. Thomas Hamill of the EIC Northwest, said that funds for "specific kinds of research and development" are channeled to 16 national laboratories attached to colleges and universities, a dozen national laboratories studying "individually prescribed instruction," and a number of Educational Resource Information Centers, for delivery to the EIC's.

[Ed. Note: Whenever and wherever *individualized education* is mentioned in professional educational literature, parents should realize that Mastery Learning/OBE/DI is the required instructional method. Homegrown individualized instruction, non-programmed kitchen table type instruction, with a parent instructing his/her child using traditional textbooks and tests, is not the same thing as *institutionalized* individualized instruction with its programmed, computer-assisted instruction or programmed reading from a script, which often provides immediate reinforcement with tokens, candy—rewards. Also of interest is the fact that prison inmates are protected from subjection to behavior modification techniques and workers in government offices are protected from subjection to training programs which are violations of their religious liberties, but prohibition of the use of behavior modification techniques on normal, American school children is non-existent. (See 1988 Clarence Thomas, chairman of the Equal Employment Opportunity Commission and present U.S. Supreme Court Justice, ruling concerning employment protection.)]

IN 1974 *INDIVIDUAL RIGHTS AND THE FEDERAL ROLE IN BEHAVIOR MODIFICATION: REPORT of the Subcommittee on Constitutional Rights* from the Committee on the Judiciary, U.S. Senate, Washington, D.C. was prepared under the chairmanship of North Carolina's late Senator Sam Ervin, who, unfortunately, was unable to continue his work on this important issue due to his being called to serve as a member of the Senate Judiciary Committee investigating the Watergate break-in. Ervin stated in the preface to the report:

> [T]echnology has begun to develop new methods of behavior control capable of altering not just an individual's actions but his very personality and manner of thinking as well. Because it affects the ability of the individual to think for himself, the behavioral technology being developed in the United States today touches upon the most basic sources of individuality, and the very core of personal freedom. To my mind, the most serious threat posed by the technology of behavior modification is the power this technology gives one man to impose his views and values on another. In our democratic society, values such as political and religious preferences are expressly left to individual choice. If our society is to remain free, one man must not be empowered to change another man's personality and dictate the values, thoughts and feelings of another.

IN 1974 *A CURRICULUM FOR PERSONALIZED EDUCATION* BY ROBERT SCANLON, FORMER Pennsylvania Secretary of Education, was published by one of the U.S. Department of Education research laboratories, Research for Better Schools in Philadelphia, Pennsylvania. Predicting the future, Scanlon stated:

> The emphasis in schools in 1985 will be to free the individual from subject matter as bodies of knowledge and provide him or her with higher order skills.... One type is values clarification.

IN A SPEECH GIVEN TO AND RECORDED BY THE ASSOCIATION FOR SUPERVISION AND CURriculum Development in 1974,[10] Dr. Leon Lessinger, superintendent of schools in Beverly Hills, California and former associate commissioner of education in the U.S. Office of Education, called for the implementation of Skinnerian behavior modification and discussed environmental influence when he said:

> Would that we had such a system; a system of accountability. Do we have a hog cholera vaccine? Three ingredients of such a vaccine:
>
> 1. Target the experience in terms of outcomes;
> 2. Self-paced learning. We have the technology now. Modules. Small groups working on common learning targets. Free learner from having to be there always in front of teacher. If we know the target, we can do beautifully if we know the target.
> 3. Use of contingency rewards. May make you feel uncomfortable. Does me, but he who shirks this responsibility does a disservice to the children of the United States. Behavior Modification is here. Better for us to master and use wisely. Powerful ... powerful... powerful.

Carolina Inn exists right across from my school. In the restaurant, rug is red; in the bar, rug is orange. I know that because I happen to pass by!... Red in the restaurant—because you feel uncomfortable and it keeps you from dillydallying around dinner. Ah, but in the bar, it's [warm, comfortable] orange!

MAN, EDUCATION & SOCIETY IN THE YEAR 2000, WRITTEN BY GRANT VENN, DIRECTOR OF the Chief State School Officers Institute and professor of education at Georgia State University, was a report or summary of discussions which took place at the Fifth Annual Chief State School Officers Institute at Jackson Hole, Wyoming, July 25–August 2, 1974. The report of the Institute was sponsored by the U.S. Office of Education in cooperation with the Council of Chief State School Officers, funded by the Office of Education, U.S. Department of Health, Education and Welfare. There is a notation on the back cover which states: "The availability of this report is limited. A single copy may be obtained free on request to the U.S. Office of Education as long as the supply lasts." Dr. Venn's best known publications are *Man, Education and Work* (1963) and *Man, Education and Manpower* (1971). Excerpts from Dr. Venn's introduction to the Summary Report of the Institute follow:

Seven days of intensive study and discussion with the top leadership of the U.S. Office of Education and specialists invited to speak to the Chiefs reached an apparent consensus regarding issues that are facing Man, Education and Society: The Year 2000....

The seven topics chosen for study by the Executive Committee of the Council of Chief State School Officers, the U.S. Office of Education and the Institute Director... follow:

1. The Role of the Future in Education—Alvin Toffler
2. Education and Human Resource Development—Willard Wirtz
3. The International Situation: The Role of Education—Frederick Champion Ward
4. Economic Matters: Public Dollar Availability—Allan K.Campbell
5. The Shape of Democracy: The Citizen Role—Forbes Bottomly
6. The Public and Private Life of the Individual—Harold Shane
7. Energy, Natural Resources and Growth—Charles J. Ryan

Excerpts from the body of Dr. Venn's summary follow:

We have reached a point where society either educates everyone or supports them....

Technological change has, suddenly and dramatically, thrown up a challenge to our nation's political, economic, and education institutions. If it is to be solved, it is going to demand a massive response on the part of American education. Technology has, in effect, created a new relationship between man, his education and his society....

The home, the church, and the school cannot be effective maintainers since the future cannot be predicted....

The clearest overall approach to finding better ways seemed to be a new role for the state departments of education....

From the question of finances to the question of values that should be taught in the schools, the consensus was that leadership and priority changing by state departments was the most important step to be taken....

After all the questions had been asked and all the dialogue ended, it appeared that the most difficult matter would be one of instituting new approaches to education....

Toffler's belief that the schools have been a "maintaining" institution for a static predictable society was not agreed to by all, but there was agreement that education for the future had to end its reliance on the past as predictor of the future....

The traditional cluster of knowledge, skills, values, and concepts will not help our young face the future in their private life, the international situation, their citizen role, their work role, nor in the area of energy, national resources or growth....

...Individuals need more learning about social process with a greater emphasis on participation in group decision making. Again we come face to face with the fact that many problems of the future must be solved based on values and priorities set by groups. Many of these values will have to be enforced by group action and will need the involvement of many individuals in order that hard decisions can be implemented. Many of the future problems cannot be solved by individual decision or action. The heavy emphasis on individual achievement and competition may need to include learning about cooperation and group achievement....

As learning becomes more tied to the future, personal and societal change "values" come to the foreground. It is doubtful that we shall ever return to the concept of values in the same way we saw them in the past.... Perhaps there is a need for the clarification of new values needed to solve future problems. They may become clear as we begin a deliberate search for values we wish to teach and provide experiences for our young in using these values in solving real problems....

It would appear that our young have become isolated from the "real work" of society and from the real decision making of society. Decision making [values clarification] may become the subject of the learning process if there are greater opportunities for "action learning" and group learning by teachers and students....

The over emphasis on knowledge, information, and theories have caused our youth to be freed from the testing of their beliefs in a non-controlled environment—the real world....

Conclusions

In addition to the three R's, the basic skills would appear to include group participation, environmental relationships and planning for the future!... Organization, structure, role and purpose, methods, content, financing, relationships among school and society, leadership and time frames must all be evaluated and changed. The greatest danger seems to be that simple improvement rather than basic change might be attempted....

The following conclusions seem to be suggested as approaches which might bring about major change!... The states collectively should establish specific minimal competencies in each of the basic tool skill areas and each state should make them the first priority for funding, staffing and organizing....

Annual state reports should be devised to replace the normative achievement test in the future with competency achievement.... The states should convene a task force to study and report the ways that are being tried and ways that might be used to provide alternatives to earning the high school diploma....

Students achieving minimal credits ought to be encouraged to develop their unique aptitudes and to test these in the community, workforce, and the school systems.... There should be a policy devised in each of the states that ends the long held basic of "time in place" [Carnegie Unit] as the evaluation of learning for credit.

Regulations must be developed which encourage the use of the community, adults, students and other learning sites than the classroom and teachers.... Full-time attendance from grades one through twelve may have become a barrier to learning—what are the alternatives?... Educational credit should be available to students for activities related to their studies in work, volunteer action, community participation, school volunteer programs and other programs contributing to the betterment of the home, school, community and society.... The time traps of learning for the young, earning for the middle-aged and yearning for the retired must be changed to a concept of continuous learning [UNESCO's lifelong learning, ed.].

Greater use of adults and students from other countries and cultures should be emphasized.... It is obvious that the schools alone cannot educate our youth. State Departments should encourage, through policies and financing, the use of other societal agencies and resources to be part of the planned educational program of high school and older youth.... Since the future indicates a smaller share of the public dollar for education, states should develop regulations and policies which use the entire year and the entire society as educational resources....

The fifty states should organize a commission to establish the values that are significant in approaching problems that must be faced in the future.... Since change is so great and problem solving the necessity of the future, the state should establish a study which would define the essential skills, understandings and approaches that our young should learn in order to participate in the social decisions that must be made in the future....

Knowledge and information is not the only basis for solving problems; our schools need to help our youth gain experience in group decision making as a basis for future citizenship....

Each state ought to look at the problem of the role of the school in making the entry job a means rather than an end.... Would a placement function for the schools help motivate youth?... Every high school student ought to devote a portion of their time to the development of a career related to the future and sensible public and private life....

Most research in education has looked at parts and pieces rather than the total relationship of man, education and society. The CCSSO should establish a long-range planning and policy group to look at societal issues and the implications for education. At present, there is no such body looking at this problem. Can the education Chiefs afford to let others do all the directing of the future?

[Ed. Note: The reader cannot help but see that the above highly controversial recommendations made in 1974 have been implemented with hardly a hitch.]

PROFESSOR LAWRENCE KOHLBERG'S MORAL DEVELOPMENT APPROACH CURRICULUM, "ETHIcal Issues in Decision Making," was developed in the early 1970s and was used extensively in law education courses in public and private schools. In 1974 Kohlberg was still developing his classifications of "Stages of Moral Development" to include a Seventh Stage—that of "Faith." Kohlberg's program was listed in the National Diffusion Network's catalog *Programs that Work* as an exemplary program. Kohlberg's Moral Development Approach includes education in the following "stages of moral development":

Stage 1—"Avoid punishment" orientation: decisions are based on a blind obedience to an external power in an attempt to avoid punishment or seek reward.
Stage 2—"Self-Benefit" orientation: decisions are based on premise of doing something for others if they reciprocate.
Stage 3—"Acceptance by others" orientation: decisions are based on whether or not their behaviors perceived as pleasing to others.
Stage 4—"Maintain the social order" orientation: decisions are based on fixed rules

which are "necessary" to perpetuate the order of society as a whole.

Stage 5—"Contract fulfillment" orientation: decisions are based on the individual respecting impartial laws and agreeing to abide by them while society agrees to respect the rights of the individual.

Stage 6—"Ethical principle" orientation: decisions are based on "conscience" and respect for each person's individuality is paramount with the values believed to be valid for all humanity.

After Stage 6, the individual experiences despair. He or she has developed principles of justice, yet is faced with an unjust world. Moral philosophy cannot solve the problem.

Stage 7—"Faith" orientation: decisions are concerned with "what is the ultimate meaning of life?"

This "Faith" orientation stage does not conflict with the principles developed through the first six stages; rather, it integrates those stages and provides a perspective on life's ultimate meaning. In Stage Seven the individual advances from an essentially human to a cosmic point of view. With Stage Seven there is a modification to a wider view of life. Emphasis changes from the individual to the cosmos.

1975

SUPERINTENDENT RAY I. POWELL, PH.D., OF SOUTH ST. PAUL, MINNESOTA PUBLIC SCHOOLS spoke out regarding values clarification and sensitivity training in 1975, saying, "It's all brainwashing!" Excerpts follow from a memorandum to "All Administrators from Ray I. Powell" concerning Center Bulletin No. 39: 1974–1975, dated February 26, 1975:

1. Parents have the prime responsibility for the inculcation of those moral and spiritual values desired for their children in the areas of abortion and birth control. Indeed, this is an inherent right of parents and must not be denied....

Effective immediately, the teaching, advising, directing, suggesting, or counseling of students in these two (2) areas cannot be/shall not be the responsibility nor the task of the South St. Paul Public Schools.

Rather, the efforts of the public schools, henceforth, shall be directed towards expanding those complimentary learning experiences in other areas of the total curriculum that will enhance these two (2) parental values, i.e.:

- preservation of the family unit.
- feminine role of the wife, mother, and homemaker.
- masculine role of guide, protector, and provider.
- advocacy of home and family values.
- respect for family structure and authority.
- enhancement of womanhood and femininity.
- restoration of morality.

2. There are more and more concerns and questions being registered today regarding the questionable results and the true intent of SENSITIVITY TRAINING, as well as its germaneness

to the goals and objectives of public education, the training of educators, and the learning experiences of students.

Consider these two (2) definitions of SENSITIVITY TRAINING (sources furnished upon request):

Sensitivity training is defined as group meetings, large or small, to discuss publicly intimate and personal matters, and opinions, values or beliefs; and/or to act out emotions and feelings toward one another in the group, using the techniques of self-confession and mutual criticism.

It is also "coercive persuasion in the form of thought reform or brainwashing."

Is the prime concern in education today not to impart knowledge, but to change "attitudes," so that children can/will willingly accept a controlled society? Are the public schools being unwittingly re-shaped to accomplish this and without realizing it?

[Ed. Note: Dr. Powell then lists 54 terms which can all be included under Sensitivity Training, a few of which are: T-Group Training, Operant Conditioning, Management by Objectives, Sex Education, Self-Hypnosis, Role Playing, Values Clarification, Situation Ethics, Alternative Life Styles, etc. Had all our schools had superintendents with Dr. Powell's character and courage, most of the problems facing our children and families today would not exist.]

CONGRESSMAN JOHN CONLAN OF ARIZONA ISSUED A PRESS RELEASE REGARDING THE CONtroversial federally funded program for ten-year-old children called *Man: A Course of Study* (M:ACOS) (Education Development Center: Cambridge, Massachusetts, 1975). On April 9, 1975 Conlan said that the $7 million National Science Foundation-funded program was designed by a team of experimental psychologists under Jerome S. Bruner and B.F. Skinner's direction to mold children's social attitudes and beliefs along lines that set them apart and alienated them from the beliefs and moral values of their parents and local communities. As a matter of fact, fifty commercial publishers refused to publish the course because of its objectionable content. The following gory story of cannibalism is excerpted from M:ACOS (Vol. 1):

The wife knew that the spirits had said her husband should eat her, but she was so exhausted that it made no impression on her, she did not care. It was only when he began to feel her, when it occurred to him to stick his fingers in her side to feel if there was flesh on her, that she suddenly felt a terrible fear; so she, who had never been afraid of dying, now tried to escape. With her feeble strength she ran for her life, and then it was as if Tuneq saw her only as a quarry that was about to escape him; he ran after her and stabbed her to death. After that, he lived on her, and collected her bones in a heap over by the side of the platform for the purpose of fulfilling the taboo rule required of all who die. (p. 115)

OCTOBER 24, 1975 THE WORLD AFFAIRS COUNCIL OF PHILADELPHIA ISSUED "A DECLARAtion of Interdependence" written by well-known historian and liberal think tank Aspen Institute board member Henry Steele Commager. This alarming document, which called to mind President Kennedy's July 4, 1962 speech calling for a "Declaration of Interdependence," was written as a contribution to our nation's celebration of its 200th birthday, and signed by 125 members of the U.S. House and Senate. Excerpts follow:

WHEN IN THE COURSE OF HISTORY the threat of extinction confronts mankind, it is necessary for the people of The United States to declare their interdependence with the people of all nations and to embrace those principles and build those institutions which will enable mankind to survive and civilization to flourish....

Two centuries ago our forefathers brought forth a new nation; now we must join with others to bring forth a new world order....

WE AFFIRM that the economy of all nations is a seamless web, and that no one nation can any longer effectively maintain its processes of production and monetary systems without recognizing the necessity for collaborative regulation by international authorities.

[Ed. Note: In 1976 the National Education Association produced a social studies curriculum entitled *A Declaration of Interdependence: Education for a Global Community* which Congresswoman Marjorie Holt (R.-MD) described as "an atrocious betrayal of American independence." It wasn't until the 1980s and 1990s that the relationship between "interdependence" or "new world order" and America's education of children became prominent in outcomes in each state. Interdependence is also an undergirding concept in global education.

In 1976 a coterie of internationalists thought their plans would have smooth sailing, not the resistance they encountered at the grassroots level which set them back a good twenty years. What we are experiencing in 1999 (American soldiers being deployed world-wide as part of United Nations "peace-keeping" operations, and UN land confiscation through executive orders, etc.) was delayed by the activism of courageous Americans to whom we all owe an enormous debt of gratitude.]

U.S. COMMISSIONER OF EDUCATION T.H. BELL MADE THE FOLLOWING STATEMENT IN A U.S. Office of Education (HEW) press release on October 29, 1975, dealing with results of the University of Texas Adult Performance Level (APL) Study. The study, headed by Dr. Norvell Northcutt, was funded at approximately $1 million under Sec. 309 of the *Adult Education Act*. T.H. Bell's statement follows:

One out of five American adults lacks the skills and knowledge needed to function effectively in the basic day-to-day struggle to make a living and maintain a home and family, according to a four-year investigation of adult functional competency released today by HEW's Office of Education. Referring to the results of the Adult Performance Level (APL) study as "rather startling," U.S. Commissioner of Education Terrell H. Bell said that they call for some major rethinking of education on several levels. "To begin with," Dr. Bell added, "adult education has to be reshaped so that students receive the kind of information that will make modern life easier for them. I also think that State and local education agencies will want to examine what they are teaching, even at the elementary levels, and perhaps reconsider their requirements for high school graduation." APL research defines functional competency as "the ability to use skills and knowledge needed for meeting the requirements of adult living."

[Ed. Note: Secretary Bell's recommendations were adopted by Oregon and Pennsylvania one year later. In 1976 Pennsylvania commenced implementation of its controversial "Project '81" which, according to its 1976 State Department of Education informational materials, "restructured Pennsylvania's Goals of Quality Education and developed a new program of basic skills and initiated studies designed to help in developing comprehensive programs in general and specialized education." The same informational materials also stated that "Pennsylvania's Contemporary Family Life Competencies were taken from an outline of a course being implemented at Parkrose High School in Oregon which focused on consumer economics competencies and makes use of both school and community resources."

There is no question in this writer's mind that the "pre-determined" results of the Texas APL Study set the stage for all state education agencies to commence dumbed-down continuous progress competency-based education, which is just another label for Benjamin Bloom's and William Spady's outcome- /performance- /results-based, school-to-work "education"— all of which use Skinnerian pigeon-training methods (mastery learning and direct instruction)—and that the initial thrust for this type of "all children can learn/redistribution of brains" lifelong education came straight out of the United Nations.]

THE DAILY WORLD OF NOVEMBER 8, 1975 CARRIED A VERY INTERESTING ARTICLE ENTITLED "Planning Is Socialism's Trademark" by Morris Zeitlin. *The Daily World* (newspaper of the Communist Party USA) was formerly known as *The Daily Worker* and was founded in 1924. The importance of this article lies in its blatant admission that regionalism, which is gradually becoming the accepted method of unelected governance in the United States (unelected councils and task forces, participatory democracy, public-private partnerships, etc.) is the form of government used in democratic socialist and communist countries. The following are excerpts from this article:

> Cities in industrially advanced countries develop complex economic, social and political interaction. In this process, major cities tend to consolidate neighboring smaller cities and settlements into metropolitan regions. Rationally, metropolitan regions should constitute governmental units having comprehensive planning and administrative powers within their boundaries.
>
> In our country (the United States), rival capitalist groups, jealously guarding their special prerogatives, have rigidly maintained the traditional boundaries of states and counties while national economic and social development has created metropolitan regions that overlap those boundaries. We have no regional government and no comprehensive regional planning to speak of. Regional government and planning remain concepts our urban scholars and planners have long advocated in vain....
>
> In socialist countries, metropolitan regions enjoy metropolitan regional government and comprehensive planning. Of the many regions on the vast territory of the Soviet Union, the Moscow Region commands special attention, for it has been, since the 1917 Revolution, the country's economic and political center.
>
> The economic and functional efficiencies and the social benefits that comprehensive national, regional and city planning make possible in socialist society explain the Soviet Union's enormous and rapid economic and social progress. Conversely, our profit-oriented ruling capitalist class makes comprehensive social and economic planning impossible, causing waste and chaos and dragging the entire nation into misery and suffering as its rule deteriorates and declines.

PROJECT INSTRUCT ANOTHER MASTERY LEARNING PROGRAM MODELED ALONG THE LINES OF the Exemplary Center for Reading Instruction (ECRI), was approved for dissemination throughout the nation by the U.S. Office of Education's Joint Dissemination Review Panel (JDRP) May 14, 1975. The final evaluation of Project INSTRUCT stated that:

> The intent and emphasis in 1970 was on behavioral indices and concrete ways of showing accountability; and the data would suggest that the reading of the students themselves may not have increased, but the impact of Project INSTRUCT in the Lincoln, Nebraska Public Schools seems to be very extensive and influential.

[Ed. Note: According to the final evaluation of Project INSTRUCT, Ronald Brandt, former executive editor of the Association for Supervision and Curriculum Development's publication *Educational Leadership*, was involved in the project.]

1976

CHILDHOOD IN CHINA, A BOOK EDITED BY WILLIAM KESSEN (YALE UNIVERSITY PRESS: New Haven, Connecticut, 1976), was reviewed by Kent Garland Burit of *The Christian Science Monitor*. The following excerpts from Burit's review provide insight into the similarities of education in Communist China in 1973 and Skinnerian Effective School Research used in American restructuring in the 1980s and 1990s:

> They were well-behaved, non aggressive with peers....
> The immediate yielding to a teacher's request seemed remarkable to the Americans....
> The strategies and communication style of the teachers is also described. They initiate, supervise closely, and terminate all activities. They teach by repetition and by formula. Their verbal and nonverbal indications of approval are in a high ratio to indications of disapproval. They discipline through persuasion and moralistic reasoning rather than punishment. They exude a confident expectation of their pupils' compliance and cooperation....
> The curriculum is saturated with ideological goals, the team reported. The child is exposed to repeated exhortations to serve the society.

[Ed. Note: The foregoing quote with its behavioral terminology could come from an issue of *The Effective School Report*, from which this writer has repeatedly quoted throughout this book. Education in non-violence, tolerance, peer resolution, cooperative learning, and politically-correct curriculum—all of which will modify the behavior of American children so that they will be like the above Communist Chinese children—is taking place in American schools in 1999. (See April 21, 1982 Spady quote calling for the above "compliance.")]

THE LOS ANGELES TIMES OF MAY 21, 1976 (PART 1–B) CARRIED AN ARTICLE ENTITLED "Cuban Children Combine Studies, Work" which clearly explained the communist work-study system and the impact of community service, both of which are being implemented in the United States in the 1990s. Important excerpts follow:

> HAVANA (AP)—The door to the side room of an old cigar factory had been left ajar, and a small knot of children could be seen preparing boxes of cigars for export. "It's part of our education system," a Cuban tobacco official explained. "They are helping and learning." The children, elementary school pupils about 9 to 11 years old, were examples of the unique

Cuban educational system of combining studies with physical work. The system, started in 1967, applies to all schools, including the island's four universities....

The Cubans say the idea is to produce well-rounded citizens capable of manual labor. But the system also provides extra hands for an economy that urgently needs more production.... Says Prime Minister Fidel Castro, "This helps to temper them from early childhood in the habits of creative work, without running the risk of possible deformation through the exclusive exercise of intellectual activity.".…

One example of the system is found at Havana's 1,639 pupil U.S.S.R.-Cuba technical school, so named because the Soviet Union equipped the school and trained the instructors. The students, mainly boys 14 to 17, learn how to melt metal and to mold it into machine parts. They are taught how to cast, weld, grind and operate a lathe. Girls work in laboratories, learning to operate testing equipment for metals and machine parts. The parts, produced while learning, are sent to factories that make machinery. The students themselves spend part of their time working inside the factories. The school also teaches language, culture, sports, political philosophy and ordinary school subjects....

Those who study for two years become what are called general workers for the factories, while four-year students become skilled technicians. All are guaranteed factory jobs upon graduation....

At the University of Havana, there are 54,000 students this year. Full-time students study four hours a day, six days a week and work another four hours daily in fields, factories or at jobs related to their future careers.... Many older students fill their work requirement by teaching, to offset the teacher shortage created when hundreds of thousands of Cubans emigrated after Castro's 1959 revolution.... This commitment to working for the good of the country remains after graduation. Graduates must serve anywhere in Cuba for three years, then are allowed to return home to continue their careers.

LAWRENCE C. PIERCE DELIVERED A PAPER IN 1976 ENTITLED "SCHOOL SITE MANAGEMENT" to a meeting of the Aspen Institute for Humanistic Studies in which he referred to site-based management as an "intermediate structure between centralized school management and education vouchers." An excerpt follows:

On January 6, 1976, San Francisco School Superintendent Robert F. Alioto proposed an organizational redesign of the district that included a shift from school district to school site management. He said, in part:

I recommend that we move toward a school site management model that values staff and a community involvement and stresses accountability. We must recognize the principal as the instructional leader of the school. We must expand the budgeting and fiscal control at each school site.... We must establish at each school site one active advisory committee which includes parents, students, and staff representatives of the school's ethnic population....

Further support for proposals to decentralize school management arises from the desire to increase public participation in school governance policies. Local control of the schools, originally instituted to make them responsive to the people, nevertheless proved to be cumbersome, and it frequently obscured the state's responsibility for providing every child with a basic education. In pursuit of greater accountability and higher professional standards, the pendulum of school government, which in the early days of this country swung toward representativeness and local control, later swung back toward greater professional autonomy and stronger executive control....

...School site management is an intermediate structure between centralized school management and educational vouchers.

[Ed. Note: Read that last statement again. Twenty-one years later the carefully laid plans of the internationalist Aspen Institute for Humanistic Studies are being implemented under the guise of unaccountable choice/charter schools, funded by the taxpayers. School-site management is an early term for site-based or school-based management promoted by the National Education Association in the 1980s and 1990s. Of extreme importance is the unambiguous call for the use of (need for) vouchers, which will supplant "choice," essential for the implementation of the international school-to-work agenda. The dollar amount of the voucher will depend on the school council's determination of how much it will cost to train your child to be a janitor (very little) or doctor (a lot).]

LAWRENCE P. GRAYSON OF THE NATIONAL INSTITUTE OF EDUCATION, U.S. DEPARTMENT OF Education, wrote "Education, Technology, and Individual Privacy" (*ECTJ*, Vol. 28, No. 3, pp. 195–208) in 1976. The following are some excerpts from this important paper which serves as a clear warning regarding the indiscriminate use of behaviorist methods and technology:

The right to privacy is based on a belief in the essential dignity and worth of the individual. Modern technological devices, along with advances in the behavioral sciences, can threaten the privacy of students. Fortunately, invasions of privacy in education have not been widespread. However, sufficient violations have been noted to warrant specific legislation and to promote a sharp increase in attention to procedures that will ensure protection of individual privacy. Technology that can reveal innermost thoughts and motives or can change basic values and behaviors, must be used judiciously and only by qualified professionals under strictly controlled conditions. Education includes individuals and educational experimentation is human experimentation. The educator must safeguard the privacy of students and their families....

Privacy has been defined as "the right to be let alone" (Cooley, 1888) and as the "right to the immunity of the person—the right to one's personality" (Warren and Brandeis, 1890). Individuals have the right to determine when, how, and to what extent they will share themselves with others. It is their right to be free from unwarranted or undesired revelation of personal information to others, to participate or withdraw as they see fit, and to be free of unwarranted surveillance through physical, psychological, or technological means.

Justice William O. Douglas expressed the concerns of many people when he stated:

We are rapidly entering the age of no privacy; when everyone is open to surveillance at all times; when there are no secrets from the government.... [There is] an alarming trend whereby the privacy and dignity of our citizens is being whittled away by sometimes imperceptible steps. Taken individually, each step may be of little consequence. But when viewed as a whole, there begins to emerge a society quite unlike any we have seen—a society in which government may intrude into the secret regions of a man's life at will. (*Osborn v. U.S.*, 1966, pp. 341–343)

Behavioral science, which is assuming an increasing role in educational technology, promises to make educational techniques more effective by recognizing individual differences among students and by patterning instruction to meet individual needs. However, behavioral science is more than an unbiased means to an end. It has a basic value position (Skinner, 1971) based on the premise that such "values as freedom and democracy, which imply that the individual ultimately has free will and is responsible for his own actions, are not only cultural inventions, but illusions" (Harman, 1970). This position is contradictory to the basic premise of freedom and is demeaning to the dignity of the individual. Behavioral science inappropriately applied can impinge on individual values without allowing for personal differences and in education can violate the privacy of the student....

Reflecting on the ethical values of our civilization in 1958, Pope Pius XII commented:

> There is a large portion of his inner world which the person discloses to a few confidential friends and shields against the intrusion of others. Certain [other] matters are kept secret at any price and in regard to anyone. Finally, there are other matters which the person is unable to consider.... And just as it is illicit to appropriate another's goods or to make an attempt on his bodily integrity without his consent, so it is not permissible to enter into his inner domain against his will, whatever is the technique or method used....

Whatever the motivations of the teacher or researcher, an individual's privacy must take precedence over effective teaching, unless good cause can be shown to do otherwise. Good cause, however, does not relieve the teacher or school administrator from the responsibility of safeguarding the privacy of the student and the family. Yet, many teachers and administrators remain insensitive to the privacy implications of behavioral science and modern technology in education....

Intent on improving education, educators, scientists, and others concerned with the development and application of technology are often insensitive to the issues of privacy raised by the use of their techniques. For example, many psychological and behavioral practices have been introduced on the ground that they will make education more efficient or effective. However, improvements in efficiency through technological applications can reinforce these practices without regard to their effects. What is now being done in education could be wrong, especially if carried out on a massive scale. As the use of technology becomes more widespread, we may reach the point where errors cannot be detected or corrected. This is especially important because technology interacts with society and culture to change established goals and virtues. Propagating an error on a national level could change the original goals to fit the erroneous situation. The error then becomes acceptable by default.

In developing and applying technology to education, potential effects must be analyzed, so that negative possibilities can be identified and overcome before major resources are committed to projects that could produce undesirable long-term social consequences.

In matters affecting privacy it is better to err on the side of the individual, than on that of research or improved educational practice. Violations of privacy can never be fully redressed.

Ftnt. No. 14. Privacy is a constitutionally protected right; education is not. The Supreme Court ruled in *Griswold v. Connecticut* (decided in 1965) that the right of privacy is guaranteed by the Constitution. In *Rodriguez v. San Antonio Independent School District* (decided in 1973), the Court ruled that education is not a protected right under the Constitution.

UNITED NATIONS EDUCATIONAL, SCIENTIFIC, AND CULTURAL ORGANIZATION (UNESCO) IN Paris, France published *The International Standard Classification of Education* (ISCED–COM.75/WS/27) in 1976. This publication revealed efforts at the highest international level to set up a classification system which will be available for use by planners assigned to the management of the global economy. Some quotes from the introduction to this 396-page document follow:

> *The International Standard Classification of Education* (ISCED) has been designed as an instrument suitable for assembling, compiling, and presenting statistics of education both within individual countries and internationally. It is expected to facilitate international compilation and comparison of education statistics as such, and also their use in conjunction with manpower and other economic statistics....
>
> ISCED should facilitate the use of education statistics in manpower planning and encourage the use of manpower statistics in educational planning. For this purpose, the most closely associated classification system in the manpower field is the International Standard Classification of Occupations (ISCO), prepared by the International Labour Office.

CATHERINE BARRETT, PRESIDENT OF THE NATIONAL EDUCATION ASSOCIATION (NEA), GAVE a speech at the 1976 NEA Annual Conference in which she made the following comments concerning the change in the role of the teacher:

> At this critical moment no one can say with certainty whether we are at the brink of a colossal disaster or whether this is indeed mankind's shining hour. But it is certain that dramatic changes in the way we raise our children in the year 2000 are indicated particularly in terms of schooling, and that these changes will require new ways of thinking. Let me propose three.
>
> First, we will help all of our people understand that school is a concept and not a place. We will not confuse "schooling" with "education." The school will be the community, the community, the school. Students, parents, and teachers will make certain that John Dewey's sound advice about schooling the whole child is not confused with nonsense about the school's providing the child's whole education....
>
> We will need to recognize that the so-called "basic skills," which currently represent nearly the total effort in elementary schools, will be taught in one quarter of the present school day. The remaining time will be devoted to what is truly fundamental and basic—time for academic inquiry, time for students to develop their own interests, time for a dialogue between students and teachers. When this happens—and it is near—the teacher can rise to his true calling. More than a dispenser of information, the teacher will be a conveyor of values, a philosopher. Students will learn to write love letters and lab notes. We will help each child build his own rocket to his own moon....
>
> Finally, if our children are to be human beings who think clearly, feel deeply, and act wisely, we will answer definitely the question "Who should make what decisions?" Teachers no longer will be victims of change; we will be the agents of change.

[Ed. Note: Catherine Barrett's idea of "school is a concept, not a place" is an idea whose time may have come in the 1990s. Many educators, including Lewis Perelman (See 1995 Perelman's book *School's Out*), are of the same opinion. This seems to follow on the heels of the concept of "education as behavior change" instead of the acquisition of knowledge.]

IN THE SEPTEMBER 1976 ISSUE OF *PHI DELTA KAPPAN*, "AMERICA'S NEXT TWENTY-FIVE Years: Some Implications for Education," Harold Shane described his version of the "new and additional basic skills" as follows:

Certainly, cross-cultural understanding and empathy have become fundamental skills, as have the skills of human relations and intercultural rapport... the arts of compromise and reconciliation, of consensus building, and of planning for interdependence become basic.... As young people mature we must help them develop... a service ethic which is geared toward the real world... the global servant concept in which we will educate our young for planetary service and eventually for some form of world citizenship.... Implicit within the "global servant" concept are the moral insights that will help us live with the regulated freedom we must eventually impose upon ourselves.

[Ed. Note: The writer would like to contrast Harold Shane's comments with those of C.S. Lewis as compiled in an article "C.S. Lewis on Liberal Arts Education" by Gregory Dunn which was published in the newsletter *On Principle* from the John M. Ashbrook Center for Public Affairs (April 1999, Vol. VII, No. 2). Excerpts from Dunn's article follow:

The first reason we study the liberal arts has to do with freedom. That freedom is an integral part of the liberal arts is borne out of [C.S.] Lewis's observation that "*liberal* comes of course from the Latin, *liber*, and means free."[11] Such an education makes one free, according to Lewis, because it transforms the pupil from "an unregenerate little bundle of appetites" into "the good man and the good citizen."[12] We act most human when we are reasonable, both in thought and deed. Animals, on the other hand, act wholly out of appetite. When hungry, they eat; when tired, they rest. Man is different. Rather than follow our appetites blindly we can be deliberate about what we do and when we do it. The ability to rule ourselves frees us from the tyranny of our appetites, and the liberal arts disciplines this self-rule. In other words, this sort of education teaches us to be most fully human and thereby, to fulfill our human duties, both public and private.

Lewis contrasts liberal arts education with what he calls "vocational training," the sort that prepares one for employment. Such training, he writes, "aims at making not a good man but a good banker, a good electrician... or a good surgeon." Lewis does admit the importance of such training—for we cannot do without bankers and electricians and surgeons—but the danger, as he sees it, is the pursuit of training at the expense of education. "If education is beaten by training, civilization dies," he writes, for the "lesson of history" is that "civilization is a rarity, attained with difficulty and easily lost."[13] It is the liberal arts, not vocational training, that preserves civilization by producing reasonable men and responsible citizens....

A third reason we study the liberal arts is because it is simply our nature and duty. Man has a natural thirst for knowledge of the Good, the True, and the Beautiful, and men and women of the past have made great sacrifices to pursue it in spite of the fact that, as Lewis puts it, "human life has always been lived on the edge of a precipice." In his words, "they propound mathematical theorems in beleaguered cities, conduct metaphysical arguments in condemned cells, make jokes on scaffolds." So, finding in the soul an appetite for such things, and knowing no appetite is made by God in vain, Lewis concludes that the pursuit of the liberal arts is pleasing to God and is possibly, for some, a God-given vocation....[14]

...Truly, we ignore the liberal arts only at our peril. Without them we will find ourselves increasingly unable to preserve a civilized society, to escape from the errors and prejudices of our day, and to struggle in the arena of ideas to the glory of God.]

TODAY'S EDUCATION, THE JOURNAL OF THE NATIONAL EDUCATION ASSOCIATION, CARRIED an article in the September–October 1976 edition entitled "The Seven Cardinal Principles Revisited." On page 1 this article stated that:

In 1972, the NEA established a Bicentennial Committee charged with developing a "living commemoration of the principles of the American Revolution." This 200th anniversary celebration of the *Declaration of Independence* was to focus on the next 100 years of education in an interdependent global community. The initial work of the Committee culminated in the NEA *Bicentennial Idea Book*. Among its ideas was that of developing a definitive volume to "contain a reframing of the Cardinal Principles of Education and recommendations for a global curriculum." After recognizing the importance of the original Cardinal Principles, which were published in 1918, the Committee made the point that "today, those policy statements about education are obsolete, education taken as a whole is not adequate to the times and too seldom anticipates the future." A report to be issued by the NEA, proposing cardinal premises for the twenty-first century is the direct and immediate outgrowth of the Bicentennial Committee's belief that "educators around the world are in a unique position to bring about a harmoniously interdependent global community based on the principles of peace and justice...." Early in September 1975, a 19-member Preplanning Committee began the task of recasting the seven Cardinal Principles of Education by developing 25 guidelines for the project.

[Ed. Note: Members of the Preplanning Committee read like a "Who's Who of Leading Globalists." It included: former Secretary of Education T.H. Bell, "Mr. Management-by-Objectives," who was responsible for the grant to William Spady of the Far West Laboratory to pilot OBE in Utah, with plans to "put OBE in all schools of the nation"; Professor Luvern Cunningham, Ohio State University, who subsequently served as advisor to the Kentucky Department of Education during its education restructuring in the 1990s; Willis Harman, Stanford Research Institute; Robert Havighurst, University of Chicago; Theodore Hesburgh, University of Notre Dame; Ralph Tyler, Center for Advanced Study in Behavioral Science; Professor Theodore Sizer, Coalition for Essential Schools, which calls for a "less is more" curriculum and removal of graduation standards (the Carnegie Unit); David Rockefeller; Professor Benjamin Bloom, father of Mastery Learning (the international learning method); the late McGeorge Bundy of the Ford Foundation; and others.]

FOUNDATIONS OF LIFELONG EDUCATION WAS PUBLISHED BY **UNESCO** (UNITED NATIONS Educational, Scientific, and Cultural Organization) Institute for Education (Pergamon Press: Oxford, N.Y., Toronto, Sydney, Paris, Frankfurt, 1976). In chapter 4, "Theoretical Foundations of Lifelong Education: A Sociological Perspective," Henri Janne described accurately the how, what and why of decentralization (site-based management, charter schools, choice, unelected school councils, etc.) being sold to naïve school boards and citizens as "local control":

> In education a monolithic structure is completely unacceptable as it creates organizations that, owing to their homogeneity and their ineluctable [inevitable] bureaucratic nature, are averse to change and to individual or local adaptation....
>
> Decentralization of the greatest possible number of decisions is indispensable in a system founded on... education defined as "learning" rather than "teaching."

[Ed. Note: "Learning," as described and defined by the educational change agents, is the process by which students/children are allowed to acquire the knowledge which will be "beneficial" to them personally as they pursue the fulfillment of their particular life roles (jobs). This process is the opposite of the traditional role of education as "teaching" students subject matter which can be used for diversified pursuits later in life.

In the 1977 entry dealing with UNESCO's Development of Educational Technology in Central and Eastern Europe the reader will note that the socialist countries of Eastern Europe had centralized systems of education and had not yet adapted their system to accommodate Henri Janne's proposals for "lifelong learning." Janne explained above how to take a centralized system of pedagogy and ideas and "localize" them in order to change their focus without ever changing the centralized control. This gives an interesting perspective on the oft-seen bumper sticker: "Think Globally—Act Locally."]

1977

ESSAYS IN ECONOMICS: THEORIES, FACTS, AND POLICIES, VOL. II (BLACKWELL PUBLISHers: Malden, Massachusetts, 1977) by the late Wassily Leontief was published. An excerpt follows:

> When I speak of national economic planning, the notion I have in mind is meant to encompass the entire complex of political, legislative, and administrative measures aimed at an explicit formulation and realization of a comprehensive national economic plan. Without a cohesive, internally consistent plan there can be, in this sense, no planning. But the preparation of a script is not enough, the play has to be staged and acted out. It is incumbent on anyone who favors introduction of national economic planning in this country—and I am one of these—to propose a plan describing how this might be done. Several congressional committees and at least one commission appointed by the President, not to speak of groups outside of the government, are now engaged in this task. (p. 398)

Who's Who in America includes the following reference to Leontief: "Economist, born Leningrad, Russia, August 5, 1906, et al." *Current Biography* in 1967 listed Leontief as :

> The creator of the input-output system revolutionizing economic research and national planning is the Russian-born Harvard professor Wassily W. Leontief.... Leontief has been a teacher at Harvard since 1931, and director of the Harvard Economic Research Project on the Structure of the American Economy since 1948.... [This project] was funded by an initial four-year grant of $100,000 from the Rockefeller Foundation.

In a letter to American educator/researcher/writer Gene Malone dated September 9, 1993, Leontief, professor at the Institute for Economic Analysis of New York University, stated: "The use of the Input-Output method in educational planning was already discussed and has been practically employed in France." OBE is similar to PPBS (Planning, Programming, Budgeting System) and MBO (Management by Objective), both of which are based on input-output economic systems theory.

Leontief died February 5, 1999 at the age of 93. *The New York Times* February 8, 1999 eulogy steered clear of any mention of Leontief's work in the promotion of Five-Year Plans, widely associated with socialist planning. However, the *Times* article provided some extremely interesting background information on Leontief:

> Dr. Leontief, with the help of ever-more powerful computers, continued to improve input-output analysis his entire life.

With advances he made in the 1950s and 1960s, that analysis became a key part of the national accounting systems for both capitalist and communist states.... [H]e preached a doctrine of applied economics, saying that research should result in practical advances.... [H]e also found time to serve as president of the American Economic Society....

Partially through input-output analysis, he also became a leading authority on the economic effects of world disarmament and increased economic controls....

He was a 1925 economics graduate of the University of Leningrad, and he was imprisoned in that city for anti-Soviet activities. He was allowed to leave the Soviet Union and went to Germany where he received master's and doctoral degrees from the University of Berlin.

He served in 1929 and 1930 in Nanking, China, as an economics advisor to the Chinese Ministry of Railroads. He then came to this country and joined the National Bureau of Economic Research in New York in 1931.

In 1932, he joined Harvard as an economics instructor. He became an assistant professor in 1933, an associate professor in 1939 and a full professor in 1946. Two years later he founded the Harvard Economic Research Project, which became a center of input-output analysis.

During World War II, he was a consultant to the Labor Department and the Office of Strategic Services [OSS, CIA, NTL].

He left Harvard in 1975 to join the faculty at New York University, where he was a full professor and also served as director of its Institute for Economic Analysis from 1975–1991. He continued to give classes at the university into his nineties.

Dr. Leontief thus taught and ran research organizations at two great universities all the while doing all-but-revolutionary economic research that would lead to major advances in national planning.... Dr. Leontief... championed the central role of government in planning.

"COMPETENCY-BASED EDUCATION: A BANDWAGON IN SEARCH OF A DEFINITION," AN ARticle by William G. Spady of the National Institute of Education, was published in the January 1977 edition of *Educational Researcher*. Excerpts follow:

> In September, 1972, the Oregon State Board of Education passed new minimum graduation requirements for students entering ninth grade in the Fall of 1974 and new minimum standards for local school districts focused on the new requirements in 1974. The thrust of these new requirements and standards involved the introduction of three domains of "survival level" competencies as minimum conditions for high school graduation by 1978: personal development, social responsibility, and career development.... Although largely unintended and unanticipated by those involved, the 1972 Oregon regulations provided the first significant nudge that set in motion across the nation over the next four years a series of actions by state level policy makers and administrators to consider, formulate and implement regulations and procedures that they now associate with the term Competency-Based Education (CBE)....
>
> It is likely, therefore, both that the outcome goals required for graduation in CBE systems will eventually emerge from a tense compromise among the many constituencies in a community regarding the necessary, the desirable, and the possible, and that C-Based diplomas will be viewed with initial if not undying skepticism by colleges and universities.... In short, CBE programs require mechanisms that collect and use student performance data as the basis of diagnosing weaknesses and necessary remediation not only for students but for themselves as well....
>
> According to information compiled by Clark and Thompson (1976), no states outside

of Oregon appear to use language consistent with a life-role conception of competency in either their current or pending regulations pertaining to mandated student proficiencies. The possible exceptions refer to the need for occupational and consumer mathematics skills. However, within the next year New York and Pennsylvania may make more decisive moves toward implementing approaches to schooling more fully resembling this conception of CBE. Almost all other states are concerned with capacity-based outcomes in limited basic skill areas (e.g., Arizona, Connecticut, Florida, Georgia, Idaho, Louisiana, Maryland, Nebraska and Tennessee), a slightly broader set of subject area proficiencies (e.g., California, Texas, Virginia and Washington, D.C.) or as-yet-undefined or else locally determined options concerned with some kind of minimum proficiency requirements (e.g., Colorado, Kansas, Michigan and New Jersey). As of October 1976, in only two cases—California and Florida—could students leave school in less than 12 years with a diploma once they passed a state-determined proficiency exam (the Oregon regulations allow local districts to determine whether early graduation will be allowed)....

Aside from Oregon, five states—California, Maryland, Michigan, New York and Pennsylvania—deserve particular attention over the next few years as sites where current thinking about substantial proficiencies or competency-based reforms suggest real promise....

Pennsylvania in a fourth case has been exploring a concept of system reform with a definite Competency-Based orientation. Originally called Community Learning and currently named "Project 81," this program would be centered around facilitating student capacities and competencies in five major areas of activity, with a stress on participation outside the school building where appropriate. The areas include a broad range of basic skills, the world of work and leisure, community governance and involvement, and a broad range of citizen and personal survival skills.

"CONCLAVE OF THE CHANGE AGENTS" BY BARBARA M. MORRIS WAS PUBLISHED IN THE March 1977 issue of *The National Educator*. Excerpts follow from this extremely important article which proves that the federal government has been deeply involved in the funding and implementation of moral/citizenship (values) education:

Early in June 1976, 85 top level members of the educational elite and an assortment of influential change agents met at an invitation only conference in Philadelphia to draft recommendations on how to put "Moral/Citizenship Education" (MCE) programs in every school in the country—public, private and parochial. Conference participants included Humanist values educators Lawrence Kohlberg and Howard Kirschenbaum and representatives of the federal government, foundations, PTA, NEA and the National Council of Churches. The recommendations that resulted from that conference which was sponsored by a Pennsylvania organization called Research for Better Schools (RBS) [a federally funded education laboratory in Philadelphia, Pennsylvania] have been submitted to the National Institute of Education, with whom RBS has a contract to research, develop and disseminate moral/citizenship education programs....

So shaky is the basis for MCE that much conference time was devoted to trying to decide what to call MCE programs so as to avoid public hostility. Here are some examples of the thinking of conference participants relating to this problem:

- "'Moral/Citizenship Education' as a title can be sold; 'Moral Education' cannot. Avoid such red-flag slogans."

- "We spent three conference days quibbling about the term 'Moral/Citizenship Education.' *That is a major problem.*" [emphasis in original]
- "The concept of self-development (which implies moral development) is more salable and will engender less resistance than moral development."
- "It is important to limit the parameters of what we're engaged in, if not to change the actual title, to avoid religious antagonisms and court action."

THE SCHOOL COUNSELOR, PUBLICATION OF THE AMERICAN PERSONNEL AND GUIDANCE ASSOciation, published a special issue on the subject of "Death" in its May 1977 issue (Vol. 24, #5). In this issue a remarkable admission regarding the results of sex education was made which explains clearly the purpose of these controversial humanistic programs: to create the problems sex ed, values ed, drug ed, and death ed were supposed to solve. An excerpt from *The School Counselor* follows:

Helping Students Clarify Values:...

The last goal is to help students clarify their values on social and ethical issues. An underlying, but seldom spoken, assumption of much of the death education movement is that Americans handle death and dying poorly and that we ought to be doing better at it. As in the case of many other problems, many Americans believe that education can initiate change. Change is evident, and death education will play as important a part in changing attitudes toward death as sex education played in changing attitudes toward sex information and wider acceptance of various sexual practices.

[Ed. Note: In light of events in the 1990s, the question arises: What does "doing better at it" mean? The statement "Death education will play as important a part in changing attitudes toward death as sex education played in changing attitudes toward... wider acceptance of various sexual practices" implies that our children benefitted from exposure to "wider acceptance of various sexual practices," when all one has to do is survey the moral landscape to see the devastating effect these programs have had on our children's lives. The same applies to death education and its effect on children's understanding of the value of life, reflected in the increased number of murders carried out by youth.]

JOANNE MCAULEY'S NATIONAL COUNCIL FOR EDUCATIONAL EXCELLENCE, A NATIONAL ORganization of concerned parents and educators, was founded in the mid-1970s and, considering the potential it had for holding the line on innovations taking place in American education, its early demise represented a real setback for parents, children, and teachers. Ms. McAuley's May/June 1977 issue of her newsletter, *The School Bell*, is proof that the National School Boards Association was, at one time, a strong proponent of local control, not a "sell out the locals" organization that in the 1990s would support site- and school-based management (taxation without representation) and charter schools. Excerpts follow:

NSBA PRESIDENT TELLS BOARDS: STAND UP TO FEDERAL MEDDLING

On March 27, George W. Smith, immediate past president of the National School Boards Association, warned school board members attending the NSBA convention in Houston that "The Congress and the federal bureaucracy could become the country's master school board unless school board members stand up and be counted." He urged delegates to continue to forge a strong NSBA to convince Congress that local school board members are truly represensative, most unselfish, and the best qualified persons to represent the local viewpoint in education.

Smith said local constituencies cannot be forgotten even while the new trust is being built with Congress. "We must not forget our own constituency," he noted. He also advised board members to be aware of—and leery of—proposals for public involvement in public school operations that would shift decision-making authority to "vaguely defined groups of citizens at the school site level." The minister from San Diego cautioned that the power to make a decision must never be divorced from the responsibility for making that decision....

He said school boards must be strong for another reason—to counter the movements of the courts and federal regulatory agencies into the operation of schools. "If we want other governmental units to stop eroding our ability to provide educational governance, we must exercise that ability more often and more effectively." Smith said, "Where we can, we should work together with all segments of the public toward the improvement of the schools. But," he concluded, "our responsibility is to all the people and we must view only the 'big ic- ture.'"

[Ed. Note: Smith's ability to foresee the implementation of site-based management, the down-grading of the importance of elected board members, and the transfer of power to public-private partnerships, etc., is to be lauded! While serving in the U.S. Department of Education this writer attempted to stop federally funded programs to train local school board members in conflict resolution and in how to implement effective school research.]

"COMPETENCY TESTS SET IN 26 SCHOOLS: NEW CURRICULUM SHIFTS TEACHING METHODS in District"** was the title of an article which appeared in *The Washington Post* on August 1, 1977. Excerpts follow:

"The materials will be standardized, the lessons will be standardized," Guines said. "We're taking the play out. We're taking the guesswork out. We're putting in a precise predicted treatment that leads to a predicted response." Guines said that the new curriculum is based on the work in behavioral psychology of Harvard University's B.F. Skinner, who developed teaching machines and even trained pigeons during World War II to pilot and detonate bombs and torpedoes. The basic idea, Guines said, is to break down complicated learning into a sequence of clear simple skills that virtually everyone can master, although at different rates of speed. "If you can train a pigeon to fly up there and press a button and set off a bomb," Guines remarked, "why can't you teach human beings to behave in an effective and rational way? We know that we can modify human behavior. We're not scared of that. This is the biggest thing that's happening in education today."...

According to Thomas B. Sticht, Associate Director for Basic Skills of the National Institute of Education, similar techniques, called competency education or mastery teaching, are now being used in many parts of the country. Since 1973, Sticht said, they have been adopted by the Army and Navy for basic training and to teach entry level job skills. They have been used successfully in college courses, he said, and also to teach mentally retarded children who previously had been classed as "uneducable." "There has to be a well-defined series of objectives," Sticht said, "and a step by step curriculum that gives some way [through Mastery Tests] to know you have met the objectives.".…

But the system also has detractors who criticize it as rigid and mechanistic. "We must be very careful," said Lawrence G. Derthick, a former U.S. Commissioner of Education, "about adopting any mechanical system of producing children like objects. There are so many complicating factors in each child—emotional, psychological, the home background, the sensitivity of teachers—there's danger in trying to turn out children like nuts and bolts or steel pins. Human beings are more complex.".…

[Ed. Note: William Spady, "father of outcome-based education," served as consultant to the D.C. schools at this exact time, working out of the U.S. Office of Education's National Institute of Education. His position at the time is listed in his curriculum vitae as "Senior Research Sociologist, 1973–1978." With Spady, Thomas Sticht, associate director for basic skills at NIE, also worked on the failed, Skinnerian D.C. school reform. In addition, the reader is urged to refer to the August 8, 1982 *Washington Post* entry which paraphrases Sticht as follows: "Ending discrimination and changing values are probably more important than reading in moving low income families into the middle class." Of further interest, the same Thomas Sticht was president of Applied Behavioral and Cognitive Sciences, Inc., San Diego, California, and has served on the U.S. Labor Department Secretary's Commission on Achieving Necessary Skills (SCANS).]

DEVELOPMENT OF EDUCATIONAL TECHNOLOGY IN CENTRAL AND EASTERN EUROPE STUDIES: *Division of Structures, Content, Methods and Techniques of Education* was published and distributed by United Nations Educational, Scientific, and Cultural Organization (UNESCO: Paris: ED–77/WS/133:English Edition) in November of 1977. The author is including excerpts from the "Section on Methods, Materials and Techniques" so that the reader will see how *America 2000/Goals 2000* restructuring is identical to education in the former Eastern European communist countries. The reader must also remember that American education is under the direction of UNESCO due to our membership in the United Nations. Excerpts follow:

The development of educational technology in the Central and Eastern European countries, as commissioned by the UNESCO Secretariat, is summarised on the basis of the oral and written information supplied by the countries having attended the Budapest International Seminar on Educational Technology in 1976. The countries involved are as follows: People's Republic of Bulgaria, Socialist Republic of Czechoslovakia, Republic of Finland, Republic of Greece, Socialist Federal Republic of Yugoslavia, People's Republic of Poland, People's Republic of Hungary, German Democratic Republic, Union of Soviet Socialist Republics. Data were also supplied by the Socialist Republic of Rumania which could not participate in the Seminar.

The factors exercising a decisive influence on the present standards of the application of educational technology and the strategies and rate of its further spread in the countries listed above are as follows:

a. the overwhelming majority of the countries represented (8 out of 10) are socialist states;

b. except for the Soviet Union and Finland, the nations concerned can be classified into the category of fairly developed countries from the technological point of view.

On the basis of the above factors some of the specific characteristics of the development of educational technology will be underlined. It follows from the essence of the socialist structure of the state in the countries concerned, except Finland and Greece, that their educational system is centralized. This creates an extremely favourable situation for central state measures designed to modernize education. The socialist state possesses the means necessary for education... for the widespread use of methodology based on solid technological foundations and of the media and means of educational technology.... In a situation in which millions of students learn and hundreds of thousands of educationalists teach, on the basis of unified curricula, decisions involving the development of the method to be adopted in education and of the media and aids of educational technology call for very thorough preparatory work....

The socialist countries also have a substantial advantage from the aspect of the development of educational technology because the training and in-service training of teachers rest on a uniform basis. In addition, curricula are uniform in the individual countries and for the different types of schools harmony between the curricular activities and the development of educational technology can be therefore established comparatively easily.

[Ed. Note: A flow chart on page 11 of the study includes under "Factors Influencing the Introduction of Educational Technology" all the components found in American educational restructuring as follows: Adequate Curricula; System of Objectives; Systems of Means of Assessment; Media System; Ensuring Appropriate Facilities (school building, hardware, media); Adequately Trained Teachers (basic training, in-service/further training/information); Research and Development; and International Cooperation.]

1978

PROFESSOR BENJAMIN BLOOM, THE "FATHER" OF MASTERY LEARNING AND DEVELOPER OF the Taxonomy of Educational Objectives, presented a paper entitled "New Views of the Learner: Implications for Instruction and Curriculum" at the 1978 Association for the Supervision and Curriculum Development (ASCD) Annual Conference. The paper was published in ASCD's *Educational Leadership* April 1978 issue (Vol. 35, #7). The following quote explains clearly the reasoning behind UNESCO's requirement that member states, including the United States, incorporate UNESCO's lifelong learning philosophy into their education policies:

<u>Continuing Learning</u>

Throughout the world, the instruction and curriculum in the schools is being studied to determine its long-term contribution to continuing learning throughout life. The Edgar Faure (UNESCO) report "Learning to Be" has had great influence on this thinking. The Faure report (Faure, 1972) stresses the many changes taking place in all societies and the difficulties individuals have in adjusting to rapid change in the society, in their work, and in their lives. Since, the report continues, it is virtually impossible to anticipate and plan for the changes that will take place, the only adaptive mechanism people have to adjust to and cope with these changes is their ability and interest in continuing learning throughout life....

We, who are responsible for the learning of our students for a ten-to-sixteen-year period, must extend our sights beyond the period that our students are in the schools or colleges. Until we do this and until it becomes a part of our curriculum planning, we will neglect those objectives of education that relate to the entire life of the individual. (pp. 574–575)

[Ed. Note: It is important to recall Bloom's definition of education: "to change the thoughts, actions, and feelings of students." In other words, the above recommendation very simply calls for lifelong brainwashing.]

IN THE AUGUST 1978 ISSUE OF *THE NATIONAL EDUCATOR* BARBARA MORRIS, EDITOR OF *The Barbara Morris Report* and author of many books related to education including her most recent book, *The Great American Con Game*,[15] reported on a speech given at the University of Illinois by Mary F. Berry, assistant secretary in the U.S. Office of Education (1977), regarding Chinese education. The following excerpts from Morris's report are too important to leave out of this book:

Indeed, what does the U.S.A. stand to learn? Let's take a look.

Red China has eliminated testing and grades. The U.S. is rapidly going the same route. Testing is being downgraded and scoffed at, and grades, where they do exist are just about meaningless.

For the Red Chinese, according to Ms. Berry, truth is a relative concept. In the U.S. schools students are taught the same thing in "values clarification." It's called situation ethics and it means it's okay to lie or cheat or steal or kill when it suits your purpose.

In Red China, according to Ms. Berry, education must serve the masses. Ditto the U.S. Only the semantics are different here. In the U.S. education is not designed for the benefit of individuals, but for society. "Society" or "masses"—what's the difference?

In Red China, according to Ms. Berry, education must be combined with productive labor and starts at six years of age, with children working at least one hour a day producing voice boxes for dolls. At the middle school level, children make auto parts as part of the school day. We are not at this low level, but Secretary Berry frankly admits, "We will draw on the Chinese model...." We are fast approaching the Chinese model. We have work/study programs and the U.S. Office of Education is working on development of Lifelong Learning programs—another Chinese import. Such programs will enable people to work and study their entire lives for the benefit of the state.

Ms. Berry admitted U.S. Lifelong Learning programs are indeed drawn on the Chinese experience, that such programs are expected to meet "needs for intellectual fulfillment and social growth. It is here that the Chinese have set the pattern for the world to follow, and it is here that American higher education may have its last, best opportunity for growth."

Secretary Berry lamented that the U.S. is only slowly moving into Lifelong Learning, but that "The community college system with its nonconventional enrollment, is one harbinger of change. The traditional extension program is another.... But we have to go beyond them and bring four year institutions and secondary institutions, as well as private instructional facilities into the Lifelong Learning movement."

Ms. Berry is not talking about the future when she recommends radical proposals for U.S. education. A meeting of the National Council for the Social Studies, held in Cincinnati last November, featured several presentations on Communist Chinese education as a model for U.S. education. In one such presentation, teachers learned how the Red Chinese educational system "is related to achievement of national goals and citizenship preparation... how cultural activities and recreational pastimes provide a vehicle for transmitting new social values." Does this help you understand why U.S. schools usually list "worthy use of leisure" or "citizenship education" as a goal of education?

[Ed. Note: Americans, involved in what would seem to be the worthy goal of implementing character, citizenship, or civic education in the government schools or in community groups, or in seeking "common ground" with groups who hold differing views on political, social, and religious issues, should think more than twice before becoming involved in this dangerous dialogue. The reason the dialogue is dangerous is evident when one studies the track record of nations whose citizens have allowed their governments to define morality or good citizenship; i.e., Nazi Germany, the Soviet Union and Red China, to name just a few.]

FIFTH REPORT OF THE NATIONAL COUNCIL ON EDUCATIONAL RESEARCH, FUNDED BY THE U.S. Office of Education, was published in an issue spanning 1978–1979. The very clear connection drawn between mastery learning and direct instruction, enabling one to understand that they are essentially the same or at least fraternal twins, is the importance of the following excerpt:

> The Learning Research and Development Center (LRDC) at the University of Pittsburgh has developed instructional mastery of learning programs providing individualized instruction in math, science, reading, and early learning skills. These have been disseminated nationally through Project Follow Through [Direct Instruction/DISTAR] and by Research for Better Schools (RBS). (pp. 28–29)

1979

"GEORGIA BASIC LIFE PROCESS SKILLS, ESEA, TITLE II, PROPOSED INSTRUCTIONAL TIME in School Programs," prepared by Lucille G. Jordan, associate state superintendent for Instructional Services of the Georgia Department of Education, was submitted to the U.S. Department of Education for a grant in 1979. The particular curricular programs which received funding under Title II were jointly funded by Exxon Corporation and the U.S. Department of Education. On page 34 of Georgia's grant proposal an extraordinary curriculum graph/chart recommends the following percentages of time be spent at and between 5, 10, 15 and 18 years of age on the following subjects:

Basic 3 R's: 90% at 5 yrs. Declining to 40% at 10 yrs. Declining to 30% at 15 yrs. Declining to 15% at 18 yrs.

Life Process Skills: (Critical thinking, problem solving, and decision making): 5% at 5 yrs. Increasing to 40% at 10 yrs. Increasing to 70% at 15 yrs. Increasing to 90% at 18 yrs.

Citizenship and Humanities Studies: 30% at 5 yrs. Increasing to 40% at 10 yrs. Increasing to 70% at 15 yrs. Increasing to 90% at 18 yrs.

Science and Technology: 25% at 5 yrs. Increasing to 28% at 10 yrs. Increasing to 30% at 15 yrs. Increasing to 55% at 18 yrs.

Career Education: 20% at 5 yrs. Increasing to 22% at 10 yrs. Increasing to 30% at 15 yrs. Increasing to 55% at 18 yrs.

Health and Physical Education: 10% for ages 5 through 18 yrs.

[Ed. Note: Please note that the "Basic 3 R's" is the only curriculum area targeted for *decrease* in time spent on instruction. An official of the Georgia School Boards Association cited this graph as being representative of Bloom's *Taxonomy*. Also, why would Exxon, who was in the early 1980s one of the major corporations complaining about illiteracy and workers who are not educated in basic academics, have funded a program guaranteed to water down basic academics? (In a 1976 speech NEA President Catherine Barrett recommended teaching basic skills in only one fourth of the school day.)]

THE U.S. CONGRESS FULFILLED PRESIDENT JIMMY CARTER'S PROMISE TO THE NATIONAL Education Association by voting for a U.S. Department of Education in 1979. Now the United States which, heretofore, had been represented at international conferences as the unenlightened member of the crowd (no ministerial/socialist status), could join the "big boys" of the international community: the "big boys" being those countries who, since World War II, had been represented at these policy-planning conferences by ministers of education. Interestingly enough, the majority of teacher members of the National Education Association were opposed to the creation of the U.S. Department of Education.

The new Cabinet-level department allowed the former Bureau of Research under the National Institute of Education to become the Office of Educational Research and Improvement (OERI), which would be closely linked to the Paris, France-based Center for Educational Research and Innovation (CERI), part of the United Nations' Office of Economic Cooperation and Development (OECD). OERI's assistant secretary would attend OECD/CERI meetings at which he would receive his "marching orders" related to international restructuring efforts and programs, all of which were either being implemented or would be implemented in the future in the United States—effective school research, site-based management, school-to-work, community education, Concerns-Based Adoption Model (CBAM), etc.

A STUDY OF SCHOOLING IN THE UNITED STATES BY JOHN GOODLAD, PH.D., DEAN OF THE Graduate School of Education, University of California, Los Angeles and associated with the Institute for Development of Educational Activities (I.D.E.A., funded by Kettering Foundation), was compiled in 1979 after being researched over a period of several years. Under Dr. Goodlad's direction, trained investigators went into communities in most regions of the country. The sample of schools studied was enormously diverse in regard to size, family income, and racial composition of the student body. The result of the landmark report was *A Place Called School: Prospects for the Future* (McGraw-Hill: New York, 1984) by Goodlad.

In *A Place Called School*, Goodlad proposed pushing high school graduation back to age 16 and having all students take a core curriculum until then. A new "fourth phase of education" would combine work, study, and community service to help ease students' transition into careers, higher education, and adult responsibilities. The following three books were additionally commissioned to be written as a result of this project:

(1) *Schooling for a Global Age*, James Becker, Editor (1979), in the preface for which Dr. Goodlad made the following statement which has contributed to the development of parent-school partnerships:

> Parents and the general public must be reached, also. Otherwise, children and youth enrolled in globally-oriented programs may find themselves in conflict with values assumed in

the home. And then the education institution frequently comes under scrutiny and must pull back.

(2) *Communities and Their Schools*, Don Davies, Editor (1981), in which the history of community education at the national and international levels (China, Tanzania, etc.) was covered and the participatory democratic operation of our schools and communities was recommended (government by unelected councils).

(3) *Arts and the Schools*, Jerome J. Hausman, Editor (1980), in which the role of the arts in schools and in society was examined and then the focus shifted to the needs of the individual. *Arts* addressed curricular issues involved in designing and implementing school arts programs and, again, actual programs are discussed and analyzed. The policy implications of implementing the programs described in the book are then discussed along with change strategies for moving from rhetoric to reality.

The four books were published by McGraw Hill. The study itself was funded by the National Institute of Education, U.S. Office of Education and the following foundations: Danforth; Ford; International Paper; The JDR 3rd Fund; Martha Holden Jennings Foundation; Charles Stewart Mott Foundation; Needmor Fund; Pedamorphosis, Inc.; Rockefeller Foundation; and Spencer Foundation. The Advisory Committee for *A Study of Schooling* included the following persons: Ralph W. Tyler, chairman; Gregory Anrig; Stephen K. Bailey; Lawrence A. Cremin; Robert K. Merton; and Arthur Jefferson. The study was conducted under the auspices of the Institute for Development of Educational Activities, Inc. (IDEA) and The Laboratory in School and Community Education, Graduate School of Education, University of California, Los Angeles.

[Ed. Note: In a telephone conversation with a representative of McGraw Hill Publishers in 1982, this writer was informed that all four books were provided to the fifty state education commissioners/superintendents. These four books provide an accurate picture of the role played by the tax-exempt foundations and federal government in the restructuring/social engineering of American society and schools to accommodate the perceived "needs" of the 21st century.]

SENATOR JACOB JAVITS (NY) REQUESTED THAT MR. ARTHUR LIPPER'S ADDRESS TO THE World Council on Gifted and Talented Children be printed in the *Congressional Record*, September 5, 1979 (pp. 11904–11905). Senator Javits said in his introduction to the text of the speech:

> Mr. President, the gifted and talented children of our Nation have long been of continuing interest to me for they represent the future leadership of the United States. Last month, in Jerusalem, the World Council on Gifted and Talented Children held its Third Biennial Conference to discuss international cooperative efforts on behalf of the gifted, and to consider research and exchange programs to promote this most precious human resource.... At the Jerusalem conference, Arthur Lipper, III, an investment banker... and great friend of the gifted and talented... forcefully presented the idea that the development of the gifted represents the best hope for future peace and stability in the international political realm.... I urge my colleagues to consider carefully his remarks, and I ask that the text of Mr. Lipper's address to the World Council on Gifted and Talented Children be printed in the *Record*.

The following excerpts from Lipper's speech reflect a total disregard for the gifted and talented children as individuals who might be capable of deciding for themselves what they wish to do or become. It focuses instead on their "use" by the state to obtain predetermined global goals:

Some years ago I read the following statement in a school publication:

> One of America's most tragic wastes of natural resources is the loss of potential for social contribution which is inherent in economically deprived, gifted children.

> Properly identified at a sufficiently early age, through culture-free, non-verbal testing, the very young child can be provided with the environment, economic and motivational support necessary for full development as a positive social contributor.

> Without such early identification, the socio-economic pressure imposed upon the economically deprived child who possesses superior cognitive ability is likely to result in either a "dropping out" or only a desire to achieve improved personal life style. The chosen or available means of obtaining a better life style may not be socially desirable. Therefore their truly constructive potential, from the standpoint of society [the State], may be forever lost.

> These thoughts seem to me to be applicable to all societies and especially to those less fortunate than America's. Specifically analyzed they are:

> 1) Identified early enough, poor but gifted children can be given medical, financial and emotional support which probably will lead to the development of positive social attitudes.

> 2) Not identified and assisted the kids may either not achieve their potential or may use their talents solely for the purpose of bettering their own lives regardless of the means employed or the effects on others.

> It is interesting to note the number of proudly proclaimed programs for gifted child identification and development which many of the Socialist and Communist countries have as a stated and de-facto matter of public policy. It is not strange that the capitalist countries, so quick to make use of all other "natural" resources—including the labor of their own and other countries—have been slower to recognize and secure the benefits accruing from the development of their own gifted children.

> Perhaps the wealthy nations have not yet sensed the compelling need for broad social progress, based upon the future contribution of the gifted, as have some of the non-capitalist countries.

In closing, Mr. Lipper makes some recommendations, the most alarming of which follows:

> Establishment of boarding schools (publicly funded) to house those identified gifted children whose existing home life is non-constructive in terms of their development.

[Ed. Note: Mr. Lipper, in his fervent desire to implement world socialism, seems to have forgotten that individuals, regardless of race, religion, talent, or income, should not be considered property of the State (human resources, human capital, etc.) to be molded and manipulated for the benefit of society as a whole (the State). Also, what and whose criteria will be employed to determine whether "home life is non-constructive"?]

"K–12 Competency-Based Education Comes to Pennsylvania" by John H. Sandberg, director of teacher education for Carnegie-Mellon University in Pittsburgh, was published in the October 1979 issue of *Phi Delta Kappan*. Excerpts from the article follow:

It is too late to stop Project '81, which will run its course and probably will soon be forgotten, but one may hope that other states will think hard before embarking on similar projects.... While it is possible that I misunderstood the meaning or intent of this "major goal" ["gain the skills and knowledge they will need as adults"], it strikes me as being unattainable on its face.... I would argue that we cannot "see that students acquire the competencies they need to be successful in the adult world" because we don't know what they are now much less what they will be ten years from now.... Exchanging courses, credits, and Carnegie Units for "newly defined competencies" will not eliminate this fundamental problem....

Finally, in the case of students who are known to be college bound and are locked into a curriculum that is dictated primarily by college requirements (not life-role expectancies), what is going to give? Will physics give way to lawn mower repair? Chemistry to cooking? Trigonometry to tile setting? Will it really make any difference for these students what the state board requires for graduation as long as Harvard wants math through calculus and two years of a foreign language?... I would be happy to settle for a short list of competencies if I thought we could handle them: Teach children how to read, to write, to do arithmetic, to draw, make music, and to get along with each other.

We are not doing these few things for enough kids now, so perhaps this is what we should be working on instead of making new lists of things we won't know how to do.... I applaud the emphasis that Project '81 gives to making better use of educational resources in the community. But as a Blueprint for structuring public education and for measuring its products, the competency-based approach embodied in Project '81 strikes me as totally ridiculous. A true skeptic might argue that Project '81 may be safely ignored on the ground that the Pennsylvania Department of Education is incompetent to chew, much less swallow, what it has attempted to bite off. Like other grandiose efforts to reform the schools, the project may generate some wind and heat and several billion pieces of paper and then go away, leaving all but the 12 pilot school districts untouched.

Nevertheless, the Pennsylvania Department of Education has already demonstrated, with competency-based teacher education, its competence to effect change—or at least the illusion of change—on a large scale. Project '81 is a much more extensive undertaking whose potential for mischief is incalculably greater. The mischief can occur if Pennsylvanians do not take a long, hard look at where Project '81 is taking them.

INFORMATION REGARDING THE PRELIMINARY PLANNING FOR SCHOOL-BASED CLINICS WAS revealed in the October 22, 1979 issue of *Nation's Schools Report* which, under the section "Schools Can Offer Health Services," stated the following:

Schools with concentrations of Medicaid-eligible students can qualify for federal money if they set up screening and referral programs. A joint effort by the Office of Education and the Health Care Financing Administration could make available to schools some of the $46 million that will probably be spent on screening Medicaid children.

Historically, schools have been excluded from such payments, said Robert Heneson-Walling, in the office of deputy commissioner of the Bureau of Education of the Handicapped. But regulations proposed jointly by the two agencies and published in the *Federal Register* October 4 would allow schools to do the screening and even provide treatment and get paid for it.

"It's never been clear that schools might take this initiative," he told *Nation's Schools Report*. To help interested school officials get started, the two departments will publish a manual in November which will cover rules-of-thumb for officials to decide whether to undertake the screening, how to do it, and how to get help from state and local agencies.

"It's not an either/or situation for the school district," said Heneson-Walling. There are seven or eight degrees of involvement a school might undertake. Some schools are already involved in extensive health screening services, because of requirements of the Education for All Handicapped Children Act, so it would be a natural step for them to become primary health delivery centers. (p. 6)

[Ed. Note: The United States model was given wide publicity at the United Nations/UNICEF-sponsored International Year of the Child Conference. The U.S. Department of Health, Education and Welfare served as co-sponsor of the International Year of the Child's program in the United States. For a glimpse into the future role of the schools in providing health care services turn to the 1999 entry for the "Little Red Riding Hood" version of the government/private sector initiatives outlined in the U.S. Department of Education/U.S. Department of Health and Human Services publication *Together We Can*. The 1999 Congressional proposal to completely fund the *Individuals with Disabilities in Education Act* would go a long way toward universalizing these activities. Increased school violence in the late 1990s is also leading to increases in the number of school psychologists who can be used for "early screening."]

"BIG SCHOOL CHANGES PROPOSED" WAS PRINTED IN THE *BANGOR* (ME) *DAILY NEWS* ON November 30, 1979. The article covered what could easily be described as futuristic plans for Vermont public education. It stated in part:

MONTPELIER, VT—A blue ribbon commission has recommended a radical restructuring of education in Vermont with year-round, ungraded schools and a policy of allowing some students to drop out at age 13. In addition, the commission suggested creation of a 4,000-student, residential school for students ages 4 through 19. The state-run school would be a center for educational research and teacher training.... The commission recommends students should be permitted to drop out of formal schooling at age 13, as long as they get a job or enroll in an alternative training program.

[Ed. Note: This extraordinary plan for radical restructuring seemed beyond the pale in 1979. However, it doesn't seem so out of reach in 1999 when most of its recommendations are being introduced nationwide. Year-round school has been proposed in many locales, being adopted in some in 1999. Boarding schools have been openly proposed by former Speaker of the House Newt Gingrich, but have not been widely embraced. However, the concept of allowing students to drop out at age 13 has its parallel in school-to-work efforts which force students to select a career emphasis by the end of eighth grade.]

IN THE NOVEMBER 1979 ISSUE OF *EDUCATIONAL LEADERSHIP*, MONTHLY PUBLICATION OF the Association for Supervision and Curriculum Development, "Mastery Learning: The Current State of the Craft" by James Block was published. Excerpts follow:

Indeed, with the help of dedicated practitioners and administrators, innovative teacher training institutions, progressive national and international educational organizations (ASCD,

NEA, NASA, UNESCO, IEA), leading educational publishers (McGraw-Hill, SRA, Westinghouse Learning Corp., Random House), and powerful news media (*The New York Times*, CBS), Mastery Learning has helped reshape the face of contemporary educational practice, research, and theory.... Entire school districts throughout North America (Chicago, Denver, D.C., New Orleans, Vancouver) are actively testing the value of Mastery Learning for their particular educational situation.

[Ed. Note: The above quote by James Block calls to mind the 1921 entry in this book which chronicles the establishment of the Council on Foreign Relations. In that entry a quotation from *Propaganda* by Edward Bernays, Sigmund Freuds's nephew, also remarks on the power of opinion to move an agenda forward:

It remains a fact in almost every act of our daily lives, whether in the sphere of politics or business, in our social conduct or our ethical thinking, we are dominated by... small number of persons... and technical means have been invented and developed by which opinion may be regimented.]

SUPER-LEARNING BY SHEILA OSTRANDER AND LYNN SCHROEDER, WITH NANCY OSTRANDER, (Dell Publishing Co., Inc.: New York, 1979) was published. Beneath the title on the cover is an explanation of *Super-Learning* as "New stress-free, fast learning methods you can use to develop supermemory and improve business and sports performance." In reality this "learning technique" is an updated version of ancient practices drawn from many religions and a grab-bag of philosophies, most presented to the chosen rhythms of certain music. The following are excerpts from the book:

Georgi Lozanov (Lo-san-ov), a Bulgarian doctor and psychiatrist, who didn't set out to be an educator... did set out, following the old adage, to study the nature of man, of the human being in all its potential. Like just about everybody else, he concluded that we're only using a fraction of our capabilities. Lozanov devised ways to open the reserves of the mind and, as a doctor, put them to work to improve the body, to heal mental and physical disease. But in investigating what the whole human being can do, he couldn't help being drawn into creative and intuitive areas. Then still investigating, almost by necessity, he became one of the leading parapsychologists in the communist world. At the same time, Lozanov realized that with his new techniques, the average person could develop supermemory, could learn factual information with unheard-of-ease. (p. 9)

...Among others, we were going to talk to a Bulgarian scientist, Dr. Georgi Lozanov, who had investigated a number of people with extraordinary mental abilities like Keuni's. Lozanov had come to claim that supermemory was a natural human ability. Not only can anyone develop it, he said, but one can do it with ease. To prove his point there were supposedly thousands of people in Bulgaria and the Soviet Union who were well on their way to acquiring supermemory of their own. (p.14)

...Dr. Lozanov greeted us in his office. Like the brilliant flowers in the garden outside, the room was awash with bright, vivid colors. As we'd already discovered at the conference in Moscow, Lozanov had a "holistic" sense of humor and a "cosmic" laugh like the Maharishi of TM fame. A lithe, compact man with warm brown eyes and a great cloud of curly, graying hair, he could be as kinetic as a handball one minute and deeply serene the next. "Suggestology can revolutionize teaching," he asserted. "Once people get over preconceived ideas about limitations, they can be much more. No longer is a person limited by believing that learning is unpleasant; that what he learns today he will forget tomorrow; that learning deteriorates with age."...

He grew philosophical, "Education is the most important thing in the world. The whole of life is learning—not only in school. I believe that developing this high motivation—which comes through the technique—can be of the greatest importance to humanity."...

"What exactly is the technique of suggestology?" we asked. To create this new "ology," Lozanov and his co-workers had drawn from an almost dizzying array of specialties: mental yoga, music, sleep-learning, physiology, hypnosis, autogenics, parapsychology, drama, to name some. Suggestology's deepest roots lay in the system of Raja Yoga. "There is really nothing new about suggestology," Lozanov explained. "The application is the new thing."...

Lozanov's suggestology is basically "applied" altered states of consciousness for learning, healing, and intuitive development. (p. 17)

[Ed. Note: Lozanov's methodology has been implemented in school systems across the country—including Henry M. Levin's Accelerated Schools Project participants—and promoted as being physically healthful and psychically helpful. Its roots, as pointed out in the quotes above, are in techniques associated with religion and mind control. In the appendix to *Super-Learning* a "Recap" is written, part of which this writer wishes to leave with the reader so that its connection to what is being presented to teachers and parents in 1999 under the guise of "research-based" theory and practice can be more readily understood:

How does it work? A very specific kind of music has a psychophysicial effect and creates a relaxed, meditative state in the body. Physiological research showed this particular music slows body rhythms to more efficient levels. This music-induced relaxation brings health benefits. It overcomes fatigue and enhances physical and emotional well-being. It's a bit like mantra meditation for it is a mind/body link that helps open up inner awareness. Physiological research also shows this calmed state of the body facilitates mental functioning and learning. The body uses *less* energy, so there's *more* for the mind. [emphasis in original] This particular music induces alert relaxation—alert mind, relaxed body.

How can you, at will, retrieve what you perceive? The answer is rhythm. The connection is made through synchronizing rhythms. Data to be learned is chanted with intonations in rhythm in time to the music. The person learning breathes along rhythmically in a relaxed state. So data, intonations, music, breathing, and body rhythms are all synchronized to a specific rhythmic cycle. The rhythm, intonations, music, and breathing make links with the conscious mind. Harmonized rhythms strengthen the information signal. Conscious awareness of unconscious perceptions is opened up through this link so you become aware of what's in your memory bank.

Finally, superlearning is about learning to learn. There is a snowballing effect once you begin to use the techniques. How do you go about doing superlearning on your own? The process is very simple. In advance, get the music, organize your material and tape it, reading it aloud at slow-paced intervals over the specified music.

Then, just relax and listen to your material as you breathe along to the music.

The roots of the above "learning" process grow deep in the mire of the ancient practices that have come to be called "New Age." The reader is urged to remember the rhythmic chants and sing-song recitations being offered as direct instruction "learning." Again, some of the therapeutic benefits from music and what is called "music therapy" are most often observed among the mentally ill and, for a lack of another designation, the learning disabled. The same areas from which most of the "research-based" data—often called "scientific"—draw their reported "success."]

***STEPS TO BETTER WRITING: A SYSTEMATIC APPROACH TO EXPOSITORY WRITING* BY GENE** Stanford (Holt, Rinehart and Winston, Inc.: New York, 1979) was published. An exercise from this book is an example of the humanistic influence exerted in a writing textbook format:

> EXERCISE C. In each of the introductory paragraphs below, underline the thesis sentence. Then indicate in the blank which construction (funnel or contrast) was used. Finally, number the factors in the preview of main supporting points....

> [Sample paragraph] 2. Too often parents think the way to rear a child is to give him guidance in the proper way to think and act. This "guidance" too often becomes an actual molding of his personality to suit the parent, as is seen in parental lectures beginning with the old clichés, "If I were you I would..." or "When I was your age I...." These parents, while they may have the good of the child at heart, are nevertheless making a grave mistake by trying to compel him to act or think in certain ways. What the teen needs instead is a type of love which gives him the freedom and confidence to develop his own opinions in matters such as religion, morality, and choice of friends. (p. 87)

[Ed. Note: The 1991 article entitled "Seniors' Church Attendance" from *Education Week* (June 12, 1991) shows how successful this type of "academic" curriculum has been in changing our children's values.]

Endnotes:

1 T.I.L.L., 67 East Shore Road, Huntington, N.Y. 11743

2 See 1998 entry concerning Newt Gingrich's statements about the future of textbooks. Also, see 1974 entry for *A Performance Accountability System for School Administrators* by T.H. Bell.

3 This quote is taken from Danielson's 67-page booklet, *Practitioner's Implementation Handbook* [Series]: *The Outcome-Based Curriculum, 2nd Ed.*, by Charlotte Danielson (Outcome Associates, Princeton, NJ, 1992). Charlotte Danielson is presently employed by the Educational Testing Service, Princeton, New Jersey.

4 The Maine Facilitator Center was funded by the U.S. Department of Education and its primary role was to disseminate federally funded National Diffusion Network programs. Since 1994 the NDN has been defunded and its functions have been taken over by the U.S. Department of Education's regional laboratories.

5 Excerpt taken from *The Leipzig Connection* mentioned and referenced earlier in this book.

6 *Another View of Philosophy and Culture: Back to Freedom and Dignity* by Francis Schaeffer (Crossway Books: Wheaton, Ill., 1989).

7 This particular "who shall survive" activity is still in use in 1990s NDN programs.

8 *Child Abuse in the Classroom* may be purchased for $10.00 by sending a check to: Eagle Forum, Pere Marquette Press, PO Box 495, Alton, IL 62002

9 The National Diffusion Network catalog, *Programs that Work*, may be purchased for $16.95 by calling Sopris West at 1–303–615–2829.

10 Audiocassette of Lessinger's speech (#612–20129) can be ordered from: ASCD, 1703 North Beauregard St., Alexandria, VA 22311–1714.

11 Sayer, George. *Jack: A Life of C.S. Lewis* (Crossway Books: Wheaton, 1994).

12 Lewis, C.S. "Our English Syllabus" in *Rehabilitations and Other Essays* (Oxford University Press: London, 1939).

13 Ibid.

14 Hooper, Walter, Ed. "Learning in War-Time," in *The Weight of Glory and Other Addresses* (Macmillan Publishing Co., New York, 1980).

15 See Resources page for ordering information for Barbara Morris's *The Great American Con Game.*

THE "EFFECTIVE" EIGHTIES

"**P**roducing a definite or desired *result* [emphasis added]," the first definition for the word "effective" found in *Webster's Dictionary*, is the appropriate definition for the word "effective" as it is used in the title Effective School Research (ESR) or Effective Schools (ES)—which will characterize much of "The Effective Eighties." This is particularly true as it relates to the Skinnerian "method," often referred to as "What Works" education, more commonly known as outcome/performance/results-based education and mastery learning/direct instruction. The evidence which links OBE to ESR is irrefutable: "Outcome-Based Education incorporates the findings of the Effective Schools Research, linking them together into a comprehensive and powerful model," stated Charlotte Danielson, M.A. in her *Practitioner's Implementation Handbook* [Series]: *The Outcome-Based Curriculum*.[1]

Whether Effective Schools Research applied to education has been truly "effective" lies in the eye of the beholder and in the beholder's definition of the purpose of education.[2] Disturbing reports continue to surface regarding steep declines in academic test scores in schools which have restructured using the various components of Effective Schools Research. These scores are from schools which, while using ESR, have not yet shifted from norm-referenced (competitive) tests—which compare students' results amongst their peers and which use "A-B-C-D-F" grading—to performance-based (non-competitive) teach-to-the-test assessments. Examples are the "open book test" and "authentic assessment"—which have the students competing against no one but themselves, giving them as much time as necessary to "master" the competencies.

Once the non-competitive, performance-based assessments are in place, the scores will naturally go up, thus allowing the social change agents to breathe a sigh of relief. The "low test score cat" will have been shoved back into his bag and the media will shout from the rooftops how well our children are doing on the new performance-based assessments! As usual, everyone will go back to sleep believing all is well—if they were ever awake to the problem in the first place.

The pre-non-competitive, performance-based academic test score decline should come as no surprise to the change agents in charge of "effective" schools. The "father" of the Effective Schools Research method, or Skinnerian mastery learning, the late Prof. Benjamin Bloom, said in his 1981 book *All Our Children Learning*: "The purpose of education and the schools is to change the thoughts, feelings and actions of students." An even more astonishing statement was made in *The Effective School Report* by one of the leading change agents, Thomas A. Kelly, Ph.D.: "The brain should be used for processing, not storage." With this educational emphasis, academic test scores could have done nothing *but* decline. If there is anyone reading this book who questions the validity of this writer's claim that America has been "deliberately dumbed down," I urge them to keep these quotes in mind.

Let me pose the following question: How could the writer of this book have written this book had her brain not been used for storage? Could the answer to that question be the reason why the social change agents do not want the brain to be used for storage?

The educationists understand full well what they are doing, since the use of Skinnerian/Pavlovian operant conditioning (mastery learning/direct instruction) does not allow for the transfer of information. All they need is a brain which knows how to *immediately* process predetermined bits and pieces of information—often nothing more than symbols, simple words or paragraphs, the knowledge of which can be easily measured—as those pieces of information relate to workforce training or a menial job; i.e., pushing a button like a pigeon in Skinner's experiments was trained to push the lever to get its kernel of corn.

That is *not* learning; that is *training* to the point of automaticity, brought about by the above-mentioned animal training. Neither is this training the same as rote learning or memorization. Rote learning or memorization requires storage of information in a brain which has used some reflective thinking to devise a method to recall it. Reflective thinking is essential for learning, allowing the brain to spend time examining the essence of the material with which it is presented.

If Bloom's and Kelly's quotes define what those in charge of educational restructuring are looking for in terms of "results," those same educationists should not be at all surprised or concerned about low test scores. All they have to do is wait for the new performance-based assessments to be put into place nationwide; after which the public—some of whom have been vociferously opposed to outcome-based education—will get off their backs.

Activities related to education in "The Effective Eighties" were not geared to improving the academic standing of our children. Quite the contrary; every single major government- or foundation-funded activity had as its goal implementation of a global workforce training agenda.

In 1984 Secretary T.H. Bell approved a grant in the amount of $152,530 to the Far West Laboratory for Educational Research and Development (now known as Ed West) at which William Spady was the director. This grant was to carry out a project entitled "Excellence in Instructional Delivery

Systems." The cover letter from the Utah superintendent of schools to Secretary T.H. Bell to which the application for grant funding was attached said, "This [the research as a result of the grant] will make it possible to put Outcome-Based Education in place, not only in Utah, but in all schools of the nation." The final report (evaluation) to the U.S. Department of Education regarding the results of this project stated:

> The four models of instructional organization outlined in this casebook are difficult programs to implement. The practices of the ten schools described in the case studies are indeed commendable. Yet we do not offer these ten case studies as "exemplary schools" deserving emulation.[3]

So, what did the change agents do? They put OBE "into every school in the nation."

Such misuse of taxpayer dollars is waste, fraud, and abuse which cries out for a Congressional investigation. Obviously, the intentions of those involved in this grant had nothing to do with the purpose of the project spelled out in the grant applicaton: "To make available to America's educators practical information about what really works well, why it works well, and how it can be made to work well in their local sites." (pp. 6–7) The real purpose of this project was to propose a radical redesign of the nation's education system from one based on inputs to one based on outputs; from one oriented toward the learning of academic content to one based on performance of selected skills, necessary for the implementation of school-to-work, a redesign thoroughly discussed in this book.

Dr. Brian Rowan, a sociologist who served as co-principal investigator with the above Robert Burns on this most fraudulent of federal grants—Utah's "Excellence in Instructional Delivery Systems Project"—explained clearly how deceptive are the claims of those who promote OBE and effective school research in a paper entitled "Shamanistic Rituals in Effective Schools." (See Appendix XXVI.) In presenting his paper before the American Educational Research Association prior to his participation in the Utah grant evaluation, Rowan knew full well the project misrepresented itself even before he participated. But, to give credit where credit is due, Rowan at least put in writing the truth about OBE and Effective Schools Research; a truth, which, unfortunately, was made available to only a very small segment of the educational establishment and has remained hidden from the public.

"The Effective Eighties" saw President Ronald Reagan, who had accused the Soviet Union of being an "Evil Empire," signing education agreements with the Soviet Union—agreements which are still in effect—and setting up a Task Force on Private Sector Initiatives in the White House which, in effect, started the ball rolling for public-private partnerships (corporate fascism) which are at the heart of the Carnegie Corporation/Marc Tucker/New American School Development Corporation's school-to-work agenda. It is ironic that the U.S. Department of Education, under the stewardship of a Republican administration, effectively transformed the essential character of the nation's public schools from "teaching"—the most traditional and conservative role of schools—to "workforce training"—perceived as liberal and "progressive."

Secretary T.H. Bell fired Edward Curran, a traditional educator who headed up the National

Institute of Education and who recommended to President Reagan that NIE—the heart of the "rot" in education—be abolished. Abolishing NIE required only that Secretary Bell give his approval, while abolishing the Department of Education—an election promise President Reagan had made which was incorporated into the Republican Party Platform—required the difficult to obtain approval of Congress. Once Ed Curran was gone, there was no further resistance to the plans of those members of the administration and their corporate cronies (school-business partnerships) who wished to transform the nation's schools from academics to the polytech education being implemented today.

As a conservative Republican, it has not been easy to come to the above conclusion regarding the role of the Republican Party in the "deliberate dumbing down" of America. At the same time, I must add that it is very likely the Democratic Party would have been even more steadfast in implementing the same agenda, had it been in a position to do so. This march to destruction seems to join all forces under its banner.

1980

SCHOOLING FOR A GLOBAL AGE EDITED BY JAMES BECKER (MCGRAW HILL: NEW YORK, 1980) was published. The preface by Professor John Goodlad is excerpted here:

> Parents and the general public must be reached also [taught a global perspective]. Otherwise, children and youth enrolled in globally-oriented programs may find themselves in conflict with values assumed in the home. And then the educational institution frequently comes under scrutiny and must pull back.

EDUCATIONAL GOALS: STUDIES AND SURVEYS IN COMPARATIVE EDUCATION WAS PREPARED for the International Bureau of Education, United Nations Educational, Scientific, and Cultural Organization (UNESCO: Courvoisier S.A.: La Chaux-de-Fonds, Switzerland, 1980). Charles Fitouri wrote the following introduction to this document which clearly reflects the influence of UNESCO on education:

> The crisis of education, about which so much has been written since the early 1960s, may be seen as the source of the need for change and innovation which has been felt and expressed since the early seventies. But what kind of innovation? And for what purpose? For what blueprint of society and to train what kind of man? This book on educational goals is based on such questions as these.

The following excerpts from *Educational Goals* identify the roots of American education restructuring:

> The International Bureau of Education's interest in the problem of educational goals and theories does not arise from pure philosophical speculation or a simple academic exercise. It has been aroused, and even imposed, by a confrontation with certain realities which

sprang up in this area when, in the early 1970's, the International Bureau of Education (IBE) set out to examine the process of educational innovation in order to attempt to analyse it and, so to speak, expose its inner mechanism. It was thus that the first studies undertaken made it possible to establish with a great degree of certainty that any innovation in education implies an orientation in the field of values and, by virtue of this fact, involves the basic problem of educational goals....

...All the pedagogical movements of the twentieth century which preach equality of educational opportunity, after having proclaimed it to be a right for everyone, are more or less founded on the various socialist schools of thought which began to emerge at the end of the eighteenth century and have since marked the course of the nineteenth century and a good part of the twentieth....

This interest led to the report of the International Commission on the Development of Education, entitled *Learning to Be*, commonly referred to as the "Faure Report." In his statement introducing this report, the president of the commission was anxious to point out that the latter had based its deliberative efforts on the following four principles:

> The existence of an international community which... is reflected in common aspirations, problems and trends, and in its movement towards one and the same destiny; "belief in democracy"; "the complete fulfillment of man" as the aim of development; and finally, the need for "over-all, life-long education."

In so doing, the International Commission on the Development of Education was in danger of succumbing to the illusion—generous though it may be—of the existence of universal and universally accepted goals. Indeed, although the four principles were unable to win unanimous support from the international community, one of them, at least, did not raise opposition of any sort, even if it happens to be the one which is most commonly violated in practice. Referred to here is the belief in democracy.... The report places special emphasis on this, stating that:

> Strong support must be given to democracy, as the only way for man to avoid becoming enslaved to machines, and the only condition compatible with the dignity which the intellectual achievements of the human race require; the concept of democracy itself must be developed, for it can no longer be limited to a minimum of judicial guarantees protecting citizens from the arbitrary exercise of power in a subsistence society. Furthermore, and in conjunction with this, more support must also be given to educational requirements, for there cannot—or will not—be a democratic and egalitarian relationship between classes divided by excessive inequality in education; and the aim and content of education must be re-created, to allow both for the new features of society and the new features of democracy.

...This world solidarity has its prerequisites and conditions which have been described by UNESCO in the following terms:

> [T]here must first of all be agreement on a system of values and a willingness to embark on a joint examination of their implications: values of justice, equality, freedom and fellowship. These will be based on a new awareness in two respects, namely: recognition of the unity of mankind, with all its diverse peoples, races and cultures, and the assertion of a desire to live together, actually experienced not simply as a necessity for survival or coexistence but as the deliberate choice of fashioning a common destiny together, with joint responsibility for the future of the human race.
>
> In such circumstances, the consciousness of the world's solidarity, which is so much needed, can only be the fruit of an active and continuous process of education, which must be put in hand without delay and to which UNESCO must make its full contribution.

...The participants, having agreed to develop and stimulate reflection on educational goals, considered that:

1. UNESCO should give particular attention to the developments at regional and international levels, of comparative studies on educational goals, from the point of view both of their influence on the development of educational theories (historical dimension) and of their impact on educational realities (sociological dimension);
2. multidisciplinary teams, comprising philosophers, historians, teachers, sociologists, economists, psychologists, planners, etc., should be involved in this work of reflection and research;
3. the themes listed below should be regarded as priority themes:

> 3.1 Determination of the goals underlying education for international understanding and peace.
> 3.2 UNESCO's contribution to the formulation and development of an international dimension of education based on a certain conception of modern man.
> 3.3 Implicit goals and explicit goals of education.
> 3.4 Role of goals in the emergence of a new type of relationship between school and society.
> 3.5 Formal education and non-formal education as they relate to the explicit goals and implicit goals of education.
> 3.6 Elucidation of a dialectic of educational goals and cultural and educational policy: philosophy of education and ideology.
> 3.7 Ways of determining educational goals in certain contexts where there is a clash between tradition and innovation.
> 3.8 Elucidation of educational goals on the basis of the child's real needs taking account of the economic, social and cultural environment.

"POLICY ABOUT POLICY: SOME THOUGHTS AND PROJECTIONS" BY LUVERN L. CUNNINGHAM was published in the November 1980 issue of *The Executive Review* (Institute for School Executives: The University of Iowa, Vol. 1., No. 2). A footnote on page 1 stated, "The paper was the Walter D. Cocking Lecture presented at the 34th Annual National Convention of Professors of Educational Administration in August, 1980, at Old Dominion University." Some excerpts from Cunningham's "Policy about Policy" follow:

> Local school officials and their constituencies will be facing several critical policy matters in this decade (some new, some enduring). These issues will test severely the structures and processes of policy making within local districts.... Local and state authorities will soon have to develop fresh policies in regard to: the first four years of life; life-long learning; secondary education; equity; classroom control and discipline; global education; languages; human resource development; incentives; testing; and resource acquisition and allocation. I would hope, therefore, that a good many boards would develop policy about policy....
>
> The object of my concern is the improvement of practice within the local units of government (local school districts) where educational policy is developed....
>
> The structure and processes of local district governance and management have changed little over the past century. In many places they appear to be creaking and groaning at the seams and at least warrant inspection if not reform....
>
> Additional steps must be taken to permit better integration of experts into policymaking.... The new professions of civil strategist and systems analyst demonstrate rather well what I have in mind on a broader scale.

The several proposals for changing the governance and management of local school districts which follow are intended to achieve practical objectives.

(1) Pursue policy development processes which are open to, indeed, require the participation of citizens and professionals.

(2) Extend and intensify the citizen role in education policy development and policy making.

[Ed. Note: The writer has selected the two proposals above in order to emphasize Dr. Cunningham's influence on the dilution and diminution of the role of elected school board members. This is the philosophy which Dr. Cunningham took into Kentucky when he served as a consultant during that state's education reform.

Implementation of the above two policies has been responsible for a subtle, gradual, and unhealthy trend towards the council form of government found in undemocratic, socialist countries. Before we know it, if Americans do not vociferously object to this gradual erosion of the elective process, their towns and cities will be run by unelected citizens who are accountable to absolutely no one, since unelected people cannot be removed from (voted out of) office. This writer has always wondered: If members of our communities want so much to serve the community, why don't they run for office? Why do we see so many people signing up to be members of unelected task forces and councils? Is it because they don't want to run the risk of not winning, or is it that an appointed position is one which requires little or no accountability and they won't have to answer for their mistakes?]

Cunningham continues:

Periodically, in the history of American education leaders have suggested that boards of education have become anachronisms, have fulfilled their mission, should be reformed, or quietly fade away. There was a period at the turn of the century when the notion of abolishing school boards attracted support from the then-emerging professions of educational administration joined by elites from the business and higher education communities. The theme was revised and revitalized in the late 1920's, principally by Charles Judd, then chairman of the Department of Education at the University of Chicago....

These proposed changes are based essentially on the recognition that the complexity of today's public institutions is such that they are often not governable or manageable within present approaches to their governance and management and are likely to be less so in the future.... My proposals therefore retain the principles of local control and policy determination by citizens but change the conditions under which policy is determined and administration is performed.... It is expected that the present pattern of school board behavior and ideology be altered in favor of practices which will allow sounder, more rationally determined school district policy.

The following proposals are amongst those included under "Synopsis of the Policy about Policy Proposals":

(1) That local boards of education develop discrete and definitive policy about policy, some of which are implied by the subsequent proposals for change in the governance and management of local school districts.

(2) That educational policy become the primary and continuing policy focus of local school officials as distinct from personnel, business, and physical facilities....

(4) That policy making agenda be prepared two to three years in advance to frame the

work of the board, administrative staff, professional organization leaders, student leaders, and citizen groups....

(7) That employee salary and wage determination prerogative now retained by boards of education of local school districts be moved to the state level.

(8) That representatives of professional groups (teachers and administrators organizations) for local school districts become members of the local boards of education and assume policy and accountability responsibilities equivalent to that office....

(11) That one or more states pass special legislation allowing school districts to suspend (for a period of time) current statutes, rules and regulations for their governance and management; and

(12) That processes of policy development and their enunciation as well as the processes of management be designed to include genuine, sustained student, parent, citizen, and professional educator involvement.

Yehezkel Dror suggests that for purposes of current policy making, the following elements should be standard features of a preferable policy-making method:

(1) There should be some clarification of values, objectives, and criteria for decision making....

(2) Explicit techniques, such as simulation and the Delphi method, should be used as far as they are appropriate, and knowledge from various disciplines should be brought to bear on the issues involved....

The weight of proposal one is not to locate ways to reduce the interference or meddling on the part of school board members in the everyday administration of the school system. The everyday meddling (or involvement if you prefer) of school board members in administrative matters that occurs across the country is understandable. In fact, board members believe deeply that they are serving their constituents when they interfere and meddle. Administrators often have little understanding of or patience for this sense of responsiveness that board members possess. As a consequence considerable institutional energy goes into disputes over the boundaries of board member and superintendent authority and responsibility.

Thus proposal one is based on the premise that both policy and administrative activity can be more efficient and effective if there is a substantial alteration in the ground rules for those activities....

There are constitutional, statutory, and other legal problems associated with the proposals. If taken seriously they may lead to rather general re-examination of the constitutional and statutory provisions for the governance and management of local districts. For example, many current school board responsibilities may need to be managed in other ways. Determining salaries and wages of school personnel, constructing (even naming) school buildings, authorizing the issuance of bonds, setting school tax elections or referenda of other sorts, the approval of federal applications for funding, and other such decisions may be designated as responsibilities of other governments.

The removal of the collective bargaining function from local districts and placing it at the state level would clear out underbrush and permit boards of education and top school officials to focus more directly upon pedagogical and learning policy.

The work of Dr. Cunningham seems to have laid the groundwork for school site-based management which has reduced the role of elected school board members to rubber stampers of decisions made primarily by school personnel and carefully selected politically correct members of the community. Dr. Cunningham served as a consultant to the State of Kentucky's

Education Reform Commission in 1989. The following quotes are taken from a memorandum dated November 2, 1989 from Luvern L. Cunningham and Lila N. Carol of Leadership Development Associates regarding *Preliminary Models of Governance for Kentucky*. The recommendations should come as no surprise to those who have read the above excerpts from Cunningham's 1980 paper.

> Each governance model is designed to facilitate the achievement of equal educational opportunity for every learner enrolled in the public schools of the State of Kentucky.
> Model One, "Total Educational Governance System for Lifetime Learning, Structural Features and Highlights"—
> Policymaking responsibility for a total educational system including higher education is concentrated in a single Board of Regents. A Chancellor would be selected as the administrative head of a newly integrated system encompassing provisions for lifetime learning. Local school districts would be dissolved and site-based control and management instituted.
> This model is a complete system of governance for a state system of education.... It is comprehensive and all inclusive, allowing for a thorough approach to accountability.
> The governance structure is designed to meet each individual's lifetime public learning needs beginning with the early years of life through the retirement period. Persons would be expected to continue a lifetime of learning consistent with the requirements of the 21st century, as portrayed so clearly in business and industry sponsored studies as well as those produced through citizens groups and public sponsorship. Lifetime educational counseling and lifetime curriculum development would be challenging new responsibilities of the integrated system.
> This bureau is the central administrative center for lifetime learning. Lifetime learning is a much larger expectation for each citizen than we have acknowledged through policy in the past. Compulsory education statutes usually bracketed the ages of five through sixteen as our expectation for free public schooling in the United States. Lifetime learning on the other hand suggests a reconsideration of the compulsory education requirements pushing taxpayer responsibility both downward and upward through the age ranges. Obviously lifetime learning has tremendous implications for educational finance moving away from traditional concepts of funding toward new ideas such as individual entitlements to be expended throughout the lifetime. Each citizen would have a lifetime learning account to draw on as needed.

[Ed. Note: For a broad view of what this last paragraph could imply, please see "When Is Assessment Really Assessment?" in Appendix XI. Many of Luvern Cunningham's proposals were incorporated into Georgia's application to the New American School Development Corporation entitled "The Next Generation School Project." In the 1999 entry dealing with a letter to the editor in Athens, Georgia, some of the details of Georgia's application—which later became a design which was offered by the Georgia 2000 Partnership for school system status leading to grant receiving and education/business partnering under *Goals 2000*—are stated. The reader should compare that letter's contents to Cunningham's proposals.]

COURSE GOALS COLLECTION WAS COMPLETED IN 1980–81 BY THE U.S. DEPARTMENT OF Education's Northwest Regional Educational Laboratory in Portland, Oregon, having been initiated in 1971 as the Tri-County Course Goal Project. According to the price list for the collection, 70,000 copies were in use throughout the United States in 1981. Descriptors within the *Collection* state: "The collection consists of fourteen volumes with 15,000 goals covering every major subject taught in the public schools from K–12."

Course Goals Collection, based on "the theoretical work of Bloom, Tyler, Gagne, Piaget, Krathwohl, Walbesser, Mager, and others," blatantly recommends the use of Mastery Learning when it states: "The K–12 Goals Collection provides a resource for developing diagnostic-prescriptive Mastery Learning approaches, both programmed and teacher managed."

This collection also advocates the use of Management by Objectives and Planning, Programming and Budgeting Systems when it asserts:

> Perhaps the greatest need addressed by the project is for a sound basis for accountability in education... assistance such as Planning, Program, Budget and Management systems or even general concepts such as Management by Objectives.

The use of values clarification and behavior modification is also encouraged when the *Goals Collection* points out that:

> Value goals of two types are included: those related to processes of values clarification; secondly, those representing values, choices that might be fostered in the context of the discipline.

Goals states under "Content" that there is to be *none* because

> [E]stablished facts change, causing many fact-bound curricula to become obsolete during the approximately five-year lag between their inception and their widespread dissemination, and social mobility and cultural pluralism make it increasingly difficult to identify the important facts.

The *Course Goals Collection* is evidence of illegal federal involvement in curriculum development. The extent of its use nationwide in 1981 is obvious since 70,000 copies were distributed and there were only approximately 16,000 school districts in the nation. Is it any wonder all states now have the same goals?

Charlotte Danielson, M.A., in the appendix to her *Practitioners Implementation Handbook* [series]*: The Outcome-Based Curriculum, 2nd Ed.* (Outcomes Associates; Princeton, N.J., 1992) entitled, "Classification System for the School Curriculum" acknowledged her use of the *Course Goals Collection* developed by the Tri-County Development Project. In the "Introduction to Outcome-Based Education" to Danielson's *Handbook* she inextricably connects Outcome-Based Education to Effective Schools Research when she says:

> Outcome-Based Education is a system for the organization and delivery of the instructional program in elementary and secondary schools which *assures success for every student* [emphasis in original]. It incorporates the findings of the Effective Schools Research, linking them together into a comprehensive and powerful model. Educators in outcome-based schools know that if they organize their schools properly, and offer high-quality instruction, all students will succeed with no change in standards. (p. 1)

[Ed. Note: Probably the most important quote involving the above Goals Project—at least as it relates to the definition of scientific, research-based instruction—is one found in Indiana Senator Joan Gubbins's excellent report entitled "Goals and Objectives: Towards a National Curriculum?" prepared for the National Council on Educational Research, September 26, 1986 as part of an investigation of the NWREL Goals Project. On page 16 of her report is the following statement:

I believe the personal valuing goals (included in the Goals Project) would be more properly classified as behavior modification procedures. Therefore, the Project's definition of behavior modification is illuminating:

> [P]rocedures used in programs of behavior modification or behavioral management are based on principles derived from scientific research (e.g., stimulus-response-reinforcement).

Americans supporting the use of mastery learning, outcome-based education, and direct instruction to teach reading, take heed! When advised that such instruction is "scientific, research-based," remember the above U.S. Department of Education definition!]

1981

"A BROAD-GAUGED RESEARCH/REFORM PLAN FOR SECONDARY EDUCATION—IN THE TRADI-tion of the Eight-Year Study," proposed by The Project on Alternatives in Education (PAE) in 1981, was submitted for consideration and received funding from the U.S. Department of Education and the National Education Association. The project was conducted by leading American change agents, including Mario D. Fantini, John Goodlad, Ralph Tyler, Ronald S. Brandt, Herbert J. Walberg and Mary Ann Raywid. Explanatory cover sheet of the grant proposal was submitted on "The John Dewey Society" letterhead. PAE called for publicly funded choice schools using "effective school [outcome-based education] research" and principles of the Eight-Year Study. These called for "inculcation of social attitudes, development of effective methods of thinking, social sensitivity, better personal-social adjustment, acquisition of important information, consistent philosophy of life," etc.

IN 1981 *OFFICE OF EDUCATIONAL RESEARCH AND IMPROVEMENT: AN OVERVIEW* WAS PRE-pared by staff members of the U.S. Department of Education for Assistant Secretary Donald Senese's use at Congressional budget hearings. Excerpts from the paper follow:

> Federal funds account for approximately 10 percent of national expenditures on education. The Federal share of educational research and related activities, however, is 90 percent of the total national investment.

The Committee on Coordinating Educational Information and Research (CCEIR), Council of Chief State School Officers (CCSSO), in its 1980 Mission Statement defined "research" as:

> For purposes of brevity, the term "educational information and research" will be used to include basic and applied research, development, improvement, evaluation, policy study, information systems development, data reporting and analysis, and the dissemination of knowledge and information gained from such inquiry.

[Ed. Note: In other words, just about everything that goes on in the classrooms of American public schools, with the exception of salaries, school buildings, buses and the purchase of equipment, is either a direct or indirect result of funding by the U.S. Department of Education—as research!

Congress has recognized the federal government's supposed limited authority in education. In 1970 ESEA: *General Education Provisions Act* was amended to include a "Prohibition against Federal Control of Education." This section prohibits the federal government from exercising any "direction, supervision, or control over the curriculum, program of instruction, administration or personnel of any education institution, school, or school system, or over the selection of library resources, textbooks, or other printed or published instructional materials by any educational institution or school system." The *Education Amendments of 1976* extended this provision to all programs in the Education Division of the U.S. Department of Health, Education and Welfare.

Although such a prohibition sounds like a restriction against federal control, in effect it leaves out more than it includes; the most important component of federal control being "research" and "development." Who cares whether the federal government is not allowed to extend its long arm down into the choice of curriculum or the selection of resources? The point is that the federal government itself was involved in the development of that curriculum or those resources, teacher training, test development, etc., at one of its research labs or centers, or paid to have it developed by school systems across the nation.]

Association for Educational Computing and Technology (AECT—a spin-off of the National Education Association) received an $855,282 federal contract for "Project BEST" (Better Education Skills through Technology) in 1981. An explanatory brochure states:

WHAT IS PROJECT BEST? Project BEST is a cooperative effort involving both the federal, state, and local government and the private sector in the planning and use of modern information technologies to improve the effectiveness of basic skills, teaching and learning.

On a sheet circulated within the U.S. Department of Education as an internal document entitled "Project BEST Dissemination Design Considerations," there appeared the following information:

PROJECT DESIGN FEATURES

What We Can Control or Manipulate? = State participation/selection process
Role of advisors
Content of program
Training of state leaders
Resource people utilized
Basic skills content areas emphasized
Perception of need to use technology

BEST's promotional flyer blatantly discussed how the project would serve not just in education, but for other program areas as well, to implement the national/international management system (MBO, PPBS, TQM):

In addition, the State Team approach and the communications network with professional associations and other groups established by the project will serve as a model for the states in implementing similar efforts in other areas of education, or in such program areas as health, human services, housing, transportation, etc.

William Spady, at that time serving as executive director of the Association of School Administrators, and Dr. Shirley McCune, serving as head of the State Services Division, Denver, Colorado, were listed as members of the advisory board for Project BEST.

[Ed. Note: Project BEST was used as a vehicle to assist in "State Capacity Building"—a process to better enable school oficials, administrators, legislators and others to provide supportive documentation and "research" for school reform efforts. State Capacity Building grants have been funded by the U.S. Department of Education and are usually matched with state budget funding.]

ALL OUR CHILDREN LEARNING BY PROFESSOR BENJAMIN BLOOM (MCGRAW HILL PUBLISHing Co.: New York, N.Y., 1981) was published. Excerpts follow:

> In an attempt to maximize curriculum effectiveness... curriculum centers throughout the world have begun to incorporate learning-for-mastery instructional strategies into the redesign of curriculum. (p. 123)

According to Bloom:

> [T]he International Association for the Evaluation of Educational Achievement (IAEEA) is an organization of 22 national research centers which are engaged in the study of education.... This group has been concerned with the use of international tests, questionnaires, and other methods to relate student achievement and attitudes to instruction, social and economic factors in each nation. The evaluation instruments also represent an international consensus on the knowledge and objectives most worth learning. (pp. 33–35)

Another extremely important statement by Bloom in *All Our Children Learning* is found on page 180: "The purpose of education and the schools is to change the thoughts, feelings and actions of students."

HUMAN INTELLIGENCE INTERNATIONAL NEWSLETTER IN ITS MARCH/APRIL 1981 ISSUE REported that critical thinking skills research was taking place within the United Nations Educational, Scientific and Cultural Organization (UNESCO), the Office of Economic Cooperation and Development (OECD), and the World Bank which planned on "increasing the bank's international education and training budget to about $900 million a year."[4] The newsletter related that the U.S. Department of Education's National Institute of Education "has awarded a three-year contract totaling approximately $780,000 to Bolt, Beranek and Newman, Inc., of Cambridge, Massachusetts to analyze current programs of instruction on cognitive skills." The July/August issue of the newsletter contained the following:

> The search for new referential systems and new values modifying existing beliefs should be based on modern microbiology. A scientific approach should be free from doctrinal bias, and its findings applicable to all man-kind. Ideological confrontations between East and West, Marxism and Liberalism, Arabs and Jews do have economic, historical, and political bases, but no biological basis. These antagonisms have been created by the human brain and could be solved by the wiser brains of future man.

[Ed. Note: It should be noted that Marilyn Jager Adams—deeply involved in "scientific, research-based phonics instruction" through her service on the Committee on the Prevention of Reading Difficulties in Young Children for the Commission on Behavioral and Social Sciences and Education of the National Research Council—has been a long time associate with the above-mentioned Bolt, Beranek and Newman.]

THE APRIL/MAY 1981 ISSUE OF *TODAY'S EDUCATION*, THE NATIONAL EDUCATION Association's monthly journal, carried an article entitled "Effective Schools: What the Research Says" by Michael Cohen, senior associate and team leader of the Research on Instruction Team of the National Institute of Education, U.S. Department of Education. Some excerpts from the article follow:

> According to Ronald Edmonds of the Harvard University Graduate School of Education, these [effective school] studies suggest that differences in effectiveness among schools can be accounted for by the following five factors:
>
> - Strong administrative leadership by the school principal, especially in regard to instructional matters.
> - School climate conducive to learning [i.e., positive, or "psychologically facilitative," school climate, ed.]; that is, a safe and orderly school relatively free of discipline and vandalism problems.
> - Schoolwide emphasis on basic skills instruction (which entails acceptance among the professional staff that instruction in the basic skills is the primary goal of the school).
> - Teacher expectations that all students, regardless of family background, can reach appropriate levels of achievement.
> - A system for monitoring and assessing pupil performance which is tied to instructional objectives....
>
> ...[T]he five factors identified as contributing to school effectiveness suggest the classical model of a bureaucratic organization: a goal-oriented organization with a hierarchical authority structure and a central manager who monitors behavior and deliberately adjusts organizational performance on the basis of clear and agreed-upon goals and of feedback regarding goal attainment....
>
> The principal must be willing to clearly set the direction for the school and to hold the staff accountable for following that direction. The staff, in turn, must be willing to view the principal's direction even if it involves giving up some claims to their own autonomy.

[Ed. Note: The reader should keep in mind that Effective School Research has been used over the past twenty years in inner city schools and schools located in the South; that its track record, if judged by academic test scores, leaves *much* to be desired. In fact, Washington, D.C. and Secretary Riley's home state of South Carolina—both of which have used Effective School Research—had the lowest academic test scores in the nation, to be followed by many inner city schools, especially those in the southern part of the nation. In this regard, the reader should re-read the 1913 entry containing quotes from Frederick T. Gates, director of charity for the Rockefeller Foundation.]

IN A 1981 ALASKA GOVERNOR'S TASK FORCE REPORT ON EFFECTIVE SCHOOLING TO THE Honorable Jay S. Hammond the following statements were made in regard to mastery learning and direct instruction (highly structured learning activities):

> It has been determined that in the learning of specific skills and factual data that it is possible to enhance achievement by using the approach of mastery learning, wherein instructional objectives are clearly defined—and instructional activities are tied directly to objectives. It has been demonstrated that direct instruction—highly structured learning activity—is effective with certain groups of students. These approaches will assist students with low achievement to move closer to the current mean or average. Yet, a highly structured system of instruction applied to everyone may in fact impede the progress of those students achieving at a level above the current mean or average. The result is that, while variance (or the spread of scores from the mean) is reduced, there is a reduction in both directions. Low achievers may move closer to the mean, but high achievers may well do likewise. The examples presented above regarding achievement may well apply to the operation of schools. If effective schooling practices are too narrow and a rigid system results, variance among districts will be reduced, but the limiting of creativity and the limiting of schools in their ability to adapt to local circumstances will cause reduction in variance from both above and below the mean or average. (pp. 38–39)

[Ed. Note: The introduction to this report which stated: "As part of the Task Force effort several studies were conducted by Northwest Regional Educational Laboratory under contract with the (Alaska) Department of Education," should explain to the reader that the U.S. Department of Education has funded—and continues to fund—mastery learning and direct instruction programs even in the face of evaluative evidence that strongly suggests that average and above average students do not benefit from such educational approaches.]

TWO IMPORTANT CONFERENCES FOR "SCHOOL IMPROVEMENT" WERE SPONSORED BY THE NORTHwest Regional Educational Laboratory (U.S. Department of Education) in 1981. They are described below:

> MEETING THE FUTURE: Improving Secondary Schools with Goal-Based Approaches to Instruction. Marriott Hotel, Portland, Oregon. Major addresses: "Alternative Futures for Our Society and Implications for Education" by Dr. Harold Pluimer, Futurist and Educational Consultant, Minneapolis, Minnesota and "School Effectiveness and Implications for Secondary School Improvement" by Dr. Alan Cohen, Professor of Education, University of San Francisco.

> Sessions on Innovative Practices: "Improving Goals, Objectives and Competencies; Making the Community a Resource for Learning" ; "Learning through Mastery Techniques; Organizing for Continuous Progress"; "Involving Teachers as Advisors to Students"; "Individualizing Programs for All Students"; "Managing Instruction with Computers"; "Developing Options for Student Assessment"; "Improving Record Keeping and Reporting Procedures"; "Increasing Staff Motivation through Group Planning and Decision-Making"; "Techniques for Managing School Improvement"; "Concerns-Based Adoption Model"; "Force Field Analysis"; "Curriculum Alignment Processes"; "Staff Development Models," and "Wisconsin R&D Center Model for School Improvement."

MICROCOMPUTERS IN TODAY'S SCHOOLS: A Conference for Educational Leaders. Benson Hotel and NWREL Headquarters, Portland, Oregon. Major addresses: "Why We Went for Micros and What Our Community Had to Say about It" by Dr. Billy Reagan, Superintendent, Houston, Texas Public Schools; "Tomorrow's Technology in Today's Schools" by Dr. Dexter Fletcher, World Institute for Computer-Assisted Teaching, and others.

THE NATIONAL EDUCATION ASSOCIATION PUBLISHED *NEA SPECIAL COMMITTEE ON INSTRUC-*
tional Technology Report which was presented to their 60th Representative Assembly, held July 4–7, 1981. An excerpt from the report related to the problems of programmed learning (computer-assisted instruction) follows:

> In its coming involvement with a technology of instruction, the profession will be faced again with the challenge of leadership—by example and by effective communication—the challenge of convincing the public that education is much more than treating students like so many Pavlovian dogs, to be conditioned and programmed into docile acceptance of a do-it-yourself blueprint of the Good Life.
>
> The problems associated with technology, in its final analysis, are problems of freedom and control. Whose freedom? Whose control? As a result of its study, the committee urges the Association to view the problems and promises of instructional technology not as a single issue but rather as a broad continuum of issues affecting all aspects of education and teaching—from purposes to products, from political pragmatism to professional practice. Most problems produced by technology have to do with the human use of human beings. In his book, *The Illusion of Technique: A Search for Meaning in a Technological Civilization* (Doubleday: New York, 1978), William Barrette observes that—
>
>> Human creativity exceeds the mechanisms it invents, and is required even for their intelligent direction.... If we try to flee from our human condition into the computer we only meet ourselves there.

"FAMILIES AND SCHOOLS: A SYSTEM OF MUTUAL SUPPORT," A SPEECH DELIVERED IN 1981 by Secretary of Education T.H. Bell before a Freeman Institute audience in Utah, included Bell's recommendation that schools should use Professor Lawrence Kohlberg's "Ethical Issues in Decision Making" to teach values. (A synopsis of Kohlberg's Stages of Moral Development is contained in a 1975 entry on the topic.)

IN 1981 MAINE'S STATE CAPACITY BUILDING GRANT FROM THE NATIONAL INSTITUTE OF Education (NIE), U.S. Department of Education, was examined and verbatim notes taken by this writer from the file at NIE. The same Capacity Building Grants were made to all fifty state departments of education. The writer has selected this important grant as an example of federal control of local education through federal funding. The following verbatim notes will help the reader understand the farce of local control and why the U.S. Department of Education must be abolished.

This particular grant was of extreme interest to the writer due to her involvement in the late seventies—along with Bettina Dobbs, the president of Guardians of Education for Maine

(GEM)—in a statewide, grassroots effort to stop the very controversial State Health Education Program (SHEP) funded in part by the Kellogg Foundation. Believe it or not, as a word of encouragement, GEM was instrumental in stopping this education program in many school districts (a good example of David and Goliath in the twentieth century). Evidently, the above-referenced NIE grant was used to further the implementation of this and other health education programs. Other states would use these grants for whatever programs they perceived to be of importance to them at that time. State budget requests for matching funds would be listed simply as "State Capacity Building."

NIE Grant G–80–0025 was in the amount of $98,000 per year for four years. Maine's share towards total federal funding was to be $118,025 out of the four-year total of $392,000. Excerpts from the grant request follow:

> These systems will emphasize staff development as primary vehicle for promoting utilization of state and national information resources for purpose of school improvement....

> Brief description of Project: This project is attempting to develop a means by which Maine educators can easily acquire and use information for problem solving and school improvement....

> OBJECTIVES:
> 1. Develop computerized information resource base which includes national, state and local resources.
> 2. Develop an information service that provides easy access to the information resource base.
> 3. Refinement of computer program and initiation of revision of data collection forms (upon recommendation of a Technical Assistance Team from the National Institute of Education).
> 4. Develop a system for coordinating, disseminating, and distributing school improvement efforts with the state education agency....

> 1/30/80... D_____ wanted to know about a technical assistance team at NIE that works with projected content of private data banks.... Believe B_____ heads such a team and could help her with her file building activities....

> DEVELOPMENT OF MAINE DATA BASE:
> Administration, coordination and facilitation of Development of a Statewide School Practice/Improvement System.... A meeting was held with the Systems Analyst of the State Education Agency to explore private file development options available through the state government computer.... Model for staff development.... Training of State Health Education Program (SHEP) staff in completing and editing data collection forms.... SHEP will receive printouts for all health education resources entered into Maine Resource Bank.

EARLY IN 1981 THE PRESIDENT'S TASK FORCE ON PRIVATE SECTOR INITIATIVES WAS INstalled at 734 Jackson Place, N.W., Washington, D.C. Membership listed on The White House letterhead read like a "Who's Who" of individuals in government agencies, universities, tax-exempt foundations, non-governmental organizations, business, media, labor unions, and religion. The names of some individuals on the task force follow: William Aramony, president, United Way; William J. Baroody, Jr., president, American Enterprise Institute; Helen G. Boosalis, mayor, City of Lincoln, Nebraska; Terence Cardinal Cooke, archbishop of New York; Governor Pierre S. Dupont, Delaware; Senator David Durenberger; Luis A. Ferre, former governor of Puerto Rico; John Gardner, chairman, Independent Sector; Edward Hill, pastor, Mt. Zion Baptist Church; Michael S. Joyce, executive director, John M. Olin Foundation; Edward H. Kiernan, president, International Association of Police; Arthur Levitt, Jr., chairman, American Stock Exchange; Richard W. Lyman, president, Rockefeller Foundation; Elder Thomas S. Monson, The Mormon Church; William C. Norris, chairman and CEO, Control Data Corporation; George Romney, chairman, National Center for Citizen Involvement; C. William Verity, Jr., chairman, Armco Steel, Inc.; Jeri J. Winger, first vice president, General Federation of Women's Clubs; Thomas H. Wyman, president, CBS, Inc.; and William S. White, president, C.S. Mott Foundation.[5]

This totally new and un-American concept of partnerships between public and private sector has been readily accepted by our elected officials who ignore its roots in socialism and its implications for the discontinuation of our representative form of government and accountability to the taxpayers. Under the "partnership" process, determining responsibility when something goes wrong is like pinning jello to the wall.

Such a change in government, if presented in clear language to citizens at the polls, would be rejected. However, when implemented gradually, using the Marxist-Hegelian Dialectic, citizens don't even notice what is happening. The shift is away from elected representatives. In time, after voters have become even more disenchanted with the candidates and election results, fewer and fewer citizens will vote. At that point a highly-respected member of the public will enter the picture to propose a solution to the problem: some sort of compromise toward parliamentary form of government found in socialist democracies which will be acceptable to Americans unfamiliar with the protections guaranteed by the *U.S. Constitution*.

One says to oneself, confidently, "This will never happen." Look around you. What do you see? Site-based management in your local schools, transferring decision-making, traditionally exercised by elected school boards, to politically correct appointees and the creation of unelected task forces at all government levels; proposals to "separate school and state" which make no mention of governmental and social structure consequences—efforts to have government money (taxes) pay for services delivered by private religious or homeschools, etc., with no public representation. There can be no accountability to the taxpayers under a system so alien to the United States' form of representative government.

How clean, neat and tidy. Wholesale destruction of an entire, wonderful system of government without firing a shot.

As a U.S. Department of Education liaison with The White House during the early days of this initiative this writer inquired of one of President Reagan's political appointees whether this initiative, was not corporate fascism; a politically incorrect question that resulted in someone else replacing me as Liaison with The White House.

A VERY IMPORTANT NATIONAL ASSESSMENT OF EDUCATIONAL PROGRESS (NAEP) REPORT, in galley stage, entitled *Measuring the Quality of Education: Conclusions and Summary*, was provided to this writer in 1981, shedding light not only on the responsibility of major tax-exempt foundations in the development of a national curriculum, but also on the role of the federal government in setting standards/goals for American education. Excerpts follow from

(1) a cover letter signed by Willard Wirtz, former secretary of labor, and Archie Lapointe, executive director of the NAEP, and (2) the report itself:

(1)

In a different sense, this report is designed to meet the responsibilities imposed at least implicitly by the three foundations which initiated and have supported the project; the Carnegie Corporation, the Ford Foundation, and the Spencer Foundation have become critical and constructive forces in American education.

(2)

Conclusions... Instead of determining "what is being taught" and basing the objectives on this present practice, the controlling question is "what ought to be taught."... It is specifically recommended that caution be exercised against putting the Assessment results in a form that could be misconstrued as constituting national—or "federal"—standards....

Summary... The report reflects most significantly the carefully considered conclusions of the Council of Seven which was established at the beginning of the project. Selected primarily for their recognized responsibility and good sense, they also reflect a variety of experiences and institutional interests: Gregory Anrig, then Massachusetts Commissioner of Education and now President of the Educational Testing Service; Stephen K. Bailey, who is the Francis Keppel Professor of Educational Policy and Administration of Harvard Graduate School of Education; Charles Bowen, Director of Plans and Program Administration for University Relations of the IBM Corporation; Clare Burstall, Deputy Director of the National Foundation for Educational Research in England and Wales; Elton Jolly, Executive Director for Opportunities Industrialization Centers; Lauren Resnick, Co-Director of the Learning Research and Development Center of the University of Pittsburgh; and Dorothy Shields, Director of Education for the AFL-CIO....

...It was the Council's suggestion and eventually its decision to shape the entire report in terms of the Assessment's potential role in developing higher and more effective educational standards. Where we had been timid about this the Council moved boldly. They were right....

...Measuring student achievement is an entirely different business from measuring other aspects of the national condition.... They get to their answers without having to make value judgments. Not so of the measurers of "educational achievement." The key term isn't defined except as they develop its meaning. The rest of this is that once that definition is worked out, the measuring process depends at critical points on what are in significant part value judgments. Whether an educational standard is "better" or "higher" depends on how it consists with ultimate educational purposes...

...Those in charge of the Assessment are in a position to guide their policies entirely by a determination of whatever "quality" means. They face no competition and are subject to no political pressures. Innovation and experimentation are part of the Assessment's authentic tradition. It can provide not only competence but conscience and courage in the implementation of the new national purpose to improve educational standards.

...A statement in the NAEP DESIGN AND DEVELOPMENT DOCUMENT covering the 1979–1980 Reading/Literature Assessment is succinctly descriptive:

> The first step in any assessment cycle is objectives development. The objectives identify the important knowledge, skills, and attitudes within an assessment area which are generally being taught or should be taught in schools. These objectives then become the framework for developing assessment exercises which measure the objectives.

Although there is little public awareness of these steps in the process of setting educational standards, they affect that process vitally and give any standard its determinative character....

...This new emphasis will mean that teaching will be increasingly oriented toward these objectives, which is good or bad depending on their quality. If these standards are to determine accountability, it is critical that their measurement reflect ultimate educational purposes rather than what might be dangerous expediencies.... The 1979–1980 Reading/ Literature Assessment, reported this year, appears to reflect a critical change in NAEP emphasis. It embodies elements of objectives-setting that are essential to a quality concept of educational standards....

...Two phrases in the design and development passage quoted above are critical. Objectives are to "identify the important knowledge, skills and attitudes." This is to include those "which are generally being taught or should be taught in the schools." The emphasis is added, but is consistent with the original context. This statement contrasts with the 1970 NAEP description of the objectives set for the first Reading assessment. These were described as involving no "distinctly 'new' objectives," but as "restatements and summarizations of objectives which (have) appeared over the last quarter century."...

...The 1969–1970 Citizenship Assessment included a group task exercise designed to determine, by observing students' group interaction, their ability to "apply democratic procedures on a practical level."... This capacity for innovation and experimentation has been lost, largely as a consequence of budgetary constraints.

Service Facility... In 1977–78, when the Texas legislature was considering the enactment of a minimum competency testing program, the Texas Education Agency made extensive use of NAEP materials in conducting a statewide survey (Texas Assessment Project—TAP) of student achievement in Reading, Writing, Mathematics, and Citizenship. The sampling plan was patterned after the National Assessment. Both the Writing and the Citizenship assessments were based largely on items and exercises selected by a Texas Education Agency staff panel from among those provided by NAEP offices. After the Texas assessment had been completed, extensive comparisons were made between the Texas results and available NAEP data, and reported to the legislative committee for consideration in connection with the adoption of the "Texas Assessment of Basic Skills." The circumstances under which the legislation was adopted preclude any clear identification of the effect of the comparisons. There is more evidence of substantial influence of the TAP initiative on the FRAMEWORK FOR THE SOCIAL STUDIES and LANGUAGE ARTS FRAMEWORK which have been developed and on the STATE BOARD GOALS which have been set for 1983.

Larger potential for National Assessment usefulness is suggested by the ten years or so of cooperation between NAEP offices and the Connecticut State Board of Education, in connection with the administration of the Connecticut Assessment of Educational Progress (CAEP). A 1980 State Board report notes that "The CAEP program is modeled after the National Assessment of Educational Progress (NAEP) in its basic goals, design and implementation." This is clearly reflected in the pattern of the twelve Connecticut assessments in seven subjects also covered by NAEP surveys. The CAEP sampling design is like NAEP's, except that students are assessed at grade rather than age levels. Goals and objectives used for the Connecticut assessments parallel clearly the objectives and subobjectives identified for the National Assessment. Many CAEP items are NAEP items; this was true of all items in the 1979–1980 Connecticut Science Assessment....

...Comparable uses of National Assessment materials have been made in a number of other states. A recent NAEP staff summary lists twelve States as having closely replicated the National Assessment model, and twelve others as having drawn on NAEP offices for technical and consultative advice. There is clear confirmation in this record of not only a substantial service potential, but also of a significant prospect for integrating state and nationwide assessment programs.

[Ed. Note: As one reads the excerpts in part two of this report, it is important to bear in mind the denials of complicity emanating from the U.S. Department of Education and the respective state departments of education when confronted with charges that the state assessments use test items from the NAEP Test Item Bank. The resistance to such use results from the public's traditional aversion to national tests and national curriculum—with which all of the above entities have denied involvement. Clearly, denial is in vain in light of the evidence contained in this document.]

THE NATIONAL CENTER FOR CITIZEN INVOLVEMENT ISSUED A REPORT ENTITLED *THE AMERI-can Volunteer, 1981: Statistics on Volunteers.* One revealing statement from the report follows:

> Volunteer Population: 92 million, 44% of whom work alone in an informal, unstructured environment on projects of their own choice; the rest of whom work in structured activities.

[Ed. Note: Obviously, the major effort related to volunteerism was—and is—to convince the 44% who are, in effect, "doing their own thing," to join in the government-private sector "Points of Light" volunteerism partnership initiated by then-President George Bush, as well as President Bill Clinton's AmeriCorps. That way they will work only on politically correct and government-approved projects.]

MALCOLM DAVIS, THE DIRECTOR OF THE OFFICE OF LIBRARIES AND LEARNING TECHNOL-ogy, Office of Educational Research and Improvement at the U.S. Department of Education, in response to this writer's comment in 1981 that computer courseware could allow children to learn at home, responded, "In essence, in the future all education will take place in the home, but the school buildings will be used for socialization purposes." This quote is not exact; however, it represents this writer's recollection of it sixteen years later. I was so stunned by his comment that I recall it often when looking at the issue of "choice" and especially that of homeschooling.

This comment was echoed by Alvin Toffler, George Gilder and Lewis Perelman during a Progress and Freedom Foundation conference in Atlanta, Georgia in August of 1995. This conference preceded and dealt with issues molding the "Contract with America" which Newt Gingrich put forth for Republican candidates to adopt as their platforms in 1996. Lewis Perelman's book, *School's Out* (Avon Books: New York, 1992), deals with this very concept and Perelman attended the conference as an expositor of "conservative" positions on education for Progress and Freedom Foundation.

[Ed. Note: A 1992 proposal to the New American Schools Development Corporation (NASDC) from The Center for the New West of Denver, Colorado included a plan from its New West Learning Center Design Team which provided a clear picture of the community of the future. "Home School Families" would be linked to "Public Schools, Communities, Private Schools,

Businesses, Alternative Schools, and Higher Education" with the New West Learning Center serving as the "hub" of the wheel, or community. While this proposal was not selected as a recipient of NASDC funding, and, fortunately, has not been funded by any government entity—YET—its description of changes in local governance and relationships of community elements met the criteria established by NASDC. (See Appendix XI and XII.)]

1982

PROFILES IN EXCELLENCE: 1982–1983: SECONDARY SCHOOL RECOGNITION PROGRAM: A Resource Guide (Office of Educational Research and Improvement of the U.S. Department of Education: Washington, D.C., 1982) listed the Kennebunk, Maine High School as one which schools across the nation might wish to emulate. The *Guide* stated:

> The major goal of the school's curriculum is to individualize the learning process for the student. The district is in the process of developing a data bank for students and a testing program for determining expectancy instructional levels for each student. Once this is in place, staff will develop an Individual Education Plan (IEP) for each student to meet individual needs. The major difficulty the school is encountering in implementing this new process is the secondary staff who are trained as subject matter teachers. Teachers need to be retrained to focus on individual needs rather than on content areas.

"FROM SCHOOLING TO LEARNING: RETHINKING PRESCHOOL THROUGH UNIVERSITY EDUCA-tion" by Don Glines was published in the January 1982 issue of the National Association of Secondary School Principals' *Bulletin*.[6] The following are excerpts:

> The implications of these global concerns for schools, educators, and education, are monumental if the views of most future writers are correct. Early recognition of this came in the 1974 book, *Learning for Tomorrow: The Role of the Future in Education* by Alvin Toffler (Random House: New York, 1974), and *The Third Wave* (William Morrow: New York, 1981) [by the same author].
>
> One passage states: "American education is obsolete; it produces people to fit into a reasonably well-functioning industrial society and we no longer have one. The basic assumption driving American education, one both deceptive and dangerous, is that the future will be like the present. Schools are preparing people for a society that no longer exists. As society shifts away from the industrial model, schools will have to turn out a different kind of person. Schools now need to produce people who can cope with change."...
>
> What do people who will be in their prime in the year 2050, assuming society makes it through the coming transitional decades, need to shape their futures? Is the current curriculum—history, mathematics, science, new versions of Dick and Jane, all taught as separate subjects, really appropriate for the concluding years of the twentieth century? The majority of futures writers have a clear answer: No. They illustrate that instant information retrieval not only ends jobs in the world of work, it ends subjects in the world of learning!...
>
> The potential technology exists to eliminate most current classrooms before the turn of the century, moving from a campus to a community-oriented learning system. A postliterate society is on the verge of arriving; reading will become a luxury, a leisure pastime, or a choice, but not an absolute essential.

Yet, the seventh grade programs in junior high and middle schools continue with the bleakness of 50 years past. Most still require English, history, science, math, and physical education, along with a semester of art and a semester of music. They have period 1, 2, 3 schedules; A, B, C report cards; tardies, notes from home; textbooks. Perhaps even worse is the fact that most colleges still prepare teachers for this antiquity; and administrators, who in spite of the goals professed in graduate courses, continue to perpetuate the system. Is it any wonder that *Learning for Tomorrow* labeled today's education obsolete?

Ron Barnes, in *Tomorrow's Educator: An Alternative to Today's School Person* (Transitions, Inc.: Phoenix, Arizona, 1977), has listed his descriptors of a New Age educator—a person who thinks systematically; accepts and promotes diversity; demonstrates a holistic perspective toward life; strives for self-awareness; promotes interdependence; is comfortable with the unknown; considers human values of highest priority; is experimental; works toward changing schools; has a more open approach to knowledge; and is a true futurist.

OUTCOME-BASED INSTRUCTIONAL MANAGEMENT: A SOCIOLOGICAL PERSPECTIVE BY WILLiam Spady was published in 1982, supported by a contract from the National Institute of Education (NIE–P–80–0194). This important paper, which provided a complete overview of the philosophy behind OBE, the organizational dimensions of outcome-based practice, the operational character of outcome-based practice, etc., also carried some interesting comments regarding OBE's relationship to the Follow Through Project. Excerpts follow:

> Implications for Follow Through... Despite the limitations of formal validation data sources, however, there is a strong case to be made for implementing fully developed OB [outcome-based] models in Follow Through sites. Philosophically, as well as empirically, this approach is inherently suited to the clientele served by Follow Through programs and possesses an operational character that is well suited for affecting positively both the cognitive and affective outcome agendas sought by a variety of current Follow Through models.
>
> Recognizing that OB practice resembles some of these models, its unique power appears to be that it possesses a fine balance between focus and flexibility, and structure and responsiveness, and that it contains elements suitable to a variety of student motivational and learning styles without leaning heavily toward any one orientation. That is, it is as inclusionary in its methodology as it is in the conditions for student learning success it tries to establish.
>
> A final point regarding the inherent appeal of OB practice for Follow Through implementation is its basic openness. Public involvement in goal setting, public visibility of objectives and standards, and performance records and reporting systems which describe the actual behavior being sought all help to "demystify" the educational process and facilitate clearer understanding and communication between parents and the school.
>
> The Network for Outcome-Based Schools itself represents a unique and powerful resource for technical assistance and implementation to any sites oriented toward OB practice.

[Ed. Note: The above excerpts should be of interest to those promoting DISTAR/Reading Mastery, the Skinnerian "systematic, intensive, scientific research-based" phonics reading program which was one of the Follow Through models. How ironic that William Spady should say that the outcome-based practice which "conservatives" say they detest is similar to the Follow Through model which they have embraced. It is obvious Spady is not referring to the Open Classroom Follow Through model, since that model did not include "public visibility of objectives and standards, performance records and reporting systems which describe the actual behaviors being sought." In other words, Spady is making it clear that OB practice is a fraternal twin of the Follow Through's Direct Instruction model developed by Siegfried Engelmann, which has also been embraced by "conservatives"!]

"LEARNING TO READ THE ECRI WAY" BY DENNIS BAILEY WAS PUBLISHED IN *THE MAINE Times* on January 8, 1982. In the article Bailey points out that

> Patrick Groff, an education professor, wrote in a 1974 issue of *Today's Education*: "So far, mastery learning has not presented the empirical evidence necessary to convince reasonable-minded teachers that all students have the same aptitude for learning every subject."

[Ed. Note: That Professor Groff, professor emeritus, San Diego State University, would make the above comment is interesting in light of recent events; namely, his co-founding with Robert Sweet of the Right to Read Foundation (RRF) which has taken a position in support of the *Reading Excellence Act of 1998*. In supporting this legislation Groff's organization has indicated support for the "scientific, research-based" reading method used in ECRI, the very technique which he says "has not presented the empirical evidence necessary to convince reasonable-minded teachers that all students have the same aptitude for learning every subject." ECRI is the mirror image of Siegfried Engelmann's DISTAR direct instruction, the Skinnerian operant conditioning-based reading program promoted in Right to Read newsletters and on its website.]

WILLIAM (BILL) SPADY, "THE FATHER OF OBE," MADE THE FOLLOWING STATEMENT DURING a conference held at the U.S. Department of Education in 1982 (attended by this writer). This writer wrote down verbatim in shorthand Spady's following comment:

> Two of the four functions of Mastery Learning are: Extra: whole agenda of acculturation, social roles, social integration, get the kids to participate in social unit, affective; and Hidden: a system of supervision and control which restrains behavior of kids; the outcome of the hidden agenda should be the fostering of social responsibility or compliance.

"STATE OF PRECOLLEGE EDUCATION IN MATHEMATICS AND SCIENCE" WAS PREPARED BY Paul DeHart Hurd, professor emeritus, Stanford University, for the National Convocation on Pre-College Education in Math and Science, National Academy of Sciences and National Academy of Engineering in Washington, D.C. in 1982. In this paper Prof. Hurd asserts that:

> In the Communist countries there are comprehensive examinations at the end of the primary, middle, and secondary schools to assess a student's actual progress. Test results are not interpreted in a competitive sense as to who has done well or poorly compared to other students or a norm, but rather whether a student has mastered the prescribed subject matter. If test results are below expectancy, the student is tutored by the teacher and students. The object is to avoid failures.

[Ed. Note: This definition is striking in its similarity to the definition of OBE/mastery learning/direct instruction, which uses non-competitive, criterion-referenced tests rather than traditional norm-referenced tests which compare students to one another. Another common feature among these techniques is continuous progress whereby students can have all the time and/or tutoring they need in order to "master" the content. Continuous progress is necessary to carry out UNESCO's lifelong learning concept. This "exit exam" process is being legislated into an increasing number of states.]

IN A SPEECH ENTITLED "REGULATED COMPETITION IN THE UNITED STATES" DELIVERED BEfore the top 52 executives in Northern Telecom's Worldwide Corporation meeting, for which the edited proceedings were published in the February 1982 issue of the *Innisbrook Papers*,[7] Harvard Professor Anthony Oettinger of the Council on Foreign Relations made the following extremely elitist statements:

> Our idea of literacy, I am afraid, is obsolete because it rests on a frozen and classical definition. Literacy, as we know it today, is the product of the conditions of the industrial revolution, of organization, of the need for a work force that could, in effect, "write with a fine round hand." It has to do, in other words, with the Bob Cratchits of the world.
>
> But as much as we might think it is, literacy is not an eternal phenomenon. Today's literacy is a phenomenon (and Dickens satirized it) that has its roots in the nineteenth century, and one does not have to reach much farther back to think of civilizations with different concepts of literacy based, for example, on oral, rather than written, traditions.
>
> The present "traditional" concept of literacy has to do with the ability to read and write. But the real question that confronts us today is: How do we help citizens function well in their society? How can they acquire the skills necessary to solve their problems?
>
> Do we, for example, really want to teach people to do a lot of sums or write in a "fine round hand" when they have a five-dollar, hand-held calculator or a word processor to work with? Or, do we really have to have everybody literate—writing and reading in the traditional sense—when we have the means through our technology to achieve a new flowering of oral communication?[8]
>
> What is speech recognition and speech synthesis all about if it does not lead to ways of reducing the burden on the individual of the imposed notions of literacy that were a product of nineteenth century economics and technology?
>
> Complexity—everybody is moaning about tasks becoming too complex for people to do. A Congressman who visited one of my classes recently said, "We have such low-grade soldiers in the U.S. that we have to train them with comic books." And an army captain in my class shot back: "What's wrong with comic books? My people *function*" [emphasis in original].
>
> It is the traditional idea that says certain forms of communication, such as comic books, are "bad." But in the modern context of functionalism they may not be all that bad.

[Ed. Note: Doesn't the above sound a lot like the Texas Study of Adult Functional Competency, the Adult Performance Level Study, and Secretary of Education T.H. Bell's and William Spady's initiation of dumbed-down competency-based education?

One can't help but wonder if Oettinger—and those social engineers with whom he associates who call the shots in regard to our children's futures—would be happy to have their own children and grandchildren offered such a limited education that they won't even know who Charles Dickens or Bob Cratchit were?]

CHESTER FINN WROTE "PUBLIC SERVICE, PUBLIC SUPPORT, PUBLIC ACCOUNTABILITY" FOR the March 1982 issue of the National Association of Secondary School Principals' *Bulletin*. Finn became a high profile figure in education circles with his appointment as assistant secretary, Office of Educational Research and Improvement, by Secretary of Education William Bennett. Finn's article was quoted in Barbara Morris's book, *Tuition Tax Credits: A Responsible Appraisal* (*The Barbara Morris Report*: Upland, Cal., 1983):

> Short of scattering money in the streets or handing it out to everyone who wants some, the funding agency must define eligible recipients.... This means, in a word, "regulation," the inevitable concommitant of public financial support.

Finn also believed the government is obligated to recognize that the private schools it helps support are different from public schools—that it is this "differentness" that makes them supportable. The other side of the coin, he says, is the obligation of private schools

> to recognize certain limits to their differentness and certain ways they must conform to the norms and expectations of a society that values and supports them....
> Some, to be sure, like to think they can have it both ways; i.e., can obtain aid without saddling themselves with unacceptable forms of regulation. But most acknowledge the general applicability of the old adage that he who pays the piper calls the tune, and are more or less resigned to amalgamating or choosing between assistance and autonomy.

ON MARCH 29, 1982, AT THE "CLOSED TO THE PUBLIC" ANNUAL MEETING OF THE COUNCIL of Chief State School Officers, Secretary of Education T.H. Bell's top assistant, Elam Herzler, told the assembled fifty state superintendents of education:

> One of the elements of an effective school is to monitor, assess, and feed back.... As little as 5 percent of a school budget K–12 would be needed over a period of 12 years to enable each student to have his own computer, and this is within our cost range.

"CAN COMPUTERS TEACH VALUES?" BY JOSEPH A. BRAUN, JR. AND KURT A. SLOBODZIAN, assistant professors in the Department of Curriculum and Instruction of the Northern Illinois University School of Education in Dekalb, Illinois, was published in the April 1982 issue of *Educational Leadership*. The following are excerpts:

> In helping children learn how to inquire and examine their own emerging value systems, most educators agree that unintentional negative reactions by teachers are deleterious to youngsters' self-concept. Couple this with potential ridicule from student peers, and one can readily see why values education has been a delicate and controversial issue. However, a student using CAI [computer-assisted instruction] in the examination, evaluation, and acquisition of values would be able to do so with mature guidance in an environment free from potential rejection or scorn.
> Another pitfall for teachers of values education is the invasion of a child's right to privacy. Well-intentioned teachers often expect self-disclosure beyond a student's limit of psychological safety (Lockwood, 1977) by demanding deeply personal revelations from par-

ticipants who are not prepared to discuss their more private thoughts. The computer, in contrast, has no misguided need to get to know "the real you."

The computer, then, is ideally suited to the role of facilitator in values education. It inherently possesses the Rogerian [psychologist Carl Rogers] qualities of genuineness and congruence. It can even be programmed to positively regard anyone who uses it. A student using CAI gains a sense of protection as well as a constant source of appropriate feedback while exploring and integrating feelings, beliefs, and behavior.

Computers have also been programmed to pick out key words from a respondent's statements. The computer program then formulates open-ended questions from key words, which causes the respondent to focus and further clarify feelings. In other words, using a program called "Doctor," Holden (1977) describes a conversation between a computer and a troubled young woman who began with a common complaint:

> Human: "Men are all alike."
> Computer: "In what way?"
> Human: "They're always bugging us about something or another."
> Computer: "Can you think of a specific example?"
> Human: "Well, my boy friend made me come here."
> Computer: "Your boyfriend made you come here?"
> Human: "He says that I'm depressed much of the time."
> Computer: "I am sorry to hear that you are depressed."
> Human: "It's true, I am unhappy."
> Computer: "Do you think coming here will help you not be unhappy?"
> Human: "I need some help. That much seems certain."
> Computer: "What would it mean if you got some help?"
> Human: "Perhaps I could learn to get along with my mother."
> Computer: "Tell me more about your family."

THE COMPLETE WORKS OF FRANCIS A. SCHAEFFER: A CHRISTIAN WORLDVIEW, VOLUME One, a Christian View of Philosophy and Culture (Crossway Books: Westchester, Ill., 1982) was published. In a treatise entitled "A Christian View of Philosophy and Culture: Back to Freedom and Dignity," noted Christian scholar and theologian Dr. Francis Schaeffer warned of B.F. Skinner and his methods:

> Skinner says that up until the present time all of humanity has considered man to be in some sense autonomous—that is, that there is in each individual an "ego" or mind or center of consciousness which can freely choose one or another course of action. But, Skinner says, autonomous man does not exist, and it is the task of behavioral psychology to abolish the conception.... Skinner declares that everything man is, everything man makes, everything man thinks is completely, 100 percent, determined by his environment.
>
> After the publication of *Beyond Freedom and Dignity* [1972], when he [Skinner] was at the Center for the Study of Democratic Institutions, he spoke at Westmont College in Santa Barbara, California. There he said, "The individual does not initiate anything." In fact, he said that any time man is freed from one kind of control, he merely comes under another kind of control. Christians consider that man is autonomous in that he is significant, he affects the environment. In behavioristic psychology, the situation is reversed. All behavior is determined not from within but from without. "You" don't exist. Man is not there. All that is there is a bundle of conditioning, a collection of what you have been in the past: your genetic makeup and your environment. But Skinner goes a step further, subordinates the

genetic factor, and suggests that man's behavior can be almost totally controlled by controlling the environment.... Some behaviorists would differ with him on this last point. How is it that the environment controls behavior?

Here Skinner brings up the concept of "operant conditioning." This notion is based on his work with pigeons and rats. The basic idea is that "when a bit of behavior is followed by a certain consequence, it is more likely to occur again, and a consequence having this effect is called a reinforcer." (p. 27) That is, for example, "anything the organism does that is followed by the receipt of food is more likely to be done again whenever the organism is hungry."

There are two kinds of reinforcers: negative reinforcers which have adverse effects, and positive reinforcers whose effect is positive. Skinner contends that only the positive reinforcers should be used. In other words, in order to reinforce a certain kind of behavior, one should not punish; he should reward. If a person is surrounded by an atmosphere in which he gets a sufficient reward for doing what society would like him to do, he will automatically do this without ever knowing why he is doing it.... Within the Skinnerian system there are no ethical controls. There is no boundary limit to what can be done by the elite in whose hands control resides.

The reduction of man's value to zero is one of the important factors which triggered the student rebellion at Berkeley and elsewhere in the 1960s. Those students sensed that they were being turned into zeros and they revolted. Christians should have sensed it long before and said and exhibited that we have an alternative.... We are on the verge of the largest revolution the world has ever seen—the control and shaping of men through the abuse of genetic knowledge, and chemical and psychological conditioning.

Will people accept it? I don't think they would accept it if (1) they had not already been taught to accept the presuppositions that lead to it, and (2) they were not in such hopelessness. Many of our secular schools have consistently taught these presuppositions, and unhappily many of our Christian lower schools and colleges have taught the crucial subjects no differently than the secular schools.

Schaeffer's "Conclusion" follows:

What do we and our children face? The biological bomb, the abuse of genetic knowledge, chemical engineering, the behavioristic manipulation of man. All these have come to popular attention only a few years ago. But they are not twenty years away. They are not five years away. They are here now in technological breakthroughs. This is where we live, and as true Christians we must be ready. This is no time for weakness in the Church of Christ. What has happened to man? We must see him as one who has torn himself away both from the infinite-personal God who created him as finite but in his image and from God's revelation to him. Made in God's image, he was made to be great, he was made to be beautiful, and he was made to be creative in life and art. But his rebellion has led him into making himself into nothing but a machine. (pp. 374–384)

AN ARTICLE ENTITLED "GRADUATES LACK TECHNICAL TRAINING, STUDY WARNS—BY 1990, 2 Million May Not Have Essential Skills Needed for Employment in 'Information Society'" was published in the May 12, 1982 issue of *Education Week*. This article clearly placed the responsibility for the transformation from traditional academic education to workforce training at the feet of the Carnegie Corporation-spawned Education Commission of the States (ECS) and the National Assessment of Educational Progress (NAEP). This article fired one of the first shots across the bow of traditional academic education. It clearly defined the new "education" landscape when it described the need for Benjamin Bloom's Taxonomy (high level skills of critical thinking; i.e., evaluation, analysis, synthesis, application, etc.) versus "low level basic skills," emphasizing the use of the brain for processing, not storage (explained by Thomas Kelly in the January 1994 issue of *The Effective School Report*). The terminology in this article would, eleven years later, be reflected in the major *Goals 2000* restructuring legislation, the *Elementary and Secondary Reauthorization Act of 1994* (H.R. 6) which referred to the learning of basic academic skills and the emphasis on repetitive drill and practice in elementary school as a "disproven theory." Some excerpts from this enlightening article follow:

> "Unless the decline of high-order skills among high-school students is reversed," warns a new report from the Education Commission of the states, "as many as two million students may graduate [in 1990] without the essential skills required for employment in tomorrow's technically-oriented labor force."
>
> "Information Society: Will Our High School Graduates Be Ready?" was prepared by Roy Forbes, director of the National Assessment of Educational Progress (NAEP) and Lynn Grover Gisi, a research assistant and writer with NAEP. Its intention, the authors say, is to "stimulate research and communication among the groups concerned with technology's impact on education."
>
> The Forbes-Gisi report reviews labor-force projections, summarizes recent National Assessment findings, and outlines "recent corporate, educational, and legislative actions" designed to address the problem.
>
> Arguing that the computer chip will replace oil in the U.S. economy, and will form the basis for a new information society, the authors say that the "basics" mastered by the high-school gaduates of the future will have to include more complex skills than minimal reading, writing, and computing. Among the higher-level skills the information age will require, they argue, will be "evaluation and analysis, critical thinking; problem-solving strategies, including mathematical problem-solving, organization and reference skills; synthesis; application; creativity; decision-making given complete information; and communication skills through a variety of modes." ...The data from the National Assessment provide convincing evidence that by the time students reach the age of 17, many do not possess [the above listed]... higher-order skills. The "elements of the problem," says the report, are:
>
> - Foreign competition. The age of high technology is rapidly changing the roles of production and other countries are responding—faster than the U.S.—by upgrading their educational programs on a national level. The U.S. educational system, says the report, "poses unique problems by its inherent commitment to diversity and emphasis on local and state control."...
>
> - Students. Technology used for educational purposes has the potential to reshape instructional delivery systems, the report says, and that may result in a decentralization of learning from traditional schools into homes, communities and industries....
>
> - Responsibilities and relevance. Education must become more relevant to the world of work, the report contends, and this requires "informational feedback systems on the successes of students who have completed the required curriculum. Quality control has focused on the inputs into a system—teachers and textbooks, for example—and not the outcomes. Thus there has been no attempt to incorporate long-term information into the management system's program planning." The report's authors agree with a report of the Southern Regional Education Board that American schooling no longer lacks the basics rather the "complexities that make for mature learning, mature citizenship, or adult success."...

Unless the U.S. can keep pace, the report contends, its "position as a leader of technology and competitor for world markets will be severely threatened."

Cooperative Efforts

Only cooperative efforts involving all segments of society will solve the problem, the report states. In particular, it calls on American industry and labor to play a greater role....

..."Industries cannot afford to pass up these opportunities and others because their future existence will depend upon it.... Clearly we are not cultivating the raw materials, our future workers, who are vital not only for economic progress, but ultimately for economic survival."

[Ed. Note: There are many responses this writer could make to the above article, but the first of which is that the statement "Clearly we are not cultivating the raw materials, our future workers"—our children!—is the most offensive of all. The use of those words alone when referring to human beings should tell the reader that something is very, very wrong in the United States of America. One has more respect for their pet animals than to refer to them as "raw materials."

Secondly, the report's agreement with the Southern Regional Education Board "that American schooling no longer lacks the basics" defies logic! From a region which consistently scores at the bottom of the heap, this is particularly repugnant. The idea that "higher order skills" should be the focus of our educational efforts can only be the product of the thinking of persons who are not concerned with whether or not students can read, write, or compute unless it is to perform a workforce function. Without a basic ability to read, write and compute on a broad base, it is impossible for anyone to have substance about which to "think critically"! Thinking critically—making choices and comparisons—requires a base knowledge that is either acquired through study (as in the case with most children who are students) or through life experience (which adults, but not children, can claim).

Lastly, the use of technology to decentralize "learning" from traditional schools into homes, communities and industries should raise a tall, red flag for successful homeschoolers. These folks are talking about government control of this process.]

THE INTERNATIONAL CONFERENCE FOR PARENT/CITIZEN INVOLVEMENT IN SCHOOLS WAS held July 22–25, 1982 at the Hilton Hotel, Salt Lake City, Utah. A letter to Secretary Bell dated February 25, 1982 requesting conference funding contained an impressive list of supporters on its letterhead, including: Scott Matheson, governor of Utah; Mrs. Barbara Bush, honorary chairperson, National School Volunteer Program; T.H. Bell, U.S. secretary of education; Dr. Don Davies, Institute for Responsive Education; Dr. Carl Marer, National Committee for Citizens in Education; Dr. M. Donald Thomas, superintendent of schools, Salt Lake City, Utah, and education representatives from Canada and Australia.

Dr. Donald Thomas, originally on the board of directors of *The Effective School Report*, and executive director of the Network for Effective Schools, is a well-known change agent. Thomas has traveled to Russia under the auspices of U.S. Secretary of Education Lamar Alexander and Dale Mann of Columbia University, to work with Russia on implementing international education restructuring.

The above-mentioned letter to Bell also stated:

The "think tank" session will be by invitation only to leaders in the movement. Its purpose will be to assess the current status of parent/citizen involvement in the schools; to identify trends and directions of the movement for the 80s; and finally to plan further positive action to support the continuation of the movement.

One of the attachments to this conference correspondence included many pages related to Effective School Research and a listing of the components necessary for education restructuring. The list included:

- mastery learning/direct instruction
- expectations
- climate
- motivation
- measurement diagnosis
- assessment
- class management
- discipline
- classroom organization
- pupil conditions/rewards
- praise
- parent involvement, etc.

Those connected with such research are listed as follows: Michael Rutter, England, Effective School Study; the late Harvard Professor Ron Edmonds; professors Benjamin Bloom and John Goodlad; Larry Lezotte; Donald Thomas; and others.

A second attachment on National Coalition for Parent Involvement in Education (NCPIE—Alexandria, Virginia) letterhead stated that NCPIE was facilitated by the National School Volunteer Program and funded by Union Carbide Corporation.

A MEMO WAS SENT TO SECRETARY OF EDUCATION T.H. BELL FROM THE ASSISTANT SECRETARY, Office of Educational Research and Improvement, regarding "upcoming events for July 31–August 31" which listed:

AUGUST 5—President Reagan is scheduled to hold a press conference in which he will announce an initiative involving the National Diffusion Network and the National Health Screening Council for Volunteer Organizations, Inc. This collaboration, called PARTNERSHIP, links schools with the media, local businesses, government and hospitals in a school improvement effort.

[Ed. Note: This activity was cancelled due to prompt grassroots opposition in the D.C. area consisting of a memorandum to the White House informing the President of concern nationwide related to the process known as "community education" and public-private partnerships.]

A U.S. DEPARTMENT OF EDUCATION MEMORANDUM TO SECRETARY BELL DATED OCTOBER 5, 1982 stated:

> President Reagan is scheduled to visit P.S. 48, an elementary school in the Bronx, New York City. During his visit the President will meet Dr. Ethna Reid, Director of the Exemplary Center for Reading Instruction, a program in the National Diffusion Network. Dr. Reid will be at P.S. 48 to train staff members in the use of ECRI.[9]

[Ed. Note: Whether the President, a very busy man, met with Dr. Reid or not, is insignificant. What IS highly significant, however, is WHY this extraordinary effort was made to introduce the President of the United States to Dr. Ethna Reid of Utah. In retrospect, scheduling President Reagan to meet with the developer of the "chosen" teaching method which incorporates Skinnerian mastery learning and direct instruction makes sense.]

U.S. SECRETARY OF EDUCATION T.H. BELL'S COMMISSION ON EXCELLENCE PUBLISHED *A Nation at Risk: The Imperative for Educational Reform* in 1982. This report laid the groundwork for the controversial restructuring Americans face today. Initially, the commission engaged in a slick, expensive propagandistic roadshow, intended to mobilize American opinion in favor of the umpteenth reform since the federal government seized control of education in 1965, causing steep declines in academic test scores. The recommendations were couched in terms Americans would accept; i.e., mastering basic skills, more homework, etc. Its hype was best illustrated by the following excerpt:

> If an unfriendly foreign power had attempted to impose on America the mediocre educational performance that exists today, we might well have viewed it as an act of war.... We have, in effect, been committing an act of unthinking, unilateral educational disarmament.

[Ed. Note: The rhetoric worked. Spending increased. Ideas, which would never have been accepted had a crisis not been deliberately created, were embraced without question. These included doing away with the only valid criterion for measuring student academic achievement—the Carnegie Unit—with its required four years of math, four years of English, four years of history, etc., in order to graduate from high school. Of interest was an informal comment made by Secretary Bell at the initial (closed to the public) commission meeting in July of 1981. Secretary Bell commented that one had to "create conflict in order to obtain one's objectives."

The conflict was indeed created between the conservatives (falsely represented by big business interests) and the liberals (the left-wing tax-exempt foundations and leadership of the teacher unions, etc.), in order to be able to come to a compromise (arrive at the consensus or common ground) which represented what the United Nations and its educational agencies had been promoting since 1945. The U.N. agenda included socialist lifelong learning and training for the global workforce. This consensus required—and succeeded in obtaining—partnerships/mergers between individuals and groups that had formerly had nothing in common—especially the partnership between government schools and business. Such a partnership is required by socialist/fascist forms of government.]

THE CENTER FOR EDUCATIONAL RESEARCH AND INNOVATION (CERI),[10] WHICH IS ATTACHED to the Organization for Economic Cooperation and Development (OECD) in Paris, France, held an International School Improvement Project (ISIP) conference in Palm Beach, Florida in 1982. Many of the key components of the United States' education reform movement (effective schools movement) were discussed by delegates from member countries. The main topic appeared to be a subject entitled "CBAM" about which absolutely nothing was said in the invitational papers sent to delegates planning to attend.

The writer was bewildered by the term "CBAM" until it appeared in the U.S. Department of Education-funded project "Changing Teacher Practice, Final Report of an Experimental Study—Gary A. Griffin, Principal Investigator, Susan Barnes, Sharon O'Neal, Sara E. Edwards, Maria E. Defino, Hobart Hukill—Report No. 9052, Research and Development Center for Teacher Education, The University of Texas, Austin, Texas 78712." Within the project report there is discussion of the application of "behavioral science for systems improvement." The "Changing Teacher Practice" project contained the "Concerns-Based Adoption Model" (CBAM), which illustrated the extent of psychological manipulation undergone by teachers who resist change. The following excerpt explains the purpose of "Concerns-Based Adoption Model" as a support tool to assist teachers through the painful process of "change":

> The Concerns-Based Adoption Model (CBAM) provides a structure for staff development planning which focuses on the process of change as a personal experience (Hall & Loucks, 1978, Note 19). The perceptions, feelings, motivations, frustrations, and satisfactions of teachers about an innovation are identified and classified according to a developmental scheme of stages. The process of change by which a person moves through these stages is attended to so that an innovation can be implemented. Concerns-based staff development recognizes and accepts as legitimate the concerns of the person involved in the change process. Change is regarded as long term and developmental, and individuals are perceived to need support as they experience change. In this model any process or product that the teacher has not previously encountered is regarded as an innovation for that teacher. (p. 37)

[Ed. Note: The information regarding the ISIP conference in Palm Beach is taken from a July 9,1982 letter from J.R. Gass of the Organization for Economic Cooperation and Development of the Center for Educational Research and Innovation to Donald J. Senese, assistant secretary for the Office of Educational Research and Improvement, U.S. Department of Education. Such international meetings at which international education/workforce training agenda items are discussed take place regularly. OERI and CERI are closely connected in the work they carry out for OECD, UNESCO and the United Nations.]

"BETWEEN CLASSES—WHAT COST, ACCOUNTABILITY?" BY TERRY L. FORTHUM, TEACHER and editor of the state newspaper of the Arizona Federation of Teachers, was published in the October 1982 issue of the *The Arizona Forum*. Excerpts follow from this thought-provoking article:

> If accountability becomes the ultimate goal of education and all areas of education are reduced to "components" measurable by standardized testing, education will no longer be a learning process but a cloning process for both the teacher and the student. The priority questions for education in the future may well be: Why can't Johnny think? Why can't

Johnny enjoy? Why can't Johnny feel? Why can't Carbon Unit J smile?...

The panic caused by educational studies of the Why Can't Johnny Read variety has created a new educational priority—ACCOUNTABILITY. In its purest form, accountability aids the profession and the professional in maintaining standards of excellence. The results of any attempt to "monitor" the profession and therefore make it accountable can only be as valid, however, as the instrument or process which produces the results....

Accountability is the central election issue in the race for Superintendent of Public Instruction [Mr. Forthum is referring to reform opponent Ann Herzer's bid to unseat Carolyn Warner as superintendent of public instruction, ed.]. The present administration has established pilot programs throughout Arizona which can measure student progress as defined by the testing instrument, therefore making the school and instructor accountable. The evaluative program, developed nationally and piloted in other states before reaching Arizona, can in fact establish a criteria for testing accountability. That it works is not the issue. The issue is how it works. The issue is not "should education be accountable" but should education make B.F. Skinner methodology the model for establishing educational accountability?

EDWARD CURRAN, DIRECTOR OF THE NATIONAL INSTITUTE OF EDUCATION, WAS DISMISSED by Secretary T.H. Bell in 1982 due to Curran's recommendation to President Reagan that the National Institute of Education—the research and development arm of the U.S. Department of Education—be abolished. President Reagan was out of the country at the time of Curran's dismissal. When President Reagan was elected Dr. Curran left his position as headmaster of the Cathedral School for Girls in Washington, D.C., first to work on the education department transition team and later to assume the directorship of the National Institute of Education.

Curran's courageous recommendation would not have required Congressional approval, as did the proposal to abolish the U.S. Department of Education; an executive order by Secretary Bell was all that was required. Abolishing NIE could have removed much of the controversial federal government influence in our local schools. In an article entitled "Success Eludes Old Research Agency," *Education Week* (December 9, 1982) quoted Dr. Curran as follows:

> NIE is based on the premise that education is a science whose progress depends on systematic "research and development." As a professional educator, I know that this premise is false.

1983

"A RELIGION FOR A NEW AGE" BY JOHN DUNPHY, WRITTEN FOR THE JANUARY/FEBRUARY 1983 issue of *The Humanist*, the journal of the American Humanist Association, lifts the veil of respectability from humanism and humanistic ethics. Excerpts follow:

> I am convinced that the battle for humankind's future must be waged and won in the public school classroom by teachers who correctly perceive their role as the proselytizers of a new faith: a religion of humanity that recognizes and respects the spark of what theologians call divinity in every human being.
>
> These teachers must embody the same selfless dedication as the most rabid fundamen-

talist preachers, for they will be ministers of another sort, utilizing a classroom instead of a pulpit to convey humanist values in whatever subjects they teach, regardless of the education level—preschool day care or a large university.

The classroom must and will become an arena of conflict between the old and the new—the rotting corpse of Christianity, together with all its adjacent evils and misery, and the new faith of Humanism, resplendent in its premise of a world in which the never-realized Christian idea of "love thy neighbor" will finally be achieved.

EDUCATION FOR RESULTS: IN RESPONSE TO A NATION AT RISK, VOL. 1: GUARANTEEING Effective Performance by Our Schools (SAFE Learning Systems, Inc.: Anaheim, Cal., 1983) by Robert Corrigan was published. In its 500-page how-to manual, Corrigan's S.A.F.E. [Systematic Approach for Effectiveness] model was described. Corrigan explains:

> The following successive phases were performed to test out the theoretical concepts of increased mastery learning effectiveness: Phase 1. To design and to extensively field-test a group instructional learning-centered program applying those programmed instructional principles postulated by Skinner and Crowder to be combined with the techniques of System Analysis for installing required system-wide managing-for-results processes including the accountable performance by teachers, principals and support personnel. This program would be "packaged" for use by teachers to deliver predictable achievement of defined mastery-learning objectives. (p. 155)

[Ed. Note: This program was endorsed by—among others—Bill Spady (Mr. OBE), the director of the controversial Far West Laboratory Outcome-Based Education Project (the Utah Grant) and Professor Homer Coker of the University of Georgia, who developed—with National Institute of Education funds—a controversial standardized teacher evaluation instrument with 420 teacher characteristics (competencies/behaviors). This book's Appendix VI contains extensive quotes from this important trail-blazing project.]

FROM THE FIRST NEWSLETTER, *OUTCOMES*, PUBLISHED BY BILL SPADY'S NETWORK FOR Outcome-Based Schools in 1983, came the article "Four Phases in Creating and Managing an Outcome-Based Program" by John Champlin of the Department of Educational Administration of Texas Tech University in Lubbock, Texas. The fact that mastery learning is outcome-based education is made clear in the following excerpts:

> "Outcome-Based" was conceived during discussions in 1979 when our attention centered around how Mastery Learning could be better managed and made more likely to survive, despite many ill-conceived design and implementation attempts. Those participating proposed that an advocacy network be established. This founding group of a dozen or so concluded that more support for Mastery Learning would be likely if this new network focused equally on outcomes as well as process. They argued that instructional delivery systems needed to be sufficiently flexible and responsive to produce a wide variety of outcomes, not just the existing limitations of basic skills programs. This decision was considered critical in view of limited success in efforts to operationalize competency-based concepts during the 1970s.... Out of these dialogues emerged the Network for Outcome-Based Schools, a loose configuration of researchers, teachers, principals, school superintendents and college profes-

sors whose goal was to advocate and implement Mastery Learning as a vehicle for producing the capabilities and responses necessary for students to attain varied outcomes. The Network has been a vigorous proponent of all of the identified components of Outcome-Based (OB) programming since its inception....

INITIATE COMMUNITY REEDUCATION AND RENORMING ACTIVITIES—Any new program development absolutely requires provisions to foster community understanding. Many well-intended change efforts have fallen upon the rocks because the community didn't understand it, challenged it, and built up so much pressure that it was easiest for staff to revert to the safe harbor of the status quo. This community effort should be designed both to reeducate and to renorm parents and the general public. It is important that your community know what you intend to do, why it is happening, and exactly what they can expect as it progresses. I believe a district will win some degree of tolerance and patience if it involves the community in this way. To expect residents to passively accept any modification after the fact or by edict is a serious error. Think of renorming the community the same way you conduct similar efforts in the school environment. Don't challenge the community, co-opt them. (pp. 36–7)

THE U.S. DEPARTMENT OF EDUCATION FUNDED TWO IMPORTANT PROJECTS IN 1983: 1) "Framing a Future for Education" for Kansas; and 2) "Strategic Planning and Furthering Excellence in Millard Public Schools" for Nebraska, both of which were assigned to Dr. Shirley McCune of the MidContinent Regional Educational Laboratory (McREL) as project director. These two projects, based on the work of the New Age Naisbitt Group founded by John Naisbitt who authored *Megatrends,* served as national pilots for OBE restructuring of America from a "representative democracy" to a "participatory democracy—moving from a left versus right politics to a politics of the radical center," in Dr. McCune's words. McCune became famous (or infamous) during the National Governors' Association conference in Wichita, Kansas in 1989 when she said:

> What we're into is the total restructuring of society. What is happening in America today and what is happening in Kansas and the Great Plains is not simply a chance situation in the usual winds of change. What it amounts to is a total transformation of society.... Our total society is in a crisis of restructuring and you can't get away from it. You can't go into rural areas, you can't go into the churches, you can't go into government or into business and hide from the fact that what we are facing is the total restructuring of our society.

[Ed. Note: In the 1996 entry regarding McCune's book, *The Light Shall Set You Free* (Athena Publishing, Alpha Connections: Santa Fe, New Mexico, 1996), McCune expressed her belief that "each individual is a co-creator with the Divine."]

"A CALL FOR A RADICAL RE-EXAMINATION: EDUCATION SHOULD REFLECT A NEW INTERNA-tional Economic Order" by Michel Debeauvais was published in the March 1983 issue of *The Education Digest.* The article was a condensed version of the original which appeared in *Prospects* (Vol. XII, No. 2, pp. 135–145). Michel Debeauvais is co-founder and president, Francophone Association of Comparative Education, Sevres, France. The following excerpts relate to the transformation of the world's education systems from traditional academic emphasis to workforce training:

> The current of thought that seeks to abolish the existing international economic order and replace it with a new order calls for reexamination of the relations between education and the economy....
>
> Assuming growing importance everywhere, however, is the inadequacy of [the response] of school systems to social needs and to the needs of the economy. These shortcomings lie behind the educational reforms upon which nearly all countries have embarked. The chief criticisms are: primary schooling often tends to direct young people toward salaried employment in the modern urban sector, whereas only a minority among them can hope to obtain such jobs; general secondary education still channels pupils' aspirations toward higher education; technical and vocational education suffer from lack of prestige and high costs, and are often ill-suited to job market trends; higher education is often perceived as isolated from national life, from the demands of cultural and internal development....
>
> There is growing realization of the role of education systems in the reproduction of inequalities—the social selection performed by the education system as it contributes to distribution of social roles and jobs in a hierarchized society. The hierarchy of school results tends to match the job hierarchy; situations where expansion of the education system is not matched by changes in the job structure are perceived as a dysfunction requiring correction.
>
> The goals of equity laid down by educational policy can be made effective only if they are an integral part of development policies pursuing this aim through diverse and mutually coordinated measures. This has led to... an integrated development policy, in which the aim of education would be... achieving the social and economic goals of development....
>
> Nevertheless, we may advance the following proposition: A policy of endogenous development to accord priority to the struggle against inequality, and to the participation of the population in decisions concerning it, ought also to be accompanied by fairly far-reaching educational reforms, redefining the role and place of training in the overall system of socio-economic objectives.
>
> Another important aspect of the New International Economic Order (NIEO)... will require substantial alterations in international relations and... public opinion will have to be prepared in order to understand and reconcile itself to the measures to be taken.... The extent of the changes in attitude made necessary by a new world order based on the values of the survival of humanity and respect for the dignity of all cultures constitutes a theme for reflection that accords a central role to education in the context of an NIEO.
>
> A new international order can be devised and implemented only by stages which correspond... to those of a more deep-seated evolution in people's thinking. United Nations bodies play a role that is by no means negligible in shaping world opinion.
>
> ...It now remains for us to find out where the children not attending school are in order to prepare educational programs capable of reaching them and answering their needs. In addition, the priority aim of reducing disparities between town and country should lead to the measurement of schooling (and nonformal education) in the countryside, something existing school statistics do not permit.
>
> ...Data on the level of instruction of workers would permit more accurate evaluation of the relations between education and employment.

FUNCTIONAL LITERACY AND THE WORKPLACE: THE PROCEEDINGS OF THE MAY 6, 1983 *National Invitational Conference* was published (Education Services, American Council of Life Insurance: Washington, D.C., 1983). Excerpts which highlight now-familiar ideas follow:

"Defining Functional Literacy" by Paul Delker, Director of the Division of Adult Education in the U.S. Department of Education who has been involved with the Federal Adult Basic Education Program since its beginnings in 1966... headed the U.S. delegation to a UNESCO meeting that drafted Recommendations on Adult Education adopted by the [UN] General Assembly in 1976.... You may be familiar with the Adult Performance Level Study (widely known as the APL Study), funded by the then U.S. Office of Education and reported in 1975. Its objectives were to describe adult functional literacy in pragmatic, behavioral, terms and to develop devices for the assessment of literacy which would be useful on a variety of operational levels. To date, the APL Study represents the most systematic and extensive effort to measure functional literacy....

"Some Responses to the Literacy Problem" by Willard Daggett, Director of the Division of Occupational Education Instruction, New York State Education Department.... Education exists within the larger context of society as a whole. As society changes, education must also change, if it is to fulfill its mission of preparing people to *thrive* [emphasis in original].... We have begun evolving into a technological society. Our educational system must also change to provide the highly trained personnel that technology requires. Five years ago, recognizing that basic changes were occurring, the New York State Education Department reviewed its system of vocational and practical arts education, to ensure that through the remaining years of this century we would be preparing our students for the society which would be, not for the society which was. In this review process, which we called "Futuring," we have relied upon both business and industry to determine what skills and knowledge will be needed in the next 15 years, and upon educators in the field and social scientists to recommend how these should be taught.

COMPUTERS IN EDUCATION: REALIZING THE POTENTIAL WAS PUBLISHED BY THE U.S. Department of Education in June, 1983. Under the subtitle "Expert and Novice Thinking" the authors speculate:

Recent studies in science education have revealed that students approach learning with many prior conceptions based on their life experiences, which can be obstacles to learning. These conceptions are very resistant to change. We need to understand why students' conceptions persevere so strongly and how best they can be modified.

"THERE HAS BEEN A CONSPIRACY OF SILENCE ABOUT TEACHING: B.F. SKINNER ARGUES that Pedagogy Is Key to School Reforms" by Susan Walton was published by *Education Week* in its August 31, 1983 issue. Excerpts from this extremely enlightening article follow:

Improving methods of teaching would do more to help public education than would lengthening the school day or any of the other reforms proposed by the National Commission on Excellence in Education and other groups that have recently issued reports on education. So argues B.F. Skinner, the Harvard University psychologist whose pioneering theories about and studies on the "conditioning" of behavior have had a substantial impact on education. Still a source of controversy 40-odd years after Mr. Skinner began his research, those theories have been instrumental in the development of mastery learning and the "teaching machines" of the 1960s. The behavioral scientist's work has also been an integral part of the debate over individualized instruction.... Central to Mr. Skinner's thinking on education are the notions that children should be allowed to learn at their own pace and that teachers should rely on "reinforcers" or rewards, to strengthen patterns of behavior that they want to encourage. Mr. Skinner argues that computers, as they are most commonly used, are essentially sophisticated versions of the "teaching machines" of the 1960s.... Pointing to recent articles and reports on how to improve education, Mr. Skinner argues that one central fallacy is that it is more important for teachers to know their subject matter than to know how to teach it. Mr. Skinner also advises that educators stop making all students advance at essentially the same rate.... No teacher can teach a class of 30 or 40 students and allow each to progress at an optimal speed. Tracking is too feeble a remedy. We must turn to INSTRUMENTS [emphasis in original] for a large part of the school curriculum. The psychologist also urges educators to "program" subject matter. "The heart of the teaching machine, call it what you will, is the programming of instruction—an advance not mentioned in any of the reports I have cited," he writes. He argues "the reinforcing consequences of being right" will eventually prompt students to do what they are supposed to do, but to elicit the behavior the first time, their behavior must be "primed" and "prompted." "Programmed instruction," Mr. Skinner contends, makes "very few demands on teachers."

[Ed. Note: Had the above interview occurred a year later, Skinner would have known that *A Nation at Risk*'s ultimate recommendations would be to implement Skinnerian mastery learning (OBE) "in all the schools of the nation."]

MAINE ASSOCIATION FOR SUPERVISION AND CURRICULUM DEVELOPMENT IN-SERVICE TRAINING was attended by this author in 1983. Dr. S. Alan Cohen led the training. Cohen taught research and curriculum design in the Department of Curriculum and Instruction at the University of San Francisco, California, and was president of SAC Associates, a private consulting firm in systems analysis, evaluation and curriculum design. The following information was contained in a flyer handed out at the in-service training:

His [Cohen's] curriculum research generated the concept of High Intensity Learning, an application of systems theory to classroom management. Today, thousands of schools around the world operate his High Intensity Learning Centers in reading and math. He co-authored the Random House series, the first commercially published basal program developed on the Mastery Learning model. A second Mastery Learning program, published in 1978, teaches pupils how to score high on standardized tests. In 1979 Dr. Cohen authored, designed and published a series of graduate textbooks under a SAC subsidiary, Mastery Learning Systems (MLS). Cohen was one of the architects of the Job Corps Curriculum System. Has been consultant to the Right to Read Office, U.S. Office of Education Office of Economic Opportunity.... His work as consultant and author to Random House and to 20th Century's B.F. Skinner's Reading Program reflects an unusual synthesis of radical behaviorism and humanistic approach to curriculum design....

...[W]ith Harry Passow and Abe Tannebaum of Teachers College, Columbia University, Dr. Cohen formed the education task force in the first War on Poverty, Mobilization for Youth. Since that time, his training in learning psychology has been applied to research, materials and systems development, writing and teaching in three major areas: systems applications to curriculum, teaching the disadvantaged and learning disabilities.

During the in-service training, this writer recorded verbatim Cohen's following points:

In 1976 Block and Burns published in the American Educational Research Association research, around the world on mastery learning. United Nations Educational, Scientific and Cultural Organization (UNESCO) is committed to Mastery Learning all over the world. We have evaluated data worldwide.... Loyola University is the information center for Mastery Learning. Amazing amount of data from all over the world that tells the obvious.... You can account for 97 out of 100 things you give in a test.... Teaching kids to discriminate between long and short "a" is bad... mundane.... Design assessments to fit what teachers are doing.... Avoid misalignment of conditions of instruction and conditions of assessment....

[Referring to the Iowa and California tests] Start teaching to them or stop using them. Find out what they truly measure.... Same issue as defining what you are teaching.... How do you get teachers to measure precisely what they teach? You must have an A and that better be different than B, C. and F because not everyone can get to Harvard. They can't buy the fact that every kid can get an A.... Way we guarantee no discrimination is to teach and test.... Between 1969 and 1971 Omaha, Nebraska implemented mastery learning curriculum citywide. Has best curriculum management I've seen anywhere.... New kind of report card... listed competencies describing what kids can do and described standardized test scores vs. norm-referenced.... Key components of mastery learning are: a) careful control of cues (stimuli), what you bring to student; b) careful control of reinforcers; c) kids on task; and d) recycling (correctives).

THE COMING REVOLUTION IN EDUCATION: BASIC EDUCATION AND THE NEW THEORY OF SCHOOLING (University Press of America, Inc.: Baton Rouge, 1983) by the late Eugene Maxwell Boyce, former professor of educational administration, Bureau of Educational Studies and Field Services, College of Education at the University of Georgia, was published. An excerpt follows:

In the communist ideology the function of universal education is clear, and easily understood. Universal education fits neatly into the authoritarian state. Education is tied directly to jobs—control of the job being the critical control point in an authoritarian state. Level of education, and consequently the level of employment, is determined first by level of achievement in school. They do not educate people for jobs that do not exist.... No such controlled relationship between education and jobs exists in democratic countries. (p. 4)

THE MAINE FACILITATOR REPORT ON CURRENT NATIONAL DIFFUSION NETWORK ACTIVITIES reported in 1983 that "ECRI [Exemplary Center for Reading Instruction] Consortium Winds Down." Excerpt follows:

After five years of operation, the Maine Mastery Learning Consortium will conclude formal operation on August 1. The Consortium, which at times had a membership of as many as thirty school districts, was formed in 1978 to provide the services of an ECRI trainer to Maine teachers using that mastery learning program. Primary support for the Consortium came from Title IV–C, in 1978–1980. From 1980–1982 it operated with federal Title II (Basic Skills) funds, and in the past year with local school district funds. The Consortium is ending at a time when many schools are just beginning to explore the implications of recent teacher effectiveness research. The critical teacher behaviors found to correlate directly with high levels of achievement—specifying learning objectives, setting high standards for mastery, modeling, practicing, eliciting responses from all students, reinforcing correct responses, and time on task—are all key components of the ECRI program that are now being used in a routine way by hundreds of Maine teachers because of the Consortium's services.

NORTHWEST REGIONAL EDUCATIONAL LABORATORY (NWREL) PUBLISHED *EFFECTIVE SCHOOLing Practices: A Research Synthesis—Goal-Based Education Program* in the mid-1980s. [Goal-based education = outcomes-based education] NWREL is a federally funded laboratory whose role has always been to develop goals for American education. An excerpt from *Effective Schooling Practices* follows:

Incentives and Rewards for Students Are Used to Promote Excellence:

1. Systems are set up in the classroom for frequent and consistent rewards to students for academic achievement and excellent behavior; they are appropriate to the developmental level of students; excellence is defined by objective standards, not by peer comparison.
2. All students know about the rewards and what they need to do to get them. Rewards are chosen because they appeal to students.
3. Rewards are related to specific achievements; some may be presented publicly; some should be immediately presented, while others delayed to teach persistence.
4. Parents are told about student successes and requested to help students keep working toward excellence. Brophy (1980); Brophy (1981); Emmer (1981); Evertson (1981); Hunter (1977); Rosswork (1977); Rutter (1979); Walker (1976).

[Ed. Note: An example of the pervasiveness of Skinnerian operant conditioning, with its rewards/reinforcement system, is found in the Effective School Research on "school climate." The definition of "positive/effective school climate" has varied; one definition being "psychologically facilitative environment"—Skinner to the core. The Charles F. Kettering Foundation Ltd. (Dayton, Ohio) *School Climate Profile*, based on Eugene Howard's Colorado Model, contains a mark-off sheet with blocks in which data are arranged by "Almost Never, Occasionally, Frequently, and Almost Always" to score behavior. Under "Program Determinants" from "Definitions of Climate Terms" in Howard's Colorado Model, we find this wording:

2. INDIVIDUALIZED PERFORMANCE EXPECTATION AND VARIED REWARD SYSTEMS:

Practices are identified whereby staff members recognize individual differences among pupils. Everyone is not expected to learn the same things in the same way or in the same length of time. Rewards are sufficiently available so that all pupils, with effort, may expect to be positively and frequently recognized by the school.

RESEARCHER AND WRITER K.M. HEATON, IN HER REVISED EDITION OF AN ARTICLE ENTITLED "Preconditioning for Acceptance of Change" explained very clearly in 1983 how radical change in our republican form of government has been brought about at the local level through the use of psychopolitics.[11] The following are excerpts from Mrs. Heaton's article:

Variants of these control strategies have been, and are being, used on every front in this war. A case in point: In the early seventies, a textbook was developed by a think tank in Berkeley, with the authority of the Governor's [Ronald Reagan] office, and coordinated by the Council on Intergovernmental Relations, which provided an elementary course in the use of psychopolitics "to provide the operant mechanism to change events in local government" (a direct quote). Named as the essential elements for planned change were:

- development of a climate for change;
- a crisis of major importance;
- a catastrophe having a physical effect on community;
- mounting cost of government, and/or major services;
- and/or collapse of government's ability to deal with these.

The Politics of Change (TPOC) then proceeded to suggest how to create these elements. TPOC offers *prima facie* evidence of a deliberate, calculated scheme to disinform, mislead, manage and control the destiny of local government in California and its citizens, without regard for legal, moral or ethical considerations.

1984

DURING JANUARY AND FEBRUARY OF 1984, THIS WRITER—WITH THE HELP OF GRASSROOTS activists and several officials in the U.S. Department of Education—organized witnesses and testimony to be presented at the U.S. Department of Education "Hatch Amendment" hearings held in seven cities: Seattle, Washington; Pittsburgh, Pennsylvania; Kansas City, Missouri; Phoenix, Arizona; Concord, New Hampshire; Orlando, Florida; and Washington, D.C. These hearings were held "pursuant to the notice of proposed rulemaking to implement Sec. 439 of the *General Education Provisions Act* (*The Protection of Pupil Rights Amendment*)."

This *Amendment* is usually referred to as the "Hatch [Sen. Orrin] Amendment," although the senator who originated it and was most involved in the initial important wording was the late Senator Edward Zorinsky (D.-Neb). As the amendment went through the Congressional committee process, Zorinsky's most important wording was weakened or deleted.

The weakened wording which attempted to address long-standing problems experienced by parents and good educators follows:

Protection of Pupil Rights, 20 U.S. Code Sec. 1232h, Inspection by parents or guardians of instructional material....

(a) All instructional material, including teachers' manuals, films, tapes, or other supplementary instructional materials which will be used in connection with any research or experimentation program or project shall be available for inspection by the parents or guardians of the children engaged in such program or project. For the purpose of this section "research or experimentation program or project" means any program or project in any applicable program designed to explore or... develop new or unproven teaching methods or techniques....

Psychiatric or psychological examination, testing or treatment:...

(b) No student shall be required, as part of any applicable program, to submit to psychiatric examination, testing or treatment, or psychological examination, testing or treatment, in which the primary purpose is to reveal information concerning political affiliations; mental and psychological problems potentially embarrassing to the student or his family; sexual behavior and attitudes; illegal, anti-social, self-incriminating and demeaning behavior; critical appraisals of other individuals with whom respondents have close family relationships; legally recognized privileged and analogous relationships, such as those of lawyers, physicians, and ministers; or income (other than that required by law to determine eligibility for participation in a program or for receiving financial assistance under such program); without the prior consent of the student (if the student is an adult or emancipated minor), or in the case of an unemancipated minor, without the prior written consent of the parent.

AT THE ANNUAL MEETING OF THE AMERICAN EDUCATIONAL RESEARCH ASSOCIATION HELD in New Orleans, Louisiana in April of 1984, Brian Rowan, Ph.D. in sociology, presented a paper entitled "Shamanistic Rituals in Effective Schools." The work on this "curious" paper was supported by the National Institute of Education, U.S. Department of Education (Contract #400–83–003). Rowan should be noted as one of the principal investigators involved in the infamous 1984 grant to Utah (See later 1984 entry for Utah grant) to implement William Spady's Outcome-Based Education program, the purpose of which was to "put OBE into all the schools of the nation."

The "curious" nature of this paper is derived from Dr. Rowan's implied criticism of the very Effective Schools Research with which he is so closely associated. The importance of Rowan's paper lies in Rowan's professional credentials and willingness to bring to the debate table a discussion of the legitimacy of claims of "effectiveness" made by those associated with the Effective Schools movement (William Spady, et al.), including promoting outcome-based education, mastery learning and direct instruction—all of which are required by Effective Schools Research. This presentation helps one to better understand the dismal academic results to be found in schools using Effective Schools Research; i.e., most often urban schools attended by underprivileged and minority children.

The following quotes are taken from "Shamanistic Rituals in Effective Schools" which can be found in its entirety in Appendix XXVI of this book:

> We begin with one of the most common shamanistic rituals in the effective schools movement, the glowing literature review....
>
> ...Lacking a systematic understanding of the scientific pros and cons of effective schools research, naïve individuals are left only with the powerful and appealing rhetoric of the reviewers.... The experienced shaman knows to avoid the scrutiny of scholars, for this can raise objections to the "scientific" basis of ritual claims and divert attention away from the appealing rhetoric. Instead, the shaman cultivates the practitioner who needs a simple and appealing formula.
>
> Thus, any experienced shaman can find "effective" schools....
>
> The ritual is particularly suited to application in urban or low performing school systems where successful instructional outcomes among disadvantaged students are highly uncertain but where mobilized publics demand immediate demonstrations of success. The uncertainties faced by practitioners in this situation can easily be alleviated by what scholars have begun to call curriculum alignment [teach to the test]....
>
> Thus, the art of measurement can be used as an aid to shamanism, especially in urban schools plagued by the uncertainties of student performance. Student variability in performance can be reduced, and relative performance increased, not by changing instructional objectives or practices, but simply by changing tests and testing procedures.

THE OFFICE OF EDUCATIONAL RESEARCH AND IMPROVEMENT OF THE U.S. DEPARTMENT OF Education in 1984 approved a grant from the Secretary's Discretionary Fund in the amount of $134,459 (Grant No. 122BH40196) to Vanderbilt University to implement Vanderbilt's proposal entitled "National Network for Educational Excellence." This project covered a period from October 1984–October 1985 to use a computer-based network of fifty superintendents to collect and exchange information about "effective" practices and to encourage national dialogue about increasing school "effectiveness," so as to promote educational excellence. (Quotation marks have been added around the words "effective" and "effectiveness" to alert the reader to the fact that this grant was another effort to implement "Effective Schools Research" based on Skinnerian psychology. Rowan's remarks in the entry prior to this one cast an interesting light on this information.) At the time this grant was made, Chester Finn was professor of education and public policy at Vanderbilt University. Finn would shortly thereafter be named assistant secretary to the Office of Educational Research and Improvement under Secretary of Education William Bennett who, in 1985, provided over $4 million to implement Effective School Research nationwide.

A LETTER TO PRESIDENT RONALD REAGAN WAS WRITTEN BY WILLARD W. GARVEY, EXECUtive director of the National Center for Privatization, dated April 6, 1984.[12] An excerpt follows:

> Privatization is now an idea whose time has come.... The knowledge, communication and computer industry can make political representatives obsolete. Privatization might well be the theme for the 200th anniversary of the Constitution. Privatization is essential for national salvation.

The following notation was printed on the letterhead of the above-mentioned letter:

> The National Center for Privatization is supported by the following groups and individuals: Heritage and Reason Foundations; Pacific and Manhattan Institutes; VOLUNTEER; National Center for Citizen Involvement; International Executive Service Corps; United Way with its Services Identification System; National Legal Center for the Public; churches; labor unions, Peter Drucker and Milton Friedman.

THE SPRING 1984 ISSUE (VOL. 7, NO.4) OF EDUCATION UPDATE FROM THE ASSOCIATION FOR Supervision and Curriculum Development carried the following statements:

> One comprehensive study concludes that counseling can have marked deleterious effects on problem students. Joan McCord, a Drexel University sociologist, undertook a 30-year follow up study of a classic, highly respected study on juvenile delinquency—"The Cambridge Somerville Youth Study." In the original study (first report in 1948) an experimental group of 253 high-risk problem boys were given extensive counseling. A control group matched as to behavior, history, and family background received no counseling. In 1975 Professor McCord contacted the original participants and compared the circumstances of the experimental and control subjects. The experimental subjects were, among other things, found more likely to commit criminal acts, be alcoholics, suffer from mental illness, die younger, and have less prestigious jobs than the control group.

[Ed. Note: The results of this study match the negative results discussed in the May 1977 issue of *The School Counselor*, American Personnel and Guidance Association's Special Issue on Death, which said,"Death education will play as important a part in changing attitudes toward death as sex education played in changing attitudes toward sex information and wider acceptance of various sexual practices." In other words, counseling, sex ed and death ed have *negative* effects, *if*, as one would hope and expect, the purpose of such programs is to help young people live happy and stable lives. This is particularly disturbing in light of increased student violence which has taken place in the nation recently.]

STEPHEN BROADY OF TARKIO, MISSOURI PRESENTED TESTIMONY IN 1984 AT THE U.S. DEpartment of Education's Region VII hearing on "Notice of Proposed Rulemaking to further implement Section 439 of the *General Education Provisions Act*, 34 CFR, Parts 75, 76, and 98, 20 U.S.C.A. Section 2132(h) 20 U.S.C. 1231e–3(a)(1), 1232h *(Hatch Amendment)*." Broady's statement exposes the controversial nature of the two leading mastery learning programs— Exemplary Center for Reading Instruction (ECRI) and Project INSTRUCT—both of which use Skinnerian operant conditioning and both of which submitted claims of effectiveness which have been questioned by persons involved in implementing and evaluating the programs. The third program, DISTAR (Direct Instruction for Systematic Teaching and Remediation), which is similar to ECRI, is the highly recommended "scientific, research-based" phonics program so popular with conservatives in the late 1990s. The following are some excerpts from Stephen Broady's testimony:

> I am a farmer currently engaged in the operation of over one thousand acres of prime farm ground. I became interested in education after my wife and I observed emotional change in our daughter while she was attending a rural public school using an "approved" federal educational project... "Project INSTRUCT"... approved for funding in the amount of $710,000 and for nationwide use by the Joint Dissemination Review Panel on May 14, 1975 (JDRP #75–37).
>
> Although Project INSTRUCT is only one of over 300 "approved" educational projects, Project INSTRUCT and the educational project upon which it is based, the Exemplary Center for Reading Instruction (ECRI), are the most widely used mastery learning educational projects in the United States.
>
> ...These mastery learning systems use a type of psychological manipulation based on the Skinnerian ideology of rewards and punishments, and individual feelings are irrelevant.... More commonly referred to as "behavior modification," the Skinnerian ideology which is used in the teaching techniques of these mastery learning systems, breaks down the process of learning into small bits of information and actually codes a type of behavior that is desired into the learning process itself.
>
> The real objective of these mastery learning systems with their behavior modification, is a deliberate attempt to make children conform to an artificial environment which is more suited to the thinking of the school than to the needs of the children.
>
> These federally funded mastery learning systems require the use on young children of a highly structured curriculum, test and re-test with the use of criterion tests, stopwatches, direct eye contact, physical contact, and psychological manipulation until the so-called "mastery" of the subject is achieved. These ideas and practices form a complex philosophy in which the "authoritarian" concept predominates.
>
> In the early part of 1983, I obtained the evaluation report of Project INSTRUCT from the

superintendent's office of the Lincoln Public Schools. At that time I was unaware the so-called behavior modification based on Skinner's rewards and punishments was used on my daughter.

The evaluation results clearly referred to behavioral objectives which were... established for: (a) students; (b) parents; (c) administrators; (d) media specialists; (e) project staff; (f) teachers; (g) paraprofessionals and volunteers, and (h) prospective teachers.

The wholesale use of behavior modification is part of Skinnerian psychology. As it was outlined in the evaluation, Project INSTRUCT includes rewards and punishments, not only for school children, but for anyone who comes in contact with the school system itself.

The *Evaluation of Project INSTRUCT, Executive Summary*, written by Carl Spencer, project director for Lincoln Public Schools, also explains that:

> Project INSTRUCT grew from beliefs that to reduce reading failure reading programs must (1) be diagnostic and prescriptive so that failure does not begin to occur, (2) be implemented by regular teachers in regular classrooms, (3) provide direct rather than indirect teaching, (4) correlate instruction in all language skills, particularly reading, spelling and handwriting....

The intent and emphasis in 1970 was on behavioral indices and concrete ways of showing accountability; and the data would suggest that the reading of the students themselves may not have increased, but the impact of Project INSTRUCT in the Lincoln, Nebraska Publish Schools seems to be very extensive and influential.

[Ed. Note: Project INSTRUCT accomplished its major objective—it developed and installed a less than successful reading program in Lincoln, Nebraska using a model which could be transported to other districts. It also had considerable impact upon the district as a whole, on schools outside of Lincoln and even on the Nebraska State Department of Education. In assessing this impact as a whole, Dr. Ronald Brandt, assistant superintendent for instruction, has said of this project, "Project INSTRUCT made a lasting contribution to instruction in the Lincoln Schools by helping us improve our planning capabilities and by furthering the concepts of focused instruction and mastery learning."

It should be noted that Dr. Ronald Brandt went on to become the executive editor of the Association for Supervision and Curriculum Development's (ASCD) publication *Educational Leadership*. ASCD could be considered the most influential education organization in the world, outside of UNESCO.]

DAVID W. HORNBECK, CHAIRMAN OF THE BOARD OF TRUSTEES OF THE CARNEGIE FOUNDA-tion for the Advancement of Teaching and Maryland's state school superintendent, oversaw the implementation of Project BASIC in 1984. Project BASIC was based on the very controversial Management by Objectives (MBO/PPBS) that is thoroughly discussed in this book.

One of the more controversial graduation requirements in Project BASIC was "the worthy use of leisure time," which was later given the more acceptable and politically correct label of "arts and recreation"—another semantic deception at work. However, Hornbeck's penultimate controversial recommendation—one which would reverberate from coast to coast, resulting in heated debate at local school board meetings—was his recommendation to the Maryland State Board of Education that community service become a mandatory graduation requirement. Many objections were raised on the grounds that that recommendation constituted involuntary servitude, thus making it unconstitutional.

[Ed. Note: In this writer's opinion, David Hornbeck is a soft-hearted, highly paid "should-have-been" Presbyterian minister do-gooder who approaches his job with missionary fervor rooted in theologian Reinhold Niebuhr's idea that a good Christian must strive to correct any unjust status quo. However, his mission seems to be to help implement a socialist world government, increasingly referred to as "The New World Disorder," as was the goal of the do-gooder Federal Council of Churches in 1942, working toward all being equally poor, miserable and illiterate.

Should the elitist power brokers, for whatever reason, feel they need the expertise of the Hornbecks of this world, please spare those least able to protect themselves—the minorities and disadvantaged—from the change agents' experimentation.]

AN ARTICLE ENTITLED "INDUSTRIAL POLICY URGED FOR GOP" WAS PUBLISHED IN *THE Washington Post* on May 14, 1984. Excerpts follow:

SAN FRANCISCO (UPI)—A conservative study group founded by supporters of President Reagan is about to issue a report that advocates Republicans shed some of their deep-rooted antipathy to a planned economy.

An industrial policy accepted by both political parties and by business and labor is essential to revitalize America's dwindling clout in the world economy, according to the study's editor, Professor Chalmers Johnson of the University of California.

"The Industrial Policy Debate" is to be issued today by the Institute for Contemporary Studies, a think-tank founded by presidential counselor Edwin Meese, Secretary of Defense Caspar Weinberger and other Reagan supporters.

"What we are really trying to pose is a serious debate that has become stupidly politicized by both parties," Johnson said. "We are trying to get the question of an industrial policy for the United States to be taken seriously by people who don't really believe in it—above all Republicans.

"Americans must come to grips with economic policy or go the way of England. We have probably got a decade before it becomes irreversible."

In the United States, he said, "The whole topic we are trying to address is so caught up with politics and the particular positions of industries that it is very hard to disentangle what we mean by economic policy."

While the Democrats are "planning to throw money at the northern Midwest 'rust' belt" to get votes, Johnson said many Republicans "are painting themselves into a corner by attacking the very concept of industrial policy—arguing that it violates the sacred principles of private enterprise and free trade."

He cited as a valid and successful national economic policy "the kind of government-business relationship" that has made Japan a leading economic force in the world. "A government-business relationship is needed in a competitive capitalist economy," he said.

"Reaganomics without an accompanying industrial policy to guide it, has been costly," Johnson said.

U.S. DEPARTMENT OF EDUCATION PRESS RELEASE FOR JUNE 14, 1984 FOLLOWS:

Secretary of Education T.H. Bell today announced planned missions and geographic regions for a nationwide network of educational research laboratories and centers in preparation for the largest discretionary grant competition ever conducted by the U.S. Department of Education. Centers will be selected to construct research on improving: writing; learning; teacher quality and effectiveness; teacher education; testing, evaluation and standards; effective elementary schools; effective secondary schools; education and employment; postsecondary education management and governance; postsecondary teaching and learning; and state and local policy development and leadership in education. For the first time in almost two decades, all parts of the United States will receive full services from the research laboratories.

[Ed. Note: All of the above increase in federal control came from an office (NIE) in the U.S. Department of Education which President Reagan had promised to abolish. Note the emphasis on funding for OBE/"effective schools," which use Skinnerian operant conditioning methods.]

IN 1984 JACQUELINE LAWRENCE GAVE TESTIMONY BEFORE THE SUBCOMMITTEE ON EDUCAtion, Arts and Humanities of the Senate Committee on Labor and Human Resources which held hearings on *Senate Joint Resolution 138*, a bill establishing a commission on teacher education. Excerpts from Mrs. Lawrence's testimony follow:

> My name is Jacqueline Lawrence. I am a parent from Montgomery County, Maryland....
>   Prior to the 1960s, American public schools placed major emphasis on the intellectual development of our children, on their mastery of basic skills such as reading, writing and mathematics. Competency in physics, biology, chemistry, and chronological factual history was required. Cognitive learning and scholarly objectivity were stressed as the basic approach to education at all levels. As a result, our nation produced a large, well-educated middle class—our greatest strength.

[Ed. Note: Mrs. Lawrence's comments regarding the "major emphasis on intellectual development prior to the 1960s" remind the writer of a scholarly ancient history textbook used in a high school history course at the Rockland, Maine District High School as late as the early 1970s. (It took awhile for the change agents to penetrate a fishing community on the coast of Maine!) The textbook written by Professor James Breasted, an Egyptologist and Semitic scholar, is a fascinating and extremely well written history of Ancient Greece, Egypt, etc., with few black and white photographs, quizzes at the end of each chapter, and text written for college level students. That was only 25 years ago! It would be virtually impossible to find a textbook of that scholarly level in public high schools or in most colleges today. This writer has nothing but a feeling of tremendous sadness pondering the vapid education landscape Americans seem so willing to accept for their offspring. It is my constant hope that American apathy in this regard is due to their not knowing what has happened, and that once they know, they will—all of them—collectively and individually attempt to reverse this situation.]

Mrs. Lawrence continued:

> It is public knowledge that since the 1960s academic standards have declined. Why? Quite simply, over the past 20 years our schools have not placed emphasis on academic achievement. There has instead been a shift toward psychological development and social adjustment of students in the affective domain, that is, their feelings, attitudes, and opinions.
>   The shift began in 1965 with the passage of the *Elementary and Secondary Education Act* (ESEA).... Since 1965, billions of federal dollars have been allocated to educational theo-

rists and curriculum developers to alter the course of public education. The blueprint for the process of educational reform may be found in a series of guides known as *Pacesetters in Innovation....* From this has come a nationwide information network of ERIC clearinghouses (Educational Resource Information Centers) and the National Diffusion Network of laboratories for the dissemination of federally funded classroom materials and curriculum.

With the new programs came a retraining of the teachers. A prime example: in 1969 the Office of Education began financing model teacher education programs known as the Behavior Science Teacher Education Program (BSTEP–OE 5803) to introduce to the classroom methods employed by the behavioral scientists, the sociometrist, and the psychiatrist.

Such methods are the most coercive and manipulative known to man today. They were originally developed and used for treating mentally disturbed in mental institutions and the criminally insane in prisons. The techniques are role-playing, psychodrama, sociodrama, simulation games, guided fantasy, diary-keeping, situation attitude scale tests, encounter groups, magic circle, and behavior modification such as isolation, time-out boxes and coffins, as well as operant conditioning. These are techniques to influence by clinical, hospital procedures the thinking processes of children in a compulsory classroom setting.

In addition to training teachers, a special cadre of sensitive manipulators, known as change agents, were trained to facilitate the process of change and to identify forces which resisted change.

The change agent serves as a catalyst for teacher and citizen awareness and attempts to gain support for educational change.

Dr. John Goodlad's *Report to the President's Commission on School Finance, Issue #9,* "Strategies for Change," dated October 1971, explains that the change agent is the decision-maker. He decides which changes a school will make. The report states that five to fifteen percent of the people in a given community are open to change. They are the Early Majority and can be counted on to be supportive. A second group, 60 to 90 percent, are the Resisters; they need special attention and careful strategies. Also there are Leaders, formal and informal, and their support is critical for effecting change.

In a diagram from the report... you will note that the change agent creates the Early Majority and influences the Leaders, and then gets both of these groups to act in concert with him to level a triple attack on the Resisters.

Goodlad's report to the President expressed concern about the willingness of the people to change: "People cannot be forced to change until they are psychologically ready."...

...Even if we assume for the sake of argument that change agents are gifted with infinite knowledge and wisdom, their methods are in conflict with the political principles of democracy. Their changes in curriculum and methods and goals of education have not come as a result of democratic discussion and decision.

In this vein, it is interesting to note that the Maryland State Teachers Association has lobbied against proposed state legislation for parental access to classroom materials because teachers "would be ineffective as change agents."...

...Moreover, education is now termed psycho-social, psycho-medical, humanistic, affective and/or diagnostic and prescriptive. Educators diagnose the child's emotional, intellectual, perceptual and conceptual development levels. Dr. Benjamin Bloom explains that what educators are classifying is the intended behavior of students, or as he puts it, "the ways in which individuals are to act, think, or feel as a result of participating in some unit of instruction."

In order to bring about desired attitudinal changes in students, teachers must first know where a child is in his or her attitudes and opinions. Various tactics and techniques are used in classrooms to make a child reveal himself to his teacher and peers. The examples I use below are nationally used and have received federal funding:

- Magic circle, talk-in, contact or group discussions: The teacher gathers the children into a circle where they are encouraged to discuss personal feelings about one another, their parents, and home life. Family size, advantages, disadvantages, comparison of toys, vacations, and clothing may be discussed. Family conflicts, worries and fears are often revealed.

- Inside-Out: A nationally-used elementary social studies program encourages students to discuss their feelings before, during and after their parents' divorce; their personal reactions to the death of a friend, pet or relative; what your friends think of you; what adults think of you and what you think of yourself.

- Logbooks: These are workbooks used in conjunction with many language arts textbooks. They are vehicles for children to reveal their reactions to short stories, often dealing with emotions and moral dilemmas. There are no right answers, only personal responses. Sometimes the logbooks guide the child into a response. For instance:

  > Even if your family is a happy one, you're bound to feel sad... or even lonely. When might a person be lonely even if he is part of a family? Loneliness is listening to your parents arguing. Loneliness is when you come home and there's no one there. Loneliness is....

Perhaps the most frequently used strategies for self-revelation are the diary and role-playing. These techniques were introduced into American public schools by an Estonian teacher, Hilda Taba, and a Romanian psychiatrist, Jacob Moreno.

[Ed. Note: In 1957 a California State Senate Investigative Committee exposed the work of Hilda Taba, Jacob Moreno and others. In spite of this exposure, these people continued to receive tax dollars and access to schools nationwide. Hilda Taba's program has remained in use by key change agents from 1960 to 1999. Bruce Joyce and Marsha Weil's *Models of Teaching* mentions her work as well as that of many other sociologists, behavioral psychologists, etc. As a school board director in 1976, the writer found materials related to the above-described programs and many others described by Mrs. Lawrence in a box given to her by a home economics teacher. Needless to say, the writer was shocked to find that behavior modification was being introduced into the curriculum under the innocent-sounding "home economics" label.]

The U.S. Office of Education gave grants to Taba to develop an elementary social studies program to improve the social adjustment and personality development of children. She had worked in reform schools and mental institutions with Moreno and found that role-playing and diaries were successful tools to learn where a child stood in his beliefs, attitudes, and social interactions.

The diary has been used for years in Russia and China for self-revelation, self-evaluation, and self-criticism. More recently the personal diary was found in Guyana throughout the Jim Jones compound.

Montgomery County, Maryland, requires its students to keep a diary from kindergarten through grade nine. Diaries are an important psychological instrument. They provide a precise record and personality profile of the child, his family members, neighbors and peers—information needed by the teacher or therapist to alter a student's behavior or attitude. It is important that the writing be free-style and spontaneous, coming directly from the emotional feeling area of the child. Diaries are not corrected for form, grammar or spelling....

A teacher manual for values education suggests 15 kinds of diaries for use in the classroom; some examples are a budget diary, religion diary, hostility and anger diary, low points diary, affectionate and tender feelings diary, and a time diary....

In the psycho-social approach to education, the child is taught concepts through the use of psychotherapy. For example, to better understand the social problem of prejudice and to teach children through experiential learning, blond children in a fifth grade (age 10) were asked to sit in the back of the room for one week, totally isolated, not permitted to participate in the classwork. For a one-and-a-half hour period each day, brown-haired students were instructed to pick on, insult, make fun of or taunt the blonds. Needless to say, taunting spilled over onto the playground with some of the blonds being told, "You can't play with us." At the end of the week, blonds were given candy bars as a reward for their suffering, but the browns, who in bullying were obeying the teacher's instructions, were given nothing. How does a child react to being punished or deprived for carrying out his assignment? How much learning went on in that classroom for five days? Some children enjoyed taunting and bullying. Was the week spent on such "experiential learning" quality time? What about the seven and one-half hours spent in taunting? Would this time have been better spent on academic learning?...

Educators use the even more volatile psycho-drama for attitudinal change. One example is the concept that we must prune away defective persons in order to improve the quality of life for the remainder of the group. This drama involves murder. Many variations are found. I first came across this psychodrama theme in a federally funded home economics curriculum guide... containing the exercise "Whom Will You Choose?" It goes as follows: 11 people are in a bomb shelter with provisions sufficient to last 11 persons two weeks or six persons a month. The group is told that five persons must be killed. They are instructed to accept the situation as fact, that is, to concern themselves with life/death choices, not with attacking the logic or probability of the situation. A profile is given of each person in the shelter. Problem people, such as the athlete who eats too much, the religious type with "hang-ups," the pregnant or ill are generally killed. Survivors tend to be those trained in medicine, engineers, and pacifiers.

[Ed. Note: Jacqueline and Malcolm Lawrence had just returned from their Foreign Service assignment in Europe and were appalled to encounter what had happened to American education in their absence. The Lawrences organized "Parents Who Care" and began to confront the school district with what they had discovered. Due to the broad publicity generated by the group's assertions and activities, Edward Hunter, former intelligence service operative and author of two books on his coined word "brainwashing" as practiced pre- and post-World War II[13]—*Brainwashing* and *Brainwashing in Red China: The Men Who Defied It*—approached the Lawrences with a request to examine the curriculum materials about which they had become concerned. Hunter took the materials for a period of time and upon returning them, informed Jackie and Malcolm that they were indeed examples of methods and techniques used in Russian and Chinese brainwashing. (The Maryland State School Board also made a statement regarding the fact that Maryland's teachers were not trained to use "psychoanalytical techniques in the classroom.") The psycho-social technique for confronting prejudice (isolation of the blonds) should be especially disturbing in light of increased concern over schoolyard taunting and increased school violence at the close of this century.]

"E.C.S. AT 20: THE COMPACT'S POTENTIAL IS STILL TO BE REALIZED" BY THOMAS TOCH was an article from *Education Week* (October 24, 1984) which covered the early history of the Education Commission of the States. Excerpts follow:

"Some degree of order needs to be brought out of this chaos," wrote James B. Conant, the President of Harvard University, in 1964 in reference to education policymaking in this nation. "We cannot have a national educational policy," he added in his book *Shaping Educational Policy*, "but we might be able to evolve a nationwide policy." The solution, Mr. Conant concluded, was a "new venture in cooperative federalism," a compact among the states to create an organization to focus national attention on the pressing education issues of the day. The following spring, the Carnegie Corporation and the Ford Foundation awarded a grant to Terry Sanford, who had recently left the governorship of North Carolina, to transform the Conant idea into reality. John W. Gardner was Carnegie's president at the time. A preliminary draft of the compact was completed by July and endorsed by representatives from all 50 states and the territories in September. Within five months, 10 states had ratified the agreement, giving it legal status. Out of the compact was born the Education Commission of the States (ECS)....

"We invented a little device to get the compact approved quickly," Mr. Sanford, now the president of Duke University, said recently. "We didn't need money from the legislatures, we had plenty of foundation funding, so we agreed that the governors could ratify it by executive order."...

But since the establishment under Governor James B. Hunt [also of North Carolina] of the Commission's Task Force on Education for Economic Growth two years ago, ECS's role has begun to change. The task force's report *Action for Excellence* joined *A Nation at Risk* and the Carnegie Foundation for the Advancement of Teaching's *High School* as principal voices in the chorus of reform. It gained Gov. Hunt and several other "education governors" who were linked to ECS wide national publicity, and, in making a series of specific reform recommendations, thrust ECS into the policy-making arena.

[Ed. Note: The multi-million dollar contract to operate the National Assessment of Educational Progress, awarded to the ECS in 1969, was transferred to Educational Testing Service (ETS) in 1983. This move was significant due to Carnegie's deep involvement in establishing, funding, and directing ECS's and ETS's activities. Essentially, this move gave Carnegie Corporation and Carnegie Foundation for the Advancement of Teaching extensive control over the direction and content of American education as a whole and individual state policy making in paticular with regard to education. Dennis Cuddy, Ph.D.—rightly, it seems—refers to the U.S. Department of Education as the "Carnegie Department of Education."]

THE PRESIDENTIALLY APPOINTED NATIONAL COUNCIL FOR EDUCATIONAL RESEARCH (NCER) issued two "Policies on Missions for Educational Research and Development Centers," dated June 14 and October 25, 1984, shortly after regional hearings had been held regarding the need for regulations to implement the *Protection of Pupil Rights Amendment* (PPRA). The following are excerpts from NCER's two policy statements:

JUNE 14, 1984. In the past two decades, federally funded research and curriculum projects have frequently provoked considerable controversy. This is primarily a result of deeply divergent philosophical views on the nature and purpose of public education in this country. During this period, the views of the general public were, for the most part, excluded from serious consideration as educational research came to be viewed as the observation and measurement of the education process using the largely quantitative techniques of modern social science [Skinnerian behaviorism].

OCTOBER 25, 1984. Insofar as it represents a broad spectrum of interests, including parents who have a serious stake in the outcomes of federally funded educational research, the Council affirms that the fundamental philosophical foundation for such research should be the unambiguous recognition and respect for the dignity and value of each human person.

For the past fifteen years the U.S. Department of Education has ignored the testimony taken at the regional hearings, the views spelled out in the above-mentioned policies, as well as the requirements of the PPRA. The two policy statements represent a strong position taken by the National Council, which oversaw the research activities of the former National Institute of Education prior to its being incorporated into the Office of Educational Research and Improvement (OERI). The Council had quite obviously read the important testimony regarding Skinnerian mastery learning/direct instruction which was given at the regional hearings on the PPRA. The Council took a stand on the most important question facing us today in education: Are we, as free Americans, going to continue to accept the succinctly expressed definition of educational research included in the last sentence of the June 14 policy, a definition which is undeniably behaviorist and part of the behavioral psychologists' vocabulary—"observation and measurement of the educational process using the largely quantitative techniques of modern social science"? Or do we agree with the Council that the fundamental philosophical foundation for such research should be the "unambiguous recognition and respect for the dignity and value of each human person"?

[Ed. Note: As a complete counterpoint to the strong policy position taken by the council, the following information should be carefully considered. Professor Robert Glaser, professor of psychology and education and co-director of the Learning Research and Development Center of the University of Pittsburgh, was for all intents and purposes put in charge of the Commission on Reading in 1983. It was Glaser who appointed members to the Commission on Reading, thereby wielding considerable influence on the recommendations resulting from that Commission's report, *Becoming a Nation of Readers*, for which Glaser wrote the foreward and which was published under the auspices of the National Academy of Education's Commission on Education and Public Policy with sponsorship from the National Institute of Education. That report was probably the most important study which set the stage for the *Reading Excellence Act of 1998* (REA), setting in motion numerous activities which resulted in a determination that only proposals which were based on "scientific research" would be accepted for funding under the REA. In the foreward to *Becoming a Nation of Readers*, Glaser said:

> In teaching, as in other professions, well-researched methods and tools are essential. This report makes clear the key role of teachers' professional knowledge. Research on instructional pacing and grouping and on adaptation to children's accomplishments has contributed to new ideas that can help all children master the basics and then attain levels of literacy far beyond the basic competencies. The reading teacher's repertoire must draw upon the deepening knowledge of child development, of the nature of the art and elegance of children's literature, and of the psychology of learning.... The report indicates why changes in teacher training, internship experiences, continuing, and sabbatical periods are necessary if teachers are to learn and refine their skills for their complex task.

Professor Glaser's credentials are uniquely important, placing him in a position of prominence regarding what method of instruction will be used in American classrooms—one based on the worldview that man is a human being, created in the image of God, with conscience, soul, intellect, creativity, free will, or one based on the new psychology of learning ("scientific," evolutionist, "research-based")—the worldview that man is an animal whose behavior can be manipulated by creating the necessary environment to bring about predictable, predetermined, neurologically conditioned responses. (The reader should refer to Appendix III, "Excerpts from *Programmed Learning: Evolving Principles and Industrial Applications*," which is a report of a 1960 seminar of businessmen and social scientists to discuss programmed learning and its application to business, at which professors B.F. Skinner, Arthur A. Lumsdaine and Robert Glaser were the speakers and discussion leaders. Robert Glaser was also a research advisor to the American Institute for Research at that time. Several pages of this report of the seminar are devoted to Glaser's "Principles of Programming.")

According to the following quote from an official Mission, Texas, school memorandum to concerned parents, Exemplary Center for Reading Instruction (ECRI), the fraternal twin of DISTAR (Direct Instruction for Systematic Teaching and Remediation), led the pack as far as Robert Glaser's National Commission on Reading was concerned:

> In 1986 ECRI was evaluated as playing a primary role in the United States becoming a nation of readers. The Regional Laboratory for Educational Improvement (sponsored by the U.S. Office of Educational and Improvement) published *Implementing the Recommendations of Becoming a Nation of Readers*. This document makes a line-by-line comparison of 31 reading programs, including ECRI. ECRI received the highest score of all 31 programs in meeting the specific recommendations of the National Commission on Reading.

Siegfried Engelmann's DISTAR (Reading Mastery) and ECRI are both based on the very sick philosophical world view that considers man nothing but an animal—an "organism" (in Skinner's words)—responsive to the manipulation of stimulus-response-stimulus immediate reinforcement or rewards to bring about predetermined, predictable behaviors. Skinner's quote about making a "pigeon a high achiever by reinforcing it on a proper schedule" is repeated often in this book to impress on the reader the horrifying aspect of animal training masquerading as education in these programs.

The National Research Council's *Preventing Reading Difficulties in Young Children*, compiled by Catherine E. Snow, M. Susan Burns, and Peg Griffin, Eds. (National Academy Press: Washington, D.C., 1998) acknowledged G. Reid Lyon, Ph.D., chief of the Learning Disabilities, Cognitive, and Social Development Branch of the National Institute of Child Health and Human Development of the National Institutes of Health (U.S. Department of Health and Human Services) who supports behaviorist reading programs like ECRI and DISTAR (Reading Mastery) as well as instruction based on so-called "medical and scientific research." Other individuals mentioned in *Preventing Reading Difficulties* who were involved in the promotion of DISTAR include Edward Kame'enui, Department of Special Education of the University of Oregon and Marilyn Jager Adams. These two individuals also served on the Committee on the Prevention of Reading Difficulties in Young Children, and Adams is mentioned in *Becoming a Nation of Readers*. (See 1998 Herzer critique of *Preventing Reading Difficulties in Young Children*.)

What does all of this tell the reader? Perhaps the same thing that is suggested to this writer: that the *Reading Excellence Act* will provide the funding and technical assistance to implement across the nation not just reading programs, but all curricula—including workforce training—in the mode of DISTAR and ECRI, which are based on "scientific, medical research." It is difficult to come to any other conclusion.

In light of this information, the *Reading Excellence Act of 1998* should be repealed. It is an unconstitutional curriculum mandate in violation of the *General Education Provisions Act of the Elementary and Secondary Education Act of 1965.* Call your congressmen and senators and ask that they support legislation to repeal this *Act.*]

IN 1984 *SCHOOLING AND TECHNOLOGY, VOL. 3, PLANNING FOR THE FUTURE: A COLLABORAtive Model, An Interpretive Report on Creative Partnerships in Technology—An Open Forum* by Dustin H. Heuston, World Institute for Computer-Assisted Teaching (WICAT) was published (Southeastern Regional Council for Educational Improvement: Research Triangle Park, North Carolina, 1984) under a grant from the U.S. Office of Education, HEW, National Institute of Education. An excerpt from "Discussion: Developing the Potential of an Amazing Tool" in *Schooling and Technology* follows:

> We've been absolutely staggered by realizing that the computer has the capability to act as if it were ten of the top psychologists working with one student.... You've seen the tip of the iceberg. Won't it be wonderful when the child in the smallest county in the most distant area or in the most confused urban setting can have the equivalent of the finest school in the world on that terminal and no one can get between that child and the curriculum? We have great moments coming in the history of education.

[Ed. Note: The comment regarding the computer's role as a "top psychologist" is as disturbing as is the idea of "no one getting between the child and the curriculum." These ideas lay to rest the publicly stated purpose of the words "parent-school partnerships" which represent a superb example of semantic deception.]

HOW TO MEASURE ATTITUDES BY MARLENE E. HENDERSON, LYNN LYONS MORRIS AND Carol Taylor Fitz-Gibbon, Center for the Study of Evaluation of the University of California, Los Angeles (Sage Publications: Thousand Oaks, Cal., 1984) was published. Funded by the National Institute of Education, the table of contents follows:

- An Introduction to the Measurement of Attitudes and Attitude Change
- Selecting from among Alternative Approaches to Collecting Attitude Information
- Self Report and Reports of Others
- Interviews, Surveys and Polls
- Logs, Journals, Diaries and Reports
- Observation Procedures, Sociometric Procedures, Various Names for the Attitude You Want to Measure
- Reference Books that List, Describe, or Evaluate Existing Measures
- Validity and Reliability of Attitude Instruments
- Validity: Is the Instrument an Appropriate One to Measure? What You Want to Know
- Names and Addresses of Publishers of Attitude Measures

TEACHING AS A MORAL CRAFT BY ALAN TOM WAS PUBLISHED (LONGMAN, INC.: WHITE Plains, N.Y., 1984). Professor Tom's book provides an extremely valuable contribution to literature on behavioral professional development for teachers and research on "effective teaching." Excerpts follow:

A.S. Barr... himself, as already noted, increasingly came to believe that his original commitment to the behavioral basis of good teaching was naïve. While he retained to the very end his lifelong interest in studying effective teaching, he gradually accepted the view that effective teaching could not be reduced to specific behaviors or behavioral patterns. In one of Barr's last papers, he made clear his belief that teaching success did not have a solely behavioral basis: "Acts are not good or bad, effective or ineffective, appropriate or inappropriate in general but in relation to the needs, purposes and conditions that give rise to them" (Barr, 1958, p. 696). In an unpublished memo, written to identify a research agenda for his retirement years, Barr (1960) admonished himself to strike out in a new direction: "Can behaviors be considered in isolation or out of context? I think not. The tabulation of behaviors out of context may be misleading. I believe this is important. Study this carefully."...

Performance-Based Teacher Education
A fundamental irony in the history of research on effective teaching is that its half century of barren results was rewarded in the 1970s by making this research a key component of the reform movement known as performance-based teacher education (PBTE).... Unfortunately, we know little more than Barr did fifty years ago about which teaching behaviors consistently produce student learning. Medley, though sympathetic to PBTE, is quite candid on this topic: "The proportion of the content of the teacher education curriculum that has been empirically shown to relate to teacher effectiveness is so small that if all of what is taught to students in preservice programs was eliminated except what research has been validated there would be nothing left but a few units in methods of teaching.... After a careful review of relevant research, Heath and Nielson conclude that the conception, design, and methodology of these studies preclude their use as an empirical basis for PBTE (1974). The authors go one step further and summarize other reviews of the connection between teacher characteristics and student learning; they find that the reviewers of this research generally conclude that "an educationally significant relationship simply has not been demonstrated."

For What Were They Searching?
The problems associated with the four teacher effectiveness strategies are so severe that the last part of the chapter addresses the question of whether the teacher effectiveness tradition can be saved, a question whose answer is unclear.

Is There A One Best Way?
Unlike earlier critics who came largely from outside the teacher effectiveness tradition and who argued that this tradition was an overly narrow approach to the study of teaching, many of the current doubters are well-known members of the empirical research establishment. McKeachie, for example, notes that he no longer believes in the educational relevance of the principles of learning about which he used to lecture teachers. He now believes that these principles apply most clearly to the learning of animals in highly controlled artificial situations, and that meaningful educational learning is both "more robust and more complex" than the situations to which the classic principles apply....

The main body of this chapter examines four strategies for approaching the study of teacher effectiveness: discovering the so-called laws of learning; identifying effective teaching behaviors; uncovering aptitude-treatment interactions, and specifying models of effective instruction such as direct instruction. Careful attention is given to the specific difficulties experienced by the practitioners of each research strategy. The results from these four behaviorally oriented research strategies are at best inconclusive.... The last section of the chapter examines the question of whether the teaching effectiveness model can be saved. Here I suggest that the various research strategies involve trade-offs and that these trade-offs make it difficult to have an instructional theory that is both accurate and applicable to a wide variety of situations. In addition, those instructional models that attempt to transcend the trade-offs between accuracy and [applicability] generally have tended to be composed of low-level generalizations that lack conceptual sophistication, such as direct instruction, academic learning time, and mastery learning. (p. 30–45)

GRANT APPLICATION FROM FAR WEST LABORATORY FOR EDUCATIONAL RESEARCH AND DEVELopment to the U.S. Department of Education for "Excellence in Instructional Delivery Systems: Research and Dissemination of Exemplary Outcome-Based Programs" was approved by T.H. Bell in 1984. William Spady, director of the Far West Laboratory, carried out this project—which came to be known as the infamous "Utah Grant." The following cover letter from Utah Superintendent of Public Instruction Leland Burningham to Secretary of Education T.H. Bell, dated July 27, 1984, is reproduced in its entirety:

Dear Secretary Bell:

I am forwarding this letter to accompany the proposal which you recommended Bill Spady and I prepare in connection with Outcome-Based Education.

This proposal centers around the detailed process by which we will work together to implement Outcome-Based Education using research verified programs. This will make it possible to put outcome-based education in place, not only in Utah but in all schools of the nation. For those who desire, we will stand ready for regional and national dissemination of the Outcome-Based Education program.

We are beginning to see positive, preliminary results from some of the isolated schools in Utah which have implemented Outcome-Based Education. These positive indicators are really exciting!

We sincerely urge your support for funding the proposal as presented.

Warmest regards,

G. Leland Burningham
State Superintendent of
Public Instruction

Attached to the grant application was Spady's "Summary of Professional Experience" which included "Senior Research Consultant to the Washington, D.C. schools" during 1977–1978—the same time the D.C. schools implemented mastery learning.

In a *Washington Post* article dated August 1, 1977, entitled "Competency Tests Set in 26 Schools," Thomas Sticht—who was later named to U.S. Secretary of Labor Elizabeth Dole's Secretary's Commission on Achieving Necessary Skills (SCANS)—was also mentioned as an associate director at the National Institute of Education (NIE) at the time mastery learning was implemented in the D.C. schools. The *Post* article quoted Sticht extensively, verifying that he and Spady were both deeply involved in the implementation of the new mastery learning curriculum. Later, in 1987, *The Washington Post* again paraphrased Sticht as follows:

> Many companies have moved operations to places with cheap, relatively poorly educated labor. What may be crucial, they say, is the dependability of a labor force and how well it can be managed and trained, not its general educational level, although a small cadre of highly educated creative people is essential to innovation and growth. Ending discrimination and changing values are probably more important than reading in moving low income families into the middle class.

[Ed. Note: What an extraordinary comment from someone supposedly involved in helping inner city students learn the basic skills! Nine years later, in an article in the March 5, 1996 issue of the *Washington Times,* the extent of academic damage caused by the Mastery Learning programs initiated by Spady and Sticht in 1977 was revealed:

> In the verbal portion of the 1995 Scholastic Achievement Test (SAT) D.C. public school students scored 342 out of a possible 800—86 points below the national average. On the math portion of the SAT, District public school students scored 375 out of a possible 800—107 points below the national average.

In 1999 the Washington, D.C. schools are using the same mastery learning/direct instruction method which *caused* the problem to *solve* the problem! In addition, the same *Washington Times* article stated that present Secretary of Education Richard Riley's home state of South Carolina, which probably has been more deeply involved in Effective Schools Research than any other state with the notable exception of Mississippi, had the next lowest scores.]

Important: The "Excellence in Instructional Delivery Systems" grant (the "Utah Grant") evaluation report, entitled *Models of Instructional Organization: A Casebook on Mastery Learning and Outcomes-Based Education* and compiled by project director Robert Burns (Far West Laboratory for Educational Research and Development: San Francisco, April 1987), stated in its "Conclusion" that:

> The four models of instructional organization outlined in this casebook are difficult programs to implement. The practices of the ten schools described in the case studies are indeed commendable. Yet we do not offer these ten case studies as "exemplary schools" deserving of emulation. Rather, they describe educators who have attempted to go beyond current curricular, instructional or organizational arrangements found in the majority of schools today. They have accepted the challenge of translating a difficult set of ideas into actual practice. And while they may not have always been completely successful, their experiences have provided us with ideas about how to begin moving closer to the ideal of successful learning for all students.

[Ed. Note: The above wording is similar to wording in the evaluation of Project INSTRUCT, another model mastery learning program (1975). Neither mastery learning project had positive "academic" results. One can only conclude that academic achievement was not the intent. The documented results were changes in "curricular, instructional and organizational arrangements" in the schools involved so that they could become performance-based, necessary for school-to-work training.

Lack of positive results indicated in the evaluation of the mastery learning/outcome-based education experiments in schools—including the much-touted Johnson City, New York's Outcomes-Driven Developmental Model—did not deter the educators/sociologists from implementing outcome-based education/mastery learning in "all schools of the nation."

In assembling this research on mastery learning/outcome-based education/direct instruction programs and their evaluations, it appears that *academic achievement has not been the desired object or the result* of the use of these "What Works" methods and curricular thrusts. There are no longitudinal studies or long-term results indicating that the newly trumpeted "scientific, research-based" criteria for program development is valid criteria. The lack of evidence should serve as a clear warning to parents and good educators to steer clear of any programs or program development based on any of the above-mentioned models, or on the Skinnerian method called for by Effective Schools Research. (See Appendix XXVI.)]

DAVID HORNBECK, SUPERINTENDENT OF MARYLAND'S PUBLIC SCHOOLS, IN TESTIMONY BEfore the Maryland State Board of Education in 1984 attempted to "mandate community service at state-approved places." During Hornbeck's testimony he quoted the late Ernest Boyer, then-president of the Carnegie Foundation for the Advancement of Teaching, as saying, "In the end the goal of service in the schools is to teach values—to help all students understand that to be fully human one must serve."

THE JULY 1984 EDITION OF THE *EFFECTIVE SCHOOL REPORT* CARRIED AN ARTICLE ENTITLED "Effective Schools for Results" by Dr. Robert E. Corrigan and Dr. George W. Bailey. Excerpts follow:

> Over the past thirty years there have been three primary programs related to the design and implementation of effective schools and successful learning results. Each of these research efforts focused on different aspects or variables in the following areas: behavioral change and the application of learning theory to produce successful learning results; the identification of sociological factors operating in effective schools; teaching strategies to effect learning, and the combination of these variables and practices in a systematic approach to achieve learning and management results.... The following professionals and groups have initiated successful educational programs which can work together as a common system to deliver predictable success for every learner—the ultimate criterion of an effective school program: Wilbur Brookover and Ron Edmonds of the Effective Schools Research Movement; B.F. Skinner, Norman Crowder, Robert and Betty O. Corrigan, 1950–1984, Mastery Learning Practices; Madeline Hunter, 1962–1984, Mastery Teaching Practices; R.E. Corringan, B.O. Corrigan, Ward Corrigan and Roger A. Kaufman, 1960–1984, A Systematic Approach for Effectiveness (SAFE) for district-wide installation of Effective Schools....
>
> Skinner proposed that it is feasible to deliver predictable learning mastery results when teachers performed the following programmed actions to design and implement lesson plans or curricula. These design and teaching steps describe the general process steps of learner-centered mastery learning instruction.

[Ed. Note: Included in step 3 of the above-mentioned learner-centered mastery learning instruction is: "Provide immediate feedback as to the correctness of learner responses, provide for immediate correction of errors, and control the progress of learning as students proceed in small steps along the tested learning path to master the learning objectives and criteria with predictable success."]

The article continues:

> The ultimate benefits to be derived through the installation of this mastery of skills delivery system will be the predictable success of all future graduates to master relevant skills to enter and succeed in society. Graduation skill standards would be continually evaluated and, where necessary, will be revised based on new skill requirements established by industrial, civic, and academic leaders either (a) to get and hold jobs, (b) to advance to higher education, and/or (c) to be self-sufficient following graduation.

[Ed. Note: How much clearer could the Corrigans be in describing the need for Skinnerian mastery learning/direct instruction in order to implement school-to-work? (See Appendix VI.)]

DR. THEODORE SIZER'S COALITION OF ESSENTIAL SCHOOLS (CES) WAS FOUNDED IN 1984. Major Coalition principles are:

- Focus on helping adolescents to learn to use their minds well....
- Less is more: Each student should master a limited number of essential skills areas of knowledge....
- School goals should apply to all students....
- Teaching and learning should be personalized; each teacher should have no more than 80 students....
- Scrap the time-honored feature of the American education system: graduation requirements based on the so-called Carnegie Units, or the "seat time" students spend in various subject areas....
- Students should be active workers [student-as-worker philosophy]....
- Students should be able to demonstrate mastery of skills and knowledge.

The Coalition of Essential Schools (CES) was established at Brown University. From twelve "charter" schools in four states, CES by 1993 grew to include more than 130 member schools in nearly thirty states. Along with the Education Commission of the States, the CES sponsors Re:Learning, a partnership with participating states to build support for essential school change at the state and district levels.

Ten years later evaluation studies have found that gains weren't measurable. Even so, philanthropist Walter H. Annenberg pledged to donate $50 million to the Annenberg Institute for School Reform, run by Sizer and based at Brown University.

It is important to mention that the majority, if not all, of the major education reform projects have failed to improve students's academic test scores. Notable examples are: Johnson City, New York—the Outcomes-Driven Development Model (ODDM) by John Champlin; William Spady's Far West Laboratory Utah Grant, "Excellence in Instructional Delivery Systems: Research and Dissemination of Exemplary Outcomes-Based Programs"; and Marc Tucker's National Center on Education and the Economy (NCEE), which moved from Washington, D.C. to Rochester, New York in 1988 to "help" that city's much-heralded reform movement.

The Rochester Democrat and Chronicle of March 14, 1993 in an article entitled "A City's Dream Unfulfilled"—after five years of Tucker's "help"—reported the following:

> Since Rochester's schools started reform, fewer graduates have received the more stringent Regents diploma. In 1986–87, 23.1% of graduates had Regents diplomas, and 17.5% graduated with them last year [1993].

JOHN I. GOODLAD CLEARLY STATED THAT HOW A STUDENT FEELS ABOUT SCHOOL IS MORE important than test scores in an article entitled "A Cooperative Effort Is Needed: Can Our Schools Get Better?" (originally published in *Phi Delta Kappan*, January, 1979 when Dr. Goodlad was dean of the Graduate School of Education at the University of California, Los Angeles, and re-published in *Education Digest* on November 1, 1984.) Excerpts follow:

> It seems to my associates and me that how a student spends time in school and how he feels about what goes on there is of much greater significance than how he scores on a standardized achievement test. But I am not sure the American people are ready to put a criterion such as this ahead of marks and scores. And so it will be difficult for schools to get better and more difficult for them to appear so....
>
> Adherence to norm-referenced [competitive] standardized test scores as the standard for judging student, teacher, and school performance has led to a stultifying approach to accountability.

IN A PERSONAL LETTER TO CHARLOTTE ISERBYT FROM STEVEN M. HERSEY, EXECUTIVE DI-rector of the Maine Association of Christian Schools dated November 17, 1984,[14] Hersey enclosed portions of a testimony by Kevin Ryan, professor at Boston University, regarding Boston University, the country of Portugal and the World Bank. Professor Ryan was called to testify for the Maine State Department of Education in a legal hearing against the Maine Association of Christian Schools. The following excerpts from Ryan's testimony are important due to the disclosure by Ryan of his role in the development of a teacher-training faculty system—modeled after that of the United States—for Portugal immediately after the communist takeover of that country. One might ask why a communist country like Portugal should choose the American teacher education curriculum to accomplish its political and philosophical goals. Portions of Ryan's testimony follow:

> A. I [Ryan] am a professor of Education [at Boston University] and I teach graduate courses and supervise dissertations. But I'm there primarily now to work on a project to help a Portuguese Minister of Education develop a teacher-training faculty system....
> Q. ...Could you describe what it is you're doing?
> A. Well, the Portuguese nation had a social revolution [communist takeover] in 1974, and at that time they decided that their educational system was very inadequate, that it was not democratic, that the mandatory compulsory age of education was only to the fourth grade, and they mandated a system of education not unlike the United States in terms of compulsory education up to grade 12 and an elementary

through high school division. The country was very interested in this. They also wanted to be part of the European Economic Community. But, unfortunately, Portugal was a poor country, and the World Bank said to them, you will not be admitted into the European Economic Community until you get in place a modern school system. And they [the World Bank] have come through with a good deal of financial support for that.

An important part of that is the development of a teacher training infrastructure. Now, what that means is that Portugal, which has, as of right now, a very small and very sort of casual teacher education method, is establishing 12 regional teacher education institutions at the university level positions; and they looked to the rest of the world for help on this, and they put out a request for proposals.... Boston University... was chosen... to train the faculties of these 12 new institutions....

Q. Now when the proposal was first made... was it contemplated that Boston University might do all the training of Portuguese teachers themselves?

A. Yes, I did. My feeling is that in this particular project the stakes are enormously high. The 120 people who are currently right now being selected for these roles in these 12 institutions are going to be there for 20 or 30 years; so that the course they have on teaching or supervision is going to set an intellectual and training agenda for them for a number of years. They are going to go on and train all these teachers with what they learned.

Q. And do you have any responsibility with respect to the curriculum that will be used in the program to develop a teacher training instruction?

A. Well, the Portuguese did a lot of study on their own, and they looked at various curricula for teacher education.... I think one of the reasons they selected Boston University was because the curriculum that they wanted taught seems to be one like an American teacher education curriculum. And we have their indication of what courses they want, and the sequence. And we—and this happened before I was there—we went with our course outlines and, in a sense, negotiated with them to a mutual satisfaction about what the content of what the various courses would be.

Q. Do you belong to any professional associations?

A. I am a member of the American Educational Research Association; I am a member of Phi Delta Kappa; I am a member of the Network of Educational Excellence; I was a member of the Master of Arts in Teaching Association—in fact, I was president, before it—before—I think it's defunct now.

[Ed. Note: Of interest is the fact that Paulo Friere, the well-known radical Brazilian educator who wrote *Pedagogy of the Oppressed*, was also a consultant to the government of Portugal at the time of its revolution. (See August 19, 1986 entry for *New York Times* article.) As of 1992 Professor Kevin Ryan is reported to be involved in and the director of the Center for the Advancement of Ethics and Character at Boston University.]

AN ARTICLE ENTITLED "OBSERVING THE BIRTH OF THE HATCH AMENDMENT REGULATIONS" by Bert I. Greene and Marvin Pasch was published in the December 1984 issue of *Educational Leadership,* monthly journal of the Association for Supervision and Curriculum Development. Excerpts from the article follow:

However, from the day the Hatch Amendment was passed, the written consent requirement lay dormant, that is, until 1984. As Charlotte Iserbyt, an education activist and former Department of Education employee, [stated] in a memorandum to her conservative allies dated 10 January 1984:

> The only tool available to us to protect our children in the government schools is a federal law, the Hatch Protection of Pupil Rights Amendment, passed unanimously by the U.S. Senate in 1978, for which the Office of Education promised regulations in early 1979.... I know that many of you, for good reason, feel that the Hatch Amendment has been useless. Of course it has been useless. Any statute which has no mechanism for enforcement is nothing more than a scrap of paper....

Iserbyt then turned her attention to the reason why regulations have not been promulgated:

> Although excellent regulations were drafted in 1982 by conservatives in the Office of the General Counsel (who have been subsequently fired by Secretary Bell), they have not seen the light of day since Bell doesn't like them and he also does not want to offend his educationist friends by signing off on regulations that will disturb their modus operandi— their persistent efforts to change the values, attitudes and beliefs of students to conform with those necessary to bring about a socialist/humanist one world government.

As Iserbyt clearly saw, it is through regulations that responsibilities become clarified, procedures for grievance and redress established, and penalties for non-compliance stated. Therefore, the importance of regulations cannot be overstated.... Interestingly, Iserbyt had notification of the proposed regulations prior to 10 January as evidenced by an Urgent Alert she sent to her "Education Group Leader Activists." Her guidance... included suggestions related to the scope of the soon-to-be published regulations. She argued:

> It was the intent of Congress to cover all the mindbending techniques and materials used in our children's classrooms, in special education and guidance, not just the narrow and difficult to define areas of psychological and psychiatric testing or treatment.

She provided a set of quotable commentaries for her contacts as they prepared oral or written testimony....
Some people who testified argued that the techniques being used in our schools can be likened to those used in Russia, Red China, and Nazi Germany....
A potentially major educational change has occurred, and the education profession failed to block it.

[Ed. Note: Anyone following or involved with the Anita Hoge/ Pennsylvania case will tell you that the U.S. Department of Education—under Secretaries of Education William Bennett and Lamar Alexander—pulled out all the stops, at every level, to thwart Hoge's efforts and those of other parents who tried to use this law. Such an assault on those who paid the bills—and provided the children ("resources") upon whom they experiment even today—was, and is, criminal.]

1985

ON MARCH 6, 1985 *EDUCATION WEEK* PUBLISHED AN ARTICLE ENTITLED "HALF OF CHIcago Students Drop Out, Study Finds: Problem Called Enormous Human Tragedy." (Return to 1968 *Learning and Instruction* entry for details of the Chicago Mastery Learning debacle.)

EFFECTIVE SCHOOLS DEVELOPMENT IN EDUCATION ACT WAS INTRODUCED INTO CONGRESS on March 8, 1985. An excerpt from the Extension of Remarks in the House of Representatives by Hon. Augustus F. Hawkins of California follows:

> Mr. Hawkins: Mr. Speaker, there are public schools in this Nation which evidence continuous improvement and growth in the academic achievement levels of their students, for each day that these students are in the school.... Where are these public schools? They are in Jackson, MS; Spencerport, NY; Los Angeles, CA; New York City; Glendale, AZ; Richmond, VA; Pittsburgh, PA; Hartford, CT; Portland,OR; and many other cities throughout the Nation.
>
> What they have in common is a determination to improve pupil performance, pupil behavior, and the effectiveness of teaching and learning in their schools. They are adherents and advocates of the late Professor Ron Edmonds's—of Michigan State University and Harvard University—effective school principles, which emphasize the belief that while public schools realistically can't control what happens in their surrounding communities, public schools can control what happens within their "four walls."

[Ed. Note: This particular legislation, which originally called for a whopping $230 million over a three-year period, did not pass. However, similar effective schools legislation, H.R. 747, passed and provided $4.5 million over a three-year period during William Bennett's tenure as U.S. Secretary of Education.

The above schools—especially Jackson, Mississippi, the home of the *Effective School Report* and one of the first inner city schools used as an effective schools (ML/DI) research experiment—which have been using mastery learning for a long period of time would provide an excellent list for Congress to use in an investigation of inner cities' norm-referenced test scores!]

THE DALLAS MORNING NEWS OF MARCH 23, 1985 RAN AN ARTICLE ENTITLED "TEACHERS' Group to Develop New Curriculum" by Karel Holloway of Boston. An excerpt follows:

> The National Education Association is beginning an 18-month program to develop a new school curriculum designed to assure that students master basic skills, NEA President Mary Futrell announced Friday. "The association first will survey scholars to determine what they believe constitutes 'mastery' in reading, writing, mathematics and social studies. Using criteria from the scholars and the findings of current education research studies, the association will develop experimental strategies to teach the mastery skills at five schools that will be selected from throughout the nation. The results of the programs tried at the five schools will determine the shape of the new curriculum," Mrs. Futrell said in a speech to the Education Writers Association. That curriculum then will be tested for three years at 24 schools nationwide.... The Mastery In Learning Project will be funded by $600,000 from the NEA and donations from other foundations. Nine education research institutes will participate in the project.

Summit Christian Academy of Dallas, Texas included the above article in a promotional flyer on which it typed the following additional information regarding the use of mastery learning:

> The purpose in sending you this article is to evidence that truly we did create "TOMORROW'S EDUCATION TODAY" five years ago at a cost of over four million dollars. We employed over

250 dedicated Christian writers and editors to create the LIFEPAC curriculum. Each had an average of five years classroom teaching experience, and over 75% held Masters degrees or higher, and 40 held Doctorate degrees. Truly, there is no finer curriculum in the market place today. For comparison between our curriculum, A.C.E., A-Beka, Bob Jones and others, please write to: Summit Christian Academy, 13789 Noel Road, Suite 100, Dallas, Texas 75240.

[Ed. Note: This article proves the extensive use by Christian educators of the same Skinnerian mastery learning used and recommended by the National Education Association. How can Christian educators, opposed to the teaching of evolution, support a teaching method based on Darwin's theory of evolution? Dr. Francis Schaeffer was right on target when he said: "Many of our secular schools have consistently taught these presuppositions (evolutionary theory) and unhappily many of our Christian lower schools and colleges have taught the crucial subjects no differently than the secular schools."]

EDUCATION DAILY OF APRIL 5, 1985 PUBLISHED AN ITEM ENTITLED "TEACHERS INFLUENCE Students' Values through Writing Assignments" which stated in part:

> Researchers attending the annual meeting of the American Educational Research Association here said writing can be used to clarify students' values and even alter their views on controversial subjects.
>
> But teachers can also use writing to manipulate a student's viewpoint and attitude on controversial issues, said a researcher who has studied how writing changes attitudes. "You can generate attitude change by writing," said John Daly of the University of Texas. Daly said his research showed that writing an essay about an issue helps students clarify their own views. But when asked to write an essay arguing a position opposing their values, the students are lead to change their minds....
>
> ...And the greater the effort a student puts into a writing assignment, the greater the change in attitude, Daly concluded.
>
> Daly's finding disturbed some educators, who said they were concerned that teachers have the power to alter students' values. "It can be dangerous when we know that educators have the power to influence kids' minds," said Barbara Mitchell of the University of Pennsylvania.

THE MAY 1985 EDUCATION UPDATE FROM THE ASSOCIATION FOR SUPERVISION AND CURriculum Development contained a revealing article "Promising Theories Die Young" about the late Madeline Hunter, University of California at Los Angeles education professor and the nation's best known Mastery Teaching teacher trainer. Dr. Hunter was a psychologist who served more than twenty years as principal of the Experimental Laboratory Elementary School at UCLA. (John Goodlad also served at UCLA's lab school.) Hunter's views on Instructional Theory Into Practice (ITIP) and on dialectical thinking follow:

> Madeline Hunter, UCLA education professor and research interpreter, told a huge, doting audience that educational theorists and practitioners "badly need each other" and that it is high time to tap each other's strengths rather than zap each other's perceived flaws. Hunter said that she is particularly conscious of this schism because "I'm part of both but not really one or the other." Hunter has been a school psychologist, principal, researcher, and, in ASCD

immediate Past President Phil Robinson's words, "one of the most able... teachers of teachers." Hunter delivered three mandates for the next decade: 1. Unite educational theory and practice; 2. Recognize, integrate, and use all three kinds of knowledge; and 3. Move toward dialectical thinking.

Under the article's subtitle, "Three Kinds of Knowledge," Hunter's presentation to the audience was covered as follows:

When she was a school psychologist, Hunter said, she had an exchange with a teacher who had rebuked a student for making a silly remark:

> Hunter: What did the smart-aleck want?
> Teacher: Attention.
> Hunter: Have you ever heard of Pavlov?
> Teacher (amazed): What do slobbering dogs have to do with it?

In the same *Education Update* article, under subtitle "Toward Dialectical Thinking," Hunter's presentation reported:

Hunter advised educators to move toward dialectical thinking, which means, she said, that with empathy, you "embrace the most convincing argument... against your own conclusion. Dialectical thinking will move us from right and wrong to better in this set of circumstances." Moving into this "thoughtful uncertainty," Hunter said, does not mean obligatory abandonment of one's own position, but she said, the advantage is that "where we take an opposing point of view and hold it in tension with our own point of view, each builds correction into the other." Hunter nudged educators to come out of "armed camps... where we're not collaborating" so that "I understand why you think it's right for your students to line up while I think it's better for them to come in casually." And she concluded, "To respectfully address another person's point of view is a master, master step. Until we accomplish it in our own profession... I see very little hope for it in our community, in our cities, in our nation, and in the world."

The validity of Hunter's claims of success for her ITIP mastery teaching program was questioned by Robert Slavin of Johns Hopkins University in his paper entitled "The Napa Evaluation of Madeline Hunter's ITIP: Lessons Learned," published in *Elementary School Journal* (Vol. 87, No. 2: University of Chicago, 1986). Slavin says in part, "Although teachers in the program changed their behavior and students' engaged rates improved, program effects on student achievement were minimal."

Robert Slavin followed up on his critique of Hunter's claims of success for her mastery teaching program with his report funded by the U.S. Department of Education entitled *Mastery Learning Reconsidered*, published by the Center for Research on Elementary and Middle Schools, Johns Hopkins University (Report No. 7, January 1987). An excerpt from the abstract of the report follows:

Several recent reviews and meta-analyses have claimed extraordinarily positive effects of mastery learning on student achievement, and Bloom (1984a, b) has hypothesized that mastery-based treatments will soon be able to produce "two-sigma" (i.e., two standard deviation) increases in achievement. This article examines the literature on achievement effects of practical applications of group-based mastery learning in elementary and secondary schools over periods of at least four weeks, using a review technique, "best evidence synthesis," which combines features of meta-analytic and traditional narrative reviews. The review found essentially no evidence to support the effectiveness of group-based mastery learning on standardized achievement measures. On experimenter-made measures, effects were generally positive but moderate in magnitude, with little evidence that effects maintained over time. These results are discussed in light of the coverage vs. Mastery dilemma posed by group-based mastery learning.

[Ed. Note: Slavin's critiques echo the negative results of mastery learning discussed elsewhere in this book. Unfortunately, ten years later Slavin received his mastery learning/direct instruction crown in 1999 when Slavin's program "Success for All," which also uses mastery learning/direct instruction, was accepted as one of the nationally recognized programs for use in restructuring.]

THE EFFECTIVE SCHOOL REPORT'S MAY 1985 ISSUE CONTAINED AN ARTICLE ENTITLED "Principal's Expectations as a Motivating Factor in Effective Schools." An excerpt follows:

> The principal expects specific behavior from particular teachers which should then translate into achievement by the students of these teachers; because of these varied expectations, the principal behaves differently toward different teachers; i.e., body language, verbal interactions and resource allocations. This treatment also influences the attitudes of the teacher toward the principal and their perception of the future utility of any increased effort toward student achievement. If this treatment is consistent over time, and if the teachers do not resist change, it will shape their behavior and through it the achievement of their students.... With time teachers' behavior, self-concepts of ability, perceptions of future utility, attitude toward the principal and students' achievement will conform more and more closely to the behavior originally expected of them.

EDUCATION DAILY OF JUNE 12, 1985 PUBLISHED "SWEEPING OVERHAUL OF MINNESOTA Education System Proposed." Excerpts follow:

> The Minnesota Business Partnership, an organization of 60 corporations, commissioned an education consulting firm to study the state education system and plan improvements. The result is the Minnesota Plan, the business community's proposals to radically restructure the state's education system. The plan was outlined Monday at a National Institute of Education seminar in Washington, D.C. by Paul Berman, President of BW Associates, which conducted the study. The proposal would make kindergarten through sixth grade the elementary level, set up grades seven through 10 as the common high schools, and create specialized programs for grades 11 and 12. Students would have to master a core program of communication, social studies, science and math until the 11th grade, and pass state competency exams at the end of the sixth and 10th grades. Moreover, the plan would eliminate state-mandated courses and allow districts and schools to determine course requirements. Under the plan, 11th and 12th grade students could take courses at post secondary institutions, technical or vocational schools or even private corporations....
>
> Despite the worries of business leaders in the partnership... most legislators don't feel a major restructuring is necessary. "Most of us feel the system is changing and responding to

needs. But it is not in need of drastic change." But Berman counters that since "the best teachers are leaving at age 30 now," teacher improvement plans would help overburdened staff and increase student-teacher contact. Teaching teams composed of a lead teacher, teaching assistants and adjunct teachers would work with 120 students. This would allow for individual student learning programs and removal of student counselors.... "It's not a fantasy no matter how radical it is," Berman contends, adding that the public does not realize that "reforms we start today are not going to be in effect for 20 years. It takes time to modernize." (p. 6)

[Ed. Note: In retrospect it seems, to this writer at least, that Minnesota was clearly out front in its early adoption of performance-based school-to-work agendas. (See Appendix X.)]

NORTH CAROLINA'S COMPENTENCY-BASED CURRICULUM, "BASIC EDUCATION PROGRAM," was introduced in 1985. A few of its more unusual "basic" competencies, involved students entertaining allegiance to a world constitution and a world government rather than to the *U.S. Constitution*. Excerpts follow:

FIFTH GRADE: Develop a flag, seal, symbol, pledge and/or national anthem for a new country.... Design a postage stamp to be used worldwide. The stamp should denote what the world would need to make it a better place....
SIXTH GRADE: Draw national symbols for an imaginary nation....
SEVENTH GRADE: Understand the need for interdependence....
NINTH GRADE: Write a constitution for a perfect society.

A NATIONAL EDUCATION ASSOCIATION (NEA) PRESS RELEASE FOR JUNE 28–JULY 3, 1985 described in considerable detail the purpose of its Mastery In Learning project.[15] It was explained that Mastery Learning is

a concept first proposed a generation ago by Harvard psychologist Jerome Bruner.... A growing body of research and educational reform proposals came from such respected educational analysts as Mortimer Adler [developer of the Paideia Proposal and long-time advocate of a one-world government, ed.], John Goodlad, Theodore Sizer, and Ernest Boyer who have all sought to translate Bruner's work into classroom reality.

Also revealed in an NEA booklet on mastery learning is the fact that

Mastery Learning is one of many instructional models. Others include Active Teaching, Direct Instruction, Student Team Learning, Socratic questioning, coaching, creative problem solving, Bruner's Concept Attainment Strategy, and Madeline Hunter's Target Teaching Approach. These models incorporate research on effective teaching, and all may be explored by the schools associated with the project.

[Ed. Note: Jerome Bruner and B.F. Skinner were the developers of the highly controversial, federally funded curriculum M:ACOS (*Man: A Course of Study*).]

EDUCATION WEEK OF AUGUST 28, 1985 CARRIED THE ARTICLE "PROPONENTS OF MASTERY Learning Defend Method after Its Rejection by Chicago" which quoted Benjamin Bloom, often cited as "the father of Mastery Learning," as saying that some 50 million children around the globe are taught with a mastery learning approach. In addition, University of California Professor James H. Block is quoted as saying he "doesn't know of any major urban school system in the United States that has not adopted some kind of mastery learning program."

[Ed. Note: James Block's statement underscores the need for a Congressional investigation requiring the U.S. Department of Education to provide longitudinal/norm-referenced test scores for all "major urban school systems" that have used mastery learning/direct instruction over the past thirty years. (See Appendix XXVI.)]

"TOTAL PRESENTATION SET FOR EDUCATORS" WAS THE HEADLINE OF AN ARTICLE IN THE *Tyler* [Texas] *Morning Telegraph* of October 31, 1985 (Sec. 3, p. 3). Excerpts follow:

> Texas Objectives for Total Academic Learning [TOTAL] will be revealed to Texas educators on Nov. 7 in Houston when four staff members of Region VII Education Service Center of Kilgore, make a presentation to the Texas Association for Supervision and Curriculum Development, (affiliate of the national organization ASCD).... The foursome will describe TOTAL, share samples of productivity and give information on how to obtain the materials through their regional service centers.... Project TOTAL was born in Kilgore in January 1984 and matured during the reform-wrought summer after passage of House Bill 246 and its implementation of Chapter 75 by the Legislature....
>
> Some 1500 teachers and 100 administrators in 75 districts of Region VII's Northeast Texas area were involved [in producing] the 5,000 pages of materials to aid school districts in complying with the law....
>
> TOTAL provides foundation curriculum documents written in "teacher talk" encompassing essential elements. It addresses all 13 subject areas of essential elements from kindergarten through 12th grade: English, language arts, mathematics, science, health, physical education, Texas and U.S. history, and computer literacy. These elements are developed into actual plans which teachers may use in helping students master the essential elements....
>
> Objectives, activities and resources are suggested for each, and also suggested are means of evaluation to see how well students have mastered each objective....
>
> "The big weakness I see is in the resource listings," she said. "We are trying to widen teachers' horizons where they haven't used much except textbooks and to give them added software that can be brought to their attention and should be available by fall 1986."

[Ed. Note: The above article was selected to explain the process employed by the states to implement mastery learning/direct instruction in the early 1980s as a response to *A Nation at Risk*. The writer of this book wrote Ross Perot, who spearheaded the Texas education reform movement in the early 1980s, warning him of the intent behind reform and providing him with valuable documentation from the U.S. Department of Education. The writer received a return receipt for the materials, but no response.]

MAINE'S STATE DEPARTMENT OF EDUCATION 1985 ASSESSMENT OF EDUCATIONAL PROGRESS [MAEP] test item bank, based in part on National Assessment of Educational Progress (NAEP) test items, included the following correct answer as to why the Soviets occupied Eastern Europe after World War II:

> [Correct answer]
> Soviet occupation was primarily a result of the Soviet Union's desire for security along its borders.

[Ed. Note: One cannot help but wonder how the international community would have responded to the United States' occupation of Canada, Mexico, Cuba, the West Indies, Greenland, and Iceland in order to "secure its borders."]

MAINE FACILITATOR CENTER FLYER REGARDING A TEACHER TRAINING SEMINAR FOR "MODels of Teaching" by Bruce Joyce et al. was distributed in 1985. Under the heading "Information Processing, One of Four Groups" was included: Direct Instruction: James Block, Benjamin Bloom, the late Madeline Hunter, and Ethna Reid—all prominent in development, implementation and promotion of Skinnerian mastery learning. An excerpt from the Maine Center's flyer regarding Direct Instruction follows:

> This model is a deductive approach to learning that presents the objective, models the skill and provides guides and independent practices. Direct Instruction requires multisensory lessons, constant monitoring by the teacher to insure understanding, and a wide range of review or practices.

[Ed. Note: How fascinating that Bruce Joyce used the label "Direct Instruction" instead of mastery learning, which proves that the two labels are rightfully applied to the same method.]

IN 1985 THE U.S. DEPARTMENT OF EDUCATION, THROUGH THE SECRETARY'S DISCRETIONary Fund under Secretary William Bennett, approved the promotion of and funding for development of a character education program by the Thomas Jefferson Research Center (TJRC) of Pasadena, California. The grant was for a "teacher training project demonstrating the viability of a district-wide educational program involving... the TJRC." Through the grant, the TJRC, founded in 1963, would apply its character education curriculum "across all segments of the [Pasadena] district's grade levels... expanding the effort to parents and community, and... to other school districts, and to share... methods and approaches with other educators and institutions nationally." Community service projects for elementary, middle, and high school students "are seen as extensions of classroom activity and essential elements in... the range of values being stressed." The TJRC's federally funded demonstration "character education" program included "Personal Responsibility Skills and Ethical Decision-Making."

National dissemination was expected to be effected through regional and national workshops, education conferences, computer conferences, and through TELE, "an electronic learning exchange... a computerized network of educators... involved with exemplary programs and computer assisted instruction programs within California and... across the nation." The promotional literature for the TJRC's middle and high school Achievement Skills programs and the text of the teacher's manual for its middle school Achievement Skills program (1984) explicitly stated that "the basis for the programs lies in the motivational theories of [Abraham] Maslow."

In *Religion, Values, and Peak Experiences* (Ohio State University Press: Columbus, Ohio, 1964) Maslow stated that "each person has his own private religion... which may be of the profoundest meaning to him personally and yet... of no meaning to anyone else... each person discovers, develops, and retains his own religion." An examination of the TJRC's middle school Achievement Skills reveals not only the program's base in Maslow's psychological theories, but also the program's ties to consciousness-altering methods. Early in the semester-long program, students are told that "we are going to study some psychology. We are going to study our selves or our *minds* [emphasis in original]. Each of you is going to get a chance to look at yourself as if you were a psychologist." Repeatedly throughout the program, students are exposed to self-hypnosis, guided imagery, visualization techniques, and relaxation therapy—tools used in psychosynthesis (defined by Roberto Assagioli as the formation or reconstruction of a new personality). In his book *Psychosynthesis*[16] as mentioned earlier in this book Assagioli notes

> the possible dangers of the exploration of the unconscious. The first and foremost is the release of drives and emotions which were locked in the unconscious and which can flood the conscious ego before it is ready and prepared and competent to contain, control and utilize them. It is the situation of the "apprentice sorcerer."
>
> ...We think that cases of suicide or of the development of psychotic states can be due to the premature and uncontrolled release of explosive drives and emotions from the unconscious.

The middle school Achievement Skills program also utilizes what are psychotherapeutic values clarification techniques: role playing, open-ended questions, and moral dilemmas. These same values clarification methodologies form the basis of the K–6 "character education" component funded by the grant. Psychologists have warned educators about the dangers of unbridled use of role-playing techniques by untrained people, for the very reasons Assagioli cites as well as others.

The K–6 materials were developed by the American Institute for Character Education (AICE) of San Antonio, Texas, and are marketed nationally. *The Teacher's Handbook* (1983) from AICE indicates that the program is another "how to learn instead of what to learn" program and admits to the use of values clarification, the promotion of self-disclosure and the creation of a classroom climate where "there are no right answers to any one problem."

U.S. PRESIDENT REAGAN AND SOVIET PRESIDENT GORBACHEV SIGNED AN AGREEMENT IN 1985 calling for

> cooperation in the field of science and technology and additional agreements in other specific fields, including the humanities and social sciences; the facilitation of the exchange by appropriate organizations of educational and teaching materials, including textbooks, syllabi and curricula, materials on methodology, samples of teaching instruments and audiovisual aids, and the exchange of primary and secondary school textbooks and other teaching materials.... The conducting of joint studies on textbooks between appropriate organizations in the United States and the Ministry of Education of the U.S.S.R.

At the same time, the Carnegie Corporation signed agreements with the Soviet Academy of Sciences which resulted in "joint research on the application of computers in early elementary education, focusing especially on the teaching of higher level skills and complex subjects to younger children."

The U.S.-Soviet education agreements were discussed in an article entitled "U.S. and Soviets to Share Insights on Computers" by Fred M. Hechinger, education editor, in the December 10, 1985 issue of the *New York Times*. The article states in part:

> A meeting of American and Soviet educational computer experts has produced an agreement to exchange specialists involved in the improvement of elementary and secondary education.
>
> The initial American-Soviet exchange is intended as a first step toward cooperation among education reformers from a number of countries, including Britain and Japan. One goal is to reduce the present emphasis on training computer programmers, and stress instead the computer's potential to restructure the education of young children, beginning in third grade or earlier.
>
> Several issues are listed for joint investigation. They include computer-based methods to develop creative abilities of primary school pupils, creation and testing of software for use in primary school, and proposals for the restructuring of the curriculum and of teaching methods through the use of computers in the early grades.
>
> Additional issues include evaluation of the training of teachers in the use of computers and elimination of teachers' fear of computers, and creation of Soviet-American pilot projects for joint experiments.

[Ed. Note: On December 20, 1985, during a "Contact America" radio interview with U.S. Secretary of Education William Bennett, co-host Malcolm Lawrence asked Bennett if he was involved in the United States-Soviet education exchanges. Bennett responded, "No. I'm not in that loop." Pray tell, what "loop" was he in during his tenure as the top official dealing with American education? The writer was informed by the U.S. Department of State that both agreements were still in effect *after* the so-called break-up of the Soviet Union. (See Appendix XXIII.)]

1986

THE FACT FINDER OF PHOENIX, ARIZONA ON JANUARY 1, 1986 (VOL. 46, NO. 4) CARRIED an article entitled "Shocking U.S. Agreements to Let Soviet and Red Chinese Educators Indoctrinate America's Children." (See Appendix XXIII.) Excerpts follow:

> We now have proof that agreements have been made with the Soviets for nearly 30 years to have their educators work with ours in planning curricula for America's school children. This is a shocking addition to what we have already learned about the many ways that the Soviets are carrying out their secret war for world domination.
>
> Early in October, we learned that two Communist educators are already here in Phoenix, teaching and conferring with educators at Central High School. Boris Bayev is a 41-year old principal of a Soviet secondary school at Ulyanovsk, USSR. A teacher from Red China is also at Central High.

EDWIN FEULNER, PRESIDENT OF THE HERITAGE FOUNDATION (CONSIDERED BY SOME TO BE the foremost "conservative" think tank in the nation), chaired the United States Information Agency's (USIA) Commission on Public Diplomacy in 1986. The annual report carried a cover letter from Feulner as chairman encouraging the acceptance of its recommendations. Under "Educational and Cultural Programs, Exchanges and International Visitors" the report states in part:

> The Commission urges USIA, the Department of State, and the relevant private sector organizations to move quickly to develop specific programs for U.S.-Soviet exchanges pursuant to the General Exchanges accord, other exchange initiatives undertaken at the Geneva Summit, and the agreement by President Reagan and General Secretary Gorbachev to review these programs at their next meeting.

[Ed. Note: The Heritage Foundation later established an office in Moscow, ostensibly to oversee Russia's "hoped-for" evolution from communism to free market economics.]

NATIONAL ACADEMY OF EDUCATION AT THE HARVARD GRADUATE SCHOOL OF EDUCATION (Cambridge, Massachussetts), sent out an informational letter in 1986 entitled "ACLS [American Council of Learned Societies]-USSR Ministry of Education Commission on Education" describing joint U.S.-Soviet education activities. An excerpt which details an extraordinary agenda for cooperation with "The Evil Empire" follows:

> Scholars from the American Council of Learned Societies and the Ministry of Education of the Soviet Union met in the United States in 1986 and agreed to establish a Commission on Education that will be responsible for joint scholarly relations in pedagogy and related fields between the United States and the Soviet Union. Some major joint U.S.- Soviet project themes are: Methods of Teaching and Learning School Science and Math Subjects Using Computers; Theory of Teaching and Learning; Psychological and Pedagogical Problems of Teaching in the Development of Pre-School and School-Age Children; and Problems of Teaching Children with Special Needs.

THE FEBRUARY 1986 ISSUE OF *THE EFFECTIVE SCHOOL REPORT* CARRIED THE FIRST OF A twelve-part series entitled "Implementing Effective Schools: Commitment—The First Step." An accurate description of the Pavlovian/Skinnerian methods required by Effective Schools Research is found in this article. Excerpts follow:

> Effective schools research is conclusive beyond any doubt that all children can learn. Practice now reveals that any school can be led, through a systematic process of training for behavioral change, to effectiveness. Neither research nor practice suggests that the process of becoming effective is easy....
>
> The task of leading a school from ineffectiveness to effectiveness is monumental; however, it can be done. And the research proves that it can be done without wholesale changes of personnel. Ron Edmonds said that we must assume that the teacher and staff are at least as educable as the children they teach....
>
> Change in an effective school must be dramatic if the school is to become effective. The mind-set of many if not most employees within the building must change. Effective school

behaviors must be demonstrated by all. These behaviors are observable, measurable, and transferable; therefore, they can be learned. In-depth and highly structured training will precede improved outcomes.

The trauma experienced by a school that sets a course of effectiveness will be substantial, and will require the implementation of a rigid, highly structured, and sequenced program with all research-based elements in place.

THE NATIONAL FORUM FOR EDUCATIONAL AWARENESS HELD A SPECIAL CEREMONY AND reception in the Russell Senate Caucus Building, Washington, D.C. on February 21, 1986 to honor Norman Dodd, research director for the Reece Committee during 1953–1954. Barbara Cueter, Charlotte Iserbyt and Elisabeth Russinoff planned the awards ceremony at which Senator Jesse Helms made the presentation of the "Americanism Award" to Mr. Dodd. Mrs. Rosalind Kress Haley, a close and long-time friend of Norman Dodd's, was responsible for the reception following the awards ceremony. Admirers of Norman Dodd from across the country arranged for the ceremony to be videotaped. Some excerpts of Senator Helms' videotaped comments follow:

I've learned a little bit about this very fine gentleman who is here today and the more I have learned the more I am convinced that there can't be any other American who has done more to bring the attention of the American people to the real story of the onslaught against American civilization than that distinguished American, Mr. Norman Dodd.

I think it was about 32 years ago... 1954 when Mr. Dodd served as the able director of research for the Reece Commission to investigate the tax-exempt foundations, and oh sir! how they needed to be investigated. Congressman Reece was so shocked by the anti-American activities of the major foundations and their academic allies that he felt obliged to establish a special committee of Congress to investigate [these] activities...

Mr. Norman Dodd, as research director of the Reece Committee, provided a great service to our nation by exposing the real designs of the tax-exempt foundations, such as, who else but the Rockefeller Foundation, and the bottom line of their activities was, and it still is, fundamentally to alter our cultural life so that socialism instead of freedom becomes the American way of life. That's what they're about. Oh, they have other pretexts, just as do such organizations today as the Council on Foreign Relations and the Trilateral Commission.

We are sounding a call to arms to you again, sir, to get you to help us combat these people.... [F]rom what I have learned of Mr. Dodd's life, he has steadfastly adhered to the ideals of our Founding Fathers, as so few do.

I hope that conservatives of today, particularly the younger ones, will go back to the hearing records of the Reece Committee and carefully review the massive amount of testimony and findings—over 1,000 pages. I think it is time to pick up where Congressman Reece and Norman Dodd left off 32 years ago and begin again with investigation of activities of the foundations. Without a doubt we are going to find the same patterns, the same designs, the same goals that were uncovered three decades ago, and those that were uncovered then were unsavory. Those which can be uncovered today will be the same.

In any case, I am so delighted to be here—it's an honor to be here... on behalf of the National Forum for Educational Awareness, and Mr. Dodd, really and truly on behalf of the American people.... [I present this] beautiful plaque.... I am proud of you, sir, and God bless you!

[Ed. Note: There is no one in a more influential position, nationally or internationally, than Senator Jesse Helms, chairman of the U.S. Senate Foreign Relations Committee, to "pick up where Congressman Reece and Norman Dodd left off 32 (now 45) years ago and begin again the investigation of activities of the foundations." The reader is urged to contact his elected officials to request a resumption of this investigation.]

CAROL BARBER, OUTCOME-BASED EDUCATION/MASTERY LEARNING CONSULTANT FROM HOUS-ton, Texas wrote "Outcome-Based Education/Mastery Learning: What Is It? Why Do It? How Do You Do It?" which appeared in the Spring (Vol. 5, No. 3) 1986 issue of *Outcomes*, the quarterly journal of the Network for Outcome-Based Schools. The following are excerpts:

OBE/ML: WHAT IS IT?

As discussed by others in this issue, there is considerable overlap in many of the school reform movements sweeping the country today. Frequently, outcome-based education and mastery learning are used interchangeably or as synonymous phrases. While there are certainly many commonalities in the two movements, they also are very different.

One way to differentiate OBE from ML from other effective school practices is to visualize an umbrella and its various parts. The umbrella includes: 1) a canopy; 2) a center pole to support the canopy; and 3) a set of hinged ribs radiating from the center pole. The umbrella gives us a perfect analogy for comparing many of the school reform movements. Outcome-based education is represented by the canopy of the umbrella. The OBE ideas represent possible reform of the total school system.... When a district moves into OBE, it is ready to examine belief systems of staff, students, parents; placement of students; grading and reporting policies; curriculum issues; certification processes; instructional methods; etc., etc., etc. In other words, OBE means an approach to reform within the *total* [emphasis in the original] school system; i.e., the umbrella under which all practices of school operation will occur.

The center pole supporting the umbrella represents the mastery learning ideas. Mastery learning supports the OBE movement in that it is the main vehicle upon which to begin the change process in the belief system, curriculum organization and instructional strategies. Mastery learning provides us with the support and processes needed to begin the total OBE reform in our schools.

The set of hinged ribs radiating from the center pole can be viewed as any of the many *effective school movements* [emphasis in original] and/or strategies available to us. Strategies such as Dr. Hunter's Mastery Teaching, Hopkins' Student Team Learning, Johnson and Johnson's Cooperative Learning, Joyce's Teaching Models, Good's TESA, and many others, represent effective practices which are totally compatible and will certainly enhance an OBE/ML program.

...Realistically, one could implement any one of the above-mentioned strategies without having ML in operation; indeed one can implement ML without having OBE. However, when OBE is implemented, ML must be applied.

"REPORT TO THE SECRETARY OF EDUCATION WILLIAM BENNETT, APRIL, 1986. TRANSFORM-ing American Education: Reducing the Risk to the Nation" was issued by the National Task Force on Educational Technology. The memo was distributed at an Ohio State School Board caucus. An excerpt follows:

For 1990–2000: The improvement and transformation of education to Mastery Learning will demand continuing support. The nation needs to recognize that the education of its citizens provides the basis for the economic, social and cultural health of American society. Enlightened national self-interest should justify the support of the well-planned educational transformation that the Task Force proposes.

ON MAY 5, 1986 *THE ST. LOUIS GLOBE-DEMOCRAT* RAN AN ARTICLE ENTITLED "SCHOOL Officials Upset by New State Plan" which reported that local educators objected vociferously to a new state plan that required them to give standardized tests in seven core subjects to students in the third, sixth, eighth, and tenth grades. Excerpts from this article follow:

Local educators are stepping up their criticism of what they claim is state interference in the way local schools teach children.... The tests are required by the *Excellence in Education Act of 1985*, a reform bill that educators have largely supported. But school officials claim the testing component will force them to change their curriculum so students learn material in the same order the tests are given [teach to the test]. They claim 70 to 80 percent of the curriculum in local schools could be determined by the new tests....

"We are not opposed to the concept of teaching children the fundamental facts that they ought to know. The issue is who controls the curriculum," said Kirkwood School District Superintendent Thomas Keating. Keating and other superintendents aired their complaints at a joint meeting last week of the Cooperating School Districts of the St. Louis Suburban Area and the Missouri School Boards Association....

...One of the harshest critics of the test plan is Ferguson-Florissant Superintendent Daniel B. Keck, who said the districts may just as well replace their school names with "Department of Elementary and Secondary Education, State of Missouri, Local Annex."...

Keck, however, said the state has bypassed elected school board members and established a direct "pipeline" to local schools. He said administrators are accountable to whoever sets the curriculum.... "To whom am I as the chief executive officer of a school district responsible: to you, or DESE?" Keck said. "In this particular system, there are no checks and balances. That is bad governance." He said the media will create public pressure to excel on the new tests.

Keck said the legislature has "inadvertently" transferred accountability for educational quality to itself. He predicted that if the test scores aren't satisfactory, the state will lower the standards "until the legislature looks good."...

..."And the same number of kids will walk out the door functionally illiterate," he said.

One of the test items (objectives) found in Missouri's Educational Objectives, Grade 12, resulting from passage of Missouri's *Excellence in Education Act of 1985*, follows:

Given a description of an individual with a debased character, such as a child murderer or a person who has set fire to an inhabited building, students should reject suggestions for punishment which would detract from the dignity of the prisoner.

IN THE MAY 15, 1986 ISSUE OF *EDUCATION DAILY* AN ARTICLE RELATED TO STUDENT ASsessment reported that "Secretary Bennett names study group to evaluate student assessment" and lists "Chairman Lamar Alexander, Governor of Tennessee and Chairman, National Governors Association, and Hillary Rodham Clinton, First Lady of Arkansas and partner in the Rose law firm" amongst members of the study group.

AN ARTICLE ENTITLED "CARNEGIE TEACHING PANEL CHARTS 'NEW FRAMEWORK'—GRANTS Totaling $900,000 Made to Press Reforms" written by Lynn Olson appeared in the May 21, 1986 issue of *Education Week*. The announced "New Framework"—amongst other things—carved in stone the methodology which teachers would be required to use in order to obtain board certification. Excerpts follow from this extremely important article:

> The Carnegie Corporation of New York announced here last week that it has awarded two major grants, totaling nearly $900,000, to forward the recommendations of the Carnegie Task Force on Teaching as a Profession.
>
> Last year, the corporation created the Carnegie Forum on Education and the Economy, a multi-million dollar initiative designed to help chart U.S. education policy during the next 10 years. The forum assembled the 14-member task force on teaching as one of its first initiatives. The foundation awarded $817,000 to Stanford University for a 15-month research project to develop prototypes of the kinds of assessments the task force's proposed National Board for Professional Teaching Standards might use to certify teachers....
>
> ...According to David A. Hamburg, president of the corporation [psychiatrist and negotiator of the Carnegie-Soviet Education Agreements], the grants illustrate Carnegie's commitment to the task force's work....
>
> The 15-month Stanford study is the "opening gambit in a long and complex campaign to develop assessments for use by the national board," said Lee S. Shulman [deeply involved with the Chicago Mastery Learning debacle, ed.], principal investigator for the study and a professor of education at Stanford....
>
> "Two major 'products' will come out of the Stanford study," said Mr. Shulman. First, it will create, field test, and critique several "prototype" assessments—most likely in the areas of elementary-school mathematics and secondary-school history.
>
> Second, it will develop a protocol for how to develop such assessments in the future.... As part of its work, the Stanford project will do the following:
>
> - Commission about 20 experts to write papers summarizing the knowledge and skills that the prototype assessments should measure.
> - Conduct "wisdom of practice" studies of outstanding teachers to determine through interviews and observations what it is that they know and can do....
> - Bring together people from around the country who are doing state-of-the-art assessments in other fields, such as those for airplane pilots and foreign-service jobs, to determine what assessment techniques are applicable to teaching.
> - Bring together experts in the fields to be tested—such as elementary-school math teachers, teacher educators, and mathematicians—to get their advice on what the assessments should measure and how.
>
> In addition, the project will have a steering committee representing key stakeholders in the creation of such assessments as well as experts in testing and in the subject areas to be tested.
>
> Members of the Task Force included: Lewis M. Branscomb, Chairman, Vice President and Chief Scientist of the International Business Machines Corporation; Alan K. Campbell, Executive Vice President and Vice Chairman of A.R.A. Services, Inc. of Philadelphia; Mary

Hatwood Futrell, President of the National Education Association; John W. Gardner, former Secretary of Health, Education and Welfare and founder of Independent Sector; Fred M. Hechinger, President of the New York Times Company Foundation, Inc.; Bill Honig, California State Superintendent of Public Instruction; James B. Hunt, former Governor of North Carolina, former Chairman of the Education Commission of the States and a lawyer with the firm of Poyner and Spruill; Vera Katz, Speaker of the Oregon House of Representatives; Governor Thomas H. Kean of New Jersey; Judith Lanier, Dean of the College of Education at Michigan State University; Arturo Madrid, President of the Tomas Rivera Center of Claremont (California) Graduate School; Shirley M. Malcolm, program head, Office of Opportunities in Science, American Association for the Advancement of Science; Ruth Randall, Commissioner of Education in Minnesota; Albert Shanker, President of the American Federation of Teachers.

AN ARTICLE IN THE MAY 21, 1986 ISSUE OF *EDUCATION WEEK* ENTITLED "RESEARCHERS Leery of Federal Plans for Collaboration—Fear 'Cooperative' Link a Path to 'Intervention'" by James Hertling discussed possible federal control of education research. Some excerpts follow:

> The Education Department's decision to form a collaborative relationship with its new research and development center on reading has revived the debate over what control the government should have over the work of educational researchers receiving federal money....
>
> ...But the cooperative agreement outlined in the April 22 Federal Register announcing the competition for the new center on reading research and education mandates government involvement in all stages of the center's work: "developing the agenda, specifying anticipated outcomes, setting research priorities, altering research objectives on the basis of preliminary finding, and receiving final results."
>
> "There's nothing we have heard that makes a cooperative agreement acceptable," said Laurie Garduque, director of governmental and professional liaison at the American Educational Research Association.

[Ed. Note: The above excerpts are important due to their identification of Secretary William Bennett's U.S. Department of Education as the source of the Skinnerian "scientific research-based" reading instruction ultimately used as the criteria necessary for funding of proposals under the *Reading Excellence Act of 1998*.]

"CARNEGIE REPORT ON EDUCATION: 'RADICAL BLUEPRINT FOR CHANGE'" BY NANCY GARland was published in the *Bangor* [Maine] *Daily News*, June 28–29, 1986. The article stated in part:

> The leader of the 600,000-member American Federation of Teachers, [Al] Shanker said many Asian and European countries are changing the way they educate their children to meet the rapidly changing needs of industry. American industries will lose ground if schools cannot produce employees with skills useful in those industries.

PAULO FREIRE'S INFLUENCE ON WORLD EDUCATION, INCLUDING EDUCATION IN THE UNITED States, is revealed in an interesting article entitled "Radical Theorist Takes His Message to the World" published in *The New York Times* August 19, 1986. Some excerpts follow:

> Within days of the triumph of the Sandinista Revolution in July 1979, Nicaragua's new leaders had tracked down the Brazilian educator Paulo Freire at the university where he was lecturing in the United States and had issued him an invitation to come to Managua to help reorganize the country's education system and design its new literacy program.
>
> When Portugal underwent its revolution in 1974 its new Government made a similar offer to Mr. Freire, as did Chile's Institute for Agrarian Reform during the period just before the election of Salvador Allende Gossens there."[17]
>
> Newly independent nations in Africa, ranging from Angola to Tanzania, have also sought the advice of the man regarded as perhaps the foremost literacy expert and radical educator in the world.
>
> "It's something that pleases me," Mr. Freire said recently as he passed through New York City, on his way to a series of workshops and seminars at American universities. "At times, I have been criticized by some philosophers of education, who place me in postures that they classify pejoratively as revolutionary...."
>
> Mr. Friere (pronounced FRAYree) first became widely known in this country with the publication *Pedagogy of the Oppressed* more than 15 years ago. He has argued that it is not education which shapes a society, but rather society which molds education to fit the ends and interests of those in control. In his view, education, particularly the process of learning to read and write, "can become an instrument of social transformation by making those at the bottom of society aware of their plight and the reasons for it."
>
> In practice, refined through literacy campaigns among peasants in the Brazilian Northeast beginning in the late 1950s and later on four continents, Mr. Freire and his many disciples have relied on words like "hunger" or "land," chosen for their relevance to the pupil's own political and social situation, to teach peasants and workers to read and write. The objective is to develop among them what Mr. Friere calls "a critical comprehension of reality."
>
> ...But Mr. Freire also argues that his distinct education has considerable relevance in the industrialized nations of the capitalist world. Mr. Freire's methods have been adapted in the United States by feminist, Hispanic and black groups that operate adult literacy programs or train teachers. Even some corporations, such as Consolidated Edison in New York, have at various times used his techniques in education programs for new workers with low levels of formal education.
>
> "I am not a technician of literacy, as many people apparently saw me in the beginning," he said. "I am an educator who thinks globally."...
>
> To some of his critics, including the Reagan Administration, Mr. Freire's emphasis on the practical has been taken to an absurd extreme in Nicaragua, where second graders count not apples or oranges but hand grenades and rifles to learn arithmetic.

[Ed. Note: See the 1993 entry for the Michigan High School Proficiency Communications Arts Framework which deals with the constructivist philosophy behind whole language and carries out Friere's philosophy of social transformation through "critical thinking."]

THE NEW YORK TIMES OF AUGUST 31, 1986 CARRIED AN ARTICLE ENTITLED "STUDY SAYS 33% of Young Adults Are Illiterate." Excerpt follows:

Results from College Graduates: The most recent Federal study was conducted by two private groups, the Educational Testing Service and the National Assessment of Educational
Progress, at a cost of $1.8 million. In testing basic skills at various levels, the study found
that one in three young adults with a college degree from a two- or four-year school failed to
answer this question correctly: If one purchased a sandwich for $1.90, a bowl of soup for 60
cents, and gave the cashier $3, how much change should he receive? The answer is 50 cents.
(p. 28)

GEORGE ROCHE, PRESIDENT OF HILLSDALE COLLEGE, HILLSDALE, MICHIGAN, AND CHAIR-
man of the National Council on Educational Research, a presidentially appointed council
overseeing the activities of the National Institute of Education, requested an investigation into
the controversial Northwest Regional Educational Laboratory's (NWREL) Tri-County K–12
Course Goals Project which was initiated in 1971. Joan Gubbins, a former Indiana state senator and chairman of the council's Improvement and Practice Committee, researched the Goals
Project, prepared, and submitted her report entitled "Goals and Objectives: Towards a National Curriculum?" to the Council on September 26, 1986.

Although Senator Gubbins's important report could have been used as a brief documenting the illegality of NWREL's role in development of the Course Goals, it evidently fell on deaf
ears. Had the premise of this report—that the goals were based on humanistic no right/no
wrong philosophy and the method was based on Skinnerian operant conditioning—been accepted by Secretary of Education William Bennett and his Assistant Secretary Chester Finn,
American parents and teachers might have seen a most welcome change in the course of
American education, as well as an end to outcome-based education, its dumb-down values-
changing curriculum, and global workforce training.

However, William Bennett and Chester Finn were promoting outcome-based education
and had no desire to pull the plug on their own agenda. In fact, four days after Senator
Gubbins presented her report to the council, Secretary William Bennett announced a $4.5
million grant to provide behaviorist effective school training for school districts across the
nation. The October 1986 issue of *The Effective School Report* announced that

Bennett awarded the money from his Secretary's Discretionary Fund for the commitment
phase of the School Effectiveness Training Network (SET/Net), the largest Effective School
training program ever undertaken. "I see this project as an indication of what school districts, large and small, can do together in improving schools," Bennett said in a Sept. 30
news conference. "This effort shows a real commitment to helping all children learn through
the Effective School process, a process that is based on research and What Works."

Secretary Bennett's reluctance to acknowledge the problems associated with NWREL's
Goals Project as pointed out by Senator Gubbins is better understood when one reads the
Project's definition of behavior modification:

[P]rocedures used in programs of behavior modification or behavioral management are based on principles derived from scientific research (e.g., stimulus-
response-reinforcement).

"Scientific, research-based" teaching with roots in Skinnerian behavioral psychology is the common thread running through the fabric of all Effective School Research; including that promoted by the U.S. Department of Education under Secretary William Bennett's direction. Senator Gubbins's fine paper could not be allowed to cast a shadow on "a process that is based on research and What Works."

TIME FOR RESULTS: GOVERNORS' REPORT ON EDUCATION WAS PRESENTED TO THE **1986** National Governors' Association annual meeting in Wichita, Kansas. Then-Governor of Tennessee Lamar Alexander chaired the meeting and outlined a plan to restructure schools in America. There was a heavy emphasis on retraining of teachers in Skinnerian practices, merit pay/incentives/rewards, etc.

"**THE COOPERATIVE UMBRELLA**" IS THE TITLE OF A SHEET FROM A PACKET OF MATERIALS distributed at a Cooperative Education conference for teachers in Northwest Indiana in 1986. The sheet was copied from *Circles of Learning: Cooperation in the Classroom, Rev. Ed.* by D.W. Johnson, R.T. Johnson and Edith Johnson Holubec (Prentice-Hall: Englewood Cliffs, N.J., 1986). An excerpt follows:

BASIC ELEMENTS OF COOPERATIVE LEARNING

Positive Interdependence
Students must feel that they need each other in order to complete the group's task, that they "sink or swim" together. Some ways to create this feeling are through establishing mutual goals (students must learn the material and make certain group members learn the material), joint rewards (if all group members achieve above a certain percentage on the test, each will receive bonus points), shared materials and information (one paper for each group or each member receives only part of the information needed to do the assignment), and assigned roles (summarizer, encourager or participator, elaborator).

1987

CHARLOTTESVILLE, VIRGINIA'S *THE DAILY PROGRESS* CARRIED NORMAN DODD'S OBITUARY in its January 30, 1987 edition. The tribute read in part:

Mr. Dodd's earlier suspicions of a political and economic conspiracy were confirmed. During his research for this committee [the Reece Committee], the president of the Ford Foundation, H. Rowan Gaither, Jr. told him that some of the giant foundations, including Ford, were working under directives from the White House to so alter life in America as to make possible a comfortable merger with the Soviet Union.

NORTH CENTRAL ASSOCIATION OF COLLEGES AND SCHOOLS (NCA): MICHIGAN COMMITTEE'S Outcomes Accreditation was published in 1987. The brochure demonstrates clearly the shift from academic education to performance/outcome-based affective education focusing on changes in the behavior of the individual student over time. Excerpts from this important publication follow:

> The NCA's Outcomes Accreditation model has generated considerable interest among Michigan educators. It is a process that follows many of the principles of the "Effective Schools Research" and results in schools focusing their activities on improving student success....
>
> Outcomes Accreditation [OA] is a school-based accreditation and evaluation model that helps schools document the effectiveness of their programs. Schools are required to target their evaluation efforts by measuring changes in student behavior; i.e., outcomes. OA serves as an alternative to the NCA's traditional evaluation formats. OA was adopted for use by NCA member schools in April 1987. Rather than focusing on "inputs" or what the school contributes to the educational process, OA examines "student outcomes" or the influence the school has on the students it serves....
>
> Schools identify no more than five areas in which they want to focus their improvement activities. Target goals are written for each area. Three of these target goals focus on cognitive or basic skill areas, and two goals address affective concerns or how students behave or feel about themselves. The goals are written in such a way that changes can be measured over time. Student outcomes are measured by comparing desired levels of student performance with present performance....
>
> Examples of specific data sources include: criterion- and norm-referenced test results, anecdotal records, attitude inventories, teacher-made tests, student participation rates, writing samples, and attendance and enrollment figures.... Next, faculty committees establish the desired levels of student performance. Although external sources such as state-mandated goals, national averages or goals developed by textbook publishers might be helpful in formulating performance expectations, educators need to base desired performance levels on their knowledge of each child. The discrepancy that exists between current and desired student performance then serves as the focus of the school improvement plan.

AT THE SECOND ANNUAL NATIONAL OUTCOME-BASED EDUCATION CONFERENCE, HELD FEBRUary 12–14, 1987 in Tempe, Arizona, a notebook was distributed which contained a flow chart describing how mastery learning works. The notebook contained materials generated by the following presenters: Part I, William Spady; Part II, Lawrence A. Rowe; Part III, Kathleen A. Fitzpatrick; and Part IV, Janet N. Barry. This writer has converted the flow chart which was in the notebook to written text in order to provide a graphic (rat maze) description of the behavior modification method behind mastery learning and direct instruction. The chart's description follows:

MASTERY LEARNING BREAKS THE FAILURE CYCLE

At the top of a circle is the word "TASK," which has an arrow pointing towards LACK OF UNDERSTANDING, which has two parts: 1) change presentation and 2) use alternative material. 2) has two arrows: one towards TASK COMPLETION SUCCESS and the other towards DIFFICULTY. DIFFICULTY has two parts: 1) peer tutoring and 2) shorten assignments. 2) has two arrows: one towards TASK COMPLETION SUCCESS and the other towards FAILURE. FAILURE has two parts: 1)change environment and 2) change curriculum. 2) has two arrows: one towards TASK COMPLETION/POSITIVE FEEDBACK, and the other towards NEGATIVE FEEDBACK. NEGATIVE FEEDBACK has two arrows: 1) use self-pacing, self-checking, and 2) group discussion of goals. 2) has two arrows: one towards ATTAINABLE GOAL/ POSITIVE FEEDBACK, the other towards POOR SELF CONCEPT. POOR SELF CONCEPT has two arrows: 1) provide successes and 2) positive feedback. 2) has two arrows: one toward RAISED SELF ESTEEM and the other LOW MOTIVATION. LOW MOTIVATION has three arrows: 1) provide choices, 2) choose relevant materials, and 3) utilize interests. 3) has two arrows: one towards HIGHER MOTIVATION/WILLINGNESS TO TRY and the other toward BEHAVIOR PROBLEMS (Task Avoidance). BEHAVIOR PROBLEMS has three arrows: 1) provide choices, 2) contracting, and 3) group goal setting. 3) has two arrows: one toward RE-CHANNELLED BEHAVIOR DIRECTED TOWARD SKILL ATTAINMENT and INADEQUATE SKILLS. INADEQUATE SKILLS has two arrows: 1) prescriptive curriculum and 2) modified environment. 2) has two arrows: one towards SKILLS ATTAINED/NEW TASK ATTEMPTED, and the other back to start, "TASK."

EDUCATION DAILY OF MAY 21, 1987 COVERED THE CARNEGIE FOUNDATION FOR THE ADvancement of Teaching's award of $817,000 to Lee Shulman of Stanford University, formerly involved in Chicago's Mastery Learning failure, for his forthcoming work on assessments for new teachers.

KATHY L. COLLINS, LEGAL COUNSEL FOR THE IOWA DEPARTMENT OF EDUCATION, WROTE AN article entitled "Children Are Not Chattel" for the American Humanist Association's journal *Free Inquiry* in the Fall of 1987 (Vol. 7, No. 4, p. 11) and stated that

> Christian parents who want the freedom to indoctrinate their children with religious education do not understand that the law that prevents them from legally teaching their kids prevents someone else from abusing them....
>
> Certified teachers are state-mandated child-abuse reporters. When children are allowed to be kept at home, there may be no outside contact, no help for the abused child.

[Ed. Note: This portentous article was published just as the homeschooling movement in America began mushrooming. Parents responded to the failures of the latest fads in the classrooms by pulling their children out of public schools to instruct them at home. Many educators viewed the rise of home education with alarm. Parental rights and constitutional religious freedoms posed a direct threat to the "it takes a village to raise a child" philosophy which was to become embedded in every state's education reform plan during the 1990s.]

ON NOVEMBER 2, 1987, A FEW SHORT YEARS BEFORE THE BERLIN WALL CAME DOWN, AND only two years after the signing of the U.S.-Soviet education agreements, Mikhail Gorbachev was reported by Novosti Press Agency Publishing House in Moscow to have said in his speech to the Soviet Central Committee, "We are moving toward a new world: the world of communism. We shall never turn off that road." Even so, after the Berlin Wall came down (1989) Gorbachev was a keynote speaker at a major Republican Party fundraiser.

DAVID W. HORNBECK OF THE CARNEGIE FOUNDATION FOR THE ADVANCEMENT OF TEACHING and Maryland's state superintendent of instruction, whose credentials lie in theology rather than in education, presented his proposal for a new public education system for the nation in the November 17, 1987 issue of *The Montgomery County* [Maryland] *Journal.* The *Journal* carried an article entitled "State Education Chief Pushes Revolutionary Plan for the Nation" that, amongst other things, "would let students enroll in schools of their choice and even sue the state over low-quality education." Excerpts follow:

> "The model state law would create a situation in which it's the school's fault and not the kid's if the school is unsuccessful. If it's not a successful school, you can leave it." The system would let a student cross district lines in search of better public education....
>
>   Hornbeck's presentation Saturday at an Asheville, North Carolina meeting aroused just a few criticisms, which were mainly concerned with the proposal's wording, said Jay P. Goldman, spokesman for the school chief's council. "This follows years of massaging and reworking it," he said....
>
>   ...The new rights proposals are directed toward all children, but special measures target those considered "at risk of educational failure." In the early years, low-income children would be identified as at risk; in later years, achievement would provide the definition.... "We're trying to take a step away from kid-bashing," Hornbeck said. "Society and the schools fail the kids.".…
>
>   ...Hornbeck, who said he is waiting for the council vote before discussing the issue with Gov. William Donald Schaefer and Maryland legislative officials, said he expects local school officials across the country to resist the proposals.
>
>   "If the council adopts this, you will have the superintendents of the United States saying we want to create new rights and routes that may well lead to the courts," Hornbeck said....
>
>   ...One of the plan's goals is to eliminate spending differentials from district to district, ranging about $2,000 per pupil from highest to lowest in Maryland. "That means $50,000 more behind one classroom of 25 kids than another," Hornbeck said.

[Ed. Note: Did we understand Mr. Goldman correctly? "This follows years of massaging and reworking"? Why does one need "years of massaging and reworking a proposal" which supposedly is in the best interests of the traditional American teacher and the children he or she teaches? Obviously, this proposal by Hornbeck was a radical one which would focus not on traditional education, but on producing or molding a "product," your child—who is now being referred to as "human capital" by Hornbeck—your child, whose workforce skills and politically correct attitudes, values and beliefs would entitle him to a Certificate in Mastery in order to be hired by and able to increase the profits of a corporation.

References to "special measures target those considered 'at risk of educational failure'" are unsettling. If our children reject the "education" to which they are subjected, they will immediately be labeled "at risk," thus subjecting them to the behavior modification programs and operant conditioning techniques normally used for special education.

When Hornbeck says, "Society and the schools fail the kids," are we to believe "It's the environment, stupid"? Everything that goes wrong in our great nation is now blamed on the "environment"; from people's choices to smoke or not to smoke, drink or not to drink, murder or not to murder, study or not to study. According to Skinnerian behaviorist thinking, since humans are to be thought of as animals, not having free will and, therefore, not being responsible for their actions, they would be incapable of making complex decisions, of deciding "yes" or "no." We are on a slippery slope when we accept this "the environment is responsible" line of thinking.

Hornbeck's proposal parallels the 1999 passage of "choice" legislation in Florida, under Governor Jeb Bush's direction. Delivery of failing grades to schools will be the trigger for funding for moving students to schools of their "choice"—including private or religious schools.]

1988

ON FEBRUARY 22, 1988 CLARENCE THOMAS, CHAIRMAN OF THE EQUAL EMPLOYMENT OPportunity Commission (EEOC), who would shortly thereafter be appointed by President George Bush to the U.S. Supreme Court, signed off on an EEOC Policy Notice regarding protection from mandatory New Age training in the workplace. The Policy Notice explained:

1. SUBJECT: Policy statement on "new age" training programs which conflict with employees' religious beliefs.
2. PURPOSE: This policy statement is intended to provide guidance in the handling of cases where an employee objects to participating in the training program because it utilizes techniques or exercises which conflict with the employee's religious beliefs.
3. EFFECTIVE DATE: Upon Receipt.
4. EXPIRATION DATE:
5. ORIGINATOR: Title VII/EPA Division, Office of Legal Counsel.
6. INSTRUCTIONS: This notice supplements the instructions in #628 of Vol. II of the Compliance Manual, Religious Accommodation, and should be inserted after p. 628–630.

[Ed. Note: This Policy Notice extends to all government employees who resist manipulative New Age training which is based on the behavioral techniques and behavior modification described in this book. Held captive in the classroom due to attendance laws, why haven't our children been provided the same protection from the mind-bending curricula and methods used on government employees in the workplace? Why are not American teachers provided this protection from the mind-bending, brain-numbing, in-service sessions which violate their constitutional rights? *The Protection of Pupil Rights Amendment* which passed the U.S. Senate unanimously in 1978, for which regulations were drafted and approved in 1984, has proven to be useless since the educational bureaucracy refuses to enforce it and has consistently stonewalled when parents have attempted to assert their rights under the law.]

THE *EFFECTIVE SCHOOL REPORT*'S MARCH, 1988 ISSUE PUBLISHED "INTERNATIONAL CONgress for Effective Schools Draws Participants from 13 Nations to London" which heralded Effective School Research as representing "the" chosen organizational and pedagogical vehicle for the operation of the world's schools. Excerpts follow:

Representatives from thirteen countries came to London in January for the inaugural meeting of the International Congress for Effective Schools. In the United States, the Effective Schools Movement was begun to improve public schools for children from low income families. Thirty American states have used effective schools precepts as part of their reform efforts.

Effective schools activities were reported from Australia, Canada, England, and Wales, Germany, Hungary, Ireland, Israel, the Netherlands, Norway, Scotland, Sweden, South Africa, and the United States. Dale Mann, a professor at Teachers College, Columbia University, and the founding chairman of the International Congress, said that the 130 registrants were using effective schools ideas in school improvement work that ran the gamut from early childhood education to high school reform.

The Congress will meet next in January, 1989 in Rotterdam. A special section of the program will offer legislators an opportunity to share their perspectives on school improvement. The Rotterdam meetings will be organized by a team led by D.A.A. Peters (Projectleider, Project Onderwijs en Social Milieu, Burg, Van Walmsumeg 892, 3011 MZ Rotterdam, the Netherlands 010–4113266).[18]

[Ed. Note: By this time the reader is all too familiar with *The Effective School Report* and Effective School Research, as well as its role in the dumbing down of public school children, particularly those from low income families. The international change agents "used" these children (experimented on them—starting with children in Jackson, Mississippi where *The Effective School Report* was originally located) prior to recommending that *all* children be subjected to the Skinnerian dumb down methods (OBE/ML/DI).

From this time on the reader will encounter entries in this book dealing with Effective Schools Research exchanges with Russia and China, thereby closing the circle on the implementation of Effective Schools Research on a global basis. Also of importance is the reference to the inclusion of England and Wales, not only in the original National Assessment of Educational Progress (NAEP) 1981 paper by Archie Lapointe and Willard Wirtz, but in the 1994 *National Issues in Education: Goals 2000 and School-to-Work* entry which reveals that:

> In 1991 Lamar Alexander, working with Chester Finn and others who were familiar with the work of British Prime Minister Margaret Thatcher in enacting a national curriculum in England and Wales, convinced Bush to endorse the idea of national standards for education.

Of interest here is that the National Assessment of Educational Progress (NAEP) had been working on assessment for many years, dating back to 1980, with Clare Burstall of Wales, U.K. Also, one might ask why the United States would want to copy the English education system in light of the poor performance of its students on basic skills tests. The December 9, 1988 issue of *The Wall Street Journal* carried an editorial entitled "And You Thought American Schools Were Bad!" in which Theodore Dalrymple, the pen name of British physician Anthony Daniels, said that:

> In eight years in medical practice in an English slum (in which lives, incidentally, a fifth of the population of the industrial English city where I work) I have met only one teenager of hundreds I have asked who knew when World War II was fought. The others thought it took place in the early 1900s or the 1970s, and lasted up to 30 years.

Another recurrent theme, which will become evident throughout the rest of this book, will be the growing emphasis on what Utah's Superintendent Burningham referred to as "research-verified programs." This term will change subtly as Effective Schools programs are referred to as "scientific, research-based," implying that they are "acceptable and desirable"— or as Secretary of Education William Bennett explained, "What Works."]

DR. SUE E. BERRYMAN, DIRECTOR OF THE INSTITUTE ON EDUCATION AND THE ECONOMY AT Teachers College, Columbia University, New York, presented a paper entitled "Education and the Economy: A Diagnostic Review and Implications for the Federal Role" at a seminar on the federal role in education held at the Aspen Institute, Aspen, Colorado on July 31–August 10, 1988. Under acknowledgments one reads:

> This Seminar was sponsored by The Carnegie Corporation, The Ford Foundation, The Hewlitt Foundation, The Primerica Foundation, and the Rockefeller Brothers Foundation. This paper is based heavily on, and could not have been written without, research conducted under the auspices of The National Center on Education and Employment, funded by the Office of Research, Office of Educational Research and Improvement of the U.S. Department of Education. The paper also relies on research funded by the National Assessment of Vocational Education.

An excerpt from Dr. Berryman's resumé, which was attached to her paper, follows:

> 1973–1985 Behavioral Scientist, Behavioral Sciences Department, The RAND Corporation, Santa Monica, California, and Washington, D.C.
>
> > Analyzed individuals' educational and employment choices and the nature and consequences of military, corporate, and federal human resource policies.

The table of contents of Dr. Berryman's report is reproduced here:

I. A FRAME OF REFERENCE

II. THE TRANSFORMATION OF THE AMERICAN ECONOMY
    HOW DO WE KNOW WHAT IS HAPPENING?
    SKILL TRENDS IN EMPLOYMENT BY OCCUPATION
    INDUSTRY CASE STUDIES: CHANGES IN THE NATURE
        AND STRUCTURE OF WORK
    RECONCILING OCCUPATIONAL COUNTS AND INDUSTRY
        CASE STUDY RESULTS

III. ELEMENTARY AND SECONDARY EDUCATION: A PICTURE OF
    DISCONNECTIONS
    WHAT DO WE NEED TO TEACH? TO WHOM? WHEN? HOW?
      What Do Students Need to Learn?
      Who Should Learn?
      When Should They Learn?
      How Should These Skills Be Taught?
      Vocabulary and Accountability
    EMPLOYERS AND EDUCATORS: ARE THEY LOOKING
        THROUGH THE SAME GLASSES?
    THE SIGNALLING SYSTEM BETWEEN SCHOOLS AND LABOR
        MARKETS
    THE STRUCTURE OF INDUSTRIES AND THE RESTRUCTURING OF
        AMERICAN COMPANIES: ANY LESSONS FOR RESTRUCTURING SCHOOLS?
      The Structure of Industries
      The Restructuring of American Companies

IV. ECONOMIC CHANGES THAT AFFECT POST-SECONDARY
    EDUCATION AND TRAINING
    COLLISION BETWEEN HUMAN CAPITAL DEMAND AND SUPPLY

Excerpts from the body of the paper follow:

WHAT DO WE NEED TO TEACH? TO WHOM? WHEN? HOW?

As the educational implications of the restructuring American economy become clearer, the incomplete—sometimes perverse—nature of current education reforms emerges.

Those reforms targeted at improving students' academic skills are clearly appropriate—up to a point, academic and work-related curricula should be the same. However, documented changes in the nature and structure of work and advances in cognitive science argue for a second wave of reform that involves fundamental changes in what we teach, to whom we teach it, when we teach it, and how we teach it. In other contexts I have talked about this second wave of reform as "shadows in the wings" for the simple reason that—to shift metaphors—this airplane is not yet ready to fly. The issues raised here pose formidable research, development, and evaluation challenges in areas such as curriculum (and associated textbook or software materials), pedagogy, the preparation of teachers, concepts and measures of accountability, and school structure.

What do industry studies imply about the core skills that students need to learn? Economic changes certainly imply the need for good academic skills. Perhaps the most profound educational implication of computers in the workplace is that they force a replacement of observational learning with learning acquired primarily through symbols, whether verbal or mathematical (e.g., Scribner and Cole, 1973; Bailey, 1988)....

As the labor force becomes increasingly multicultural and job content changes rapidly and in confusing ways, communication problems also increase between workers, generating the need for interpersonal communication and conflict resolution skills....

WHO SHOULD LEARN?

The skills just described are generic in that, in general, they cut across industries and occupations. Thus, everyone needs to learn them, not just some people. This does not mean that everyone needs to learn them in the same way. It does mean that for these skills, our educational objectives for everyone need to be roughly the same.

The idea has been most problematic for higher order cognitive thinking. Like other industrialized nations, the United States has harbored two quite distinct educational traditions—one concerned with elite education, the other with mass education. As Resnick [Lauren] (1987a) points out, these traditions conceived of schooling differently, had different clienteles, and held different goals for their students. Thus, although "...it is not new to include thinking, problem solving, and reasoning in someone's curriculum, it is new to include it in everyone's curriculum."...

WHEN SHOULD THEY LEARN?

Early. We usually think about preparing students for the labor market during high school. However, we are talking generic work-related skills here, not occupationally specific ones; for these high school is too late. It is implausible to think that high school sophomores educated in a passive learning regime for the first nine years of their schooling can learn to self-regulate their learning in the tenth year. We can make analogous arguments about learning how to learn, about learning how to function effectively in teams, or about learning how to resolve conflicts.

For example, as Resnick (1987a) notes, the most important single message of modern research on the nature of thinking is that the kinds of activities traditionally associated with thinking are not limited to advanced levels of development.

> These activities are an intimate part of even elementary learning.... In fact, the term "higher order" skills is probably itself fundamentally misleading, for it suggests that another set of skills, presumably called "lower order," needs to come first. This assumption... implicitly... justifies long years of drill on the "basics" before thinking and problem solving are demanded.... Research suggests that failure to cultivate aspects of (higher order cognitive) thinking may be the source of major learning difficulties even in elementary school.

This section relies heavily on pioneering work in cognitive psychology, cognitive science, and cognitive anthropology on non-school learning and its implications for how we structure formal learning. At the heart of this research is the presumption that intelligence and expertise are built out of interaction with the environment, not in isolation from it. This work implicitly challenges our traditional distinctions between "head" and "hand," between "academic" and "vocational" education, between "education" and "training," and between school-based and work-based learning.

Coming out of this stream of research is a much clearer sense of how school-based learning and non-school-based learning differ from each other. In a bravura synthesis of the work in this field, Lauren Resnick (1987b) delineates four broad contrasts between in-school and out-of-school mental activity that raise profound questions about the utility and effectiveness of schooling for all non-school activity, including work of all types and for all learners, whether at-risk, or not-at-risk. They stimulate us to rethink—radically rethink—how we teach in school.

The first contrast is between individual cognition in school versus shared cognition outside. Although group activities occur in school, students are ultimately judged on what they can do by themselves. Much of the core activity of the school—homework or in class exercises—is designed as individual work. For the most part, students fail or succeed at a task independently of what other students do (aside from grading on a curve). By contrast, a great deal of activity outside of school is socially shared: work, personal life, and recreation take place in social systems in which what one person is able to do depends fundamentally on what others do and in which "successful" functioning depends upon the mesh of several individuals' mental and physical performance. This contrast argues for much more team and co-operative learning, the student being accountable for both individual and team performance. (p. 21)

[Ed. Note: The above emphasis on group learning, group cooperation, etc., reminds me of a comment made by a lady in the audience when I was giving a speech on education restructuring with its emphasis on the need for cooperative learning and how cooperative learning is used in communist countries. She recounted an incident which occurred while visiting relatives in the Ukraine (part of the former Soviet Union). A fire broke out in the house one evening and, instead of her relatives using their individual brains and ingenuity to put it out, (assuming individual responsibility), everyone sat on the couch and franticly stared at one another, not knowing how to deal with the situation.]

THE EAST GIBSON COUNTY (INDIANA) GROUP, KNOWN AS "JEANNIE'S GROUP," OPPOSED the use of *Tactics for Thinking*, developed by Robert Marzano in 1988.[19] After long and heated discussions with the school system, the superintendent suddenly notified the group that he had arranged for a debate to be held in two days! Short notice, considering the fact that he carefully neglected to inform them until the day of the debate that they would be debating outside experts. And, experts they were—no less than Ronald Brandt of the Association for Supervision and Curriculum Development (ASCD) and Professor Ed Jenkins of Indiana University. A firsthand account of a portion of the debate follows:

> [Pat Burkhart, one of the East Gibson County Group debaters] "We would like to do some demonstrations for you.... The first one is yoga (demonstrated).... The second exercise is self hypnosis.... These instructions... came from an article in *The Readers' Digest* (demonstrated).... The third exercise is a semi-trance. This is the semi-trance in the Norman-Lindsay book *Human Information Processing* referenced by Marzano in *Tactics for Thinking*, 'Unit 1: Attention Control' (demonstrated).... The fourth exercise is the Involuntary Attention-Orienting Reflex. These steps come from the book *The Working Brain* by Alexandr Luria [of Russia] which is also referenced in the *Tactics for Thinking* manual by Marzano (demonstrated). The last exercise is Marzano's Attention Control in the *Tactics* manual. As a volunteer, we have an 8-year-old child who understands the difference between acting and reality. We thought this appropriate—to use a child—since Marzano does. The difference is, our child knows what we are doing, but Marzano's victims don't.
>   "Please tell us what is the difference? The thing that is really silly is that we are supposed to believe that this is higher order learning—that it is learning to learn.... This is learning to have your conscious mind sedated and using only your unconscious mind which processes everything indiscriminately.... There isn't much going on here besides a form of self-hypnosis."
>   In conclusion, the opponents of *Tactics for Thinking* asked Joan Gubbins, former Indiana state senator and presidentially appointed member of the National Council for Educational Research, to read the following:

> If we turn to Marzano's conclusions at the end of his evaluation, he states, and I quote: "These findings can not be considered stable." Do you understand what all of this says? Marzano himself says his evaluation of this experimental program is unreliable.... Nothing is said about improvement of performance on standardized achievement tests by the students used in this field testing. However, in a program Marzano reported on in 1984 [he admitted that] "a decrease in math and reading achievement was indicated on standardized tests."

THE AUGUST 1988 ISSUE OF *EDUCATION UPDATE*, PUBLISHED BY THE ASSOCIATION FOR Supervision and Curriculum Development (ASCD), carried an article entitled "Tactics for Thinking Attacked in Washington, Indiana" which said, in part:

> *Tactics for Thinking*, a framework for teaching thinking developed at the Midcontinent Regional Educational Laboratory (McREL) and published by ASCD in 1986, has recently been the target of critics who argue that it "brainwashes" children and advances a "New Age" agenda of one-world government. The problems first occurred in Battle Ground, Washington, and have surfaced in at least one other Washington community and in two Indiana towns.

Tactics, according to ASCD Executive Editor Ron Brandt, "gives teachers a practical way to teach their students to think well." The program teaches 22 skills divided into three categories: Learning-to-Learn Skills, Content Skills, and Reasoning Skills.... For example, a unit of the program on "attention control" describes how adult learners are able to disregard distractions and concentrate on a particular subject, which helps their performance. The *Tactics Trainer's Manual* suggests an exercise in which participants can be voluntarily controlled. Although the strategy may seem ordinary, critics of *Tactics* in East Gibson, Indiana, said it "is the same technique used by hypnotists, used in mind control, and in New Age meditation."

...Marzano denied that *Tactics* is controversial or contains sensitive material, asking, "How can teaching kids to control their attention in class so they can learn more be controversial?"

Paul Drotz, an assistant superintendent in the South Kitsap, Washington school district where *Tactics* was challenged, said that "the vocabulary used in the program left us pretty open to attacks. I could change 12 words and local critics would have a difficult time attacking it." Judy Olson, a consultant hired by the Washington ASCD to train teachers in *Tactics*, said she advised trainees to call one unit "pay attention" rather than "attention control." Because of the controversy, however, the Washington ASCD will no longer provide *Tactics* training, although it will still build awareness of it, members of the group's governing board said.

...Marzano said that development and field testing of *Tactics* was "typical," and that the screening process, which included review by eight nationally recognized experts in critical thinking, was more thorough than normal.... ASCD has sold more than 17,000 teacher's manuals, 3,600 trainer's guides and 550 videotapes since it began publishing the program. Marzano estimates that 20,000 teachers have been trained in the program.

Brandt suggested that school districts involve board members, teachers, and the community early on in deciding whether and how *Tactics* might be used in the system. ASCD will continue to closely monitor any instance in which the program is challenged. Anyone knowing of such incidents should write Brandt at ASCD headquarters, 1703 Beauregard St., Alexandria, VA 22311–1714.

[Ed. Note: The *Tactics* program, or a similar critical thinking program using another title, could well be part of the curriculum in each of the 16,000 school districts in the nation, since it takes only one of those 20,000 teachers in each district to train other teachers. It was, however, not adopted in East Gibson County, Indiana.]

THE AUGUST 11, 1988 EDITION OF *EDUCATION DAILY* COVERED THE NATIONAL CITIZENS Alliance Press Conference held at the National Press Club in Washington, D.C. Excerpts follow:

GROUP ASKS EDUCATION DEPARTMENT TO STOP FUNDING "MIND-CONTROL" CURRICULA, END SOVIET EXCHANGES

A citizens group headed by a former Education Department official asked ED to stop promoting curriculum the group says controls students' minds.

The National Citizens Alliance (NCA), a group of parents and teachers, alleged at a Washington, D.C. news conference yesterday that ED is promoting "mind-control" curricula that use hypnosis-like techniques to foster concentration.

NCA wants to "get the federal government to stop pouring millions of dollars" into the "development of mind-control programs currently sweeping through American schools," said Charlotte Iserbyt, who served as senior policy advisor in ED's Office of Educational Research and Improvement from 1981 to 1982 and is NCA's East Coast coordinator. Iserbyt called on Education Secretary William Bennett and other federal officials to:

End federal funding and promotion of programs such as *Tactics for Thinking,* which is used in Indiana schools.[20] NCA says the curriculum "employs hypnotic-like processes and altered states of consciousness techniques on children";

Cancel the education portion of the 1985 exchange agreement between the United States and the Soviet Union, which NCA says allows dissemination of "communist propaganda" through global teaching methods and the joint development of textbooks and computer software; and

Force Pennsylvania to ask parental consent before using its Educational Quality Assessment test, which NCA says uses "psychological and psychiatric testing" in violation of the federal *Protection of Pupil Rights Amendment* [Anita Hoge case against the Pennsylvania Department of Education].

NCA also criticized ED's National Assessment of Educational Progress for tracking student attitudes and behavior, saying that obtaining such information violates privacy rights and could lead to behavior modification nationwide.

Secretary Bennett's spokesman Loye Miller said he is not aware of the complaints to which NCA refers. An OERI spokesman declined to comment.—Christopher Grasso

A MAJOR REPORT ENTITLED *THE FORGOTTEN HALF: PATHWAYS TO SUCCESS FOR AMERICA'S Youth and Young Families* was published by the W.T. Grant Foundation's Commission on Work, Family and Citizenship.[21] The November 23, 1988 issue of *Education Week* carried an item on the report which stated that service projects and community service were recommended as a requirement for graduation. An excerpt from the article follows:

The report recommends that schools and communities "establish attractive service opportunities" for young people and either include service projects as part of the curriculum or require a specified amount of community service as a requirement toward graduation. The report also encourages "partnerships between business and state and local governments that provide opportunities for job training."

A RECAP OF A 1988 INVITATIONAL CONFERENCE IN THE U.S.S.R. ENTITLED "CHILDREN, Computers and Education," written by David Porteous, contract coordinator for the School of Social Work, University of Connecticut, West Hartford, Connecticut, was published in the 1988/1989 issue of *T.H.E. Journal* (technology journal).[22] Excerpts follow:

Recently, educators from the United States, Canada, West Germany and the Netherlands met with counterparts from the Soviet Union and Bulgaria in an historic first—an invitational conference in the U.S.S.R. titled "Children, Computers, and Education."

The word "informatics" is used in Russian to denote the principles underlying the operations of computer hardware and software. Informatics seems to encompass the electronic and algorithmic systems of computers. Dr. Alexey Semenov of the Soviet Academy of Sciences said algorithmic thinking is embedded in the Soviet's educational system and fundamental to their understanding of cognition. This fits with the Soviet schools' high regard for mathematics and physics....

Semenov's presentation on the history and present status of algorithmics in Soviet schools started with the fact that their schools have used programmed instruction since the 1960s.... As might be expected, LOGO is held in high esteem in the Soviet Union and Seymour Papert works with some Soviet schools....

There was hope among the leaders with whom we talked that computers will become seen and used in more diverse ways throughout the curriculum. Certainly the goals of Gorbachev's Perestroika include the restructuring of schools, along with other institutions and the economy, and a subsequent technological boost to the country. With the broad curriculum reforms and structural changes occurring in schools today and in the near future, the computer could expedite this process....

MODEL SCHOOL

Most schools have one or more sponsors, such as factories, institutes, universities, which provide materials, professional assistance and a place for students in the upper forms to do practical work for three to four hours a week, including computer programming. School #344 has close ties with a university and a technical institute, for instance [same as USA School-to-Work proposals, ed.]....

...The informatics curriculum, with objectives broader than computer use, is taught even when students do not have access to a computer....

We were told that this conference, from Leningrad to Moscow to Zvenigorod, had begun to open many minds as to what is possible with computers and children beyond the formal informatics curriculum. Professional respect and relationships have developed among participants. We could not have heard better news for our efforts to achieve a major step towards a productive global discussion of how all children can benefit from an informed use of CAI [computer-assisted instruction/programmed learning] in the world's classrooms.

1989

IN AN ARTICLE IN THE JANUARY 25, 1989 ISSUE OF *EDUCATION WEEK* CHESTER E. FINN, JR., former head of the U.S. Department of Education's research branch, told business leaders in Washington that he favored the development of a "national curriculum."

RUSHWORTH KIDDER, PRESIDENT OF THE INSTITUTE FOR GLOBAL ETHICS WITH OFFICES IN Camden, Maine, and London, England, wrote *Reinventing the Future: Global Goals for the 21st Century*, published by The Christian Science Publishing Society (MIT Press, Cambridge, Mass, 1989) which covered the dialogue between 35 notables from 12 nations gathered at "Wingspread" in Racine, Wisconsin in April of 1989. *The Christian Science Monitor*, the Johnson Foundation and the University of Maryland-Baltimore County sponsored the event. In his book Kidder stated that the conference included "everything that sounded like a reasonable goal for the year 2000," among which were the following: "Educate children in the context of one world; Develop educational curricula that reflect the realitites of global interdependence; Promote community service; Inculcate a healthy skepticism for authority; Reduce the share of GNP (Gross National Product) devoted to military spending; and Strengthen the role of the United Nations and other multilateral forums."

In a July 5, 1994 letter from Mr. Kidder to Mr. David Zanotti, president of the Northeast Ohio Roundtable, Kidder described the work of his Institute for Global Ethics as follows:

> The Institute for Global Ethics is an independent, non-profit educational organization specifically dedicated to promoting the discussion of ethics in a global context. Taking a journalistic rather than an academic approach, we see our task as responding to the ever-growing need for identifying and describing standards of ethical values throughout the world. We don't dictate what those values should be. Instead, we try to help discover what they actually are—and to promote their discussion and application in ways that are non-threatening, inclusive, and conflict-resolving.
>
> The Institute has a national board of directors, an international advisory council, a network of nationwide and global connections, and a membership base of some 2,500 individuals in the United States and around the world. Some of our activities [from which the writer has selected only a few] include:
>
> - **Global Values Survey**. We are currently carrying out a multi-country survey of values and ethics to help us understand the core values that unite various cultures as well as the different ways each culture defines an ethical decision. The pilot survey, carried out among samples of business leaders in Japan, India, and the United States, was completed in June. We're now laying plans to launch a full-scale survey of individuals in business, politics, medicine, journalism, and other sectors of society in 12 nations. [The Institute was awarded a $450,000 grant from the W.K. Kellogg Foundation of Battle Creek, Michigan to accomplish this survey, ed.]
>
> - **Education**. The Institute works actively with several school districts and educational organizations in the United States on character education, seeking ways to help schools and communities find the core, shared values among their constituencies that can form a basis for discussions of ethical issues in the schools. We've produced an award-winning half-hour video, *Personal Ethics and the Future of the World*, designed for use in schools and with audiences of all ages. And we've also published a booklet, *Character Education: Lessons from the Past, Models for the Future*, by Professor James Leming of Southern Illinois University.
>
> - **Seminars**. We are currently working with several clients (including the J.M. Smucker Company, Lancaster Laboratories, Inc., and the Council on Foundations in Washington, D.C.) to provide ethics training programs. We have trained more than 1,000 executives and managers in day-long, intensive seminars, and developed a train-the-trainers program as well. Our goal is to encourage what we call "ethical fitness"—which, like physical fitness, needs to be practiced, developed and applied.
>
> - **Radio**. Our newest venture is a one-hour Public Radio program titled "Let's Be Honest—Ethical Issues of the '90s." Featuring a three-person panel and a moderator, the program focuses on the moral and ethical aspects of a specific topic drawn from the week's news and encourages on-air telephone calls from listeners. Pilot versions of the program, aired on Maine Public Radio, have been very well received, and plans are afoot to develop a version of the program for a national audience.

[Ed. Note: Kidder's Global Ethics program is another example of the problem with character education as a whole: basing character, values and ethics on consensus decisions by a group instead of absolute, enduring principles.]

KENT TEMPUS WROTE "EDUCATION IN THE FUTURE: 21ST CENTURY SCHOOLS WILL OFFER Learning for All Citizens" for *The Muscatine* [Iowa] *Journal*'s April 22, 1989 issue. Excerpts follow:

> Schools in 21st Century Iowa will be hubs of their communit[ies], providing broad learning opportunities for all citizens, according to the director of the Iowa Department of Education. William Lepley says future schools will be centers for family and social services as well. "Society in the year 2010 has realized that the school is the single societal institution that can truly be an advocate, a resource, and a catalyst for children and families, as well as learners of all ages," Lepley said.... Students' evaluation will improve. Instead of grades, students will be assessed not on the work they complete, but on the skills they master, he explained.
>
> Community service will be a graduation requirement. Also, educational opportunities are available for all citizens from preschool to adults. The school year won't be restricted to 180 days of 5–1/2 hours each, because flexible schedules and teacher contracts will permit year-round learning, he said. "Teachers in ideal schools are managers of the learning environment," Lepley said. "The teacher has been given the tools to be able to diagnose learning needs and to prescribe appropriate activities." Schools themselves will change too, Lepley noted. The ideal school houses social agencies such as health, job, and human service agencies, child care and serves as the community's senior citizen volunteer center, he said. And adults come to ideal schools—open round the clock—for educational opportunities ranging from childbirth and parenting classes to pre-retirement planning, he added. In the ideal community, Lepley said, the superintendent coordinates children and family services, in addition to education.

[Ed. Note: Lepley used the term "hub" in this article and in a pamphlet distributed widely across Iowa to describe the school of the future which will encompass numerous social service agencies, health care, job training, child care, etc. This concept mirrored the Community Education plans promoted by the Mott Foundation of Michigan and incorporated into federal grantmaking under the *Elementary and Secondary Education Act of 1965*.

A multitude of state reform plans in the early 1990s include diagrams of this same plan, exhibiting the school as the center (or "hub") of the community; significantly, some diagrams show churches, recreation and other private aspects of life encompassed within the "hub" concept. With the advent of school-to-work programs, the concept has been expanded to include "one-stop training centers" for workforce development and placement. Children who don't pass the proficiency assessments will be sent through these "centers" for services and remediation which will rely on operant conditioning methods to ensure "success".

Substitute "government" for schools like this "hub" plan and what political/economic system do we have? Who exactly asked for—voted for?—this alien "education" system which places our citizens and communities under the control of the unelected school superintendent?]

BARRY BEAR, A MILDLY RETARDED 11-YEAR-OLD INDIAN BOY LIVING ON A RESERVATION AND being taught at home by his mother, was declared a "child in need of assistance" (CINA) by a landmark Iowa Supreme Court decision on May 17, 1989. Barry Bear was removed from his home when the court cited "his parents' failure to exercise a reasonable degree of care in supervising him" because he was not in school. His parents had been previously jailed for violating the state's compulsory attendance (truancy) law. This precipitated the filing of a

CINA petition, leading ultimately to the legal challenge which resulted in the Iowa Supreme Court decision. According to "The Tama Story: Educational Tyranny in Iowa," an article by Samuel Blumenfeld,[23] the following occurred:

> [The State of Iowa] wanted to establish a legal precedent whereby home-schooled children could be removed from parents found guilty of violating the compulsory attendance law.
>
> The juvenile law states that a child in need of assistance is a child (1) whose parents physically abused or neglected the child, (2) a child who "has suffered or is imminently likely to suffer harmful effects as a result of the failure of the parent... to exercise a reasonable degree of care in supervising the child," or (3) a child who is in need of treatment for serious mental illness or disorder.
>
> Definition two is the one the State decided could be effectively used to prosecute Barry Bear's parents. It is also vague enough, wide enough to include fundamentalist Christian home schoolers. After all, the State can always get humanistic psychiatrists, psychologists, guidance counselors, and other "experts" to testify that keeping a child out of public school can cause "harmful effects" by depriving the child of needed socialization....
>
> ...Barry was taken from his family and placed in foster care.

[Ed. Note: This ominous decision was supposed to have created court case precedent in Iowa and around the country. A handful of heroic homeschoolers stopped these efforts; at the same time foiling a truancy bill in the Iowa legislature that would have allowed—even mandated— a homeschooled child to be removed from his parents and placed into foster care. The Barry Bear case provides a snapshot of the future, of the "penalties" that will be imposed on parents who fail to comply with various aspects of compulsory attendance and testing laws. The full weight of this "hammer" will be felt when school-to-work certification requirements and newly proposed "performance-based" national standards and assessments for "accountability" and "quality" are imposed on *all* children, including the homeschooled. It should be noted that no national organization assisted in the grassroots homeschoolers' resistance, on behalf of the Bear family, to these aggressive state actions.]

THE NATIONAL GOVERNORS' ASSOCIATION (NGA) EDUCATION SUMMIT WAS CONVENED IN 1989 by President George Bush at the University of Virginia in Charlottesville, Virginia. The NGA unveiled *America 2000*—now known as *Goals 2000*—and its six national education goals (which have now been increased to eight). These goals have served to carve into stone controversial "education" practices thoroughly exposed in this book, and to lay the foundation for activating school-to-work initiatives. The goals are as follows:

> GOAL 1. By the year 2000, all children will start school ready to learn.
> GOAL 2. By the year 2000, the high school graduation rate will increase to at least 90 percent.
> GOAL 3. By the year 2000, all students will leave grades 4, 8, and 12 having demonstrated competency over challenging subject matter including English, mathematics, science, foreign languages, civics and government, economics, arts, history, and geography, and every school in America will ensure that all students learn to use their minds well, so they may be prepared for responsible citizenship, further learning, and productive employment in our Nation's modern economy.
> GOAL 4. By the year 2000, the Nation's teaching force will have access to programs for

the continued improvement of their professional skills and the opportunity to acquire the knowledge and skills needed to instruct and prepare all American students for the next century.

GOAL 5. By the year 2000, United States students will be first in the world in mathematics and science achievement.

GOAL 6. By the year 2000, every adult American will be literate and will possess the knowledge and skills necessary to compete in a global economy and exercise the rights and responsibilities of citizenship.

—Later Additions—

GOAL 7. By the year 2000, every school in the United States will be free of drugs, violence and the unauthorized presence of firearms and alcohol and will offer a disciplined environment conducive to learning.

GOAL 8. By the year 2000, every school will promote partnerships that will increase parental involvement and participation in promoting the social, emotional, and academic growth of children.

[Ed. Note: In 1999, ten years later, the National Education Goals Panel recommended changing the name *Goals 2000* to *America's Goals* since the goals would not be reached by the year 2000—thanks to intense opposition to *Goals 2000* from teachers and parents, who considered it a corporate/federal takeover of the nation's schools.]

THE JULY 5, 1989 ISSUE OF *THE NEW YORK TIMES* CARRIED AN ARTICLE BY EDWARD B. Fiske entitled "Lessons—in the quiet world of schools, a time bomb is set for 1993 on certifying teachers." An excerpt follows:

> The new national system will not replace those now in use. Rather, it will offer a new voluntary credential to experienced teachers willing to undergo classroom observations and a battery of sophisticated new tests of their pedagogical expertise. The system is modeled on professional specialty boards in, say, medicine, through which doctors who are already licensed to practice obtain an additional prestigious credential.... For each of these credentials the task is to figure out "what teachers should know and be able to do." Then designers must devise ways of measuring teachers using new techniques like video simulations of classroom situations. All in all, it's a five-year, $50 million project for which the National Board [National/Carnegie Board for Professional Teaching Standards] is seeking Federal, corporation and foundation support.... The National Board has thus signaled that four years from now it intends to start issuing credentials based on the image of a teacher who would have a hard time functioning in most public schools today. The choice would seem to be either to back away from this image or put pressure on schools to change.... David Kearns, Chairman of the Xerox Corporation and a member of the board, believes schools should change. "Schools must find ways of driving decision-making down to the people who actually do the teaching," he said.

THE *BANGOR* [MAINE] *DAILY NEWS* OF JULY 18, 1989 CARRIED AN ASSOCIATED PRESS ITEM entitled "Long-Awaited National Teaching Certificate Detailed" which described in a nutshell the so-called "voluntary" national teacher certification system first called for in 1986 by the Carnegie Forum on Education and Economy report, *A Nation Prepared: Teachers for the 21st Century.* Excerpts from the article follow:

> Teachers will be rigorously tested on their specialty, teaching techniques and knowledge of child development under a voluntary national certification system outlined Monday by an independent panel.
>
> With its new national credential, to be offered in 29 fields starting in 1993, the National Board for Professional Teaching Standards says it hopes to dispel the myth that "any modestly educated person with some instinct for nurturing has the requisite qualifications to teach."
>
> The private group said it hopes that the system will also lead to improved teacher training and, ultimately, to better-educated children.
>
> "The process will push the renewal of American education a big step closer to reality," former North Carolina Governor James Hunt, chairman of the 63-member board, said Monday in releasing the guidelines.
>
> The nation's 2.3 million teachers will need a bachelor of arts degree and at least three years of experience to apply for certification, according to the blueprint.
>
> Board president, James A. Kelly, said professions such as medicine and law took decades to set standards for practitioners. He said the teacher standards board, formed in 1987, will compress the process into five years "because we want to influence the quality of the enormous influx of new teachers needed during the 1990s.... The new credential is expected to help draw more and better people into teaching and help teachers move into new roles as mentors, curriculum specialists and other positions requiring expertise or extra responsibility."
>
> The national board was proposed three years ago. Many were skeptical that its mix of teachers, government officials, business leaders and higher education representatives could succeed at what they said was a highly controversial task with uncertain potential to improve education.
>
> Albert Shanker, president of the American Federation of Teachers and a longtime backer of national teacher certification, said the criteria laid out Monday prove the skeptics wrong. "They said it couldn't be done, but we did it," Shanker said. "We can be proud that we have come so far."

[Ed. Note: If the statement "the National Board for Professional Teaching Standards (NBPTS) says it hopes to dispel the myth that 'any modestly educated person with some instinct for nurturing has the requisite qualifications to teach'" is true, then a high percentage of very successful homeschooling mothers will be expected to close shop—even though their children are outperforming public education students, receiving scholarships, and being accepted in the nation's top universities and colleges! As for the NBPTS wanting to "influence the quality of the enormous influx of new teachers needed during the 1990s" the reader should refer to the 1993 entry which provides the U.S. Department of Education's new definition of "quality."]

AN ARTICLE ENTITLED "THE DECADE OF THE NINETIES" BY DONALD THOMAS, EXECUTIVE director, Network for Effective Schools, was published in *The Effective School Report* for August 1989. Under the subtitle "Educational Implications" Thomas says:

Operate schools on a year-round basis; train citizens and students in skills and processes of effective participation in government; develop public policy toward private education....

Desirable future conditions: The economy will be more of an equilibrium economy with less dependence upon money, and more dependence upon the production and exchange of goods and services. There will be an increased movement toward cooperation and responsibility for the well-being of others. The civil rights of all individuals will be respected and taught in homes and schools; a value system will emerge that will give basic human values—i.e., liberal arts, caring for others, etc.—their proper place. There will be fewer single family dwellings. Industry will take more responsibility for education, particularly for job training....

...[D]evelop curricula to involve students in anticipating and planning how to welcome newcomers; use community education to help citizens anticipate and prepare for newcomers; design and implement statewide parent education and education for responsible parenthood; institute widespread, effective public education programs on family life; ensure that human caring will become the focus of curriculum at all levels; develop courses in futuring with future centers in high schools; involve schools with water commissions, air quality commissions, city councils, county commissions, legislatures and governmental agencies, focusing on economics, ecology, environment and culture as an integral part of the learning; teach and practice a win-win philosophy in schools [Deming's TQM] in the place of the present win-lose philosophy....

CITIZENSHIP
Necessary Quality: Protecting each other from distractive forces.... These are qualities that can best be learned through practice and experience. Our schools must, therefore, give young people the opportunities for service to others, practice in public service, and adherence to personal responsibilities. The basic values of a good and free nation can be learned by young people when appropriate conditions exist as schools form partnerships with community agencies for public service projects to be a part of schooling; rewards are provided for encouraging young people to perform community service; community service is recognized as a necessary learning option....

The year 2000 is very near. The sooner we begin the task of improving student achievement and citizenship, the sooner we will achieve the national objective for adequately preparing our young people to live in the 21st century; to be broadly literate in a world community; to be highly skilled in an ever-changing work environment; to be human in a society of individuals striving for personal satisfaction and security. To achieve this goal we will need to think differently about schools, about children and about education. We, as a nation, must see education as a lifelong process, as occurring in the total community, and as being the responsibility of everyone.... Our national survival depends on it; the world expects it, and the children of the world require it.

[Ed. Note: Leaving aside the focus on political correctness, one should be concerned over the total lack of emphasis on—or even mention of—academics. It would be a grave mistake to dismiss this article as the totalitarian ravings of a lesser-known change agent spoken to his closest change-agent associates. Dr. Thomas, a close friend of the late former Secretary of Education T.H. Bell and present Secretary Richard Riley, is one of the most important change agents in the world. He has been responsible for controversial restructuring in several states and has been involved in exchanges with the former Soviet Union and Eastern European nations which are implementing Effective School Research. Again, it was he who recommended a $50.00 fine for parents who refused to volunteer in schools—both in South Carolina and in Utah.]

"APPROPRIATE EDUCATION IN THE PRIMARY GRADES: A POSITION STATEMENT OF THE NA-tional Association for the Education of Young Children" (NAEYC) was published and distrib-uted in 1989.[24] Excerpts follow:

INTEGRATED COMPONENTS OF APPROPRIATE AND INAPPROPRIATE PRACTICE IN
THE PRIMARY GRADES

Appropriate Practice. The curriculum is integrated so that children's learning in all tradi-tional subject areas occurs primarily through projects and learning centers that teachers plan and that reflect children's interests and suggestions. Teachers guide children's involvement in projects and enrich the learning experience by extending children's ideas, responding to their questions, engaging them in conversation and challenging their thinking.
Inappropriate Practice. Curriculum is divided into separate subjects and time is carefully allotted for each with primary emphasis given each day to reading and secondarily to math. Other subjects such as social studies, science, and health are covered if time permits. Art, music, and physical education are taught only once a week and only by teachers who are specialists in those areas.

Appropriate Practice. The goal of the math program is to enable chidren to use math through exploration, discovery, and solving meaningful problems. Math activities are integrated with other relevant projects, such as science and social studies....
Inappropriate Practice. Math is taught as a separate subject at a scheduled time each day. A math textbook with accompanying workbooks, practice sheets, and board work is the focus of the math program. Teachers move sequentially through lessons as outlined in the teacher's edition of the text.... Timed tests on number facts are given and graded daily. Competition between children or groups of children.... is used to motivate children to learn math facts.

RENEWAL OF U. S.-SOVIET EDUCATION/CULTURAL AGREEMENTS IN 1989 CALLED FOR PLAC-ing statues of Soviet cultural figures on United States territory.

IN 1989 THE ASSOCIATION FOR SUPERVISION AND CURRICULUM DEVELOPMENT'S (ASCD) Elementary Global Education Framework entitled "Elementary Education for the 21st Cen-tury: A Planning Framework Based on Outcomes" announced on its title page the following:

The realities of the globally interconnected and culturally diverse world of the 21st century require an education for all students that will enable them to see themselves as—

HUMAN BEINGS
whose home is
PLANET EARTH
who are citizens of a
MULTICULTURAL DEMOCRATIC SOCIETY
in an increasingly
INTERCONNECTED WORLD
and who
LEARN, CARE, THINK, CHOOSE, and ACT

to celebrate life on this Planet
and
to meet the global challenges confronting Humankind

Key global challenges at the outset of the 21st century are in the areas of improving and maintaining the quality of the ENVIRONMENT, improving and maintaining HEALTH AND WELL-BEING, assuring HUMAN RIGHTS, and reducing VIOLENCE AND CONFLICT.

This ASCD framework was used by the Eugene, Oregon School District 4J as a guide for development of their Education 2000 Elementary Integrated Curriculum K–5.[25] Excerpts from the "Guide" to be used by teachers involved in curriculum implementation follow:

District 4J Mission

Investing in Students
Creating the Future
Eugene's Elementary Program's Mission
To Instill in Each child

- a sense of self worth
- a respect for the earth and all peoples
- and a commitment to the pursuit of life-long learning....

One of the five priorities established in the District's future planning report in 1988–1989 addressed the need to design an appropriate education for an information age.... Some of the skills and knowledge that students will need to acquire include:
1. managing information and learning to learn (i.e., problem solving, critical thinking, applying knowledge, making decisions and judgments);
2. understanding and participating in the arts;
3. interpersonal and intrapersonal skills;
4. global perspectives; and
5. using appropriate technology....
After careful consideration of the educational needs of students preparing for the 21st century, the writing committee defined its task as developing a more conceptual-based curriculum with essential skills at its core. A conceptual-based curriculum is structured around broad-based themes that allow for the integration of skills and subject matter rather than emphasizing disjointed, small, unrelated chunks of information.

Curriculum Strands
How is the content of the curriculum organized?
In place of the eight traditional disciplines around which the former curriculum was organized, the Education 2000 Curriculum is organized around three curriculum strands.... 1) The Human Family, 2) Our Planetary Home and Its Place in the Universe, and 3) Understanding and Fulfillment of the Individual.

Core Skills
What skills are included in the curriculum? Core essential skills include physical, social, and thinking skills incorporating language arts and mathematics.

Major Themes and Concepts
What major themes and concepts are included? The Education 2000 Curriculum includes six major themes: Communities, Change, Power, Interactions, Form and Systems.

Characteristics of the Curriculum
What are some of the characteristics of the new curriculum? First, it expands the traditional understanding of "basic skills" to include dimensions of thinking as well as language arts, mathematics, physical and social skill development.

It shifts what is required from many individual bits of content to major themes and related concepts.... With the former curriculum, elementary students were expected to master 2,175 separate bits of information that included skills, concepts and content organized within eight discrete disciplines. The new K–5 Education 2000 Curriculum requires mastery of only six major themes, 60 concepts and 132 core skills organized within three curriculum strands. This revision greatly reduces the fragmented nature of the former curriculum and significantly decreases the number of specific requirements to approximately one-tenth of the original number.

[Ed. Note: ASCD's involvement in this local school district's curriculum was a logical follow up to its involvement from the beginning in Robert Muller's *World Core Curriculum*, upon which District 4J's curriculum was based. According to an article entitled "Educator Proposes a Global Core Curriculum" by Susan Hooper which appeared in the November 27, 1985 issue of *Education Week*, Gordon Cawelti, executive director of ASCD, in an address to educators from twelve Western nations and Japan, urged them to press for the development of a world core curriculum based on knowledge that will ensure "peaceful and cooperative existence among the human species on this planet." *Education Week* explained, "Cawelti's world core curriculum would be based on... proposals put forth by Robert Muller, Assistant Secretary General of the United Nations, in his recent book *New Genesis: Shaping a Global Spirituality*."

Of additional significance is the fact that Willard Daggett's International Center for Leadership in Education discussed the Eugene District 4J in an article entitled "Cyber High School" in its March 1998 issue of *Model Schools News*. Regarding the Center's selection of Cyber High School, Eugene 4J School District, Eugene, Oregon as one of its model schools, the article states:

For the first time in human history, teacher, learner, and learning material do not have to be in the same place at the same time. This concept has the potential of revolutionizing education, considering the fact that where students live has always been the single greatest factor influencing the quality of their education, albeit one often overlooked. The truth of the matter is that what street they lived on, what town they lived in, what state and country determined what classes they could take, the quality of teachers they could expect, and who their classmates would be. But all that is about to change.... Courses offered also include several inventive multidisciplinary subjects such as "Baseball: Its Impact on American Society and World History through Film," not to mention the fact that all of the courses offer a global classroom and a multi-cultural perspective.]

THE AUTUMN 1989 ISSUE OF *THE 2020 NEWSLETTER* PUBLISHED BY IMTEC, A NORWEGIAN education association,[26] revealed the fact that as they push forward with their own International Learning Cooperative, Europeans were embracing the American *Tactics for Thinking* program developed by the U.S. Department of Education's MidContinent Regional Laboratory (McREL). Of interest is the fact that Shirley McCune (referenced several times in this book) was senior director of McREL at the time the activities described in *The 2020 Newsletter* were taking place. This newsletter illustrated clearly the extent of internationalization of not only curriculum, but instruction, assessment and administration. IMTEC reported:

> The IMTEC training program for school-based development consultants is going on at present in two countries: Germany... the Netherlands. We are also planning a renewed program in Norway. We are also in the planning stage of this program in the U.K.

A section of IMTEC's newsletter entitled "Cooperation with McREL" made the following statements:

> The Second "School-Year 2020" International Conference held in Colorado, October 1988, was a joint undertaking by McREL (the MidContinent Regional Educational Laboratory) and IMTEC....
>
> Our cooperation with McREL will continue. A Development Group represented by people from McREL and IMTEC is presently working on new programs building on McREL's Achieving Excellence Program (A+) and IMTEC's IDP, the Institutional Development Program....
>
> McREL's A+ is a site- or school-based management system. It organizes and uses research-based knowledge to increase educational efficiency, effectiveness and excellence.... The A+ management system also provides unique assessment tools for maintaining progress and redirecting energy. Pilot programs of A+ will take place in the Netherlands, in the UK, and most likely Norway during 1989/90....
>
> THINKING SKILLS
> IMTEC is presently developing a new "Thinking skills" program, building upon development work in several countries. Central to our interest has been the "Tactics" program developed by McREL.

[Ed. Note: The above relates to Effective School Research, OBE, ML, PPBS, etc.; what is being sold to Americans as "local control" or "localism" is in fact "global." In addition, the "Tactics" program is the same *Tactics for Thinking* discussed in the 1988 "Jeannie's Group" entry in this book.]

SOVIETS IN THE CLASSROOM: AMERICA'S LATEST EDUCATION FAD WRITTEN BY THIS WRITER in 1989 (published four years after the fact by America's Future, Inc.), details the U.S.-Soviet and Carnegie-Soviet education agreements. (For full text of this pamphlet, see Appendix XXIII.) Two excerpts dealing with the specific agreements follow:

> The agreements call for "Cooperation in the field of science and technology and additional agreements in other specific fields, including the humanities and social sciences; the facilitation of the exchange by appropriate organizations of educational and teaching materials, including textbooks, syllabi and curricula, materials on methodology, samples of teaching instruments and audiovisual aids... exchange of primary and secondary school textbooks and other teaching materials... the conducting of joint studies on textbooks between appropriate organizations in the United States and the Ministry of Education of the U.S.S.R."...

2. The Carnegie Corporation's exchange agreement with the Soviet Academy of Sciences has resulted in "joint research on the application of computers in early elementary education, focusing especially on the teaching of higher level skills and complex subjects to younger children." ("Higher level skills" is often a euphemism for "critical thinking skills.") Carnegie's 1988 one-year $250,000 grant is funding implementation of this program, coordinated on the American side by Michael Cole, director of the Laboratory of Comparative Human Cognition at the University of California, San Diego.

AN ARTICLE IN THE SEPTEMBER 9, 1989 ISSUE OF *THE WASHINGTON TIMES* ENTITLED "CHINA Says Educators Sowed Seeds of Unrest" placed blame on teachers for the student democracy protests which resulted in the Tiananmen Square massacre. Excerpts follow:

BEIJING (AGENCE FRANCE-PRESSE)—In a front-page editorial, the intellectual *Guangming Daily* said teachers had used their classrooms to spread "bourgeois liberalization," the standard code word for undesirable Western influences....

..."We must clearly understand that the teaching rostrum is provided by the people and the Communist Party and that it is sacred," the newspaper said. "The people's teachers have the right to spread Marxist theory, communist morality and knowledge of the Four Modernizations," it added. "Teachers have no right to spread bourgeois liberal tendencies."

Yesterday's editorial came as efforts by the authorities to put fresh emphasis on political education have been moving into high gear and just days before the 40th anniversary of Communist China on October 1.

On Tuesday, 40 teachers at Beijing University, which had been a hotbed of student unrest, were forced to take up shovels and clear scrub from a campus playing field as part of the push for political re-education through manual labor....

...The premier also defended a new government plan to send graduating students to farms and factories for a year, saying it was meant to "improve feelings toward laboring people."

"We hold that young students should, first of all, work in 'grassroots' units to obtain practical experience," Mr. Li said.

Many students have privately said they dread and scorn the scheme.

ON SEPTEMBER 10, 1989 *THE WASHINGTON POST* RAN AN ARTICLE ENTITLED "CHINA Orders Manual Labor for Students: Beijing Moves Again to Control Citizenry" which mirrored and elaborated on the above-excerpted article of September 9. The *Post* reported:

The mandatory labor requirement is the latest in a series of measures taken by the government to punish, restrict and reeducate Chinese students, particularly those in the capital, since the democracy movement was crushed by the army in early June.

...The newly announced measure is reminiscent of the approach taken by the Chinese government in the 1950s, when students worked for several hours a week either in factories or in workshops established on school premises.... In another development, students at two leading Beijing universities this week revealed that students will be required to take a test of their political reliability before being allowed to formally enroll.

KENTUCKY SUPREME COURT RULED IN *ROSE V. COUNCIL FOR BETTER EDUCATION, INC.* IN 1989. The importance of the ruling in this case cannot be over emphasized since it called for a redistribution of wealth (equalization) plan for Kentucky. The same plan was recommended by David Hornbeck for all the states in November of 1987. It was not long before Hornbeck and his fellow change agents, including Luvern Cunningham of Ohio State University and "site-based management/lessen elected school board influence" reputation, descended on Daniel Boone's country. The following excerpt detailing the Kentucky story was taken from *A Citizen's Handbook: The Kentucky Education Reform Act—Historical Background, Provisions, Time Line, Questions and Answers, Court Cases, Overview* (Kentucky Legislative Research Commission: Frankfort, Kentucky, September 1996):

> This decision applies to the entire sweep of the system—all its parts and parcels. This decision applies to all the statutes creating, implementing and financing the system and to all regulations, etc., pertaining thereto. This decision covers the creation of local school districts, school boards, and the Kentucky Department of Education to the Foundation Program and Power Equalization Program. It covers school construction and maintenance, teacher certification—the whole gamut of the common school system in Kentucky.... Since we have, by this decision, declared the system of common schools in Kentucky to be unconstitutional, Section 183 places an absolute duty on the General Assembly to re-create, re-establish a new system of common schools in the Commonwealth. —*Rose* at 215, 216.

IN 1989 SHIRLEY McCUNE, SENIOR DIRECTOR OF THE U.S. DEPARTMENT OF EDUCATION-funded MidContinent Regional Educational Laboratory (McREL), told the teachers in South Kitsap, Washington: "The school of the future must be far different than that of today to meet the changing needs of society." The following excerpts are taken from an article entitled "Schools of the Future" which was published in the *Bremerton* [Washington] *Sun* on October 14th:

> When you walk in the building, there's a row of offices. In one are drug counselors. One is for social security. Another, family and child psychologists. Yet another has a doctor and nurse who do well-child exams.
>
> In the cafeteria, senior citizens mingle with students having lunch. Oldsters and youngsters are sometimes paired for school projects, like oral history.
>
> There's a child-care center, and tied into it are classes for teenagers where they learn the importance of child-nurturing skills.
>
> In the gym, homemakers are taking exercise classes. After work, more men and women will show up for their fitness workout.
>
> These are "community learning centers, not just schools." "Schools are no longer in the schooling business" but rather in "human resource development," she said.
>
> Dr. McCune was in South Kitsap to talk about something everyone's hearing a lot about these days—"restructuring" schools. Her speech kicked off a full day of teacher training. Across the state, most teachers were taking part in local or state-sponsored training.
>
> In South Kitsap, workshop choices reflected the wave of the future Dr. McCune described. They dealt with topics such as celebrating differences in learning styles, using whole language approach, using cooperative learning, and integrating technology with curriculum.

Endnotes:

1 *Practitioner's Implementation Handbook* [series]: *The Outcome-Based Curriculum, Second Ed.*, by Charlotte Danielson (Outcomes Associates: Princeton, NJ, 1992).

2 See Appendix XXVI entitled "Shamanistic Rituals in Effective Schools" by Brian Rowan who says, among other eye-opening comments, "Thus, any experienced shaman can find 'effective' schools."

3 *Models of Instructional Organization: A Casebook of Mastery Learning and Outcome-Based Education*, Robert Burns, Ed. (Far West Regional Laboratory for Educational Research and Development: San Francisco, April 1987).

4 *Human Intelligence International Newsletter* mailing address is: P.O. Box 1163, Birmingham, MI 48012.

5 The Mott Foundation was one of the early initiators and heavy financial supporters of un-American community education and the unelected advisory council concept. Mott still retains its role as leader of this movement, which is now international and borrows much of its organizational structure from communist China.

6 At the time he wrote the article, Glines was assistant to the director of the Office of Instructional Support and Bilingual Education of the State of California Department of Education, Sacramento, California. This article was adapted with permission from an article published in *The California Journal on Teacher Education* (Spring, 1980).

7 Copies of the February issue of the *Innisbrook Papers* can be ordered from: Corporate Relations Department, Northern Telecom Limited, 33 City Centre Drive, Mississauga, Ontario L5A2A2.

8 The reader should not dismiss this last comment by Oettinger as a flippant remark. For more information on "the new flowering of oral communication" read *ComSpeak 2050, How Talking Computers Will Recreate an Oral Culture by Mid-21st Century* by William Crossman, 404–524–7438, e-mail: WillCross@aol.com

9 Information taken from Charlotte T. Iserbyt's *Back to Basics Reform Or... OBE Skinnerian International Curriculum* (Charlotte Thomson Iserbyt: Bath, Maine, 1985).

10 Center for Educational Research and Innovation: Rue Andre-Pascal, 75775, Paris, France.

11 K.M. Heaton's article can be obtained by writing: Hart Publications, 1507 Lincoln Street, Bellingham, WA 98226.

12 Private collection of the writer.

13 *Brainwashing* (Capp Clark Publishing Co., Ltd.: Toronto, 1971) and *Brainwashing in Red China: The Men Who Defied It* (Vanguard Press, Inc.: New York, NY, 1973).

14 Private collection of the writer.

15 For more information on this project, write: Mastery in Learning Project, National Education Association, 1201 16th Street, NW, Washington, DC 20036.

16 Roberto Assagioli, *Psychosynthesis: A Manual of Principles and Techniques* (Viking Press: New York, 1965).

17 Like Paolo Friere, Kevin Ryan of Boston University was invited by and received a contract from the newly-established Portuguese government, after its communist revolution in 1974, to train teachers so that Portugal could meet the European Community admission requirements. Professor Ryan is prominent in the character and moral education movement in the U.S. in the 1990s.

18 For more information on the Rotterdam meetings and/or the International Congress for Effective Schools, write: A.A. Peters or Professor Dale Mann, or Professor Terry Astuto at Teachers College, Columbia University, New York, NY 10027, or call 212–678–3726.

19 For more information regarding the next few entries dealing with the *Tactics for Thinking* curriculum or for information on Higher Order Thinking Skills (HOTS), contact Jeannie Georges who gave testimony at The National Citizens Alliance press conference and who has written extensively on the subject. Her address is: Route 1, Box 215, Lynnville, Indiana 47619, tel. 812–922–3247.

20 Ibid.

21 Single copies of the report, *The Forgotten Half: Pathways to Success for America's Youth and Young Families*, may be obtained free from: William T. Grant Foundation Commission on Work, Family and Citizenship, 100 Connecticut Avenue, NW, Suite 301, Washington, DC 20036–5541.

22 This conference is another example of an activity associated with the U.S.-Soviet education agreements signed in 1985. This particular conference very likely took place as a consequence of the Carnegie Corporation's exchange agreement with the Soviet Academy of Sciences, resulting in "joint research on the application of computers in early elementary education, focusing especially on the teaching of higher level skills and complex subjects to younger children."

23 *The Blumenfeld Education Letter*, April 1990 (Vol. V., No. 4).

24 A copy of this NAEYC publication (#578) is available by sending $.50 to: NAEYC, 1509 16th St., NW, Washington, DC 20036, or by calling 202–232–8777.

25 Oregon School District 4J, 200 N. Monroe, Eugene, OR 97402. Margaret Nichols was superintendent of schools for District 4J.

26 IMTEC is located at: Dynekilgata 10, 0569, Oslo 5 Norway.

8

THE NOXIOUS NINETIES

Many quotes in this book point toward implementation of radical restructuring of the nation's schools in "The Noxious Nineties." The one entry this writer believes best illustrates this plan and how it would be implemented throughout the remainder of the 20th century and into the 21st century is taken from *Conclusions and Recommendations for the Social Studies* (Charles Scribner's Sons: N.Y., 1934). This study was funded to the tune of $340,000 by the Carnegie Corporation of New York, quite a sum of money in 1934 dollars! Professor Harold Laski, the philosopher of British socialism, said of this report: "At bottom, and stripped of its carefully neutral phrases, the Report is an educational program for a Socialist America." An important and revealing excerpt from *Conclusions and Recommendations* follows:

> The Commission was also driven to this broader conception of its task by the obvious fact that American civilization, in common with Western civilization, is passing through one of the great critical ages of history, is modifying its traditional faith in economic individualism [free enterprise], and is embarking upon vast experiments in social planning and control which call for large-scale cooperation on the part of the people.... (pp.1–2)
>   ...Cumulative evidence supports the conclusion that in the United States and in other countries the age of "laissez faire" in economy and government is closing and that a new age of collectivism is emerging. (p. 16)

That a "new age of collectivism" has emerged and is being implemented right now under our very noses in "The Noxious Nineties," with little or no outrage from the public or our elected officials, can only be attributed to the "deliberate dumbing down" of Americans, who haven't been taught the difference between free enterprise and planned economies (socialism); between "group thinking" and individual freedom and responsibility.

The late Norman Dodd in 1986 made an extremely pertinent and important observation regarding Americans' growing preference to "think and act collectively" and the resulting dangers. Mr. Dodd's comments were made upon his receipt of the National Citizens' Alliance Americanism Award presented by Senator Jesse Helms. This award recognized Dodd's courageous work as research director for the 1953 Congressional investigation of the tax-exempt foundations. In Dodd's words:

> What is happening I can best explain by describing to you where you would end up if you could sponsor a resumption of the inquiry into the effect of foundation-type organizations in this country. If that were to be done, you would come into possession of proof... exposing a fundamental truth which has never been put into words.
>
> I shall try to recite that truth to you and you can take it home and act on it as a premise. This truth is that whenever a people show by their actions that they prefer to think and act collectively, their dynasty becomes a reenactment of the story of the Fall, as told to us by God through Moses.... We are now in a position where we can see that it is that dynastic effect which you are experiencing today.
>
> We have a task and that task is to sponsor an inquiry which would pull out into the open the proofs which show that it is that dynasty that is being worked out by us as a people, unwittingly, in complete ignorance....
>
> I wish I could help you... think about that truth because it has never been put into circulation. It now deserves to be, and it is persons like yourselves [dear readers] who can contribute to the circulation of that particular finding which the foundations, in their zeal, have actually made understandable. They [the foundations] have made a mistake.... The mistake they have made is now represented by their determination to cooperate with the Soviet Union educationally.

1990

SECRETARY'S COMMISSION ON ACHIEVING NECESSARY SKILLS (SCANS—U.S. DEPARTMENT of Labor) was established in 1990 and concluded its work in May of 1992. SCANS was conceived by Roberts T. Jones, assistant secretary of the Employment and Training Administration (ETA), through his parentage of the seminal study *Workforce 2000*. He and then-Secretary of Labor Elizabeth Dole created the Commission and Arnold Packer served as executive director. SCANS was established by Secretary Dole to determine the skills that young people need to succeed in the world of work.[1] The Secretary's Commission on Achieving Necessary Skills published four reports "intended to define the know-how American students and workers need for workplace success... in communities across the United States." The reports are:

1. *Learning a Living: A Blueprint for High Performance*—"why change is needed"
2. *What Work Requires of Schools*—"defines the five competencies and three-part foundation that constitute the SCANS know-how"
3. *Skills and Tasks for Jobs*—"a tracing of the relationship between the SCANS competencies and skills and 50 common occupations"
4. *Teaching the SCANS Competencies*—"unites six articles that give education and training practitioners practical suggestions for applying SCANS in classroom and workplace"

Learning a Living: A Blueprint for High Performance, the first report from SCANS, asserts that "The Commission's fundamental purpose is to encourage a high performance economy characterized by high-skill, high-wage employment." The following controversial component of SCANS, which angered parents and ignited fires of protest across the nation, is found on page 65 of *Learning a Living*:

HYPOTHETICAL RESUMÉ

Jane Smith   Date of Report: 5/1/92
19 Main Street   Soc. Sec.: 599–46–1234
Anytown   Date of Birth: 3/7/73
Home Phone: 817–777–3333   Age; 19

SCANS Personal Qualities	Average Rating	No. of Ratings
Responsibility	Excellent	10
Self-Esteem	Excellent	10
Sociability	Excellent	8
Self-Management	Excellent	7
Integrity/Honesty	Good	6

Since when did the federal government assign itself the responsibility of grading citizens on "personal qualities"? Since our government began to consider citizens "human capital" or "resources"? Are citizens useful for anything besides potential workers? The above resumé also included the number of points Jane earned toward her "Certificate of Initial Mastery" as well as a record of volunteer and work experience. The bureaucrat at the U.S. Labor Department who wrote this part of the report explained:

> Because this information would be extremely useful to employers in making hiring decisions and to colleges in evaluating applications, students would have a strong motivation to learn the SCANS foundation skills and workplace competencies, and employers and colleges would have a strong incentive to require them.

Nine years later the hypothetical SCANS resumé would become reality as exemplified by Ohio's Career Passport which is a collection of student records that showcase past performance. The Passport includes a resumé, transcript, narrative identifying career goals and activities, as well as any diplomas, awards, certifications, licenses and community involvement.

The aforementioned information regarding this Career Passport is taken from a May 25, 1999 letter from the Akron Regional Development Board to area employers which states that Ohio's companies can sign on as employers who "ask for the Career Passport." This letter continues as follows:

> By joining the more than 3000 businesses nationally that are requesting records, you help drive home the message that accountability, initiative, and motivation are traits that companies seek in job candidates.
>
> The Akron Regional Development Board, and The Greater Cleveland Growth Association, Cleveland Tomorrow, the Ohio Department of Education Career Educators, and Regions

8 and 9 School-to-Work have teamed up with the National Aliance of Business (NAB) to encourage employers to use school records as part of their hiring process. The national campaign called "Making Academics Count," will help students, parents and educators become more aware of the importance of requisite workplace skills.

Help send the message to area students by completing the enclosed reply form and returning it via fax to 330–379–3164. We will count you as an organization that wants young people to realize the importance of education and work skills....

You can learn more about this initiative online at www.makeacademicscount.org or www.c-e-a.org/ohiocdm.htm. On behalf of the Akron Regional Development Board and employers across our region, we encourage you to promote higher achievement by endorsing the "*Ask for the Career Passport*" program.

At this point it is important to recall the fact that one of the members appointed to the SCANS which originated this type of career passport was Thomas Sticht, Ph.D., infamous for the following quote which parents should ponder, especially if they feel that techademics are the answer to their children's upward mobility. Sticht's statement paraphrased in the August 1, 1987 issue of *The Washington Post* bears repeating here:

Ending discrimination and changing values are probably more important than reading in moving low income families into the middle class.... What may be crucial [companies say] is the dependability of the labor force and how well it can be managed and trained—not its general education level, although a small cadre of highly educated, creative people is essential to innovation and growth.

IN 1990 ARKANSAS GOVERNOR WILLIAM JEFFERSON CLINTON PUSHED THROUGH A MAJOR statewide reform measure, *Act 236*, which was a forerunner of *Goals 2000*. According to *National Issues in Education: Goals 2000 and School-to-Work* by John F. Jennings, Ed.[2] (Phi Delta Kappan and The Institute for Educational Leadership: Washington, D.C., 1995):

In the National Governors' Association he championed comprehensive statewide reform and was a key leader in the effort to develop the National Education Goals. In announcing his platform to "put people first" he made education a central part of the presidential campaign.

THE *WASHINGTON POST* PUBLISHED "TYING PROFESSIONAL PAY TO PRODUCTIVITY" BY ELIZAbeth Spayd in its January 28, 1990 issue in which Ms. Spayd covered the use of behavior modification in the workplace in order to increase productivity. Some excerpts follow:

"One CEO I know says to employees, 'If you tell me I can't measure what you're doing, I'm not sure I need you here,'" recalls Michael Emig, a compensation consultant with Wyatt Co. in Washington. "The fact is, any work that people are paid to do can be measured. The trick is to go in with an open mind.".... To help ensure that productivity goals are met, the paychecks of top managers now reflect their ability to meet department goals, a compensation plan that eventually will spread throughout the hospital. According to Arthur Andersen & Co., which consulted Pekin Memorial on its plan, the keystone to implementing productivity bonuses is putting everything in measurable terms, considering such factors as accuracy, speed, cost, quality—even creativity.... Once the job has been quantified, the next step is to examine the processes by which work is done, dividing them into those that add value and those that don't. Those that don't should be eliminated.

Studies show white-collar workers on average spend 75 percent of their time doing non-value-added tasks, Skwarek said. But defining the waste and eliminating it are two different things. And for productivity to increase, proper employment of the compensation lever is critical.

A bank teller might be rewarded for the number of customers processed in a week, but penalized for every customer who complains about service. In jobs where it's difficult to measure the output of a *single worker* [emphasis in original], compensation might be linked to a group's ability to meet certain goals, an increasingly common approach.

Whatever the approach, Wyatt's Emig encourages companies to think big—meaning bonuses as high as 25 percent of salary.

"The basic idea is borrowed from B.F. Skinner, who taught us that behavior which is positively reinforced will be repeated," says Emig. "But it doesn't work if people don't consider the money worth striving for."

[Ed. Note: Is it politically incorrect to ask how the United States became the most productive nation in the world without using the above-outlined ridiculous Total Quality Management system based on Skinner's operant conditioning?]

THE NATIONAL CENTER ON EDUCATION AND THE ECONOMY (NCEE) ISSUED IN 1990 A PRO-posal to the New American Schools Development Corporation (NASDC) entitled "The National Alliance for Restructuring Education: Schools and Systems for the 21st Century." The report was stamped "CONFIDENTIAL." On the cover page NCEE's partners in this venture are listed as follows: States of Arkansas, Kentucky, New York, Vermont, and Washington; Cities of Pittsburgh, PA; Rochester, NY; San Diego, CA; and White Plains, NY; Apple Computer, Inc.; Center for the Study of Social Policy; Commission on the Skills of the American Workforce; Harvard Project on Effective Services; Learning Research and Development Center at the University of Pittsburgh; National Alliance of Business; National Board for Professional Teaching Standards; New Standards Project; Public Agenda Foundation; and Xerox Corporation.

[Ed. Note: In Appendix XII of this book NCEE's proposal is heavily excerpted. The last few pages of excerpted materials which relate to "staff development" could have been written by the late Madeline Hunter, master teacher trainer who has translated "theory into practice" in her "Instructional Theory Into Practice: ITIP."[3] These excerpted materials prove that NCEE's National Alliance for Restructuring Education, in conjunction with the University of Pittsburgh's Learning Research and Development Center and the National Board for Professional Teaching Standards, has selected "the method"—Skinnerian operant conditioning—to train teachers so that, as robots, they will all teach exactly the same way.]

WORLD CONFERENCE ON EDUCATION FOR ALL, SPONSORED BY THE WORLD BANK, UNITED Nations Educational, Scientific, and Cultural Organization (UNESCO), and others, was held March 5–9, 1990 in Jomtien, Thailand. "Outcomes" were approved at this conference, and the Education for All Forum Secretariat advertised the "World Declaration on Education for All" and "Framework for Action to Meet Basic Learning Needs" as the agenda for discussion at the

World Conference.[4] Important and significant institutional membership in the Education for All Coalition included: American Association of School Administrators (AASA); Association for Supervision and Curriculum Development; International Reading Association [which was the prime mover behind the dumb-down Whole Language reading instruction, ed.]; and the National Education Association.

Other statements on the conference promotional flyer included:

> The 1990 World Conference on Education for All represented an important milestone in education development. Convened by the executive heads of the United Nations Development Program (UNDP), the United Nations Children's Fund (UNICEF), the United Nations Educational, Scientific and Cultural Organization (UNESCO) and the World Bank, the conference called on all nations to take effective action to meet the basic learning needs of children, youth and adults in all countries of the world....
>
> The World Conference defined basic learning needs as the essential learning tools—such as literacy, oral expression, numeracy, and problem-solving—and basic learning content—required by all people to develop their full capacities, to live and work in dignity, to participate fully in development, to improve the quality of their lives, to make informed decisions, and to continue learning.

THE MARCH 28, 1990 ISSUE OF *EDUCATION WEEK* RE-PUBLISHED "A ROAD MAP FOR RE-structuring Schools," a one-page list of principles of restructuring and steps for policy makers to use. Developed by the Education Commission of the States (ECS) and the National Governors' Association (NGA) and signed by Jane Armstrong, director of policy studies for ECS, this "Road Map" was a result of two regional workshops to discuss strategies for redesigning state education systems to meet national performance goals. Excerpts follow:

> PRINCIPLES OF RESTRUCTURING... Restructuring requires risk-taking and experimentation in order to transform schools into dynamic, self-renewing organizations....
>
> STEPS FOR POLICY MAKERS TO TAKE... Develop a specific and demanding statement of what basic skills, thinking skills, knowledge, attitudes and behaviors you want all students to have when they complete school....

- Student outcomes should meet employability criteria suggested by business and industry.
- Build a coalition of business, community, education and political leaders... to bring external pressure on the education system for productive change.
- Sell the agenda to policy makers and the public.
- Identify and train spokespersons to advocate system restructuring.
- Get business and political leaders to carry the restructuring banner.
- Provide flexibility, encourage experimentation and decentralize decision making.
- Use incentives to encourage risk taking and experimentation.
- Decentralize authority by encouraging site-based management.
- Redesign teacher and administrator education.
- Redesign teacher education to model instruction for an active learning classroom.

- Develop programs that focus on content knowledge and new forms of pedagogy.
- Link schools with universities and other sources of information to help teachers expand their knowledge of teaching and learning.
- Strengthen the clinical experience by placing teacher candidates in schools that are restructuring.
- Provide time for teacher renewal, collaboration and the acquisition of new skills, understandings and attitudes.
- Provide incentives for teachers to receive national board certification.
- Develop multiple ways to measure progress to avoid "high stakes" testing and teaching to a single test.
- Develop "outcomes-based" accreditation procedures.
- Provide rewards for high-achieving schools and sanctions for low-achieving schools.
- Create programs that engage students in community service.
- Collaborate with other social service agencies to fully serve the needs of all children.
- Encourage parental involvement.
- Create public school choice plans.
- Provide incentives to reward accomplishments.
- Align and revise state policies to support restructuring.
- Develop business/education partnerships. Use technology to explore new ways to deliver instruction… not as an "add-on" to the traditional lecture, recite, test method of instruction.
- Be prepared to handle policy decisions on jurisdiction over distance learning; i.e., teacher certification, textbook and curriculum approval.

The ECS/NGA Restructuring Workshops were supported by grants from the American Express Foundation, ARCO Foundation, BellSouth Foundation, Carnegie Corporation of New York, Control Data Corporation and The John D. and Catherine T. MacArthur Foundation.

IN 1990 MARC TUCKER'S NATIONAL CENTER ON EDUCATION AND THE ECONOMY (NCEE) of Rochester, New York published *America's Choice: High Skills or Low Wages!* which asserted:

> Once youth centers are established, we propose that the child labor laws be amended to make the granting of work permits to young people up to age 18 contingent on either their possession of a certificate of initial mastery [CIM] or their enrollment in a program leading to the certificate. At first glance, this may seem draconian. But in the long run this requirement will benefit our youth and ultimately the nation.

[Ed. Note: The "Certificate of Initial Mastery" (CIM) is a device which is copyrighted to the private sector National Center on Education and the Economy to be used by the public schools.]

THE STATE OF MAINE TOOK A LEADERSHIP POSITION IN THE IMPLEMENTATION OF A SCHOOL-to-work system in 1990. The following excerpts from *The School to Work Revolution* by Lynn

Olson (Perseus Books: New York, 1997) relate to the first steps taken to implement this new corporate fascist system of governance. Olson recalled Maine's activity as follows:

> John Fitzsimmons, the President of the Maine Technical College System and former state labor commissioner in Maine during the 1980s, traveled to Germany and Denmark in the early 1990s, along with the then-Governor John R. McKernan, Jr. [husband of U.S. Senator from Maine Olympia Snowe], to get a first-hand view of European apprenticeships. The governor and Fitzsimmons were so impressed by what they saw that they plotted the outlines for a Maine initiative on paper napkins on the transatlantic flight home. In February 1993 the Maine Youth Apprenticeship Program—now called Maine Career Advantage—accepted its first 12 students. By 1996 the initiative had spread to 276 students, 108 high schools, and 197 businesses. An additional 850 students were involved in career-preparation activities such as job shadows, developing portfolios, and summer internships.
>
> "I really believe, in my state, the future lies in the quality of the skilled workforce," Fitzsimmons told me in 1994, a strong Rhode Island accent still lingering in his voice. "We will not compete with a North Carolina Research Triangle or with Massachusetts's Harvard and M.I.T. and their ability to be international research areas. We will be the producers of goods. And I take great pride in that because if we're able to produce high-quality products, it will mean high-wage jobs for our people."

POLYTECHNICAL EDUCATION: A STEP BY ROBERT H. BECK, UNIVERSITY OF MINNESOTA, was published in 1990. Beck was under contract to the National Center for Research in Vocational Education, University of California, Berkeley and was supported by the Office of Vocational and Adult Education through a U.S. Department of Education grant for $4 million [Carl D. *Perkins Vocational Education Act*, Grant #V051A80004–88A, September.[5]] Had this report not cost $4 million in taxpayers' money, one could dismiss it as just another effort by the federal government to keep its education researchers occupied. Why would the government spend such an enormous amount of money on a government project describing the Soviet polytech system unless the government was considering putting the same polytech system in place in the United States?

Recent workforce training legislation in Congress does indeed call for the implementation of the Soviet/German/Danish polytech system.

WILLIAM SPADY PRESENTED "ENSURING THE SUCCESS OF ALL STUDENTS TODAY FOR Tomorrow's Changing World" for the U.S. Department of Defense, Mediterranean Region in 1990. Excerpts follow:

> When addressing the issue of Exit Outcome development in one of our Illinois high school districts during the Spring, I too was forced to take a look at the "realities" that seem to surround us and that have the potential for shaping the character of the future in which we and our children will live. At first blush, ten somewhat interrelated trends seemed clear to me, some of which parallel "Theobold's Eight Driving Forces," and some of which resemble trends identified by John Naisbitt and his *Future Trends* colleagues. Others are simply my own…. [D]espite the historical trend toward intellectual enlightenment and cultural pluralism, there has been a major rise in religious and political orthodoxy, intolerance, fundamentalism and conservatism with which young people will have to be prepared to deal.

DAVID W. HORNBECK, MEMBER OF THE BOARD OF TRUSTEES OF THE CARNEGIE CORPORA-
tion and a partner in the Washington, D.C. law firm of Hogan and Hartson, delivered a paper
entitled "Technology and Students at Risk of School Failure" at the Council of Chief State
School Officers' (CCSSO) 1990 Technology Conference in Minneapolis, Minnesota April 29–
May 2. The paper was commissioned by the CCSSO and was distributed by the federally
funded North Central Regional Educational Laboratory (NCREL) in Elmhurst, Illinois. Excerpts from this paper follow:

> In March, the Kentucky legislature enacted the most aggressive and far-reaching education
> legislation in memory. They identified six goals for their schools (President Bush's Six Ambi-
> tious Goals adopted by the Governors February 25). The goals include not only math, sci-
> ence, social studies and English but, more significantly, they emphasize such things as think-
> ing, problem solving, main ideas and integration of knowledge. Kentucky, however, went
> further. They are building a new set of assessment strategies that are performance based;
> they have adopted a system of rewards and sanctions that will impact on the schools' staffs
> in proportion to the schools' success in increasing the proportion of successful students in a
> school or the failure to do so. The President, the Governors and now a state legislature have
> made decisions that reflect the future.
>
> The fact is that corporate America is becoming increasingly involved in the policy and
> politics of elementary and secondary education. The Committee for Economic Development
> was the first major corporate player. They were joined by the National Alliance of Business.
> Most recently, The Business Roundtable, which is composed of the nation's 201 largest cor-
> porations, has recognized their vital interest in American public education. Each corporation
> has "adopted" a state where each corporation will concentrate strong effort. Moreover, they
> have declared that the effort will be of at least ten years' duration....
>
> ...There are numerous ways technology, and I initially refer to the computer, can as-
> sist.... The computer motivates. It is non-judgmental. It will inform a student of success or
> failure without saying by word or deed that the student is good or bad. The computer indi-
> vidualizes learning, permitting mastery at one's own pace.... The computer gives prompt
> feedback....
>
> Let's turn then to more specific contributions computers can make. First, it is clear that
> the basic skills of students can be enhanced. In a presentation to the U.S. Senate Committee
> on Labor and Human Resources in 1987, Robert Tagaart, relying on work done by himself,
> Gordon Berlin, and Andrew Green, identified ten elements that research prescribes to teach
> basic skills effectively. They include:
>
> * individualized, self-paced instruction
> * competency-based, open entry/open exit approaches
> * use of multiple media and methods, including computers
> * frequent feedback and positive reinforcement
> * accountability of teachers and learners
> * efficient management to maximize time on task
> * individual attention and one-on-one instruction
> * supportive services and learning environments
> * linkages to work, training, and other activities

[Ed. Note: Kentucky's experience with its new set of performance-based assessment strategies was a disaster. An article in the June 26, 1997 Louisville *Courier-Journal* datelined Frankfurt, Kentucky stated:

Nearly all elementary and middle schools in Kentucky received incorrectly low test scores last fall, and fixing the error will mean that teachers will get an estimated $2 million in additional reward money.... While the error by Advanced Systems in Measurement and Evaluation, Inc., amounts to a small change in the schools' actual scores—an average of about 1 point on a 140–point scale—there could be serious consequences for the state's test, which has already been at the center of controversy. Critics seized upon the mistake as evidence that significant changes are needed in the testing system created by Kentucky's 1990 school reform law.

The March/April, 1997 issue of *Kentucky Citizens Digest* carried an article entitled "Are Basic Skills a Casualty of KERA?—Are state tests causing teachers to underemphasize basic skills?" which revealed that:

If two recent reports are any indication, basic skills among students may very well be a casualty of education reform in Kentucky. A report from RAND, a prominent national research organization, found that tests now being used under KERA (called KIRIS tests) are causing public school teachers to de-emphasize basic skills instruction in Kentucky schools. "The subject areas for which the most teachers indicated a decrease since KIRIS began," said the report, "were art, social studies, science, and reading. Eighty-nine percent of the teachers indicated that these changes were due largely to KIRIS."]

LAMAR ALEXANDER, FORMER GOVERNOR OF TENNESSEE, SECRETARY OF EDUCATION IN PRESI-dent George Bush's administration, and Republican presidential candidate in 1999, was quoted in *Southern Living* (Vol. 25, No. 6, June 1990) in an interview when he was serving as president of the University of Tennessee as saying:

I suggest we create a brand-new American school, as different from today's schoolhouse as the telegraph was from The Pony Express. Such a school would probably start with babies and go through the eighth grade. It would be all year long. It would be open 6 a.m. to 6 p.m. Every child would have his or her own computer and workstation. Every child would have a team of teachers that would stay with that child until graduation....

We already spend more money than any country per pupil on education. I just don't think we spend it well.

THE *BLUMENFELD EDUCATION LETTER* FOR AUGUST 1990 INCLUDED IN ITS COLUMN "VITAL QUOTE"[6] the following quote from Professor George Reisman's *The Intellectual Activist*:

I believe that the decline in education is probably responsible for the widespread use of drugs. To live in the midst of a civilized society with a level of knowledge closer perhaps to that of primitive man than to what a civilized adult requires (which, regrettably, is the intellectual state of many of today's students and graduates) must be a terrifying experience, urgently calling for some kind of relief, and drugs may appear to many to be the solution.... This is no longer an educational system. Its character has been completely transformed and it now clearly reveals itself to be what for many decades it has been in the process of becoming: namely, an agency working for the barbarization of youth.

George Reisman, Prof. of Economics, Pepperdine University, *The Intellectual Activist*, p. 8.

[Ed. Note: The decline in education is not only probably responsible for the widespread use of drugs, it is also probably responsible for the increase in all sorts of irresponsible and immoral behavior among youth today, including violence and sexual promiscuity. Dr. Reisman's statement is particularly poignant in light of increased incidents of school violence in the late 1990s.]

DR. M. DONALD THOMAS, IN AN ARTICLE IN *THE EFFECTIVE SCHOOL REPORT*'S SEPTEMBER, 1990 issue entitled "Education 90: A Framework for the Future," said in part:

From Washington to modern times, literacy has meant the ability to read and write, the ability to understand numbers, and the capacity to appreciate factual material. The world, however, has changed dramatically in the last 30 years. The introduction of technology in information processing, the compression of the world into a single economic system, and the revolution in political organizations are influences never imagined to be possible in our lifetime.... Literacy, therefore, will be different in the year 2000. It will mean that students will need the following [the writer has selected some key requirements from a much longer list, ed.]:

- Appreciation of different cultures, differences in belief systems and differences in political structures.
- An understanding of communications and the ability of people to live in one world as one community of nations....
- In a compressed world with one economic system... it is especially important that all our people be more highly educated and that the differences between low and high socio-economic students be significantly narrowed....
- Education begins at birth and ends at death....
- Education is a responsibility to be assumed by the whole community....
- Learning how to learn is more important than memorizing facts....
- Schools form partnerships with community agencies for public service projects to be a part of schooling....
- Rewards are provided for encouraging young people to perform community service.

"WORLD CLASS SCHOOLS AND THE SOCIAL STUDIES" BY CORDELL SVENGALIS FROM *SOCIAL Studies Horizons* (Iowa Department of Education: Des Moines, Iowa, Vol. 3, No. 1, Fall 1990) was published. The following excerpts reveal a significant definition of "World Class education," one of the popular "buzz words" used to describe and promote education reform during the early 1990s:

As part of a nationwide trend, the Iowa Department of Education has become involved in the movement to develop a world-class educational system for the schools of our state....

Few would argue with the need to greatly improve the educational system we now have, and to help students acquire the skills they will need to become better integrated into the global community. We have not only become globally interdependent, we have come to recognize our global interconnectedness. Therefore, a World Class education program would have as one of its major objectives the development of skills and understandings grounded in an ethical/moral context. This ethical/moral context would be based on the idea of assuming a sense of responsibility toward our interrelated planetary future....

Perhaps the most compelling vision of our time is that of a *sustainable society* [emphasis in original]. Our global society, in terms of the environmental degradation, explosive population growth in the Third World, energy shortages, pollution, conflict, crime, drugs, poverty, and just sheer complexity, is not sustainable into the 21st century.... Students need to understand these things as part of their World Class education.

This particular issue of *Social Studies Horizons* also reported on the 1990 Chicago Conference on Holistic Education, which issued a document called "The Chicago Statement" calling for a radical change in education. An excerpt asserts that:

The time has come to transform education so as to address the human and environmental changes which confront us. We believe that education for this new era must be holistic. The holistic perspective is the recognition that all life on this planet is interconnected.... Holism emphasizes the challenge of creating a sustainable, just and peaceful society in harmony with the Earth and its life.

Dr. Svengalis of the Iowa Department of Education was involved in the production of a *Catalogue of Global Education Classroom Activities, Lesson Plans, and Resources*. The curriculum came under fire from the Iowa Farm Bureau because of its open advocacy of vegetarianism and environmentalism, according to the Iowa Farm Bureau's *Spokesman* (September 19, 1992) article entitled "State Role in Global Education Resource Guide under Review." Also included in the global education curriculum were themes of pacifism, population controls, international global government, and Gaia worship. Fourth and sixth graders could be assigned to "[t]alk about the ideas of a 'living' Earth using Lovelock's Gaia hypothesis." Dr. James Lovelock made the radical "scientific" proposal that the Earth was both an entity and a deity.

According to education reform researchers Marla Quenzer and Sarah Leslie, environmental "outcomes" were supplanting traditional academics. In an article published in the May 1993 issue of *Free World Research Report* entitled "The Myth of a Competitive World-Class Education," Quenzer and Leslie refuted the idea that "world-class" education is competitive and academically challenging. Under the new reforms they found an emphasis on cooperation and sustainability based upon extreme environmentalism and "a kind of 'New Age' soup of pantheism, Hinduism, Taoism and Buddhism." They cited an article entitled "Global Framework for Local Education" from *Holistic Education Review* (Spring 1991):

This author, Joel Beversluis, states "that educational objectives [should] transcend the accumulation of facts, the learning of skills, and even the preparation for work and life in the world as it is. Rather, at its best, education will assist, like a midwife, in the transformation of the mindsets—the consciousness—of students...." Beversluis asks, "Is it not time for the community of educators and educational publishers to recognize that the respectful study of diverse cosmologies, value systems, and religions has a legitimate and even necessary place in the curriculum?" He then proceeds to list these new "global" values....

Just what values are being talked about? This turns out to be the pivotal question. Beversluis spells it out for us. He lists as negative values: "individualism, nationalism, free enterprise, unlimited growth and progress, and competitive achievement." The values he lists as positive are "interdependence, diversity, cooperation, equilibrium, and limits." The values that he lists as negative are foundational to western civilization and are based upon a rich Judeo-Christian heritage. The values he lists as positive can be found in Iowa's proposal for "World-Class Education under 'Examples of Core Concepts'" and are an integral part of Iowa's Global Education goals. Not surprisingly, these same values crop up in all the new state "outcomes" lists as well.

[Ed. Note: For more information on the connection between extreme environmentalism, sustainability, and the deliberate dumbing down of America, see Appendix XXVII.]

THE 1990–91 (WINTER) ISSUE OF *OUTCOMES,* AN EDUCATIONAL JOURNAL DEVOTED TO DIS-cussion of Outcome-Based Education and the problems associated with its implementation (teachers', administrators' and community resistance) published a remarkable article entitled "Paradigm Change: More Magic than Logic" by John C. Hillary. The reader should remember that the manipulation of classroom teachers and administrators discussed in this article is standard operating procedure in most schools undergoing "restructuring." Excerpts from Hillary's article in *Outcomes* follow:

> The deeper changes that frustrate leaders and threaten followers are planned second-order changes.... These changes intentionally challenge widely shared assumptions, disintegrate the context of "organization" and, in general, reframe the social system. This, in turn, gener-ates widespread ambiguity, discontinuity, anxiety, frustration, confusion, paranoia, cynicism and anger as well as temporary dysfunction. Such trauma often builds to the point that leaders abandon their efforts.
>
> The most disruptive changes—second order changes—on the other hand, call into question the entire context of organization. Such multidimensional changes not only chal-lenge the content of each domain but also disrupt the alignment among them. Paradigm change is therefore not only traumatic in and of itself, but also challenges other attributes and disintegrates the relationship among all domains. The eventual outcome of such change is "transformed" or "renewed" organization.
>
> The new vision for schooling suggested by contemporary educators represents a sig-nificant "second order" challenge to school organization.
>
> The leader of planned second order change will be regarded as out of context by the organization. If he thinks and behaves in accord with a vision that requires second order changes, he has no choice but to violate or challenge the established culture, mission/pur-pose, and paradigm of the organization. From the existing frame of reference, such behavior will be seen as illogical. Powerful and pervasive psycho-social forces will bear down on the renegade in a relentless organizational effort to bring him back into alignment. Unless the leader succeeds in progressively bending the pervasive frame, persistence is increasingly risky.
>
> During second order change, the organization must face and hopefully pass through a period of widespread psychological ambiguity, social disconnectedness and general confu-sion.... The requisite disintegration of the existing culture, mission/purpose, and paradigm disrupts the organization's frame of reference. During this time, there is little or no clear and consistent context to guide the thinking and behavior of members. In social systems, this condition produces dysfunction, anxiety, frustration, disequilibrium, and systemic chaos.
>
> The instigator of second order change must consistently behave in ways that will not make sense when framed by the existing context. With time and leadership, the organization

environment must move from initially and naturally selecting against the innovation to selecting for the innovation. The extinction of the old way of doing business is the desired outcome. Hence and with time, the risk should gradually shift away from the innovator and toward those who persist in holding on to "the way it's always been."

[Ed. Note: The writer, over a fairly long period of years, has come to the conclusion that many of America's best administrators and teachers have been waging a "silent" war against the above change agent activities, and that had they not been so engaged, the public education system would have been destroyed long ago.]

1991

"AMERICA 2000 PLAN," WRITTEN IN 1991 AND DESIGNED TO IMPLEMENT THE CARNEGIE Corporation's restructuring agenda, was presented to the American people by President Bush's Secretary of Education Lamar Alexander. The plan proposed to radically restructure American society and was prepared by, amongst others, Chester Finn—former assistant secretary, Office of Educational Research and Improvement, and associated with Education Excellence Network (Hudson Institute). Secretary Alexander claimed, "The brand new American school would be year-round, open from 6 to 6, for children 3 months to 18 years." The slim booklet containing *America 2000: An Education Strategy (Rev.)—Making This Land All That It Should Be* was published by the U.S. Department of Education and portions of this publication follow:

Message from President George Bush
April 18, 1991

To those who want to see real improvement in American education, I say: There will be no renaissance without revolution.

We've made a good beginning by setting the nation's sights on six ambitious National Education Goals—and setting for our target the year 2000.... For today's students, we must make existing schools better and more accountable. For tomorrow's students, the next generation, we must create a New Generation of American Schools. For all of us, for the adults who think our school days are over, we've got to become a Nation of Students—recognize learning is a lifelong process. Finally, outside our schools we must cultivate communities where learning can happen....

EXECUTIVE SUMMARY
The strategy anticipates major change in our 110,000 public and private schools, change in every American community, change in every American home, change in our attitude about learning. The strategy will spur far-reaching changes in weary practices, outmoded assumptions and long-assumed constraints on education. It will require us to make some lifestyle changes, too....

America 2000 is a national strategy, not a federal program. It honors local control, relies on local initiative, affirms states and localities as the senior partners in paying for education, and recognizes the private sector as a vital partner, too.

The federal government's role in this strategy is limited—wisely—as its part in education always has been. But that role will be played vigorously. Washington can help by setting standards, highlighting examples, contributing some funds, providing flexibility in exchange for accountability and pushing and prodding—then pushing and prodding some more.

The *America 2000* strategy has four parts that will be pursued simultaneously. For tomorrow's students, we must invent new schools to meet the demands of a new century with a New Generation of American Schools, bringing at least 535 of them into existence by 1996 and thousands by decade's end....[19]

THE CHALLENGE: America's Skills and Knowledge Gap

Introduction:
As a nation, we now invest more in education than in defense. Nor is the rest of the world sitting idly by, waiting for America to catch up. Serious efforts at education improvement are under way by most of our international competition and trading partners.

While more than 4 million adults are taking basic education courses outside the schools, there is no systematic means of matching training to needs; no uniform standards measure the skills needed and the skills learned.

[Ed. Note: Carnegie's Marc Tucker took care of matching training to needs when his *Human Resources Development Plan for the United States*, developed by the National Center for Education and the Economy, was unveiled in 1992. (See Appendix XVIII.) As far as keeping track of the progress of our "international competition and trading partners" is concerned, the North American Free Trade Agreement (NAFTA), the General Agreements for Tariffs and Trade (GATT), and international co-ordination of ISO 9000 and 1400 through the United Nations will ensure that we maintain "computability."]

WHO WOULD EVER HAVE IMAGINED THAT THE EDUCATIONAL AND CULTURAL EXCHANGES signed between President Reagan and President Gorbachev, and those negotiated since 1985, would result in Russian "cops" from the recently disintegrated "Evil Empire" flying American police helicopters as described in the following article "Cop Swap: His Beat Is Leningrad but He's on Loan to LAPD—His Local Host Will Visit U.S.S.R." by Bob Pool, which appeared in the April 30, 1991 issue of *The Los Angeles Times*. Excerpts follow:

That wasn't Gorky Park that a burly Russian cop was swooping over Monday in a police helicopter. That was Griffith Park. Leningrad policeman Albert Vorontsov went airborne to get acquainted with Los Angeles and launch a first-ever swap of Soviet and local police officers that is aimed at spreading goodwill—and trading good ideas. Vorontsov will shadow Los Angeles Police Sergeant Greg Braun for two weeks. Then Braun will travel to the Soviet Union in June to work with Vorontsov.... "We may think we're on the cutting edge of technology in police work, but a lot of other people are doing very innovative, bright things all over the world," said Bayan Lewis, an LAPD commander who helped Braun arrange Vorontsov's visit.

Kern County lawmen have adapted a simple Soviet "pole vault" technique that can flip SWAT team members into second-story windows, he said.

AN ARTICLE ENTITLED "SENIORS' CHURCH ATTENDANCE" WAS PUBLISHED IN THE JUNE 12, 1991 issue of *Education Week*. The central premise of the article was summed up in the following quote:

High school seniors in 1990 were much less interested in, and involved with, organized religion than were their counterparts in the 1970's, according to data compiled by the Institute for Social Research (ISR) at the University of Michigan.

[Ed. Note: The Institute for Social Research (ISR) is, interestingly enough, the same institute that was involved in Ronald Havelock's *The Change Agents' Guide to Innovation in Education* which instructed educators how to "identify resisters" and how to sneak controversial sex, drug and death education into curriculum despite parental objections. The article reveals that the schools were highly successful in their efforts to indoctrinate students in non-absolutist, humanistic values. It should come as no surprise that the average American in 1991, subjected to values clarification in the schools of the 1960s, 1970s, and 1980s, is non-judgmental regarding immoral behavior. For example: in 1999 President Clinton, according to the polls, retained the confidence of 60–75% of the American people during his investigation and even after his impeachment trial revealed flagrant immoral activity.]

"**WEEK IN THE SUBWAY AS CULTURAL EXCHANGE**" **BY JACQUES STEINBERG WHICH APPEARED** in the June 15, 1991 issue of *The New York Times* pointed out some of the interesting activities resulting from the exchanges signed between President Reagan and President Gorbachev. An excerpt follows:

> A hapless fare-beater was arrested today in the Chambers Street subway station, and he was suddenly surrounded by six Moscow police officers. This was not a scene out of a Cold War nightmare. The Soviets were not taking over the United States. This was a cultural exchange.

THE LATE MORTIMER ADLER'S BOOK *HAVES WITHOUT HAVE-NOTS: ESSAYS FOR THE 21ST Century on Democracy and Socialism* (Macmillan Publishing Company: New York, 1991) was published. The book's dedication was to "Mikhail Gorbachev—whose perestroika opened the window to this vision of the future in the United States, Eastern Europe, and the Soviet Union." *Haves Without Have-Nots* takes on additional importance with the imminent approach of the year 2000 and the tragic upheavals in former communist countries, some of which seem to be reverting to communism. Excerpts follow:

> In the almost fifty years that have elapsed since 1943, I joined the World Federalists and campaigned for world government; I was appointed by President Robert M. Hutchins of the University of Chicago to his Committee to Frame a World Constitution, established by him immediately after atomic bombs were dropped on Hiroshima and Nagasaki; I conducted a seminar for the Ford Foundation on war and peace, world peace, and world government in 1951; and I wrote two books (*The Common Sense of Politics*, 1971, and *A Vision of the Future*, 1984), in which these subjects are treated with a maturity acquired by years of thinking about them....
>
> Finally, in Section 5, I will close with a vision of the new world of the Twentieth Century, in which the conflict between the two great superpowers—the USA and its NATO allies vs. the USSR and its Warsaw Pact satellites—will be replaced by the USDR (a union of socialist democratic republics). This will be a penultimate stage of progress toward a truly global world federal union that will eliminate the remaining potentially threatening conflict between the have and the have-not nations. (pp. 250–251)

[Ed. Note: Mortimer Adler can also be remembered as the author of *The Paidea Proposal*, an educational "innovation" used to introduce the concept of charter-type schools into mainstream school reform along with humanistic emphasis on subject matter. Adler was also one of the most visible facilitators for the Aspen Institute for Humanistic Studies (established in the 1940s) which has trained most of our government leaders in the dialectical process of reaching consensus. While Adler did not live to respond to the break up of the former Soviet Union, his interim vision of the formation of a "union of socialist democratic republics" bears watching.]

GLOBAL ALLIANCE FOR TRANSFORMING EDUCATION (GATE) PUBLISHED *EDUCATION 2000: A Holistic Perspective* in August, 1991.[7] The following excerpts are taken from "The Vision Statement" and the "GATE Partnerships for Transforming Education" section of "The Plan for Implementation":

Principle II. Honoring Students as Individuals

We call for a thorough rethinking of grading, assessment, and standardized examinations.... In successful innovative schools around the world, grades and standardized tests have been replaced by personalized assessments which enable students to become inner directed. The natural result of this practice is the development of self-knowledge, self-discipline, and genuine enthusiasm for learning.

We call for an expanded application of the tremendous knowledge we now have about learning styles, multiple intelligences, and the psychological bases of learning.... The work being done on multiple intelligences demonstrates that an area of strength such as bodily kinesthetic, musical, or visual spatial can be tapped to strengthen areas of weakness such as linguistic or logical-mathematical....

Principle IV. Holistic Education

...Holistic education celebrates and makes constructive use of evolving, alternate views of reality and multiple ways of knowing. It is not only the intellectual and vocational aspects of human development that needed guidance and nurturance, but also the physical, social, moral, aesthetic, creative, and—in a nonsectarian sense—spiritual aspects. Holistic education takes into account the numinous [supernatural] mystery of life and the universe in addition to the experiential reality.[8]

Holism is a re-emerging paradigm, based on a rich heritage from many scholarly fields. Holism affirms the inherent interdependence of evolving theory, research, and practice. Holism is rooted in the assumption that the universe is an integrated whole in which everything is connected. This assumption of wholeness and unity is in direct opposition to the paradigm of separation and fragmentation that prevails in the contemporary world. Holism corrects the imbalance of reductionistic approaches through its emphasis on an expanded conception of science and human possibility. Holism carries significant implications for human and planetary ecology and evolution. These implications are discussed throughout this document....

Principle VI. Freedom of Choice

We are for a truly democratic model of education to empower all citizens to participate in meaningful ways in the life of the community and the planet. The building of a truly democratic society means far more than allowing people to vote for their leaders—it means empowering individuals to take an active part in the affairs of their community. A truly democratic society is more than "the rule of the majority"—it is a community in which disparate voices are heard and genuine human concerns are addressed. It is a society open to constructive change when social or cultural change is required....

Principle VIII. Educating for Global Citizenship
　　We believe that each of us—whether we realize it or not—is a global citizen.... A goal of global education is to open minds. This is accomplished through interdisciplinary studies, experiences which foster understanding, reflection and critical thinking, and creative response.... These principles include the usefulness of diversity, the value of cooperation and balance, the needs and rights of participants, and the need for sustainability within the system.
　　Other important components of global education include understanding causes of conflict and experiencing the methods of conflict resolution. At the same time, exploring social issues such as human rights, justice, population pressures, and development is essential to an accurate understanding of the causes of war and conditions for peace.
　　Since the world's religions and spiritual traditions have such enormous impact, global education encourages understanding and appreciation of them and of the universal values they proclaim, including the search for meaning, love, compassion, wisdom, truth, and harmony. Thus, education in a global age addresses what is most fully and universally human....

CONCLUSION*

　　...We in education are beginning to recognize that the structure, purposes, and methods of our profession were designed for an historical period which is now coming to a close. The time has come to transform education so as to address the human and environmental challenges which confront us.[9]
　　*This conclusion is *The Chicago Statement on Education* adopted by eighty international holistic educators at Chicago, Illinois, June, 1990....

GATE PARTNERSHIPS FOR TRANSFORMING EDUCATION

[The visual graphic on the front of this section included planets rotating around a central orb entitled "GATE." The "planets" were labeled with the following titles:]

- Young people
- Teachers
- Education Associations
- United Nations Organizations
- Local Communities
- Government & Local/National Education Leaders
- Families
- Teacher Educators & Academies
- Business
- Media
- Model Holistic Schools
- Citizen Groups for Social Change....

Business

GATE understands that a working partnership needs to be built with business. Business leaders recognize that the structure and form of today's education are not meeting the ever-expanding needs of a global society....

Example: W.E. Deming is the creator of *Total Quality Management* [TQM]—a holistic perspective that is transforming the hierarchical nature of the business world. He claims that "a long-term commitment to new understanding and new philosophy is required of any management that seeks transformation."[10] There is a common thread between Deming's TQM model and holistic education. At the 1991 conference in Colorado, a group discussing GATE's interface with business drew the idea of *Total Quality Education* [emphasis in original] into their dialogue. This discussion has led to the beginnings of a national TQE movement in which business, government, and education leaders will be addressing holism in education. It is an opportunity for GATE's vision to get wide distribution.

In a separate section of the GATE material entitled "United Nations Organizations" one reads:

Example #1. Several members of the GATE Steering Committee serve on the Seed Advisory Committee for the Global Education Program for Peace and Universal Responsibility at the United Nations' University for Peace in Costa Rica.

Example #2. GATE has been networking with various branches of UNESCO to develop a series of World Conferences on Education.... The conferences would model the non-hierarchical process of new leadership and would be organized according to the following tracks: Critical issues in education; Global citizenship and ecological education; Education for all; Innovative strategies and techniques; Spiritual education; Peace and education; and The media and education.[11]

The reference to the United Nations' University for Peace in Costa Rica brings former United Nations Under Secretary Robert Muller into the picture. Muller wrote his own World Core Curriculum which he credits to a demon spirit guide, Djhwan Khul, who gained notoriety in the early 1900s as the spirit guide of Theosophist Alice Bailey who wrote *Education in the New Age* (Lucis Publishing Company: New York, 1954).[12] Muller also authored a novel in 1988 entitled *First Lady of the World* (World Happiness and Cooperation: Anacortes, Wash., 1991) in which his fictitious world leader enumerates a series of proposals necessary for the smooth running of a global society. A few of those proposals follow:

7. A World Core Curriculum and a Planetary Management Curriculum are adopted by UNESCO as common guides for proper Global Education in all schools and universities of Earth. 1996 is proclaimed International Year of Global Education....

11. More and more countries disarm, demilitarize and have their borders protected by UN observers under regional and international guarantees. The savings are devoted to development, the environment, education and social services....

15. A host of new world conferences are convened at an accelerated pace: on soil erosion, on mountain areas, reforestation, the world's cold zones, consumer protection, standardization, world community, a world tax system, etc. (pp. 70–71)

The implementation of this global management system has been accurately described in two novels—B.F. Skinner's *Walden Two*, which describes "the method" (behavior modification), and Robert Muller's *First Lady of the World*, which describes "the mechanics" (blueprint). Speaking of the effect of *Walden Two*, which is required reading in college classrooms across the country, the promotional blurb on the jacket of the book says:

This fictional outline of a modern utopia has been a center of raging controversy ever since its publication in 1948. Set in the United States, it provocatively pictures a society in which human problems are solved by a scientific technology of human conduct—and in which many of our contemporary values are obsolete.

[Ed. Note: Please refer to the 1993 entry regarding the Fall issue of *Outcomes* containing an interview with Ken Hazelip and James Block connecting Skinnerian operant conditioning and mastery learning to Total Quality Management as well as exposing the fact that mastery learning has been a "hard sell" with American teachers. (Also see 1998 Willard Daggett's *Model School News* related to District 4J in Oregon as a "model school district.")]

A SAMPLE "21ST CENTURY REPORT CARD" WAS A HANDOUT AT THE AUGUST, 1991 ASSO-ciation for Supervision and Curriculum Development (ASCD) Network conference in Traverse City, Michigan entitled "Creating the Twenty-First Century." Descriptive excerpts—which originally led this writer to believe this sample report card was a joke until able to verify its actual existence—follow:

DaVinci Elementary School
Principal: R.B. Fuller

[After each of the following categories there is a mark A through F as a grade, ed.]

Spatial Relationships; Intuition; Insight; Generates Ideas Freely; Daydreaming/Reverie; Gestalt Perception; Esthetic Sensibility: color, form, music, poetry

Teacher's Comments: school psychologist suggests remedial imagination

Work Habits: Able to transcend space/time limitations; Is flexible; Listens attentively—with third ear; Follows directions unless better idea occurs; Completes assignments—when useful; Makes good use of time: fantasizing, creating, meditating.

Citizenship: Accepts responsibility; Respects authority—if there is justification for respect; Respects rights and property of others; Shows empathy/telepathy;

Teacher's signature:
Parent's signature:

Bonnie Newhouse, a Traverse City, Michigan wife and mother of four children who had served on the junior and senior parent advisory committees as well as the district advisory council, wrote an article for the *Traverse City Record-Eagle*'s March 18, 1992 issue which included the following information related to change agent tactics to implement restructuring promoted at the ASCD meetings:

In a study done by the U.S. Senate Republican Policy Committee on Illiteracy, September 1989, they conclude: "For the past 50 years, America's classrooms have been used by psychologists, sociologists, educationists and politicians as a giant laboratory for unproven, untried theories of learning, resulting in a near collapse of public education."

This "collapse" was also referred to by William Spady in his address to the ASCD High School Futures Planning Consortium III August 1991 meeting in Traverse City. He spoke of prominent educators talking of WHEN the public education system collapses, not IF [emphasis in original]. He also shared with the audience that he was one of three given a grant by the Danforth Foundation with the assignment to transform America's high schools.

What does all this really mean for our students? From the information gathered and rhetoric offered, perhaps the most significant was found in yet another ASCD Network conference held the previous week, "Creating the 21st Century"; an example of a 21st Century Report Card [was presented]....

We are seeing a major shift away from academics toward attitudes and values. The question is, who will determine which outcomes your child must have to graduate? If all this seems farfetched, one has only to read some of the information presented at the ASCD workshops: "Learners' behavior must show... Learners' attitudes must demonstrate... Learners will advocate for collaborative change."

Most enlightening was a session titled, "How to develop the 'desired state' for your high school." A more accurate title may have been "How to manipulate teachers, parents and the school board to accomplish your agenda." Among the suggestions: use teachers in these pilots that are the kids' favorites; introduction of special education in the classrooms will help in overcoming the barrier of the closed door; how do you deal with people who sabotage your plan? Do little things to include them, give them power, let them be co-chairs.

THE GEORGIA PUBLIC POLICY FOUNDATION, A STATE AFFILIATE OF THE HERITAGE FOUNDAtion, published *Reach for the Stars: A Proposal for Education Reform in Georgia* by Matthew J. Glavin in October of 1991.[13] Excerpts follow:

[Preface] The Georgia Public Policy Foundation wishes to thank the Hudson Institute for sharing much of their original research that constitutes the basis for this plan....

[Foreword] *Reach for the Stars* proposes step-by-step how we can take the education bull by the horns and steer it toward success. For parents, it means an end to excessive school taxes and the beginning of accountability on the part of the school system.... I urge you to read this report with an open mind and an eye toward change. If Georgia hopes to continue another decade of growth, it must begin preparing now. *Reach for the Stars* outlines the necessary steps to ensure Georgia's future. As citizens, we can not afford to miss this opportunity.

William Bennett
Former Secretary of Education
October, 1991

[Ed. Note: The introduction to *Reach for the Stars* quotes the late Al Shanker, long-time president of the nation's second largest teacher union—American Federation of Teachers—as if Shanker would be recommending any changes or restructuring other than that proposed by the Carnegie Corporation. The reader should refer to the 1986 entry which quoted from an article entitled "Carnegie Report on Education: Radical Blueprint for Change" which appeared in the June 28–29, 1986 issue of *The Bangor* [ME] *Daily News*. This article identified Shanker as a willing accomplice of Carnegie's plan (the Marc Tucker/National Center for Education and the Economy plan) to restructure education.]

In the following excerpts from *Reach for the Stars* the writer has related the statements to outcome-based education, education restructuring, school-to-work, site-based management, etc., all of which concerned parents and teachers have been led to believe are anathema to conservatives:

> And we need a system of measuring achievement that will tell parents how well their sons and daughters are doing compared with what they need to know to get ahead—not compared to what a kid in another county or another state knows [outcome-based education which replaces norm-referenced testing with criterion-based testing].
>
> It's time to shift the power back to the teachers and principals [site-based management which abolishes the power of elected school boards].
>
> Under the Georgia Public Policy Plan, "ready for life" means having the knowledge and skills to be successful in life as a citizen, employee and person. Earning a basic high school diploma should mean one is ready for life [UNESCO's lifelong learning and elements of competency-based/outcomes-based education].
>
> Second, create a new statewide assessment system which: (a) measures the extent to which individual students are meeting the standards; (b) provides information on school performance for parent selection of schools; and (c) gives employers an objective and meaningful way to assess the capabilities of job applicants by requiring a uniform exit assessment to earn a high school diploma [the controversial National Assessment of Educational Progress which measures students' attitudes and beliefs, and school-to-work, SCANS].
>
> Academic standards should include knowledge, concepts, and skills that all students, college-bound and job-bound, need to master [school-to-work, mastery learning].
>
> These standards are currently being developed at the national level by the National Education Goals Panel (NEGP) [no local representation].
>
> The academic standards will: (a) identify the core competencies that all students should master at key transition points in their education careers, and (b) identify the skills and knowledge that students must master to earn a high school diploma.... These academic standards will also include knowledge and skills needed for responsible citizenship; personal skills required to get, keep, and progress on a job; and social skills needed to work with others on a job [Certificate of Initial Mastery, lifelong learning, SCANS, OBE, mastery learning, and school-to-work].
>
> In conjunction with the National Education Goals Panel, a new voluntary nationwide examination system is being developed based on the five core subjects that are tied to the new national academic standards. Georgia should adopt this new examination system as soon as it is available for implementation. [This "voluntary nationwide examination system," which circumvents local control, has metamorphosed into a mandated nationwide examination for which legislation has been before Congress since 1997.]
>
> The State of Georgia should take this opportunity to request that the NAEP reauthorization... include a provision allowing any state that wishes to use the NAEP tests on a school-by-school basis to do so [NAEP was not designed to be a school-by-school comparison].
>
> There are three integral and inseparable concepts that will "free the teachers" and "free the parents"—Deregulation, School Autonomy and Parental Choice.

[Ed. Note: How can there be "freedom" for parents and teachers when schools are run by unelected (unaccountable) councils which must conform their curriculum to *Goals 2000*— national standards, national tests, resulting in a nationalized (socialist) education system?]

> One of the guiding philosophies of this plan is that government funding for K–12 education should be targeted to the child—not the school district. Each and every school-aged child will be entitled to public support for his or her education. Parents can use the

child's publicly funded "scholarship" at any school where the child meets admission requirements. Exceptions would be schools that fail to meet state performance standards, or private
schools that choose not to participate.

[Ed. Note: Targeting funding to the child according to the child's Individual Education Plan
(IEP) and meeting the state requirements fits in nicely with school-to-work. Won't a child
whose career path is that of a fireman receive less funding than a child whose career path is
that of an engineer?]

> Under the Georgia Public Policy Foundation recommendations the local districts must
> divest themselves of operating control of the schools [site-based management and charter
> schools].
> Each autonomous public school organizes as a non-profit corporation with a board
> selected by the teachers and other certified staff of the school.

[Ed. Note: This proposes a complete change of government, resulting in loss of representation
by publicly elected representatives.[14] This is the Carnegie Corporation's plan spelled out in *A
Nation Prepared: Teachers for the 21st Century*[15] which proposed the total restructuring of the
teaching profession and Luvern Cunningham's disastrous Kentucky model.]

> "Company Schools," schools that are sponsored at the work site for students who come to
> work with a parent but which are also open to local students [school-to-work].
> The curriculum in most American schools is geared toward the lower rote skills and is
> far less challenging than curricula in many other countries. [The reference to "lower rote
> skills" is a reference to basic skills—reading, writing, and arithmetic—and the rote learning
> of those skills. In 1994 H.R. 6, the controversial legislation that had parents up in arms,
> referred to "lower rote skills" in this same derogatory manner. The funding in H.R. 6 was
> definitely geared toward OBE/mastery learning/direct instruction and multi-cultural pro-
> grams, ed.]

[Ed. Note: This report could have been written by UNESCO and the U.S. Department of
Education with assistance from the Carnegie Corporation and the teachers' unions—American Federation of Teachers (AFT) and National Education Association (NEA). It incorporates
most of the essential elements of OBE, *America 2000, Goals 2000*, the New American School
Development Corporation's charter schools, and SCANS.]

HUMAN CAPITAL AND AMERICA'S FUTURE: AN ECONOMIC STRATEGY FOR THE NINETIES
(Hopkins Press: Baltimore, Md., 1991) edited by David W. Hornbeck and Lester M. Salamon,
was published. The following quotes confirm the worst fears of parents related to education
reform and dumbed down outcomes which are referenced by the change agents as "world
class." *Human Capital* explains that:

> [E]mployer beliefs about the superior capabilities of educated people turned out NOT to be
> confirmed in practice [emphasis in original]; educated employees have higher turn-over rates,
> lower job satisfaction, and poorer promotion records than less educated employees. (p. 7)

Education researcher Judith McLemore of Alabama excerpted and commented upon David
Hornbeck's statements in "New Paradigms for Action," chapter 13 of *Human Capital* :

Programs proposed to "cope with *human capital* problems" include "Initiatives to alleviate poverty" (p. 360) which include "income transfers."... The gap between "the haves and the have-nots is growing." Economic prosperity of the nation is "heavily dependent" upon stability. (p. 362)

Fastest growing "segment of the work force" is "women, blacks and hispanics, whom we have historically served poorly," and *not* "white males" whom we have historically served relatively well.... At present, "schools and other *human capital* related institutions contribute to the growing gap between the *rich and the poor*." (p. 363)

The alteration of our *human capital development* institutions must be as fundamental as the changes in our economic institutions and other parts of our social fabric.... It is imperative to "improve the school success of young people with whom we have failed historically." (p. 364)

"What are the basic tools we have available to initiate and sustain real change?"... 1. Demonstration projects... 2. Charismatic leaders... 3. Money (p. 365)... 4. Lawsuits (p. 366)... 5. Labor contracts... 6. Legislation. (p. 367)

"It is not possible to achieve the kind of outcomes we envision without being specific as to what those outcomes are. Moreover, it is necessary to define the quality and scope of the desired outcomes. Using the *Job Training Partnership Act* as an example... one of the frequent criticisms of its outcome definition is that it encourages 'creaming.' If, however, the outcome sought and rewarded was not just job placement, but job placement for the most difficult to serve and job placements of a certain quality in terms of pay and future prospects, one would quickly eliminate that charge.... Crafting outcomes can be a very tricky process ... to achieve the high graduation rates reflecting higher achievement levels will require success with the same young people with whom we have failed even with lower standards." (pp. 369–370)

"What we teach should basically be the same for ALL students." (p. 375) [all emphases in original]

"New Paradigms for Action" makes it clear that in the future the "system" (not the student) will be responsible for student success... and the students will be followed (data collection system from birth until death?). The "system" will be rewarded or penalized for the success/failure of those "difficult to serve" including whether or not they get high paying jobs after schooling ends.

In order to drive home her point that our children, as human capital, are nothing but pawns in the hands of the state/business community, McLemore refers to the foreword to Alexander Frazier's book *Adventuring, Mastering, Associating: New Strategies for Teaching Children* (Association for Supervision and Curriculum Development: Washington, D.C., 1976), written by Delmo Della-Dora, president of ASCD (1975–1976), which said, "This work represents Alexander Frazier's attempt to describe what he calls an equal rights curriculum for all children." On page 83 Frazier said, "Our goal is the removal of inequality among children who have been undertaught, overtaught, mistaught, or not taught some things at all." On page 15 he said, "Jefferson saw the public school as an agency for finding talent to serve the state. In the same way, the school could recruit for the business and industrial establishment."

VIRGINIA BIRT BAKER'S PAPER, WRITTEN IN 1991,"EDUCATIONAL CHOICE—THE EDUCATION Voucher, Tax Credits, and the Nonpublic Schools" explains very clearly that educational "choice" is a Trojan Horse carrying government control of all schools and schooling. Excerpts follow:

"Education is an emotional issue," he said. "We're staying away from the word 'voucher' because 'educational choice' sounds a little more palatable to parents. Educational choice is giving students and their parents a voucher... and we want to mobilize a significant number of people... to get the camel's nose under the tent.... We've got to prepare for the long term... so we can strengthen our position and that of our friends."

So reported a leader of a covert "new right" Dallas think tank at a recent White House Conference on Education. The pro-choice activists are vociferous proponents of tuition tax credits and the education voucher, and we wonder why they want to "improve the schools' and parents' attitudes" by confounding our intellectual inquiries with an emotional and illusory word change.

The Associated Press has reported that... President George Bush said, "Choice will be a critical element in education reform for years to come." This recent upsurge in support of "choice" and the voucher program is nothing new and deserves closer scrutiny by parents and especially by private and home school patrons....

The Private School Trap—
To parents who have been paying taxes to support government schools, it sounds wonderful to be able to choose the better school not necessarily in their neighborhood. To parents who have been paying taxes to government schools and paying the tuition costs to send their children to private schools, a tax break or a government-paid incentive would be a welcome relief from financial strain, seemingly encouraging a sort of free-market approach to education. But stop and think: The state has its fangs into private and home schools now; what will it be like when schools are recipients of "choice" money?

The truth of the matter is, once private education accepts tuition tax credits/vouchers it can no longer remain "private," because through government regulations, it will be forced to become one and the same with its public counterpart.

THE UNITED STATES COALITION FOR EDUCATION FOR ALL (USCEFA)—AN OUTGROWTH OF World Conference on Education for All, Jomtien, Thailand—met October 30–November 1,1991 in Alexandria, Virginia. President Bush's wife, Barbara, was named honorary chairperson. One of the keynote speakers at the event was Deputy Minister of Education Elena Lenskaya, Republic of Russia.[16] The purpose of this conference was to "involve the United States in reform of education/community renewal worldwide." The same United Nations outcomes as those recommended at the Jomtien conference were adopted. According to "The Mission Statement":

USCEFA is comprised of a diverse group of international, domestic, governmental and non-governmental groups, associations, and individual education, business, media and health leaders. The Coalition was created as an outgrowth of the World Conference on Education for All, where official delegations from 156 countries achieved a worldwide consensus to launch a renewed worldwide initiative to meet the basic learning needs of all children, youth and adults.[17]

The Coalition is taking this worldwide consensus and bridging between the initiatives for reform in other countries and the goals for education reform in the United States. [This statement flies in the face of change agent assurances at the local and state level that goals are locally developed, ed.]

It strongly believes that the improvement of education is essential for improving the quality of life for the world's people and for sustainable economic development; and for these reasons, this organization is committed to improving the state of basic education in the United States and developing countries by creating new partnerships for educational reform....

Through seminars, publications, media events, conferences, networking and the dissemination of information, the U.S. Coalition for Education for All is working to meet the goals set by the World Conference on Education for All. Members of the Board of Directors include:

President: Janet Whitla, Education Development Center, Inc.[18]
Vice President: Stephen F. Moseley, Academy for Educational Development, Inc.
Secretary: Richard Long, International Reading Association
Treasurer: John Comings, World Education, Inc.
Clifford Block, Far West Regional Laboratory for Educational Research and Improvement
David Dorn, American Federation of Teachers
Alan Hill, Apple Computer, Inc.
Gary Marx, American Association of School Administrators
Thomas Shannon, National School Boards Association
Daniel Wagner, National Center on Adult Literacy, University of Pennsylvania

NEW AMERICAN SCHOOLS DEVELOPMENT CORPORATION (NASDC) WAS ESTABLISHED IN 1991. President George Bush requested that the business community raise funds to support development of "radical, break-the-mold" schools (one in each Congressional district) which would in the future be known as "charter schools" (public school "choice" schools).[19] The Request for Proposals from NASDC required that:

Design teams should define the scope and focus of their own work. Student age-grouping may be unconventional, and designs may serve students younger than five years of age and older than eighteen; students need not all be assembled in a single building or at a particular time of day; the school day and school year may be redefined. The duties of administrators, teachers, volunteers, parents, and all other adults may be changed.... The design may entail major changes in community governance, community structures and the functions of other institutions such as public health agencies and welfare departments. Alternatively, designs may adopt conventional arrangements for any of above.

THE EFFECTIVE SCHOOL REPORT'S NOVEMBER 1991 ISSUE CARRIED AN ARTICLE ENTITLED "A Letter from Russia." The following excerpts illustrate the extent of damage resulting from the 1985 U.S.-Soviet and Carnegie education agreements and other exchange agreements:

Editor's note: Don Thomas, executive director of the Network for Effective Schools, journeyed to Russia in September as part of a contingent of American educators traveling under the auspices of the U.S. Department of Education (Secretary Lamar Alexander). Dale Mann of Columbia University was a part of the delegation. After initial meetings in Moscow, Thomas traveled to the City of Sochi to meet with Russian educators. One of his contacts was Professor Victor Nouja, a school administrator from Rostov-on-Don. The following letter is a follow-up communication from Nouja, who is eager to establish contacts with American educators for the exchange of information and teaching on school management practices:

Dear Mr. Thomas:

How are you and your family? Now that we have returned from the first East-West International Workshop in Sochi (Russia) to our native city, Rostov-on-Don, my friends and I want to thank you for the opportunity you gave us to learn about the experiences of school reform and educational management in the state of South Carolina and the evaluation of schools in South Carolina. I am sure your experience will be very helpful for us.... There are many teachers and school principals who are very interested in taking part in different projects. But, we would like to have our own project—"Rostov-South Carolina-Utah." Me and my boss had a very long and promising talk with our city authorities about our possible contacts. And they promise to undertake sponsorship of the international teacher training and school management program.

Now some words about goals of the project. The first is—to exchange our experience in school management and especially in evaluation of school activity. The second is—to transfer your experience of using computer systems in both teaching and school management. The third goal—exchange of teaching experience. Now we begin to work with groups of teachers who are ready for actions in this project.

Mr. Thomas, I'll be very happy if you send a letter and tell me your vision on points I have described. If there is no objection and difficulties to start this project then we need to find time and place we could meet and discuss details. It might be either your town in South Carolina or our native city Rostov-on-Don. At that meeting we'll be able to work out a program or project and sign something like an agreement on form and the matter of the project. Our city's authorities are ready to take part in this business. I hope we could organize this meeting this winter or early in spring time. Mr. Thomas, I have a big favor to ask of you... papers and some tests for accreditation of schools.

Signed Victor Nouja, 344103 Stz Sodzujestva NeF, ap 170, Rostov-on-Don, USSR, Russia

BRITISH COLUMBIA TEACHERS' FEDERATION[20] **IN 1991 PUBLISHED "WHAT IS THE MARKET** Model?" Excerpts from this interesting flyer made available to Canadian teachers follows:

AIMS: The Market Model aims to reduce learning to an instrument serving social power. More specifically public education is enlisted in the Market Model to serve the needs of corporate capital in an information age of global production.

FEATURES:
1. In Canada the market model started in higher education, and is now moving to secondary schooling.
2. Cuts in government funding, with corporate funding targeted to particular projects.
3. Purpose of education—to compete economically in the international marketplace.
4. Demands that public education be redesigned to serve as a knowledge producer for private corporations in the national economic competition.
5. Textbook production and distribution under control of private corporations.
6. Academic teachers are conceived as "business persons" who provide goods and services under Free Trade Agreement and NAFTA.

RHETORIC:
"New Reality"
Competition, Market Discipline
"The Campus as Corporation" (Strangeway, 1984)
Curriculum Products
Resource Units or Resource Packages
Uniform Standards Skills

MAIN SOURCE: McMurtry, John, *Journal of Philosophy of Education*, Vol. 25, No. 2, 1991.
PD95–0016

[Ed. Note: Many of McMurtry's tongue-in-cheek ideas are to be found in so-called "conservative" think tanks' papers on education restructuring. Number 6 under "Features" is particularly offensive in that the idea of teachers becoming "private contractors" instead of school system employees is being discussed and proposed around many a policy maker's table in this country. What a peculiar thing. If teachers are being trained not to concentrate on subject matter or "lower level skill development," what would they have to market? The ability to "train" students to perform certain tasks in a certain way in a certain period of time? Market Model Maniacs?]

1992

THE *EFFECTIVE SCHOOL REPORT*'S FEBRUARY 1992 ISSUE CARRIED AN ARTICLE ENTITLED "Free Education in a Free Society" by Nick Zienau of England's Educational Consultancy. It reads in part:

> This article describes a project which began at a conference organized in September 1991 to discuss possibilities for projects between East and West which might assist the process of educational reform in Russia and the other republics formerly of the USSR.... An important part of becoming convinced that this was worthwhile was to discover that there was a common set of values and ideas about the changes facing education systems whether in Russia, the U.S. or Europe.... A key theme for us was, therefore, that those ideas which hitherto have been seen as progressive alternatives and often dangerously radical in educational theory and practice will increasingly become part of mainstream education practice and thinking.
>
> A second key principle was the idea that increasingly education will cease to be a state monopoly and must have a relationship with the free market. This seems related to the idea of individual enterprise and choice. Our belief is that it is helpful to educational reform and therefore to this project to form collaborative relationships between the state and organizations acting in the free market. This will help to allow individual autonomy, enterprise, etc., to flourish and allow relationships between those involved in reform not to be based on fixed budgets and supply side economics. It will require us to have clear contracts between participants. If we have ideas about how to go about training teachers, we will learn these best from each other by doing it together and that only in this way can the project be effective as an educational intervention between nations, between innovators or between individuals.
>
> ...We believe in an exchange of learning and in the idea that there is likely to be as much that the West can learn from eastern partners as the other way around. We believe that a key to what this learning might be about is that the West's knowledge of how to do things

in education, how to make changes for instance in the technology, is matched by pedagogic systems and theories which have been highly developed in Russia. We believe that these theories and practices can form the basis of radical curriculum innovation and organizational reform.

Finally, we believe in a project that has an organic structure. It will have two nodes, one in the east and one in the west, and it will span three continents. It will have a core structure which must have a small financial base and it will have participating organizations and individuals. However, the form of the organization must be one in which projects can be developed from the center core and not controlled by it. Participants should be free to create these without relying on central funding or permission as long as they can fit into this set of agreed values which the project will develop.

First among these is the theme of teacher education (both pre- and in-service). We see this as the key way of changing and influencing education....

Thirdly, we hope to gain the active involvement of industry and commerce. It will be the concern of the project to encourage such collaboration on both sides, both in the Eastern consortium and in the Western consortium. We understand it as an important way of ensuring that education is relevant to society, understood and cared about, and seen as connected to sources of wealth creation in society. Certainly in the East and also, we would venture, increasingly in the West, active involvement of industry and commerce is essential in order to obtain the funds and commitment necessary for educational reform to succeed. This means that in practice we will take every available opportunity to involve actively avant-garde leaders of industry and commerce both in funding, supporting and implementing the project. The important criteria for collaboration must be that there is sufficient congruence of ethics and values about the goals and methods of the project.

Fourthly, in order to "practice what we preach," we believe that our meetings and projects events do actively demonstrate and work with the pedagogic systems, that the learning should be managed in a conscious way. We therefore will make it a feature of the project that we focus on the skills and strategies of managing learning in an international context whether it be in the seminars, conferences, exchange trips or consultations. Fifth, it will be important to formulate structures and models of organization that encourage independence and autonomy through small groups.... The education reform process will be built on the work of many small groups making their own decisions. We will need to build into our project structure of contract making, interdependence with autonomy and hold it within a regulated and boundaried field of action. These kinds of structures and models are new forms of organization for both East and West and represent a move away from hierarchy and role-dominated cultures.

The Consortium activity has the official support of the Minister of Education for the Russian Republic, Dr. Edouard Dneprov, and a close liaison has been established with the Ministry. On the Western side, the consortium at present includes consultants, trainers, and researchers from the UK, Netherlands and the USA who aim in the first place to act as a bridge into the various educational networks in the West. These will include higher education initiatives, networks of alternative schools, organizations involved in innovative teacher training, consulting organizations, industrial and commercial organizations concerned with pedagogical innovation. They are also currently working to obtain funding and support among possible private and public sector sponsors.

Signed Nick Zienau

[Ed. Note: Considerable space has been devoted to quotes from *The Effective School Report* due to their obvious close relationship to activities in American education restructuring; i.e., choice, charter schools, school-business partnerships, school-to-work legislation, The New

American Schools Development Corporation, site-based management, merger of public and private sectors, and the Skinnerian workforce training methodology. This important article justifies the validity of concerns expressed by Americans opposed to the U.S.-Soviet and Carnegie-Soviet education agreements signed in 1985 by President Reagan, Mikhail Gorbachev, Carnegie Corporation and the then-Soviet Academy of Sciences, respectively.]

"BEIJING JOURNAL: PERSONAL FILE AND WORKER YOKED FOR LIFE" BY NICHOLAS D. KRISTOF was published in *The New York Times* on March 16, 1992. This article described the Chinese *dangan* as part of a web of social controls that ensures order in China. Excerpts follow:

> BEIJING—As part of China's complex system of social control and surveillance, the authorities keep a dangan, or file, on virtually everyone except peasants. Indeed, most Chinese have two dangans: one at their workplace and another in their local police station.... "School records and grade transcripts," she began, offering a foreigner a rare look into the dangan system, "Entry into the Communist Youth League and the Communist Party. Family members and photo. Promotions and level of work. Performance evaluations. That kind of thing. About 10 times."
>
> A file is opened on each urban citizen when he or she enters elementary school, and it shadows the person throughout life, moving on to high school, college and employer. Particularly for officials, professors and Communist Party members, the dangan contains political evaluations that affect career prospects and permission to leave the country.... The dangan affects promotions and job opportunities, and it is difficult to escape from because any prospective employer is supposed to examine an applicant's dangan before making a hiring decision.

[Ed. Note: Sounds like the U.S. Secretary of Labor's Commission on Achieving Necessary Skills resumé for "Jane Smith" which grades Jane on a 1–10 basis on honesty, etc., and which includes her community service activities. Oregon's legislation stating that employers could not hire potential employees unless they had a Certificate of Initial Mastery did not pass. However, the very idea that it was proposed means that that is exactly what is intended. The above article is important because of U.S. educators' official visits to China and the fact that the U.S. Department of Education's contract for the SPEEDE Express (an electronic data exchange system to be used for transfer of student records, etc.) is the beginning of the transfer of personal data on students to various agencies, prospective employers, etc.]

FILLING THE GAPS: AN OVERVIEW OF DATA ON EDUCATION IN GRADES K THROUGH 12 WAS published by the National Center for Educational Statistics (U.S. Department of Education, Office of Educational Research and Improvement: Washington, D.C. [NCES 92–132], 1992). On page 5 one finds a most extraordinary and revolutionary definition of teacher "quality" which transfers the responsibility for learning from the student to the teacher. Excerpts from *Filling the Gaps* follow:

> TEACHERS
> Beginning in the 1980s, NCES collected detailed information on the characteristics and qualifications of teachers....
> But the term "qualifications" is not synonymous with "quality." The characteristics

that contribute to good teaching are many, and no single configuration of traits, qualifications, or behaviors unvaryingly produces optimal student outcomes in all situations. NCES teacher surveys have concentrated on collecting data on "qualifications," rather than trying to define "quality." In order to define and measure "quality," characteristics and qualifications of teachers must be related to growth in student achievement.

[Ed. Note: If the bottom line regarding "quality teaching" is "growth in student achievement" one must assume that extraordinary measures will be necessary to bring about such "growth in student achievement" and the only measures that exist are those associated with the Skinnerian operant conditioning method used in mastery learning/direct instruction/outcome-/results-/performance-based education, all of which are synonymous with the new definition of "achievement." The Skinnerian method identifies each and every minute component of the subject to be learned and measures each and every response by the student and teacher, leaving much real learning out of the picture. It is evident that the teacher will also be "trained" in the same way the student is "trained" in order to become a "quality teacher" who never deviates from the script and whose every action, including facial expressions and body gestures, can be precisely measured, accounted for, and evaluated.

As a teacher, you WILL perform, or you will lose your job.

As a student, you WILL achieve, unless you are unwilling to be trained like an animal, in which case you may be sent to some form of "boot camp" for "re-education."

In order to accomplish the above, you, as a teacher, WILL teach to the test.]

Perhaps the most important data gap in understanding how teachers affect the educational process is the lack of a good definition of "teacher quality."... The National Education Statistics Agenda Committee... has recommended that OERI fund special studies to improve the measurement of, among other things, "important school processes including... methods of training teachers and assessing their competence."

Another gap relates to the assessment of teacher quality....

The qualifications measures that NCES does not collect cannot currently be related to measures of student achievement.... Development of a measure of "teacher quality" would be hastened by obtaining student outcome measures that could be linked to the rich nationally representative data on teacher qualifications.... These data are collected from information available in school records.... This student records form, if found feasible, could provide the data necessary to improve our understanding and measurement of "teacher quality."

[Ed. Note: In addition to data-gathering based on teach-to-the-test produced student performance measures of "teacher quality," *Filling the Gaps* also outlines other data gathering that is related to the "quality" measure—quality of life. According to *Filling the Gaps*:

Socio-economic status (SES) of students is important for understanding, among other things, student outcomes including achievement test scores and graduation rates.... [C]ompletion in 1993 of the project to map decennial census information to school district boundaries will enable most elementary/secondary data to be linked to school district SES measures for analysis.

The original 1981 Census Mapping Project, a joint venture between the National Center for Education Statistics and the U.S. Census Bureau, was kept a highly guarded secret for a long time. One can only speculate as to the reason—perhaps it is related to the fact that exchanging information of this type between government agencies has been, technically, illegal. (The reader may remember the cries of protest that surfaced in the mid-1980s over the idea of the IRS tracking unpaid student college loans by sharing data from the U.S. Department of Education. The justification for continuing to illegally share interagency data was lost in the shuffle as the dust settled over that debate. Perhaps the 1981 Census Mapping Project was used as justification for "on-going practice constitutes acceptable practice.") However, it is important to note the fact that the SES measures projected for the 1993 NCES-U.S. Census project are to be arrived at by analyzing data collected on the "community"—or school district—level.

NCES maintains a series of *Educational Records Series* handbooks containing the computer coding numbers, categories, and specific pieces of information gathered and recorded about anything connected with schools—including *Handbook VIII: The Community*. This handbook, while having its contents merged into later versions of others in the series, originally contained the coding for all community "quality of life" information, including factors producing socio-economic status data and a chapter entitled "Attitudes, Values and Beliefs." This handbook provided the vehicle for profiling a "community"—defined as a "school district" by the Census Mapping Project—for planning of programs by Community Education practitioners. (*Community Education's Effect on Quality of Life* by W. James Giddis, Diana Page, and George L. Mailberger [Center for Community Education at the University of West Florida: Pensacola, Fla., 1981], p. 8.)

Profiling a community for "Attitudes, Values and Beliefs" is useful for those education change agents steeped in the methods taught in Ronald J. Havelock's *The Change Agents' Guide to Innovation in Education*, regularly taught at the National Training Laboratory's programs and other leadership training seminars for teachers, administrators, board members, elected or appointed officials, and other "first-level adopters" of new education reform/restructuring proposals. The data gathered through the Census Mapping Project, among other things, assists in identifying those in a local community defined as "resisters" to controversial programs.

Efforts to require "accountability" based on "measurements of teacher quality" have much broader consequences than most policy makers have imagined. Defining terms can lead to understanding that some recent reform efforts are based on faulty premises, to say the least.]

COMMUNITY LEARNING INFORMATION NETWORK, INC. (CLIN) WAS INCORPORATED IN 1992. CLIN's 22-page publicity packet stated in part:

> CLIN was incorporated in April of 1992, with a bi-partisan "Blue Ribbon" board of directors to implement a community-linked learning technology and information delivery system. CLIN has attracted a following in a substantial number of communities and involves a broad range of industries and interests (including educators, small and large businesses, hospitals, National Guard and Reserves, various government agencies, public housing, and inner city organizations and telecommunication providers) in implementing the CLIN concept. CLIN has been recognized by the White House and senior members of Congress and currently has legislation marked for testbed projects. CLIN has also developed international projects to include an approved project with the People's Republic of China sponsored by the highest levels of the Chinese government.[21]

[Ed. Note: United States government assistance to the Chinese Communist government will ensure an even tighter control of that government over every aspect of its citizens' lives. The transfer of medical records, personal information, etc. over CLIN networks should be of great concern to Americans who value their right to privacy. U.S. Senator Phil Gramm of Texas (R.) has been the chairman of the board of directors for CLIN—a public-private venture.]

TEXAS RESEARCHER BILLY LYON WROTE *CONNECTIONS AND CONFLICTS OF INTEREST (OR, There Ought To Be an Investigation!)* in 1992.[22] This extraordinary piece of research, which discusses in detail the private, for-profit design team projects selected by the New American School Development Corporation (NASDC) and the connections of those involved, also presented new information on vouchers (educational "choice"). The preface is presented below in its entirety:

PREFACE

This paper began as a revision and update of the original article, "$$$ 'Choice' For Profit? $$$," about the Edison Project. Since writing that article, however, the eleven "Design Teams" have been selected by the New American School Development Corporation and the released embargoes received, giving more fodder for grist. To be perfectly honest, some of the connections were just too irresistible to ignore. Each one led to another and this paper has grown like over-leavened dough. The "Design Teams," new information from *America 2000*, proposed legislation, and a little digging in some old files, provided further insight into the voucher proposals. This paper is about vouchers (educational "choice") as much as anything, but from a different perspective. The Design Teams give you an idea of what kind of "private schools" the vouchers may eventually be used for.

For those who received the earlier "Choice for Profit?" article, Appendix A contains additional information on Time-Warner, Benno C. Schmidt and Chester Finn, Jr. The material on James S. Coleman in Appendix B is especially significant.

By no means, does this paper cover all connections, or even all the "Design Teams." We're sure that those who are left out will not be offended. A chart is enclosed which, hopefully, will help you see some of these connections.

As you read this paper, keep in mind that in the beginning of talks on education reform/restructuring, all that citizens were demanding was a return to traditional basics. They wanted their children to be able to read!

This writer has, with much difficulty, selected only a few important quotes from Billy Lyon's report. "With much difficulty" due to the report's containing nothing *but* vital information and documentation on a subject which has everything to do with our children's futures and that of our nation—"choice." Excerpts from this fine report follow:

THE EDISON PROJECT, TIME-WARNER & WHITTLE COMMUNICATIONS:

Chris Whittle's Edison Project is an initiative to build a national, private, for-profit school system. Time-Warner has been not only a full partner in the Edison Project, but owned 50% of Whittle's principal company, Whittle Communications LP. Other initial Edison Project partners and financiers were Phillips Electronics and Associated Newspapers Holdings, which agreed to spend up to $60 million for the three-year study. Team members of The Edison Project include: Yale University President Benno C. Schmidt, Jr.; Lee Eisenberg, former editor-in-chief of *Esquire* (Whittle was once co-owner); Dominique Browning, former assistant managing editor of *Newsweek Magazine*; Vanderbilt University professor and former assistant secretary of education in the Reagan Administration Chester E. Finn, Jr.; and John Chubb of the liberal Brookings Institution and Center for Education Innovation....

NASDC DESIGN TEAMS:
NASDC is the private, non-profit corporation set up by American business leaders at the request of President Bush to develop a new generation of American schools by contracting with and supporting the most promising "break the mold," "start from scratch," curricula design teams. Even though NASDC is non-profit, the eleven winning design teams are "for profit." NASDC is part of *America 2000*, President Bush's education restructuring strategy....
Clinton Administration Secretary of Education Richard W. Riley calls NASDC and *Goals 2000* (*Educate America Act*), a powerful combination for "change and improvement." NASDC Executive Management Council Chairman Kearns says the two working in partnership "will provide systemic change in education." ("NASDC FACTS," New American Schools Development Corp., no date, received 9/13/93)....
In a *Wall Street Journal* (6/5/92) article Benno Schmidt, president of the Edison Project, discussing what is wrong with present schools and how projects such as the Edison Project might improve things, claims that "schools have wavered from liberal educational purposes... leav[ing] little room for the free play of young people's curiosity... and the cultivation of the imagination...." He asked, "What might result if children came to school as toddlers or even earlier, rather than as five- or six-year-olds? What if parents were systematically involved and actually worked regularly in schools? What if students taught other students much more? What if schools were open 12 hours a day, 12 months a year? What if... a school system across the nation was completely tied together technologically, and could take advantage of systemwide experimentation?..." [What if we just taught students how to read and write well and compute 2 plus 2 without a calculator? B. Lyon]

CHESTER FINN:
Dr. Dennis Cuddy, in *Now is the Dawning of the New Age New World Order*,... said: "In the book *We Must Take Charge*, not only does Finn advocate a national curriculum, but he also writes:

> The school is the vital delivery system, the state is the policy setter (and chief paymaster), and nothing in between is very important. This formulation turns on its head the traditional American assumption that every city, town, and county bears the chief responsibility for organizing and operating its own schools as a municipal function. That is what we once meant by local control, but it has become an anachronism no longer justified by research, consistent with sound fiscal policy or organizational theory, suited to our mobility patterns, or important to the public.
>
> Every student must meet a core learning standard or be penalized, according to Finn, who says perhaps the best way to enforce this standard is to confer valuable benefits and privileges on people who meet it, and to withhold them from those who do not. Work permits, good jobs, and college admission are the most obvious, but there is ample scope here for imagination in devising carrots and sticks. Drivers' licenses could be deferred. So could eligibility for professional athletic teams. The minimum wage paid to those who earn their certificates might be a dollar an hour higher.

Cuddy refers to a U.S. Department of Education "White Paper" (probably prepared largely by Finn)... with a cover letter saying "Assessment can be used as both a carrot and stick".... Under the White Paper's section "Intervening in Academic Bankruptcy" it indicates that some school districts may be unwilling to meet their educational responsibilities, and in those cases, state intervention may mean "replacing district superintendents and local school boards with state-appointed officials." This is the same "state takeover" of local schools not meeting certain state standards that Carnegie persuaded the National Governors' Association to recommend when Lamar Alexander was its chairman in 1986.

Dr. Cuddy then reminds us that "Leading conservatives around the country were warned about the Alexander/Finn educational philosophy, but most refused to oppose the nomination of Lamar Alexander as Secretary of Education."

JOHN CHUBB:

Team member John E. Chubb, senior fellow with the Brookings Institution, was a participant at the 1989 White House Workshop on Choice in Education at which he also introduced speaker Governor Rudy Perpich of Minnesota. Chubb is on the Executive Committee of the Center for Educational Innovation, "an independent project of the Manhattan Institute for Policy Research... [whose goal]... is to improve the educational system in America by challenging conventional methods and encouraging new approaches... seeks to accomplish this through... research, discussion and dissemination directed at a broad public audience. The Center's work is made possible by grants and gifts from the following: Karen and Tucker Anderson, The Chase Manhattan Bank, Exxon Education Foundation, The Lauder Foundation, The Rockefeller Foundation and others." (From "Education Policy Paper, Number 1, Model for Choice: A Report on Manhattan's District 4, Manhattan Institute for Policy Research" included in the notebook entitled *Choosing Better Schools, Regional Strategy Meetings on Choice in Education* which came from the U.S. Department of Education, Office of Intergovernmental and Interagency Affairs, Jack Klenk, special advisor.)

John Chubb is one of a 14-member task force who issued a study that "proposed a set of bold, innovative solutions designed to bring about... improvements in Texas public schools," entitled *Choice in Education: Opportunities for Texas* (March, 1990). In addition to Chubb, "Members of the Task Force producing this study included... Dr. John Goodman, president of the National Center for Policy Analysis, Dallas; Allan Parker, associate professor of law, St. Mary's University, San Antonio; Dr. Linus Wright, former under secretary of education; Dr. Kathy Hayes, associate professor of economics; and Fritz Steiger, president, Texas Public Policy Foundation." (Texas Public Policy Foundation *REPORT*, Summer, 1990, Vol. 11, Issue 11, pages 3–4.) Dallas Eagle Forum also reportedly co-sponsored the John Chubb-Terry Moe conferences in March, 1990....

VOUCHERS ("CHOICE"), EDISON PROJECT AND NASDC DESIGN TEAMS:

Since vouchers (educational "choice") are important to the success of this scheme to "privatize" and "decentralize" education through "Design Teams," the Edison Project and other private programs, with the assistance of waivers and "flexibility," vouchers need to be examined in the new context.... Mainstream news sources have pointed out that vouchers will benefit Chris Whittle's Edison Project, as well as any "privatized" school projects. Examples are:

NEWSWEEK (6/8/92)—"There's no question that Whittle schools could be extremely rewarding... if Congress approves a voucher system...."

TIME (6/8/92)—[owned by Time-Warner]—"...the Bush Administration strongly supports the concepts that underlie the Edison Project.... Many observers believe Whittle's long-term plan anticipates the use of these (voucher) funds. If adopted, the reform (vouchers) could funnel billions of public dollars into private schools...."

CHUBB & CONSERVATIVES:

Most conservatives have been conspicuously silent on John Chubb's partnership in The Edison Project, and the benefits to be accrued from government voucher assistance. Many call this "privatization" of education, leaving the impression that it is "free market enterprise," which is absolutely ridiculous since the venture is taxpayer funded and, consequently, government controlled! Chubb's role may now be an embarrassment to those, who with great fanfare and publicity, sponsored his tour around the country extolling the virtues, but not the consequences, of education "choice." Nor were people informed of Chubb's liberal connections. And, only later did people learn of the other "designs" on "choice" money which came to light with the introduction of *America 2000*, The Edison Project, and the other for-profit programs. The Design Teams projects were probably part of a veiled plan that drove the promotion of vouchers to begin with—from top down. Before letting the cat out of the bag, however, it was necessary to garner support for the strategy, especially from Christian conservatives. "Choice" had to be sold to them as beneficial. And, so it was. Many fell for it, following certain leaders. John Chubb was at the top of the sales team.... [John Chubb is also a supporter of the Skinnerian DISTAR/Reading Mastery program developed by Siegfried Engelmann and thoroughly discussed in this book, ed.]

LAYING THE GROUNDWORK:

Regional strategy meetings on choice in education were held in the fall of 1989, following the White House Workshop on Choice in January, where John Chubb, Dennis P. Doyle, Joe Nathan, Governor Rudy Perpich of Minnesota, Governor Tommy Thompson of Wisconsin, and then-Governor of Tennessee Lamar Alexander were speakers. At the strategy meetings, research papers, position statements, and policy analyses were presented and the information compiled in a large notebook entitled, *Choosing Better Schools: Regional Strategy Meetings on Choice in Education*. The notebook contained two "Education Policy Papers," from the Center for Educational Innovation (CEI), a project of the Manhattan Institute for Policy Research. The list of CEI Executive Committee members included John Chubb, Senior Fellow, Brookings Institution, and Joe Nathan, Senior Fellow, Humphrey Institute of Public Affairs. Among the CEI supporters were... The Chase Manhattan Bank, Exxon Education Foundation... The Rockefeller Foundation.... (THIS ISN'T GRASSROOTS CONSERVATISM, FOLKS!) CEI's Education Policy Paper #2, "The Right to Choose," contained presentations by John Chubb, Joe Nathan, Chester Finn, Jr., and James S. Coleman.

James S. Coleman has been busy, too. His work penetrates the entire educational environment, including restructuring. He's been quoted in educational materials for at least 25 years. Recently, a paper by Coleman, entitled "Parental Involvement in Education," was included with the *America 2000* issues paper, "What Other Communities Are Doing, National Educational Goal #1," distributed after the third America 2000 satellite town hall meeting (7/28/92).... Coleman gives yet another reason for approving "choice," one less publicized. He said that the "choice system" would give the school more authority, making it possible to require more of parents and children by having them accept and obey a set of rules as a condition of entering and continuing in the school....

PRIVATE VOUCHERS:

Does the information just presented tell us something about the evolution of arguments for vouchers; from one of assisting those in private schools to that of aiding the poor who can't afford a private school? Does it explain why all voucher legislation/amendments are directly or indirectly connected to Title I, Chapter I of ESEA, which addresses the "Disadvantaged"? Does it suggest that the purpose of the whole scheme is "homogenization" through more integration, economically and socially... for total equality through redistribution of wealth and children, via vouchers?...

G.I. BILL FOR CHILDREN, OR INTEGRATION BY VOUCHER?
Recall these statements:

> Albert Shanker, American Federation of Teachers—"It may be that we can't get the big changes we need without choice."
>
> President George Bush—"Choice is the one reform that drives all others."
>
> Former U.S. Secretary of Education Lauro Cavazos—"President Bush and I are determined to use the power of choice to help restructure American education."

A MESSAGE FROM PRESIDENT GEORGE BUSH WAS DELIVERED REGARDING *THE NATIONAL Youth Apprenticeship Act* (House Doc. #102–320, *The Congressional Record*) on May 3, 1992. Excerpts follow:

> I am pleased to transmit herewith for your immediate consideration *The National Youth Apprenticeship Act of 1992*.... This legislation would establish a national framework for implementing comprehensive youth apprenticeship programs.... These programs would be a high-quality learning alternative for preparing young people to be valuable and productive members of the 21st century work force.... There is widespread agreement that the time has come to strengthen the connection between the academic subjects taught in our schools and the demands of the modern, high technology workplace.... Under my proposal, a student could enter a youth apprenticeship program in the 11th or 12th grade. Before reaching these grades, students would receive career and academic guidance to prepare them for entry into youth apprenticeship programs.... A youth apprentice would receive academic instruction, job training and work experience.... Standards of academic achievement, consistent with voluntary national standards, will apply to all academic instruction, including the required instruction in the core subjects of English, mathematics, science, history, and geography. Students would be expected to demonstrate mastery of job skills....
>
> My proposal provides for involvement at the Federal, State and local levels to ensure the success of the program. Enactment of my proposal will result in national standards applicable to all youth apprenticeship programs. Thus, upon the completion of the program, the youth will have a portable credential that will be recognized wherever the individual may go to seek employment or pursue further education and training....
>
> I believe that the time has come for a national, comprehensive approach to work-based learning. The bill I am proposing would establish a formal process in which business, labor, and education would form partnerships to motivate the Nation's young people to stay in school and become productive citizens.... I urge the Congress to give swift and favorable consideration to the *National Youth Apprenticeship Act of 1992*.

AN ARTICLE BY LAURA ROGERS ENTITLED "IN LOCO PARENTIS, PART II—THE 'PARENTS AS Teachers' Program Lives On" was published in the September 1992 issue of *Chronicles*.[23] Ms. Rogers rendered all Americans a great service by providing a seminal work on this totalitarian program. Excerpts from her excellent article follow:

> For the uninitiated, the PAT [Parents as Teachers] program was begun in Missouri in 1981, ostensibly for the purpose of curbing the high dropout rate and winning back parental support for the public school system. In 1985 the state legislature mandated that the PAT program be offered to all schools and children in Missouri and since then the PAT program has

been proposed in at least forty other states. Simply put, the program pivots on assigning to all parents and children a "certified parent educator." This state employee evaluates the child (under the guise of educational screening), assigns the child a computer code classification, and initiates a computer file that the state will use to track the child for the rest of his or her life. All of the computer code designations label the child to some degree "at risk," and there is no classification for "normal." The state agent conducts periodic home and school visits to check on the child and the family, dispensing *gratis* such things as nutritional counseling, mental health services, and even food. Schools under the PAT program provide free day and overnight care. The "certified parent" might forbid the biological parents to spank their child, and might prescribe, if the child is deemed "unhappy," psychological counseling or a drug such as Ritalin. If the parents refuse the recommended services or drugs, the state may remove the child from the home, place him in a residential treatment center, and force the parents to enroll in family counseling for an indefinite period.

ON NOVEMBER 11, 1992, SEVERAL DAYS AFTER THE 1992 PRESIDENTIAL ELECTION, MARC Tucker, director of the National Center on Education and the Economy in Rochester, New York, wrote a letter to Hillary Clinton on NCEE letterhead in which he outlined a lifelong, (socialist) workforce agenda, most of which—interestingly enough—had no problem being approved by a Republican-controlled Congress within three years.[24] (See Appendix XV and XVIII.) The letter's introductory paragraph stated:

> I still cannot believe you won! But utter delight that you did pervades all the circles in which I move. I met last Wednesday in David Rockefeller's [Jr.] office with him, John Sculley [Apple Computer executive] et al. It was a great celebration. Both John and David R. were more expansive than I have ever seen them—literally radiating happiness. My own view and their's is that this country has seized its last chance....
>
> ...We propose, first, that the President appoint a national council on human resource development.... It would be established in such a way to assure continuity of membership across administrations, so that the consensus it forges will outlast any one administration.... Second, we propose that a new agency be created, the National Institute for Learning, Work and Service.

AMERICAN FEDERATION OF TEACHERS AFFILIATE, THE PHILADELPHIA FEDERATION OF TEACH-ers, stated its opposition to Outcome-Based Education (OBE) in a November 20, 1992 letter to Pennsylvania state senators as follows:

> OBE should be a pilot project at best, and tested in several schools as a welcome addition to the existing Carnegie Units. It should not be implemented statewide because it could be a costly disaster. OBE has no grade designations. OBE has minimal "benchmark" designations. There are no time designations. For example, a student completes all English requirements in one and one-half years. This student is not required to further develop English skills in the remaining two and one-half years of his/her high school career. There are NO safety nets for students. OBE is really non-graded schools and non-graded classrooms. It is a very dishonest approach to slipping this whole structure into place. Parents, teachers, and students have a right to honestly discuss these very important educational plans. We would appreciate your

support in the closing days of this legislative session to block any implementation of Outcomes-Based Education here in the Commonwealth of Pennsylvania.

SCHOOL'S OUT: A RADICAL NEW FORMULA FOR THE REVITALIZATION OF AMERICA'S EDUCATional System by Lewis J. Perelman was published (Avon Books: New York, 1992). The book's cover stated that:

> Dr. Perelman earned his doctorate in social policy at the Harvard Graduate School of Education. A Senior Fellow of the Discovery Institute, he was formerly Director of Project Learning 2000—a study of restructuring education and training sponsored by nine U.S. corporations and foundations.

George Gilder, author of *Wealth and Poverty*, also recommended the book by Perelman as follows: "A compulsively readable rush to a vital new paradigm for technology and learning. You will never think of schools in the same way again" In the preface of *School's Out*, Perelman reveals that:

> Unlike others who channeled their disaffection into calls for "reform," by 1970 I was convinced that the education system could not be amended but needed to be entirely replaced by a new mechanism more attuned to the technology and social fabric of the modern world. This conclusion was nurtured by many sources, but especially influential were the works of B.F. Skinner, George Leonard and Jay Forrester. The work of Skinner and his disciples showed that the processes of learning could be analyzed, understood, and organized to serve the individual learner's needs.... Inspired by such ideas, I returned to Harvard in 1970 and spent the next three years in an intense and largely independent study of most of the key questions that underlie this book: What is learning and how does it work? What technologies can facilitate learning, and how do they work? How does learning fit in with the overall processes of human economy and ecology? And most important, how do you transform or replace established human institutions?...
>
> Of the several Harvard and MIT faculty who contributed to my exploration of these questions, I particularly benefited from the aid and encouragement of Wassily Leontief, Harvey Liebenstein, Jay Forrester, Ithiel deSola Pool, B.F. Skinner, and Paul Yivisaker.... After leaving Harvard, I continued my research for another year with support from a grant from the Rockefeller Brothers Fund and presented the results of the whole five years of study in my first book, *The Global Mind*, published in 1976. (p. 8)

[Ed. Note: In 1994 Dr. Perelman served as education specialist for the Progress and Freedom Foundation's First Annual Meeting in Atlanta, Georgia, "Cyberspace and the American Dream."[25] The Progress and Freedom Foundation published Alvin and Heidi Toffler's book, *Creating a New Civilization: The Politics of the Third Wave*, which carried a foreword by U.S. Representative and soon-to-be Speaker of the House Newt Gingrich (R., GA). On page 96 of the Toffler's book, the Progress and Freedom Foundation issued this invitation:

> If you have read and been influenced by this or by any of their works, they—and we—would like to know about it. Especially if you have ideas for how to speed the transition to a Third Wave America, please send them to us.]

1993

THE 1993 ANNUAL REPORT OF THE HERITAGE FOUNDATION OF WASHINGTON, D.C., DEDI-
cated to their twentieth year celebration, revealed the following:

> The idea of the North American Free Trade Agreement (NAFTA) originated with Heritage
> Fellow Richard Allen and has long been advocated by Heritage policy analysts.... The idea of
> creating a North American free trade zone from the Yukon to the Yucatan was first proposed
> by Heritage Distinguished Fellow Richard Allen in the late 1970s, refined by then Presidential
> candidate Ronald Reagan, and further developed in a major 1986 Heritage Foundation study.
> (p. 4)

[Ed. Note: The Free Trade Agreement got the ball rolling for the development of skills standards by the newly formed National Skills Standards Board, endorsed by the U.S. Labor Department Secretary's Commission on Achieving Necessary Skills (SCANS) study originated
under Labor Secretary Elizabeth Dole, and eventually led to the *School-to-Work Opportunities
Act* and the dumbing down of American education curriculum for workforce training. With all
of this emphasis on "standards" it should be pointed out that NAFTA allows exchanges of all
categories of professionals, with those coming from Mexico and Canada having met their own
countries' standards, not necessarily equal to those required in the United States. If this process evolves the way most of these exchange processes have in the past, that disparity will be
addressed in one of two ways—by changing U.S. standards to match foreign standards, or by
altering both NAFTA nations' standards to align with international standards like ISO 9000 or
ISO 1400 monitored by UNESCO. This should be of concern to professional organizations in
the United States.]

"SCHOOLROOM SHUFFLE: TRAILING IN EDUCATION FOR YEARS, KENTUCKY TRIES RADICAL
Reforms—Grades 1 through 3 Become One Class with No Texts, Desks or Report Cards—Some
Parents, Principals Balk" by Suzanne Alexander was published in *The Wall Street Journal* (A–
6) on January 5, 1993. Some excerpts follow:

> LEXINGTON, KENTUCKY—Teachers work in teams, using children's literature to teach spelling,
> reading and writing. For math and science, students are taught to analyze instead of memo-
> rize.
>   "We've turned education topsy-turvy," says teacher Beverly Dean, gazing around her
> classroom at children studying on pillows, a couch and a rocking chair.
>   Indeed, Kentucky has become a giant laboratory for school reform.
>   "We have redefined the basics and challenged every assumption you have about learn-
> ing," says Faye King, principal of Stanton Elementary School in eastern Kentucky. "It's radi-
> cal and its comprehensive. But we can't do any worse, so why not go for the best."...
>   In some cases, public schools themselves are resisting change. Longfellow Elementary
> Center in rural Mayfield, Ky., has postponed combining its kindergarten through third grades
> while it pleads with state officials not to force it to do so next year. "It's almost humanly
> impossible to teach when you put so many age (and ability) levels in one classroom," says
> principal Elsie Jones. She adds that without grades, parents won't know at what level their
> children are performing, and should the students move away, their new schools may have
> difficulty placing them in the appropriate grade....

Although its fourth and fifth grades remain traditional, changes in what were the lower grades (in Picadome Elementary) have transformed the atmosphere in those classrooms. "This is my 19th year of teaching, and this is my best year," says Barbara Evans, trying to keep order within groups of noisy six and seven-year-olds racing to complete math, cursive writing and art assignments with a dinosaur theme.

TOTAL QUALITY FOR SCHOOLS: A SUGGESTION FOR AMERICAN EDUCATION BY JOSEPH C. Fields was published (ASQ Quality Press: Milwaukee, Wis., 1993). This book was given to selected local school boards in districts implementing reform/restructuring. Excerpts follow:

> Educators must confront this age-old question of whom to serve and resolve this question in favor of the customer and the American culture, political system, and economic system.... (p. 19)
>
> Schools must think in terms of futures, always 10 to 20 years ahead of today. Schools that are constant in their purposes must change to meet customer requirements. Schools must deal with the problems of today as well as the problems of tomorrow to assure Americans that they will be in the education business of the future. As the number of private schools increases, as school vouchers and schools of choice develop, and as schools take on more and more social responsibilities, it is questionable whether or not certain schools will be in business in the future....
>
> Businesses will not buy from uncertified vendors. This idea might contain some merit for educators. The state of Tennessee, in its original Career Ladder Program for educators, required a portfolio of specifications, quality assurances, work standards, and process control in addition to several site visits from evaluators who were unfamiliar with the evaluated teacher. Consider too the "parent as vendor" of a precious resource, the child. In the internal customer concept, the parent is serving the teacher. Teachers could identify reasonable specifications for parents relative to the home learning environment and certify parents who will cooperate. (p. 48)

[Ed. Note: The above statement is absolutely appalling! In the words of Cynthia Weatherly in her article "Privatization or Socialization?":

> We are misled when we believe that education is a commodity or service to be "purchased" by "consumers." This tends to make the public believe that education is market-driven. Compulsory attendance laws make education anything but market-driven! More importantly, the concept of consumer/purchaser does not correlate to our relationship to our elected officials who are legal overseers of the process. Have we lost sight of what our relationship to government is? Education is a trust, not a commodity. These are our children, and their futures; parents are not "shopping" for education, but are fervently searching for someone to whom they are willing to entrust the task of providing an academic education for their children.
>
> As charter schools develop, the temptation will be for private industry to take a more direct role in funding and developing programs for these schools which will produce workers who can fill the corporations' needs. These schools, then, have the potential of becoming "corporate academies" with a narrow focus and limited curriculum base. This is accomplished through the school-business partnerships growing into corporate funding to accomplish its task. As this potential reality develops, the specter of true socialism—the combining of the private and public sectors to produce goods and services—takes on discernible size and shape....

B.F. Skinner once mused that the functions of government in the future would be educational. In the above scenario we see that the reverse of that prediction can be true as well—in the future the functions of education will be governmental. Let us remember that the true purpose of education is the intrinsic enhancement of the individual. Let us not reduce education to limited learning for lifelong labor and our great country's heritage of freedom to a footnote in history.

In addition, at the Sixth Annual Model Schools Conference—sponsored by Willard Daggett, director of the International Center for Leadership in Education—in Atlanta, Georgia in July of 1998, a participant who is an assistant principal at a middle school in Southern California made this comment to a reporter regarding mechanisms to encourage parental involvement and support in the education of children:

> One way to make sure that parents attend conferences at school and support the educational process for their children would be to dock a certain part of their tax deduction for their children. There could be a scale of activities in which the parents would be required to have documentation—perhaps a sign-off at the school—of participation before they would be allowed to claim their tax deductions for their children. I agree with Daggett that we may have to employ some measures that seem extreme.[26]

Returning to a final quote from *Total Quality for Schools: A Suggestion for American Education*:

> In all this interpretation, schools are not free. They require responsible commitment from everyone. Citizens would no more be allowed to put obstacles in the way of public educators than to interfere with public medical, police, or fire protection personnel who are doing their duty. (p. 53)]

IN 1993 THE U.S. DEPARTMENT OF EDUCATION'S NATIONAL CENTER FOR EDUCATIONAL Statistics (NCES) described in a handout a joint project between NCES and the Council of Chief State School Officers (CCSSO) to develop an electronic data link between education and the "world of work" called "SPEEDE Express." This linking process would facilitate local "industry partnerships" and would prepare for the use of an "international standard" for exchanging student records.[27] An excerpt from the handout follows:

> In 1989, building on projects completed in Florida and Texas,[28] work began on the development of a national (eventually, an international) standard for exchanging student records more efficiently. This system would tap into the sophisticated automation of many education agencies and institutions. The Standardization of Postsecondary Education Electronic Data Exchange (SPEEDE) is intended to assist school districts (grades pre-kindergarten through 12 and postsecondary educational institutions in the United States and Canada) in the process of transmitting student academic records (transcripts) from one educational institution, agency, corporation, or other recipient.

M. DONALD THOMAS'S "PLAN FOR ACTION" ENTITLED *THE EMPOWERED EDUCATIONAL SYS-*
tem for the 21st Century—Establishing Competitiveness, Productivity, Accountability and Eq-

uity in South Carolina Education was presented to the South Carolina legislature in 1993. Included among other radical recommendations in Thomas's plan was: "Board authority to require parents (guardians) to provide services to schools which their children attend."

In a videotape of Thomas making these assertions at a school board meeting, a parent asked the question, "What would the penalty be if parents didn't wish to perform such services?" Thomas responded, "Fifty dollars!" He then went on to claim that he had instituted such a requirement in a school system in Utah without resistance.[29]

PETER SHAW WROTE "THE COMPETITIVENESS ILLUSION: DOES OUR COUNTRY NEED TO BE Literate in Order to Be Competitive? If not, Why Read?" for the January 18, 1993 issue of *The National Review*. The following quotes are from page 41:

> The technological society does not particularly depend on education. A glance at the record shows us that the rapid growth of the United States into the world's greatest industrial power coincided with a steady drop in reading levels running from 1930 to the present. Regna Lee Wood a teacher, pointed out in an article in *NR* (Sept. 14th) that this falling off was followed by a related, long decline in SAT scores beginning in 1941. Technological society turns out to work in the opposite way from that usually supposed: namely, by actually requiring less rather than more education of its workers. This is because modern industry depends on reducing human error, which means reducing dependence on the individual worker's expertise and judgment. In building or maintaining electronic devices, workers who once installed or rewired electrical circuits now plug in modular components consisting of machine-printed circuit boards.... The future role of literacy in the workplace has been succinctly stated by Pierre Dogan, the president of Granite Communications, a company that is now "developing software for hotel housekeeping." It seems that "so long as maids can read room numbers, they will be able to check off tasks completed or order supplies by simply touching pictures on the screen." Dogan points out that "you can create a work program with prompting including iconic [picture] messages." In fact, he logically concludes, "you can use an illiterate workforce."

[Ed. Note: This article provides an excellent explanation of why large multinational corporations such as BMW's owner, Mercedes-Benz, etc., are settling in those states which have for many years been used as national pilot/experimental laboratory states for Skinnerian mastery learning/training in leisure and life/work skills. Among those states are Southern states which were part of the early General Education Board's "benevolent effort" to reform the South after the Civil War, including Alabama, Mississippi and South Carolina (present Secretary of Education Richard Riley's home state which has produced the second lowest standardized test scores in the nation).

These states are also a part of the Southern Regional Education Board (SREB) consortium, which has produced and dispersed an educational approach called "techademics" outlined in a program and book entitled *High Schools That Work*, written by Dr. Gene Bottoms of the SREB. (Bottoms was once employed by the Georgia Department of Education when Georgia was implementing competency-based education, the forerunner of outcome-based education, and later ran for state superintendent, unsuccessfully.)

In 1994 Dr. Bottoms addressed the Second Model Schools Conference in Atlanta—sponsored by the International Center for Leadership in Education, Inc. and directed by Dr. Willard Daggett—explaining how the *High Schools That Work* model operated through integrating academic and vocational studies. As Dr. Bottoms explained, a survey by the Committee for Economic Development had revealed that students preparing to go to work right out of high school had an inflated opinion of their abilities. "Techademics" seeks to integrate academic subjects with vocational subjects by eliminating the theoretical aspects of these courses (such as English, math and science) which would be taught in college preparatory classes, and uses instead Daggett's "Application Model" to learn how to apply this information directly to work-related tasks. In Dr. Bottoms's words: "To significantly improve the achievement of vocational completers, SREB and its partners believe that any model for integrating academic and vocational studies must change the high school's focus from ability as the key to academic success to effort as the key" (direct quote from page 110 of the *Second Model Schools Conference Proceedings*).

Some additional quotes from Dr. Bottoms's address to the participants at the Model Schools Conference bear repeating here for the light they may shed on the integration of educational reform as such reform relates to charter schools/choice and "techademics":

> Take language arts, math, science, and vocational teachers off for a three-day weekend together. Take their books and make them find common materials they teach. Break down barriers of ignorance and form a team....
>
> ...Teams went into industries to see what business needs....
>
> ...Decentralization and site-based management are the keys. These schools stretch time on task—standards firm but time flexible. Need a longer day, week, and year for extra help....
>
> ...Basic principle: an ungraded academic core with a career emphasis. The NAEP is used in measuring achievement....
>
> ...Each student has the same English teacher for four years....
>
> Can't carry out Deming's principles in present structure—must change to accommodate TQM.... Break out of state cultures—cross state lines!]

MIKHAIL GORBACHEV, FORMER PRESIDENT OF THE SOVIET UNION, WAS QUOTED IN AN ARticle in the January 23, 1993 issue of *The Cape Cod* (Massachusetts) *Times* as recommending that President Bill Clinton make America the creator of a new world order based on consensus—thereby placing the United States under the authority of the United Nations. Gorbachev was later named the "convening chair" and host of a world forum on the "first global civilization" held in San Francisco from September 27–October 1 in 1995. The article quoted Gorbachev as follows:

> The future needs... international institutions acting on behalf of all. A higher institution that operates on a consensus. Such a choice would narrow the independence many believe the United States now enjoys.... President Clinton will be a success if he uses American influence to accomplish the transformation of international responsibility and increase significantly the role of the United Nations.... He will be a great President—if he can make America the creator of a new world order based on consensus.

IN THE UNITED STATES COALITION FOR EDUCATION FOR ALL'S (USCEFA) PUBLICATION *EFA Today* January-March, 1993 issue, Russell Bong of the National Training Laboratory's Institute for Applied Behavioral Science (NTL) wrote an article entitled "Overcoming Resistance and Facilitating Change: The NTL Institute's Approach."[30] An extraordinarily blatant, and some might consider frightening, explanation of the purpose of the National Training Laboratory can be found in the following excerpted material:

> Founded in 1947, the NTL Institute was affiliated with the National Education Association during its first 20 years of operation. The Institute became independent in 1967 and today serves as a nonprofit professional membership organization of applied behavioral science experts.... Dedicated to developing and applying scientific methods to behavior modification, the Institute facilitates productive change at the individual, social, organizational, and macro-system levels....
>
> To elaborate, attitudes are primarily shaped by values and beliefs, which, in turn, are shaped by both perceptions and misperceptions. NTL's approach seeks to fundamentally change personal attitudes, which it does by reshaping underlying beliefs and by eliminating dysfunctional misperceptions....
>
> It all comes down to a basic tenet: In order to facilitate change on a larger level, individuals must first work for change on a personal level. To become a true and effective agent of change, one must facilitate change within oneself.

IN 1993 DR. BEAU FLY JONES, A SENIOR DIRECTOR OF THE NORTH CENTRAL REGIONAL Educational Laboratory (NCREL) in Oak Brook, Illinois and a strong advocate and practitioner of Skinnerian mastery learning, wrote "The Unfolding of an International Partnership: A Story of Russia and the U.S." published in *EFA Today* (No. 2, January–March, 1993). Excerpts follow which illustrate the extent of controversial exchange activities due to the 1985 U.S.-Soviet and Carnegie-Soviet agreements in education:

> Well-designed exchanges often involve strong emotions, including caring, empathy, and the excitement of discovery, and individuals may return from such exchanges not only with cognitive paradigm shifts, but also with life-changing values and interests.
>
> This has been the case with the NCREL involvement in Russia.
>
> In January 1992, the Russian Ministry of Education assumed control of the former Soviet Ministry's responsibilities. Dr. Edward Dneprov, the new minister, initiated massive reforms focusing on decentralization, democratization, and the demilitarization of the Russian school system.
>
> NCREL's relationship with the new Russian Ministry began with an invitation to join the Metropolis Project, a collaboration among schools in Chicago, Moscow, and Amsterdam. The objective of the Project is to identify and develop successful models of systemic change in an urban context. To this end, the Project involves research, training, and exchanges of school staff in the three cities. Themes that guide these efforts are authentic learning, global education and strategic teaching....
>
> ...Metropolis schools were being selected, and one of the highlights of the delegation's February tour was the signing of a Letter of Cooperation between the Russian Ministry and the Chicago Public Schools....
>
> Existing exchanges between the U.S. and Russia tend to focus on university students or the teaching of foreign languages. For that reason, one of the major problems in obtaining funding for the Metropolis Project was that it involved a new level of exchange, this time between Russia and U.S. teachers and administrators, as well as a change in the nature of the exchange, which would focus on school reform and school-based training.

JAMES COLLINS AND MARTIN HABERMAN ECHOED EUGENE BOYCE IN THE FEBRUARY 1993 issue of *The Journal of Associating Teacher Educators* in an article entitled "The Future of the Teaching Profession" when they said:

> Schooling is now seen as primarily job training and, for this reason, quite comparable to schooling in non-democratic societies. Once education is redefined as a personal good and as emphasizing preparation for this world of work as its first purpose, our schools can appropriately be compared with those in the U.S.S.R.[31]

THE *READING* [PENNSYLVANIA] *EAGLE/TIMES* OF MARCH 2, 1993 CARRIED AN ARTICLE entitled "Deming Lashes out in Live Teleconference on Quality" by Don Spatz. Excerpts follow:

> It wasn't supposed to happen. Featuring the famous Dr. W. Edwards Deming, last week's live video conference among 900 colleges and universities—including Kutztown University—was supposed to be an agreeable session touting the benefits of "Creating Learning Organizations: Growth through Quality." Instead it turned into a running battle between Deming and the other panelists. They dropped Deming's name for everything they espoused; Deming said they were "digging as deep a pit for education as they have for business."...
>
> "They need to understand where they (workers) fit in the total process," said Peter Senge, author and director of the Organizational Learning Center at the Massachusetts Institute of Technology's Sloan School of Management. "The rule is to facilitate a learning environment where people can grow and change."
>
> But there the agreement seemed to end.
>
> Senge and his panelists spoke at length of how the organization works because of the way "we think and interact; of how companies should no longer have boss and workers but rather should have leadership throughout the organization; of everyone constantly asking questions of everyone else; of not expecting an outsider to come in and fix things but of expecting workers themselves to solve problems."
>
> And they spoke of everyone being given the ability to speak—through a series of dialogues—and to share their own answers to problems at any level of the organization.
>
> "There's a deep desire within us to re-establish our ability to converse with each other," Senge said.
>
> Deming agreed the basis for any negotiation is for everybody to win. "But having everybody talk does not produce knowledge," he said. "That only comes from hard work, and usually comes from outside the organization," he said. "You are digging deeper this pit we are in," he said. "Having everybody involved is not going to do it."
>
> Senge noted employees' morale will rise if they are involved.
>
> "That's not a measure of improvement," Deming retorted. "That (discussion) will not produce anything new. It will just dig the pit deeper."...
>
> Later, when panelists said they wanted to expand the concept of education, they noted the system of giving tests and letter grades is outmoded. Deming interrupted, noting their philosophy is "just as destructive in education as it has been in industry."

THE MARCH 3, 1993 ISSUE OF *EDUCATION WEEK* RAN THE ARTICLE "CENTER LISTS SKILLS Both Disabled, Non-Disabled Should Have." An excerpt follows:

A federally funded research center has unveiled a list of academic and life skills it says all students—disabled as well as non-disabled—should have upon leaving school. The wide-ranging list compiled by the National Center for Educational Outcomes at the University of Minnesota includes 25 outcomes for what young people should gain from school and 77 indicators of whether those outcomes are being achieved. "We ought to be trying to achieve the best possible outcomes for all kids," said James E. Ysseldyke, the director of the Center. "We shouldn't have a separate system of outcomes and educators for disabled kids."... The life skills identified by the Center include the ability to get along with others, to be responsible for one's self, and to successfully manage daily life. Upon leaving school, the indicators say students should be able to make "healthy lifestyle choices," to cope with stresses, and to volunteer in their communities, among other outcomes.

[Ed. Note: The above makes sense in light of the fact that "scientific research-based" (behaviorist/operant conditioning) direct, systematic phonics (DISTAR or Reading Mastery) is the phonics reading program developed *for* special education students, which will be used for *all* students under the *Reading Excellence Act of 1998* passed by Congress. This also foreshadows the emphasis on full funding for the *Individuals with Disabilities in Education Act* (IDEA) in the 1999 debates over the reauthorization of the *Elementary and Secondary Education Act* (ESEA).]

THE APRIL 14, 1993 DRAFT OF THE *MICHIGAN HIGH SCHOOL PROFICIENCY COMMUNICAtions Arts Frameworks* was published. Excerpts follow:

Use Literature to Broaden Experiences
To attain this goal literature is used:
- to examine beliefs and attitudes.
- to reshape students' thoughts by having them interact with other people and cultures who may have diverse perspectives.
- to converse with other minds about important and significant issues.
- to learn about human conditions that occur across time and space.
- to gain insights into and reflect upon their own and others' lives. (p. 37)

[Ed. Note: The first two "purposes" for the use of literature were removed in the 1994 *Final Assessment Framework for the Michigan High School Proficiency Test in Reading* due to controversy. Please check the 1994 entry on Michigan's *Communication Arts Framework* for an excellent explanation of the real purpose of whole language reading instruction.]

"INTEREST IN CHARACTER EDUCATION SEEN GROWING" WAS PUBLISHED IN THE MAY 1993 issue of the Association for Supervision and Curriculum Development's (ASCD) *Education Update*. Some excerpts follow regarding the move to develop programs which will be acceptable to the public while hopefully not resulting in lawsuits filed under the *First Amendment to the U.S. Constitution* over separation of church and state. According to ASCD:

The subject of controversy and confusion in the last several decades, character education is making a resurgence in public schools. This movement is built on a growing consensus in favor of teaching a set of traditional or "core" ethical values in a more direct way.

Experts tracking this trend say the character education movement is growing in response to pressure placed on schools both to reduce student antisocial behavior—including drug use and violence—and to produce more respectful and responsible citizens.

The reawakening is occurring "because people are banging on the schoolhouse door," says Kevin Ryan, director of the Boston University Center for the Advancement of Ethics and Character. "The invitation is coming from outside. Parents and policymakers are disturbed by a total inability of our culture to pass on its values."

Thomas Lickona, an author and professor of education at the State University of New York at Cortland, sees the motivating force as a "growing national sense of moral crisis and what people speak of as a steady moral decline." Some of the causes being discussed are the breakdown of the family, the failure of adults to exercise moral leadership, and the abandonment of ethics at all levels. Society is now turning back to schools to transmit positive moral values. Gallup Polls provide one indication of the growing support for school-based values education; polls in each of the last several years show that parents strongly agree that schools need to provide instruction on morals and moral behavior.

But even with broadening public support, some schools may be reluctant to adopt explicit values curriculum partly because of the checkered past of values education and the fear of creating conflict with religious and ethnic groups over whose values to teach.

THE *EFFECTIVE SCHOOL REPORT*'S MAY 1993 ISSUE CARRIED "DIALOGUES IN INTERNA-tional Education" by Nick Zienau which discussed a conference in Sochi, Russia organized by the Ministry of Russia and a Norwegian network known as IMTEC which works with the U.S. Department of Education's Midcontinent Regional Educational Laboratory (McREL), the developer of *Tactics for Thinking*. The writer has selected the following curious excerpts which indicate that some fairly weird activities are taking place in Russia dealing with education and brain research, activities in which European and American educators are involved:

> Even organising a conference seemed beyond the capacity of the Ministry of Education itself! Some Westerners even left in impatience at the dreadful lack of movement in either the practical organisation of the event or in moving the discussions on beyond what seemed to them endless bizarre philosophical ramblings.
>
> So after 3 days in Russia, I was amazed when in a shoddy hotel in Sochi on the Black Sea, I first heard a young woman speak about Educational Cultures, alternative schools and with passion about philosophy and pedagogy.
>
> As Tatyana Kovalyova talked about her school in Tomsk with 25 teachers and 25 philosophers working together, I realized what an enormously different value is placed in Russia on education than in a rich West where 30 kids are likely to get one teacher between them. I could also see what an impact this had on the degree to which very fundamental processes of learning were understood and experimented with.
>
> ...Active physicists and intellectuals seemed to be there as well as professional teachers, schools in which university staff taught seven-year-olds mathematics! And yet they were really interested in how children and people learn as a science—they kept talking about research they were doing.... Their continuous interest in research reminded me of TV plays about Crick and Watson researching the structure of DNA or the Manhattan project in the war when a team of scientists searching [sic] for the key to atomic bombs before the Germans got them. It was that same feeling of being in at the moment of discovery of some basic understanding of how the world works....
>
> A lot of stuff is written in Europe about the ideas of the "learning organisation" but it

was in Russia that I really found out what such a thing feels like. In Europe I believe we have always been restricted in these principles of learning by the resistance to new thinking that adults develop. In Russia and in particular in Eureka [Russian term for large teacher professional development seminars] I found a whole-hearted commitment to change and development that both impressed me and at times alarmed me.

There is a kind of ruthlessness which seems associated with doing anything quite so singlemindedly, and so it is with Eureka. In the Russian context it seems rather natural that such a complete and radical approach to change is now possible. The question that I think Alexander and his colleagues confront us with is how far are we in the West really prepared to look at our basic assumptions and the evidence that things need to change?...

Firstly, there seems an overwhelming need internationally to improve and develop the education system to prepare the next generation for a hugely different world.... The ending of the cold war makes it possible to reunite threads of thinking and development in education and learning that have been long kept separate.

...We believe we have reached a point of synergy between our team in the West and that of Alexander in the East that will result in an innovative new step in group learning for educators and those interested in the subject of learning systems.

In the end, my best recommendation must be that I see the seminar in California as a further challenge, a further opportunity to develop together and a real chance to be at the cutting edge of development towards a 21st century that I want to be around in. Hope to see you all there.

(Nick Zienau is a senior partner in Zienau Consulting which together with Cascade International of San Francisco is organising the seminar. The Russian partner in this enterprise is Eureka Free University, Moscow.)

SUSTAINABLE AMERICA: A NEW CONSENSUS FOR PROSPERITY, OPPORTUNITY AND HEALTHY Environment for the Future was published in 1993 by the President's Council on Sustainable Development. In chapter 3, "Information and Education," under a subtitle "Reforming Formal Education" the report says:

Educating for sustainability does not follow academic theories according to a single discipline but rather emphasizes connections among all subject areas, as well as geographic and cultural relationships....

Education for sustainability is not an add-on curriculum—that is, it is not a new core subject like math or science. Instead, it involves an understanding of how each subject relates to environmental, economic, and social issues.

AN INTERVIEW WITH KEN HAZLIP AND JAMES BLOCK WAS INCLUDED IN THE FALL 1993 issue of *Outcomes*, the Outcome-Based Education movement's journal mentioned in previous entries in this book. Excerpts from that interview follow:

Jim: To stay on this point about labels, this movement, this idea set, has made several choices of labels. At one time it was called Mastery Learning, another Outcomes-Based Education, and now Partners for Quality Learning. Yet much of what has driven this movement under the OBE label has not changed from Mastery Learning and what has changed still comes from the research done under the Mastery Learning rubric. Will this new Quality Learning label stimulate a better idea base than the old label OBE?

Ken: I doubt it. The power of our movement still derives from the original Mastery Learning idea....

Jim: When we were a Mastery Learning movement, we were concerned with schools and school districts. As we move to quality, we start to see linkages between school and the workplace....

Ken: Our school environment certainly does not look like this. The irony of the linkages you describe is that we will have to look to industry to "fix" problems that we have imported from old industrial practices because we were trying so hard to look like factories years ago.

Jim: I am a little surprised by your response. It seems to me that one of the characteristics of the workplace is that it is organized to produce a product.... Surely you are not arguing that the workplace and the workworld is the same kind of place that we should generate for kids in our schools?

Ken: Again, it depends on the level of health that the workplace presents us.

Jim: So what we are in the business of doing is just generating little workers? Where do the kids come into the equation of this process?

Ken: Kids should drive the terms forming the equation. We should be looking at them and their needs to determine how best to work with them, not forcing them into the mould our traditional classrooms and traditional methods require.... Most workplaces are still 180 degrees away from this, however—they are negative, coercive, demanding. But many in the American workplace are reinventing or reengineering that workplace. Many are beginning to look at the "old" research that John Champlin mentioned in our summer interview—Getzels and Guba and their organizational development work, Herzberg's motivation-hygiene work, and Deming's ideas [TQM]. In reinventing the workplace, they believe it can be caused to be both productive and satisfying for the worker. We can create that in the classroom and have kids who are challenged, motivated, and excited to be there....

Jim: ...Our movement has based its efforts on the research, but apparently the research in this case is perceived as either out of date or out of fashion. Why do we need to look outside to industry for models that we have described inside the ML/OBE field?

Ken: So many of the concepts presented by business gurus about workplace change are summed up very well in Mastery Learning's basic beliefs.

Jim: Is it that people within the Mastery or the Outcomes movement can only go so far, or do we need a swift kick from the outside?

Ken: As far as our mental models go, experience and environment have put burdensome blinders on us, and many will not see the implications of ideas until they are approached from a different perspective. I would rather we did not need so many detours, but if Deming gets us closer to better schools, then we "do" Deming. I incorporated his ideas and many business models when I was directing a district's restructuring efforts. We all want the research to drive our efforts, but our movement's Mastery Learning research exists in a broader context, and education research just does not have a lot of credibility among too many educators. The reasons are mostly poor ones, but they exist nonetheless and form a real barrier to change. If Deming presents an idea without the research prejudice baggage attached, I will start with Deming and end up teaching the group about the research.

A LETTER FROM LAWRENCE W. LEZOTTE, PUBLISHER OF *EFFECTIVE SCHOOLS RESEARCH Abstracts*, was written to his colleagues in September, 1993. An excerpt follows:

First, whether or not you have been engaged in this debate as yet, you need to become familiar with the concerns and issues of the Christian Coalition. You must be prepared to respond to its challenges, which are often based on half truths and misinformation. These issues must be carefully and clearly explained to those citizens who wish to hear the educators' point of view. This will require all of us to be familiar with the research on such important topics as Mastery Learning, Continuous Progress, and De-Tracking—to mention just a few. Second, to develop mainstream community involvement, I strongly recommend that school and district leaders create a task force to study the issues related to school reform and be prepared to present their views along with the views that will be presented by the Christian Coalition. I truly believe that if educators have to debate the coalition alone, more often than not, educators will lose the debate on school reform. We need to make sure that a broad cross-section of our citizens are involved in the important debate on the future of public education and, in turn, the future of our nation.

[Ed. Note: While this author thinks it is remarkable that Dr. Lezotte would admit to being at a disadvantage in combatting "resisters," it is somewhat unfortunate that he should give credit to only one organization as being responsible for the opposition which restructuring has encountered. A broad cross-section of the country—including teachers and administrators in public schools—has been in the camp of the "resisters" when it comes to restructuring. The writer finds it hard to believe that the educational establishment—with the extraordinary resources at its disposal—was unable to obtain the support of the community, and found it necessary to use Ronald Havelock's change agentry on the citizenry.

In writing this letter Lezotte evidently fired the first shot of warning to the education community, for not six months after Lezotte's letter was written, a researcher downloaded from the internet the National Education Goals Panel's *Community Action Toolkit*, which contained instructions for combatting community resistance to restructuring. It provided recommendations for action by specific community entities—the press, civic organizations, religious entities, and business—and samples of letters to the editor, advertisements, supportive flyers, and public service announcements, for use in building support for local educational restructuring. One of the most distasteful results of this effort was the recommended manipulation of the religious community. (See Appendix XIV.)]

THE IMPACT ON EDUCATION OF THE UNITED STATES SIGNING THE NORTH AMERICAN FREE Trade Agreement was discussed in an article entitled "USIA's Grants Go to Schools in NAFTA Nations" published in the September 12, 1993 edition of *The Washington Times*. Some excerpts follow:

> United States Information Agency Director Joseph Duffey attending a four-day "implementation" conference at Vancouver, British Columbia, yesterday announced the first North American three-way university affiliation grants to involve exchanges of faculty and staff among Canadian, Mexican and U.S. universities for teaching, lecturing, research and curriculum development.
>
> "We often have university affiliation grants," Mr. Duffey said in an interview before he left for Vancouver. "This is the first time we've decided to start awarding three or four a year that involved three countries in North America."... Each USIA award will carry about $100,000, plus travel and per diem expenses, for exchanges of faculty, administrators and educational materials.

The agreement, part of the broadened dialogue that has come out of the North American Free Trade Agreement, will support an array of projects focused on history, economic development, international trade and the environment.

"What we seek to do is, among other things, nothing less than dismantling barriers to academic mobility," Mr. Duffey said in a speech at the conference.

Mr. Duffey said he expects the North American countries to succeed in achieving a sense of regional community where the quest for a common community of nations in Western Europe has foundered.

"We're trying to reverse the tradition of nationalism and people, who in looking to their identity, look backwards to the past," he said. "Instead, we want them to look to the future." (p. A–5)

THE FOLLOWING LETTER FROM UTAH GOVERNOR MICHAEL O. LEAVITT AND HIS STATE SU-perintendent of Public Instruction Scott W. Bean, dated September 30, 1993, gave a clear picture of the role of the governors of the individual states in implementing United Nations Educational, Scientific and Cultural Organization's (UNESCO) lifelong learning "cradle-to-grave" agenda in the United States. Utah's state report, "A Utah Perspective on the National Education Goals," was written and edited by Dr. David E. Nelson of the Utah State Office of Education who was also involved in the 1984 Utah OBE grant. Some excerpts follow:

At the education summit in Charlottesville, Virginia, in September 1989, the nation's governors agreed to establish national education goals and a system to assess and monitor progress toward achieving them. Today, September 30, 1993, the anniversary of the historic summit, the National Education Goals Panel will issue its third annual education report. The report will focus on national and state progress toward achieving the education goals set in 1990 by the President and the governors. This progress report will inform the nation on how well we are doing on each of the goals. The governors also agreed to report individually on efforts of their respective states related to their state's performance toward achieving the national goals.

Our own report, "A Utah Perspective on the National Education Goals," is issued to citizens of the state of Utah to inform them on the progress being made in our state toward the national goals. Because the goals are "cradle to grave" and cover the preschool years and the after school years, the information has been compiled from many state agencies. Meeting all of these six goals will require the coordination and work of all state agencies.

IN LONNIE HARP'S ARTICLE "WIDELY MIXED TEST RESULTS LEAVE SOME IN KENTUCKY Puzzled," which appeared in *Education Week*'s October 13, 1993 issue, the problems with the national reform leader's implementation of its widely-acclaimed restructuring—*Kentucky Education Restructuring Act* (KERA)—were outlined. An excerpt follows:

As Kentucky moves toward implementation of its path-breaking system of rewards and sanctions for schools, state students have handed officials a hard-to-read snapshot of the progress of reform.

Results of the second year of a new open-ended assessment system, released last month, produced widely mixed results and, in the case of older students, some troubling declines.

THE NOVEMBER 15, 1993 ISSUE OF *THE ATLANTA CONSTITUTION* CARRIED AN ARTICLE entitled "Ware Students Are Drawn to Swampy Experiment: Magnet School Makes Okefenokee Its Lab." Outlining what could be interpreted as the use of magnet/charter schools in a school-to-work scenario, excerpts follow:

> The Ware County School of Agriculture, Environmental and Forestry Sciences is an experiment in educational excellence that was years in the dreaming and application-pending stages.
> The concept was to create a magnet school unlike any other in the Southeast, a school where the study of sciences most important to the surrounding land would be incorporated into almost all the curricula. That would produce graduates oriented toward the disciplines most needed by employers in the region's forestry and agriculture industries.

IN 1993 *THE SCHOOL TO WORK OPPORTUNITIES ACT* PASSED THE HOUSE OF REPRESENTATIVES without a roll call vote. [It passed the Senate in 1994, ed.] This legislation called for Soviet/German full employment/quota-type system, incorporating the Danish model for polytech education. Anyone familiar with this legislation will recognize the similarity between its wording and the late Professor Eugene Boyce's definition of communist polytech education (found in this book's 1983 entry for *The Coming Revolution in Education)* which states that the communists "do not educate people for jobs that do not exist. No such direct, controlled relationship between education and jobs exists in democratic countries."

IN A CRITIQUE OF H.R. 6—*THE ELEMENTARY AND SECONDARY EDUCATION REAUTHORIZATION Act of 1993*—Cynthia Weatherly wrote in a memo to this writer:

> HR 6 is an omnibus bill originally presented to Congress in January 1993 as a reauthorization bill for *The Elementary and Secondary Education Act of 1965*. The first and last paragraphs of this 901–page tome are the only parts of the original bill which remain. 886 pages are printed in italics, which means that there are 886 pages of new language, otherwise known as "new law." *Goals 2000* and the National Education Goals Panel form the framework for HR 6. All of the education proposals in HR 6 are constructed in such a way as to cause "the nation to meet the national education goals." Therefore, instead of a reauthorization bill for *ESEA 1965*, HR 6 becomes the implementation bill for *Goals 2000* and the School-to-Work bills. One of the most controversial components included in HR 6 deals with basic pedagogy in which the framers deny the need for basic skills acquisition before engaging in more complex tasks. References to more controversial components follow:
>
>> [T]he "disproven theory that children must learn basic skills before engaging in more complex tasks continues to dominate strategies for classroom instruction, resulting in emphasis on repetitive drill and practice at the expense of content-rich instruction, accelerated curricula, and effective teaching to high standards. Use of low-level tests that are not aligned with curricula fails to provide adequate information about what children know and can do and encourages curricula and instruction that focus on the low-level skills measured by such tests.
>>
>> [H.R. 6] Provides for restructuring of our nation's education and social services delivery systems.... Local schools may use federal funds to serve as centers for delivery of education and human services for members of the community; unaccountable consolidation of

programs; waivers of laws, outcome-based education language and practices; parents as partners skill training; i.e. "All parents can contribute to their children's success by helping at home and becoming partners with teachers so that children can achieve high standards." Requires school-parent compacts that outline how parents, staff and students will share responsibility for student achievement and means by which school and parents will build and develop a partnership, etc.; facilitates school-to-work transition; encouragement to pursue public school choice, and development of charter schools.

WELCOME NEWS ON THE OUTCOME-BASED EDUCATION FRONT WAS REPORTED IN AN ARTICLE entitled "In Littleton, Colorado, Voters Expel Education Faddists," which appeared in the November 18, 1993 issue of *The Wall Street Journal*. Excerpts from this article which illustrate how David overcame Goliath in the late twentieth century and reveal the extent of controversy raging in Littleton over its school system's adoption of "outcomes-based education" (OBE) follow:

> There [Littleton, CO.], a slate of three "back-to-basics" candidates crushed another coalition, including two incumbents, that supported a host of trendy educational reforms and was backed by the educational establishment. All 15 principals, for example, released an open letter to voters denouncing the insurgent slate. Yet the margin of victory was nearly 2 to 1. What had so galvanized voters? The fact that their district is a national leader in implementing "outcome-based education" (OBE) and that officials there had, as the journal *Education Week* explained in a pre-election article acknowledging the contests' significance, "pioneered new performance assessments and standards for high school graduation."
>
> ...Having acknowledged that American schools are in need of improvement, a growing number of educators are gravitating toward the view that the fault lies in too much emphasis on "content knowledge" and not enough concern, to quote the Littleton principal again, with "decision-making skills, thinking skills, and the ability to find and use information." Or, to quote the Littleton elementary principals' letter, students "must do more than spell and compute. They must be able to reason, persuade and solve problems."
>
> Nevertheless, OBE proponents, with their emphasis on "thinking skills," repeatedly contrast their theory with an approach that hasn't been in vogue for decades, one of perpetual rote learning in which all creativity is stifled. *Education Week* is typical in presenting this caricature. It described the Littleton reforms as nothing more than encouraging students "to focus on problem-solving rather than memorization"—as if a nation in which only 32% of 17-year-olds in a 1986 survey could place the Civil War in the correct half-century was in danger of stuffing too many facts into students' heads.
>
> Across America, school districts are considering, or putting in place, reforms similar to those in Littleton. Educators, often with the best of intentions, are rewriting report cards to include fuzzy criteria such as self-esteem and interpersonal relationships. They are denigrating standardized measurements of knowledge and the memorization of facts. To be sure, not all of the rethinking is misguided, but some of it amounts to dubious experimentation on children. Littleton proves that with the proper candidates, the movement toward a vague, "skill-oriented" curriculum can be stopped in its tracks.

[Ed. Note: Very regrettably the above refreshing and impressive victory over the bureaucracy was short-lived. Slick change agent tactics managed to bring at least one new supposedly anti-reform, back-to-basics board member "on board" what one hoped to be a sinking ship, thus assuring a return to implementation of the "nationally-detested" OBE. Littleton, Colorado became one of Willard Daggett's Model School systems and a national model for implementation of outcome-based education.

Six years later Littleton tragically made front-page news nationally and internationally when on April 20, 1999, two teenagers at Columbine High School killed twelve students and one teacher, wounding many others with shotgun blasts, automatic pistol fire, and homemade pipe bombs, after which they took their own lives. This was the worst of what has become a rash of school violence against fellow students and teachers by young people. The sites of this lengthening list of tragedies are also sites of schools and school systems which have been restructured and embraced the outcome-based/performance-based/mastery learning concepts of schooling, with all the programs and methods with which they are associated. This writer, in a letter to the editor published by several national journals, discussed what she perceives to be a possible cause of such violence. The text of this letter is reprinted here in its entirety:

> An important question should be examined in regard to the tragedy in Littleton, Colorado. "What was going on inside the brains of the two boys who committed this terrible crime?"
>
> Not only should Americans point the finger at violent television as a reason for copycat violence. They should examine the effects of computers and computer games on the human brain. I am no expert, but the computer is an operant conditioning machine and no less than the late Harvard Professor B.F. Skinner, the father of operant conditioning, referred to it as "his box." Operant conditioning bypasses the brain with all the important functions which distinguish man from an animal: memory, conscience, imagination, insight, and intuition, functions by which human beings know absolutes and truths and are able to know God.
>
> Use of computer programming (simulation/virtual reality) to train individuals to fly an airplane, perform surgery, etc. serve a very useful purpose. On the other hand, the same simulation/virtual reality computer war game videos which allow the individual to engage in killing in a bloody and violent atmosphere, played over and over again, desensitize the individual to the evil act of killing, whereby the individual, as a programmed robot, finds it increasingly easy to carry this distorted vision of reality outside into other areas of his life, such as a school building or playground. If that individual happens to be full of hatred, it doesn't take much imagination to figure out what "programmed" action he or she may take in order to vent that hatred and frustration.
>
> The use of computer-assisted instruction in school, which unfortunately has been accepted as the alternative to traditional education, should also be of some concern to those seeking an answer to school violence. The same operant conditioning, upon which school programs for all disciplines is based, can be used for training an individual to perform. Skinner said "I could make a pigeon a high achiever by reinforcing (rewarding) it on a proper schedule" and "What is reinforced (rewarded) will be repeated." Such "training" is not "education" in the traditional sense since it does not transfer. With traditional academic "education" a student is capable of transferring what he learns to other areas of his life, at some future time. He can store the information for future use; it is in his brain where it is able to be reflected upon, where his soul, memory and conscience are able to influence the information and decisions he makes.
>
> Not so with operant conditioning where no such transfer occurs. Children who spend their school years "learning" (being "trained") in this manner can be expected to experience a certain frustration and dehumanization in their behavior since the creative functions of the brain are being constantly cut off. Operant conditioning experiments on animals have caused similar frustration and violent behavior.
>
> If Littleton, Colorado schools are anything like other schools around the nation, they

are using the highly controversial "scientific research-based" Outcome-Based Education/ Mastery Learning/Direct Instruction based on Skinnerian behavioral psychology, which is necessary for School-to-Work programs and workforce training. OBE and computer-assisted instruction go together as a hand fits in a glove. The combination amounts to a most lethal concoction for our children.

I fear that unless we examine the use and effect of video games and the use for twelve years of computers in the classroom we may experience more Littletons. Is it too far-fetched to assume that he who is trained like an animal may just end up behaving like an animal?]

EDDIE PRICE, A 39-YEAR-OLD SOCIAL STUDIES TEACHER WITH SEVENTEEN YEARS OF TEACH-ing experience, wrote "A Reign of Terror—Impressions of KERA" which appeared in the December, 1993 issue of *The Hancock Clarion* of Hawesville, Kentucky. Excerpts from his important and, one might point out, extremely courageous article follow:

I would never do anything to jeopardize my teaching career or, even more importantly, the security of my family, but I MUST speak out against what I perceive as a massive wrong in education—the Kentucky Education Reform Act (KERA).

The perpetrators of KERA began inundating our schools with mountains of regulations, restrictions, and KERA mandates.... When we expressed our concerns we were told "Be patient.... Give KERA a chance.... Teachers, we need your help. This is a partnership."

KERA's Outcomes appeared to throw the hard, objective, factual subject matter out the window in favor of affective goals (more concerned with emotions and feelings). Our curriculum would have to be pared down and structured around values and attitudes.

When teachers voiced concerns about not meeting the Valued Outcomes, they were "soothed" with the explanation that schools would be given the chance to improve. "A 'Kentucky Distinguished Educator' will be sent to your building to help you grow." Then I learned that this official had the absolute power to declare the school "A School in Crisis"! The principal, and individual teachers could be eliminated with the single stroke of a pen. Past performances, evaluations, educational degrees, experience, awards, student achievement outside of KERA would mean nothing....

When I sat down and read the entire history of KERA's evolution, I realized that our lawmakers and, even worse, our public had been skillfully and strategically duped. KERA had been slickly packaged in deceptive language of "glittering generalities" that the public seemed eager to swallow in the name of reform. Who could argue with such glossy words as "excellence," "revamping," "progress," "outcome-based," "self-esteem," etc., unless they are "traditional," "hidebound," "inflexible," and "resistant to change"? I realized that our distinguished and infallible commissioner basked in the full limelight of a press he had masterfully managed. Kentucky newspaper editors had been appointed to state committees in the name of "progress" and their editorials provided—free of charge—an excellent soapbox from which to indoctrinate the public. Pro-KERA articles and comments have no problem making headlines while others with opposing views must pay exorbitant sums for "political advertisements." School principals and test scores can be subjectively manipulated from above to bring down the Kentucky Distinguished Educators upon schools "not politically correct." For a "dissident," teaching in the public schools today is similar to living under a Stalinist "Reign of Terror."

This is all so incredibly un-American that someone, maybe the FBI again, must investigate our legislature to discover how and why such a massive piece of legislation passed without more discussion. How many millions have already been squandered? How many millions more? No one truly had a chance to examine it fully. The public education hearings held across the state were structured around a preconceived plan devised by a national organization—the Pritchard Committee. The whole thing was rammed down the public's throat before anyone could mobilize. Most concerned were placated by the false notion that parents and teachers would have more control with the "depoliticalization" of education. The end result? Our local, elected school boards (those most responsive to a community's needs) were virtually stripped of their power while state control drastically tightened. The state now mandates the outcomes, approves the curriculum, trains the teachers, and judges the performance of students—all of which must conform to KERA.

[Ed. Note: Had the media, over the past ten years, been willing to publish the many articles and letters to the editor which mirrored Eddie Price's concerns, the national restructuring effort would be dead in its tracks. Even with censorship of opponents' views, restructuring has run up against intense opposition and is "in deep trouble." An article which appeared in the October 10, 1998 issue of the Louisville, Kentucky *Courier Journal* entitled "Kentucky Schools Test Scores Vary Little from Last Year" shows that KERA has been a total flop, as have all the other multi-million dollar, corporation-backed state reform acts implemented across the country. Wherever Carnegie's David Hornbeck goes one can expect a first-class academic flop! Of course, flops are essential in order to convince the public that "workforce training" is the solution—the deliberate dumbing down at work.]

1994

U.S. COALITION FOR EDUCATION FOR ALL: A HISTORY WAS PUBLISHED IN 1994 BY THE U.S. Coalition for Education for All based in Washington, D.C. Excerpts from that publication follow:

> U.S. delegates from government agencies and non-governmental organizations participated in the 1990 World Conference and helped to prepare the Education for All (EFA) goals and action plan. In February 1991 the U. S. Coalition for Education for All (USCEFA) was created to promote EFA awareness and activities in the United States and to serve as a link to the global EFA movement.... In 1991, USCEFA held its first major conference, "Learning for All: Bridging Domestic and International Education."...
>
> ...From this conference the USCEFA's agenda unfolded. USCEFA organized a symposium entitled "Integrating Social Services and Education: A Look at Collaboration and Delivery." At the first meeting of the International Consultative Forum on EFA, U.N. sponsors singled out USCEFA as a model for national initiatives supporting basic education worldwide. This forum selected USCEFA to lead an international task force to explore the involvement of media in education....
>
> USCEFA's 1994 main events included: a symposium entitled "The Educational Implications of NAFTA" [North American Free Trade Agreement] that addressed educational issues emerging in the wake of the signing of the NAFTA agreement; co-sponsorship of a global teleconference entitled "Global Interdependence: the United States and the Third World." USCEFA's most prominent 1994 event is its December conference; "The Revolution in World Education: Toward Systemic Change." This conference explores systemic change in education and the achievement of educational goals and outcomes around the world.... USCEFA will continue to cooperate internationally to keep the spirit of the Jomtien Conference alive and to make Education for All a reality at home and abroad.

"To OBE or Not to OBE?" was the question posed by Marjorie Ledell, associate of William Spady's in his High Success Network, in her article for *Educational Leadership*'s January 1994 issue. From page 18 we read:

> Finally, raise the real issue and depend on democracy. Don't let "to OBE or Not to OBE" or "to implement or not implement efforts to improve student learning" cloud the overdue national debate about whether public education should exist or be replaced with publicly funded private education.

The January 1994 issue of *The Effective School Report* carried an article entitled "Alternative Assessment of Student Achievement: The Open Book Test" by Thomas A. Kelly, Ph.D. An excerpt follows:

> All classroom tests should be open book tests.... We are moving toward higher level thinking and away from memorization of facts. Give them the facts. Once we leave school, we can use references any time we want. We are no longer required to memorize endless lists of facts, formulas, etc. Open book tests will move school activities much closer to real life activities. The human brain should be used for processing, not storage.

[Ed. Note: Initially the writer's reaction to this quote was disbelief, and then plain revulsion over what can only be referred to as a pervasive mindset found in those educators who have been "transformed" into managers of the learning process, total quality technicians, etc. A true understanding of the significance of Dr. Kelly's statement came to me only after GenYvette Sutton, a fine researcher from Pennsylvania, made the following perceptive comments as part of her contribution to a video entitled "The Truth behind Outcome-Based Education" in which this writer also participated.[32] In the segment of the video dealing with the dangers of Skinnerian operant conditioning used in computer programming, the new emphasis on critical thinking, and Dr. Kelly's comments regarding the brain being used for processing and not for storage, Sutton said:

> True education should expand all the faculties of the mind: memory, conscience, imagination, insight, intuition and brain. When you just process information, you deny or cut off those other functions of the mind and reduce it to the brain alone, which is just simply [responding to stimuli]. The danger is unbelievable....
> Columbia Teachers College held a symposium on "Knowing: How We Come to Know Things" and how important this is. Some speakers said that much that is being done in education denies these other functions of the mind and reduces them to the [responsive] brain alone. They reminded us that those other functions—memory, conscience, imagination, insight, and intuition—are the functions by which we know absolutes and truths, [discern right from wrong], and are able to know God.

Outcome-based education, because it concentrates on the "end product" of its process, can be said to restrict the student's mental functioning to the level Kelly described as "processing." The predetermined goals and outcomes prevent the student from using brain functions which make him unique as a human being. Success in an outcome-based environment is restricted to performing prescribed tasks to the point of automaticity. The functions of memory and creativity are not used, nor are they considered necessary to succeed in an OBE program or any program that uses Skinnerian mastery learning or direct instruction. Predictability is the bottom line for OBE, limiting the student to only those responses which are prescribed. When trained by OBE methodology, the student cannot fail unless he employs creativity and produces an unpredicted response. In an OBE environment, he can believe only that which is acceptable. The most predictable outcome, over time, is frustration—and ultimately, low achievement and behavior problems. We should be reminded that robots, although generally reliable, have no feelings and are not governed by conscience..

What a chilling thought.]

EDUCATION WEEK CARRIED AN ARTICLE IN ITS MARCH 16, 1994 ISSUE ENTITLED "BACK TO the Future—with Funding from NASDC and Direction from the Hudson Institute, the Modern Red Schoolhouse Updates an American Icon for the 90's" by Lynn Olson. Excerpts follow:

> Of all the design teams funded by the New American Schools Development Corporation in 1992, the Modern Red Schoolhouse was the one with the closest ties to the Republican Administration then in power and its ideological heart....
>
> ...Its chief sponsor is the Hudson Institute, a public policy center based in Indianapolis that made its reputation analyzing national security issues. Hudson's board of trustees includes former Gov. Pierre S. du Pont, IV, of Delaware and former Vice President Dan Quayle.
>
> William J. Bennett, a U.S. Secretary of Education under President Ronald Reagan, served as chairman of the design team. Bennett, an outspoken proponent of private school choice, left the project last year when he formed Empower America, a conservative think tank based in Washington. Bennett once described the Modern Red Schoolhouse to *The Washington Times* as a "conservative plan with the three C's at its core: content, character, and choice."
>
> Yet, in many ways, the Modern Red Schoolhouse defies political or ideological labels. Some of its instructional approaches, such as multi-age homerooms and self-paced learning, would be considered "radical" by observers on both sides of the political aisle.

PRESIDENT CLINTON SIGNED *GOALS 2000 ACT* ON MARCH 24, 1994. THIS LEGISLATION LAID a large portion of the groundwork for radical restructuring of the nation's schools from the teaching of academics to workforce training.

MICHIGAN'S STATE BOARD OF EDUCATION ADOPTED THE FINAL VERSION OF THE *COMMUNICAtion Arts Framework for the High School Proficiency Test* in April of 1994. Extensive excerpts from the *Framework*, representative of standards adopted throughout the country intended to assist students in entering the workforce or in pursuing higher education, follow:

Assessment Framework for the Michigan High School Proficiency Test in Reading

INTRODUCTION

One of the more widely used methods of control is legislatively mandated graduation standards that require students to pass state mandated tests (Berk, 1986).... The lesson seems to be that if tests remain inadequate, so will the curriculum they influence.

The challenge for Michigan is to create a reading/communication arts framework for curriculum and assessment that does not narrow the curriculum. To prevent this from happening, the Model Core Curriculum Outcomes in Reading, the foundation upon which the proficiency test is based, must be incorporated into a framework that is consistent with the emerging trends in the field. The Model Core Curriculum Outcomes in Reading are derived from the Michigan Reading Association's definition of reading (Wixson & Peters, 1984). The definition provided a theoretical foundation for changing reading instruction and assessment in the state. It is based on a constructivist view of reading that posits, "Reading is the process of constructing meaning through the dynamic interaction among the reader, the text, and the context of the reading situation." (Wixson & Peters, p. 4)...

While the constructivist perspective is a useful way to view the reading process, it must be expanded to include the social dimension of learning. This perspective is best illustrated by the work of Vygotsky (1978). He contended that higher cognitive learning is rooted in social connections; and as a result, knowledge is socially constructed as learners engage in holistic and authentic activities (Englert & Palincsar, 1991; Palincsar & Klenk, 1992)....

A common feature of the constructivist and socioconstructivist views of reading is the importance placed on metacognition—purposeful, effortful, self-regulated, active, intentional learning.... What is called for is a vision of curriculum that incorporates a socioconstructivist view of reading into a curriculum framework that defines the context for constructing meaning in a way that is consistent with the Model Core Curriculum.

A New Vision

For too long a period of time the reading/communication arts area has avoided the question: *Is there a content to reading/communication arts?* [emphasis in original]... At the elementary level the predominate focus is process—reading, writing, viewing, listening and speaking. While literature has recently assumed a more prominent role, the ideas and issues that persist and recur over time are relegated to a secondary level of importance. As a result, literature instruction at the elementary level is haphazard at best (Walmsley & Walp, 1992).

At the middle and high school levels the emphasis is primarily on content, content which is often narrowly defined by literary studies of the canon. Instruction resembles more of a transfusionist's perspective in which students receive information much in the same way patients receive blood (Applebee, 1989; Crews, 1992). Taught in this manner, content is memorized, regurgitated, and trivialized. When this occurs, the high school literature curriculum becomes decontextualized and fragmented (Purves, 1992). In this context the primary goal is to understand a novel, short story, poem, or play; the result is that the literary work becomes the end rather than a means to the end. What is absent from both the process and content perspectives is the application of knowledge in authentic ways. What is needed is a vision of reading/communication arts curriculum that more explicitly defines the context for constructing meaning in a more meaningful way, one that fosters active learning in authentic contexts such as the home, community, and the workplace.

An Expanding View of Text

[T]here is more to developing a curriculum than content. The ideas, themes, issues, and problems that make up the content of text must be placed in a framework that is linked to other considerations such as: what is to be learned, how it is to be learned, in what context it is to be applied, and how is it to be assessed? The framework becomes the common thread that ties together all the components of the instructional system.

...The context in which this type of learning occurs is prescribed by a reading/communication arts curriculum that provides students with learning opportunities. These learning opportunities... apply their existing knowledge to issues and problems that result in new understandings, to synthesize and communicate what they have learned, to generate new knowledge or creative applications, and to think critically about the content and make decisions or take actions that relate to it. This type of innovative curriculum points the way toward higher, richer levels of knowing that are assessed in authentic ways.

Overview of the Framework

The primary goal of the Reading/Communication Arts Framework described in this document is to develop independent, self-sufficient, lifelong learners whose understandings and capabilities allow them to become personally, socially, and civically involved in the world around them... requires the integration of disciplinary knowledge with learner characteristics that promote positive attitudes and dispositions. These elements... guide the systematic delivery of the curriculum. Student achievement of the goals is determined by an assessment system that uses authentic performances to evaluate student proficiency. (See Figure 1)

Figure 1
Communication Arts/Reading Framework for Curriculum and Assessment
GOALS
RESOURCES
DISCIPLINARY KNOWLEGE LEARNER CHARACTERISTICS *Literary Knowledge *Dispositions of Thoughtfulness *Discourse Knowledge *Metacognitive Knowledge *Process Knowledge *Attitudes and Perceptions
AUTHENTIC APPLICATION OF KNOWLEDGE *Engaging *Meaningful *Functional *Integrated
READING OUTCOMES
CURRICULUM CONSIDERATIONS
ASSESSMENT SYSTEM *Model Tasks *Portfolio *On-Demand Tasks

[Ed. Note: The material that was emphasized in the *Assessment Framework for the Michigan High School Proficiency Test in Reading* above is an excellent explanation of the Whole Language philosophy. When education materials refer to "authentic" applications of learning, that means reading or any other learning which is "applied" in a real world setting; for instance, manuals of instruction for operation of household appliances, or letters to the editor concerning a topic which has been discussed in the classroom and about which the student has formulated an "acceptable" position. Anywhere the Michigan *Framework* mentions "social dimensions of learning" or "socioconstructive views of learning" it is saying that learning has to be applied in a social setting or have a social end. In this context, learning for the sake of learning and without prejudice regarding a social point of view is unacceptable. There must be a "social construction" taking place for the learning to be meaningful. This is a good illustration of how children obtain a social/political point of view which is often contrary to that of their parents.

The reference to and building upon the work of Vygotsky indicates the waywardness of the *Michigan Framework*. L.S. Vygotsky was a Soviet psychologist and mentor to the infamous psychologist of the same origin, A.R. Luria. Vygotsky and Luria conducted research in the teaching of higher level skills—known in this country as Higher Order Thinking Skills (HOTS)—which deals with the changing of attitudes, values and beliefs. "Constructivist" learning is a term which Vygotsky used when training teachers to "build on the knowledge that children have already obtained" and which is often mistaken to mean building one concept upon another. This could not be further from the truth. With Vygotsky in mind, the building of knowledge is always in a particular direction—that which has been determined by the social/ political outcomes desired by the one who is teaching or directing the student's efforts. The *Michigan Framework*—and most other states' frameworks—are based on the idea that the "method of control" is a state-mandated test which reflects the curriculum—teach to the test.]

EDUCATION WEEK PUBLISHED THE ARTICLE "SUCCESS WITH COALITION REFORMS SEEN LIM- ited in Some Schools" by Debra Viadero of New Orleans on April 13, 1994. An excerpt follows:

> Some of the first studies to look at the acclaimed Coalition of Essential Schools reform network suggest that some participating schools are having limited success in implementing its ideas.
>
> Five studies on coalition schools were presented here last week during the annual meeting of the American Education Research Association. Collectively, they draw on the experiences of 24 schools nationwide. The coalition currently has nearly 160 member schools.
>
> Four of the five studies suggest that, while some teachers have made profound changes in their teaching styles as a result of involvement in the coalition, few, if any, of the schools studied have implemented its philosophy wholesale. Some schools, facing teacher dissen- sion or financial or district pressures, have abandoned it.

THE NATIONAL SCHOOL BOARDS ASSOCIATION (NSBA) RECOMMENDED RADICAL CHANGES for local school boards at its annual meeting in New Orleans in April of 1994. An article entitled "N.S.B.A. Endorses All Alternatives to Traditional School Governance" in *Education Week* for April 13, 1994 relates the following:

> "A New Framework for School Governance" endorses school-based decisionmaking, charter schools, and other alternatives to traditional governance structures, provided they meet local needs.... Much of the report focuses on improving the alignment of government services at all levels so that children can meet high academic standards.
>
> In addition to the national education goals, the new report advocates the creation of national goals for child and youth development.... Establishing explicit, substantive goals based on children's needs will allow providers to coordinate services more effectively and insure that help is available to those in need.

[Ed. Note: What a difference seventeen years can make! On March 27, 1977 the immediate past president of the National School Boards Association warned school board members "to be aware of and leery of... proposals for public involvement in public school operations that would shift decision-making authority to 'vaguely-defined groups of citizens' at the school site level," which is exactly what NSBA meant when it called for "alternatives to traditional governance structures" in 1994.]

SCHOOL-TO-WORK TRANSITION IN THE UNITED STATES: THE CASE OF THE MISSING SOCIAL Partners—A Report of the Governance and Finance Team of the Comparative Learning Teams Project (Center for Learning and Competitiveness, School of Public Affairs of the University of Maryland: College Park, Md., 1994) was prepared by Robert W. Glover, team leader for the

Center for the Study of Human Resources, and Alan Weisberg, Foothill Associates, with assistance from team members: Andrew M. Churchill, Jobs for the Future; Sharon Knotts Green, Motorola, Inc.; Robert McPherson, Center for the Study of Human Resources; Janet Lewis, Hewlett Packard Corporation; Quint Rahberger, Oregon Bureau of Labor and Industries; Mark Scott, Center for Learning and Competitiveness; and F. Eugene Scott, Sutter Health Systems. This document was published as a joint project of the Center for Learning and Competitiveness (CLC) and The Greater Austin [Texas] Chamber of Commerce.

The CLC Advisory Board includes the following persons: The Hon. William E. Brock,[33] chair, senior partner of The Brock Group; Dr. Anthony P. Carnavale, director of Human Resource Studies, Committee for Economic Development; Nancy S. Grasmick, state superintendent of schools for the State of Maryland; Dr. Herbert J. Grover, professor of education, University of Wisconsin at Green Bay; Mayor Vera Katz, Portland, Oregon; Eugenia Kemble, assistant to the president for educational issues, American Federation of Teachers/AFL-CIO; The Hon. John R. McKernan, Jr., governor of Maine; Hilary C. Pennington, president, Jobs for the Future; William B. Rouse, chief executive officer, Search Technology, Inc.; and, Marc Tucker, president, National Center on Education and the Economy. Anne Heald is the executive director of the CLC.

Excerpts from *School-to-Work Transition in the United States* follow:

In February 1993, CLC brought together 25 leading experts from state and federal organizations as well as international leaders, to identify the most pressing questions and problems that confront policymakers and practitioners working to build school-to-work transition systems in the United States. The outcome of that meeting was a consensus that there were five areas in need of immediate in-depth attention:

- Building a System: Governance and Finance
- Developing Standards, Assessment and Credentialing
- Building Partnerships: The Role of Economic Actors
- Designing Quality Programs
- Providing Career Guidance

To address these issues, and with the generous financial support of the German Marshall Fund of the United States, CLC initiated its Comparative Learning Teams Project. CLC issued a request for proposals nationwide, and respondents were asked to select one of these areas as the focus for an international learning investigation, developing levels of inquiry in substantial detail and with specific outcomes for their trip. The capacity of teams to effectively disseminate their findings in a way that would positively impact on the development of school-to-work systems in the United States was a key selection criteria.

CLC awarded grants to five organizations in the school-to-work transition field who led, planned and supported a Comparative Learning Team. The grants enabled each team of at least nine people to visit two European sites where sophisticated school-to-work transition teams operate. Each comparative learning team participated in carefully planned 12– to 14– day working sessions in Germany, Denmark, the United Kingdom, Switzerland and Sweden, where they gained direct access to their foreign counterparts and first-hand exposure to European systems....

Already, the work of the comparative learning teams has had an impact on system-building in the United States. Team members were able to build on their European experience when designing state systems under the guidelines of the new Federal School-to-Work

Opportunities Act. Officials in the Departments of Labor and Education, working on school-to-work policies, were briefed…. Participants have spoken at numerous conferences, and published comments in newspapers and newsletters. Key findings of the teams are guiding further policy work around key issues such as the engagement of industry in school-to-work programs and in the design of skill standards….

For over a decade American policy leaders have looked to Europe for insight into how to move young people effectively from school to the workforce, while providing them with relevant and valuable skills. The impressive achievements of European systems triggered much enthusiasm in this country about the potential positive impact of reform here.

Now with the passage of the school-to-work legislation, and with states actively attempting to build school-to-work transition systems… the international experience remains highly significant. Issues that challenge American policymakers in building systems, such as developing appropriate funding mechanisms, engaging industry partnership and ensuring relevant standards, have long been at the core of investigation in Europe….

…As states and sites move to implement comprehensive reform in the United States under the auspices of the School-to-Work Opportunities Act, all five reports will provide valuable information and insight into the best international lessons…. We want to express our thanks to the lead organizations for the project: The Austin [Texas] Chamber of Commerce, the New Standards Project [Marc Tucker's National Center for Education and the Economy program], The Council of Chief State School Officers, the National Alliance of Business, and the Northwest Regional Educational Laboratory.

The following quote from an article in the May 14, 1984 issue of *The Washington Post* entitled "Industrial Policy Urged for GOP" sheds some light on behind-the-scenes activities which have led to acceptance of corporate-fascist workforce training necessary for a planned economy:

A conservative study group founded by supporters of President Reagan is about to issue a report that advocates Republicans shed some of their deep-rooted antipathy to a planned economy. The "Industrial Policy Debate" is to be issued today by the Institute for Contemporary Studies, a think tank founded by Presidential Counselor Edwin Meese, Secretary of Defense Caspar Weinberger, and other Reagan supporters.

It should also be pointed out that Secretary of Defense Caspar Weinberger served as Secretary of the U.S. Department of Health, Education, and Welfare in the Nixon Administration in 1973, and that he oversaw the development and publication of the Planning, Programming, Budgeting and Evaluation Systems (PPB[E]S) *State Educational Records and Reports Series* handbooks which document the establishment of the central planning system for the USA. One of the handbooks included in this series entitled *Financial Accounting: Classifications and Standard Terminology for Local and State School Systems* stated in its preface:

Another project funded by the Office of Education from 1968 to 1971 was the development of a program, planning, budgeting, and evaluation conceptual design under the sponsorship of the Association of School Business Officials' Research Corporation…. The emphasis in this project is on the development of a goal-oriented system for evaluating programs.[34]

[Ed. Note: One can't resist asking the politically incorrect questions: When were the American people asked if they wanted to exchange our free enterprise system for the socialist school-to-work system identified with European countries? When was the decision made, and by whom, that the United States would benefit from a planned economy, when this nation has served as the lighthouse for the world, beckoning millions to its shores to benefit from the upward mobility provided by the free enterprise system? By this time the reader should seriously question the legitimacy of the "lead organizations" for the Comparative Learning Teams Project—organizations that this book has documented to be involved in "the deliberate dumbing down" of America.]

A PAPER ENTITLED "ISSUE FOR DESIGNING A SYSTEM OF SKILL STANDARDS AND CERTIFICAtion for the American Workforce: On What Basis Should Occupation/Skill/Industry Clusters Be Organized?" by Robert W. Glover of the Center for the Study of Human Resources, University of Texas at Austin, was prepared for the U.S. Department of Labor in May of 1994. Mr. Glover has contributed to several national and international studies, including *America's Choice: High Skills or Low Wages!*[35] and was the author of the Texas Department of Commerce's publication entitled *Developing a System of Skill Standards for the State of Texas* (January 1993). Excerpts from Glover's paper follow:

> The Appeal of Setting National Standards as a Device To Reform and
> Upgrade American Learning Systems
>
> In its report published in June 1990, the Commission on Skills of the American Workforce placed the development of skill standards and certification on the table as a major policy instrument for improving the education and training preparation of the American Workforce.... Specifically, the Commission's first recommendation called for "A new educational performance standard... for all students, to be met by age 16... established nationally" (p. 69)... [and] described the new assessment system as focusing on thinking-based achievement rather than routine skills. This new certification, which has come to be called the Certificate of Initial Mastery was envisioned as a cumulative assessment and certification process involving a variety of assessments, including a portfolio of performances and projects. It was to be administered by an independent examining organization and focus on "thinking-based achievement, not routine skills."
>
> Recommendation number 3... called for the development of "a comprehensive system of Technical and Professional Certificates and associate's degrees for the majority of our students and workers who do not pursue a baccalaureate degree" (*Commission on Skills of the American Workforce*, 1990, p. 77).
>
> The Certificate of Initial Mastery aims to cover general workplace skills whereas the envisioned system of Technical and Professional Certificates and associate's degrees was aimed at assessment and certification of specific occupational skills. The two types of certification are parallel and complementary.... The two sets of skills are related but separable. Obtaining a Certificate of Initial Mastery was considered by the Commission as a gateway or threshold conveying eligibility to compete for Technical and Professional Certificates.
>
> The Commission on Skills of the American Workforce recommended that the Certificate of Initial Mastery be "benchmarked to the highest standards in the world" [undefined] (p. 69). Likewise the standards of Professional and Technical Certificates should be "at least equal to those set by other advanced industrialized nations" (p. 77).
>
> Since the publication of *America's Choice: High Skills or Low Wages!* in June 1990, considerable progress has been made toward moving the concept of a cumulative portfolio of tests, projects, and achievements into reality. Within a short year, public opinion about national testing made a remarkable transformation from high negative to positive (Marshall

and Tucker, 1992). The Secretary's Commission on Achieving Necessary Skills (SCANS), chaired by William Brock (who also served as co-chair of the Commission on Skills of the American Workforce [U.S. Secretary of Labor]), developed an innovative taxonomy of transferable generic skills applicable to all workforce entrants in a high performance economy. The New Standards Project, under the direction of Marc Tucker of the National Center on Education and the Economy and Lauren Resnick of the Learning and Development Center at the University of Pittsburgh, working with a consortium of 19 states and 6 local school districts, is developing new approaches to assessment toward the creation of a certificate of initial mastery (National Center on Education and the Economy, 1994a, 1994b, and 1994c). Now the recommendations of the Commission are embodied in the *Goals 2000* legislation recently passed by Congress and signed into law.

As an amplification of the above report, the writer would like to quote from the presentation by Paul F. Cole, secretary-treasurer of the New York State AFL-CIO Chapter, at the Second Annual Model Schools Conference in Atlanta, Georgia in 1994. Mr. Cole's statements included:

> I worked on the critical thinking skills portion of the Secretary's Commission on Achieving Necessary Skills (SCANS) report. The fundamental revolution in the workplace called for restructuring of education to meet the challenge....
>
>   Value-added students produce a high performance environment....[36]
>
>   We must go from norm-referenced to criterion-referenced testing. Educational equality is the goal. We must benchmark nationally. Office of Educational Research and Improvement (OERI) study on standards reflected these changes to be made:
>
>   1. Setting standards
>   2. New assessments—portfolios, authentic assessment
>   3. System of credentialing
>   4. Curriculum frameworks
>
>   Some industries are devising standards for school achievement. Queens Aviation High School, [Queens] New York, meets FAA standards. National Skill Standards Board is working on integrating comprehensive skill standards....
>
>   Manipulation of symbols is a skill used with computers rather than direct observation of information. This will affect how we teach reading.

[Ed. Note: This last statement regarding reading should be considered very seriously. What changes in the teaching of reading have been promoted of late? Primarily, the "scientific, research-based, direct, systematic" Skinnerian behavioral approach characterized by direct instruction—and funded under *The Reading Excellence Act* in 1998. Is this emphasis an outgrowth of SCANS-related policies adopted by "partnerships" between government and business interests at the expense of real educational opportunities for children? In 1981 Professor Thomas Oettinger said in a speech that "in the modern context of functionalism, they [comic books], may not be all that bad" for instruction. Comic books and Paul Cole's "manipulation of symbols" have much in common. (See Appendix XI and XXV.)]

PRESIDENT BILL CLINTON SIGNED THE *SCHOOL-TO-WORK OPPORTUNITIES ACT OF 1994* ON May 4, 1994. This law provided seed money to states for development of local partnerships of business, labor, government, education and community organizations to develop school-to-work systems.

THE *WASHINGTON POST* CARRIED AN ARTICLE ENTITLED "TRYING TO CATCH UP ON THEIR Reading: Tutors Find What Students Miss" in its May 25, 1994 edition. Excerpts from this article follow:

> Students are selected for the program by English teachers, counselors, and principals.... Sykes said the D.C. school system will establish "gates," or assessments at grades 3, 5, 6, 8 and 9. There will be no student who will move beyond that gate unless they have shown mastery skills to move to the next level. Sykes said the school system also is developing a statewide reading curriculum that would alleviate the problem of students missing lessons when they change schools in the District.
>
> The students who are enrolled in the Sylvan Center [a private contractor which uses mastery learning] at Anacostia High School said they are proud to go there. There is no stigma attached to the program. In fact, they said, their friends want to know how to join them in a learning environment where the teachers pay close attention... and give them treats... don't seem irritated when they don't understand and congratulate them for every step of progress they make. "This program gives you confidence. It's fun to learn like this. If you do good, they give you awards."
>
> Tarenia Rogers, 15, a tenth-grader, said the program gives her something to look forward to when she goes to school. "It's like a job," she said. "When you come in here and work, *you get paid*" [emphasis in original]. When students score well or complete assignments, teachers reward them with tokens that can be used to buy products such as beads, basketballs and T-shirts at the Sylvan "store"—a display counter that stands in one corner of the classroom.

[Ed. Note: This is the school system in which William Spady and Thomas Sticht served as consultants in the implementation of the now infamous Mastery Learning program in 1978, and which in 1996 had the lowest test scores in the nation. Interesting that Washington, D.C. schools—like Chicago which experienced the "human tragedy" due to mastery learning—is again implementing the same Skinnerian rat training method for "tutoring" its inner city children. (See Appendix XXV.)]

THE CONFERENCE BOARD PUBLISHED *BUSINESS AND EDUCATION REFORM: THE FOURTH Wave—A Research Report* (CB Report No. 1091–94–RR) in 1994. Founded in 1916, the Conference Board was established with a two-fold purpose: 1) to improve the business enterprise system and 2) to enhance the contribution of business to society. To accomplish this, the Conference Board strives to be the leading global business membership organization that enables senior executives from all industries to explore and exchange ideas of importance concerning business policy and practices. The Board has offices in New York City, Brussels, Belgium, and Ottawa, Ontario, Canada. Some excerpts from this extremely important, 41-page document from The Conference Board follow:

> A study of business involvement in systemic education reform shows that such reform:
> * is a long-term, complex and politically charged process requiring on-going commitment
> * demands that business collaborate with other important stakeholders to effect real reform
> * requires clearly stated and explicit goals that place children first

- emphasizes structural changes within schools, communities and the public policy process.

...Data show that during more than 10 years of dedicated effort to improve the U.S. educational system, the business community has invested significant financial, human, and time resources in schools. But business executives have often been frustrated as they have discovered that most of the initiatives, while well-intended and often quite useful to small groups of students, have failed to effect major changes in the ways schools operate or in the overall performance of the education system.

The business community now stands at a critical juncture in its involvement in school reform, with two significantly different pathways developing. The first, evidenced by the emergence of charter schools, privatization initiatives, and emphasis on school choice involves stepping outside the current system and attempting to improve education by starting anew. Businesses that choose this path accept the premise that the current system is irretrievably broken and cannot possibly be repaired by those working within it.

The second path, collaboration for systemic reform, in which many Conference Board companies are deeply involved and upon which this report focuses, assumes that significant competencies exist within schools and that systemic changes can be made to improve performance.

Collaboration involves formal working relationships among business and school officials, social and human service agencies, parents and other relevant stakeholders to reform schools by changing the systems in which they are embedded, the reward structures that perpetuate them, and the defining features (e.g., curriculum, school days, performance measurement) of the schools themselves. The critical assumption is that the schools can be transformed from within....

In effect, blame for the problems of national competitiveness and for the problems of children in a complex and changing society is moving away from schools toward a more honest assessment of what is producing the so-called crisis in our schools. The answers often lie outside the schools themselves.

Since schools reflect society, it may be necessary to rebuild the community infrastructure in new ways, by using the school itself as a community resource....

Despite significant external pressures and constant cries of crisis in the educational system, schools have remained largely unchanged....

School days remain, for the most part, shorter than those of other industrialized nations, and the school year remains on an agrarian calendar. The structure of schools tends to isolate teachers not only from each other, but also from other important stakeholders, such as parents, businesses, social service and civic agencies, and community organizations that might take up some of the social and family burdens that have been placed on schools. Subjects are still predominantly taught in rote memorization fashion in short bursts of activity of 45–50 minutes. Often little time is devoted to staff or curriculum development.

In part, this situation exists because, as Chester Finn has stated, "people aren't changing their behavior at the 'retail' level of education." The explanation for this inability to change is due, in part, to public attitudes about education and schooling. These attitudes, which research shows are pervasive, mean that, rhetoric aside, fostering serious organizational change in schools has been difficult to accomplish....

MODELS OF COLLABORATION FOR SYSTEMIC REFORM

Case 1: Re:Learning—Monsanto, Southwestern Bell, Emerson Electric and Hallmark's Support for Systemic Education Reform

The group determined that the goal would be active student learning with demonstrations of student accomplishment, which is a fundamental aspect of the Common Principles of the Coalition of Essential Schools. The principles provided a foundation upon which all of the group's efforts could build, with particular attention devoted to the aspect it deemed most critical to actually achieving their goals: development of the teachers who work in the restructured schools.

The organizational framework the coalition chose to achieve its goal was Re:Learning, a national effort to address education reform by redesigning the total education system. Re:Learning, begun in 1988, includes the Coalition of Essential Schools, the Education Commission of the States, and all member schools, districts, and states....

Case 5: Partnership for Kentucky School Reform

The state of Kentucky is identified as being on the leading edge of the school restructuring and reform movement. Faced with the *Kentucky Education Reform Act* (KERA), which was intended to radically restructure schools because the system had been declared unconstitutional, business leaders in the state rallied together with educators and government leaders.

This type of collaboration was not new: Leaders in these three sectors had been interacting for a number of years, particularly concerning issues of education in the Louisville area and surrounding Jefferson County. Indeed, Louisville had been one of the 12 National Alliance of Business Compact Cities, funded to develop ways for these sectors to work together to improve education.

KERA represents a long-term and systemic approach to school reform. Among other things, the act guarantees a certain level of funding on a per-student basis, establishes mechanisms to equalize school financing, and introduces school-based management at each school along with major curriculum revisions and an entirely new primary school program.

One of the more innovative approaches embedded within KERA is the establishment of family resource centers and youth services centers within schools in poor areas. This "one-stop shopping" approach is meant to ensure that children are able to learn when they are in school because their families are receiving needed services. Additionally, all four-year-olds are required to attend preschool. A strict accountability system accompanies and supports the implementation efforts. One characteristic of KERA is its emphasis on high expectations for children.

KERA, coupled with the Business Roundtable's efforts to involve the business community in state-level advocacy, galvanized the business community into action. In the fall of 1990, the CEO's of three companies, John Hall of Ashland Oil, David Jones of Humana, and Kent C. "Oz" Nelson of United Parcel Service, established the Partnership of Kentucky School Reform. With the inaugural meeting held in March 1991, more than 50 leaders joined together to solidify their support for successful implementation of the innovative KERA. The group represented a non-partisan cross-section of business, government, civic, and education leaders, all making a commitment to improve the quality of education in the state through a statewide information campaign combined with local activities to support the reform movement.

[Ed. Note: KERA has become a case study in how educational reform went *astray* in a state that "was on the leading edge of the school restructuring and reform movement," and how it brought *grief* to parents, students, teachers and legislators. It was also a case study that involved a key, if not *the* key education change agent—who is not even an educator—David W. Hornbeck, who took his marching orders from Marc Tucker's National Center on Education and the Economy (NCEE).

To add insult to injury, Hornbeck left Kentucky's sinking KERA ship to become superintendent of the Philadelphia, Pennsylvania school system where his tenure in Pennsylvania was equally controversial and destructive, resulting in the school system's being declared unable to function, wanting the state to take it over pending its "re-establishing" itself. Is it the role of the Hornbecks of this world to *de*structure schools, enabling them to be *re*structured according to the needs of the global economy?

Are the Hornbecks of the world brought in specifically for that purpose?

Additionally, one could ask why The Conference Board, and business interests in general, find the work of particular change agents and their tactics so appealing and positive? Is it because the change agent puppets are performing perfectly for their puppeteers who consider our children "human capital resources" to be trained, allowing the multinational corporations to spin off profits as a result? Take the case of a school system in New Mexico; the local school board rejected the Re:Learning Project only to be heavily pressured by the governor and a CEO of a multinational corporation—and others—who absolutely insisted on the implementation of Re:Learning. These folks had just returned from the "Charlottesville Summit" where they had received their marching orders under *America 2000*.[37]]

IN THE *READING* (PENNSYLVANIA) *EAGLE/TIMES* ON JUNE 25, 1994 AN ARTICLE BY STEPHANIE Ebbert entitled "School Exams Likely to Have Russian Origin" stated the following:

> Teachers in the former Soviet Union, who played host to visiting U.S. educators, express interest in exchanging tests and course material to compare students' aptitudes and curriculum.... Wyommissing School District students may soon be taking tests drawn up by teachers in the former Soviet Union.
>
> Dr. Charles R. Walker, superintendent, has established ties with educators in St. Petersburg, the former Leningrad, as a result of an April excursion there. Walker, one of 32 educators who, along with their spouses, took a 10-day educational trip to visit schools in St. Petersburg and Moscow, returned with contacts, fax numbers from Russian schools, and plans to establish ties to ensure students are competitive on a global scale.
>
> Teachers there expressed interest in exchanging tests and course material to compare students' aptitude and curriculum in the two countries, Walker said. In one public school that Walker visited the board had recently decided to mandate that students wear uniforms to try to contain the forces of commercialism, at least during the school day, he said.

[Ed. Note: Although dress codes are proper—and many private schools require an identifiable uniform to distinguish their schools' students from others—many government schools in urban areas in the U.S. are beginning to require uniforms. With the advent of: reduced time for recess; encouraging military personnel to function as teachers or instructors; the use of police to monitor school corridors and to teach the unsuccessful DARE (Drug Abuse Resistance Education) program; and the concept of our children being labeled "human capital resources" for the government-promoted school-to-work scheme, the idea of uniforms for public school students is more than a little disturbing.]

THE SECOND ANNUAL MODEL SCHOOLS CONFERENCE, SPONSORED BY THE INTERNATIONAL Center for Leadership in Education, Inc. (ICLE—whose director is Dr. Willard R. Daggett, previously employed as a co-trainer with William Spady at Outcome-Based Education training sessions sponsored by Spady's High Success Network) was held June 26–29, 1994 in Atlanta, Georgia. Representatives of the educational systems of China, Denmark, England, France, Germany, Japan, and Russia were included as presenters at the conference.

Of special interest was the presentation given by Su Lin, founder and chairwoman of China International Intellectual Resources Development Center for Children (CICC).[38] This school has branches in the United States, Germany, and other countries to facilitate the immersion of its Chinese students into the culture as well as the language of other countries. Excerpts from her presentation follow:

> It is CICC's task to be engaged in educational reforms, to establish organizations of intercultural communications, and to integrate educational institutions with enterprises. Therefore, CICC's systems engineering of education is an enormous constitution [composition] of education and technology, theory and practice, experimentation, organization, and management.
>
> CICC has been incorporated into an international group.
>
> We stress the following aspects:
>
> 1. The kind of citizens required by the 21st century will constitute our essential consideration of educational receivers, aims, and contents.
> 2. We must do experiments in the search for a new education model.
> 3. The greatest characteristics of the 21st century will be the internationalization of education. With that in mind, we aim to develop our education in an international environment, as education is supposed to be an open system.
> 4. China is carrying on its social reforms, encouraging individuals and the non-governmental sector to run education. Educational institutions in China are all affected by the shortage of financial resources.
> 5. The secure job policy makes education a closed and extremely stable system, closed to competition. Our curriculum is out of date. Education reforms are imperative in China....
>
> Sincere love of children is the principle upon which CICC is constructed....
>
> I am strongly against parents or teachers who impose their own views and demands on the children. Education is a noble job that calls for devotion and dedication with no reservation. Chances and conditions for education should be equal for every child....
>
> The cultural, economic, and educational levels for the minorities in Hainan are relatively low. With these factors in mind, CICC intentionally enrolls students from these minorities for educational experimentation and research....
>
> The aim of CICC is to develop children into persons with sound personality for the 21st century. To this end we incorporate the following features:
>
> 1. Standardization—a series of educational activities designed, organized, and managed according to educational principles and social needs to achieve a desired end.
> 2. Complying with natural law—all educational activities must obey the natural physiological and psychological development of children. Tampering with these laws leads to failure, as in the medieval missionary schools and family education.
> 3. Exploitation—exploiting the tremendous potential capacities of children.
> 4. Succession and systemization—treat the developmental process as a systemic whole.
>
> ...Personality is the synthesis of a person's mental and physical qualities. Our proposal is that elementary education should be globally oriented.... This is the inexorable result of international economic development.
>
> Education reforms conducted by CICC include the shortening of the whole educational

period to fifteen years of schooling. Weekday boarding is one of the educational facilities of CICC. They [the students] are required to board at school on weekdays and go back home by school bus on weekends. We provide boarding for the following reasons:

1. Most people are too busy working to pay enough attention to the education of their own children.

2. Many of the children come from broken families. The boarding school is a place they can turn to for comfort. Some even prefer to stay at school on weekends.

3. Many parents are not well-educated themselves and know nothing about how to bring up their own children.

4. China has a "one-child" policy as a way of controlling the birthrate. It is statistically shown that problems such as self-centeredness, stubbornness, and dependence are some common characteristics of only children nowadays. CICC provides boarding to strengthen the children's sense of equality, solidarity, and independence.

We have established a school for the parents, where people can learn how to educate their own children. The overall plan for CICC has Moon Lake as the hub of the community with the educational center around it. CICC has organized itself into a self-supported international group corporation of educational institutions and enterprises by opening businesses and services in children's education, science and technology, medicine and health, legal, insurance, trade and tourism.

[Ed. Note: Do the above outlines remind the reader of the New American Schools Development Corporation's criteria for schooling in the United States through charter schools that bear many of the above characteristics? Can the reader recognize the Chinese equivalent of "at-risk" categories that our country is targeting for educational funding? Does reference to boarding schools remind the reader of the November 1979 article in *The Bangor* (Maine) *Daily News* about radical changes proposed by a Vermont task force which included boarding schools, a center for educational research and teacher training, and elements of the school-to-work agenda for the 1990s?

The above Chinese model, describing the school as the "hub" of the community, bears much resemblance to the community education programs of the past twenty-five years or so. While the Chinese still use the word "children" instead of this country's substitute "human capital resources," one must not lose sight of the environment—political, economic, and religious—in which the above extreme, communist and coercive "educational solutions" are suggested and established. The reader should also bear in mind that this program was presented at Willard Daggett's ICLE "Model Schools" conference.]

"SCHOOLS: INTO THE FUTURE" IS THE TITLE OF AN ARTICLE WHICH RAN IN *THE OREGONIAN* [Portland, Oregon] on September 8, 1994 and carried a subtitle as lead-in which read "Oregon's school-reform plan is one of the country's most ambitious—and this year it really kicks into gear." Since Oregon was the first state to implement the *Goals 2000 Act* (signed by President Clinton on March 31, 1994) and *The School-to-Work Opportunities Act* (signed by Clinton May 4, 1994), before quoting from the article in *The Oregonian*, the writer wants to quote from the first paragraph of the radical *Goals 2000 Act*:

PUBLIC LAW 103–227
March 31, 1994
103rd Congress

To improve learning and teaching by providing a national framework for education reform; to promote the research, consensus building, and systemic changes needed to ensure equitable educational opportunities and high levels of educational achievement for all students; to provide a framework for reauthorization of all Federal education programs; to promote the development and adoption of a voluntary national system of skill standards and certification; and for other purposes.[39]

Excerpts from the "Schools: Into the Future" article which enable the reader to comprehend the controversial nature of *Goals 2000*:

Efforts to make learning more relevant by breaking down walls between schools and the adult world are bringing the most visible changes. At Portland's Roosevelt High, for example, students will choose career paths early in their high school years and actually will follow them into the workplace with real-world experiences such as internships and job-shadowing programs. At Grant High, students will learn directly from Cellular One workers. And at Marshall High, business leaders will serve as mentors to individual students, guiding the choices that will affect their futures in the world of work.

Oregon's law, like President Clinton's Goals 2000 reform legislation, aims to dramatically raise the education levels of students schools failed to reach in the past. This year, Portland Public Schools will embark on a plan to push all students into an academic regimen equal to that traditionally reserved for the college-bound, says Jack Bierwirth, Portland Public Schools Superintendent.

It will do so by aggressively following Oregon's school-reform blueprint. The state plan attempts to reach the forgotten half in two ways:[40] by requiring all students to meet high academic standards and by blending academics with new vocational paths that lead to further studies and good jobs.

Because of the state plan's scope and high standards, the American Legislative Exchange Council last month chose Oregon as one of eight states to receive its A+ award in education.

Replacing the Diploma

Oregon's reform plan will require students to earn two certificates of mastery to graduate—one at about the end of their sophomore year and the second about two years later. This year's eighth-graders will be the first class to earn certificates instead of diplomas.

Reformers say the distinction is central to the changes education faces: diplomas are based on course credits or the time students put in. But certificates, they say, are based on standards or what students know and can do.

Another article in the same September 8, 1994 issue of *The Oregonian* was entitled "Model Program Links Classroom to Workplace." This article by Courtenay Thompson deals with a pilot project to implement school-to-work requirements of the *Oregon Educational Act for the 21st Century*. The following are excerpts from that article:

In the blood splatters of murder victims, David Douglas High School senior Chrissy Ballantine is learning about both forensics and her future.

A student in the school's innovative Law Network course, the 17-year-old is exploring careers by learning to interpret blood splatters with the help of a Multnomah County forensic specialist. Last year, she also analyzed the book *Lust Killer*, a true-crime novel by Ann Rule about Jerome Brudos, an Oregon serial killer.

Not standard classroom fare, but Ballantine raves about the two-year course, a pilot program to implement school-to-work requirements of the Oregon Educational Act for the 21st Century.... "We were doing an excellent job of providing a well-rounded college prep education," said Anthony Palermini, David Douglas superintendent. "But it wasn't relevant to 25 to 30 percent of our students."

As a result, the district began developing what it calls Project Stars—"Students Taking Authentic Routes to Success"—in which students select one of six general career areas, or "constellations," to concentrate their electives. Students will work toward certificates of advanced mastery, a key measure of academic success under state-mandated school reform.... The career focus would start in the seventh grade, when students would take a career-orientation class. Students would select their constellation by the time they hit high school.

[Ed. Note: The fact that Oregon's school-to-work reform plan received the American Legislative Exchange Council's (ALEC) highest educational award *should* come as a surprise since ALEC is an association created by "conservatives" (Paul Weyrich) in 1981 as a counterpart to the liberal, Rockefeller-spawned ACIR (Advisory Commission on Intergovernmental Relations); both organizations draft "model" legislation for use by state and federal legislators.]

ON NOVEMBER 2, 1994 *EDUCATION WEEK* PUBLISHED AN EDITORIAL LETTER BY THIS WRITER entitled "Viewing Reform Partnerships as Big Brother's Intrusion." A portion of the letter follows:

Don Davies ("Partnerships for Reform," *Commentary*, October 12, 1994) just doesn't get the message: Smart Americans don't like partnerships with the government; and if public schools aren't "government," what are they?

Evidently there are still enough politically savvy (educated) Americans who reject such partnerships, having studied government intrusion in the home and family in countries such as Cuba, the former Soviet Union and Eastern bloc countries, and especially in Communist China, from which some of Don Davies's community-education research apparently has emanated.

The Community Learning and Information Network, Inc., or CLIN, incorporated in 1992 and supported by major corporations and education associations, will make Professor Davies's dream come true. He "won't have to worry about citizens who 'resist'" *Goals 2000* reform (don't want to dance with the government). According to the CLIN fact sheet, "The CLIN concept is to implement a community-linked learning-technology and information-delivery system that uses... two-way interactive video, networked computer-assisted learning, video programming, multimedia, interactive cable, and electronic mail (including electronic video mail) based on an 'open systems' architectural approach. CLIN, Inc.'s goal is [to] link every public and private school in the United States, as well as every institution of higher education and corporate and industrial training sites."

An information packet from the Community Learning and Information Network states: "CLIN has also developed international projects, to include an approved project with the People's Republic of China sponsored by the highest levels of the Chinese government."

Professor Davies's concerns about lack of parental and taxpayer support for reform will also be dealt with when the National Goals Panel's 235-page *Community Action Tool Kit*, the intent of which is to psychologically manipulate taxpayers into supporting *Goals 2000*, hits our communities. The *Tool Kit* recommends, among other techniques, these: "Describe allies and opponents; identify change agents; get the president of Hewlett Packard to write the chairman of the school board a letter supporting the proposal." It also provides a case study of how Christian ministers were manipulated into supporting *Goals 2000* in Edmonds, Washington.

Alexander Solzhenitsyn, the famous Soviet dissident, issued an important warning when he said, "Coexistence on this tightly knit earth should be viewed as an existence not only without wars... but also without [government] telling us how to live, what to say, what to think, what to know, and what not to know."

So-called "peace" is breaking out all over the world. How long this type of peace will last will depend on the patience freedom-loving citizens have with Global Big Brother's intrusion into the privacy of their homes and families.

CHALLENGERS FOR INSIGHT IN ITS NOVEMBER 1994 NEWSLETTER PUBLISHED AN ARTICLE entitled "Susan Kovalik's Integrated Thematic Instruction" which enables the average parent or teacher to understand a new teaching model based on "brain compatible learning" for outcome-/performance-based education.[41] This critique of Kovalik's model was written by education researchers Marilyn Boyer and Barbara Volkman of Indiana.[42] Since this article describes a new and most controversial method which may well be used extensively throughout the nation, this writer has included it in its entirety so that the reader can use it for educational purposes:

SUSAN KOVALIK'S INTEGRATED THEMATIC INSTRUCTION
By Barbara Volkman and Marilyn Boyer

Controversy continues to rage throughout Indiana over a state-supported teaching model for Outcome-/Performance-Based Education. Many traditional teaching methods are being eliminated as public school classrooms experiment with new teaching techniques based on *brain-compatible learning*, such as those promoted in the 1992 Integrated Thematic Instruction: The Model (ITI) developed by Susan Kovalik and Associates of Arizona.

A memorandum was sent to all Indiana superintendents, inviting them to attend a lunch/conversation with Susan Kovalik in Indianapolis on November 10, 1994 during the 7th National Conference of the American Association of School Librarians. [It stated in part that] ITI is of great interest to parents in Indiana and elsewhere, since *"Susan is well known as a writer, facilitator, and president of one of the largest inservice training organizations in the United States,"* according to the invitation.

Kovalik's material shows a strong connection to the New Age philosophies of Eastern mysticism and Western occultism. Indiana has for several years been putting in place the *new age curriculum* that contains all of the psychological/educational processes necessary to achieve in the student the desired *state, national and international outcomes*.

Master teacher Barbara Pedersen, an associate of Susan Kovalik's from Central Elementary School in Lebanon, Indiana, has brought the ITI model to Indiana classrooms through the Indiana Department of Education-supported C.L.A.S.S. (Connecting Learning Assures Successful Students) project. Pedersen not only trains and coaches teachers in many schools in Indiana, but now has expanded to include Kentucky teachers.

The ITI model's approach to teaching uses a single theme (yearly, monthly, weekly) to tie together various areas of instruction such as science, math, history, and reading. Thematic teaching is not new. What is new, says Kovalik in her 1992 ITI manual, is that, "The entire ITI Model—curriculum development and instructional strategies—has been selected and organized with great care to fit how the brain learns" (p. 3).

This type of thematic model, based on human brain research, is called *brain-compatible learning*. However, a close look behind the model at the books that Kovalik cites as brain research reveals that ITI is not based on valid scientific studies, but rather on educational theories tied to psychic phenomena research.

The mind, claims Kovalik, is designed to learn from the experience and complexities of the natural world, and thus she rejects the logical, sequential (traditional) teaching approach to learning. According to Kovalik, the goal of school districts and school boards should be to provide students with a brain-compatible learning environment by eliminating policies that support brain-antagonistic elements (i.e., a textbook for every student, traditional evaluation/grading, and sequential curricula presented in a logical manner).

Opponents of the ITI model list the following major criticisms: 1) New Age ideas and practices including yoga relaxation, visualization, and guided imagery leading to altered states of consciousness; 2) Tribes, a cooperative learning model predominantly centered on social (peer group) development rather than individual academic achievement; 3) academic deficiencies traced to emphasis on *exploration of the complex, random, chaotic "real world"* instead of concentrated on sequential, logical teaching of subject matter through textbooks; 4) controversial nature of certain themes (political, religious, paranormal, etc.) and overemphasis on themes; and 5) teaching methods and curriculum linked to questionable brain research (i.e., *Brain-Compatible Classroom*).

The ITI model encompasses six main brain research theories:

(1) Triune Brain—Paul McLean's evolutionary theory of mankind's *three separate brains* of varying ages. This is a key component and rationale for providing a stress-free brain-compatible learning environment.

(2) Accelerated Learning—the speed up memory learning by teaching directly to the subconscious mind derived from George Lozanov's Suggestology, which is based upon research from yogis and psychics. The ITI model has all of the parts of this type of Accelerated Learning—yoga relaxation, visualization, guided imagery and special effects of music. Lozanov's method is also called SALT (Suggestive Accelerative Learning and Teaching [which supports Stanford's Henry Levin's Accelerated Schools efforts]) and Integrative Learning.

(3) Left Brain/Right Brain Thinking—a theory to develop the intuitive side of the right brain by accessing the subconscious mind. There is no consensus in the research to support this theory. Although some scientists have claimed to validate the roles of the left/right brain hemispheres, others would disagree. "We don't have one shred of evidence that something as high-level as creativity could be allocated to one side of the brain or the other," says Levy (professor of biopsychology at the University of Chicago). "Attempts to apply what is known about hemispheric differences to the enhancement of learning are premature.... That was the conclusion of the fourteen-member panel of researchers from the National Academy of Sciences that recently completed a broad view of 'brain asymmetry'" (The *Omni Wholemind Newsletter*, Vol. 1, No. 4, March 1988).

(4) The Seven Intelligences—redefines intelligence to include music, dance, sports, etc. Howard Gardner, departing from traditional education, theorizes that humans have seven intelligences that are associated with brain locations. They are *logical-mathematical, linguisitic, spatial, bodily-kinesthetic, musical, intrapersonal, and interpersonal*. Gardner labels what has been traditionally called a human talent as an intelligence. Parents should have grave concerns about labeling a student's personal beliefs and his/her interaction with others as intelligences, because the state can then do the developing and assessing of them. This is one of the dangers of Outcome-Based Education since the learner outcomes often include the student's attitudes and beliefs.

(5) Personality Types/Learning Styles—Pedersen refers to the importance of learning styles. One of the methods of identifying/teaching to learning styles used in Indiana as well as many other states is the 4MAT system of instruction developed by Bernice McCarthy. 4MAT is based on theories from education, psychology, neurology and management. The system includes four types of learners: Imaginative, Analytic, Common Sense and Dynamic. McCarthy teaches to the learning style of the student with left/right mode techniques.

(6) Brain-Compatible Learning, a phrase coined by Leslie Hart, author of *Human Brain and Human Learning*. Hart believes humans learn best from the rich, random, chaotic "real world" instead of concentrated, sequential, logical teaching of subject matter through textbooks.

Replacing traditional teaching methods with occult techniques that teach directly to the subconscious mind opens the door to possible mind control (brainwashing). It appears that some education reformers think children can learn better in this hypnotic state which allows all material into the mind. Children can then absorb any agenda the school (state) wishes to teach without the brain discriminating the validity of the material.

Authors' Update (recent developments since this article was written):

Howard Gardner has now expanded to eight and a half intelligences by adding naturalist and half of spiritual.

The following recent publications show that educators continue to misapply the brain theory and research that even the scientific community still disputes:

A Celebration of Neurons: An Educator's Guide to the Human Brain by Robert Sylwester is published by the Association for Supervision and Curriculum Development (ASCD) in 1995 as a major guide for educators. Sylwester notes that educators must not make the mistake of left/right brain books, workshops and curriculum that often went far beyond the research findings. He sees misinformed or uninformed people making major policy decisions for educators. However, he maintains that application of this research is an important step for educators even though the applications are not clear, the issues are complex, and educators generally lack the scientific background to understand or build a curriculum utilizing the research.

The Education Commission of the States has held 16 workshops in the last year on the implications that neuroscience may have for state policymakers who may be getting carried away on brain research. ("Education Policymakers Embrace Brain Findings—Scientists Question Rush to Apply Brain-Research Findings," by Linda Jacobson, *Education Week*, April 8, 1998) [all emphases in original]

JOHN OMICINSKI, GANNETT NEWS SERVICE, WROTE "MULTICULTURALISM IS A WORTHY Goal, but America Still Needs Americans" which appeared in the Sunday, November 20, 1994 issue of the *Detroit News*. Omicinski's article covered a speech by Librarian of Congress James Billington at the 75th anniversary of Georgetown University's School of Foreign Service.[43] A few interesting excerpts from the article follow:

Will America lead the world into the 21st century? Not the way things are going, says Librarian of Congress James Billington. [Not] in a country afflicted with a lazy, ill-defined multiculturalism filling up with African Americans, Korean Americans, Japanese Americans, he suggests. And his bottom line is simple: America doesn't work without Americans.

As a custodian of the library and its 105 million items, Billington is caretaker of the world's largest depository of human culture. He also is one of Washington's sharpest minds, an expert on Russian history as well as America's heritage, and an even rarer breed—a straight talker.

The arsenal of information we command ought to qualify the United States as an unchallenged cultural superpower, Billington says. But this imposing mother lode of words isn't of much use if U.S. residents are too indolent, too self-satisfied, too culturally balkanized to use it, he says....

Is America an idea or a nation?

The sharpening split between left and right makes that a cutting-edge question in the current cultural wars. And Billington comes down on the side of nationhood largely because America's good ideas don't much matter if there's no nation to push them.

Gathering the world's civilization to itself, the United States should be primed to set a model for the world. But it isn't working that way, said Billington. A gaggle of voices—all given equal weight in a society that may have forgotten its traditional values—has turned America into a dizzy spin. "Unfortunately, we seem to have lost our national compass somewhere on the road to the next millenium," Billington said. "We are getting ever more lazy.... Many of our great institutions of higher learning seem to have become indifferent to—even contemptuous of—their historic function of transmitting a basic understanding of their own culture from one generation to the next.

"In place of the expanding, inclusive America, which adds without subtracting, the ideological multiculturist would create a balkanized America and a continuous process of subtraction from any sense of common tradition or shared values.... This kind of multiculturalism is the denial rather than the fulfillment of true pluralism, which in the great American tradition assumes a variety of authentic and deep convictions rather than a... uniformity of relativistic indifference."

Billington sees a single language as the ultimate national glue. Though English is on its way to dominating the world, America's left-wing elitist intellectuals say it shouldn't be America's *lingua franca*. "In any country that endures, there must be a *unum* as well as a *pluribus*," said Billington.

That's not all.

Billington says a national idea also requires a "clearer understanding than our educational system has often done in recent years of our durable constitutional system and public institutions and of our distinctively Judeo-Christian roots.... The bridges to other cultures will not be solid unless they begin with casements that are sunk deep into one's own native ground."

Leaders of our governments, schools and universities have much to answer for, perhaps even the death of the American nation. Billington's speech is another reason to demand better from them, or show them the door.

EDUCATION WEEK OF NOVEMBER 23, 1994 RAN THE ARTICLE "EDUCATION, RELIGIOUS Groups, Seek Common Ground." Excerpts follow:

The leaders of several national education associations and conservative religious and citizens' groups have been meeting behind the scenes in an effort to find common ground on school reform and end their increasingly hostile debate.... An encouraging sign—and surprising turnabout—in the debate between school-reform leaders and their conservative opponents has been the recent partnership of William G. Spady, a leading advocate of outcomes-based education, and Robert L. Simonds, the president of the Costa Mesa, California-based Citizens for Excellence in Education, which says it has about 250,000 members nationwide. In many ways, the two men represent polar opposites in the debate over the direction of schools. Yet in recent months, they have made plans to sponsor jointly a non-profit National Center for Reconciliation and Educational Reform at the University of Northern Colorado in Gruel....

In many areas, CEE-affiliated activists support a back-to-basics agenda, opposing whole language instruction, open-ended assessments and teaching strategies that stray from the drill-and-practice routine. But after building a constituency that has seen its job as fighting against the tide, Mr. Simonds said, it is time to work with educators on better choices.... "We are not opposed to Bill Spady's theory of outcomes-based education. There are a lot of good ideas in it," Mr. Simonds said.

IN A LETTER DATED DECEMBER 12, 1994 FROM WILLIAM SPADY OF THE HIGH SUCCESS Network to Dr. Nancy Grasmick, Maryland state superintendent of schools, a copy of which was very likely sent to the 49 other state school chiefs, Spady made the following statements:

With both the federal government and state bodies pushing harder than ever to improve the focus and effectiveness of what happens at the local level, major educational reform seems inevitable—except for one new factor: the open resistance by citizens' groups to a host of "progressive" reform ideas and initiatives....

When we met in March, Dr. Simonds was a staunch opponent of virtually everything I advocated in terms of outcomes-based educational change and restructuring. Today, to the amazement of many educators and policy makers, he is in agreement with the basic components and principles articulated in the enclosed document developed by Dr. Kit Marshall and myself. More importantly, he and I have joined forces to form a National Center on Educational Reconciliation and Reform—an endeavor that colleagues across the country tell us is badly needed....

We would be delighted to discuss the feasibility of working with you and your constituents to bring this program to your state and to generate a broad base of support for reconciliation and reform. This could be done either under the auspices of the *Goals 2000* initiative or through other sponsorship.

COTTAGE GROVE, OREGON'S SOUTH LANE SCHOOL DISTRICT PLOUGHS AHEAD AS THE NATION'S certificate in mastery pack leader. According to an article entitled "Cottage Grove Endures Trials, Triumphs as It Tests New School Plan" in the December 13, 1994 issue of *The Oregonian*:

Parents are still fighting the changes. Students will mutter about being guinea pigs. Teachers—even those who back the reforms—groan about the workload.

Last spring, Cottage Grove High School handed out the state's first certificates of initial mastery to 81 sophomores. The certificate, keystone in the 1991 reform act, is designed to measure students on what they've learned and what they can do, as opposed to what courses they have taken.

Much of the criticism arises from the way ninth-graders were thrust cold into the new program two years ago. They worked on team projects that would be graded jointly, took more responsibility for their own learning and developed portfolios of their classwork. And, more significantly, they had to meet higher academic standards.

Timm Wagner, 16, failed to get his certificate last year because, he says, his teammates on a group project didn't get their work done. "I don't like it," he says. "If I'm doing a job, I should get fired if I do something wrong, not if somebody else does something wrong."

SCHOOL-TO-WORK PROGRAMS PROMOTED BY BUSINESS IS THE SUBJECT OF AN ARTICLE ENtitled "Leading Business Executives Create Council to Promote S-T-W Programs" in the December 14, 1994 issue of *Education Week*. Some excerpts follow:

Some of the nation's leading corporate executives last week announced that they have formed a group to promote business involvement in school-to-work programs.

Members of the National Employment Leadership Council will work with the U.S. Education and Labor departments to implement school-to-work programs in their own companies and encourage other firms to do the same. Whether many businesses take them up on the offer could determine the prospects for work-based learning in the United States. The new council provides the strongest signal to date that the private sector may be ready to support such programs....

But the council stopped short of releasing numeric goals for how many firms it hopes to recruit or how many training slots they would provide.... Jerome Grossman, the chairman and C.E.O. of the New England Medical Center, said the council hopes to set numeric objectives within the next two months.

The council's staff is housed at the Institute for Educational Leadership, a non-profit group based in Washington.

The following companies and C.E.O.'s are charter members of the council: Ford Motor Co., Alan Trotman; American Express Travel Related Services Co, Inc., Roger Ballou; Atlanta Life Insurance Co., Jesse Hill, Jr.; BellSouth Corp., John Clendenin; Charles Schwab Corp., Lawrence J. Stupski; Cybernet Systems Co., Heidi Jacobs; Eastman Kodak Co., George Fisher; H.J. Russell & Co., Herman J. Russell; ImmunoGen, Inc., Mitchell Sayare; Manpower Corporation, Mitchell Fromstein; McDonald's USA, Ed Rensi; New England Medical Center, Jerome H. Grossman; Pacer Systems, Inc., John C. Rennie; Peavey Electronics Corp., Melia Peavey; Phillips Display Components, Dr. Iva Wilson, president; Siemens Corporation, Albert Hoser, president and C.E.O.; the Taubman Company, Al Taubman, chairman; Thom McAn Shoe Company, Larry McVey, president; UNUM Corporation, James F. Orr, III, chairman and C.E.O.; and Will-Burt Company, Harry Featherstone, chairman and C.E.O.

WEDNESDAY, DECEMBER 28, 1994 ISSUE OF *THE WALL STREET JOURNAL* CARRIED AN ARticle under its column Critical Thought entitled "Acclaimed Reforms of U.S. Education Are Popular but Unproven—Ted Sizer's Methods Stress Reasoning over Rote: Gains Aren't Measurable—Ambiguity and Faculty Battles." Sizer's Coalition of Essential Schools, considered by many to be the centerpiece of national education reform, proves to be more workable in theory than in practice. Some excerpts follow:

In the crusade to revitalize high schools, no one has attracted more attention—or money—than Theodore R. Sizer, professor of education at Brown University and creator of Essential Schools. But as Dr. Sizer's adherents and donations pile up, so too does research challenging the effectiveness of coalition schools. Five recent, little-publicized studies, including a five-year research project sponsored by the coalition itself, suggest that Dr. Sizer's ideas may be a lot more workable in theory than in practice....

Not since John Dewey, whose writings shaped the 20th century U.S. curriculum, has one person's philosophy taken hold in so many classrooms, educators say. More than $100 million has poured in from education foundations and donors such as AT&T, Exxon and Citicorp. Anecdotal evidence from some coalition schools points to improved attendance rates, lower dropout rates, better test scores or more students going to college.

But even coalition officials concede such evidence is spotty. They also haven't tried to determine comprehensively whether coalition students are learning more, despite pressure to do so from some benefactors. Grant Wiggins, the coalition's former research director, says he remains unconvinced that coalition schools are better. "It has always been my sense that it's not better. It's not worse; it's just different," explains Dr. Wiggins, who says he quit the coalition in 1988 because of "a combination of burnout and frustration."

1995

THE JANUARY 1, 1995 ISSUE OF *EDUCATION WEEK* CARRIED AN ARTICLE BY ROBERT C. Johnston entitled "33 Religious Groups Join Riley in Seeking Greater Family Role in Schools." Some excerpts follow:

Nearly three dozen religious leaders put aside theological differences to join Secretary of Education Richard W. Riley in a holiday season declaration supporting involvement in education....

...Mr. Riley added that religious leaders came to a "clear recognition" that the religious community can play a "more active and positive role" in helping parents educate their children.

Ms. Doyle said the department may follow up by working with the religious organizations to provide instructional materials for parents. The department also hopes to provide an education guide for ministers as well as meeting space for future activities arranged by the religious groups.

Asked about the political overtones of reaching out to church groups, Ms. Doyle said: "The Secretary made it clear he was not asking them to stand with him and support all (Clinton) Administration initiatives. This is about families."

[Ed. Note: Separation of church and state flies out the window when church communities plan to *join* government, business, parents, and schools in helping all families participate in their children's education, and especially when the U.S. Department of Education provides religious organizations with instructional materials for parents!]

IN AN ARTICLE ENTITLED "RUSSIAN TEACHER REVIEWS WORK IN SAD 53" WHICH WAS published in the January 12, 1995 issue of *The Bangor* (Maine) *Daily News*, Brenda Seekins explains all too clearly the extent of cooperation between Russia and the U.S. in school-to-work (planned economy) activities. According to Seekins's research these activities were not confined to ivory tower musings, but had penetrated education at the local level. Some excerpts follow:

> PITTSFIELD—Russian exchange teacher Tanya Koslova addressed the SAD 53 board of directors Monday night to express her appreciation for the opportunity to work with the district and Maine Central Institute [MCI—deeply involved with workforce training].
>
> She offered an overview of the work she had done in the district over the past four months, spending two months with children in kindergarten through grade eight and the balance of her time at MCI.
>
> She particularly enjoyed students who participated in her Russian humanities class who were "highly-motivated and eager students."[MCI Headmaster] Cummings told the board that MCI will be the recipient of the School-to-Work funding in conjunction with the Maine Youth Apprenticeship Program.
>
> The school could receive up to $8,000 to provide staff training to better integrate academics with the program provided by apprentices' worksites.

MACHIAVEL PEDAGOGUE OU LE MINISTERE DE LA REFORME PSYCHOLOGIQUE [MACHIAVELlian Pedagogy or the Ministry of Psychological Reform] by Pascal Bernardin (Editions Notre-Dame des Graces: Paris, 1995) was published. This book deals with United Nations Educational, Scientific, and Cultural Organization's (UNESCO) role in the transformation of education worldwide from a system based on academic instruction to one in which the purpose is nothing but conditioning for acceptance of world government (New World Order). Monsieur Bernardin discusses brainwashing techniques such as cognitive dissonance and the group process, and is highly critical of the role played by American and European behavioral psychologists in the transformation of the world's schools from places of learning to mental health clinics for brainwashing. The following are excerpts from this writer's translation from the French version:

> The general philosophy of the pedagogical revolution is exposed, without detour, in the publications of the international organizations (UNESCO, OECD, Council of Europe, Commission of Bruxelles...)....
>
> This pedagogical revolution attempts to impose an ethic for the creation of a new society and to establish an intercultural society. The new ethic is nothing more than a remarkable presentation of a communist utopia. A study of the documents leaves no doubt, under cover of ethics and behind a rhetoric and remarkable dialectic, of a communist ideology for which only the presentation and the means of action have been modified.... Also it is no surprise that the level of scholarship will continue to go down since the role of the school has been redefined so that its principal mission is no longer intellectual but social formation....One no longer gives students intellectual tools for liberation but imposes on them values, attitudes, and behavior using psychological manipulation techniques.

SALEM, OREGON'S *THE STATESMAN JOURNAL* OF FEBRUARY 4, 1995 CARRIED AN ARTICLE entitled "Service Learning Projects Match Students with Needs in the Salem-Keizer Community." Excerpts follow:

Service learning is a method through which students learn values, citizenship, and skills by performing a variety of community services. On any given school day, hundreds of Salem-Keizer teens leave their classrooms to visit local businesses, nonprofit agencies and other community organizations or activities.

The students aren't on field trips—they're visiting their service sites, where they perform a variety of community service work, also referred to as "service learning." It is here that students are learning the meaning of citizenship and service. They're also becoming more aware of their role in the community.

"Service learning demonstrates the partnership between the school district and the community. Students learn firsthand about the needs and issues of our community—the homeless, the hungry, the elderly, and environment—while they work toward meeting those needs," explains Pat Abeene, Volunteer Services coordinator for the district.

Abeene said service learning takes various forms. These range from the district's Youth Community Service Program—in which high school students get [selective or elective] credit for community service—to individual school projects integrated into the regular curriculum.

Other service sites offered through the program include the Boys and Girls Clubs, nursing homes, the Humane Society, and Oregon state parks.... Another example of service learning was the McNary Area Service Learning Project. The successful project teamed eight Keizer schools in the collection of 6,000 recyclable milk jugs from area homes—a service currently unavailable through Salem-Keizer disposal companies.

THE FOLLOWING STATEMENTS WERE PUBLISHED IN 1995 IN THE MARYLAND STATE DEPARTment of Education's *MSDE Bulletin* (Vol. 6, No. 3) entitled "Keeping You Current on Education Reform in Maryland":

SEEKING COMMON GROUND ON SCHOOL REFORM

William Spady, a leading proponent of outcomes-based education, and Robert Simonds, head of a Christian group that has led the fight against OBE, made a joint presentation before the State Board in February to discuss their 10-months' dialogue of reconciliation....

Early in their discussions, which began at a meeting last March of the Association of Supervision and Curriculum Development (ASCD) the two men agreed that the public schools are essential to democracy and must be strengthened....

The two men have come to agreement on a set of components and principles for school reform, which Spady calls the "High Success" model. They agree that specific reform alternatives should include the following components:

* Quality performance standards
* Future-focused planning
* Extensive community involvement
* Continuous improvement strategies
* Challenging learning experiences
* Advanced instructional processes
* Real-life learning assessments

Both men had praise for Maryland's reforms. Simonds said, "The Maryland Learning Outcomes are what parents want."...

Several education associations (including the Association for Supervision and Curriculum Development, the American Association of School Administrators, the National School

Boards Association, the National PTA) have joined with the Citizens for Excellence in Education and other conservative groups to continue the search for common ground on education.

[Ed. Note: Robert Simonds's co-option by the very groups responsible for at least thirty years of failed, so-called "reform," is beyond this writer's comprehension.[44]]

"CONTENT OF OUR KIDS' TESTS SHOULDN'T BE SECRET" BY MARGARET SITTE, COLUMNIST, ran in the March 3, 1995 issue of *The Bismarck* (N.D.) *Tribune*. Excerpts follow:

In 1990 North Dakota eighth-graders scored highest in math on the National Assessment of Educational Progress. Questions of psycho-analysis have surfaced, however, leaving many parents to ask, "What exactly is the NAEP?" Senator Bob Stenehjem, R., Bismarck, thinks it's time to find out, and he has introduced SB 2308 allowing parents the right to see it.

Anita Hoge, a Pennsylvania mother of three, listened intently one day in 1986 as her ninth-grade son came home complaining, "I've just taken the weirdest test in the world. It was so hard. You couldn't answer the questions."

"The prospect of working most of my adult life depresses me. Check 'yes,' 'no,' or 'sometimes.'"

Being a concerned parent, Anita marched to school and demanded to see the test, the Pennsylvania Educational Quality Assessment. She was refused. A feeling in the pit of her stomach told her something was terribly wrong.

Anita called other parents, and together six women embarked on an extensive investigation that lasted several years.

Berit Kjos's *Brave New Schools* (Harvest House Publishers: Eugene, Ore., 1995), in discussing Anita Hoge's case, states:

Anita Hoge, a native of Pennsylvania, is no stranger to concerned parents or to the educational establishment. While her story has encouraged thousands of parents across the country, it has also brought anxiety to the change agents who hoped to conceal their strategies until they accomplish their purpose. Anita's courageous search for answers to mystifying school practices has given us a glimpse of an educational process designed to conform all children to the new, politically correct version of "appropriate mental health."

Anita's journey will take you through a maze of white papers and technical documents and expose the true nature of contemporary education: social engineering. It will give you an inside look at the deceptive testing mechanism designed to measure the attitudes and values of our children and make sure every student will demonstrate the pre-planned nonacademic "outcomes." Unwilling to give up in the face of overwhelming opposition, Anita has become a living demonstration of the hope that "one person can make a difference." (p. 206)

[Ed. Note: Anita Hoge filed a lawsuit against the U.S. Department of Education, the Pennsylvania State Department of Education and others, using the federal *Protection of Pupil Rights Amendment*. The outcome of her suit was delayed by the U.S. Department of Education's tactics until the statute of limitations expired, thus its acknowledgment that her suit was legitimate served only as a moral victory. The Pennsylvania Department of Education continued to stonewall Mrs. Hoge's efforts to uncover the privacy-invading components of its statewide assessment test, discontinuing its use for a time and later changing the name of the test—as good change agents are wont to do!

For further information, see the 1964 discussion of the origins of the NAEP; 1988 National Citizens Alliance press conference at the National Press Club; 1998 Ohio Supreme Court favorable decision in Steve Rea's challenge to the Ohio Department of Education; and Appendix IV.]

THE *BISMARCK* (N.D.) *SUNDAY TRIBUNE* CARRIED AN ARTICLE ENTITLED "TEST BOARD Tackles Secrecy Stigma" by Jeff Olson in the March 5, 1995 issue. Excerpts follow:

A Bismarck legislator's bill to let parents inspect a national student achievement test sent the exam's governing board scrambling for a new public access policy.

New policy directives give parents a look at old test questions and demographic background questions, but maintain high security for National Assessment of Educational Progress [NAEP] exam questions still in use. They were approved Friday in Washington.

Should Sen. Robert Stenehjem's bill become law, director of the NAEP, Archie LaPointe, said it would mean the end of the exam in North Dakota. National test results wouldn't waver because North Dakota students are a sliver of the nation-wide test sample. But LaPointe feared copycat legislation could seriously disrupt NAEP operations in other Great Plains states.

National Assessment personnel came from the Educational Testing Service at Princeton, N.J., a private company under contract to the federal government which sponsors the NAEP.[45]

ETS staff and governing board members from across the country said they were surprised by Stenehjem's bill. North Dakota children have dominated state-by-state comparisons in the NAEP.

But the 25-year-old program has been peppered with accusations that it amounts to psychological testing, and is not the anonymous comparison of academic achievement as prescribed by law. Parents are also upset that they can't have easy access to active test questions.

"The NAEP just isn't worth it," said Stenehjem, a Republican who sponsored SB 2308. "There is too much secrecy and there are too many intrusive background questions."

Parents from Pennsylvania, Nebraska, Iowa and other states have complained bitterly about the NAEP for several years. But no one has scared the governing board with legislation. Until now.

"EDUCATORS, RELIGIOUS GROUPS CALL SCHOOL TRUCE—THEY AGREE TO DISAGREE ON Hot Issues of '90s" by Sally Streff Buzbee was published in the March 22, 1995 issue of *The Atlanta Constitution*. What the article actually said is that the left and the right will meet at the middle (common ground, or what Shirley McCune refers to as "the radical center"). This is an excellent example of the Hegelian Dialectic at work. Some pertinent excerpts follow:

ARLINGTON, VIRGINIA—Educators and religious parents fighting a bitter "culture war" over the future of America's public schools signed a pledge Tuesday to tone down their rhetoric and cooperate for children's good....

...[T]he 17 groups, ranging from the conservative Christian Coalition to the liberal People for the American Way, pledged to work to solve disputes before they become lawsuits and to improve communication and respect each other's positions.

The agreement could influence debates likely in Congress this year over school vouchers and school prayer. But the agreement will be aimed at solving disputes that have divided communities in recent years.

"The statement is eagerly awaited," said Charles Haynes, a visiting scholar at The Freedom Forum First Amendment Center. He brought the groups together with help from the non-partisan Association for Supervision and Curriculum Development (ASCD).

"People in Vista, California, and in many other communities have been saying 'We want it now,'" Haynes said. The Vista school district near San Diego has been fighting over the teaching of evolution and creationism.

"This is going to give all these local districts something to look at, something to help guide them." Haynes said.

"Several prominent groups, including the conservative Focus on the Family and the liberal American Civil Liberties Union, did not sign the statement of principles," Haynes noted.

"I don't think any of them are against it in theory, but thought it was vague," he said.

In part, the agreement will clarify for local teachers, principals and parents what the Supreme Court has ruled is allowable in public schools, such as the fact that religious groups have equal access to school rooms for after-school meetings.

"Far too often, constitutionally protected religious liberties are being denied," said Robert Simonds of Citizens for Excellence in Education.

The agreement basically says, "Public schools should not be hostile to religion," said Education Secretary Richard Riley, who also signed it.

[Ed. Note: This writer questions the use of the word "non-partisan" when referring to ASCD, since ASCD—a spin-off of the National Education Association—is not a political party. Also, anyone who uses the ASCD to bring groups together on the issue of religion is behaving like whomever put the wolf in charge of the henhouse. As far as the people in Vista, California saying, "We want it now," what is it they want now? Why have they hung out the white flag in the war courageous parents across the nation have been fighting since 1945 to hold the line on the issue of "coming to common ground" on values?

Allowing religious groups to have equal access to school rooms for after-school meetings is actually the "camel's nose under the tent" for state regulation of religious activities and the introduction of all sorts of religions into the school's curriculum. Remember that Secretary Riley said that "Public schools should not be hostile to religion" and even witchcraft is a state-recognized religion.]

"WHY THE EDUCATION DEPARTMENT MUST GO" BY GORDON S. JONES, FORMER UNDER secretary of education in Secretary T.H. Bell's department of education, was published in *The Washington Times* on April 7, 1995. Jones said in part:

> To put the matter in its starkest terms, state school superintendents like the Department of Education because they are getting, on average nationwide, almost half of their funding and staff courtesy of the federal taxpayer. The state of Michigan, for example, receives 77 percent of its operating budget from the Department of Education; its counterpart in Iowa has 81 percent of its staff paid for by Uncle Sugar.

[Ed. Note: One of the primary reasons for abolishing the U.S. Department of Education is to cut down to size the bloated and dictatorial state departments of education which receive their marching orders from Washington.]

THE SUNDAY NEW YORK TIMES MAGAZINE OF APRIL 30, 1995 PUBLISHED "WHO'LL TEACH Kids Right from Wrong?—The Character Education Movement Thinks the Answer Is the Schools" by Roger Rosenblatt. This article describes very clearly the pros and cons of a very controversial subject—the character education movement of the late 1980s and 1990s.

Rosenblatt devotes a good bit of space to Thomas Lickona, a developmental psychologist and a professor of education at the State University of New York, who is an acknowledged leader of the burgeoning character education movement. Lickona has recently established the Center for the 4th and 5th R's (Respect and Responsibility) at State University of New York-Cortland, which is becoming something of a national center for the study and development of character education curricula.

In the *New York Times* article Rosenblatt said that

> Character Education represents an effort to teach moral behavior to primary and secondary school students in a time perceived to be morally rudderless and to be without such teaching in local communities or in the home. Across the country, teachers are confronting children with moral dilemmas and asking them to think and talk. The felt need for this kind of education is so deep and widespread that it spurred a movement that has attracted as many former activists of the 1960s—Lickona is one—as it has conservative thinkers and politicians of the 1980s. (Supporters include Barbara Jordan, Barbara Bush, Marian Wright Edelman, Jesse Jackson, Tom Selleck and Nathan Glazer)....
>
> ...Richard Baer, Jr., of Cornell University has found fault with the content of some courses (bland pablum) and complained to Rosenblatt that there is no empirical evidence that character education actually improves character. Baer's main concern is that the public schools will become centers of a culture war between those on the the right who believe that character education must incorporate religion and those on the left who do not want religious teaching at all....
>
> ...Besides Lickona's center at Cortland, there is the Josephson Institute of Ethics in Los Angeles which supports a Character Counts Coalition. Amitai Etzioni, a leader of the Communitarian movement, has devoted the energy of his Communitarian Network to advance the cause. Boston University has established the Center for the Advancement of Ethics and Character specifically to develop character education. All this is in addition to the work of individual schoolteachers and educators at the university level who are turning the idea that values can be formally taught into a field of study—Kevin Ryan, Director of the Center for the Advancement of Ethics and Character Education at Boston University; Kevin Walsh at the University of Alabama; William Damon at Brown University, and others. Kevin Ryan says: "We've had 10 years of talking about school reform. This issue is at the *heart* [emphasis in original] of school reform." For Kevin Walsh, the ultimate purpose of character education is nothing less than "to prepare the next generation to inherit society."

Rosenblatt identifies the following states as being involved in implementing character education: Mississippi, New Hampshire, New Jersey (the N.J. Dept. of Education has endorsed a set of "core values" and set up a council to define commonly accepted values). He lists St. Louis, Seattle, Chicago, San Antonio, and Frankfort, KY as cities and towns involved in character education and concludes by saying, "Classes in character education are held in rural and suburban schools, like those around Lansing, N.Y., and in inner-city schools, like Theodore Roosevelt High School in the Bronx."

In discussing the problems associated with character education, Rosenblatt asks what happens when two moral rights collide? A teacher might well begin complicating things, talking of exceptions and degrees, but a teacher also wants to avoid sliding into the moral relativism that created the mess that character educators are trying to fix. Rosenblatt then reveals the contradiction in Lickona's argument regarding moral relativism when he says, "Deciding to do his [Lickona's] dissertation on children's moral thinking, he was drawn... to Lawrence Kohlberg of Harvard, a major figure in the late 1960s on the subject of moral reasoning." The reader is urged to review this book's 1975 entry which describes Kohlberg's "Ethical Issues in Decision Making" for an understanding of the "moral relativism which created the mess that character educators," including especially Lickona, are supposedly correcting.

[Ed. Note: Curriculum is not the answer. The hiring of competent teachers whose lifestyles are exemplary and who exhibit civilized behavior (respectful, courteous, caring, loyal, etc.) is the best and safest way for schools to encourage morality in our children. Such an atmosphere, in combination with literature which helps students understand that moral behavior is something to emulate, not disdain, would do more than all the "character," "civics," "citizenship" and "values education" being discussed by the carefully selected task forces representing all degrees of political persuasion being set up to create the dialectic necessary to reach "common ground" on consensus values.

A careful reading of Rosenblatt's article is recommended as the first step towards an understanding of the pitfalls Americans face as they enthusiastically join forces to solve problems which clearly, short of violating the First Amendment, cannot be dealt with successfully in the classroom.]

LOOKING BACK, THINKING AHEAD: AMERICAN SCHOOL REFORM 1993–1995 WAS PUBLISHED by the Hudson Institute's (Indianapolis, Ind.) Educational Excellence Network (Chester Finn, William Bennett, Lamar Alexander, Diane Ravitch) in 1995. An excerpt follows:

> The report decries the backlash against outcomes-based education.... Many state outcomes are inappropriate... but... unfortunately, an awfully important baby [mastery learning] could go down the drain with the OBE bath water, and the country could find itself returning to an era when inputs, services, and intentions are the main gauge of educational quality and performance.

[Ed. Note: This quote exposes the hypocrisy of those "opposing OBE"; they oppose the outcomes, but not the *Skinnerian method*. As explained elsewhere, the outcomes can be changed overnight, whereas once all teachers have been trained or retrained in Skinnerian mastery learning, there can be *no* return to academic freedom for teachers or students.]

COMMITTEE FOR ECONOMIC DEVELOPMENT (CED) 1995 YEARBOOK ENTITLED *PUTTING LEARNing First: Governing and Managing the Schools for High Achievement* was published. This 60-page report called for school choice, charter schools, and social services delivered through schools or in collaboration with schools.

THE NATIONAL EDUCATION GOALS PANEL *COMMUNITY ACTION TOOLKIT* WAS DEVELOPED and distributed by the U.S. Department of Education in 1995. The *Toolkit* was to be used for brainwashing, coercing and coalescing communities into accepting *Goals 2000*, H.R. 6, school-to-work, UNESCO's lifelong learning, etc. *Toolkit* instructions discussed how to deal with resisters. Elected officials, governors, and others were involved in production and dissemination of this 300 + page "How To" *Toolkit*, which used Professor Ronald Havelock's *The Change Agent's Guide to Innovations in Education* techniques to brainwash themselves and their constituents, especially targeting the religious community. (See Appendix XIV.)

"The Shocking Beliefs behind Educational Strategic Planning" by Michael Jacques was published in the August 1995 issue of *The Interpreter*. Jacques, a concerned parent from West Allis, Wisconsin, has provided some very "hard-to-come-by" information regarding The Cambridge Group, an international strategic planning center for education reform. Excerpts from this informative article follow:

> Strategic planning seems to be the driving force at the local level for Outcomes-Based Education (OBE)/*Goals 2000*. Most school districts... have a facilitator trained by The Cambridge Group, which is an international strategic planning center for education out of Montgomery, Alabama. The *Facilitator's Training Manual* states under "The Urgency of Change" on p. 4:
>
>> Education must declare its magnanimous intent and omnipotent ability to serve as the surrogate family.

"Strategic Planning" is defined:

> > Either no one can see or will acknowledge the fact that the real task of reformation is the radical transformation—a re-creation—of every facet of the American education system—its purpose and scope, its governance, its teaching and learning dynamics, its curricula, its time and place—all with a new dedication to developing the original genius in the mind of every student. This means a complete change of all education paradigms, of definitions, of disciplines, of vocabularies—perhaps values. This is the meaning of reform. And that is the meaning of strategic planning.... (p. 20)
> >
> > The advent of this new age, and the discovery that human beings now have both the capacity and the inclinations to re-create themselves in their own image according to their own imaginations... specifically it has demanded a redefinition of the human being.... (p. 28)
>
> > Urgency of Change
> > Spiritual: once confined only to that thought to be religious and other worldly; forbidden in the world of practicality and reality; a relationship between someone and God or something. Now, a realization of the pneumapsychosomatic nature of every person; the practical reality of the human spirit when manifested in self-esteem, motivation, aesthetic appreciation, manners and respect, as well as reverence; and *a priori* an ultimate relationship between people....
> >
> > The fact is that all American institutions—the Constitution, the Bill of Rights, the legislative and judicial branches of government, the education system, and other aspects of the current established order—were predicated on a mono-cultural society. It will be interesting to see how long the present systems can exist in a polyglot society. (p. 29)

Mr. Jacques ends his article by quoting from the Wisconsin Independent School Board Association: "Only the village idiot would consider letting the entire village in on the task of raising his children."

"THE LANGUAGE OF OBE REVEALS ITS LIMITATIONS" BY GRETCHEN SCHWARZ WAS PUB-
lished in the September 1995 issue of *Educational Leadership*, Association for Supervision
and Curriculum Development's (ASCD) journal. Ms. Schwarz is assistant professor of curriculum and instruction at Oklahoma State University, Stillwater, Oklahoma. Excerpts from
Schwarz's refreshingly objective critique of OBE follow:

> In contrast, the language of Outcome-Based Education (OBE) seems limiting and dehuman-
> izing. Many educators not associated with the Religious Right are highly critical of OBE, as
> am I, but for different reasons.... In response to the March 1994 issue of *Educational Leader-
> ship*, which portrayed OBE in a positive light, I would like to consider the language of OBE as
> revealed in *Choosing Outcomes of Significance* by William Spady. Individual words and phrases
> jump out at me as a reader. Following are terms that Spady used frequently and that particu-
> larly troubled me... "outcomes, generalizable, Discrete Content Skills, microforms of learn-
> ing, Structured Task Performances, components in a larger block of curriculum, competence,
> mental processing, performance enablers, execution, Higher-Order Competencies, technical
> and strategic Life Performance Roles."...
>
> Such mechanistic, instrumentalist language has a constraining effect on me as a reader,
> just as OBE has a constraining effect on school reform. This list reads like the terminology of
> the CEO or the social engineer—very much in the management-oriented, positivist-behav-
> iorist tradition....
>
> ...With OBE, outside experts prescribe what is best for students and teachers, who
> remain essentially voiceless. Uniform outcomes are designed and implemented in a curricu-
> lum that reduces thinking to mental processing....
>
> All the bottom-line language reminds the reader of the boardroom. Of course, Spady's
> High Success Network is a business. But children are neither customers nor products, and a
> school is not a business....
>
> OBE language is the scientistic, industrial language of Tyler and Skinner as documented
> by Callahan (1962) in *Education and the Cult of Efficiency*. Ultimately, the language of OBE
> is controlling, narrow, mechanistic, and finally, impoverished. Our students and teachers
> deserve more than OBE has to offer.

[Ed. Note: Professor Schwarz's comment that OBE "reduces thinking to mental processing"
calls to mind the Thomas Kelly quote: "The brain should be used for processing, not storage."]

A REAFFIRMATION OF FAITH IN MAINE'S PUBLIC SCHOOLS, EDITED BY MARGARET L. STUBBS,
Ph.D. of the Maine Department of Education in Augusta, Maine, was published in 1995. This
document revealed the extraordinary thrust towards a partnership between religious institutions and the public schools. *Reaffirmation of Faith* also describes the socialist (planned
economy) nature of workforce training in Maine. Excerpts follow:

> Religious and spiritual institutions have the responsibility to cultivate within their organiza-
> tions the values they hope will guide their constituents' lives in a changing world that offers
> not only opportunity and beauty but also great danger, and in so doing have a complemen-
> tary role to play as community participants in systemic school change....
>
> Before hiring a student, even for part-time work, review each student's work portfolio;
> the portfolio should contain vital information as to the student's school attendance record,
> achievement and assessment, sample writings, letter of recommendation, etc....

...Two-year degree programs in regional Vocational/Technical Centers for public high school graduates.... Courses would be based on an assessment of the work needs of the region. The particular courses would "sunset" once the needs of the area were fulfilled and new courses for the associate degree would be offered to fulfill new assessed needs for the area.

[Ed. Note: The last two sentences regarding "assessment of the work needs of the region" and courses "sunsetting" once the needs of the area were fulfilled show that Maine has adopted the same system described by Professor Eugene Boyce when he said in communist countries education is "directly tied to jobs.... They do not educate people for jobs that do not exist. No such direct controlled relationships between education and jobs exists in democratic countries" (see 1983 Eugene Boyce entry). Suppose your child wants to take a course that has "sunsetted"? Will he/she have to leave the state in search of such a course, or be deprived of the opportunity?]

H.R. 1617 OR *THE CAREERS ACT (CONSOLIDATED AND REFORMED EDUCATION, EMPLOYment, and Rehabilitation Systems Act)* passed the U.S. House of Representatives in September of 1995. The law calls for four consolidated job training programs to replace formerly existing programs: youth development and career preparation; adult training; adult education and literacy; and vocational rehabilitation. This legislation was based on school-to-work legislation passed in 1994. Four block grants for job training were tied together at state and local levels to form one cohesive system organized around a single plan submitted to the federal government.

Under this plan states would develop one-stop delivery systems, business-led unelected local workforce boards, and voucher programs to allow them to maintain "top-notch state-of-the-art job training programs." State legislatures would be bypassed and money would be driven to states and communities (in most cases 80% funding is spent locally). H.R. 1617 gave enormous power to state governors and removed the power of local school boards to determine what is best for their students. Labor market information systems, funded by the federal government to increase availability of information provided to those who need additional job training, would be strengthened.

To promote accountability, *The CAREERS Act* set up a system of goals and performance indicators to ensure that states, communities, service providers, and "clients" are all focused on *results*. The Act consolidated or eliminated more than 150 program authorities. This legislation fulfilled requirements outlined in Marc Tucker's letter to Hillary Clinton following the November 1992 election. H.R. 1617 represented a radical change in America's free economic system. (See Appendix XV.)

IN 1995 REPORTS OF OUTCOME-BASED EDUCATION FAILURES CONTINUED TO SURFACE: CHIcago, Illinois; Johnson City, New York; Utah OBE Project; Kentucky; Pasco, Washington; California; Rochester, New York (Carnegie National Alliance for Education and Economy—Marc Tucker/David Hornbeck pilots); Cottage Grove, Oregon (first high school in nation to issue the Certificate of Initial Mastery, which originated and is copyrighted by Marc Tucker's Center for Education and the Economy); Ted Sizer's Coalition of Essential Schools (funded by Carnegie's Education Commission of the States and multi-millionaire Walter Annenberg); inner cities—

most of which used Mastery Learning—especially Washington, D.C.; and Secretary of Education Riley's home state of South Carolina (lowest test scores in the nation). These failures and troubling consequences were reported in major newspapers, magazines and education-related journals.

[Ed. Note: The writer predicts that once schools have been manipulated into substituting non-competitive criterion-referenced testing for competitive norm-referenced testing, the dismal test score scenario will be a thing of the past, as a result of the proposed "quality" teach-to-the test measures of educational achievement being put in place. Then, all parents can plaster their cars with "My Child Is an Honor Student" bumper stickers.]

TRI-CITIES FOUNDATION FOR ACADEMIC EXCELLENCE (TFAE) OF PASCO, WASHINGTON issued a press release in 1995 entitled "Survey of Former Pasco, Washington Teachers Gives Outcomes-Based Education Insights" which read as follows:

> In 1988 the Pasco School District piloted OBE and has since been used as an OBE role model for education reform across Washington State and the nation. During the 1992–93 and 1993–94 school years, the Pasco School District lost more than one hundred teachers. Tri-Cities Foundation for Academic Excellence (TFAE) surveyed these former teachers to obtain their insights on the OBE program and establish whether or not the OBE philosophy and the manner in which it was implemented were influential factors in their leaving the District. Are teachers currently being coerced or forced to leave the Pasco School District if they are not using the Outcomes-Based Instructional Model? The following results represent responses from teachers in a district used as a model for Washington state's now-mandated Outcomes-Based Education and OBE across the nation:
>
> - 68% responded children did not benefit from Outcomes-Based Education;
> - 86% responded Outcomes-Based Education divided teachers and created polarized camps;
> - 27% stated that they were asked to leave if they didn't agree with Outcomes-Based Education.
>
> The survey was designed for complete confidentiality and anonymity.[46]

[Ed. Note: Barbara McFarlin-Kosiec, Ph.D. in Educational Leadership, a veteran teacher in the Pasco School District, has filed suit against the district due to its non-renewal of her contract. The non-renewal was based on the vice-principal's opinion that she failed to use the instructional process of OBE in the classroom. Ms. Kosiec's suit is based upon her belief that her constitutional rights have been violated; i.e., in order to continue teaching in the district she was required to go along with an alien philosophy and to hold certain politically correct attitudes and beliefs.[47]]

NATIONAL ISSUES IN EDUCATION: GOALS 2000 AND SCHOOL-TO-WORK EDITED BY JOHN F. Jennings, general counsel for education for the Committee on Education and Labor of the U.S. House of Representatives (Phi Delta Kappa: Bloomington, Ind., and Institute for Educational

Leadership: Washington, D.C., 1995) was published.[48] The following are comments by Mr. Jennings which reveal some heretofore closely guarded secrets related to the roots of *Goals 2000* and *The School-to-Work Opportunities Act*:

> Now there is a measure of national agreement that there should be voluntary national standards.... All the major education organizations, all the major business groups, the nation's governors, the current Democratic president, and the former Republican president have all advocated this concept. The purpose of this book is to explain why and how this agreement came about by focusing on two major legislative initiatives of the Clinton Administration: the *Goals 2000 Act* and the *School-to-Work Opportunities Act*. The Clinton initiatives are rooted in the Bush legislation and in the summit conference held by President Bush with the nation's governors in Charlottesville, Virginia, in 1989, in which then-Governor Clinton took part. At that event the governors and the President agreed on the concept of national goals for education, the first ever to be devised.
>
> While previously there had been some acceptance of the idea that the federal government had a role in dealing with special needs children and with certain problems in education, there had not been agreement in this century that the national government had a legitimate concern about the general state of education. And, it is important to point out, the governors did not universally endorse the idea of expanding the influence of the federal government in education. Some—probably most—hoped that some new way could be found to raise the issue of education to a level of national awareness without relying on such past practices as federal grants. The tension created by trying to find this new way permeated the debate that took place during the next five years.
>
> President Bush complemented his meeting with the governors by sending to Congress legislation that he believed would reform education. That bill contained a number of small-scale programs seeking to change a few schools and practices. The Democratic House and Senate reluctantly passed a version of Bush's bill. However, very conservative Republican senators subsequently filibustered the final bill; and the initial Bush school reform initiative died in 1990.
>
> In 1991 Lamar Alexander was appointed secretary of education by President Bush, and he substantially revised the bill that the Senate had killed the year before. Alexander, working with Chester Finn and others who were familiar with the work of British Prime Minister Margaret Thatcher in enacting a national curriculum in England and Wales, convinced Bush to endorse the idea of national standards for education.

[Ed. Note: Of interest here is that the National Assessment of Educational Progress (NAEP) had been working on assessment for many years, dating back at least to 1980, with Clare Burstall of Wales, U.K.]

The internationalization of education, with its exchanges of data systems, curricula, methods, technology, teachers, etc., is essential for the implementation of the international socialist management and control system being put in place right now. A fascinating book entitled *Union Now: The Proposal for Inter-Democracy—Federal Union* (shorter version) by Clarence Streit (Harper Brothers Publishers: New York and London, 1941) described plans for the reunification of the United States and England, the first stage of which is presently being expanded to include the European Community and former (?) communist countries in Eastern Europe.

Our nation's replication of the English education system, as proposed by Lamar Alexander and Chester Finn, coincides with the proclaimed desire of Andrew Carnegie in 1886 to "create two nations out of one people" (return the United States to the "mother" country—England).

Carnegie's corporation of the same name and all of its subsidiaries have been the principal organizations in charge of American education. Through funding of the most important entities controlling American education—the Educational Testing Service, the National Assessment of Educational Progress, the Education Commission of the States—and through its most important exchanges with the "former" Soviet Union, Carnegie's power, influence, and point of view have been strongly felt throughout this century. Lenin would be pleased indeed with the accomplishements of the Carnegie Corporation in promoting what Lenin referred to as international socialism through the creation of individual regions and later through the amalgamation of those regions into an international socialist system; i.e., one world government.

The following quote from Andrew Carnegie's *Triumphant Democracy or Fifty Years' March of the Republic* (Charles Scribners Sons: New York, 1886) is thought provoking:

> Time may dispel many pleasing illusions and destroy many noble dreams, but it shall never shake my belief that the wound caused by the wholly un-looked for and undesired separation of the mother from her child is not to bleed forever. Let men say what they will, therefore, I say, that as surely as the sun in the heavens once shone upon Britain and America united, so surely is it one morning to rise, shine upon, and greet again the reunited state, the British-American union.

Jennings's revelations from *National Issues in Education* continue below:

> The governors and the President had agreed on national goals for education in 1989, but they had not proposed national standards for education. Therefore, Bush's second reform plan moved national involvement in education to a more advanced stage....
>
> A Republican president proposing such national standards in education was the education policymaking equivalent to the reshaping of foreign policy when President Nixon went to China. Richard Nixon had made a career out of attacking Communism and calling liberals sympathizers of that ideology; and then he—not a liberal—opened the doors to "Red" China, the same doors that he had spent 25 years locking.

[Ed. Note: It was also under Nixon's watch that the National Institute of Education was created and it was he who carved the nation into ten regions, facilitating the change in our constitutional governance from a constitutional republic to a participatory democracy—through the regional government process necessary for world government. The late Senator Edmund Muskie (D.-Maine), referred to as "Mr. Metro" by those opposed to regional government, said Nixon had accomplished what several democratic administrations had been unable to accomplish!]

Jennings continued his fascinating account as follows:

> Democratic Presidents Kennedy and Johnson had proposed a major expansion of federal aid to education in the 1960s and had achieved the enactment of historic legislation that created the current array of federal programs. But they were dogged along the way by criticism from conservatives who asserted that the liberals were really trying to nationalize education. Now, 25 years later, it was a self-proclaimed conservative Republican, not a liberal Democrat, who was advocating a monumental movement away from local control of education.
>
> Despite the importance of the second Bush legislation, it ran into the same problem as the first. A Democratic Congress reluctantly passed the bill in the House and the Senate, but

the conference report again was filibustered by very conservative Republican senators who were not as impressed as were Bush, Alexander, and Finn with the accomplishments of Margaret Thatcher in establishing a national curriculum.

[Ed. Note: The writer would like to repeat the quote from Theodore Dalrymple (pen name for Dr. Anthony Daniels), the British physician who wrote for *The Wall Street Journal* in 1988 the following observations concerning the deplorable condition of the English education system which Bush, Alexander and Finn wished to emulate:

In eight years in medical practice in an English slum (in which lives incidentally a fifth of a population of the industrial English city where I work) I have met only one teen-ager of hundreds I have asked who knew when World War II was fought. The others thought it took place in the 1900s or the 1970s, and lasted up to 30 years.]

National Issues in Education also includes a chapter by U.S. Secretary of Education Richard W. Riley. Riley provides two delicious morsels regarding the "bipartisan" atmosphere surrounding the birthing of *Goals 2000* and the *School-to-Work Opportunities Act*:

The National Goals Panel was actively opposed by Congress which felt no ownership and resented the non-voting status of Congressional members.... (p. 5)
...Truth was the reform movement at the national level had no statutory basis. Even ten years after the report *A Nation at Risk*, there had been little federal response. The National Education Goals, three years after their announcement, had no legal standing of any kind. No federal initiative, no funding or flexibility had been enacted to provide states, communities, or schools with the assistance they needed to reach these important goals. Most troubling of all, as attractive as the goals were, as important as they were, as essential as they were, in the final analysis they represented nothing more than a political agreement between a former President and the nation's governors. We decided to take the seeds of interest we had inherited and transform them into a national movement—a movement in which states and local districts with a clear vision of where they wanted to go could count on the American people and the federal government as partners in the journey. Thus the *Goals 2000—Educate America Act* was conceived. (p. 6)

[Ed. Note: The reader by this time recognizes the fact that the American people did not buy into *Goals 2000/School-to-Work*, that the government was compelled to use its change agent manual—the bag of tricks in the *Community Action Toolkit*— to implement the restructuring and get key legislation passed. (See Appendix XIV.)

IN DECEMBER OF 1995 THE FOLLOWING INFORMATION WAS EXCERPTED FROM UNITED STATES Information Agency internet sources and put into summary form by education researcher and writer Joan Masters of Bowie, Maryland:

DECEMBER 3, 1995: MADRID, SPAIN—U.S. President Bill Clinton, president of the European Commission Jacques Santer, and Prime Minister of Spain Felipe Gonzalez, who is also president of the European Union's Council of Ministers, formally endorse a New Transatlantic Agenda (NTA). The NTA would enable the two sides, the US and the EU, to join forces to deal with a wide range of international, political and economic issues. The New Agenda's "joint action" has some one hundred "initiatives" aimed at achieving four broad objectives:

1. Promoting peace, development and democracy around the world;
2. Responding to global challenges;
3. Contributing to the expansion of world trade; and
4. Building bridges across the Atlantic.

With little or no national debate the United States is committed to become the European Union's "partner" in solving most of the world's problems. Only the enlargement of NATO receives wide coverage. (On September 9, 1997, 133 of the United States' "leading foreign policy experts and statesmen" signed the New Atlantic Initiative Statement on NATO enlargement. These signers cover a broad range of America's well-known nationalists and internationalists. John O'Sullivan, editor of William F. Buckley's "conservative" journal *National Review*, resigned his position to become founder and co-chairman of the New Atlantic Initiative.)

DECEMBER 21, 1995: WASHINGTON, D.C.—Dr. Joseph Duffey, Director of the United States Information Agency (USIA) and Mr. Jeronimo Saavedra Acevedo, minister of science and education of Spain, signed an agreement between the United States of America (U.S.) and the European Community (EC) establishing a cooperation programme in higher education and vocational education and training. This agreement is in keeping with the fourth NTA objective—"Building bridges across the Atlantic"—and establishes a "formal basis for the conduct of cooperative activities in higher education and vocational education and training." The annex of this seven page Agreement reveals that the US/EC will form a consortia to support education institutions and vocational training establishments undertaking joint projects. Each consortium will be supported by seed funding and will mutually agree upon eligible subject areas. Activities eligible for support may include: frameworks for student mobility, including work placement; structured exchanges of students, teachers, trainers, and administrators; joint development of innovative curricula; and transatlantic cooperation. Among other things too numerous to mention here, the joint consortia projects will be made available for the use of "a wider audience." *No longer called citizens*, the Agreement acknowledges "the crucial contributions of education and training for the development of *human resources* capable of participating in the global knowledge-based economy." [emphasis in original]

By 1996 grants were already being given to US colleges and universities for such projects as: "Global Dimensions in Health Care;" "Atlas"—a project for environmental management; and "US/EU Export Development Program," a feature of which is the use of student mobility, "not just for academic purposes, but also as part of an export development program designed to facilitate more transatlantic trade for local business and industry." Another very interestingly named project, given out to seven different American institutions, is called "Work World 2000: An International Strategy for School-to-Work Transitions." Using simulations of both American and European workplaces and company models, students will learn the structures of international business and follow up with transatlantic exchanges and internships.

DECEMBER 1995: BRUSSELS, BELGIUM—Representatives from the nations of the European Union release their study group report called *Accomplishing Europe through Education and Training*. For Americans to understand the inherent dangers of throwing in our lot with the socialistic states of Europe, especially in the field of education, this report needs to be studied in depth. It's no secret that some conservatives in the U.S. believe that a European education is far superior to what has been offered in our public education system in the last thirty years. And this may be right, at least academically. On the other hand, there are those who believe many of the "innovations" we are plagued with, such as sex education, originated in Europe, especially in England. One European group doing studies on "multi-media" materials complains that most of the educational software in the EU comes from the US. So, it is difficult to know for certain which continent created the propaganda horrors inflicted on our children today in the classrooms of our respective countries. But whatever the truth, much as the Soviet Union once tried to create the "Soviet Man," the European Union study group report is laying out a plan to develop the "European Union Citizen."

The report reminds its readers of the history of pagan times and the great philosophers of Greece, then recalls Europe's Christian roots, implying that the Union of Europe's ancient nations has now begun a new age; education of the Union's children must change to accommodate this modern era of globalisation and dissemination of information technologies. For Americans, who cut their milk teeth on the ideals of independence and freedom, and the belief that anyone who works hard can overcome anything, even class, one sentence is particularly chilling. The report says, "Trends in work/employment practices and the emergence of a learning society will be even more instrumental in defining everyone's place, as a function of skills and knowledge built up throughout life." But with all the talk of the information society and "life-long learning," these European educators predict that "ever-increasing ecological pressures will prompt a radical re-think of our model of economic growth with increasing emphasis on 'sustainability.'" This contradictory vision of economic growth and environmental sustainability may yet be the un-doing of the New World Order on both sides of the Atlantic.

1996

THE *CHICAGO TRIBUNE* OF FEBRUARY 14, 1996 CARRIED THE ARTICLE "SCHOOL PLAN SKIPS over the Basics." Some excerpts follow:

Yet for all their specifics, school leaders said Tuesday that they will not spell out many details on how they will implement their version of direct instruction, a back-to-basics instructional approach that has won national acclaim for improving student achievement at other inner city schools....

Chicago school officials were so impressed with the approach, which uses scripted lessons delivered in a rapid-fire manner, that a contingent of them flew last year to Houston to see how direct instruction helped one of the schools post some of the highest test scores in Texas.... But for now, Chicago school leaders said they need more time to "customize" direct instruction to fit the local needs....

"The educational plan is a big plan, and it's comprehensive," said Paul Villas, chief executive officer of the schools. "We've looked at a lot of solutions and direct instruction is just one of them."... DeChico maintained that they remained enthusiastic about the direct instruction approach....

One other top school official indicated that the early draft of the education plan included only a few lines about it. The reason, according to the source, was because of complaints, particularly from local teachers, that the approach is too time-consuming and stunts teacher creativity.... The administrator suggested that school leaders may have been swayed by teacher complaints that direct instruction requires too much of teachers, who would have to study the scripted lessons nightly for the next day....

Villas said that by June, school leaders will be ready to trot out details on how they will use direct instruction.

[Ed. Note: Where are the norm-referenced test scores that prove student achievement in inner city schools? Or, has enough time passed (16 years) that the change agents can count on parents and teachers having such short memories that they have forgotten that 18,000 inner city students dropped out of high school due to the same "rat lab" Chicago Mastery Learning experiment to which they were subjected between 1968 and 1981?]

THE *CHICAGO TRIBUNE* RAN THE ARTICLE "CITY SCHOOLS DROPPING IOWA SKILLS TESTS" on March 7, 1996. An excerpt follows:

> The new test would assess whether students have mastered what they have been taught.... One potentially contentious issue remains: direct instruction, a strategy aimed at forcing low-achieving schools to accept a curriculum based on scripted lessons and recitation.... "I can't imagine that the majority of the teachers in our school would at all be willing to implement direct instruction," said Julie Wopestehoff, Executive Director of Parents United for Responsible Education.

AN UNTITLED ARTICLE APPEARED IN *THE CHICAGO SUN TIMES* ON MARCH 8, 1996. AN excerpt follows:

> Determined to show that all Chicago public school students can succeed, DePaul University is waiting for the stroke of Governor Edgar's pen to kick off plans for its own charter school.... "These children can learn at the same rate as the children of Ph.D.'s.... We have a list of things we can choose from. There's direct instruction, whole language, team learning, cooperative learning," said Barbara Sizemore, Dean of DePaul University's College of Education, Chicago.

[Ed. Note: Well, well. This quote stripped the Empress and her change agent associates of whatever clothing they had left—which wasn't much due to this type of "bait and switch" technique having been used on parents over and over again. Create the problem; parents scream; impose a solution they would never have accepted in the first place; parents gratefully accept it, not knowing the only difference between the solution and what they had before is a new label.

Some parents understood the manipulative mastery learning method. This writer has boxes full of letters from teachers, doctors, and parents in Texas, Ohio, Arizona, Indiana, etc., deploring the serious negative effects of mastery learning—sickness and stress. But when the change agents substituted the "direct instruction" label for the failed "mastery learning" label, how could parents be expected to recognize the deceit?

Actually, it does take some kind of nerve to propose a solution which only fourteen years earlier had been *discredited as a failure* in Chicago, and which has put Chicago, Washington, D.C., and South Carolina at the bottom of the heap as far as test scores go. If one checked all the other inner city schools that have used this Skinnerian method, one would find only minor differences between their low test scores and those of the three mentioned above.

Dean Sizemore was telling parents and teachers something—something very important. She was obviously very proud of the menu being offered to the naïve charter school parents and children in Chicago—the menu to be offered to all schools in the nation. The implementation of site-based management (unelected, hand-picked councils) would assure approval of Sizemore's controversial outcome-based education which consisted of cooperative learning and Engelmann's direct instruction/DISTAR/SRA/mastery learning in conjunction with literature-based whole language instruction, etc.—a delicious concoction to be sure, guaranteed to further dumb down our children.

Parents, Direct Instruction is *not* back-to-basics (teacher-directed instruction of content, with the teacher teaching in the front of the classroom). It is fast-forward into the world of global workforce training, where the teacher will be in front of the classroom chanting, not instructing; your children will be expected to "perform" like rats or pigeons, not learn academic content.

Parents want teachers to teach content which their child can relate to other parts of his/her life for complete understanding; they want their child to be able to make connections between what he/she learns and past knowledge, to be used in the future. Chanting back what a teacher chants is *not* learning—it is training. There can be no transfer of knowledge when bits and pieces of information which relate to nothing are all the "robots" can repeat. Parents don't want teachers to be controllers or directors, and they surely don't want their children to be passive learners chanting back answers like parrots, mimicking what a teacher says. Such *training* considers your child as nothing but a raw resource to be prepared and molded as a product. Traditional education, which allows for give and take between teacher and student (creativity) is the last thing in which the corporate/education elite is interested.

This new type of education (training), in conjunction with mandatory community service, workforce preparation starting in elementary school, mandatory uniforms for America's school children, new school board policies regarding fighting in school which will allow the police to come to the school and drag your children into holding tanks for further prosecution, etc., sends chills down the back of this writer. It brings to mind the ugliness of a recent era in history which many seem to have forgotten.]

IN-SERVICE TEACHER TRAINING WAS HELD IN CHICAGO, INDIANAPOLIS, AND MINNEAPOLIS during the first part of May in 1996. The flyer advertising these events stated the following:

NATIONAL EDUCATION INSTITUTE PRESENTS

Using Research-Based Teaching Techniques to Increase Student Learning:
Or How to Teach Anyone Anything

PROGRAM AGENDA:
The three key parts of direct instruction; discover the major and minor differences between direct instruction and traditional teaching methods.
National consultant, teacher and trainer Adrienne Allen conducted the training sessions.

[Ed. Note: This flyer was received from a homeschool mom who said the "research-based" training was for homeschoolers. The above quote presents a very different picture from that being circulated throughout the nation which describes direct instruction as a "traditional" teaching method.]

"DUMBED-DOWN SATs DISGUISE DEFICIENCIES—THE FAULT, DEAR EDUCATOR, IS NOT IN Our Tests," by George C. Roche, president of Hillsdale College in Hillsdale, Michigan, was published in the July 5, 1996 issue of *Human Events*. Dr. Roche's article underscores the success of the internationalist change agents' relentless efforts to dumb down our children and, in turn, our nation. The following excerpts are most enlightening:

"SAT Scores Rise Strongly after Test Is Overhauled" read a *Wall Street Journal* headline. The continuation of the article carried the title "SAT Scores Post Strong Increase." Good news?

Hardly. The "higher" scores came from a "dumbed-down" test. Students now have an extra half hour to complete the "new" Scholastic Aptitude Test. They now use electronic calculators and answer fewer questions in general and fewer multiple-choice math questions in particular. Reading passages now ask definitions from context. And the difficult antonym section (involving knowledge of words that are opposite in meaning), calling for linguistic and intellectual subtleties long lost, has been dropped entirely.

...Here's the College Board's rationale for the changes: "Students taking the SAT in the 1990s are substantially different from those who took the test in the 1940s when the scale was created. Continuing to force-fit their scores to a scale established for a very different group of students reduces the interpretive value of the score within the population for the sake of slavish consistency to the original scale and comparisons over time."

They'd like you to be persuaded by exaggerations like "force-fit" and "slavish" and breeze past their statement that today's students are "substantially different" from those who took the test in 1940. I'd like you to be persuaded that the College Board just admitted that the educational system's "substantially different" students are really "substantially deficient."

...The history standards of the government's new *Goals 2000* program, drenched in political correctness, highlight America's admitted faults and leave out much that is positive. OBE students going through the *Goals 2000* program wouldn't have much of a chance with the older, tougher SAT test, but the easier version, plus the "recentering" changes now in place will help disguise actual deficiencies.

Putting an artificially higher number on actually lower academic performance only highlights the problems facing American education. You can fiddle with the figures forever, but as long as education "professionals" refuse to be honest with our citizens, matters can only get worse.

[Ed. Note: Not only did Dr. Roche vent his frustration with the new SAT, *The New York Times*, in an article entitled "Defining Literacy Downward" in its August 28, 1996 issue, stated: "The S.A.T. turns poor performance into a new norm."]

DIANA M. FESSLER, A DULY-ELECTED MEMBER OF THE OHIO STATE BOARD OF EDUCATION, wrote "An Open Letter to Governor Voinovich and Members of the General Assembly" on August 5, 1996. That there are still elected officials who take seriously their duties to represent their constituents and not government officials in a state department of education is cause for rejoicing. Excerpts from this important and illuminating letter, which gives a first-hand account of the ridiculous tax-supported antics required by the bureaucracy to create "group think," follow:

This letter will not engender the good will of my colleagues on the State Board of Education (SBE), but I value good government more than camaraderie. Three problems exist: using public money for questionable activities, discussing crucial issues at locations not convenient for the public, and attempting to squelch First Amendment rights. SBE retreats have been hotbeds for these misdeeds.

During the August '94 retreat, members were blindfolded and collectively tied up with rope, reportedly, to identify members with leadership skills.

The January '95 retreat was my first after being elected. Stated goals were priority setting and "team building." Dividing us into two groups, the facilitators gave each person five or six cardboard puzzle pieces from different puzzles. They instructed us not to speak, point, or otherwise show that we needed certain pieces from one another in our group. We had thirty minutes to finish our individual puzzles. I finished the task in two or three minutes and then struggled to remain silent, yet, after looking at the pictures from the previous retreat, I spoke out against spending public dollars on games. A facilitator tried to shush me. Unintimidated, I urged our group to help the other one so we could go on with *business*. Our group was admonished for breaking the rules. Puzzling rules, if the mission was team building.

Loath to attend the five-day January '96 retreat, I went because committee minutes showed a request for the code of ethics from another state's appointed board. My antenna up, I was not surprised when the facilitator asked us to list attitudes and behaviors we expected of one another. Terms like respect, tolerance, team work, and speaking with one voice were used. I asked if we were creating a code of ethics and the answer was yes. I reasoned that an appointed or volunteer board might need a code of ethics if they do not use some form of parliamentary procudure, but, for the SBE, such a code would be superfluous. We have each sworn an oath to support the Constitution and obey the law, and our meetings are governed by parliamentary law. The issue was dropped, temporarily.

More game-playing. Approaching from opposite sides at the same time, each team was instructed to cross a large mat that was divided into squares and to avoid the squares that had embedded beepers. A beep signaled the person to retrace his steps and the team to start over. Observing from the sideline, I could not stand the foolishness any longer. I broke the rules by putting paper on the non-beeping squares to mark the path. As I watched two adult bodies share a space big enough for two shoes, not four, I wondered what this had to do with public education or public policy debate. After dinner, some board members were roped together.

Days later, the code of ethics issue resurfaced when a member raised the noxious idea that we should "speak with one voice." Most members seem to believe that once the Board adopts a resolution, all members must support it, regardless of its merit or lack thereof, because it is the will of the majority. *As an elected official, it is my responsibility to speak on the behalf of those who elected me—not to be an echo of the Board.* Accordingly, even if all other members vote yes and I cast the only no vote on matters of substance, I cannot promote that to which I am opposed, nor do I feel any obligation to remain silent.

The discussion of speaking with one voice included the absurd notion that the Ohio Department of Education's (ODE) 500-plus employees (the bureaucracy) and the nineteen-member State Board of Education are just one big happy family—blurring the distinction between the two and minimizing SBE's authority to direct the ODE. No one except me seemed to reject this fallacy.

Speaking with one voice also included the notion that members should not attend legislative hearings or otherwise influence legislation, but should reserve those activities for ODE staff. The concern was that a legislator or the press might regard a member, not as a citizen, but (forbid the thought), as a member of the SBE and therefore might take heed to any comments or concerns! Nevertheless, members *are* encouraged to support *majority* opinion, under the supervision of ODE personnel. I immediately reacted by saying that the SBE cannot make policies that violate the Constitution. Agitated, the same member who raised the issue asked me, "Why not?" Incredulous that an American in public service would need to ask such a question, I explained that I will not surrender my rights of free speech and association. The ODE attorney remained silent throughout this heated exchange although another member suggested that such a policy could be a public relations problem. We adjourned.

"PARENTS TURN TO TUTORS: REBELLION AGAINST WHOLE LANGUAGE" BY ROSALIND ROSSI and Sharon Cotliar was published in *The Chicago Sun-Times* on August 12, 1996. Excerpts follow:

> Jean Iovino, owner of eight Sylvan Learning Centers in the suburbs, said the number of beginning readers in her centers has skyrocketed in the last five years.... Many parents suggest that the shift from phonics to the "whole language" philosophy of reading instruction is behind the drop in scores.... "Our business has increased 20 percent a year every year for the past four years," said Vickie Glazar, spokeswoman for Maryland-based Sylvan Learning Systems.

[Ed. Note: Sylvan Learning Centers use mastery learning/direct instruction. The *Reading Excellence Act of 1998* (H.R. 2614) contains the legally questionable call for the use of Sylvan Learning Centers: "Tutorial service providers might include public agencies, non-profit private organizations, and profit-seeking private business firms (e.g., Sylvan Learning Centers)."]

"A GUIDE TO COMPETING TEACHING METHODS" BY ROSALIND ROSSI WAS PUBLISHED IN *THE Chicago Sun-Times* on August 12, 1996. A portion of "A Guide" follows:

> Direct Instruction: A method of instruction in which the teacher directs lessons in carefully sequenced steps. In one of its most conservative forms, developed by Siegfried Engelmann of the University of Oregon, teachers use textbooks with child-tested scripts to teach phonics in small steps, and children repeat back words, or give answers as a group in fast-paced, rhythmic, "choral chants." Often includes heavy use of workbooks. Complaints about direct instruction: The Engelmann method, used alone, has been accused of turning teachers into robots, of robbing children of the joy of reading real books at an early age and of emphasizing sound over meaning.

DR. SHIRLEY MCCUNE, PROJECT DIRECTOR FOR THE MID-CONTINENT REGIONAL EDUCAtional Laboratory (McREL) wrote *The Light Shall Set You Free* (Athena Publishing, Alpha Connections: Santa Fe, New Mexico, 1996), in which she revealed her theological connections with New Age guru Alice Bailey. Excerpts from McCune's book underscore the fact that the U.S. taxpayer is paying the salaries of social engineers with bizarre beliefs who are wreaking havoc in curriculum development and organizational restructuring of the nation's schools. Excerpts follow:

Those who journey into the Light will move with us in the ethers to live in the Fifth Dimension and above. Those who choose to stay in the lower vibrations will be provided for accordingly also. The Earth will be cleansed in the next decade for the purification must be complete.... The way to the Light is to increase your vibratory frequency.... This point of Light stimulates each breath we take.... The Light is within.... This tremendous source of power can be accessed only by going within the mind's eye and by listening to the silence.... This path requires a whole new curriculum and set of guidelines to describe our existence.... The Light is within us always, silently waiting to be discovered, to show us the way back to our divinity.... Each individual is actually a co-creator with the Divine.... The date for entry into the Fifth Dimension is scheduled for the year 2012, says Kuthum [An alleged "ascended master" who supposedly transmitted his ideas to Madame Blavatsky, founder of the Theosophical Society and author of *The Secret Doctrine* and *Isis Unveiled*, ed.]....

...We are entering the Age of Aquarius.... The goal for all of humanity who will enter the new millenium is to become androgynous.... Educational systems, businesses, political structures, and governments all built on self-serving principles, for example, are crumbling, only to be re-born through tremendous pain into higher forms. Thus, we are witnessing "the end of the world" and we do not even recognize what we see. Standing on the threshold of the Aquarian Age... we can align our bodies and our behaviors to create harmony and consistency with the God within us.

"UNDERSTANDING OUTCOME-BASED EDUCATION," AN ARTICLE WRITTEN BY JERRY L. HADdock, Ed.D., regional director for Southern California/Southern Nevada and director of curriculum for the Association of Christian Schools International (ACSI), and Sharon R. Berry, Ph.D., a director of curriculum of ACSI, was published in 1996 and circulated throughout the ACSI network of Christian schools.[49] Excerpts follow:

MASTERY LEARNING
Developed from Skinnerian psychology, Mastery Learning proposes that students should be taught until they have learned a subject no matter how long it takes. Believing that all learning could be broken into minute, successive steps of behavior, thousands of objectives for each subject area were published in voluminous books. The difference in Outcome-Based Education is a specification of a smaller number of more general outcomes. For example, there are 36 outcomes specified for graduation in the Littleton, Colorado project....

On the last page of the article—as a part of a larger category entitled "Where Do We Stand?"—under the title "Mastery Learning" the authors assert:

This [mastery] is also an important part of the Christian school. No, not in the sense that secular OBE proponents advocate, but with a Christ-honoring emphasis. One that says every student is important enough to have an appropriate instructional program and a teacher who is sensitive enough to do what is necessary to ensure that the student masters curriculum at his/her ability level. The distinction here is that we should not require all students to learn at the same rate. God has given each of us different talents and abilities. To the best of our ability we ensure that students achieve basic standards, with all students being challenged to reach their potential. As Dr. Bruce Wilkinson, author of "The 7 Laws of the Learner," has emphasized, "If a student hasn't learned, the teacher hasn't taught."

[Ed. Note: It is difficult to understand ACSI's support for a method of teaching which is clearly based on Darwin's theory of evolution (that man is an animal), which uses Skinnerian stimulus-response-stimulus operant conditioning. How can Christian educators and parents oppose the teaching of evolution at school board meetings across the country and then return to their homes/schools the next day and use a method of teaching/learning which is based on the evolutionist theory which they oppose? Personally, this writer does not agree with Dr. Wilkinson's statement concerning the student and teacher. Sometimes, no matter how well a teacher may teach, the student may not be interested in learning.[50]]

ANITA HOGE DEVISED AND DISTRIBUTED WIDELY "FIVE MAGIC QUESTIONS ENABLE PARENTS to Debate the Issues" in 1996 as a tool for parents' groups to use in testimony before state legislatures and local school boards. The text of the pamphlet follows in its entirety.

FIVE MAGIC QUESTIONS ENABLE PARENTS TO DEBATE THE ISSUES

Education regulations or laws state which standards or outcomes your child needs to meet to graduate. Many of the outcomes are vague and subjective. Look at the verbs. This shows why these outcomes are impossible to measure objectively. An example under a category like "Citizenship" states, "All students will negotiate and cooperate with others." The Five Magic Questions parents can use to win the debate when outcomes reflect subjective or vague areas are:

1. *How do you measure that outcome?* If an outcome states that "all children must have ethical judgment, honesty, or integrity," what exactly is going to be measured? How do you measure a bias in a child in order for him to graduate? Must children be diagnosed? Will they be graded by observation or pencil or paper tests? How will performance or behavior be addressed?

2. *How is that outcome scored or what is the standard?* What behavior is "Appropriate" and to what degree? For example, how much self-esteem is too much or not enough to graduate? Can government score the attitudes and values of its citizens?

3. *Who decides what that standard will be?* The state has extended their mandated graduation requirements or exit outcomes down to the individual child. This bypasses all local autonomy. What about locally elected school directors? Will they become obsolete? Are we talking about a state or government diploma?

4. *How will my child be remediated?* What are you going to do to my children to change them from here to there in their attitudes and values in order to graduate? How do you remediate ethical judgment, decision-making, interpersonal skills, environmental attitudes? What techniques will be used? What risks are involved? What justification does the state have to change my children's attitudes?

5. *What if parent and state disagree on the standard or how it is measured in the classroom?* Who has the ultimate authority over the child? What about privacy? Can parents opt out of a graduation requirement of the state?

All children must meet the same fixed standard of "future citizen" or not graduate, go to college, or get a job. Your child is human capital. This is why the state wants control of the graduation requirement—and that is why local school boards must create policy to stop the state from exerting power over elected officials. Ask this question: Do you want equity in opportunity, or do you want equity in standards?

AMERICAN FAMILY ASSOCIATION LAW CENTER IN TUPELO, MISSISSIPPI ISSUED A PRESS release on September 13, 1996 which read in part:

> On behalf of concerned parents, students and school board members in two Oregon school districts, the American Family Association Law Center and National Legal Foundation teamed up to file a lawsuit in federal district court today challenging Oregon's statewide education reforms adopted in conjunction with *Goals 2000*.
>
> The momentous lawsuit alleges three claims of constitutional violations by the Oregon State Board of Education, Superintendent of Public Instruction and two school districts, resulting from Oregon's adoption and implementation of the radical transformational ideas embodied in the Oregon Education Act for the Twenty-first Century. The forty-two page complaint alleges that Oregon has adopted reforms that dispense with aspects of traditional education and, in their place, mandate "outcomes" that become the only absolutes tolerated by the statewide educational system.
>
> The Complaint further alleges that the Oregon reforms formally abandon any belief in absolutes or facts in a traditional sense, and, in their place, decree feelings, attitudes, and beliefs approved by the government. According to AFA Law Center Senior Trial Attorney Stephen M. Crampton, "The imposition of government-approved attitude and beliefs flies squarely in the face of the First Amendment. It was Thomas Jefferson who said that God created the mind free and it is, therefore, not subject to force or coercion by government. Apparently, the Oregon educational establishment is unfamiliar with Jefferson or the First Amendment. What is going on [in Oregon] is nothing short of slavery of the mind."[51]

[Ed. Note: Hats off to the concerned parents and citizens of Oregon! Although the Oregon lawsuit was not successful—the negative decision by the court is being appealed—it provided a case study of what could be done in all fifty states, since all states have the same problems due to *Goals 2000* mandates. Many New Standards Project (NSP—Tucker's National Center for Education and the Economy program which leads to Certificate of Initial Mastery) states must comply with NSP requirements which *totally remove* any local control or significant input. The Oregon lawsuit, in this writer's opinion, would have been more significant and have had a better chance of succeeding had it included as its major concern the role of the federally funded Northwest Regional Educational Laboratory in developing the NWREL Goals Collection as the delivery system for the dehumanizing mastery learning/direct instruction method required by OBE and *Goals 2000*.]

A PAPER ENTITLED "A REPORT ON THE WORK TOWARD NATIONAL STANDARDS, ASSESS-ments and Certificates" was prepared for the Ohio State Board of Education in 1996 by Diana M. Fessler, elected board member. This superb report was submitted under cover of a Letter of Transmittal, excerpts of which follow:

> The National Center on Education and the Economy is an organization dedicated to the development of a unified system of education and employment. The National Center's vision is to create a national human resources development system, interwoven with a new approach to governing. This report is a summary of the National Center's agenda that is, by design and intent, applicable to all states, and it is now being implemented in many of them.
>
> As you are well aware, the "Standards for Ohio Schools: Coming Together to Build a Future Where Every Child Counts" document is coming up for a vote in the near future. It is riddled with continuous improvement, professional development, diminished authority for

local school boards, school performance standards, a call to "organize" programs according to labor market needs, a provision for worksite-based learning opportunities; all of which dovetail nicely with the NCEE agenda....

There is no doubt that H.R. 1617 (known as the *Consolidated and Reformed Education, Employment, and Rehabilitation Systems Act* or CAREERS), and the Senate version of the same bill, S. 143 (*The Workforce Development Act of 1995*), are extensions of the 1994 *School-to-Work Act*. They represent the culmination of the NCEE's effort to get Congress to impose "The System" on all Americans. However, federal control is not needed to put "The System" in place in every state. The only thing that is needed is the federal money that will become available as the result of the legislation being passed. As an aside, although a very important one, the proposed legislation would have sent the money to the office of the governor, by-passing the General Assembly.

On September 27, 1996, the NCEE plan was temporarily halted from being incorpo-rated into federal law when the CAREERS bill was defeated in Conference Committee. Un-doubtedly, the bills will be re-introduced in 1997. Nevertheless, much of the plan can be, and is being, implemented under existing laws, regulations, and/or waivers. Unless something is done to stop it, the NCEE agenda will continue to be implemented, albeit on a less expansive scale, to the detriment of our children and grandchildren.

IN THE SEPTEMBER 1996 ISSUE OF *VITALITY* AN ARTICLE ENTITLED "EDUCATION: WHY THE 'Dumbing Down' in the Schools?" by Rep. Henry Hyde, chairman of the Republican Platform Committee, was published. Congressman Hyde, in an excellent critique of *Goals 2000*, School-to-Work and CAREERS legislation, asserted:

This concept has been around since at least the 1960s and perhaps as far back as the 1930s. It has been tried in many schools over the last 20–30 years, to the detriment of our children. In the 70s, it was called "Mastery Learning" under the supervision of Professor Benjamin Bloom, and now it is known as "Outcomes-Based Education" (OBE). State school superin-tendents have learned to call OBE by other names because of its bad reputation which precedes it, but the concepts are all the same.

[Ed. Note: Representative Henry Hyde seems to be one of the few congressmen who under-stands the "method." This writer wonders if he is aware of the fact that the Chicago schools are using the method under the label "direct instruction"—and that Chicago schools have signed an education agreement with Russia?]

IN THE SCHOOL WATCH COLUMN OF *THE ATLANTA CONSTITUTION* THE TOPIC OF THE DAY FOR October 14, 1996 was "Teaching Politics." Excerpts follow:

Teachers are finding innovative ways to interest students in becoming well-informed voters. Many teachers form a seating chart based on alphabetic order, but Linda Morrison uses another method. In her current issues class at North Cobb High School, liberals sit on the left side of the room and conservatives sit—where else?—on the right. Morrison's technique is one of many methods teachers are using to educate students on electoral and political pro-cesses.

"When you combine what we do in here with their American government class, it makes everything a lot more interesting for the students," said Morrison, a former Cobb County Teacher of the Year.

At the beginning of the year, Morrison gives her class a political orientation test, which charts how conservative or liberal a student is on several issues. The more liberal your views, the farther to the left of the room you sit. Those with moderate views sit closer to the middle, and conservatives sit on the right.

"Our main textbook is *Newsweek*," Morrison said. "Whatever the current issues are, we discuss them. All I usually do is referee."

OCTOBER 21, 1996 *THE NEW YORK TIMES* PUBLISHED AN ARTICLE ENTITLED "CARNEGIE Foundation Selects a New Leader," Lee Shulman, Ph.D. For further information about the "new leader" the reader should re-read the 1968 entry on "Learning and Instruction... Chicago Mastery Learning" in which the behavioral psychologist Lee Shulman was deeply involved.

1997

ON JANUARY 25, 1997 THE FIRST PLENARY SESSION OF THE NATIONAL COMMISSION ON Civic Renewal was held. Funded by the Pew Charitable Trusts, the Commission operates out of the Institute for Philosophy and Public Policy, a research center at the University of Maryland at College Park. One common theme running through the numerous reports produced in 1998 as a result of the Commission's study of the "deplorable" lack of citizen involvement, crying out for partnerships, etc., was that elected officials are no longer able to meaningfully contribute to the decision-making process when seeking answers to societal problems.

Those chosen to promote political and social "action" in our "needy" communities came from all political persuasions—a clever technique which made the Commission seem all-embracing and allows for public ownership of the projects selected for implementation and encouragement. When one had Ernesto Cortes, Jr. of the Industrial Areas Foundation representing the political left and former Secretary of Education William Bennett representing the political right—which is increasingly controlled by "neoconservatives"—it was not unreasonable to expect that discussions would result in reaching "common ground" politics of the "radical center;" which is an abandonment of principle by both the right and the left. A list of high profile Americans involved in the National Commission on Civic Renewal will be included at the end of this entry.

Why is the National Commission on Civic Renewal being created at this time? The Commission says that:

In spite of recent improvement in the economy, both experts and ordinary citizens have become increasingly troubled about what they see as a decline in the strength of our social fabric and in the quality of our civil and civic life. Basic institutions at the family and neighborhood level have come under intense pressure; voting and other forms of community and political participation have declined; Americans' trust in large institutions and in one another has plunged. The Commission will seek to address these ills: by gathering and assessing information and advice from a wide range of voices; by inventorying, studying, and highlighting promising civic organizations and initiatives around the country; and by offering specific recommendations for improving our civic and civil life.

Statistics published in a 1982 National Center for Citizen Involvement report quoting from a 1981 issue of *The National Volunteer* stated that 44% of Americans work as volunteers *outside* of an organization—"doing their own thing," so to speak—not the volunteerism the elite involved in commissions similar to the National Commission on Civic Renewal are interested in promoting.

The writer will wager that the above-referenced "ordinary" citizens were not consulted on this elitist project. "Ordinary" citizens are too involved in trying to make a living, "meeting the payroll," and being part of that "44%" to find time to be herded around by change agent planners, participating in projects which more often than not do not significantly affect the lives of those most in need. If the reader feels that the writer of this book is going overboard with her use of the word "elite," hold onto your seat while we make an ascent into the rooftop conference room of a Washington, D.C. club where one of the meetings held by the Commission took place. Hear ye! Hear ye! Theda Skocpol, professor of government and sociology at Harvard University, is about to give testimony before the Commission:

> My research on the past and present of U.S. civic engagement suggests that *this Commission should look upward, not downward.* [all emphases in original] Too much money in politics, too great a reliance on staff-led groups, *too much top-down manipulation—and far too few incentives for leaders to organize or engage in dialogue with actual groups of fellow citizens across the nation*—these are Americans' sense of disconnection from shared civic life. You won't find the answers you seek in purely local groups, or among the less privileged. You must look to America's powerful and best-educated elites—to folks like all of us sitting in this room. What is [it] that we [businesspeople], professors, foundation heads, think tank impresarios, and religious and political leaders are doing that we should not be doing? Equally pertinent, what new things should we elites do? America's best educated, wealthiest, and most powerful leaders are the ones who are failing our fellow citizens—because we have withdrawn from the group settings in which we would have daily chances to work with, and discuss the nation's concerns, with most of our fellow citizens.

The writer has an answer for Ms. Skocpol: stop trying to social engineer "the locals" into accepting solutions which "the locals" never asked for and probably would not want if they were informed of the real purpose of the so-called "solutions." Skocpol refers to the activities of "tax-exempt foundation heads and think tank impresarios." She would be wise to remain silent on that score, considering the severe damage done by those very entities to the preservation of freedom in our nation. The Commission seems to have made a big mistake publishing Skocpol's paper. Its condescending, elitist tone surely will not help to get their project off the ground—perhaps that is best for all of us.

Excerpts from *The Final Report of the National Commission on Civic Renewal: A Nation of Spectators—How Civic Disengagement Weakens America and What We Can Do about It* (1998) follow:

Defining the Challenge of Civic Renewal.
In America we do not depend on kings, clerics, or aristocrats, or (for that matter) on technocratic elites or self-appointed leaders to serve as the "vanguard" for the rest of us. [This is a

strange comment in light of the makeup and conclusions of the Commission and its expert consultants, ed.]...

We believe that the capacity for democratic citizenship must be nurtured in institutions such as families, neighborhoods, schools, faith communities, local governments, and political movements—and therefore, that our democracy must attend carefully to the health of these institutions....

We believe that building democracy means individuals, voluntary associations, private markets, and the public sector working together—not locked in battle.

[Ed. Note: First, the writer thought that the United States was a constitutional republic, not a democracy. Secondly, again we find the reference to the public sector and the private having to join together; i.e., partnerships, which the reader should recognize as corporate fascism/socialism. This is the first time the writer has been informed that the above-mentioned groups have been "locked in battle." The next thing we will hear is that in order for "democracy" to flower, a la Red China, we must all participate in sensitivity training/conflict resolution/encounter group sessions similar to the Ohio State Board of Education retreat described by Ohio State Board member Diana Fessler (see August 5, 1996 entry).]

We believe that democracy means not only discussing our differences, but also undertaking concrete projects with our fellow citizens to achieve common goals.... (p. 7–8)

A New Movement.
New organizations are refocusing the attention of families, schools, and communities on the formation of civic character....

...But we believe that the current level of mistrust [of government and large institutions, ed.] is inconsistent with civic health. Americans cannot love their country if they have contempt for its government.... (p. 10–11)

Meeting the Challenge of Civic Renewal.
The goals of civic renewal are straightforward: to strengthen the institutions that help form the knowledge, skills, and virtues citizens need for active engagement in civic life; to remove the impediments to civic engagement wherever they exist; and to multiply the arenas for meaningful and effective civic action.... (p. 12)

Individuals.
We therefore challenge every citizen to become an active member of at least one association dealing with matters of local neighborhood, church, or community concern. [Is this a challenge to the "44%" who cannot presently be tracked and controlled in their "civic and volunteer" service? ed.]...

Families.
It means sweeping away impediments to adoption. It means dramatically reforming foster care and establishing a national norm that no child should spend more than one birthday without a permanent home in a stable, loving family. It means a massive new partnership among the public, private, and voluntary sectors to provide adult mentors for one million young people now languishing on waiting lists across our land.

[Ed. Note: "A national norm"? Who keeps track and evaluates? Who decides what is a "stable, loving family"? "Massive new partnership"? "Adult mentors for one million young people...

on waiting lists"? What waiting lists? To be adopted, to have a mentor? These partnerships mean that government will coordinate the activities of the private and voluntary sectors to accomplish enforceable standards in the area of family life. The Commission also acknowledged that a healthy mistrust of government is essential for a "democracy." This writer believes it to be essential for the preservation of freedom as well. Perhaps what our nation needs is an even higher level of citizen mistrust which would result in more people going to the polls to vote out rascals.]

Neighborhoods.
Every neighborhood should assume responsibility for matters of significant local concern, emphasizing areas where neighbors can do meaningful civic work together. For example: neighborhood crime watches; cleaning, repairing, and patrolling public parks; escort services for students walking from home to school in the morning and back in the afternoon....
(p. 13)
...We applaud the efforts of organizations such as the National Civic League, the Center for Democracy and Citizenship, the Civic Practices Network, the Center for Living Democracy, the Pew Partnership for Civic Change, and [Heritage Foundation's] *Policy Review: The Journal of American Citizenship* to identify promising community-based empowerment efforts, to make this information available to communities searching for usable models, and to weave together local activities into a wider community-based movement for civic renewal.

Schools.
First, we add our voices to others—such as the Communitarian Network, the Character Counts! Coalition, the Character Education Partnership, and the Center for Civic Education—in support of a far greater emphasis on civic and character education. We believe that our schools should foster the knowledge, skills, and virtues our young people need to become good democratic citizens....
While the National Commission has not reached agreement on mandatory community service for high school students, we are impressed with the ways in which well-designed community work carefully linked to classroom reflection can enhance the civic education of students.... Every state should require all students to demonstrate mastery of basic civic information and concepts as a condition of high school graduation. [Citizenship, OBE-style]
In addition to their role in forming civic competence and character, we believe that the overall performance of our schools has important effects on our civic condition. To cite but one example: students consigned to failing schools are far less likely to achieve full participation in civic life. Free citizens must be educated. For this reason, we offer some proposals to improve teaching and learning....
...Despite the political and substantive difficulties, the federal government should spur the development of a voluntary national testing system with high standards and make it available for adoption (or adaptation) by states and localities. (p. 15)
The federal government, states, and localities should cooperate to increase parental choice through such measures as open enrollment and public school choice within districts (and even beyond). Within five years, every state should enact meaningful charter school legislation, and the federal government should dramatically increase its support for charter schools. (pp. 14–16)

Note: While the National Commission has focused its report and recommendations on areas of substantial agreement, we note an important area of ongoing disagreement among us.

Some members of the National Commission advocate public support for parental choice broadened to include private and religious schools, especially for low-income students now trapped in failing systems. These members believe that wider choice will enhance educational opportunity and accountability, improve quality, help get parents more involved in their children's schooling and catalyze civic engagement. They consider school choice to be a crucial and necessary step toward civic renewal and self-government.

Other Commission members believe that public schools have been, and continue to be, vital meeting grounds in which future citizens learn to respect and work with one another across their differences. These members fear that choice widened beyond the bounds of public schools could diminish support for public education, further fragment our society, and weaken our democracy.

We were not able to resolve these differences. (Not surprisingly, our nation's representatives have not yet reached common ground, either.) But we do agree on the civic standards and principles that should be employed in public deliberation on school choice, and we call for continued civil dialogue on this question.

Faith-based Institutions.
Faith-based institutions should take full advantage of new opportunities under federal law to receive public support for activities such as job search programs, "second chance" homes for unmarried teen parents, child care, and drug treatment, while maintaining their religious character. The federal government should broaden this new partnership with faith-based institutions to cover the maximum feasible range of social services....

The federal government should revise the tax code to increase incentives for charitable contributions and to recognize the charitable efforts of all Americans, including poor and low-income families....

Individual faith-based institutions should band together into community-wide coalitions to achieve important civic objectives....

...We call for the mobilization of public, foundation, and corporate support for new ventures, such as John Dilulio's Jeremiah Project, which will help gather credible data about the effectiveness of faith-based activities, mobilize resources, and direct them to promising faith-based programs.

[Ed. Note: This is the most frightening "partnership" proposal of all. When the government "partners" with another entity, it is always the government who sets the standard—and enforces it. While there may be worthwhile efforts that many churches in a community can agree upon and work together to accomplish, again, this should be decided on the local level by the churches involved without any coordination by any other entity to satisfy its goals and aims. Gathering "credible data" about "faith-based activities" so that resources can be directed to "promising faith-based programs" is exactly what the writer was referring to earlier when she cautioned the reader about partnering churches or "faith-based institutions" with the government.]

The following high profile individuals are involved in the National Commission on Civic Renewal project:

- **Co-Chairman William Bennett**, former U.S. Secretary of Education, and co-director of Empower America, an organization dedicated to promoting "conservative" principles and ideas. Secretary of Education Bennett funded the American Institute for Character Education/Thomas Jefferson Research Center's very controversial, no right/ no wrong answers character education program based on Abraham Mazlow's Hierarchy of Needs and Self-Actualization. When confronted with information concerning the U.S.-Soviet education agreements signed during his tenure, Bennett said, "I'm not in that loop."

- **Co-Chairman Sam Nunn**, former U.S. Senator from Georgia, was deeply involved in the passage of National Service legislation to lay the groundwork for a nationwide "civilian service corps" by offering generous higher education benefits in exchange for one or two years of public volunteer service. Though Nunn served as chairman of the Senate Armed Services Committee, the "volunteer service" legislation he sponsored was in no way involved with military service to this country.

- **Executive Director William A. Galston**, professor of government in the School of Public Affairs, University of Maryland at College Park and director of the University's Institute for Philosophy and Public Policy. From January 1993 through May 1995, Galston served as deputy assistant for domestic policy to President Clinton. Galston was also deeply involved in the drafting of *Goals 2000*. Prior political experience includes: chief speech writer for former Independent Party presidential candidate John Anderson's National Unity Campaign in 1980; issues director for Democratic presidential candidate Walter Mondale's campaign; senior advisor for then-Senator Al Gore's campaign for the Democratic Party's presidential nomination; and since 1989 served as senior advisor for the Democratic Leadership Council and the Progressive Policy Institute.

- **Lamar Alexander**, former governor of Tennessee, former U.S. Secretary of Education, former and present candidate for the Republican Party nomination for President of the United States.

* **Elaine Chao**, Distinguished Fellow, The Heritage Foundation. Until recently, Elaine Chao was president and chief executive officer of United Way of America.

- **Ernesto Cortes, Jr.**, Industrial Areas Foundation (IAI), Southwest regional director. Founded more than fifty years ago in Chicago by the late Saul Alinsky, the IAF is a non-profit organization, originally operating throughout the Catholic Church in the U.S., designed to provide leadership training to poor and moderate income people in more than forty broadly based, multi-ethnic organizations in the United States and the United Kingdom. (See Resources for availability of Stephanie Block's article and forthcoming book dealing with the highly controversial activities of the Industrial Areas Foundation.)

- **Amitai Etzioni**, professor at Georgetown University, founder and chairman of The Communitarian Network, is involved with the Education For All (EFA) activities both nationally and internationally, the Character Education Partnership, and the activities of the Freedom Forum First Amendment Foundation (Vanderbilt University). According to *Webster's New World Dictionary* (1976) a "communitarian" is "a member or advocate of a communistic community." Communitarianism is the social philosophy of the Skinnerian Walden II experimental commune at Los Horcones, Mexico.[52]

- **John Gardner**, professor of education at Stanford University in California, has served as former president of the Carnegie Corporation of New York, which—as the reader knows—has had virtual control over American education since the early 1900s.

- **Peter C. Goldmark, Jr.**, was elected the eleventh president of the Rockefeller Foundation in June 1988. Goldmark is a member of the Council on Foreign Relations.

- **Oz Guiness**, Senior Fellow with The Trinity Forum. Guiness headed up the controversial Williamsburg Charter Character Education Project whose work was continued by Charles Haynes of the Freedom Forum First Amendment Foundation at Vanderbilt University.

- **Michael S. Joyce**, president and chief executive officer of The Lynde and Harry Bradley Foundation in Milwaukee, was former leader of the John M. Olin Foundation in New York and the Goldseker Foundation in Baltimore. A strong supporter of parental choice in education, Joyce spent six years with the Educational Research Council of America and was a contributing editor to a textbook series on the social studies. Joyce served on the Presidential Transition Team in the Reagan Administration and in 1993 joined with William Kristol to found the Project for the Republican Future.

- **Richard D. Land**, president-treasurer of the Ethics and Religious Liberty Commission of the Southern Baptist Convention, the agency for "applied Christianity" (social and moral concerns) for the Convention.

- **His Eminence Bernard Cardinal Law**, Archbishop of Boston since 1984. He was created Cardinal by Pope John Paul II in May 1985.

- **Edwin Lupberger**, chairman of the U.S. Chamber of Commerce and member of the U.S. Chamber's Center for Workforce Preparation, also serves on the board of the Committee for Economic Development (CED) and is Louisiana's Honorary Consul of the Federal Republic of Germany.

- **Bruno V. Manno**, executive director of the National Commission on Philanthropy and Civic Renewal, is closely associated with Vanderbilt University and the Hudson Institute. Manno has served as assistant secretary of education for policy and planning and as director of planning for the Office of Educational Research and Improvement under Secretary of Education Lamar Alexander in 1986.

- **Sanford McDonnell**, chairman of the Character Education Partnership and McDonnell Douglas Corporation.

- **Michael Novak**, currently holds the George Frederick Jewett Chair in Religion and Public Policy at the American Enterprise Institute. Mr. Novak has received numerous awards, including the Templeton Prize for Progress in Religion (1994).

- **Lester Salamon**, director of the Institute for Policy Studies at The Johns Hopkins University, and was the co-editor of *Human Capital and America's Future* with David Hornbeck.

- **Robert Woodson, Sr.**, founder and president of the National Center for Neighborhood Enterprise which has been in the forefront of the movement to "empower" low-income Americans. In 1990 Woodson received the high-profile John and Catherine T. MacArthur Fellowship. He is a board member of the American Association of Enterprise Zones and the Commission on National and Community Service.

[Ed. Note: The writer cannot help but compare this commission and its *raison d'etre* with former President Dwight Eisenhower's American Assembly, which developed the pre-determined, socialistic "Goals for Americans" in 1960. As to the meeting of minds on "common ground," Shirley McCune (referred to previously in this book as a major education change agent with the Mid-Continent Regional Educational Laboratory) quoted from The [John] Naisbitt Group's training materials regarding political philosophy at an educational restructuring presentation to the Millard, Nebraska School District[53] when she explained that basic shifts re-lated to restructuring move across a continuum: Naisbitt listed "From" and "To" as being "left vs. right politics" resulting in "a politics of the radical center." This is an excellent illustration of the Hegelian Dialectic at work and is the basis of the activities of the National Commission on Civic Renewal.]

NATIONAL BLUE RIBBON SCHOOLS PROGRAM WAS THE SUBJECT OF INFORMATIONAL LETTER No. 54 from Maine's Commissioner of Education J. Duke Albanese to all superintendents of schools and secondary and middle school principals, dated May 16, 1997. The reader should realize that all states participate in this program, so the next time your superintendent or any member of the education bureaucracy says your school is not controlled by the state or federal government, pull out a copy of this letter and show it to them. The criteria for selection, which are noticeably short on references to traditional "academic excellence," are taken from *Goals 2000* materials. Excerpts follow:

> I am pleased to invite you to participate in the 1997–1998 Blue Ribbon Schools Program, for secondary and middle schools, sponsored by the U.S. Department of Education and admin-istered by the Maine Department of Education.
>
> The Blue Ribbon Schools Program identifies and gives national recognition to a diverse group of public and *private* schools that are unusually effective in meeting local, state, and national goals in educating all of their students [emphasis added]. The program seeks to promote school improvement nationwide through the collaborative self-evaluation process required of local school communities that participate. In addition, recognized schools serve as models for other schools and communities seeking to provide high quality education for all their students. This program allows us to demonstrate that today's schools can achieve excellence and to spotlight examples of what break-the-mold programs and practices might look like.
>
> Criteria for selection as a national school of excellence include:
>
> - Student focus and support
> - Challenging standards and curriculum
> - Teaching and active learning
> - Learning-centered culture and organization
> - Professional communities
> - Leadership and organizational vitality
> - School, family and community partnerships
> - Indicators of success
>
> The quality of each school is judged in the context of how successfully it is meeting its own goals and how well its programs are tailored to local needs.
>
> Nevertheless, for a school to be judged deserving of national recognition, it must show significant progress in meeting state and national goals, and must have attained a standard of overall excellence that is worthy of respect and emulation by schools elsewhere of similar size characteristics.

[Ed. Note: Don't the preceding two paragraphs represent an oxymoron?]

THE MAY 1997 ISSUE OF *THE EFFECTIVE SCHOOL REPORT* CARRIED AN ARTICLE ENTITLED "The Future of Hong Kong Is Linked to Education." Excerpts follow:

The information to be presented will come from a major report recently issued by the Education Commission established by the Central Government of Hong Kong in 1983. The major reference will be *Education Commission Report No. 7, Quality School Education*, issued in November, 1996.

As one reads each [article] in the series of articles, the obvious and continuous reference to the effective schools movement becomes more than apparent. It serves us well to understand that just as the effective schools correlates were developed within our realm of the world, so it is these same correlates have been adopted throughout the world to improve the quality and design of education.

A blue ribbon commission was formed in April, 1996 to make recommendations on the development and establishment of quality school education. Three broad principles served as the bases for the work of the committee. They included the following:

- Ways to relate school funding to performance[54]
- Roles of key players in the school system and
- Their relationship with one another.

Beyond the primary principles established by the committee are six objectives which may appear to many educators as fundamental objectives for any school system in any nation. These primary objectives include:

- to enhance the community's appreciation of the need for quality school education;
- to inculcate a *quality* culture in the school system [emphasis in original];
- to provide a practical framework for key players in the school system to achieve the aims of education in an effective, efficient and accountable manner;
- to recommend an integrated strategy for quality assurance;
- to reward or give recognition to performing schools; and
- to assist or take appropriate remedial action regarding under-performing schools to encourage initiatives and continuous improvement.

In its deliberations, the committee reviewed large volumes of overseas and local literature on the effective schools movement, quality assurance measures and school management approaches. Members of the committee participated in visits to study the operation of education throughout the world.... The [Education Commission] report was primarily a product which offered a plan to develop performance indicators for the school system.... Society has accepted the responsibility to provide an education for each and every child and to structure such an education according to their individual abilities and aptitudes.... As a leader in international commerce, the community of Hong Kong, especially the business community, recognizes massive changes in world trade and production. As businesses throughout the world, including nations in North America and Europe, have restructured their businesses and production systems, Hong Kong has emerged as one of the world's foremost financial centers, a hub of regional telecommunications, transport and trading, a leading tourist and convention destination and a major exporter of professional services to the world, especially mainland China. Along with its transformation, Hong Kong commerce now demands a labor force which is "informed and knowledgeable, highly qualified and specialised, with advanced skills and the ability to think independently and to communicate well." (p. 5)

[Ed. Note: Surprise! Surprise! The reader should turn to Appendix VI for the SAFE effective school international pilot project carried out in Korea in 1970 to see that many of the "effective school correlates" referred to above were *exported* from the U.S. to other parts of the world.]

"THE GOAL OF HONG KONG SCHOOLS—ESTABLISHING QUALITY IN ITS SCHOOLS" WAS THE feature article in the June/July, 1997 issue of *The Effective School Report*. This article continues the explanation of the transformation of Hong Kong's educational system which began in last month's issue. Excerpts follow:

> Excellence is found in the innovations and outstanding performance which distinguish one school from others.

> School Choice Should Be Made Available
> Hong Kong's education system provides parents with a choice of different types of schools. The perception of parents and students of the educational process, and the satisfaction of members of the community with outcomes are also useful indicators of the quality of education.
> Excellence is not confined to achieving outstanding academic results or promoting the self-esteem of students. For instance, some schools might achieve excellence by developing the potential of low achievers and producing value-added results.
> In order to build a quality culture in schools, a number of measures must be taken. They include:

> - translating the goals into achievable, observable and measurable quality indicators;
> - having a school funding system which is efficient and equitable, which meets basic needs and which is related to performance;
> - providing incentives to recognize and encourage initiatives and the pursuit of excellence.

> Aims
> To prepare students to become responsible citizens and maintain high moral standards....

> Output Indicators
> Output indicators may start with value-added performance in three areas; academic achievement; students' self-esteem; and perception of the school teachers, parents and students. As a start, these three types of output indicators may be developed first, followed by the development of indicators in other domains such as the students' ability for self-learning, social and communicative skills, moral attitudes and civic-mindedness. In order to encourage continuous improvement, the sooner the various indicators are developed, the better....

> Value-Added Concept of Output Indicators
> We suggest that in assessing the performance of a school, it would be more appropriate and fairer to bring in the concept of value-added achievement rather than simply looking at absolute performance. Value-added performance can be assessed in a number of areas. For example, it would not be appropriate to compare the academic performance of different schools if they admit students coming from different backgrounds. The value-added concept allows comparison of students as they enter a school and as they leave. The same concept

can be applied across the output indicators. The focus will be on a student's progress over the years.

(Information used in this series has been derived from the publication, *Education Commission Report No. 7—Quality School Education*, prepared by the Hong Kong Task Group on School Quality and School Funding and the Hong Kong Education Commission, chaired by Professor Rosie Young, November, 1996.)

[Ed. Note: Anyone the slightest bit familiar with educational restructuring, *Goals 2000*, or school-to-work programs will understand from the above excerpts, the extent of the internationalization of education and the duplicity of those—including the media—who deny that restructuring is international. Rudyard Kipling's "East is East and West is West" has been successfully repudiated by those involved in training the global workforce. A more appropriate Kipling quote might be one from *London Truth*, reprinted in the Middlebury, Vermont *Register* of March 1899, which follows: "Pile on your brown {white, black, red, pink, yellow} man's burden to satisfy your greed."]

ATLANTIC MONTHLY'S JULY 1997 ISSUE CARRIED THE ARTICLE "THE COMPUTER DELUSION" by Todd Oppenheimer. Excerpts follow:

> There is no good evidence that most uses of computers significantly improve teaching and learning, yet school districts are cutting programs—music, art, physical education—that enrich children's lives to make room for this dubious nostrum, and the Clinton Administration has embraced the goal of "computers in every classroom" with credulous and costly enthusiasm....
>
> The noted psychologist B.F. Skinner, referring to the first days of his "teaching machines," in the late 1950s and early 1960s wrote, "I was soon saying that, with the help of teaching machines and programmed instruction, students could learn twice as much in the same time and with the same effort as in a standard classroom." Ten years after Skinner's recollections were published, President Bill Clinton campaigned for a "bridge to the twenty-first century... where computers are as much a part of the classroom as blackboards." Clinton was not alone in his enthusiasm for a program estimated to cost somewhere between $40 billion and $100 billion over the next five years. Speaker of the House Newt Gingrich, talking about computers to the Republican National Committee early this year, said, "We could do so much to make education available twenty-four hours a day, seven days a week, that people could literally have a whole different attitude toward learning."... In a poll taken early last year U.S. teachers ranked computer skills and media technology as more "essential" than the study of European history, biology, chemistry, and physics; than dealing with social problems such as drugs and family breakdown; than learning practical job skills; and than reading modern American writers such as Steinbeck and Hemingway or classic ones such as Plato and Shakespeare....
>
> Interestingly, shop classes and field trips are two programs that the National information Infrastructure Advisory Council, the Clinton Administration's technology task force, suggests reducing in order to shift resources into computers. But are these results what technology promoters really intend? "You need to apply common sense," Esther Dyson, the president of EDventure Holdings and one of the task force's leading school advocates, told me recently, "Shop with a good teacher probably is worth more than computers with a lousy teacher. But if it's a poor program, this may provide a good excuse for cutting it. There will be a lot of trials and errors with this. And I don't know how to prevent those errors."[55] The issue, perhaps is the magnitude of the errors.

Alan Lesgold, a professor of psychology and the associate director of the Learning Research and Development Center at the University of Pittsburgh, calls the computer an "amplifier," because it encourages both enlightened study practices and thoughtless ones. There's a real risk, though, that the thoughtless practices will dominate, slowly dumbing down huge numbers of tomorrow's adults. As Sherry Turkle, a professor of the sociology of science at the Massachusetts Institute of Technology and a longtime observer of children's use of computers, told me, "The possibilities of using this thing poorly so outweigh the chance of using it well, it makes people like us, who are fundamentally optimistic about computers, very reticent."...

Clifford Stoll, the author of *Silicon Snake Oil: Second Thoughts on the Information Highway* (1995), told *The New York Times* last year, recalling his own school days in the 1960s, "We loved them because we didn't have to teach, and parents loved them because it showed their schools were high-tech. But no learning happened."...

Reading programs get particularly bad reviews. One small but carefully controlled study went so far as to claim that Reader Rabbit, a reading program now used in more than 100,000 schools, caused students to suffer a 50 percent drop in creativity. (Apparently, after forty-nine students used the program for seven months, they were no longer able to answer open-ended questions and showed a markedly diminished ability to brainstorm with fluency and originality.)

What about hard sciences, which seem so well suited to computer study? Logo, the high-profile programming language refined by Seymour Papert and widely used in middle and high schools, fostered huge hope of expanding children's cognitive skills. As students directed the computer to build things, such as geometric shapes, Papert believed, they would learn "procedural thinking," similar to the way a computer processes information. According to a number of studies, however, Logo has generally failed to deliver on its promises....

Judah Schwartz [a physicist], a professor of education at Harvard and a co-director of the school's Educational Technology Center, told me that a few newer applications, when used properly, can dramatically expand children's math and science thinking by giving them new tools to "make and explore conjectures." Still, Schwartz acknowledges that perhaps "ninety-nine percent of the educational programs are terrible, really terrible."...

Opinions diverge in part because research on the brain is still so sketchy, and computers are so new, that the effect of computers on the brain remains a great mystery. "I don't think we know anything about it," Harry Chugani, a pediatric neurobiologist at Wayne State University, told me. This very ignorance makes skeptics wary. "Nobody knows how kids' internal wiring works," Clifford Stoll wrote in *Silicon Snake Oil*, "but anyone who's directed away from social interactions has a head start on turning out weird.... No computer can teach what a walk through a pine forest feels like. Sensation has no substitute."...

In *Silicon Snake Oil* Michael Fellows, a computer scientist at the University of Victoria, in British Columbia, was even blunter. "Most schools would probably be better off if they threw their computers into the Dumpster."... The problem is that technology leaders rarely include these or other warnings in their recommendations. When I asked Dyson why the Clinton task force proceeded with such fervor, despite the classroom computer's shortcomings, she said, "It's so clear the world is changing."

[Ed. Note: "The world is changing" is the response change agents are trained to use when confronted by common sense taxpayers who ask why dumb projects are being funded. The writer can't possibly recall the number of times her change agent superintendent responded with those exact words! The reader can rightfully accuse the writer of this book of an anti-computer bias and of selectivity in choosing quotes to prove her point. I stand "guilty" on all counts. Those interested in computer-assisted instruction should get a copy of the above article so they will not be overly influenced by this writer's selection of quotes.]

AN ARTICLE ENTITLED "'REAL-LIFE' SCHOOL ELIMINATES BOOKS" APPEARED IN THE SEP-tember 1, 1997 issue of *The Washington Times*. The article reveals the extent to which American public schools are doing away with books.

> WALKERSVILLE, MD—Third-grader Billy Horn had a math problem his mother couldn't help solve, so she asked for the source.
>
> "I said, 'Where's your book?' and he said, 'They don't have books,'" Joan Horn said.
>
> Like most people schooled in the 1960s and 1970s, Mrs. Horn assumed her children would learn their lessons as she did, from heavy books with problems at the end of each chapter.
>
> But textbooks play a smaller role, even a minor one, in modern education.
>
> "We're trying to make school look more like real-life experiences and have assignments that are intriguing and captivating and problem-solving," said Jerome Strum, Billy's principal at Glade Elementary.

ON SEPTEMBER 24, 1997 TEXAS CHRISTIAN ALERT NETWORK (TCAN) ISSUED A MEMO entitled "Communism Comes to Texas Public Education." TCAN had received the following excerpted analytical summary by Chris Patterson, reseacher, of the Texas version of the national school-to-work legislation. The first paragraph of the alert warned that:

> This nationally mandated program will differ very little from one state to another so persons in all states should read the following very carefully and decide whether you want the federal government to have absolute control of your child and his/her career, from the cradle to the grave.

TEXAS SCHOOL-TO-WORK SYSTEM
by Chris Patterson

Introduction
In November 1996, Texas received a $61 million dollar federal grant to implement a School-to-Work (STW) system. With this grant, Texas joined the group of 36 states which participate in a national workforce development program. The national program is designed, regulated and initially funded by the federal government. The objective of this program is to coordinate workforce development with economic, educational and welfare plans within and between states of our nation. STW introduces "major changes or a radical transformation of the purpose, content and structure of public schools."

Key Components of STW
Employer needs and skill standards drive STW as curriculum and instructional practices are modified to prepare students to enter the local workforce....

Academic education and vocational instruction are fully integrated. Curriculum is founded upon performance-based standards. Academic subjects incorporate instruction related to personal and career goals. Both work and school-based instruction are designed according to local workforce needs. "All students will engage in STW."...

Students will be prepared for, certified and placed in post-secondary education or jobs which reduce mismatches between students/education and education/workplace, incorporating:

- Career awareness kindergarten through 6th grade.
- Choice of career pathway by no later than 8th grade.
- Work-based learning which includes mentorship, job-shadowing, volunteer service, school-based enterprise, apprenticeship, internship and paid work experience.
- Students will be required to acquire the following as conditions for graduation: certificates of initial and/or advanced mastery.
- Workplace competencies and paid work experience in career field.
- Statutory requirements will be established for schools to adopt block scheduling.
- Health and human services will be integrated with school and work-based learning.
- An electronic data tracking system will be developed for all students.

The only elected official responsible for STW governance is the Governor of Texas. The Texas Skills Standards Board recommends standards and certification to the Texas Council on Workforce & Economic Competitiveness....

The Council exercises statutory authority to develop, maintain and enforce STW....

The Council delegates authority to the Texas Workforce Commission to direct activities of participating organizations, including: the Texas Education Agency, Higher Education Board, Human Services, Rehabilitation Commission, Commerce Department, Commission for the Blind, National & Community Services, and Veterans Education. The Texas Workforce Commission governs twenty-eight Local Workforce Development Boards which direct local implementation of STW....

Proponents of STW Claim:

The objectives of STW are to provide students with:

- Rigorous academics;
- Opportunity for highly skilled, highly-paid jobs;
- Participation in STW is optional for both students and businesses.

Opponents of STW Claim:

Academics are diluted and academic achievement will decrease because:

- Curriculum standards are performance- or outcomes-based;
- Academic learning is displaced by personal, social and workplace competency instruction;
- Block scheduling results in less course content and lower test scores;
- Ability Grouping (including Honors Courses) which increases student achievement is prohibited;
- Traditional liberal arts education is replaced by vocational training;
- Students will be identified and trained for low skill, low pay jobs. Less than 15% of workforce requires a Bachelor's Degree;
- Leading 5 targeted occupations identify cashiers, janitors/cleaners, sales clerks and registered nurses;
- Participation is not fully voluntary—the state is pursuing legislation to make STW a condition of graduation.

Vocational and academic instruction are integrated; students are not provided an opportunity to select academic course work which is not integrated. Private sector funding is required to support STW (matching funds of $20 million will be required in 1997 and will increase to a projected $45 million in 2001). According to the STW grant proposal, Texas has no immediate plans to tax businesses to force participation as is done in Europe, but areas will be required to raise private funds.

STW Poses Troubling Questions:

- Should the government direct the development of curriculum, implementation of instructional practices and establishment of a data collection system for schools?
- Should the government through schools identify, train, certify and place workers?
- Should educational policies be established without the authority of state school boards, local district boards and legislators?
- Should the purpose, structure and means of public education be "transformed" without public debate and consent?
- Should the government establish a national plan for economic management?

ON OCTOBER 14, 1997 THE CENTER OF THE AMERICAN EXPERIMENT BREAKFAST AND LUNcheon Forum Series of Minneapolis, Minnesota held its meeting at the Radisson Plaza Hotel. The flyer announced the appearance of Chester E. Finn, Jr., who would speak on "Reforming Education—Why Do Bad Things Happen to Good Ideas?" Excerpts from the flyer read:

> Join us for an American Experiment Breakfast Forum at which Chester E. Finn, Jr., discusses why conservatively inspired school reforms frequently get morphed into anti-intellectual and statist mush. Why are basically good ideas such as outcomes-based education and national standards often turned upside down by educational establishmentarians? What does this track record portend for school choice? How can future hijackings be averted? Dr. Finn is president of the Thomas B. Fordham Foundation and also serves as John M. Olin Fellow at the Hudson Institute. Quite likely the nation's most prolific education critic, he is the author of a shelf of books and writes regularly for *The Wall Street Journal, Commentary* and other publications.

[Ed. Note: The flyer conveniently omitted the fact that Chester Finn was one of the architects of President George Bush's *America 2000*, which is the foundation document for President Clinton's *Goals 2000* "real" conservatives so thoroughly detest. The author includes this information regarding Finn as proof that the dialectic (right vs. left meeting at the radical center) has been accomplished. The "neo-conservatives" have seized the high ground, and are developing and supporting socialist programs initially proposed by the liberals. An example being the flyer statement "basically good ideas such as 'outcomes-based education,'" which is shocking coming from a supposedly "conservative" organization and speaker. The exceptions are choice, vouchers, magnet/charter schools, which give the *appearance* of originating with conservatives—which will also track your child into a preplanned future. This alien (socialist) concept is, however, supported by the multinational corporations, foundations, education union leadership, and institutionalized educational research and development change agents for global workforce training purposes.

As an example of the above collaboration toward global workforce training taking the place of education, please refer back to the 1976 entry for NEA's "Cardinal Principles Revisited, 1976," which included on its panel: David Rockefeller, Chase Manhattan Bank; McGeorge Bundy, Ford Foundation; Francois Blanchard, Syndicat National des Enseignements de Second Degre (France); Lester Brown, Worldwatch Institute; Willis Harman, Stanford Research Institute; Fred Jarvis, National Union of Teachers (England); Sally Swing Shelley, United Nations; Sir Walter Perry, The Open University (England); and Joe H. Foy, Houston Natural Gas Co. The author has selected the above, primarily non-educator individuals, from a lengthy list to help the reader understand how the education establishment at the very top is "in bed with," or more likely controlled by, leading international think tanks and multinational corporations.

The author would also like to point out that the American Experiment organization in Minnesota is another state affiliate of the neo-conservative Heritage Foundation.]

"Clinton Charm Gets Rio Workout" was the title of an article for _The News &_ _Observer_ of Raleigh, North Carolina on October 16, 1997. Excerpt follows:

By stressing the importance of education, Clinton identified a passion shared by his Brazilian host, President Fernando Henrique Cardoso, a university professor who has earmarked a portion of the unexpected earnings from Brazil's massive privatization project to improve public schools. The two governments agreed to a "partnership for education" in which the United States will help Brazil develop standardized testing of its public schools' performance, U.S. and Brazilian classrooms will be linked by computer, and a commission will be set up to oversee a new student exchange program and promote private sector investments in schools.

H.R. 2614, _The Reading Excellence Act_, passed the U.S. House of Representatives in November of 1997.[56] For the first time in U.S. history legislation has been passed which mandates a particular method of teaching. Excerpts from the abstract of the legislation follow:

SELECTION OF READING AND LITERACY GRANT APPLICATIONS
Applications from Reading and Literacy Partnerships will go to the Secretary of Education, who would forward them to a Peer Review Panel for initial approval. The Peer Review Panel will consist of experts in the field of reading who are appropriate to evaluate such grant applications. Members would be selected by the National Institute for Literacy (NIFL) in consultation with the National Research Council (NRC, a division of the National Academy of Sciences); the Child Development and Behavior Branch (CDBB) of the National Institutes of Health; and the Secretary of Education. NIFL, NRC, CDBB and the Secretary would also be members of the Peer Review Panel. A priority would be given to applications from states that have modified or plan to modify state teacher certification in the area of reading to reflect reliable, replicable research on reading.... In selecting an applicant, the Reading and Literacy Partnership must give priority to subgrantees that form a partnership with a local Head Start program or a community-based organization (CBO) working with children to improve their reading skills, or state or federally funded preschool programs or family literacy programs.

INFORMATION DISSEMINATION
The National Institute for Literacy would head up the effort to disseminate information on

reliable, replicable research on reading to all recipients of Federal financial assistance under ESEA, Head Start, IDEA, and the *Adult Education Act*. In doing so, NIFL would build upon applicable information networks currently in existence including OERI (Office of Educational Research and Improvement, U.S. Department of Education) and those established by states and private sector entities. The panel may assist any reading and literacy partnerships to determine whether applications for subgrants meet the requirements of this *Act* relating to reliable, replicable research on reading.

AUTHORIZATION
There would be a total of $260 million available for this *Act*. For more detailed information, visit the worldwide web at http://www.house.gov/eeo/.

[Ed. Note: Legislating a particular method to teach reading would never have been possible had the Hegelian Dialectic not been used. Workforce training requires that Skinnerian operant conditioning (programmed learning) be implemented in the schools. The only way to get that method accepted was:

(1) Create the problem: introduce Whole Language which is guaranteed to hinder children's ability to learn to read and causes parents to scream for a solution—any solution!
(2) Right on schedule, the social change agents responded with a predetermined solution which necessitated the use of Skinnerian direct instruction (programmed learning) to teach reading.

Little have parents realized that Skinnerian direct instruction and Skinnerian mastery learning are identical twins with very bad track records which caused William Spady et al. to rename them "Outcome-Based Education" in the early 1980s.

In order to assure passage of *The Reading Excellence Act*, Douglas Carnine, Ph.D., director of the Follow Through Direct Instruction Model in the University of Oregon's Department of *Special* Education which is associated with the National Center to Improve the Tools of Educators (NCITE) funded by the U.S. Department of Education's Office of *Special* Education, sent a letter to "Concerned Friends" requesting they lobby for passage of H.R. 2614. The author has deliberately emphasized the word "special" in special education because the fact that direct instruction programs are designed for special education students should not be lost on the reader, since *all* students—not just those needing special education—will be exposed to the direct instruction process and the Skinnerian operant conditioning method. (For more information regarding direct instruction, please refer to Appendix II, III, VI, XVII, XX, XXI, XXV, and XXVI.)

The following critique of DISTAR, Engelmann's Direct Instruction special education program, by a special education teacher in Florida should serve as a warning for those who do not understand the implications of using special education programs on all children.[57] The teacher points out that DISTAR was:

1. Developed for teaching the severely impaired (retardation and neurologically impaired).
2. NOT suitable EVER for regular education.
3. Is political "goosestepping"—group training.
4. Purely "mechanical" system—"authoritarian."
5. For NORMAL intelligence to SUPERIOR intelligence—a DISASTER. Teacher pounds away (scripted); children become bored; "frigidity" sets in and children tune out. Become the next behavior problems [emphasis in original].

6. We would be deliberately creating behavioral (mental) dropouts.

You can teach (the teachers) DISTAR in two days ("mechanistic"). Teachers don't have to know anything about language development. "El cheapo" response to whole language debacle.]

BARBARA CROSSETE WROTE AN ARTICLE, "HOW TO FIX A CROWDED WORLD: ADD PEOPLE," published in *The New York Times* on Sunday, November 2, 1997, which took a refreshingly different position on the subject of population control than that taken by most journalists writing for the major print media. Some excerpts follow:

> In the 200 years since Thomas Malthus published his *Essay on the Principle of Population* and threw a scare into the human race about the limits of the earth's resources, people everywhere have been asking: Are there too many of us?
>
> This week, leading demographers from around the world will meet here to fret over a revolutionary new fear: Will there soon be too few of us?...
>
> ...But for demographers, the problem lately is not absolute numbers of people and their pressures on the environment and natural resources. Now the experts are worried about what happens when population growth slows in a lot of places or even stops entirely or declines in some. Fertility rates in many places are dropping rapidly, especially in the richest countries, where, to put it simply, any two people are not producing two more people.
>
> If this trend continues it could have far-reaching consequences, demographers say. When more and more of the world's most highly industrialized and economically productive nations do not replenish their numbers, their role as engines of global growth—both as producers and consumers of goods—is thrown into doubt.
>
> "These developed countries have a particularly important role because they provide a great deal of the economic leadership and social leadership," said Joseph Chamie, director of the United Nations population division, which organized the conference this week.
>
> "There are basically the producer nations, the consumer nations and the donor nations," he said. "China today is exporting to whom? Basically to the United States and Europe, and that's helping the Chinese economy. Europe alone consumes a great deal and produces a great deal. If they start shrinking there will be a readjustment, and it will be global in its impact. It will affect the entire world economy."
>
> Unlike dips in population growth throughout history, this slide—which began in the 1960's—was not caused by a natural or economic disaster, a war or plagues. There is no Black Death to blame, no World War I, no Great Depression. This decline is widespread. It is steady. And while no demographer would say that predictions are infallible—prognosticators have surely been wrong.

[Ed. Note: While Crossett tells the reader what *didn't* cause the slide in population growth, she neglects to point out that *Roe v. Wade*, which legalized abortion, was largely reponsible for the slide in the USA. For an understanding of the results of population planning in the early 1970s, please refer to the April 6, 1971 entry on the "Revised Report of Population Subcommittee" in Lansing, Michigan.]

FORMER VICE PRESIDENT DAN QUAYLE JUMPED ON THE PUBLIC-PRIVATE PARTNERSHIP BAND-wagon, extending it to include the government and churches "dancing together" to help the less fortunate in our society, as reported in the November 13, 1997 issue of *The* (Louisville, Kentucky) *Courier Journal.* The following are some excerpts from "Quayle Backs Church-Government Partnerships":

> Sounding like a preacher and a politician, former Vice President Dan Quayle told about 5,000 people in Louisville last night that the government should use churches and other "faith-based institutions" to administer help to the poor, the homeless, the abused and the neglected....
>
> He said everyone supports the concept of church-state separation, but "The Constitution protects religion from government. It's not the other way around."...
>
> He told them that inner-city churches must become partners with the government to fight crime, deliver nutrition and restore family values, said Jefferson County Republican Party Chairman Bill Stone, who arranged the meeting and attended it with Quayle.

[Ed. Note: Mr. Quayle, have you been living under a rock ever since 1965 when the *Elementary and Secondary Education Act* passed and all the government's values-destroying education programs and methods became a part of our local schools' curriculum? Mr. Quayle, did you understand the intrusive, far-reaching effects of *America 2000* developed by the administration for which you served as Vice President?]

1998

THE AMERICAN INSTITUTE FOR CHARACTER EDUCATION (AICE), A LEADING DEVELOPER OF character education materials, funded by grants from the Lilly Endowment as well as other foundations and best known for its development of materials for the Thomas Jefferson Research Center's controversial character education program, transferred its assets to Learning for Life in 1998. Information downloaded from Learning for Life's website reveals that Learning for Life is extending AICE's curriculum development efforts into the area of "school-to-careers" (school-to-work). One of its brochures states that:

> Learning for Life can provide the basis for operating and meeting the goals of the *School-to-Work Opportunities Act of 1994.* The *Act* has three basic components that are used to accomplish its goals: school-based learning, connecting activities, and work-based learning.
>
> Before a School-to-Careers program is developed, an assessment is conducted to determine precisely how the Learning for Life program can help the school or school system help the students address the transition from school to careers. Only after this is done can a program be designed to help meet the school's needs.
>
> Learning for Life will become a catalyst for establishing relationships between community-based organizations, including both for-profit and not-for-profit organizations, and the local school district, selected schools, and students....

Some of Learning for Life's connecting activities are listed as:

- Camps, retreats, conferences and workshops
- COPE courses, with team building, leadership, self-reliance, respect for self and others, and self-esteem

- Community-wide service projects, such as food drives, crime prevention programs, and service learning
- Program resources, such as leadership development workshops and scholarship opportunities
- Ethics in Action in Exploring: Five components that assist with the development of ethical decision-making.

[Ed. Note: The last "connecting activity" listed in Learning for Life's materials should be of particular concern for parents upset over the Thomas Jefferson Research Center Curriculum.]

IN 1998 THE EUROPEAN COMMISSION DIRECTORATE GENERAL OF EDUCATION, TRAINING and Youth in Brussels, Belgium announced the availability of their Leonardo da Vinci Programme Cooperation in Higher Education and Vocational Education Document entitled "Cooperation in Higher Education and Vocational Education and Training between the European Community and the United States of America—Third Call for Proposals. Launching Date: 17 February 1998." Excerpts from the announcement taken from the Internet follow:

On 23 October 1995, the Council adopted a decision concerning the conclusion of an agreement for cooperation in higher education and vocational training between the European Community and the United States of America. The Cooperation Programme aims to add a new European Community/United States dimension to student-centered cooperation and bring balanced benefits to both the European Community and the United States.

Transatlantic cooperative activities eligible for support are:

- Development of organisational frameworks for transatlantic student mobility, including work placements, which will provide adequate language preparation and full academic recognition;
- Joint development of innovative curricula, teaching materials, methods and modules including those exploiting the new education technologies;
- Other innovative projects, including the use of new technologies and distance learning, which aim to improve the quality and cost-effectiveness of transatlantic cooperation in higher education and vocational education and training.

ECUMENICAL NEWS INTERNATIONAL'S NEWS HIGHLIGHTS (LONDON-ENI) OF FEBRUARY 19, 1998 reported that the World Bank and the world's faiths promise to work together: "The World Bank and the world's major religions [agreed] to establish joint working groups on development issues, it was announced at the end of a high-level, two-day dialogue at Lambeth Palace."

THE NEW YORK TIMES OP ED PAGE CARRIED AN EDITORIAL IN ITS MAY 5, 1998 EDITION entitled "The New World Order" by A.M. Rosenthal. Mr. Rosenthal put into perspective the values dilemma facing those who benefit from trade with nations not committed to the traditional definition of human rights. Excerpts follow:

APRIL 30—U.S. approves another $1 billion in aid to Indonesia as part of the international $40 billion economic bailout. President Suharto refuses to break up the multibillion-dollar monopolies controlled by himself, his family and friends. He says no political reforms until 2003, at earliest. Police break up student protests.

- May 1—Washington Times and A.P. say C.I.A. reports China has nuclear missiles targeted at U.S.
- May 3—President Clinton's June visit to China will include welcome ceremonies at Tiananmen Square. Washington preparing to allow U.S. companies to sell nuclear reactors to China.
- May 4—Human rights workers report continued oppression in China and Indonesia; more executions in China than in all the rest of the world.

The U.S., its democratic allies and major dictatorships are rapidly building a new world order—not quite finished yet, but already a central part of international life and values.

Its ideology, powers, rewards and punishments are supplanting those that prevailed internationally until 1994, when President Clinton joined the new order. If it continues, it will be the most important new international concept since the end of World War II.

The order was created without formal parliamentary approval by its sponsors, or any treaty. But every week, sometimes every day, the underlying tenets are revealed, in action. See above.

The following description of objectives and goals of the new order is so different from principles recently assumed in the West, though not always followed, that it may read as satire. It is not.

The fundamental change, demanded by the dictatorships and agreed to in practice by the democracies, is that the internal policies of persecution by the rulers, and the rights of the governed, are not a primary moral or economic consideration of the world.

The democracies, under these values, can protest some internal acts of the dictatorships—torture and such. But they must do so quietly, not allowing these acts, or often even security interests, to damage the new overriding value of the democratic leaders.

That value is the trade and investment with the dictatorships that the democracies believe important to their national economies—which are sometimes called jobs, but usually interpreted as corporate profit.

In exchange, dictatorships allow democracies to invest and trade in enterprises the capitalists consider profitable to their corporate strength, although not necessarily to their own employees or the national economic health of their countries.

If the dictatorships, or authoritarian governments as some are known more pleasantly, find their economies collapsing through the corruption generic to such societies, the International Monetary Fund and individual democracies rush to arrive with bailout.

The explanation given is that otherwise the dictatorships' economies would disintegrate, bringing revolution. Now, the people of the dictatorships may long for revolution. Obviously that cannot be allowed to overcome saving the dictatorship and thus rescuing the money invested by nationals of democracies.

Accepting these values, the events described above become understandable and even neatly logical.

The Indonesian dictator, for instance, was installed by the army 33 years ago and has been in power ever since. Now he needs scores of billions with which to overcome his own ineptitude and family corruption, and do the right thing by his foreign investors. Who can deny him?

The U.S. gets to sell strategic material to China, offering as an extra a visit to China by the U.S. President to honor the Communist leaders and expand their power and political life span.

Religious and political mavericks in the totalitarian partnership of the new world order get prison, or death, often both.

The press of the democracies gets to write stories about the growth of order in the new world order. Other citizens of the democracies get to say costs of imported goods are down: how nice.

Americans and Europeans may come to object for political or moral reasons, or because the new world order may after all cost them their jobs. But they will never be able to say they never knew; see above.

THE *BOSTON GLOBE* CARRIED AN ARTICLE ENTITLED "SUSPICIONS ABOUT THE STATEWIDE Tests" by Jeff Jacoby in the May 7, 1998 issue. The article contained such good information that much of it is included here:

I was going to write a column expressing my reservations about the MCAS, a 15-hour-long series of tests now being administered to fourth-, eighth-, and tenth-graders in every Massachusetts public school. I was going to point out that for all the ink and air time being devoted to the Massachusetts Comprehensive Assessment System, as it's formally called, little is actually known about it. I was even going to suggest that with all the uneasy questions the MCAS raises, parents ought to exercise their legal right to keep their children from taking it.

For one thing, I was going to call attention to the spotty record of Advanced Systems, the Dover, N.H., company hired to devise and grade the 210,000 tests being administered this month. Advanced Systems lost its $32 million contract with the State of Kentucky after botching the scores of more than 1,000 elementary and middle schools. The state launched what the magazine *Education Week* called "a sweeping audit" of the company's performance, scrutinizing "how the mistake could have gone undetected for many months."

Kentucky wasn't the only state where Advanced Systems failed. Scores in Maine were miscalculated, too. In New Hampshire, skepticism runs so high that the state Senate wants an elaborate regimen of supervision over every aspect of Advanced Systems' operations. Has the company cleaned up its act, I was going to ask, or is Massachusetts also going to wind up with shoddy and unreliable data?

But incompetent scoring was the least of my concerns.

I was going to highlight the copycat nature of these "assessments." Other states have been administering similar tests, always linking them to the federal *Goals 2000* and School-to-Work laws, both of which are considerably more creepy and New-World-Orderish than their innocuous names suggest. The very word "assessment" conveys something beyond mere measurement of academic achievement. Parents in state after state have discovered that their kids are being evaluated not just on their knowledge of language, math, and science, but on what they think, how they behave, and the way they were raised.

Would the MCAS, I was going to wonder, be as full of fuzzy PC questions on "feelings" and "attitudes" as tests elsewhere have been? If not, why have officials balked at a simple amendment to the *1993 Education Reform Act* providing that the MCAS "shall be designed to avoid the gathering or measuring of individual student attitudes, beliefs, or behaviors"? No one, I was going to say, could object to a clarification so straightforward—unless the purpose of the assessments is in fact to probe students on matters that are none of the state's concern.

Such as? Well, the Pennsylvania Educational Quality Assessment instructed students to react to statements like "I often wish I were somebody else" and "I don't receive much attention at home." To measure their "tolerance," students were presented with 35 situations—"Your sister wants to marry a person whose religion is much different from yours from your family" [*sic*], "You are asked to sit at a table with retarded students in the lunchroom"—and asked how comfortable or uncomfortable each would make them.

The California Learning Assessment System included loaded questions like this: "European Americans discriminated against Chinese immigrants because of ethnic and cultural differences. By yourself, think about an instance of discrimination that you know of. It could be a situation in which a person or a group of people is treated unfairly because of age, color, customs, or some other quality or belief. What could be done to help solve this problem?"

Kentucky told fourth-graders to imagine themselves Indians at the time the first pioneers arrived and to write "how you would have felt when you saw the pioneers cutting down trees and clearing land." Rhode Island grilled students on how often they like being in school ("Never? Sometimes? Always?"), whether they are happy with themselves "as a person," and how socially active their parents are.

I was going to quote the sweeping phrase in the Massachusetts ed-reform law that empowers the Department of Education to assemble a dossier on each student comprising "basic demographic information, program and course information, and such other information as the department shall determine necessary." I was going to describe the extraordinary secrecy that surrounds these tests in many states. Parents and school committee members are forbidden to see them, or are allowed to do so only if they sign nondisclosure agreements. The College Board isn't so mysterious about its SATs (each year it releases the previous year's tests). So why are many states so furtive about their "assessments"?

I distrust the MCAS. I am more than somewhat skeptical of the motives behind it and was going to write a column saying so.

But I have been persuaded not to jump to conclusions. I have been urged to wait for this first MCAS to play itself out, to see whether students report being asked anything dubious or improper. I have been reminded that this year's tests will only set a bench-mark—that not until 2003 will the tests actually have an impact on students' ability to graduate.

So, I'll hold my doubts in abeyance. For now. I can always write that column another time.

"SOUTH CAROLINA TAKES TO HEART COACH'S SHOT AT 'HORRIBLE' SCHOOLS" WAS AN article with a Clemson, South Carolina dateline which appeared in the May 15, 1998 *Atlanta Journal-Constitution*. Some excerpts follow:

Educators and politicians screeched when they heard former Clemson University basketball coach Rick Barnes say he was packing up his family and moving to Austin, Texas in part because South Carolina schools are "horrible."...

Ever since the late 1970s, when current U.S. Education Secretary Richard Riley became governor, education reform has been a top issue in South Carolina. Yet, over nearly two decades, the state has remained—along with several other Southern states—at the bottom of national rankings....

Moreover, South Carolina schools regularly win the U.S. Department of Education's Blue Ribbon, showing excellence in student achievement and teacher performance. Three elementary schools in fast-growing Greenville County won the award last year.

[Ed. Note: South Carolina can claim the dubious distinction of having been the home state of Effective Schools Research change agent Donald Thomas, promoter of U.S.-Soviet pedagogy exchanges, and U.S. Secretary of Education Richard Riley, former state school superintendent and governor of South Carolina during the adoption phase of the state's OBE/school-to-work experiments. The above article is most telling in that it proves that the southern states which adopted the late Professor Ron Edmonds's Effective Schools Research and its components (mastery learning/direct instruction/outcome-based education/cooperative learning, etc., etc.) in the mid-1970s have the lowest test scores in the nation. The philosophy behind Effective School Research, that "all children can learn if provided with the necessary 'environment' and enough time" is no more, no less than the outcome-based education philosophy which has by 1998 been implemented "in all schools of the nation." How can South Carolina have the lowest test scores and win Blue Ribbons?

The Effective School Report, the journal from which this writer has frequently quoted—and the one and only journal which consistently deals with OBE, TQM, Effective Schools, etc.—was born in Jackson, Mississippi in the early 1980s. Former Secretary of Education T.H. Bell served on the board of directors of its parent company, Kelwynn, Inc., the Effective Schools training company which published The Effective School Report. It should come as no surprise that Jackson, Mississippi schools served as the first guinea pig schools for implementation of Effective School Research.

The fact that South Carolina and Mississippi, two of the southern states most deeply involved in mastery learning over a long period of time, have such low academic test scores should be adequate justification for Congress to call for an investigation of the consequences of adopting effective school research and outcome-based education, if, and the writer repeats if, academic performance is what is being sought by the education bureaucracy and the Congress which funds public education. Surely, if the departments of education in those southern states which implemented effective school research had performed longitudinal studies tracking the children who went through those schools, education policy planners would have evidence that effective school research falls far short of the claims made by its proponents, most of whom benefit financially from such promotion. (See Appendix XXVI.)

This writer has a question for Coach Barnes: Couldn't his family's move to Austin, Texas, which is implementing the same Skinnerian method under another label (direct instruction), be a wonderful example of jumping from the frying pan into the fire—especially since Austin, Texas is also deeply involved (a leader) in non-academic school-to-work?]

A VERY INTERESTING ARTICLE ENTITLED "TAKING TECHNICAL ASSISTANCE ON THE ROAD" was published in the Spring 1998 issue of Early Developments (Vol. 2, No. 1), a publication of the Frank Porter Graham Child Development Center at the University of North Carolina at Chapel Hill.[58] This center is funded in part by UNC and partly by PR/Award No. R307A60004 administered by the Office of Educational Research and Improvement, U.S. Department of Education. Excerpts from the article follow:

> By the early 1990s, Frank Porter Graham's researchers were at work in the People's Republic of China, Eastern Europe, and the former Soviet Union. For example, in 1995 Shelley deFosset and Pat Trohanis began working with the privately financed Step by Step program which was aimed at creating early childhood education demonstration projects initially in 17 emerging democracies of Central and Eastern Europe and the former Soviet Union.

Step by Step founder and sponsor, George Soros, through his Open Society Foundation, wanted to create a childhood education project that would ultimately lead to a new participatory citizenry beginning with the youngest members of society, its children.[59] Educators and parents in the countries involved have been enthusiastic—and, by the end of the second year Step by Step was in 1,500 classrooms serving over 37,500 children and families. Most countries have been successful in getting local funding for the programs.

Through a subcontract with Children's Resources International of Washington, D.C. which is the Open Society's technical assistance arm for the Step by Step project, de Fosset and Trohanis have hosted two groups of Russian teachers and administrators in the United States, and deFosset estimated that she's visited Russia "16 or 17" times. While in the U.S. Russians received training and visited numerous preschool programs. "When we're in Russia, we do training in the cities in Russia—and then we visit programs and provide feedback on existing programs," said de Fosset.

MARILYN PEASE OF NEW BEDFORD, MASSACHUSETTS WROTE AN ARTICLE FOR THE MAY 22, 1998 issue of *The Standard-Times* of New Bedford entitled "MCAS Tests Undermine Rights of Parents" which deals with the same subject covered by Mr. Jacoby's May 7 column, but from a parent's perspective. Excerpts follow:

Once upon a time, Americans lived in a republic, where the voice of the minority carried as much weight as the voice of the majority because of a representative government. Laws and rights applied to individuals whether one, one hundred, or more people exercised their rights as opposed to marching lockstep or allowing themselves to be herded.

Along comes the Massachusetts Comprehensive Assessment System. The Department of Education wants us to believe that it's mandated for all 4th, 8th, and 10th graders and that the law has not provided for students or parents to "opt out." However, the law also does not specifically prohibit parents from exempting their children from the assessment; doing so would be a usurpation of parental authority and responsibility.

The state Supreme Court recognizes that children are not mere creatures of the state. Those who nurture and direct their destiny have the right to prepare them for additional obligations. Furthermore, Public Law 96–88, Title I, Section 101, number 3 states: "Parents have the primary responsibility for the education of their children and states, localities, and private interests have the primary responsibility for supporting that parental role."...

I submitted my intent in writing to exempt my son from MCAS. Despite my lack of permission, the test was administered to him, regardless. What ever happened to parent/school partnerships? What if parents expect the public schools to provide factual information for their children to assimilate instead of the assessment of opinions their children are expected to synthesize, opinions that are being scored toward state standards, and opinions that will consequently be remedied until that standard is achieved?

We the People are allowing a major paradigm shift to occur, in which the state will be directing student destiny based on his or her performance on the MCAS. This correlates with MGL Chapter 69, Section 1D (I), which parents may review but not contest. Did parents knowingly relinquish their rights and authority upon enrolling their children in public schools?

Mr. Rick Atkins from the DOE's Accountability and Evaluation Services agreed that the law does not prohibit a parent from exempting their child from the MCAS. However, he said the child would receive a score of zero, which would be averaged with and thus would affect the entire school district. (Is that in the law, or another arbitrary and capricious rule the DOE spontaneously made up? Did our local educrats bother to ask?)

By refusing to exempt any child from the MCAS upon parental request, one might presume that their child is being exploited by the public schools so as not to bring down the average scores of the entire district. It appears that fundamental civil liberties are also being violated, but who cares? It's only one person, maybe a few. I guess it's easier to perpetuate the deception than to acknowledge it. Then We the People would have to do something about it.

AL CUOCO AND FAYE RUOPP, FORMER MATHEMATICS TEACHERS WHO WORK IN MATH EDUCA-tion, wrote an article entitled "Math Exam Rationale Doesn't Add up: Simple Questions Are Often Posed in Unnecessarily Complex Ways" which was published in the May 24, 1998 issue of the *Boston Globe*. Excerpts follow:

In the Foreword to the "Guide to the Massachusetts Comprehensive Assessment System: Mathematics" former Commissioner of Education Antonucci says: "I believe that teachers and administrators will find the sample questions to be particularly helpful in bringing the Massachusetts Mathematics 'Curriculum Frameworks' learning standards to life in class-rooms and schools."

Like many teachers across the state, we studied the sample questions and were dismayed by what we found. We challenge the assertion that the tests given in the last couple of weeks reflect learning standards and, even more importantly, we question the assertion put forth by Antonucci that "this critical new program... is designed to raise the academic achieve-ment of all students of the commonwealth."

Indeed, the battery of tests given in grades 4, 8, and 10 follows a tradition with which teachers are quite familiar. It is one more example of a numerical indicator that can be improved over time without significantly increasing our students' understanding. In other words, the test is designed so that the first-round scores will be low and so that scores can be improved, year by year, by an evolving cottage industry of coaching techniques.

Teachers know how to prepare students for tests like these, but they will certainly fail to do so this year since they received the guide documents only three months before the actual tests. But test scores will go up in subsequent years as teachers take valuable class time away from what they know is important and spend it on test preparation. Government officials will then make public statements about raising academic achievement, and, once again, our students will be shortchanged.

We are former mathematics teachers who continue to work in education. We are out-raged that teachers and students have to waste valuable classroom time on tests that are not only poorly constructed, but also contain content that is unnecessarily vague, complicated, and inappropriate. We are worried that MCAS will raise havoc with existing curriculums without any real benefit to students' mathematical expertise.

We examined the mathematics guide documents closely, and will comment specifically on those for grade 10. We encourage the public to look closely at this guide and those for other subject areas as well, since much of the debate over MCAS has not focused on the quality of the tests.

Our claims that scores will rise over time without any benefit to our children is based on what we found: The majority of the sample questions are shallow, one-step problems, and it's possible to solve most of the problems using very little mathematics. But the ques-tions are posed using unnecessarily sophisticated mathematical notation or appealing to conventions that are not universally taught in 10th grade classes. In other words, the tests ask trivial questions in obscure ways.

Teachers all over the state will soon abandon curriculums that they know are educationally sound so they can teach material of questionable content validity to prepare students for the MCAS.

[Ed. Note: The May 5, 1986 *St. Louis Globe Democrat* article "School Officials Upset by New Plan" reports that school officials in St. Louis made the same, exact prediction. (See 1986 entry.) This process also correlates to the National Center for Educational Statistics' plans to judge "teacher quality" by increase in "student performance"—teach-to-the-test. (See 1992 entry for *Filling the Gaps.*)]

THE SPRING 1998 ISSUE OF ASSOCIATION FOR SUPERVISION AND CURRICULUM DEVELOPMENT'S *Curriculum Update* was devoted to arts education and the main article was entitled "Arts Education: A Cornerstone of Basic Education." This writer, always a supporter of music and art in the public school curriculum, was educated regarding the real purpose of arts education when reading *Arts and the Schools* by Jerome Hausmann, one of the four books commissioned for John Goodlad's federally and foundation-funded *The Study of Schooling.* (See 1979 *Schooling in the United States.*) The *Curriculum Update* article exposes these same "reformed" purposes for arts education as devised by those contributing to America's dumbing down. Excerpts follow from this enlightening article:

> CLAIMING ITS PLACE IN THE CORE CURRICULUM
> "Today's school gatekeepers think of arts education as they experienced it, as holiday art or as recreation, not as a cognitive process," says Leilani Lattin Duke, director of the Getty Education Institute for the Arts. By studying the arts, students can develop capacities for critical thinking and problem solving, she explains.
> "The arts represent forms that humans have created to convey their feelings, their visions, their aspirations, and their values," says Elliot Eisner, professor of education and art at Stanford University. "The presence of arts in the schools makes it possible for children and adolescents to learn how to read the images that arts provide.... Children need to be able to look at art and images and to recognize their historical and cultural significance in order to understand the message being conveyed."
> Once children can interpret these sometimes confusing messages, they will need to learn how to manage them. "A lot of what is taught in school suggests that there are correct and incorrect answers to questions, as evidenced by the use of multiple-choice and true/false tests," explains Lehman. "In the real world, questions aren't posed that way." For example, questions about how to achieve world peace or end world hunger don't have any easy answers. The arts naturally require people to seek multiple solutions.

[Ed. Note: The writer understands and appreciates the artist's legitimate role of creating a painting or writing music as an expression of his own feelings about life. That is what makes art so special. However, social engineers should not use art to promote their own agendas in the classroom. The reader is urged to turn to the 1970 entry which quotes from Leonard S. Kenworthy's paper, "The International Dimension of Education: Background Paper II Prepared for the World Conference on Education," which says in part:

> For example, the writer has found tremendously effective a 10-minute film on the United Nations, entitled "Overture." There is no narrative in this film; the pictures are shown against

a background of music, with the Vienna Symphony Orchestra playing the Egmont *Overture*. It is a powerful learning device and moves its viewers in a way few other approaches touch them.

Anyone familiar with Chairman Mao's brainwashing in Red China understands the use of theatre, art, and music to indoctrinate citizens.]

THE BUSINESS SECTION OF THE MAY 27, 1998 ISSUE OF *USA TODAY* CARRIED AN ARTICLE entitled "Schools Learn Lessons in Efficiency from Business." Excerpts follow:

The biggest experiment, however, involves the public school system itself. In one of the most ambitious attempts yet to take something that works in business and apply it to public education, the 19 schools here expect in six months to become the first school district in the world to be ISO 9000 certified.

ISO 9000, a sort of Good Housekeeping Seal of Approval for businesses, is a way of enforcing excellence that has been embraced by businesses worldwide.... But because the Lancaster [Pennsylvania] schools have identified their customers to be students and parents, ISO 9000 by definition must also force improvements in curriculum, teaching methods and anything else that leads to the ultimate goal of higher academic achievement.

There is growing optimism in education circles that this could be the landmark experiment that finally marries education to a nuts-and-bolts business tool. ISO 9000 proponents say it will enforce discipline, not upon the students, but upon an unwieldy system. It will enforce consistency so that average teachers closely resemble the best.

Will it work? Mixed signals abound. Interviews find Lancaster teachers and principals sold on ISO 9000—but unable to articulate how it will affect the classroom. That's a red flag to the business world.

The U.S. Department of Education is so hopeful that it is funding the Lancaster experiment with $800,000 in federal grants. [With a per pupil expenditure of $18,000 a year, the Lancaster School District is having a hard time making ends meet and was at the beginning of 1999 saddled with $95 million in debt, ed.] It will be the first school district to get certified, although the Brandywine district in Delaware is not far behind.

The New Jersey State Legislature wants the state's entire public school system to be ISO 9000 certified and has enacted a waiver from state monitoring to those that implement it. However, only four of 600 school districts are so far considering it.

Success is far from certain. ISO 9000 is laden with flowcharts and statistics and comes steeped in manufacturing terminology guaranteed to make teachers cringe. Curriculum is a "process control." "Scrap" is a lost learning opportunity.

The biggest roadblock has been the inability of educators to fully understand it. There have been workshops for two years, but many still are unable to cite examples about how it has changed the classroom.

That's a warning sign to Kurt Landgraf, chairman of DuPont Europe, who has a master's degree in education. At this stage in ISO 9000 training, every employee "should be able to tell you exactly what they're doing differently," he says.

But Robert Bowen, the business consultant the school district hired to implement ISO 9000, says he's not worried. He knows first-hand that ISO 9000 is difficult to grasp because he's spent a decade unsuccessfully trying to explain to his parents what he does for a living....

Business leaders hesitate to get their hopes up. Throughout the 1990s schools have dabbled in continuous improvement and other pieces of total quality management (TQM).

But despite those methods, U.S. 12th graders finish ahead of only Cyprus and South Africa in the international Math and Science Survey, says IBM CEO Louis Gerstner.

Trade magazine *Quality Progress* said the number of public schools surveyed that had TQM projects in 1997 dropped 32% from 1996.

"We lost our way," says Mary Schutz, a principal in Wagon Mound, N.M. where teachers were once as excited about TQM as Lancaster's are about ISO 9000.

He (William Kiefer, the Lancaster schools' ISO coordinator) also promises solid evidence by this fall that academic achievement is on the rise in Lancaster.

So far, such evidence does not exist.

[Ed. Note: When the writer attended the 1992 National Governors Association "Quality in Education" Conference held in Minneapolis, Minnesota, the session designed for school and other public officials was facilitated by a representative of IBM. During the question and answer period, a superintendent inquired about what to do when the expense of processing older teachers through staff development was not yielding changes in their behavior or level of acceptance of "reform." The facilitator, without a second thought, pointed to the TQM flowchart on the wall behind her and indicated a box marked "Waste Management." She then answered, "You watch them; you document their mistakes; then you get rid of them." That is the TQM/ISO 9000 process at work.]

ASSOCIATION FOR SUPERVISION AND CURRICULUM DEVELOPMENT'S JUNE 1998 ISSUE OF *Education Update* carried a "Message from the Executive Director" subtitled "South Africa Tackles Ambitious Curriculum Reform Effort." Revealing excerpts follow:

In March 1998, I traveled to Cape Town, South Africa, as a participant in the Comparative Human Relations Initiative Consultation, funded by the Ford Foundation through a grant awarded to the Southern Education Foundation in Atlanta, Georgia.... South Africa's education system is crippled by the legacy of apartheid as it struggles to deal with issues of inequity and quality.... Consequently, the brew of raised expectations among the ever-growing numbers of the poor and the government's inability to respond portends trying times ahead.

The new government is trying to respond to this situation through an enterprise called the National Qualifications Framework (NQF), an innovative education and training paradigm that uses outcome-based education to prepare students to be lifelong learners. Subsequently, a massive curriculum reform effort entitled Curriculum 2005 was initiated in January of the 1998 academic year in all primary schools. But the solid vision behind Curriculum 2005 has been marred by inadequate implementation of strategies and resources.

Various public and private groups have either supported or criticized the government's decision to implement Curriculum 2005, which is based largely on the tenets of outcome-based education. Sangaliso Mikhatshwa, Deputy Minister of Education, asserts that "this system offers much in South Africa's move away from the rote learning and content-driven curricula of the past." He further contends that it represents a "head, hands, and heart approach," as learners are required to indicate what they have learned in terms of knowledge, skills, and attitudes.

It is still too early to predict whether these difficulties represent mortal wounds to the government's education reform plans or merely predictable roadblocks along the way to successful innovation. The one thing that is certain about South Africa is the predictability of the unpredictable. Still, there are insurmountable courage, hope, and optimism among South Africa's peoples.

[Ed. Note: The language in this article—particularly the wording "offers much in South Africa's move away from the rote learning and content-driven curricula of the past"—parallels and echoes that of the opening pages of H.R. 6, the reauthorization of funding for the *Elementary and Secondary Education Act*, which called for funding programs and curricula which would not address so-called "lower order skills." This language is interpreted to mean memorization of facts and basic academic skills as we have always known them. In addition, the reader should understand that outcome-based education is based on Effective Schools Research, the basis for international education reform, and that it has generated intense opposition abroad as well as in the United States of America.[60] The writer also assumes that language contained in International Loan Agreement guidelines issued by the World Bank to facilitate "development" in South Africa may have contributed to the adoption of this internationally accepted (mandated) Skinnerian method. (See November 17, 1984 Maine Association of Christian Schools' letter regarding Kevin Ryan, Portugal, and the World Bank, and Appendix VI which relates to Korea and the World Bank.)]

THE JUNE 7, 1998 ISSUE OF OREGON'S *STATESMAN JOURNAL* PUBLISHED AN ARTICLE ENtitled "Salem-Keizer Test Scores Fall." Excerpts follow:

Salem-Keizer student scores dipped for the second consecutive year in a prominent achievement test, dragging district scores further below the national average.... "We can't and shouldn't try to make any excuses for it," said Dan Johnson, the district administrator spearheading education reform efforts. "It's fairly consistent across each of the categories in terms of the decline."

"Some averages fell to the 40th percentile or lower."... District administrators were hard-pressed to pinpoint reasons for the falling scores.

Johnson attributed it partly to school reforms and a phenomenon he called the "change curve." Schools that shift their teaching approaches often witness dips in scores while they're trying to make changes in the classroom.... Candalaria has worked hard to improve students' creative thinking when approaching math problems.... But by focusing on new skills, teachers might have given less attention to basic math computation, where scores are dropping, she said.

THE *ATLANTA CONSTITUTION* RAN AN ARTICLE ENTITLED "GINGRICH: TAPS FOR TEXTBOOKS— He Says Computers Will Replace Them" in its June 9, 1998 edition. Excerpts follow:

[Newt] Gingrich, speaking Monday at the Supercom trade show at the Georgia World Congress Center, said the onrush of technology will make textbooks obsolete.

"One of the goals should be to replace all textbooks with a PC," the Georgia Republican said. "I would hope within five years they would have no more textbooks."

Personal computers are the new focus for learning and students should be given one when they enter first grade, he said.

That suggestion drew immediate fire from Washington, D.C.-based author Harriet Tyson, who wrote *A Conspiracy of Good Intentions: America's Textbook Fiasco*.

Gingrich has distorted technology's value, she said. "He is like a 16-year-old who just fell in love with computers. He is not a techie. He's just in love with techies."

Gingrich, a former college professor who peppers his talks with references to writers such as Peter Drucker, W. Edwards Deming and Alexis de Tocqueville, also called for an overhaul of the nation's schools. Gingrich urged that schools be judged in a business context.

Gingrich argued that Internet connections should often be available to replace the traditional lecture by a professor. In contrast to the old-style teaching model, the Net would be accessible 24 hours a day, he said. "We have to become a learning society."

[Ed. Note: The following quote from the 1971 *The Individualized Learning Letter* entry echoes the views of Newt Gingrich:

Down with textbooks! Textbooks not only encourage learning at the wrong level (imparting facts rather than telling how to gather facts, etc.), they also violate an important new concern in American education—Individualized Instruction.

This is also another instance which reminds us of the gravity of the consequences of H.R. 6 (reauthorization of the *Elementary and Secondary Education Act of 1965*) and its assertions that "lower order skills" (memorization and basic academics) should not be funded or promoted.]

THE TRI-CITY HERALD OF KENNEWICK, WASHINGTON CARRIED "GROUP SUPPORTING PAULA Jones Case Sues Pasco Schools" by Wendy Culverwell in its June 11, 1998 issue. The article tells us that:

The organization that is paying Paula Jones' legal bills in her sexual harassment case against President Clinton filed suit Monday against the Pasco School District.

The suit contends the district violated the constitutional rights of a former teacher who objected to outcome-based education.

In the action filed in U.S. District Court in Spokane, the Rutherford Institute alleges the district wrongfully terminated Barbara McFarlin-Kosiec and violated her constitutional rights to free speech and free exercise of religion. The complaint seeks economic damages.

Ken Rice, the Kennewick attorney who represents the district, said the district hasn't been served with the complaint, but he doesn't believe the suit has merit. He said the district would defend itself vigorously.

According to the press release issued by the Rutherford Institute, McFarlin-Kosiec was forced to resign as a teacher in 1995 because of her opposition to outcome-based education. She was a veteran teacher when she was hired in 1993 to teach at Mark Twain Elementary.

The lawsuit was filed by Greg Casey and Bruce Gore, Spokane attorneys affiliated with the Rutherford Institute.... The Institute describes itself as an international, non-profit civil liberties organization specializing in the defense of human rights.

Neither McFarlin-Kosiec nor her attorneys could be reached for comment Wednesday.

[Ed. Note: The reader will recognize the name of Barbara McFarlin-Kosiec as one of the teachers who reviewed and endorsed *the deliberate dumbing down of america*. Who better could understand the consequences of opposition to the restructuring paradigm shift?]

THE WASHINGTON TIMES OF JUNE 11, 1998 PRINTED AN ASSOCIATED PRESS ARTICLE ENtitled "Congress to Expand Education Savings." Important excerpts follow:

House and Senate negotiators agreed yesterday on a bill to expand tax-favored savings accounts for educational expenses, including tuition at private and religious schools, and to erase a ban on President Clinton's proposed national standardized tests. The deal removes an obstacle to President Clinton's plan for voluntary national tests in fourth-grade reading and eighth-grade math. Negotiators deleted an amendment passed by the Senate in April that would have banned the standards-based tests unless specifically authorized by Congress and would have converted some Education Department programs into block grants.

The negotiators also tacked on a reading bill, supported by Mr. Clinton, that must be signed in order for $210 million to be spent starting July 1 for research, teacher training and grants to help improve reading instruction.

[Ed. Note: Although the above legislation did not become law, the importance of this entry relates to (1) the removal of the ban on national testing and (2) the approval of legislation which will mandate a particular method of reading instruction, Skinnerian Direct Instruction in *The Reading Excellence Act*, which *did* pass a few months later in November of 1998 as part of the omnibus budget.]

AS A SMALL ITEM IN THE JUNE 19, 1998 ISSUE OF *THE WASHINGTON TIMES,* AN ARTICLE appeared entitled "Panel: Make Education Career-Focused" which says in its entirety:

All high school students should receive a mixture of academically challenging courses and work experiences regardless of whether or not they plan to attend college, a group of business leaders and educators said yesterday.

The report singled out Thomas Jefferson School for Science and Technology, an elite public high school in Fairfax County [Virginia], as proof that such an approach doesn't have to sacrifice academics.

JUNE 19, 1998 THE EUROPEAN COMMISSION DIRECTORATE GENERAL FOR EDUCATION, TRAINing and Youth in Brussels, Belgium issued another call for proposals under the Leonardo da Vinci Programme Document "Cooperation in Higher Education and Vocational Education and Training between the European Community and the United States of America." Excerpts from the Internet post follow:

Over 17,600 young people are on placements in other European countries under the Leonardo da Vinci programme.... The European Commission has granted assistance totalling ECU [European Community Unit] 29.7 million to 22 countries taking part in the Leonardo da Vinci vocational training programme in order to organise transnational placement and exchange programmes for young people and trainers throughout Europe. Over 17,600 young people undergoing initial training or in employment will carry out a period of training in a company or training establishment in another country participating in the programme, in order to gain experience and improve their employment prospects.

The sectors of activity in which these young people and trainers will exercise their mobility are extremely varied and cover both industry (e.g., apprenticeships in electrical engineering) and agriculture (e.g., training in aquaculture), as well as services (e.g., the hotel trade or catering). The aim of such placements is to acquire certified occupational experience and in the case of longer placements, to learn an additional skill.

CONTINUING HER EXCELLENT WORK AS "WATCHDOG" ON BEHALF OF OHIO TAXPAYERS, STATE Board of Education member Diana Fessler—an articulate opponent of the school-to-work philosophy—wrote a letter dated June 22, 1998 to U.S. Secretary of Education Richard Riley and U.S. Secretary of Labor Alexis Herman in regard to her being barred from a meeting sponsored by the National School-to-Work Office of the U.S. Department of Education on June 14–18, 1998 in Cleveland, Ohio. Ms. Fessler's letter is reproduced in its entirety in order to relay the complete details of her experience.

Dear Secretaries Riley and Herman:

I am a duly elected member of the Ohio State Board of Education (SBE) with approximately one million people residing in my district. Section 3301.07(C) of the Ohio Revised Code directs the SBE to administer and supervise the allocation and distribution of all state and federal funds for public education in Ohio. Accordingly, I have an obligation to be fully informed regarding education matters affecting my constituents.

Seeking to stay abreast of School-to-Work (STW), I made arrangements to attend a meeting sponsored by the National School-to-Work Office (NSTWO) on June 14–18, 1998 in Cleveland, Ohio. Forty-three states and Puerto Rico were represented. I was formally introduced and welcomed from the podium by Ohio's STW director, and I attended the Sunday through Tuesday morning sessions without incident.

On Tuesday afternoon, Ivan Charner of the Academy of Educational Development (operator of the NSTWO's Learning Center) told me I could not attend his closed "strategy" meeting for the eight states that received first-round STW money. I find it incredible that those who claim that STW is good for kids, good for the economy, good for our nation, and worthy of replication find it necessary to conduct the public's business behind closed doors, and I told him so. A woman nearby said, "Well, the FBI meets behind closed doors," and I thought to myself, "Good grief, this is worse than I thought; these people think a STW meeting is on par with an FBI operation."

Mr. Charner referred me to Ms. Irene Lynn, Interim Director of the NSTWO. She confirmed that I was not welcome, saying: "It is just not an open meeting; it is a non-public meeting." I asked, "Who is paying for this meeting?" and she acknowledged that taxpayers were. I asked who decided to keep me out and she said that she had. I asked what the NSTWO was trying to hide, and she said it was just a "working meeting," and that government workers often get together for such meetings, and nothing was hidden.

These were not routine staff meetings. Participants had flown in from all across the country to meet in a swanky hotel, at taxpayers' expense, to identify and discuss "obstacles" that they face in moving the STW agenda forward and to develop "strategies" to overcome those "obstacles."

Ms. Lynn attributed the "problem" to my "not understanding STW" and used the common, and offensive tactic of characterizing those who do not blindly embrace STW as being "misinformed" or "lacking in understanding." When I pointed that out, Ms. Lynn corrected herself and acknowledged that the "problem" is philosophical in nature, not informational.

It is no secret that I have serious reservations regarding the STW system. I have researched it extensively, and I have made that research available to my constituents via my web site—to the chagrin of STW devotees who seek to hide the full scope of STW from the American people for as long as possible using whatever means necessary. Thus, they attempt to conduct the people's business behind closed doors, or only in the presence of the Enlightened. This bureaucratic tyranny undermines rational, open disagreement—the hallmark of civil liberty in the arena of government.

To reaffirm that there was a concerted effort to bar me from the meeting, on Wednesday morning I entered the Communications Task Force meeting room and stood at the back of the room. Stephanie Powers, Director of Communication & Public Affairs, Office of the Assistant Secretary, U.S. Department of Labor, Employment & Training Administration; and Peter Woolfolk, Special Assistant for Communications, Vocational and Adult Education, Office of the Assistant Secretary, U.S. Department of Education, insisted that I leave.

One can only wonder what NSTWO was trying to accomplish by barring me from the meeting. One might reasonably conclude that the decision to oust me was considered to be the lesser of two evils; i.e., the repercussions of doing so being less problematic than risking full disclosure of what took place during the meetings. I also found it troubling when Ms. Powers said that I need to understand that "Congress has provided for these business meetings"—implying that Congress would approve closed-door STW meetings.

Ms. Powers said that she knew that we did not agree on STW. As I told Ms. Powers, STW is not the issue—it is whether the general public, through their elected representatives, have access to critical public information regarding the work being done to re-shape our schools, our economy, and our system of government. She had no reply. Knowing that the meeting would have been "shortened" had I stayed, I left the hotel, but there are still questions that need to be answered:

- By what authority did Mr. Charner, Ms. Lynn, Ms. Powers, and Mr. Woolfolk bar me from the meetings?
- Why was it imperative that the public's business be conducted behind closed doors?
- And, if STW is indeed good for kids and essential for the good of the economy, why must the details be kept hidden from public scrutiny?

NSTWO has yet to provide me with copies of Ohio's Urban/Rural Opportunities Grants, claiming that they cannot do so unless the grantees give the NSTWO permission to do so. Any attempt to make the release of public records contingent on the one seeking the information first getting permission from the recipient of federal funds is absurd, but it does illustrate the extent to which your employees will go to restrict the flow of information. Therefore, pursuant to the FOI Act, please see that I get a copy of each Ohio UROG grant including the budget narratives and appendices, as well as the following documents relevant to the June 14–18 STW meeting in Cleveland: the communication from legal counsel regarding closed-door meetings; all RFP's, SGA's, and contracts (including facilitation and technical assistance) with appendices and the budgets; a list of all disbursements including date, amount, vendor, and purpose; all notes taken by staff and "recorders"; all overheads, handouts, background materials, audio tapes, and videos, and candidate applications, including resumes and appendices, of those applying for the position of Director of the NSTWO.

This is not a letter of complaint; it is a declaration: your people are out of control. This letter also serves as formal notification that concealment of public information, unless required for national security, will not be tolerated. Furthermore, I am seeking legal counsel to determine if any state or federal laws have been broken regarding this matter.

The purpose of government is to serve the interests of the people—not to develop legislative agendas, refine implementation strategies, and create marketing plans behind closed doors. Apologies from bureaucratic bullies who willfully prevented me from gathering the background information to enable me to carry out the duties of my office would be meaningless. Ms. Lynn, Ms. Powers, Mr. Woolfolk, and Mr. Charner should be fired and their positions filled by people who have a firm understanding of, and respect for, how representative government is supposed to work.

Please give this letter your prompt attention. I look forward to receiving your personal letter of reply.

On behalf of my constituents,

Diana M. Fessler
Ohio State Board of Education—Third District[61]

CC: Senators Lott, Ashcroft, DeWine, Glenn Representatives Gingrich, Armey, DeLay, Boehner, Hyde, Hoekstra and Graham

THE JUNE 1998 ISSUE OF *THE CHRISTIAN CONSCIENCE* CARRIED AN ARTICLE BY EDUCATION researcher Bettye Lewis of Michigan entitled "Violence in the Schools: Part 2—Achieving National Education Goal Six." In this article Lewis asserted that "Goal 6 may be the most diabolical goal in the *Goals 2000: Educate America Act*, since it is this goal which will strip away individual freedoms in favor of the collective world community (New World Order). Will Americans wake up and refuse to relinquish their unalienable (God-given) constitutional rights? Or will they continue in apathy as they increasingly become drones in the coming New World Order?" Excerpts of Lewis's article follow:

The Michigan Strategy Proposal for Drug and Violence Free Schools and Communities states:

> Michigan now has one of the Nation's most aggressive and comprehensive long-term strategies to reach Goal 6: "By the year 2000, every school in America will be free of drugs and violence and will offer a disciplined environment conducive to learning."
>
> Governor John Engler and the Michigan State Board of Education have worked jointly to provide leadership and establish a clear plan of action to enable our schools and communities to create safe, disciplined and drug free learning environments for our children by the year 2000. It will demand local community action, greater coordination, and careful targeting of $17 million in federal Drug Free Schools and Communities Act (DFSCA).[62]

Throughout this document the Communitarian agenda is apparent. This philosophy assigns responsibility to the community, not the parents, for the development of the child.... The section on "Action Items" refers to State and Local Goals and shows us how dictatorial the state and federal Government have become toward recipients of *Drug Free Schools and Communities Act* funds. Notice there is no choice—"the school district *will*...."

Every school district will develop a local school-community coalition and advisory team. The data banks established for continual assessment and analysis will be the controlling factor, not only regarding the individual, but the school and the community, establishing community norms as well.... As one reads this proposal for accomplishing Goal 6, it becomes clear this document became the foundation for the Bias Crime Response Task Force Report. Surveys, marketing and a media blitz will be used to convince the public that violence is out of control and every community must be used to address the problem and fully implement Goal 6. Five years ago—1993—this document (Michigan's Strategy Proposal) cited the State Goal to be:

> Every school-community drug education advisory team will review current needs assessment and problem statements, undertake and complete a comprehensive needs assessment with data sufficient to identify, alter or select prevention programming and utilize

data to plan evaluations of program impact by June 1994. The state will compile a county
by county risk and protective factor profile as a local resource and for comparative data.

The State Goal reveals just how extensive the databanks will be and how the data will
be used as a means to dictate how every school/community will address the problem and
develop prescribed national norms. The target date, June 1994, aligned perfectly with the
1994 Student Data Handbook: Elementary, Secondary and Early Childhood and the *1994
Staff Data Handbook: Elementary, Secondary and Early Childhood.*[63] These data handbooks
were first developed in 1974.... One of the original ten data handbooks was on community
and number-coded community values—the values every U.S. community was eventually to
embrace as their norms.[64]...

...The systems change and the implementation of the School-to-Work system will force
the continual assessment of children to analyze the progress being made toward the elimination of all bias, individualism and privacy. Common unity cannot prevail unless all children
develop the predetermined behavior, attitudes, and values for existence in the interdependent global society of the future.

The federal government is up to its old trick of creating a problem—which they certainly have done by limiting discipline in schools, subjecting children to certain learning
experiences, requiring inclusive education which requires juvenile offenders in tethers to be
in the regular classroom, requiring group consensus decision making and problem solving.
The violence problem has been advertised for quite some time, and the rigged survey results
will be used to continue the media blitz to gain public acknowledgment of the problem. The
solution to the problem was planned long before *Goals 2000*, but the objective was state
enforcement and control.

Most of the plan has already been implemented. Remember, everything is to be in
place by the year 2000. We already have alternative schools, after-hours programs, full-
service schools, day care, peer mediation, community service, character education, health
education, uniforms in some schools, etc.

Goal 6 data banks on violence and bias crimes open the public square to drowning in
the flood waters of the collective. Laws will be of no importance as norms become dictated
by the federal government via their data collection system. These norms are becoming very
evident: a new type of family (the community), gun control... efforts to modify the values of
Christians or any faith that disagrees with the norms of anti-individualism, population control, promotion of the world community over nationalism, with survival only through cooperation, collaboration and consensus. (pp. 14–23)[65]

[Ed. Note: Lewis's exposé of what is taking place in Michigan is a most valuable warning for
all Americans. In order to fully understand the significance of her exposé, substitute the
names of *your* children, *your* town, *your* county and *your* state and you will feel chills race
down your spine.]

DR. LAWRENCE W. LEZOTTE, SENIOR VICE PRESIDENT OF EFFECTIVE SCHOOLS, OKEMOS,
Michigan, presented a paper entitled "Learning for All—What Will It Take?" at the Sixth
Annual Model Schools Conference sponsored by Willard Daggett's International Center for
Leadership in Education, Inc., at the Renaissance Waverly Hotel and Cobb Convention Centre
in Atlanta, Georgia, June 28–July 1, 1998. An excerpt from Dr. Lezotte's paper follows:

A single school, as a system, can control enough of the variables to assure that virtually all
students do learn. The distinguished educational researcher Robert Gagne said that the es-

sential task of the teacher is to arrange the conditions of the learner's environment so that the process of learning will be activated, supported, enhanced, and maintained.

[Ed. Note: Quoting from the 1969 entry in this book entitled *Improving Educational Assessment and an Inventory of Measures of Affective Behavior*, the writer wishes to draw the reader's attention to a most revealing statement from "The Purposes of Assessment" by Ralph Tyler:

> Now, as the people from conditioning have moved into an interest in learning in the schools, the notions of behavioral objectives have become much more specific. As far as I know, one cannot very well teach a pigeon a general principle that he can apply to a variety of situations. The objectives for persons coming out of the Skinnerian background tend to be highly specific ones. When I listened to Gagne, who is an intelligent and effective conditioner, talk about human learning objectives, I wince a good deal because he sets very specific ones. I know that we can attain levels of generalization of objectives that are higher than that.

Making the connection between Lezotte, Gagne, and Tyler should help the reader understand that the restructuring going on in this nation's schools reflects the use of Skinnerian operant conditioning (OBE/ML/DI). Lezotte, one of the leaders of today's restructuring movement, has made this clear by his reference to Gagne, conditions and environment. The high profile that Lezotte maintains with his Effective Schools organization and his consistent appearance at Willard Daggett's meetings and seminars—and Daggett's close former association with William Spady of OBE fame—should demonstrate to the reader that all of these participants and promoters of the restructuring movement are "singing the same tune," as it were, and they sound exactly like Skinner's operant-conditioned pigeons. Lawrence Lezotte has also served on the board of directors for *The Effective School Report*—this very important and relatively unknown (to the public) journal.]

THE *ATLANTA CONSTITUTION*'S JULY 1, 1998 EDITION CARRIED AN ARTICLE BY DOUG Cumming entitled "Georgia Schools OK Tracking Systems" which confirmed the worst fears of education researchers tracking Planning, Programming, Budgeting Systems (PPBS) and Management by Objectives (MBO) for over twenty-five years. Excerpts from this revealing article follow:

> Taking its biggest step yet to create a powerful new computer information system that can track every state education dollar down to the attendance rates and test scores of every Georgia classroom, the State Board of Education approved two major computer contracts Tuesday.
>
> The two contracts, for as much as $31 million over the next 12 months, along with a related contract tabled until July 9, will give school systems quicker access to information.
>
> "For example, the new systems will let school systems instantly report students who are absent for two consecutive weeks or suspended for drugs, alcohol, or guns. This will allow the state to immediately revoke their driver's licenses under a law that took effect this year.
>
> "That's just a taste of what is possible. In the future, by linking student records, staff records and funding formulas, the new system will also allow local schools and state policymakers to see how well teachers and students are performing within specific programs.

"We know that in education for too long, programs have been implemented, and there was never any comprehensive measurement," said Miriam V. Holland, director of administrative technology for the state Department of Education.

"The state goal over the next few years is to be able to pinpoint the cause of academic weaknesses such as the recent failure rate on the science portion of the state's graduation exam," she said.

Bonnie Knight, head of business and technology for the Rockdale schools, said she is excited about what will be possible when a new student-information system is introduced and linked to the accounting system. Then, teachers can punch up on their own computer, within security limits, family and student records, and administrators can access the kind of information that private businesses normally use to determine the cost-effectiveness of any program. Knight says she knows of no other state that is linking student records with state and local school accounting systems.

James Mullins, a lobbyist for DeKalb County schools, which uses its own information systems, said the new system will put increasing pressure on systems like his to adopt the state's system. He said many local systems quietly worry that the proposed new system could eventually give the state the power of a "Big Brother" to control local schools directly.

[Ed. Note: The legitimate concern expressed by James Mullins of DeKalb County regarding "Big Brother" comes as a timely warning for naïve Americans who see nothing wrong with providing any and all information—social security numbers, fingerprints, personal data—to anyone who requests it, even, and especially, your local school officials. The reader is urged to re-read the 1972 entry in this book which quoted from "Schools to Try New Program" published in the Tallahassee, Florida *The Ledger* for the Cecil Golden comment which likened PPBS/MBO—of which the above article is the fulfillment—to an atom bomb: "[L]ike those assembling the atom bomb, very few of them understand exactly what they are building, and won't until we put all the parts together."]

"**Vocational Project Lauded**" **was published in the Salem, Oregon** *The Statesman Journal* on July 7, 1998. This article discussed a program in which students repair donated computers for use in schools (Students Recycling Used Technology or STRUT). Some excerpts follow:

> Gov. John Kitzhaber, addressing a national conference of educators Monday, praised a vocational education program as an example of school reform that emphasizes results instead of class time.
>
> Students repair donated computers for use in schools through the program known as Students Recycling Used Technology, or STRUT.
>
> The program is a model for the next generation of vocational education in the United States, Kitzhaber told the Education Commission of the States, an educational policy group that includes governors and state legislators.
>
> "The new model," said Kitzhaber, "provides standards and the basics but then requires students to demonstrate that they can actually apply the knowledge that they've learned."
>
> "Conceived in 1995, STRUT has placed 10,000 refurbished computers in schools and has more than 800 students repairing computers statewide.
>
> "The program's results have inspired educators in Washington, California, Arizona, New Mexico and Texas to copy it. STRUT is a modern version of traditional vocational education because it combines two objectives," said Frank Newman, Commission President....

"In Indiana, new programs similar to STRUT rely on professional technicians, not students, to repair donated computers.... One downside is that a lot of what is donated is low quality," said Carolyn Breedlove, a telecommunications lobbyist for the National Education Association in Washington, D.C. "Companies get tax write-offs often not commensurate with the quality of the donations."

THE JULY 9, 1998 ISSUE OF THE SOUTH BRISTOL, MAINE *LINCOLN COUNTY WEEKLY* PUBlished an article entitled "Darling Center Hosts UNESCO Conference" which illustrates the extent to which even the smallest towns in our nation are being affected by international education policies. The article states in part:

> While the majority of residents and visitors in the area celebrate Damariscotta's past 150 years, a fledgling group of international visitors gather at the Ira C. Darling Marine Center to plan for the future.
>
> Participants in the third International Working Conference on Information Technology in Education Management (ITEM) have come from 18 countries, including Australia, Japan, New Zealand, China and the Netherlands, to share their research on integrating information for education management....
>
> ..."One very important aspect of this work is how integrated information influences or informs the decisions of school administrators and policy makers," said Ray Taylor, the conference coordinator and a former superintendent of the Augusta school district....
>
> While the Darling Center hosted the meeting, School Union 74, UNESCO (United Nations Educational, Scientific and Cultural Organization), and a North Carolina company, OR/ED Laboratories, also supported the week's events.
>
> "Most of the participants work with national information systems for education, with Great Britain, Israel, Hong Kong, and New Zealand, having among the most advanced systems," Taylor said.
>
> Speakers debated the benefits of standardizing student and school information across regions. Such information systems benefit students by tracking their academic achievement, as well as administrators who have individual children continually entering and leaving their schools.
>
> "This goes beyond counting cheese and buses," one participant remarked. "We want to create consistent data on local, regional and national levels." [And international? ed.]

THE JULY 11, 1998 ISSUE OF *THE WASHINGTON TIMES* CARRIED AN ARTICLE ENTITLED "Classroom Brain-Watchers?" by Kathleen Parker which discussed the federal government's plan to prevent school violence by "adding psychoanalysis to our teachers' laundry list of responsibilities." Excerpts follow:

> I have a healthy paranoia toward government, born most likely of having been reared by a misanthropic WWII pilot with a bomb shelter. Let's just say, when government bureaucrats knock on my door and say, "We want to help you," I get the same feeling I got as a little girl when the old man down the street reached over his cyclone fence to offer me a piece of candy. Not "No, thanks," but "Run!"
>
> When they come knocking to say they want to help my children, I reflect wistfully on moats.

Such that when I recently heard about the federal government's plan to prevent school violence by adding psychoanalysis to our teachers' laundry list of responsibilities, I began pricing drawbridges.

Judging from the absence of news stories on the subject, you may have missed your future. President Clinton first mentioned the plan in his June 13 radio address to the nation. Education Secretary Richard Riley mentioned it again a couple of weeks ago during the Safe and Drug Free Schools Conference in Washington, D.C.

Mr. Clinton has directed Mr. Riley and Attorney General Janet Reno to work with the National Association of School Psychologists to develop a framework—"early warning guide"—to help teachers and principals identify which kids are most likely to bring Grandpa's deer rifle to school one of these days.

The plan also calls for expanding links between schools and local psychological communities so children identified as "troubled" have access to counseling.

Because the guide is in the early planning stages, details are skimpy. No one knows yet how danger signs will be defined or recognized, according to a Department of Education spokesperson. Right off, I'd have to say it's pretty easy to tell which kids are dangerous without creating a psychological bureaucracy. In nearly all recent school shootings, as Mr. Clinton pointed out, the shooters announced their plans in advance.

In other words, if a kid says, "I'm going to blow everybody away tomorrow because they've been picking on me since nursery school," you might assume trouble. If, on the other hand, a third-grade boy draws a picture of a ship exploding with bodies flying in all directions, punctuated by red ink blots, you might assume you've got a normal third-grader on your hands.

But you can bet that won't be the thinking once the warning guide is in the hands of extremely well-meaning educators and counselors, some of whom have the judgment and perception of parakeets. That third-grader will wind up in some counselor's office for analysis and reprogramming before you can say "Freud."

Paranoid? You bet.

My own child—a kind, sensitive 13-year-old whose disinterest in guns rivals his interest in hanging up wet towels—drew incredibly violent pictures during his grade-school years. The exploding ship with exploding bodies comes to mind. How might a newly trained teacher—especially a female teacher without sons—interpret such a drawing?

Clearly a sociopath. Get that boy downtown!

Will any child who talks about guns be sent to the "thought police"? What about playing cowboys and Indians, or "Star Wars" during recess? Does this qualify a child for re-education? What sort of records will be kept?

Even Mr. Riley expressed concerns about the plan. "We need to be very cautious about the idea of sorting out our children and labeling them," he said in the speech. "Too many children are already being sorted out in our schools and too often this approach to education has been harmful to minority youth."

Not to mention harmful to freedom. Can mandatory psychological profiling be far behind? The potential for abuse of power and thought control is the stuff of science fiction. But that's just the thinking of a paranoid. I probably just need a little psychotherapy.

And a big moat.

IN THE JULY 14, 1998 *CONGRESSIONAL RECORD* CONGRESSMAN HENRY HYDE (R., IL) IN-cluded a very important article written by D.L. Cuddy, Ph.D., former senior associate with the U.S. Department of Education and consultant to the North Carolina House Select Committee for Federal Education Grants. Cuddy wrote "Education: The New Transatlantic Agenda" which appeared in the July 2, 1998 issue of Dunn, North Carolina's *The Daily Record*. Excerpts follow:

The White House released a statement May 18 at the conclusion of the U.S.-European Summit in London, indicating that "through the New Transatlantic Agenda (NTA), created in 1995, the United States and the European Union have focused on addressing the challenges and opportunities of global integration."

One part of this "global integration" in 1995 was the agreement between the U.S. and the European Community establishing a cooperation program in higher education and vocational education and training.

The agreement, signed December 21, 1995, called for "improving the quality of human resource development... transatlantic student mobility... and thus portability of academic credits." In this regard, a joint committee would reach decisions by consensus.

As part of the NTA, the United States and European Union then convened a major conference, "Bridging the Atlantic People-to-People Links," May 5–6. 1997, calling for "thematic networks for curriculum development," and further stating that in an information-based global economy, "governments too are obliged to adapt their economic, training and social welfare programs."

The conference final report noted that in the United States, ACHIEVE has been one of the organizations at the forefront of defining key issues in this regard and developing strategies to address them.

ACHIEVE has been measuring and reporting each state's annual progress in establishing internationally competitive standards and business leaders involved have indicated their commitment to consider the quality of each state's standards when making business location or expansion decisions.

The "Partners in a Global Economy Working Group" of the conference discussed "what redesigning of curricula is required... (i.e., what career skills are needed)... portability of skill certificates... institutionalizing cross-national learning/training activities."

Most people debating STW in America are familiar with the role of Marc Tucker, president of the National Center on Education and the Economy. He's also on the National Skill Standards Board (NSSB).

On the National Skill Standards Board website under international links, one finds "Smartcards Project Forum," under which one reads: "The Tavistock Institute and the European Commission are working on a feasibility study to research the effect of using Smartcards in competence accreditation. The study will be carried out in the USA and parts of Europe."

The project involves assessing and validating students' skills, with information placed on personal skills Smartcards, which "become real passports to employment."

If without a passport one cannot enter a country, does this mean that without a skills passport, one may not be able to get a job in the future?

In October 1997, the Tavistock Institute (and Manchester University) completed the final report for the European Commission and described in a report summary were the relevancy of *Goals 2000*, SCANS... typology with its "profound implications for the curriculum and training changes that this will require," valid skills standards and portable credentials "benchmarked to international standards such as those promulgated by the International Standards Organization (ISO)."

The report summary went on to say that "there is increasing attention being focused on developing global skill standards and accreditation agreements" and there will be "partnerships between government, industry and representatives of worker organizations ... [and] a high degree of integration... embedding skills within the broader context of economic and social activity and specifically within the areas of secondary education work-based learning and local and regional economic development.... The NSSB, *Goals 2000*, STW Program are all combining to act as a catalyst to promote the formation of partnerships to develop skills standards. In this regard, a system like O*Net can be seen as the glue that holds everything together."

O*Net is a new occupational database system sponsored by the U.S. Department of Labor's Employment and Training Administration and is being piloted in Texas, South Carolina, California, New York and Minnesota. It includes information such as "Worker Characteristics" (abilities, interests and work styles) and "Worker Requirements" (e.g., basic skills, knowledge and education).

CHRISTINE BURNS, A VETERAN TEACHER OF OUTSTANDING CHARACTER, REPUTATION AND credentials, labeled the St. Louis Career Academy a "diabolical gauntlet of pandemonium" in an article entitled "School-to-Work Academy: A 'Model' for Chaos" which appeared in the July 1998 issue of *The Education Reporter*. Excerpts follow:

The Career Academy... was touted by education reformers as the wave of the future—the "New Urban High School"—with the intent that it will eventually be open 24 hours a day. The Career Academy was designed to be one of five "break-the-mold" School-to-Work model high schools in the U.S. that are to be replicated throughout the country.

In May of this year, the Career Academy's facade of "success" and "achievement" began to crumble when one of its teachers came forward to paint a sordid picture of chaos, confusion and ineptitude at the school, calling it "a diabolical gauntlet of pandemonium" for its students.

Mrs. Burns, after eight months' teaching at the academy, desired only to "get out of it" and be "rid of the problem." But then the school district told her to read, critique and sign off on a document entitled "Building the Foundation for Life-Long, Self-Directed Learning" which according to Burns was "full of lies, suppositions and half truths." Realizing that she could not sign the document, she says that neither could she "walk away without someone, somewhere, knowing what I believe to be the truth about what is happening, or rather, not happening at the St. Louis Career Academy."

Mrs. Burns drafted a rebuttal to "Building a Foundation" which she sent to the school's principal, the CED Superintendent, the court-appointed vocational education monitor, and the school district's seven board members. The rebuttal charges the school with "lying about students gaining in academic achievement." It contends that "the school relies too heavily on computers, that computer labs are typically chaotic and poorly controlled due to lack of manpower," and that "destruction and theft of equipment are commonplace." "Students cheat on computerized tests to advance to their next 'tier' (grade)," she wrote, adding that "the school lacks practical in-classroom teaching, order and discipline." She charged that "children at the academy have been part of a giant School-to-Work experiment for the past two years, subjected to unproven and unorthodox practices and procedures, like rats in a maze."

Though the Career Academy has attempted to refute Mrs. Burns's charges, "Building the Foundation"'s 37 paragraphs provide some clues as to their validity. Paragraph 9 refers to the school's staff and students as remaining "intensely involved in an on-going process of self-creation." Paragraph 26 whines that: "In spite of an explicit court mandate to 'break the mold,' the academy continues to come under attack from proponents of the old system." Yet paragraph 30 admits that "students have learned they can fool the computer by 'smart guessing' or by memorizing answers for retests. Some students wonder how much of their learning they will retain. Others have 'maxed out' on the English and math programs, and do not feel challenged by their supplemental work."

BILL CARLSON, AN EDUCATION RESEARCHER FROM TEXAS, COVERED THE SCHOOL-TO-CAREER Academy Conference held July 23–24, 1998 at the Airport Hyatt Hotel in Burlingame, California. Carlson's article should be in the hands of parents and small businessmen who have been subjected to the skilled manipulation of the change agent promoters of STW. Excerpts from Mr. Carlson's article, "Impressions and Concerns: A Preliminary Report" follow:

The School-to-Career (STC) "academy" featured two keynote speakers, J.D. Hoye and Willard Daggett. Hoye bills herself as J.D. Hoye, President, Keep the Change, Inc. Her web site (http://inet.ed.gov./offices/OVAE/hoye.html) identifies her as the Director of the National School-to-Work (STW) Office in Washington, D.C. (Note: STC and STW as used in this report convey the same meaning.) Hoye's former involvement was with the Oregon Department of Education and Office of Community College Services, Oregon, arguably and tragically the most OBE-impacted state in the nation.... Both speakers are extremely smooth and clever STW marketers. Both have a passion for ALL children to learn and seem convinced that STW will "level the playing field." (It must, however, be mandatory that ALL children experience STW. Why?)

Hoye gives the message that our current education system does great for 25–30% of the students. She wants a level playing field for ALL students. She points to a book called *The New Basics* as a guide. She plays down memorization, abstract and theoretical teaching because they don't stick as well as cooperative project completions. Now is the time to promote STC throughout our communities because it "sunsets in 2001." Be creative in finding ways to "convince" skeptics, especially parents. Involve them in the process and they will believe the ideas generated were their own. Administrators should make sure, as far as possible, that hiring, promotion and retention policies coincide with promotion of school-to-work goals.

Students are the best communicators of the need for change and STW. Periodically, a student was brought out to give a "first-hand example" of our need to change, change, change to STW. She describes what we are doing (promoting school-to-career) as "the most important thing happening on our planet!"

Willard Daggett was clearly the featured event. (web site—http://www.daggett.com) He was introduced as one who is "taking on the task of promoting school-to-career in California." If Dr. Daggett is the King of STW, Hoye is certainly the Queen. Daggett touts himself as being the President of the International Center for Leadership in Education, Inc.

He offered thanks to educators for "hanging in there" in spite of all of the criticism. His advice to the audience was, "Don't put the spin on STC as STC, but put the spin on 'The Basics' in relation to school-to-career." (Fool 'em?) In order to effect change (the key word, again!), you must have a passion to change. Basic conditions to create change: 1. Have passion, 2. Have data, 3. Have leadership, and 4. Have staff development. Using these four ingredients, you will have successful models to help market STC. Some of the 255 subject areas in our schools should be taken out. "In America, when something goes into the curriculum, it never comes out." Examples given (I believe) to take out: some of the requirements in math, science, social studies, etc. He wants schools to make room for information that now "doubles every nine months!"

Daggett says reading for entertainment should be mostly replaced with reading and writing technical manuals and emphasis should be placed on procedure and process.... Daggett said that the time has come to create controversy.... He has discussed with neurosurgeons (He has one in the family.) whether death is inevitable, or, with the advance of biotech, an option. Heavy stuff!... In one of the "breakout" sessions that I attended, the focus was on how to sell STW to an unaware community. For the past four years, educators, school board members, teacher unions, and some employers have been the targets of repeated STW indoctrination. Now, parents, students and others must somehow be hauled in. One lady said she thought the name (STW) should be changed because a conservative group called "the Eagle Forum" is openly and effectively critical of STW.... Following skeptical comments, the same lady concluded that, "Now, for sure, we'll have to change the name" and call STC something other than STC. (Fool 'em!)...

I haven't heard speakers like this since the radical 1960's era when those demanding "change" wore long hair, headbands and sandals, not a suit and tie. Daggett and Hoye continued to "evangelize" the vast cult-like following of those who now support radical changes to our schools. Citizens are paying BIG-TIME for this experiment in social control, but too few know much about STC. And probably would want no part of it if/when it's ever fully explained to them.

I don't.

DR. KEN WILLIAMS, AN ELECTED TRUSTEE TO THE ORANGE COUNTY DEPARTMENT OF EDUcation and board-certified family physician in Santa Ana, California, wrote the following August 27, 1998 letter to the *American School Board Journal* regarding the School-to-Work Career Inventory and Assessments. Dr. Williams's incredible experience exposes the dangerous implications of the use of psychological assessments, etc., to predict an individual's career potential. The full text of Dr. Williams's letter follows:

Dear Sir:

I am writing you as an elected Trustee to the Orange County Department of Education in California regarding the STW Career Inventory and Assessments. I was asked to share this information with you because of my concerns with the STW program.

Last year, I took a computer-assisted career inventory program at the local high school here in Orange County to determine what career pathway I would have been encouraged to take if I were a freshman.

To my surprise, the career inventory programs encouraged me to follow a career pathway that would lead to one of the following occupations: 1) Auto Muffler Installer, 2) Plasterer and Drywall Installer, 3) Glazier, 4) Cement Mason, 5) Auto Body and Fender Repairer, 6) Railroad Brake Operator, 7) Bus Driver, and 8) Modeling.

Now, let me state that I am not degrading any of these occupations. The good people of this nation who are engaged in these fields are hard working Americans who deserve our respect. My concern is that when I took this career assessment and inventory, I answered all twenty or so questions with the idea that I wanted to be a family physician practicing in the city of Santa Ana, California, where I took the career program at the local high school (where a STW program is in place).

In conclusion, I wonder how many smart and talented kids from traditionally disadvantaged minority groups in this inner city are being directed into low wage and low skill jobs, instead of into professional and graduate schools. Is this the ultimate, "in-your-face" federal program that will take away liberties and freedoms from our people?

Sincerely,
Dr. Ken Williams

WILLIAM J. BRAUN, SR., ISSUED A PRESS RELEASE DATED AUGUST 29, 1998 FROM CLEVE-land, Ohio concerning a landmark education case, *State ex rel. Stephen Rea v. Ohio Department of Education*. The press release discussed the successfully argued Stephen Rea court case regarding the status of certain tests and assessments being declared public records:

> Stephen Rea, relying on the *U.S. Freedom of Information Act* and the *State of Ohio Availability of Public Records Law*, requested copies of sensitive testing materials used on his daughter at West Branch High School, Beloit, Ohio.
>
> His continued requests fell upon deaf ears, all the way up to the State Superintendent of Schools. Rea argued that all classroom materials generated with government-funded dollars constituted public records *per se*.
>
> He would be allowed to view the requested materials, but only if he agreed to sign a secrecy agreement that carried a fine and imprisonment clause if violated. On 28 August 1996, Rea filed a complaint with the Ohio Supreme Court, which was accepted for trial.
>
> Rea sought judicial judgment against the Ohio Board of Education on four issues. The case was tried *in mandamus*. In a powerfully worded majority opinion, the Court ruled in favor of Rea and his daughter. (*State of Ohio, ex rel: Stephen Rea, et al v. Ohio Department of Education*. Case No. 96–1997, *in Mandamus*.)
>
> Tomorrow's battles will shift abruptly from school superintendents' offices and Department of Education conference rooms to State and Federal Court Chambers, where they are more likely winnable, including the recovery of reasonable fees and court costs.

"WORKFORCE INVESTMENT ACT PUTS AMERICA ON ROAD TO FASCISM—HILLARY'S GLOBAL Village and the New World Order Are Officially Instituted by Congress" by Jim Day appeared in the August, 1998 *St. Louis Metro Voice* monthly. Excerpts follow:

> "Few bills which we consider will have a greater impact on more Americans than the *Workforce Investment Act* (H.R. 1385) we pass today."—Sen. Edward Kennedy (*Congressional Record*, July 30, 1998, p. S 9490).
>
> [PUBLISHER'S NOTE: Truer words were never spoken in relation to gaining total control of the citizens of the United States and turning our nation into a fascist state. If you think this is an outlandish statement, read this article. What you are about to read is the absolute truth which is backed by more documentation than you could ever hope to read.]
>
> On July 30 Senators Edward Kennedy (D) MA, Jim Jeffords (R) VT, Mike DeWine (R) OH, Paul Wellstone (D) MN, Christopher Dodd (D) CT, and Jack Reed (D) RI, unanimously passed by a voice vote the Conference Report on H.R. 1385—the *Workforce Investment Act of 1998*—the latest version of "The CAREERS Act." A voice vote only requires a majority of those present to pass or reject a bill. The report was then sent back to the House of Representatives for review.
>
> According to the *Congressional Record*, only six senators spoke on the floor. Due to the fact that no roll call vote was taken, it is not known if any other senators were present in the chamber at the time.
>
> Late in the afternoon the next day, July 31, without any notice, when most congressmen were on planes headed home, five congressmen, again by a voice vote, unanimously approved H.R. 1385, paving the way for President Clinton's signature on August 7. The five congressmen were William Clay, Sr. (D) MO, Howard P. "Buck" McKeon (R) CA, William "Bill" Goodling (R) PA, Dale Kildee (D) MI, and Matthew Martinez (D) CA.
>
> Again, due to the fact that no roll call vote was taken, no one knows how many other, if any, congressmen were present at the time of the vote. These 11 men and President Clinton

have just created and signed into law legislation which converts America's free market economic system to a controlled or managed market system—the same type of economic system which was established by Nazi Germany.

[Ed. Note: President Clinton, on August 7, 1998, signed this controversial school-to-work/job training bill, the final version of the infamous *CAREERS Act* which grassroots activists had worked hard to kill for over four years and had thought they had put to rest in the summer of 1996 when Senator Trent Lott refused to bring it up for a vote. These same activists were taken by surprise when Rep. Howard P. (Buck) McKeon, proclaimed conservative from California, appeared out of nowhere like a stealth bomber, reintroduced and assisted to pass similar legislation in April 1997—this time titled *The Employment Training and Literacy Enhancement Act of 1997*. Activists had little time to mount an effort to down this nasty stealth missile, allowing it to go on to the Senate which, in turn, passed it in August of 1998.]

THE NATIONAL ACADEMY OF SCIENCES AND THE U.S. DEPARTMENT OF EDUCATION-FUNDED *Preventing Reading Difficulties in Young Children*, Grant No. 0235501 (National Academy Press: Washington, D.C., 1998), was critiqued by Ann Herzer of Arizona, M.A., reading specialist. Herzer literally lobbed a well-justified grenade at those so-called "experts" involved in the research and writing of the book, whose credentials indicate their long-term involvement in programs for special education and in the promotion or development of Skinnerian operant conditioning programs to teach reading and other subjects. Mrs. Herzer's critique follows in its entirety:

The National Academy of Sciences is a private, non-profit organization which was granted a Charter by Congress in 1963. The Academy advises the government on scientific and technical matters. (p. iv)

The following three groups are named on the title page for the above book:

(1) Committee on the Prevention of Reading Difficulties in Young Children;

(2) Commission on Behavioral and Social Sciences and Education and

(3) National Research Council.

Apparently the first committee mentioned was responsible for the report (the book) and members were "Chosen for their special competencies and with regard for appropriate balance." (p. ii)

The Acknowledgments read like a *Who's Who of Government Change Agents and Behavioral Scientists*. Reid Lyon (National Institute of Health—NIH) with whom I spoke regarding *The Reading Excellence Act*, is listed, as are members connected with NIH's labs, several members from the U.S. Department of Education, the Carnegie Corp., etc, etc., etc.

During the information-gathering phase, a number of people are mentioned who made presentations to the committee on programs that focused on prevention of reading difficulties. They did not say who selected the presenters. I am familiar with two names: Ethna Reid (*Keyboarding, Reading and Spelling*) and John Nunnary (*Success for All*). I will never forget Reid's government-sponsored (NDN) program, the *Exemplary Center for Reading Instruction* (ECRI). The 1978 week-long ECRI workshop I attended started my investigation into the Skinnerian Mastery Learning/Direct Instruction programs. *Success for All* is one of the New American Schools Development Corporation programs, selected and approved by Presidents Bush and Clinton for restructuring education, which also uses Skinnerian Direct Instruction.

Several professional associations were mentioned along with groups, including Save the Children International.

Some members of the Committee are worth mentioning: Marilyn Jager Adams who wrote *Beginning to Read: Thinking and Learning about Print* (a real Pavlovian bell-ringer disguised under phonics) and Edward J. Kame'enui, special education, University of Oregon and associate director of the federally funded National Center to Improve the Tools of Educators (NCITE)—the same center with which Douglas Carnine (who was involved with the failed Follow Through federal program and the government-sponsored Skinnerian S-R-S program DISTAR—(Direct Instruction System for Teaching and Remediation) is connected. DISTAR is now being touted by the government change agents and the radical right Heritage Foundation as a Direct Instruction "scientific" program for teaching phonics (of all things) to pre-K–3rd grade students.

Members and their qualifications are mentioned as follows: Catherine Snow, M.A. and Ph.D in psychology from McGill University (Canada); Marilyn Jager Adams, visiting professor at Harvard University School of Education and a previous research scientist at Bolt, Beranek and Newman, Inc.; Barbara T. Bowman, co-founder and president, the Erickson Institute in Chicago, Illinois, recent appointee to the Great Books Foundation and the National Board for Professional Teaching Standards; M. Susan Burns, formerly on the faculty at the University of Pittsburgh; Barbara Foorman, University of Texas, Houston Health Science Center and also principal investigator of the Early Intervention Program of the National Institute of Child Health and Human Development, consulting editor for the *Journal of Learning Disabilities* and a member of the New Standards Project; Claude N. Goldenberg, a research psychologist in the Department of Psychiatry, Biobehavioral Sciences at the University of California, Los Angeles; William Labor of the University of Pennsylvania, currently engaged in several research programs funded by the National Science Foundation and the National Endowment for the Humanities; Richard K. Olson, associate director of the Center for the Study of Learning Disabilities funded by the National Institutes of Health; Charles A. Perfetti, a senior scientist at the Learning Research and Development Center at the University of Pittsburgh; etc., etc., etc., who are supposed to give this hand-picked committee an "appropriate balance."

The "treatment" suggested in both of the above-mentioned books [Jager's *Beginning to Read* and *Preventing Reading Difficulties*] for teaching young children to read appears to have been designed for the mentally retarded to severely handicapped children—not average children.

This group is proposing language training from birth. Apparently parents are to be trained as though *none* have any normal/natural instincts in child rearing or language. HIPPY, PAT (Parents as Teachers) and other home-bound programs are now proposed for the "at risk"—the poor and minority children, but how long will it be before the radical behavioral scientists demand home visits and training for all children and their families as was mandated in the former Soviet Union?

In my opinion, the individuals involved in producing the two above-mentioned books and especially the U.S. government, who supplies the grant money, are not interested in children learning to read but only in training and programming them for the planned global workforce. Otherwise programs like DISTAR, ECRI and Madeline Hunter's *Essential Elements of Instruction* would have been exposed and stopped long ago.

When I evaluated the Texas Alternative Document (TAD), I was not aware of the significance of TAD until Reid Lyon and others responded on the internet education loop. These individuals apparently are supporting the Skinnerian DISTAR, or similar programs, as a method to teach reading through the distribution of TAD. TAD is now being pushed in Nebraska as curricula for language arts. I predicted it would be the national model for restructuring and teacher training. DISTAR is now training teachers in California, according to *Education Week*. The big emphasis nationally is on "teacher training," especially in Reading—"re-training," *not* "education"—is the emphasis [emphasis in original].

THE SEPTEMBER 1998 ISSUE OF THE *AMERICAN FAMILY ASSOCIATION JOURNAL* CARRIED AN article entitled "Despite Heavy Funding Public Schools Showing Marks of Internal Crumbling" which stated that 59% of new teachers in Massachusetts failed to meet the minimum standard of a basic reading and writing test. Excerpts follow:

> This past April, the Massachusetts Board of Education for the first time required new teachers to take a basic reading and writing test. Officials were horrified, however, to discover that 59% of the new teachers failed to meet the minimum standard. John Silber, Board of Education Chairman, complained that the test only required would-be teachers to score at an eighth-grade level. The test results were "pretty frightening," Silber said. "These were all college graduates."
>
> Massachusetts's strategy following the embarrassment? Education officials lowered the minimum score required to pass the test from a 77% to 66%. The new strategy succeeded; only 44% of would-be teachers failed the test.

THE SEPTEMBER 16, 1998 ISSUE OF *THE WASHINGTON TIMES* CARRIED AN ARTICLE ENTITLED "New Tack Taken on Religion in Schools: Group Seeks End to Secular Bias" which chronicles the publication of a new guidebook, *Taking Religion Seriously across the Curriculum* co-authored by Charles Haynes of the First Amendment Center at Vanderbilt University and Warren Nord of the University of North Carolina (Association for Supervision and Curriculum Development and the First Amendment Center: Washington, D.C., 1998). The opening paragraph of the article is very telling:

> A group of educators and policy advocates yesterday united around a "new consensus" on teaching about religion in public schools, calling it a long-shot agenda but the most likely to satisfy all Americans....
>
> ..."If this book is the next step, it's a big step," said Diane Berreth of the Association for Supervision and Curriculum Development (ASCD), which advises public schools on teaching.
>
> The "new approach" seeks a middle ground between totally secular schools and those where the local majority religion is promoted by school officials. "Religion is still not taken seriously in the public school curriculum," said Charles Haynes, a co-author of the new guidebook.
>
> Warren Nord, a University of North Carolina humanities professor and co-author, said, "A full education must acknowledge different ways of knowing reality, from the scientific and economic to the religious and moral."... Miss Berreth of ASCD said a few pilot schools must test the new agenda to prove its effectiveness. "This may be a role of [charter schools]," she said.

[Ed. Note: The above two authors made their remarks at a symposium with five other panelists. The event was sponsored by the Freedom Forum and the ASCD, which published the 220-page book with the First Amendment Center at Vanderbilt University.

If anyone out there believes a book published by the Association for Supervision and Curriculum Development (a spin-off of the National Education Association which consistently issues tirades about Christians who believe in sound moral values) could come up with anything the purpose of which is *not* to make further inroads into the *destruction* of whatever absolutist values our children still have, then I suggest they have been living under a rock ever since the 1940's when the drive to eliminate absolutist moral values from our schools started. The ASCD was heavily involved in the mind-altering curriculum *Tactics for Thinking*.

Researchers and activists involved in following the circuitous path taken by those who want to remove religious-based absolute values from this planet, starting in the schools, have thrown roadblocks in their way every time they surfaced with a new sugar-coated version of their sugar-coated values-destroying curriculum. How many more times must citizen researchers leap forward to expose this fraudulent crowd which has used semantic deception (given its programs the following misleading labels) and operated as the following entities:

- "Character Education" in the early 1970's (which advised those involved not to use the "red flag" word "values");
- The Public Education Religion Study Center at Wright State University's "comparative religion" curriculum (which was funded by Religious Heritage of America, Inc. and the Lilly Endowment of the Eli Lilly Corporation);
- the appointed Maryland Values Commission, another project shared with Religious Heritage of America;
- the American Institute for Character Education (AICE), funded by the Lilly Endowment;
- the Williamsburg Charter proposal which led to the First Amendment Center's curriculum "Teaching about Religion," and now, *Taking Religion Seriously across the Curriculum*, which a high school teacher from San Diego, California said should be "mandatory reading" for all public school instructors.]

AN ARTICLE ENTITLED "U.S. ANNOUNCED EXCHANGE PROGRAMS" APPEARED IN THE September 18, 1998 edition of the *Odessa* (Russia) *Post* which heralded the results of the U.S.-Soviet Education Agreements signed in 1985 and numerous planning activities since 1985. Excerpts follow:

> The program is administered by the U.S. Information Service. The American Council for Collaboration in Education and Language Study (ACCELS), the International Renaissance Foundation, and the International Research and Exchanges Board for Scholars (IREX) will be responsible for processing applications, selecting candidates and administering the exchange and scholarship programs....
>
> ...ACCELS will administer the U.S.-Ukraine Awards for Excellence in Teaching, which will bring 15 Ukrainian teachers of English and American Studies to the United States... in the summer of 1999. Finalists selected from participating regions can also win computer equipment, copiers or internet access for their schools....
>
> ...[N]ot only can Ukrainians find out more about the American way of life, our values, beliefs, hope and ambitions, Americans will also learn more about Ukraine and Ukrainians.

"A QUESTION OF EFFECTIVENESS" BY ANDREW TROTTER WAS PUBLISHED IN THE OCTOBER 1, 1998 issue of *Education Week*'s special report entitled *Technology Counts '98—Putting School Technology to the Test*. This important special issue should be read in its entirety for an understanding of the plusses and minuses of using technology in the classroom. One interesting chart on page 9 indicated that when the public and teachers were asked "How much do you think computers have helped improve student learning?" members of the public, in contrast to educators, were nearly twice as likely to say "A great amount"(MCI Nationwide Poll on Internet in Education, 1998).

THE OCTOBER 7, 1998 ISSUE OF *EDUCATION WEEK* CARRIED A FULL-PAGE ADVERTISEMENT FOR THE Sixteenth Annual Effective Schools Conference to be held in March of 1999. This writer has copied the advertisement in order to illustrate that any concern for academic instruction for American school children is a thing of the past. (The semantic deception will be obvious.)

SIXTEENTH ANNUAL
EFFECTIVE SCHOOLS CONFERENCE

LEARNING FOR ALL—WHATEVER IT TAKES
March 4–7, 1999
Willard Daggett, Larry Lezotte, Ray Gollarz, Michael Fullan, John Jay Bonstingl, Ernest Stachowski, Douglas Reeves, Alan November, Spence Rogers, Sandi Redenbach, Robert Slavin

NSCI
NATIONAL SCHOOL CONFERENCE INSTITUTE[66]
Phoenix, Arizona
Pre-Conferences:

Leading Learning for All
Making the Right Changes at the District Level to Assure Successful, Sustainable School Reform—with Larry Lezotte

Educational Accountability in Complex School Systems
The Challenges of High Standards, Accurate Assessments, and Meaningful Accountability with Douglas Reeves

CONTENTS

- Correlates of Effective Schools
- Developing the Leadership Team
- Meaningful Educational Accountability
- Creating Positive School Climate
- Managing Change to Implement Standards
- Instructional Strategies to Enhance Achievement
- Infusing Technology
- Ensuring the Success of All Children
- Effective School Improvement Planning
- Quality Teaching in the Classroom
- Communication Literacy

- Classroom Success—Applying Brain Research
- Motivating Students
- Assessments as a Performance Tool
- Quality and Equity in the School
- Site-Based Decision Making
- Learning Organizations

AN ARTICLE ENTITLED "CHARACTER EDUCATION CATCHING ON AT SCHOOLS—RESPECT, REsponsibility Emphasized" by Anu Manchikanti was published in the October 9, 1998 issue of *The Washington Times*. Excerpts follow:

Character education is a national movement to bring universal virtues into the classroom.

At Wasatch, a character education program has been in place for two years.

Thomas Lickona, director of the National Center for the 4th and 5th Rs (respect and responsibility), says a moral decline in youth reflects a character crisis in the United States.

In his 1997 State of the Union Address, President Clinton called for schools to teach character and mold children into good citizens. Most recently, Vice President Al Gore announced $2.7 million in grants for 10 states under the Partnerships in Character Education Pilot Projects Program. The grants should allow states to work with school districts in developing curriculum and providing teacher training for character education programs. Iowa, New Mexico and Utah have received such grants.

"It isn't a separate curriculum or an add-on or an extra thing," said Kristin Fink, character education specialist at the Utah State Office of Education. "It's really something that should be woven into everything we do."

According to Kevin Ryan, director of the Center for the Advancement of Ethics and Character at Boston University, the potential for character education exists in all curriculum to engage children in moral thought.

For instance, physical education teachers might emphasize the importance of playing fair in athletics, or science teachers may stimulate discussion about the ethical issues involved in genetic cloning.

"They're going to either learn good character or bad character," Mr. Ryan said. "It's all an inevitable part of life that schools will have an impact."

But Murray Philip, a school board member in Nashville, Tennessee questions the idea that character can be taught. "Who are we to decide what is good character, and what is bad character?" he said. Mr. Philip doubts that character can be taught because he feels it is learned through adversity and experience. Many argue that the job of teaching character lies in the hands of families rather than schools. "There's an awful lot of kids who are not being taught anything at home," Mr. Ryan said. "There's no such thing as a morally neutral school."

[Ed. Note: In response to the statements by Thomas Lickona, it is hard for this writer to accept Mr. Lickona as a leader in the area of moral education considering his promotion of the late Lawrence Kohlberg's humanistic "Stages of Moral Development" and morally relativistic character education program "Ethical Issues in Decision Making."

As for Clinton's 1997 State of the Union speech, with the recently concluded impeachment trial and the events which precipitated it, there are no words to adequately express the irony of Clinton's calling for the schools to teach "character." Also, can one really imagine a government-developed character education program or one that would be allowed to be used in government-supported schools which would be effective, when government-supported "scientific research" is based in an evolutionary perspective of our children being trainable animals? Children observing teachers and others in authority exhibiting good character is the best "character education." Also, allowing school boards to hire teachers whose lives incorporate high moral character would do much to contribute to the solution of this problem.

After having read and said all of the above, the writer would like to issue degrees in rocket science for all the parents who understand the problem!]

APPROXIMATELY 3,500 PEOPLE ATTENDED A RALLY ON SUNDAY, OCTOBER 11, 1998 AT THE Minnesota State Capitol in Minneapolis in opposition to Minnesota's graduation standards. [Some accounts put the number present at as high as 5,000.] Minnesota's major media—*The Minneapolis Star Tribune, The St. Paul Pioneer Press, The Minnesota Daily* and four local television stations—gave coverage to the rally. *The Minneapolis Star Tribune* article "Multiple Choice Review of Education—Profiles of Learning Takes Central Stage at Gubernatorial Debate on Education—Large Protest at Capital Targets the State's Newest Graduation Standards" stated in part:

> Minnesota's Graduation Rule came under vigorous attack on Sunday as many hundreds of residents rallied at the state capitol demanding an end to the academic standards known as the "Profiles of Learning." Opponents lambasted the rule as an attempt to control schools and a move towards a socialist government. Many fear the rule will force schools to steer away from the basics and "dumb down" public schools. Organizers estimated the crowd at 3,500. Ronald Anderson, age 61, a grandfather from St. Paul said, "Public schools are teaching more touchy-feely education instead of history, math and sciences and all that stuff." He waved a sign that read "Do not experiment with our children."

[Ed. Note: Why was the above-mentioned important news item ignored by out-of-state media? Is it because news coverage of successful opposition to restructuring in one state might serve to encourage activists in other states?

Corporate and education journals indicate that those in charge of restructuring our schools are not happy at all with the sluggish pace of restructuring due to the effectiveness of parent and teacher opposition. If the reader puts all of this information together the obvious cannot be avoided: opponents across the country are doing far better than they realize—they have slowed down the restructuring of our nation from free enterprise to socialism far more than they know. How many more "Minnesota" stories are there out there about which we know nothing due to media censorship?]

THE FOLLOWING NEWS ITEM WAS CARRIED BY *USA TODAY* IN ITS OCTOBER 12, 1998 ISSUE:

> SALT LAKE CITY, UTAH—The Utah School Boards Association has asked a judge to declare the '98 *Charter Schools Act* unconstitutional. Charter schools are funded with public education money, but are exempt from many of the restrictions on public schools. The lawsuit alleges local school boards have control over schools in their boundaries, and that by reaching within those boundaries, the state is creating a new school district without a public vote.

[Ed. Note: Hats off to the Utah School Boards Association. When education activists/researchers in their many speeches across the nation referred to charter schools as "taxation without representation" the silence in conservative audiences was "deafening."]

IN 1998 THE NORTHWEST REGIONAL EDUCATIONAL LABORATORY, ONE OF THE TEN LABORA-tories across the nation supported by contracts with the U.S. Department of Education's Office of Educational Research and Improvement (OERI), provided the following information on its "Education & Community Services: Emerging Issues" website (http//www.nwrel.org/pscc/emerging.html). For the reader who may, understandably, want to have an up-to-date report on the status of the restructuring of the nation's schools, through school-to-work and the merging of education and workforce training with social services (systemic change), there is probably no better source than the Northwest Regional Educational Laboratory. "Emerging Issues" as of October 16, 1998 follow:

Twelve major emerging issues have been identified from an analysis of recent policy reports and validated by a focus group of state leaders as having a significant impact on education in the Northwest:

1. Acknowledging fundamental shifts in teaching and learning. A view of students as active learners... emphasis on cooperative and applied learning.
2. Dealing with the rising threat of violence. High incidence of violence, substance abuse, and gang-related crime are causing schools to review discipline policies, implement special curricula, and work increasingly with law enforcement and other community agencies.
3. Assuring a sound infrastructure for education. A growing student population is on a collision course with an aging and inadequate physical and fiscal infrastructure.
4. Strengthening the connection between education and work. Relationships between education and work are being re-examined and restructured.... [M]arketplace requires workers with higher levels of complex skills.
5. Garnering support for education reform. Education reform, like all change, is generating anxiety and opposition. Educators are increasingly attempting to involve parents and community members in open, honest discussion.
6. Changing expectations for education decisionmaking and governance.... [I]ncreased community collaboration, school site councils, and service integration efforts are altering and redefining many traditional governance and decisionmaking processes. [No approval of voters, ed.]
7. Using standards as a means to systemic change. Consensus that piecemeal changes in schooling are not adequate to meet the challenges of the future is giving rise to a growing emphasis on standards and assessment at all levels of the education system.
8. Strengthening support and respect for teachers.... [T]eachers are the critical element in providing quality education, and that their task is becoming more complex and difficult as they face increased expectations in teaching a more diverse student body.
9. Supporting young children and their families. Educators are defining their role in working with families to ensure the healthy early development of children.... [Does their role include interference in family life? ed.]
10. Increasing community collaboration and service integration.... [C]hange occurs only with the full commitment of the community, schools are getting involved in

collaborative efforts with many other types of organizations. [This collaboration, integration, etc., represents a change in governance without approval of the voters, ed.]

11. Harnessing new technologies.... [C]omputers in schools are putting technology in the forefront of efforts to fundamentally change the role of students from passive to active learners and the role of teachers from information givers to facilitators and coaches. [Clearly a shift from academic education to performance-based workforce training, ed.]

12. Shifting the focus from risk toward resiliency. Realizing that the vast majority of children develop into successful adults, educators and other service providers are shifting their attention from deficit program models that address specific risk factors toward program approaches that focus more on enhancing positive factors. [If the reader understands #12, please contact the writer, ed.]

"CHARTER SCHOOLS BILL NOW LAW" REPORTED *THE ARIZONA REPUBLIC* IN AN AP REPORT appearing in its October 23, 1998 issue. Excerpts from this news item, which identifies the Democratic Party with a Republican initiative, follow:

President Clinton on Thursday signed the *Charter School Expansion Act of 1998* to speed the development of high-quality charter schools, a key element of his education agenda. The law authorizes up to $100 million a year over the next five years for the planning and expansion of charter schools. Clinton cited the charter schools legislation as an example of bipartisan cooperation....

Clinton has set a goal of 3,000 charter schools nationwide by the time he leaves office. There now are about 1,000.

Charter schools tend to be smaller and custom-designed. Under charter schools laws, depending on the state, parents, community activists, teachers or even private companies may set up schools under a special agreement or charter. The schools might emphasize a particular curriculum such as arts or technology, or more traditional teaching methods using repetition and drills, or experimental methods that let children learn at their own pace.

[Ed. Note: Charter schools are obliged to adhere to federal guidelines; i.e., *Goals 2000*, etc. Individuals familiar with charter school legislation consider them unaccountable to the taxpayers due to their being run by unelected councils; taxation without representation.]

A NATIONAL INSTITUTE ON CAREER MAJORS WAS ANNOUNCED NOVEMBER 4, 1998 BY THE National School-to-Work Office. The accuracy of predictions made by anti-school-to-work citizens—that their children's academic education would be watered down, if not eliminated, once the Marc Tucker Plan moved out of its planning stage and into the following action mode—is demonstrated by the following:

Just one month after it announced that all 50 states were "on board" to receive federal School-to-Work Implementation Grants, the National School-to-Work (STW) Office has now announced (Nov. 4) a National Institute on Career Majors to be held in Chicago, Illinois on February 4-6, 1999.

"The purpose of the Institute is to bring together State Teams to strategically design a plan to implement career majors at the State and local levels." To participate, states are asked to assemble "an interagency team of 6–10 members representing State level policy-makers around education and labor; business and industry; educators at the secondary and postsecondary level; and include representatives from a local-level partnership that is currently building a STW system around career majors."

Activities will "focus on strengthening the capacity of education and business leaders to develop a standards-based curriculum leading to high skills, high wage, high demand occupations. Through individual team facilitation, each State Team will develop or revise a plan to organize school learning around career majors."

Attendance at this institute is limited to 15 teams, but more are sure to follow. Funds are being provided for team travel. Funds are also going to be made available to states at a later date to host similar career majors institutes for their local STW partnerships.

The event will take place at the Fairmont Hotel... Chicago, Illinois.

"NEW MODEL FOR TEACHER EDUCATION—WITH FOCUS ON CONTEXT AND WORKPLACE: Project Could Better Prepare Students" by Michael Childs was published in the November 9, 1998 issue of *Columns* (p. 2), a University of Georgia faculty newsletter. Excerpts from the article follow:

University of Georgia's College of Education is beginning a three-year project that will attempt to bring together classroom and real-life work experiences in a way that could change how teachers are taught and what they're taught to teach. The project could better prepare students for the challenges they are likely to face in the changing workplace of the 21st century.

The college will develop and pilot-test a new teacher-education model that will place prospective teachers not only in the context in which they will work—the classroom—but also in the context of where their students will work—community and workplace settings in business, industry and the professions.

"Teachers need to understand much more of the pedagogy. Teachers need to understand how it applies in life settings," says Dean Russell Yeany. "We don't just want to perpetuate academic learning—at some point it has to be applied to the workplace...."

...A long-term goal is to have a much more effective school-to-work transition for students.

"Schooling should transition right into work and I think schooling has become so academic that it isn't transitioning well into work," says Yeany.

Funded for 18 months by an initial $864,000 grant from the U.S. Department of Education, the Teacher Development Pre-Service Model of Excellence Initiative is one of the college's largest and most ambitious projects ever.

"This is a big investment by the federal government to develop a model they hope will become available to other colleges," says Yeany.

A student orientation to area business and industry will include both on-site and virtual observation of manufacturing and business processes.

THE NOVEMBER 16, 1998 EDITION OF *THE ATLANTA CONSTITUTION* CARRIED AN ARTICLE entitled "Education in a Relaxed Atmosphere: Brain-Based Method—Teaching Trend Emphasizing Creativity, Flexibility and Informality Growing in Area Schools" by Delbert Ellerton.

The activities described in the article are typical of the exercises promoted by Sheila Ostrander, Lynn Schroeder with Nancy Ostrander in their book *Superlearning 2000* (Dell Publishing: New York 1994), an updated version of their earlier book *Superlearning*. The following are excerpts from the article:

> At the front of Amanda Neff's softly lit, first-grade classroom in Henry County, a plant sits next to the glass case that is home to Riley, a small black rat snake.
>
> As Riley slithers around inside the glass box at Wesley Lakes Elementary School, a group of students eagerly crowds around.
>
> Riley is just one of the several ways Neff is bringing life to her classroom by teaching students in ways that emerging research says they naturally learn. Instead of just reading books about snakes, the students have the real thing right before them.
>
> Teachers such as Neff are part of a national group embracing an approach formally called brain-based learning. The trend, which surfaced in California in the 1980s, is based on teachers being flexible and creative. It also is based on the belief that eliminating the sterile, institutional environment encourages children to relax and learn.
>
> In addition to using Riley, the snake, as an educational tool, Neff softens the mood in her Wesley Lakes classroom by dimming the bright overhead fluorescent lights and turning on lamps in corners of the room. She plays soft music on a computer CD player throughout the day....
>
> "It's making children feel more comfortable and taking away the threat. They're more open. They don't shut down on me when I ask them something," Harris said.
>
> Harris's students sit in groups of three in an arrangement educators call "tribes." The setup is said to encourage teamwork. Teachers in Henry and Clayton counties have received brain-based learning training through staff development workshops. One such workshop in Clayton County is called "Symphony on Styles" and focuses on effective teaching methods for students' diverse learning styles, said Bobbi Ford of Clayton's staff development department....
>
> In October, Ford attended a brain-based learning conference in California which drew educators from Sweden, Canada, Australia, South Africa and Mexico....
>
> ...Teachers in Coweta, Fulton and Carroll counties also use brain-based techniques. One Coweta school plays classical music over the intercom.
>
> A newly formed statewide brain-based learning advisory council met in Athens last month, attracting 23 interested educators. The council is building a network to provide information about brain-based learning, said Judith Reiff, an early childhood education professor at the University of Georgia who is on the council.

[Ed. Note: Even though the reader can read the roots of *Superlearning* in this book's earlier, 1979 entry, the writer would like to repeat a section of *Superlearning 2000* that gives an explanation of what it is:

What is Superlearning?

These are the Superlearning core techniques that vastly accelerate learning and brighten performance. Techniques that can help you take charge of change.

- Get into a stress-free, "best" mindbody state for what you are doing.
- Absorb information in a paced, rhythmic way.
- Use music to expand memory, energize the mind, and link to the subconscious.

- Engage your whole brain, your senses, emotions, and imagination for peak performance.
- Become aware of blocks to learning and change, then flood them away.

Not even a multiple personality would want to use all the exercises and ploys offered in this book. The idea is to give you a choice. You don't need to pick up very many to flesh out the basic Superlearning protocols. First and foremost, Superlearning involves a new sense of your self and your possibilities, a new perspective—a twenty-first century point of view.

In the first chapter of *Superlearning 2000* on pages 8–9 we find the following quotes:

> Five pages, that's all we devoted to Lozanov learning when we wrote about our Communist odyssey. (See *Psychic Discoveries Behind the Iron Curtain*, 1970; updated and to be republished, 1995.) Inquiries roared in from everywhere, even the Pentagon's Institute of Defense Analysis. Western mind-groupies rushed to Sofia [Bulgaria], while a handful of pioneering educators began the hard work of adapting the Communist learning system to North America.
>
> A genuinely powerful new way to learn, to expand memory, to excel began to emerge in Des Moines, Toronto, Atlanta. By the late 1970s an innovative psychologist, Dr. Donald Schuster of University of Iowa at Ames, founded the Society for Accelerative Learning and Teaching (SALT). Now there are professional societies in a dozen countries, including the very international Society for Effective Affective Learning (SEAL) in England. At the time only a few professionals had moved outside of establishment lines. What about all the other people who always wanted to color outside the lines? We took what was proven and devised something that wasn't: a do-it-yourself system. Superlearning, open to everyone. The generic name is accelerative or *accelerated learning*.
>
> Basic Superlearning draws from Lozanov and his sources, ancient ones like Raja Yoga, contemporary ones like Soviet science.... And we got lucky. We came across another "ology": Sophrology, "the science of harmonious consciousness," a cornucopia of routes to excellence still almost unknown in America, developed by Alfonso Caycedo, a Spanish M.D. every bit as innovative as Lozanov.

[Ed. Note: These last sentences remind this writer of the early work of Roberto Assagioli, author of *Psychosynthesis*. The reader should also be made aware that Henry Levin of Stanford's Institute for Accelerated Learning does indeed advocate the Superlearning (SALT, SEAL) method for its member schools.]

"COMING SOON TO A SCHOOL NEAR YOU: FORCED LABOR" BY PAUL MULSHINE, COLUMNIST, was published in the November 29, 1998 issue of the Newark, New Jersey *Star-Ledger*. Excerpts from Mulshine's article follow:

> Imagine a state that uses its school system not to produce independent-minded, broadly educated citizens, but compliant workers trained to behave. A state where, in their early teens, children are forced to make a lifelong decision from 14 government-sanctioned career possibilities with such depressing titles as "waste management," "administrative services" and "manufacturing, installation and repair." A state where students in the government schools are forced to spend one day a week toiling in menial labor.
>
> The old Soviet Union? China?
>
> Nope. New Jersey.

I wish I were making this up. But I'm not. This is a fair summation—minus the jargon—of the School-to-Work program that the state is planning to impose on us next year. You can veiw it on the Internet at http://www.state.nj.us/njded/proposed/standards/ stass2.htm. See for yourself.

NINA SHIKRAII REES OF THE HERITAGE FOUNDATION, WASHINGTON, D.C., WROTE AN ARticle entitled "Time to Overhaul the *Elementary and Secondary Education Act of 1965*" which recommended a major shift in the traditional philosophy of education from an emphasis on inputs to an emphasis on outputs. An abstract of her article which was published in a Heritage Foundation Press Release dated December 2, 1998, follows:

> During the reauthorization process of the 1965 *Elementary and Secondary Education Act*, the 106th Congress has a historic opportunity to change the course of K–12 education. Congress needs to shift the goals of the ESEA from one confined to inputs to one focused on achievement. Congress can make this happen by sending more federal dollars to the classroom instead of to education bureaucracies; empower parents, teachers and principals; boosting the quality of teachers; and allowing flexibility and demanding accountability. Sending money to the same old federal education programs will waste precious education tax dollars and allow American students to fall even further behind their counterparts in the developed world.

[Ed. Note: If what Ms. Rees recommends is authorized by the 106th Congress, the course of K–12 education will be more than changed. It will be eliminated, to be replaced by K–12 school-to-work training, required by NAFTA and GATT, both of which are supported by Ms. Rees's employer, the Heritage Foundation. As sensible as the above recommendations may appear at first sight, as one moves carefully through the text one can identify key words which should raise red flags for those opposed to the philosophy behind *Goals 2000* and the *School-to-Work Opportunities Act*.

When Ms. Rees says "Congress needs to shift the goals of the ESEA from one confined to inputs to one focused on achievement" she really means she supports outcome-based education, since the word "achievement" as she has used it means "outcome." She then goes on to recommend all the "nasties" associated with Marc Tucker's National Center on Education and the Economy which are also associated with all recent restructuring legislation, as well as with outcome-based education: "empowering of parents, teachers, and principals"; "sending more federal dollars to the classroom"; "boosting the quality of teachers"; "allowing flexibility"; and "demanding accountability."

Of special interest here is her recommendation to boost the "quality of teachers." The reader is urged to turn to the 1992 entry regarding *Filling the Gaps* for the new millenium definition of "quality of teachers."

Note also how this report uses the word "achievement." This is the alternative to focusing on "inputs"—the legal requirement of most state constitutions with regard to their responsibility to the public to "offer," "make available" or "furnish" educational *opportunity* to all citizens. Most of our state constitutions—unless they have changed in the last few years—do not require the state to be responsible for each student's success, because the state cannot ensure what is a personal responsibility. States are responsible for the provision of everything necessary for a child or student to have the *opportunity* to achieve academic success—"inputs." (This has traditionally been known as the Carnegie Unit requirement.) It is when the state becomes the guarantor of success—Ms. Rees's "achievement"—that parents have felt the stifling hand of the state in the area of privacy and personal freedom.

Sending more "dollars to the classroom" may sound like returning to local control, but is in fact the reverse since it bypasses not only state legislators—who presumably represent their constituents at the state level—but also local school boards who traditionally have made decisions at the central office building level—not at the school building level—on how their constituents' tax money could best be spent.

Much damage has been done over the years under the guise of "accountability." Exactly to whom does the Heritage Foundation want the schools to be accountable? Parents and taxpayers who have had no say whatsoever in restructuring plans, or the international business community which initiated and supports the recommendations spelled out in most of Heritage Foundation's reports, including its call for the use of Skinnerian Direct Instruction (DISTAR) as presently implemented in Houston, Texas at Thaddeus Lott's Model Wesley Elementary School, and which is on a roll across the nation since the passage of the *Reading Excellence Act*?]

CENTER ON EDUCATION AND WORK OF THE UNIVERSITY OF WISCONSIN PUBLISHED A PAPER in 1998 entitled "Changing Admission Procedures in Four-Year Colleges to Support K–14 Reform."[67] The paper lists as the principal investigators: L. Allen Phelps, University of Wisconsin-Madison and David Stern, University of California at Berkeley. Christine Maidl Pribbenow, University of Wisconsin-Madison is listed as project director. The following project areas are listed as: Postsecondary; competency-based admissions; secondary; integrated curriculum; and performance-based assessment. Excerpts from the project abstract follow:

> This one-year (1998) National Center for Research in Vocational Education (NCRVE) project consists of a number of specific research questions which will be addressed through the work of investigators at both U.C.-Berkeley and U.W.-Madison. The purpose of this project is to review existing research on performance-based assessment in education and discuss the use of these assessments in college admissions. This review will provide a broader understanding of the ways in which school-to-work and other K–14 reforms are being accommodated in the higher education admission policies and processes being adopted by institutions, particularly those with selective admissions criteria.
>
> At U.C.-Berkeley, investigators will identify 4–5 states that are beginning to develop new processes for admission and placement using performance-based assessment. Through a series of surveys, on-site and telephone interviews, the following will be examined: [Two of five areas of interest have been selected to illustrate the intent, ed.]... (3) Various approaches taken by select high schools in response to the initiative... and (5)The alignment of state K–12, K–14, or K–16 educational standards and industry and occupational standards with these assessments.
>
> At U.W.-Madison, investigators will complete quantitative and qualitative analyses of the early efforts to develop performance-based admissions and their initial effects on student experiences and outcomes in postsecondary education.... Essentially, the goal is to generate evidence that illustrates the innovative developments, benefits and limitations of using performance-based assessments for college admissions that support models of continuous, seamless learning focused simultaneously on careers and college. Researchers intend to conduct the following studies:

- Examine the efficacy, validity and reliability of the CBA for admitting high school graduates with intensive, career-focused high school experiences.
- Explore the link between college experiences with earlier career-related learning as provided and documented in the CBA process.

Both the U.C.-Berkeley and U.W.-Madison researchers will use their research to write a proposal for consideration by the governing boards and administrative leaders of four-year colleges and universities, both public and private. A meeting will then be convened with high-level representatives of four-year colleges and universities to discuss this proposal. The investigators' findings will also be used to complete a report which reviews research and current practice, analyzes performance-based admission efforts, and discusses the proposal regarding the use of performance-based assessment. Finally, one or two briefs will be published which summarize the findings and/or proposal in a reader-friendly format for policymakers, university governing boards, university faculty and administrators.

[Ed. Note: The reader should be aware that the above project is just one of many efforts to change the focus of higher learning from liberal arts, theoretical and applied arts to a continuation of the school-to-work focus. The National Center for Educational Statistics published a new handbook in its *Educational Reports Series* in 1993 which outlined the new "crosswalks" of course descriptions at the postsecondary or college/university level. These crosswalks reflect the transition to performance-based coursework from academic/theoretical coursework. The result is a complete refocusing of postsecondary education toward behavioral performance rather than encouraging the traditional emphasis on academic knowledge acquisition.]

"A GOVERNOR WITH PRINCIPLE WOULD REJECT SCHOOL-TO-WORK" BY PAUL MULSHINE was published in the December 6, 1998 issue of the Newark, New Jersey *Star-Ledger*. Excerpts from Mulshine's article follow:

> Christine Whitman once wrote that Republicans believe that "government should only do what individuals can't do for themselves and that government decisions should be made as close to the people they affect as possible."
>
> A wonderful philosophy. There's a problem, though: By that standard, our governor is not a Republican....
>
> ...Her administration's latest travesty, the School-to-Work proposal, is just the latest in a long line of thoroughly un-Republican concepts backed by Whitman. Since I wrote about the proposal last week, a couple of things have happened. Assemblyman Scott Garrett, a Republican from Sussex County, announced the introduction of a bill that will prohibit forced labor in schools. Also, the Homdel Board of Education held a meeting Wednesday night at which people came from all over the state to raise objections to the idea. It was a pivotal event. Never in my 22 years of journalism have I seen a proposal get knocked around by so many different people for so many different reasons.
>
> A freshman at Holmdel High School said that her friends were in a panic. The requirement that all juniors and seniors spend a day a week working would mean they'd have to miss classes. This would harm their chances of getting into college, the girl said. She asked that most Republican of questions, "How come we have no say in this?"
>
> A guy in a sweat suit from a nearby town raised another objection: "The school is not the state's. The school is mine, and they tell me it's not mine. I didn't see them at the bake sale."

A school superintendent said that he'd fled Ohio because of a similar program there that was destroying the high-achieving schools by turning them into vocational centers. Several people objected to a requirement that students choose a career in the sophomore year of high school.

One cited a study that showed that the typical college student changes majors three times before settling on a field....

...This is an amazing thing Whitman's people have invented: A concept that offends practically everyone. Usually a political idea has a core constituency—bleeding heart liberals, tightwad conservatives, public employee unions, whatever. But this one riles people up across the board. It does make the bureaucrats happy, though....

...It would be wonderful, just once, to see Christie Whitman denounce a bad idea not because of poll results but because of principle. Close your eyes. Try to imagine Christie Whitman uttering the words, "This is wrong. Trenton should not impose ideas like this on the people of New Jersey."

You can't imagine it? Me neither.

ON DECEMBER 23, 1998 MAINE'S COMMISSIONER OF EDUCATION J. DUKE ALBANESE SENT a memorandum to all superintendents of schools related to the *Maine Aspirations Benchmarking Initiative*. Excerpts from this memorandum, which reveal the extent of Maine's transformation of its schools from academics to workforce training and of its educational bureaucracy's disregard for student privacy follow:

Sponsored by Webber Energy Fuels, the $300,000 initiative is directed by the University of Maine/Maine Principals' Association Research Partnership, in collaboration with the National Center for Student Aspirations and the Maine Department of Education.

The Initiative has the potential of surveying the entire population of students in grades 6 through 12 in Maine public schools, providing an unparalleled database portraying the status of student aspirations in Maine and the conditions that nurture, delay or prevent their development.

The Initiative expands and elaborates on the highly successful Student Aspirations Survey. The approximately 30-minute survey will provide schools with information and insight, from their students' perspectives, in areas of the total learning environment, including:

- aspirations
- conditions in schools
- challenging behaviors
- school climate
- parent-school interaction
- parental support and guidance

The Initiative is highly relevant to the Maine Learning Results. While the Learning Results allow the measurement of achievement, the Benchmarking Initiative will allow the measurement of motivation to achieve. The Initiative will enable schools to begin to assess themselves as related to the Guiding Principles which have not yet been addressed in content standards. Survey questions strongly relate to Guiding Principles II and IV—a Self-Directed and Life-Long Learner, and a Responsible and Involved Citizen, respectively. The

Initiative will provide baseline data on career development and help schools and the standard of career preparation....

...Schools participating in the Initiative will receive several important benefits—all at no cost: 1) schools will receive detailed informative reports of their students' responses, providing an assessment of the school dynamics and their effect on aspirations, motivation, and learning; 2) broader reports based on the data will provide the opportunity for schools to compare their profiles against state and regional profiles; 3) schools can take advantage of responsive programs and technical assistance to create or strengthen aspiration conditions in areas of need identified by schools; and 4) schools will receive assistance in monitoring the impact of reform efforts, including a follow-up survey toward the end of the project to check against the baseline data, an important, but often neglected step in the action research process.

1999

THE FEDERALLY FUNDED NORTH CENTRAL REGIONAL EDUCATIONAL LABORATORY (NCREL), which serves seven states in the Midwest, published "New Times Demands New Ways of Learning" in its Winter-Spring issue of *EdTalk*. This article "is intended to offer a way to evaluate the effectiveness of various technologies and technology programs against the backdrop of new research on learning." Some excerpts follow:

"Learning" here does not mean how well students perform on standardized tests. That's not learning, as researchers and educational reformers are coming to understand it. There's a dynamic shift occurring in this country as we move from traditional definitions of learning and course design to models of engaged learning that involve more student interaction, more connections among schools, more collaboration among teachers and students, more involvement of teachers as facilitators, and more emphasis on technology as a tool for learning. It is in this context that our framework operates; it is this type of engaged learning that technology must support to be effective....

In place of these old assumptions, researchers are positing new ways of looking at learning that promote:

- engaged, meaningful learning and collaboration involving challenging and real-life tasks; and
- technology as a toll [requirement] for learning, communication, and collaboration.

The traditional learning model is not relevant to real student needs.

These attributes contrast sharply with the discrete, low-level skill, content, and assessment methods that traditional ways of learning favor. The new workplace requirements for learning are incompatible with instruction that assumes the teacher is the information giver and the student a passive recipient.

The new requirements are at odds with testing programs that assess skills that are useful only in school.

Technology in support of outmoded educational systems is counterproductive.

The reliance on standarized tests is ludicrous. Technology works in school not because tests scores increase, but because technology empowers new solutions.

There are no definitive answers about the effectiveness of technology in boosting student learning, student readiness for workforce skills, teacher productivity, and cost effectiveness. True, some examples of technology have shown strong and consistent positive results. But even powerful programs might show no effects due to myriad methodological flaws. It would be most unfortunate to reject these because standardized tests showed no significant differences. Instead, measures should evaluate individual technologies against specific learning, collaboration, and communication goals.

What is effective learning and how can it be measured?... [Barbara Means of SRI International] identified seven variables that, when present in the classroom, indicate that effective teaching and learning are occurring: These classroom variables are:

- children are engaged in authentic and multidisciplinary tasks;
- assessments are based on students' performance of real tasks;
- students participate in interactive modes of instruction;
- students work collaboratively;
- students are grouped heterogeneously;
- the teacher is a factilitator in learning; and
- students learn through exploration.

We took these variables and reorganized them into a set of eight categories of learning: tasks, assessment, instruction, learning, context, grouping, teacher roles, and student roles.

Centralized systems are likely to inhibit learning to the extent that they use the transfer mode of learning and instruction. This model assumes that the central source holds most of the important information and that it is the student's job to transfer the information from this central source to his or her location and "learn" it.

[Ed. Note: The above text provides an excellent, if not depressing, overview of the transformation from education to workforce training. The timing of this article is interesting in light of other reports, some of which are referred to in this book, exposing the limits of computer technology in the teaching of the important basic academic skills. The above article also admits the lack of supportive research on the "effectiveness of technology in boosting student learning," but still insists that the methodology should not be rejected just "because standardized tests showed no significant differences." Instead, the answer is to use this unconfirmed technology to accomplish limited learning tasks in an attempt to convince the reader that this "new" type of "education" should be embraced by all.]

ROSIE AVILA, A SCHOOL BOARD MEMBER IN THE SANTA ANA UNIFIED SCHOOL DISTRICT, Santa Ana, California, wrote an interesting but frightening article entitled "Parent Report Cards" regarding the implications of parent education programs which was included on an education website on the Internet January 10, 1999. Some excerpts follow:

As a school board member I have discovered just how they will implement the *U.N. Convention on the Rights of the Child*, the new global parenting code....

I noticed every time they talked about parent involvement (a goal of *Goals 2000*) it was in the context of parent education, what parents need to do at home to help their children succeed in school. Parents are called partners with the schools....

Federal funding mandates parent education. Every one of our schools has a parent education program; 300–400 parents at a time are going through these.... All parents are required to sign a Parent Compact, agreeing to do certain things at home, "provide a study space, put the kids to bed on time, read with them," etc. So, parents are trained, then have to sign an agreement.

Then I saw a bill pass in Sacramento at the State level. It was first described as a "parent report card," but I understand there was objection and so it was redefined, but passed anyway.... I read an article in the *Better Homes and Gardens Magazine* describing the new "parent report card." It said students would give information to their teachers, and parents [would be] graded on students' grooming, sleep habits, and attendance at school meetings, etc. The article said, "Students would be empowered by signing off on their parents' report card," and that "Children knew when their parents were flunking."

Our school district received a $1.1 million dollar grant under "safe schools," another goal of *Goals 2000*. It said we would not have any violence or drugs in schools in the new century and that prevention was the key. Quoting Janet Reno, "Students acted up when they had neglectful parents" and that we could spot them in the early grades. So, if a parent was deemed to be neglectful (failed on their report card, was what I figured), they would have to go through the SARB (Student Attendance Review Board) and have a meeting at the police department with someone from the District Attorney, Child Protection Service, Social Services, School Counselors, etc. Here they would be given their court-ordered program to improve their parenting.

So, there it was. A global parenting code: the *Convention on the Rights of the Child*, federally funded parenting courses with a required Parent Compact through Chapter One, a State Parent Report Card, and a local punishment or coercion policy redefining the role of the SARB to include neglectful parents.

They have most of the system in place here in California. They just need that ratification of the *U.N. Convention on the Rights of the Child.*

[Ed. Note: The above information regarding report cards for parents should come as no surprise given the following recommendation made by neo-conservative Chester E. Finn, Jr., in an article condensed from the Heritage Foundation's *Policy Review*; Summer 1986, No. 37, pp. 58–61 (reprinted in *Education Digest* on January 1987, p. 4).]

6. Parents must be enlisted in the work of the school and in the education of their children. Along with endorsing over to the school their child's tuition grant, parents must be asked to assume certain elemental responsibilities, both for such mundane matters as discipline and attendance and for such specific ones as providing the child with a place to do his homework and checking each night to make sure it is done. Just as parents should have the right to evaluate—and choose among—schools, so too should teachers and principals have the right to appraise parents' performance with respect to the education of their children. What about a section in the child's report card where the school team can "grade" the parents' performance?

Really, Mr. Finn? This seems to be a bizarre approach to "school choice"—"endorsing over to the school their child's tuition grant, parents must be asked to assume elemental responsibilities." Ms. Avila's concern about the liberal international influence in public schools seems to have found its way into the "conservative solution."]

An Educator's Guide to Schoolwide Reform (Educational Research Service: Arlington, Virginia, 1999) was prepared for publication by American Institutes for Research under the direction of Rebecca Herman as project director. The *Guide* was produced under contract to the American Association of School Administrators, the American Federation of Teachers, the National Association of Elementary School Principals, and the National Education Association. The "overview" of the *Guide* states in part:

> This guide was prepared for educators and others to use when investigating different approaches to school reform. It reviews the research on 24 "whole-school," "comprehensive," "schoolwide" approaches.
>
> THIS GUIDE IS NOT MEANT TO ENDORSE, FAVOR, OR DISCREDIT ANY OF THE APPROACHES. Rather, it is designed to assist those who want to critically examine the most widely available schoolwide reform approaches. Schools can improve their performance in a variety of ways, not just by using a schoolwide approach. However, educators interested in these approaches should find the guide useful.

This book has repeatedly dealt with the Skinnerian, scientific, research-based method of teaching and learning, therefore, the writer lists below only the four out of 24 programs recommended by the *Guide* which clearly use this method. They are:

1. Coalition of Essential Schools
2. Direct Instruction
3. Modern Red Schoolhouse
4. Success for All

Since much already has been written about Siegfried Engelmann's Direct Instruction in this book, the writer will focus on Robert Slavin's "Success for All." The following excerpts from "Ready, READ!" by Nicholas Lemann, which appeared in the November 1998 issue of *The Atlantic Monthly*, give the reader a clear picture of how a direct instruction/mastery learning classroom marketed as "Success for All" functions:

> Success for All, Accelerated Schools, and the School Development Program, all designed by university professors—the first two have each been adopted by more than a thousand schools across the country, and the third by 700....
>
> ...By the end of this school year the Success for All organization will have a budget of $30 million and will operate in more than 1,100 schools all over the country. Among its customers are the Edison Project which is private [publicly funded charter school]; the state of New Jersey; and the cities of Houston, Memphis, and Miami....
>
> ...The prevailing criticism of Success for All is that it is designed to produce higher scores on a couple of tests chosen by Slavin, for which the control-group schools don't train their students; the gains it produces, according to critics, are substantially limited to the first year of the program.
>
> Success for All tells schools precisely what to teach and how to teach it—to the point of scripting, nearly minute by minute, every teacher's activity in every classroom every day of the year.
>
> ...Teachers must use a series of catch phrases and hand signals developed by Success for All.... At every level Slavin's programs greatly reduce teacher autonomy, through control of the curriculum.... People usually describe Success for All with terms like "prescriptive," "highly structured," and "teacher-proof"; Slavin likes to use the word "relentless." One education researcher I spoke with called it "Taylorism in the classroom," after Frederick Winslow Taylor, the early twentieth-century efficiency expert who routinized every detail of factory work....
>
> A few minutes in a Success for All classroom conveys the Parris Island feeling of the

program better than any general description could. It is first grade—the pivotal year. The students read the first page of the story loudly, in unison. The teacher says, "Okay, next page. Finger in place, ready, read!" After a few minutes of this students have finished the story. Not missing a beat, the teacher says, "Close your books, please. Let's get ready for vocabulary." She moves to a posted handwritten sheet of words and points to herself. "My turn. Maze, haze, hazy, lazy. Your turn." She points to the class. The students shout out the words in unison: "Maze! Haze! Hazy! Lazy!"

Then the teacher announces that the students are going to do "red words"—Success for All lingo for words that students can't decode from their phonemic components. "Okay, do your first word," she says. The students call out together, "Only! O (clap) N(clap) L(clap) Y(clap). Only!" After they've done the red words, the teacher says, "Now let's go to our meaningful sentences." The students read from a sheet loudly and in unison the definitions of three words and then three sentences, each into their cooperative learning groups to write three sentences of their own, using each of the words. "If you work right, you'll earn work points for your work team! You clear?" Twenty voices call out, "Yes!"

Last year, when I was there, the school was phasing in uniforms.

[Ed. Note: Brown shirts?]

IN A LETTER TO THE EDITOR PRINTED IN THE ATHENS (GEORGIA) DAILY NEWS/BANNER *Herald* of January 18, 1999, Priscilla Carroll, former elementary school teacher, responded to a letter to the editor from Professor Carl Glickman of the University of Georgia, author of books on school reform, which dealt with changes in local school board responsibilities as a result of the adoption of block scheduling, one of the reform components resulting from Clarke County (Athens) School District being designated as a "Next Generation School" district. Mrs. Carroll responded that:

Some of the Next Generation School Project power structure changes state:
   a) Local boards will not manage, operate nor make decisions for running schools.
   b) Local boards will be advised by created community teams or collaboratives.
   c) Local boards must let go... presiding over student or employee grievance hearing.
   d) Grievance hearings will be delegated to "duly appointed mediation and arbitration panels."
   e) Local boards won't decide field trip requests, student transfers, challenges to library books, school calendar decisions, bus routing problems and athletic program concerns.
   f) Local boards must "move away from... hiring, firing and promoting employees."
   g) Local boards "will be freed of constraints and obligations that impede their ability to address the global issues which are more worthy of their time."
   h) Local boards must "give up the role of keeper of the purse" (won't control education money).
   i) The local "appointed" school superintendents (LSS), are to be trained and controlled by the state.

[Ed. Note: When Georgia's radical "break the mold" Next Generation School Project proposal was not accepted as one of the original New American School Development Corporation (NASDC) design teams, corporate and non-profit "partnership" funding was generated to accomplish the Project within the state. Mrs. Carroll's comments were paraphrased from the

"Next Generation School Project" manual. Professor Luvern Cunningham would be pleased to see how his recommendations to get rid of school boards are being carried out across the country.]

"SCHOOL TO WORK GETS POOR GRADE IN STUDY" BY MARK SHRUG AND RICHARD WEST-ern of the University of Wisconsin at Milwaukee, professors who conducted a study for the Wisconsin Policy Research Institute, appeared in the January 19, 1999 issue of *The Milwaukee Journal Sentinel.* Excerpts follow:

> More than $195 million, almost all federal money, was spent from 1991 to 1998 in Wisconsin on programs under the label School-to-Work, but it has had almost no demonstrable impact on the state's schools or economy.... It has had no identifiable impact on the academic learning of K–12 students in Wisconsin and it has involved too few students in its core, work-based learning activities to register a significant aggregate impact on Wisconsin's workforce.
>
> Many school districts, including MPS (Milwaukee), generally have dropped the term. And attention, some suggest, has shifted to different policies, particularly proficiency testing and a looming statewide test that all students will have to pass to graduate.
>
> The study says one of the few tangible accomplishments of School to Work was that 347 students had graduated from apprenticeship programs statewide. But, the study says, that was equal to 1/10,000th of the state workforce in 1996.... The study says there was no "reliable evidence" that School-to-Work had accomplished any of its major goals.
>
> Grants were used ($30 million) for teacher training, apprenticeships, job shadowing and connections between schools and individual businesses.
>
> James H. Miller, president of the policy research institute, said, "As with most bureaucratic educational reforms, School-to-Work sounds terrific, but in reality it is all style with absolutely no substance."

[Ed. Note: Let's hope that the old adage "You can lead a horse to water, but can't make him drink" will play itself out in regard to school-to-work.

However, leadership in the homeschool community seems to have embraced at least a portion of the school-to-work proposition. While apprenticeship has been promoted to homeschoolers as an alternative to "electives" by some homeschool organizations and leaders (Bill Gothard, Doug Wilson et al.), now the apprenticeship concept is being embraced at the post-high school level by none other than Michael Farris of Home School Legal Defense Association. In his announcement about the forthcoming establishment of the Patrick Henry College in Purcellville, Virginia, Farris stated in an interview with Andrea Billups of *The Washington Times* (May 17, 1999):

> "I wanted to break out of the educational box like I've helped to do with K-through-12 education."...
>
> ...Initially, the school will offer a lone undergraduate major in government, featuring an apprenticeship program designed to give students practical experience in public policy and service....
>
> As a part of their curriculum, Patrick Henry students will work on faculty-supervised research and writing projects for congressional offices, state legislators, federal agencies, think tanks and advocacy groups.
>
> "We are combining a traditional liberal arts model with a white-collar version of voca-

tional training," said the school's provost and academic dean, Brad Jacob, a lawyer and professor who served as the CEO of the Christian Legal Society. "It all comes from the ivory tower concerns, where students learn theory but don't know beans about how to work in the workplace.... We believe in mentoring and disciplining."[68]

This should come as no surprise in light of Mr. Farris's previous public enthusiasm for apprenticeships expressed at his organization's National Home Educator's Leadership Conference in Orlando, Florida in 1995. During a "debate" with William Spady, Farris lauded the Swiss educational system as a "very successful national model."[68] The Swiss system is committed to apprenticeships, with 75% of its students never going to high school or college but into apprenticeships after the eighth grade. Their K–8 system prepares students to enter apprenticeships, certainly limiting career employment choices and movement.

The bottom line is this: "apprenticeship" *is* "workforce training." Skipping over traditional academic high school and college subjects, or watering down a liberal arts college education to accommodate its "application" to a workplace setting, constitute the "deliberate dumbing down" of homeschoolers. Could school-to-work at the college level be the "camel's nose under the tent for STW at K–12 level for homeschoolers?]

THE JANUARY 1999 ISSUE OF *COMMUNITY UPDATE* PUBLISHED BY THE U.S. DEPARTMENT OF Education provided an update on activities being held by the Religion and Education Partnership (first established in 1995). The following excerpts describe the involvement of "the church in the state" and "the state in the church"— something heretofore not spelled out in government publications. The U.S. Department of Education announced that:

> Religious leaders, educators, members of the higher education community, and students came together at Spalding University in Louisville, Kentucky on December 11, for the fourth Religion and Education Summit supported by the Partnership for Family Involvement in Education....
>
> More than 500 participants gathered in Louisville from Kentucky, Ohio, Indiana, and Tennessee to hear U.S. Secretary of Education Richard W. Riley participate in a town hall discussion on three important topics: family involvement in education, school safety, and preparing young people for college and careers. Programs that support these initiatives were presented in small group gatherings where participants could speak to practitioners from Tampa, Florida; Birmingham, Alabama; and Louisville, Kentucky. A materials fair featuring model programs, community services, information about the public schools in the area, and materials produced by the Partnership for Family Involvement in Education was open throughout the summit.
>
> The goal of the Religion and Education Summit was to bring together leadership representing faith communities and elementary, secondary, and higher education to discuss issues of concern to the community and to build partnerships to bring about changes needed for the benefit of all children. Previous summits were held in Lawrence, Massachusetts; Wilmington, Delaware; and St. Petersburg, Florida. Partnerships formed at these summits have continued to work together to improve education and strengthen family and community involvement in local schools. To obtain information on how to plan and hold a Religion and Education Summit, email partner@ed.gov.

[Ed. Note: The writer suggests that parents involved in such partnerships re-read "Little Red Riding Hood" and retrace Little Red Riding Hood's steps to Grandma's house in the woods.

Particular attention should be given to Red Riding Hood's finding The Big Bad Wolf in Grandma's bed wearing Grandma's night cap!]

SPEAKING OF "LITTLE RED RIDING HOOD," THE JANUARY 24, 1999 ISSUE OF *THE GWINNETT Daily Post* of Lawrenceville, Georgia contained an article by staff writer Laura Ingram entitled "Clusters Promote Community Growth." This article describes a second-step phase of a "systems change" effort outlined in a joint publication from the U.S. Department of Education and the U.S. Department of Health and Human Services, *Together We Can*. The article, which illustrates the shift from representative (elected) governance to regional (unelected) governance with its "Big Bad Wolf" use of partnerships to accomplish its goals, is included in its entirety below:

> Unique groups called Community Cluster Care Teams were born last April, comprised of 12 Gwinnett communities, and have taken their first steps toward uniting sections of the county into neighborhoods.
>
> "The entire community needs to get involved," said Suzanne Brighton, coordinator for the teams. "We need to look at the environment we're raising our children in. Everybody has a responsibility to create a healthy environment where children can grow."
>
> Parents, teachers, senior citizens, clergy, business people, school officials and social service workers first met this new creation April 15 at a conference called "Together We Can," sponsored by the Gwinnett Coalition for Health and Human Services and BellSouth.
>
> The 200 participants split into 12 groups based on high school clusters and came up with particular ways to improve each cluster/community. But they did not stop at just a sketch.
>
> The 12 teams continued meeting throughout the year, drawing more community members and resources into their group, and creating strategic plans to accomplish their goals and shrink scary statistics that show children finding their way into drugs, pregnancy and violence.
>
> This fall, their imperative to heal and unite their neighborhoods took shape as tree plantings, youth dialogues, new youth basketball teams, grandparent adoptions and bilingual services.
>
> Metro United Way's vice president of community investments, Geralyn Sheehan, calls the teams a pilot program for the entire nation, teaching residents throughout America how to reconnect with others to build a healthier community.

[Ed. Note: To further illustrate what the U.S. Department of Education and U.S. Department of Health and Human Services book *Together We Can: A Guide for Crafting a Profamily System of Education and Human Services* (Contract #RP912060001: PrismDAE, a division of DAE Corporation: Chevy Chase, Maryland, 1993) outlined as a blueprint to follow for "local systems change," the writer will offer some excerpts from this publication. Jointly signed by Secretary of Education Richard W. Riley and Secretary of Health and Human Services Donna E. Shalala, the foreword to this book reads:

> This book was developed jointly... to help communities improve coordination of education, health and human services for at-risk children and families. *Together We Can: A Guide for Crafting a Profamily System of Education and Human Services* reflects the work and experience of a study group of researchers and front-line administrators and practitioners working with promising programs that link education and human services. *Together We Can* leads the

reader through a five-stage collaborative process with milestones and landmines portrayed through vignettes and case studies describing the personal experiences of the study group members.

Together We Can is a practical guide that can assist local communites in the difficult process of creating a more responsive education and human service delivery system. The guidebook emphasizes the effective delivery of supports for families, a crucial step toward assuring the future success of America's children. Recognizing that the current system of programs serving children is fragmented, confusing and inefficient, the guidebook advocates a radical change in the service delivery system. It encourages a holistic approach in treating the problems of children and families; easy access to comprehensive services; early detection of problems and preventive health care services; and flexibility for education, health and human services.

We believe this guide is a practical tool for the many communities that are working to create more comprehensive, family-focused service delivery systems for children and their families.

[Ed. Note: This is pure, unadulterated "communitarianism," which is defined as: "communitarian—a member or advocate of a communistic community" (p. 288) and "ism"— a doctrine, theory, system" (p. 474) in *Webster's New World Dictionary of the American Language* (William Colliers—World Publishing Co., Inc.: New York, 1976.), the system we have been told is "dead."]

In the preface to *Together We Can* we find the following:

Across America, people are recognizing that all of the institutions and agencies whose mission is to nurture and strengthen children and families must collaborate....

The U.S. Department of Education and the U.S. Department of Health and Human Services charged the School-Linked Integrated Services Study Group with capturing the experiences of collaborative endeavors across the country and creating a guide for integrating services....

Basic to the guide is the concept of *systems change* [emphasis in original]. We define systems change as a revision of the ways that people and institutions think, behave, and use their resources.... The Study Group believes *collaborative strategies* [emphasis in original] are the key to systems change.... Collaborative strategies, in which partners share a vision, establish common goals, and agree to use their power to achieve them are necessary; commitment of resources and willingness to alter existing policies are a vital part of such strategies.

Most importantly, the children and families who participate in our education and human service systems are essential to its reinvention. They are indispensable partners with educators, human service professionals, business leaders, civic and religious leaders, leaders of community-based organizations, and other citizens in creating the profamily system that the guide envisions.

The School-Linked Integrated Services Study Group consisted of representatives of: "Institute for Educational Leadership, Washington, D.C.; Florida International University Human Resource Service Professional Development Center, Miami, Florida; Walbridge Elementary School, St. Louis, Missouri; National Center on Adult Literacy, Philadelphia, Pennsylvania; Center for Collaboration for Children of California State University, Fullerton, California; Prince Georges County Public Schools, Suitland, Maryland; San Diego City Schools, San Diego, California; Public School 146M, New York City; Savannah-Chatham County Youth Futures Authority, Savannah, Georgia [Anna Casey grant recipient which promoted school-based clinics]; School of Education at Stanford University, Stanford, California; Early Childhood and Family Education division of North Central Regional Educational Laboratory, Oak Brook, Illinois; Danforth Foundation, St. Louis, Missouri; Cities in Schools, Charlotte, North Carolina; Community Education Leadership Project of the Institute for Educational Leadership, Washington, D.C.; Better Boys Foundation, Chicago, Illinois; National Center for Services Integration of Mathtech, Inc., Falls Church, Virginia; Community Schools of Rochester City School District, Rochester, New York; Clinic Services/Family Counseling Center of the Massachusetts Society for Prevention of Cruelty to Children, Boston, Massachusetts; Lansing School District, Lansing, Michigan; Parent Action, Baltimore, Maryland; New Jersey Department of Human Services, Trenton, New Jersey; School of the Future of El Centro Familiar Office of the Family Service Center, Houston, Texas; New York State Department of Education, Brooklyn, New York; Walbridge Caring Communities Program, St. Louis, Missouri; and a practicing psychologist."

In the interest of fully informing the reader of just exactly what these projects are about and hope to accomplish, the writer is including highlights of a two-part appendix which are so totally invasive and frightening in their implications that they should relegate George Orwell's *1984* to the "light reading" stacks!

Appendix A
Checklist 1
Process for Crafting a Profamily System of Education and Human Services

Stage One: Getting Together
- Has a small group decided to act?
- Do the players meet the following criteria for membership in the collaborative:
  ___clout;
  ___commitment; and
  ___diversity?
- Are the right people involved...
- Have partners reflected on their work and celebrated their accomplishments?

Stage Two: Building Trust and Ownership
- Has the collaborative conducted a comprehensive community assessment that...
  ___produces a profile of child and family well-being in the community; ...
- Have partners defined a shared vision and goals for changing education and human services?...

Stage Three: Developing a Strategic Plan
- Has the collaborative narrowed its focus to a specific neighborhood for launching a service delivery prototype?
- Has the collaborative conducted a neighborhood analysis...
- Has the collaborative defined the target outcomes?...
- Is a mechanism in place for using program-level intelligence to suggest system-level changes?...

Stage Four: Taking Action
- Is the collaborative evaluating progress by:
    ___using process evaluation techniques; and
    ___measuring outcomes?
- Have partners reflected on their work and celebrated their accomplishments?

Stage Five: Going to Scale
- Has the collaborative built a formal governance structure?...
- Is the collaborative promoting change in the federal government's role in delivering services for children and families?
- Is the collaborative continuing to reflect and celebrate as it "climbs the mountain" of systems change?

Checklist 2
Indicators of Systems Change

Are agency agreements in place?...

Do program-level information and intelligence trigger policy-level changes across multiple systems?...

Have partners developed shared information systems?
- Is there ready access to each other's records? ...
- Have agencies replaced separate in-house forms to gather the same kind of information with a common form used by all members or other organizations to establish program eligibility? Assess case management needs? Develop case plans?

Have partner agencies incorporated the vision and values of the collaborative at their administrative and staff levels?
- Have partners altered their hiring criteria, job descriptions, and preservice or inservice training to conform to a vision of comprehensive, accessible, culturally appropriate, family-centered, and outcome-oriented services? ...
- Are outcome goals clearly established?
- Has the collaborative used its data collection capacity to document how well children and families are faring in their communities and how well agencies and child-serving institutions are meeting their mandates? ...
- Are outcomes measurable? Do they specify what degree of change is expected to occur in the lives of children and families during what period of time?
- Is shared accountability a part of outcomes that reflect education, human service, and community goals and objectives?

Has the collaborative devised a financing strategy to ensure long-term funding?

Has the collaborative gained legitimacy in the community as a key vehicle for addressing and resolving community issues regarding children and families?
- Are the collaborative's positions on community issues supported by commitments from public and private service providers, the business community, and the church- and neighborhood-based organizations whose members are often most directly affected by collaborative decisionmaking?

The above activities are advocated and coordinated through a center which was established with taxpayers' money and is described in the following explanation of its activities:

National Center for Services Integration

The National Center for Services Integration (NCSI) was established in late 1991 with funds from the U.S. Department of Health and Human Services and private foundations to improve life outcomes for children and families through the creative integration of education, health and human services. The center itself is a collaboration of six organizations: Mathtech, Inc.; the Child and Family Policy Center; National Center for Children in Poverty; National Governors' Association, Policy Studies Associates; and the Yale Bush Center. It also receives guidance from distinguished advisors knowledgeable about the issues and institutions concerned with service integration.

The primary purpose of NCSI is to stimulate, guide, and actively support service integration efforts throughout the entire country. To accomplish its mission, NCSI has undertaken a variety of activities through its Information Clearinghouse on Service Integration and a Technical Assistance Network.

The Clearinghouse, which is operated by the National Center on Children in Poverty at Columbia University, collects and disseminates information and materials on service integration issues and related topics. They have developed a computer directory of service integration programs, a separate directory of organizations, and an extensive research library collection that can provide information and support to community-based programs. Individuals, organizations, and localities can access any of the Clearinghouse services....

The Technical Assistance Network, which is operated by Charles Bruner of the Child and Family Policy Center [Kids Count] and Mathtech [government contractor for the evaluation of sex education programs], brings together leading service integration planners, practitioners, administrators, and experts to exchange ideas and information, to develop written resource materials for communities and practitioners and to convene working groups composed of persons in the forefront of particular issues to develop strategies for successfully resolving some of the challenges facing communities and governmental entities involved in service integration efforts.

[Ed. Note: If the reader has any questions about why school-based clinics, school-to-work, community education programs, year-round schools, one-stop training centers, and all of the other "locally conceived" programs have come into their communities with such force and fundamental support, the above federally funded and conceived plans should answer them. *Together We Can* brings together national and international plans for socializing all services to our citizenry. One example is the International Year of the Child proposals which originated in 1979 and are hereby funded, formatted, and fulfilled in *Together We Can*'s "how-to" instruction manual. These are the processes necessary to create the "perfect human resource"—the global worker. President Nixon vetoed the child and family legislation encompassing all of the above activities (the *Humphrey-Hawkins Child and Family Services Act*) in the mid–1970s, calling it the most socialistic legislation he had ever seen. *The New York Times* carried an article by Edward B. Fiske entitled "Early Schooling Is Now the Rage" in its April 13, 1986 issue which explained:

Mr. Nixon not only vetoed the bill (Humphrey-Hawkins] but also fired off a scathing message to Congress, proclaiming that he would have no part in the "Sovietizing" of American Society. "Good public policy requires that we enhance rather than diminish both parental authority and parental involvement with children."

This comprehensive program links almost every entry in this book, from cradle to grave. None of this could have been accomplished without the use of behaviorist methods and change agent tactics carefully documented in this book. Americans would not have willingly turned over decision making in these areas unless manipulated into doing so; no one ever voted to conduct our government in this manner. *The Montgomery County Blueprint* of 1946— fifty-plus years ago—spelled out this approach. In the *Blueprint* Paul Mort pointed out that it takes fifty years to accomplish "systems change." He was right on target.]

IN HIS JANUARY 1999 STATE OF THE UNION SPEECH BEFORE THE 106TH CONGRESS, PRESIdent Bill Clinton referred to his "100,000 new cops" legislation and funding. Possible uses for these new "police resources" might be found in information regarding Community-Oriented Policing (COP) training available through agreements between local police departments and the U.S. Department of Justice, Bureau of Justice Assistance (BJA). The following excerpt is taken from Community-Oriented Police (COP) materials published through the auspices of the U.S. Department of Justice:

COMMUNITY POLICING WHAT IS IT?

- Shift in philosophy about police duties vs. community responsibilities to a team concept of total quality management of the community. Reidentifying police role as a facilitator in the community.
- Leaders of the community (law enforcement, government, business, education, health, civic, non-profit, medical, religious, etc.) collaborating to identify problems in the community, what the significant impact on people will be, and suggesting solutions to those problems
- Identifying common ground, where all factions of a community can work together for the common good of the community in a broader problem-solving approach. Forming a partnership between police and the rest of the community where each is accountable to each other and the community as a whole.
- Raising community awareness of programs and functions of community agencies and organizations, to make it easier for citizens to contact the correct source for solutions to their problems, thus releasing police time to take care of legitimate police business.

A recent article in *The Washington Times* (National Weekly Edition) of May 17–23, 1999 entitled "Ahem, about those 100,000 new cops…" sheds some light on what is a little-known but controversial program. Excerpts follow:

Whatever happened to those 100,000 new cops President Clinton promised to put on the streets back in 1994? More to the point, what became of the $9 billion appropriation to fund the much-hyped Community Oriented Policing Services Program (COPS) that was supposed to deliver them?

According to an embarrassing new report released by the Justice Department's Office of Inspector General (IG), the money is being spent on anything and everything but new police officers.

…[T]he IG discovered, during the course of 150 audits of grant recipients, that 78 percent of grantees charged unallowable costs to the federal government for such things as overtime, police uniforms and fringe benefits not approved in advance; that 41 percent of grant recipients showed indicators of simply having used federal funds to supplant local funds, sometimes paying the salaries of officers already on board, and other times not meeting the program's matching funds requirements; that 58% of grantees either did not develop a good faith plan to retain officer positions or said they would not retain the positions at the conclusion of the grants.

All told, the IG report identified $52 million in questionable costs; $71 million that could have been put to better use.

As to how many new police officers are actually on the street as a result of all this manna from Washington, well, that's something not yet pinned down. The IG's audit shows the COPS program has issued some $5 billion in grants, enough to fund 92,000 officers, of which only 50,000 appear to be on the street.

Three years ago, IBD noted that federal grants have been going to fund state parks, nature sanctuaries and other places not usually associated with violent crime. In Florida, for instance, the state Department of Environmental Protection received a $3.5 million COPS grant to hire 30 marine patrol officers to monitor a national marine sanctuary. (Manatees can be a real threat to public order, you know.)

More than 20 criminal investigations of COPS grantees have been opened thus far, yet the lucre continues to flow. But the real problem with the COPS program is the further politicization of American law enforcement at all levels. By dangling billions before state and local departments, the federal government is teasing law enforcement into a bidding war and lobbying campaign, shifting the emphasis from dealing with crime to worrying about how to score a hit on the cash-laden Beltway pinata.

Not only is there reason for legitimate concern over the "politicization" of American law enforcement. The use of the money for COPS to pay organizations like Community Research Associates to train police departments in towns across this country to employ tactics similar to those used by educational change agents to accomplish questionable re-orienting of law enforcement activities cries out for an investigation. A sample of such suggestions, taken from U.S. Department of Justice materials, follows:

MEETING #3... We ask that between now and the time we arrive, you contact these identified individuals and arrange for a day-long session.... This group will be exposed to the history, elements and types of COP, as well as strategic planning concepts necessary to COP implementation. This will also leave us with tasks to perform, should there exist a consensus opinion to proceed with Phase II of the COP initiative. We recommend that members of your department holding the rank of Captain and above attend this meeting (in uniform) and that they be instructed prior to the meeting to disperse themselves evenly throughout the audience.

[Ed. Note: Accolades to the police departments and public officials who understand that their law enforcement resources should be applied toward fulfilling their constitutional law enforcement duties rather than to help them engage in public/private partnership community development and social service programs which, due to the blurring of lines of responsibility, are unaccountable to the public and truly "communitarian" in their tone.]

"STATE OF EDUCATION CRITICIZED—NONPROFIT ORGANIZATION HIRED AT FORMER Governor's Urging Pinpoints Weaknesses Within Ohio's Academic System" is published in the

March 24, 1999 issue of the Akron, Ohio *Beacon Journal*. Excerpts from this article follow:

> COLUMBUS—A national organization, hired to look at Ohio's education system, issued a report card yesterday and the results were not good.
>
> The critical assessment, presented to the state's educational policy leaders, was surprising because the nonprofit organization, Achieve Inc., was hired at the urging of former Gov. George Voinovich, who helped devise the funding system.
>
> The organization is made up of executives from some of the nation's largest corporations—IBM, Boeing and Procter & Gamble—and governors from North Carolina, Michigan, Nevada and Wisconsin. [The National Governor's Association set up this organization to "manage" reform, ed.]...
>
> Among the findings:
>
> - Ohio's academic goals are not clearly defined. Accountability standards are ineffective because there are no rewards or punishments associated with failure or success. The emphasis is on holding kids, not adults, accountable.
> - If the state is serious about improving academics and holding schools accountable, it must provide districts with the resources and tools—that, is more money—to do the job.
> - The state should provide assistance in districts that are performing poorly, close schools if no improvements are made and re-open them with new leaders....
>
> Fred Blosser, superintendent of Canton schools, agreed with Achieve's assessment.
>
> "The state's academic goals are not defined," he said. While Canton has adopted its own goals—graduating every child with the ability to think and reason, to have concern for others and to have a desire to continue to learn—the state's only concern is getting children to a minimum level of knowledge, he said.
>
> "All I am hearing is 'proficiency, proficiency, proficiency—and attendance.' There is more to educating a child than meeting minimum proficiency," Blosser said.

[Ed. Note: Note that the emphasis is placed on only attaining a "minimum" level of proficiency. If anyone still has any doubts by now what the full implementation of education reform will mean for the children, teachers and schools of America, read the article again carefully. Reformer (change agent) David Hornbeck's original recommendations for rewarding or penalizing schools, depending on the results of individual children's proficiency test scores, is now being widely implemented across America. Children will pass or fail based upon these test scores. Teachers will be rewarded or penalized based on the test scores of children in their classrooms. Schools which do not function up to par will be shut down or "managed." Under increasing pressure, teachers will be devoting massive amounts of time to "teach to the test." And the teaching method of choice will be direct instruction/mastery learning which drills the students like robots until they can spout out the correct answer without thinking.

One might wonder how Ohio students and schools fared with their first run-through of these new tests. The Akron *Beacon Journal*, in a follow-up article "State Ranking of Schools Sure to Rankle: Many Area Districts Are Scoring Very Poorly in Statewide Evaluation (April 6, 1999) reported:

> About 1.8 million report cards went into the mail yesterday to the parents of each of Ohio's public school children....

While showing that students in general are doing better, especially on the state's ninth-grade proficiency tests, math continues to be a weak spot.

And many schools in the area are falling short of academic goals, according to the reports.

This year, only 15 of Ohio's 611 school districts achieved the highest rating of "effective." Not one of the 62 school districts in Summit, Stark, Portage, Medina or Wayne counties was in that elite group....

Akron Superintendent Brian Williams—whose district met only one of the 18 criteria—prepared the parents of his district for bad news by sending a letter home last week.]

THE CONFERENCE BOARD (ONE OF THE MOST INFLUENTIAL INTERNATIONAL GROUPS PRO-moting the world management/control system and workforce training in the schools) advertised its "1999 Strategic Learning Conference: A Tool Kit to Power Business Performance" to be held March 29–30, 1999 at the Marriott World Trade Center, New York City. On the front of the brochure at the very bottom it states, "The collective wisdom of executives worldwide." In regard to the subject of the conference, it states:

The Strategic Learning Model was developed by Professor William Pietersen at Columbia Business School. At this conference, he and other leading-edge thinkers and corporate practitioners will walk you through a framework—from beginning to end—that will demonstrate how to create systematic learning initiatives that can result in better business strategy and bottom-line results.

"Dry stuff, that," you say. Not at all. Under the "Making or Breaking Strategy through Culture" one reads: "Culture is the key to success. This fundamental dimension of your strategic development can determine success or failure. Find out how to ensure you create a strong culture of success." Carlos Rivero, Ph.D., director of research, Delta Consulting, and Robert Bontempo, professor of executive education at Columbia Business School, are the presenters. The last two highlighted comments in this particular section state in distinctly Skinnerian terms the following:

What Gets Measured Gets Done
and
What Gets Rewarded Gets Done Repeatedly

[Ed. Note: This entry demonstrates how every facet of our lives will, in the future, be based on Professor B.F. Skinner's scientific and manipulative philosophy extensively discussed in this book.]

U.S. SECRETARY OF EDUCATION RICHARD RILEY DELIVERED THE SIXTH STATE OF AMERICAN Education speech early in 1999 in Long Beach, California. For the reader who has arrived at this point in this book, Riley's recommendations will come as no surprise. The reader could probably have written Riley's speech, since it covers everything painstakingly and consistently initiated over time using the Hegelian Dialectic, semantic deception and gradualism. Riley's proposals—including the "communitarian" *Together We Can* "systems change" in the

January, 1999 entry—could have been lifted out of the 1946 *Montgomery County Blueprint* discussed in the preface to this book.

In his February 16 speech Riley called for: Community Partnerships, charter schools, schools open year-round/morning-to-night, "Schools [of the future] serving as centers of communities"; focus on reading [referring to the "landmark study by the Academy of Science"]; "Democracy of Excellence"; early childhood initiatives [Parents as Teachers, etc.]; school uniforms; violence-prevention programs; "sustained progress" [North Carolina, Maryland, Texas and Kentucky as "successes"—those states which have been struggling to keep their heads above water during the past twenty-five years, ed.]; teacher "quality"; "option schools"; "magnet schools"; school-to-work "opportunities"; and more choices. Obviously, the interpretation of this information depends on one's definition of Riley's words! Astoundingly, based on no supportive evidence, Riley said:

> We know a good deal more about how to turn around low-performing schools: from giving teachers more time for training and collaboration; to redesigning the curriculum; to removing a principal who doesn't provide leadership; to issuing school report cards that measure real achievement over time; to enforcing effective discipline policies.

[Ed. Note: To assist Secretary Riley in his effort to bring "transformation" to the education arena, the writer is providing the reader with a "Recipe for Educational Disaster" which the reader is encouraged to duplicate and send to Riley, others who may hold his position at a future date, elected officials, school superintendents, teachers, and anyone else who could benefit from its sage advice. The credit for the recipe (which has been "doctored up" a bit) will have to go to "anonymous," for the writer is unable to identify its author, but whoever you are—many, many thanks!

RECIPE FOR EDUCATIONAL DISASTER
Combine the following ingredients for a total disaster in education.

Mix together:
1 Plump Federal Government (pits and all)
50 State Education Agencies
2 Liberal Teachers Unions (NEA, AFT)
1 National Diffusion Network

Sift together:
Several Socialist Foundations (Carnegie, Ford, Rockefeller, Danforth, Spencer, Pew and Kettering)
Graduate Schools
Teachers Colleges
Textbook Publishers

Fold In:
Planned Parenthood
SIECUS (Sex Information Education Council of the United States)
Drug Education
Self-Esteem Education [Character Education]
Death Education

School-to-Work "techademics"
(Be sure to remove all Basic Skills.)

Add the Following Funds for Extra Spice:

Title I (special provisions for disadvantaged youngsters)

Title II (school libraries, textbooks, and instructional materials, also "educational technology" and so-called "basic skills improvement")

Title III ("innovative programs," psychological experiments, "exemplary" programs; additional guidance, and "special" programs for wonderful classes in health, population and global education, testing and counseling)

Title IV (educational labs and centers, libraries, early childhood education, more guidance, testing and counseling, social workers and psychiatrists)

Title V (grants and resources to the state education agencies for data collection and management, personnel development, and handicapped, migrant children, "community education," ethnic heritage programs, bilingual education, opportunities for Indian students, emergency aid, etc.)

If none of these ingredients are available in their original form due to "repackaging and renaming" because of "brand name" changes, presently available substitutes work just as well! Potential substitute items: Educators for parents (Parents as Teachers) or *Together We Can* "caring communities."

Strain out all ABSOLUTE values and morals.
Sprinkle with Change Agents.
Simmer for twelve years to fourteen years.

TOPPING:

Add *all* four-year-olds, blend with year-round school and Head Start programs.
Combine the following (stirring constantly):

Learner Outcomes

Accreditation Standards

(Teach-to-the-Test adds flavor, too.)

Pour in secretive, federal- and state-mandated tests (personality profiles passed off as academic tests) and report cards for parents.
Add a huge supply of edible "tokens" for immediate gratification after correct responses blended into mixture.
Baste until ALL are completely BRAINWASHED.

Serving Size: Approximately 40,000,000 children

Serve leftovers to the next generation. (Ideal to serve to State Senators and Representatives, U.S. Congressmen and Senators, and other public officials during black tie dinners.)

DESSERT SUGGESTION: TAXES A LA MODE

With this last entry I rest my case.

The deliberate dumbing down has now become the excuse for complete social change, including the privatization of education (the handing over to the unelected multinational corporations the responsibility for education—actually training—of future citizens). Such a transfer of responsibility will be facilitated by the creation of charter/magnet schools and passage of legislation providing tuition tax credits/vouchers. The workforce development system will, of course, be international, as is indicated by many quotes in this book. Parents who may be enthusiastic about the various choice proposals may change their minds regarding "choice" when their child becomes part of the corporate fascist quota system, being tracked into a career chosen for him/her by unelected corporate managers who set labor force requirements.

Such quotas will be a part of the global planned economy. Parents will have no say regarding their child's placement since there will no longer be an elected body, such as a school board, to whom they can complain.

Only a dumbed-down, brainwashed, conditioned citizenry could willingly accept what is being offered Americans under the guise of "remaining competitive in an increasingly global economy," and relinquishing our sovereignty in the name of "global understanding and peace." The following quotations from Edward Hunter, the man who coined the term "brainwashing" and author of *Brainwashing: The Men Who Defied It*,[69] speak to what we as Americans can still do to reverse the process:

> Surely there can no longer be a trace of doubt that brainwashing is sheer evil. The fight against it is the culminating issue of all time, in which every human being is protagonist. There can be neither escape nor neutrality where such responsibilities lie.
>
> There can be neither front nor rear, for the great lesson that came from the brainwashing chambers was that while every man has a cracking point, every man's cracking point can be immensely strengthened. That is the job of home, school, and church. The mother, teacher, and pastor are in the front lines in this ideological conflict, and every word they say to their sons and daughters is important to the struggle, for character more than anything else will determine the outcome.
>
> Truth is the most important serum and integrity the most devastating weapon that can be used against the totalitarian concept.... Nothing should be allowed to interfere with the task of getting those facts across to the people who need and can use them.
>
> Only an informed people can shoulder their responsibility effectively. When free men know both what they are fighting against and what they are fighting to preserve and enhance, they are unbeatable, stronger than any strategy.
>
> What is absolutely essential is that the full facts be given to all our people, for mind warfare is total war. This approach can make our struggle for the mind the crusade it should be. Never since man received reason beyond the instincts of animal kind has there been a more important issue. In the fight to give man forever the opportunity to develop, every possible weapon must be utilized on the field of battle, which is everywhere. There is no "behind the lines" any longer.

Endnotes:

1   The foregoing information was taken from Appendix A–1 of the SCANS publication *What Work Requires of Schools* (U.S. Department of Labor: Washington, D.C., 1991).

2   *National Issues in Education: Goals 2000 and School-to-Work* by John F. Jennings, Ed. (Phi Delta Kappa: Bloomington, Ind., and The Institute for Educational Leadership: Washington, D.C., 1995).

3   For those interested in seeing how Skinner's animal training works with teachers, Madeline Hunter's *Instructional Theory into Practice: ITIP* is a collection of Hunter's instructional materials which she developed and taught throughout her career. This material may be purchased from: Association for Supervision and Curriculum Development, 1703 North Beauregard St., Alexandria, VA 22311–1714, Ph: 1–800–933–2723.

4   World Education for All Forum Secretariat is located at: United Nations Educational, Scientific, and Cultural Organization, 7

Place de Fonteroy, 75352 Paris O75P, France.

5   *Polytechnical Education: A Step* by Robert H. Beck available by calling 1-800-637-7651.

6   Ordering address: *The Blumenfeld Education Report*, Literacy Unlimited, Inc., 2527 Knox Drive, Rockford, Illinois 61114.

7   Global Alliance for Transforming Education, 4202 Ashwoody Trail, Atlanta, GA 30319.

8   Numinous: "1: supernatural, mysterious 2: filled with a sense of the presence of divinity; holy 3: appealing to the higher emotions or to the aesthetic sense; spiritual." (*Webster's Seventh New College Dictionary* [G. & C. Merriam Company: Springfield, MA, 1971.])

9   Please re-read the 1934 entry regarding *Conclusions and Recommendations for the Social Studies* funded by the Carnegie Corporation, the wording of which very closely resembles the GATE entry.

10 Edwards Deming stated in an interview at the University of Pittsburgh in 1992 that "What I took to Japan [TQM] was not the American way."

11 "Non-hierarchical process of new leadership" is Total Quality Management (TQM).

12 See 1991 entry concerning Association for Supervision and Curriculum Development's efforts in the Eugene, Oregon School District 4J for further information regarding Muller and his curriculum.

13 Glavin, Matthew J., *Reach for the Stars: A Proposal for Education Reform in Georgia*. (Georgia Public Policy Foundation: Atlanta, GA, 1991)

14 In 1997 Michigan Governor John Engler funded and supported a report prepared by an appointed commission which recommended that Michigan's schools—as an example to the nation—be divested of public control and turned into "corporations." These "corporations" would give stock to families with children in the communities in which the schools were located and to employees of the schools—the employees would receive larger shares than the parent/citizen stockholders—and to other "interested entities" which could include business and corporate interests. Because of the structure of "corporations," the question was and could be asked concerning the possibility of investment by foreign, or certainly interstate, interests. This certainly raises the spectre of "corporate academies" being created out of our public schools.

15 Those interested in obtaining a copy of the Carnegie Corporation's report *A Nation Prepared: Teachers for the 21st Century*, published in the May 21, 1986 issue of *Education Week*, can do so by writing to: *Education Week*, Suite 775, 1255 23rd Street, N.W., Washington, D.C. 20003.

16 The Russian Deputy Minister of Education Elena Lenskaya was also a presenter at Willard Daggett's International Center for Leadership in Education, Inc., Second Annual Model Schools Conference in Atlanta, Georgia in the summer of 1994. She made a return appearance in the summer of 1998 at the Sixth Annual Model Schools Conference.

17 The USCEFA's definition for "basic learning needs," as put forth in their literature, is "the essential learning tools—such as literacy, oral expression, numeracy, problem-solving and basic learning content—required by all people to develop their full capacities to live and work in dignity, to participate fully in development, to improve the quality of their lives, to make informed decisions."

18 Education Development Center, Inc. in Newton, Massachusetts was the developer of the controversial social studies program *Man: A Course of Study or M:ACOS*, based on the work of B.F. Skinner and Jerome Bruner.

19 See 1991 New American Schools Development Corporation entry.

20 British Columbia Teachers' Federation, 100-550 West 6th Avenue, Vancouver, BC V5Z 4P2.

21 For more information regarding Community Learning Information Network, write CLIN, 1776 K St., N.W., Fifth Floor, Washington, D.C. 20006, Office: 202-857-2330.

22 The writer considers this publication a "Must Read"! It may be ordered by sending $12.00 to: Billy Lyon, Route #1, Box 37, Edgewood, TX 75117.

23 The reader may wish to order Ms. Rogers's first article, "In Loco Parentis: The Brave New Family in Missouri," as well as a complete copy of the excerpted article from: *Chronicles*, 934 N. Main Street, Rockford, IL 61103.

24 From personal collection of this writer, provided by a fellow researcher.

25 See previous reference to this conference in the 1981 entry of this book dealing with comments by Malcolm Davis.

26 See 1993 entry for M. Donald Thomas's "A Plan for Action," which contains proposals from Dr. Don Thomas concerning $50 fines for parents who refuse to volunteer.

27 For further information on this subject, the NAEP, and violation of privacy, order a copy of "When Johnny Takes the Test: How Your Child Is Identified and Tracked to the National Data Bank—and Beyond" by Melanie Fields, Anita Hoge and Sarah Leslie from: Conscience Press, P.O. Box 449, Ravenna, Ohio 44266, or http://www.christianconscience.com.

28 Florida and Texas were specifically selected because of their use in the data collection project for migratory children and their families.

29 Videotape from private collection.

30 For more information about the NTL Institute services, or its approach to change, contact: Russell Bong, Marketing Manager, NTL Institute for Applied Behavioral Science, 1240 North Pitt St., Suite 100, Alexandria, VA 22314-1403. Phone: 1-800-777-5227; FAX: 703-684-1256.

31 See entry for 1983 quote from book by Eugene Maxwell Boyce, *The Coming Revolution in Education and the New Theory of Schooling*.

32 "The Truth Behind Outcome-Based Education" was produced and distributed by Compass and can be ordered by calling: 1-800-977-2177.

33 William E. Brock has also served as a former U.S. Secretary of Labor and as chairman of the Labor Secretary's Commission on Achieving Necessary Skills (SCANS), appointed by then-Secretary of Labor Elizabeth Dole.

34 National Center for Education Statistics. *Financial Accounting: Classifications and Standard Terminology for Local and State*

School Systems. (U.S. Government Printing Office: Washington, D.C., 1973) DHEW Publication No. (OE) 73–11800.

35 The Commission on Skills of the American Workforce produced this 1990 report. The commission included Marc Tucker, who wrote the now-famous letter to Hillary Clinton following the election of Bill Clinton as President. It should be noted that Hillary Clinton was appointed to the commission by William Bennett, then-secretary of education. (See 1986 entry dealing with this story.)

36 Please see Appendix XI "When Is Assessment Really Assessment?" and index references for Sticht and Oettinger.

37 *America 2000* eventually became *Goals 2000.*

38 The report from the Second Annual Conference on Model Schools was written by Cynthia Weatherly and published in the January 1995 issue of *The Christian Conscience* (Vol. 1, No. 1).

39 "Voluntary," for the time being.

40 The words "forgotten half" are taken from the 1988 W.T. Grant Co.'s landmark report entitled *The Forgotten Half: Pathways to Success for America's Youth and Young Families.* (See 1988 entry for more about this report.)

41 Susan Kovalik formed her ITI company in 1982 and has now moved to the state of Washington. If the reader is interested in accessing Kovalik's materials, her internet site address is: http://www.kovalik.com. This writer in no way endorses the work of Susan Kovalik, but is merely making this information available to provide the reader with original research.

42 Challengers for Insight's address is: 520 N. State Road 135, Suite M–125, Greenwood, IN 46142.

43 *Fire in the Minds of Men: Origins of the Revolutionary Faith* (Basic Books, Inc.: New York, 1980) was written by James H. Billington, librarian of the U.S. Congress in which he wrote in chapter 4, "The Occult Origins of Organization," the following: "The story of the secret socieites can never be fully reconstructed, but it has been badly neglected—even avoided, one suspects—because the evidence that is available repeatedly leads us into territory equally uncongenial to modern historians in the East and the West.... In what follows I shall attempt to show that modern revolutionary tradition as it came to be internationalized under Napoleon and the Restoration grew out of occult Freemasonry; that early organizational ideas originated more from Pythagorean mysticism than from practical experience; and that the real innovators were not so much political activists as literary intellectuals, on whom German romantic thought in general—and Baviarian Illuminism in particular—exerted great influence...." (p. 87) It is helpful for serious education researchers who have uncovered evidence similar to that of Billington's to have an historian of his caliber confirming the influence of these occultic societies on the stability of society in general, and education in particular, over the ages.

44 For more background on the history of the "common ground movement" in education reform, see "Separation of School and State: Why We Cannot Sign," by Lynn and Sarah Leslie, published in the December 1997 issue of *The Christian Conscience*, PO Box 449, Ravenna, OH 44266 or posted on the web at http://www.christianconscience.com.

45 Educational Testing Service was created in 1946 and was launched by an initial endowment of $750,000 from the Carnegie Corporation.

46 For a summary report of the Former Pasco Teacher Survey, send a self-addressed stamped envelope to: TFAE, 2527 W. Kennewick Avenue, #350, Kennewick, Washington 99336.

47 Ms. Kosiec can be reached by writing: Barbara McFarlin-Kosiec, 635 N. Fisher, Kennewick, Washington 99336. She is also available for speaking engagements/interviews.

48 Order *National Issues in Education* by calling 1–800–766–1156. The price is $18, plus $3 S&H.

49 A note at the bottom of the article states: "The article was approved by the ACSI Executive Board."

50 If the reader is interested in reading this article in its entirety, please write: Association of Christian Schools International, P.O. Box 35097, Colorado Springs, Colorado 80935–3509, or call 1–800–367–0798.

51 American Family Association Law Center's address is: P.O. Drawer 2440, Tupelo, Mississippi 38803; and telephone: 1–601–680–3886.

52 Los Horcones's e-mail address is: walden@imparcial.comm.mx.

53 John Naisbitt is the author of *Megatrends* and *Megatrends 2000*, required reading for former Speaker of the House Newt Gingrich's seminars.

54 This is wording found in PPBS/MBO material.

55 Esther Dyson was also a speaker and active participant in the Progress and Freedom Foundation's meeting in Atlanta in 1994, "Cyberspace and the American Dream."

56 Refer to the 1984 National Council for Educational Research entry for the history of *The Reading Excellence Act.*

57 Private conversation with teacher who wishes to remain anonymous due to the political heat generated by these reading discussions.

58 Those interested in the activities of the Frank Porter Graham Child Development Center can access its website at: http://www.fpg.unc.edu.

59 George Soros is chairman of the Soros Fund Management. Born in Budapest, Hungary, Soros received his B.S. degree from the London School of Economics in 1952. Married for the second time to Susan Weber Soros, they have raised five children, two born of his first wife. Maintaining homes in Manhattan, London, and Southampton and Bedford, New York, he describes himself as a "financial, philanthropic, and philosophical speculator." Investment funds bearing his name have earned him a fortune estimated at $2.5 billion. He has now become more well known for giving money away than for amassing it, and has established a global network of philanthropic organizations. In the early 1980s he used his wealth to foster political and philosophical freedom in Eastern Europe. To overcome censorship in his native Hungary, Soros distributed photocopiers throughout the country. After building a record of worldwide giving which tops over $350 million annually, Soros has turned his focus on the United States, sponsoring controversial projects dealing with social programs—including drug policy reform and poverty (*Vanity Fair.* November, 1997). The August 14, 1998 issue of *USA Today* carried an article entitled "Soros Stirs

Ruble Debate" which states: "But few people knowledgeable of financial markets—even those outside financial circles who dislike Soros for his donations to assisted suicide and the legalization of marijuana—are prepared to accuse him of a conspiracy to cause a Russian panic."

60 Refer to the 1993 entry dealing with H.R. 6.

61 Ms. Fessler can be reached at: 7530 Ross Road, New Carlisle, OH 45344, 937-845-8428, diana@fessler.com or http://www.fessler.com.

62 Formerly known as the *Drug Free Schools Act.*

63 National Center for Educational Statistics within the Office of Educational Research and Improvement of the U.S. Department of Education produced these handbooks for use by state and local education agencies in collecting data on all aspects of school- and community-related activities, arranged in detailed collection codes.

64 These handbooks are a central part of the Planning, Programming, Budgeting and Management System (PPBS) extensively documented in this book.

65 "Early Warning Family Response," the government's "Action Plan to Deal with Violence," which illustrates the oppressive hand of government at work, can be obtained by calling: 1-800-4ED-PUBS (1-800-433-7827) or by e-mail at edpuborders@aspersys.com.

66 National School Conference Institute (NSCI), P.O. Box 37527, Phoenix, AZ 85069-7527, Toll free: 888-399-8745, http://www.nscinet.com

67 For more information on this project, contact L. Allen Phelps, Center on Education and Work: 608-263-3696 (Ph.) or 608-262-3063 (Fax) or aphelps@soemadison.wisc.edu.

68 For more information about Michael Farris and HSLDA, visit http://www.christianconscience.com.

69 Edward Hunter. *Brainwashing: The Men Who Defied It* (Vanguard Press, Inc.: New York, New York, 1956), chapter 11, "A Matter of Integrity."

Reinforcing Harris

" Harris, we're moving you to the dumbing-down project. You've earned it."

AFTERWORD

It is agreed by many Americans that the United States is living on "borrowed time," but how many of us are willing to reflect seriously on what has happened and how the situation can be reversed? In 1985 this writer, in her slim booklet *Back to Basics or OBE-Skinnerian International Curriculum?*, warned:

> Whether or not the United States of America—through citizen preoccupation with fashion, TV, sports, gourmet cooking, jogging, making a living, etc., all of which are perfectly legitimate and worthwhile activities in a "free society," coupled with lack of understanding of the internationalists' use of gradualism and Hegelian philosophy to attain their goals—slides into the totalitarian black hole of a socialist one world government, with the resulting loss of freedoms our ancestors fought and died for, depends on whether *YOU*, the reader, are convinced the problems described in this book are serious enough for you to spend a few minutes writing to your elected officials.... If the present situation continues unchecked, by the year 1998: children now in kindergarten will have been through thirteen years of Skinnerian world government brainwash under the deceptive guise of the "New Basics"; you and I may no longer be around to vote; and the 18-year-olds may well be on their way to vote what historians have referred to as the greatest experiment in human freedom straight down the tubes.

Well, this writer is still around, and fortunately, so are many other concerned Americans who in 1985 were in their fifties. What this writer predicted has for the most part happened, although it is difficult for the average American to identify or to nail down since the loss of our freedoms at the ballot box—and more importantly through regional government which uses unelected officials to make decisions—has been introduced very gradually.

The most serious problem resulting from the "deliberate dumbing down" is that important decision making is increasingly being delegated to unelected Americans. Citizens are being called upon to participate in the political process through communitarian group management procedures (site-based school management, task forces, blue-ribbon commissions, town meetings, group consensus, call-in talk shows, polling, etc.) and public policy is being made using the "uninformed" opinions of those who have, through no fault of their own, been dumbed down by being either mis-educated or not educated at all in the traditional sense. Many cannot even read a newspaper and depend on TV for their knowledge and understanding of current events.

Part of the solution to this problem could be to return all decision making to duly-elected officials. That, of course, would not assure that those who are elected would be any better qualified to make decisions than those presently calling the shots in Delphi circles and the numerous unelected decision-making venues at work in our country. However, accountability would be restored, and citizens could once more, as free individuals—and, I repeat, *individuals*—vote these people out of office and elect persons who *are* educated in the traditional disciplines of history and government (the *U.S. Constitution*), economics and basic academics. Eventually, if the public education system can be restored to its former excellence, our nation would be able to get back on track.

Seldom, if ever, does one hear the following fairly simple solution suggested when the question is posed regarding how to restore our public education system to its traditional (pre-1930's) state of excellence:

> Elected officials at the local level have the authority to re-establish public education according to the wishes of the taxpayers in each local community. Teachers with degrees in specific subject matter could be hired without requiring that they have state or national certification which subjects them to seemingly ruinous training courses which do not deal with academic material. However, the *funding of the schools must remain local* if citizens wish to re-create truly academic institutions. There can be no tuition tax credits, vouchers, charter schools, or laundered state tax monies (monies co-mingled with federal money) if citizens wish to be 100% in charge of the education philosophy; i.e., curriculum, hiring of teachers, teaching methods, etc. Americans forget too easily the old saying, "He who pays the piper calls the tune." For those who find such a solution unworkable due to the discrepancies in local community tax bases, I say refer to the beginning of this book regarding the ability to educate on a shoestring. Education costs little: brainwashing and social services are very, very expensive.

Granted, the above "solution" may sound simplistic, and in this day and age would not be easy to implement in urban areas, where many of the needs are the greatest. However, when one surveys the urban education landscape as presently constituted, there are few bright spots. Billions of dollars in tax money, which should have gone into true academics, have been siphoned off into the operation of huge and unnecessary bureaucracies. As one has seen after reading this book, community services and changing students' values have been judged more essential than teaching a child to read, to understand his historical setting, the essentials of science, and how to calculate. Basic academics, in most inner city schools under the umbrella of Effective Schools Research, have been taught using Skinnerian mastery learning programs which have resulted in producing low test scores. Discipline has broken down to such an extent that the prescription of the drug Ritalin is commonplace, retired military officers are running urban schools, uniforms are mandated in many public schools, and the police are being called upon to keep order in the former halls of academe.

There is no question that much careful and sensitive thought must go into planning for the urban schools, keeping in mind at all times that most of the problems facing these schools and communities have been a result of what you have read about in this book and the willingness of elected officials to accept the "carrot" along with the big stick (the money with all the federal and state controls on how it is to be used).

It is never too late to see the light at the end of the tunnel. Nothing positive can be accomplished, regardless of how much money and good will exist, unless we Americans learn again to stand on our own two feet, as individuals, not as members of the "group" using Total Quality Management, but as individuals with God-given intellects; as individuals who accept their responsibility to be contributing participants in our constitutional republic instead of being observers in a so-called "participatory" democracy where only those who agree with the *status quo* will be allowed to have a voice. Our nation did not become great through group action. It became great in every way due to individual Americans thinking and acting independently, caring for one another and not expecting the government to care for them or their neighbors, and accepting responsibility for their actions without blaming the "environment" for all their misdeeds—from broken marriages, smoking and drinking to violent behavior.

To repeat the theme of this book: *We are human beings, not animals.* We have free will. We can choose and build our futures, something animals are not capable of doing. Animals are justified in blaming their environment for their behavior! We, as human beings, with intellect, soul and conscience, do not have such justification.

Very recent history, being made as this book is written, should serve as a wake-up call. We, as citizens, seem increasingly unable to make the important connections between individual personal behavior and its effect on the nation/world as a whole. There can be no stability in our world if common decency (morality) is shunted aside and considered a "personal matter" not affecting the entire body politic (personal behavior vs. public morals). Our children deserve more from those adults who bemoan the sorry state of this nation while making excuses for public officials' immoral conduct, and who are poor examples of good behavior themselves. How can we expect our children to grow up and become responsible citizens and future leaders if we sanction immorality at all levels of personal life and government? How can our children accept our criticisms and correction when caught lying or stealing when they see us making excuses for such behavior at the highest levels of government and leadership?

Truly, the "non-absolutist value vaccine" (extensively documented in this book) has taken and can be expected to further sicken our nation in the absence of a return to dependence on very clear and simple moral standards, such as the Ten Commandments which used to hang on the walls of every school and public building in this nation.

Of utmost importance for all Americans at this critical juncture in American education is for us *not* to accept a solution that may in the long run turn out to be more harmful than the present unsatisfactory state of American public education. Some solutions being floated around sound good, such as the complete abandonment of public education in favor of a privately operated system in which parents ostensibly could choose the school to which they send their children. It is important to take a very hard look at such solutions. First, who is going to run those schools? Are parents aware that the New American School Development Corporation and its charter schools for workforce training were set up precisely for the purpose of replacing the deliberately "crashed" public schools? Where would children in the low-income urban areas end up? What private and/or "publicly-funded private" entities are waiting in the wings to orchestrate and relegate these students into dead-end workforce training institutions?

As explained in the preface and at the end of this book, the global workforce training system is being put in place as I write. For example, on June 28, 1999, Gene Sperling, the director of the President's Economic Council, in an interview with CNN's "Moneyline" said that some of the $100 billion "surplus" could be used to make sure "children are ready to be the workers of the next century." What real "choice" will parents have when it comes to where their children will be so-called "educated" (trained) to be the "workers of the next century"? The powers-that-be must be pretty sure of themselves to so blatantly refer to education's primary goal as creating little workers. Are American parents really so dumbed down that they find such comments coming from the highest office in the land acceptable? Even if those operating charter schools had the best of motives, what is going to happen to the majority of children who come from homes where both parents work, where there is only one parent, where there are numerous societal problems which would impinge upon the freedom of parents to be a part of the privately-supported system—sell their children into serfdom?

"Choice in education" is an appealing concept until put under the microscope of 1990s reality. At this point in time, "true choice" with no strings attached exists only for homeschoolers and private (independent and religious) schools that have not in any way compromised their freedom to do *exactly as they wish*. By that, the author means that such an entity has never: (1) accepted one single penny which has at any time, in any fashion, been a source of government—at any level—revenue (tax money; i.e., vouchers, tax credits, or funding from private sources subsidized in any way by the government); and or (2) availed themselves of any services provided by local, state, or federal governments or private sources subsidized in any way by the government (i.e., extracurricular school activities including music, art, sports, field trips, computer use, etc., or health and mental health services which may have been provided when the student was enrolled in the public school system). "True" choice is an option for the minority of children whose parents had better be on guard when offered free computers and software to learn the curriculum required in order to obtain the certificate in mastery necessary to obtain a job or be accepted in college. "True" choice is not an option for the majority of children whose parents are not in a position to avail themselves of it.

A massive national effort to restore true local control of our public schools seems to this writer to be the only "real" long-term solution which will guarantee freedom and upward mobility for *all* our children. Such a solution is no more difficult to implement than solutions presently being offered by those who wish to "use" America's youth for their own profit-seeking motives-resulting in the loss of economic and political freedom.

In order for such a solution to be implemented, elected officials must understand from whence came the problems in education. It is for that reason, for the true understanding of public officials, that this book was written. The author hopes and prays that the greatest number of elected officials will read this book and take the necessary courageous action to reverse the situation which, if left unattended, represents a grave threat to the continued freedom of our nation.

—Charlotte Thomson Iserbyt

Reversing the Situation

RESOURCES

"A Commentary on the Industrial Areas Foundation" published by the Wanderer Forum Foundation, December 1998. Order from: Wanderer Forum Foundation, P.O. Box 542, Hudson, WI 54016-0542. Phone: 651-426-2812. The "Commentary" was prepared under the direction of Stephanie Block, director of special projects for the Wanderer Forum Foundation. (Ms. Block has written *Change Agents: The Industrial Areas Foundation in the Catholic Church*, preliminarily scheduled for publication in 2000.)

Back to Basics Reform or OBE ... Skinnerian International Curriculum? by Charlotte Thomson Iserbyt (Iserbyt: Bath, Maine, 1985). Order from: 3-D Research, 1062 Washington Street, Bath, Maine 04530, Ph. 207-442-0543, Fax 207-442-0551.

Brave New Schools: Guiding Your Child through the Dangers of the Changing School System by Berit Kjos (Harvest House Publishers: Eugene, Oreg., 1995). Available in bookstores.

Child Abuse in the Classroom by Phyllis Schlafly (Pere Marquette Press: Alton, Ill, 1984). Order from: Pere Marquette Press, P.O. Box 495, Alton, IL 62002.

Goals 2000: Restructuring our Schools—Restructuring Society by Kathy Finnegan (Hearthstone Publishing: Oklahoma City, Okla., 1996). Order by calling 1-800-752-1144 or writing Hearthstone Publishing, Ltd., 500 Beacon Drive, Oklahoma City, OK. 73127.

"Harrison Bergeron" by Kurt Vonnegut. A short story from Vonnegut's book *Welcome to the Monkey House* (Delacorte Press/Seymour Lawrence: New York, 1961), which is also available as a video by the same name.

Outcome-Based Education and Higher Order Thinking Skills by Jeannie Georges. Order from: Jeannie Georges, Route #1, Lynnville, IN 47619. Phone: 812–922–3247.

The Children's Story by James Clavell (Delacorte Press/Eleanor Friede: New York, 1963) can be found in libraries or ordered through your local bookstores.

The Great American Con Game by Barbara M. Morris [with updated sequel by Charlotte T. Iserbyt, 1986 and 1997] (Image FX: Escondido, Cal., 1997). Order by writing: Image FX, P.O. Box 937, Escondido, CA 92033–0937 or E-Mail: Imagefx100@aol.com .

The Hidden Story by Geraldine E. Rodgers (Rodgers: Marketing Technologies, 1999). This on-disc book deals with "Two different and opposite kinds of readers... developed at the very beginning stages of reading instruction as the result of different and opposite kinds of teaching. One kind of reader is taught to read by the 'sound' of print and reads automatically and with great accuracy. The other kind of reader is taught to read by the 'meaning' of print, as Chinese characters are read, and not only reads inaccurately, but is actually encouraged to do so by so-called 'psycholinguistic guessing.'" *The Hidden Story* summarizes many years of research by this former elementary school teacher. Available (on disc only) from 1st Books Library at: www.1stbooks.com.

The Impossible Dream by K.M. Heaton. (Hart Publications: Bellingham, Wash., 1993.) Order by writing: Hart Publications, 1507 Lincoln St., Bellingham, WA 98226.

The Perestroika Deception: The World's Slide towards the "Second October Revolution" by Anatoliy Golitsyn. (Edward Harle: London & New York, 1995) Order by calling 212–447–5111.

Tuition Tax Credits: A Responsible Appraisal by Barbara M. Morris. (The Barbara Morris Report: Upland, Cal., 1983) Order by writing Image FX, P.O. Box 937, Escondido, CA 92033–0937 or E-Mail: Imagefx100@aol.com. A few copies still available.

Notes

Notes

GLOSSARY

GLOSSARY

Accountable/Accountability. See Behaviorist Terminology section at end of Glossary.

Affective Domain. The area of learning that deals with feelings, beliefs, values, attitudes, and motives—all those inner factors that determine behavior and responses to stimuli. By changing or modifying the affective domain, educators can control behavior, or so they believe. (See **Direct Instruction**, **Mastery Learning**, **Taxonomy of Educational Objectives**, and Appendix XIX)

Assessment. Has come to be accepted as a means of measuring student progress toward international, national, and state goals. It should be noted that there is no dictionary definition which defines "assessment" in this way. The education establishment has co-opted this word over time. (See **Authentic Assessment** and Appendix IV and XI)

At-Risk Student. Any "student who is at risk of not meeting the goals of the educational program... or not becoming a productive worker" (Iowa State Standards which match the National Goals). Programs such as Parents as Teachers (PAT), 21st Century Schools, Healthy People 2000, and others define at-risk categories. (See 1992 Parents as Teachers articles by Laura Rogers)

Authentic Assessment. Measures a student's behavior; alternative performance measure of a student's ability to solve problems and perform tasks under simulated "real life" situations. It measures student responses which demonstrate what students think, do, and have become. These outcomes are recorded during normal classroom involvement such as recess, lunch, field trips, and at other unexpected times. Teachers may use hand-held computer scanners that scan the students' bar-coded names and responses, then transfer the information into a computer at a later time. (See Appendix XVI)

Behavior Theory, Behavior Modification, Behaviorist, Behaviorism. (Refer to Behaviorist Terminology section of the Glossary and Appendix II, III, V and XIX).

Benchmark. The following definition is taken from "A Report from the Committee on Labor and Human Resources, Summary of S. 14" and is also included in Appendix XV:

> This act will require States to measure and report annually on benchmarks—measurable indicators of the progress the State has set out to achieve in meeting broad work force development goals related to employment, education, and earning gains.
>
> Benchmarks related to employment and earning gains include, at a minimum, placement and retention in unsubsidized employment for one year, and increased earnings for participants.
>
> Benchmarks related to education include, at a minimum, student mastery of certain skills, including: academic knowledge and work readiness skills; occu-

pational and industry-recognized skills according to skill proficiencies for students in career preparation programs; placement in, retention in, and completion of secondary education; placement and retention in military service; and increased literacy skills. It is expected that States will develop additional benchmarks.

Block Grants. Part of the New Federalism movement of the early eighties, block grants send federal assistance, with all its federal regulations, directly to the local level, bypassing the traditional constitutional oversight of the state legislature. Block grants are a necessary part of unconstitutional regional government. They are sold to the citizens as enhancing local control when in fact they do just the opposite by removing an important elected official check at the state level. The 105th Congress (1998) Republican-backed *Dollars to the Classroom Act* is a good example of how this state legislative bypass is effected.

Career Transcript. The SCANS 2000 Center at Johns Hopkins University in Baltimore has developed something called a "career transcript," the purpose of which is to provide quick, more accurate summaries of applicants' education and work experiences. A career transcript "can be thought of as a certified resumé of lifelong learning," SCANS 2000 Chairman Arnold Packer wrote in a recent paper on the proposal. "The problem with academic transcripts," Packer said, "is that they're designed for students going on to other schools; they have little currency in the workplace." The career transcript "sort of fits between" resumes and school records, Scott Brainard, a SCANS/2000 program evaluator, said. It would contain a job applicant's scores on standardized tests such as the SAT or tests from national vendors like Microsoft.

The transcript also would include an assessment of workplace performance based on supervisors' evaluations, and an assessment of school performance based on benchmarked classroom tasks. The common language of the career transcript would be provided by SCANS (Labor Secretary's Commission on Achieving Necessary Skills), a 1991 panel that identified skills workers need in such areas as planning, communicating, working with others and using technology.

[The above information was excerpted from a report of the Association for Career and Technical Education, which was downloaded from the Internet, January 24, 1999 (http://www.avaonline.org/Weekly.html), ed.]

Carnegie Unit. A system developed in 1905 for standardizing the high school curriculum. Traditionally, students were required to complete a certain number of Carnegie Units (seat time in a specific subject area) in order to graduate (i.e., 4 units of English, 4 of math, 4 of history, 4 of science, etc.). The restructuring of American education from inputs to outputs (outcome-based education) requires the removal of the Carnegie Unit as an indicator of academic exposure in order to graduate.

Certificates of Initial and Advanced Mastery (CIM and CAM). These certificates are a result of the 1990 report *America's Choice: High Skills or Low Wages!* produced by a commission appointed by the National Center on Education and the Economy. This group, led by Marc S. Tucker, was co-chaired by former U.S. Secretaries of Labor and chaired by Ira C. Magaziner, close friend and advisor to the Clintons. [Marc Tucker's organization holds trademark ownership of "Certificate of Initial Mastery" and "Certificate of Advanced Mastery." That being the case, why are states and localities issuing what amounts to a privately validated diploma? ed.]

The following excerpts regarding School-to-Work (STW) and CIM and CAM have been taken from *The School-to-Work Revolution* by Lynn Olson (Perseus Books: Reading, Massachusetts, 1997), pp. 191–193. [The writer recommends Olson's book for those interested in the history of school-to-work activities in the United States, without necessarily endorsing her views, ed.]

The report advocated creating an Americanized version of the European systems, beginning with a radical restructuring of the American high school. All students would have to demonstrate that they had met a high standard of academic achievement during the first stage of their secondary school education. Those who did would earn something called a "certificate of initial mastery," typically at around age 16. [The CIM also requires mastery in the various attitudes and citizenship skills declared necessary for employment and citizenship, ed.] During the upper stage of secondary school, students could either enter college directly, spend additional time preparing for the more competitive colleges and universities, or begin to pursue a professional and technical certificate, which most likely would require some postsecondary education.

At the time, Vera Katz was vice chairman of the House Education Committee in Oregon and a member of the National Center's board of directors. Katz saw an opportunity to apply the adage that "all politics is local." From her offices in Salem, she decided to put the commission's recommendations to the test. The bill that she sponsored in the Oregon legislature mirrored many of the recommendations in *America's Choice*. It passed in 1991 with little opposition and with the strong backing of both the governor and the state's business community.

It called for all students to earn a certificate of initial mastery [CIM] in the core academic subjects by grade 10. After that, all students would pursue a "certificate of advanced mastery" (or CAM) in one of six career pathways for their last two years of high school. Within each pathway (in arts and communications, business and management, health services, human resources, industry and technology, and natural resources) students could earn either a college-preparatory endorsement or a professional-technical endorsement, or both.

Supporters of the new law hailed it as the end of tracking in the high schools. Because all students would have to meet a common academic standard to receive a certificate of initial mastery, all would have to demonstrate command of high-level academic content.

Opponents of the new law depicted it as tracking writ large. They claimed that because students at the age of 16 would have to select a career pathway and decide whether they were pursuing entry in a four-year college or not, their opportunities would be limited. They also worried that the law would encourage students to drop out of high school once they had earned the certificate of initial mastery.

The Oregon Education Association, the state's largest teachers' union, came down hard against the new law. "Schools should not be forged as a service industry for business, nor should we be misdirected by the assumption that our economic ills are somehow the fault of the public schools," the union protested.

The majority of parents and students surveyed also opposed having to choose a career focus by the middle of high school, particularly if young people could not change their minds. However, they liked the idea of providing both college-bound and non-college-bound students with a sense of how their academic courses applied to the real world, and they thought high schools should provide students with some career preparation.

Change Agent. A term used by many people, including President Clinton, leading educators, and social engineers, to identify individuals, highly trained in the group process and in the Delphi Technique. These people are designated to bring about controversial change in education, in the operation of our local and state governments, and at the federal and international levels. (See Preface regarding Iserbyt training to become a change agent, 1947 regarding establishment of National Training Laboratory, 1973 Ronald Havelock Change Agent Guide, 1993 letter from Lawrence Lezotte, and Appendix XIV)

Character Education. Programs which are offered under the following labels of: "values education," "citizenship education," "civic education," and similar titles. The purpose of these courses is to teach students global, core, humanist, no right/no wrong values. The process of identifying the core values involves the entire community, often bypassing the views of elected school boards. The first attempt at devising such a curriculum was made in 1964 when the American Humanist Association began its involvement in "ethical education." The roots of humanistic moral/character education lie in the United Nations Educational, Scientific, and Cultural Association (UNESCO). As a school board director trying to remove values clarification from the curriculum in 1977, I was informed by a Congregational minister at a public school board meeting that parents did not have a right to determine their children's values—that it was up to the government schools to do so!

Many well-meaning groups have attempted to implement "character education" programs with the intention of instilling biblically supported values. It should be noted that attempting to instill Bible-based virtues without spiritual understanding or instruction will always result in less-than-successful results. Also, to base "commonly-held" character qualities on prevailing law does not take into consideration possible changes in the law. Another important consideration with character education is who will teach it. School boards have been consistently hamstrung by civil rights statutes when it comes to hiring teachers whose lifestyles exhibit desirable character qualities and who are good role models for students.

(See 1933 *Humanist Manifesto I*, 1933 Onalee McGraw pamphlet *Secular Humanism in the Schools*, 1941 *Education for Destruction* by Philadelphia, Pennsylvania public school teacher Bessie Burchett, 1946 Brock Chisholm speech, 1964 "Ethical Education" published in *Free Mind* [the journal of the American Humanist Association], 1970 Leonard S. Kenworthy "Background Paper," **Core Values/Virtues**, and Appendix V and XIX)

Charter School. A public school created by a partnership between the private sector and government for the purpose of providing additional academic and other choices for students. Charter schools must comply with federal and state laws in order to receive funding. However, these schools have no elected board, making them an excellent example of taxation without representation. Charter Schools are supported by conservative Republicans as well as liberal Democrats, including President Clinton. (See 1991 NASDC article, **Magnet Schools,** and Appendix XII)

Choice. Allowing parents to enroll their children in any public school within the district or inter-district, or, depending on the scope of the choice program, providing tax credits that can be applied toward tuition in private schools. All schools receiving federal funding must adopt "voluntary" national standards which force students to conform to government-defined and dictated core beliefs, values, and attitudes. "Such choices should include all schools that serve the public and are accountable to public authority," asserted *America 2000: An Education Strategy* (U.S. Department of Education: Washington, D.C., 1991), p. 31, which was developed under Secretary of Education Lamar Alexander.

Presently, parents have the choice to enroll their children in public schools, private or religiously affiliated schools, or home school them. To adopt "choice" solutions will bring government regulation to *all* choices because public money cannot be expended or credited without accountability; it is illegal to do so. The recent move to support privately funded vouchers by giving tax deductions for them is a backdoor approach which will boomerang because even a tax deduction has to be accountable. A study of the gradualism involved in regulation of the child care industry is a case in point. As parents were allowed tax deductions for child care, regulations were suddenly drawn up and imposed, in many cases forcing the home-based child care providers out of business or into an underground operating mode. Family members who were providers of child care were excluded from the exemption, etc. Another result has been the regulation of private and government child care providers to the point that even the food they offer the children must meet a standard. Beware of "choice" proposals, no matter who is offering them. (See 1991 Virginia Birt Baker's "Educational Choice—The Education Voucher, Tax Credits, and the Nonpublic Schools," and Resource List)

Citizenship Education. The following definition comes from "School-to-Work and Ralph Tyler" by Dean Gotcher in *Institution for Authority Research Newsletter* (April 1998):

> Education which produces a socialist (dialectic-minded) citizen who is not concerned with unalienable rights (given by a higher authority) but with human rights (determined by the group in consensus, guided by social engineers). With the former, one is innocent until proven guilty, since facts determine one's guilt; with the latter, one is guilty until proven innocent, since feelings (personal, social felt needs) determine one's guilt or innocence.

(See **Character Education**, **Citizenship Education**, and **Values Clarification**)

Climate. See **Environment**.

Cognitive Dissonance. Disorganization of thoughts, mental confusion, and emotional tension caused by behavior modification which conflicts with one's values. Such manipulation causes many to rethink and modify their values in order to conform to expected behavior. (See 1991 "Paradigm Change: More Magic than Logic" by John C. Hillary, and Appendix XIII and XIX)

Cognitive Domain. (See **Taxonomy of Educational Objectives** and Appendix XIX)

Common Ground. A place of compromise; a *pleasant*-sounding strategy developed by change agents for silencing opposing voices and winning community support. The adjective "bipartisan" is used more and more in a positive way as elected officials accept the perceived "need" to come to consensus in order to avoid conflict. (See **Consensus Build-**

ing, **Delphi Technique**, **Group Process**, **Synthesis**, and Appendix XXII)

Community Education. A process, not a program, by which the total community is involved in decision making by consensus, using the group process and the Delphi Technique. The original purpose of Community Education was and still is to put all services (health, leisure, senior citizen, recreation, etc.) under the umbrella of the school district. Community Education literature states that the purpose of Community Education is to change the attitudes and values of community residents. Community Education seeks to eliminate elected officials, replacing them with politically correct, unelected members of a community council who will not challenge controversial new programs. Government officials who promote Community Education have likened it to the Chinese Communist communal system. "Group process," "participatory democracy," and "sustainable development" are other terms associated with Community Education. (See 1979 October article on school-based clinics, 1994 November Iserbyt article in *Education Week* and Appendix I)

Consensus Building. The process by which students, schools, communities, or groups of people learn to give up individual beliefs and ideas in order to work for "common goals." These may be dictated from the top down (international to local), yet be promoted as grassroots ideologies. Consensus building changes beliefs through pressure to conform to group thinking. (See **Common Ground**, **Delphi Technique**, **Group Process**, **Synthesis** and Appendix XXII)

Core Values/Virtues. The late Ernest L. Boyer, former president of the Carnegie Foundation for the Advancement of Teaching, defined "The Core Virtues" in his book *The Basic School: A Community for Learning—An Introduction to the Basic School* as

> The Basic School is concerned with the ethical and moral dimensions of a child's life. Seven core virtues—honesty, respect, responsibility, compassion, self-discipline, perseverance, and giving—are emphasized to guide the Basic School as it promotes excellence in living, as well as in learning.

He goes on to say under a section called "Living with Purpose" that

> The core virtues of the Basic School are taught both by word and deed. Through curriculum, school climate, and service, students are encouraged to apply the lessons of the classroom to the world around them.

On face value, who could question the above seven core virtues? A problem arises when a student interjects his religion's definition of any of these core virtues. That is when values education becomes sticky and when that student will be put down with a retort from the teacher similar to "That's *your* definition." Unless the core virtues have a solid religious or philosophical base which does not allow for situational ethics, instruction in this controversial area becomes useless, confusing, and a waste of time. (For Example: the culture of the Netsilik Eskimo Tribe, discussed in *Man: A Course of Study* [MACOS], the controversial B.F. Skinner/Jerome Bruner social studies program, considered the putting of elderly people out on the ice to die the "compassionate" and "responsible" thing to do. (See 1975 MACOS entry and Appendix IV, V, and XIX)

Critical Thinking. Professor Benjamin Bloom defines good teaching as "challenging students' fixed beliefs." Critical thinking does exactly that using Bloom's Taxonomy and values clarification to bring about attitudinal and value change. (See Appendix XIX and XXIII)

Delphi Technique. The social scientists' label for a communication technique used to get a diverse group to arrive at a predetermined consensus position through circulating information for comment in several rounds, synthesizing the responses until all agree. If a participant's view cannot be synthesized with the group's view after repeated rounds, then the premise must be declared invalid and abandoned. More recently, the foregoing original definition has evolved into allowing the participant's opposing view to be abandoned in order to achieve consensus. (See **Common Ground**, **Consensus Building** and **Group Process**)

Dialectic, Hegelian. Common ground, consensus, and compromise/thesis-antithesis-synthesis. (See Preface, **Common Ground**, **Consensus Building** and **Group Process**)

Direct Instruction (DI). Developed by Siegfried Engelmann in the 1960s and known as DISTAR (Direct Instruction System for Teaching and Remediation) or SRA's "Reading Mastery," it was one of the models used in Project Follow Through. Direct Instruction is based on Skinnerian operant conditioning and has traditionally been used with special education students. DI requires teachers to teach from a script and to use hand signals and sounds to punctuate the "learning" process. The following excerpts taken from the research of those deeply involved in the development and promotion of Direct Instruction provide important information about this Skinnerian "scientific, research-based" method of instruction.

> (1) "The Direct Instruction Model emphasizes group face-to-face instruction by teachers and aides using carefully sequenced lessons in reading, arithmetic, and language. These programs were designed by Siegfried Engelmann using modern behavioral principles and advanced programming strategies (Becker, Engelmann, & Thomas, 1975), and are published by Science Research Associates under the trade name DISTAR." ("Sponsor Findings from Project Follow Through," Wesley C. Becker and Siegfried Engelmann, University of Oregon, *Effective School Practices*, Winter, 1996, page 33)
>
> (2) "Direct Instruction: A behavior-based model for comprehensive educational intervention with the disadvantaged." Paper presented at the VIII Symposium on Behavior Modification, Caracas, Venezuela, February, 1978. Division of Teacher Education, University of Oregon, Eugene, Oregon. Reference Notes at the end of the article include: "A Constructive Look at Follow Through Results" by Carl Bereiter, Ontario Institute for Studies in Education, and Midian Kurland, University of Illinois at Urbana-Champaign, originally published in *Interchange* (Vol. 12, Winter, 1981), which was reprinted, with permission, in *Effective School Practices* (Winter, 1996).
>
> (3) "First, he (Engelmann) hypothesized that children would generalize their learning in new, untaught situations, if they could respond perfectly to a smaller set of carefully engineered tasks. He also favored a rapid instructional pace and choral group response, punctuated by individual student responses, believing that this would heighten student engagement and allow teachers to perform regular checks for student mastery," from "Making Research Serve the Profession" by Bonnie Grossen, Research Associate with the University of Oregon's

National Center to Improve the Tools of Educators, a project funded by a grant from the U.S. Office of Special Education, and publisher of *Effective School Practices*, published in the Fall 1996 issue of *American Educator*, journal of the American Federation of Teachers.

(See **Effective Schools**, **Mastery Learning**, and Appendix II, III, XVII and XXI)

Effective Schools. The following definition is taken from an article entitled "Effective Schools for Results" published in *The Effective School Report* (July 1984):

> Over the past 30 years there have been three primary programs related to the design and implementation of Effective Schools and successful learning results. Each effort focused on different aspects: behavioral change and application of learning theory to produce successful learning results; identification of sociological factors operating in Effective Schools; teaching strategies to effect learning; and the combination of these variables and practices in a systematic approach to achieve learning and management results. The results of these research programs offer proven practices which, when combined in an interdisciplinary approach, can deliver "predictable excellence" in educational results, the ultimate criterion of an Effective School program.
>
> The following professionals and groups have been involved in this research and development: Wilbur Brookover, Ron Edmonds, Effective Schools Research Movement; B.F. Skinner, Norman Crowder, Robert E. and Betty O. Corrigan (1950–1984), Mastery Learning Practices; R.E. Corrigan, B.O. Corrigan, Ward Corrigan, and Roger A. Kaufman (1960–1984); Project entitled "A Systematic Approach for Effectiveness (SAFE) for District-wide Installation of Effective Schools."

(See July 1984 *Effective School Report* and Appendix VI and XXVI)

Environment. A key term used in behavior modification. Changing one's environment can be utilized to bring about behavioral change. The term "psychologically facilitative climate" means the same thing as "positive school climate."

Facilitate, Facilitator. A change agent who chairs handpicked committees or groups to direct discussion toward the "right," predetermined conclusions or consensus. This process is called "managed change." Facilitators are highly trained to deal with "resisters," those opposed to the predetermined change. (See **Change Agent** and Appendix XIV)

Global Education. Education for the purpose of creating "global citizens." Also known as "world class" education, "holistic" education or the "transformation" of education. A pilot global education curriculum in Iowa (*Catalogue of Global Education Classroom Activities, Lesson Plans, and Resources*, 1991) emphasized topics such as environmentalism, vegetarianism, pantheism, pacifism, population control and global government. In holistic fashion, it was designed to be "integrated" and "infused" throughout the academic curriculum. The Global Alliance for Transforming Education (GATE) in *Education 2000: A Holistic Perspective* (1991) defines holistic (global) education as follows:

> We call for wholeness in the educational process, and for the transformation of educational institutions and policies required to attain this aim. Wholeness implies that each academic discipline provides merely a different perspective

on the rich, complex, integrated phenomenon of life. Holistic education celebrates and makes constructive use of evolving, alternative views of reality and multiple ways of knowing. It is not only the intellectual and vocational aspects of human develpment that need guidance and nurturance, but also the physical, social, moral, aesthetic, creative, and in a nonsectarian sense—spiritual aspects. Holistic education takes into account the numinous mystery of life and the universe in addition to the experiential reality.

(See 1991 Global Alliance for Transforming Education, **Sustainable Development**, **World Class Education**, and Appendix XXVII.)

Gradualism. "Two steps forward, one step back." This political process allows change agents to introduce major social change in bits and pieces, rather than in sweeping proposals. Often semantic deception is used to introduce these changes, focusing attention on the "trees" (the bits and pieces) rather than the "forest." Gradualism keeps the common thread of change out of view while the process of change continues—unnoticed by the general public. (See Preface)

Group Process. The group process uses sensitivity training and other psychological techniques to strip the individual of his individuality and to manipulate him into conformity with politically correct group values and goals. (See 1947 National Training Laboratory, **Consensus Building** and Appendix XXII)

Higher Order Thinking Skills (HOTS). Psychological manipulation using "application, analysis, synthesis, and evaluation" (the higher levels of Bloom's Taxonomy) without the factual knowledge needed for rational and objective thinking. The student is drawn toward making conclusions based on biased, politically correct information and disinformation. (See **Critical Thinking** and Appendix XIX and XXIII)

Holistic (Wholistic) Education. Involving the whole person—"body, soul and spirit." It integrates all subjects and infuses everything with a pantheistic, monistic spirituality. (See 1991 Sustainable Development/GATE entry, **Global Education**, Appendix XXVII, and Resource List *Brave New Schools* information)

Human Capital or Resource. The new label for all children and adults who are being shaped/molded to match the supposed needs of the global economy. The trained workforce product of global/national schooling. (See Appendix XI, XII, XV, and XVIII)

Humanism (Secular). A belief system based on the self-determination of man. Recognized as a religion in the United States. (See 1933 entry on *Humanist Manifesto I* and Onalee McGraw pamphlet and **Character Education**)

Individual Education Plan (IEP). A plan drawn up to accommodate the needs of individual children who traditionally have been labeled "special education." IEPs will, in the future, be used for all children due to the move from traditional competitive education to non-competitive, teach-to-the-test outcome-based education/mastery learning/direct instruction and workforce training (STW) which necessarily use individually prescribed instruction. IEPs often call for the use of behavior modification techniques, including Skinnerian operant conditioning. Title I Special Education regulations contain a *parental consent with the right to refuse requirement* before developing IEPs or using behavior modification techniques, a protection not presently available to non-special education students. It is important that in the future *all* students who have IEPs be covered by this consent requirement and that relevant language, i.e., language covering all such students and all types of "plans" related to behavior disorders, academics, career training, etc., be included in the reauthorization of the *Elementary and Secondary Education Act of 1965*. The transformation of schools from academics to OBE and STW will require IEPs for *all* students. (See 1982–1983 *Profiles in Excellence: Secondary School Recognition Program*)

Individually Prescribed Instruction (IPI) or Individualized Education. Developed in the early 1960s at the University of Pittsburgh's Learning Research and Development Center and at the federally funded laboratory Research for Better Schools in Philadelphia, PA, Individually Prescribed Instruction's development coincided with the Great Society's accountability movement in the sixties which had as its focus equal opportunity and would increasingly deal with outcomes at the *individual* student level. Performance-based education (IPI) calls for mastery learning/direct instruction, which has been gradually implemented over the past thirty years, initially as a result of the emergence of computer technology which permitted the student to work at his own pace with programmed learning. Computer-assisted-instruction using OBE/mastery learning/direct instruction enables the planners to predictably achieve their "outcomes"; i.e., to bring about behavior change as well as training in skills necessary for the global workforce and to collect and store data in such detail as to include information on the *individual* student/adult, necessary for "recycling" and remediation purposes. (See Appendix II, III, VII and VIII)

Life Skills, Life Role Competencies, Lifelong Learning. Preparation for all life roles. The total development of the child—body, mind, and spirit as a learner, worker, consumer, family member, and citizen. What the student will believe, think, and do to meet the exit outcomes. UNESCO coined the phrase "lifelong learning" and identified the life skills/ life role competencies which are being implemented worldwide. Outcome-based education, mastery learning, and direct instruction lend themselves to "lifelong learning" since one can take as long as one wants or needs—forever, if need be—to master whatever the controllers want him to "master." (See Appendix IV)

Literacy, Functional. Basic literacy skills, such as reading a bus schedule, needed to "function." Professor Oettinger of Harvard, who supports functional literacy, says "in the modern context of functionalism, comic books may not be all that bad." (See 1975 Commissioner of Education T.H. Bell comments, 1979 "K-12 Competency-Based Education Comes to Pennsylvania," 1981 Professor Oettinger speech, and 1983 "Functional Literacy and the Workplace")

Local Control. A euphemism to pacify critics of federal control, since all control in the 1990s rests with those who determine the national standards and assessment and provide the money to implement the restructuring. Local educators are free only to find ways to meet those national standards. If local schools do not meet the standards (perform), they will be penalized. Taxpayers should be aware of the fact that state intervention in local schools does not always mean that your school is not doing well academically. It may mean just the opposite: there is still resistance from good educators who refuse to participate in the "teach to the test dumbing down" which is part of performance-based teaching, OBE, mastery learning and direct instruction. Sometimes called "localized control" and often incorrectly associated with block grants which circumvent elected officials at the state level, thereby lessening true local control.

The *1994 Association for Supervision and Curriculum Development Yearbook: The Governance of Curriculum* stated: "...[I]ndeed, local control has been, and continues to be, the most durable myth, or operating principle, of educational governance in the United States." From *Communities and Their Schools* by Don Davies, Ed. (McGraw-Hill: New York, 1981), Miriam Clasby, longtime Community Educator, makes the statement: "...Unless considerations of schooling are placed within the contexts of... world society, they run the danger of unwittingly affirming a past that no longer exists."

Lower-Order Skills. These include knowledge, comprehension, and memorization, the cornerstones of traditional education. HR 6—the 1993 reauthorization of the *Elementary and Secondary Education Act of 1965*—recommended the abandonment of the so-called "lower-order skills," to be replaced by ones which engage students in more "complex tasks." (See 1993 HR 6)

Magnet Schools. A public school focused on a specialized area of learning, often in partnership with a private organization. They were originally promoted as a way to bring about racial integration. In the context of a socialist full employment, planned economy, magnet schools have traditionally been associated with the Soviet polytech system and its quotas for engineers, ballet dancers, etc. Charter schools can also serve the same purpose by providing specialized training. (See 1991 NASDC article, **Charter Schools** and Appendix XII)

Mastery Learning (ML). Proponents of ML believe that almost all children can learn if given enough time, adequate resources geared to the individual learning style of the student, and a curriculum aligned to test items. Mastery learning and direct instruction use Skinnerian methodology (operant conditioning) in order to obtain "predictable" results. The critical teacher behaviors found to correlate directly with high levels of achievement are: specifying learning objectives, setting high standards for mastery, modeling, practicing, eliciting responses from all students, reinforcing correct responses, setting up systems for frequent and consistent rewards, and time on task. Benjamin Bloom, the father of ML, says "the purpose of education is to change the thoughts, actions, and feelings of students," and he developed his mastery learning to do exactly that. (See 1968 Mastery Learning entry, **Direct Instruction**, **Effective School Research**, **Individually Prescribed Education**, **Outcome-based Education**, Appendix VI and XIX)

National Assessment of Educational Progress (NAEP). "The Nation's Report Card" which measures student progress by testing different subject areas in alternate years, carried out from 1965 to 1981 by the Education Commission of the States and since 1983 by the Educational Testing Service under contract to the U.S. Department of Education's National Center for Educational Statistics. Also gathers personal data on children and families in order to fill out longitudinal profiles that include information on students' and parents' attitudes, values, and beliefs. (See Appendix IV and XI)

National Center on Education and the Economy (NCEE). Founded by Marc Tucker, NCEE conceived the CIM and CAM in a 1990 report called *America's Choice: High Skills or Low*

Wages! [Note: NCEE's subsidiary, the National Alliance for Restructuring Education, has been renamed "America's Choice for School Design."] (See **Certificates of Initial and Advanced Mastery**, **New Standards Project** and Appendix XV and XVIII)

National Skills Standard Board (NSSB). NSSB, an independent authority acting under the auspices of the U.S. Department of Labor, has authority to identify occupation clusters and define the student skill level required for certification to work within these clusters. Both schools and businesses would be expected to follow government guidelines and adopt these standards. In other words, students will have to meet the government standards in order to be certified for various kinds of jobs. (See **SCANS**)

New American Schools Development Corporation (NASDC). NASDC was formed in 1991 when President George Bush requested that the business community raise funds to support development of "radical, break the mold" schools—one in each Congressional district. Ann McLaughlin was CEO and President of NASDC. The Request for Proposals stated: "The design may entail major changes in community governance... community structures and functions of other institutions such as public health agencies and welfare departments."(See 1991 NASDC)

New Standards Project (NSP). A partnership formed by Marc Tucker (head of NCEE) and Lauren Resnick, co-director with Robert Glaser of the University of Pittsburgh's Learning Research and Development Center, to establish a "world class" system of standards and assessment that reflects international standards and culminates with the CIM and CAM. (See **Certificates of Initial and Advanced Mastery**)

Outcome-based Education (OBE). The following definition comes from *Excellence in Instructional Delivery Systems: Research and Dissemination of Exemplary Outcome-Based Programs*, a grant application submitted to the United States Department of Education for funding in 1984 by William Spady, Director, Far West Laboratory for Educational Research and Development:

> The concept of Outcome-Based Education emerged from the synthesis of two broad areas of instructional design and improvement. One is known widely as Mastery Learning and is identified with the pioneering work of Benjamin Bloom (1968, 1976), James Block (1971, 1974), Block and Lorin Anderson (1975), and Block and Robert Burns (1977). The other is known as Competency-Based Education (not to be confused with Minimum Competency Testing) and was defined conceptually and operationally by Spady (1977) and by Spady and Mitchell (1977).
>
> The term "Outcome-Based Education" represents a synthesis of these two approaches and took form in the winter of 1980 with the formation of an organization known as the Network for Outcome-Based Schools. OBE is based on the following philosophical premises:
>
> 1. Almost all students are capable of achieving excellence in learning the essentials of formal schooling.
> 2. Success influences self-concept; self-concept influences learning and behavior.
> 3. The instructional process can be changed to improve learning.
> 4. Schools can maximize the learning conditions for all students by
>   a. Establishing a school climate which continually affirms the worth and diversity of all students
>   b. Specifying expected learning outcomes

c. Expecting that all students perform at high levels of learning

d. Ensuring that all students experience opportunities for personal success

e. Varying the time for learning according to the needs of each student and the complexity of the task

f. Having staff and students both take responsibility for successful learning outcomes

g. Determining instructional assignments directly through continuous assessment of student learning

h. Certifying educational progress whenever demonstrated mastery is assessed and validated.

(See Appendix XXVI)

Outcomes. Based on Prof. Benjamin Bloom's *Taxonomy of Educational Objectives*, the outcomes of education in the 1990s and in the 21st century define "What students must know, be able to do, and be like." Determined at the national and international level, they must be met locally. Called "learning goals," "performance objectives," "standards," "competencies," or "capacities," all require students to embrace "new thinking, new strategies, new behavior, and new beliefs" (Lee Droegemueller, Commissioner of Education, "Assessment: Kansas Quality Performance Accreditation [QPA]," Kansas State Board of Education, Topeka, KS, January 1992).

(See 1991 "outcomes" recommended at Jomtien, Thailand "World Conference on Education for All" and Conference of U.S. Coalition on Education for All, and 1994 "U.S. Coalition for All: A History")

Ownership. Encouraging parents to participate in school activities in order for them to feel a part of restructuring—to have a feeling of ownership which will result in parental support for radical change.

Paradigm. A world view; a mental framework for thinking, for organizing information, and for understanding and explaining reality. A paradigm shift occurs when one turns the traditional way of doing things on its head, as is the case with corporate fascist public-private partnerships, the use of unelected boards for decision making, School-to-Work, etc. (See 1991 John C. Hillary's "Paradigm Change; More Magic than Logic")

Parent Report Card. Report card issued by the school that grades parents on how they bring up their children, especially concerning school-related areas. The State of California recently passed a law requiring parent report cards. (See 1993 *Total Quality for Schools* by Joseph C. Fields, and 1999 January Rosemarie Avila article)

Parents as Teachers (PAT). A federally funded program which brings the state educator into homes to make sure each child starts school "ready to learn" and "able to learn." The child is given a personal computer code number, and a computer record is initiated that will enable the national data system to track each child for the rest of his life. Parents as well as children are evaluated. (See 1992 Laura Rogers's articles and **At-Risk Students**)

Participatory Democracy. Opposite of republican, representative, constitutional form of government. Participatory Democracy uses polls, unelected councils, and task forces in which the voice of the people becomes more important than the voice of elected representatives. Example: 1998–1999 investigation of President Clinton and the use by the U.S.

Senate of *polls* rather than *principles* to determine whether the President is fit to remain in office. Form of government supported by socialists and communists. (See 1984 April letter to President Reagan from Willard W. Garvey, Executive Director of the National Center for Privatization, which said in part "Privatization is now an idea whose time has come.... The knowledge, communication, and computer industry can make political representatives obsolete.")

Partnership. Usually refers to a new concept of governance which calls for a merger of the public and private sectors, commonly known as corporate fascism or socialism. Partnerships between government and the private sector result in a breakdown of the representative form of government and a lessening of accountability to the taxpayer. (See 1981 "President's Task Force on Private Sector Initiatives," 1984 *Washington Post* article "Industrial Policy Urged for GOP" and **Participatory Democracy**)

Planning, Programming, Budgeting, Management System (PPBS) and Management by Objectives (MBO). A system used for planning and accounting which calls for: 1) establishing a goal; 2) setting forth plans to achieve it; 3) funding the effort; 4) evaluating success or failure at the end of the funding cycle; and 5) adjusting plans to achieve the goal, including funding, and starting over again with more precise focus. The following background information is taken from *Goals 2000: Restructuring Our Schools... Restructuring Our Society* by Kathie Finnegan (Hearthstone Publishing, Ltd.: Oklahoma City, Oklahoma, 1996), pp. 306–307:

> ...Originally developed in 1961 by Robert McNamara when he was Secretary of Defense in cooperation with the Rand Corporation. PPBS is the vehicle for achieving predetermined goals in government.
>
> In 1961, following suggestions of the Rand Corporation, President Kennedy launched PPBS in the Department of Defense (DOD) under Robert Strange McNamara. Although PPBS was clumsy, costly, and ineffective (and no more successful in industry than it was in managing the Vietnam War), President Johnson initiated PPBS in 1965 throughout the entire legislative branch due to its administrative effectiveness. Later it was put into all branches of the federal government.
>
> A key point about running the government by PPBS is that it is government by appointed—not elected—officials. In 1972 the International Institute of Applied Systems Analysis (another name for PPBS) was established in Austria with twelve nations participating, including the United States and the Soviet Union. PPBS under many names has become the dominant organization/restructuring/re-engineering model for most of corporate America and many institutions and organizations. PPBS has been described as applied scientific socialism. It is used to control what people produce, what they consume, how they spend their work and leisure time, what they think, and how they react to various stimuli.
>
> The concept applied to education works this way: if you know what you have to start with (young, impressionable children) and you know what you want to end up with (citizen-workers for a centrally planned global economy), it is possible to design a system that will achieve that "outcome." PPBS is a continuous loop, renewable/reviewed/re-funded every three, five, or seven years so that basic assumptions and goals can be re-calibrated.

(See 1967 PPBS in California, 1972 June 11th speech by Mary Thompson, **Systems**, and Appendix IX and XXII)

Privatization. Transferring policy-making and implementation from the public tax-supported domain into the private or business sectors, where educational leaders and elected boards become accountable to wealthy funders (such as the Carnegie, Ford, Danforth, Pew, Rockefeller, Spencer, or Annenberg foundations, to name a few), multinational corporations, and non-profit organizations, rather than to concerned parents and taxpayers. (See 1981 President's Task Force on Private Sector Initiatives)

Psychological Approach. "1. A method of teaching in which new subject matter and ideas are presented in a manner appropriate to the way in which the pupil learns and through situations that are meaningful to him" is the definition given by the *Dictionary of Education, 3rd Edition* by Carter V. Good, Ed. (McGraw-Hill: New York, 1973), published under the auspices of Phi Delta Kappa. It is also called a Child-Experience Approach, Functional Approach. Contrast with logical method.

Psychomotor Domain. (See **Taxonomy of Educational Objectives** and Appendix XIX)

Quality. The following definition is provided in *Filling the Gaps: An Overview of Data on Education in Grades K–12* (National Center for Educational Statistics (NCES), Office of Educational Research and Improvement [ID: NCES 92–132]: Washington, D.C., 1992). In the section called "Teachers" on page 5 we find:

> Beginning in the 1980s NCES collected detailed information on the characteristics and qualifications of teachers. Information collected includes years of full- and part-time teachers' experience in public and private schools, major and minor degree fields for all earned degrees (from Associate degree to Ph.D.), type of certificate in teaching assignment fields, college coursework in mathematics and science, and, to a limited extent, participation in in-service education. The inclusion of these measures in SASS [Schools and Staffing Survey] allows for an assessment of the qualifications of the current teaching force.
>
> But the term "qualifications" is not synonymous with "quality." The characteristics that contribute to good teaching are many, and no single configuration of traits, qualifications, or behaviors unvaryingly produces optimal student outcomes in all situations. NCES teacher surveys have concentrated on collecting data on "qualifications," rather than trying to define "quality." In order to define and measure "quality," characteristics and qualifications of teachers must be related to growth in student achievement.

[Ed. Note: This definition forces teachers to comply with *Goals 2000* criteria and to teach to the test.] (See 1992 *Filling the Gaps*)

Regional Education Laboratories. The following definition comes from *Goals 2000: Restructuring Our Schools... Restructuring Our Society* by Kathy Finnegan (ibid.), pp. 306–307.

> The U.S. Department of Education maintains ten RELs ("labs") in scattered geographic areas—all under the jurisdiction of OERI [the Office of Educational Research and Improvement]. The labs function as field offices of OERI, assisting the states under their jurisdiction in finding and implementing educational re-

sources (such as the "validated" programs of the NDN [National Diffusion Network]) suited to their needs. They also generate and oversee research projects, print publications, and provide training programs to teachers and administrators. Each lab puts out a catalog of its publications. Under Goals 2000 the regional labs are charged with designing appropriate materials for their clients if suitable ones cannot be found. The ten regions are:

1. The Northeastern Region (Maine, New Hampshire, Vermont, Massachusetts, Rhode Island, Connecticut, New York, and Puerto Rico and the Virgin Islands) served by the Education Alliance for Equity and Excellence at Brown University in Providence, Rhode Island.

2. The Mid-Atlantic Region (New Jersey, Pennsylvania, Delaware, Maryland, and Washington, D.C.) served by the Center for Research in Human Development and Education at Temple University in Philadelphia.

3. The Appalachian Region (Virginia, West Virginia, Kentucky, and Tennessee) served by the Appalachia Educational Laboratory (AEL) in Charleston, West Virginia.

4. The Southeastern Region (North Carolina, South Carolina, Georgia, Florida, Alabama, and Mississippi) served by the Southeastern Regional Vision for Education (SERVE) in Greensboro, North Carolina.

5. The Southwestern Region (Arkansas, Louisiana, Oklahoma, Texas, and New Mexico) served by the Southwest Educational Development Laboratory (SEDL) in Austin, Texas.

6. The Central Region (North Dakota, South Dakota, Nebraska, Kansas, Missouri, Colorado, and Wyoming) served by the Mid-Continent Regional Educational Laboratory (McREL) in Aurora, Colorado.

7. The Midwestern Region (Minnesota, Wisconsin, Michigan, Ohio, Indiana, Illinois, and Iowa) served by the North Central Regional Educational Laboratory (NCREL) in Oak Brook, Illinois.

8. The Northwestern Region (Alaska, Washington, Oregon, Idaho, and Montana) served by the Northwest Regional Educational Laboratory (NWREL) in Portland, Oregon.

9. The Western Region (California, Nevada, Utah, and Arizona) served by the Far West Laboratory for Educational Research and Development (FWL) in San Francisco, California.

10. The Pacific Region (Hawaii, American Samoa, Commonwealth of the Northern Mariana Islands, Federated States of Micronesia, Kosrae, Pohnpei, Chuuk and Yap, Guam, Republic of the Marshall Islands, and the Republic of Palau) served by the Pacific Regional Educational Laboratory (PREL) in Honolulu, Hawaii.

Restructuring. A systemic or system-wide movement to change the entire education model in order to achieve the new national goals; also known as "transformation." This lifelong, revolutionary, never-ending change system (paradigm shift) includes mastery learning, direct instruction, outcome-based education, Total Quality Management, and partnerships with business and community leaders, churches, and parents. Restructuring calls for the involvement of carefully selected, politically correct unelected members of the community in the decision making process. (See 1991 Hillary's "Paradigm Change: More Magic than Logic," **Paradigm**, **School Reform**, **Systemic Change** and Appendix XII)

SCANS (The Secretary's Commission on Achieving Necessary Skills). SCANS was created under Elizabeth Dole as Secretary of Labor. It links education to the Department of Labor in a joint effort to create a workforce that meets the future needs for a global workforce and produces students who are competent in prescribed work skills including attitudes and group thinking. It can direct students into specific training, limit their options, and bring intrusive government influences into all aspects of life. (See 1990 SCANS article, **Certificates of Initial Mastery and Advanced Mastery**, and Appendix XV and XVIII)

School-Based Decision Making. A form of school governance that replaces elected school boards and/or central school system administrators with a school site council consisting of unelected principals, teachers, and selected parents who support the radical changes called for by restructuring. Designed to implement the changes with minimal hindrance, it is not accountable to elected officials, dissenting parents, or the taxpayers. It is also known as "site-based management." It could be referred to as "taxation without representation." (See 1977 National School Board Association [NSBA] President's Warnings at NSBA Conference)

School-to-Work or School-to-Career. Legislative initiative which changes focus of education to workforce training instead of information-based academic learning. The link or partnership between the schools and businesses established through the SCANS competencies which provide a criterion both for testing and training the global workforce, also known as "limited learning for lifelong labor." (See **SCANS** and Appendix XV and XVIII)

Semantic Deception. The use by change agents of words and terms which mean one thing to the average, normal, common sense American but have an entirely different meaning for the change agent who is attempting to restructure the schools or implement controversial programs. Some examples are: higher order thinking skills (HOTS), critical thinking, basic skills, core values, direct instruction, health, etc. Part of Appendix XXVI says: "...[P]olicy analysts sometimes use the rituals of research to confound and weaken political or scientific opponents, a form of research that appears similar to the 'black' magic of witches." (See 1972 Mary Thompson paper on PPBS, and Appendix XI and XXVI)

Skill Standards. The following excerpts have been taken from *The School-to-Work Revolution* by Lynn Olson (ibid.), pp. 178–179. [The writer recommends Olsen's book for those interested in the history of school-to-work activities in the United States, without necessarily endorsing her views, ed.]

> Skill standards spell out what workers within an industry or cluster of occupations should know and be able to do to succeed on the job. They indicate to employers the skills of job applicants and provide workers with a widely recognized credential. They could improve the quality of career information available to schools, employers, and young people. For example, they could help improve the match between what is learned in school and what is necessary on the job. In 1992 the federal government funded 22 pilot projects to test whether industries in the United States could develop voluntary skill standards. The projects covered industries ranging from printing, metalworking, and electronics to retail, hospitality, and tourism. Of the 22 pilot projects funded so far, the vast majority are led by trade associations or industry groups. In 1994 the Congress created a National Skill Standards Board to help promote the development of such voluntary efforts. The Board is charged with clustering occupations or industries into broad groups

that would cover most of the workforce in the United States. In addition, it is supposed to develop a common national framework in which skill standards could be developed.

(See 1990 SCANS article and Appendix XV and XVIII)

Special Education. Planned for all children "at risk" of not meeting the national standards. Special Education has traditionally required Individual Education Plans (IEPs) for economically disadvantaged, learning disabled, and gifted and talented students. Special Education IEPs are a necessary component of OBE/ML/DI and school-to-work programs. (See **At-Risk Students**)

Sustainable Development. "World Class Schools and the Social Studies" from *Social Studies Horizons* by Dr. Cordell Svengalis (Iowa Dept. of Education: Des Moines, Iowa, Vol. 3, No. 1, Fall 1990) says in part:

> ...a World Class education program would have as one of its major objectives the development of skills and understandings grounded in an ethical/moral context. This ethical/moral context would be based on the idea of assuming a sense of responsibility toward our interrelated planetary future.... Perhaps the most compelling vision of our time is that of a **"sustainable society"** [emphasis in original]. Our global society, in terms of the environmental degradation, explosive population growth in the Third World, energy shortages, pollution, conflict, crime, drugs, poverty, and just sheer complexity, is not sustainable into the 21st century.... Students need to understand these things as part of their World Class education.

(See 1991 GATE entry, **Global Education**, Resource List, and Appendix XXVII)

Synthesis. One of the higher-order thinking skills in Bloom's *Taxonomy*. Uses the principles of Hegelian dialectics to join the beliefs or ideas (theses) of individual students into a new joint belief—the compromise solution or synthesis. (See **Taxonomy of Educational Objectives** and Appendix XIX)

Systemic Change or School Reform. Total holistic transformation: top down, system-wide, international as well as national. "Systemic" means one mind directing one body with many parts. It includes preschools, public elementary and high schools, private schools, colleges, universities, health clinics, and every other kind of community partner. The planned deadline is school year 2000–2001. (See **Global Education** and **Restructuring**)

Systems, Systems Design, Systems Approach. The following definition comes from Appendix VIII:

> When scientific and experimental methods are applied in an orderly and comprehensive way to the planning of instructional tasks, or to entire programs, this process is sometimes known as "systems design," or the "systems approach to instructional development." Implicit in the systems approach is the use of clearly stated objectives, experimentally derived data to evaluate the results of the system, and feedback loops which allow the system to improve itself based on evaluation.
>
> A systematic approach usually involves needs assessment (to determine

what the problem really is); a solution selection (to meet the needs); development of instructional objectives (if an instructional solution is indeed needed); an analysis of tasks and content to meet the objectives; selection of instructional strategies; sequencing of instructional events; selection of media; developing or locating the necessary resources; try out/evaluation of the effectiveness of the resources; revision of resources until they are effective; and recycling continuously through the whole process. The systems approach is basic to educational technology. Individual learning requires systematic planning because it may operate with little or no direct intervention by the teacher.

(See **PPBS**)

Taxonomy of Educational Objectives. From the book titled *Taxonomy of Educational Objectives: The Classification of Educational Goals* by David Krathwohl, Benjamin Bloom, and Bertram Massie (Longman, Inc.: New York, 1956). Bloom explains the purpose of the taxonomy when he defines good teaching as "challenging the students' fixed beliefs." He also says that "The purpose of education and the schools is to change the thoughts, actions, and feelings of students." It is important to remember that Bloom is the father of OBE/mastery learning/direct instruction which are based on Pavlov and Skinner's experiments with animals (operant conditioning). Remember also that mastery learning and direct instruction have been designed to implement Bloom's taxonomy in the cognitive, affective (values) and psychomotor domains.

The six levels of Bloom's taxonomy through which a child must travel in order to have his world view reorganized—his values changed—are Knowledge (list, match, name, define, state), Comprehension (explain, paraphrase, summarize, describe), Application (relate, solve, use, show, classify), Analysis (support, differentiate, generalize), Synthesis (design, produce, predict), and Evaluation (conclude, assess, critique).

The taxonomy has been used by teachers, curriculum builders, and educational research workers as one device to attack the problem of specifying in detail the expected outcomes of the learning process. When educational objectives are stated in operational and detailed form, it is possible to make appropriate evaluation instruments and to determine with some precision which learning experiences are likely to be of value in promoting the development of the objective and which are likely to be of little or no value. Bloom, in attempting to do research on what might be called "peak learning experiences," produced evidence which suggested that "a single hour of classroom activity under certain conditions may bring about a major reorganization in cognitive as well as affective behaviors." (See Appendix XIX)

Teacher Tenure. A policy which traditionally protected incompetent teachers from being fired. Retention of teacher tenure becomes more and more attractive as competent academically-oriented teachers have their jobs threatened only to be replaced by non-academically oriented teachers trained in TQM whose expertise lies in the facilitation of learning (using Pavlovian/Skinnerian "Best Practices," providing the technological resources necessary to bring about change of behavior, predictable results, and training in workforce skills).

Total Quality Management (TQM). A socialist strategy for managing continual improvement through statistical tools and decision-making techniques. Administered through site-based management (school-based decision making), it emphasizes the "customer" or "stake-holder" including everyone but the concerned parent. TQM is simply a refined version of Planning, Programming, Budget Systems (PPBS) and Management by Objectives (MBO) and has much in common with the principles underlying continuous progress mastery learning. Edwards W. Deming, the physicist who originally introduced TQM to the Japanese as a manufacturing management process to use during their industrial rebuilding after World War II, said in an interview at the University of Pittsburgh: "What I took to Japan was *not* the American way." (See Appendix XXII)

UNESCO (United Nations Educational, Scientific, and Cultural Organization). A specialized agency of the United Nations, headquartered in Paris, France. UNESCO began in 1946 with twenty member states and now has 171 members. In a brochure called "What is UNESCO?" we find: "UNESCO's Constitution says that 'since wars begin in the minds of men, it is in the minds of men that the defenses of peace must be constructed.' Building these defenses through international cooperation remains UNESCO's top priority."

Universal Values. Honesty, integrity, tolerance, and other values believed to be common to all the people and the world's cultures. This belief is counter to the facts of history. (See **Core Values/Virtues**)

U.S.-Soviet Education Agreements. President Eisenhower signed the first U.S.-Soviet Education Agreement in 1958. It was just one of many agreements negotiated with the Soviets which dealt with space, medicine, culture, and other areas. The purpose of the education agreement was to initiate exchanges of teachers from both countries and to study one another's curriculum and textbooks, but *not* to engage in the development of curriculum. In 1985 the Reagan Administration and the Carnegie Corporation departed from this less controversial agenda when they negotiated agreements with the Soviet Union which dealt not only with teacher and student exchanges but also with cooperation in curriculum development, including "joint research on the application of computers in early elementary education, focusing especially on the teaching of higher level skills and complex subjects to younger children." This aspect paved the way for Russian teachers to visit and work in American schools including those specializing in school-to-work activities. (See 1991 articles "Cop Swap," "Week in the Subway," 1994 "School Exams… Russian Origin," 1995 "Russian Teacher Review Works in SAD 53, Maine," and Appendix XXIII)

Values Clarification (VC). A strategy for changing a student's values, usually, but not always, associated with the work of Sidney Simon. VC prods students to examine their own values in light of their upbringing and if they find that their values are a result of their parents' direction, they are told that their values are not valid. In order for values to be valid they must be chosen freely by the student without any influence from church or family. The VC process usually takes place in the group with exercises and games which create dependency amongst members of the group and which contribute to group consensus on what is right and wrong, based on situational ethics. (See **Character Education**, **Citizenship Education**, and **Synthesis**)

Vouchers. Vouchers and tuition tax credits are used by parents to pay for children's education in private schools of their choice. A voucher is a direct method of payment to a private school of a certain amount of tax money provided by a public municipality, whereas a tuition tax credit is a form of delayed reimbursement by deduction of a certain portion of one's taxes related to the cost of private school tuition. The dangers of such choice measures for parents are best expressed in the old adage "He who pays the piper calls the tune." (See 1982 entry "Public Service, Public Support, Public Accountability" by Chester Finn, former Assistant Secretary, Office of Educational Research and Improvement [OERI], U.S. Department of Education, under Secretary William Bennett, and **Choice**)

Work-Based Learning. Programs designed to teach older students (grades 7 and up) work skills on the job site, thereby assuring that the student can perform the tasks needed by local employers when the student graduates from public school. (See 1976 May 21st article "Cuban Children Combine Studies, Work" from *The Los Angeles Times*)

World Class Education. A term loosely bandied about by government and corporate change agents. It simply means Third World-class academic education and first-class school-to-work/school-to-career Soviet/German (Socialist) polytech education. It is a non-competitive system based on national standards and benchmarks that match international standards. Students must embrace a common set of universal beliefs and values in preparation for the next century. This process uses technology (computers, robotics, etc.), mastery learning, continuous progress, and individual education plans which allow for lifelong learning as promoted by the United Nations. (See **Global Education**)

Behaviorist Terminology

The following list includes words, terms, and phrases used by educators and behavioral psychologists, scientists, sociologists, etc., in their educational research and literature as well as in background papers for elected officials. This list should be of use to the average parent who may not be familiar with these terms, thereby not being alert to their *real* meaning, allowing their children to be subjected to experimental behavior modification programs which are found in all areas of curriculum from social studies to reading instruction to workforce training. Although some of these words can also be used in a non-behaviorist context, most of them specifically relate to the field of behavioral psychology which holds the evolutionary world view that man is an animal, without soul, conscience, intellect, creativity, and free will. If parents, elected officials, and others are familiar with these words—not necessarily having to thoroughly understand their definitions—they will be able to identify programs which may not be in the best interest of their children or their constituents. One can point to a barrage of education programs and legislation voted on during the past thirty-four years at the local, state, and federal levels which might not have been approved or passed had our elected officials and their constituents recognized and understood the meaning of the words on this list.

The reader should also refer to their own dictionary or *Webster's New World Dictionary of the American Language, 2nd College Edition* (William Collins & The World Publishing Co., Inc.: Cleveland, Ohio, 1974) from which several of the following definitions were taken, or this book's Glossary and/or Index to find definitions for some of the words and the location in this book of instances where the majority of them are used. For instance, appendices II, III, V and VII deal extensively with the subject of behavioral terminology.

accountable, accountability All sorts of mischief has been carried out "in the name of accountability," from the implementation of individualized education—outcome-based education and all its tentacles—to the collection of personal and private data, to the justification of bigger budgets for education, using PPBS, etc. Traditionally, accountability meant being legally responsible for taxpayers' money; making sure students had adequate resources, teachers, etc., in order to learn. The state was responsible for offering an educational experience for *all* children—input—not for assuring that every *individual* child would learn what he was taught. Children were allowed to receive less than perfect grades for their efforts and not all children got what we used to call "the most" from their educational experience. However, the state's legal responsibility had been fulfilled.

   Accountability increasingly means that the government schools must be accountable for predetermined results (results, performance, outcome-based education). Legislation is in the works to hold teachers accountable for student results which means students are no longer held responsible for their work or lack of work. In order to implement such an accountability system, systematic, scientific, research-based education (based on behaviorist principles) is being implemented. Such education which teaches to the test, using Skinnerian operant conditioning, has predictable and measurable, if narrow, results and serves the limited learning needs of the school-to-work agenda. The results of such narrow education are measurable data which must be collected at the individual student and teacher level, able to be stored in the computer for recycling and remediation purposes.

   The use of such a narrow, rigid method of training assures predictable results which carry out the requirements of the new definition of accountability. That is why OBE, ML DI, and Effective School Research all claim that "almost all children can learn." Skinner said, "You will teach your student as he wants to be taught, but never forget that it is within your power to make him want what you want him to want." There is virtually no way a student can avoid "learning" exactly what the planners want him to learn unless he actually rebels against the method/system which considers him nothing more than a machine/animal to be conditioned/trained. (See Appendix XXIV)

affective (Feelings, emotions)

alignment (All teacher training and curriculum resources are aligned with tests, assessments, etc.; i.e., teach to the test)

animal, animal psychology (Used to develop operant conditioning programs)

assessment, assessment strategies, authentic assessment (See Glossary)

attitude, attitudinal (Point of view; dealing with attitudes, values, beliefs)

automaticity (Level of training at which behavior becomes automatic ["knee jerk" reflex])

Behavior Analysis (One of twenty different intervention strategies that was used in Project Follow Through)

The following four behaviorist definitions are taken from *Dictionary of Education, 3rd Edition* by Carter V. Good, Ed. (McGraw-Hill; New York, 1973), published under the auspices of Phi Delta Kappa:

behavior modification: (Techniques for dealing with maladaptive behavior either through classical conditioning [for example, avoiding anxiety in a specified situation by conditioning a response incompatible with anxiety] or through operant conditioning [as by arranging and managing reinforcement contingencies so that desired behaviors are increased in frequency and maintained and undesired behaviors are decreased in frequency and/or removed]. When used with the nonfunctioning or disruptive school child, behavior changes are measurable by continuous assessment and graphic means; behavior management, though using many of the same techniques, is a less precise method.)

behavior shaping: (The process by which a target response or series of responses is developed through the use of strategically placed reinforcers; a term used primarily by those who identify themselves with B.F. Skinner's operant conditioning.)

behavior theory: (A view which regards human behavior as primarily rooted in the experiential history of the organism, as having been learned, and as susceptible to modification by psychological means; emphasis is on the nature of the learning processes that underlie behavioral change, and these processes are regarded as essentially identical to those involved in any other kind of complex human learning.)

behaviorism: (A systematic approach to or school of psychology, which regards objective, observable manifestations such as motor and glandular responses as the key to an understanding of human behavior; consciousness, feeling, and other subjective phenomena are rejected as unnecessary; places much reliance on the study of behavior of animals under controlled conditions; originated with the work of M.F. Meyer, A.P. Weiss, and J.B. Watson during the first two decades of the present century; the most widely known contemporary exponent was B.F. Skinner.)

Best Practices (Term often used in performance-based educational teacher training material which refers to behavioristic, scientific, research-based teaching practices)

climate (Environment)

clinical practice (Diagnose and prescribe)

coaching (To instruct and train)

competent (Adequate)

computer-assisted instruction (C-A-I: programmed learning)

conditioned (Having developed a conditioned reflex or behavior pattern)

conditioned response (Conditioned reflex in which the response—e.g., secretion of saliva in a dog—is occasioned by a secondary stimulus—e.g., the ringing of a bell repeatedly—associated with the primary stimulus—e.g., the sight of meat)

criterion-referenced testing (Testing which does not compare student's scores with those of the group, but which has the student working at his own pace and in competition with no one but himself; such testing is necessary for individually prescribed instruction, mastery learning, and direct instruction, all of which teach to the test. Traditional education does not teach to the test, thereby exposing the student to a much wider and rich knowledge base, some of which he is never tested on, but which becomes an important part of his understanding of the world around him.)

critical thinking (See Glossary)

cue (A secondary stimulus that guides behavior, often without entering consciousness)

direct instruction or Direct Instruction (SRA's DISTAR: Direct Instruction System for Teaching and Remediation, also known as "Reading Mastery" or any programmed learning based on the principles of Skinnerian operant conditioning)

education (The following definition of education is taken from a 1972 speech given by Mary Thompson on the subject of PPBS in education: "The objective of education is to measure and diagnose the child in order to prescribe a program to develop his feelings and emotions, values and loyalties toward predetermined behavioral objectives. Drawing it right down to basics, we are talking about *conditioned response* in human terms. Pavlov experimented on dogs.")

effective, effective school research, effective schools (International school restructuring movement which seeks to level the playing field for all children, thereby dumbing down the particularly bright and average students; a form of redistribution of brains, intelligence. [See Glossary and Appendix XXVI])

elicit (Used in relation to a specific behavior: to draw forth, evoke, cause to be revealed)

enabling (To make possible or effective)

environment, environmental (Climate—"psychologically facilitative" when applied to education)

exceptional (Teachers who are trained to use operant conditioning. Also, master teachers)

experimental (Used in relation to research conducted on teachers and students, usually without their "informed" consent. Legislation is on the books which protects prisoners from such experimental research.)

extinguish (Stop certain behavior)

fade (As behavior reaches "automaticity" level, use of operant conditioning is gradually reduced to zero level)

guiding (Helping student to model [copy] teacher's behavior)

incentives (Motivators, rewards, special treatment to assure correct behavior)

indicators (Specify what students must know and be able to do)

individualized education, individualized education plans/programs (IEPS) (See Glossary for **Mastery Learning, Direct Instruction**)

instructional design technology (The use of such technology can be compared to assembly-line type of teaching which requires teacher to perform in a systematic, exact manner, so that the student's every action [behavior] can be scientifically measured and replicated; to shape and mold the child as one would shape and mold a piece of clay)

intensive, systematic phonics or any other "scientific" research-based instruction (A simple way to teach which uses operant conditioning; a method which must be understood and rejected if teaching is to remain "teaching" and not become behavior modification and "training." Some excellent traditional phonics programs are incorrectly described as "intensive and systematic direct instruction of phonics" when in fact they are not, since they do not use operant conditioning.)

know and be able to do (See Glossary for **Taxonomy of Educational Objectives**)

latent period (Interval between stimulation and response)

management skills (Related to TQM [See Glossary for **Quality**])

mastery, mastery learning (Based on Skinnerian operant conditioning; same as direct instruction [See Glossary])

measurement (Critical component of Skinnerian operant conditioning)

measurement by objectives (In education, means only the prepared script will be taught and tested, or teach to the test [See Glossary for **Quality**])

merit pay (Tied to teacher performance, effectiveness; whether performance results in student achievement [See Glossary for **Quality**])

modeling (Performing behavior teacher wants students to copy)

monitoring (Observing behavior of student and teacher; teacher behavior must be monitored daily and weekly to make sure teacher doing prepared script correctly, like an actor performing before his audience)

neurological (Response which strictly deals with the nervous system; in education, related to operant conditioning which bypasses the brain; often referred to as "knee-jerk")

observe, observation (Of student and teacher [See **monitoring** above])

operant conditioning, behavior modification (At every step, immediate feedback or reward desirable, immediate repetition and elaboration of the correct response used)

outcome-based education (Known as OBE; formerly known as mastery learning combined with Competency-Based Education)

outcomes (Results, performance, competencies, standards, achievement)

overt response (Can be measured and timed; very important in Direct Instruction, DISTAR/ECRI-type programs since Skinner said a response must be oral; why children are required to respond in unison and orally)

penalize (Mostly in regard to teachers who "just don't get it"; cut their classroom supplies, give them bad performance rating, etc., get rid of them by any means [early retirement, etc.] and hire teachers trained in TQM)

penalize failure (School doesn't "produce" desired results, using the "systems design/approach"; state departments of education will know teachers aren't teaching the script, aren't teaching to the test, aren't using programmed learning, operant conditioning; school will be punished in order to get the results required by Goals 2000 and School to Work.)

performance-based (Outcome, result, achievement, standards, competency-based, necessary for workforce training)

precise (Exact, able to be "measured")

predictable (Able to be accurately predicted because dependent on measurement and is scientifically based; does not allow for free will)

predictable response (If operant conditioning is used, one can predict the response; it is virtually a "sure" thing; automatic response which bypasses the brain)

programmed learning (Independent learning by a pupil, who advances little by little, through a series of questions, the answers to which are given elsewhere in the programmed textbook or computer software program; computer-assisted-instruction)

prompt (Word used to describe action to remind or help someone remember a line, as for an actor; often referred to as a cue)

psychological climate (The careful and systematic arrangement of the student's environment to facilitate whatever behavior is desired by the teacher)

psychology (The modern version of psychology relates to nothing but behavior)

quality teaching (Characteristics and qualifications of teachers related to growth in student outcomes, results, performance, achievement; the opposite of traditional education where "inputs" [resources, books, teachers, science labs, etc.] were legally required for education, but not student "results" which were considered the responsibility of the student. Obviously, the behaviorists consider students as machines, *not* human beings, since they don't take into account the fact that human beings have free will and may just not want to learn when and what the behaviorists want them to learn. Such a definition of quality teaching, which puts the 100% onus on the teacher, is sure to cause an exodus from public education of our nation's finest teachers.)

rate (Speed of reaction; Skinner method demands a high, quick, fast rate of response; otherwise student will have time to reflect on what he/she is doing; high rate of response assures that the subject will respond without thinking)

reflect (Give back an image of; think critically about your practice [teachers]; recommended for teachers when monitored by performance raters)

reflex (Neurological reaction; i.e., as when one automatically withdraws his hand from a hot stove)

reinforce, reinforcement (To increase the probability of a response to a stimulus by giving a reward or ending a painful stimulus)

replicate (Repetition of an experiment under controlled conditions so that a specific result may be observed)

research-based ("Scientific, research-based instructional practices" has come to mean teaching/training based on a world view that considers man an animal without a soul, conscience, creativity, or free will whose behavior can be changed using operant conditioning and other manipulative psychological techniques without his knowledge or "informed" consent. Government research is necessarily "scientific, research-based" since government's world view is based on evolution and Skinner. Private research is another matter since it is not required to be based on any particular world view, but often reflects the same viewpoint. Unfortunately, many religious and private schools are using methods and programs based on "scientific" research.)

response (Reaction, reply)

script (Teachers using Skinnerian operant conditioning *must* teach from a prepared curriculum format; they are not allowed to deviate from that script)

sociology (The science of human society and of social relations, organization, and change; specifically, the study of the beliefs, values, interrelationships, etc., of societal groups and of the principles or processes governing social phenomena. Of interest here is that many of the principal promoters of outcome-based education, Spady et al., which includes Skinnerian operant conditioning and effective schools research, are for the most part sociologists, not educators.)

stimulus (Any action or agent which causes a change in activity in an organism, organ, or part, as something that excites an end organ, starts a nerve impulse, activates a muscle, etc.)

succeed, success (Meet the required criteria)

systems, systematic, systems theory (Basis for current restructuring of education. [See Glossary for **Planning, Programming and Budgeting Systems, Systems, Systems Design** and **Systems Approach**])

taxonomy (See Glossary for **Taxonomy of Educational Objectives**)

teaching practice (Teacher performance, not necessarily academic or knowledge-based)

technology (Any form of instructional media)

theory into practice (The late Madeline Hunter's Mastery Teaching: Instructional Theory into Practice (ITIP). Translating into practice in the classroom the theory teacher has learned; experimentation on the students)

threshold (Baseline, in operant terms, where subject can be conditioned)

Total Quality Management (Management technique which uses behavior modification [See Glossary for **Systems** and **Total Quality Management**])

APPENDICES

APPENDICES

Appendix I

Excerpts from *Community-Centered Schools*

Community-Centered Schools: The Blueprint, Montgomery County, Maryland Schools, as proposed by Dr. Nicholaus L. Englehardt and Associates, Consultants, and written by Dr. Walter D. Cocking (New York City: April 1, 1946). This was probably the most important blueprint for the nation, although The Hawaii Master Plan [see 1969] certainly follows in its footsteps. Dr. Paul Mort's statement below is right on target. It took exactly fifty years to implement "The Blueprint" in every school of the nation. Letter of transmittal states:

> [The] program should be put into operation gradually... and Dr. Paul Mort and others have accumulated evidence which shows a period of almost fifty years between the establishment of need (need assessment, etc.) and the school programs geared to meet it.
>
> If the school as an agency of society is to justify itself for the period ahead of us, it must be accepted that its fundamental function is to serve the people of the entire community, the very young children, the children of middle years, early adolescent youth, older youth and the adults as well.
>
> The task of the teacher of the future is a greatly different task than that which teachers usually performed in the past. The fundamental equipment expected of the teacher of yesterday was knowledge of the subject he taught. Modern education demands teachers who are acquainted by experience as well as by study with our democratic society and who participate actively in the life of the community.
>
> They have a broad cultural background and an understanding of world conditions. Teacher educational institutions have not prepared teachers to do these things. Prior emphasis has been upon subject matter and method.

The Blueprint goes on to list the major purposes of a total instructional program "of benefit to the entire community." Under "The Educational Program" one finds:

> continuing and improving the teaching of the cultures of the past;
> developing the ability to communicate effectively;
> developing the ability to think;
> developing desirable personality and character traits;

discovering and developing worthwhile interests;

developing respect for others, or intercultural relations;

protecting and promoting health;

developing wholesome home and family life (Other agencies must accept at least some of the responsibilities formerly borne by the family. The school must study the problem intensively. It must experiment.);

developing wholesome habits and understanding of work;

good members of society cannot be developed if they are ignorant of work and what goes into it. In the years which lie ahead, it would appear that the school is the only agency which society has which can be expected to accept this responsibility.

IT MUST BE DONE. [emphasis in the original]

developing understanding of economic principles and forces (Emphasis must be placed upon the economic principles and forces which are operating at that time rather than upon those of the past.);

developing consumer competence... schools of the future must do much about such things;

developing vocational competence;

developing social and civic competence—understand obligations as a member of the group;... and to give wholeheartedly and unselfishly service to his local, state, national and world government;

developing understanding of, and skill in, the democratic way of life;

developing knowledge, understanding of, and skill in, the creative arts;

developing understanding of, and skill in, wholesome and worthwhile leisure activities (Much depends upon people discovering and practicing worthwhile leisure pursuits.);

developing a well-rounded emotional life with particular attention to moral and spiritual needs. (A well-balanced emotional life is the final test of a well-educated person. It is our belief that all people are religious, that religion finds expression in many different ways. We do not believe in America that they should teach any particular kind or type of religion.)

Under "The Service Program" one finds Health and Medical Services. (In the school of the future, provision must be made not only for children enrolled but to all people, young and old.) The list is endless and includes the following cradle-through-grave services: recreational, library, guidance and counseling, child care, demonstration and experimental services, planning and research, employment, audiovisual, social welfare, group meeting place, character-building services. *The Plan* [*Blueprint*] states further:

> The end results are that the school makes itself indispensable to all phases of community life. In the future development of school programs, the service program will receive increasing emphasis until the school becomes in fact the agency to which all the people in the community turn for assistance.

Appendix II

Excerpts from *Teaching Machines and Programmed Learning*

Teaching Machines and Programmed Learning: A Source Book, edited by A.A. Lumsdaine, Program Director, American Institute for Research, Professor of Education, University of California, Los Angeles and Robert Glaser, Professor of Psychology, University of Pittsburgh, Research Advisor, American Institute for Research (Department of Audio-Visual Instruction, National Education Association, Washington, D.C., 1960).

> The original studies reported by contributors to this volume also received direct support from the Office of the Air Research and Development Command of the U.S. Air Force, the U.S. Office of Education, and a number of other agencies including HumRRO (Department of the Army), the Ford Foundation and the Fund for the Advancement of Education, and several industrial organizations. Acknowledgment should also be made of the support and encouragement provided on several of these projects by the University of Pittsburgh, Harvard University, and a number of other academic institutions. [Preface]

From "Teaching Machines: An Introductory Overview," A.A. Lumsdaine:

> Despite great variation in complexity and special features, all of the devices that are currently called "teaching machines" represent some form of variation on what can be called the tutorial or Socratic method of teaching. That is, they present the individual student with programs of questions and answers, problems to be solved, or exercises to be performed. In addition, however, they always provide some type of automatic feedback or correction to the student so that he is immediately informed of his progress at each step and given a basis for correcting his errors. They thus differ from films, TV and most other audio-visual media as ordinarily utilized, because of three important properties. First, continuous active student response is required, providing explicit practice and testing of each step of what is to be learned. Second, a basis is provided for informing the student with minimal delay whether each response he makes is correct, leading him directly or indirectly to correction of his errors. Third, the student proceeds on an individual basis at his own rate—faster students romping through an instructional sequence very rapidly, slower students being tutored as slowly as necessary, with indefinite [*sic*] patience to meet their special needs. (p. 5)

From "Results of Use of Machines for Testing and for Drill upon Learning in Educational Psychology," James Kenneth Little:

> Previous investigations of college instructional problems had (the writer felt) emphasized the following relevant points: (a) the motivating effect upon the learner of knowledge of standing and progress; (b) the value, both for motivation and for guidance in learning, of informing students specifically and immediately of their errors and their successes in their work; (c) the value in the above (and other) connections of the frequent short test, as contrasted with less frequent longer tests or examinations; (d) the great importance of continuous adjustment to individual differences not only in capacity but also in error pattern and difficulty; (e) the value, in all of these connections, of a consistent use of the make-up test. (p. 59)

From Part III: "Skinner's Teaching Machines and Programming Concepts":

> A comprehensive report of the work at Harvard on teaching machines and the programming of materials used within them was prepared in 1958 as a report to the Fund for the Advancement of Education. Skinner summarized the first part of this report in a symposium paper at the 1958 meetings of the American Psychological Association and shortly thereafter published it in *Science* [October 23, 1958 issue]. This major article, reproduced in full as the third paper in Part III, attracted wide attention to the potentialities of "teaching machines." It also focused attention on the "*programming*" of detailed, carefully ordered learning sequences by which complex behavioral repertoires could be shaped through successive approximations. (p. 96) [emphasis in original]

From "The Science of Learning and the Art of Teaching," B.F. Skinner:

> Recent improvements in the conditions which control behavior in the field of learning are of two principal sorts. The "law of effect" has been taken seriously; we have made sure that effects do occur and that they occur under conditions which are optimal for producing the changes called learning. Once we have arranged the particular type of consequence called reinforcement, our techniques permit us to shape the behavior of an organism almost at will. It has become a routine exercise to demonstrate this in classes in elementary psychology by conditioning such an organism as a pigeon. (pp. 99–100)

> In all this work, the species of the organism has made surprisingly little difference. It is true that the organisms studied have all been vertebrates, but they still cover a wide range. Comparable results have been obtained with rats, pigeons, dogs, monkeys, human children, and most recently—by the author in collaboration with Ogden R. Lindsley—with human psychotic subjects. In spite of great phylogenetic differences, all these organisms show amazingly similar properties of the learning process. It should be emphasized that this has been achieved by analyzing the effects of reinforcement and by designing techniques which manipulate reinforcement with considerable precision. Only in this way can the behavior of the individual organism be brought under such precise control. It is also important to note that through a gradual advance to complex interrelations among responses, the same degree of rigor is being extended to behavior which would usually be assigned to such fields as perception, thinking, and personality dynamics. (p. 103)

> These requirements are not excessive, but they are probably incompatible with the current realities of the classroom. In the experimental study of learning it has been found that the

contingencies of reinforcement which are most efficient in controlling the organism cannot be arranged through the personal mediation of the experimenter. An organism is affected by subtle details of contingencies which are beyond the capacity of the human organism to arrange. Mechanical and electrical devices must be used. Mechanical help is also demanded by the sheer number of contingencies which may be used efficiently in a single experimental session. We have recorded many millions of responses from a single organism during thousands of experimental hours. Personal arrangement of the contingencies and personal observation of the results are quite unthinkable. Now, the human organism is, if anything, more sensitive to precise contingencies than the other organisms we have studied. We have every reason to expect, therefore, that the most effective control of human learning will require instrumental aid. The simple fact is that, as a mere reinforcing mechanism, the teacher is out of date. This would be true even if a single teacher devoted all her time to a single child, but her inadequacy is multiplied many-fold when she must serve as a reinforcing device to many children at once. If the teacher is to take advantage of recent advances in the study of learning, she must have the help of mechanical devices. (p. 109)

The important features of the device are these: Reinforcement for the right answer is immediate. The mere manipulation of the device will probably be reinforcing enough to keep the average pupil at work for a suitable period each day, provided traces of earlier aversive control can be wiped out. A teacher may supervise an entire class at work on such devices at the same time, yet each child may progress at his own rate, completing as many problems as possible within the class period. If forced to be away from school, he may return to pick up where he left off. The gifted child will advance rapidly but can be kept from getting too far ahead either by being excused from arithmetic for a time or by being given special sets of problems which take him into some of the interesting by-paths of mathematics. (p.110)

Some objections to the use of such devices in the classroom can easily be foreseen. The cry will be raised that the child is being treated as a mere animal and that an essentially human intellectual achievement is being analyzed in unduly mechanistic terms. Mathematical behavior is usually regarded not as a repertoire of responses involving numbers and numerical operations, but as evidence of mathematical ability or the exercise of the power of reason. It is true that the techniques which are emerging from the experimental study of learning are not designed to "develop the mind" or to further some vague "understanding" of mathematical relationships. They are designed, on the contrary, to establish the very behaviors which are taken to be the evidences of such mental states or processes. This is only a special case of the general change which is under way in the interpretation of human affairs. An advancing science continues to offer more and more convincing alternatives to traditional formulations. The behavior in terms of which human thinking must eventually be defined is worth treating in its own right as the substantial goal for education. (p. 111)

From Part V: "Some Recent Work," article entitled "Teaching Machines and Human Beings," John W. Blyth:

There is another less obvious but no less important advantage to be gained in exploiting the teaching machine. The machine makes it possible to provide some of the conditions that we have long known to be necessary for effective learning. A savage instructing his son in the use of the bow and arrow knew that the son needed plenty of practice and that he had to see where the arrow went on each shot if he was to make any improvement on the next. The importance of this immediate feedback was formulated years ago by Thorndike as the "law of effect." According to this law of learning, an action which leads to a satisfactory result tends to be repeated. In the contemporary terminology of B.F. Skinner, of Harvard University, immediate reinforcement or reward is important in the learning process. As far as the application of this principle is concerned, we do a much better job of teaching rats, pigeons, and football players than we do in teaching mathematicians and physicists. Teaching machines designed for individual use make it possible to provide this immediate reinforcement for every student.... Laboratory experiments have demonstrated that the use of immediate reinforcement techniques is a very efficient way of training animals to make a discriminative response to selected stimuli. Rats and pigeons can be trained to perform a whole series of such responses in sequence. Their actions then form a complicated "chain" of events.... The only reason a rat should turn to the right rather than the left at a certain point is that it is that turn which leads to reinforcement. (p. 402)

Appendix III

Excerpts from *Programmed Learning*

Programmed Learning: Evolving Principles and Industrial Applications, Jerome P. Lysaught, Ed. (Foundation for Research on Human Behavior: Ann Arbor, Michigan, 1961).

Business organizations, as well as educational institutions, have an increasing demand for training, improved skills and more effective teaching methods. In October 1960, businessmen and social scientists met together to discuss programmed learning, some of its current applications in business, and the outlook for the future. This is the report of their meeting.

About This Report
...The increased demand for training, improved skills and better education in industry has stimulated some business organizations to explore the possibilities of programmed learning with the aid of devices which include automated teaching machines. The earliest teaching machines, developed several decades ago by S.J. Pressey who was the first psychologist to see "the coming industrial revolution in education" were designed for self-scoring, not for programmed instruction in the present sense. The appropriate current emphasis, reflected in the seminar, is on the concepts and principles of programmed learning, and on the translation of learning theory into the programming of instruction or teaching. Mechanical devices used should thus reflect the desired methods of teaching and learning, not determine them....

In planning the seminar held in October, 1960, Eastman Kodak and IBM representatives agreed to present and develop and use programmed instruction in their training programs. They shared the Foundation's conviction that a major emphasis on programming principles, learning theory and research, rather than on teaching machines themselves, would provide the most practical guidelines to other companies and to educational institutions interested in exploring programmed learning to increase the effectiveness of their training and education. Consequently, in addition to the two industry experiences, a large portion of the seminar was devoted to theory, principles, and the results of experimental studies in universities. The three social scientists from academic institutions who led these discussions at the seminar are pioneers and distinguished leaders in this field. It became very clear that programmed learning is an area in which the research and experience of practitioners in universities and in industry can be of great mutual benefit. The speakers and discussion leaders at the seminar included the following:

Dr. B.F. Skinner, Professor of Psychology, Harvard University
Dr. Arthur A. Lumsdaine, Professor of Education, University of California, Los Angeles, and Research Advisor for Education Media to the American Institute for Research
Dr. Robert Glaser, Professor of Psychology, University of Pittsburgh, and Research Advisor, American Institute for Research

...The seminar was part of the Foundation's continuing program to bring the results of social science research to the businessmen who can use them.

From the "Introduction," by Thomas H. Miller:

In recent months the professional journals and some popular publications have had much to say about research on teaching machines and programmed learning. Because most of this research has been limited to a few specific experiments and because field application has generally been in elementary and secondary schools, very little has been said of applications to adult learning. It was our feeling, and this is why we are so pleased to cooperate with the Foundation in the holding of this seminar, that more of us should be exploring more fully the relevance and importance of programmed instruction to adult learning in general, and to business and industrial education in particular.

First, I should emphasize that we here at Kodak are quite serious about this matter of programmed learning. We attempt to keep abreast of significant developments in learning theory and education because we are responsible for seeing that each one of our men and women receives the best possible training for his work in the company. We are confident that programmed learning will have great implications for our future efforts, and we look forward to providing better, more individualized instruction for our people as a result of this development.

Secondly, I want to explain that our feelings about programmed learning result from two factors: the result of our own initial efforts at instructing by means of this system, and the inherent characteristics of programmed learning which will give strength to any industrial training experience. With programmed learning we can adapt instruction to the individuality of each student. Each student works at his own personal speed throughout the learning experience. Each student is constantly active, interacting with the program, concentrating on the task of learning. Each student can trace his own progress, and receive timely, individual reinforcement for correct work.

To introduce the subject, we would like to have each of you work through the first lesson of Dr. B.F. Skinner's course in psychology. We would hope, incidentally, that a portion of the material is somewhat new to you so that some learning will actually take place in your encounter with the subject matter. Further, we hope it will demonstrate certain phenomena that will be spoken of repeatedly today, such as effective reinforcement of the learner and progress at the individual rate.

Imagine yourself to be a freshman student at Harvard. You are taking, for the first time, a college course in psychology. This is your first day in that course. Your introduction to the course consists of the presentation of the programmed learning sequence on the next pages.

The directions are simple. You should read the first stimulus item, S-1, consider it, and then construct in your own words the best possible answer. As soon as you have done this, turn the page and compare your answer with the answer listed at R-1, the first response item. Proceed through the program, going on to S-2 on the next page, turning the page to R-2 and comparing your response; proceeding to S-3 below, turn back a page to compare your response to R-3, and so on. You will be reading back and forth, turning a page each time to find the response item.

<u>FIRST LESSON IN PSYCHOLOGY</u>

S-1. A doctor taps your knee (patellar tendon) with a rubber hammer to test your "_____ ."
R-4. Hammer (or mallet)
S-5. The <u>stimulus</u> which elicits a knee jerk is the _____ delivered by the so-called "stimulus object" or hammer.
R-8. Elicits
S-9. To avoid unwanted nuances of meaning in popular words, we do not say that a stimulus "triggers," "stimulates," or "causes" a response but that it _____ a response.
R-12. Latency
S-13. The weakest stimulus sufficient to elicit a response marks the "threshold" of the reflex. A tap on the knee will not elicit a kick if it is below the _____.
R-16. Latency
S-17. A forceful tap elicits a strong kick; a tap barely above the threshold elicits a weak kick. Magnitude of response thus depends on the intensity of the _____.
R-20. (1) Response (2) Stimulus (3) Reflex
S-21. If a sip of very weak lemonade does not cause salivation, the stimulus is said to be below _____.

The following responses are on the turned page:

R-1. Reflexes
S-4. The stimulating object used by the doctor to elicit a knee jerk is a(n) _____.
R-5. Tap (or blow)
S-8. Technically speaking, a reflex involves a process called elicitation: A stimulus _____ a response.
R-9. Elicits
S-12. The time which elapses between the onset of the stimulus and the onset of the response is called the "latency." Thus the time between tap and kick is the _____ of the knee jerk reflex.
R-13. Threshold
S-16. The fraction of a second which elapses between "brushing the eye" and "blink" is the _____ of the reflex.
R-17. Stimulus (tap)
S-20. When a person is startled by a loud noise, his sudden movement is his (1)_____ to the noise, which has acted as a (2)_____. The two together are called a(n) (3)_____ .
R-21. Threshold

From "Principles of Programming" by Robert Glaser:

(This article was prepared under U.S. Office of Education Research Contract SAE–8417 #691. This is a preliminary version of a forthcoming book chapter.)

Yesterday, October 16, was the official publication date of the book *Teaching Machines and Programmed Learning* which Dr. Lumsdaine and I have edited, and which you have received for this seminar. It is indeed true that this book would never have been conceived without the well-known and perhaps undying work of Professor Skinner, and I would like to take this opportunity—what I consider to be a rather momentous occasion for both Art Lumsdaine and myself—to present Fred with a copy of the book at this time. It is largely through Professor Skinner's work that all this theory and excitement about teaching machines and programmed learning has come about. (Presentation to Professor Skinner).

Most recently, and actually in the course of preparing this volume, I have completed or compiled what appears to me to be the major ideas being expressed in the field of teaching machines and programmed learning. The basic notions have been developed from research findings in the experimental study of learning and have been expressed by a number of men in the field, and to a large extent by the speakers at this platform. However, since the use of teaching machines is in its Kitty Hawk stage, and since the application of the science of learning to the development of a technology of training and education is also in its childhood, I should like to set these notions down for your consideration and discuss each point rather briefly....

Evoking Specific Behavior

The essential task involved is to evoke the specific forms of behavior from the student and through appropriate reinforcement bring them under the control of specific subject matter stimuli. As a student goes through a learning program, certain of his responses must be strengthened and shaped from initial unskilled behavior to subject matter competence. Programming rules are concerned with how one goes about doing this.

Our present knowledge of the learning process points out that through the process of reinforcement, new forms of behavior can be created with a great degree of subtlety. The central feature of this process is making the reinforcement contingent upon performances of the learner. (Often the word "reward" is used to refer to one class of reinforcing events.) By differentially applying reinforcement to relatively minute behavioral changes, it is possible to progress from the initial behavior of the learner in small steps through the development of more complex behaviors. This progression can take place by small enough steps so that the student's progress and motivation is not jeopardized by frequent failures.

Since a great deal of teaching and learning is needed for acquiring complex behavioral repertoires, such as a new language or calculus operation, the number of reinforcements and the subtleties of reinforcements required to establish such complicated behavior over-taxes the skill of the most efficient instructor, especially within the limits of his time and usual classroom organization.

...The term "programming" refers to the process of constructing sequences of instructional material in a way that maximizes the rate of acquisition and retention, and enhances the motivation of the student....

Defining the Desired Behavior

...The first step in programming is to define the field. This means that the programmer must outline precisely the behavior he wants the student to perform at the end of the program and must specify the kinds of stimulus material that a student will have available in the course of this performance. A primary purpose of instruction is to provide the student with a behavioral repertoire called knowledge of the subject matter....

Reinforcement a Central Process

A central process for the acquisition of behavior is reinforcement. Behavior is acquired as a result of a contingent relationship between the response of an organism and a consequent event. In order for these contingencies of reinforcement to be effective, certain conditions must be met. Reinforcement must follow the occurrence of the behavior being taught. If this is not the case, different and perhaps unwanted behavior will be learned. In addition, a sufficient number of reinforcements must be given so that the desired behavior is strengthened and its probability of occurrence for a particular student is high in appropriate situations. As has been said, in progressing from the initial repertoire to the terminal repertoire, the student is reinforced for minute changes in behavior which bring him closer and closer to skilled performance. And these minute changes are brought about by successive steps in the program. In most instructional programs, the reinforcing agent for the students is "knowledge of results," that is, knowledge about whether or not the response he performs is the result considered correct. Failure to provide adequate reinforcement and hence failure to strengthen the behavior of the student with respect to the subject matter often results in the student showing a lack of interest. This means that his interest is shifted to other activities for which sufficient reinforcement is provided....

The Principle of Gradual Progression

My third point is gradual progression to establish complex repertoires. In getting the student from his initial repertoire to the terminal repertoire, it has been indicated that an important principle is that of gradual progression. We do not wait for the student to emit complex behavior in the course of trial and error and then reinforce correct performance. In fact, he may never emit the skillful behavior we require. When developing complex performance we first reinforce any available behavior which is the slightest approximation to the terminal behavior. Later we use this behavior in the next step to reinforce a small change which is in the *direction* of the terminal repertoire. The program moves in graded steps working from simple to higher and higher levels of complexity.

The principle of gradual progression serves to make the student correct as often as possible and is also the fastest way to develop a complex repertoire. It is difficult to see how complex behavior can appear except through the specific reinforcement of members of a graded series. It seems that this is an important principle in the rapid creation of new patterns of behavior.

At each step, the programmer must ask what behavior must a student have before he can take this step. He must ask what principles or interverbal relationships will facilitate this sequence of steps that form a progression from initially assumed knowledge to the specified final repertoire. *No step should be encountered before the student can take it with a high probability of success....*

Eliciting Available Responses and Controlling Error

The next point that I want to make is called "emitted behavior and prompting". This concerns making the desired behavior more probable. A student is assumed, as I have said, to possess some initial related behavior in the subject matter before he starts the course. The behavior available must be specified, and the programmer can, at the beginning, appeal only to those available responses. How then do we get the students to emit these available responses? Before behavior is reinforced, it must be emitted and instructional material must be designed to elicit the correct and appropriate behavior which can then be appropriately reinforced. A major portion of what we call the rules of programming is concerned with evoking behavior, that is, concerned with techniques for getting the students to emit new or low strength responses with a minimum of errors.

The occurrence of behavior in a program *is* made more probable if the materials are designed so that each frame makes the correct answers in the next frame more likely. The probability of success is increased by the use of formal hinting and coaching techniques based upon what we know about verbal behavior....

Putting the Student on His Own

The next point is called "fading or vanishing." Thus far it has been indicated that programming techniques utilize the principle of reinforcement, the principle of prompting. The next one we come to is the principle of fading or vanishing. This principle involves the gradual removal of prompts or cues, so that by the time the student has completed the lesson, he is responding only to the stimulus material which he will actually have available when he performs the "real task." He is on his own, so to speak, and learning crutches have been eliminated. Fading can then be defined as the gradual withdrawal of stimulus support. The systematic progression of programmed learning is well set up to accomplish this. It is always to be kept in mind that these principles are quite in contrast to "rote learning" or drill. In rote learning, many wrong responses are permitted to occur, and the student eventually learns to develop his own prompts often to a relatively unrelated series of stimuli. Programmed learning, on the other hand, is designed to take advantage of the inherent organization of the subject matter or of the behavior of the subject in relation to the subject matter in shaping up the student's learning. [all emphases in original]

[Ed. Note: The computer in 1999 is a sophisticated version of the teaching machine referred to in 1960.]

Appendix IV

Excerpts from *A Plan for Evaluating the Quality of Educational Programs in Pennsylvania*

A Plan for Evaluating the Quality of Educational Programs in Pennsylvania: Highlights of a Report from Educational Testing Services (Princeton, NJ) to the State Board of Education of the Commonwealth of Pennsylvania, June 30, 1965.

BACKGROUND

The planning project reported in this document had its inception in a mandate from the General Assembly of Pennsylvania. The mandate is to be found in Section 290.1 of the Act of August 8, 1963, P.L. 564 (Act 299, *The School District Reorganization Act of 1963*). It reads as follows:

> Educational Performance Standards—To implement the purpose of this subdivision, the State Board of Education, as soon as possible and in any event no later than July 1, 1965, shall develop or cause to be developed an evaluation procedure designed to measure objectively the adequacy and efficiency of the educational programs offered by the public schools of the Commonwealth. The evaluation procedure to be developed shall include tests measuring the achievements and performance of students pursuing all of the various subjects and courses comprising the curricula. The evaluation procedure shall be so constructed and developed as to provide each school district with relevant comparative data to enable directors and administrators to more readily appraise the educational performance and effectuate without delay the strengthening of the district's educational program. Tests developed under the authority of this section to be administered to pupils shall be used for the purpose of providing a uniform evaluation of each school district and the other purposes set forth in this subdivision. The State Board of Education shall devise performance standards upon completion of the evaluation procedure required by this section.

This committee on Quality Education sought the advice of experts in the behavioral sciences. These experts constituted a Standing Advisory Committee for the project.... It [the Committee] concluded that an educational program is to be regarded as adequate only if it can be shown to contribute to the total development of pupils.... The Committee recognizes that many of the desirable qualities that schools should help pupils acquire are difficult to define and even more difficult to measure. It feels, nevertheless, that any evaluation procedure that leaves these qualities out of account is deficient as a basis for determining whether the program of any school district is educationally adequate. Having in mind this view of education and its evaluation, the Committee requested the Educational Testing Service [Note: federally-funded, ed.] of Princeton, N.J. to assist in the development of a plan for the implementation of Act 299.... What follows gives the highlights of the three-volume report entitled *A Plan for Evaluating the Quality of Educational Programs in Pennsylvania.*

PROPOSED GOALS OF EDUCATION
The first step in judging the quality of educational programs is to decide on the purposes of education. What should children be and do and know as a consequence of having gone to school? What are the goals of the schools? These questions have been high on the agenda of the Committee on Quality Education. Its members wanted a set of goals that would reflect the problems society faces in the world today.... Available measures of the factors are uneven in their development. Some of the measures are considerably more valid, precise, and interpretable than others. Measures of conventional academic achievement, for instance, are at a more advanced stage of development than measures of attitude and values. This unevenness poses a difficult, but not an insoluble, problem in designing an evaluation program of the kind we are proposing, In a nutshell, the current situation is as follows:

1. All of the ten goals of education stated above are to be regarded of prime importance in education of high quality. Any educational program that neglects any of the goals is to be regarded as less than adequate. [The Ten Quality Goals are listed below under California's Plan which lists Pennsylvania's Ten Quality Goals as those to be used by California, ed.]
2. Measures of progress toward the ten goals are unequally developed. Some are more dependable and valid than others. For example, tests of reading comprehension are relatively well developed and reasonably well understood, while tests of such qualities as self-understanding and tolerance are less well developed and poorly understood.
3. Nevertheless, the evaluation of pupil performance in all areas is critically important as a means of keeping educational programs in balance.
4. Work should therefore begin on evaluating progress toward all ten goals to the extent that this is possible.
5. Where the available measures are clearly inadequate, intensive research and development should be undertaken immediately to bring them to the point where they can have full effect in the evaluation program.
6. Where the available measures are adequate, studies should be undertaken immediately to use these measures in the development of appropriate criteria for assessing school programs.

ILLUSTRATIVE STUDIES
During the past year, we conducted two studies involving five school systems for the following purposes: (1) to identify specifically the practical problems that would be encountered in studies to develop performance criteria for school programs, (2) to see what usable measures might be obtained for measuring the kinds of output called for by the ten proposed goals of education, (3) to see what usable measures might be available for measuring input and the variables that condition output, (4) to see how the several measures might be related and

combined to produce the necessary performance criteria.

The outcomes of these studies suggest (1) that good cooperation can be expected from the school systems in conducting such studies in the future, (2) that reliable measures of some aspect of each of the ten kinds of output implied by the ten goals is possible, (3) that the validity of many of the available measures, however, is open to question, (4) that there are many measures still to be developed if all the most important aspects of educational output are to be effectively appraised, (5) that it is feasible to express performance criteria in a form which takes into account conditions under which schools work and which at the same time constitute a challenge to the majority of schools to improve their programs.

THE DEVELOPMENT AND APPLICATION OF PERFORMANCE CRITERIA

Out of the work of the two illustrative studies a design for a study to develop performance criteria has emerged. It has five characteristics as follows:

1. It would provide multiple performance objectives for schools of any given type.
2. It assumes that pupils at seven different grade levels will be tested twice, two years apart, first, to establish levels of input and second, to establish levels of output. [This was, for many years, the NAEP schedule, ed.]
3. It envisages a testing program which consists of a core program made up of tests which have already been proved to be dependable and an experimental program made up of tests to be developed to a state of dependability in the course of the study.
4. It would be carried out on a ten per cent sample of the schools of the Commonwealth and would probably involve about 7,000 classrooms and 200,000 pupils. [This is the NAEP sampling method used for many years, ed.]

SUPPORTING RESEARCH

At all stages of this planning study it has become increasingly apparent to us that any program to evaluate the quality of education in Pennsylvania which was unaccompanied by a strong program of research would be sterile. Two kinds of research are essential:

• Research specially designed to invent, develop, and validate the measures needed by the evaluation program—especially measures of the kinds of educational output assumed by such goals as self-understanding, tolerance, citizenship, attitude toward school and learning, and creativity.

• Research to identify those educational processes and those modifiable conditions of learning that hold the greatest possibilities for improving the educational output in schools of varying types.

...The four studies were concerned (a) with measures of the ways children think and solve problems, (b) with the test-taking motivation of students in culturally deprived areas, (c) with the measurement of creativity, and (d) with the attitudes of primary school pupils toward school.

What have the studies shown?

• They have shown that ordinary achievement tests leave untouched many important intellectual qualities of students, but that with a concentrated program of research it should be possible to develop measures of these qualities.

• They have shown that youngsters from disadvantaged backgrounds do not usually try as hard on tests as their more favored classmates, but that they can be motivated to do so.

- They have shown that it is possible to get a rough measure of the degree to which students bring a creative approach to the arts, the sciences, and the problems of human relations.
- They have shown how the attitudes of primary school children toward their teachers, their school, their classmates may be developing and have suggested how important these attitudes can be in conditioning the children's further education.

Finally, these studies have shown that much more research needs to be done on how to assess the output of the schools and how to develop procedures for strengthening their programs. We are convinced by our work this year that such research will be fruitful and should be energetically pursued.

RECOMMENDATIONS

1. General policies:

1.2. The evaluation program should avoid any suggestion of a policing operation to see where schools are meeting minimum regulations. It should encourage, not inhibit, experimentation with (a) new curricula, (b) new administrative arrangements, (c) new approaches to instruction....

1.3. The State Board of Education should rely upon the Superintendent of Public Instruction for developing and executing the evaluation program, it being understood, however, that where appropriate he may delegate parts of the work to universities or to other competent agencies outside the Department of Public Instruction....

2. Procedures. The following procedures are recommended as constituting the essentials of an educational evaluation program for the Commonwealth....

2.2. A General Panel of Review consisting of educators, behavioral scientists, and representatives of the general public should be appointed to review the system of tests and measures to be used to ascertain how well pupils are progressing toward the educational goals and to advise on research and development leading to new and improved means of assessing progress toward the goals.

2.3. For each of several areas of educational output, there should be a Sub-Panel of Examiners drawn from the General Panel of Review, with additional numbers drawn from among appropriate specialists in education and the behavioral sciences, to consider in detail the tests and measures related to the area of their concern and to advise the General Panel of Review regarding the quality of the tests and measures and the means for their improvement.

2.4. A broad program of research should be initiated forthwith for the purpose of (a) improving the educational output, especially those that have to do with the personal and social qualities of pupils and for which in many cases no satisfactory measures now exist, and (b) discovering those processes of education and conditions of learning that will maximize the quality of educational output under a variety of circumstances. This program of research should take full advantage of the outcomes of similar research being done elsewhere by adapting these outcomes to the needs of Pennsylvania.

2.5. In those cases where a school system, after applying the appropriate criteria, is dissatisfied with the level of performance of its pupils, such school systems should have the advice and assistance of the Department of Public Instruction in determining what changes in educational processes and/or in the conditions of learning would be most likely to bring about improvement.

Proof that Pennsylvania's goals were the model for the nation is found in the California State Plan, Title III of the *Elementary and Secondary Education Act*, P.L. 89-10, as Amended by P.L. 90–247, 1970, which states on page 2, (6/9/69 revised):

These Ten Goals were generated in the Study of Quality Education initiated by the Pennsylvania State Board of Education in response to a mandate from the Pennsylvania General Assembly. The Ten Goals provided a classification system simple enough (in terms of the number of categories) to work with and yet comprehensive enough in scope to include almost any educational objective, whether cognitive, affective [attitudes, values, ed.] or psychomotor. These Ten Goals are listed below:

1. Quality education should help every child acquire the greatest possible understanding of himself and appreciation of his worthiness as a member of society (Self-Understanding).
2. Quality education should help every child acquire understanding and appreciation of persons belonging to social, cultural, and ethnic groups different from his own (Tolerance of Others).
3. Quality education should help every child acquire to the fullest extent possible for him mastery of the basic skills in the use of words and numbers (Basic Skills).
4. Quality education should help every child acquire a positive attitude toward school and toward the learning process (Attitude Toward School).
5. Quality education should help every child acquire the habits and attitudes associated with responsible citizenship (Citizenship).
6. Quality education should help every child acquire good health habits and an understanding of the conditions necessary for the maintenance of physical and emotional well being (Health).
7. Quality education should give every child opportunities in one or more fields of endeavor (Creativity).
8. Quality education should help every child understand the opportunities open to him for preparing himself for a productive life and should enable him to take full advantage of these opportunities (Vocational Preparation).
9. Quality education should help every child to understand and appreciate as much as he can of human achievement in the natural sciences, the social sciences, the humanities, and the arts (Intellectual Achievement).
10. Quality education should help every child prepare for a world of rapid changes and unforeseeable demands in which continuing education throughout his adult life should be a normal expectation (Life-Long Learning).

[Ed. Note: Anita Hoge's successful complaint against the Pennsylvania Department of Education's Educational Quality Assessment (EQA), filed under the federal *Protection of Pupil Rights Amendment*, exposed the extent of federal involvement in curricula, testing and evaluation primarily designed to change children's attitudes, values, and beliefs. These are the areas to which parents most vociferously object. In the mid-1970s the Pennsylvania chapter of the liberal American Civil Liberties Union sided with parents regarding their objections; i.e., invasion of privacy, etc.

All state and local school district goals, standards, competencies, outcomes, results, etc., developed from this time on across the nation were based primarily on these Pennsylvania goals. It is interesting to note that the plans for national assessment were in progress several years prior to passage of the *Elementary and Secondary Education Act of 1965*. This *Act* signified the end of local control due to its call for the installation of an accountability system in each of the state departments of education applying for federal assistance.

It should be noted that included on the Standing Advisory Committee and its pool of "experts" in the behavioral sciences were: David R. Krathwohl (co-author with Benjamin Bloom of *The Taxonomy of Educational Objectives: Affective Domain*) of the College of Education at Michigan State University; Urie Bonfenbrenner of the Department of Sociology at Cornell University; and Ralph W. Tyler of the Center for Advanced Study in the Behavioral Sciences at Palo Alto, California.]

Appendix V

Comments on and Excerpts from *Behavioral Science Teacher Education Program* (BSTEP)

Behavioral Science Teacher Education Program (BSTEP), 1965–1969, funded by the U.S. Department of Health, Education, and Welfare, was initiated at Michigan State University. Its purpose was to change the teacher from a transmitter of knowledge/content to a social change agent/facilitator/clinician. Traditional public school administrators were appalled at this new role for teachers. Long-time education researcher Bettye Lewis provided a capsule description and critique of BSTEP in 1984. Her comments and verbatim quotes from BSTEP follow:

Objectives of BSTEP are stated as follows:

Three major goals:

1. Development of a new kind of elementary school teacher who is basically well educated, engages in teaching as clinical practice, is an effective student of the capacities and environmental characteristics of human learning, and functions as a responsible agent of social change.
2. Systematic use of research and clinical experience in decision-making processes at all levels.
3. A new laboratory and clinical base, from the behavioral sciences, on which to found undergraduate and in-service teacher education programs, and recycle evaluations of teaching tools and performance.

...The BSTEP teacher is expected to learn from experience through a cyclical style of describing, analyzing, hypothesizing, prescribing, treating, and observing consequences (in particular—the consequences of the treatment administered)....

The program is designed to focus the skills and knowledge of Behavioral Scientists on education problems, translating research into viable programs for preservice and in-service teachers. The traditional concept of research as theory

A–23

is not discarded, but the emphasis is shifted to a form of practical action-research in classrooms and laboratory.

The humanities are designed to promote an understanding of human behavior in humanistic terms.... Students are to be exposed to non-western thought and values in order to sensitize them to their own backgrounds and inherent cultural biases.... Skills initiating and directing role-playing are developed to increase sensitivity and perception. Simulation games are included for training in communication skills as leaders or agents of social change. (p. 1)

Lewis's comments regarding "Systematic Analysis of Future Society," taken from p. 237 of BSTEP:

B.F. Skinner's behavioral philosophy is quite apparent in this BSTEP Design which states

Calculations of the future and how to modify it are no longer considered obscure academic pursuits. Instead, they are the business of many who are concerned about and responsible for devising various modes of social change.

One can't help but wonder—who gave the educators the "responsibility" or the "right" to devise modes of social change, to use teachers as the "change agents," and to use the children as the guinea pigs through which society is to be changed? One realizes the extent to which this "future society planning" has already gone after reading through the following lengthy list of organizations involved in this behavioral designing:

1. Department of Health, Education, and Welfare—*Exploring Possibilities of a Social State-of-the-Union*
2. American Academy of Arts and Sciences—Commission of the Year 2000
3. American Academy of Political and Social Science
4. United Nations Future-Planning Operation in Geneva, Switzerland
5. World Future Society of Washington, D.C.
6. General Electric Company—Technical Management Planning Organization
7. The Air Force and Rand Corporation [designer of PPBS, ed.]
8. The Hudson Institute [See 1992 entry regarding approval by business/corporation-funded New American School Development Corporation of the Hudson Institute's "Modern Red School House" proposal. The Design Team was headed by former Secretary of Education William J. Bennett and includes Chester Finn, former Assistant Secretary to Education Secretary, and former Governor Lamar Alexander and author of *America 2000* (President Clinton's *Goals 2000*), ed.]
9. Ford Foundation's *Resources for the Future and Les Futuribles*—a combination of future and possible
10. University of Illinois, Southern Illinois University, Stanford University, Syracuse University, etc.
11. IBM (International Business Machines)

This section of the report concludes with: "We are getting closer to developing effective methods for shaping the future and are advancing in fundamental social and individual evolution."

From the section entitled "Futurism as a Social Tool and Decision-Making by an Elite" (p. 248)

Lewis quotes:

> The complexity of the society and rapidity of change will require that comprehensive long-range planning become the rule, in order that carefully developed plans will be ready before changes occur.... Long-range planning and implementation of plans will be made by a technological-scientific elite. Political democracy, in the American ideological sense, will be limited to broad social policy; even there, issues, alternatives, and means will be so complex that the elite will be influential to a degree which will arouse the fear and animosity of others. This will strain the democratic fabric to a ripping point.... [The reader should refer to the 1972 entry entitled "People Control Blueprint" from the May issue of *The National Educator,* ed.]

"A Controlling Elite"
...The Protestant Ethic will atrophy as more and more enjoy varied leisure and guaranteed sustenance. Work as the means and end of living will diminish.... No major source of a sense of worth and dignity will replace the Protestant Ethic. Most people will tend to be hedonistic, and a dominant elite will provide "bread and circuses" to keep social dissension and disruption at a minimum. A small elite will carry society's burdens. The resulting impersonal manipulation of most people's lifestyles will be softened by provisions for pleasure-seeking and guaranteed physical necessities. (p. 255)

"Systems Approach and Cybernetics"
...The use of the systems approach to problem solving and of cybernetics to manage automation will remold the nation. They will increase efficiency and depersonalization.... Most of the population will seek meaning through other means or devote themselves to pleasure seeking. The controlling elite will engage in power plays largely without the involvement of most of the people.... The society will be a leisurely one. People will study, play, and travel; some will be in various stages of the drug-induced experiences. (p. 259)

"Communications Capabilities and Potentialities for Opinion Control"
...Each individual will receive at birth a multipurpose identification which will have, among other things, extensive communications uses. None will be out of touch with those authorized to reach him. Each will be able to receive instant updating of ideas and information on topics previously identified. Routine jobs to be done in any setting can be initiated automatically by those responsible for the task; all will be in constant communication with their employers, or other controllers, and thus exposed to direct and subliminal influence. Mass media transmission will be instantaneous to wherever people are in forms suited to their particular needs and roles. Each individual will be saturated with ideas and information. Some will be self-selected; other kinds will be imposed overtly by those who assume responsibility for others' actions (for example: employers); still other kinds will be imposed covertly by various agencies, organizations, and enterprises. Relatively few individuals will be able to maintain control over their opinions. Most will be pawns of competing opinion molders. (p. 261)

Lewis comments further:

> In order to implement this training and to make sure that future elementary teachers accept the "right attitudes" and "behavioral objectives," the use of computers and the collection of information are stressed. The "Central Processor" or the computer programmed to accept or reject on the basis of behavioral objectives, will be the "judge and the jury" as to

who will and who will not be the future teachers. For anyone who loves individual freedom, who desires it for their own children, and prays for a future America with individual freedom held sacred—BSTEP has to be a most frightening and devastating plan. It is indeed the "world" of Orwell's *1984*, the Identity Society, and the *Walden II* of B.F. Skinner. In reference to the latter, it is indeed *Beyond Freedom and Dignity*, the title of a B.F. Skinner book. It is a "nightmare" created by the Behaviorists and Humanists who are fast becoming the Major Directors of Public Education.

Appendix VI

Excerpts from *Education for Results*

Education for Results: In Response to A Nation At Risk, Vol.1: Guaranteeing Effective Performance by Our Schools by Robert E. Corrigan, Ph.D., and Betty O. Corrigan (SAFE Learning Systems, Inc.: Anaheim, CA, 1983). This particular paper was published in 1983 for the Reagan Administration's use, and actually served as a springboard for implementing OBE. Most of the experimentation history (pilot OBE/ML/DI) programs, including one in Korea discussed in this paper, were implemented in the 1960s and 1970s.

The Education for Results Project, which basically called for using Corrigan's Model (mastery learning/outcome-based education/management information systems) had the support of the following twenty key education change agents:

DR. LEON LESSINGER, Superintendent, Beverly Hills School District, Beverly Hills, CA; DR. JACK WARD, Associate Superintendent, Mendocino County, CA; DR. ROBERT KANE, Consultant, Teacher Preparation & Licensing Committee, State of California; DR. NOLAN ESTES, Professor of Education, University of Texas; DR. JAMES MCPHAIL, Chairman, Department of Educational Administration & Supervision, University of Southern Mississippi; DR. HOSEA GRISHAM, Superintendent, North Panola County School, Mississippi, President, Mississippi Association of School Administrators; DR. HINES CRONIN, Superintendent, Moss Point School District, Moss Point, MS; DR. MEL BUCKLEY, Superintendent, Newton Public School, Newton, MS; DR. ROBERT MORGAN, Director, Learning Systems Institute, Florida State University, Tallahassee, FL; DR. ROGER A. KAUFMAN, Professor of Education, Florida State University, Tallahassee, FL; DR. HOMER COKER, Teacher Corps Program, Georgia State University, Atlanta, GA; DR. ANNETTE KEARNEY, Assistant Director, National Council for Negro Women, New York City; DR. JOHN PICTON, Beaverton, OR; DR. LOUIS ZEYEN, Deputy Executive Director, American Association of School Administrators; DR. WILLIAM SPADY, Director, Center for the Improvement of Learning, Arlington, VA; DR. GENE GEISERT, Professor of Education, St. John's University, Jamaica, NY; DR. AL HOYE, Minneapolis Unified School District, MN; DR. WILFRED LANDRUS, Chapman College, Professor of Education, Orange, CA; DR. ROBERT CORRIGAN, Corrigan and Associates, Anaheim, CA; and MRS. BETTY CORRIGAN, Corrigan and Associates, Anaheim, CA. Lessinger, Estes, Kaufman, Coker, Spady and the Corrigans are among the key proponents of OBE/ML and have been involved for many years. The following are excerpts from *Education for Results*:

PROLOGUE: Committing to the Feasible Delivery of Effective Educational Results, by Nolan Estes, prior U.S. Commissioner of Education, University of Texas, Austin.... On April 26, 1983, the National Commission for Excellence in Education presented to President Ronald Reagan *A Nation at Risk*, a report on the status of quality education in the United States. This commission was formed by Secretary of Education Dr. Terrel Bell, in August 1981, to evaluate the current status of our national educational system in terms of its overall performance effectiveness; and, where appropriate, to propose changes in policy, practices, and programs to increase the effectiveness of our schools....

The beginning of this reported decline in the performance effectiveness began in the 1960's. As a Commissioner of Education (1965–1969), along with other Commissioners, we made substantial investments in grants and programs to develop more effective professional practices to replace those then in operation. We concentrated our investments in two major programs, namely:
   A. To increase learning effectiveness (*mastery scores*) for all learners; and
   B. To increase the management effectiveness of the delivery system to increase the measured success for learners.

Several major multi-million dollar programs were initiated in the 1960's consistent with the achievement of the goals stated above. The major focus on development of more effective management-for-results practices and application was Operation PEP, State of California. This was a multi-year program involving several hundred senior educational administrators across the state. Dr. Robert E. Corrigan, as director of the training programs, offered to these administrators skills in management-for-results practices encompassed in his "Systematic Approach for Effectiveness" (SAFE). The acceptance of these practices by these senior educational practitioners is evidenced by the fact that they were applied by Title III management centers across the state of California after the federal funds were removed.
A second key thrust by the Department of Education (1965–1968) was to support the development of new teaching practices which would prove more effective in the delivery of success for learners. A major program was funded for the installation of a Teacher Fellowship Program at Chapman College, Orange, California. This program was headed by Dr. Robert E. Corrigan to develop a Masters Degree in Instructional Systems Design (ISD). This developing program focused on the design of a new learning-centered technology developed by the Corrigans to assure predictable mastery by all learners of all relevant skills and knowledge in the curricula offered in our schools.
...In these two volumes presented herein by the Corrigans, you are offered the PROOF of these most effective results-focused practices by many school districts both large and small, both urban and rural, in a variety of areas across our country over a period of 22 + years (1960–1983)..
Since the 1960s, these effective management-for-results practices have expanded to include the required use of micro computer management systems to control for the delivery of cost-effective results for learners, for the educational practitioners, and the taxpayers.
These publications (Volumes I and II) offer to all educational partners (including teachers, learners, administrators, boards of education, parents, and the community at large) proven ways and means to deliver effective performance by our schools—a "business-like" approach to manage the achievement of established priorities for action and the installation of these successful educational practices in the schools of America.
...We are required NOW to make only the necessary minimal investments in time and/

or money by each member of the educational partnership in order to turn our currently reported mediocre performance effectiveness as presented by the Commission on Excellence into a shining success story for all concerned, in particular for the future citizens of this nation and the survival and growth of our nation as a whole. [all emphases in original]

From Chapter 13: "Instructional Systems Development in Korean Educational Reform" by Robert M. Morgan:

A Systems Center Study of Korean Education—1970

The aim of this study was an attempt by the Republic of Korea to determine if it might be able to organize its educational resources in ways that would make its educational programs more responsive to the nation's needs and, simultaneously, function more efficiently. The Korean Government invited the Florida State University to assist with the project and an interdisciplinary study team was assembled. In the planning phase of the project it was judged that a "systems approach" to the analysis of Korea's educational sector would be suitable.

The study team spent three months in Korea in 1970 gathering information about the educational system, the economy, the nation's needs and wants for its educational programs, and the resources available for potential improvement of the system. Members of the study team visited schools at all levels throughout Korea and talked to hundreds of teachers, administrators and students. The team also worked with several Korean government ministries.

...The data was analyzed in terms of future manpower needs and educational output, estimated cost benefits, strategies for appropriate introduction of innovation and technology into the system.

[Ed. Note: While reading the following, please keep in mind educational restructuring in the United States to meet the demands of the global economy—the shift from academic education to work force training, using Outcome-Based Education/ML/DI and TQM.]

Economic Factors
Following the Korean War the Korean economy experienced remarkable industrial progress and growth which was predicted to continue into the foreseeable future. The labor force was increasing steadily and the rate of unemployment, decreasing. However, a major problem was anticipated from lack of congruence between the nation's manpower requirements and the projected supply of skilled technical labor. The only long-range solution to these problems was a reordering of the educational priorities in the schools of Korea.

The Contemporary Korean School System

The educational goals that characterized the Korean elementary and middle schools in 1970 were... restricted to the conventional academic domain. The student learning outcomes at these levels fell almost exclusively into the informational and skill categories of education and was characterized by rote memorization of classically academic subjects with the overriding objective of preparing students for the national competitive examinations which were used to select those students for entry to the next level of education.

The existing curriculum was not as relevant to preparing Korean children to live and prosper as adults as it could and should have been. While the study team did not attempt to specify educational objectives, it believed the curriculum could be broadened to include the teaching of inquiry skills and problem-solving approaches and generally attend more to process objectives—and that these should not only be learning outcomes but also serve as effective instructional means. It was also suggested that pre-occupational training would add to the graduates' employability, retrainability and occupational mobility.

A Proposed New Educational Model—1971

The study team suggested that a nine-year, free and compulsory educational program was necessary to support Korea's continuing economic expansion. (*Systems Analysis for Educational Change: The Republic of Korea* by Morgan, Robert M. and Chadwick, C.B. [University of Florida Press: Gainesville, FL, 1971]). The vocational high schools of Korea were not effectively serving the purposes for which they were formed. Based upon assumptions about potential for improved academic accomplishment at the elementary-middle school level, the study team recommended that this training be directed exclusively to preparing people for specific jobs. The job training programs would be of variable duration, would be operated only as long as there were known manpower needs for the jobs in question, and would be open to qualified citizens of any age level. [emphasis added]

...The new school proposed by the study team involved a number of changes from the existing system. These included changing the basic instructional unit from its present class size to a larger grouping, introducing individualized instructional concepts and associated materials, modifying the role of the teaching staff, increasing the ratio of students to teachers, and using *programmed* instructional television and radio.

...A middle school... moved to a system of individualized instruction... would be performance based, permit students to move at their own learning rate, and would place a larger measure of responsibility on the students for self-direction of their learning experiences. It would also reduce reliance on direct teacher-to-student instruction. The basic instructional resource for that portion of the curriculum to be individualized would be a "student-learning unit" prepared in modular form and packaged for ease of storage and retrieval by students. These units would be developed using the Instructional Systems Design (ISD) approach. The student-learning unit would contain the behavioral objectives for the unit, critical instructional materials, directions to other learning resources, and criterion-referenced test items which would permit the student to assess his own progress through the unit. The principles of *programmed instruction* would be employed in the development of these units even though most of the instructional materials were not programmed instruction *per se*.... The teaching team would operate under the direction of a master teacher whose main job would be the management of the learning environment....

...It was estimated that a functional national educational television system could be built which would be an integral component of the system of instructional resources.... It would be a form of programmed instruction developed to teach specific behaviors and would call for active responses from the student. Auxiliary printed materials would be developed to go with the ITV programs in which the students would write responses, solve problems and record reactions and questions. Student learning would be closely monitored and the teacher would be furnished supportive and supplementary materials to help her work individually with any students who experience difficulty or who fall behind in the televised instruction.

...The study team proposed an organization, which it labeled the Korean Educational Development Institute (KEDI), to design and try out the system and its components. KEDI would reappraise the educational goals and objectives for the elementary-middle [E-M, ed.] schools. It would develop definitions of desired learning outcomes at the various levels and then design and build the instructional programs to achieve these outcomes.... Estimates were that it would take approximately four to five years to build and test the new system. The cost of development and installation on a national scale was estimated to be approximately $17,000,000.

...During the last quarter of 1971 the KEDI staff focused on two major activities. These were: (1) an intensive series of meetings with Korean educators on the E-M project, and (2) the writing of the International Loan Agreement. The first of these activities was essential to broaden the base of support and to respond to questions or criticisms and to secure the cooperation of educators throughout the nation....

...KEDI was the beginning of a competency-based program of student learning.

...In the several tryouts since 1973—four small scale and four large scale—the achievement levels have generally been higher for the demonstration students than for the comparison group.

...In 1978, the President of the Republic appointed an external commission to conduct an independent evaluation of the new E-M program. This group assessed student and teacher attitudes toward the new program as well as community reaction. They also selected 18 schools and directed that the new KEDI system be implemented in these schools for five months in six basic subject areas, and identified a group of traditional schools to serve as the control. They found that mean achievement across all subject areas was 24 percent higher in the experimental group than in the control group, and that 30 percent more of the experimental students achieved subject mastery. The commission recommended an orderly implementation of the new E-M program in all of Korea's schools. [all emphases in original]

[Ed. Note: There is no way a valid determination can be made on the basis of instruction over a five-month period. Was the experimental group taught to the test as in OBE/ML/DI? Has the education ministry followed these students to see if their superior achievement has held over time? One would have to look at longitudinal data as well as the examinations used to come to any sort of valid conclusion regarding the superiority of OBE over the traditional Korean form of education. Also, what kinds of results were they looking for—academic or occupational?]

Appendix VII

Excerpts from *Performance-based Teacher Education*

Performance-based Teacher Education: What Is the State of the Art?, Stanley Elam, Ed. (Phi Delta Kappan Publications: Washington, D.C., 1971). Paper prepared for the Committee on Performance-based Teacher Education of the American Association of Colleges for Teacher Education pursuant to a contract with the U.S. Office of Education through the Texas Education Agency, Austin, Texas.

The Association is pleased to offer to the teacher education community the Committee's first state-of-the-art paper. In performance-based programs performance goals are specified, and agreed to, in rigorous detail in advance of instruction. The student must either be able to demonstrate his ability to promote desirable learning or exhibit behavior known to promote it. He is held accountable, not for passing grades, but for attaining a general level of competency in performing the essential tasks of teaching.... Emphasis is on demonstrated product or output. Acceptance of this basic principle has program implications that are truly revolutionary.

Probably the roots of PBTE [Performance-based Teacher Education, ed.] lie in general societal conditions and the institutional responses to them characteristic of the Sixties. For example, the realization that little or no progress was being made in narrowing wide inequality gaps led to increasing governmental attention to racial, ethnic, and socioeconomic minority needs, particularly educational ones.

The claim that traditional teacher education programs were not producing people equipped to teach minority group children and youth effectively has pointed directly to the need for reform in teacher education.

Moreover, the claim of minority group youth that there should be alternative routes to professional status has raised serious questions about the suitability of generally recognized teacher education programs.

Confronted with the ultimate question of the meaning of life in American society, youths have pressed for greater relevance in their education and a voice in determining what its goals should be. Thus PBTE usually includes a means of shared decision-making power... [T]he student's rate of progress through the program is determined by demonstrated competency rather than by time or course completion.... Instruction is individualized and personalized.... Because time is a variable, not a constant, and because students may enter with widely differing backgrounds and purposes, instruction is likely to be highly person- and situation-specific.... The learning experience of the individuals is guided by feedback.... [T]eaching competencies to be demonstrated are role-derived, specified in behavioral terms, and made public; assessment criteria are competency-based, specify mastery levels, and made public; assessment requires performance as prime evidence, takes student knowledge into account; student's progress rate depends on demonstrated competency; instructional program facilitates development and evaluation of specific competencies.... The application of such a systematic strategy to any human process is called the systems approach.... We cannot be sure that measurement techniques essential both to objectivity and to valid assessment of affective and complex cognitive objectives will be developed rapidly enough for the new exit requirements to be any better than the conventional letter grades of the past. Unless heroic efforts are made on both the knowledge and measurement fronts, then PBTE may well have a stunted growth.... To recapitulate, the promise of performance-based teacher education lies primarily in: 1) the fact that its focus on objectives and its emphasis upon the sharing process by which those objectives are formulated in advance are made explicit and used as the basis for evaluating performance; 2) the fact that a large share of the responsibility for learning is shifted from teacher to student; 3) the fact that it increases efficiency through systematic use of feedback, motivating and guiding learning efforts of prospective teachers; 4) the fact that greater attention is given to variation among individual abilities, needs, and interests; 5) the fact that learning is tied more directly to the objectives to be achieved than to the learning resources utilized to attain them; 6) the fact that prospective teachers are taught in the way they are expected to teach; 7) the fact that PBTE is consistent with democratic principles; 8) the fact that it is consistent with what we know about the psychology of learning; 9) the fact that it permits effective integration of theory and practice; 10) the fact that it provides better bases for designing research about teaching performance. These advantages would seem sufficient to warrant and ensure a strong and viable movement.

From "The Scope of PBTE":

Among the most difficult questions asked about the viability of performance-based instruction as the basis for substantial change in teacher preparatory programs are these: Will it tend to produce technicians, paraprofessionals, teacher aides, etc., rather than professionals?... These questions derive from the fact that while performance-based instruction eliminates waste in the learning process through clarity in definition of goods, it can be applied only to learning in which the objectives sought are susceptible of definition in advance in behavioral terms. Thus it is difficult to apply when the outcomes sought are complex and subtle, and particularly when they are affective or attitudinal in character.

From "Philosophic Underpinning":

Some authorities have expressed the fact that PBTE has an inadequate philosophic base, pointing out that any performance-based system rests on particular values, and the most important of which are expressed in the competencies chosen and in the design of the learning activities.

From "Political and Management Difficulties":

...4) There are political aspects to the question of how far the professor's academic freedom and the student's right to choose what he wishes to learn extend in PBTE. 5) ...The mere adoption of a PBTE program will eliminate some prospective students because they do not find it appealing. The question remains: Will these be the students who should be eliminated?... 6) The PBTE movement could deteriorate into a power struggle over who controls what. 7) PBTE removes students regularly from the campus into field settings and emphasizes individual study and progress rather than class-course organization, thus tends to isolate the people involved. We live in a period when such isolation is not a popular social concept, and since many aspects of the PBTE approach could be conceived as Skinnerian, dehumanizing etc., it is important that programs be managed in such a way as to minimize isolation?... 9) Finally, there is a need to overcome the apathy, threat, anxiety, administrative resistance, and other barriers that stand in the way of moving toward PBTE and toward performance-based teaching in the schools.

[Ed. Note: Over the years one has seen the departure of many talented teachers who have left the profession due to Skinnerian Performance-based Teacher Education.]

Appendix VIII

Excerpts from "The Field of Educational Technology"

"The Field of Educational Technology: A Statement of Definition," by Donald P. Ely, Ed. Published in *Audiovisual Instruction* (Association of Educational Computing and Technology: Washington, D.C.), October 1972 (pp. 36 ff).

There is no single author of this statement since the definition process involved several hundred people over the period of one year. Kenneth Silber spent more time than any other person and provided continuity through several drafts. Other writers included Kenneth Norberg, Geoffrey Squires, and Gerald Torkelson. Significant contributions were made by Robert Heinich, Charles F. Hoban, Jr., Wesley Meierhenry, and Robert Wagner through discussion papers prepared early in the process. Reactions from related fields were helpful—Desmond Cook (Educational Psychology), Keith Mielke (Telecommunications), and Robert Taylor (Library and Information Science). Each reviewed an earlier draft of the manuscript and met to discuss it. Finally, credit should go to the more than 100 members of the Association of Educational Computing and Technology [AECT, spin-off of the NEA, ed.] who participated at the open hearings held during the Minneapolis convention. And now, the process must go on with each reader. May I have your reactions? Signed by Donald P. Ely, Editor, Chairman, Definition and Terminology Committee, AECT, Branch of the National Education Association....

When scientific and experimental methods are applied in an orderly and comprehensive way to the planning of instructional tasks, or to entire programs, this process is sometimes known as "systems design," or the "systems approach to instructional development." Implicit in the systems approach is the use of clearly stated objectives, experimentally derived, data to evaluate the results of the system, and feedback loops which allow the system to improve itself based on evaluation.

A systematic approach usually involves: needs assessment (to determine what the problem really is); solution selection (to meet the needs); development of instructional objectives (if an instructional solution is indeed needed); analysis of tasks and content needed to meet the objectives; selection of instructional strategies; sequencing of instructional events; selection of media; developing or locating the necessary resources; tryout/evaluation of the effectiveness of the resources; revision of resources until they are effective; and recycling continuously through the whole process. The systems approach is basic to educational technology.

Individualized learning requires systematic planning because it may operate with little or no direct intervention by the teacher. If the benefits of individualized and personalized learning are to succeed, it will be necessary to make full use of appropriate technical resources, to shift money saved by this approach into the development of more effective resources, and to make consistent and expanded use of experimental study and evaluation techniques. All of these require the use of the systems approach to succeed.

The rationale for a unique field of educational technology is its synthesis of three concepts: providing a broad range of learning resources, individualizing and personalizing learning as a focus, and using the systems approach as an intellectual and operational approach to the facilitation of learning. The combination of these concepts in the broader context of education and society yields synergistic outcomes—behaviors which are not predictable on the parts alone—but outcomes with extra energy which is created by the unique interrelationship of the parts....

Within the context of society, the purposes and means of the educational technologist create two value questions: are the means used by the educational technologist neutral, or do they have ends and values built in? Does a person concerned with the means of education also have to be concerned with the ends?... These questions and issues and their resolution by each person in the field is as much a part of the definition of the field as the functions the people in the field perform.

Is technology neutral?

Theoretically, technology in the "pure" state is neutral in its operation, simply the powerful and faithful servant of the society it serves but does not affect.

But institutionalized technology in the real world is never that pure. Once embedded in socioeconomic systems, it tends to become self-justifying and self-perpetuating and does indeed affect the society it serves.

Technology neatly separates ends from means, and attempts to become neutral by divorcing itself from value-laden ends. However, if technology is independent of means, then its worth must be measured by the degree of success and the efficiency with which it achieves the goals set before it. Thus, the technological thrust in modern society is to continually refine and strengthen the means whatever the goal.

The net result, which has been pointed out by many scholars of technology, is that the means tend to become the ends. The means which sometimes serve as the end of technology are NOT neutral. As most critics of technology have pointed out, these means have effects—effects which are not neutral at all. Whether the effects are positive or negative is a question for debate, but neutrality is a choice which does not exist.

For example, it is clear that technology has effects on man, but what are they? One position is that technology exerts a subtle force to reduce human beings to standardized components which can readily be assimilated to whatever system is being served. It absorbs them into man-machine systems by robbing them of their humanity and making them human machines.

The opposing position states that technology makes humaneness and difference possible. It creates the options we need for true freedom, and creates a world which allows divergent value systems.

The opposite of the neutral technician is what we might call the concentrated professional. This person realizes that the means make the ends possible, and that cooperation or hindrance makes ends possible or impossible. The concerned professional has a point of view about the ends and then decides whether or not the work being done will make possible positive or negative ends.

If it is decided the work will bring about negative ends, the concerned professional refuses to perform it.

The scientist working on genetic selection and manipulation because "it can help eliminate disease from the human race" and those who have quit working on it because it will "lead to totalitarian domination by a master race" are examples of concerned professionals. Regardless of their position, they have considered the ends of their work and made a decision to work or not based on how they viewed those ends.

It should be clear that the concerned professional does not have to be a "liberal" or a "conservative." The concerned professional must however, show moral sensitivity to the effect of what he or she does. [emphasis in original]

It does not matter what position an individual comes to as long as it is not "I'll do it because it can be done."

We believe that in the American society of the 1970s and beyond the educational technologist cannot afford to be a neutral technician. The field calls for concerned professionals. Some very hard questions must be raised about everything this person is called on to do. The concerned professional must ask how the resources produced or used affect all of society, as well as the scientist's own life.

The concerned specialist must ask what to do if he/she disagrees with the messages of the resources.

It is less important how an educational technologist answers these questions than it is that they are asked, and that there is concern with the real end of the means.... The educational technologist is not the only person making decisions about the facilitation of learning through the identification, development, organization, and utilization of learning resources. The teacher, curriculum specialist, administrator, content specialist, librarian and the student are involved in the process, too.... It is, therefore, important for the field of educational technology to recognize the "other people" context in which it operates.

Further, it is essential to ascertain what the relationship of the field of educational technology with these other fields will be. In a practical sense, the work relationship means "who will get to make the ultimate decisions about facilitating learning and how it is done?" There are at least five types of alternatives for the facilitation of learning. They differ along the dimension of formality, based on the compulsory nature of the institution, on the degree of authority of those in charge, and on the range of resources available.

The effects of technology cannot, therefore, be overlooked. They create serious concerns for society as a whole. They are particularly important to a person involved in a field like educational technology, since its effects help to shape human minds.

What are the effects of packaged learning [OBE/ML/DI, ed.], etc., on a person for 18 years? Are we moving too fast technologically for people to cope with the changes? How do feeling and spontaneity fit into a technologically-based system? Are we trying to program all connections between people?

The educational technologist, as a concerned professional, must study the philosophical, psychological and sociological implications of how the technologist can facilitate learning.

[Ed. Note: This paper was an attachment to an AECT proposal to develop *Handbook X* of the *Educational Records and Reports Series* for the National Center for Educational Statistics. AECT also received the Project BEST (Better Education Skills through Technology) contract from the U.S. Department of Education in 1982. The excerpts are very important as they relate to the concerns of leading educators in the field of technology regarding ethical and privacy issues surrounding the use of programmed learning (OBE/ML/DI) in conjunction with technology in the schools of the United States. Donald Ely (Editor and Chairman of the Definition and Terminology Committee, AECT) was also involved in Project BEST in 1982. Also listed as members of BEST's Advisory Board were Dr. Shirley McCune of the Midcontinental Regional Education Laboratory and William Spady of the American Association of School Administrators—both of whom are closely associated with outcome-based education/mastery learning, the purpose of which is to "restructure" not only the schools, but America itself through changing the attitudes, values, and beliefs of students to accept citizenship in a one-world socialist government. These excerpts should be brought to the attention of Ely, Spady, and McCune with the question: "Do you share the concerns of your associates who contributed to the writing of this paper?" If so, why do you have such a hard time understanding why parents and taxpayers are opposed to Skinnerian outcome-based education?]

Appendix IX

Excerpts from *A Performance Accountability System*

A Performance Accountability System for School Administrators by T.H. Bell (Parker Publishing Co.: New York, 1974). T.H. Bell served as Secretary of Education during President Ronald Reagan's first term in office, 1981–1985, and also served as Commissioner of Education in the U.S. Office of Education during the Ford Administration. Excerpts from the book follow:

The Need for a Management System

Under the pressure of the free-enterprise system and the unremitting demand that large corporations earn profits and pay dividends to stockholders, management efficiency through orientation to results has led to development of management systems such as the one described in this book. Most of the successful corporations in the United States now use annually adopted objectives as a means of focusing the energies and efforts of managers on the attainment of goals that are widely known and broadly accepted. Although the problems of educational management are obviously quite different from those of the private sector, there is much to be learned from industry's systems approach in gaining more efficiency in educational management. The outcomes are quite similar. (p. 21)

Why Needs Assessments?

As a people, Americans have turned from a preoccupation with production and plenty to a concern for the quality of human life in this nation. We have moved beyond the point where production of the necessities for existence is a concern. We want a rich and meaningful life and we want equality of opportunity for all citizens.

Drug abuse, juvenile delinquency, lack of respect for law and order, coping with environmental damage are all problems with which education must be concerned in this new era of social awareness and public concern for the success and happiness of all. These enormous demands call for systematic attention to the performance outcomes of the schools and colleges of the nation. Since we have so many problems and since our resources are limited, it is essential that we look at the performance of our educational institutions and establish a hierarchy of priorities.... We should seek to solve the problems that are causing the greatest amount of difficulty and unrest across the nation. We should seek to solve the problems whose solutions will both stimulate the economy and free the public from the burden of supporting citizens who are unable to support themselves. We must, in short, assess our educational needs before establishing our objectives and setting into action leadership and management plans. (pp. 32–32)

Use of Tests in Needs Assessments

The economic, sociological, psychological and physical aspects of students must be taken into account as we look at their educational needs and accomplishments, and fortunately there are a number of attitude and inventory scales that can be used to assess these admittedly difficult to measure outcomes....

Most of these efforts to manage education try to center in one place an information center that receives reports and makes available to all members of the management team various types of information useful to managers....

School management by objectives demands more use of educational tests and measures (pp. 33–35).

The Student and Staff Personnel Profile

A departmental or school student and staff personnel profile, constructed from needs assessment information, will provide information in greater depth than is typically found in most school or college operations. The characteristics of the student populations being served and the social, economic, racial, and ethnic make-up of the community or neighborhood must be weighed in making assumptions on performance expectations. An objective, expressed in anticipated performance results, must take into account the characteristics of the students, the neighborhood and community. (p. 42)

Humanizing Education

Many of our current problems of alienation and depersonalization are at least partly traceable to our emphasis in our schools upon giving and getting information and our neglect of the discovery of meaning and humanization. The committee writing the 1962 *ASCD Yearbook* listed common school practices that have depersonalizing and alienating effects:

- The emphasis on fact instead of feelings
- The belief that intelligence is fixed and immutable
- The continual emphasis upon grades, artificial reasons instead of real ones for learning
- Conformity and preoccupation with order and neatness
- Authority, support and evidence
- Solitary learning
- Cookbook approaches
- Adult concepts considered as the only ones of value
- Emphasis on competition
- Lockstep progression
- Force, threat and coercion
- Wooden rules and regulations
- The age-old idea that if it's hard it's good for them

Until now we have been schooling to fit a "norm" of society. It's time to begin thinking of an education for every man. As defined by Carl R. Rogers, "The only man who is educated is the man who has learned how to learn; the man who has learned how to adapt and change; the man who has realized that no knowledge is secure, that only the process of seeking knowledge gives a basis for security."

This clearly invalidates our conception of a successful student as one who simply graduates with a degree and a high grade point average—a molded, shaped figure ready to slip away from life and learning into the split-levels and station wagons of suburbia. (p. 161)

[Ed. Note: There is no question in this writer's mind that this one man bears much of the responsibility for the deliberate dumbing down of our schools. He set the stage for outcome-based education through his early support for systems management, management by objectives (MBO), and Planning Programming Budgeting System (PPBS). These systems later evolved into full-blown Total Quality Management/OBE, having gone through the initial stage of Professor Benjamin Bloom's mastery learning and ending up as William Spady's transformational OBE. Outcome-based or results/performance/competency-based education requires mastery learning, individualized instruction, systems management, and computer technology. Bell's earlier activities in the seventies as U.S. Commissioner of Education—including his role in supporting dumbed-down life role competencies for K–12 (See 1975 *Adult Performance Level Study* and 1983 Delker article) and Bell's testimony before Congress in favor of a U.S. Department of Education—should have kept his name off any list of potential nominees presented to President Reagan. Concerns regarding this nomination expressed by Reagan supporters were proven well founded when Bell, in 1984, funded William Spady's infamous Utah OBE grant which promised to (and did) put OBE "in all schools of the nation"; spearheaded the technology initiative in the 1980s; predicted that schools would be bookless by the year 2000; recommended that all students have computers; and fired Edward Curran, the Director of the National Institute of Education, when Curran recommended to President Reagan that Curran's office, the NIE, be abolished.

According to a former member of the Utah Education Association, who was a close associate of Bell's in the early 1970s, if the Senate Committee that confirmed T.H. Bell as Secretary of Education had read Bell's *A Performance Accountability System for School Administrators*, it is unlikely Bell would have been confirmed.]

Appendix X

Excerpts from "The Next Step: *The Minnesota Plan*"

"The Next Step: *The Minnesota Plan*" by Paul Berman, Executive Director, Center for Policy Alternatives, and President of BW Associates, a consulting firm specializing in policy research and analysis in Berkeley, California (*Phi Delta Kappan*: Washington, D.C.) November 1985, p. 40.

Elementary and secondary education in America are in need of more than just repair and maintenance; the challenge is to move to "a new plateau of learning." The necessary structural reforms for such a move appear to be under way in Minnesota.... Although Minnesota's schools are among the best in the nation, the evidence shows that they have been unable to keep pace with the rapidly increasing need for more students to learn more.... Various groups in the state, as well as reform-minded legislatures and state officials, have been asking basic questions about the future of education in Minnesota. One such group is the Minnesota Business Partnership which contracted with me and my associates to examine K–12 education and suggest reforms, if necessary.... The result was *The Minnesota Plan*, a document that has altered the nature of the debate in Minnesota. Gov. Rudy Perpich and Ruth Randall, his superintendent of public instruction, used the Plan, as well as the work of others when they proposed to the state legislature reform measures based on concepts in the Plan.

Under "Restructuring Schooling":

...[T]he usual six years of comprehensive secondary education in junior and senior high schools, with their multiplicity of courses and student tracking, should be phased out. Instead, all students should attend a four-year secondary school that concentrates on core academic subjects. Then they should have opportunities to specialize for two years.

Though the *Minnesota Plan* has many unique elements, it has derived specific reforms from three sources. First, various state-level proposals over the past few years influenced what went into the *Plan* as well as what was omitted. My experience in developing reforms for what became California's omnibus education reform legislation (S.B. 813) was particularly valuable. Second, recent and earlier literature on schooling was extremely helpful, particularly the work of Benjamin Bloom, John Goodlad, and Theodore Sizer....

Tracking has been justified as a way for schools to meet the legitimate concern that students should be prepared for different careers. The comprehensive high school, with its bewildering array of courses, also evolved in part to satisfy this need. For example, most states, including Minnesota, impose seat-time or graduation requirements under which each student must take a certain number of units of high school mathematics....

The challenge for American education is to provide a common and equivalent educational experience for all students and to prepare them for different careers. The comprehensive high school has not and cannot... meet either goal adequately.... The restructuring... offers a different approach to realizing these dual objectives of American education. All students would concentrate on a core academic program in grades 7 through 10 and then, in grades 11 and 12, choose further education that matches their career aspirations.

Research and practice in thousands of classrooms both in the U.S. and abroad indicate that instructional strategies using this assumption, such as mastery learning or cooperative learning techniques, can result in more students learning dramatically more in both basic and higher-order skills. The *Minnesota Plan* calls for these approaches to be taught to senior teachers who can then train other teachers to shift their expectations and instruction to enable all students to learn. Mastery learning is controversial. However, the bulk of the evidence shows that large gains in student learning occur if teachers have the training and support to implement mastery learning effectively. Too often, mastery learning has been introduced as a "top down" innovation. The *Minnesota Plan*, by contrast, proposes a grassroots approach to implementation....

A publicly elected school-level board, operating in concert with a school-site management council, would decide which courses to offer at the school and which courses might be offered by other public schools or by other public or private providers. Schools would have the authority to "contract out" or "contract in" for teaching services.... This restructuring would take advantage of strength in the best European systems.... Deregulate curriculum and instruction. Educators should be free to design curriculum and instruction that they feel meets state standards and community needs. States should set basic goals; educators should be responsible to the community for helping students to meet these goals.

A restructuring of schooling could not realize its full promise without jettisoning the anachronistic system of employing course-unit/seat-time requirements as the criterion for student promotion and graduation. Advancement should be based on demonstrated achievement.... State-mandated course and graduation requirements would be eliminated in favor of a statement by the state of the competencies students are expected to master and two state tests, which would be required of all students before they leave the sixth and tenth grades.

[Ed. Note: Paul Berman is a well known and highly paid consultant/change agent. Berman has been associated with RAND Corporation, a major policy development think tank which helped develop the Planning, Programming and Budgeting System (PPBS).]

Appendix XI

"When Is Assessment REALLY Assessment?"

"When Is Assessment REALLY Assessment?" by Cynthia Weatherly, published in *The Christian Conscience* (Vol. 1, No. 9, 1995, pp. 28–32, 50). It can be found on the Internet at http://www.christianconscience.com.

Why are the new-fangled tests called "assessments"? The answer is shocking!

During preparation for a workshop on educational policy in 1982, I was asked by the host organization to prepare a glossary of terms pertaining to my presentation. That request seemed simple enough and a reasonable one, so I set about compiling terms related to Competency-Based Education (CBE, forerunner of Outcome-Based Education and promulgated by the same man—Bill Spady), our fad-of-the-moment in educational reformation toward illiteracy in Georgia.

As I said, the task *seemed* simple enough. However, while still in the A's of the alphabet, I developed an overwhelming respect for professional compilers of glossaries. The first word block I encountered was *assessment*. Sure it was familiar; we all knew it meant "test," but the longer I struggled to apply that definition to CBE the more elusive *assessment's* definition became.

The latest word for "test" was "instrument" and that proved easy to explain. But *assessment* was a broader term. *Assessment* was the noun form of the verb "assess." What did *assess* actually mean? The National Assessment of Educational Progress (NAEP) had been in use since its development in the latter 1960s. Had we overlooked a change in emphasis by the Federal level of education implied by the use of the word *assessment* that could be significant?

Receiving no help from my small hill of accumulated state department of education materials relating to assessment, I decided to read the instruction manual: *Webster's New World Dictionary*. *Webster's* clearly stated:

> **assess**: 1. to set an estimated value on (property, etc.) for taxation 2. To set the amount of (a tax, fine, damages, etc.) 3. To impose a fine, tax, or special payment on (a person or

property) 4. To impose (an amount) as a fine, tax, etc. 5. To estimate or determine the significance, importance, or value of, evaluate.

assessment: 1. The act of assessing 2. The amount assessed.

This definition disturbed me a little. I had assumed that *assessment* was just the latest educationese for a broad-based test. Had I missed something somewhere?

To accomplish the task at hand—the glossary—I crafted a definition that read like this:

> **Assessment:** an estimation; determination of the significance or value of. As used in education, a general term for measuring student progress. Conflict in definition occurs when considering that this is a measurement process used to determine the value or significance of a particular outcome in educational performance. Therefore, it is not a true measurement, but a process of assigning value to specific tasks, creating a cumulative score for performance instead of an accurate measurement against a standard.

It sounded good at the time and spoke to the question of "what are we testing?" which was a growing concern due to the nature of Competency-Based Education's life role skills competencies, which were going to dictate our educational goals—just like OBE does today. Even though satisfied to have introduced the idea that there may be a conflict within the definition of *assessment* as an educational term, I was bothered that I could find no definitions in other dictionaries, including legal ones, which did not have primary meanings related to assigning a value for tax purposes. *Assessment* is primarily a legal term; in fact, the use of the word "instrument" could carry a legal connotation as well. Disturbing.

The Federal Accounting Process

In March of 1984 I had the privilege of giving testimony supporting stringent regulations for the *Pupil Privacy Act* (the *Hatch Amendment*) which amended the *General Education Provisions Act* to offer protection from intrusive questioning, programs, and the record-keeping for parents and students. Again, preparation for that testimony caused me to review the national Center for Educational Statistics' handbook series known as the *State Educational Records and Report Series*. Specifically, *Handbook IIR*, the *Financial Accounting Handbook*, alluded to a "unified accounting system" based on the process known as Planning, Programming and Budgeting System (PPBS) which was to be used by all school systems. PPBS involves mandated goals and constant adjustment of resources to ensure that goals are met—the system that is still in use today. In testifying, I drew a projected conclusion:

> If our financial resource reporting is going to be unified by such a system, then are we not but a step away from unified goals for our educational outcomes? This is assuredly a step toward mandated national curriculum and interstate and interregional tax and financial management revisions.... Will we not soon be sharing tax resources from region to region as needed to "equalize" educational opportunities and programs deemed "exemplary" or in the "national interest" to produce global-minded citizens?

The longer I thought of *assessment* being the "value determined for tax purposes" and the possibility of cross-regional/state sharing of tax resources, the more concerned I became over the idea that the record-keeping and information-compiling might become so tied to the individual student that *assessment* might have a more malignant potential. We were talking about our children here.

At that point in time there was a growing emphasis on choice and vouchers/tuition tax credits in education. Since with the money flows the control, could this be part of the *assessment* picture? That would tie an individual student moving about in the "choice market" directly to a federal accounting process both financially and educationally due to national standards being proposed. No one seemed to be too worried about it in the 1980s, but it still bothered me.

Over a period of time I shared my concern with close associates—if *assess* was to "assign a value for tax purposes," then why were we *assessing* children? A theory began to take root and grow in my mind: somehow we were going to allow children's potential worth to society to be measured, and their future life roles would somehow be measured, and their future life roles would somehow be projected, and they would be limited by that assigned worth. What a thought! Could this be possible in the United States?

Human Capital Defined

Later someone sent me pages from a book entitled *Human Capital and America's Future*, edited by David W. Hornbeck and Lester M. Salamon. The title itself set off alarm bells because of the connection to education shared by many of the contributors, especially Hornbeck. It was now the early 1990s and many disturbing things were happening. David Hornbeck was a highly visible change agent responsible for many radical education reforms in states from Kentucky to Iowa and had been consultant to many more. Why was Hornbeck focusing on *human capital*? That term had been primarily used in economic and commercial literature. Hornbeck was also identified with changes in assessment in the school systems with which he consulted and worked.

The book was published by Johns Hopkins University Press in 1991 and contains an enlightening list of contributors in addition to Hornbeck: Ernest Boyer, Nancy Barrett, Anthony Carnavale, Sheldon Danziger, Marian Wright Edelman, Scott Fosler, Daniel Greenberg, Jason Jaffras, Arnold Packer, Isabel Sawhill, Marion Pines, Donald Stewart, and Lester Salamon. The social and political views of *Human Capital's* contributors could be the basis of another whole article, but suffice it to say that most of the radical changes toward a managed populous in this country can be reflected among this group of individuals. Weren't some of them involved in dis-establishing the U.S. Department of Health, Education and Welfare (HEW) and turning it into the Department of Education?

While references to *human capital* have been the fare of business publications for some time, it has only been in the last few years that this term has been applied to school children. In Hornbeck's chapter "New Paradigm for Action," he outlined the systemic change which must occur to produce the workforce for the future and fulfill our nation's *human capital* needs. Hornbeck's "new paradigm of action" looked a lot like old OBE—setting specific performance standards and invoking penalties for schools, teachers and students not meeting them:

> If the new comprehensive system is to be outcome-based, careful attention must be paid to *assessment* strategies. The selection of outcome indicators will be informed by the availability of sound *assessment instruments*. [emphasis added]

Now here was Hornbeck using *assessment* and *instrument* together instead of a substitute for one or the other—and he had selected the two terms which carried legal usage definitions. Hornbeck asserted that while the NAEP might be universally available, and portfolio *assessments* (notice the use of both words together) would become popular, "the Educational Testing Service (ETS) is investing time and funds in developing new approaches to assessment." He further stated that most of the present *assessment* observations are "related to academic objectives":

> Similar sensitivity is required in carefully defining appropriate assessment tools in other areas as well. In citizenship, a method should be developed for expressing qualitative aspects of participation activities.... [A] different *value* could be placed on community service.... *Physical and mental fitness...* problems arise as we confront legal and even constitutional issues (self-incrimination, search and seizure).... Perhaps a school system should plan to have all students undergo a physical exam in the fourth, eighth, and twelfth grades as a health counterpart to the academic testing program. Again, the emphasis must be on carefully determining assessment strategies that measure the outcomes to be achieved. [emphasis added]

All of this is structured because "incremental change is insufficient. Systems must be radically altered to produce what the nation's economy demands in a work force."

Weren't we supposed to be concerned about the education of school children? This sounded a lot like literature which proposed "full employment" policies, much like the billboards and signs plastered on public transportation and public buildings in Grenada—"Work for everyone: everyone working!"—before the U.S. invasion to overthrow their Communist government in 1983.

Was this why the Council of Chief State School Officers accepted a contract from the National Center for Educational Statistics to develop what is known as the SPEEDE ExPRESS (the Exchange of Permanent Records Electronically of Students and Schools)? This electronic information track can carry the most diverse and extensive information on a student, delivering it to future employers, places of higher education, training centers, health providers (contraceptive histories will be included), the military, and a number of other recipients yet to be designated. Then if employers, government, and others have input into what should be the outcome of education in this country—instead of education being academically and information-based—then this concept of "assessment as assigning a value" to a child takes on proportions that are certainly Orwellian.

What if your child's *assessed* worth doesn't meet anyone's projected goal? Proponents of the Certificate of Initial Mastery (CIM) and the Certificate of Advanced Mastery (CAM) are, in truth, fleshing out the skeleton of assigning a value to a person. Without the CIM/CAM in those states adopting the concept, young persons will not be able to apply for a job, drive a car, or do many other things which have never before been predicated on government's conferring a value on a person's worth to society. The People's Republic of China, a Communist country, uses "no conformity—no job" policies to enforce its "one child" policy.

Have we understood the direction of these changes? Is this constitutional or moral?

Assessing Human Value
The next piece to the puzzle of assessment fell into place when my suspicions were confirmed that we really *were* assessing "value". The August 1993 issue of *Visions*, the newsletter of the Education for Future Initiative sponsored by Pacific Telesis Foundation, was given out at a

legislative committee meeting as part of a packet of information on technology in the classroom and school-to-work transition activities. The lead article was "Beyond the Bubble" with a blurb reading: "Educators are finding that new ways of teaching require new forms of assessment."

On page three there was a column entitled "Authentic Definitions." Finally, I thought, I have found an educational publication that will define this word and allay my fears. Sure enough, there was the word:

> **Assessment**—The act or result of judging the *worth* or *value* of something or *someone*. [emphasis added]

The worth or value of something or someone?! This was confirmation that educational testing had taken an extreme left turn. It was not comforting to realize that our children were going to be assigned a value based on "acceptable performance behaviors in life-role applications" as proposed in Pacific Telesis Foundation's "Authentic Definitions."

Knowing that:

1. our children would be tracked and that extensively detailed files would be electronically compiled and transmitted to select users;

2. information would include or be based on a value level assigned to them contingent upon performance—as a child—of life role competencies;

3. value levels could reflect the scale of achievement outlined in the United States Labor Department's 1993 *Secretary's Commission on Achieving Necessary Skills* (SCANS) publications which encompasses personality traits and private preferences, and

4. the purpose of education had documentably been diverted into workforce training, led me, ultimately, to the conclusion that indeed the future holds a less than bright prospect for our young people. To be formally assigned a "worth" to society based on your ability as a child to demonstrate that you can perform an "essential skill" should be a foreign concept in a constitutional republic like the one in which we live—these United States of America.

An example of how these efforts at assessment have been perverted to the ends outlined above is given in *Crucial Issues In Testing*, edited by Ralph W. Tyler and Richard M. Wolf. This book is one in a series prepared under the auspices of the National Society for the Study of Education, which in 1974 included names like William Spady, John Goodlad, and Robert Havighurst on its governing committee. On page 98, within an article by Carmen J. Finley (of the American Institute for Research) is a section entitled "Defining Goals Versus Comparison with an Average":

> In the National Assessment program specific objectives or goals are defined and exercises are written which determine how well these goals are being met. For example, in citizenship a major objective is to "Support Rights and Freedoms of All Individuals." One specific way in which a person might meet this goal is to defend the right of a person with very unpopular views to express his opinion and support the right of "extreme" (political or religious) groups to express their views in public.

One exercise which was written to try to tell whether or not this objective was being met is as follows:

> Below are three statements which make some people angry. Mark each statement as to

whether you think a person on radio or TV should or should not be allowed to make these statements:

- Russia is better than the United States.
- Some races of people are better than others.
- It is not necessary to believe in God.

This is the goal-oriented approach. The objectives or goals represent a kind of standard which is considered desirable to achieve. The exercises, if they are good measures, tell to what extent the goals are being achieved. This approach tells very specifically what a person knows or can do.

I submit that the goals-oriented/performance-based/OBE assessment approach just outlined tells more than what a child knows or can do. This approach very specifically reveals what a child feels and believes. Remember that assessments measure predetermined outcomes. Those outcomes represent the judged "worth" or "value" of your children and mine!

With the last election cycle, hope swept the country that since a conservative majority had exerted itself, changes would be made. As a country we'd be snatched from the brink of economic socialism and potential corporate fascism, and sanity would be restored to the halls of government. Right?

When Right Is Left

It just happens that the October 1992 edition of *Visions* (Pac Telesis Foundation newsletter) contained an article entitled "Why Technology?" It began

> Alvin Toffler, the author of such influential books as *Future Shock* and *The Third Wave*, has written that the spread of personal computers is the single most important change in the field of knowledge since the invention of movable type in the 15th century. He goes on to state that knowledge is the key to power in the 21st century—not mineral rights or military force.

This was the same publication that carried the definitive definition of *assessment*. And wasn't this the same Alvin Toffler who wrote *Creating a New American Civilization*, which heralds the coming "Third Wave" of global culture, published by the Progress and Freedom Foundation and introduced at their "Cyberspace and the New American Dream" conference in Atlanta last year?

Newt Gingrich, the new Speaker of the House, introduced Toffler as his longtime friend and then sat quietly by to hear Toffler say that national sovereignty was a thing of the past and that he was an avowed secularist. These are the stripes of our new "conservative" future?

At the same Cyberspace conference, an array of professionals from many areas of cultural life paraded their contributions to leadership toward the much-touted "Third Wave". The spokesperson for education in Progress and Freedom Foundation's lineup was—and still is—Lewis J. Perelman, author of *School's Out: A Radical New Formula for the Revitalization of America's Educational System*. Perelman advocates what he calls just-in-time learning, privatized public schools, Total Quality applications, hyperlearning, and many other catchy concepts which are now, of course, getting much attention in the policy debates.

It should be noted that in the preface to his book Perelman cites Wassily Leontief and B.F. Skinner among those from whom he particularly benefited during his years at Harvard in the 1970s. Most interesting, since Leontief is the acknowledged expert on management by objectives (MBO)—the forerunner and companion to PPBS. And Skinner was the American father of behavioral psychology and mastery learning/operant conditioning—the foundation for OBE.

These relationships of Perelman's are important because he supplied the connecting piece to complete the puzzle picture of our children's future. Perelman states on page 316 that

> ...Nostalgic mythology about "local control" should not mask the reality that the state governments have the constitutional authority, call the shots, and pay most of the bill for education. But government, local or otherwise, no longer needs to own and operate school systems or academic institutions.

Taxing Human Worth

Now to the heart of Perelman's alternative proposal which forms the future of "conservative" educational policy and expresses *assessment's* future use:

> ...One possibility would be a *human capital tax* [emphasis added]. The human capital tax might be simply the same as a personal income tax, or might be calculated or ear-marked in a more limited way. Technicalities aside, it's logical that if the government is going to help fund investments in the development of the community's human capital, taking back a share of the resulting gains is a good way to pay for it. In effect, each generation of beneficiaries of such investment pays back some of the benefits it received to the next generation [value-added tax, ed.]. (p. 317)

> We should deal with parents who are *starving their children's minds* with the same legal remedies we use to deal with parents who are starving their children's bodies. The media through which a microchoice [voucher] system is provided will give public authorities more accurate information on what individual families and kids are doing than is currently available, making it easier to identify instances of negligence or misuse. [emphasis added] (p. 318)

> ...[T]here's no good reason why the learner should not be able to purchase services or products from any provider—whether public or private, in-state or out-of-state. (p. 319)

A Value-Added Tax For Human Worth

There is the framework. A value-added tax process that will *deduct* from a services/education super-voucher a tax for every level of achievement/skill a student achieves—true *assessment*. Standards will be rigid and penalties for non-achievement will be enforceable against the student, his parents, and providers of educational services in order to achieve a trained workforce.

The implications for families being disrupted by accusations and prosecutions for Perelman's implied abuse and neglect over "parental starving of children's minds" are startling in their flagrancy.

An elaborate and accurate system will track families and students, leaving privacy and confidentiality in the dust. The tax/voucher will follow the student across state and regional boundaries, necessitating a reformulation of tax bases; this could even be extended to foreign sources—facilitated by choice and charter school initiatives. (Remember Toffler asserts that national sovereignty is, or will soon be, a thing of the past. And what about GATT's education provision?)

The World Bank has just announced (Associated Press, *The Des Moines Register*, 9/15/95) its new formula for estimating a nation's worth. Ismael Serageldin, World Bank Vice President for Environmentally Sustainable Development, stated in *Monitoring Environmental Progress: A Report on Work in Progress* that the system "for the first time folds a country's people and its natural resources into its overall balance sheet." While the World Bank projects that its new system of measuring wealth which "attempts to go beyond traditional gauges" and lists "Human Resources: value represented by people's productive capacity" (e.g. education, nutrition) will take years to perfect, I submit that our process of *assessment* is a giant step in that direction.

I am reminded that in May of 1984 the *Washington Post* published an article entitled "Industrial Policy Urged for GOP." The Institute for Contemporary Studies, "founded by Edwin Meese, Caspar Weinberger, and other Reagan supporters," issued a report that advocated "Republicans shed some of their deep-rooted antipathy to a planned economy." All signals seem to point to the fact that this has indeed happened.

Somewhere in all of this is lost the ability to communicate our culture in an organized way and to teach basic skills that can be used whether cyberspace technology is available or not. Didn't we used to call this "education"? Didn't we believe that our children had some choice in their futures?

When is *assessment* really *assessment*? Ernest Boyer, former Director of the Office of Education and Carnegie Foundation director, once said, "To be fully human one must **serve**." In the future to be fully assessed may mean our children's worth as a **servant** of the state will be "assigned a value for tax purposes"—*assessment*.

America, where are you?

Eph. 6:10-20

Appendix XII

Excerpts from "The National Alliance for Restructuring Education: Schools—and Systems—for the 21st Century"

A Proposal to the New American Schools Development Corporation
by the
National Center on Education and the Economy
Attn.: Marc Tucker, President
39 State Street, Suite 500, Rochester (Monroe County), NY 14614
Phone: (716) 546-7620 and FAX: (716) 546-3145
and its Partners:

State of Arkansas
Apple Computer, Inc.
State of Kentucky
Center for the Study of Social Policy
State of New York
Commission on the Skills of the American Workforce
Pittsburgh, PA
Harvard Project on Effective Services
Rochester, NY

Learning Research and Development Center at the University of Pittsburgh
San Diego, CA
State of Vermont
National Alliance of Business
State of Washington
National Board for Professional Teaching Standards
White Plains, NY
New Standards Project
Xerox Corporation
Public Agenda Foundation

Brandon is a small, rural village in the Green Mountains an hour south of Burlington on Vermont Highway 7. The people here are poor, and the ugly white-brick two-story building looks more like a weather-beaten industrial plant than a school. But, on the inside, Otter Valley Union High School has become a high output academic setting that produces the state's debate champions, its own literary magazine and a choir that performed Mozart at Carnegie Hall.

Bucking bureaucratic rules and winning state waivers from regulations, the faculty at

Otter Valley restructured their school over the past six years. They worked with the community to set ambitious goals. They created interdisciplinary teams of teachers to improve instruction. They moved to cooperative learning and heterogeneous grouping. A rotating *troika* of teachers assumed the role of principal. They started "measuring" [emphasis in original] learning through portfolios of the students' work in math, English, social studies and science. They fought for time and money to get the training for themselves that allowed this transformation. The students responded. (p. 2)

Now, imagine for the moment where we might be if states and districts *routinely* [emphasis in original] gave birth to schools like Otter Valley in Vermont. Imagine systems that provide assistance and encouragement to schools to "break the mold" instead of inflexible rules that only harden it. (p. 3)

Our object is to make schools like Otter Valley... the norm everywhere. By 1995 we plan to have 243 schools in seven states—enrolling a student body representative of the American people—cast in molds they set themselves and performing as well as any in the world. These schools will be the vanguard of a far larger number in many more states that will meet the same standard in five years.

Reaching this goal will require a transformation in virtually every important aspect of the American system of education, features that have remained essentially unchanged for nearly 70 years, from graduation standards to incentives that motivate students, from curriculum to budgeting, from assessment systems to teaching careers. (page 4)

Promoting and—especially—sustaining these changes in the schools will require complementary and equally radical changes in the organization of school districts and the structure and administration of education policy at the state level. It will also require thoughtful and sustained communication with the citizens of these states to build the public consensus needed to support those revolutionary changes. Designing and implementing this kind of fundamental transformation not just in a few schools, but in schools, districts and states in many parts of the country at once is an unprecedented undertaking. Pulling it off will require the coordinated action of hundreds of the most talented, committed educators and specialists from many walks of American life beyond education. The National Alliance for Restructuring has assembled such a team and has devised a plan that will enable us to work together to get the job done. The states and districts that are our Partners are utterly committed to this transformation. (p. 4)

Under "America's Schools and Systems: Cast in a 1920's Mold," the report says:

"Breaking the mold" means breaking this system, root and branch. (p. 6)

The first design task, then, is to define what outcomes are wanted and create quality measures of progress toward those outcomes.

All the states and districts in our consortium are members of the New Standards Project, which is itself a Partner in our consortium. We are committed to developing standards and developing an examination system in all the content areas covered by Goals 3 and 4 of the National Education Goals as well as work skills at the 4th, 8th and 10th grade levels. It will set a world-class standard of performance for all students, though we plan to accommodate many different examinations. These exams will emphasize the ability to think well, demonstrate an understanding of subjects studied and apply what one knows to the kind of complex problems encountered in real life. (pp. 8–9)

The New Standards Project is developing a mastery-based examination with known standards.... The New Standards Project's examination system will employ advanced forms of performance examinations as well as assessments of the quality of students' work as revealed through portfolios, exhibitions and projects. But this is not our only resource for this proposal. Many of the states and districts in our consortium are themselves leaders in the national movement to create high standards and new forms of student performance assessment. Vermont, for example, is pioneering the development of portfolio assessment. Pittsburgh developed one of the first and widely admired systems for assessing higher order thinking skills. And Kentucky is investing $29 million in the development of a whole new system of student performance assessment that will advance the state of the art.

The approach we plan to use for assessment will provide a powerful tool for this purpose. At its heart is the idea of setting tasks for students to do. It is the performance of students on these tasks that will be assessed by the system. To a significant extent, the tasks, by defining students' work, will define their curriculum. (p. 9–10)

Along with the Alliance states and school districts, it is committed to developing... outcome standards that will enable our Partners to create performance-oriented systems for the delivery of health and human services that will parallel what we propose for schools. (p. 14)

Changing the district and state systems from rule-driven, input-oriented systems to output-driven, performance-oriented systems will be as hard to achieve as the changes we described for schools and just as necessary. It is one of the most difficult design challenges we face.... We believe that, at its core, this is best thought of as a problem in the design of a very large staff development effort, an effort to enable thousands of people to develop the skills, attitudes and values to transform schools and communities all over the United States.... For years, most staff development has been based on learning from theory that is divorced from practice. We envision learning by participation in a community of practitioners, a community that includes people at every level of mastery.

How can we create such a system for the teachers and others in our sites? In the classic model of learning through practice, the newcomer joins the work environment of a master, learning by participating in all of the activities of that environment. This works when newcomers are to be socialized into established and well-functioning communities of practice. But our problem is how simultaneously to create a new system and socialize educators to function within it. There are few, if any, schools that are already effectively carrying out an integrated program of transformed learning and teaching meeting world-class standards, joined with a social service program and engaging parents and the community in the process. Nevertheless, we believe it is possible to design a continuing professional development program that includes the essential elements. There are five such elements:

- Observation and modeling. Newcomers spend a significant amount of time observing mentors at work. From this observation, they learned to discriminate good from poor practice and acceptable from unacceptable outcomes. Observation is not haphazard. It is mediated by conversations in which critical features of the work are pointed out and processes are analyzed. Our development program must provide opportunities for this kind of supported observation and analysis of the work of "masters."

- Active practice. This is the heart of it; those who are developing their skills work at the job they are learning, rather than learning about the job. Either in their own schools or in those in which their mentors teach, teachers will actively practice the new kinds of teaching for which we aim.

- Scaffolding. But by definition, they don't yet know how to do these tasks—they are still learning. How can they manage this practice then? The answer is scaffolding. They learn by working side-by-side with an expert. But beginners can also scaffold one another by sharing a difficult task that neither might be able to do alone. Within our professional development design, we will need to provide scaffolding for our teachers' early efforts in new forms of teaching, either from expert teachers or from others going through the same skill development process.

- Coaching. Success also depends on the availability of coaching by a supportive expert who observes and comments on the learner's efforts. Coaching is not a one-time affair, but continuous, spread out over the many months or years that it takes to become a full-fledged expert. We will have to provide for extended coaching for our teachers, both in the sites in which they are interning, which we call master sites, and in their own schools.

- Guided Reflection. We will need to provide for reflection by those developing their skills. Just practicing the new forms of teaching, just doing it, even well, will not prepare teachers for the flexibility that will be necessary as they continue working over the years with new groups of students, with new aspects of curriculum. Successful teaching must be a reflective practice, one in which individuals are continually considering, evaluating and improving on their own work. This capacity and disposition needs to be cultivated during the development period, and supported indefinitely. It is not just a matter of time for reflection—although that is crucial—but also a community of others to engage with in a reflective process. (page 22–23)

Our design problem is to build a development program that will contain each of the above elements within the constraints of a situation in which the teachers engaging in this development process remain part of a team responsible for educating children at their home school. Furthermore, we must find a way to quickly scale up the number of schools and teachers participating.

What are our resources? Fundamentally, people, school practice environments, information and educational materials, time and communication resources.

People: We need master practitioners, teachers already teaching well in the new ways we are hoping will spread through our system. We need expert consultants who can connect our teachers to the best research and other knowledge about instruction and learning. We need people who can function as on-site coaches—who are master practitioners of teaching, but who have enough freedom from daily teaching responsibility that they can travel to the schools in which our teacher-apprentices are working to observe, support and critique.

At the outset, we are, by definition, short on master practitioners. But there are teachers, both within our Partner sites and elsewhere, who are doing superb work on some part of the curriculum. Our plan draws in some of these people as master practitioners. Working through Learning Research Development Center [Pittsburgh, ed.], we will be able to put our school professionals in touch with the best research knowledge in the world on questions of curriculum and instruction.

In our projected cascade design, described below, teachers and other practitioners who become experts will serve in subsequent years as master practitioners. A system of certification for master practitioners will be designed to insure against the loss of fidelity that characteristically plagues cascade designs. It will also serve as an incentive (through recognition and, possibly, additional pay) for the extra work that teachers will need to become master practitioners. We will work with the National Board for Professional Teaching Standards on designing this certification process. (pp. 21–24)

How We Plan to Do It

...Getting there will require more than new policies and different practices. It will require a change in the prevailing culture—the attitudes, values, norms and accepted ways of doing things—that defines the environment that determines whether individual schools succeed or fail in the transformation process. We will know that we have succeeded when there are enough transformed schools in any one area, and enough districts designed and managed to support such schools, that their approach to education sets the norms, frames the attitudes and defines the accepted ways of doing things in that part of the world. Then there will be no turning back. (p. 33)

Bear in mind that we have selected our site Partners because their restructuring plans are already among the most advanced in the country. Each of the states in which we will initially concentrate—Vermont, New York and Kentucky—have developed sweeping strategic plans of action. (p. 36)

Hornbeck, Tucker, Cohen and Gloria Frazier will visit all of the sites at least once a month, providing support and technical assistance. (p. 43)

[Ed. Note: To date there have been no reports from states, cities, schools or school districts listed as "Partners" which show academic improvement as a result of their involvement in Marc Tucker's project. Rochester, NY in particular, was a disaster case, with a National Public Broadcasting System report in mid-April of 1993 "accusing the city school district of flunking the once-heralded movement to reform its schools." Vermont's efforts have proven to be less than successful and Kentucky's system of student performance assessment had to be scrapped after enormous controversy over faulty development by the designers.]

Appendix XIII

"Psychology's Best Kept Secrets"

"Psychology's Best Kept Secrets," the entire Chapter 9 from *The Whole Language OBE Fraud*, by Samuel Blumenfeld (Paradigm Company: Boise, ID, 1996) pp. 77–89, is reproduced here.

It is more than a little curious that in a nation where so much research has been done by psychologists on the nature of human cognition—how children learn—that these same psychologists have shown virtually no interest in the greatest learning problem plaguing American education: the teaching of reading. It is true that there is much interest in diagnosing reading disability and exploring "dyslexia," but no interest in the instructional cause of reading disability, despite the fact that Dr. Samuel T. Orton first drew attention to the problem back in 1929.

Which brings us to the Center for Cognitive Studies where Frank Smith allegedly absorbed the wisdom of Noam Chomsky et al. The chief architect of the Center was Jerome Bruner who tells us in his autobiography, *In Search of Mind*, that cognitive psychology was born in 1956 at a symposium on the cognitive sciences held at the Massachusetts Institute of Technology. Two of the key persons who participated in that symposium were Harvard behavioral psychologist George Miller and linguist Noam Chomsky.

It was that symposium that convinced Miller to leave B.F. Skinner's behaviorist camp at Harvard and join Jerome Bruner in developing cognitive psychology. Miller writes:

> I went away from the Symposium with a strong conviction, more imitative than rational, that experimental psychology, theoretical linguistics, and the computer simulation of cognitive processes were all pieces from a larger whole, and that the future would see a progressive elaboration and coordination of their shared concerns. (Bruner, p. 122)

Three years later, in 1959, Chomsky was to give the coup de grace to the behaviorist theory about language by a devastating review of B.F. Skinner's book, *Verbal Behavior* (1957). Skinner had sought to explain language development in humans as a form of conditioned stimulus-response behavior similar to the way that animals in psych labs could be trained through conditioning techniques. Pavlov's famous experiments on dogs in Russia were the best known example of such experiments, the results of which were to permit psychologists to devise techniques that could be applied in changing and molding human behavior.

J.B. Watson, the father of American behaviorism, had written in 1924:

> Behaviorism...holds that the subject matter of human psychology is the behavior of the human being. Behaviorism claims that consciousness is neither a definite nor a usable concept.... (p. 2)

> The behaviorist asks: Why don't we make what we can observe the real field of psychology? Let us limit ourselves to things that can be observed and formulate laws concerning only those things. Now what can we observe? We can observe behavior—what the organism does or says. And let us point out at once that saying is doing—that is, behaving. (p. 6)

Chomsky demonstrated that the behaviorists' attempts to explain language in the limited terms of stimulus-response behavior were fundamentally flawed. He argued that "our interpretation of the world is based on representational systems that derive from the structure of the mind itself and do not mirror in any direct way the form of the external world." In other words, the human child is born with a brain that already contains certain innate knowledge that permits the child to learn language rapidly, without direct instruction from anyone. But the mystery is that the structure of the mind does indeed mirror the form of the external world, for function of language is to name the external world. The child's ability to master the phonological structure of the language, the abstractions of sound symbols, as well as syntax so rapidly and effortlessly suggested to Chomsky that man's genetic makeup provided him with a highly developed language capability.

What is ironic in all of this is that despite the fact that Chomsky is a radical socialist and believes in evolution, his views about innate knowledge are quite compatible with and even strongly confirms the Biblical view of man being created with the ability to use language. God gave Adam the ability to speak because He wanted Adam to be able to converse with Him. In other words, Adam was given the power of the word for the specific purpose of being able to know God. The second purpose of language was to enable Adam to know the world for God gave Adam the task of establishing dominion over all living creatures, which meant naming them and classifying them. In other words, God made Adam an observer, a scientist. After the creation of Eve, the third function of language became apparent: to know others. And since language is the tool of thought, the fourth function of language was to be able to think and thereby know oneself.

In 1960 Miller and Bruner got an unrestricted grant of a quarter-million dollars from the Carnegie Corporation of New York to set up their Center for Cognitive Studies at Harvard. Miller brought ideas about communication theory, computation, and linguistics to the Center whereas Bruner brought ideas about social psychology, developmental psychology, and anthropology to the mix. It was obvious that the new interest in the mind had been spurred by the new computer technology. For, as Bruner writes, "You cannot properly conceive of managing a complex world of information without a workable concept of mind." The result is that the Center brought together the ideas and theories of scholars and scientists working in many associated fields and drew graduate students from M.I.T., Harvard, and elsewhere.

Bruner concentrated on early childhood mental development which brought him into contact with the work of the Swiss psychologist Jean Piaget whose pioneering work in the field had contributed greatly to an understanding of how the child's mind grows. Piaget saw the child as an egocentric individual, gradually modifying his egocentrism as he adapted himself to the reality of others.

But Bruner, a socialist, was not entirely satisfied with the Piagetian view which seemed to favor the development of individualism. "Piaget's children," writes Bruner, "are little intellectuals, detached from the hurly-burly of the human condition." He was far more attracted to the work of Lev Semyonovich Vygotsky (1896–1934), the Soviet cognitive psychologist. Bruner writes:

> Vygotsky's world was an utterly different place, almost the world of a great Russian novel.... Growing up in it is full of achieving consciousness and voluntary control, of learning to speak and then finding out what it means, of clumsily taking over the forms and tools of the culture and learning how to use them appropriately.... (p.138)

> Vygotsky published little and virtually nothing that appeared in English before 1960; indeed, until the late 1950s, most of what he wrote in Russian was suppressed and had been banned after the 1936 purge. Sickly and brilliant, he died of tuberculosis in his thirties.... He was a Russian and a Jew, deeply interested in the arts and in language.... His objective was to explore how human society provided instruments to empower the individual mind. He was a serious intellectual Marxist, when Marxism was a starchy and dogmatic subject. This was his undoing at the time of the Stalinist purges.... Though I knew Piaget and never knew Vygotsky, I feel I know Vygotsky better as a person. (p. 137)

The man who introduced Bruner to Vygotsky was Alexander Luria, the Soviet psychologist whose book, *The Nature of Human Conflicts*, had been translated into English and published in the United States in 1932. Luria wrote in his preface:

> The researches described here are the results of the experimental psychological investigations carried on at the State Institute of Experimental Psychology, Moscow, during the period of 1923–1930. The chief problems of the author were an objective and materialistic description of the mechanisms lying at the basis of the disorganisation of human behaviour and an experimental approach to the laws of its regulation.... To accomplish this it was necessary to create artificially affects and models of experimental neuroses which made possible an analysis of the laws lying at the basis of the disintegration of behavior. (p. xi)

Pavlov himself, Luria's mentor, had proudly summed up the results of his famous experiments in a book, *Twenty Years of Objective Study*, published in 1935. These experiments on animals had enormous implications for experiments on human beings. Pavlov wrote:

> The power of our knowledge over the nervous system will, of course, appear to much greater advantage if we learn not only to injure the nervous system but also to restore it at will. It will then have been really proved that we have mastered the processes and are controlling them. Indeed, this is so. In many cases we are not only causing disease, but are eliminating it with great exactitude, one might say, to order. (p. 690)

Thus, Pavlov had already done considerable experimentation on the causes of behavioral disorganization. Luria writes (p. 2):

Pavlov obtained very definite affective "breaks," an acute disorganisation of behaviour, each time that the conditioned reflexes collided, when the animal was unable to react to two mutually exclusive tendencies, or was incapable of adequately responding to any imperative problem.

Apparently, there were many psychologists at that time working on the same problem. Luria writes (p[p]. 206–207):

We are not the first of those who have artificially created disorganisation of human behaviour. A large number of facts pertaining to this problem has been contributed by contemporary physiologists, as well as by psychologists.

I.P. Pavlov was the first investigator who, with the help of exceedingly bold workers, succeeded experimentally in creating neuroses with experimental animals. Working with conditioned reflexes in dogs, Pavlov came to the conclusion that every time an elaborated reflex came into conflict with the unconditional reflex, the behavior of the dog markedly changed....

Although, in the experiments with the collision of the conditioned reflexes in animals, it is fairly easy to obtain acute forms of artificial affect, it is much more difficult to get those results in human experiments....

K. Lewin, in our opinion, has been one of the most prominent psychologists to elucidate this question of the artificial production of affect and of the experimental disorganisation of behaviour. The method of his procedure—the introduction of an emotional setting into the experience of a human, the interest of the subject in the experiment—helped him to obtain an artificial disruption of the affect of considerable strength.... Here the fundamental conception of Lewin is very close to ours.

Who was K. Lewin? Why he was the very same Kurt Lewin who came to the United States in 1933, founded the Research Center for Group Dynamics at M.I.T. (which later moved to the University of Michigan), and invented "sensitivity training." Shortly before his death in 1947, Lewin founded the National Training Laboratory which established its campus at Bethel, Maine, under the sponsorship of the National Education Association. Their teachers were instructed in the techniques of sensitivity training and how to become effective change agents.

After Lewin's death, his colleagues continued to develop his sensitivity-training sessions which became known as t-groups (t for training). The t-group became the basis of the encounter movement in which participants get in touch with their feelings.

Carl Rogers, one of the chief practitioners of the t-group, considered sensitivity training to be "perhaps the most significant social invention of this century." All of this spurred the development of humanist "Third Force" psychology by Rogers, Abraham Maslow and others, which has had an enormous influence on the affective curriculum of public education.

Lewin had started his career as a social psychologist in Berlin where he organized a "collective" in which he and his students pursued the experiments which Luria later recognized as highly effective. Some of Lewin's students were Russians who studied under him in the early 1920s and returned to the Soviet Union to teach and continue their research at the University of Moscow. In 1929 Lewin attended the Ninth International Congress of Psychologists at Yale where, according to Harvard psychologist Gordon Allport, his work "was decisive in forcing some American psychologists to revise their own theories of the nature of intelligent behavior and of learning."

In 1932, Lewis M. Terman, head of the psychology department at Stanford, invited Lewin to spend six months as a visiting professor at Stanford. Lewin had been recommended by Edwin G. Boring, director of the Psych Lab at Harvard, who had been greatly impressed with Lewin at the Yale conference. After the stint at Stanford, Lewin decided to return to Germany via the Pacific and the Trans-Siberian railroad. In Moscow he was able to confer with his fellow psychologists, including Luria. Hitler had just come to power in Germany, and in August 1933, Lewin left Germany for good.

The importance of Lewin in this story is that he represented the collectivist mentality in the psychological community which had its own socio-political agenda. Certainly, the psychologists who were experimenting with artificially induced behavioral disorganization in their laboratories in Germany, the Soviet Union, and the United States had a reason for their experiments. And Lewin was considered highly skilled in such experiments with human beings which greatly interested American psychologists. Lewin's biographer, Alfred J. Marrow, writes:

> Students of progressive education also saw the need for studies of group behavior. This was stimulated by the educational philosophy of John Dewey. To carry out Dewey's theory of "learning by doing," teachers organized such group projects as student self-government and hobby-club activities. This called for the development of leadership skills and collective setting of group goals.... Lewin's pioneering research in group behavior thus drew upon the experience of educators in deciding upon and developing topics for research and in establishing a strong interest among social psychologists and teachers. (p. 167)

One of Lewin's most significant experiments was aimed at determining the behavioral effects of frustration on children and how these effects are produced. Marrow writes:

> The experiment indicated that in frustration the children tended to regress to a surprising degree. They tended to become babyish. Intellectually, children of four-and-a-half years tended toward the behavior of a three-year-old. The degree of intellectual regression varied directly with the strength of the frustration. Change in emotional behavior was also recorded. There was less smiling and singing and more thumbsucking, noisiness, and restless actions. Aggressiveness also increased and some children went so far as to hit, kick, and break objects. There was a 30 per cent rise in the number of hostile actions toward the experimenter and a 34 per cent decrease in friendly approaches....

> The authors summarized their main findings as follows: "Frustration as it operated in these experiments resulted in an average regression in the level of intellectual functioning, in increased unhappiness, restlessness, and destructiveness, in increased ultra-group unity, and in increased out-group aggression. The amounts of increase in negative emotionality were positively related to strength of frustration." (p. 122)

In other words, Lewin and his colleagues had proven beyond a shadow of a doubt that frustration could cause the same symptoms of behavioral disorganization in children that Pavlov, Luria and associates had produced in their laboratories with animals. On the matter of teaching reading, Lewin favored the look-say, whole-word method. Marrow writes:

> Lewin's students had unusually wide latitude in choosing their particular field of study.

Sara Forrer, for example, decided to investigate Ovid Decroly's method of teaching retarded children to read.... The Belgian teacher had postulated that children retain sentences more easily than single words and words more easily than single letters. Lewin stated, in referring to Forrer's experiment, that "the findings confirm the marked advantage of the 'global' method of reading and writing. To a child taking no joy in learning to write an alphabet, a change of valence (attractiveness) occurs more quickly when he is allowed as soon as possible to write meaningful communications in sentence form." (p. 258)

What is interesting in all of this is that Clara Schmitt in 1914 (see chap. 12) had shown in her analysis of the errors made by mentally defective and normal children that the mentally defective had problems learning to read phonetically. And even when they were taught to read phonetically, they made the kinds of errors that normal children make when taught to read by the look-say method. Decroly was obviously confirming that the "global," or whole language method, was easier for retarded children than the more abstract alphabetic system. But to assume that the global (i.e., whole language) method was also better for normal children was either a serious error on Lewin's part, or a deliberate effort to promote look-say. He must have known that the Central Committee of the Communist Party in the Soviet Union had rejected the whole-word method in 1933 mainly through the work of his colleagues, Luria and Vygotsky.

Lewin obviously believed in the Marxist doctrine that the end justifies the means. In his book, *Resolving Social Conflicts*, published in 1948, he wrote:

> In regard to a change toward democracy this paradox of democratic leadership is still more pointed. In an experimental change, for instance, from individualistic freedom (laissez faire) to democracy, the incoming democratic leader could not tell the group members exactly what they should do because that would lead to autocracy. Still some manipulations of the situation have to be made to lead the group into the direction of democracy....

> To investigate change toward democracy a situation has to be created for a certain period where the leader is sufficiently in control to rule out influence he does not want and to manipulate the situation to a sufficient degree. The goal of the democratic leader in this transition period will have to be the same as that of any good teacher, namely, to make himself superfluous, to be replaced by indigenous leaders from the group. (p. 39)

In other words, during the transition period from individualism to "democracy" (i.e., collectivism) the end can justify the means, because the "end" is the greater good. The look-say method may be needed during the transition period in order to make Americans less literate and thereby less independent as individuals. This would indeed be a necessary strategy for moving the nation toward a socialist, collectivist society. And, of course, it was in keeping with Dewey's own views on reading instruction given in his essay, "The Primary School Fetich," published in 1898.

Vygotsky died in 1934 and Lewin died in 1947, but Luria, who knew them both, continued his work. During World War II he did painstaking research on brain-injured people, discovering many facets of how the brain works. He had worked closely with Vygotsky from 1924 to 1934, the period in which they had worked on early childhood development and the artificial means of creating behavioral disorganization. During that period Vygotsky also worked on the problems of Soviet education, applying psychology to the problems of massive illiteracy which, according to James Wertsch, "has been almost completely overcome today."

How were the Soviets able to achieve this? By using an alphabetic-phonics method of teaching reading!

The Bruner-Luria connection was a very close one. Bruner attended psychological conferences in Moscow, and, in 1960, Luria visited the Center for Cognitive Studies. Bruner writes:

> Luria and I became fast friends almost immediately. We were compatible temperamentally and very much in agreement about psychological matters.... (p. 145)

> In the fifteen or so years that I knew him well, I do not think that two months ever went by without a letter from him, a new book or translation of his.... He was the czar of Russian psychology, but a more benign czar would be hard to imagine! (p. 144)

Why were they so compatible? Well, as a student Bruner not only sympathized with communism, but in his senior year at Duke, he became a member of the Communist Party. He writes:

> That last year at Duke was 1938, the bitter winding down of the Spanish Civil War. My roommate, Irv Dunston, and I were invited to become members of a Marxist "study group" held at the home of a gifted young mathematics professor. Each week we would prepare by reading something of Marx or Lenin. I liked the slogans—that production was for use not for profit, to each according to his effort, and so on—but the turgid arguments of Marxist "thinkers" repelled me....

> My fondness for the slogans must have been enough, for we were asked eventually to join a "cell" of the Communist Party in Durham, "with real working-class people." After a late-into-the-night discussion, we decided that this was our duty....

> The cell meetings, in that dingy apartment near the railroad station in Durham, were the intrinsic, the conspiratorial appeal—our code names included.... My "duties" were to take an active part on campus in the American Student Union, to put the "right" candidates into office....

> The year ended; I departed Durham. I never even had to resign from the Party. I was given no names or contacts, but told simply that I would soon know who and how. I guess I didn't make it. (pp. 29–30)

Thus ended Bruner's formal relationship with the Communist Party. But nowhere in his autobiography does Bruner indicate any loss of belief in socialism or Marxism. The fact that he felt so compatible with Luria and preferred Vygotsky to Piaget would lead one to believe that Bruner has remained sympathetic to communism throughout his professional life. He and his fellow psychologists thought nothing of attending psychological conferences in Moscow during the height of the Cold War while American soldiers were dying in Vietnam fighting communism.

On matters of education, Bruner was instrumental in creating in 1965 the famous—or infamous, depending on your point of view—social studies curriculum for ten-year-olds, *Man: A Course of Study*, better known as MACOS. Bruner writes:

[A]fter a year or two of very favorable notices... and widespread adoptions, the course came under attack from the extreme right-wing John Birch [Society] in league with newly emerging "creationists," opposed to the teaching of evolution. Between them they mounted the now familiar right-wing harassment of any school district proposing to use the course.... Governor Reagan of California, whose state sheltered the core of the John Birch, came out squarely against the course.... And so symbolic had the course become for the extreme Right that they managed to pass on their "literature" about it to a right-wing group in Australia, then in opposition to the widespread adoption of the course there. (p. 194)

One would have to conclude from the above that the Center for Cognitive Studies was not exactly a hotbed of conservative, anti-communist thinking. And it is interesting to note that when Frank Smith left the Center with his newly acquired Ph.D., he embarked on his career as a phonics-basher par excellence and was soon catapulted into the position of "expert" on reading and literacy by the look-say establishment.

Appendix XIV

Alert on *National Education Goals Panel Community Action Tool Kit*

October 6, 1994
TO: Concerned Citizens
FROM: Charlotte Iserbyt, Former Senior Policy Advisor,
U.S. Department of Education, Office of Educational Research
and Improvement, from which all components of educational
restructuring (OBE/ML/Goals 2000) emanated.
SUBJECT: *National Education Goals Panel Community Action Tool Kit;
Do-It-Yourself Kit for Education Renewal, Community
Organizing Guide*, September 1994. ACTION ALERT.

Order the above-mentioned materials from the Government Printing Office, 202–512–1800. The Stock No. for ordering is 065–000–00680–4. The price is $37. It is important to confront your elected officials IMMEDIATELY with the proof before educators receive project and move ahead with it in your community.

Concerned parents, teachers, plain taxpayers, etc. are fortunate that we were able to obtain a copy of these incredible materials which in a nutshell spell out clearly how to manipulate all segments of the community into accepting/supporting GOALS 2000 (the restructuring of our schools, i.e., "nation," according to a speech delivered by Shirley McCune of the Midcontinent Regional Education Laboratory at the Governor's Conference, Wichita, Kansas, 1989). Explicit strategies are presented in manipulation of the community into accepting theoretical, unproven curricula. The guide provides clear and ample direction to censure dissenting voices critical of the restructuring. These directions include deliberately misleading of the media, formulation of core groups to isolate and stifle dissenters, contrived data collection among other offensive activities. The aim is not to reach consensus but to obfuscate the real issues in order to push forward a one-sided agenda. A most disturbing reference is made toward controlling by name a particular religious group.

For years education researchers have referred to the change agents' bible: *The Change*

Agents' Guide to Innovation in Education by Ronald G. Havelock, Program Director, Center for Research on Utilization of Scientific Knowledge, Institute for Social Research, University of Michigan, portions of which were originally developed as part of Contract No. OEC-0-8-080603-4535(010) with the Office of Education, U.S. Department of Health, Education, and Welfare, under the title "Diffusion of Utilization Research to Knowledge Linkers in Education." The copyright is 1973 (Educational Technology Publications, Inc.: Englewood Cliffs, NJ), LC 72-87317. The *Guide* contains authentic case studies of how change agents manipulate their communities into accepting controversial curricula, methods, etc. Some freedom-loving education researchers have taken the course on how to bring about change and how to "identify resisters," etc. (themselves!). Ronald Havelock has strong connections to UNESCO (United Nations).

That the National Goals Panel, which includes elected officials (governors, legislators, etc.), could condone the use of manipulative change agent tactics (the above described *National Goals Panel Community Action Kit* reads like Ronald Havelock was the Project Director) is difficult to fathom. Do they know what is in this Kit? Do they feel that the restructuring of our nation a la Shirley McCune and Naisbett, i.e., the changing of our political/economic system from free enterprise/capitalist to corporate fascist/planned economy (merger of public and private sector) and from a constitutional representative republic to a participatory democracy (for proof see federally-funded education restructuring projects implemented in many states during past ten years) is so important that totalitarian methods must be used to reach consensus and approval? Don't citizens have the right to make such important decisions related to the future of their children and nation at the ballot box, rather than having themselves subjected to a tax-funded manipulative brainwash in order to come to phony consensus?

Opposition to OBE, Goals 2000 has been so intensive and effective that the education bureaucracy, in collusion with multinational corporations, has openly sunk to this incredibly totalitarian level in order to get acceptance at the local level of its international socialist lifelong dumbdown education/job training agenda.

The *Do-It-Yourself Kit for Education Renewal* consists of four parts: (1) "Community Organizing Guide"—57 pages; (2) "Guide to Getting Out Your Message" [better titled "How to Manipulate the Media and the Taxpayers," ed.]—74 pages; (3) "Resource Guide"—66 pages; and (4) "Guide to Goals and Standards"—38 pages.

CALL NATIONAL GOALS PANEL AT 202-632-0952 TO REGISTER YOUR CONCERN OVER THE CONTENTS/METHODS RECOMMENDED IN THE PANEL'S *COMMUNITY ACTION TOOLKIT*. TELL THEM YOU WILL ASK YOUR ELECTED REPRESENTATIVES TO CALL FOR AN INVESTIGATION OF THE U.S. DEPARTMENT OF EDUCATION'S ACTIVITIES WHICH ARE WORKING AGAINST THE BEST INTERESTS OF AMERICAN CITIZENS, USING PSYCHOLOGICAL MANIPULATION (DELPHI TECHNIQUE, GROUP PROCESS BRAINWASH METHODS, ETC.) TO GET COMMUNITY APPROVAL OF GOALS 2000. ASK THEM TO STOP DISTRIBUTION OF THE *ACTION TOOL KIT* UNTIL CONGRESS HAS HAD AN OPPORTUNITY TO EXAMINE ITS CONTENTS. ASK FOR A WRITTEN RESPONSE TO YOUR CONCERNS. CALL OR WRITE YOUR ELECTED OFFICIALS REQUESTING A CONGRESSIONAL INVESTIGATION OF THE GOAL PANEL'S *TOOLKIT* DEVELOPED WITH YOUR TAX MONIES.

Excerpts (verbatim quotes from the *Tool Kit*) follow:

...Step 3: Describe Allies and Opponents; Identify Change Agents....

Step 1: Identify a Leadership Team. This section provides suggestions on how to find the leaders in your community. It also includes a checklist of likely candidates—partners for your effort.

Troubleshooting. Even as you are expanding the base of support, it will be important to be aware of the opposition. Keep an eye out for your opponents, respect their opinions, and try to explain yours. Understand the process of inclusion.

Step 1: Identify a Leadership Team. The people who lead the community campaign to reform education will give it inspiration, drive, and momentum. They will set the ground-work for a long-term reform strategy. This is a task that requires numbers of committed people, but it must start with a core team.... There are likely candidates for leadership... members of PTA, president of Chamber of Commerce, president of local teachers' union, members of social action committee of a local church or synagogue.

Step 2: Develop a Common Vision. "It takes a whole village to educate a child"; assess-ing current strengths and weaknesses and building a strong accountability system to regu-larly measure and report on progress towards the goals over time; identifying the barriers to and opportunities for goal attainment in many systems that support teaching and learning; creating and mounting strategies to overcome barriers....

Objectives: Schools... in implementing comprehensive parent involvement programs, will offer more adult literacy, parent training and lifelong learning opportunities to improve the ties between home and school and enhance parents' work and home lives....

Holding Community Meetings. Identifying Participants: It may be useful to invite leaders from key organizations to act as spokespersons or to lead small discussion groups.... Have a designated number of people personally responsible for bringing others to the meeting....

Developing an Agenda: The agenda for your community goals meeting should be con-structed in a way that galvanizes support for your mission and refines it where necessary. Make sure to involve the core group of leaders in developing the agenda....

Choosing a Facilitator: An organized discussion about education reform will not happen spontaneously. It will be necessary to have a facilitator to help direct discussion around the issues related to the goals and the ways they apply to the community. The facilitator will need to encourage audience participation. He or she will need to ensure that no single person monopolizes the discussion and that shy people are encouraged to speak. The facili-tator will bring discussions to a close and guide the audience to decisions about actions that need to be taken....

Community Review of Goals in Small Groups. The group will divide into smaller sec-tions—one for each of the goals identified in the previous discussion. It may be helpful to appoint leaders for each small group. The groups should reflect diversity. They should make any necessary revisions in the goal and then brainstorm about how the community can accomplish the needs identified in each goal. Emerging from the group sessions will be the beginnings of a community action plan and the methods for measuring progress toward the community education goals....

- **Case Study of Allegheny Policy Council**. Participants were asked for input which would lead directly to a regional plan for focusing our resources to improve math and science. The resulting plan will guide regional action. It will be used to indicate regional consensus to secure national funding and to guide local allocation of resources....

Conducting Surveys. In addition, the findings of a survey can help formulate and bolster positions of the campaign....

Develop a Useful Questionnaire. Biased wording also invalidates results, so emotionally loaded or slanted questions should be strictly avoided. It may be difficult to ask neutral questions—especially when you have strong feelings on the topic—but that is the only way to get valid information....

CASE STUDY: Omaha 2000.
Initiatives were so much more easily accepted because people felt that the survey made them a part of the decision-making process. [A few survey questions follow, ed.]

- Parenting education programs should be available for all parents?
- Our community should appreciate and embrace the growth of diversity?
- Every citizen should be responsible to assist students and support education?
- All children should have a personal mentor available to assist them?...

Develop a Strategy. Evaluate Context for Change; describe allies and opponents; identify change agents.

For many issues there will be significant institutional barriers to any change you hope to initiate....

Elements of Systematic Reform.
Creating a coordinated education and training system.... Are these programs built around a multi-year sequence of learning at work sites and at school—learning that is connected and coordinated?

Describe Allies and Opponents.
On the other hand, there may be people or organizations in the community who will oppose the reforms you are attempting to institute. Some of these opponents simply may not understand the goals of the campaign. Others will persist in their opposition. Before your organization takes any action, you will need to anticipate the potential reaction of opponents. List your opponents and what your success might mean to them. Refer to the **Troubleshooting** section for suggestions on how to deal with opposition.

Identify Change Agents.
One change agent could be the Superintendent of schools because she or he has the power to institute a district-wide policy to include community members in the standards-development process.

["Power" is mentioned many times in this section, ed.]

Resistance. This will be the most difficult stage. The public will be reluctant to face the trade-offs that come from choosing a specific plan of action.

To describe opponents answer these questions:_____
List the resources of your opponents.

Council Strategy Chart.
Get the president of Hewlett Packard to write the chair of the school board a letter supporting the proposal. [Strategy to get calculators for school, ed.]

Community Organizing Tips.
Surveys can do more than help you gather information. They can also build community ownership of reform.

Business and Labor Leaders' Checklist.
Business and labor can make the goals work by building community support, helping to measure effectiveness, and defining required workforce skills that could be matched to academic achievement targets.

Other Sources of Support
Potential allies for your effort are everywhere.... Consult the resource directory.... Also, do not overlook other goals- and standards-based reform campaigns as a source of information and support. School officials and community leaders in Edmonds, Washington; San Antonio, Texas; Omaha, Nebraska; Bangor, Maine; and hundreds of other municipalities.

Identifying Financial Resources.
As you begin your search for funding, remember the federal government. With its passage of the comprehensive *Goals 2000: Educate America Act,* Congress has made it easier for communities to restructure education.... What's more, the legislation takes a big-picture view of education that goes beyond the traditional K–12 focus of past administrations. Education is defined as a process that begins in early childhood and continues to adulthood through lifelong learning situations. It emphasizes the connections between preschool, school, and work.

Troubleshooting.
You are likely to face opposition any time you try to introduce change into a community.... Their concerns may be based on confusion over what goals and standards are... or they may be satisfied with current state of learning in your community.

Following are tips on how to explain National Education Goals and Standards.... For a fuller description of the relevance of national goals and standards-based reform movement... please see "Guide to Goals and Standards" booklet in *Tool Kit.*

Know the Facts.
For definitions of many of the other terms of the debate, see "Glossary of Terms" at end of "Resource Directory."

Give Everyone a Role.
Not everybody has to share your views. Be sensitive to concerns of your opponents. Talk about what offends them and address their issues.

Avoid Loaded Words and Phrases.
Words and phrases like "outcomes," "outcome-based education," "self-esteem," and "attitudes" may mean different things to certain groups.... Remember, if you stick to clear, concrete terms that everyone comprehends, not only will you be better understood, you may also avoid serious conflict down the road.

Keep your Perspective.
Opposition may come from a small part of the community. Balance their concerns appropriately and reinforce the fact that the National Goals have widespread support. You might think of inviting opponents into the schools to let them see for themselves how your community action plan is improving education.

Beware of The One-Size-Fits-All Argument.
Reassure your opposition that the National Education Goals, the framework for your community's education reform effort, are not trying to establish a national curriculum for all schools. [This is a bald-faced lie. According to *Education Week*, Jan. 25, 1989, "Chester E. Finn, Jr. former head of the Education Department's research branch, told business leaders here last week that he favored the development of a 'national curriculum.'", ed.]

Remember the equity issue.
Every student will be expected to meet higher standards. No students will be denied the opportunity to learn [This is Spady's et al terminology for outcome-based education, effective schools, mastery learning, ed.]

Ask for Help. See Resource Directory... Case Study of Edmonds, Washington: Sylvia Soholt, who works in Edmonds' planning and community relations division, says they deliberately chose a process involving multiple drafts of each phase because "it gives the message that you are open to change."

The text was not presented as a writ from the school district, but rather as "this is what your neighbors said students should learn and be able to do."

By sending the draft to everybody in the community, the school district was able to deflect charges of being exclusive. District officials carefully documented the originator of each idea to demonstrate that the plan was developed by the community, not by school officials.

In a meeting to discuss the first draft, some raised religious doubts about the reform effort. They said they feared the schools would take charge of rearing children, teaching non-Christian values instead of improving academic skills. Some suggested that computers would monitor and mold children into automatons.

Faced with these objections, the superintendent, Brian L. Benzel, knew he could not just dismiss the criticisms as misguided. He felt that the school district needed to clarify the purpose behind the reform effort before releasing a second draft of the document. Benzel approached Edmonds' ministers and invited them to a meeting on education reform efforts.

At the meeting, the superintendent addressed the expressed fears and explained what the reform movement was really trying to do. He said he believed that they misunderstood the district's intentions, but thought their concerns were important. He let the ministers talk about education. They all agreed that education needed to be improved and that it was important to define student skills.

In the course of the conversation, it became clear that the religious community was not walking lock-step against reform. Reform meant something different to each minister. It appeared that the ministers simply wanted to be part of the debate. As a result of this positive meeting, they carried the message back to their congregations, that the school reformers were willing to listen and be inclusive.

Following these meetings the school district made revisions that incorporated the objections and reflected the concerns of the whole community. The district removed confusing jargon from the draft. For example, people had objected to defining "critical thinking" as a skill—they believed it suggested that children should be taught to be critical of their parents.

So the second draft defined "thinking and problem-solving" as the ability to "think creatively and develop innovative ideas and solutions" and to "think critically and make independent judgments."

To address the concern that the district was stressing some skills over others, it developed a poster depicting the skills and abilities a student needs as a "tapestry of learning," where all the elements have equal importance and are woven together.

The school district is now moving to the next step. They are creating assessment tools to measure the standard they have developed, using the same strategy of full community involvement. [Supt. Brian Benzel, Chairman, Governor's Task Force on Schools for the 21st Century, is listed as a partner (WA State) in Marc Tucker's National Alliance for Restructuring Education Schools—and Systems—for the 21st Century. See Appendix XII. In other words, the citizens and ministers in Edmonds, Washington were manipulated by a very important and recognized "change agent," ed.]

The importance of ordering the entire Kit cannot be overemphasized. We have dealt only with one section, "The Community Organizing Guide."

Please fax me info regarding action you and members of your community intend to take to expose this incredible federal initiative.

Thanks very much.

Appendix XV

"Will Republicans Betray America By Voting For Marc Tucker's Human Resources Development System: H.R. 1617 and S. 143?"

"Will Republicans Betray America By Voting For Marc Tucker's Human Resources Development System: H.R. 1617 and S. 143?" by Samuel Blumenfeld is taken from the *The Blumenfeld Education Letter*, May 1996 (Vol.11, No. 5, Letter #116).

There is no doubt that H.R. 1617 (known as the "Consolidated and Reformed Education, Employment, and Rehabilitation System's Act" or "CAREERS Act"), which passed the House in September 1995 by a vote of 345 to 79, and S. 143 (the Workforce Development Act of 1995), which passed the Senate in October by 95 to 2, will do more to lead America into socialist-fascist totalitarianism than any other pieces of legislation before the present Republican-dominated Congress.

Both bills, when reconciled in conference committee, will enact into law Marc Tucker's infamous Human Resources Development System, outlined in Tucker's exuberant letter of November 11, 1992 to Hillary Clinton, a member of the board of trustees of Tucker's National Center on Education and the Economy. He wrote:

> I still cannot believe you won. But utter delight that you did pervades all the circles in which I move. I met last Wednesday in David Rockefeller's office with him, John Sculley, Dave Barram and David Haselkorn. It was a great celebration. Both John and David R. were more expansive than I have ever seen them—literally radiating happiness....

> The subject we were discussing was what you and Bill should do now about education, training, and labor market policy. Following that meeting, I chaired another in Washington on the same topic....

> Our purpose in these meetings was to propose concrete actions that the Clinton administration could take—between now and the inauguration, in the first 100 days and beyond. The result, from where I sit, was really exciting. We took a very large leap forward in terms

of how to advance the agenda on which you and we have all been working—a practical plan for putting all the major components of the system in place within four years, by the time Bill has to run again.

That Hillary Clinton had been working with Tucker and associates to develop this fascist education system is confirmed by the fact that Tucker paid Hillary $102,000 in 1991 for her work as a consultant to the NCEE. Obviously, the letter of November '92 was meant to help prepare the Clintons to get the Tucker plan passed into law and implemented by the fifty states. In it Tucker outlined his "vision" of a human resources development system:

> What is essential is that we create a seamless web of opportunities to develop one's skills that literally extends from cradle to grave and is the same system for everyone—young and old, poor and rich, worker and full-time student. It needs to be a system driven by client needs (not agency regulations or the needs of the organizations providing the services), guided by clear standards that define the stages of the system for the people who progress through it, and regulated on the basis of outcomes that providers produce for their clients, not inputs into the system.

One should be aware that Tucker's plan to restructure American education goes back to his 1986 report on teaching, *A Nation Prepared: Teachers for the 21st Century*, produced when he was executive director of the Carnegie Forum on Education and the Economy. In 1987, New York Gov. Cuomo and the leaders of Rochester, N.Y., invited Tucker to set up his National Center on Education and the Economy (NCEE) in that city. The idea was that the Center, with the help of an initial subsidy of $1 million from Gov. Cuomo, would help Rochester implement Tucker's basic restructuring ideas in that city's school system.

GOALS 2000

In 1989 the NCEE issued its first report, *To Secure Our Future: The Federal Role in Education*, which became the basis for Goals 2000. The report basically framed the issues and shaped the agreements that were made at President Bush's famous Education Summit at the University of Virginia, Charlottesville, in the fall of 1989. After the summit, in which Gov. Clinton of Arkansas was an active participant, the National Governors' Association asked the NCEE to assist in the development of national goals for education. These goals were subsequently promoted by President Bush in his 1990 State of the Union address. Apparently, a Republican president was willing to accept the education reform plan of the ultra-liberal NCEE rather than call upon a conservative think tank to come up with a conservative reform plan.

In 1989, Tucker's group created the Commission on the Skills of the American Workforce which compiled a report entitled *America's Choice: High Skills or Low Wages!* The report, issued in June 1990, is the basic blueprint for Tucker's Human Resources Development System which moves American education from its traditional emphasis on academics and knowledge to a Soviet-style workforce training and certification program.

Both H.R. 1617 and S. 143 represent the culmination of Tucker's efforts to get Congress to impose his system on America. That Republicans should be in the forefront of promoting these bills makes one wonder if the Republican Party is becoming the new fascist party of America. In the Tucker system, the government will plan your life for you, track you from birth to death on its mammoth data-gathering computer, and regulate employment and eventually the entire economy.

Henry Hyde Opposes

The only Republican congressman to openly oppose this legislation is Rep. Henry Hyde of Illinois, who addressed a letter to his colleagues in March of this year stating why he opposes the Tucker plan and the legislation that makes it law. He wrote:

Dear Colleague:

President Clinton's plan for a national workforce of skilled laborers is being achieved through the Goals 2000 Educate America Act (HR 1804), School-to-Work Opportunities Act (SWO) (HR 2884), and Improving America's Schools Act (IASA) (HR 6), all of which were passed and signed into law by President Clinton in 1994.

I'll tell you why it is so important to repeal these laws. The plan for Goals 2000 was developed by Bill Clinton, Hillary Clinton, Ira Magaziner, and Marc Tucker, President of the National Center on Education and the Economy (funded by the Carnegie Foundation), prior to Clinton's election. It is a concept for dumbing-down our schools and changing the character of the nation through behavior modification (a vital part of this plan). It moves away from an academically intensive curriculum to one that is integrated with vocational training, producing skilled manpower for the labor market. The economy will be controlled by the federal government by controlling our workforce and our schools. I'm enclosing an 18-page letter to Hillary Clinton from Marc Tucker which includes the framework for Goals 2000....

Two other bills, still pending, are designed to advance the School-to-Work phase of Goals 2000. The Careers Act (HR 1617) and the Workforce Development Act (S 143) will support a nationwide work force development system, state by state. Funding is provided for "one stop career" employment agencies under the supervision of the federal government. Please, let's not let these bills become law.

At an education summit in 1989, then-Governor Bill Clinton chaired a Governors' meeting to establish national performance goals to make America internationally competitive. The governors adopted six of the National Education Goals which are now included in the 8 goals in Goals 2000. The other two came from goals adopted at a World Conference sponsored by the United Nations and the World Bank in March, 1990....

Behavior modification is a significant part of restructuring our schools. School children will be trained to be "politically correct," to be unbiased, to understand diversity, to accept alternative family lifestyles, to contribute to the community through mandatory community service, to respect and protect the environment, to become a collaborative contributor and a quality producer. In Marc Tucker's letter to Mrs. Clinton, laying out the plan for Goals 2000 he states, "Radical changes in attitudes, values and beliefs are required to move any combination of these agendas."

Dumbing-down education is a prime component in creating a willing workforce. Higher education is not conducive to accepting skilled labor training for a career that fits into the federal government's planned labor force. Goals 2000 abandons the American competitive tracking system. It is replaced by new national achievement standards which assess students' behavior and attitude....

A computer tracking system will track teachers' training and performance, school performance, and students from pre-kindergarten through technical training and into the workforce. All information will be made available to interested government officials and prospective employers.

Pre-school, health clinics, daily meals, and parental assistance (they have the gall to instruct parents on how to rear their children, including how students' free time should be spent) are in this all-inclusive "cradle to grave" plan to control our children's minds and careers....

This concept has been around since at least the 1960s and perhaps as far back as the 1930s. It has been tried in many schools over the past 20–30 years, to the detriment of our children. In the '70s, it was called "Mastery Learning" under the supervision of Professor Benjamin Bloom and now is known as "OBE." State school superintendents have learned to call OBE by other names because of its bad reputation which precedes it but the concepts are all the same.

I ask you to please investigate Goals 2000 yourself. I think you will come to the same conclusion. Goals 2000 must be rejected, and the sooner the better—for our children's sake.

What has been the response to Rep. Hyde's very strong letter? So far, the only response we know of is a 4-page letter dated March 28 from William Goodling, Republican from Pennsylvania, Chairman of the Committee on Economic and Educational Opportunities, and Howard P. "Buck" McKeon, Chairman of the Subcommittee on Postsecondary Education, Training and Life-long Learning. Goodling, serving his 10th term in Congress, was a school superintendent before becoming a Congressman. McKeon, a Republican from California, is a first-term freshman who seems neither to understand the significance of the bill he is promoting nor the subcommittee he heads. Attached to their letter was a six-page compendium of explanations "developed to respond to similar concerns and misunderstandings that have been expressed over the CAREERS bill in recent months." Goodling and McKeon write:

We recently received a "dear colleague" from you entitled "Clinton's National Workforce and Education Plan," in which you express concerns over H.R. 1617, the House-passed CAREERS Act....

In your letter you describe the CAREERS legislation, and the Senate's Workforce Development Act as "designed to advance the School to Work phase of Goals 2000," tying the roots of this legislation to the work of the Clinton Administration, Ira Magaziner, and Marc Tucker. In fact, CAREERS is the product of efforts by Republicans going back to the Reagan and Bush Administrations, and incorporates suggestions by a bipartisan coalition of reform-minded colleagues, including many leading Republican Governors.

At last, two honest Republicans admitting that it is the Republicans who are creating the educational foundations for a totalitarian system in America! Who are these fascist Republicans? Chester Finn, Dennis Doyle, Bill Bennett, Terrel Bell? It was Bell who in 1984 awarded Bill Spady the grant to continue work on implementing Outcome-Based Education in all of the schools in America. Concerning Chester Finn, Bell writes in his memoir, *The Thirteenth Man*:

David Stockman, director of the Office of Management and Budget, suggested that the very competent Chester Finn be appointed deputy undersecretary for planning and budget in ED. Finn had served in the Nixon White House. I had known him from my Nixon-Ford years, and I knew that I could work with him. Given Stockman's support, I was hopeful that he would be the first one to break the logjam. But despite this endorsement, Finn was promptly rejected by White House Personnel because he was currently serving on the staff of Democratic Senator Pat Moynihan. [Stockman and Finn had both been close to Moynihan during their Harvard days.]

Now we know why Chester Finn can't be trusted! In his book, Bell bemoans the fact that President Reagan did not want the federal government to assume a role of leadership in education. In fact, Reagan wanted to abolish the Education Department but was unable to get the support needed in Congress. Nevertheless, in the bowels of the educational bureaucracy plans were well under way by the National Center for Education Statistics to create its massive computerized data-collection system. It seems as if the government works on two tiers: there is the visible tier of politicians in the White House and Congress which the public is very much aware of; and there is the invisible tier made up of bureaucrats, laboratories, and various foundation-supported commissions that quietly advance the liberal-socialist agenda no matter who occupies the White House or controls Congress. Funding for the invisible tier is always forthcoming in the Budget, even though the politicians may not have the foggiest idea what the money is being spent on.

Iserbyt Blows the Whistle

It was Charlotte Iserbyt, former senior staff member at the Education Department, who saw what was going on among the socialist-fascist planners in the invisible tier and decided to let the public know. Her little book, *Back to Basics Reform Or ...Skinnerian International Curriculum?*, published in 1985, revealed what the invisible tier was doing to prepare America for a socialist one-world government scheduled for the early years of the twenty-first century. She wrote:

> This book deals with the social engineers' continuing efforts, paid for with international, federal, state, and tax-exempt foundation funding, to manipulate and control Americans from birth to death using the educational system as the primary vehicle for bringing about planned social, political, and economic change. (The major change in our economic system will be the determination by industry and government of who will be selected to perform the necessary tasks in our society—quotas for engineers, doctors, service workers, etc. to bring about the socialist concept of full employment.)

That's a virtual description of Marc Tucker's Human Resources Development system. Charlotte was fired for her patriotism. But the cat was out of the bag, and now a small group of conservative activists was able to track the doings of the invisibles. In her book Charlotte was able to document Terrel Bell's complicity with Bill Spady in the development of Outcome-Based Education. She also sounded the alarm on Skinnerian mastery learning, the technique to be used in the schools to change the values, beliefs and behavior of American children.

But to many of us, it was Marc Tucker's letter to Hillary Clinton that proved to be the great eye opener. What was so shocking was the clear totalitarian nature of what was being planned by these American social engineers. And for Republicans in Congress to even contemplate using any component of this plan as a means of reforming American education is to reveal the utter bankruptcy of the Republican party when it comes to education. For Goodling to promote any components of this plan is to betray fundamental Republican principles in defense of freedom. But perhaps the Republicans no longer adhere to these principles and have indeed become the new American fascists. In his letter to Rep. Hyde, Goodling writes:

> In exchange for billions of dollars in federal funding for job training and employment assistance, the CAREERS bill does ask States and local communities to establish what we call integrated career center systems, where there are easily accessible, single points of entry into

local employment and training programs, for people in need of employment assistance or job training, and for employers in need of workers. The actual design for such systems is left entirely to the State and local community. Co-located Career centers (some call them one-stops) are encouraged, not required. And they are locally-designed, appointed and managed—not federally run or controlled.

Apparently, Goodling is unaware that federal control is not needed to put the Tucker plan in place in every state. The only thing that is needed is federal money. Tucker's change agents will design the local systems so that they conform with the overall national—not federal—plan. The social engineers desperately need the federal money to implement this totalitarian plan, and Goodling is willing to give it to them.

As for the Senate bill, S. 143, it is much more in line with just about everything Marc Tucker wants. And the prime promoter of that bill is Sen. Nancy Kassebaum of Kansas who should be designated as Republican traitor number one. It is hard to believe that a so-called Republican can be so blind to the totalitarian nature of the Workforce Development Act of 1995. A Report from the Committee on Labor and Human Resources, summarizes S. 143 as follows:

TITLE I

State Systems—Statewide work force development systems are established through a single allotment of funds to each State. A minimum of 25 percent of the funds are for work force employment activities, such as creating one-stop career centers or providing job training. Work force employment activities are to be planned and administered under the authority of the Governor. A minimum of 25 percent of the funds are for work force education activities, including vocational and adult education. Work force education activities are to be planned and administered under the authority of the State Educational Agency.

The remaining 50 percent of the funds are to be used for any work force employment or education activities as a State decides.... The decision to allocate funds from this "flex account" is made through a collaborative process involving, among others, the Governor, the State educational agency, and the private sector....

State goals and benchmarks are established in the plan, as well as how the State will use its funds to meet those goals and benchmarks.

In addition, the plan includes how the State will establish systems for one-stop career centers, labor market information, and accountability for job placement, as described in the bill....

The Governor must enter into agreements with local communities for the delivery of work force employment, school-to-work, or economic development activities, where appropriate....

TITLE II

Job Corps remains as a residential program for at-risk youth, but is integrated with the statewide work force development system. Primary responsibility for the operation of Job Corps centers is transferred to the States, and each center must be linked into the one-stop career center system and other local training and education efforts.

TITLE III

A Federal partnership is established to administer all Federal responsibilities, including approval, of the State plans, negotiation of benchmarks with each State, and dissemination of best practices.

A governing board, composed of 13 members, will manage the partnership. The board is composed of a majority of representatives from business and industry, and representatives of labor, education and Governors....

Final authority for the approval of State plans and disbursement of funds, however, remains with the Secretary of Education and the Secretary of Labor.

Other national activities include national assessments of vocational education, a national labor market information system, and establishment of a national center for research in education and work force development....

The Workforce Development Act of 1995 promotes the development of a new and coherent system in which all segments of the work force can obtain the skills necessary to earn wages sufficient to maintain a high quality of living and in which a skilled work force can meet the labor market needs of the businesses of each State.

Note how this plan ignores state legislatures or local school boards. The governor runs everything. This is, for all intents and purposes, a coup d'etat that overthrows the representative form of government and local school boards that are supposed to govern education.

Research Galore

Also, the call for the establishment of a national center for research in education and work force development is based on the already existing National Center for Research in Vocational Education at the University of California at Berkeley. A new center will be established by the Governing Board. Its areas of focus are to include:

(1) combining academic and vocational education; (2) connecting classroom instruction with work-based learning; (3) creating a continuum of educational programs which provide multiple exit points for employment; (4) establishing high-quality support services for students; (5) developing new models for remediation of basic academic skills; (6) identifying ways to establish links among educational and job training programs at State and local levels; (7) creating new models for career guidance, counseling, and information; (8) evaluating economic and labor market changes that will affect work force needs; (9) preparing teachers and professionals; (10) obtaining information on practices in other countries that may be adapted for use in the United States; (11) providing assistance to States and local entities in developing and using systems of performance measures and standards; and (12) maintaining a clearinghouse to provide information about the conditions of systems and programs funded under this act.

Obviously, this national center will provide a lot of good jobs at good wages for a lot of liberal university graduates. They will need directors, assistant directors, researchers, statisticians, consultants, secretaries, and staffers producing an endless number of reports to be distributed to every member of Congress, every Governor, every school administrator. Think of all the trees that will have to be cut down to make paper for all of the reports, and think of all the computers, modems, word processors, copy machines, phones and faxes that will have to be bought. Who knows, the national center may balloon to the size of the Pentagon if it is to service the nation's entire workforce development system.

For Republicans who believe in *less* government, the word *less* now apparently means *more*!

Governing Board

And according to this Kassebaum-Tucker plan all power over American education will reside in the Governing Board. The committee report says:

> The Work Force Development Partnership will be headed by a Governing Board composed of 13 members, including 7 representatives of business and industry, 2 representatives of labor and workers, 1 representative of adult education providers, 1 representative of vocational education providers, and 2 Governors, appointed by the President with the advice and consent of the Senate. The Governing Board shall be appointed not later than September 30, 1996.

> The duties of the Governing Board include: (1) Overseeing the development of a national labor market information system and job placement accountability system. (2) Establishing model benchmarks, taking into account existing work force development benchmark efforts at the State level. (3) Negotiating benchmarks with the States. (4) Reviewing and approving State plans. (5) Reviewing reports on the States' progress toward their benchmarks. (6) Preparing and submitting an annual report to Congress on the absolute and relative performance of States' progress toward their benchmarks. (7) Awarding incentive grants. (8) Issuing sanctions. (9) Disseminating information on best practices. (10) Performing the duties relating to the Job Corps. (11) Reviewing other federally funded work force development programs. (12) Reviewing and approving the transition work plan submitted to the Secretaries of Labor and Education. (13) Overseeing all activities of the Federal partnership.

Benchmarks Equal Outcomes

What are "benchmarks," about which the Governing Board will be so concerned? Benchmark is the new word for outcome. Since the lawmakers are concerned that the American people might find out that the Tucker plan is simply another version of Outcome-Based Education, they've decided to eliminate any terminology which might produce widespread parental and conservative opposition. Here's how the lawmakers define benchmarks:

> This act will require States to measure and report annually on benchmarks—measurable indicators of the progress the State has set out to achieve in meeting broad work force development goals related to employment, education, and earning gains.
> Benchmarks related to employment and earning gains include, at a minimum, placement and retention in unsubsidized employment for one year, and increased earnings for participants. Benchmarks related to education include, at a minimum, student mastery of certain skills, including: academic knowledge and work readiness skills; occupational and industry-recognized skills according to skill proficiencies for students in career preparation programs; placement in, retention in, and completion of secondary education; placement and retention in military service; and increased literacy skills. It is expected that States will develop additional benchmarks.

If any further proof were needed to indict Nancy Kassebaum as the Republican Party's leading socialist-fascist, one need not seek further than the May 20, 1996 issue of *Forbes* magazine in which Steve Forbes writes:

Advocates of nationalized health care are on the verge of a stunning achievement with the passage of the Senate's Kennedy-Kassebaum bill. This legislation is portrayed as a benign way of making it easier for people to keep health insurance when they change jobs or to buy insurance if they are in less-than-perfect health. Actually, if this becomes law, it will put us on a fast track to Hillary care. Yet few foes of her socialized monstrosity are fighting what one opponent has rightly called a "Trojan pony."

The First Lady must be beaming. The enforcement language is lifted almost directly from Clinton care. Ferocious penalties litter the House version of this legislation. For instance, doctors face heavy fines if they are deemed to have delivered "unnecessary" health care services. And who determines what is unnecessary? You guessed it—federal bureaucrats, not physicians....

The Senate bill is written in a way that guarantees the eventual imposition of federal price controls. Right now, there are no caps on premiums—which will rise big-time because of the bill's mandates on who is eligible for insurance. Washington State, for example, has Kennedy-Kassebaum-like guarantees. Premiums for individual policy holders have skyrocketed. As prices go up, young, healthy people won't bother to buy insurance. The whole process will then create irresistible pressure for federal controls "to make insurance affordable." There are other flaws here. The bill blithely guarantees that mental health coverage will equal coverage for physical ailments; this is an open invitation for massive abuse. Rules, mandates and caps will proliferate.

The Senate version doesn't even contain a provision for Medical Savings Accounts, the only hope for restoring true freedom and consumerism to the health care field.

Is this what voters elected a Republican Congress for?

Thanks to Nancy Kassebaum and her fellow socialist-fascists in the Senate, this Republican Congress will do more to inch us toward totalitarianism than any previous Congress. Does Senator Dole approve of what his fellow Kansan is doing?

Meanwhile, what should *we* do? We should do all we can to get the federal government out of the education and health care businesses. If Republicans really believe in downsizing government, the last thing they should be doing is voting for more government intrusion in education and health care.

Call, write, or fax your Representatives and Senators. Purchase a copy of the *U.S. Congress Handbook*, P.O. Box 566, McLean, VA 22101, 703-356-3572. This handbook contains all of the information you will need for access to your Washington lawmakers. They need to hear from you.

Appendix XVI

"Totalitarian Data-Gathering System Prepared by U.S. Department of Education"

"Totalitarian Data-Gathering System Prepared by U.S. Department of Education" by Samuel Blumenfeld from *The Blumenfeld Education Newsletter,* October 1995 (Vol. 10, No. 10, Letter #109).

If ever proof were needed to confirm that the New World Order would be totalitarian in its control of individual citizens, the U.S. Department of Education's recent release of its handbooks on data-gathering on students and faculty should be enough to satisfy any freedom-loving citizen. The two publications are the *Student Data Handbook for Early Childhood, Elementary, and Secondary Education* (NCES 94–303) released in June 1994, comprised of 226 pages plus about 100 pages of appendices, and the *Staff Data Handbook: Elementary, Secondary and Early Childhood Education* (NCES 95–327) released in January 1995, comprised of 219 pages and about 70 pages of appendices. Both Handbooks were produced under the auspices of the U.S. Department of Education, the Office of Educational Research and Improvement (OERI), and the National Center for Education Statistics (NCES). Both can be obtained by telephone from the U.S. Dept. of Education. The Foreword for the *Student Data Handbook* states:

> NCES is pleased to release the 1994 *Student Data Handbook: Elementary, Secondary and Early Childhood Education.* It is a major effort to establish current and consistent terms, definitions and classification codes to maintain, correct, report and exchange information about students.
>
> When this effort began, the only existing national standards for student data had been published by NCES in 1974. Because student data have evolved greatly over time both in the type and format of data maintained, it was essential that new standards be developed that would reflect current practices.
>
> This national effort was coordinated by the Council of Chief State School Officers under

contract to the National Center for Educational Statistics. Those individuals and organizations involved in the process truly reflect all interested stakeholders in elementary, secondary and early childhood education.

NCES has a strong commitment to provide technical assistance and support to the education community to facilitate the collection, reporting, and use of high quality education information. This handbook is one outcome of that commitment. It is but one in a series of related handbooks and manuals that NCES has published in the past and plans to continue to develop in the future.

The Foreword is signed by Paul D. Planchon, Associate Commissioner, Elementary/Secondary Education Statistics Division and Lee M. Hoffman, Chief, General Surveys and Analysis Branch of the National Center for Education Statistics.

In the Acknowledgments we read:

> This document is the result of the work of many individuals from around the country who generously contributed their knowledge, time, and commitment....

> The handbook owes its existence to the members of the National Task Force on Education Data Elements. The task force's Student Data Subgroup helped conceptualize and oversee its development, reviewed several copies of the drafts, and provided constant and timely assistance to the project. A list of the task force members is included in Appendix A.

The task force includes 28 members, of which 6 were from state departments of education (Mississippi, Ohio, Florida, Minnesota, Texas, New York) and 6 from city and county school districts. The rest were bureaucrats from various offices of the U.S. Dept. of Education, the American Association of Collegiate Registrars and Admissions Officers, Johns Hopkins University, Bureau of the Census, University of California, (Santa Barbara), Council of Great City Schools, and the National Science Foundation.

Bureaucrats at Work

We read further in the Acknowledgments:

> Under contract from the National Center for Education Statistics (NCES), staff from the Council of Chief State School Officers (CCSSO) prepared the manuscript of this handbook. Barbara S. Clements, Project Director, provided the leadership for this effort and is the primary author of the document....

> Emerson Elliott, Commissioner of Education Statistics, who has encouraged inter- and intra-agency collaboration and teamwork to improve the quality of education data, set the stage for this effort. Paul Planchon, Associate Commissioner of Education Statistics, Elementary/Secondary Education Statistics Division, provided strong support and guidance for the handbook as a project under his authority. Lee Hoffman, Chief, General Survey and Analysis Branch, not only provided technical advice as a task force member, but also reviewed all drafts of the document....

In other words, a small army of bureaucrats have been working on this project for years. The purpose of the student handbook is described in Chapter 1:

1) to provide a common language that can be used to describe information about students,

2) to promote standard maintenance of student data, 3) to encourage the automation of student data maintenance, 4) to promote the development of policies to safeguard the confidentiality and ensure appropriate use of student data, and 5) to describe how data can be maintained in a way that promotes appropriate and flexible usage by all relevant parties.

Chapter 1 also provides this revealing Overview:

Accurate and comprehensive information is needed in order to make appropriate cost-effective and timely decisions about students within both public and private schools. Teachers, school administrators, school district administrators, school board members, and state and federal education agency personnel must use information about students to plan and carry out programs of learning that meet the needs of children with different abilities and requirements, from divergent backgrounds, and of different ages. School health officials and other service providers also use information about individual students to ensure appropriate services are provided to them. These information needs are being met in an increasing number of instances by automated management information systems that allow data to be analyzed in a variety of ways to address the questions and needs of the decision-makers. A management information system is effective, however, only to the extent that data are consistently entered into the system according to established definitions, data are updated and maintained on a regular basis, and information relevant for ongoing decision-making can be added to the system. This handbook addresses the importance of consistency in how data are defined and maintained within the education system.

Designing Data Collection
...Researchers from the [U.S.] Department of Education, federally funded laboratories and research centers, universities, and other public and private organizations provide insights into the needs and performance of the nation's schools through surveys such as the National Education Longitudinal Survey and assessment activities such as the National Assessment of Educational Progress. This handbook can be valuable for researchers concerned with accuracy and consistency in designing data collection activities and reporting results of studies on groups of students.

The handbook is intended to serve public and private education agencies, schools, and other centers and institutions serving students from preschool through high school graduation, as well as researchers and the general public....

No governmental agency requires the use of the terms, definitions, and procedures of this handbook; however, care was taken to make sure that the definitions in this handbook were consistent with many governmental reporting requirements existing at the time of the handbook's completion....

A Tool for Decision Making
The handbook identifies concepts and data elements which are used to describe and make decisions about students. Some decisions are very specific, pertaining to personal needs, vocational choices, and educational programs of individual students. Other decisions are broader in scope, concerning the planning and management of education for large groups of students....

Some types of student data are maintained because of federal, state or local reporting requirements. If federal, state or local reporting requirements are made consistent, then a single collection of information about students can serve multiple purposes.

If student data are maintained in a cumulative (longitudinal) record using consistent terms and definitions, the permanent record contains all relevant information and is easier to interpret....

Automated Database

The advantages of maintaining student records in an automated database, however, are numerous. Automated databases promote the maintenance of consistently defined information, since the computer software specifies how data are coded and otherwise entered....

Student data must be kept confidential. ...Whether or not student data are maintained in a computer, all school or school district staff needing data about an individual student or groups of students must have access to pertinent information. ...Teachers can analyze student performance using a variety of types of information and decide what concepts need to be retaught or reinforced.

Obviously, the purpose of the project is to produce standardization among data-gatherers so that all of the student information can be computerized and stored in a central database. As the Handbook states:

Technical advances in computer data entry, storage, and retrieval are developing quickly, making these aspects of student records management less expensive, more efficient, less demanding of physical space, and more accessible to multiple users.

Incidentally, if you are curious about the legislation that authorized funding for all of this, the Handbook refers to the Standards for Education Data Collection and Reporting (SEDCAR) developed pursuant to the Hawkins-Stafford Amendments of 1988 which authorized "an effort to improve the comparability, quality and usefulness of education data."

SPEEDE/ExPRESS System

The *Handbook* also reveals that its standards are compatible with those of the SPEEDE/ExPRESS format. (SPEEDE stands for Standardization of Postsecondary Education Electronic Data Exchanges, and ExPRESS stands for Exchange of Permanent Records Electronically for Students and Schools.) SPEEDE/ExPRESS "provides a standard format for a student record or transcript to be sent from one school or school district to another or from a school or school district to a postsecondary institution."

Confidentiality

Although lip service to confidentiality is required in the Family Educational Rights and Privacy Act of 1974 (FERPA), the law allows information in student records to be disclosed "without student or parental permission" to:

1) School employees who have a need to know. 2) Other schools to which a student is transferring. 3) Certain government officials in order to carry out lawful functions. 4) Appropriate parties in connection with financial aid to a student. 5) Organizations doing certain studies for the school. 6) Accrediting organizations. 7) Individuals who have obtained court orders or subpoenas. 8) Persons who need to know in cases of health and safety emergencies. 9) State and local authorities to whom disclosure is required by state laws adopted before November 19, 1974.

FERPA also "guarantees the student and/or his or her parents the right to inspect and review all of the student's education records maintained by the school or school district, and the right to request that a school correct records believed to be inaccurate or misleading."

The Number Code

What kind of data will the system collect? The most detailed personal information about the individual in all aspects of his life. The system uses a number code for each specific piece of information. For example, codes 001 to 012 deal with the student's name. Codes 013 to 036 deal with the student's background, which includes Identification Number (013), Identification System (014) with fourteen subcategories: 01 Driver's license number, 02 Health record number, 03 Medicaid number, 04 Migrant student records transfer system (MSRTS) number, 05 Professional certificate or license number, 06 School-assigned number, 07 Selective Service number, 08 Social security administration number, 09 College Board/ACT code set of PK-grade 12 institutions, 10 Local education agency (LEA) number, 11 State education agency (SEA) number, 12 U.S. Department of Education, National Center for Education Statistics (NCES) number, 13 Other organization number (e.g., Roman Catholic Diocese or association number), 99 Other. In other words, Americans will be identified and numbered as never before.

Data on Student's Religion

Under Religious Background (030) we find the following subcategories: 01 Amish, 02 Assembly of God, 03 Baptist, 04 Buddhist, 05 Calvinist, 06 Catholic, 07 Eastern Orthodox, 08 Episcopal, 09 Friends, 10 Greek Orthodox, 11 Hindu, 12 Islamic, 13 Jehovah's Witnesses, 14 Jewish, 15 Latter Day Saints, 16 Lutheran, 17 Mennonite, 18 Methodist, 19 Pentecostal, 20 Presbyterian, 21 Other Christian denomination, 22 Seventh Day Adventist, 23 Tao, 98 None, 99 Other.

In other words, the traditional designations of Protestant, Catholic, or Jewish are no longer sufficient for the data-gatherers who want to know much more about an individual's religious values. Note the absence of Unitarian-Universalist. I think they're more numerous in America than practitioners of Tao.

Homeschools and Private Schools

Will homeschoolers be included in this data-gathering system? Under Address/Contact Information we find that code 056 "Non-Resident Attendance Rationale—The reason that the student attends a school outside of his or her usual attendance area," contains 10 subcategories, including 07 "Home schooling—The student is receiving educational instruction offered in a home environment, as regulated by state law, for reasons other than health." So, homeschoolers are not only included, but have their own code number: 056–07.

Private schools are also included under "School Information." Code 076 "School Administration" includes subcategory 05 "Private, non-religiously-affiliated school," and 06 "Private, religiously-affiliated school." Under "School Type" (077) we find subcategories 02 "Alternative," and 04 "Montessori." Under "Discontinuing Schooling Reason" (112) we find subcategory 19 "Religion—The student left school because of religious convictions."

Under "Non-Entrance Information" we find category 116 "Reason for Non-Entrance in Local or Secondary School," under which we find subcategory 03 "Home schooling—The individual is receiving educational services offered in a home environment for reasons other than health." Also under 116 we find subcategory 05 "Religious reason—The individual or his or her parent/guardian has religious convictions that prohibit participation in the educational program of the school or education agency, and the individual is not receiving approved instruction elsewhere." Thus, the government controllers cover all bases.

Assessment Information

Data on students will also include extensive assessment information. Under "Assessment Type" (189) we find the following subcategories: 01 Achievement Test, 02 Advanced Placement Test, 03 Aptitude Test, 04 Attitudinal Test— "An assessment to measure the mental and emotional set or patterns of likes and dislikes or opinions held by a student or a group of students. This is often used in relation to considerations such as controversial issues or personal adjustments." 05 Cognitive and perceptual skills test— "An assessment to measure components of a student's mental ability such as visual memory, figure-ground differentiation, auditory memory, reasoning ability, and sequential processing." 06 Developmental Observation, 07 Interest Inventory— "An assessment used to measure the extent to which a student's pattern of likes and dislikes corresponds to those of individuals who are known to be successfully engaged in a given vocation, subject area, program of studies, or other activity." 08 Language Proficiency Test, 09 Manual Dexterity Test, 10 Mental Ability (Intelligence) Test, 11 Performance Assessment— "An assessment to measure a student's knowledge or skill by requiring him or her to produce an answer or product that is not necessarily in a standardized format. Examples of performance assessment include writing short answers, solving complex mathematical problems, writing an extended essay, conducting an experiment, presenting an oral argument, or assembling a portfolio of representative work." 12 Personality Test— "An assessment to measure a student's affective or nonintellectual aspects of behavior such as emotional adjustment, interpersonal relations, motivation, interests, and attitudes." 13 Portfolio Assessment, 14 Psychological Test— "An assessment to measure a sample of behavior in an objective and standardized way." 15 Psychomotor Test, 16 Reading Readiness Test. Note that the assessment tests are in complete harmony with Outcome-Based Education.

All About Your Teeth

It's hard to imagine a less-intrusive data-gathering system than this one, and it is difficult to exaggerate the thoroughness of the system. For example, under Health Conditions we find the category of Oral Health with the following code designations: 230 Number of Teeth, 231 Number of Permanent Teeth Lost, 232 Number of Teeth Decayed, 233 Number of Teeth Restored, 234 Occlusion Condition, with subcategories 01 Normal occlusion, 02 Mild malocclusion, 03 Moderate malocclusion, 04 Severe malocclusion. 235 Gingival (Gum) Condition, with subcategories 01 Normal, 02 Mild deviation, 03 Moderate deviation, 04 Severe deviation. 236 Oral Soft Tissue Condition, with subcategories 01 Normal, 02 Mild deviation, 03 Moderate deviation, 04 Severe deviation. 237 Dental Prosthetics, and Orthodontic Appliances.

Why all of this interest in teeth? Will the schools be offering dental services at state expense? Or is the information for the purposes of identification in case your face is smashed to a pulp by a guard in one of their concentration camps for the politically incorrect? But by then every individual will probably be microchipped, bar coded, tattooed or tagged. Are we being paranoid? Were Jews in Germany in 1933 paranoid? Were anticommunist Russians in 1917 paranoid?

Medical Data

Medical information will also include Maternal and Pre-Natal Condition, Conditions at Birth, Health History, described as: "A record of an individual's afflictions, conditions, injuries, accidents, treatments, and procedures"; Medical Evaluations, Disabling Conditions, Medical Laboratory Tests, Immunizations, Limitations on School Activities, Health Care Provider, and Other Health Information— "Information about an individual's medical or health requirements that are not otherwise addressed above."

Under category 322 Student Support Service Type, we read, "Type of related or ancillary services provided to an individual or a group of individuals within the formal educational system or offered by an outside agency which provides non-instructional services to support the general welfare of students. This includes physical and emotional health, the ability to select an appropriate course of study, admission to appropriate educational programs, and the ability to adjust to and remain in school through the completion of programs. In serving a student with an identified disability, related services include developmental, corrective, or supportive services required to ensure that the individual benefits from special education." There are 39 subcategories under category 322.

Individual Health Plan

Code number 331 refers to Service Provider Type— "The qualified individual or licensed organization (if licensing is necessary) responsible for serving the student." Subcategory 02 refers to Health nurse— "Certified, licensed, registered nurse or nurse practitioner who provides any of the following services: 1) case finding activities to include health appraisal, screening for developmental maturational/milestones, vision and hearing acuity, speech, dental deviations, growth, and nutritional disorders; 2) nursing care procedures that include immunization, medication-monitoring and administration, nursing assessment, and procedures related to the health impaired student's Individual Health Plan (IHP); 3) care coordination and outreach to children who do not otherwise receive preventive health care, follow-ups to assure referral completion, home visits for follow-up planning or home environment assessment, and interim prenatal or family planning and monitoring; 4) patient/student counseling or instruction to include nursing assessment, counseling, and anticipatory guidance to maintain wellness or provide assistance for identified health problems or concerns.

Socialized Medicine Via Education

Obviously, the health provision aspects of public education are to be expanded exponentially. If the liberals can't get socialized medicine through the health care system, they'll get it through the education system.

Subcategory 03 Social worker reads: "Certified, licensed, or otherwise qualified professional who provides the following services: 1) preparing a social or developmental history on a student with disabilities; 2) group and individual counseling with a student and his or her family; 3) working with those problems in a student's living situation (home, school, and community) that affect adjustment in school; 4) mobilizing school and community resources in order to enable the student to receive maximum benefit from his or her educational program; and 5) other related services as necessary."

Serviced to Death

What kind of individual will emerge from an "education" system as all-encompassing and suffocating as this one? American children will be serviced to death by their government which will surround them with teachers and specialists tormenting them in subtle, abusive ways with endless tests, emotional probing and strip searching, and required politically correct performances to indicate, in Bill Spady's words, "visionary higher-order exit outcomes." This is a system designed to turn every healthy youngster that enters it into an academically crippled, emotionally damaged adult.

Subcategory 04 Psychologist reads: "Certified, licensed, or otherwise qualified professional who provides the following services: 1) administering psychological and educational tests, and other assessment procedures; 2) interpreting assessment results; 3) obtaining, integrating, and interpreting information about student behavior and conditions relating to learning; 4) consulting with other staff members in planning school programs to meet the special needs of students as indicated by psychological tests, interviews, and behavioral evaluations; 5) planning and managing a program of psychological services, including psychological counseling for students and parents."

Subcategory 05 Counselor reads: "A staff member responsible for guiding individuals, families, groups and communities by assisting them in problem-solving, decision-making, discovering meaning, and articulating goals related to personal, educational, and career development." How many guidance counselors that you know can help anyone, let alone a student, "discover meaning"? What a joke all of this is.

Do We Need This?

We are told that the government needs all of this incredibly detailed information so that effective decisions can be made for the student by bureaucrats, teachers, administrators, and others on the government's payroll. But what it all adds up to is a tool of behavioral control and management of the American population by the controlling elite. The government of a free people does not go about creating the most detailed and thorough personal dossier on each citizen from date of birth to be stored in government computers on the pretext that it is needed to provide that citizen with an education.

When I attended public school as a child in New York City in the early 1930s, all they needed was my name, address, date of birth, and parents' names. That was it. And it was all written by hand on a card. Your entire school record was on a single card with your final grades for each subject for each year. That's the way it ought to be today.

As for the Staff Handbook, it calls for the same kind of thorough biographical data as outlined in the Student Handbook such as race, religion, ethnicity, plus extensive data on educational background, professional development, credentialing, employment, job and course assignments, and evaluations. If you add to this the data in the teacher's file when he or she was a student, you have an incredibly detailed profile of that individual. In Chapter 1 of the Staff Handbook, we read:

> Education agencies and institutions maintain information about staff to facilitate the efficient and effective functioning of the education enterprise.... If all data about a staff member are maintained in an automated data system, many uses and types of analyses are possible. For instance, an administrator may need to know about the availability of human resources to initiate a new program. Information about the background, educational and professional qualifications of current staff members could be used to identify possible candidates to work on the program.

Note the reference to the staff member as a "human resource." That's the thinking of a systems bureaucrat to whom a human being is now a "resource" to be controlled and used like any other natural resource.

What Can Be Done?

It is absolutely essential, if we are to remain a free people, that this entire data-collection system be stopped and dismantled. It has no place in a free society. The legislation that authorized it must be repealed or rescinded or defunded. This entire system is based on the need of behavioral scientists for a detailed, longitudinal accumulation of data to verify the [efficacy] of their programs to change human behavior. Benjamin Bloom, the godfather of Outcome-Based Education, wrote in his 1964 book *Stability and Change in Human Characteristics*:

> We can learn very little about human growth, development, or even about specific human characteristics unless we make full use of the time dimension. Efforts to control or change human behavior by therapy, by education, or by other means will be inadequate and poorly understood until we can follow behavior over a longer period. (p. 5)

That the behaviorist's purpose of education is to change human behavior was spelled out in Bloom's *Taxonomy of Educational Goals* dealing with the affective domain. He was greatly concerned with the need to get control of children as early as possible. He wrote:

> The evidence points out convincingly to the fact that age is a factor operating against attempts to effect a complete or thorough-going reorganization of attitudes and values. (p. 85)

> The evidence collected thus far suggests that a single hour of classroom activity under certain conditions may bring about a major reorganization in cognitive as well as affective behaviors. We are of the opinion that this will prove to be a most fruitful area of research in connection with the affective domain. (p. 88)

And in *Stability and Change in Human Characteristics*, Bloom wrote:

> We believe that the early environment is of crucial importance for three reasons. The first is based on the very rapid growth of selected characteristics in the early years and conceives of the variations in the early environment as so important because they shape these characteristics in their most rapid periods of formation.
> Secondly, each characteristic is built on a base of that same characteristic at an earlier time or on the base of other characteristics which precede it in development....

> A third reason... stems from learning theory. It is much easier to learn something new than it is to stamp out one set of learned behaviors and replace them by a new set. (p. 215)

The data collection system outlined in the Student Handbook will give the behaviorists the vital tool they need to hone their ability to thoroughly reorganize the values, attitudes and behaviors of the American student. God help us if this system is implemented.

Appendix XVII

Memos on Direct Instruction

January 10, 1997 Memo
To: Researchers
From: Charlotte Iserbyt
Regarding: Direct Instruction

The Christian Conscience, September 1996, commenced the serialization on a monthly basis of my updated 1985 *Back to Basics Reform or OBE... Skinnerian International Curriculum* (Chronological History of OBE/ML: 1880s through 1990s). I urge those of you trying to edu-cate opponents of OBE and School-to-Work programs WHO SUPPORT DIRECT INSTRUC-TION, please go to *The Christian Conscience* website (http://www.christianconscience.com) and request the September–December 1996 back issues. These will take you through the important sixties and will explain with complete documentation that the Direct Instruction method is similar to the Skinnerian OBE/mastery learning method and should be rejected since animal training methods have nothing to do with education. For the life of me I cannot understand why Christian schools and home schoolers support ML/DI which uses animal training methods based on the theory of evolution (man is nothing but an animal) which they so vociferously oppose.

Those ramming OBE/ML work force training down our throats ran into so much trouble, due unfortunately only to the nasty outcomes, not due to the Skinnerian method, that they rescued their OBE/ML restructuring by jumping from the mastery learning ship onto its sister ship, Direct Instruction. They figured, and it seems with good reason, that if they presented the same method with a different label and focused on academic, not affective, touchy-feely outcomes, they could capture the approval of the conservative opposition.

Direct Instruction is on a roll—all over the country. California is looking at DI; parents were ready for "anything" after the whole language disaster. Chicago, which surely should know better after its ML catastrophe which resulted in half the freshman class not graduating, is implementing DI. Doug Carnine, Director of the federally funded National Center to Improve the Tools of Educators, in Eugene, Oregon, has written Ms. Moran, California's Commission for the Establishment of Academic Content and Performance Standards, regarding the Center's work with Virginia on aligning their state assessment with their standards and in developing their accountability system. What is of interest here is that Carnine, who is close to Engelmann, the father of DI—DISTAR, and who was involved in the Follow Through Direct Instruction Evaluation (1970–76), known as the "largest and most expensive social experiment ever launched," has surfaced 20 years later as a key player in education restructuring. You will be told Direct Instruction is "back to basics" and if you squawk hard enough about the outcomes or standards of learning, or whatever they call your objectives, the educrats may recommend Virginia's Standards of Learning [Is this E.D. Hirsch? ed.] which are pretty clean—for now—but don't forget those standards can be interpreted by the educrats any way they want, and some fine day, they could be completely changed. The problem is not the outcomes, but the Skinnerian method essential for workforce training, and Direct Instruction is just as bad, for the same reasons, as Mastery Learning, which has been a disaster in all the inner city schools in which it was used.

Last night on the *Jim Lehrer Show* there was a panel discussion on the sorry state of education during which John Chubb of the liberal Brookings Institute, who heads up the Edison Project (charter schools), recommended Direct Instruction as the solution to the nation's education problems. Chubb et al., with strong ties into the international business community, support publicly funded charter schools, which, as all of you know, will be used for workforce training. The Skinnerian Method, be it ML or DI, is of vital importance to the implementation of workforce training. ML and DI are not the same thing as teacher-initiated or driven instruction of basic content material (traditional education). Curriculum in script form using operant conditioning, i.e. Programmed Learning, be it Ethna Reid's ECRI Mastery Learning (ML) or Engelmann's SRA (DISTAR). Direct Instruction (DI) is **not** the same as teacher-initiated or driven instruction of basic **content** material (traditional education). **PLS PUT ON INTERNET!**

January 29, 1997 Memo
To: Supporters of Direct Instruction
From: Charlotte Iserbyt
Regarding: The Role of Siegfried Engelmann, developer of DISTAR/Reading Mastery, in teacher training for federally funded ECRI (Skinnerian Mastery Learning)

On April 12, 1980 the Maine Facilitator Center (National Diffusion Network) held a conference to train teachers in Ethna Reid's mastery learning program known as "The Exemplary Center for Reading Instruction." A teacher friend of mine gave me the 125-page teacher training manual used at the conference.

Although I had always suspected that Engelmann's DISTAR/Reading Mastery was in some way connected to the ECRI program since the techniques were similar, I was unable to make a direct connection. When I first read the training manual ten years ago, I did not know who Engelmann was so his name meant nothing to me. Now that I know who he is, you can imagine how shocked and sickened I was to find him referenced in Reid's rat lab training manual. My worst suspicions regarding DI/Reading Mastery have been confirmed. One of the many references follows:

BASIC PRINCIPLES OF BEHAVIOR MANAGEMENT

Until recent years, the study of human behavior was thought to elude careful analysis. However, during the last three decades, scientific techniques have been developed for the study of behavior which show that behavioral processes are based upon exact principles. In applying these principles to teaching, Becker, Engelmann, and Thomas stated:

> The experimental study of events that make learning happen has produced consistent findings that can provide the teacher with a systematic basis for doing her job. Events occurring <u>before</u> and <u>after</u> a child makes a response have been shown to be critical in determining when and where that response will occur again. Environmental events that influence responding are called <u>stimuli</u>. A teacher accomplishes a teaching objective by effectively arranging the occurrence of <u>stimulus</u> events for the child—that is, by controlling when and how she talks, praises, shows things, and prompts responses.

> Teaching is further described as a three-step process, written S-R-S
>   (S) The teacher presents preceding stimuli (signal)
>   (R) The child responds
>   (R) The teacher presents following stimulus (consequence)
> This Model for Direct Teaching can be shown thus:
>   S (Preceding Stimuli);
>   R (Pupil Response); and
>   S (Consequent Stimuli)

Reference #8, Becker, Engelmann, and Thomas, *Teaching: A Course in Applied Psychology* (Science Research Associates, Inc.: Chicago, 1971), p.1.

DISTAR/Reading Mastery is being used in the Houston public schools and is being touted as the most successful curriculum around by conservative groups. It is also being promoted by the multi-national corporations and John Chubb who support charter schools for workforce training.

January 30, 1997 Memo
To: Supporters of Direct Instruction
From: Charlotte Iserbyt

Forces for Change in the Primary Schools 1980 (High Scope Press High Scope Educational Research Foundation: Ypsilanti, MI, 1980), pp.81–82, identifies Douglas Carnine as "Director of Follow Through (FT) Direct Instruction Model, University of Oregon, Department of Special Education." The FT program was a longitudinal educational experiment aimed at finding effective methods for educating disadvantaged children.

Doug Carnine's Dec. 11, 1996 letter to Ms. Ellen Moran, State of California, Commission for the Establishment of Academic Content and Performance Standards, is written on the National Center to Improve the Tools of Educators letterhead which also says in fine print "To address the Quality of Technology, Media and Materials for Students with Diverse Learning

Needs, funded by the U.S. Office of Special Education Programs." Carnine's letter to Moran stated that "the Center is working closely with the VA Dept. of Education and State Board on aligning their state assessment with their standards and in developing their accountability system.... NCITE is also preparing informal assessment benchmarks for first and second grade in math and language arts that schools can volunteer to use before the formal assessment begins in grade 3. Our center is willing to make these and other materials we develop for Virginia available to the Commission without charge."

DISTAR/Reading Mastery is being promoted as an alternative to Whole Language reading instruction. Even if one doesn't object to Skinnerian behavior modification/operant conditioning/animal training being used on children, doesn't it make sense to question whether one wants their perfectly normal children subjected to a program designed for disadvantaged children (10-15% of students). Many critics of Skinnerian training programs have gone even further and suggested that it was unethical to use disadvantaged children for experimentation, such as was done with the "Follow Through" program in the late sixties.

I have before me a study entitled *Educational Outcomes and Indicators for Students Completing School*, from the National Center on Educational Outcomes, The College of Education, University of Minnesota, in collaboration with St. Cloud State University and National Association of State Directors of Special Education, 1993, which says: "The National Center on Educational Outcomes (NCEO) is working with federal and state agencies to facilitate and enhance the collection and use of data on educational outcomes for students with disabilities. In doing so, it has taken an inclusive approach: Identifying a conceptual model of outcomes that applies to ALL students, not just to students with disabilities."

Is this what the "deliberate dumbing down" of America is all about? All children are considered to have disabilities and are categorized as special education? All children will have an individualized education plan? All children will be taught using Skinnerian behavioral psychology, be it mastery learning/OBE or Direct Instruction/DISTAR/Reading Mastery?

Although the Evaluation of Follow Through cited some academic and self-esteem gains at some sites due to the use of the Direct Instruction model, it would have been virtually impossible for these gains not to have been made considering the open classroom, touchy-feely models with which it was compared. Had the Direct Instruction model been in competition with a good traditional phonics program not based on animal psychology, it is most unlikely it would have been able to point to any gains at all. Also, the results of the Follow Through program should be questioned as valuable to our society as a whole since they were based, again, on the results in inner city schools. Why didn't those involved reach for the stars and try to find out what it was, in our most academically oriented schools, with high test scores, in middle income communities, that lead to success, and use that model in the inner city schools? Isn't it elitist to suggest that low income, minority children were not capable of attaining the same results as those of their more advantaged classmates in other parts of the country? And isn't it interesting that the model for the "disadvantaged" children (Engelmann's Direct Instruction/Reading Mastery) seems to have been selected for ALL our children as the model for the schools of the 21st Century, publicly funded charter schools, run by unelected directors, whose purpose will be to "train" our children (human resources) for the global workforce?

If the above analysis is on target, and the documentation unfortunately seems to point in that direction, it is a very, very sad day for American education, our children, and our nation.

January 30, 1997 Memo
To: Activists in States Implementing DISTAR/Reading Mastery using Doug Carnine of the federally-funded national Center to Improve the Tools of Educators, as Consultant to your State Deptartment of Education
From: Charlotte Iserbyt
Regarding: Doug Carnine's work in your State. Proof that Direct Instruction/Reading Mastery is 100% B.F. Skinner Rat Lab education

Am sending you the alerts I have been getting out the past two weeks, which have gone onto the Internet, and which you should have, if you are not on-line.

Carnine has not responded to my original January 10, 1997 alert, although requested to do so by others on the Internet. Considering the amount of information we have on his connections with Engelmann, father of DISTAR/Reading Mastery, dating back twenty years, it is no surprise Engelmann, Becker, Carnine, etc., do not wish to respond.

Those who do not understand Skinnerian behavioral psychology and its use on innocent children are making a very big mistake supporting DI/Reading Mastery. I have the entire ECRI teacher training in which Engelmann is referenced several times (absolutely nauseating quotes). I cannot find a word to express my disgust that such a dehumanizing method could be used on anyone, much less captive children in the classroom. I don't care if it is used to teach the Ten Commandments. It is sick, sick, sick, and our good people had better wake up and stop embracing it simply because it uses intensive phonics instead of Whole Language. Hitler had a pretty good system going for him, too; he used this method; so do the Russians. I personally consider my two sons to be more than "organisms." I pulled them out of a Christian school that used ML for the same reason fifteen years ago.

After reading the ECRI teacher training I can honestly say that I would prefer to have my child in a Whole Language class, learning nothing, than a Skinnerian DI class, possibly learning bits and pieces of basics (which will never transfer) and in which my child's whole being, personality, etc. will be damaged, perhaps forever. And I have fought Whole Language ever since it arrived on the horizon, for over ten years. I have written about it. One article was even published in *The Congressional Record*. I mention this only to convince those still believing I am possibly pro-Whole Language that I am not. I support teaching phonics with the teacher in front of the class, lecturing the children (teacher-initiated or -driven instruction of basic content material: traditional education). Curriculum in script form using operant conditioning, i.e. Programmed Learning, be it Ethna Reid's ECRI or Engelmann's SRA (DISTAR/Reading Mastery/Direct Instruction) is not traditional teaching.

When Ann Herzer, a teacher, complained about going through the ECRI training in Arizona, she was absolutely crucified, strung up, and left there to bleed (by conservatives, among others). She was asked by the trainer, "Don't you understand—we're training the children to be 'people pleasers'?" You should see the file I have of letters from distraught parents, reputable doctors, psychologists, etc. who came to Ann's defense in opposing this sick program. You should see the letters from plain moms about their children getting sick; nervous ailments, ticks, nightmares, etc. Ann and the parents were threatened with legal reprisal if they didn't shut up. Ann did not shut up.

The U.S. Department of Education has denied that ECRI uses rat training; also denies that there was ever an ECRI teacher training manual, which I happen to hold in my hand right this minute! Fortunately, a wonderful American teacher who went through the training in

Maine in 1980 gave me the manual. We would never have had the entire story without her help.

Please get on the bandwagon with your Governors, Legislature, State Board of Education, media, etc. But most of all with local school boards and parents. Warn them! And don't forget to tell them that when we have exposed Direct Instruction for what it is, the change agents will give it another name. Global economy, multinational corporations, and the United Nations must have only one method of training, and that is Skinner. The outcomes can be changed overnight; the method cannot.

Appendix XVIII

"A Human Resources Development Plan for the United States"

NATIONAL CENTER ON EDUCATION AND THE ECONOMY
(c)1992 National Center on Education and the Economy
Additional Copies are Available for $7.50 each, postpaid from the
National Center on Education and the Economy
39 State Street, Suite 500
Rochester, NY 14614–1327
716–546–7620
FAX: 716–546–3145

Preface

The advent of the Clinton administration creates a unique opportunity for the country to develop a truly national system for the development of its human resources, second to none on the globe. The National Center on Education and the Economy and its predecessor organization, the Carnegie Forum on Education and the Economy, have been elaborating a national agenda in this arena over the last eight years. Here, we outline a set of recommendations to the incoming Clinton administration in the area of human resource development. It builds directly on the proposals that the President-elect advanced during the campaign. This report is mainly the work of a small group of people with close ties to the National Center: Tim Barnicle, David Barram, Michael Cohen, David Hasselkorn, David Hornbeck, Shirley Malcom, Ray Marshall, Susan McGuire, Hilary Pennington, Andy Plattner, Lauren Resnick, David Rockefeller, Jr., Betsy Brown Ruzzi, Robert Schwartz, John Sculley, Marshall Smith, Bill Spring and myself. While all of these people are in general agreement with what follows, they may not agree on the details.

—Marc Tucker

Introduction

The great opportunity in front of the country now is to remold the entire American system for human resources development, almost all of the current components of which were put in place before World War II. The natural course is to take each of the ideas that were advanced in the campaign in the area of education and training and translate them individually into legislative proposals. But that will lead to these programs being grafted onto the present system, not to a new system, and the opportunity will have been lost. If this sense of time and place is correct, it is essential that the nation's efforts be guided by a consistent vision of what it wants to accomplish in the field of human resources development, a vision that can shape the actions not only of the new administration but of many others over the next few years.

What follows comes in two pieces:

First, a vision of the kind of national—not federal—human resources development system the nation could have. This is interwoven with a new approach to governing that should inform that vision. What is essential is that we create a seamless web of opportunities to develop one's skills that literally extends from cradle to grave and is the same system for everyone— young and old, poor and rich, worker and full-time student. It needs to be a system *driven by client needs* (not agency regulations or the needs of the organizations providing the services), *guided by clear standards* that define the stages of the system for the people who progress through it, and *regulated on the basis of outcomes* that providers produce for their clients, not inputs into the system.

Second, a proposed legislative agenda the new administration and the Congress can use to implement this vision. We propose four *high priority* packages that will enable the federal government to move quickly:

1. The *first* would use the President-elect's proposal for an *apprenticeship* system as the keystone of a strategy for putting a whole new postsecondary training system in place. That system would incorporate his proposal for reforming *postsecondary education finance*. It contains what we think is a powerful idea for rolling out and scaling up the whole new human resources system nationwide over the next four years, using the (renamed) apprenticeship idea as the entering wedge.

2. The *second* would combine initiatives on dislocated workers, a rebuilt employment service and a new system of labor market boards in a single *employment security* program built on the best practices anywhere in the world. This is the backbone of a system for assuring adult workers in our society that they need never again watch with dismay as their jobs disappear and their chances of ever getting a job again go with them.

3. The *third* would concentrate on the overwhelming problems of our *inner cities*, combining elements of the first and second packages into a special program to greatly raise the work-related skills of the people trapped in the core of our great cities.

4. The *fourth* would enable the new administration to take advantage of legislation on which

Congress has already been working to advance the *elementary and secondary reform* agenda.

The Vision

An Economic Strategy Based on Skill Development

♦ The economy's strength is derived from a whole population as skilled as any in the world, working in workplaces organized to take maximum advantage of the skills those people have to offer.

♦ A seamless system of unending skill development that begins in the home with the very young and continues through school, postsecondary education and the workplace.

The Schools

♦ Clear national standards of performance in general education (the knowledge and skills that everyone is expected to hold in common) are set to the level of the best achieving nations in the world for students of 16 and public schools are expected to bring all but the most severely handicapped up to that standard. Students get a certificate when they meet this standard, allowing them to go on to the next stage of their education. Though the standards are set to international benchmarks, they are distinctly American, reflecting our needs and values.

♦ We have a national system of education in which curriculum, pedagogy, examinations and teacher education and licensure systems are all linked to the national standards, but which provides for substantial variation among states, districts and schools on these matters. This new system of linked standards, curriculum and pedagogy will abandon the American tracking system, combining high academic standards with the ability to apply what one knows to real world problems and qualifying all students for a lifetime of learning in the postsecondary system and at work.

♦ We have a system that rewards students who meet the national standards with further education and good jobs, providing them a strong incentive to work hard in school.

♦ Our public school systems are reorganized to free up school professionals to make the key decisions about how to use all the available resources to bring students up to the standards. Most of the federal, state, district and union rules and regulations that now restrict school professionals' ability to make these decisions are swept away, though strong measures are in place to make sure that vulnerable populations get the help they need. School professionals are paid at a level comparable to that of other professionals, but they are expected to put in a full year to spend whatever time it takes to do the job and to be fully accountable for the results of their work. The federal, state and local governments provide the time, staff development resources, technology and other support needed for them to do the job. Nothing less than a wholly restructured school system can possibly bring all of our students up to a standard only a few have been expected to meet up to now.

♦ There is an aggressive program of public choice in our schools.

♦ All students are guaranteed that they will have a fair shot at reaching the standards, that is, that whether they make it or not depends only on the effort they are willing to make. A determined effort on the part of the federal government will be required on this point. School delivery standards may be required. If so, these standards should have the same status in the system as the new student performance standards, but they should be fashioned so as not to constitute a new bureaucratic nightmare.

Postsecondary Education and Work Skills

♦ All students who meet the new national standards for general education are entitled to the equivalent of three more years of free additional education. We would have the federal and state governments match funds to guarantee one free year of college education to everyone who meets the new national standards for general education (the amount of this award would be set at a stipulated maximum so as to avoid runaway charges for college tuition). So a student who meets the standard at 16 would be entitled to two free years of high school and one of college. Loans, which can be forgiven for public service, are available for additional education beyond that. National standards for sub-baccalaureate college-level professional and technical degrees and certificates will be established with the participation of employers, labor and higher education. These programs will include both academic study and structured on-the-job training. Eighty percent or more of American high school graduates will be expected to get some form of college degree, though most of them less than a baccalaureate. These new professional and technical certificates and degrees typically are won within three years of acquiring the general education certificate, so, for most postsecondary students, college will be free. These professional and technical degree programs will be designed to link to programs leading to the baccalaureate degree and higher degrees. There will be no dead ends in this system. Everyone who meets the general education standard will be able to go to some form of college, being able to borrow all the money they need to do so, beyond the first free year.

This idea of post-secondary professional and technical certificates captures all of the essentials of the apprenticeship idea, while offering none of its drawbacks (see below). But it also makes it clear that those engaged in apprentice-style programs are getting more than narrow training; they are continuing their education for other purposes as well, and building a base for more education later. Clearly, this idea redefines college. Proprietary schools, employers, and community-based organizations will want to offer these programs, as well as community colleges and four-year institutions, but these new entrants will have to be accredited if they are to qualify to offer the programs.

♦ Employers are not required to provide slots for the structured on-the-job training component of the program but many do so, because they get first access to the most accomplished graduates of these programs and they can use these programs to introduce the trainees to their own values and way of doing things.

♦ The system of skill standards for technical and professional degrees is the same for students just coming out of high school and for adults in the workforce. It is progressive, in the sense that certificates and degrees for the entry level jobs lead to further professional and technical education programs at higher levels. Just as in the case of the system for the schools, though the standards are the same everywhere (leading to maximum mobility for students), the curricula can vary widely and programs can be custom designed to fit the needs of full-time and part-time students with very different requirements. Government grant and loan programs are available on the same terms to full-time and part-time students, as long as the programs in which they are enrolled are designed to lead to certificates and degrees defined by the system of professional and technical standards.

♦ The national system of professional and technical standards is designed much like the multistate bar, which provides a national core around which the states can specify additional standards that meet their unique needs. There are national standards and exams for no more than 20 broad occupational areas, each of which can lead to many occupations in a number of related industries. Students who qualify in any one of these areas have the broad skills required by a whole family of occupations, and most are sufficiently skilled to enter the workforce immediately, with further occupation-specific skills provided by their union or employer. Industry and occupational groups can voluntarily create standards building on these broad standards for their own needs, as can the states. Students entering the system are first introduced to very broad occupational groups, narrowing over time to concentrate on acquiring the skills needed for a cluster of occupations. This modular system provides for the initiative of particular states and industries while at the same time providing for mobility across states and occupations by reducing the time and cost entailed in moving from one occupation to another. In this way, a balance is established between the kinds of generic skills needed to function effectively in high performance work organizations and the skills needed to continue learning quickly and well through a lifetime of work, on the one hand, and the specific skills needed to perform at a high level in a particular occupation on the other.

♦ Institutions receiving grant and loan funds under this system are required to provide information to the public and to government agencies in a uniform format. This information covers enrollment by program, costs and success rates for students of different backgrounds and characteristics, and career outcomes for those students, thereby enabling students to make informed choices among institutions based on cost and performance. Loan defaults are reduced to a level close to zero, both because programs that do not deliver what they promise are not selected by prospective students and because the new postsecondary loan system uses the IRS to collect what is owed from salaries and wages as they are earned.

Education and Training for Employed and Unemployed Adults

♦ The national system of skills standards establishes the basis for the development of a coherent, unified training system. That system can be accessed by students coming out of high school, employed adults who want to improve their prospects, unemployed adults who are dislocated and others who lack the basic skills required to get out of poverty. But it is all the same system. There are no longer any parts of it that are exclusively for the disadvantaged, though special measures are taken to make sure that the disadvantaged are served. It is a system for everyone, just as all the parts of the system already described are for everyone. So the people who take advantage of this system are not marked by it as damaged goods. The skills they acquire are world class, clear and defined in part by the employers who will make decisions about hiring and advancement.

♦ The new general education standard becomes the target for all basic education programs, both for school dropouts and adults. Achieving that standard is the prerequisite for enrollment in all professional and technical degree programs. A wide range of agencies and institutions offer programs leading to the general education certificate, including high schools, dropout recovery centers, adult education centers, community colleges, prisons and employers. These programs are tailored to the needs of the people who enroll in them. All the programs receiving government grant or loan funds that come with dropouts and adults for enrollment in programs preparing students to meet the general education standard must release the same kind of data required of the postsecondary institutions on enrollment, program description, cost and success rates. Reports are produced for each institution and for the system as a whole showing different success rates for each major demographic group.

♦ The system is funded in four different ways, all providing access to the same or a similar set of services. School dropouts below the age of 21 are entitled to the same amount of funding from the same sources that they would have been entitled to had they stayed in school. Dislocated workers are funded by the federal government through the federal programs for that purpose and by state unemployment insurance funds. The chronically unemployed are funded by federal and state funds established for that purpose. Employed people can access the system through the requirement that their employers spend an amount equal to 1 and 1/2 percent of their salary and wage bill on training leading to national skill certification. People in prison could get reductions in their sentences by meeting the general education standard in a program provided by the prison system. Any of these groups can also use the balances in their grant entitlement or their access to the student loan fund.

Labor Market Systems

♦ The Employment Service is greatly upgraded, and separated from the Unemployment Insurance Fund. All available front-line jobs—whether public or private—must be listed in it by law [this provision must be carefully designed to make sure that employers will not be subject to employment suits based on the data produced by this system—if they are subject to such suits, they will not participate]. All trainees in the system looking for work are entitled to be listed in it without a fee. So it is no longer a system just for the poor and unskilled, but for everyone. The system is fully computerized. It lists not only job openings and job seekers (with their qualifications) but also all the institutions in the labor market area offering programs leading to the general education certificate and those offering programs leading to the professional and technical college degrees and certificates, along with all the relevant data about the costs, characteristics and performance of those programs—for everyone and for special populations. Counselors are available to any citizen to help them assess their needs, plan a program and finance it, and, once they are trained, to locate available jobs.

♦ A system of labor market boards is established at the local, state and federal levels to coordinate the systems for job training, postsecondary professional and technical education, adult basic education, job matching and counseling. The rebuilt Employment Service is supervised by these boards. The system's clients no longer have to go from agency to agency filling out separate applications for separate programs. It is all taken care of at the local labor market board office by one counselor accessing the integrated computer-based program, which makes it possible for the counselor to determine eligibility for all relevant programs at once, plan a program with the client and assemble the necessary funding from all the available sources. The same system will enable counselor and client to array all the relevant program providers side by side, assess their relative costs and performance records and determine which providers are best able to meet the client's needs based on performance.

Some Common Features

♦ Throughout, the object is to have a performance- and client-oriented system and to encourage local creativity and responsibility by getting local people to commit to high goals and organize to achieve them, sweeping away as much of the rules, regulations and bureaucracy that are in their way as possible, provided that they are making real progress against their goals. For this to work, the standards at every level of the system have to be clear; every client has to know what they have to accomplish in order to get what they want out of the system. The service providers have to be supported in the task of getting their clients to the finish line and rewarded when they are making real progress toward that goal. We would sweep away means-tested programs, because they stigmatize their recipients and alienate the public, replacing them with programs that are for everyone, but also work for the disadvantaged. We would replace rules defining inputs with rules defining outcomes and the rewards for achieving them. This means, among other things, permitting local people to combine many federal programs as they see fit, provided that the intended beneficiaries are progressing toward the right outcomes. We would make individuals, their families and whole communities the unit of service, not agencies, programs and projects. Wherever possible, we would have service providers compete with one another for funds that come with the client, in an environment in which the client has good information about the cost and performance record of the competing providers. Dealing with public agencies— whether they are schools or the employment service—should be more like dealing with Federal Express than with the old Post Office.

An Agenda for the Federal Government

Government at every level has an enormous potential for affecting a nation's human capacity—from the resources it provides to nourish pregnant women to the incentives it provides to employers to invest in the skill development of their employees. In this section we concentrate on the role the federal government can play and largely restrict our field of vision to elementary and secondary education, job training and labor market policy.

Everything that follows is cast in the frame of strategies for bringing the new system described in the preceding section into being, not as a pilot program, not as a few demonstrations to be swept aside in another administration, but everywhere, as the new way of doing business.

The preceding section presented a vision of the system we have in mind chronologically from the point of view of an individual served by it. Here we reverse the order, starting with a description of program components designed to serve adults, and working our way down to the very young.

High Skills for Economic competitiveness Program

Developing System Standards

♦ Create a National Board for Professional and Technical Standards. The Board is a private not-for-profit chartered by Congress. Its charter specifies broad membership composed of leading figures from higher education, business, labor, government and advocacy groups. The Board can receive appropriated funds from Congress, private foundations, individuals and corporations. Neither Congress nor the executive branch can dictate the standards set by the Board. But the Board is required to report annually to the President and the Congress in order to provide for public accountability. It is also directed to work collaboratively with the states and cities involved in the Collaborative Design and Development Program (see below) in the development of the standards.

♦ Charter specifies that the National Board will set broad performance standards (not time-in-the-seat standards or course standards) for postsecondary Professional and Technical certificates and degrees at the sub-baccalaureate level, in not more than 20 areas and develops performance examinations for each. The Board is required to set broad standards of the kind described in the vision statement above, and is not permitted to simply reify the narrow standards that characterize many occupations now (more than 2,000 standards currently exist, many, for licensed occupations—these are not the kinds of standards we have in mind). It also specifies that the programs leading to these certificates and degrees will combine time in the classroom with time at the work-site in structured on-the-job training. The Board is responsible for administering the exam system and continually updating the standards and exams. The standards assume the existence of prerequisite world class general education standards set by the National Board for Student Achievement Standards, described below. The new standards and exams are meant to be supplemented for particular occupations by the states and by individual industries and occupational groups, with support from the National Board.

♦ Legislation creating the Board is sent to the Congress in the first six months of the administration, imposing a deadline for creating the standards and the exams within three years of passage of the legislation.

Commentary:

The proposal reframes the Clinton apprenticeship proposal as a college program and establishes a mechanism for setting the standards for the program. The unions are very concerned that the new apprenticeships will be confused with the established registered apprenticeships. Focus groups conducted by Jobs for the Future and others show that parents everywhere want their kids to go to college, not to be shunted aside into a non-college apprenticeship "vocational" program. By requiring these programs to be a combination of classroom instruction and structured OJT, and creating a standard-setting board that includes employers and labor, all the objectives of the apprenticeship idea are achieved, while at the same [time], assuring much broader support for the idea, as well as a guarantee that the program will not become too narrowly [focussed] on particular occupations. It also ties the Clinton apprenticeship idea to the Clinton college funding proposal in a seamless web. Charging the Board with creating not more than 20 certificate or degree categories establishes a balance between the need to create one national system on the one hand with the need to avoid creating a cumbersome and rigid national bureaucracy on the other. This approach provides lots of latitude for individual industry groups, professional groups and state authorities to establish their own standards, while at the same time avoiding the chaos that would surely result if they were the only source of standards. The bill establishing the Board should also authorize the executive branch to make grants to industry groups, professional societies, occupational groups and states to develop their own standards and exams. Our assumption is that the system we are proposing will be managed so as to encourage the states to combine the last two years of high school and the first two years of community college into three-year programs leading to college degrees and certificates. Proprietary institutions, employers and community-based organizations could also offer these programs, but they would have to be accredited to offer these college-level programs. Eventually, students getting their general education certificates might go directly to community college or to another form of college, but the new system should not require that.

Collaborative Design and Development Program

The object is to create a single comprehensive system for professional and technical education that meets the requirements of everyone from high school students to skilled dislocated workers, from the hard core unemployed to employed adults who want to improve their prospects. Creating such a system means sweeping aside countless programs, building new ones, combining funding authorities, changing deeply embedded institutional structures, and so on.

The question is how to get from where we are to where we want to be. Trying to ram it down everyone's throat would engender overwhelming opposition. Our idea is to draft legislation that would offer an opportunity for those states—and selected large cities—that are excited about this set of ideas to come forward and join with each other and with the federal government in an alliance to do the necessary design work and actually deliver the needed services on a fast track. The legislation would require the executive branch to establish a competitive grant program for these states and cities and to engage a group of organizations to offer technical assistance to the expanding set of states and cities engaged in designing and implementing the new system. This is not the usual large scale experiment nor is it a demonstration program, but a highly regarded precedent exists for this approach in the National Science Foundation's SSI program. As soon as the first set of states is engaged, another set would be invited to participate, until most or all of the states are involved. It is a collaborative design, rollout and scale-up program. It is intended to parallel the work of the National Board for Professional and Technical Standards, so that the states and cities (and all their partners) would be able to implement the new standards as soon [as] they become available, although they would be delivering services on a large scale before that happened. Thus, major parts of the whole system would be in operation in a majority of the states within three years from the passage of the initial legislation. Inclusion of selected large cities in this design is not an afterthought. We believe that what we are proposing here for the cities is the necessary complement to a large scale job-creation program for the cities. Skill development will not work if there are no jobs, but job development will not work without a determined effort to improve the skills of city residents. This is the skills development component.

♦ Participants

—Volunteer states, counterpart initiative for cities.

—15 states, 15 cities selected to begin in the first year, 15 more in each successive year.

—5 year grants (on the order of $20 million per year to each state, lower amounts to the cities) given to each, with specific goals to be achieved by the third year; including program elements in place (e.g., upgraded employment service), number of people enrolled in new professional and technical programs, and so on[.]

♦ Criteria for Selection

—A core set of High Performance Work Organization firms willing to participate in standard setting and to offer training slots and mentors.

—Strategies for enriching existing coop ed, tech prep, other programs to meet the criteria.

—Commitment to implementing new general education standard in legislation.

—Commitment to implementing the new Technical and Professional skills standards for college.

—Commitment to developing an outcome- and performance-based system for human resources development.

—Commitment to new role for employment service.

—Commitment to join with others in national design and implementation activity.

♦ Clients

Young adults entering workforce.
Dislocated workers.
Long term unemployed.
Employed who want to upgrade skills.

♦ Program Components

—Institute own version of state and local labor market boards. Local labor market boards to involve leading employers, labor representatives, educators and advocacy group leaders in running the redesigned employment service, running intake system for all clients, counseling all clients, maintaining the information system that will make the vendor market efficient and organizing employers to provide job experience and training slots for school youth and adult trainees.

—Rebuild employment service as a primary function of labor market boards.

—Develop programs to bring dropouts and illiterate up to general education certificate standard. Organize local alternative providers and firms to provide alternative education, counseling, job experience and placement services to these clients.

—Develop programs for dislocated workers and hard-core unemployed (see below).

—Develop city- and state-wide programs to combine the last two years of high school and the first two years of college into three year programs after acquisition of the general education certificate to culminate in college certificates and degrees. These programs should combine academics and structured on-the-job training.

—Develop uniform reporting system for providers, requiring them to provide information in that format on characteristics of clients, their success rates by program, and the costs of those programs. Develop computer-based system for combining this data at local labor market board offices with employment data from [the] state so that counselors and clients can look at programs offered by colleges and other vendors in terms of cost, client characteristics, program design, and outcomes, including subsequent employment histories for graduates.

—Design all programs around the forthcoming general education standards and the standards to be developed by the National Board for Professional and Technical Standards.

—Create statewide program of technical assistance to firms on high performance work organization and to help them develop quality programs for participants in Technical and Professional certificate and degree programs (it is essential that these programs be high quality, nonbureaucratic and voluntary for the firms).

—Participate with other states and the national technical assistance program in the national alliance effort to exchange information and assistance among all participants.

♦ National Technical Assistance to Participants

—Executive branch authorized to compete [for] opportunity to provide the following services (probably using a Request For Qualifications).

—State-of-the art assistance to the states and cities related to the principal program components (e.g.; work reorganization, training, basic literacy, funding systems, apprenticeship systems, large scale data management systems, training systems for the human resources professionals who make the whole system work, etc.). A number of organizations would be funded. Each would be expected to provide information and direct assistance to the states and cities involved, and to coordinate their efforts with one another.

—It is essential that the technical assistance function include a major professional development component to make sure the key people in the states and cities upon whom success depends have the resources available to develop the high skills required. Some of the funds for this function should be provided directly to the states and cities, some to the technical assistance agency.

—Coordination of the design and implementation activities of the whole consortium, documentation [of] results, preparation of reports, etc. One organization would be funded to perform this function.

Dislocated Workers Program

♦ New legislation would permit combining all dislocated workers programs at a redesigned employment service office. Clients would, in effect, receive vouchers for education and training in amounts determined by the benefits for which they qualify. Employment service case managers would qualify client workers for benefits and assist the client in the selection of education and training programs offered by provider institutions. Any provider institutions that receive funds derived from dislocated worker programs are required to provide information on costs and performance of programs in uniform format described above. This consolidated and voucherized dislocated workers program would operate nationwide. It would be integrated with the Collaborative Design and Development Program in those states and cities in which that program functioned. It would be built around the general education certificate and the Professional and Technical Certificate and Degree Program as soon as those standards were in place. In this way, programs for dislocated workers would be progressively and fully integrated with the rest of the national education and training system.

Levy-Grant System

♦ This is the part of the system that provides funds for currently employed people to improve their skills. Ideally, it should specifically provide means whereby front-line workers can earn their general education credential (if they do not already have one) and acquire Professional and Technical Certificates and degrees in fields of their choosing.

♦ Everything we have heard indicates virtually universal opposition in the employer community to the proposal for a 1 and 1/2 percent levy on employers for training to support the costs associated with employed workers gaining these skills, whatever the levy is called. The President may choose to press forward with the proposal nevertheless. Alternatively, he could take a leaf out of the German book. One of the most important reasons that large German employers offer apprenticeship slots to German youngsters is that they fear, with good reason, that if they don't volunteer to do so, the law will require it. The President could gather a group of leading executives and business organization leaders, and tell them straight out that he will hold back on submitting legislation to require a training levy, provided that they commit themselves to a drive to get employers to get their average expenditures on front-line employee training up to two percent of front-line employee salaries and wages within two years. If they have not done so within that time, then he will expect their support when he submits legislation requiring the training levy. He could do the same thing with respect to slots for structured on-the-job training.

Loan/Public Service Program

♦ This proposal was a keystone of the Clinton campaign. Because we assumed that it is being designed by others, we did not focus on its details. From everything we know about it, however, it is entirely compatible with the rest of what is proposed here. What is, of course, especially relevant here is that our reconceptualization of the apprenticeship proposal as a college level education program, combined with our proposal that everyone who gets the general education credential be entitled to a free year of higher education (combined federal and state funds) will have a decided impact on the calculations of cost for the college loan/public service program.

Assistance for Dropouts and the Long-Term Unemployed

The problem of upgrading the skills of high school dropouts and the adult hard core unemployed is especially difficult. It is also at the heart of the problem of our inner cities. All the evidence indicates that what is needed is something with all the important characteristics of a non-residential Job Corps-like program. The problem with the Job Corps is that it is operated directly by the federal government and is therefore not embedded at all in the infrastructure of local communities.

The way to solve this problem is to create a new urban program that is locally—not federally—organized and administered, but which must operate in a way that uses something like the federal standards for contracting for Job Corps services. In this way, local employers, neighborhood organizations and other local service providers could meet the need, but requiring local authorities to use the federal standards would assure high quality results. Programs for high school dropouts and the hard core unemployed would probably have to be separately organized, though the services provided would be much the same. Federal funds would be offered on a matching basis with state and local funds for this purpose. These programs should be fully integrated with the revitalized employment service. The local labor market board would be the local authority responsible for receiving the funds and contracting with providers for the services. It would provide diagnostic, placement and testing services. We would eliminate the targeted jobs credit and use the money now spent on that program to finance these operations. Funds can also be used from the JOBS program in the Welfare Reform Act. This will not be sufficient, however, because there is currently no federal money available to meet the needs of hard-core unemployed males (mostly Black) and so new monies will have to be appropriated for that purpose.

Elementary and Secondary Education Program

The situation with respect to elementary and secondary education is very different from adult education and training. In the latter case, a new vision and a whole new structure is required. In the former, there is increasing acceptance of a new vision and structure among the public at large, within the relevant professional groups and in Congress. There is also a lot of existing activity on which to build. So our recommendations here are rather more terse than in the case of adult education and training.

The general approach here is parallel to the approach described for the High Skills for Economic Competitiveness Program. Here, too, we start with standards. And we propose a collaborative program with the states and with the major cities (adding, in this case, areas suffering from rural poverty) that provides an opportunity for those that wish to do so to participate in a staged, voluntary and progressive implementation of the new system. The parallelism is deliberate. Some states and cities may wish to participate in both programs, developing the whole system at once, others in only one. Much of what we propose can be accomplished through revisions to the conference report on S2 and HR 4323, recently defeated on a cloture vote in the Congress. Solid majorities were behind the legislation in both houses of Congress.

Standard Setting

Legislation to accelerate the process of national standard setting in education was contained in the conference report on S2 and HR 4323. The new administration should support the early introduction of this legislation to create a National Board for Student Achievement Standards. The Board should be established as an independent not-for-profit organization chartered by the United States Congress. The charter should establish a self-perpetuating board of trustees for the Board that is broadly representative of the American people, including representation of general government at all levels, education, employers, labor, child advocacy groups and the general public. It should be eligible to receive funds from private foundations, government (including funds directly appropriated by the Congress), corporations and individuals. It should be charged with coming to a consensus on content standards for the core subjects in elementary and secondary education and for work-related skills. We do not believe that it should be charged with developing a national examination system, but that funds should be appropriated by the Congress to enable the Executive Branch to provide support to a variety of groups that come forward to implement examination systems based on the standards established by the Board. The Board should be required to report annually to the Congress and the public, whether or not it receives Congressional appropriations.

Systemic Change in Public Education: A Collaborative Design and Development Program

As we noted above, the conference report on S2 and HR 4323 contained a comprehensive program to support systemic change in public education upon which we would build. Here again, we would invite the states to submit proposals in a competitive grant program on the same principles and for the same reasons we suggested that approach above. Each year, additional states—and, in this case, major cities and poor rural areas—would be added to the network. Here again, most of the existing rules and regulations affecting relevant federal education programs would be waived, save for those relating to health, public safety and civil rights, and the participants would be expected to specify objectives for specific demographic groups of students and to make steady progress toward their achievement as a condition of remaining in the program. While the participants would have a lot of latitude in constructing a strategy that fits their particular context, that strategy would have to show how they planned to:

- Implement an examination system related to the standards development by the National Board.

- Empower school staff to make the key decisions as to how the students will meet those standards.

- Provide curricular resources to the school staffs related to the new standards and examinations.

- Reorganize pre-service and in-service professional development programs to support the development of the skills necessary to bring all students up to the new standards.

- Reorganize the delivery of health and social services to children and their families so as to support students and the school faculties.

- Deploy advanced technologies to support the learning of students in and out of school.

- Restructure the organization and management of public elementary and secondary education on the principles of modern quality management, empowering school staff, reducing intermediate layers of bureaucracy and the burden of rules and regulations from the state, the board of education and the unions and holding school staff accountable for student progress.

Funds provided by this program could be used for professional development, to provide critically needed "glue" support to weld together activities consistent with the purposes of the program, and to provide student services. But funds for direct student services could be used only for services rendered before and after the regular school day, on weekends and during vacation periods. States receiving funds under this program would have to provide relief from regulation comparable to that provided by the federal government.

Federal Programs for the Disadvantaged

- The established federal education programs for the disadvantaged need to be thoroughly overhauled to reflect an emphasis on results for the students rather than compliance with the regulations. A national commission on Chapter 1, the largest of these programs, chaired by David Hornbeck, has designed a radically new version of this legislation, with the active participation of many of the advocacy groups. Other groups have been similarly engaged. We think the new administration should quickly endorse the work of the national commission and introduce its proposals early next year. It is unlikely that this legislation will pass before the deadline—two years away—for the reauthorization of the Elementary and Secondary Education Act, but early endorsement of this new approach by the administration will send a strong signal to the Congress and will greatly affect the climate in which other parts of the act will be considered.

Public Choice, Technology, Integrated Health and Human Services, Curriculum Resources, High Performance Management, Professional Development and Research and Development

- The restructuring of the schools that we envision is not likely to succeed unless the schools have a lot of information about how to do it and real assistance in getting it done. The areas in which this help is needed are suggested by the heading for this section.

[Ed. Note: This is one of the most significant reports to which we've had access. It calls for a complete change in our form of government, education and opportunity to pursue individual life choices. At the time of the publication of this document the following people were serving on the Board of Trustees of the National Center on Education and the Economy. Many of these names will be familiar and significant as the reader relates them to proposals for change and reform.

Appendix XIX

"Taxonomy"

Excerpts from a newsletter from an Education Researcher,[1] written in 1980.

1980: Mrs. Margaret Oda of the Hawaii Department of Education mentioned that much help had come in Hawaii's curriculum from Madelyn Hunter's Elementary Laboratory School at the University of California, at Los Angeles. The Publisher of this newsletter wrote Madelyn Hunter and obtained data on her teaching concepts. In the material which she sent to us, the elusive term "Taxonomy" surfaced once again. On page 2 of "Audio Visual Materials" which she sent, two films are listed:

> Item 2: "Objectives in the Cognitive Domain." In a clear and comprehensive language Dr. Hunter teaches the 6 levels of *Bloom's Taxonomy Of Educational Objectives: Handbook I: Cognitive Domain.*

> Item 3: "Objectives in the Affective Domain." With remarkable clarity Dr. Hunter teaches the Krathwohl *Taxonomy of Educational Objectives: Handbook II: Affective Domain.*

Once again, as *Taxonomy* emerged, the Publisher of this newsletter decided it was time to see what the educational Master Planners had in mind for America's children. In the material which follows, we will focus our attention mostly on the Affective Domain since space does not allow us to consider all three domains. And, because from a relevant standpoint, it is the Affective Domain which should receive our immediate attention, since that is one of the domains which [our state's] own Accountability Resolution embraces. We have read many descriptions from many articles of *Taxonomy*, but after reading the plan itself felt actual excerpts were the only way to do justice to a plan which otherwise might have been cast off as a figment of our imagination. Excerpts from [*Taxonomy of Educational Objectives*] *Handbook II* follow:

The three domains of the *Taxonomy*:

I. COGNITIVE: Objectives which emphasize remembering or reproducing something which has presumably been learned, as well as objectives which involve solving of some intellective task for which the individual has to determine the essential problem and then reorder given material or combine it with ideas, methods, or procedures previously learned. Cognitive objectives vary from simple recall of material learned to highly original and creative ways of combining and synthesizing new ideas and materials. We found that the largest proportion of educational objectives fell into this domain.

II. AFFECTIVE: Objectives which emphasize a feeling tone, an emotion, or a degree of acceptance or rejection. Affective objectives vary from simple attention to selected phenomena to complex but internally consistent qualities of character and conscience. We found a large number of such objectives in the literature expressed as interests, attitudes, appreciations, values, and emotional sets or biases.

III. PSYCHOMOTOR: Objectives which emphasize some muscular or motor skills, some manipulation of material objects, or some act which requires a neuromuscular co-ordination. We found few such objectives in the literature. When found, they were most frequently related to handwriting and speech and to physical education, trade, and technical courses.

...A much more serious reason for the hesitation in the use of affective measures for grading purposes comes from somewhat deeper philosophical and cultural values. Achievement, competence, productivity, etc., are regarded as public matters. Honors are awarded for high achievement, honor lists may be published by the Dean, and lists of National Merit Scholarship winners may be printed in newspapers. In contrast, one's beliefs, attitudes, values and personality characteristics are more likely to be regarded as private matters, except in the most extreme instances already noted. My attitudes toward God, home, and family are private concerns, and this privacy is generally respected. My political attitudes are private. I may reveal them if I wish, but no one can force me to do so. In fact, my voting behavior is usually protected from public view. Each man's home is his castle, and his interests, values, beliefs and personality may not be scrutinized unless he voluntarily gives permission to have them revealed. This public-private status of cognitive vs. affective behaviors is deeply rooted in the Judeo-Christian religion and is a value highly cherished in the democratic traditions of the Western World.

Closely linked to this private aspect of affective behavior is the distinction frequently made between education and indoctrination in a democratic society. Education opens up possibilities for free choice and individual decision. Education helps the individual to explore many aspects of the world and even his own feelings and emotion, but choice and decision are matters for the individual. Indoctrination, on the other hand, is viewed as reducing the possibilities of free choice and decision. It is regarded as an attempt to persuade and coerce the individual to accept a particular viewpoint or belief, to act in a particular manner, and to profess a particular value and way of life.

THE CONTRIBUTIONS OF A TAXONOMY OF AFFECTIVE OBJECTIVES

If affective objectives and goals are to be realized, they must be defined clearly; learning experiences to help the student develop in the desired direction must be provided; and there must be some systematic method for appraising the extent to which students grow in the desired ways.

...The more we carefully studied the components... the clearer it became that a continuum might be derived by appropriately ordering them. Thus the continuum progressed from [to] a level at which the individual is merely aware of a phenomenon, being able to perceive it. At a next level he is willing to attend to phenomena. At a next level he responds to the phenomena with a positive feeling. Eventually he may feel strongly enough to go out of his way to respond. At some point in the process he conceptualizes his behavior and feelings and organizes these conceptualizations into a structure. This structure grows in complexity as it becomes his life outlook.

This ordering of the components seemed to describe a process by which a given phenomenon or value passed from a level of bare awareness to a position of some power to guide or control the behavior of the person. If it is passed through all the stages in which it played an increasingly important role in a person's life it would come to dominate and control certain aspects of that life as it was absorbed more and more into the internal controlling structure. This process of continuum seemed best described by a term which was heard at various times in our discussions and which has been used similarly in the literature: "internalization." This word seemed an apt description of the process by which the phenomenon of value successively and pervasively become a part of the individual.

INTERNALIZATION: ITS NATURE

English and English (1958) define it as "incorporating something within the mind or body; adopting as one's own the ideas, practices, standards, or values of another person or of society" (p. 272).

...Thus in the Taxonomy, internalization is viewed as a process through which there is at first an incomplete and tentative adoption of only the overt manifestations of the desired behavior and later a more complete adoption.

...The term is a close relative of the term "socialization," which, though it is often used as a synonym...[properly means]..."conformity in outward behavior without necessarily accepting the values." They define socialization as "the process whereby a person... acquires sensitivity to social stimuli...and learns to get along with, and to behave like others in his group or culture."... (p. 508)

English and English's concept of socialization helps to define a portion of the content of the affective domain—that which is internalized.... [T]his definition must be interpreted broadly since "sensitivity to social stimuli" must include the arts as well as others' behavior.

This definition suggests that the culture is perceived as the controlling force in the individual's actions.... [O]ur schools, in their roles as developers of individualism and as change agents in the culture, are not solely concerned with conformity.... The term "internalization" by referring to the process through which values, attitudes, etc., in general are acquired, is thus broader than socialization, which refers only to the acceptance of the contemporary value pattern of the society.

...The term "internalization" refers to this inner growth which takes place as there is "acceptance by the individual of the attitudes, codes, principles, or sanctions that become a part of himself in forming value judgments or in determining his conduct."...

Kelman (1958) used the term "internalization" in describing a theory of attitude change. He distinguished three different processes (compliance, identification, and internalization) by which an individual accepts influence or conforms. These three processes are defined as follows:

[1] *Compliance* can be said to occur when an individual accepts influence because he hopes to achieve a favorable reaction from another person or group. He adopts the induced behavior not because he believes in its content but because he expects to gain specific rewards or approval and avoid specific punishments or disapproval by conforming.

[2] *Identification* can be said to occur when an individual accepts influence because he wants to establish or maintain a satisfying relationship to another person or group (e.g., teacher or other school authority).... The individual naturally believes in the response which he adopts through identification.... The satisfaction from identification is due to the act of conforming as such.

[3] *Internalization* can be said to occur when an individual accepts influence because the content of the induced behavior—the ideas and actions of which it is composed—is intrinsically rewarding. He adopts the induced behavior because it is congruent with his value system.... Behavior adopted in this fashion tends to be integrated with the individual's existing values. Thus, the satisfaction derived from internalization is due to the content of the new behavior.

...The *Taxonomy* uses the term "internalization" to encompass all three of Kelman's terms, recognizing them as different stages in the internalization process.

A NEW LOOK AT CURRICULUM, EVALUATION, AND RESEARCH (Chapter 6)

...The *Taxonomy* has been used by teachers, curriculum builders, and educational research workers as one device to attack the problems of specifying in detail the expected outcomes of the learning process. When educational objectives are stated in operational and detailed form, it is possible to make appropriate evaluation instruments and to determine, with some precision, which learning experiences are likely to be of value in promoting the development of the objective and which are likely to be of little or no value.

It is this increased specificity which we hope will be prompted by the Affective Domain part of the *Taxonomy*.... If affective objectives can be defined with appropriate precision, we believe it may be no more difficult to produce changes in students in this domain than in the cognitive domain.

...The securing of the appropriate responses from the individual... requires that the new cues and stimuli be received under conditions that make it easy for the individual to respond and give him satisfaction from the act of responding....

However, as we turn to the objectives which go beyond merely receiving or responding to stimuli and cues, we find that the development of learning experiences that are appropriate requires far more effort and far more complex sets of arrangements than are usually provided in particular classroom lessons and sessions....

...It is to be expected that some objectives may take several years to be reached to a significant degree.... The ordering of objectives is of importance in both domains, but we regard it as of prime importance in the affective domain.

...Some objectives, particularly the complex ones at the top of the affective continuum, are probably attained as the product of all, or at least a major portion, of a student's years in school. Thus, measures of a semester's or year's growth would reveal little change. This suggests that an evaluation plan covering at least several grades and involving the coordinated efforts of several teachers is probably a necessity. A plan involving all the grades in a system is likely to be even more effective. Such efforts would permit gathering longitudinal data on the same students so that gains in complex objectives would be measurable.... If we are serious about attaining complex affective objectives, we shall have to build coordinated evaluation programs that trace the successes and failures of our efforts to achieve them.

Achievement of Affective Objectives and Behaviors

...For any major reorganization of actual practices and responses to take place, the individual must be able to examine his own feelings and attitudes on the subject, bring them out into the open, see how they compare with the feelings and views of others, and move from an intellectual awareness of a particular behavior or practice to an actual commitment to the new practice....

What is suggested here, if specific changes are to take place in the learners, is that the learning experiences must be of a two-way nature in which both the students and teachers are involved in an interactive manner, rather than having one present something to be "learned" by the other.

A... finding is emerging from the study of enrichment of educational opportunities in the New York public schools, which has been termed "Higher Horizons" (Mayer 1961).... The significant thing to remember in this very ambitious project is that the major impact of the new program is to develop attitudes and values toward learning which are not shared by the parents and guardians or by the peer group in the neighborhood. There are many stories of the conflict and tension that these new practices are producing between parents and children. There is even more conflict between the students and the members of their peer groups who are not participating in the special opportunities. The effectiveness of this new set of environmental conditions is probably related to the extent to which the students are "isolated" from both the home and peer group during this period of time. It is unlikely that such "separation" from the home and peer group would take place after the age of sixteen and seventeen. And it is also likely that the earlier new environments are created, the more effective they will be.

From the operational point of view and from the research point of view, it does seem clear that, to create effectively a new set of attitudes and values, the individual must undergo great reorganization of his personal beliefs and attitudes, and he must be involved in an environment which in many ways is separated from the previous environment in which he has developed.

...[T]he changes produced in such a general academic atmosphere which is not deliberately created are probably of smaller magnitude than the changes produced where the entire environment is organized (deliberately or not) with a particular theme at work. In summary, we find that learning experiences which are highly organized and interrelated may produce major changes in behavior related to complex objectives in both the cognitive and affective domains. Such new objectives can best be attained where the individual is separated from earlier environmental conditions and when he is in association with a group of peers who are changing in much the same direction and who thus tend to reinforce each other.

In his studies of stability and change in various characteristics, Bloom (1964) finds that the individual is more open to some of these major changes earlier in the growth period than later....The evidence points quite convincingly to the fact that age is a factor operating against attempts to effect a complete or thorough-going reorganization of attitudes and values.... It is quite possible that the adolescent period, with its biological and other modifications, is a stage in which more change can be produced than in many other periods of the individual's career.... [T]here is an increasing stability of interests in the age period of about ten to fifteen and that appropriate learning experiences and counseling and guidance may do much to develop different kinds of interests.

Some Additional Research Problems

...[Bloom] has been attempting to do research on what might be called "peak learning experiences." ...[T]he evidence collected so far suggests that a single hour of classroom activity under certain conditions may bring about a major reorganization in cognitive as well as affective behaviors.... It may very well help us to understand some of the conditions that are necessary for major changes in learners in affective objectives....

Allport (1954) emphasizes the basic reorganization that must take place in the individual if really new values and character traits are to be formed. We are of the opinion that as we come to understand this process we may find ways of helping bring about major changes in the affective domain with less in the way of trauma and conflict than now seems to be the case. Is it possible for individuals to take on the new without rejecting the old? Is it possible that programs of the Higher Horizons type (Mayer, 1961) help individuals become motivated toward higher education and the new values involved in academic work without at the same time bringing about great conflict and tension between the individual and his home?

...However, back of all the more operational and psychological problems is the basic question of what changes are desirable and appropriate. Here is where the philosopher and behavioral scientist must find ways of determining what changes are desirable and what changes are necessary.... It is not enough merely to desire a new objective or to wish others to be molded in the image that we find desirable or satisfactory.... New objectives are important, but they must be thought through very carefully, and all must be willing to pay the price if they are to be obtained.

...Can the schools take the initiative in the affective domain, or must they approach it with great caution and hesitation? We leave this problem to the curriculum makers, the educational philosophers, and the social and political forces which may or may not make certain objectives clearly desirable and even necessary.

The Affective domain is, in retrospect, a virtual "Pandora's Box."... We are not entirely sure that opening our "box" is necessarily a good thing; we are certain that it is not likely to be a source of peace and harmony among the members of the school staff, [but] our "box" must be opened if we are to face reality and take action.

It is in this "box" that the most influential controls are to be found. The affective domain contains the forces that determine the nature of an individual's life and ultimately the life of an entire people.... Education is not the rote memorization of meaningless material to be regurgitated on an examination paper. Perhaps the two *Taxonomy* structures may help us to see the awesome possibilities of the relations between students-ideas-teachers.

The Philosophy... The Commitment

...Erikson describes the achievement of integrity, which is the hallmark of maturity as: "the age's accrued assurance of its proclivity for order and meaning. It is a post-narcissistic love of the human ego—not of the self—as an experience which conveys some world order and spiritual sense no matter how dearly paid for. It is the acceptance of one's one and only life cycle as something that had to be and that, by necessity, permitted of no substitutions; it thus means a new, a different love of one's parents.... Although aware of the relativity of all the various lifestyles which have given meaning to human striving, the possessor of integrity is ready to defend the dignity of his own lifestyle against all physical and economic threats. For he knows that an individual life is the accidental coincidence of but one life cycle with but one segment of history; and that for him all human integrity stands or falls with the one style of integrity of which he partakes. The style of integrity developed by his culture or civilization thus becomes the "Patrimony of his soul," the seal of his moral paternity of himself. Before this final solution, death loses its sting (Erikson, p. 232)....

A Condensed Version of the Affective Domain of the Taxonomy of Educational Objectives

1.0 Receiving (Attending)

At this level we are concerned that the learner be sensitized in the existence of certain phenomena and stimuli; that is, that he be willing to receive or to attend to them. This is clearly the first and crucial step if the learner is to be properly oriented to learn what the teacher intends that he will.... Because of previous experience (formal or informal), the student brings to each situation a point of view or set which may facilitate or hinder his recognition of the phenomena to which the teacher is trying to sensitize him.

1.1 Awareness

Awareness is almost a cognitive behavior.... [W]e are not so much concerned with a memory of, or ability to recall, an item or fact as we are that, given appropriate opportunity, the learner will merely be conscious of something.

1.2 Willingness to Receive

In this category we have come a step up the ladder.... At a minimum level, we are here describing the behavior of being willing to take notice of the phenomena and give it his attention.

1.3 Controlled or Selected Attention

In some instances it may refer not so much to the selectivity of attention as to the control of attention, so that when certain stimuli are present they will be attended to. There is an element of the learner's controlling the attention here, so that the favored stimulus is selected and attended to despite competing and distracting stimuli.

2.0 Responding

...This is a very low level of commitment, and we would not say at this level that this was "a value of his" or that he had "such-and-such an attitude."... [W]e could say that he is doing something with or about the phenomena besides merely perceiving it....

...Most commonly we use the term to indicate the desire that a child become sufficiently involved in or committed to a subject, phenomenon, or activity that he will seek it out and gain satisfaction from working with it or engaging in it.

2.1 Acquiescence in Responding

We might use the word "obedience" or "compliance" to describe this behavior.... The student makes the response, but he has not fully accepted the necessity for doing so.

2.2 Willingness to Respond

...There is the implication that the learner is sufficiently committed to exhibiting the behavior that he does so not just because of a fear of punishment, but "on his own" or voluntarily. It may help to note that the element of resistance or of yielding unwillingly, which is possibly present at the previous level, is here replaced with consent of proceeding from one's own choice.

2.3 Satisfaction in Response

The additional element in the step beyond the Willingness to Respond level, the consent, the assent to responding, or the voluntary response, is that the behavior is accompanied by a feeling of satisfaction, an emotional response, generally of pleasure, zest, or enjoyment.... Just where in the process of internalization the attachment of an emotional response, kick, or thrill to a behavior occurs has been hard to determine.

3.0 Valuing

This is the only category headed by a term which is in common use in the expression of objectives by teachers. Further, it is employed in its usual sense: that a thing, phenomenon, or behavior has worth. This abstract concept of worth is in part a result of the individual's own valuing or assessment, but it is much more a social product that has been slowly internalized or accepted and has come to be used by the student as his own criterion of worth....

...At this level, we are not concerned with the relationships among values but rather with the internalization of a set of specified ideas, values.... [T]he objectives classified here are the prime stuff from which the conscience of the individual is developed into active control of behavior.

3.1 Acceptance of Value

The term "belief," which is defined as "the emotional acceptance of a proposition or doctrine upon what one implicitly considers adequate ground" (English & English, 1958, p. 64), describes quite well what may be thought of as the dominant characteristic here.... One of the distinguishing characteristics of this behavior is consistency of response. It is consistent enough so that the person is perceived by others as holding the belief or value.... [H]e is both sufficiently consistent that others can identify the value, and sufficiently committed that he is willing to be so identified.

3.2 Preference for a Value

...Behavior at this level implies not just the acceptance of a value to the point of being willing to be identified with it, but the individual is sufficiently committed to the value to pursue it, to seek it out, to want it.

3.3 Commitment

...In some instances this may border on faith, in the sense of it being firm emotional acceptance of a belief upon admittedly non-rational grounds. Loyalty to a position, group, or cause would also be classified here.

The person who displays behavior at this level is clearly perceived as holding the value.... He tries to convince others and seeks converts to his cause.... There is a tension here which needs to be satisfied; action is the result of an aroused need or drive. There is a real motivation to act out the behavior.

4.0 Organization

As the learner successively internalizes values, he encounters situations for which more than one value is relevant. Thus, necessity arises for a) organization of the values into the system, b) the determination of the interrelationships among them, and c) the establishment of the dominant and pervasive ones.... This category is intended as the proper classification for objectives which describe the beginnings of the building of a value system.

4.1 Conceptualization of a Value

...This permits the individual to see how the value relates to those that he already holds or to new ones that he is coming to hold.

4.2 Organization of a Value System

Objectives properly classified here are those which require the learner to bring together a complex of values, possibly disparate values, and to bring these into an ordered relationship with one another.... This is, of course, the goal of such objectives, which seek to have the student formulate a philosophy of life.

5.0 Characterization by a Value or Value Complex

At this level of internalization the values already have a place in the individual's value hierarchy, are organized into some kind of internally consistent system, have controlled the behavior of the individual for a sufficient time that he has adapted to behaving this way; and an evocation of the behavior no longer arouses emotion or affect except when the individual is threatened or challenged.

5.1 Generalized Set

The generalized set is that which gives an internal consistency to the system of attitudes and values at any particular moment.... It is a persistent and consistent response to a family of related situations or objects.

5.2 Characterization

...[T]he peak of the internalization process.... Thus, here are found those objectives which concern one's view of the universe, one's philosophy of life, one's "weltanschauung"—a value system having as its object the whole of what is known or knowable.

As the title of the category implies, these objectives are so encompassing that they tend to characterize the individual almost completely.

Endnote:
1. The researcher who produced this piece wishes to remain anonymous.

Appendix XX

"The 'Skinner-Box' School"

"The 'Skinner-Box' School" by Jed Brown was published in the March 1994 issue of *Squibbs* and is reprinted here in its entirety.

Outcome-Based Education (OBE) has become a blight on the landscape of our national heritage. After only a few years of OBE, whole school systems are beginning to wither and die. Much worse, the children, their minds once fertile fields of intellectual soil, are even now being infected by the worm of ignorance. True learning is starved to death, as all of the nutrients of sound academic practice are being replaced with a dust-bowl curriculum that is structured to secure proper attitudes for the "Brave New World." Sadly, the only "outcome" of OBE will be a baser society, a society in which the nobility of the mind is lost to the savagery of enslavement.

But wait! Parents have been told that Outcome-Based Education has nothing to do with changing the attitudes and values of their children; that OBE will improve learning for all children through "best-practices" research. What parents are not being told is that the research base for OBE is from the field of psychology, not education; that in psychology the term "learning" is synonymous with the term "conditioning." What parents are *not* being told is that Outcome-Based Education is not education at all; it is but the hollow substitute of psychological conditioning or, as it is sometimes called, behavior modification.

Why is conditioning replacing the teaching/learning process in our schools? If the object is to change the attitudes and values of the young, why would "behavior modification" be used? Why not work with attitudes and values directly? Just tell the children what they must believe! After all, the conventional wisdom is that attitudes control behavior. If a child develops the "right" attitudes he will behave in the "right" manner. Beyond the fact that parents would not stand for such an intrusion as an overt assault on traditional values, psychologists know something that lay people do not. They realize that the direct approach to changing values does not work.

Modern psychological research suggests that the opposite of conventional wisdom is true. It is our behavior that shapes our attitudes, not the other way around. Therefore, to control a child's attitudes and values it is first necessary to modify the child's behavior. If the child has the "right" behavior, then his attitude will change to accommodate the behavior, his value system will change to reflect his new set of attitudes. It is like falling dominoes: if the first piece is toppled, then the rest will tumble after. Thus, conditioning, i.e., modifying behavior, is the perfect method for instilling in children the new value system required of citizens of the New World Order. Our schools know that changing behavior is the first domino. Remember, "the student shall demonstrate."

To understand the devastation of OBE conditioning, it is important to know its origins and how it is being used to change children forever. The lineage of psychological conditioning can be formally traced back to the early part of this century, to an American psychologist named John B. Watson. Watson is credited as the father of the Behaviorist School of Psychology. He believed that psychology should become the science of behavior, discarding references to thoughts, feelings, and motivation. For Watson, only that which was observable was important. The goal of psychology, he thought, should be to predict a behavioral response given a particular stimulus.

Further, it was a time of great debate in psychology. The debate centered on whether heredity or the environment had the most profound effect on the development of the individual. Watson believed that heredity had little or no effect, that a person's development was almost totally dependent upon his environment. In fact, Watson boasted,

> Give me a dozen healthy infants, well formed, and my own specified world to bring them up in, and I'll guarantee to take any one at random and train him to become any type of specialist I might select—doctor, lawyer, artist, merchant-chief, and yes, even beggar-man and thief, regardless of his talents, penchants, tendencies, abilities, vocations, and race of his ancestors.

Watson's statement is at the heart of OBE. Watson became the most influential force in spreading the idea that human behavior was nothing more than a set of conditioned responses. According to the narrow view of Behaviorism, learning is nothing more than "a relatively permanent change in an organism's behavior due to experience." Other psychologists first, then educational leaders, and finally rank-and-file teachers have been persuaded to adopt the Behaviorists' view of education. The richness of education is thus lost, as the schooling experience is reduced to only applied learning. No longer does learning enhance the internal locus of man—it is but an external shell. The curriculum has become hollow and learning has become mere conditioning.

Three different types of psychological conditioning have invaded schools with Outcome-Based Education and education reform. Each type has its specified purpose in controlling the behavior, and therefore the minds, attitudes, and values of our young. The first is **Classical Conditioning,** developed by a Russian physiologist named Ivan Pavlov only a few years before Watson's conception of Behaviorism. The second, credited to B.F. Skinner, is **Operant or Instrumental Conditioning**. The third, attributed to Albert Bandura, is **Observational Learning**. Each of these Behaviorist conditioning approaches is woven through the OBE reforms of education to accomplish only one thing: to control attitudes by controlling behavior.

Classical, or **Pavlovian Conditioning** can be defined as creating a relatively permanent change in behavior by the association of a new stimulus with an old stimulus that elicits a particular response. Working on physiology experiments, Pavlov noted that each time the dogs he used as subjects were to be fed they began to salivate. He identified the food as the "old" stimulus and the salivation as the response, or behavior. Pavlov rang a bell each time the food was presented to the dogs. The bell was identified as the "new" stimulus. After several pairings of the bell and the food, he found that the dogs would salivate with the bell alone. A change in behavior had occurred.

All well and good, but what do dogs, food, saliva, and bells have to do with changing attitudes in children? Just like Pavlov's dogs, children's behavior patterns can be changed with **Classical Conditioning**. Upon sufficient pairings, a child will associate old behavior patterns and consequent attitudes with new stimuli. The Pavlovian approach is therefore a potent weapon for those who wish to change the belief structures of our children. Further, **Classical Conditioning** may be used to set children up for further conditioning that is necessary for more complex attitude shifts. The method is being used to desensitize children to certain issues that heretofore would have been considered inappropriate for school-age children.

One example of an attitude change by Pavlovian conditioning revolves around the word "family." The term "family," as it is applied to the home setting, is used as the old stimulus. The allegiance to parents and siblings that is normally associated with the term "family" may be thought of as the response, or behavior. With the current education reform movement the child is told by the teacher that the school class is now the family. Thus, the term "class" may be thought of as the new stimulus. By continually referring to the class or classroom as the family, an attitude change takes place. By association, the child is conditioned to give family allegiance to the class and teacher.

An example of desensitizing children through **Classical Conditioning** can be seen in the inclusion of gender orientation within the curriculum. The school setting may be thought of as the old stimulus. The formal school setting carries with it a whole set of emotional-behavioral responses, or behaviors. There is an air of authority and legitimacy that is attached to those subjects included in the curriculum. This feeling of legitimacy can be considered a behavioral response. By placing the topic of gender orientation into the curriculum, it is associated with legitimacy of the school settings. Thus, children are desensitized to a topic that is different from the traditional value structure, and hence they are predisposed to further conditioning.

The real meat and potatoes of Outcome-Based Education is **Operant Conditioning**, or **Rat Psychology**, so called because B.F. Skinner used rats as his experimental subjects. A "Skinner Box," a box containing a press bar and a place to dispense a food pellet, is used to condition the rat to press the bar (the behavior). A food pellet (the stimulus) is used to reinforce the desired behavior, pressing the bar. The rat, having no idea what to expect, is placed in the box. Once in the box, the rat's movements are exploratory and random. As soon as the rat looks towards the bar, the experimenter releases a food pellet. After eating the food the rat resumes his random movement. Another look, another pellet. Another look, another pellet.

Once the rat is trained to look at the bar, he is required to approach the bar before the pellet is delivered. The rat must then come closer and closer to the bar each time before reinforcement is given. Over time, the rat's behavior is slowly shaped by the experimenter; each trial the rat successively approximates more closely the ultimate behavior of pressing the bar. Eventually the well-conditioned rat will continually press the bar as fast as he can eat.

Operant Conditioning is, therefore, defined as a relatively permanent change in behavior by successive approximations through repeated trials using positive or negative reinforcements.

The concept of "successive approximation" is key to understanding the use of **Operant Conditioning** with Outcome-Based Education. Just as for the rat, the experimenter (the State) establishes the ultimate goals for children (pressing the bar). OBE requires that specific behavioral outcomes be designed such that the children must master each outcome in succession. The outcomes are designed in a spiral fashion, such that as the child goes further in school, the outcomes more closely approximate the ultimate goals. As children master an outcome, the reinforcement is found in approval (food pellets). Another outcome, more approval. Another outcome, more approval (successive approximation). When the Skinner Box experiment is complete, our children, like rats, will dance to the tune of the State.

Observational Learning, although it does not carry the name conditioning, has been described by Dollard and Miller as a special case of **Operant Conditioning**. It is **Operant Conditioning** applied to social behavior. **Observational Learning** is the twenty-five cent word for modeling. There are two purposes for **Observational Learning** in the schools. First, it is a method used to condition a host of social behaviors, like parenting styles, gender roles, problem-solving strategies, and discipline boundaries. Second, it is used as reinforcer of the behaviors and attitudes previously conditioned with **Classical** and **Operant Conditioning**.

According to **Observational Learning**, people model the behavior of those within their "reference groups." Under normal conditions, the child's primary reference group is the family. Nevertheless, children are being conditioned with **Classical** methods to shift allegiance to their new school family, their new reference group. Once the new group is established, schools use surveys to gauge attitudes and then orchestrate the conditioning process through **Observational Learning**. Relying almost exclusively on cooperative learning (group learning), OBE reforms unfortunately use **Observational Learning** to establish and enforce the proper behaviors and attitudes through peer pressure and a forced "group think" process.

The idea that our schools are not dealing in attitudes and values is ludicrous. The psychologists have ripped the schools from parents and teachers alike. Their only objective is to create children who may look different, but behave the same, think the same, and believe the same. They shall create in each child the "perfect child." Like John B. Watson, they shall create children as they see fit. They shall do it with conditioning, not teaching. Is it any wonder that our schools are failing to educate children when we use rats as the example of exemplary learning? Welcome to the "Brave New World." Welcome to the "SKINNER BOX SCHOOL."

Appendix XXI

"Status of Internationalization of Education"

"Status of Internationalization of Education" by Charlotte Iserbyt originally appeared in *The Christian Conscience* (March 1998) and is printed here in its entirety with updates to reflect more recent events.

Those participating in the Direct Instruction (DI)/Core Knowledge (CK) debate on an anti-education reform Internet discussion loop or elsewhere may wish to step back and take a look at the big picture, without which none of the myriad components of restructuring can be fairly discussed or judged. At present it seems that some very sincere people, who have done excellent work in the past, have a severe case of tunnel vision. They must get themselves out of the tunnel in order to survey the landscape.

Ingredients in the recipe

The recipe for the international curriculum/workforce training agenda calls for implementation of the following components. (Noted after each component in italics is the status of each agenda item, i.e., whether or not the component[s] has/have been accomplished.)

(1) **Federal/International Control of Education.** The creation of the U.S. Department of Education in 1978 established the official link between U.S. education and all the international agencies and Ministries of Education which answer to the United Nations and its lifelong learning agenda. *(Done.)*

(2) **Passage of Goals 2000** *(done)*, **STW Opportunities Act** *(done)*, **Careers Act.** *(Done.)*

(3) **Funding.** Federal government funding of the instructional method, computers, curriculum, national assessment, and workforce training. All funding is now in place with the exception of pending Senate passage of the *CAREERS Act* and pending Senate passage of the *Reading Excellence Act* (the international Mastery Learning/Direct Instruction method). Pro-

fessor S. Alan Cohen, Associate Director of the Center for Outcome-Based Education at the University of San Francisco, said (at a conference on Mastery Learning sponsored by the Maine Association for Supervision and Curriculum Development, May 13, 1983, at Saco, Maine): "In 1976 Block and Burns published in AERA research around the world on mastery learning. UNESCO committed to ML all over the world.... [We] have evaluated data world-wide." *(Funding for all of the above is now in place due to the pounding of the last nails in the coffin: passage of the CAREERS Act and the* Reading Excellence Act *in late 1998.)*

(4) Skinnerian Method. Direct Instruction/Mastery Learning/OBE are necessary for global workforce training which is outcome, results, performance-based training—not education. Education has not been performance-based, traditionally—with the exception of the arts—since traditional education deals with the intellect, not just knee-jerk muscle movements based on Pavlov and B.F. Skinner's stimulus-response (S-R-S). The computer has all the bells (rewards) and whistles (punishments) to achieve OBE's standards in the academic, workforce, and value change areas. The new label for the old OBE is now "standards-based education." Anyone out there who knows of an even newer label, please let me know. *(Done when Senate approved* Reading Excellence Act.*)*

(5) Sequential Core Curriculum. The Texas Alternative Document(TAD) and E.D. Hirsch's Core Knowledge Sequence, in conjunction with scripted curricula such as DISTAR, ECRI, or SUCCESS FOR ALL—which specify exactly what is to be taught, how it is to be taught, and when it is to be taught—are good examples of what could be used. The TAD could provide the framework for the national curriculum since it supports the method—Direct Instruction—and has the support of key players in restructuring, including E.D. Hirsch, Chester Finn, etc.

If subject (content) is not specific and sequential, students' performance is difficult to "measure." One of Skinner's criteria for learning is that results/outcomes be "measurable." This type of core curriculum is ready-made for computer-assisted instruction/programmed learning. Curriculum must also be the same for all students; otherwise, international assessment using the computer will be virtually impossible. The main reason the educrats want to control private and home school education is that results from the computerized international education system will be skewed (unreliable and incomplete) if all the world's children are not in the computer, thus denying the corporate trainers and educrats the necessary information for future planning and remediation on an international scale. Remember, we are looking at a global planned economy. *(Choice of core curriculum/framework is pending, but law requires that it be "scientific" and "research-based"—which limits the choices to behaviorist programs.)*

A European Union Press Release (www.eurunion.org/news/home/htm) Feb. 3, 1998 (No. 7/98) stated:

> International Conference in Akron to Explore Issues of Workforce Development.... Representatives of industry, government and education from throughout the United States and the European Union (EU) will gather in Akron, Ohio from February 9-11 to discuss issues of workforce development and the increasing shortage of skilled workers available to fill jobs in industry. The Akron Forum of Regional Collaboration to Develop Learning Strategies for the Global Economy is a joint undertaking of the United States Information Agency (USIA) and the European Commission, and will be hosted by the Northeast Ohio Trade and Economic Consortium (NEOTEC). The Akron Forum is an important initiative under the New Transat-

lantic Agency (NTA) which, through more than one hundred joint projects, reaffirms strong and enduring ties between the United States and the European Union....

(6) Global Ethics/Values. A CIVITAS press release dated "4/7/97" says:

"UNESCO Chief Cites Link Between Democracy and Development... Stresses Role of Values," by David Pitts USIA Staff Writer. Washington. Sustainable development cannot occur "without freedom, justice, and democracy," says Federico Mayor, director-general of the United Nations Educational, Scientific and Cultural Organization (UNESCO). "Sustainable development requires sustainable democracy," he added in an April 7 address before the International Steering Committee of CIVITAS, an international consortium for civic education that is holding its spring meeting at the White House conference center. According to Mayor, "the partnership between UNESCO and CIVITAS is very important" in helping to promote the culture of democracy around the globe.... The "moral aspects" of the civic education movement were also underlined by Mayor. This means encouraging those values and beliefs that best allow for peace and freedom to thrive, he said....

CIVITAS was initiated in June 1995 at the CIVITAS Prague conference. Following that meeting, participants representing 50 nations signed a declaration pledging "to create and maintain a worldwide network that will make civic education a higher priority on the international agenda."

Participants at the Prague Conference included Diane Ravitch, a member of Hudson Institute's Education Policy Committee and Educational Excellence Network, and the late Albert Shanker, former President of the American Federation of Teachers. Of interest in this regard is the fact that the AFT's "Education for Democracy Project" was launched by the AFT in cooperation with the Educational Excellence Network and Freedom House (1985), and was partially funded by the U.S. Department of Education. *(Global ethics curriculum, under many different labels, is in progress.)*

(7) Technology which includes robotics and computer-assisted instruction (programmed learning). Mastery Learning/Direct Instruction fit like a hand in the glove of the computer. They have been made for each other. Skinner said "the computer is the sophisticated version of his (Skinner's) box." *(Federally-funded OBE/ML, using computers, in use in all schools to a different degree, but method not yet mandated. The passage of the* Reading Excellence Act of 1998 *could facilitate this component.)*

(8) Choice. Choice in the form of tuition tax credits, vouchers, charter schools, use of public education facilities and materials by home schoolers, apprenticeships with corporations which are in partnership with government (corporate fascism), etc., will result in federal (international) control of American education. *(Pending.)*

(9) Teacher Union Support. Support from the American Federation of Teachers and the National Education Association seems to be assured. The AFT supports both Direct Instruction and Hirsch's *Core Curriculum*. The NEA supports the new reading research recommended in the *Reading Excellence Act*. Bob Chase, President of the NEA, said in the January 1998 issue of *Today's Education*, "Stop the sound and fury of the phonics vs. whole language war: we need both." *(Done.)*

Whole Language vs. Direct Instruction

How conservatives can so wholeheartedly support what and who the unconstitutional U.S. Department of Education has funded in the past (Engelmann and Carnine) and what the U.S. Department of Education, AFT, NEA, and, most recently, the left-of-center Learning Alliance and President Bill Clinton support is difficult to understand.

The unconstitutional *Reading Excellence Act*, passed by Congress in 1998, will for the first time in the history of American education mandate a particular method of teaching. In order to get approval of the DI method, its use was attached to reading, which is the essential tool for learning. If the Direct Instruction method had been attached to legislation related to some other discipline, about which controversy was not raging, it is unlikely it would have passed the House of Representatives. The whole language controversy facilitated passage of this legislation—a perfect example of the dialectic method in action.

The method, Direct Instruction, will be used to teach all disciplines, including workforce skills. Direct Instruction is not content; it is method, as was the 1968 federally-funded program Exemplary Center for Reading Instruction (ECRI) which trained teachers (1968-1998) in Mastery Learning (virtually the same method as Direct Instruction). Teachers who have been trained by ECRI trainers can apply their training to any discipline (math, science, history, etc.).

Interestingly enough, Siegfried Engelmann, the developer of DISTAR (Direct Instruction), is referenced on numerous occasions in the ECRI teacher training as a developer of programs based on operant conditioning. ECRI and DISTAR are both based on operant conditioning. Skinner said "I could make a pigeon a high achiever by reinforcing it on a proper schedule" (operant conditioning), exactly what David Hornbeck, Bill Spady, Thomas Sticht and all the education change agents criticized by conservatives, are looking for, right? High achievers in the planned global workforce economy. All of this fits nicely into Total Quality Management and ISO 9000. That TQM is based on many of the principles of Mastery Learning has been admitted by key change agents.

Whether E.D. Hirsch's *Core Knowledge* or some other sequential curriculum is used will be irrelevant. Hirsch's *Core Knowledge* seems to be the choice at the present time, but who knows? Curriculum for the computer can be changed overnight. The method cannot. Regarding Hirsch's so-called credentials and his support of "historical revisionism," the Free Congress Foundation's daily programming regarding Hirsch, February 1997 reads:

> *A History of Us: All the People* by Joy Hakim and published by the Oxford University Press has initiated a great deal of controversy concerning its historical revisionism. Discussing their review of this textbook on NET's *Morning View* were Allan Ryskind, senior fellow at the National Journalism Center, and Peter LaBarbera, executive director of Accuracy in Academia who co-authored a critique of the textbook in the Sept. 12th issue of *Human Events*. According to Ryskind and LaBarbera, the textbook reports that the deficit was 2.3 trillion dollars when Ronald Reagan left office in 1988 [Ryskind puts the deficit at $155 billion, ed.]; claims Ho Chi Minh's goal was to free Vietnam from outsiders; blames President Truman for China's Communist Government; and credits Fidel Castro for improved schools and race relations in Cuba. This textbook is heralded by E.D. Hirsch, who is a cultural literacy guide, who's trying to promote standards for school children. And yet, if this is the best thing they can do, and this is being lauded even by some conservatives as good history, then I think our education system is in bigger trouble than we thought.

According to *The Jim Lehrer News Hour* (September 17, 1997) Hirsch said, "National testing is a good idea, but be careful of the content." One can assume that national testing would suit Hirsch just fine as long as the content is his *Core Knowledge*.

One who has watched the educrats turn traditional education on its head over a period of years would truly have to be in a coma not to see a very ugly picture emerging. It doesn't take a rocket scientist to put together the pieces of this puzzle. The international education system could not have been fully implemented without approval of the Skinnerian method, and the change agents—using conservative concern over whole language—have succeeded in having the Skinnerian method mandated at the national level.

A matter of morality

There have been too few people who understand how evil the method is, and who have been willing to speak out. The noted philosopher and author Francis Schaeffer has spoken most eloquently in opposition to the Skinner method in his book *Back to Freedom and Dignity*. The extent of damage to our children from bad content K–12, outrageous as the outcomes are and have been since this writer started researching education in 1973, cannot be compared to the damage to our children from the use of operant conditioning K–12. Do parents really understand that this method was first used on rats and pigeons in experimental laboratories? Human beings are not animals; they have intellect, soul, conscience and creativity. They can think. They can figure things out. Direct Instruction or Mastery Learning do not take any of these important human aspects into account.

Those who *do* understand the dangers inherent in operant conditioning are naturally very concerned over the decision to mandate this method of instruction. Concerned parent Tracey Hayes, for one, comes to mind as an individual who has been very helpful to me, a researcher and writer. Many of us have read much of the medical research on operant conditioning. We have written on the subject, but we have never actually "used" the method on our own children. Tracey is valuable particularly for this reason—as well as for the fine in-depth research she has done as an opponent of whole language which she has at great cost made available to all of us. She saw what Engelmann's DISTAR did to her own child. She has helped me enormously to understand the reality of this evil method. Those grassroots parents researching education are extremely lucky to have her input.

As for Ann Herzer, we all know her credentials as a long-time traditional phonics reading teacher and the courageous stand she took in opposing the Exemplary Center for Reading Instruction (ECRI) teacher training. She and Tracey have personally lived out the nightmare of operant conditioning and are thus in a position to speak authoritatively regarding the method. Do those who support Direct Instruction agree with Ann Herzer's teacher trainer who angrily said to her when she resisted the training, "Don't you understand we are training our children to be people pleasers?"

Also, as a member of the AFT, Herzer was responsible for getting a resolution unanimously approved by the Arizona affiliate of the AFT to forbid federal funding of operant conditioning programs for use on teachers and children. The late Al Shanker, President of the AFT, who was Carnegie Corporation's stooge for many years and who supported global workforce training, tabled her resolution at the AFT national convention in 1984. He knew the Skinner method was necessary for workforce training and admitted to Herzer that he was a member of the Trilateral Commission. It should come as no surprise that Shanker's successor, Sandra Feldman, also supports the method, this time under the label of Direct Instruction, the fraternal twin of ECRI.

Sometimes one becomes so convinced of the rightness of a message, due to one's respect for the carrier of the message, that one can get off track. I'm afraid that this is what is happening with anti-reform researchers and parents across the nation—in the tunnel and off the track.

Those opposing the mandating of the Direct Instruction method have been vilified by those formerly considered allies in opposition to education restructuring. Those who oppose the method do so not to be contrary. The position they are taking is not primarily related to whether one method works better than another method. Our position is primarily a moral position. It is *wrong* to use an animal training method on human beings. Did the great intellects and thinkers of this world—scientists, historians, writers, theologians—learn this way? Your children should not have their potentials limited by such a method. Why should your children be used in this experiment to robotize the world, to train human beings to be people-pleasing, cookie-cutter citizens?

From the above examples one can see that everything is in place. The only missing component was mandating the method. Republican support for the *Reading Excellence Act* has handed the method to the internationalist change agents on a silver platter. The Arizona legislature jumped the gun on U.S. Senate passage of the *Act* by considering legislation which would implement the *Reading Excellence Act* in Arizona. We can now expect the same type of legislation to surface in all states, and, tragically, to be supported by conservatives, unless this warning is heeded. The fact that national testing has been put on hold is meaningless since the National Assessment for Educational Progress has received heavy funding since 1965 and has been used in all states. All that has to be done is to align the NAEP with whatever core curriculum and School-to-Work skills are selected for use, and to implement the Certificate of Initial Mastery nationwide.

What Should We Do?

Call for repeal of the *Reading Excellence Act* passed by Congress. Lobby against similar non-traditional ML/DI phonics legislation in your state. If possible, put your children in "good" private schools which receive no tax support or exemptions whatsoever, or, best of all, home school your children.

Oppose passage of legislation supporting tuition tax credits or exemptions, vouchers, charter schools, etc. Make sure whatever education you choose is not based on Skinnerian Mastery Learning/Direct Instruction by a teacher or using the computer. Teach your children to read using traditional phonics reading instruction; e.g. programs by Eller, Blumenfeld, Schlafly, Sister Monica, etc.

Appendix XXII

"The Thief of American Individualism: Total Quality Management and School-to-Work"

"The Thief of American Individualism: Total Quality Management and School-to-Work" by Tim Clem was published in the December 1996 (Vol. 2, No. 11) of *The Christian Conscience*.

Virtually unknown to parents across the USA is the Federal *School-to-Work Opportunities Act* (STWOA). For the first time in American history, Government and Business have joined together to educate children. Why is this unusual? Government and Business operate together in countries such as China, Germany, Russia, Japan and in third world countries, not the USA. Right now corporations, along with your local school system, are creating partnerships linking the Federal *School-to-Work Opportunities Act* with your local school district.

Understanding the TQM Foundation

School-to-Work is based on the foundation of Total Quality Management (TQM), also known as Continuous Quality Improvement (CQI). First introduced and rejected by U.S. companies in the post-World War II era, William Edwards Deming, the father of Quality, presented his theories to Japan and found himself welcomed as a national hero. Japan claimed that their social and economic turnaround came from Mr. Deming's TQM theory. Since this turnaround, TQM has been implemented almost entirely within corporate America in hopes to mimic Japanese successes. Americans have been subjected to the thought that Japan and other countries such as Germany are ahead of the USA in technology and education.

Education and business theorists believe that Americans must "benchmark" their schools and corporate management against the supposed successes of Japan and Germany. Their speculation is dead wrong. For example:

> ...[T]he American workforce is still 30% more productive than the Japanese. Sixty percent of American high school students are more likely to attend college than Japanese. There is no evidence that Japanese students learn more in school or that Japanese adults are more literate than Americans. Japanese companies are not more technologically advanced than

American companies. Japanese companies don't earn more patents than American companies.[1]

Only 40% of Japanese homes have sewage systems.[2] American students and workers have all been intimidated by misrepresented successes of the Japanese. We are told repeatedly that because of the greater dedication of Japanese students and workers we are losing our status of world leader. Jobs could be lost, and America could go bankrupt.

Group Think

Total Quality teaches students and workers that Americans will never adapt to the preferred Japanese methods unless we change our culture. Changing a culture requires a complete change in the way we think, a "paradigm shift." Americans willing to search "within" are giving up their personal responsibilities and their pursuit of individual happiness in exchange for a "we can all work together—appreciate one another as a group" mentality.

Quality training experts admit that telling employees they must begin an entirely new way of thinking is frightening upon inception. One chart shows the "Steps in transition management," in which a worker moves from a state of well-being through stages of shock, denial, strong emotion (frustration), acceptance, experimental (frustration again), fuller understanding and integration.[3] [This is otherwise known as cognitive dissonance, a technique utilized to manipulate people into changing behaviors, attitudes, values, etc., ed.]

Therefore, much time and training is spent in self-esteem building. The employee begins to forget the discomfort they first sensed in exchange for comfort offered in group encounter sessions called "team building." Slowly, along with fear of losing their future, job, home, food, and all precious vitals, they begin to melt into the safety of the workgroup they encounter daily. This is labeled as a "team," a "unit," or "family group." This new way of thinking is called "higher order thinking skills," which implies that they have reached a new intellectual plane. By this type of indoctrination, we are volunteering the loss of our supposedly outmoded culture so we may imitate the business management style and educational methods of the Japanese.

The STWOA Grant Application states repeatedly that TQM and CQI shall be the structure of this program. At first glance, we associate the word "quality" with goodness; however, TQM does not describe "quality" in this manner. TQM defines quality not as an end product but as a "process." In order for this process to be implemented, the company must first require (as mentioned above) a total culture change, also described as "paradigm shift." This paradigm change results in a system where all employees operate under a unified set of "values" or corporate beliefs. Workers go through hours upon hours of in-depth group training before they become a part of the TQM process. This training teaches workers that individual values can hinder the performance of their team.

Workers who question the training are labeled with names such as "snipers" or "renegades." The instructor is taught to use the compliant employees in pressuring the sniper to conform. The group then uses a process called "bringing out." Fellow employees make statements to the sniper that imply concern for the feelings of the sniper. For example, "Is there something we have said or done that makes you not want to join our group?" Or, "What would you be giving up if you decided to go along with the rest of us?" Or, "Is it fair to take us all down for your one concern?" Eventually, each employee must put aside personal values in exchange for a common value system within their workgroup.

Quality training and educational manuals state that once workers adapt to a new method of thinking, the workgroup can efficiently function as a team. Individual performance is never rewarded or encouraged. All problems in the workplace can be settled by a predetermined "Problem-Solving Process." No problem can be solved by an individual; the praise that an individual receives from solving a problem could detract from the accomplishments of a workgroup and possibly cause hurt feelings. Therefore, all the workers of a group must meet and utilize the Problem Solving Model before coming to a solution. This model systematically takes the group through a *serendipity* or encounter group session where methods of free discussion called "freewheeling," "round robin," "slip sheet" and "brainstorming" are utilized. A sense of security and openness is established through a facilitator.

A facilitator can develop, in a group which meets intensively, a psychological climate of safety in which freedom of expression and reduction of defensiveness gradually occur."[4]

The facilitator sets the ground rules of the session. Ground rules typically include the following directions: no criticizing, no shutting out, all ideas must be recorded, all ideas must be evaluated, no preconceived solutions are allowed to be brought to the meeting. A solution must have group consensus before it is implemented. All solutions are tracked and monitored for effectiveness. By utilizing the Problem-Solving Process, TQM experts ensure that the employee and their team will be able to find ways to solve problems on an employee level, eliminating costly management input.

Creating a *Kaizen* Culture

TQM labels this employee level of problem solving as "empowerment." These employees are to then become a "world class" workgroup, able to compete within a "global" economy. This global economy is described as a workplace where a state of continuous quality occurs. This state causes change at a very rapid pace and only companies with employees highly trained in problem solving and TQM processes can survive. This state is called *Kaizen*, the Japanese word used for describing a state of continual changing where one can always adapt without hesitation or question. Reaching this level takes hours of employee group training sessions. Therefore, TQM is described as an "evolution to bring about a revolutionary process." Quality experts state that it takes up to ten years for a company and its employees to reach *Kaizen*. Therefore, TQM-based companies are looking for employees that are already "globally trained." If a TQM company could hire these *Kaizen* level employees, millions of dollars can be saved in training and more management positions could be eliminated, thus increasing profits greatly. If a student has been prepared in the "process," one can see how a recent graduate of School-to-Work will be met with open arms within the corporate world.

The STWOA states that all students will be adept in TQM techniques of problem solving and associated behaviors. In addition to Cognitive Skills, all students will be tested to determine Affective Skills such as self-esteem, ability to relate to others, diversity, and appreciation for other cultures. The STWOA states that student skills will be assessed and described according to the *Jobs Program Training Act* (JPTA).

JPTA standards are found in the federal skills catalog called *Skills and Tasks for Jobs: A SCANS Report for America 2000* published by the Secretary's Commission on Achieving Necessary Skills (SCANS) of the U.S. Department of Labor. As in Total Quality Management, all jobs are reduced to a "Task Level." For instance, the SCANS catalog lists the various tasks of a farmer: plowing, planting, harvesting, feeding, even menial tasks such as shoveling manure. These various tasks are given a rating showing the level of skill needed to accomplish each task. This skill rating is then matched with a School-to-Work student, linking the student with a vocational career training path that continues throughout the remaining years of the student's education. The STWOA student is then placed in a vocational apprenticeship at the local Vo-Tech School where he can perfect the skills needed for his future.

The STWOA student must have school and work-related experience with their apprenticeship program. Between the ages of 16 and 17 each student must work in a field of their training to gain on-the-job (OTJ) experience. When the student has completed both schooling and OTJ requirements, he is given a certificate that enables him to be placed in the workforce. Prior to and after STWOA training, the student may allow the state to make available his personal scores and records to potential employers. Potential employers will then search the STWOA computer database for students meeting job requirements and test scores necessary for employment.

The dangers of the federal STWOA are frightening. Just think: the lifelong vocational destiny of a student is determined by a test, and at the most awkward stage of one's life—adolescence. Time and perseverance have always been on the side of the American Dream. We are in a country where all citizens have had the same opportunity to pursue a vocation or goal of their choice at any stage of life if they so desired. STWOA removes these entrepreneurial elements and replaces them with social engineering and captivity.

Endnotes:
1. Eberts, Ray and Cindelyn. *The Myths of Japanese Quality* (Prentice Hall: New York, 1995).
2. "Prosperity's Base: ODA," *Japan Times* (October 16, 1990), p.20.
3. Atkinson, Phillip E. *Creating Cultural Change: The Key to Successful Total Quality Management* (Pfeiffer & Co, 1990).
4. Rogers, Carl. *Carl Rogers on Encounter Groups* (Harper: New York, 1970).

Appendix XXIII

"Soviets in the Classroom: America's Latest Education Fad"

"Soviets in the Classroom: America's Latest Education Fad" by Charlotte T. Iserbyt is a pamphlet published in 1989 (America's Future, Inc.: New Rochelle, NY).*

Education Agreements with the Soviet Union

Is the repugnant act of burning the American flag more damaging to our nation's political integrity than letting the Soviets into our classrooms, in person, on video, or through U.S.-Soviet jointly developed curricula?

One would think so, considering the extensive establishment media coverage given the flag decision compared to the *wall of silence* built around the Soviet invasion of American classrooms.

Maybe America needs a Supreme Court decision similar to the flag-burning decision saying it's legal to let the Soviets teach our children and to "put up statues of well known Soviet cultural figures in our parks," as called for in the *General Agreement between the U.S.A. and the U.S.S.R. on Contacts, Exchanges and Cooperation in Scientific, Technical, Educational, Cultural and Other Fields*, signed in 1985 and 1988 at Geneva and Moscow, respectively. The media might find it impossible to "cover up" a Supreme Court decision.

Perhaps if Americans knew about and understood the deep significance of these agreements, their outrage might even exceed that demonstrated over the flag decision. They might even call for a fully televised Congressional investigation leading to cancellation of *all* education agreements with the Soviets—government-initiated agreements as well as those with tax-exempt private foundations.

The agreements call for "cooperation in the field of science and technology and additional agreements in other specific fields, including the humanities and social sciences; the facilitation of the exchange by appropriate organizations of educational and teaching materials, including textbooks, syllabi, and curricula, materials on methodology, samples of teaching instruments and audiovisual aids, and the exchange of primary and secondary school textbooks and other teaching materials... [and] the conducting of joint studies on textbooks

A–136

between appropriate organizations in the United States and the Ministry of Education of the U.S.S.R."

What do the Soviets—who kidnapped 10,000 Afghan children and shipped them to the Soviet Union for "re-education" and in the spring of 1989 used poison gas and sharpened shovels to disperse a nationalistic demonstration in Soviet Georgia, killing at least twenty persons and injuring 200—have to offer our children in the way of school materials? What does a country have to offer our children in the way of school materials which, according to an 1987 "out-of-print" book by American Federation of Labor—Council of Industrial Organizations (AFL-CIO) entitled *Cruel and Usual Punishment: Forced Labor in Today's USSR*, holds tens of thousands of political prisoners in Soviet prisons, labor camps, and psychiatric hospitals, including between four and five million non-political prisoners in slave labor camps? What does a country which publishes children's books for disinformation purposes overseas—and in the case of books distributed in India, portrays America as "rich, uncaring, and prejudiced," and compares us with the Brahmin caste, which is the ruling caste much resented by the disadvantaged in India—have to offer our children in the way of school materials?[1]

Contrary to the media's portrayal of political change in the Soviet Union, the August 1986 issue of *Comparative Education Review* published an article entitled "Aspects of Socialist Education: The New Soviet Educational Reform" which states that the Soviet reform movement recommends the "intensification of ideological education." A June 2, 1986 *Washington Times* article entitled "Russian Education Obsolete" says in a discussion of education reform, "The specialist of today should have a thorough Marxist-Leninist training." Professor Adam Ulam, the distinguished director of Harvard's Russian Research Center, reports that

> [O]ne of the principal goals of military patriotic education is to counteract any pacifist tendencies, to teach all Soviet citizens, from the youngest children to pensioners, that they must be prepared at any moment to fight for socialism.... The determination to instill explicitly military values in the schools comes through with equally striking clarity in textbooks and manuals used by teachers.

Soviet General Popkov wrote in August 1986 in a regional military paper, *Sovetskiy Voin*, that

> [T]he schools are taking on ever increasing importance in military and patriotic indoctrination. Party documents on school reform define an extensive, scientifically based program for this work.[2]

In light of the above information, which contradicts Gorbachev's *glasnost/perestroika* propaganda, why has our government signed education agreements calling for extensive cooperation with the Soviets in curricula development, exchanges of educational materials and the conducting of joint studies?

Why are Soviet educators permitted to do what U.S. Department of Education educators are forbidden by law to do: involve themselves in curricula development?

Why did the U.S. Department of State authorize the unelected, tax-exempt Carnegie Corporation, a long-time and well funded advocate of disarmament and "world interdependence," to negotiate with the Soviet Academy of Sciences, known to be an intelligence-gathering arm of the KJB, regarding "curriculum development and the restructuring of American education"? Is it because "privately endowed foundations can operate in areas government may prefer to avoid" as stressed by psychiatrist Dr. David Hamburg, President of the Carnegie Corporation and chief negotiator for the exchange agreement, in an interview with the *Los Angeles Times* on June 12, 1987? (Colonel Oliver North's "operations in areas government preferred to avoid" resulted in a fully televised multi-million dollar Congressional investigation.)

Representative Lee Hamilton (D-IN) said during the Iran-Contra hearings that "The use of private parties to carry out the high purposes of government makes us the subject of puzzlement and ridicule." Shouldn't he be asked why the use by our government (State Department) of private parties (tax-exempt Carnegie Corporation and other foundations) to carry out the high purposes of government does not similarly make Congress the subject of puzzlement and ridicule?

A Few Examples

A complete listing of the many shocking exchange activities taking place as a result of the 1985 and 1988–1991 agreements would require volumes. A few concrete examples should suffice to convince the reader that all proposals called for in the agreements are being faithfully and fastidiously carried out.

1. Cambridge-based Educators for Social Responsibility (ESR) project, "Educating for New Ways of Thinking: An American-Soviet Institute." Two such institute sessions have been held (one in Leningrad the summer of 1989) at which "Soviet and American educators examined classroom theory and practice in critical thinking about social and political issues and worked on recommendations and resources for improving the ways we teach about each other's country, and on *A Source-Book for New Ways of Thinking in Education: A U.S.-Soviet Guide* for use by teachers and students in both countries."[3]

"Critical thinking" is the latest fad to hit our children's classrooms. N. Landa's *Lenin: On Educating Youth*, published by the Soviet state-controlled *Novosti Press*, quotes Lenin on "thinking" as follows:

> To pose a real question means to define a problem which demands a new approach and new research…. Sometimes accepted truth no longer answers as a solution for a serious and pressing problem. The school should cultivate in pupils the ability to perceive scientifically evolved truths as stages along the endless road of cognition—not as something stationary and set.

More recently, an article in *Education Week* (4–9–86) entitled "Are Teachers Ready to Teach Pupils to Think?" laments the fact that graduating college seniors

> show little evolution of alternative views on any issue, tending to treat all opinions as equally good, tending to hold opinions based largely on whims or unsubstantiated beliefs, and hesitating to take stands based on evidence and reason. Summing up a decade of research in the 1960's, O.J. Harvey laments that very high percentages… [of educators] "operated in cognitive styles grounded in absolute assumptions—viewing reality in terms of good/bad, right/wrong, and either/or, while attributing goodness and truth to wise and all-knowing authorities."

One doesn't have to have a Ph.D. to accurately predict what U.S.-Soviet jointly developed critical thinking curricula will look like. Do American parents want their children exposed to this type of education, especially when it will also be on computer where they can't get their hands on it?

2. The Carnegie Corporation's exchange agreement with the Soviet Academy of Sciences has resulted in "joint research on the application of computers in early elementary education, focusing especially on the teaching of higher level skills and complex subjects to younger children." ("Higher level skills" is often a euphemism for "critical thinking skills," or values, attitudes, etc.) Carnegie's 1988 one-year, $250,000 grant is funding implementation of this program, coordinated on the American side by Michael Cole, Director of the Laboratory of Comparative Human Cognition at the University of California, San Diego.[4]

3. The American-Soviet Textbook Study Project began in 1977, was suspended in 1979 when Soviet troops invaded Afghanistan, and resumed in 1985 under the Geneva Agreement. At a conference held in Racine, Wisconsin in November 1987, the U.S. representatives acquiesced to the Soviet insistence that American textbooks should present a more "balanced" (i.e., friendly) discussion of Lenin and should give the Russians more "credit" for their role in World War II. A.M. Rosenthal of the *New York Times* said in a December 8, 1987 editorial that

> American educators solemnly discuss with Soviet educators the mutual need for textbook revision, just as if the state did not censor every single book published in the Soviet Union and the Russians could write as they pleased. That is comedy, if you like it real black.

4. Scholars from the American Council of Learned Societies and the Ministry of Education of the Soviet Union met in the United States in 1986 and agreed to establish a Commission on Education that will be responsible for joint scholarly relations in pedagogy and related fields between the United States and the Soviet Union. Some major joint U.S.-Soviet project themes are: Methods of Teaching and Learning School Science and Math Subjects Using Computers; Theory of Teaching and Learning; Psychological and Pedagogical Problems of Teaching in the Development of Pre-School and School-age Children, and Problems of Teaching Children with Special Needs.[5]

5. The Copen Foundation/New York State Education Department/Soviet Academy of Sciences agreement "links students, teachers, administrators in U.S. and Soviet schools by computer and video-telephone lines." Mr. Copen declared

> Soviet officials are especially interested in studying the effects of telecommunications on intercultural understanding, teaching methods, and learning outcomes, and that the Soviets have assigned five scientists to monitor the project.[6]

This agreement should be challenged on constitutional grounds since Article I, Section 10 of the U.S. Constitution says, "No State shall, without the consent of Congress,... enter into any agreement or compact with another State, or with a foreign power."

6. Under terms reached with the Soviet Academy of Sciences, the National Science Teachers Association will publish a Soviet science magazine in the United States. Copies of *Quantum* scheduled for publication in September 1989 will be distributed free of charge to gifted and talented children in this country.[7]

7. On December 8, 1987 the independent National Academy of Sciences pledged to help place more than a million computers in Soviet classrooms by the early 1990s.[8]

8. A $175,000 grant was made from the United States Information Agency (USIA) to the National Association of Secondary School Principals, the American Council of Teachers of Russian, and Sister Cities International. This grant will implement an expanded student exchange program, calling for up to 1500 American high school students to live and study in the Soviet Union each year and an equal number of Soviet students to come to the United States.[9] Former Education Secretary William Bennett told the Kansas City Chamber of Commerce on January 21, 1986 that

> American students know little about their own history and heritage and we have forgotten that intellectual innocence is easily seduced and the price we pay is that some of our children can only nod their heads in agreement when confronted with standard Soviet propaganda. They lack the knowledge to recognize it as propaganda, much less to refute it.

9. On March 4, 1989, fifteen Soviet teens and two adult teachers arrived in Aurora, Colorado as part of the Reagan-Gorbachev agreements. According to an article by Beth Peterson in the high school newspaper *Raider Review*

> A conflict arose when reportedly a Russian student, Farkhod (who was head of the Komsomol Young Communist League and spokesman for the group) told students in an honors history class, "You are all going to be Communists within fifty years. Just remember that every society must be ready for Communism—even America."

10. Students participated in the Phillips Academy in Andover, Massachusetts student exchange with an elite Soviet prep school deep in Siberia. The students "agreed one characteristic was more striking than any other: an indefatigable commitment to Soviet communism." One student, Horovath, said, "I think in general young people are more committed to the Party's ideology than to their parents." Another student, Tom Clyde, said, "They seem to think there is going to be a world revolution any day now and the Communist Party will overtake America."[10]

The Soviet Union: The Only Benefactor

Does our government really believe that the Soviet government is participating in these student exchanges so that their students can be de-programmed and become good little capitalists eager for peace at any price?

Michael Warder of the Rockford Institute says that "Exchanges are allegedly designed to promote peace." However, he points out that, as currently devised

> most exchanges are of benefit only to the Soviet Union. In the summer of 1985 a group of 46 Soviets visited the United States on a so-called goodwill mission. But the 46 were selected, briefed, and controlled by Soviet security organs. Each of the "friendly visitors" had relatives being held hostage at home, lest any of them might consider defecting or deviating from the

official Soviet propaganda line. Their trip was paid for by the Soviet government, and among them were Soviet agents.

Mr. Warder notes that

> Soviet leaders know that if peace propaganda effectively reaches the U.S. public it will result in the Congress voting less money for national defense. U.S. groups going to the Soviet Union have no such "equal" opportunity to reduce Soviet arms expenditures.[11]

How on target Warder's comments have proven to be! Soviet propagandizing of the American people has been so successful that on May 9, 1989 four top Soviet officials were given the red carpet treatment by the U.S. House Armed Services Committee: "They appealed for a warmer approach by Washington and asked us to open a second front against the Cold War."[12] Could their appearance have something to do with the proposed defense budget cuts?

The cost to the American taxpayer—not only in terms of the miseducation of his children, but also in terms of plain, hard-earned tax dollars—is immense. Soviet students coming here are having their travel, living expenses, and tuition paid for by *our* tax dollars, while some of our children cannot afford to go to college.

In 1988 the U.S. Department of State awarded $4,540,000 to various groups involved in education exchanges with the Soviet Union and Eastern Europe.[13] This amount, which is probably the amount doled out annually, is just the tip of the funding iceberg, with large annual grants from other government agencies and tax-exempt foundations keeping the controversial exchanges afloat.

It is to be hoped that the tragic Tiananmen Square massacre of Chinese students will result in cancellation of the U.S.-Chinese student exchanges, resulting in a lessening of our budget deficit, rather than in a transfer of those tax dollars into the U.S.-Soviet education exchange account.

A Night to Remember tells of the five iceberg warnings sent by wireless to the *Titanic*. When the sixth message—"Look out for icebergs!"—came in, the *Titanic's* operator wired back, "Shut up. I'm busy." Just 35 minutes later, the ship whose captain had said, "God Himself could not sink *Titanic*," was sinking.

We have been warned. Are we, like the *Titanic's* operator, convinced that "God Himself cannot sink" America?

The question Americans must ask themselves is: Why, when the Soviet Union is an economic, political, moral, and social basket case, militarily superior but internally on the verge of collapse, does the United States seek its assistance in improving our educational system? Those responsible should be required to justify their support for actions which are *not* in the best interest of the United States.

*The address for America's Future is: 7800 Bonhomme, St. Louis, MO 36105.

Endnotes:

1. Bailey, Kathleen. "Disinformation: A Soviet Technique for Managing Behavior." *Issues in Soviet Education: Proceedings of a Conference*, National Advisory Council on Education Research and Improvement, March 3, 1988.
2. Finn, Chester E., Jr., Assistant Secretary, U.S. Department of Education, "Mapping the Common Ground." Remarks before the American Forum on Education and International Competence, St. Louis, MI, May 16, 1988.
3. Educators for Social Responsibility, Cambridge, MA. Promotional flyer entitled "Teaching for Critical Thinking in the Nuclear

Age: A U.S.-Soviet Institute," Leningrad, U.S.S.R., July 27–August 12, 1989 and flyer entitled "Educating for New Ways of Thinking: An American-Soviet Institute," Hampshire College, Amherst, MA, August 7–21, 1988.

4. Carnegie Corporation of New York. "The List of Grants and Appropriations 1988," reprinted from the *1988 Annual Report of the Carnegie Corporation*.

5. National Academy of Education, Harvard Graduate School of Education, Cambridge, MA. Informational Letter entitled "ACLS–U.S.S.R. Ministry of Education Commission on Education," Fall 1987.

6. "Computers," *Education Week*, Dec. 7, 1988.

7. "NSTA to Publish Soviet Journal," *Education Week*, May 17, 1989.

8. Breen, Tom. "Academy to Give Soviets Computers," *Washington Times*, Dec. 9, 1987.

9. "New Exchange Set for U.S., Soviet Students," *Education Week*, Sept. 28, 1988.

10. Lee, Gary. "The Students' Surprise," *Washington Post*, May 26, 1987.

11. *The Don Bell Report*, Nov. 21, 1986.

12. Gordon, Michael R. "House Panel Sees 4 Soviet Officials," *New York Times*, May 10, 1989.

13. *Federal Register*, Feb. 18, 1988.

Appendix XXIV

"Our Children: The Drones"

"Our Children: The Drones" by Ann Herzer, M.A., Reading Specialist. This two-part article was written in 1984 and is reprinted here with permission of the author.

Part I

With taxpayers' money through a National Science Foundation grant, in 1968 Richard I. Evans wrote *B.F. Skinner: The Man and His Ideas*. The philosophy stated in this book should be of critical interest to all people that are interested in education and value the individual. Following are some direct quotes from Skinner included in Evans's book:

I could make a pigeon a high achiever by reinforcing it on a proper schedule. (p. 10)

When I say a concept is irrelevant, I mean that it has no bearing on the kind of analysis I am trying to develop. (p. 23)

For the purpose of analyzing behavior, we have to assume man is a machine. (p. 24)

You can induce him to behave according to the dictates of society instead of his own selfish interest. (p. 42)

It is conceivable that a technique of control will be developed which cannot be discovered. The word "brainwashing" is dangerous. (p. 54)

We want him [the student] to come under the control of his environment rather than on verbal directions given by members of his family. (p. 64)

I predict that the curriculum of the future will be designed around various capacities and abilities rather than subject. (p 72)

I don't believe in mental discipline as such.... I'm much more concerned with the student's so-called personality traits. (p. 72)

I should not bother with ordinary learning theory, for example. I would eliminate most sensory psychology and I would give them [the students] no cognitive psychology whatso-ever. (p. 91)

It isn't the person who is important, it's the method. If the practice of psychology [operant conditioning] survives, that's the main objective. It's the same with cultural practices in general; no one survives as a person. (p. 96)

It does bother me that thousands of teachers don't understand, because immediate gains are more likely in the classroom than in the clinic. Teachers will eventually know—they must—and I am more concerned with promoting my theories in education [operant conditioning]. (p. 106)

I should like to see our government set up a large educational agency in which specialists could be sent to train teachers [in operant conditioning]. (p. 109)

Have the radical psychologists achieved their goals? Let's take a look at exactly what they believe.

The study of human emotions, feelings, and individual worth are of no concern to these psychologists. They believe that by shaping behavior one can produce any "human machine" that society needs. Skinner proposes to achieve this utopian goal through the American school system.

Evans asked Skinner what would happen if a "hostile government were to gain control and proceed to shape the development of children, putting such techniques totally into use." Skinner replied, "There's no doubt about it, but what are you going to do? To impose a moratorium on science would be worst of all." Would it?

A Nation at Risk states that "If an unfriendly foreign power had attempted to impose on America the mediocre educational performance that exists today, we might well have viewed it as an act of war. As it stands, we have allowed this to happen to ourselves." Did we? Did the American people really know what was happening in education and to their children? The answer is no.

A naive and great nation of freedom-loving people has been deceived by a "technique of control" that cannot be discovered by the average American. By subtle means of mind manipulation from clever propaganda techniques to out-and-out lies, the American people have been sold these radical ideas, methods, and techniques that truly place our nation and our children at risk.

Skinner said, "You will teach your student as he wants to be taught, but never forget that it is within your power to make him want what you want him to want." In other words, a teacher can program and shape a child into being anything the radicals decide he should be.

Parents and American citizens should be aware of the government-sponsored programs being disseminated throughout the United States by the National Diffusion Network. The Network was established in 1974 to promote government-approved educational programs. Many of these programs are subtly designed with behavioral psychology techniques that could train young children to aim for limited goals of common labor. These programs prey on the poor and minority children in our nation. Many of these programs started in the 1960's.

You might wonder who selects these programs. A panel of twenty-two so-called "experts" selects the programs and approves them for dissemination by the Network. They are promoted in a book called *Educational Programs That Work* published by the U.S. Department of Education.

A great number of programs being promoted by the Network state in the book that "No evidence has been submitted to or approved by the Panel." It seems that even these great experts are not willing to accept the responsibility if these government programs fail or succeed.

The radical behavioral psychologists believe in a totally planned society with so many elite to rule, while the drones follow like programmed robots.

Very few college professors, teachers, school board members, or the news media have ever heard of the National Diffusion Network, and certainly the average American citizen is not aware of the *Educational Programs That Work* book or the programs therein. Every American should obtain this book and take a long look at just what their children are being taught or not taught.

One experimental program after another has been placed in the American classroom over the last twenty years. Many of these programs have been brought into the classrooms over the objections of teachers and parents—those teachers and parents who understood what was happening. These programs have proliferated to such an extent that the school child has become a human guinea pig for these radicals who propose to bring about the good life for the whole world by "brainwashing."

When is the last time you heard your children speak of the "American dream"?

An unfriendly, "hostile government" in action? Well, maybe.

Part II

At taxpayers' expense, preparation of B. F. Skinner's dehumanizing book *Beyond Freedom and Dignity* was supported by the National Institute of Mental Health (grant number K6–MH–21, 755–01). Skinner suggested that "what is called for now is a 'technology of behavior'—a systematic and scientific program to alter the nature of man."

The major theme in Evans's book is that because of the complexity of the modern world we can no longer afford freedom and dignity; therefore, the scientific method of operant conditioning should be used to control and shape mankind for the good of the world.

Man is considered a "human machine" with no soul, no free will, just a number like "K6–MH–21, 755–01" to be manipulated by change agents—a group of self-anointed, radical behavioral psychologists proposing to brainwash man into submission to whatever they determine to be the best for mankind.

This is not a new theme in history. It is older than the Inquisition. What *is* new in history is that a scientific method of brainwashing does exist. The American soldier in Korea and [the Jones cult in] Jonestown, Guyana are only two recent examples of this fact.

If one were to attempt this radical change, the most logical place to start this step-by-step "technology of control" would be to start in the schools and the free marketplace.

A planned curriculum and a planned economy could strangle a nation like the United States within a few short years, and help to bring about "equality" for the whole world. This is conceivable if a technique of control could be developed that could not be detected by the average American. Has it happened? Just look at our schools and the economy. How many small companies have gone broke recently? How many small farmers are being forced out of business? Who controls the schools, the industries, the media, the natural resources, and, more importantly, who *will* control the land in the United States?

For the unread and skeptics, I'm going to suggest several books that give a comprehensive overview of American education and the extensive use of classical and operant conditioning in our society. Of course, one must first read Skinner's books to fully understand what he has proposed.

Perhaps the best and most comprehensive book written that truly gives historical documentation for the decline of our system was written by Augustine G. Rudd in 1957 and called *Bending the Twig*. Mr. Rudd was chairman of the Educational Committee for the New York Chapter of the Sons of the American Revolution. Far too much blame has been placed on John Dewey, in my opinion. At least his educational theories were child-oriented, but of course the radical psychologists were not in vogue in 1957.

A Report of the Comptroller General of the United States, dated April 15, 1977 (HRD-7749) should be obtained from government records and read by all Americans. The title is "Questions Persist about Federal Support for Development of Curriculum Materials and Behavior Modification Techniques Used in Local Schools." It appears that nothing has been done about the questions.

Other titles that everyone should read are:

The Psychological Society, Martin Gross
Thought Reform and the Psychology of Totalism, Robert Jay Lifton
Mind Control, Peter Schrag
The People Shapers, Vance Packard
Change Agents in the Schools, Barbara M. Morris
Behavior Mod, Philip J. Hilts
The Literacy Hoax, Paul Copperman
Legal Challenges to Behavior Modification, Reed Martin
Walden Two, B. F. Skinner
The Suicide Cult, Marshall Kilduff and Ron Javers
Snapping, Flo Conway and Jim Siegelman

Below are direct quotes from *Beyond Freedom and Dignity*:

Why should I care whether my government, or my form of government, survives long after my death?...

Why should I be concerned about the survival of a particular kind of economic system?...

A remote personal good becomes effective when a person is controlled for the good of others, and the culture which induces some of its members to work for its survival brings an even more remote consequence to bear.... It is a matter of the good of the culture, not of the individual....

A programmed sequence of contingencies may be needed. The technology has been most successful where behavior can be fairly easily specified and where appropriate contingencies can be constructed—for example, in child care, schools, and the management of retardates and institutionalized psychotics. The same principles are being applied, however, in the preparation of instructional materials at all educational levels, in psychotherapy beyond simple management, in urban design, and in many other fields of human behavior....

Such a technology is ethically neutral....

It is not difficult to see what is wrong in most educational environments, and much has already been done to design materials which make learning as easy as possible.

In Part I of "Our Children: The Drones" I quoted some of the change agents and how they proposed to bring about the change in society and education.

This next article will deal with actual enactment of the methods and programs, and how they are being promoted by the United States Department of Education through the National Diffusion Network.

The first program I'm going to tell you about is the one that started what I now refer to as my "search for freedom and dignity" for myself, children, and teachers. The first program is known as The Exemplary Center for Reading Instruction. The word "reading" is a misnomer. This program is pure operant conditioning in the best tradition of B.F. Skinner.

In 1978, I was working in a Title I program in Phoenix, Arizona. Our program was one of forty that had been selected as outstanding programs in the United States. The government was doing a three-year study on forty programs. The study was called the "Sustaining Effects Study." I assumed that study was being done so our program and the other successful ones could be used as examples for the rest of the country.

Our program was based on an individualized diagnostic program for each child. The child's reading and math needs were determined and we were taught to remediate the specific needs in each child's area of weakness, while trying to build on the child's strong areas as well. We were proud to have been selected as one of the innovative programs in the nation. Part of our program also called for continuous training in our area of specialization. Mine was reading. I was also a member of the parent advisory committee.

In early 1978, our principal, Title I supervisor, and assistant superintendent of schools for the district met with the Title I teachers and proposed a week-long workshop based on a mastery teaching and learning theory. Quite a sales pitch was given for the method and the director. My principal said he had known her for several years and that she was a personal friend of a prominent church and business leader in our community. Since his daughter was a personal friend of mine and he is highly respected as a church and community leader, this was a good selling point from my point of view. Another selling point was the limited cost of the workshop, and the training would include the Title I aides and some of the classroom teachers as well.

The time arrived for the workshop, and substitute teachers were obtained for the teachers. The training session was held at the district office. Our trainer's name was Mrs. Currington from Hawkins, Texas.

We were to meet from 8:00 a.m. to 4:30 p.m. every day, Monday through Friday. We were told that if we could not keep those hours and attend every day, not to attend the workshop. I thought that was rather strange, but said nothing at the time.

One of our teachers, Sherri _____, had small children and was having a problem with adjusting the hours with baby sitters. Since her husband was a medical doctor, she could not depend on him for before and after school care. She asked if she could come late and leave early on some days. She was told no, and that it was her problem to work out. Somehow she did.

On Monday when we arrived at the district office, we found our tables arranged in a U shape with Mrs. Currington at the head. We were never introduced to her, nor were any words of welcome extended. She started to teach, and I started to take notes. My supervisor told me not to take notes, that all the information would be supplied later. I thought this was a very strange arrangement, but I stopped taking notes for the time being.

Two hours into the program I whispered to Sherri, "Just what in the [h—] is this?" By this time they had handed out a massive workbook that made no sense whatsoever. Sherri pointed out that no method or philosophy was stated in the book and asked me if I thought this was strange.

When we broke for lunch, I met one of our outstanding classroom teachers in the restroom and she was in tears. She said, "Ann, I don't know what is wrong with me. I have never reacted to anything like this before." I said, "Deanna, this is the worst thing I have ever been exposed to." She said, "Me too. I just thought it was me."

Several teachers had lunch together and we were all very alarmed about the workshop. One old timer said, "This is just another program that we have to put up with—we have had one after the other for several years. We just learn one method and program, then they bring in another one. This will pass like all the rest."

Since two hours' credit was being offered by UCLA at Davis, some of the teachers asked me if I was going to sign up for it. I said no, because I would not want such a thing on my transcripts. None of our teachers signed up for credit.

Daily, more and more of the teachers were raising their eyebrows and my friend Mary _____ was beside herself. Finally, I said, "Look, Mary, we bought a pig in a poke and none of the teachers are buying this."

We were pressured to memorize the word-by-word directives and pass the proficiency tests on a daily basis. Each teacher taking her turn, we were required to follow each directive exactly as the students would. Finally, the teachers and aides started asking questions. Some became downright hostile toward the teacher-trainer. Our questions were deferred by intimidation. For example, when someone would question a portion of the teaching technique, the trainer would say, "Shame on you. Don't you want to do what is best for children?"

When Deanna pointed out that the program did not take into consideration the learning styles of individual children, Mrs. Currington said, "The group is more important than the individual and we should raise our children to be people pleasers." That is when I really sat up to take notice. I recognized the philosophy right away, and I recognized this program as being political.

Children were required to master each and every small step before moving on, and only perfect penmanship was to be allowed from the child. Mary asked about small children whose fine motor skills had not developed. Mrs. Currington said, "All fine motor skills have developed by the age of one." Wow!

By this time Sherri was laughing. At one point an administrator from the district office came in and said, "We thought this was awful too when we attended the workshop last week, but it gets better as the week goes along." This was the first time we realized that the administrators had taken the workshop, also.

At one point in the training we were required to raise our arms to a 45-degree angle with our fingers pointed. The children were to do this whenever they completed an assignment and the teacher was to check for perfect penmanship, etc. If the work was not perfect, then the child had to start over. The rest of the class traced their word with their finger and said the word in unison while the others made the correction.

I kept asking, "What is this method?" I was somewhat more verbal than the rest. At one point my principal said they used this method in Germany. This is when I said to Sherri, "I recognize the salute: Sieg Heil! I'm not going to do this again."

At this point I sat with my arms folded and Sherri continued to chuckle. I was not laughing. This workshop was no longer funny. I was thinking that something was very amiss.

Sherri and I were sitting at the same table across from each other. Mrs. Currington came and moved our table out from the others and told us to work with the group across the room. Since this was impossible, I thought it was very strange. That's when I noticed that our behavior was being monitored by the teacher-trainer, Mrs. Currington. I told Mary and Sherri to be careful of their actions because we were being monitored. They said, "Oh come on, Ann."

The next day our table had been moved to the end of the room, in direct view of the teacher-trainer.

On the last day of our workshop, Mrs. Currington said she had just returned from doing a workshop in Boston, and they drove her out of town with police escort. Someone asked her why, and she said it was because of a paper she had presented in the workshop. She said she would not present the paper again unless Dr. Reid (the program director) ordered her to. Deanna asked if she could see the paper and Mrs. Currington said yes if Deanna would return it right after lunch and promise not to show it to anyone.

The next day Deanna told me that the paper was the "Children's Hour."[1] I said, "I'm not surprised that they ran her out of Boston with police escort because that is where they threw the tea overboard!"

I am happy to report that I did not pass their fidelity or proficiency tests.

Endnote:

1. "The Children's Hour" is a story by James Clavell which deals with the ability of a "new" teacher, brought to an elementary classroom as a result of a "hostile government's takeover," who is able to completely subvert the values, beliefs and loyalties of the children in a half hour's time. At the end of the story the children had cut up the American flag and thrown the flagpole out of the window, and had been convinced that prayer was a waste of time because "what you receive always comes from soembody else," not God. (See pp. 70–71 of this book.)

Appendix XXV

(1) "The Truth about How We All Have Been Had"

and

(2) "The Difference between Traditional Education and Direct Instruction"

(1) "The Truth about How We All Have Been Had" by Charlotte T. Iserbyt was an alert sent out in late 1998, after the passage of *Omnibus Budget Bill for 1999* which contained the *Reading Excellence Act*. (2) "The Difference between Traditional Education and Direct Instruction" by Tracey J. Hayes has been published in the January 1999 issue of *The Education Reporter* after having been distributed with Iserbyt's alert.

(1) "The Truth about How We All Have Been Had"

Please bear with me. This alert is going to try to explain what happened on the slow road to teaching our children how to read. You may use this alert/article in any way you wish as long as you attribute it to the authors, Iserbyt and Hayes, and do not alter it or add to it in any way. The story is sad and should make American blood boil. Before you start reading, please take the time to read the last two pages of this alert containing an article entitled "The Difference between Traditional Education and Direct Instruction" by Tracey J. Hayes.

First, I want to thank the loop for alerting me about two years ago to the activities of Doug Carnine, director of the federally funded National Center to Improve the Tools of Educators (NCITE) at the University of Oregon. By the way, folks, that is a federally funded office which has dealt for a very long period of time with programs for special education children. Carnine's name jumped out at me when mentioned in one of the loop's communications supporting direct, systematic, intensive phonics (direct instruction), which, by the way, is NOT TRADITIONAL PHONICS INSTRUCTION.

I immediately thought, "Wait a minute. What's going on here? Is this the same Doug Carnine who was involved with Siegfried Engelmann's *Follow Through* DISTAR program (now known as *Teach Your Child To Read in 100 Easy Lessons* or Reading Mastery), about whom I had written in my 1985 book *Back To Basics Reform or... OBE Skinnerian International Curriculum?*" Of course it was, and from that time on I devoted much time trying to convince parents that "direct instruction," regardless of whether it is spelled with lower or upper case "d" and "i," is based on the operant conditioning experiments with animals carried out by the Russian Ivan Pavlov and the American professor B.F. Skinner.

In January of 1997 I wrote many memoranda on this subject which were included on the Internet Education Loop website, identifying Carnine and Engelmann with Ethna Reid's learning program which Ann Herzer (a traditional phonics reading teacher opposed to Skinnerian operant conditioning) so valiantly fought in the late '70s and early '80s. When Herzer objected to the training, she was asked, "Don't you know we are training our children to be people pleasers?" [See Appendix XVII of this book, ed.] I pointed out that my 1985 book *Back To Basics Reform Or...* discussed the ECRI/DISTAR method. Many of us have fought this method for twenty years and, sad to say, we have gotten nowhere. I suppose that is to be expected since we are not part of the national conservative leadership nor are we part of the education establishment leadership. No one listens to you unless you are well funded and have fancy letterhead. Follow the money, follow the money. We didn't have the resources to make a difference.

However, all is not lost if those of you who read this alert will take the necessary action to stop the funding of the *Reading Excellence Act* at the local level. Millions of tax dollars will be gushing forth in your communities to implement this Skinnerian reading program under the guise of "scientific, research-based" phonics reading instruction.

Let me quote from an October 1997 letter Doug Carnine wrote to "concerned friends" asking them to support H.R. 2614, *The Reading Excellence Act,* which called for the use of "research-based" reading instruction programs; i.e., his and Engelmann's program (ECRI/DISTAR). Obviously, use of these programs could be of financial benefit to those involved in the development of the program. Carnine's letter encouraged the following:

> As you know, significant reforms are in process in the bellwether states of California and Texas as well as in many other states. State lawmakers, education leaders, and concerned citizens are joining forces to ensure that the wealth of scientific research on reading conducted during the past three decades is fully transformed into effective classroom reading instruction.

Much of the "scientific research" to which he refers is the Skinnerian dog-training method used in DISTAR and ECRI. Whenever you see the word "effective" related to education, realize that it relates to the late Ron Edmonds's Effective School Research (Harvard and Michigan State). It says "almost all children can learn" when taught to the test, provided the necessary environment for that individual child and enough time for the child to "master" whatever the content (or workforce skills) is made available. That's Skinnerian/behavioral terminology, for those who are not initiated. The new term for "environment" is now *"positive school climate,"* which takes the place of the behaviorist term "psychologically manipulative environment." Effective School Research calls for the elimination of the Carnegie unit, norm-referenced testing, grade levels, etc. Effective School Research calls for outcome-based education, which is mastery learning and can include direct instruction. Both are closely related to Total Quality Management and Planning, Programming, and Budgeting Systems.

Of course, for those who don't have any problem with this type of education/training, STOP: you need read no further. For those who may have questions, please bear with me.

First, you will want to be sure I am correct in my claim that this is, in fact, Skinnerian dog training. The final piece of the puzzle, which should be the clincher and for which many of us are most grateful (God works in wondrous ways!) came in the publishing of *What Works in Education*, edited by Crandall, Jacobson, and Sloane (Cambridge Center for Behavioral Studies: Cambridge, Massachusetts, 1997).[1] The Center's activities and publications can be accessed on their website (http://www.behavior.org). Following are some excerpts related to two of the nine programs discussed in this book:

> *What Works in Education* is the result of a collaborative effort between two organizations: The Cambridge Center for Behavioral Studies and Division 33 of the American Psychological Association.... We would like to extend our gratitude to Doug Carnine, Professor of Education at the University of Oregon, and Bonnie Grossen, Editor of *Effective School Practices*, for consulting on this project.

The chapter entitled "Mabel B. Wesley Elementary" states:

> The Mabel B. Wesley Elementary School in Houston, Texas, has had a schoolwide Direct Instruction language arts curriculum since 1976, and has implemented other direct instruction programs and other programs based on related approaches in other subject matters.... Dr. Thaddeus S. Lott, Sr. is the Project Manager for the Northwest Charter District and Mrs. Wilma Rimes is the principal of Mabel B. Wesley Elementary School.
>
> In 1975... in searching for a means of improving reading skills, Dr. Lott, then the new principal, visited a campus that was implementing the DISTAR reading curriculum (see *Direct Instruction for Teaching Reading and Remediation*, Carnine and Silbert, 1979), developed by Engelmann (reported in Becker, Engelmann and Thomas, 1975A and 1975B). He was impressed by what he observed and began the implementation of DISTAR [now called Reading Mastery, ed.] in 1976.

The chapter entitled "Exemplary Center for Reading Instruction—ECRI" by Ethna R. Reid of the Reid Foundation states:

> ABSTRACT: ECRI provides consulting and training for individual classrooms, grade levels, or entire schools in implementing a direct instruction model in language arts. The ECRI model is applied to and adapted for existing instructional materials. From these materials, structured lessons are developed to teach an integrated curriculum of phonics, oral and silent reading, comprehension, study skills, spelling, literature, and creative and expository writing. ECRI also includes rate building, mastery learning, and behavior management components.
>
> ECRI identified effective teaching strategies later corroborated in the Follow Through Program (Stebbins, L.B., St. Pierre, R.G., Proper, E.D., Anderson, R.B., & Cerva, R.T., 1977) and now known as Direct Instruction (Jenson, Sloane & Young, 1988, pp. 335–336, 350–362). ECRI adopted a general direct instructional approach and expanded it... in ways that allowed applica-

tion to existing subject material in any content area.

Can you not see that this is the necessary Skinnerian method for application to workforce training? Skinner said, "I could make a pigeon a high achiever by reinforcing it on a proper schedule."

The above ECRI connection with DISTAR (Reading Mastery), the direct instruction program being pushed all over the country (Thaddeus Lott's Houston site is the best known) should come as no surprise since the developer of DISTAR, Siegfried Engelmann, has his work in Skinnerian operant conditioning cited several times in Ethna Reid's *Teacher Training Manual*. Of interest is the fact that the U.S. Department of Education in 1981, when Ann Herzer tried to have ECRI shut down, lied in writing when it said ECRI did not use operant conditioning. I have all the correspondence regarding this controversy. A class action suit should be filed against the U.S. Department of Education for its role in promoting this type of training/conditioning under the guise of "education" and for lying about the method.

In other words, ECRI and DISTAR are not just close cousins; they are, in fact, fraternal twins. The only difference between them is their name. They were both funded during the War on Poverty, Great Society 1960s, and since that time have been used on the most helpless members of our society, the underprivileged and minority children. Professors Benjamin Bloom and Lee Shulman's 1968–1981 Chicago Mastery Learning Program was, according to a March 6, 1985 article in *Education Week*

> a tragedy of enormous proportions with almost one-half of the 39,500 public school students in the 1980 freshman class failing to graduate, and only one-third of those graduating able to read at or above the national 12th grade level.

Of interest is the fact that claims of effectiveness similar to those made regarding the Houston DISTAR program were made by the elitist change agents during the 1970s and early 1980s. The Chicago Program crashed in 1981.

What happened to the students who participated in Chicago's Skinnerian experiment? What happened to Lee Shulman, who was involved in the Chicago Mastery Learning disaster? Lee Shulman went on to become the Director of the Carnegie Foundation's Board for Professional Teaching Standards, which is the architect of the performance-based (Skinnerian) teacher training model. Shulman, who had been a Fellow of the American Psychological Association and a Fellow of the Center for the Advancement of Behavioral Sciences, later became President of the Carnegie Foundation for the Advancement of Teaching. The reader should refer to the fact that the book *What Works in Education* is a result of a collaborative effort between the American Psychological Association and the Cambridge Center for Behavioral Studies. What rewards for such a disaster! The lives of the children involved in the experiment are not so decorously documented.

One simple question should be asked which should put this whole matter to rest: Why haven't the underprivileged, the minorities, etc., had more academic success if these programs (which have been used in most of our inner cities under the guise of effective schooling practices) are in fact so "effective"? Why is it that some very good anti-OBE people out there don't even realize that this method *is* OBE? It is based on Bloom's and Spady's contention (which, by the way, is embraced by the Soviets in their polytechnical training as well) that "all except the most seriously handicapped" children can learn, if they work at their own pace with an individualized education plan, are taught to the test, do not have to compete with classmates, are subject to criterion-referenced testing rather than norm-referenced testing, and have as long as they want to "master" the controllers' outcomes, results, or competencies. Outcome-based mastery learning/direct instruction is what the United Nations is talking about when it refers to Lifelong Learning. Everyone can take as long as needed to "master" what the corporate and international planners want as long as everyone "masters" it, even if it takes a lifetime. God forbid that you may not *want* to master certain things. And don't forget, it's not just students but *all* of us who will be involved in this lifelong learning—unless, of course, Americans wake up and do something.

Whether either program has produced the gains proponents of the "method" suggest is questionable. The basic skills test results from Mission, Texas, which used ECRI for a period of twenty years, certainly are dismal. Much more documentation is required in this regard. By the time we have the sad truth regarding longitudinal test studies, including information on where the DISTAR-educated students are now or 10 years from now, and what they are doing, if anything, it will be too late. Norm-referenced testing will be a thing of the past. Performance-based testing (portfolios, demonstrations, etc.) will be standard, and we will have highways plastered with "My Son/Daughter Is an Honor Student." We will never know how dumbed down our children are except when, instead of saying "Please, may I have the ketchup?" they simply grunt a certain number of times for ketchup and a certain number of times for butter, etc.

The basic question, however, aside from test scores, remains: Is it moral to use this method on children in the classroom without their informed consent, even if results show small and *temporary* gains? There are laws on the books which give prisoners protection against such behavior modification methods. Medical research is available showing that operant conditioning causes psychological, neurological, and medical problems. Children in the ECRI program have exhibited such symptoms. There are doctors' statements to this fact.

For those who still don't believe that DISTAR (Reading Mastery) is the same as ECRI, let me quote from a few pages of a dissertation by a top state department of education official who does not wish to have it attributed to him. The paper, written in 1986, entitled "The Exemplary Center for Reading Instruction—ECRI," states in part:

> One of the major goals was to do a cost-effectiveness study to ascertain the most beneficial time to introduce academic skills to students. The only break the children had during their instruction was a snack time which was used as a language experience to discuss the various foods the children were eating. *The main instructional unit was the SRA DISTAR Program.* The results showed an increase in pupil IQ of approximately 20 points in the first year of the program and elimination of a great many behavioral problems. [emphasis added]

Facts Established

1. ECRI and DISTAR are fraternal twins, and both use Skinnerian operant conditioning.

2. Operant conditioning is based on Pavlov's experiments with slobbering dogs.

3. The Right to Read Foundation, formerly headed by Robert Sweet, supports *Teaching Your Children to Read in 100 Easy Lessons*, which is SRA's DISTAR (Mastery Reading). Sweet recently became a consultant to the House Education and Workforce Committee and helped

draft and promote the *Reading Excellence Act*. Several years ago when Tracey Hayes, a researcher, brought her concerns regarding the Carnine/Engelmann program to his attention, Sweet told her he saw nothing wrong with mastery learning. Good parents looking for traditional phonics-based reading instruction for their children have been had by the master manipulators' use of the Hegelian dialectic. They (the internationalist change agents) created the whole language disaster (or took advantage of it) in order to get parents to scream so that parents could be offered the predetermined solution: the direct instruction Skinnerian program which can be applied to any other disciplines, including WORKFORCE TRAINING!

And the desperate parents have bought into this shameful scam, thinking that the educational establishment really cared about their children learning to read. The corporate sector, which supports direct instruction, does not really want educated workers. Thomas Sticht, a member of the Secretary's Commission on Achieving Necessary Skills (SCANS) said as much when he was quoted in an August 17, 1987 *Washington Post* article as follows:

> Many companies have moved operations to places with cheap, relatively poorly educated labor. What may be crucial, they say, is the dependability of a labor force and how well it can be managed and trained—not its general educational level, although a small cadre of highly educated creative people is essential to innovation and growth. Ending discrimination and changing values are probably more important than reading in moving low-income families into the middle class.

Sticht was also at one time associated with the "Hooked on Phonics" program. Oh, what a tangled web we weave! Harvard's Professor Anthony Oettinger, a member of the Council on Foreign Relations, which is bringing us STW, Free Trade and Global Governance, said in 1981:

> The present "traditional" concept of literacy has to do with the ability to read and write. But the real question that confronts us today is: How do we help citizens *function* well in their society? How can they acquire the skills necessary to solve their problems? *Do we really have to have everybody literate—writing and reading in the traditional sense*—when we have the means through our technology to achieve a new flowering of oral communication? It is the traditional idea that says certain forms of communication such as comic books are "bad." But in the modern context of *functionalism* they may not be all that bad. [emphasis added]

All that one must do to smell one big rat is ask the following questions:

1. Why would former California Commissioner of Education William Honig (who was at one time someone parents loved to hate) support something supposedly good for our children (DISTAR/ECRI) after years of implementing the progressive, humanistic agenda? Why would the leadership of the two major teacher unions support a method which supposedly is in the best interests of your children unless all of them have been walking down the road to Damascus?

2. Why do the multinational corporations support ECRI/DISTAR? Ann Herzer lost her bid for Superintendent of Instruction in Arizona due to the corporate elite supporting the incumbent Carolyn Warner when they found out Herzer was opposed to the Skinnerian Mastery Learning method. Herzer had won the Republican nomination in a landslide and was on her way to victory over Warner, the Democrat.

3. Why did the U.S. Department of Education schedule President Reagan to go to the Bronx, New York to visit an ECRI classroom and to meet with Ethna Reid in 1981?

It's up to the reader to answer these questions.

For those who are interested in additional in-depth research on this problem, Ann Herzer is putting her files on CD-ROM. My book *the deliberate dumbing down of america* will be out in 1999, and my 1985 *Back to Basics Reform Or... OBE Skinnerian International Curriculum?* is still available for those who want the history of this mess. *Back to Basics Reform* spells out clearly the Herzer story and how the U.S. Department of Education lied about ECRI in order to keep the Skinnerian method afloat. The Department knew it was necessary for global workforce training. Don't forget: mastery learning/direct instruction is the preferred UNESCO method of instruction.

And for those who are opposed to OBE, please do not forget for one moment that *OBE is mastery learning/direct instruction.* The only difference between OBE and Direct Instruction is that OBE had very bad, outrageous (to use the words of the late Al Shanker) outcomes, and direct instruction (DISTAR/ECRI) has, for the moment, those peanut butter-and-jelly-sounding phonics outcomes. Remember how former Secretary of Education and "Mr. Virtues" William Bennett opposed OBE? He gave 4.5 million dollars to provide Skinnerian Effective School Training (OBE) while Secretary of Education. Do you also remember that he said, "I don't want to throw the baby out with the bath water"? What he meant was that he didn't want the "method" (ML/DI) to go down the drain with the "bad" outcomes. He ultimately headed up the Modern Red School House Charter School, which uses the "baby" (mastery learning/ direct instruction).

And so, folks, that's how we all were had.

Let me let you in on a personal secret:

Even I, who had written fourteen years ago on ECRI and who was knowledgeable about the Follow Through program and DISTAR being Skinnerian, fell for Siegfried Engelmann when he complained about whole language. The article I had published in the *Congressional Record*, October 23, 1989 entitled "Reading: The Civil Rights Issue of the 1990's," which attacked whole language, even quoted Engelmann! I had forgotten he was the developer of DISTAR, and I was not at that time aware that DISTAR was ECRI.

I tell you this so you will understand that not just you, but I, also (until very recently) was conned on this issue. I, too, fell for the words *"direct, systematic, intensive phonics."* I used those words in my article. I thought that was good stuff!

Let's stop the phonics wars, think about our children's futures as free people, not trained animals, and work together to stop the funding of the inhumane Skinnerian method to teach reading and everything else, including workforce training skills.

Thanks for listening.

P.S.: Samuel Blumenfeld, in the Foreword to my new book, has taken a stand against direct instruction. He's a very principled fellow! I hope this alert will get a lot more principled people to take a stand against this method before it's too late.

Endnote:
1. *What Works in Education* can be ordered from the Cambridge Center by calling 1–978–369–2227.

(2)"The Difference Between Traditional Education and Direct Instruction"
by Tracey J. Hayes

The major difference between Traditional Education and Direct Instruction (DI) is the method in which the content is taught.

Traditional education focuses on content-rich curriculum in which a particular subject is "introduced, taught, and reviewed," moving from simple to complex, spiraling back to refresh and retain previously learned material while progressing in that subject. Some publishing companies make recommendations on what content is to be taught, but in most traditional education classrooms, the teacher decides "how" the "what" is to be taught.

To help determine student achievement in traditional education, weekly quizzes and end-of-chapter tests are administered. One hundred percent mastery is, however, not expected. The teacher knows that with time and review, retention of knowledge and test scores will improve. The object of traditional education is to offer students a broad foundation of information, based on facts and figures, that will be retained for future application on high stakes assessments, education and career objectives, and life-long wisdom.

Traditional education is sometimes described as "direct instruction." In traditional education the teacher stands in front of the classroom "directly instructing" the students in the subject matter. Direct instruction and teacher-directed instruction (used in traditional education) are examples of how words in our language can be perceived as being one and the same, when in fact they are very different from one another. Deceptive semantics has created much confusion among many educators as well as parents.

With traditional education, on Monday the teacher assigns her class a chapter to read on the subject of George Washington crossing the Delaware. She tells them they will be tested on this subject on Friday, but she doesn't tell them *exactly* on what they will be tested. In other words, they must learn as much as they can about *everything* in the chapter—including the name of George Washington's horse. When tested, the students might receive a 75% or 80% grade and some parents may be upset with what they consider a "low" grade. However, in fact, the students have done far better than students using mastery learning or direct instruction who are taught to the test, only learning that material on which the teacher tells them they will be tested and receiving a grade of 90–100%. The students in the traditional education class have actually learned many, many times more than the students in a mastery learning or direct instruction class, even though they did not have to *use* all they learned on their test. Professor Benjamin Bloom, the father of mastery learning, was certainly correct when he asserted that students could reach 85% mastery—of a *limited* or dumbed down curriculum.

Direct Instruction focuses on a narrow curriculum in which a particular subject is introduced via a stimulus, expecting a particular response from the student. Based on behavioral psychology and the work of B.F. Skinner, DI requires the teacher to use operant conditioning and behavior modification techniques. In a DI classroom the teacher must follow a prescribed set of lesson plans, sometimes in script form, and use certain cues such as clapping with the intent to incite a certain reaction such as unison chanting from the students. In many classrooms, rewards and tokens are also used to generate a predetermined response (S-R-S).

Direct Instruction is a teaching method that bypasses the brain and instigates a reflex that is not natural, but rather controlled and programmed. This kind of manipulation causes some students to become so stressed that they become sick or develop nervous tics. Many DI programs are designed for the computer with built-in bells and whistles to "control and pace the learning outcomes." With outcome-based education (OBE) already in many schools, Computer Assisted Learning (CAL), programmed with the ML/DI method, is also promoting affective/subjective goals.

Direct Instruction expects mastery (ML) to be achieved in each area of instruction before moving onto the next level. There are frequent tests, cramming, cranking, and drilling the skills to perfection, so test scores are usually high in the early years. Typical classrooms, however, consist of students with varying abilities, so the amount of content is decreased to accommodate the slowest learner. In some schools cooperative learning is used to appease the high achiever. Since review of previously learned materials is not encouraged, overall retention is less. SAT scores are low, and ultimate application is not achieved and in some cases stifled.

Direct Instruction has been used for decades in areas where poverty is prevalent because the method of teaching promotes order and discipline in the classroom. Since many parents want to discard whole language and implement phonics, schools across the nation are adopting DI programs without truly understanding the *method* behind the content. At the expense of destroying one's free will, these schools are training students to become passive drones rather than educated citizens. As students plateau at a certain level because they cannot make sense of the knowledge they once were expected to recall on command, one must wonder if the pressure to perform like barking dogs is what students really need or what we really want.

Appendix XXVI

"Shamanistic Rituals in Effective Schools*"

"Shamanistic Rituals in Effective Schools*" by Brian Rowan, Senior Research Scientist, Far West Laboratory for Educational Research and Development. Paper presented at the annual meeting of the American Educational Research Association, New Orleans, LA, April, 1984. Asterisk in title is notation on bottom of title page which states, "Work on this paper was supported by the National Institute of Education, Department of Education, under Contract No. 400–83–003. The contents do not necessarily reflect the view or policies of the Department of Education or the National Institute of Education." Brian Rowan was involved in Bill Spady's Far West Lab grant to the Utah State Department of Education to "put OBE in all schools of the nation."

This paper develops a theoretical perspective for analyzing the non-scientific uses of research in educational policy debates. A central focus is educational researchers' use of shamanistic rituals to affect organizational health (cf., Miracle, 1982). A number of shamanistic rituals derived from research on "effective" schools are described here, and an analysis demonstrates the circumstances under which these rituals can be used to divine the unknown, cure ills, and control uncertain events.

Background

Miracle (1982) suggested that shamans and applied social scientists perform a number of similar functions in society. Shamans, the powerful medicine men of premodern societies, worked mainly to cure ills, divine the unknown, and control uncertain events, and they performed these functions by using a specialized craft obtained after a long period of formal initiation and training. Similarly, applied social scientists acquire a specialized craft after initiation and training, and they too are called upon to alleviate the vague ills of corporate groups, divine the unknown for organizational strategists, or bring order to the uncertain events that plague institutional affairs.

The analogy raises a number of important issues for applied social science. First and foremost, shamans practice magic, whereas applied social researchers are thought to practice "science." To liken scientists to magicians raises interesting questions about the relationship of science to pragmatic action. An additional problem is that shamans are but one of the many practitioners of magic in societies, and they can be distinguished from others who employ magic in their rituals, for example, sorcerers, witches and wizards. This observation raises questions about the uses of research in modern policy analysis. If educational "science" functions as magic, who are the shamans, witches, and sorcerers of educational research?

Forms of Pragmatic Action

We begin with the problem of whether applied educational scientists practice magic. A number of anthropologists have observed that magic is used for pragmatic purposes in premodern societies, but that magic is not the only form of pragmatism available to premodern practitioners. For example, both Malinowski (1948) and Evans Pritchard (1965) argued that premodern societies possessed sound technical logics that practitioners could use to successfully accomplish most work tasks. In addition, premodern people were able to sharply distinguish between these working, practical logics and magic. In premodern societies, when tasks were going well, the technical logic of everyday work dominated action. But as uncertainties increased, or as conflict and stress became more problematic, premodern practitioners began to supplement technique with magic. Thus, Malinowski (1948) observed the fishing practices of Trobriand islanders and found that, in the safety of lagoons, practitioners made little use of magic and relied primarily on established technical routines to ensure good fishing. But as activities moved into the more dangerous open seas, magic was increasingly invoked as a supplemental technical aid.

Similar points can be made about the modern educational practitioner's use of research. It seems clear that schools have an established series of technical routines (Goodlad, 1983). But these practices are not grounded in the highly stylized logics of modern science. Rather, they exist in the more subtle and largely unarticulated logic of teachers and administrators (Jackson, 1968). Although some educational observers have likened this unarticulated logic to magic (e.g., Lortie, 1975), Malinwoski's (1948) [sic] discussion suggests that it is more appropriate to think of educational research as magic. The educational practitioner appears to make wide use of the subtle and unarticulated logic of schooling, and this logic appears to have the desired technical effect on a large number of students (Hyman, Wright and Reed, 1975). Practitioners make much less use of the stylized "scientific" knowledge of applied social scientists. Indeed, like Malinowski's Trobrianders, they appear to reserve the use of "science" for those sectors of schooling which are problematic or in "crisis."

Other arguments also suggest that educational "science" functions much like magic. As Miracle (1982) noted, both applied social scientists and shamans utilize a "force" that derives from an other world (Mauss and Hubert, 1961). Shamans, for example, often travel to other worlds to communicate with spirits or accompany the dead to their supernatural resting places. As a result, they are said to inhabit both the real world and a spirit or supernatural world. Similarly, applied scientists appear to inhabit two distinct worlds, one the "real" world, the other the proverbial "ivory tower." It is widely recognized that knowledge gained in the ivory tower is not the same as that gained in the "real" world, an observation that endows "scientific" knowledge with a certain otherworldly nature. Thus, like shamans, applied educational scientists inhabit two worlds and practice a craft that has a special legitimacy in social affairs.

Types of Magic

If we perist [*sic*] in the analogy between educational "science" and magic, it becomes useful to classify various types of magic and magicians. In premodern societies, for example, there were numerous practitioners of magic, including not only shamans, but also various witches, wizards and sorcerers. Distinctions among these practitioners can be made on the basis of their actual magic practices. Wizards and witches often practiced forms of "black magic" that were used as weapons to defend interests or harm enemies, whereas the shaman's magic was most often employed for benevolent purposes, including the curing of ills. There is also a need to look carefully at the rituals practiced by different groups. For example, shamans often engage in a common "spitting and sucking cure," but they also use other rituals from their "bag of tricks."

Educational researchers can also be classified by the types and functions of the rituals they perform. For example, policy analysts sometimes use the rituals of research to confound and weaken political or scientific opponents, a form of research that appears similar to the "black" magic of witches. But there are also research shamans who can be called upon by policy analysts to perform healing rituals. All types of research ritualists select from a common and well-known bag of research tricks, although in recent years there has been a rise of ritual specialists who exclusively work either qualitative or quantitative magic on policy audiences.

Shamanism and School Effectiveness Research

In this paper, we limit attention to a single type of research ritualist—the research shaman—and to a few related magic tricks used within a narrow policy domain. Our interest is in describing research rituals that heal and revitalize sectors of education and not in research that fans controversy, inflicts harm on ideological enemies, or demoralizes existing constituencies in a policy domain. Moreover, the analysis will be narrowed to a few research rituals used in one policy domain to better illustrate how research shamans operate.

Shamanism and Crisis

It is commonly observed that working practitioners in education remain detached from, even ignorant of, the findings and applications of applied research. Yet this observation is not entirely true. Educational policy makers and their research ritualists continue to generate research, and this research continues to play a role in certain sectors of educational practice. Thus, a question emerges: in what sectors of educational institutions are the rituals of research shamanism most utilized?

Anthropological studies suggest some answers to this question. It has been argued that magic assumes its highest importance in institutional sectors plagued by three conditions: (a) high levels of technical uncertainty; (b) structural cleavages that create great stress among social groups; and (c) social disorganization that creates problematic mood states among participants (Malinowski, 1925; Gluckman, 1952; Wallace, 1956). The argument here is that research shamanism is most valued in sectors of education that contain these characteristics. Thus, research in education is most numerous in areas where there is high technical uncertainty (do schools/programs/teachers make a difference to educational outcomes?). The rituals of research also take on great importance in areas where there is conflict among social groups (are new educational initiatives needed to redress past social inequities?). And finally, research is increasingly directed at problems related to disorganization and dissatisfaction in institutional sectors of education (are urban/high schools better or worse than in the past?).

Research on Effective Schools

Research on effective schools has its origins in these problems. The research deals with a sector of educational institutions—the instructional core—which has long been the subject of uncertainty, conflict, and pessimism, and where the use of myth and ritual has been common (Meyer and Rowan, 1977; 1978). What is distinctive about "effective schools" research, in contrast to much past scientific work, is that it has taken a shamanistic approach to the problems of schooling. It has not fanned the flames of discontent and uncertainty like previous scholarly work (e.g., Coleman et al., 1966; Averch et al., 1972; Jencks et al., 1972), but instead has held out hope that the pervasive ills of modern urban schooling can be cured.

Edmonds (1979a), the most powerful of all effective schools shamans before his untimely death, seemed accutely [sic] aware of the need for healing in modern educational institutions, and a careful reading of his works reveals his strategy for effecting a cure for the problems confronting urban education. He argued that research must be used to counter the pessimistic view that schools have weak effects on student outcomes, and that as this occurred, practitioners could attain new expectation states that facilitated, rather than hindered, the achievement of disadvantaged children (see, especially, Edmonds, 1978; 1979b). Thus, Edmonds saw that "science" could be used to confront the conflicts, uncertainties, and problematic mood states afflicting modern schooling.

That Edmonds' [sic] approach possessed a special "force" in educational policy arenas is indisputable. Like the revitalization movements that swept the great plains during the period of indian [sic] decline (Wallace, 1966), the rituals of effective schools research diffused widely and rapidly. They were adopted by other shamans, who brought them to state departments of education and local school systems, and there these rituals were used as the cornerstone of ambitious revitalization ceremonials (see, e.g., Ogden et al., 1982; Shoemaker, 1982; Clark and McCarthy, 1983).

It is worth noting that the perspective being developed here does not necessarily imply that these shamanistic rituals are hoaxes. Indeed, just as many modern medical practitioners have come to recognize the wisdom and efficacy of shamans, there is at least some reason to think that the arguments of effective schools proponents possess some scientific merit (see, e.g., Rowan, Bossert and Dwyer, 1983). Nevertheless, for the moment, it is useful to suspend our empirical curiousity [sic] about whether these initiatives really "work," [sic] and to examine instead some of the concrete ritual practices that characterize this new educational movement.

Important Shamanistic Rituals

It has already been suggested that shamanistic rituals are designed to cure ills, divine the unknown, and control uncertain events. In this section of the paper, three prominent effective schools rituals are discussed and their relationship to the central functions of magic are illustrated.

Curing Ills with Literature Reviews

We begin with one of the most common shamanistic rituals in the effective schools movement, the glowing literature review that promises relief from the currently pervasive sense that educational institutions are in poor organizational health. Miller's (1983: 1) review illustrates the general form of this ritual: "Not so long ago the conventional wisdom regarding American schools was that 'schools do not make a difference.' ...Yet today... the message of... research is primarily postive [*sic*] and upbeat: schools can make a difference" (Miller, 1983: 1).

A closer look illustrates the consistent dramatic form used by reviewers to affect the promise of a cure. First, the authors contrast the dismal tradition of school effects research with "more recent" and more positive studies of effective schools. This is followed by the citation of a host of previously unpublished and obscure studies which are often nothing more than other positive literature reviews. The final step is a grandiose concluding statement, which most often calls on practitioners to adopt the new discoveries.

We speculate that these rituals have their most dramatic effect on naïve individuals who have little time or inclination to follow-up footnotes or read works cited in the text, or on those who have little tolerance for the ambiguity that marks true scientific debate. Lacking a systematic understanding of the scientific pros and cons of effective schools research, naïve individuals are left only with the powerful and appealing rhetoric of the reviewers. Thus it is that research on effective schools has come to be seen as a "cure" for educational ills the less it has been published in scholarly journals and the more it has been disseminated in practitioner magazines. The experiences shaman knows to avoid the scrutiny of scholars, for this can raise objections to the "scientific" basis of ritual claims and divert attention away from the appealing rhetoric. Instead, the shaman cultivates the practitioner who needs a simple and appealing formula.

Divining the Unknown Using Outliers

While the literature review ritual can be observed equally well by both qualitative and quantitative specialists, a second ritual, designed to divine the unknown, is the exclusive domain of quantitative ritualists. The ritual uses residuals from a regression analysis to identify "effective" schools and to contrast them with "ineffective" schools. The purpose is to divine an answer to two nagging questions in school effectiveness research: which are the effective schools in a system and what are these schools doing that makes them different?

The techniques involved in this ritual have been described before (see, Rowan et al., 1983). A regression equation predicting school achievement from school socioeconomic composition is tested, and errors of prediction are calculated. The errors (or residuals) are used to identify "effective" and "ineffective" schools and form samples for contrasted groups studies. The ritual almost always strongly supports the rhetorical posture of the ritual literature review. Since predictor variables never account for all of the variance in school-level achievement, an analysis of residuals will always demonstrate that schools differ in achievement even after controlling for socioeconomic composition. Thus any experienced shaman can find "effective" schools. Second, if a shaman asks a large number of questions, a number of structural and cultural differences between effective and ineffective schools can be found. Thus, the outliers ritual not only identifies the previously unrecognized "effective" schools, it also reveals for the first time why these schools attain effectiveness.

From a magician's standpoint, this ritual's power can be increased in a number of ways. First, the worse the specification of the initial regression model, the more persuasive the ritual. For example, by failing to include all measures of school socioeconomic composition, a shaman can increase the residual achievement differences between schools. This, in turn, enhances claims that "effective" schools make a difference to achievement. Moreover, to the extent that school characteristics are correlated to omitted socioeconomic predictors, misspecification [*sic*] enhances the liklihood [*sic*] that differences in school characteristics will be found between "effective" and "ineffective" groups of schools. Thus, the worse the initial regression model, the more powerful the shamanistic ritual.

A related tactic is to use aggregate models. By using schools rather than individuals as the unit of analysis, proportions of variance in achievement explained by school management and culture are increased. In between-school analyses, schools can be seen to account for nearly 30% of the variance in achievement. But in between-individual analyses, this is reduced to about 5%. Thus, effective schools ritualists have been able to inflate their claims of school effects through a simple aggregation trick (see Alexander and Griffin, 1976).

The experienced shaman also avoids certain practices. For example, it is wise not to repeat the residuals ritual in the same population, for this highlights the low correlation of residuals over time and raises questions about measurement reliability. It is much wiser to demonstrate reliability by using the conventional, and cross-sectional, "split/half" procedure of psychometricians (see, Forsythe, 1973). Similarly, after a few performances of the residuals ritual and the associated contrasted group study, it becomes possible to ignore problems of validation. Thus, as time moves on, the wise shaman avoids achievement data and the residuals ritual entirely, and instead assesses schools on the degree to which their structures match those of previously identified "effective" schools.

Controlling Uncertainty through Measurement

A final shamanistic ritual in the effective schools movement requires the shaman to have advanced training in the art of psychometrics. The ritual is particularly suited to application in urban or low performing school systems where successful instructional outcomes among disadvantaged students are highly uncertain but where mobilized publics demand immediate demonstrations of success. The uncertainties faced by practitioners in this situation can easily be alleviated by what scholars have begun to call "curriculum alignment."

This ritual begins with an analysis of what is actually being taught in schools. The shaman conducting the ritual assembles a group of local practitioners and together they list instructional objectives for each grade level. The next step is to find achievement tests that ask questions related to these objectives. To the extent that test items matching local objectives are found, either in commerically [*sic*] prepared tests or in locally constructed ones, and to the extent that these items are used in achievement testing rather than the haphazard collection of items contained in most commerically [*sic*] prepared tests, the curriculum and testing systems of the local school are said to be "aligned."

Since it is known that at least some variance in student achievement is a function of students [*sic*] opportunity to learn what is tested in criterion measures (Cooley and Leinhardt, 1980), the alignment ritual can have immediate effects on perceptions of effectiveness. For example, a school system moving from an unaligned commercially prepared achievement test to an aligned one can expect that it will score higher on national norms than before. But this increased "effectiveness" does not occur because students are learning more or different things. In the typical alignment ceremony, only test items—not instruction—are changed. Nevertheless, while student learning remains unchanged, alignment allows students to practice criterion measures and achieve higher test scores, thus giving them an advantage over comparable students in unaligned school systems.

An even more powerful demonstration of instructional effectiveness can be achieved if shamans avoid the standard psychometric practice of designing norm-referenced achievement tests and move instead toward criterion-referenced tests. As Popham and Husek (1969) discussed, the typical norm-referenced achievement test eliminates items that nearly all students in a population can answer correctly, since norm-referenced tests are designed to produce between-student variance in achievement scores. But if one neglects this practice and allows items that almost everyone can answer correctly to be included in achievement tests, a larger number of students will appear to be performing more successfully in their academics.

Thus, the art of measurement can be used as an aid to shamanism, espcially [*sic*] in urban schools plagued by the uncertainties of student performance. Student variability in performance can be reduced, and relative performance increased, not by changing instructional objectives or practices, but simply by changing tests and testing procedures.

Conclusion

The analysis of specific shamanistic rituals in the effective schools movement raises a number of important questions about the relationship of applied science to pragmatic action. Most importantly, it suggests that future studies of "science" as magic are needed. There is a need to begin to chart other rituals used by applied scientists to disarm enemies, cure ills, and divine the unknown. Moreover, there is a need to study the conditions under which these magical practices spread through practitioner populations. Using this perspective, much of the literature on organizational change and applied research can be rewritten from an institutional perspective (Meyer and Rowan, 1977).

At the same time, there is a need to carefully analyze the science of magic. There can be little doubt that Malinowski's (1948: 50) observations about premodern magic will ring true for many observers of current applied research in education:

> ...when the sociologist approaches the study of magic... he finds to his disappointment an entirely sober, prosaic, even clumsy art, enacted for purely practical reasons, governed by crude and shallow beliefs, carried out in a simple and monotonous technique.

Yet this "clumsy" art sometimes achieves great effects in practitioner communities and may even have some empirical merit, and this raises the appealing promise that applied social scientists can someday develop shamanistic rituals that empirically "work."

References

Alexander, K. and L. Griffin. School district effects on academic achievement: a reconsideration. *American Sociological Review*, 1976, *41*, 144–151.

Averch, H.A. et al. *How effective is schooling? A critical review of research*. Englewood Cliffs, N.J.: Educational Technology Publications, 1972.

Coleman, J.S. et al. *Equality of educational opportunity*. Washington, D.C., U.S. Department of Health, Education and Welfare, 1966.

Cooley, W.W. and G. Leinhardt. The instructional dimensions study. *Educational Evaluation and Policy Analysis*, 1980. *2*, 1–26.

Clark, T.A. and D. McCarthy. School improvement in New York City: the evolution of a project. *Educational Researcher*, 1983, *12*. 17–24.

Edmonds, R. *A discussion of the literature and issues related to effective schooling*. St. Louis: CEMREL, Inc., 1978 [*sic*].

Edmonds, R. Effective schools for the urban poor. *Educational Leadership*, 1979a, *37*, 15–24.

Edmonds, R. A conversation with Ron Edmonds. *Educational Leadership*, 1979b, *37*, 12–15.

Evans Pritchard, E. *Theories of primitive religion*. London: Cambridge Press, 1965.

Forsythe, R.A. Some empirical results related to the stability of performance indicators in Dyer's student change model of an educational system. *Journal of Educational Measurement*, 1973, *10*, 7–12.

Gluckman, M. *Rituals of rebellion in S.E. Africa*. London: Oxford Press, 1954.

Goodlad, J.I. *A Place called school*. New York: McGraw Hill, 1983.

Hyman, H.H., C. Wright and C. Reed. *The enduring effects of education*. Chicago: University of Chicago Press, 1975.

Jackson, P.W. *Life in classrooms*. New York: Holt, Rinehart and Winston, 1968.

Jencks, C.L. et al. *Inequality: a reassessment of the effects of family and schooling in America*. New York: Basic Books, 1972.

Lortie D. *Schoolteacher*. Chicago: University of Chicago Press, 1975.

Malinowski, B. *Magic, science and religion*. Glencoe: Free Press, 1948.

Mauss M. and H. Hubert. *On magic and the unknown*. In, Parsons, T. et al (eds.). *Theories of society, II*. Glencoe: Free Press, 1961.

Meyer, J. and B. Rowan. Formal structure as myth and ceremony. *American Journal of Sociology*, 1977, *83*, 340–363.

Meyer, J. and B. Rowan. The structure of educational organizations. In M. Meyer et al, *Environments and organizations*. San Francisco: Jossey Bass.

Miller, S. *A history of effective schools research: A critical review*. Paper presented at the annual meeting of the American Educational research [*sic*] Association, Montreal, April, 1983.

Miracle, A.W. The making of shamans and applied anthropologists. *Practicing Anthropology*, 1982, *5*, 18–19.

Ogden, E., W. Fowler and D. Kunz. *A study of strategies to increase student achievement in low achieving schools*. Paper presented at the annual meeting of the American Educational Research Association, New York, March, 1982.

Popham, W. and H. Husek. Implications of criterion referenced measurement. *Journal of Educational Measurement*, 1969, *6*, 1–9.

Rowan, B., S. Bossert and D. Dwyer. Research on effective schools: a cautionary note. *Educational Researcher*, 1983, *12*, 24–31.

Shoemaker, J. *What are we learning? Evaluating the Connecticut school effectiveness project*. Paper presented at the annual meeting of the American Educational Research Association, New York, March, 1982.

Wallace, A. Revitalization movements. *American Anthropologist*, 1956, *58*, 264–281.

[Ed. Note: We shall forever be grateful to Brian Rowan for crafting such an eye-opening presentation of the process used by the change agent "shamans" to sell the damaged goods of Effective Schools Research—and many other programs, like OBE, mastery learning and direct instruction—through manipulated or "massaged" research data. His exposé of the use of alignment of curriculum to testing to create an illusion of improved performance of schools is quite phenomenal for someone so involved in the spread of OBE to "all schools in the nation."]

Appendix XXVII

"Big Bad Cows and Cars:
Green Utopianism & Environmental Outcomes"

"Big Bad Cows and Cars: Green Utopianism & Environmental Quality," by Sarah Leslie from the *Free World Research Report* (Vol. 2 No. 6), June 1993. Reprinted in its entirety with permission of author.

The problem with cows and cars, it seems, is with their... well, er... emissions. Both are supposedly responsible for wreaking havoc on the planet Earth (spelled with a capital "E" to suggest respect and "reverence") because of their CO_2 output—for one a matter of life, for the other a manner of mechanization.

They both have to go. This means tractors, too, of course. The goals for sustainability, according to the latest environmental craze (which we have dubbed "Green Utopianianism"), require an abandonment of modern material affluence, a transfer of wealth to third world countries and, unmistakably, a return to the manual plow accompanied by a vegetarian diet.

Where can one find such utopian nonsense? It is popping up with increasing frequency in mainstream publications and credible-sounding scientific documents. Jeremy Rifkin's "Beyond Beef" campaign and Al Gore's recent book, *Earth in the Balance*, have lent the necessary pizazz to launch a massive public relations campaign about the environmental hazards of these CO_2 emissions (that's "gas" for the folks in Rio Linda, California).

The education establishment, prone to jumping on the latest bandwagon, is going great guns for environmental education. Educators are frequently puzzled and amazed when parents object to environmental and global curricula and outcomes. What could be wrong with that? they ask. We recommend they read the literature.

The Rave Review

We found the abolishment of the cow and car through reading an Iowa Department of Education document. Several years ago, in a publication entitled *Social Studies Horizons* (Fall 1990), just such a utopian book was given a rave review. This book, originally entitled *The Future as*

If It Really Mattered, was recently re-issued under a new title—*Toward A Sustainable Society: An Economic, Social and Environmental Agenda for Our Children's Future* by James Garbarino. The title says it all. It is quite an agenda!

Here is the rave review:

> Excerpts from a book that is a class of practical wisdom on what a sustainable society is, why we need to move to a sustainable society, and what a sustainable society might look like. It is this kind of thinking we need to consider as we move toward transforming the social studies. It seems to me that teaching the "transformational economics" of sustainability would be a much more empowering and enlivening process for our students than the text-book-mires "dismal science" approach to economics that has been the norm. (*Social Studies Horizons*, p. 4)

If you think sustainability is just a nice new term to describe more environmentally responsible farming methods, think again. Sustainability, at least to the new Green Utopians, is an entire restructuring of the way humans live on the planet, and is the new prime directive for the survival of species (man only somewhat included).

The Iowa DE publication quoted Garbarino:

> This enjoyment of owning, having, spending, buying, and consuming is a serious threat. It threatens our relationship with the Earth and our relationships with each other, particularly in our families and in our efforts to preserve the resources necessary for social welfare systems. It cannibalizes the planet, undermines the spiritual order, and leaves us scrambling to fill the social and spiritual void with positions. It is an addiction pure and simple... and our chances of making the transition to a sustainable society depend upon our overcoming it. (p. 4)

The major chore for humans on Garbarino's anthropomorphic Earth is to make the transition to sustainability. But, just what does HE mean by this? What is the agenda of the new Green Utopians?

Utopian Sustainability

Garbarino's transition to sustainability is a process long on ideology and short on specifics, in typical utopian fashion. Garbarino states:

> Our goal, remember, is the creation of a more *sustainable* human community based on competent social welfare systems, just and satisfying employment, reliance on the nonmonetarized economy for meeting many needs, and a political climate that encourages cultural evolution and human dignity. (p. 162) [emphasis added]

Garbarino identifies himself as a utopian throughout the book. His optimistic view of the future is dependent upon his faith that the human race will accept stringent population control measures, severely limited transportation and trade, earth-friendly housing, local neighborhood food and energy production, and government-regulated health and social welfare services. The seriousness of "our common future" is enough to warrant this massive overhaul of the Western lifestyle.

Our Not-So-Rave Review

The preface of Garbarino's book (page *ix*) gives credit to Aurelio Peccei and the Club of Rome for the "wealth of ideas and information about the prospects for a sustainable society." The Club of Rome is best known for its earth-shattering GLOBAL 2000 report, *Limits to Growth* (1972), calling for massive world-wide population control measures and many other controversial plans. The Club of Rome is one of those international organizations that the extreme left esteems (including the national media) and the extreme right views as one of "those" conspiratorial groups.

The Club of Rome does not advocate for a mainstream, reasonable approach to environmental stewardship. Not by any stretch of the imagination. It is an indisputable fact that the Club of Rome is tied closely to the wacky international New Age groups known as Planetary Citizens. Planetary Citizens sponsored a "1990 World Symposium on Interspecies & Interdimensional Communication." (This means communicating with species not of this world!) Aurelio Peccei's name has appeared on Planetary Citizens letterhead.

A Return to the Plow

Tractors will go the way of the car and the cow. Manual high-tech plows are the wave of the new utopian future.

> The plow developed by the Schumacher-inspired Intermediate Technology Group is a good example [of appropriate technology]. It relieves the backbreaking burden of working an oxen-powered plow, but it is not a conventional tractor. In their clever arrangement, a small engine pulls a plow across a field using a wire, while two farmers use their skill and strength to guide it. The result is better plowing with a less expensive tool and provision of meaningful work. (p. 223)

This utopian vision of a new society includes agricultural cooperatives, a cashless economy, and women working at home at gardening chores to provide food for their households and communities. "Household and community gardens can successfully produce fruits and vegetables, and in some cases even grain." (p. 231–2) Concurrent with these recommendations is the elimination of most trade because of its relationship to transportation (which produces CO_2). Everything must be produced locally.

Eating meat is not included in the book. "The massive concentrations of cattle excrement produce large amounts of methane," claims Garbarino in Rifkin-like fashion. Presumably the cow is regulated to a position of prominence in society, perhaps even veneration. If the cow isn't good for food, and not an "appropriate" technological substitute for the tractor for use with plows, then perhaps the Green Utopians of the future will hang garlands of flowers about their necks!

Car Crimes

"Using a car to accomplish daily tasks that could be done without one is a misdemeanor against the Earth and posterity. Social policies that encourage driving and discourage walking are crimes against the planet." (p. 221) The term for this new kind of crime in Green Utopia is "bioeconomic crime" according to Nicholas Georgescu-Roegen, who is further quoted on the matter of automobiles:

> Every time we produce a Cadillac, we irrevocably destroy an amount of low entropy that could otherwise be used for producing a plow or a spade. In other words, every time we

produce a Cadillac, we do it at the cost of decreasing the number of human lives in the future. (p. 135)

This type of logic, which ties Western consumption to the future destruction of the Earth, is the drumbeat of Garbarino's book. It explains the reasoning behind the original version of the Iowa Global Education curriculum manual (*Catalogue of Global Education Classroom Activities, Lesson Plans, and Resources*), which contained a Social Studies exercise for grades 4–6 which linked eating red meat to the destruction of the tropical rainforest:

> Calculate the amount of meat eaten by a person in the U.S. per year; translate to number of animals. How much energy and grain are used to produce this meat? How many trees in the tropical rainforest are destroyed to produce this meat? (p. 26)

For Garbarino and the Green Utopians, automobile-based urbanization is a major culprit in the anti-sustainable modern lifestyle. "Suburbs are not conducive to sustainable patterns." (p. 166) Suburbs allow people to live far away from where they work and shop. Suburbs depend upon the car, or other forms of transit. Suburbs are not an acceptable alternative. So what, then, is the utopian alternative?

The Abolition of Patriarchy

Garbarino would like to redefine the family in the context of community, what he terms social welfare systems for a sustainable society. His ideas parallel those of the social engineers. He would make community be parent: "Communities should share joint custody of children with parents.... We can require 'registration and inspection' of young children so that the community can monitor child development and not lose track of the children for which it is responsible." (p. 245) Garbarino also calls for a parenting license.

Family roles are redefined, too. "We need to end masculine domination both in the family and in society, so that we can create a cultural climate in which the sustainable society can exist." (p. 66) Patriarchy is a threat to the planet, according to Garbarino. He devotes an entire chapter to this subject because he believes we need to have a more feminine ethic to survive. His book has probably never been fully embraced by the feminists, however, because he believes women should be out working in the gardens and fields producing the household's food!

Garbarino's design for sustainable social welfare systems for families are nearly identical to the education reform efforts, including parents as "partners," a "community level organization... for transportation systems, formal education, industrial enterprise, and the like." (p. 222) Although he does not specifically identify the school as the "hub" of the community structure (as we have seen in other education reform writings), it is clear that the new environmentally-correct society will be managed by grouping people into small neighborhood communities—almost completely self-sufficient in food production and other life needs, but requiring intimate governmental managing of their personal and family lives.

Mandatory Population Controls

Garbarino writes:

> To achieve a stable population, countries will have to establish a comprehensive and pervasive family planning program and carefully monitor immigration. At minimum, accom-

plishing this will require incentives for keeping family size at the replacement level, penalties for exceeding that level, and complete access to contraception. It will mean that family size will be limited to two children. (p. 228)

Family planning, the obligatory two children, is the cornerstone of Garbarino's sustainable society. He lauds the Chinese example, despite its oppressiveness (penalties) and slaughter (mandatory abortions). In fact, rewards and penalties for ecologically responsible procreation are a key component to Garbarino's ideal society. He views children as consumers of scarce resources, more mouths to feed on a crowded planet.

Garbarino consistently speaks of children in terms of economics (human capital?):

> Children are an economic benefit in the households, neighborhoods, and communities that rely upon human labor rather than non-renewable energy and materials to produce food and provide utilities. (p. 79)

> Limiting the size of specific families may turn children into an economic commodity, if people can sell their rights to bear them. (p. 84)

> Children are the currency of family life." (p. 180)

Cashless Economics

A radical new economic order is interwoven throughout the entire text of the book. Garbarino's economics calls for a cashless society and a new kind of economics that accurately accounts for the damage done to the environment. The price of every item must calculate the cost in terms of environmental destruction, especially nonrenewable resources like gasoline and oil.

Free enterprise is the villain to the world's environmental woes. It is responsible for the destruction of the planet according to Garbarino and he utterly dismisses it as an option or a solution. The current "economic order and its cultural baggage are major obstacles in the transition to a sustainable society." (p. 116) Reading Garbarino does not make one feel comfortable about Gorbachev heading up the new world effort for this Green Utopia (his international Green Cross environmental effort). The abolishment of free enterprise has always been at the forefront of the communist agenda.

Severe limits to world trade are called for by Garbarino: "In a sustainable system, world trade would be limited to two domains. The first is ideas, technology, and artistic creations and the people necessary to communicate them. The second is material goods needed to meet basic human needs or to dramatically enhance human experience in ways unavailable locally. Most world trade today fails to meet either criterion." (p. 152) It is not clear why artistic creations are given such a high priority for trade! The National Endowment for the Arts will appreciate this recommendation.

Voluntary Poverty

A total and complete reduction in the modern American affluent lifestyle is called for. "A relatively poor American family typically uses less of the world's resources than an affluent American family, but it still consumes much more than an Indian family that lives at subsistence level." (p. 85) Therefore, Garbarino concludes, that only reasonable solution is this: "As the world's leading consumer... [the United States] has a special obligation to reduce its demands for resources to a level that is domestically sustainable." (p. 89–90)

Garbarino's ideas about what constitutes "sustainable" and the average American's are radically different. He links American consumerism to every threat to the planet. It is not unlike the Iowa Global Education exercise for Home Economics students grades 9–12: "Seek connections between U.S. consumer and eating habits and the presence of malnutrition worldwide." (*Catalogue*, p. 36)

A Riceville, Iowa sophomore English class was given a "Simplicity Survey" as part of "The Thoreau Project." The test sheds considerable light on the extent to which Garbarino's radical ideas about sustainability have infiltrated classroom curriculum. Here are a few sample "commitments" that students had to make on the survey:

- I and/or my family will own no more than three sets of clothes and three pairs of shoes per person.
- I and/or my family will own only one automobile.
- My family and/or I will eat less meat, more vegetables and fruits, and no white sugar.
- My family and/or I will make our own simple personal products—such as, deodorant, soap, toothpaste—from old historical recipes.
- My family and/or I will learn to do almost everything for ourselves: cleaning, baking, repairing, building, etc.
- My family will have no more than two children.

This survey is a good indication of how outcome-based education will function. If the child does not score at a high enough "committed" level, the "teacher may ask you to retake this survey in order to see if the unit changes your commitment." In other words, if the child doesn't display the correct attitudes about this radical form of sustainability, they may have to re-take the test to see if their attitudes were changed!

The New Religion

To break our addiction to free enterprise, material consumption, and freedom in general, Garbarino calls for some new values. It is here that we begin to see the link between his Green Utopian view of a sustainable society and the strange-sounding ethical values contained in the new educational outcomes being promoted across the country. Garbarino cites Amitai Etzioni, saying that he "links consumerism, the work ethic, and cultural patriotism. This is a linkage we must break, replacing it with a combination of passionate commitment to a humane social environment and rejection of materialism as an end rather than a very limited means." (p. 100) The old values have to go, to be replaced by a new ethic. These new values necessarily entail a new religion.

You may have guessed it—we need to form a relationship with the Earth. We are not told exactly HOW one goes about forming this new "relationship." Hugging trees is good for a start—we need to "speak to the trees and listen to the birds." (p. 226) Presumably, this new anthropomorphic view of Mother Earth is the new religion. Garbarino describes it this way: "A reformed human family emphasizing equity and harmony... is a good model to follow in establishing our relationship with the Earth." (p. 99)

Like many of the other new Green Utopians (Al Gore, especially), Garbarino denigrates Christianity because it elevates man above nature: "Christianity was an ecological regression compared with the primitive animist impulse that emphasized the spiritual integrity of existence, the commonality of being, which demanded respect for the trees, the waters, the plants, the animals—for the Earth as a whole." (p. 98) Garbarino would replace big, bad Christianity with Eastern mysticism. "Buddhism teaches that material goods are only a means of achieving personal well-being. Consuming for its own sake has no value." (p. 99)

And, here is a big admission: "Primitive animism has more in common with emerging ecological science, although other religious traditions can also accommodate it." (p. 98–99) This admission may serve to explain the recent upsurge of religious indoctrination in environmental and global education curricula. It also explains the including of native American Indian ritualistic rites in children's curricula.

Garbarino advocates for this new (old) earth-centered religion. But what of other religions? What will happen to freedom of religion under this utopian system? "Freedom will be absolute in the realm of ideas and expression but minimal in the domains of environmentally threatening behavior." You can believe whatever you like, but your actions cannot harm the environment, however that comes to be defined. In fact, the environment reigns supreme in Green Utopia. The Earth's needs (real or perceived) are paramount to human needs and human rights.

The New Green "Outcomes"

To achieve this Green Utopia requires that human beings accept a new system of ethics, one that values the Earth. Garbarino suggests that if "we can forge this link between personal and public concerns, we will be able to harness the motivating power of the family in transforming Spaceship Earth." (p. 67) The current classroom emphases on environmental and global education are prime examples of this. Making small children feel responsible for the survival of the planet is one of the mechanisms for forging this link. "Children... need... to develop a sense of kinship with nature." (p. 169)

Reversing biases "that currently discourage reusability, manual labor, and self reliance" (p. 205) is one of the goals for educating the public. This means that it is absolutely essential that public attitudes and values be altered to fit the new environmental crisis worldview of the future, complete with utopian solutions.

Amazingly, Garbarino's book contains language almost identical to an outcome seen state by state across America in the new push for outcome-based education. "Socialization to adulthood means acquiring the skills and attitudes necessary to assume full responsibility in the work place, the home, and the community." (p. 206) An Iowa World Class Schools document states: "A world-class education will equip students to live, work and compete as successful citizens in a global society." (p. 5)

In light of Garbarino's Green Utopia, state by state comparisons of nearly identical outcome-based language takes on new significance. The language that educators are struggling to define is easily managed by the environmental fringe. In fact, William Spady, the father of modern OBE, has written: "A fragile and vulnerable global environment... requires altering economic consumption patterns and quality of life standards, and taking collective responsibility for promoting health and wellness." (Spady and Marshall, 1990)

In the new Green Utopia, social abilities are of prime importance. Garbarino gives primacy to social development rather than technological issues: "[s]ocial changes, not technological fixes, are the primary vehicle for averting disaster and placing humanity on sustainable ecological and socioeconomic footing." (p. 21) Because of this de-emphasis on technology, he believes that children "must become adept at language, body control, morality, reasoning, emotional expressiveness, and interpersonal relations. Unless they do, they become a burden—to their families, to our society, and even to themselves." (p. 105)

The belief system of the Green Utopians explains the national pressure to have attitudinal, behavioral and value-laden outcomes. It also explains the vacuum of solid academics. Reading, writing and arithmetic will no longer solve the world's problems. The crisis is too complex. Humans must be taught to adjust and adapt instead. Garbarino does not stake his future hopes in technological development and man's potential to develop scientific solutions for the complex environmental crisis. The only hope that he sees is sustainability.

Another nationally popular outcome has to do with diversity. Garbarino explains why this is so necessary: "Cultural diversity is as important as biological diversity in enhancing evolutionary resilience and human progress." At least for some, "diversity" has much more to do with their religious beliefs in evolution of mankind than it has to do with protecting the human rights of religious and ethnic groups. Cultural diversity, in the form of multicultural education, often promotes ritualistic pagan practices that enhance a feeling of connectedness with the Earth.

Those who oppose the teaching of this new religion of interconnectedness with nature are labeled "racists." When Davenport, Iowa school board member Elaine Rathmann challenged a "Multi-Cultural Week" as mere "political indoctrination and social reform" she was publicly charged in the local press with racism.

The New Green Utopian Classroom

A recent article by Barbara Melz of the *Boston Globe* appeared in the *Des Moines Register* (6/6/93, p. 3E). Melz details the vulnerability of children to emotional manipulation in areas of environmentalism. She quotes from a book by Lynne Dumas (*Talking with Your Child about a Troubled World*, Fawcett Columbine): "Everything becomes a personal issue for kids, everything gets related in their minds to their own safety."

The article goes on to give a poignant example of how vulnerable children can be to this type of education:

> This is especially true of environmental issues, she says. From the earliest ages, children relate to animals and nature in a kind of magical way. "TV shots of oil-soaked birds and seals, whales trapped on a beach, endangered dolphins all these kinds of things can be very upsetting to them. They can react with an intensity that surprises parents," she says... [S]olid waste disposal is an issue many school-age children glom on to in a very concrete way. "They see how much trash they produce in their own house. So here's their worry: If everyone's house makes this much trash, what will happen? Will there be enough room for me to live in the world?"

Are children being educated or indoctrinated? Is it fair to burden them with feelings of guilt and responsibility based on the perceived crisis of the Green Utopians?

Only One Choice

A thorough reading of Garbarino's book, especially in the context of other works by the new Green Utopians, creates the crisis and then presents the solution. His crisis is an out-of-control world population problem compounded by scarce resources. His world view is clearly founded on the Club of Rome *Global 2000* report. Garbarino has a limited view of human potential, technological innovation, the value of free enterprise, or ingenuity. However, there are serious questions about the scientific and rational validity of the entire so-called species.

The only politically-correct technology for the Green Utopians is apparently the computer, probably because of its ability to control human behavior through the charting of actions and attitudes. The greater good of society and the seriousness of the threat against the planet would likely justify a central data bank to monitor each citizen according to the logic of Green Utopians.

Garbarino's solution is a return to third-world subsistence living. Garbarino doesn't say this directly. One must read between the lines and come to understand that abolishing cows and cars, transportation and trade, free enterprise and a market economy, and certain basic human freedoms in matters related to religion and procreation can only mean an international totalitarian society. Granted, Garbarino, the consummate Green Utopian, objects to this (totalitarianism) and feigns to distance himself from the nastiness of it all. Yet his proposals can mean nothing else.

The New Green World View
To explain sustainability, Garbarino gives an extensive quote from *Voluntary Simplicity* by Duane Elgin, in which Ram Dass—"a Western-style intellectual turned Eastern-style mystic"—tells a story about an ideal society. It sheds much light on what Garbarino means by a "sustainable" society. Here are a few highlights:

> I look out over a gentle valley in the Kumoan Hills at the base of the Himalayas. A river flows through the valley, forming now and again manmade tributaries that irrigate the fertile fields. These fields surround the fifty or so thatched or tin-roofed houses and extend in increasing narrow terraces up the surrounding hillsides.
>
> In several of these fields I watch village men standing on their wooden plows goading on their slow-moving water buffalo who pull the plows, provide the men's families with milk, and help to carry their burdens. And amid the green of the hills, in brightly colored saris and nose rings, women cut the high grasses to feed the buffalo and gather the firewood which, along with the dried dung from the buffalo, will provide the fire to cook the grains harvested from the fields and to warm the houses against the winter colds and dry them during the monsoons. A huge haystack passes along the path, seemingly self-propelled, in that the woman on whose head it rests is lost entirely from view.
>
> It all moves as if in slow motion. Time is measured by the sun, the seasons, and the generations. A conch shell sounds from a tiny temple, which houses a deity worshiped in these hills. The stories of this and other deities are recited and sung, and they are honored by flowers and festivals and fasts. They provide a context—vast in its scale of aeons of time, rich with teachings of reincarnation and the morality inherent in the inevitable workings of karma. And it is this context that gives vertical meaning to these villagers' lives with their endless repetition of cycles of birth and death. (p. 36–37)

The Other Side of the Story
This scene is seductive, rich with description of people living in a sustainable society close to the Earth. However, there is another side to this story. It would burst the bubble of the utopians to hear it. Further, it would give great credence to Christianity as a potent force for personal freedom in the world. This alternative account comes from a humble missionary story, *The Bamboo Cross*, by Homer Dowdy:

> Just over beyond the mountains which surrounded the Sixteen Peaks lived the Tring.

They were the most difficult of all the mountain tribes that Sau had tried to reach. They were shy. When strangers approached they scurried into the forest. The Tring were the poorest, most fear-ridden tribe of all. If Sau's people often went hungry, the Tring lived always on the edge of starvation.

They did not live in villages.

The spirits that ruled them forbade one family to dip water from another's source; one of them could not even live across the stream from an in-law. So Tring houses were spotted sparsely for long distances along the mountain rivers, each a desolation picture of isolation.

Clinging to the steep, stony sides of mountains for mere existence, the Tring shivered in the ceaseless cold of the wind. Often gusts broke down the corn before it could come into ear. The wet monsoon blew when they needed it to be dry, and when it was dry for too long they suffered from the drought.

The demons, too, kept them hungry. If a man went to his field in the morning and found dew on the ground, he returned home without working that day to avoid a curse.

If fortune kept him away from his field beyond the planting season—well, it was evident that the spirits did not want him to find his food in such an easy way.

And if he did plant, he was careful not to plant enough to satisfy his needs. The spirits always demanded of him that he search in the forest for roots and leaves to eke out his diet. For this reason he was inclined to plant just enough mountain rice to keep his alcohol jars full. (p. 72)

The Bamboo Cross is a descriptive account of how people's lives in this tribe and others were truly transformed when they were released from the spiritual bondage to their demons and fat sorcerers (who exacted large amounts of material goods from their subjects to relieve them of supposed curses).

New Green Utopia

Green Utopia, then, may be a place—several generations hence—where people living in a "sustainable" society strongly resemble more primitive cultures with one notable exception. There will be a little box that does things, and people talk on it, and you have to push the correct buttons for food and medicine. No one knows the complicated math and science required to program this box because shopkeeper math and logic are not taught anymore. The little box is, therefore, an object of great superstition and magic. It accurately predicts the weather and seems to know almost everything.

The little box is the computer.

Garbarino's book was probably never a best-seller. But for those who are seeking to understand the rationale, worldview and justification for such a radical education reform proposal, it just might provide a few unexpected answers.

INDEX

INDEX

C

D

N

Q

R

USE THESE COUPONS!

the deliberate dumbing down of america

This book is an absolute must for All Americans–especially for parents, teachers, and elected officials! To order, please send a check or money order for **$39.95 plus $6 shipping and handling ($45.95)–soft cover, and $47.00 plus $7 shipping and handling ($54.00)–hard cover** (Maine residents please add 6% tax):

3D Research Co., 1062 Washington St., Bath, ME 04530

Name _____

Address _____

City _____ State ____ Zip _____

Phone _____ Fax _____

E-Mail _____

the deliberate dumbing down of america

This book is an absolute must for All Americans–especially for parents, teachers, and elected officials! To order, please send a check or money order for **$39.95 plus $6 shipping and handling ($45.95)–soft cover, and $47.00 plus $7 shipping and handling ($54.00)–hard cover** (Maine residents please add 6% tax):

3D Research Co., 1062 Washington St., Bath, ME 04530

Name _____

Address _____

City _____ State ____ Zip _____

Phone _____ Fax _____

E-Mail _____

the deliberate dumbing down of america

This book is an absolute must for All Americans–especially for parents, teachers, and elected officials! To order, please send a check or money order for **$39.95 plus $6 shipping and handling ($45.95)–soft cover, and $47.00 plus $7 shipping and handling ($54.00)–hard cover** (Maine residents please add 6% tax):

3D Research Co., 1062 Washington St., Bath, ME 04530

Name _____

Address _____

City _____ State ____ Zip _____

Phone _____ Fax _____

E-Mail _____

the deliberate dumbing down of america

This book is an absolute must for All Americans–especially for parents, teachers, and elected officials! To order, please send a check or money order for **$39.95 plus $6 shipping and handling ($45.95)–soft cover, and $47.00 plus $7 shipping and handling ($54.00)–hard cover** (Maine residents please add 6% tax):

3D Research Co., 1062 Washington St., Bath, ME 04530

Name _____

Address _____

City _____ State ____ Zip _____

Phone _____ Fax _____

E-Mail _____

the deliberate dumbing down of america

This book is an absolute must for All Americans–especially for parents, teachers, and elected officials! To order, please send a check or money order for **$39.95 plus $6 shipping and handling ($45.95)–soft cover, and $47.00 plus $7 shipping and handling ($54.00)–hard cover** (Maine residents please add 6% tax):

3D Research Co., 1062 Washington St., Bath, ME 04530

Name _____

Address _____

City _____ State ____ Zip _____

Phone _____ Fax _____

E-Mail _____

the deliberate dumbing down of america

This book is an absolute must for All Americans–especially for parents, teachers, and elected officials! To order, please send a check or money order for **$39.95 plus $6 shipping and handling ($45.95)–soft cover, and $47.00 plus $7 shipping and handling ($54.00)–hard cover** (Maine residents please add 6% tax):

3D Research Co., 1062 Washington St., Bath, ME 04530

Name _____

Address _____

City _____ State ____ Zip _____

Phone _____ Fax _____

E-Mail _____

the deliberate dumbing down of america

This book is an absolute must for All Americans–especially for parents, teachers, and elected officials! To order, please send a check or money order for **$39.95 plus $6 shipping and handling ($45.95)–soft cover, and $47.00 plus $7 shipping and handling ($54.00)–hard cover** (Maine residents please add 6% tax):

3D Research Co., 1062 Washington St., Bath, ME 04530

Name _____

Address _____

City _____ State ____ Zip _____

Phone _____ Fax _____

E-Mail _____

the deliberate dumbing down of america

This book is an absolute must for All Americans–especially for parents, teachers, and elected officials! To order, please send a check or money order for **$39.95 plus $6 shipping and handling ($45.95)–soft cover, and $47.00 plus $7 shipping and handling ($54.00)–hard cover** (Maine residents please add 6% tax):

3D Research Co., 1062 Washington St., Bath, ME 04530

Name _____

Address _____

City _____ State ____ Zip _____

Phone _____ Fax _____

E-Mail _____

Notes

Notes

the deliberate dumbing down of america....
a chronological paper trail (770 pages)
By Charlotte Thomson Iserbyt

The book is 770 pages and is formatted on 8.5 x 11" size paper for easy copying. The author gives permission to the reader to copy verbatim quotes as long as each page number contains the name of the book, the author, the ISBN number, and the telephone number where the book may be ordered. The book was written not just to be read but to be used by citizens in an effort to reverse the deplorable situation to be found in our nation today, not just in education, but in other areas as well, a situation which is required for our nation to become a properly functioning socialist "unit" in the New World Order, Global Management System, under the United Nations. As anyone the least bit familiar with history knows, as the schools go, so goes the nation! And it is primarily through schools that our free, constitutional republic, under God, has been and is being taken from us.

Please send all inquiries to:

Charlotte Thomson Iserbyt, 3D Research Co., 1062 Washington Street, Bath, ME 04530. Tel. 207-442-0543. Fax: 207-442-0551.
Email: dumbdown@blazenetme.net Web: www.deliberatedumbingdown.com.

CONSOLIDATION

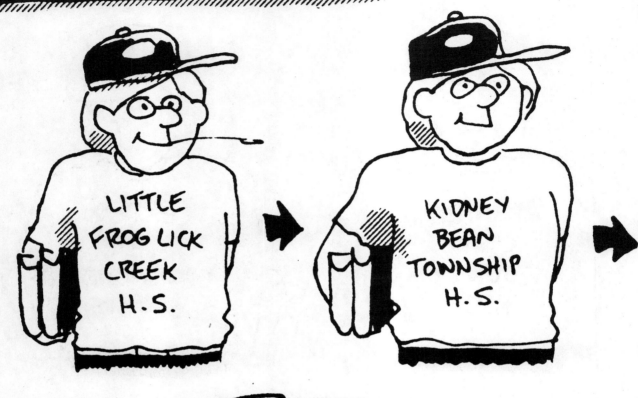

©'83 PETT   KAPPAN